The Little Oxford Dictionary

The Little Oxford Dictionary

First edited by George Ostler

Revised Seventh Edition

Edited by Maurice Waite

OXFORD
UNIVERSITY PRESS

YMCA Library Building, Jai Singh Road, New Delhi 110001

Oxford University Press is a department of the University of Oxford.
It furthers the University's objective of excellence in research, scholarship
and education by publishing worldwide in

Oxford   New York
Athens Auckland Bangkok Bogota Buenos Aires Calcutta
Cape Town Chennai Dar es Salaam Delhi Florence Hong Kong Istanbul
Karachi Kuala Lumpur Madrid Melbourne Mexico City Mumbai
Nairobi Paris São Paulo Singapore Taipei Tokyo Toronto Warsaw

with associated companies in

Berlin Ibadan

First Edition, 1930
Second Edition 1937
Third Edition 1941
Fourth Edition 1969
Fifth Edition 1980
Sixth Edition 1986
Seventh Edition 1994
Revised Seventh Edition 1998

This edition first published in India 1998 by arrangement with
Oxford University Press, Oxford
Third Impression 1999

ISBN 0 19 564784 X

For sale in India, Bangladesh, Myanmar, Bhutan, Sri Lanka and Nepal

Printed in India by Rekha Printers Pvt. Ltd., New Delhi 110020
and published by Manzar Khan, Oxford University Press
YMCA Library Building, Jai Singh Road, New Delhi 110001

Contents

Editorial staff

Editor Maurice Waite

Assistant Editor Andrew Hodgson

Contributing Editors Anna Howes
Louise Jones
Bernadette Paton
Anne St John-Hall

Keyboarders Anne Whear

Pam Marjara
Kay Pepler

Schools English Consultant Elaine Ashmore-Short

Features of the dictionary

Headwords (words given their own entries) are in bold type:

> **abandon** /əˈbænd(ə)n/ ● *verb* desert …

or in bold italic type if they are borrowed from another language and are usually printed in italics:

> ***autobahn***

Variant spellings are shown:

> **almanac** … (also **almanack**)

Words that are different but are spelt the same way (homographs) are printed with raised numbers:

> **abode¹**
> **abode²**

Variant American spellings are labelled *US*:

> **anaemia** … (*US* **anemia**)

Pronunciations are given in the International Phonetic Alphabet. See p. xi for an explanation.

Parts of speech are shown in italic:

> **abhor** … *verb*
> **abhorrence** … *noun*

If a word is used as more than one part of speech, each comes after a ●:

> **abandon** … ● *noun* … ● *verb* …

For explanations of parts of speech, see the panels at the dictionary entries for *noun*, *verb*, etc.

Inflections Irregular and difficult forms are given for:

nouns:
> **ability** … (*plural* **-ies**)
> **sheep** … (*plural* same)
> **tomato** … (*plural* **-es**)

> (Irregular plurals are not given for compounds such as *footman* and *schoolchild*.)

Features of the dictionary

verbs:	**abate** ... (-ting)
	abut ... (-tt-) [indicating **abutted**, **abutting**]
	ring ... (*past tense* **rang**; *past participle* **rung**)
adjectives:	**good** ... (**better**, **best**)
	narrow ... (-er, -est)
	able ... (-r, -st)
adverbs:	**well** ... (**better**, **best**)

Definitions Round brackets are used for

a optional words, e.g. at

  back ... *verb* (cause to) go backwards

  (because *back* can mean either 'go backwards'
  or 'cause to go backwards')

b typical objects of verbs:

  bank ... *verb* deposit (money) at bank

c typical subjects of verbs:

  break ... *verb* (of waves) curl over and foam

d typical nouns qualified by an adjective:

  catchy ... (of tune) easily remembered

Subject labels are sometimes used to help define a word:

  sharp ... *Music* above true pitch

Register labels are used if a word is slang, colloquial, or
formal:

  ace ... *adjective slang* excellent

  Coarse slang means that a word, although widely used,
  is still unacceptable to many people.

  Offensive means that a word is offensive to members of a
  particular ethnic, religious, or other group.

Phrases are entered under their main word:

  company ... **in company with**

A comma in a phrase indicates alternatives:

in, to excess

means that *in excess* and *to excess* are both phrases.

Compounds are entered under their main word or element
(usually the first):

air ... air speed ... airstrip

unless they need entries of their own:

broad
broadcast
broadside

A comma in a compound indicates alternatives:

block capitals, letters

means that *block capitals* and *block letters* are both
compounds.

Derivatives are put at the end of the entry for the word they are
derived from:

rob ... robber *noun*

unless they need defining:

drive ...
driver *noun* person who drives; golf club
for driving from tee.

Cross-references are printed in small capitals:

anatto = ANNATTO.
arose *past* of ARISE.

Definitions will be found at the entries referred to.

Note on proprietary terms

This dictionary includes some words which are, or are asserted to be, proprietary names or trade marks. Their inclusion does not imply that they have acquired for legal purposes a non-proprietary or general significance, nor is any other judgement implied concerning their legal status. In cases where the editor has some evidence that a word is used as a proprietary name or trade mark this is indicated by the label *proprietary term*, but no judgement concerning the legal status of such words is made or implied thereby.

Pronunciation symbols

Consonants

b	*but*	n	*no*	ʃ	*she*
d	*dog*	p	*pen*	ʒ	*vision*
f	*few*	r	*red*	θ	*thin*
g	*get*	s	*sit*	ð	*this*
h	*he*	t	*top*	ŋ	*ring*
j	*yes*	v	*voice*	x	*loch*
k	*cat*	w	*we*	tʃ	*chip*
l	*leg*	z	*zoo*	dʒ	*jar*
m	*man*				

Vowels

æ	*cat*	ʌ	*run*	əʊ	*no*
ɑ:	*arm*	ʊ	*put*	eə	*hair*
e	*bed*	u:	*too*	ɪə	*near*
ɜ:	*her*	ə	*ago*	ɔɪ	*boy*
ɪ	*sit*	aɪ	*my*	ʊə	*poor*
i:	*see*	aʊ	*how*	aɪə	*fire*
ɒ	*hot*	eɪ	*day*	aʊə	*sour*
ɔ:	*saw*				

(ə) signifies the indeterminate sound in gard*e*n, carn*a*l, and rhyth*m*.

The mark ˜ indicates a nasalized sound, as in the following vowels that are not natural in English:

> æ̃ (*ingénue*)
> ɑ̃ (*élan*)
> ɔ̃ (*bon voyage*)

The main or primary stress of a word is shown by ' before the relevant syllable.

Aa

A *abbreviation* ampere(s). □ **A-bomb** atomic bomb; **A level** advanced level in GCE exam.

a /ə, eɪ/ *adjective* (called the indefinite article) (also **an** /æn, ən/ before vowel sound) one, some, any; per.

AA *abbreviation* Automobile Association; Alcoholics Anonymous; anti-aircraft.

aardvark /'ɑːdvɑːk/ *noun* mammal with tubular snout and long tongue.

aback /ə'bæk/ *adverb* □ **taken aback** disconcerted, surprised.

abacus /'æbəkəs/ *noun* (*plural* **-es**) frame with wires along which beads are slid for calculating.

abaft /ə'bɑːft/ *Nautical* ● *adverb* in or towards stern of ship. ● *preposition* nearer stern than.

abandon /ə'bændən/ ● *verb* desert; give up (hope etc.). ● *noun* freedom from inhibitions. □ **abandonment** *noun*.

abandoned *adjective* deserted; unrestrained.

abase /ə'beɪs/ *verb* (**-sing**) humiliate; degrade. □ **abasement** *noun*.

abashed /ə'bæʃt/ *adjective* embarrassed; disconcerted.

abate /ə'beɪt/ *verb* (**-ting**) make or become less strong etc. □ **abatement** *noun*.

abattoir /'æbətwɑː/ *noun* slaughterhouse.

abbess /'æbɪs/ *noun* female head of abbey of nuns.

abbey /'æbɪ/ *noun* (*plural* **-s**) (building occupied by) community of monks or nuns.

abbot /'æbət/ *noun* head of community of monks.

abbreviate /ə'briːvɪeɪt/ *verb* shorten. □ **abbreviation** *noun*.

ABC /eɪbiː'siː/ *noun* alphabet; rudiments of subject; alphabetical guide.

abdicate /'æbdɪkeɪt/ *verb* renounce or resign from (throne etc.). □ **abdication** *noun*.

abdomen /'æbdəmən/ *noun* belly; rear part of insect etc. □ **abdominal** /æb'dɒmɪn(ə)l/ *adjective*.

abduct /əb'dʌkt/ *verb* carry off illegally, kidnap. □ **abduction** *noun*; **abductor** *noun*.

aberrant /æ'berənt/ *adjective* showing aberration.

aberration /æbə'reɪʃ(ə)n/ *noun* deviation from normal type or accepted standard; distortion.

abet /ə'bet/ *verb* encourage (offender), assist (offence). □ **abetter**, *Law* **abettor** *noun*.

abeyance /ə'beɪəns/ *noun* (usually after *in*, *into*) temporary disuse; suspension.

abhor /əb'hɔː/ *verb* (**-rr-**) detest; regard with disgust.

abhorrence /əb'hɒrəns/ *noun* disgust, detestation.

abhorrent *adjective* (often + *to*) disgusting.

abide /ə'baɪd/ *verb* (**-ding**, *past & past participle* **abode** /ə'bəʊd/ or **abided**) tolerate; (+ *by*) act in accordance with (rule); keep (promise).

abiding /ə'baɪdɪŋ/ *adjective* enduring, permanent.

ability /ə'bɪlɪtɪ/ *noun* (*plural* **-ies**) (often + *to do*) capacity, power; cleverness, talent.

abject /'æbdʒekt/ *adjective* miserable; degraded; despicable. □ **abjection** /-'dʒek-/ *noun*.

abjure /əb'dʒʊə/ *verb* renounce on oath. □ **abjuration** /-dʒʊ'reɪ-/ *noun*.

ablaze /ə'bleɪz/ *adjective & adverb* on fire; glittering; excited.

able /'eɪb(ə)l/ *adjective* (**-r**, **-st**) (+ *to do*) having power; talented. □ **able-bodied** healthy, fit. □ **ably** *adverb*.

ablution /ə'bluːʃ(ə)n/ *noun* (usually in *plural*) ceremonial washing of hands etc.; *colloquial* washing oneself.

abnegate /'æbnɪɡeɪt/ *verb* (**-ting**) give up, renounce. □ **abnegation** *noun*.

abnormal /æb'nɔːm(ə)l/ *adjective* exceptional; deviating from the norm. □ **abnormality** /-'mæl-/ *noun*; **abnormally** *adverb*.

aboard /ə'bɔːd/ *adverb & preposition* on or into (ship, aircraft, etc.).

abode¹ /ə'bəʊd/ *noun* dwelling place.

abode² *past & past participle* of ABIDE.

abolish /ə'bɒlɪʃ/ *verb* end existence of. □ **abolition** /æbə'lɪʃ(ə)n/ *noun*; **abolitionist** /æbə'lɪʃənɪst/ *noun*.

abominable /ə'bɒmɪnəb(ə)l/ *adjective* detestable, loathsome; *colloquial* very unpleasant. □ **Abominable Snowman** yeti. □ **abominably** *adverb*.

abominate /ə'bɒmɪneɪt/ *verb* (**-ting**) detest, loathe. □ **abomination** *noun*.

aboriginal /æbə'rɪdʒɪn(ə)l/ ● *adjective* indigenous; (usually **Aboriginal**) of the Australian Aborigines. ● *noun* aboriginal inhabitant, esp. (usually **Aboriginal**) of Australia.

aborigines /æbə'rɪdʒɪnɪz/ *plural noun* aboriginal inhabitants, esp. (usually **Aborigines**) of Australia.

■ **Usage** It is best to refer to one *Aboriginal* but several *Aborigines*, although *Aboriginals* is also acceptable.

abort /ə'bɔːt/ *verb* miscarry; effect abortion of; (cause to) end before completion.

abortion /ə'bɔːʃ(ə)n/ *noun* natural or (esp.) induced expulsion of foetus before it can survive; stunted or misshapen creature. □ **abortionist** *noun*.

abortive /ə'bɔːtɪv/ *adjective* fruitless, unsuccessful.

abound /ə'baʊnd/ *verb* be plentiful; (+ *in, with*) be rich in, teem with.

about /ə'baʊt/ ● *preposition* on subject of; relating to, in relation to; at a time near to; around (in); surrounding; here and there in. ● *adverb* approximately; nearby; in every direction; on the move, in action; all around. □ **about-face, -turn** turn made so as to face opposite direction, change of policy etc.; **be about to** be on the point of doing.

above /ə'bʌv/ ● *preposition* over, on top of, higher than; more than; higher in rank, importance, etc. than; too great or good for; beyond reach of. ● *adverb* at or to higher point, overhead; earlier on page or in book. □ **above all** more than anything else; **above-board** without concealment.

abracadabra /æbrəkə'dæbrə/ *interjection* supposedly magic word.

abrade /ə'breɪd/ *verb* (**-ding**) scrape or wear away by rubbing.

abrasion /ə'breɪʒ(ə)n/ *noun* rubbing or scraping away; resulting damaged area.

abrasive /ə'breɪsɪv/ ● *adjective* capable of rubbing or grinding down; harsh or hurtful in manner. ● *noun* abrasive substance.

abreast /ə'brest/ *adverb* side by side and facing same way; (+ *of*) up to date with.

abridge /ə'brɪdʒ/ *verb* (**-ging**) shorten (a book etc.). □ **abridgement** *noun*.

abroad /ə'brɔːd/ *adverb* in or to foreign country; widely; in circulation.

abrogate /'æbrəgeɪt/ *verb* (**-ting**) repeal, abolish (law etc.). □ **abrogation** *noun*.

abrupt /ə'brʌpt/ *adjective* sudden, hasty; curt; steep. □ **abruptly** *adverb*; **abruptness** *noun*.

abscess /'æbsɪs/ *noun* (*plural* **-es**) swelling containing pus.

abscond /əb'skɒnd/ *verb* flee, esp. to avoid arrest; escape.

abseil /'æbseɪl/ ● *verb* descend (building etc.) by using doubled rope fixed at higher point. ● *noun* such a descent.

absence /'æbsəns/ *noun* being away; duration of this; (+ *of*) lack. □ **absence of mind** inattentiveness.

absent ● *adjective* /'æbsənt/ not present or existing; lacking; inattentive. ● *verb* /əb'sent/ (**absent oneself**) go or stay away. □ **absently** *adverb*.

absentee /æbsən'tiː/ *noun* person not present.

absenteeism /æbsən'tiːɪz(ə)m/ *noun* absenting oneself from work, school, etc.

absent-minded *adjective* forgetful, inattentive. □ **absent-mindedly** *adverb*; **absent-mindedness** *noun*.

absinthe /'æbsɪnθ/ *noun* wormwood-based, aniseed-flavoured liqueur.

absolute /'æbsəluːt/ *adjective* complete, utter; unconditional; despotic; not relative; (of adjective or transitive verb) without expressed noun or object; (of decree etc.) final. □ **absolute majority** one over all rivals combined; **absolute temperature** one measured from absolute zero; **absolute zero** lowest possible temperature (− 273.15°C or 0°K).

absolutely adverb completely; in an absolute sense; colloquial quite so, yes.

absolution /æbsə'luːʃ(ə)n/ noun formal forgiveness of sins.

absolutism /'æbsəluːtɪz(ə)m/ noun absolute government. □ **absolutist** noun.

absolve /əb'zɒlv/ verb (**-ving**) (often + from, of) free from blame or obligation.

absorb /əb'sɔːb/ verb incorporate; assimilate; take in (heat etc.); deal with easily, reduce intensity of; (often as **absorbing** adjective) engross attention of; consume (resources).

absorbent /əb'sɔːbənt/ ● adjective tending to absorb. ● noun absorbent substance.

absorption /əb'sɔːpʃ(ə)n/ noun absorbing, being absorbed. □ **absorptive** adjective.

abstain /əb'steɪn/ verb (usually + from) refrain (from indulging); decline to vote.

abstemious /əb'stiːmɪəs/ adjective moderate or ascetic, esp. in eating and drinking. □ **abstemiously** adverb.

abstention /əb'stenʃ(ə)n/ noun abstaining, esp. from voting.

abstinence /'æbstɪnəns/ noun abstaining, esp. from food or alcohol. □ **abstinent** adjective.

abstract ● adjective /'æbstrækt/ of or existing in theory rather than practice, not concrete; (of art etc.) not representational. ● verb /əb'strækt/ (often + from) remove; summarize. ● noun /'æbstrækt/ summary; abstract idea, work of art, etc.

abstracted adjective inattentive. □ **abstractedly** adverb.

abstraction /əb'strækʃ(ə)n/ noun abstracting; abstract idea; abstract qualities in art; absent-mindedness.

abstruse /əb'struːs/ adjective hard to understand; profound.

absurd /əb'sɜːd/ adjective wildly inappropriate; ridiculous. □ **absurdity** noun (plural **-ies**); **absurdly** adverb.

ABTA /'æbtə/ abbreviation Association of British Travel Agents.

abundance /ə'bʌnd(ə)ns/ noun plenty; more than enough; wealth.

abundant adjective plentiful; (+ in) rich. □ **abundantly** adverb.

abuse ● verb /ə'bjuːz/ (**-sing**) use improperly; misuse; maltreat; insult verbally. ● noun /ə'bjuːs/ misuse; insulting language; corrupt practice. □ **abuser** /ə'bjuːzə/ noun.

abusive /ə'bjuːsɪv/ adjective insulting, offensive. □ **abusively** adverb.

abut /ə'bʌt/ verb (**-tt-**) (+ on) border on; (+ on, against) touch or lean on.

abysmal /ə'bɪzm(ə)l/ adjective very bad; dire. □ **abysmally** adverb.

abyss /ə'bɪs/ noun deep chasm.

AC abbreviation alternating current.

a/c abbreviation account.

acacia /ə'keɪʃə/ noun tree with yellow or white flowers.

academia /ækə'diːmɪə/ noun the world of scholars.

academic /ækə'demɪk/ ● adjective scholarly; of learning; of no practical relevance. ● noun teacher or scholar in university etc. □ **academically** adverb.

academician /əkædə'mɪʃ(ə)n/ noun member of Academy.

academy /ə'kædəmɪ/ noun (plural **-ies**) place of specialized training; (**Academy**) society of distinguished scholars, artists, scientists, etc.; Scottish secondary school.

acanthus /ə'kænθəs/ noun (plural **-es**) spring herbaceous plant with spiny leaves.

ACAS /'eɪkæs/ abbreviation Advisory, Conciliation, and Arbitration Service.

accede /æk'siːd/ verb (**-ding**) (+ to) take office, esp. as monarch; assent to.

accelerate /ək'seləreɪt/ verb (**-ting**) increase speed (of); (cause to) happen earlier. □ **acceleration** noun.

accelerator noun device for increasing speed, esp. pedal in vehicle; Physics apparatus for imparting high speeds to charged particles.

accent ● noun /'æksənt/ style of pronunciation of region or social group (see panel); emphasis; prominence given to syllable by stress or pitch; mark on letter indicating pronunciation (see panel). ● *verb* /æk'sent/ emphasize; write or print accents on.

accentuate /æk'sentʃʊeɪt/ *verb* (**-ting**) emphasize, make prominent. □ **accentuation** *noun*.

accept /ək'sept/ *verb* willingly receive; answer (invitation etc.) affirmatively; regard favourably; receive as valid or suitable. □ **acceptance** *noun*.

acceptable *adjective* worth accepting; tolerable. □ **acceptability** *noun*, **acceptably** *adverb*.

access /'ækses/ ● *noun* way of approach or entry; right or opportunity to reach, use, or visit. ● *verb* gain access to (data) in computer.

accessible /ək'sesɪb(ə)l/ *adjective* reachable or obtainable; easy to understand. □ **accessibility** *noun*.

accession /ək'seʃ(ə)n/ *noun* taking office, esp. as monarch; thing added.

accessory /ək'sesərɪ/ *noun* (*plural* **-ies**) additional or extra thing (usually in *plural*) small attachment or item of dress; (*often* + *to*) person who abets in or is privy to illegal act.

accident /'æksɪd(ə)nt/ *noun* unintentional unfortunate esp. harmful event; event without apparent cause; unexpected event. □ **accident-prone** clumsy; **by accident** unintentionally.

accidental /æksɪ'dent(ə)l/ ● *adjective* happening or done by chance or accident. ● *noun Music* sharp, flat, or natural indicating momentary departure of note from key signature. □ **accidentally** *adverb*.

acclaim /ə'kleɪm/ ● *verb* welcome or applaud enthusiastically. ● *noun* applause; welcome; public praise. □ **acclamation** /æklə-/ *noun*.

acclimatize /ə'klaɪmətaɪz/ *verb* (*also* **-ise**) (**-zing** *or* **-sing**) adapt to new climate or conditions. □ **acclimatization** *noun*.

accolade /'ækəleɪd/ *noun* praise given; touch made with sword at conferring of knighthood.

accommodate /ə'kɒmədeɪt/ *verb* (**-ting**) provide lodging or room for; adapt, harmonize, reconcile; do favour to; (+ *with*) supply.

■ **Usage** *Accommodate, accommodation,* etc. are spelt with two *m*s, not one.

accommodating *adjective* obliging.

accommodation *noun* lodgings; adjustment, adaptation; convenient arrangement. □ **accommodation address** postal address used instead of permanent one.

Accent

1 A person's accent is the way he or she pronounces words, and people from different regions and different groups in society have different accents. For instance, most people in northern England say *path* with a 'short' *a*, while most people in southern England say it with a 'long' *a*, and in America and Canada the *r* in *far* and *port* is generally pronounced, while in south-eastern England, for example, it is not. Everyone speaks with an accent, although some accents may be regarded as having more prestige, such as 'Received Pronunciation' (RP) in the UK.

2 An accent on a letter is a mark added to it to alter the sound it stands for. In French, for example, there are

    ´(acute), as in *état*   ¨(diaeresis), as in *Noël*
    `(grave), as in *mère*   ¸(cedilla), as in *français*
    ˆ(circumflex), as in *guêpe*

and German has

    ¨(umlaut), as in *München*.

There are no accents on native English words, but many words borrowed from other languages still have them, such as *blasé* and *façade*.

accompaniment /əˈkʌmpənɪmənt/ noun instrumental or orchestral support for solo instrument, voice, or group; accompanying thing.

accompany /əˈkʌmpənɪ/ verb (-ies, -ied) go with, attend; (usually in passive; + with, by) be done or found with; Music play accompaniment for. □ **accompanist** noun Music.

accomplice /əˈkʌmplɪs/ noun partner in crime.

accomplish /əˈkʌmplɪʃ/ verb succeed in doing; achieve, complete.

accomplished adjective clever, skilled.

accomplishment noun completion (of task etc.); acquired esp. social skill; thing achieved.

accord /əˈkɔːd/ • verb (often + with) be consistent or in harmony; grant, give. • noun agreement; consent. □ **of one's own accord** on one's own initiative.

accordance noun □ **in accordance with** in conformity to.

according adverb (+ to) as stated by; (+ to, as) in proportion to or as.

accordingly adverb as circumstances suggest or require; consequently.

accordion /əˈkɔːdɪən/ noun musical reed instrument with concertina-like bellows, keys, and buttons.

accost /əˈkɒst/ verb approach and speak boldly to.

account /əˈkaʊnt/ • noun narration, description; arrangement at bank etc. for depositing and withdrawing money etc.; statement of financial transactions with balance; importance; behalf. • verb consider as. □ **account for** explain, answer for; kill, destroy; **on account** to be paid for later, in part payment; **on account of** because of; **on no account** under no circumstances; **take account of, take into account** consider.

accountable adjective responsible, required to account for one's conduct; explicable. □ **accountability** noun.

accountant noun professional keeper or verifier of financial accounts. □ **accountancy** noun; **accounting** noun.

accoutrements /əˈkuːtrəmənts/ plural noun equipment, trappings.

accredit /əˈkredɪt/ verb (-t-) (+ to) attribute; (+ with) credit; (usually + to, at) send (ambassador etc.) with credentials.

accredited adjective officially recognized; generally accepted.

accretion /əˈkriːʃ(ə)n/ noun growth by accumulation or organic enlargement; the resulting whole; matter so added.

accrue /əˈkruː/ verb (-ues, -ued, -uing) (often + to) come as natural increase or advantage, esp. financial.

accumulate /əˈkjuːmjʊleɪt/ verb (-ting) acquire increasing number or quantity of; amass, collect; grow numerous; increase. □ **accumulation** noun; **accumulative** /-lətɪv/ adjective.

accumulator noun rechargeable electric cell; bet placed on sequence of events, with winnings and stake from each placed on next.

accurate /ˈækjʊrət/ adjective precise; conforming exactly with truth etc. □ **accuracy** noun; **accurately** adverb.

accursed /əˈkɜːsɪd/ adjective under a curse; colloquial detestable, annoying.

accusative /əˈkjuːzətɪv/ Grammar • noun case expressing object of action. • adjective of or in an accusative.

accuse /əˈkjuːz/ verb (-sing) (often + of) charge with fault or crime; blame. □ **accusation** /æk-/ noun; **accusatory** adjective.

accustom /əˈkʌstəm/ verb (+ to) make used to.

accustomed adjective (usually + to) used (to a thing); customary.

ace • noun playing card with single spot; person who excels in some activity; Tennis unreturnable service. • adjective slang excellent. □ **within an ace of** on the verge of.

acerbic /əˈsɜːbɪk/ adjective harsh and sharp, esp. in speech or manner. □ **acerbity** noun (plural -ies).

acetate /ˈæsɪteɪt/ noun compound of acetic acid, esp. the cellulose ester; fabric made from this.

acetic /əˈsiːtɪk/ adjective of or like vinegar. □ **acetic acid** clear liquid acid in vinegar.

acetone /ˈæsɪtəʊn/ noun colourless volatile solvent of organic compounds.

acetylene /əˈsetɪliːn/ noun inflammable hydrocarbon gas, used esp. in welding.

ache /eɪk/ ● *noun* continuous dull pain; mental distress. ● *verb* (**aching**) suffer from or be the source of an ache.

achieve /ə'tʃiːv/ *verb* (**-ving**) reach or attain by effort; accomplish (task etc.); be successful. □ **achiever** *noun;* **achievement** *noun.*

Achilles /ə'kɪliːz/ *noun* □ **Achilles heel** vulnerable point; **Achilles tendon** tendon attaching calf muscles to heel.

achromatic /ækrəʊ'mætɪk/ *adjective* transmitting light without separating it into colours; free from colour. □ **achromatically** *adverb.*

achy /'eɪkɪ/ *adjective* (**-ier, -iest**) suffering from aches.

acid /'æsɪd/ ● *noun Chemistry* substance that neutralizes alkalis, turns litmus red, and usually contains hydrogen and is sour; *slang* drug LSD. ● *adjective* having properties of acid; sour; biting, sharp. □ **acid drop** sharp-tasting boiled sweet; **acid house** synthesized music with simple beat, associated with hallucinogenic drugs; **acid rain** rain containing acid formed from industrial waste in atmosphere; **acid test** severe or conclusive test. □ **acidic** /ə'sɪd-/ *adjective;* **acidify** /ə'sɪd-/ *verb* (**-ies, -ied**); **acidity** /-'sɪd-/ *noun.*

acidulous /ə'sɪdjʊləs/ *adjective* somewhat acid.

acknowledge /ək'nɒlɪdʒ/ *verb* (**-ging**) recognize, accept truth of; confirm receipt of (letter etc.); show that one has noticed; express gratitude for.

acknowledgement *noun* (also **acknowledgment**) acknowledging; thing given or done in gratitude; letter etc. confirming receipt; (usually in *plural*) author's thanks, prefacing book.

acme /'ækmɪ/ *noun* highest point.

acne /'æknɪ/ *noun* skin condition with red pimples.

acolyte /'ækəlaɪt/ *noun* assistant, esp. of priest.

aconite /'ækənaɪt/ *noun* any of various poisonous plants, esp. monkshood; drug made from these.

acorn /'eɪkɔːn/ *noun* fruit of oak.

acoustic /ə'kuːstɪk/ *adjective* of sound or sense of hearing; (of musical instrument etc.) without electrical amplification. □ **acoustically** *adverb.*

acoustics *plural noun* properties (of a room etc.) in transmitting sound; (treated as *singular*) science of sound.

acquaint /ə'kweɪnt/ *verb* (+ *with*) make aware of or familiar with. □ **be acquainted with** know.

acquaintance *noun* being acquainted; person one knows slightly. □ **acquaintanceship** *noun.*

acquiesce /ækwɪ'es/ *verb* (**-cing**) agree, esp. tacitly. □ **acquiescence** *noun;* **acquiescent** *adjective.*

acquire /ə'kwaɪə/ *verb* (**-ring**) gain possession of. □ **acquired immune deficiency syndrome** = AIDS; **acquired taste** liking developed by experience.

acquirement *noun* thing acquired or attained.

acquisition /ækwɪ'zɪʃ(ə)n/ *noun* (esp. useful) thing acquired; acquiring, being acquired.

acquisitive /ə'kwɪzɪtɪv/ *adjective* keen to acquire things.

acquit /ə'kwɪt/ *verb* (**-tt-**) (often + *of*) declare not guilty; (**acquit oneself**) behave, perform, (+ *of*) discharge (duty etc.). □ **acquittal** *noun.*

acre /'eɪkə/ *noun* measure of land, 4840 sq. yards, 0.405 ha.

acreage /'eɪkərɪdʒ/ *noun* number of acres.

acrid /'ækrɪd/ *adjective* bitterly pungent. □ **acridity** /-'krɪd-/ *noun.*

acrimonious /ækrɪ'məʊnɪəs/ *adjective* bitter in manner or temper. □ **acrimony** /'ækrɪmənɪ/ *noun.*

acrobat /'ækrəbæt/ *noun* performer of acrobatics. □ **acrobatic** /-'bæt-/ *adjective.*

acrobatics /ækrə'bætɪks/ *plural noun* gymnastic feats.

acronym /'ækrənɪm/ *noun* word formed from initial letters of other words (e.g. *laser, NATO*).

acropolis /ə'krɒpəlɪs/ *noun* citadel of ancient Greek city.

across /ə'krɒs/ ● *preposition* to or on other side of; from one side to another side of. ● *adverb* to or on other side; from one side to another. □ **across the board** applying to all.

acrostic /ə'krɒstɪk/ *noun* poem etc. in which first (or first and last) letters of lines form word(s).

acrylic /ə'krɪlɪk/ ● *adjective* made from acrylic acid. ● *noun* acrylic fibre, fabric, or paint.

acrylic acid *noun* a pungent liquid organic acid.

act ● *noun* thing done, deed; process of doing; item of entertainment; pretence; main division of play; decree of legislative body. ● *verb* behave; perform actions or functions; (often + *on*) have effect; perform in play etc.; pretend; play part of. □ **act for** be (legal) representative of; **act up** *colloquial* misbehave, give trouble.

acting *adjective* serving temporarily as.

actinism /'æktɪnɪz(ə)m/ *noun* property of short-wave radiation that produces chemical changes, as in photography.

action /'ækʃ(ə)n/ *noun* process of doing or acting; forcefulness, energy; exertion of energy or influence; deed, act; (**the action**) series of events in story, play, etc., *slang* exciting activity; battle; mechanism of instrument; style of movement; lawsuit. □ **action-packed** full of action or excitement; **action replay** playback of part of television broadcast; **out of action** not functioning.

actionable *adjective* providing grounds for legal action.

activate /'æktɪveɪt/ *verb* (**-ting**) make active or radioactive. □ **activation** *noun*.

active /'æktɪv/ ● *adjective* marked by action; energetic, diligent; working, operative; *Grammar* (of verb) of which subject performs action (e.g. *saw* in *he saw a film*). ● *noun Grammar* active form or voice. □ **active service** military service in wartime. □ **actively** *adverb*.

activism *noun* policy of vigorous action, esp. for a political cause. □ **activist** *noun*.

activity /æk'tɪvɪtɪ/ *noun* (*plural* **-ies**) being active; busy or energetic action; (often in *plural*) occupation, pursuit.

actor /'æktə/ *noun* person who acts in play, film, etc.

actress /'æktrɪs/ *noun* female actor.

actual /'æktʃʊəl/ *adjective* existing, real; current. □ **actuality** /-'æl-/ *noun* (*plural* **-ies**).

actually *adverb* in fact, really.

actuary /'æktʃʊərɪ/ *noun* (*plural* **-ies**) statistician, esp. one calculating insurance risks and premiums. □ **actuarial** /-'eər-/ *adjective*.

actuate /'æktʃʊeɪt/ *verb* (**-ting**) cause to move, function, act.

acuity /ə'kju:ɪtɪ/ *noun* acuteness.

acumen /'ækjʊmen/ *noun* keen insight or discernment.

acupuncture /'ækjʊpʌŋktʃə/ *noun* medical treatment using needles in parts of the body. □ **acupuncturist** *noun*.

acute /ə'kju:t/ *adjective* (**-r**, **-st**) keen, penetrating; shrewd; (of disease) coming quickly to crisis; (of angle) less than 90°. □ **acute (accent)** mark (ˊ) over letter indicating pronunciation. □ **acutely** *adverb*.

AD *abbreviation* of the Christian era (*Anno Domini*).

ad *noun colloquial* advertisement.

adage /'ædɪdʒ/ *noun* proverb, maxim.

adagio /ə'dɑ:ʒɪəʊ/ *Music* ● *adverb & adjective* in slow time. ● *noun* (*plural* **-s**) adagio passage.

adamant /'ædəmənt/ *adjective* stubbornly resolute. □ **adamantly** *adverb*.

Adam's apple /'ædəmz/ *noun* cartilaginous projection at front of neck.

adapt /ə'dæpt/ *verb* (+ *to*) fit, adjust; (+ *to*, *for*) make suitable, modify; (usually + *to*) adjust to new conditions. □ **adaptable** *adjective*; **adaptation** /æd-/ *noun*.

adaptor *noun* device for making equipment compatible; *Electricity* device for connecting several electrical plugs to one socket.

add *verb* join as increase or supplement; unite (numbers) to get their total; say further. □ **add up** find total of; (+ *to*) amount to.

addendum /ə'dendəm/ *noun* (*plural* **-da**) thing to be added; material added at end of book.

adder /'ædə/ *noun* small venomous snake.

addict /'ædɪkt/ *noun* person addicted, esp. to drug; *colloquial* devotee.

addicted /ə'dɪktɪd/ *adjective* (usually + *to*) dependent on a drug as a habit;

devoted to an interest. □ **addiction**
noun.

addictive /ə'dɪktɪv/ *adjective* causing addiction.

addition /ə'dɪʃ(ə)n/ *noun* adding; person or thing added. □ **in addition** (often + *to*) also, as well.

additional *adjective* added, extra. □ **additionally** *adverb.*

additive /'ædɪtɪv/ *noun* substance added, esp. to colour, flavour, or preserve food.

addle /'æd(ə)l/ *verb* (**-ling**) muddle, confuse; (usually as **addled** *adjective*) (of egg) become rotten.

address /ə'dres/ ● *noun* place where person lives or organization is situated; particulars of this, esp. for postal purposes; speech delivered to an audience. ● *verb* write postal directions on; direct (remarks etc.); speak or write to; direct one's attention to.

addressee /ædre'si:/ *noun* person to whom letter etc. is addressed.

adduce /ə'dju:s/ *verb* (**-cing**) cite as proof or instance. □ **adducible** *adjective.*

adenoids /'ædɪnɔɪdz/ *plural noun* enlarged lymphatic tissue between nose and throat, often hindering breathing. □ **adenoidal** /-'nɔɪ-/ *adjective.*

adept ● *adjective* /ə'dept, 'ædept/ (+ *at, in*) skilful. ● *noun* /'ædept/ adept person.

adequate /'ædɪkwət/ *adjective* sufficient, satisfactory. □ **adequacy** *noun;* **adequately** *adverb.*

adhere /əd'hɪə/ *verb* (**-ring**) (usually + *to*) stick fast; behave according to (rule etc.); give allegiance.

adherent ● *noun* supporter. ● *adjective* adhering. □ **adherence** *noun.*

adhesion /əd'hi:ʒ(ə)n/ *noun* adhering.

adhesive /əd'hi:sɪv/ ● *adjective* sticky, causing adhesion. ● *noun* adhesive substance.

ad hoc /æd 'hɒk/ *adverb & adjective* for one particular occasion or use.

adieu /ə'dju:/ *interjection* goodbye.

ad infinitum /æd ɪnfɪ'naɪtəm/ *adverb* without limit; for ever.

adipose /'ædɪpəʊz/ *adjective* of fat, fatty. □ **adiposity** /-'pɒs-/ *noun.*

adjacent /ə'dʒeɪs(ə)nt/ *adjective* lying near; adjoining. □ **adjacency** *noun.*

adjective /'ædʒɪktɪv/ *noun* word indicating quality of noun or pronoun (see panel). □ **adjectival** /-'taɪv-/ *adjective.*

adjoin /ə'dʒɔɪn/ *verb* be next to and joined with.

adjourn /ə'dʒɜ:n/ *verb* postpone, break off; (+ *to*) transfer to (another place). □ **adjournment** *noun.*

....

Adjective

An adjective is a word that describes a noun or pronoun, e.g.
    red, clever, German, depressed, battered, sticky, shining

Most can be used either before a noun, e.g.
    the red *house*   *a* clever *woman*

or after a verb like *be, seem,* or *call,* e.g.
    The house is red.   *I wouldn't call him* lazy.
    She seems very clever.

Some can be used only before a noun, e.g.
    the chief *reason* (one cannot say **the reason is chief*)

Some can be used only after a verb, e.g.
    The ship is still afloat. (one cannot say *an afloat ship)

A few can be used only immediately after a noun, e.g.
    the president elect (one cannot say either **an elect president* or
    **The president is elect*)

....

adjudge /ə'dʒʌdʒ/ verb (**-ging**) pronounce judgement on; pronounce or award judicially. □ **adjudg(e)ment** noun.

adjudicate /ə'dʒuːdɪkeɪt/ verb (**-ting**) act as judge; adjudge. □ **adjudication** noun; **adjudicator** noun.

adjunct /'ædʒʌŋkt/ noun (+ to, of) subordinate or incidental thing.

adjure /ə'dʒʊə/ verb (**-ring**) (usually + to do) beg or command. □ **adjuration** noun.

adjust /ə'dʒʌst/ verb order, position; regulate; arrange; (usually + to) adapt; harmonize. □ **adjustable** adjective; **adjustment** noun.

adjutant /'ædʒʊt(ə)nt/ noun army officer assisting superior in administrative duties.

ad lib /æd 'lɪb/ ● verb (**-bb-**) improvise. ● adjective improvised. ● adverb to any desired extent.

Adm. abbreviation Admiral.

administer /əd'mɪnɪstə/ verb manage (affairs); formally deliver, dispense.

administration /ədmɪnɪ'streɪʃ(ə)n/ noun administering, esp. public affairs; government in power.

administrative /əd'mɪnɪstrətɪv/ adjective of the management of affairs.

administrator /əd'mɪnɪstreɪtə/ noun manager of business, public affairs, or person's estate.

admirable /'ædmərəb(ə)l/ adjective deserving admiration; excellent. □ **admirably** adverb.

admiral /'ædmər(ə)l/ noun commander-in-chief of navy; high-ranking naval officer, commander.

Admiralty noun (plural **-ies**) (in full **Admiralty Board**) historical committee superintending Royal Navy.

admire /əd'maɪə/ verb regard with approval, respect, or satisfaction; express admiration of. □ **admiration** /ædmə-'reɪ-/ noun; **admirer** noun; **admiring** adjective; **admiringly** adverb.

admissible /əd'mɪsɪb(ə)l/ adjective worth accepting or considering; allowable. □ **admissibility** noun.

admission /əd'mɪʃ(ə)n/ noun acknowledgement (of error etc.); (right of) entering; entrance charge.

admit /əd'mɪt/ verb (**-tt-**) (often + to be, that) acknowledge, recognize as true; (+ to) confess to; let in; accommodate; take (patient) into hospital; (+ of) allow as possible.

admittance noun admitting or being admitted, usually to a place.

admittedly adverb as must be admitted.

admixture /æd'mɪkstʃə/ noun thing added, esp. minor ingredient; adding of this.

admonish /əd'mɒnɪʃ/ verb reprove; urge; (+ of) warn. □ **admonishment** noun; **admonition** /ædmə'nɪ-/ noun; **admonitory** adjective.

ad nauseam /æd 'nɔːzɪæm/ adverb to a sickening extent.

ado /ə'duː/ noun fuss; trouble.

adobe /ə'dəʊbɪ/ noun sun-dried brick.

adolescent /ædə'lesənt/ ● adjective between childhood and adulthood. ● noun adolescent person. □ **adolescence** noun.

adopt /ə'dɒpt/ verb legally take (child) as one's own; take over (another's idea etc.); choose; accept responsibility for; approve (report etc.). □ **adoption** noun.

adoptive adjective because of adoption.

adorable /ə'dɔːrəb(ə)l/ adjective deserving adoration; colloquial delightful, charming.

adore /ə'dɔː/ verb (**-ring**) love intensely; worship; colloquial like very much. □ **adoration** /ædə'reɪ-/ noun; **adorer** noun.

adorn /ə'dɔːn/ verb add beauty to, decorate. □ **adornment** noun.

adrenal /ə'driːn(ə)l/ ● adjective of adrenal glands. ● noun (in full **adrenal gland**) either of two ductless glands above the kidneys.

adrenalin /ə'drenəlɪn/ noun stimulative hormone secreted by adrenal glands.

adrift /ə'drɪft/ adverb & adjective drifting; colloquial unfastened, out of order.

adroit /ə'drɔɪt/ adjective dexterous, skilful.

adsorb /əd'sɔːb/ verb attract and hold thin layer of (gas or liquid) on its surface. □ **adsorbent** adjective & noun; **adsorption** noun.

adulation /ædjʊ'leɪʃ(ə)n/ *noun* obsequious flattery.

adult /'ædʌlt/ ● *adjective* grown-up, mature; of or for adults. ● *noun* adult person. □ **adulthood** *noun*.

adulterate /ə'dʌltəreɪt/ *verb* (**-ting**) debase (esp. food) by adding other substances. □ **adulteration** *noun*.

adultery /ə'dʌltərɪ/ *noun* voluntary sexual intercourse of married person other than with spouse. □ **adulterer**, **adulteress** *noun*; **adulterous** *adjective*.

adumbrate /'ædʌmbreɪt/ *verb* (**-ting**) indicate faintly or in outline; foreshadow. □ **adumbration** *noun*.

advance /əd'vɑːns/ ● *verb* (**-cing**) move or put forward; progress; pay or lend beforehand; promote; present (idea etc.). ● *noun* going forward; progress; prepayment, loan; payment beforehand; (in *plural*) amorous approaches; rise in price. ● *adjective* done etc. beforehand. □ **advance on** approach threateningly; **in advance** ahead, beforehand.

advanced *adjective* well ahead; socially progressive. □ **advanced level** high level GCE exam.

advancement *noun* promotion of person, cause, etc.

advantage /əd'vɑːntɪdʒ/ ● *noun* beneficial feature; benefit, profit; (often + *over*) superiority; *Tennis* next point after deuce. ● *verb* (**-ging**) benefit, favour. □ **take advantage of** make good use of; exploit. □ **advantageous** /ædvən-'teɪdʒəs/ *adjective*.

Advent /'ædvent/ *noun* season before Christmas; coming of Christ; (**advent**) arrival.

Adventist *noun* member of sect believing in imminent second coming of Christ.

adventure /əd'ventʃə/ ● *noun* unusual and exciting experience; enterprise. ● *verb* (**-ring**) dare, venture. □ **adventure playground** one with climbing frames etc.

adventurer *noun* (*feminine* **adventuress**) person who seeks adventure esp. for personal gain or pleasure; financial speculator.

adventurous *adjective* venturesome, enterprising.

adverb /'ædvɜːb/ *noun* word indicating manner, degree, circumstance, etc. used to modify verb, adjective, or other adverb (see panel). □ **adverbial** /əd'vɜː-/ *adjective*.

adversary /'ædvəsərɪ/ *noun* (*plural* **-ies**) enemy; opponent. □ **adversarial** /-'seə-/ *adjective*.

adverse /'ædvɜːs/ *adjective* unfavourable; harmful. □ **adversely** *adverb*.

adversity /əd'vɜːsɪtɪ/ *noun* misfortune.

advert /'ædvɜːt/ *noun colloquial* advertisement.

advertise /'ædvətaɪz/ *verb* (**-sing**) promote publicly to increase sales; make generally known; seek to sell, fill (vacancy), or (+ *for*) buy or employ by notice in newspaper etc.

advertisement /əd'vɜːtɪsmənt/ *noun* public announcement advertising something; advertising.

advice /əd'vaɪs/ *noun* recommendation on how to act; information; notice of transaction.

advisable /əd'vaɪzəb(ə)l/ *adjective* to be recommended; expedient. □ **advisability** *noun*.

advise /əd'vaɪz/ *verb* (**-sing**) give advice (to); recommend; (usually + *of*, *that*) inform.

advisedly /əd'vaɪzɪdlɪ/ *adverb* deliberately.

adviser *noun* person who advises, esp. officially.

advisory /əd'vaɪzərɪ/ *adjective* giving advice.

advocaat /ædvə'kɑːt/ *noun* liqueur of eggs, sugar, and brandy.

advocacy /'ædvəkəsɪ/ *noun* support or argument for cause etc.

advocate ● *noun* /'ædvəkət/ (+ *of*) person who speaks in favour; person who pleads for another, esp. in law court. ● *verb* /'ædvəkeɪt/ (**-ting**) recommend by argument.

adze /ædz/ *noun* (*US* **adz**) axe with arched blade at right angles to handle.

aegis /'iːdʒɪs/ *noun* protection; support.

aeolian harp /iː'əʊliən/ *noun* (*US* **eolian harp**) stringed instrument sounding when wind passes through it.

aeon /'iːɒn/ *noun* (also **eon**) long or indefinite period; an age.

aerate /'eəreɪt/ *verb* (**-ting**) charge with carbon dioxide; expose to air. □ **aeration** *noun.*

aerial /'eərɪəl/ ● *noun* device for transmitting or receiving radio signals. ● *adjective* from the air; existing in the air; like air.

aero- *combining form* air; aircraft.

aerobatics /eərə'bætɪks/ *plural noun* feats of spectacular flying of aircraft; (treated as *singular*) performance of these.

aerobics /eə'rəʊbɪks/ *plural noun* vigorous exercises designed to increase oxygen intake. □ **aerobic** *adjective.*

aerodrome /'eərədrəʊm/ *noun* small airport or airfield.

aerodynamics /ˌeərəʊdaɪ'næmɪks/ *plural noun* (usually treated as *singular*) dynamics of solid bodies moving through air. □ **aerodynamic** *adjective.*

aerofoil /'eərəfɔɪl/ *noun* structure with curved surfaces (e.g. aircraft wing), designed to give lift in flight.

aeronautics /ˌeərəʊ'nɔːtɪks/ *plural noun* (usually treated as *singular*) science or practice of motion in the air. □ **aeronautical** *adjective.*

aeroplane /'eərəpleɪn/ *noun* powered heavier-than-air aircraft with wings.

aerosol /'eərəsɒl/ *noun* pressurized container releasing substance as fine spray.

aerospace /'eərəʊspeɪs/ *noun* earth's atmosphere and outer space; aviation in this.

aesthete /'iːsθiːt/ *noun* person who appreciates beauty.

aesthetic /iːs'θetɪk/ *adjective* of or sensitive to beauty; tasteful. □ **aesthetically** *adverb;* **aestheticism** /-sɪz(ə)m/ *noun.*

aetiology /iːtɪ'ɒlədʒɪ/ *noun* (*US* **etiology**) study of causation or of causes of disease. □ **aetiological** /-ə'lɒdʒ-/ *adjective.*

afar /ə'fɑː/ *adverb* at or to a distance.

affable /'æfəb(ə)l/ *adjective* friendly; courteous. □ **affability** *noun;* **affably** *adverb.*

....

Adverb

An adverb is used:

1 with a verb, to say:
    a how something happens, e.g. *He walks* quickly.
    b where something happens, e.g. *I live* here.
    c when something happens, e.g. *They visited us* yesterday.
    d how often something happens, e.g. *We usually have coffee.*

2 to strengthen or weaken the meaning of:
    a a verb, e.g. *He* really *meant it. I* almost *fell asleep.*
    b an adjective, e.g. *She is* very *clever. This is a* slightly *better result.*
    c another adverb, e.g. *It comes off* terribly *easily. The boys* nearly always *get home late.*

3 to add to the meaning of a whole sentence, e.g.
    He is probably *our best player.* Luckily, *no one was hurt.*

In writing or in formal speech, it is **incorrect** to use an adjective instead of an adverb. For example, use

    Do it *properly.*   and not   **Do it* proper.

but note that many words are both an adjective and an adverb, e.g.

adjective	adverb
a fast *horse*	He ran fast.
a long *time*	Have you been here long?

....

affair /əˈfeə/ *noun* matter, concern; love affair; *colloquial* thing, event; (in *plural*) business.

affect /əˈfekt/ *verb* produce effect on; (of disease etc.) attack; move emotionally; use for effect; pretend to feel; (+ *to do*) pretend.

■ **Usage** *Affect* is often confused with *effect*, which means 'to bring about'.

affectation /æfekˈteɪʃ(ə)n/ *noun* artificial manner; pretentious display.

affected *adjective* pretended; full of affectation.

affection /əˈfekʃ(ə)n/ *noun* goodwill, fond feeling; disease.

affectionate /əˈfekʃənət/ *adjective* loving. □ **affectionately** *adverb*.

affidavit /æfɪˈdeɪvɪt/ *noun* written statement on oath.

affiliate /əˈfɪlɪeɪt/ *verb* (**-ting**) (+ *to, with*) attach to, connect to, or adopt as member or branch.

affiliation *noun* affiliating, being affiliated. □ **affiliation order** legal order compelling supposed father to support illegitimate child.

affinity /əˈfɪnɪtɪ/ *noun* (*plural* **-ies**) attraction; relationship; resemblance; *Chemistry* tendency of substances to combine with others.

affirm /əˈfɜːm/ *verb* state as fact; make solemn declaration in place of oath. □ **affirmation** /æfəˈmeɪʃ(ə)n/ *noun*.

affirmative /əˈfɜːmətɪv/ ● *adjective* affirming, expressing approval. ● *noun* affirmative statement.

affix ● *verb* /əˈfɪks/ attach, fasten; add in writing. ● *noun* /ˈæfɪks/ addition; prefix; suffix.

afflict /əˈflɪkt/ *verb* distress physically or mentally.

affliction *noun* distress, suffering; cause of this.

affluent /ˈæfluənt/ *adjective* rich. □ **affluence** *noun*.

afford /əˈfɔːd/ *verb* (after *can, be able to*) have enough money, time, etc., for; be able to spare (time etc.); (+ *to do*) be in a position; provide.

afforest /əˈfɒrɪst/ *verb* convert into forest; plant with trees. □ **afforestation** *noun*.

affray /əˈfreɪ/ *noun* breach of peace by fighting or rioting in public.

affront /əˈfrʌnt/ ● *noun* open insult. ● *verb* insult openly; embarrass.

Afghan /ˈæfgæn/ ● *noun* native, national, or language of Afghanistan. ● *adjective* of Afghanistan. □ **Afghan hound** tall dog with long silky hair.

afield /əˈfiːld/ *adverb* to or at a distance.

aflame /əˈfleɪm/ *adverb & adjective* in flames; very excited.

afloat /əˈfləʊt/ *adverb & adjective* floating; at sea; out of debt.

afoot /əˈfʊt/ *adverb & adjective* in operation; progressing.

afore /əˈfɔː/ *preposition & adverb* archaic before.

afore- *combining form* previously.

aforethought *adjective* (after noun) premeditated.

a fortiori /eɪ fɔːtɪˈɔːraɪ/ *adverb & adjective* with stronger reason. [Latin]

afraid /əˈfreɪd/ *adjective* alarmed, frightened. □ **be afraid** *colloquial* politely regret.

afresh /əˈfreʃ/ *adverb* anew; with fresh start.

African /ˈæfrɪkən/ ● *noun* native of Africa; person of African descent. ● *adjective* of Africa.

Afrikaans /æfrɪˈkɑːns/ *noun* language derived from Dutch, used in S. Africa.

Afrikaner /æfrɪˈkɑːnə/ *noun* Afrikaans-speaking white person in S. Africa.

Afro /ˈæfrəʊ/ ● *adjective* (of hair) tightly-curled and bushy. ● *noun* (*plural* **-s**) Afro hairstyle.

Afro- *combining form* African.

aft /ɑːft/ *adverb* at or towards stern or tail.

after /ˈɑːftə/ ● *preposition* following in time; in view of; despite; behind; in pursuit or quest of; about, concerning; in allusion to or imitation of. ● *conjunction* later than. ● *adverb* later; behind. ● *adjective* later. □ **after all** in spite of everything; **afterbirth** placenta etc. discharged after childbirth; **aftercare** attention after leaving hospital etc.; **after-effect** delayed effect of accident etc.; **afterlife** life after death; **afters** *colloquial* sweet dessert; **aftershave** lotion applied to face after shaving; **afterthought** thing thought of or added later.

aftermath /'ɑːftəmæθ/ *noun* consequences.

afternoon /ɑːftə'nuːn/ *noun* time between midday and evening.

afterwards /'ɑːftəwədz/ *adverb* later, subsequently.

again /ə'gen/ *adverb* another time; as previously; in addition; on the other hand. □ **again and again** repeatedly.

against /ə'genst/ *preposition* in opposition to; into collision or in contact with; to the disadvantage of; in contrast to; in anticipation of; as compensating factor to; in return for.

agape /ə'geɪp/ *adjective* gaping.

agate /'ægət/ *noun* usually hard streaked chalcedony.

agave /ə'geɪvɪ/ *noun* spiny-leaved plant.

age • *noun* length of past life or existence; *colloquial* (often in *plural*) a long time; historical period; old age. • *verb* (**ageing**) (cause to) show signs of age; grow old; mature. □ **come of age** reach legal adult status; **under age** not old enough.

aged *adjective* /eɪdʒd/ of the age of; /'eɪdʒɪd/ old.

ageism /'eɪdʒɪz(ə)m/ *noun* prejudice or discrimination on grounds of age.

ageless /'eɪdʒlɪs/ *adjective* never growing or appearing old.

agency /'eɪdʒənsɪ/ *noun* (*plural* **-ies**) business or premises of agent; action; intervention.

agenda /ə'dʒendə/ *noun* (*plural* **-s**) list of items to be considered at meeting; things to be done.

agent /'eɪdʒ(ə)nt/ *noun* person acting for another in business etc.; person or thing producing effect.

agent provocateur /ɑːʒɑ̃ prəvɒkə'tɜː/ *noun* (*plural* **agents provocateurs** same pronunciation) person tempting suspected offenders to self-incriminating action. [French]

agglomerate /ə'glɒməreɪt/ *verb* (**-ting**) collect into mass. □ **agglomeration** *noun.*

agglutinate /ə'gluːtɪneɪt/ *verb* (**-ting**) stick as with glue. □ **agglutination** *noun;* **agglutinative** /-nətɪv/ *adjective.*

aggrandize /ə'grændaɪz/ *verb* (also **-ise**) (**-zing** or **-sing**) increase power, rank, or wealth of; make seem greater. □ **aggrandizement** /-dɪz-/ *noun.*

aggravate /'ægrəveɪt/ *verb* (**-ting**) increase seriousness of; *colloquial* annoy. □ **aggravation** *noun.*

■ **Usage** The use of *aggravate* to mean 'annoy' is considered incorrect by some people, but it is common in informal use.

aggregate • *noun* /'ægrɪgət/ sum total; crushed stone etc. used in making concrete. • *adjective* /'ægrɪgət/ collective, total. • *verb* /'ægrɪgeɪt/ collect together, unite; *colloquial* amount to. □ **aggregation** *noun.*

aggression /ə'greʃ(ə)n/ *noun* unprovoked attack; hostile act or feeling. □ **aggressor** *noun.*

aggressive /ə'gresɪv/ *adjective* given to aggression; forceful, self-assertive. □ **aggressively** *adverb.*

aggrieved /ə'griːvd/ *adjective* having grievance.

aggro /'ægrəʊ/ *noun slang* aggression; difficulty.

aghast /ə'gɑːst/ *adjective* amazed and horrified.

agile /'ædʒaɪl/ *adjective* quick-moving; nimble. □ **agility** /ə'dʒɪlɪtɪ/ *noun.*

agitate /'ædʒɪteɪt/ *verb* (**-ting**) disturb, excite; (often + *for, against*) campaign, esp. politically; shake briskly. □ **agitation** *noun*; **agitator** *noun.*

AGM *abbreviation* annual general meeting.

agnail /'ægneɪl/ *noun* torn skin at root of fingernail; resulting soreness.

agnostic /æg'nɒstɪk/ • *noun* person who believes that existence of God is not provable. • *adjective* of agnosticism. □ **agnosticism** /-sɪz(ə)m/ *noun.*

ago /ə'gəʊ/ *adverb* in the past.

agog /ə'gɒg/ *adjective* eager, expectant.

agonize /'ægənaɪz/ *verb* (also **-ise**) (**-zing** or **-sing**) undergo mental anguish; (cause to) suffer agony; (as **agonized** *adjective*) expressing agony.

agony /'ægənɪ/ *noun* (*plural* **-ies**) extreme physical or mental suffering; severe struggle. □ **agony aunt** *colloquial* writer answering letters in **agony column** *colloquial*, section of magazine etc. offering personal advice.

agoraphobia /ˌægərəˈfəʊbɪə/ *noun* extreme fear of open spaces. □ **agoraphobic** *adjective*.

agrarian /əˈgreərɪən/ • *adjective* of land or its cultivation. • *noun* advocate of redistribution of land.

agree /əˈgriː/ *verb* (**-ees, -eed,**) (often + *with*) hold similar opinion, be or become in harmony, suit, be compatible; (+ *to do*) consent; reach agreement about.

agreeable *adjective* pleasing; willing to agree. □ **agreeably** *adverb*.

agreement *noun* act or state of agreeing; arrangement, contract.

agriculture /ˈægrɪkʌltʃə/ *noun* cultivation of the soil and rearing of animals. □ **agricultural** /-ˈkʌl-/ *adjective*; **agriculturalist** /-ˈkʌl-/ *noun*.

agronomy /əˈgrɒnəmɪ/ *noun* science of soil management and crop production. □ **agronomist** *noun*.

aground /əˈgraʊnd/ *adjective & adverb* on(to) bottom of shallow water.

ague /ˈeɪgjuː/ *noun* shivering fit; *historical* malarial fever.

ah /ɑː/ *interjection expressing surprise, pleasure, or realization.*

aha /ɑːˈhɑː/ *interjection expressing surprise, triumph, mockery, etc.*

ahead /əˈhed/ *adverb* in advance, in front; (often + *on*) in the lead (on points etc.).

ahoy /əˈhɔɪ/ *interjection Nautical* call used in hailing.

AI *abbreviation* artificial insemination; artificial intelligence.

aid • *noun* help; person or thing that helps. • *verb* help; promote (recovery etc.). □ **in aid of** in support of, *colloquial* for purpose of.

aide /eɪd/ *noun* aide-de-camp; assistant.

aide-de-camp /eɪd də ˈkɑ̃/ *noun* (*plural* **aides-** same pronunciation) officer assisting senior officer.

Aids *noun* (also **AIDS**) acquired immune deficiency syndrome.

ail *verb* be ill or in poor condition.

aileron /ˈeɪlərɒn/ *noun* hinged flap on aircraft wing.

ailment *noun* illness, esp. minor one.

aim • *verb* intend, try; (usually + *at*) direct, point; take aim. • *noun* purpose, object; directing of weapon etc. at object. □ **take aim** direct weapon etc. at object.

aimless *adjective* purposeless. □ **aimlessly** *adverb*.

ain't /eɪnt/ *colloquial* am not, is not, are not; has not, have not.

■ **Usage** The use of *ain't* is incorrect in standard English.

air • *noun* mixture chiefly of oxygen and nitrogen surrounding earth; open space; earth's atmosphere, often as place where aircraft operate; appearance, manner; (in *plural*) affected manner; tune. • *verb* expose (room, clothes, etc.) to air, ventilate; express and discuss publicly. □ **airbase** base for military aircraft; **air-bed** inflatable mattress; **airborne** transported by air, (of aircraft) in the air; **airbrick** brick perforated for ventilation; **Air Commodore** RAF officer next above Group Captain; **air-conditioned** *adjective* equipped with **air-conditioning**, regulation of humidity and temperature in building, apparatus for this; **airfield** area with runway(s) for aircraft; **air force** branch of armed forces fighting in the air; **airgun** gun using compressed air to fire pellets; **air hostess** stewardess in aircraft; **air letter** sheet of paper forming airmail letter; **airlift** *noun* emergency transport of supplies etc. by air, *verb* transport thus; **airline** public air transport company; **airliner** large passenger aircraft; **airlock** stoppage of flow by air bubble in pipe etc., compartment giving access to pressurized chamber; **airmail** system of transporting mail by air, mail carried thus; **airman** pilot or member of aircraft crew; **Air (Chief, Vice-) Marshal** high ranks in RAF; **airplane** *US* aeroplane; **airport** airfield with facilities for passengers and cargo; **air raid** attack by aircraft; **air rifle** rifle using compressed air to fire pellets; **airs and graces** affected manner; **airship** powered aircraft lighter than air; **airsick** nauseous from air travel; **airspace** air above a country; **air speed** aircraft's speed relative to air; **airstrip** strip of ground for take-off and landing of aircraft; **air terminal** building with transport to and from airport; **air traffic**

controller official who controls air traffic by radio; **airway** recognized route of aircraft, passage for air into lungs; **airwoman** woman pilot or member of aircraft crew; **by air** by or in aircraft; **on the air** being broadcast.

aircraft noun (plural same) aeroplane, helicopter. □ **aircraft carrier** warship that carries and acts as base for aircraft; **aircraftman, aircraftwoman** lowest rank in RAF.

Airedale /'eədeɪl/ noun terrier of large rough-coated breed.

airless adjective stuffy; still, calm.

airtight adjective impermeable to air.

airworthy adjective (of aircraft) fit to fly. □ **airworthiness** noun.

airy adjective (**-ier, -iest**) well-ventilated; flippant; light as air. □ **airy-fairy** colloquial unrealistic, impractical.

aisle /aɪl/ noun side part of church divided by pillars from nave; passage between rows of pews, seats, etc.

aitchbone /'eɪtʃbəʊn/ noun rump bone of animal; cut of beef over this.

ajar /ə'dʒɑː/ adverb & adjective (of door etc.) slightly open.

Akela /ɑː'keɪlə/ noun adult leader of Cub Scouts.

akimbo /ə'kɪmbəʊ/ adverb (of arms) with hands on hips and elbows out.

akin /ə'kɪn/ adjective related; similar.

alabaster /'æləbɑːstə/ ● noun translucent usually white form of gypsum. ● adjective of alabaster; white, smooth.

à la carte /æ lɑː 'kɑːt/ adverb & adjective with individually priced dishes.

alacrity /ə'lækrɪtɪ/ noun briskness; readiness.

à la mode /æ lɑː 'məʊd/ adverb & adjective in fashion; fashionable.

alarm /ə'lɑːm/ ● noun warning of danger etc.; warning sound or device; alarm clock; apprehension. ● verb frighten, disturb; warn. □ **alarm clock** clock that rings at set time. □ **alarming** adjective.

alarmist /ə'lɑːmɪst/ noun person spreading unnecessary alarm.

alas /ə'læs/ interjection expressing grief or regret.

alb noun long white vestment worn by Christian priests.

albatross /'ælbətrɒs/ noun long-winged seabird related to petrel; Golf score of 3 strokes under par for hole.

albeit /ɔːl'biːɪt/ conjunction although.

albino /æl'biːnəʊ/ noun (plural **-s**) person or animal lacking pigment in skin, hair, and eyes. □ **albinism** /'ælbɪnɪz(ə)m/ noun.

album /'ælbəm/ noun book for displaying photographs etc.; long-playing gramophone record; set of these.

albumen /'ælbjʊmɪn/ noun egg white.

albumin /'ælbjʊmɪn/ noun water-soluble protein found in egg white, milk, blood, etc.

alchemy /'ælkəmɪ/ noun medieval chemistry, esp. seeking to turn base metals into gold. □ **alchemist** noun.

alcohol /'ælkəhɒl/ noun colourless volatile liquid, esp. as intoxicant present in wine, beer, spirits, etc. and as a solvent, fuel, etc.; liquor containing this; other compound of this type.

alcoholic /ælkə'hɒlɪk/ ● adjective of, like, containing, or caused by alcohol. ● noun person suffering from alcoholism.

alcoholism /'ælkəhɒlɪz(ə)m/ noun condition resulting from addiction to alcohol.

alcove /'ælkəʊv/ noun recess in wall of room, garden, etc.

alder /'ɔːldə/ noun tree related to birch.

alderman /'ɔːldəmən/ noun esp. historical civic dignitary next in rank to mayor.

ale noun beer.

alert /ə'lɜːt/ ● adjective watchful. ● noun alarm; state or period of special vigilance. ● verb (often + to) warn.

alfalfa /æl'fælfə/ noun clover-like plant used for fodder.

alfresco /æl'freskəʊ/ adjective & adverb in the open air.

alga /'ælgə/ noun (plural **-gae** /-dʒiː/) (usually in plural) non-flowering stemless water plant.

algebra /'ældʒɪbrə/ noun branch of mathematics using letters to represent numbers. □ **algebraic** /-'breɪk/ adjective.

Algol /'ælgɒl/ noun high-level computer-programming language.

algorithm /'ælgərɪð(ə)m/ noun process or rules for (esp. computer) calculation etc.

alias /'eɪlɪəs/ ● *adverb* also known as. ● *noun* assumed name.

alibi /'ælɪbaɪ/ *noun* (*plural* **-s**) proof that one was elsewhere; excuse.

■ **Usage** The use of *alibi* to mean 'an excuse' is considered incorrect by some people.

alien /'eɪlɪən/ ● *adjective* (often + *to*) unfamiliar, repugnant; foreign; of beings from another world. ● *noun* non-naturalized foreigner; a being from another world.

alienate /'eɪlɪəneɪt/ *verb* (**-ting**) estrange; transfer ownership of. □ **alienation** *noun*.

alight¹ /ə'laɪt/ *adjective* on fire; lit up.

alight² /ə'laɪt/ *verb* (often + *from*) get down or off; come to earth, settle.

align /ə'laɪn/ *verb* place in or bring into line; (usually + *with*) ally (oneself etc.). □ **alignment** *noun*.

alike /ə'laɪk/ ● *adjective* similar, like. ● *adverb* in similar way.

alimentary /ælɪ'mentərɪ/ *adjective* concerning nutrition; nourishing. □ **alimentary canal** channel through which food passes during digestion.

alimony /'ælɪmənɪ/ *noun* money payable to a divorced or separated spouse.

alive /ə'laɪv/ *adjective* living; lively, active; (usually + *to*) alert to; (usually + *with*) swarming with.

alkali /'ælkəlaɪ/ *noun* (*plural* **-s**) substance that neutralizes acids, turns litmus blue, and forms caustic solutions in water. □ **alkaline** *adjective*; **alkalinity** /-'lɪn-/ *noun*.

alkaloid /'ælkəlɔɪd/ *noun* plant-based compound often used as drug, e.g. morphine, quinine.

all /ɔːl/ ● *adjective* whole amount, number, or extent of. ● *noun* all people or things concerned; (+ *of*) the whole of. ● *adverb* entirely, quite. □ **all along** from the beginning; **all but** very nearly; **all for** *colloquial* strongly in favour of; **all-clear** signal that danger or difficulty is over; **all fours** hands and knees; **all in** exhausted; **all-in** inclusive of all; **all in all** everything considered; **all out** (**all-out** before noun) involving all one's strength etc.; **all over** completely finished, in or on all parts of one's body;

all-purpose having many uses; **all right** satisfactory, safe and sound, in good condition, satisfactorily, I consent; **all-right** (before noun) *colloquial* acceptable; **all round** in all respects, for each person; **all-round** (of person) versatile; **all-rounder** versatile person; **All Saints' Day** 1 Nov.; **all the same** nevertheless; **all there** *colloquial* mentally alert or normal; **all together** all at once, all in one place; **at all** (with negative or in questions) in any way, to any extent; **in all** in total, altogether.

■ **Usage** See note at ALTOGETHER.

Allah /'ælə/ *noun*: Muslim name of God.

allay /ə'leɪ/ *verb* lessen; alleviate.

allege /ə'ledʒ/ *verb* declare, esp. without proof. □ **allegation** /ælɪ'geɪʃ(ə)n/ *noun*; **allegedly** /ə'ledʒɪdlɪ/ *adverb*.

allegiance /ə'liːdʒ(ə)ns/ *noun* loyalty; duty of subject.

allegory /'ælɪgərɪ/ *noun* (*plural* **-ies**) story with moral represented symbolically. □ **allegorical** /-'gɒr-/ *adjective*; **allegorize** *verb* (also **-ise**) (**-zing** or **-sing**).

allegretto /ælɪ'gretəʊ/ *Music* ● *adverb & adjective* in fairly brisk tempo. ● *noun* (*plural* **-s**) allegretto movement or passage.

allegro /ə'legrəʊ/ *Music* ● *adverb & adjective* in lively tempo. ● *noun* (*plural* **-s**) allegro movement or passage.

alleluia /ælɪ'luːjə/ (also **hallelujah** /hæl-/) ● *interjection* God be praised. ● *noun* (*plural* **-s**) song of praise to God.

allergic /ə'lɜːdʒɪk/ *adjective* (+ *to*) having allergy to, *colloquial* having strong dislike for; caused by allergy.

allergy /'ælədʒɪ/ *noun* (*plural* **-ies**) reaction to certain substances.

alleviate /ə'liːvɪeɪt/ *verb* (**-ting**) make (pain etc.) less severe. □ **alleviation** *noun*.

alley /'ælɪ/ *noun* (*plural* **-s**) narrow street or passage; enclosure for skittles, bowling, etc.

alliance /ə'laɪəns/ *noun* formal union or association of states, political parties, etc. or of families by marriage.

allied /'ælaɪd/ *adjective* connected or related; (also **Allied**) associated in an alliance.

alligator /'ælɪgeɪtə/ *noun* large reptile of crocodile family.

alliteration /əlɪtə'reɪʃ(ə)n/ noun recurrence of same initial letter or sound in adjacent or nearby words, as in *The fair breeze blew, the white foam flew, the furrow followed free.* □ **alliterate** /-'lɪt-/ verb; **alliterative** /ə'lɪtərətɪv/ adjective.

allocate /'æləkeɪt/ verb (**-ting**) (usually + *to*) assign. □ **allocation** noun.

allot /ə'lɒt/ verb (**-tt-**) apportion or distribute to (person).

allotment /ə'lɒtmənt/ noun small plot of land rented for cultivation; share; allotting.

allow /ə'laʊ/ verb (often + *to do*) permit; assign fixed sum to; (usually + *for*) provide or set aside for a purpose. □ **allow for** take into consideration.

allowance noun amount or sum allowed, esp. regularly; deduction, discount. □ **make allowances** (often + *for*) judge leniently.

alloy /'ælɔɪ/ ● noun mixture of metals; inferior metal mixed esp. with gold or silver. ● verb mix (metals); /ə'lɔɪ/ debase by admixture; spoil (pleasure).

allspice /'ɔːlspaɪs/ noun spice made from berry of pimento plant; this berry.

allude /ə'luːd/ verb (**-ding**) (+ *to*) make allusion to.

allure /ə'ljʊə/ ● verb (**-ring**) attract, charm, entice. ● noun attractiveness, charm. □ **allurement** noun.

allusion /ə'luːʒ(ə)n/ noun (often + *to*) passing or indirect reference. □ **allusive** /-sɪv/ adjective.

alluvium /ə'luːvɪəm/ noun (plural **-via**) deposit left by flood, esp. in river valley. □ **alluvial** adjective.

ally ● noun /'ælaɪ/ (plural **-ies**) state or person formally cooperating or united with another, esp. in war. ● verb (also /ə'laɪ/) (**-ies, -ied**) (often **ally oneself with**) combine in alliance (with).

Alma Mater /ælmə 'mɑːtə/ noun one's university, school, or college.

almanac /'ɔːlmənæk/ noun (also **almanack**) calendar, usually with astronomical data.

almighty /ɔːl'maɪtɪ/ ● adjective infinitely powerful; very great. ● noun (**the Almighty**) God.

almond /'ɑːmənd/ noun kernel of nutlike fruit related to plum; tree bearing this.

almoner /'ɑːmənə/ noun social worker attached to hospital.

almost /'ɔːlməʊst/ adverb all but, very nearly.

alms /ɑːmz/ plural noun historical donation of money or food to the poor. □ **almshouse** charitable institution for the poor.

aloe /'æləʊ/ noun plant with toothed fleshy leaves; (in plural) strong laxative from aloe juice. □ **aloe vera** /'vɪərə/ variety yielding substance used in cosmetics; this substance.

aloft /ə'lɒft/ adjective & adverb high up, overhead.

alone /ə'ləʊn/ ● adjective without company or help; lonely. ● adverb only, exclusively.

along /ə'lɒŋ/ ● preposition beside or through (part of) the length of. ● adverb onward, into more advanced state; with oneself or others; beside or through (part of) thing's length. □ **alongside** at or close to side (of); **along with** in addition to.

aloof /ə'luːf/ ● adjective unconcerned, unsympathetic. ● adverb away, apart.

aloud /ə'laʊd/ adverb audibly.

alp noun high mountain, esp. (**the Alps**) those in Switzerland and adjacent countries.

alpaca /æl'pækə/ noun S. American llama-like animal; its long wool; fabric made from this.

alpha /'ælfə/ noun first letter of Greek alphabet (A, α). □ **alpha and omega** beginning and end; **alpha particle** helium nucleus emitted by radioactive substance.

alphabet /'ælfəbet/ noun set of letters or signs used in a language. □ **alphabetical** /-'bet-/ adjective.

alphanumeric /ælfənjuː'merɪk/ adjective containing both letters and numbers.

alpine /'ælpaɪn/ ● adjective of high mountains or (**Alpine**) the Alps. ● noun plant suited to mountain regions; = rock plant.

already /ɔːl'redɪ/ adverb before the time in question; as early as this.

alright adverb = ALL RIGHT.

■ **Usage** Although *alright* is widely used, it is not correct in standard English.

Alsatian /æl'seɪʃ(ə)n/ noun large dog of a breed of wolfhound.

also /'ɔːlsəʊ/ adverb in addition, besides. □ **also-ran** loser in race, undistinguished person.

altar /'ɔːltə/ noun flat table or block for offerings to deity; Communion table.

alter /'ɔːltə/ verb change in character, shape, etc. □ **alteration** noun.

altercation /ɔːltə'keɪʃ(ə)n/ noun dispute, wrangle.

alternate • adjective /ɔːl'tɜːnət/ (with noun in plural) every other; (of things of two kinds) alternating. • verb /'ɔːltəneɪt/ (-ting) (often + with) arrange or occur by turns; (+ between) go repeatedly from one to another. □ **alternating current** electric current regularly reversing direction. □ **alternately** adverb; **alternation** noun.

■ **Usage** See note at ALTERNATIVE.

alternative /ɔːl'tɜːnətɪv/ • adjective available as another choice; unconventional. • noun any of two or more possibilities; choice. □ **alternatively** adverb.

■ **Usage** The adjective alternative is often confused with alternate, which is correctly used in 'there will be a dance on alternate Saturdays'.

alternator /'ɔːltəneɪtə/ noun dynamo generating alternating current.

although /ɔːl'ðəʊ/ conjunction though.

altimeter /'æltɪmiːtə/ noun instrument measuring altitude.

altitude /'æltɪtjuːd/ noun height, esp. of object above sea level or horizon.

alto /'æltəʊ/ • noun (plural **-s**) = CONTRALTO; highest adult male singing voice; singer with this. • adjective having range of alto.

altogether /ɔːltə'geðə/ adverb totally; on the whole; in total.

■ **Usage** Note that altogether means 'in total', as in six rooms altogether, whereas all together means 'all at once' or 'all in one place' as in six rooms all together.

altruism /'æltruːɪz(ə)m/ noun unselfishness as principle of action. □ **altruist** noun; **altruistic** /-'ɪs-/ adjective.

alumina /ə'luːmɪnə/ noun aluminium oxide; emery.

aluminium /æljʊ'mɪnɪəm/ noun (US **aluminum** /ə'luːmɪnəm/) a light silvery metallic element.

alumnus /ə'lʌmnəs/ noun (plural **-ni** /-naɪ/) former pupil or student.

always /'ɔːlweɪz/ adverb at all times; whatever the circumstances; repeatedly.

Alzheimer's disease /'æltshaɪməz/ noun brain disorder causing senility.

AM abbreviation amplitude modulation.

am 1st singular present of BE.

a.m. abbreviation before noon (ante meridiem).

amalgam /ə'mælgəm/ noun mixture, blend; alloy of any metal with mercury.

amalgamate /ə'mælgəmeɪt/ verb (-ting) mix; unite. □ **amalgamation** noun.

amanuensis /əmænjʊ'ensɪs/ noun (plural **-enses** /-siːz/) assistant, esp. writing from dictation.

amaranth /'æmərænθ/ noun plant with green, red, or purple flowers; imaginary unfading flower. □ **amaranthine** /-'rænθaɪn/ adjective.

amaryllis /æmə'rɪlɪs/ noun plant with lily-like flowers.

amass /ə'mæs/ verb heap together, accumulate.

amateur /'æmətə/ noun person engaging in pursuit as pastime not profession; person with limited skill. □ **amateurish** adjective; **amateurism** noun.

amatory /'æmətərɪ/ adjective of sexual love.

amaze /ə'meɪz/ verb (-zing) fill with surprise or wonder. □ **amazement** noun; **amazing** adjective.

Amazon /'æməzən/ noun one of a mythical race of female warriors; (**amazon**) strong or athletic woman. □ **Amazonian** /-'zəʊ-/ adjective.

ambassador /æm'bæsədə/ noun diplomat living abroad as representative of his or her country; promoter. □ **ambassadorial** /-'dɔː-/ adjective.

amber /'æmbə/ • noun yellow translucent fossil resin; colour of this. • adjective of or like amber.

ambergris /'æmbəgriːs/ noun waxlike substance from sperm whale, used in perfumes.

ambidextrous /æmbɪ'dekstrəs/ *adjective* able to use either hand equally well.

ambience /'æmbɪəns/ *noun* surroundings, atmosphere.

ambient /'æmbɪənt/ *adjective* surrounding.

ambiguous /æm'bɪgjʊəs/ *adjective* having a double meaning; difficult to classify. □ **ambiguity** /-'gju:-/ *noun* (*plural* **-ies**).

ambit /'æmbɪt/ *noun* scope, bounds.

ambition /æm'bɪʃ(ə)n/ *noun* determination to succeed; object of this.

ambitious *adjective* full of ambition.

ambivalent /æm'bɪvələnt/ *adjective* having mixed feelings towards person or thing. □ **ambivalence** *noun*.

amble /'æmb(ə)l/ ● *verb* (**-ling**) walk at leisurely pace. ● *noun* leisurely pace.

ambrosia /æm'brəʊzɪə/ *noun* food of the gods in classical mythology; delicious food etc.

ambulance /'æmbjʊləns/ *noun* vehicle for taking patients to hospital; mobile army hospital.

ambulatory /'æmbjʊlətərɪ/ *adjective* of or for walking.

ambuscade /æmbəs'keɪd/ *noun & verb* (**-ding**) ambush.

ambush /'æmbʊʃ/ ● *noun* surprise attack by people hiding; hiding place for this. ● *verb* attack from ambush; waylay.

ameliorate /ə'mi:lɪəreɪt/ *verb* (**-ting**) make or become better. □ **amelioration** *noun*, **ameliorative** /-rətɪv/ *adjective*.

amen /ɑ:'men/ *interjection* (esp. at end of prayer) so be it.

amenable /ə'mi:nəb(ə)l/ *adjective* responsive, docile; (often + *to*) answerable (to law etc.).

amend /ə'mend/ *verb* correct error in; make minor alterations in.

amendment *noun* minor alteration or addition in document etc.

amends *noun* □ **make amends** (often + *for*) give compensation.

amenity /ə'mi:nɪtɪ/ *noun* (*plural* **-ies**) pleasant or useful feature or facility; pleasantness (of a place etc.).

American /ə'merɪkən/ ● *adjective* of America, esp. the US. ● *noun* native, citizen, or inhabitant of America, esp. the US; English as spoken in the US.

□ **Americanize** *verb* (also **-ise**) (**-zing** or **-sing**).

Americanism *noun* word etc. of US origin or usage.

amethyst /'æməθɪst/ *noun* purple or violet semiprecious stone.

amiable /'eɪmɪəb(ə)l/ *adjective* friendly and pleasant, likeable. □ **amiability** *noun*; **amiably** *adverb*.

amicable /'æmɪkəb(ə)l/ *adjective* friendly. □ **amicably** *adverb*.

amid /ə'mɪd/ *preposition* in the middle of.

amidships /ə'mɪdʃɪps/ *adverb* in(to) the middle of a ship.

amidst /ə'mɪdst/ = AMID.

amino acid /ə'mi:nəʊ/ *noun* organic acid found in proteins.

amir = EMIR.

amiss /ə'mɪs/ ● *adjective* out of order, wrong. ● *adverb* wrong(ly), inappropriately. □ **take amiss** be offended by.

amity /'æmɪtɪ/ *noun* friendship.

ammeter /'æmɪtə/ *noun* instrument for measuring electric current.

ammo /'æməʊ/ *noun* slang ammunition.

ammonia /ə'məʊnɪə/ *noun* pungent strongly alkaline gas; solution of this in water.

ammonite /'æmənaɪt/ *noun* coil-shaped fossil shell.

ammunition /æmjʊ'nɪʃ(ə)n/ *noun* bullets, shells, grenades, etc.; information usable in argument.

amnesia /æm'ni:zɪə/ *noun* loss of memory. □ **amnesiac** *adjective & noun*.

amnesty /'æmnɪstɪ/ *noun* (*plural* **-ies**) general pardon, esp. for political offences.

amniocentesis /æmnɪəʊsen'ti:sɪs/ *noun* (*plural* **-teses** /-si:z/) sampling of amniotic fluid to detect foetal abnormality.

amniotic fluid /æmnɪ'ɒtɪk/ *noun* fluid surrounding embryo.

amoeba /ə'mi:bə/ *noun* (*plural* **-s**) microscopic single-celled organism living in water.

amok /ə'mɒk/ *adverb* □ **run amok**, **amuck** /ə'mʌk/ run wild.

among /ə'mʌŋ/ *preposition* (also **amongst**) surrounded by; included in or in the category of; from the joint resources of; between.

amoral /eɪˈmɒr(ə)l/ *adjective* beyond morality; without moral principles.

amorous /ˈæmərəs/ *adjective* showing or feeling sexual love.

amorphous /əˈmɔːfəs/ *adjective* of no definite shape; vague; non-crystalline.

amount /əˈmaʊnt/ • *noun* total number, size, value, extent, etc. • *verb* (+ *to*) be equivalent in number, size, etc. to.

amour /əˈmʊə/ *noun* (esp. secret) love affair.

amp *noun* ampere; *colloquial* amplifier.

ampere /ˈæmpeə/ *noun* SI unit of electric current.

ampersand /ˈæmpəsænd/ *noun* the sign '&' (= *and*).

amphetamine /æmˈfetəmiːn/ *noun* synthetic stimulant drug.

amphibian /æmˈfɪbɪən/ *noun* amphibious animal or vehicle.

amphibious /æmˈfɪbɪəs/ *adjective* living or operating on land and in water; involving military forces landed from the sea.

amphitheatre /ˈæmfɪθɪətə/ *noun* round open building with tiers of seats surrounding central space.

amphora /ˈæmfərə/ *noun* (*plural* -rae /-riː/) Greek or Roman two-handled jar.

ample /ˈæmp(ə)l/ *adjective* (-r, -st) plentiful, extensive; more than enough. □ **amply** *adverb*.

amplifier /ˈæmplɪfaɪə/ *noun* device for amplifying sounds or electrical signals.

amplify /ˈæmplɪfaɪ/ *verb* (-ies, -ied) increase strength of (sound or electrical signal); add details to (story etc.). □ **amplification** *noun*.

amplitude /ˈæmplɪtjuːd/ *noun* spaciousness; maximum departure from average of oscillation, alternating current, etc. □ **amplitude modulation** modulation of a wave by variation of its amplitude.

ampoule /ˈæmpuːl/ *noun* small sealed capsule holding solution for injection.

amputate /ˈæmpjʊteɪt/ *verb* (-ting) cut off surgically (limb etc.). □ **amputation** *noun*; **amputee** /-ˈtiː/ *noun*.

amuck = AMOK.

amulet /ˈæmjʊlɪt/ *noun* charm worn against evil.

amuse /əˈmjuːz/ *verb* (-sing) cause to laugh or smile; interest, occupy. □ **amusing** *adjective*.

amusement *noun* being amused; thing that amuses, esp. device for entertainment at fairground etc. □ **amusement arcade** indoor area with slot machines etc.

an see A.

anabolic steroid /ænəˈbɒlɪk/ *noun* synthetic steroid hormone used to build muscle.

anachronism /əˈnækrənɪz(ə)m/ *noun* attribution of custom, event, etc. to wrong period; thing thus attributed; out-of-date person or thing. □ **anachronistic** /-ˈnɪs-/ *adjective*.

anaconda /ænəˈkɒndə/ *noun* large S. American constrictor.

anaemia /əˈniːmɪə/ *noun* (*US* **anemia**) deficiency of red blood cells or their haemoglobin, causing pallor and listlessness. □ **anaemic** *adjective*.

anaesthesia /ænɪsˈθiːzɪə/ *noun* (*US* **anes-**) artificially induced insensibility to pain.

anaesthetic /ænɪsˈθetɪk/ (*US* **anes-**) • *noun* drug, gas, etc., producing anaesthesia. • *adjective* producing anaesthesia.

anaesthetist /əˈniːsθətɪst/ *noun* (*US* **anes-**) person who administers anaesthetics.

anaesthetize /əˈniːsθətaɪz/ *verb* (also **-ise**; *US* also **anes-**) (-zing or -sing) administer anaesthetic to.

anagram /ˈænəgræm/ *noun* word or phrase formed by transposing letters of another.

anal /ˈeɪn(ə)l/ *adjective* of the anus.

analgesia /ænəlˈdʒiːzɪə/ *noun* absence or relief of pain.

analgesic /ænəlˈdʒiːsɪk/ • *noun* pain-killing drug. • *adjective* pain-killing.

analogous /əˈnæləgəs/ *adjective* (usually + *to*) partially similar or parallel.

analogue /ˈænəlɒg/ (*US* **analog**) • *noun* analogous thing. • *adjective* (of computer (usually **analog**), watch, etc.) using physical variables (e.g. voltage, position of hands) to represent numbers.

analogy /əˈnælədʒɪ/ *noun* (*plural* **-ies**) correspondence, similarity; reasoning from parallel cases.

analyse /ˈænəlaɪz/ *verb* (**-sing**) (*US* **analyze**; **-zing**) perform analysis on.

analysis /əˈnælɪsɪs/ *noun* (*plural* **-lyses** /-siːz/) detailed examination; *Chemistry* determination of constituent parts; psychoanalysis.

analyst /ˈænəlɪst/ *noun* person who analyses.

analytical /ænəˈlɪtɪkəl/ *adjective* (also **analytic**) of or using analysis.

analyze *US* = ANALYSE.

anarchism /ˈænəkɪz(ə)m/ *noun* belief that government and law should be abolished. □ **anarchist** *noun*; **anarchistic** /-ˈkɪstɪk/ *adjective*.

anarchy /ˈænəkɪ/ *noun* disorder, esp. political. □ **anarchic** /əˈnɑːkɪk/ *adjective*.

anathema /əˈnæθəmə/ *noun* (*plural* **-s**) detested thing; Church's curse.

anatomy /əˈnætəmɪ/ *noun* (*plural* **-ies**) (science of) animal or plant structure. □ **anatomical** /ænəˈtɒmɪk(ə)l/ *adjective*; **anatomist** *noun*.

anatto = ANNATTO.

ANC *abbreviation* African National Congress.

ancestor /ˈænsestə/ *noun* person, animal, or plant from which another has descended or evolved; prototype.

ancestral /ænˈsestr(ə)l/ *adjective* inherited from ancestors.

ancestry /ˈænsestrɪ/ *noun* (*plural* **-ies**) lineage; ancestors collectively.

anchor /ˈæŋkə/ ● *noun* metal device used to moor ship to sea-bottom. ● *verb* secure with anchor; fix firmly; cast anchor. □ **anchorman** coordinator, esp. compère in broadcast.

anchorage /ˈæŋkərɪdʒ/ *noun* place for anchoring; lying at anchor.

anchorite /ˈæŋkəraɪt/ *noun* hermit, recluse.

anchovy /ˈæntʃəvɪ/ *noun* (*plural* **-ies**) small strong-flavoured fish of herring family.

ancien régime /ɑ̃sjæ̃ reˈʒiːm/ *noun* superseded regime, esp. that of pre-Revolutionary France. [French]

ancient /ˈeɪnʃ(ə)nt/ *adjective* of times long past; very old.

ancillary /ænˈsɪlərɪ/ ● *adjective* subsidiary, auxiliary; (esp. of health workers) providing essential support.

● *noun* (*plural* **-ies**) auxiliary; ancillary worker.

and *conjunction* connecting words, clauses, or sentences.

andante /ænˈdæntɪ/ *Music* ● *adverb & adjective* in moderately slow time. ● *noun* andante movement or passage.

androgynous /ænˈdrɒdʒɪnəs/ *adjective* hermaphrodite.

android /ˈændrɔɪd/ *noun* robot with human appearance.

anecdote /ˈænɪkdəʊt/ *noun* short, esp. true, story. □ **anecdotal** /-ˈdəʊt(ə)l/ *adjective*.

anemia *US* = ANAEMIA.

anemic *US* = ANAEMIC.

anemometer /ænɪˈmɒmɪtə/ *noun* instrument for measuring wind force.

anemone /əˈneməni/ *noun* plant related to buttercup.

aneroid barometer /ˈænərɔɪd/ *noun* barometer that measures air pressure by registering its action on lid of box containing vacuum.

anesthesia etc. *US* = ANAESTHESIA etc.

aneurysm /ˈænjʊrɪz(ə)m/ *noun* (also **aneurism**) excessive enlargement of artery.

anew /əˈnjuː/ *adverb* again; in different way.

angel /ˈeɪndʒ(ə)l/ *noun* attendant or messenger of God usually represented as human with wings; kind or virtuous person. □ **angel cake** light sponge cake; **angelfish** small fish with winglike fins. □ **angelic** /ænˈdʒelɪk/ *adjective*; **angelically** *adverb*.

angelica /ænˈdʒelɪkə/ *noun* aromatic plant; its candied stalks.

angelus /ˈændʒɪləs/ *noun* RC prayers said at morning, noon, and sunset; bell rung for this.

anger /ˈæŋgə/ ● *noun* extreme displeasure. ● *verb* make angry.

angina /ænˈdʒaɪnə/ *noun* (in full **angina pectoris**) chest pain brought on by exertion, owing to poor blood supply to heart.

angle[1] /ˈæŋg(ə)l/ ● *noun* space between two meeting lines or surfaces, esp. as measured in degrees; corner; point of view. ● *verb* (**-ling**) move or place obliquely; present (information) in biased way.

angle² /'æŋg(ə)l/ *verb* (**-ling**) fish with line and hook; (+ *for*) seek objective indirectly. □ **angler** *noun*.

Anglican /'æŋglɪkən/ ● *adjective* of Church of England. ● *noun* member of Anglican Church. □ **Anglicanism** *noun*.

Anglicism /'æŋglɪsɪz(ə)m/ *noun* English expression or custom.

Anglicize /'æŋglɪsaɪz/ *verb* (also **-ise**) (**-zing** or **-sing**) make English in character etc.

Anglo- *combining form* English or British (and).

Anglo-Catholic /æŋgləʊ'kæθəlɪk/ ● *adjective* of High Church Anglican group emphasizing its Catholic tradition. ● *noun* member of this group.

Anglo-Indian /æŋgləʊ'ɪndɪən/ ● *adjective* of England and India; of British descent but Indian residence. ● *noun* Anglo-Indian person.

Anglophile /'æŋgləʊfaɪl/ *noun* admirer of England or the English.

Anglo-Saxon /æŋgləʊ'sæks(ə)n/ ● *adjective* of English Saxons before Norman Conquest; of English descent. ● *noun* Anglo-Saxon person or language; *colloquial* plain (esp. crude) English.

angora /æŋ'gɔːrə/ *noun* fabric made from hair of angora goat or rabbit. □ **angora cat**, **goat**, **rabbit** long-haired varieties.

angostura /æŋgə'stjʊərə/ *noun* aromatic bitter bark of S. American tree.

angry /'æŋgrɪ/ *adjective* (**-ier**, **-iest**) feeling or showing anger; (of wound etc.) inflamed, painful. □ **angrily** *adverb*.

angst /æŋst/ *noun* anxiety, neurotic fear; guilt.

angstrom /'æŋstrəm/ *noun* unit of wavelength measurement.

anguish /'æŋgwɪʃ/ *noun* severe mental or physical pain. □ **anguished** *adjective*.

angular /'æŋgjʊlə/ *adjective* having sharp corners or (of person) features; (of distance) measured by angle. □ **angularity** /-'lær-/ *noun*.

aniline /'ænɪliːn/ *noun* colourless oily liquid used in dyes, drugs, and plastics.

animadvert /ænɪmæd'vɜːt/ *verb* (+ *on*) *literary* criticize, censure. □ **animadversion** *noun*.

animal /'ænɪm(ə)l/ ● *noun* living organism, esp. other than man, having sensation and usually ability to move; brutish person. ● *adjective* of or like animal; carnal.

animality /ænɪ'mælɪtɪ/ *noun* the animal world; animal behaviour.

animate ● *adjective* /'ænɪmət/ having life; lively. ● *verb* /'ænɪmeɪt/ (**-ting**) enliven; give life to.

animated /'ænɪmeɪtɪd/ *adjective* lively; living; (of film) using animation.

animation /ænɪ'meɪʃ(ə)n/ *noun* liveliness; being alive; technique of film-making by photographing sequence of drawings or positions of puppets etc. to create illusion of movement.

animator /'ænɪmeɪtə/ *noun* artist who prepares animated films.

animism /'ænɪmɪz(ə)m/ *noun* belief that inanimate objects and natural phenomena have souls. □ **animist** *noun*; **animistic** /-'mɪs-/ *adjective*.

animosity /ænɪ'mɒsɪtɪ/ *noun* (*plural* **-ies**) hostility.

animus /'ænɪməs/ *noun* hostility, ill feeling.

anion /'ænaɪən/ *noun* negatively charged ion.

anise /'ænɪs/ *noun* plant with aromatic seeds.

aniseed /'ænɪsiːd/ *noun* seed of anise.

ankle /'æŋk(ə)l/ *noun* joint connecting foot with leg.

anklet /'æŋklɪt/ *noun* ornament worn round ankle.

ankylosis /æŋkɪ'ləʊsɪs/ *noun* stiffening of joint by fusing of bones.

annals /'æn(ə)lz/ *plural noun* narrative of events year by year; historical records. □ **annalist** *noun*.

annatto /ə'nætəʊ/ *noun* (also **anatto**) orange-red food colouring made from tropical fruit.

anneal /ə'niːl/ *verb* heat (metal, glass) and cool slowly, esp. to toughen.

annelid /'ænəlɪd/ *noun* segmented worm, e.g. earthworm.

annex /æ'neks/ *verb* (often + *to*) add as subordinate part; take possession of. □ **annexation** *noun*.

annexe /'æneks/ *noun* supplementary building.

annihilate /əˈnaɪəleɪt/ *verb* (**-ting**) destroy utterly. □ **annihilation** *noun*.

anniversary /ænɪˈvɜːsərɪ/ *noun* (*plural* **-ies**) yearly return of date of event; celebration of this.

Anno Domini /ænəʊ ˈdɒmɪnaɪ/ see AD.

annotate /ˈænəteɪt/ *verb* (**-ting**) add explanatory notes to. □ **annotation** *noun*.

announce /əˈnaʊns/ *verb* (**-cing**) make publicly known; make known the approach of. □ **announcement** *noun*.

announcer *noun* person who announces, esp. in broadcasting.

annoy /əˈnɔɪ/ *verb* (often in *passive* + *at*, *with*) anger or distress slightly; harass. □ **annoyance** *noun*.

annual /ˈænjʊəl/ ● *adjective* reckoned by the year; recurring yearly. ● *noun* book etc. published yearly; plant living only one year. □ **annually** *adverb*.

annuity /əˈnjuːɪtɪ/ *noun* (*plural* **-ies**) yearly grant or allowance; investment yielding fixed annual sum for stated period.

annul /əˈnʌl/ *verb* (**-ll-**) declare invalid; cancel, abolish. □ **annulment** *noun*.

annular /ˈænjʊlə/ *adjective* ring-shaped.

annulate /ˈænjʊlət/ *adjective* marked with or formed of rings.

annunciation /ənʌnsɪˈeɪʃ(ə)n/ *noun* announcement, esp. (**Annunciation**) that made by the angel Gabriel to Mary.

anode /ˈænəʊd/ *noun* positive electrode.

anodize /ˈænədaɪz/ *verb* (also **-ise**) (**-zing** or **-sing**) coat (metal) with protective layer by electrolysis.

anodyne /ˈænədaɪn/ ● *adjective* pain-relieving; soothing. ● *noun* anodyne drug etc.

anoint /əˈnɔɪnt/ *verb* apply oil or ointment to, esp. ritually.

anomalous /əˈnɒmələs/ *adjective* irregular, abnormal.

anomaly /əˈnɒməlɪ/ *noun* (*plural* **-ies**) anomalous thing.

anon /əˈnɒn/ *adverb archaic* soon.

anon. *abbreviation* anonymous.

anonymous /əˈnɒnɪməs/ *adjective* of unknown name or authorship; featureless. □ **anonymity** /ænəˈnɪm-/ *noun*.

anorak /ˈænəræk/ *noun* waterproof usually hooded jacket.

anorexia /ænəˈreksɪə/ *noun* lack of appetite, esp. (in full **anorexia nervosa** /nɜːˈvəʊsə/) obsessive desire to lose weight by refusing to eat. □ **anorexic** *adjective & noun*.

another /əˈnʌðə/ ● *adjective* an additional or different. ● *pronoun* an additional or different person or thing.

answer /ˈɑːnsə/ ● *noun* something said or done in reaction to a question, statement, or circumstance; solution to problem. ● *verb* make an answer or response (to); suit; (+ *to*, *for*) be responsible to or for; (+ *to*) correspond to (esp. description). □ **answer back** answer insolently; **answering machine**, **answerphone** tape recorder which answers telephone calls and takes messages.

answerable *adjective* (usually + *to*, *for*) responsible; that can be answered.

ant *noun* small usually wingless insect living in complex social group. □ **anteater** mammal feeding on ants; **anthill** moundlike ants' nest.

antacid /ænˈtæsɪd/ *noun & adjective* preventive or corrective of acidity.

antagonism /ænˈtæɡənɪz(ə)m/ *noun* active hostility.

antagonist /ænˈtæɡənɪst/ *noun* opponent. □ **antagonistic** /-ˈnɪs-/ *adjective*.

antagonize /ænˈtæɡənaɪz/ *verb* (also **-ise**) (**-zing** or **-sing**) provoke.

Antarctic /ænˈtɑːktɪk/ ● *adjective* of south polar region. ● *noun* this region.

ante /ˈæntɪ/ *noun* stake put up by poker player before receiving cards; amount payable in advance.

ante- /ˈæntɪ/ *prefix* before.

antecedent /æntɪˈsiːd(ə)nt/ ● *noun* preceding thing or circumstance; *Grammar* word, phrase, etc., to which another word refers; (in *plural*) person's ancestors. ● *adjective* previous.

antechamber /ˈæntɪtʃeɪmbə/ *noun* ante-room.

antedate /æntɪˈdeɪt/ *verb* (**-ting**) precede in time; give earlier than true date to.

antediluvian /æntɪdɪˈluːvɪən/ *adjective* before the Flood; *colloquial* very old.

antelope /ˈæntɪləʊp/ *noun* (*plural* same or **-s**) swift deerlike animal.

antenatal /æntɪˈneɪt(ə)l/ *adjective* before birth; of pregnancy.

antenna /æn'tenə/ noun (plural **-tennae** /-niː/) each of pair of feelers on head of insect or crustacean; (plural **-s**) aerial.

anterior /æn'tɪərɪə/ adjective nearer the front; (often + to) prior.

ante-room /'æntɪruːm/ noun small room leading to main one.

anthem /'ænθəm/ noun choral composition for church use; song of praise, esp. for nation.

anther /'ænθə/ noun part of stamen containing pollen.

anthology /æn'θɒlədʒɪ/ noun (plural **-ies**) collection of poems, essays, stories, etc.

anthracite /'ænθrəsaɪt/ noun hard kind of coal.

anthrax /'ænθræks/ noun disease of sheep and cattle transmissible to humans.

anthropocentric /ænθrəpəʊ'sentrɪk/ adjective regarding humankind as centre of existence.

anthropoid /'ænθrəpɔɪd/ ● adjective human in form. ● noun anthropoid ape.

anthropology /ænθrə'pɒlədʒɪ/ noun study of humankind, esp. societies and customs. □ **anthropological** /-pə'lɒdʒ-/ adjective; **anthropologist** noun.

anthropomorphism /ænθrəpə'mɔːfɪz(ə)m/ noun attributing of human characteristics to god, animal, or thing. □ **anthropomorphic** adjective; **anthropomorphize** verb (also **-ise**) (**-zing** or **-sing**).

anti- /'æntɪ/ prefix opposed to; preventing; opposite of; unconventional.

anti-abortion /-ə'bɔːʃ(ə)n/ adjective opposing abortion. □ **anti-abortionist** noun.

anti-aircraft /-'eəkrɑːft/ adjective for defence against enemy aircraft.

antibiotic /-baɪ'ɒtɪk/ ● noun substance that can inhibit or destroy bacteria etc. ● adjective functioning as antibiotic.

antibody /'æntɪbɒdɪ/ noun (plural **-ies**) blood protein produced in reaction to antigens.

antic /'æntɪk/ noun (usually in plural) foolish behaviour.

anticipate /æn'tɪsɪpeɪt/ verb (**-ting**) deal with or use before proper time; expect; forestall. □ **anticipation** noun; **anticipatory** adjective.

anticlimax /-'klaɪmæks/ noun disappointing conclusion to something significant.

anticlockwise /-'klɒkwaɪz/ ● adverb in opposite direction to hands of clock. ● adjective moving anticlockwise.

anticyclone /-'saɪkləʊn/ noun system of winds outwards from area of high pressure, producing fine weather.

antidepressant /-dɪ'pres(ə)nt/ ● noun drug etc. alleviating depression. ● adjective alleviating depression.

antidote /'æntɪdəʊt/ noun medicine used to counteract poison.

antifreeze /'æntɪfriːz/ noun substance added to water (esp. in vehicle's radiator) to lower its freezing point.

antigen /'æntɪdʒ(ə)n/ noun foreign substance causing body to produce antibodies.

anti-hero /'æntɪhɪərəʊ/ noun (plural **-es**) central character in story, lacking conventional heroic qualities.

antihistamine /-'hɪstəmiːn/ noun drug that counteracts effect of histamine, used esp. to treat allergies.

antiknock /æntɪ'nɒk/ noun substance added to motor fuel to prevent premature combustion.

anti-lock /'æntɪlɒk/ adjective (of brakes) not locking when applied suddenly.

antimony /'æntɪmənɪ/ noun brittle silvery metallic element.

anti-nuclear /-'njuːklɪə/ adjective opposed to development of nuclear weapons or power.

antipathy /æn'tɪpəθɪ/ noun (plural **-ies**) (often + to, for, between) strong aversion or dislike. □ **antipathetic** /-'θet-/ adjective.

antiperspirant /-'pɜːspərənt/ noun substance inhibiting perspiration.

antiphon /'æntɪf(ə)n/ noun hymn sung alternately by two groups. □ **antiphonal** /-'tɪf-/ adjective.

antipodes /æn'tɪpədiːz/ plural noun places diametrically opposite each other on the earth, esp. (also **Antipodes**) Australasia in relation to Europe. □ **antipodean** /-'diːən/ adjective & noun.

antiquarian /æntɪ'kweərɪən/ ● adjective of or dealing in rare books. ● noun antiquary.

antiquary /'æntɪkwərɪ/ *noun* (*plural* **-ies**) student or collector of antiques etc.

antiquated /'æntɪkweɪtɪd/ *adjective* old-fashioned.

antique /æn'tiːk/ • *noun* old valuable object, esp. piece of furniture etc. • *adjective* of or existing since old times; old-fashioned.

antiquity /æn'tɪkwətɪ/ *noun* (*plural* **-ies**) ancient times, esp. before Middle Ages; (in *plural*) great age; remains from ancient times.

antirrhinum /æntɪ'raɪnəm/ *noun* snapdragon.

anti-Semitic /-sɪ'mɪtɪk/ *adjective* prejudiced against Jews. □ **anti-Semite** /-'siːmaɪt/ *noun*; **anti-Semitism** /-'semɪ-/ *noun*.

antiseptic /-'septɪk/ • *adjective* counteracting sepsis by destroying germs. • *noun* antiseptic substance.

antisocial /-'səʊʃ(ə)l/ *adjective* not sociable; opposed or harmful to society.

■ **Usage** It is a mistake to use *antisocial* instead of *unsocial* in the phrase *unsocial hours.*

antistatic /-'stætɪk/ *adjective* counteracting effect of static electricity.

antithesis /æn'tɪθəsɪs/ *noun* (*plural* **-theses** /-siːz/) (often + *of*, *to*) direct opposite; contrast; rhetorical use of strongly contrasted words. □ **antithetical** /-'θet-/ *adjective*.

antitoxin /-'tɒksɪn/ *noun* antibody counteracting toxin. □ **antitoxic** *adjective*.

antitrades /-'treɪdz/ *plural noun* winds blowing above and in opposite direction to trade winds.

antiviral /-'vaɪər(ə)l/ *adjective* effective against viruses.

antler /'æntlə/ *noun* branched horn of deer.

antonym /'æntənɪm/ *noun* word opposite in meaning to another, e.g. *wet* is an antonym of *dry.*

anus /'eɪnəs/ *noun* (*plural* **-es**) excretory opening at end of alimentary canal.

anvil /'ænvɪl/ *noun* iron block on which metals are worked.

anxiety /æŋ'zaɪətɪ/ *noun* (*plural* **-ies**) troubled state of mind; worry; eagerness.

anxious /'æŋkʃəs/ *adjective* mentally troubled; marked by anxiety; (+ *to do*) uneasily wanting. □ **anxiously** *adverb*.

any /'enɪ/ • *adjective* one or some, no matter which. • *pronoun* any one; any number or amount. • *adverb* at all. □ **anybody** *pronoun* any person, *noun* an important person; **anyhow** anyway, at random; **anyone** anybody; **anything** any thing, a thing of any kind; **anyway** in any way, in any case; **anywhere** (in or to) any place.

AOB *abbreviation* any other business.

aorta /eɪ'ɔːtə/ *noun* (*plural* **-s**) main artery carrying blood from heart.

apace /ə'peɪs/ *adverb* literary swiftly.

apart /ə'pɑːt/ *adverb* separately; into pieces; at or to a distance.

apartheid /ə'pɑːteɪt/ *noun* racial segregation, esp. in S. Africa.

apartment /ə'pɑːtmənt/ *noun* (*US* or esp. for holidays) flat; (usually in *plural*) room.

apathy /'æpəθɪ/ *noun* lack of interest, indifference. □ **apathetic** /-'θet-/ *adjective*.

apatosaurus /əpætə'sɔːrəs/ *noun* (*plural* **-ruses**) large long-necked plant-eating dinosaur.

ape • *noun* tailless monkey; imitator. • *verb* (**-ping**) imitate.

aperient /ə'pɪərɪənt/ *adjective* & *noun* laxative.

aperitif /əperɪ'tiːf/ *noun* alcoholic drink before meal.

aperture /'æpətʃə/ *noun* opening or gap, esp. variable one letting light into camera.

apex /'eɪpeks/ *noun* (*plural* **-es**) highest point; tip.

aphasia /ə'feɪzɪə/ *noun* loss of verbal understanding or expression.

aphelion /ə'fiːlɪən/ *noun* (*plural* **-lia**) point of orbit farthest from sun.

aphid /'eɪfɪd/ *noun* insect infesting plants.

aphis /'eɪfɪs/ *noun* (*plural* **aphides** /-diːz/) aphid.

aphorism /'æfərɪz(ə)m/ *noun* short wise saying. □ **aphoristic** /-'rɪs-/ *adjective*.

aphrodisiac /æfrə'dɪzɪæk/ • *adjective* arousing sexual desire. • *noun* aphrodisiac substance.

apiary /'eɪpɪərɪ/ *noun* (*plural* **-ies**) place where bees are kept. □ **apiarist** *noun*.

apiculture /ˈeɪpɪkʌltʃə/ noun bee-keeping.

apiece /əˈpiːs/ adverb for each one.

aplomb /əˈplɒm/ noun self-assurance.

apocalypse /əˈpɒkəlɪps/ noun destructive event; revelation, esp. about the end of the world. □ **apocalyptic** /-ˈlɪp-/ adjective.

Apocrypha /əˈpɒkrɪfə/ plural noun Old Testament books not in Hebrew Bible; (**apocrypha**) writings etc. not considered genuine. □ **apocryphal** adjective.

apogee /ˈæpədʒiː/ noun highest point; point farthest from earth in orbit of moon etc.

apolitical /eɪpəˈlɪtɪk(ə)l/ adjective not interested or involved in politics.

apologetic /əpɒləˈdʒetɪk/ adjective expressing regret. □ **apologetically** adverb.

apologia /æpəˈləʊdʒə/ noun formal defence of conduct or opinions.

apologist /əˈpɒlədʒɪst/ noun person who defends by argument.

apologize /əˈpɒlədʒaɪz/ verb (also **-ise**) (**-zing** or **-sing**) make apology.

apology /əˈpɒlədʒɪ/ noun (plural **-ies**) regretful acknowledgement of offence or failure; explanation.

apophthegm /ˈæpəθem/ noun short wise saying.

apoplexy /ˈæpəpleksɪ/ noun sudden paralysis caused by blockage or rupture of brain artery. □ **apoplectic** /-ˈplek-/ adjective.

apostasy /əˈpɒstəsɪ/ noun (plural **-ies**) abandonment of belief, faith, etc.

apostate /əˈpɒsteɪt/ noun person who renounces belief. □ **apostatize** /-tət-/ verb (also **-ise**) (**-zing** or **-sing**).

a posteriori /eɪ pɒsteriˈɔːraɪ/ adjective & adverb from effects to causes.

Apostle /əˈpɒs(ə)l/ noun any of twelve men sent by Christ to preach gospel; (**apostle**) leader of reform.

apostolic /æpəsˈtɒlɪk/ adjective of Apostles; of the Pope.

apostrophe /əˈpɒstrəfɪ/ noun punctuation mark (') indicating possession or marking omission of letter(s) or number(s) (see panel).

apostrophize verb (also **-ise**) (**-zing** or **-sing**) address (esp. absent person or thing).

apothecary /əˈpɒθəkərɪ/ noun (plural **-ies**) archaic pharmacist.

apotheosis /əpɒθɪˈəʊsɪs/ noun (plural **-oses** /-siːz/) deification; glorification or sublime example (of thing).

appal /əˈpɔːl/ verb (**-ll-**) dismay; horrify.

apparatus /æpəˈreɪtəs/ noun equipment for scientific or other work.

apparel /əˈpær(ə)l/ noun formal clothing. □ **apparelled** adjective.

apparent /əˈpærənt/ adjective obvious; seeming. □ **apparently** adverb.

apparition /æpəˈrɪʃ(ə)n/ noun thing that appears, esp. of startling kind; ghost.

appeal /əˈpiːl/ ● verb make earnest or formal request; (usually + to) be attractive; (+ to) resort to for support; (often + to) apply to higher court for revision of judicial decision; Cricket ask umpire to declare batsman out. ● noun appealing; request for aid; attractiveness.

appear /əˈpɪə/ verb become or be visible; seem; present oneself; be published.

appearance noun appearing; outward form; (in plural) outward show of prosperity, virtue, etc.

appease /əˈpiːz/ verb (**-sing**) make calm or quiet, esp. conciliate (aggressor) with concessions; satisfy (appetite etc.). □ **appeasement** noun.

appellant /əˈpelənt/ noun person who appeals to higher court.

appellation /æpəˈleɪʃ(ə)n/ noun formal name, title.

append /əˈpend/ verb (usually + to) attach, affix; add.

appendage /əˈpendɪdʒ/ noun thing attached; addition.

appendectomy /æpenˈdektəmɪ/ noun (also **appendicectomy** /əpendɪˈsektəmɪ/) (plural **-ies**) surgical removal of appendix.

appendicitis /əpendɪˈsaɪtɪs/ noun inflammation of appendix.

appendix /əˈpendɪks/ noun (plural **-dices** /-siːz/) tubular sac attached to large intestine; addition to book etc.

appertain /æpəˈteɪn/ verb (+ to) belong, relate to.

appetite /ˈæpɪtaɪt/ noun (usually + for) desire (esp. for food); inclination, desire.

appetizer /ˈæpɪtaɪzə/ *noun* (also **-iser**) thing eaten or drunk to stimulate appetite.

appetizing /ˈæpɪtaɪzɪŋ/ *adjective* (also **-ising**) (esp. of food) stimulating appetite.

applaud /əˈplɔːd/ *verb* express approval (of), esp. by clapping; commend.

applause /əˈplɔːz/ *noun* warm approval, esp. clapping.

apple /ˈæp(ə)l/ *noun* roundish firm fruit. □ **apple of one's eye** cherished person or thing; **apple-pie bed** bed with sheets folded so that one cannot stretch out one's legs; **apple-pie order** extreme neatness.

appliance /əˈplaɪəns/ *noun* device etc. for specific task.

applicable /ˈæplɪkəb(ə)l/ *adjective* (often + *to*) that may be applied. □ **applicability** *noun*.

applicant /ˈæplɪkənt/ *noun* person who applies for job etc.

application /æplɪˈkeɪʃ(ə)n/ *noun* formal request; applying; thing applied; diligence; relevance; use.

applicator /ˈæplɪkeɪtə/ *noun* device for applying ointment etc.

appliqué /æˈpliːkeɪ/ ● *noun* work in which cut-out fabric is fixed on to other fabric. ● *verb* (**-qués, -quéd, -quéing**) decorate with appliqué.

....

Apostrophe '

This is used:

1 to indicate possession:

with a singular noun:

   a boy's book; a week's work; the boss's salary.

with a plural already ending with *s*:

   a girls' school; two weeks' newspapers; the bosses' salaries.

with a plural not already ending with *s*:

   the children's books; women's liberation.

with a singular name:

   Bill's book; John's coat; Barnabas' (or *Barnabas's*) *book; Nicholas'* (or *Nicholas's*) *coat.*

with a name ending in *-es* that is pronounced /-ɪz/:

   Bridges' poems; Moses' mother

and before the word *sake*:

   for God's sake; for goodness' sake; for Nicholas' sake

but it is often omitted in a business name:

   Barclays Bank.

2 to mark an omission of one or more letters or numbers:

   he's (he is or *he has)*   *haven't (have not)*
   can't (cannot)   *we'll (we shall)*
   won't (will not)   *o'clock (of the clock)*
   the summer of '68 (1968)

3 when letters or numbers are referred to in plural form:

   mind your p's and q's; find all the number 7's.

but it is unnecessary in, e.g.

   MPs; the 1940s.

....

apply /ə'plaɪ/ *verb* (**-ies, -ied**) (often + *for, to, to do*) make formal request; (often + *to*) be relevant; make use of; (often + *to*) put or spread (on); (**apply oneself**; often + *to*) devote oneself.

appoint /ə'pɔɪnt/ *verb* assign job or office to; (often + *for*) fix (time etc.); (as **appointed** *adjective*) equipped, furnished.

appointment *noun* appointing, being appointed; arrangement for meeting; job available; (in *plural*) equipment, fittings.

apportion /ə'pɔːʃ(ə)n/ *verb* (often + *to*) share out. □ **apportionment** *noun*.

apposite /'æpəzɪt/ *adjective* (often + *to*) well expressed, appropriate.

apposition /æpə'zɪʃ(ə)n/ *noun* juxtaposition, esp. of syntactically parallel words etc. (e.g. *my friend Sue*).

appraise /ə'preɪz/ *verb* (**-sing**) estimate value or quality of. □ **appraisal** *noun*.

appreciable /ə'priːʃəb(ə)l/ *adjective* significant; considerable.

appreciate /ə'priːʃɪeɪt/ *verb* (**-ting**) (highly) value; be grateful for; understand, recognize; rise in value. □ **appreciation** *noun*; **appreciative** /-ʃətɪv/ *adjective*.

apprehend /æprɪ'hend/ *verb* arrest; understand.

apprehension /æprɪ'henʃ(ə)n/ *noun* fearful anticipation; arrest; understanding.

apprehensive /æprɪ'hensɪv/ *adjective* uneasy, fearful. □ **apprehensively** *adverb*.

apprentice /ə'prentɪs/ ● *noun* person learning trade by working for agreed period. ● *verb* (usually + *to*) engage as apprentice. □ **apprenticeship** *noun*.

apprise /ə'praɪz/ *verb* (**-sing**) (usually + *of*) inform.

approach /ə'prəʊtʃ/ ● *verb* come nearer (to) in space or time; be similar to; approximate to; set about; make tentative proposal to. ● *noun* act or means of approaching; approximation; technique; part of aircraft's flight before landing.

approachable /ə'prəʊtʃəb(ə)l/ *adjective* friendly; able to be approached.

approbation /æprə'beɪʃ(ə)n/ *noun* approval, consent.

appropriate ● *adjective* /ə'prəʊprɪət/ suitable, proper. ● *verb* (**-ting**) /ə'prəʊprɪeɪt/ take possession of; devote (money etc.) to special purpose. □ **appropriately** *adverb*; **appropriation** *noun*.

approval /ə'pruːv(ə)l/ *noun* approving; consent. □ **on approval** returnable if not satisfactory.

approve /ə'pruːv/ *verb* (**-ving**) sanction; (often + *of*) regard with favour.

approx. *abbreviation* approximate(ly).

approximate ● *adjective* /ə'prɒksɪmət/ fairly correct; near to the actual. ● *verb* /ə'prɒksɪmeɪt/ (**-ting**) (often + *to*) be or make near. □ **approximately** *adverb*; **approximation** *noun*.

appurtenances /ə'pɜːtɪnənsɪz/ *plural noun* accessories; belongings.

APR *abbreviation* annual(ized) percentage rate.

Apr. *abbreviation* April.

après-ski /æprer'skiː/ ● *noun* activities after a day's skiing. ● *adjective* suitable for these. [French]

apricot /'eɪprɪkɒt/ ● *noun* small orange-yellow peachlike fruit; its colour. ● *adjective* orange-yellow.

April /'eɪpr(ə)l/ *noun* fourth month of year. □ **April Fool** victim of hoax on 1 Apr.

a priori /eɪ praɪ'ɔːraɪ/ ● *adjective* from cause to effect; not derived from experience; assumed without investigation. ● *adverb* deductively; as far as one knows.

apron /'eɪprən/ *noun* garment protecting front of clothes; area on airfield for manoeuvring or loading; part of stage in front of curtain.

apropos /æprə'pəʊ/ ● *adjective* appropriate; *colloquial* (often + *of*) in respect of. ● *adverb* appropriately; incidentally.

apse /æps/ *noun* arched or domed recess esp. at end of church.

apsis /'æpsɪs/ *noun* (*plural* **apsides** /-diːz/) aphelion or perihelion of planet, apogee or perigee of moon.

apt *adjective* suitable, appropriate; (+ *to do*) having a tendency; quick to learn.

aptitude /'æptɪtjuːd/ *noun* talent; ability, esp. specified.

aqualung /'ækwəlʌŋ/ *noun* portable underwater breathing-apparatus.

aquamarine /ækwəmə'ri:n/ ● noun bluish-green beryl; its colour. ● adjective bluish-green.

aquaplane /'ækwəpleɪn/ ● noun board for riding on water, pulled by speedboat. ● verb (-ning) ride on this; (of vehicle) glide uncontrollably on wet surface.

aquarelle /ækwə'rel/ noun painting in transparent water-colours.

aquarium /ə'kweərɪəm/ noun (plural -s) tank for keeping fish etc.

Aquarius /ə'kweərɪəs/ noun eleventh sign of zodiac.

aquatic /ə'kwætɪk/ adjective growing or living in water; done in or on water.

aquatint /'ækwətɪnt/ noun etched print like water colour.

aqueduct /'ækwɪdʌkt/ noun water channel, esp. raised structure across valley.

aqueous /'eɪkwɪəs/ adjective of or like water.

aquiline /'ækwɪlaɪn/ adjective of or like an eagle; (of nose) curved.

Arab /'ærəb/ ● noun member of Semitic people inhabiting originally Saudi Arabia, now Middle East generally; horse of breed originally native to Arabia. ● adjective of Arabia or Arabs.

arabesque /ærə'besk/ noun decoration with intertwined leaves, scrollwork, etc.; ballet posture with one leg extended horizontally backwards.

Arabian /ə'reɪbɪən/ ● adjective of Arabia. ● noun Arab.

Arabic /'ærəbɪk/ ● noun language of Arabs. ● adjective of Arabs or their language. □ **arabic numerals** 1, 2, 3, etc.

arable /'ærəb(ə)l/ adjective fit for growing crops.

arachnid /ə'ræknɪd/ noun creature of class comprising spiders, scorpions, etc.

Aramaic /ærə'meɪɪk/ ● noun language of Syria at time of Christ. ● adjective of or in Aramaic.

arbiter /'ɑːbɪtə/ noun arbitrator; person influential in specific field.

arbitrary /'ɑːbɪtrərɪ/ adjective random; capricious, despotic. □ **arbitrarily** adverb.

arbitrate /'ɑːbɪtreɪt/ verb (-ting) settle dispute between others. □ **arbitration** noun; **arbitrator** noun.

arboreal /ɑː'bɔːrɪəl/ adjective of or living in trees.

arboretum /ɑːbə'riːtəm/ noun (plural -ta) tree-garden.

arboriculture /'ɑːbərɪkʌltʃə/ noun cultivation of trees and shrubs.

arbour /'ɑːbə/ noun (US **arbor**) shady garden alcove enclosed by trees etc.

arc noun part of circumference of circle or other curve; luminous discharge between two electrodes. □ **arc lamp** one using electric arc; **arc welding** using electric arc to melt metals to be welded.

arcade /ɑː'keɪd/ noun covered walk, esp. lined with shops; series of arches supporting or along wall.

Arcadian /ɑː'keɪdɪən/ adjective ideally rustic.

arcane /ɑː'keɪn/ adjective mysterious, secret.

arch¹ ● noun curved structure supporting bridge, floor, etc. as opening or ornament. ● verb form arch; provide with or form into arch.

arch² adjective self-consciously or affectedly playful.

archaeology /ɑːkɪ'ɒlədʒɪ/ noun (US **archeology**) study of ancient cultures, esp. by excavation of physical remains. □ **archaeological** /-ə'lɒdʒ-/ adjective; **archaeologist** noun.

archaic /ɑː'keɪɪk/ adjective antiquated; (of word) no longer in ordinary use; of early period in culture.

archaism /'ɑːkeɪɪz(ə)m/ noun archaic word etc.; use of the archaic. □ **archaistic** /-'ɪst-/ adjective.

archangel /'ɑːkeɪndʒ(ə)l/ noun angel of highest rank.

archbishop /ɑːtʃ'bɪʃəp/ noun chief bishop.

archbishopric noun office or diocese of archbishop.

archdeacon /ɑːtʃ'diːkən/ noun church dignitary next below bishop. □ **archdeaconry** noun (plural -ies).

archdiocese /ɑːtʃ'daɪəsɪs/ noun archbishop's diocese. □ **archdiocesan** /-daɪ'ɒsɪs(ə)n/ adjective.

arch-enemy /ɑːtʃ'enəmɪ/ noun (plural -ies) chief enemy.

archeology US = ARCHAEOLOGY.

archer /'ɑːtʃə/ *noun* person who shoots with bow and arrows.

archery /'ɑːtʃərɪ/ *noun* shooting with bow and arrows.

archetype /'ɑːkɪtaɪp/ *noun* original model, typical specimen. □ **archetypal** /-'taɪp-/ *adjective*.

archipelago /ɑːkɪ'pelagəʊ/ *noun* (*plural* **-s**) group of islands; sea with many islands.

architect /'ɑːkɪtekt/ *noun* designer of buildings etc.; (+ *of*) person who brings about specified thing.

architectonic /ɑːkɪtek'tɒnɪk/ *adjective* of architecture.

architecture /'ɑːkɪtektʃə/ *noun* design and construction of buildings; style of building. □ **architectural** /-'tek-/ *adjective*.

architrave /'ɑːkɪtreɪv/ *noun* moulded frame round doorway or window; main beam laid across tops of classical columns.

archive /'ɑːkaɪv/ *noun* (usually in *plural*) collection of documents or records; place where these are kept.

archivist /'ɑːkɪvɪst/ *noun* keeper of archives.

archway /'ɑːtʃweɪ/ *noun* arched entrance or passage.

Arctic /'ɑːktɪk/ ● *adjective* of north polar region; (**arctic**) very cold. ● *noun* Arctic region.

ardent /'ɑːd(ə)nt/ *adjective* eager, fervent, passionate; burning. □ **ardently** *adverb*.

ardour /'ɑːdə/ *noun* zeal, enthusiasm.

arduous /'ɑːdjʊəs/ *adjective* hard to accomplish; strenuous.

are see BE.

area /'eərɪə/ *noun* extent or measure of surface; region; space set aside for a purpose; scope, range; space in front of house basement.

arena /ə'riːnə/ *noun* centre of amphitheatre; scene of conflict; sphere of action.

aren't /ɑːnt/ are not; (in questions) am not.

arête /æ'reɪt/ *noun* sharp mountain ridge.

argon /'ɑːgɒn/ *noun* inert gaseous element.

argot /'ɑːgəʊ/ *noun* jargon of group or class.

argue /'ɑːgjuː/ *verb* (**-ues, -ued, -uing**) exchange views, esp. heatedly; (often + *that*) maintain by reasoning; (+ *for, against*) reason. □ **arguable** *adjective*; **arguably** *adverb*.

argument /'ɑːgjʊmənt/ *noun* (esp. heated) exchange of views; reason given; reasoning; summary of book etc. □ **argumentation** /-men-/ *noun*.

argumentative /ɑːgjʊ'mentətɪv/ *adjective* fond of arguing.

argy-bargy /ɑːdʒɪ'bɑːdʒɪ/ *noun* jocular dispute, wrangle.

aria /'ɑːrɪə/ *noun* song for one voice in opera, oratorio, etc.

arid /'ærɪd/ *noun* dry, parched. □ **aridity** /ə'rɪd-/ *noun*.

Aries /'eəriːz/ *noun* first sign of zodiac.

aright /ə'raɪt/ *adverb* rightly.

arise /ə'raɪz/ *verb* (**-sing**; *past* **arose** /ə'rəʊz/; *past participle* **arisen** /ə'rɪz(ə)n/) originate; (usually + *from, out of*) result; emerge; rise.

aristocracy /ærɪ'stɒkrəsɪ/ *noun* (*plural* **-ies**) ruling class, nobility.

aristocrat /'ærɪstəkræt/ *noun* member of aristocracy.

aristocratic /ærɪstə'krætɪk/ *adjective* of the aristocracy; grand, distinguished.

arithmetic ● *noun* /ə'rɪθmətɪk/ science of numbers; computation; use of numbers. ● *adjective* /ærɪθ'metɪk/ (also **arithmetical**) of arithmetic.

ark *noun* ship in which Noah escaped the Flood. □ **Ark of the Covenant** wooden chest containing tables of Jewish law.

arm[1] *noun* upper limb of human body; sleeve; raised side part of chair; branch; armlike thing. □ **armchair** chair with arms, theoretical rather than active; **arm in arm** with arms linked; **armpit** hollow under arm at shoulder; **at arm's length** at a distance; **with open arms** cordially. □ **armful** *noun*.

arm[2] ● *noun* (usually in *plural*) weapon; branch of military forces; (in *plural*) heraldic devices. ● *verb* equip with arms; equip oneself with arms; make (bomb) ready. □ **up in arms** (usually + *against, about*) actively resisting.

armada /ɑːˈmɑːdə/ noun fleet of warships.

armadillo /ɑːməˈdɪləʊ/ noun (plural -s) S. American burrowing mammal with plated body.

Armageddon /ɑːməˈgedə)n/ noun huge battle at end of world.

armament /ˈɑːməmənt/ noun military weapon etc.; equipping for war.

armature /ˈɑːmətʃə/ noun rotating coil or coils of dynamo or electric motor; iron bar placed across poles of magnet; framework on which sculpture is moulded.

armistice /ˈɑːmɪstɪs/ noun truce.

armlet /ˈɑːmlɪt/ noun band worn round arm.

armorial /ɑːˈmɔːrɪəl/ adjective of heraldic arms.

armour /ˈɑːmə/ noun protective covering formerly worn in fighting; metal plates etc. protecting ship, car, tank, etc.; armoured vehicles. □ **armoured** adjective.

armourer noun maker of arms or armour; official in charge of arms.

armoury /ˈɑːmərɪ/ noun (plural -ies) arsenal.

army /ˈɑːmɪ/ noun (plural -ies) organized armed land force; vast number; organized body.

arnica /ˈɑːnɪkə/ noun plant with yellow flowers; medicine made from it.

aroma /əˈrəʊmə/ noun pleasing smell; subtle quality. □ **aromatic** /ærəˈmætɪk/ adjective.

aromatherapy noun use of plant extracts and oils in massage. □ **aromatherapist** noun.

arose past of ARISE.

around /əˈraʊnd/ ● adverb on every side; all round; colloquial in existence, near at hand. ● preposition on or along the circuit of; on every side of; here and there in or near; about.

arouse /əˈraʊz/ verb (-sing) induce (esp. emotion); awake from sleep; stir into activity; stimulate sexually. □ **arousal** noun.

arpeggio /ɑːˈpedʒɪəʊ/ noun (plural -s) notes of chord played in rapid succession.

arrack /ˈærək/ noun alcoholic spirit made esp. from rice.

arraign /əˈreɪn/ verb indict, accuse; find fault with. □ **arraignment** noun.

arrange /əˈreɪndʒ/ verb (-ging) put in order; plan or provide for; (+ to do, for) take measures; (+ with person) agree about procedure for; Music adapt (piece). □ **arrangement** noun.

arrant /ˈærənt/ adjective downright, utter.

arras /ˈærəs/ noun tapestry wall-hanging.

array /əˈreɪ/ ● noun imposing series; ordered arrangement, esp. of troops. ● verb deck, adorn; set in order; marshal (forces).

arrears /əˈrɪəz/ plural noun outstanding debt; what remains undone. □ **in arrears** behindhand, esp. in payment.

arrest /əˈrest/ ● verb lawfully seize; stop; catch attention of. ● noun arresting, being arrested; stoppage.

arrival /əˈraɪv(ə)l/ noun arriving; person or thing arriving.

arrive /əˈraɪv/ verb (-ving) come to destination; (+ at) reach (conclusion); colloquial become successful, be born.

arrogant /ˈærəgənt/ adjective aggressively assertive or presumptuous. □ **arrogance** noun, **arrogantly** adverb.

arrogate /ˈærəgeɪt/ verb (-ting) claim without right. □ **arrogation** noun.

arrow /ˈærəʊ/ noun pointed missile shot from bow; representation of this, esp. to show direction. □ **arrowhead** pointed tip of arrow.

arrowroot /ˈærəʊruːt/ noun nutritious starch.

arsenal /ˈɑːsən(ə)l/ noun place where weapons and ammunition are made or stored.

arsenic /ˈɑːsənɪk/ noun brittle semi-metallic element; its highly poisonous trioxide.

arson /ˈɑːsən/ noun crime of deliberately setting property on fire. □ **arsonist** noun.

art noun human creative skill, its application; branch of creative activity concerned with imitative and imaginative designs, sounds, or ideas, e.g. painting, music, writing; creative activity resulting in visual representation; thing in which skill can be exercised; (in *plural*) certain branches of learning (esp. languages, literature, history, etc.) as distinct from sciences; knack; cunning. □ **art nouveau** /ɑː nuːˈvəʊ/ art style of late 19th c., with flowing lines.

artefact /ˈɑːtɪfækt/ *noun* (also **artifact**) man-made object.

arterial /ɑːˈtɪərɪəl/ *adjective* of or like artery. □ **arterial road** important main road.

arteriosclerosis /ɑːtɪərɪəʊskliəˈrəʊsɪs/ *noun* hardening and thickening of artery walls.

artery /ˈɑːtərɪ/ *noun* (*plural* **-ies**) blood vessel carrying blood from heart; main road or railway line.

artesian well /ɑːˈtiːzɪən/ well in which water rises by natural pressure through vertically drilled hole.

artful /ˈɑːtfʊl/ *adjective* sly, crafty. □ **artfully** *adverb*.

arthritis /ɑːˈθraɪtɪs/ *noun* inflammation of joint. □ **arthritic** /-ˈθrɪt-/ *adjective & noun*.

arthropod /ˈɑːθrəpɒd/ *noun* animal with segmented body and jointed limbs, e.g. insect, spider, crustacean.

artichoke /ˈɑːtɪtʃəʊk/ *noun* plant allied to thistle; its partly edible flower; Jerusalem artichoke.

article /ˈɑːtɪk(ə)l/ ● *noun* item or thing; short piece of non-fiction in newspaper etc.; clause of agreement etc.; = DEFINITE ARTICLE, INDEFINITE ARTICLE. ● *verb* employ under contract as trainee.

articular /ɑːˈtɪkjʊlə/ *adjective* of joints.

articulate ● *adjective* /ɑːˈtɪkjʊlət/ fluent and clear in speech; (of speech) in which separate sounds and words are clear; having joints. ● *verb* /ɑːˈtɪkjʊleɪt/ (**-ting**) speak distinctly; express clearly; connect with joints. □ **articulated lorry** one with sections connected by flexible joint. □ **articulately** *adverb*; **articulation** *noun*.

artifact = ARTEFACT.

artifice /ˈɑːtɪfɪs/ *noun* trick; cunning; skill.

artificer /ɑːˈtɪfɪsə/ *noun* craftsman.

artificial /ɑːtɪˈfɪʃ(ə)l/ *adjective* not natural; imitating nature; insincere. □ **artificial insemination** non-sexual injection of semen into uterus; **artificial intelligence** (use of) computers replacing human intelligence; **artificial respiration** manual or mechanical stimulation of breathing. □ **artificiality** /-ʃɪˈæl-/ *noun*; **artificially** *adverb*.

artillery /ɑːˈtɪlərɪ/ *noun* large guns used in fighting on land; branch of army using these. □ **artilleryman** *noun*.

artisan /ɑːtɪˈzæn/ *noun* skilled worker or craftsman.

artist /ˈɑːtɪst/ *noun* person who practises any art, esp. painting; artiste. □ **artistic** *adjective*; **artistically** *adverb*; **artistry** *noun*.

artiste /ɑːˈtiːst/ *noun* professional singer, dancer, etc.

artless *adjective* guileless, ingenuous; natural; clumsy. □ **artlessly** *adverb*.

arty *adjective* (**-ier, -iest**) pretentiously or affectedly artistic.

arum /ˈeərəm/ *noun* plant with arrow-shaped leaves.

Aryan /ˈeərɪən/ ● *noun* speaker of any Indo-European language. ● *adjective* of Aryans.

as /æz, əz/ ● *adverb* to the same extent. ● *conjunction* in the same way that; while, when; since, seeing that; although. ● *preposition* in the capacity or form of. □ **as ... as ...** to the same extent that ... is, does, etc.

asafoetida /æsəˈfetɪdə/ *noun* (*US* **asafetida**) resinous pungent gum.

asbestos /æsˈbestɒs/ *noun* fibrous silicate mineral; heat-resistant or insulating substance made from this.

ascend /əˈsend/ *verb* slope upwards; go or come up, climb.

ascendancy *noun* (often + *over*) dominant control.

ascendant *adjective* rising. □ **in the ascendant** gaining or having power or authority.

ascension /əˈsenʃ(ə)n/ *noun* ascent, esp. (**Ascension**) of Christ into heaven.

ascent /əˈsent/ *noun* ascending, rising; upward path or slope.

ascertain /æsəˈteɪn/ *verb* find out for certain. □ **ascertainment** *noun*.

ascetic /əˈsetɪk/ ● *adjective* severely abstinent; self-denying. ● *noun* ascetic person. □ **asceticism** /-tɪs-/ *noun*.

ascorbic acid /əˈskɔːbɪk/ *noun* vitamin C.

ascribe /əˈskraɪb/ *verb* (**-bing**) (usually + *to*) attribute; regard as belonging. □ **ascription** /-ˈskrɪp-/ *noun*.

asepsis /eɪˈsepsɪs/ *noun* absence of sepsis or harmful bacteria; aseptic method in surgery. □ **aseptic** *adjective*.

asexual /eɪˈseksjʊəl/ *adjective* without sex or sexuality; (of reproduction) not involving fusion of gametes. □ **asexually** *adverb*.

ash[1] *noun* (often in *plural*) powdery residue left after burning; (in *plural*) human remains after cremation; (**the Ashes**) trophy in cricket between England and Australia. □ **ashcan** *US* dustbin; **ashtray** receptacle for tobacco ash; **Ash Wednesday** first day of Lent.

ash[2] *noun* tree with silver-grey bark; its wood.

ashamed /əˈʃeɪmd/ *adjective* embarrassed by shame; (+ *to do*) reluctant owing to shame.

ashen /ˈæʃ(ə)n/ *adjective* grey, pale.

ashore /əˈʃɔː/ *adverb* to or on shore.

ashram /ˈæʃræm/ *noun* religious retreat for Hindus.

Asian /ˈeɪʃ(ə)n/ • *adjective* of Asia. • *noun* native of Asia; person of Asian descent.

aside /əˈsaɪd/ • *adverb* to or on one side; away, apart. • *noun* words spoken aside, esp. by actor to audience.

asinine /ˈæsɪnaɪn/ *adjective* asslike; stupid.

ask /ɑːsk/ *verb* call for answer to or about; seek to obtain from another person; invite; (+ *for*) seek to obtain or meet. □ **ask after** inquire about (esp. person).

askance /əˈskæns/ *adverb* sideways. □ **look askance at** regard suspiciously.

askew /əˈskjuː/ • *adverb* crookedly. • *adjective* oblique; awry.

aslant /əˈslɑːnt/ • *adverb* at a slant. • *preposition* obliquely across.

asleep /əˈsliːp/ • *adjective* sleeping; *colloquial* inattentive; (of limb) numb. • *adverb* into state of sleep.

asp *noun* small venomous snake.

asparagus /əsˈpærəgəs/ *noun* plant of lily family; its edible shoots.

aspect /ˈæspekt/ *noun* feature, viewpoint, etc. to be considered; appearance, look; side facing specified direction.

aspen /ˈæspən/ *noun* poplar with fluttering leaves.

asperity /æsˈperɪtɪ/ *noun* sharpness of temper or tone; roughness.

aspersion /əsˈpɜːʃ(ə)n/ *noun* □ **cast aspersions on** defame.

asphalt /ˈæsfælt/ • *noun* bituminous pitch; mixture of this with gravel etc. for surfacing roads etc. • *verb* surface with asphalt.

asphodel /ˈæsfədel/ *noun* kind of lily.

asphyxia /æsˈfɪksɪə/ *noun* lack of oxygen in blood; suffocation.

asphyxiate /əsˈfɪksɪeɪt/ *verb* (**-ting**) suffocate. □ **asphyxiation** *noun*.

aspic /ˈæspɪk/ *noun* clear savoury jelly.

aspidistra /æspɪˈdɪstrə/ *noun* house plant with broad tapering leaves.

aspirant /ˈæspɪrənt/ • *adjective* aspiring. • *noun* person who aspires.

aspirate • *noun* /ˈæspərət/ sound of *h*; consonant blended with this. • *verb* /ˈæspəreɪt/ (**-ting**) pronounce with *h*; draw (fluid) by suction from cavity.

aspiration /æspəˈreɪʃ(ə)n/ *noun* ambition, desire; aspirating.

aspire /əˈspaɪə/ *verb* (**-ring**) (usually + *to, after, to do*) have ambition or strong desire.

aspirin /ˈæsprɪn/ *noun* (*plural* same or **-s**) white powder used to reduce pain and fever; tablet of this.

ass *noun* 4-legged animal with long ears, related to horse; donkey; stupid person.

assail /əˈseɪl/ *verb* attack physically or verbally. □ **assailant** *noun*.

assassin /əˈsæsɪn/ *noun* killer, esp. of political or religious leader.

assassinate /əˈsæsɪneɪt/ *verb* (**-ting**) kill for political or religious motives. □ **assassination** *noun*.

assault /əˈsɔːlt/ • *noun* violent physical or verbal attack; *Law* threat or display of violence against person. • *verb* make assault on. □ **assault and battery** *Law* threatening act resulting in physical harm to person.

assay /ə'seɪ/ ● *noun* test of metal or ore for ingredients and quality. ● *verb* make assay of.

assegai /'æsɪgaɪ/ *noun* light iron-tipped S. African spear.

assemblage /ə'semblɪdʒ/ *noun* assembled group.

assemble /ə'semb(ə)l/ *verb* (**-ling**) fit together parts of; fit (parts) together; bring or come together.

assembly /ə'semblɪ/ *noun* (*plural* **-ies**) assembling; assembled group, esp. as parliament etc.; fitting together of parts. □ **assembly line** machinery arranged so that product can be progressively assembled.

assent /ə'sent/ ● *noun* consent, approval. ● *verb* (usually + *to*) agree, consent.

assert /ə'sɜːt/ *verb* declare; enforce claim to; (**assert oneself**) insist on one's rights.

assertion /ə'sɜːʃ(ə)n/ *noun* declaration; forthright statement.

assertive *adjective* asserting oneself; forthright, positive. □ **assertively** *adverb*; **assertiveness** *noun*.

assess /ə'ses/ *verb* estimate size or quality of; estimate value of (property etc.) for taxation. □ **assessment** *noun*.

assessor *noun* person who assesses taxes etc.; judge's technical adviser in court.

asset /'æset/ *noun* useful or valuable person or thing; (usually in *plural*) property and possessions.

assiduous /ə'sɪdjʊəs/ *adjective* persevering, hard-working. □ **assiduity** /æsɪ'djuːɪtɪ/ *noun*; **assiduously** *adverb*.

assign /ə'saɪn/ *verb* allot; appoint; fix (time, place, etc.); (+ *to*) ascribe to, *Law* transfer formally to.

assignation /æsɪg'neɪʃ(ə)n/ *noun* appointment, esp. made by lovers; assigning, being assigned.

assignee /əsaɪ'niː/ *noun Law* person to whom property or right is assigned.

assignment /ə'saɪnmənt/ *noun* task or mission; assigning, being assigned.

assimilate /ə'sɪmɪleɪt/ *verb* (**-ting**) absorb or be absorbed into system; (usually + *to*) make like. □ **assimilable** *adjective*; **assimilation** *noun*; **assimilative** /-lətɪv/ *adjective*.

assist /ə'sɪst/ *verb* (often + *in*) help. □ **assistance** *noun*.

assistant *noun* helper; subordinate worker; = SHOP ASSISTANT.

assizes /ə'saɪzɪz/ *plural noun historical* court periodically administering civil and criminal law.

Assoc. *abbreviation* Association.

associate ● *verb* /ə'səʊʃɪeɪt/ (**-ting**) connect mentally; join, combine; (usually + *with*) have frequent dealings. ● *noun* /ə'səʊʃɪət/ partner, colleague; friend, companion. ● *adjective* /ə'səʊʃɪət/ joined, allied.

association /əsəʊsɪ'eɪʃ(ə)n/ *noun* group organized for joint purpose; associating, being associated; connection of ideas. □ **association football** kind played with round ball which may be handled only by goalkeeper.

assonance /'æsənəns/ *noun* partial resemblance of sound between syllables, as in *run-up*, or *wary* and *barely*. □ **assonant** *adjective*.

assorted /ə'sɔːtɪd/ *adjective* of various sorts, mixed.

assortment /ə'sɔːtmənt/ *noun* diverse group or mixture.

assuage /ə'sweɪdʒ/ *verb* (**-ging**) soothe; appease.

assume /ə'sjuːm/ *verb* (**-ming**) take to be true; undertake; simulate; take on (aspect, attribute, etc.).

assumption /ə'sʌmpʃ(ə)n/ *noun* assuming; thing assumed; (**Assumption**) reception of Virgin Mary bodily into heaven.

assurance *noun* declaration; insurance, esp. of life; certainty; self-confidence.

assure /ə'ʃʊə/ *verb* (**-ring**) (often + *of*) convince; tell (person) confidently; ensure, guarantee (result etc.); insure (esp. life).

assuredly /ə'ʃʊərɪdlɪ/ *adverb* certainly.

aster /'æstə/ *noun* plant with bright daisy-like flowers.

asterisk /'æstərɪsk/ *noun* symbol (*) used to indicate omission etc.

astern /ə'stɜːn/ *adverb* in or to rear of ship or aircraft; backwards.

asteroid /'æstərɔɪd/ *noun* any of numerous small planets between orbits of Mars and Jupiter.

asthma /ˈæsmə/ noun condition marked by difficulty in breathing. □ **asthmatic** /-ˈmæt-/ adjective & noun.

astigmatism /əˈstɪgmətɪz(ə)m/ noun eye or lens defect resulting in distorted images. □ **astigmatic** /æstɪgˈmætɪk/ adjective.

astir /əˈstɜː/ adverb & adjective in motion; out of bed.

astonish /əˈstɒnɪʃ/ verb amaze, surprise. □ **astonishment** noun.

astound /əˈstaʊnd/ verb astonish greatly.

astrakhan /æstrəˈkæn/ noun dark curly fleece of Astrakhan lamb; cloth imitating this.

astral /ˈæstr(ə)l/ adjective of stars; starry.

astray /əˈstreɪ/ adverb & adjective away from right way. □ **go astray** be lost.

astride /əˈstraɪd/ • adverb (often + of) with one leg on each side. • preposition astride of.

astringent /əˈstrɪndʒənt/ • adjective contracting body tissue, esp. to check bleeding; austere, severe. • noun astringent substance. □ **astringency** noun.

astrolabe /ˈæstrəleɪb/ noun instrument for measuring altitude of stars etc.

astrology /əˈstrɒlədʒɪ/ noun study of supposed planetary influence on human affairs. □ **astrologer** noun; **astrological** /æstrəˈlɒdʒ-/ adjective.

astronaut /ˈæstrənɔːt/ noun space traveller.

astronautics /æstrəˈnɔːtɪks/ plural noun (treated as singular) science of space travel. □ **astronautical** adjective.

astronomical /æstrəˈnɒmɪk(ə)l/ adjective (also **astronomic**) of astronomy; vast. □ **astronomically** adverb.

astronomy /əˈstrɒnəmɪ/ noun science of celestial bodies. □ **astronomer** noun.

astrophysics /æstrəʊˈfɪzɪks/ plural noun (treated as singular) study of physics and chemistry of celestial bodies. □ **astrophysical** adjective; **astrophysicist** noun.

astute /əˈstjuːt/ adjective shrewd. □ **astutely** adverb; **astuteness** noun.

asunder /əˈsʌndə/ adverb literary apart.

asylum /əˈsaɪləm/ noun sanctuary; = POLITICAL ASYLUM; historical mental institution.

asymmetry /eɪˈsɪmətrɪ/ noun lack of symmetry. □ **asymmetric(al)** /-ˈmet-/ adjective.

at /æt, ət/ preposition expressing position, point in time or on scale, engagement in activity, value or rate, or motion or aim towards.

atavism /ˈætəvɪz(ə)m/ noun resemblance to remote ancestors; reversion to earlier type. □ **atavistic** /-ˈvɪs-/ adjective.

ate past of EAT.

atelier /əˈtelɪeɪ/ noun workshop; artist's studio.

atheism /ˈeɪθɪɪz(ə)m/ noun belief that no God exists. □ **atheist** noun; **atheistic** /-ˈɪst-/ adjective.

atherosclerosis /æθərəʊskləˈrəʊsɪs/ noun formation of fatty deposits in the arteries.

athlete /ˈæθliːt/ noun person who engages in athletics, exercises, etc. □ **athlete's foot** fungal foot disease.

athletic /æθˈletɪk/ adjective of athletes or athletics; physically strong or agile. □ **athletically** adverb; **athleticism** noun.

athletics plural noun (usually treated as singular) physical exercises, esp. track and field events.

atlas /ˈætləs/ noun book of maps.

atmosphere /ˈætməsfɪə/ noun gases enveloping earth, other planet, etc.; tone, mood, etc., of place, book, etc.; unit of pressure. □ **atmospheric** /-ˈfer-/ adjective.

atmospherics /ætməsˈferɪks/ plural noun electrical disturbance in atmosphere; interference with telecommunications caused by this.

atoll /ˈætɒl/ noun ring-shaped coral reef enclosing lagoon.

atom /ˈætəm/ noun smallest particle of chemical element that can take part in chemical reaction; this as source of nuclear energy; minute portion or thing. □ **atom bomb** bomb in which energy is released by nuclear fission.

atomic /əˈtɒmɪk/ adjective of atoms; of or using atomic energy or atom bombs. □ **atomic bomb** atom bomb; **atomic energy** nuclear energy; **atomic number** number of protons in nucleus of atom; **atomic weight** ratio of mass of one atom of element to 1/12 mass of atom of carbon-12.

atomize /ˈætəmaɪz/ verb (also **-ise**) (**-zing** or **-sing**) reduce to atoms or fine spray.

atomizer noun (also **-iser**) aerosol.

atonal /eɪˈtəʊn(ə)l/ adjective Music not written in any key. □ **atonality** /-ˈnæl-/ noun.

atone /əˈtəʊn/ verb (**-ning**) (usually + for) make amends. □ **atonement** noun.

atrium /ˈeɪtrɪəm/ noun (plural **-s** or **atria**) either of upper cavities of heart.

atrocious /əˈtrəʊʃəs/ adjective very bad; wicked. □ **atrociously** adverb.

atrocity /əˈtrɒsɪtɪ/ noun (plural **-ies**) wicked or cruel act.

atrophy /ˈætrəfɪ/ ● noun wasting away, esp. through disuse. ● verb (**-ies**, **-ied**) suffer atrophy; cause atrophy in.

atropine /ˈætrəpiːn/ noun poisonous alkaloid in deadly nightshade.

attach /əˈtætʃ/ verb fasten, affix, join; (in passive; + to) be very fond of; (+ to) attribute or be attributable to.

attaché /əˈtæʃeɪ/ noun specialist member of ambassador's staff. □ **attaché case** small rectangular document case.

attachment noun thing attached, esp. for particular purpose; affection, devotion; attaching, being attached.

attack /əˈtæk/ ● verb try to hurt or deflect using force; criticize adversely; act harmfully on; Sport try to score against; vigorously apply oneself to. ● noun act of attacking; sudden onset of illness. □ **attacker** noun.

attain /əˈteɪn/ verb gain, accomplish; reach; (+ to) arrive at (goal etc.).

attainment noun attaining; (often in plural) skill, achievement.

attar /ˈætɑː/ noun perfume made from rose-petals.

attempt /əˈtempt/ ● verb try; try to accomplish or conquer. ● noun (often + at, on) attempting; endeavour.

attend /əˈtend/ verb be present at; go regularly to; (often + to) apply mind or oneself; (+ to) deal with; accompany, wait on. □ **attender** noun.

attendance noun attending; number of people present.

attendant ● noun person attending, esp. to provide service. ● adjective accompanying; (often + on) waiting.

attention /əˈtenʃ(ə)n/ noun act or faculty of applying one's mind, notice; consideration, care; Military erect attitude of readiness; (in plural) courtesies.

attentive /əˈtentɪv/ adjective (+ to) paying attention. □ **attentively** adverb.

attenuate /əˈtenjʊeɪt/ verb (**-ting**) make thin; reduce in force or value. □ **attenuation** noun.

attest /əˈtest/ verb certify validity of; (+ to) bear witness to. □ **attestation** /æt-/ noun.

attic /ˈætɪk/ noun room or space immediately under roof of house.

attire /əˈtaɪə/ noun clothes, esp. formal.

attired adjective dressed, esp. formally.

attitude /ˈætɪtjuːd/ noun opinion, way of thinking; (often + to) behaviour reflecting this; bodily posture.

attitudinize /ætɪˈtjuːdɪnaɪz/ verb (also **-ise**) (**-zing** or **-sing**) adopt attitudes.

attorney /əˈtɜːnɪ/ noun person, esp. lawyer, appointed to act for another in business or legal matters; US qualified lawyer. □ **Attorney-General** chief legal officer of government.

attract /əˈtrækt/ verb (of magnet etc.) draw to itself or oneself; arouse interest or admiration in.

attraction /əˈtrækʃ(ə)n/ noun attracting, being attracted; attractive quality; person or thing that attracts.

attractive /əˈtræktɪv/ adjective attracting esp. interest or admiration; pleasing. □ **attractively** adverb.

attribute ● verb /əˈtrɪbjuːt/ (**-ting**) (usually + to) regard as belonging to or as written, said, or caused by, etc. ● noun /ˈætrɪbjuːt/ quality ascribed to person or thing; characteristic quality; object frequently associated with person, office, or status. □ **attributable** /əˈtrɪbjʊtəb(ə)l/ adjective, **attribution** /ætrɪˈbjuːʃ(ə)n/ noun.

attributive /əˈtrɪbjʊtɪv/ adjective expressing an attribute; (of adjective or noun) preceding word it describes.

attrition /əˈtrɪʃ(ə)n/ noun gradual wearing down; friction, abrasion.

attune /əˈtjuːn/ verb (**-ning**) (usually + to) adjust; Music tune.

atypical /eɪˈtɪpɪk(ə)l/ adjective not typical. □ **atypically** adverb.

aubergine /ˈəʊbəʒiːn/ *noun* (plant with) oval usually purple fruit used as vegetable.

aubrietia /ɔːˈbriːʃə/ *noun* (also **aubretia**) dwarf perennial rock plant.

auburn /ˈɔːbən/ *adjective* (usually of hair) reddish-brown.

auction /ˈɔːkʃ(ə)n/ ● *noun* sale in which each article is sold to highest bidder. ● *verb* sell by auction.

auctioneer /ɔːkʃəˈnɪə/ *noun* person who conducts auctions.

audacious /ɔːˈdeɪʃəs/ *adjective* daring, bold; impudent. □ **audacity** /-ˈdæs-/ *noun*.

audible /ˈɔːdɪb(ə)l/ *adjective* that can be heard. □ **audibility** *noun*; **audibly** *adverb*.

audience /ˈɔːdɪəns/ *noun* group of listeners or spectators; group of people reached by any spoken or written message; formal interview.

audio /ˈɔːdɪəʊ/ *noun* (reproduction of) sound. □ **audiotape** magnetic tape for recording sound; **audio typist** person who types from tape recording; **audio-visual** using both sight and sound.

audit /ˈɔːdɪt/ ● *noun* official scrutiny of accounts. ● *verb* (**-t-**) conduct audit of. □ **auditor** *noun*.

audition /ɔːˈdɪʃ(ə)n/ ● *noun* test of performer's ability. ● *verb* assess or be assessed at audition.

auditorium /ɔːdɪˈtɔːrɪəm/ *noun* (*plural* **-s**) part of theatre etc. for audience.

auditory /ˈɔːdɪtərɪ/ *adjective* of hearing.

au fait /əʊ ˈfeɪ/ *adjective* (usually + *with*) conversant.

Aug. *abbreviation* August.

auger /ˈɔːgə/ *noun* tool with screw point for boring holes in wood.

aught /ɔːt/ *noun archaic* anything.

augment /ɔːgˈment/ *verb* make greater, increase. □ **augmentation** *noun*.

augur /ˈɔːgə/ *verb* portend; serve as omen.

augury /ˈɔːgjʊrɪ/ *noun* (*plural* **-ies**) omen; interpretation of omens.

August /ˈɔːgəst/ *noun* eighth month of year.

august /ɔːˈgʌst/ *adjective* venerable, imposing.

auk /ɔːk/ *noun* black and white seabird with small wings.

aunt /ɑːnt/ *noun* parent's sister; uncle's wife. □ **Aunt Sally** game in which sticks or balls are thrown at dummy, target of general abuse.

aunty /ˈɑːntɪ/ *noun* (also **auntie**) (*plural* **-ies**) *colloquial* aunt.

au pair /əʊ ˈpeə/ *noun* young foreign woman who helps with housework in return for room and board.

aura /ˈɔːrə/ *noun* distinctive atmosphere; subtle emanation.

aural /ˈɔːr(ə)l/ *adjective* of ear or hearing. □ **aurally** *adverb*.

aureole /ˈɔːrɪəʊl/ *noun* (also **aureola** /ɔːˈriːələ/) halo.

au revoir /əʊ rəˈvwɑː/ *interjection & noun* goodbye (until we meet again). [French]

auricle /ˈɔːrɪk(ə)l/ *noun* external ear of animal; atrium of heart.

auriferous /ɔːˈrɪfərəs/ *adjective* yielding gold.

aurora /ɔːˈrɔːrə/ *noun* (*plural* **-s** or **-rae** /-riː/) streamers of light above northern (**aurora borealis** /bɒrɪˈeɪlɪs/) or southern (**aurora australis** /ɔːˈstreɪlɪs/) polar region.

auscultation /ɔːskəlˈteɪʃ(ə)n/ *noun* listening to sound of heart etc. to help diagnosis.

auspice /ˈɔːspɪs/ *noun* omen; (in *plural*) patronage.

auspicious /ɔːˈspɪʃəs/ *adjective* promising; favourable.

Aussie /ˈɒzɪ/ *noun & adjective slang* Australian.

austere /ɔːˈstɪə/ *adjective* (**-r**, **-st**) severely simple; stern; morally strict. □ **austerity** /-ˈter-/ *noun*.

austral /ˈɔːstr(ə)l/ *adjective* southern.

Australasian /ɒstrəˈleɪʒ(ə)n/ *adjective* of Australia and SW Pacific islands.

Australian /ɒˈstreɪlɪən/ ● *adjective* of Australia. ● *noun* native or national of Australia.

autarchy /ˈɔːtɑːkɪ/ *noun* absolute rule.

autarky /ˈɔːtɑːkɪ/ *noun* self-sufficiency.

authentic /ɔːˈθentɪk/ *adjective* of undisputed origin, genuine; trustworthy. □ **authentically** *adverb*; **authenticity** /-ˈtɪs-/ *noun*.

authenticate /ɔːˈθentɪkeɪt/ *verb* (**-ting**) establish as true, genuine, or valid. □ **authentication** *noun*.

author /ˈɔːθə/ *noun* (*feminine* **authoress** /ˈɔːθrɪs/) writer of book etc.; originator. □ **authorship** *noun*.

authoritarian /ɔːˌθɒrɪˈteərɪən/ ● *adjective* favouring strict obedience to authority. ● *noun* authoritarian person.

authoritative /ɔːˈθɒrɪtətɪv/ *adjective* reliable, esp. having authority.

authority /ɔːˈθɒrɪtɪ/ *noun* (*plural* **-ies**) power or right to enforce obedience; (esp. in *plural*) body having this; delegated power; influence based on recognized knowledge or expertise; expert.

authorize /ˈɔːθəraɪz/ *verb* (also **-ise**) (**-zing** or **-sing**) (+ *to do*) give authority to (person); sanction officially. □ **Authorized Version** English translation (1611) of Bible. □ **authorization** *noun*.

autism /ˈɔːtɪz(ə)m/ *noun* condition characterized by self-absorption and withdrawal. □ **autistic** /-ˈtɪs-/ *adjective*.

auto- *combining form* self; one's own; of or by oneself or itself.

autobahn /ˈɔːtəʊbɑːn/ *noun* German, Austrian, or Swiss motorway. [German]

autobiography /ɔːtəʊbaɪˈɒɡrəfɪ/ *noun* (*plural* **-ies**) story of one's own life. □ **autobiographer** *noun*, **autobiographical** /-əˈɡræf-/ *adjective*.

autocracy /ɔːˈtɒkrəsɪ/ *noun* (*plural* **-ies**) absolute rule by one person.

autocrat /ˈɔːtəkræt/ *noun* absolute ruler. □ **autocratic** /-ˈkræt-/ *adjective*; **autocratically** /-ˈkræt-/ *adverb*.

autocross /ˈɔːtəkrɒs/ *noun* motor racing across country or on unmade roads.

autograph /ˈɔːtəɡrɑːf/ ● *noun* signature, esp. of celebrity. ● *verb* write on or sign in one's own handwriting.

automate /ˈɔːtəmeɪt/ *verb* (**-ting**) convert to or operate by automation.

automatic /ɔːtəˈmætɪk/ ● *adjective* working by itself, without direct human involvement; done spontaneously; following inevitably; (of firearm) that can be loaded and fired continuously; (of vehicle or its transmission) using gears

that change automatically. ● *noun* automatic firearm, vehicle, etc. □ **automatically** *adverb*.

automation *noun* use of automatic equipment in place of manual labour.

automaton /ɔːˈtɒmət(ə)n/ *noun* (*plural* **-mata** or **-s**) machine controlled automatically.

automobile /ˈɔːtəməbiːl/ *noun* US motor car.

automotive /ɔːtəˈməʊtɪv/ *adjective* of motor vehicles.

autonomous /ɔːˈtɒnəməs/ *adjective* self-governing; free to act independently. □ **autonomy** *noun*.

autopsy /ˈɔːtɒpsɪ/ *noun* (*plural* **-ies**) post-mortem.

auto-suggestion /ɔːtəʊsəˈdʒestʃ(ə)n/ *noun* hypnotic or subconscious suggestion made to oneself.

autumn /ˈɔːtəm/ *noun* season between summer and winter. □ **autumnal** /ɔːˈtʌmn(ə)l/ *adjective*.

auxiliary /ɔːɡˈzɪljərɪ/ ● *adjective* giving help; additional, subsidiary. ● *noun* (*plural* **-ies**) auxiliary person or thing; (in *plural*) foreign or allied troops in service of nation at war; auxiliary verb. □ **auxiliary verb** one used with another verb to form tenses etc. (see panel).

avail /əˈveɪl/ ● *verb* (often + *to*) be of use; help; (**avail oneself of**) use, profit by. ● *noun* use, profit.

available *adjective* at one's disposal; (of person) free, able to be contacted. □ **availability** *noun*.

avalanche /ˈævəlɑːntʃ/ *noun* mass of snow and ice rapidly sliding down mountain; sudden abundance.

avant-garde /ævãˈɡɑːd/ ● *noun* innovators, esp. in the arts. ● *adjective* new, pioneering.

avarice /ˈævərɪs/ *noun* greed for wealth. □ **avaricious** /-ˈrɪʃ-/ *adjective*.

avatar /ˈævətɑː/ *noun Hindu Mythology* descent of god to earth in bodily form.

avenge /əˈvendʒ/ *verb* (**-ging**) inflict retribution on behalf of; exact retribution for.

avenue /ˈævənjuː/ *noun* road or path, usually tree-lined; way of approach.

aver /əˈvɜː/ *verb* (**-rr-**) *formal* assert, affirm.

average /'ævərɪdʒ/ ● *noun* usual amount, extent, or rate; number obtained by dividing sum of given numbers by how many there are. ● *adjective* usual, ordinary; mediocre; constituting average. ● *verb* (**-ging**) amount on average to; do on average; estimate average of. □ **average out (at)** result in average (of); **on average** as an average rate etc.

averse /ə'vɜ:s/ *adjective* (usually + *to*) opposed, disinclined.

aversion /ə'vɜ:ʃ(ə)n/ *noun* (usually + *to, for*) dislike, unwillingness; object of this.

avert /ə'vɜ:t/ *verb* prevent; (often + *from*) turn away.

aviary /'eɪvɪərɪ/ *noun* (*plural* **-ies**) large cage or building for keeping birds.

aviation /eɪvɪ'eɪʃ(ə)n/ *noun* the flying of aircraft.

aviator /'eɪvɪeɪtə/ *noun* person who flies aircraft.

avid /'ævɪd/ *adjective* eager; greedy. □ **avidity** /-'vɪd-/ *noun*; **avidly** *adverb*.

avocado /ævə'kɑːdəʊ/ *noun* (*plural* **-s**) (in full **avocado pear**) dark green pear-shaped fruit with creamy flesh.

avocet /'ævəset/ *noun* wading bird with long upturned bill.

avoid /ə'vɔɪd/ *verb* keep away or refrain from; escape; evade. □ **avoidable** *adjective*; **avoidance** *noun*.

avoirdupois /ævədə'pɔɪz/ *noun* system of weights based on pound of 16 ounces.

avow /ə'vaʊ/ *verb formal* declare; confess. □ **avowal** *noun*; **avowedly** /ə'vaʊɪdlɪ/ *adverb*.

avuncular /ə'vʌŋkjʊlə/ *adjective* of or like an uncle.

await /ə'weɪt/ *verb* wait for; be in store for.

awake /ə'weɪk/ ● *verb* (**-king**; *past* **awoke**; *past participle* **awoken**) (also **awaken**) rouse from sleep; cease to sleep; (often + *to*) become alert, aware, or active. ● *adjective* not asleep; alert.

award /ə'wɔ:d/ ● *verb* give or order to be given as payment, penalty, or prize. ● *noun* thing awarded; judicial decision.

aware /ə'weə/ *adjective* (often + *of, that*) conscious, having knowledge. □ **awareness** *noun*.

awash /ə'wɒʃ/ *adjective* at surface of and just covered by water; (+ *with*) abounding.

away ● *adverb* to or at distance; into non-existence; constantly, persistently. ● *adjective* (of match etc.) played on opponent's ground.

awe /ɔː/ ● *noun* reverential fear or wonder. ● *verb* (**awing**) inspire with awe. □ **awe-inspiring** awesome, magnificent.

aweigh /ə'weɪ/ *adjective* (of anchor) just lifted from sea bottom.

awesome *adjective* inspiring awe.

Auxiliary verb

An auxiliary verb is used in front of another verb to alter its meaning. Mainly, it expresses:

1 when something happens, by forming a tense of the main verb, e.g. *I shall go. He was going.*

2 permission, obligation, or ability to do something, e.g. *They may go. You must go. I can't go.*

3 the likelihood of something happening, e.g. *I might go. She would go if she could.*

The principal auxiliary verbs are:

be	have	must	will
can	let	ought	would
could	may	shall	
do	might	should	

---

awful /'ɔ:fʊl/ *adjective colloquial* very bad; very great; *poetical* inspiring awe.

awfully *adverb colloquial* badly; very.

awhile /ə'waɪl/ *adverb* for a short time.

awkward /'ɔ:kwəd/ *adjective* difficult to use; clumsy; embarrassing, embarrassed; hard to deal with.

awl /ɔ:l/ *noun* small tool for pricking holes, esp. in leather.

awning /'ɔ:nɪŋ/ *noun* fabric roof, shelter.

awoke *past* of AWAKE.

awoken *past participle* of AWAKE.

AWOL /'eɪwɒl/ *abbreviation colloquial* absent without leave.

awry /ə'raɪ/ ● *adverb* crookedly; amiss. ● *adjective* crooked; unsound.

axe /æks/ ● *noun* (*US* **ax**) chopping-tool with heavy blade; (**the axe**) dismissal (of employees), abandonment of project etc. ● *verb* (**axing**) cut (staff, services, etc.); abandon (project).

axial /'æksɪəl/ *adjective* of, forming, or placed round axis.

axiom /'æksɪəm/ *noun* established principle; self-evident truth. □ **axiomatic** /-'mæt-/ *adjective*.

axis /'æksɪs/ *noun* (*plural* **axes** /-si:z/) imaginary line about which object rotates; line dividing regular figure symmetrically; reference line for measurement of coordinates etc.

axle /'æks(ə)l/ *noun* spindle on which wheel turns or is fixed.

ayatollah /aɪə'tɒlə/ *noun* religious leader in Iran.

aye /aɪ/ ● *adverb archaic or dialect* yes. ● *noun* affirmative answer or vote.

azalea /ə'zeɪlɪə/ *noun* kind of rhododendron.

azimuth /'æzɪməθ/ *noun* angular distance between point below star etc. and north or south. □ **azimuthal** *adjective*.

azure /'æʒə/ *adjective & noun* sky-blue.

Bb

B *abbreviation* black (pencil lead).

b. *abbreviation* born.

BA *abbreviation* Bachelor of Arts.

baa /bɑ:/ *noun & verb* (**baas, baaed** or **baa'd**) bleat.

babble /'bæb(ə)l/ ● *verb* (**-ling**) talk, chatter, or say incoherently or excessively; (of stream) murmur; repeat foolishly. ● *noun* babbling; murmur of water etc.

babe *noun* baby.

babel /'beɪb(ə)l/ *noun* confused noise, esp. of voices.

baboon /bə'bu:n/ *noun* large kind of monkey.

baby /'beɪbɪ/ *noun* (*plural* **-ies**) very young child; childish person; youngest member of family etc.; very young animal; small specimen. □ **baby boom** *colloquial* temporary increase in birth rate; **baby grand** small grand piano.

babysit *verb* (**-tt-**; *past & past participle* **-sat**) look after child while parents are out. □ **babysitter** *noun*.

baccarat /'bækərɑ:/ *noun* gambling card game.

bachelor /'bætʃələ/ *noun* unmarried man; person with a university first degree.

bacillus /bə'sɪləs/ *noun* (*plural* **bacilli** /-laɪ/) rod-shaped bacterium. □ **bacillary** *adjective*.

back ● *noun* rear surface of human body from shoulders to hips; upper surface of animal's body; spine; reverse or more distant part; part of garment covering back; defensive player in football etc. ● *adverb* away from front; in(to) the past or an earlier or normal position or condition; in return; at a distance. ● *verb* help with money or moral support; (often + *up*) (cause to) go backwards; bet on; provide with or serve as back, support, or backing to; *Music* accompany. ● *adjective* situated to rear; past, not current; reversed. □ **backache** ache in back; **backbencher** MP without senior office; **backbiting** malicious talk; **back boiler** one behind domestic fire etc.; **backbone** spine, main support, firmness of character; **backchat** *colloquial* verbal insolence; **backcloth** painted cloth at back of stage; **backdate** make retrospectively valid, put earlier date to; **back door** secret or ingenious means; **back down** withdraw from confrontation; **backdrop** backcloth; **backfire** (of engine or vehicle) undergo premature explosion in cylinder or exhaust pipe, (of plan etc.) have opposite of intended effect; **backhand** *Tennis etc.* (stroke) made with hand across body; **backhanded** indirect, ambiguous; **backhander** *slang* bribe; **backlash** violent, usually hostile, reaction; **backlog** arrears (of work etc.); **back number** old issue of magazine etc.; **back out** (often + *of*) withdraw; **backpack** rucksack; **back-pedal** reverse previous action or opinion; **back room** place where (esp. secret) work goes on; **back seat** less prominent or important position; **backside** *colloquial* buttocks; **backslide** return to bad ways; **backstage** behind the scenes; **backstreet** *noun* sidestreet, alley, *adjective* illicit, illegal; **backstroke** stroke made by swimmer lying on back; **back to front** with back and front reversed; **backtrack** retrace one's steps, reverse one's policy or opinion; **back up** give (esp. moral) support to, *Computing* make backup of; **backup** support, *Computing* (making of) spare copy of data; **backwash** receding waves, repercussions; **backwater** peaceful, secluded, or dull place, stagnant water fed from stream; **backwoods** remote uncleared forest land.

backgammon /ˈbækgæmən/ *noun* board game with pieces moved according to throw of dice.

background /ˈbækgraʊnd/ *noun* back part of scene etc.; inconspicuous position; person's education, social circumstances, etc.; explanatory information etc.

backing *noun* help or support; material used for thing's back or support; musical accompaniment.

backward *adjective* directed backwards; slow in learning; shy.

backwards *adverb* away from one's front; back foremost; in reverse of usual way; into worse state; into past; back towards starting point □ **bend over backwards** *colloquial* make every effort.

bacon /ˈbeɪkən/ *noun* cured meat from back and sides of pig.

bacteriology /bæktɪərɪˈɒlədʒɪ/ *noun* study of bacteria.

bacterium /bækˈtɪərɪəm/ *noun* (*plural* **-ria**) single-celled micro-organism. □ **bacterial** *adjective*.

■ **Usage** It is a mistake to use the plural form *bacteria* when only one bacterium is meant.

bad *adjective* (**worse**, **worst**) inadequate, defective; unpleasant; harmful; decayed; ill, injured; regretful, guilty; serious, severe; wicked; naughty; incorrect, not valid. □ **bad debt** debt that is not recoverable; **bad-tempered** irritable.

bade *archaic past* of BID.

badge *noun* small flat emblem worn as sign of office, membership, etc. or bearing slogan etc.

badger /ˈbædʒə/ ● *noun* nocturnal burrowing mammal with black and white striped head. ● *verb* pester.

badinage /ˈbædɪnɑːʒ/ *noun* banter. [French]

badly *adverb* (**worse**, **worst**) in bad manner; severely; very much.

badminton /ˈbædmɪnt(ə)n/ *noun* game played with rackets and shuttlecock.

baffle /ˈbæf(ə)l/ ● *verb* perplex; frustrate. ● *noun* device that hinders flow of fluid or sound. □ **bafflement** *noun*.

bag ● *noun* soft open-topped receptacle; piece of luggage; (in *plural*, usually + *of*) *colloquial* large amount; animal's sac; amount of game shot by one person. ● *verb* secure, take possession of; bulge, hang loosely; put in bag; shoot (game).

bagatelle /bægəˈtel/ *noun* game in which small balls are struck into holes on inclined board; mere trifle.

bagel /ˈbeɪg(ə)l/ *noun* ring-shaped bread roll.

baggage /ˈbægɪdʒ/ *noun* luggage; portable equipment of army.

baggy *adjective* (**-ier**, **-iest**) hanging loosely.

bagpipes /'bægpaɪps/ *plural noun* musical instrument with windbag for pumping air through reeded pipes.

baguette /bæˈget/ *noun* long thin French loaf.

bail[1] ● *noun* security given for released prisoner's return for trial; person(s) pledging this. ● *verb* (usually + *out*) give bail for and secure release of (prisoner).

bail[2] *noun* Cricket either of two crosspieces resting on stumps.

bail[3] *verb* (also **bale**) (usually + *out*) scoop (water) out of (boat etc.). □ **bail out** = BALE OUT.

bailey /'beɪlɪ/ *noun* (*plural* **-s**) outer wall of castle; court enclosed by this.

bailiff /'beɪlɪf/ *noun* sheriff's officer who executes writs, performs distraints, etc.; landlord's agent or steward.

bailiwick /'beɪlɪwɪk/ *noun* district of bailiff.

bairn /beən/ *noun Scottish & Northern English* child.

bait ● *noun* food to entice prey; allurement. ● *verb* torment (chained animal); harass (person); put bait on or in (fishhook, trap, etc.).

baize /beɪz/ *noun* usually green felted woollen fabric used for coverings etc.

bake *verb* (**-king**) cook or become cooked by dry heat esp. in oven; *colloquial* be very hot; harden by heat. □ **baking powder** mixture used as raising agent.

Bakelite /'beɪkəlaɪt/ *noun proprietary term* kind of plastic.

baker /'beɪkə/ *noun* professional breadmaker. □ **baker's dozen** thirteen.

bakery /'beɪkərɪ/ *noun* (*plural* **-ies**) place where bread is made or sold.

baksheesh /'bækʃiːʃ/ *noun* gratuity, tip.

Balaclava /bælə'klɑːvə/ *noun* (in full **Balaclava helmet**) woollen covering for head and neck.

balalaika /bælə'laɪkə/ *noun* Russian triangular-bodied guitar-like musical instrument.

balance /'bæləns/ ● *noun* even distribution of weight or amount; stability of body or mind; weighing apparatus;

counteracting weight or force; regulating device in clock etc.; decisive weight or amount; difference between credits and debits; remainder. ● *verb* (**-cing**) bring or come into or keep in equilibrium; offset, compare; equal, neutralize; (usually as **balanced** *adjective*) make well-proportioned and harmonious; equalize debits and credits of account, have debits and credits equal. □ **balance of payments** difference between payments into and out of a country; **balance of power** position in which no country etc. predominates, power held by small group when larger groups are of (almost) equal strength; **balance of trade** difference between exports and imports; **balance sheet** statement giving balance of account; **on balance** all things considered.

balcony /'bælkənɪ/ *noun* (*plural* **-ies**) outside balustraded or railed platform with access from upper floor; upper tier of seats in theatre etc.

bald /bɔːld/ *adjective* lacking some or all hair on scalp; without fur, feathers, etc.; with surface worn away; direct. □ **baldly** *adverb*; **baldness** *noun*.

balderdash /'bɔːldədæʃ/ *noun* nonsense.

balding /'bɔːldɪŋ/ *adjective* becoming bald.

bale[1] ● *noun* bundle of merchandise or hay. ● *verb* (**-ling**) make up into bales. □ **bale out** (also **bail out**) make emergency parachute jump from aircraft.

bale[2] = BAIL[3].

baleful /'beɪlfʊl/ *adjective* menacing; destructive; malignant.

balk = BAULK.

ball[1] /bɔːl/ *noun* spherical object or mass; usually spherical object used in game; rounded part of foot or hand at base of big toe or thumb; cannon ball; delivery or pass of ball in game. □ **ball-bearing** bearing using ring of small balls between its two parts, one such ball; **ballcock** valve operated by floating ball that controls level of water in cistern; **ball game** *US* baseball game, *colloquial* affair or matter; **ballpoint (pen)** pen with tiny ball as writing point.

ball[2] /bɔːl/ *noun* formal social gathering for dancing; *slang* enjoyable time.

ballad /ˈbæləd/ *noun* poem or song narrating popular story; slow sentimental song. □ **balladry** *noun*.

ballast /ˈbæləst/ ● *noun* heavy material stabilizing ship, controlling height of balloon, etc.; coarse stone etc. as bed of road or railway. ● *verb* provide with ballast.

ballerina /bæləˈriːnə/ *noun* female ballet dancer.

ballet /ˈbæleɪ/ *noun* dramatic or representational style of dancing to music; piece or performance of ballet. □ **ballet dancer** dancer of ballet. □ **balletic** /bəˈletɪk/ *adjective*.

ballistic /bəˈlɪstɪk/ *adjective* of projectiles. □ **ballistic missile** one that is powered and guided but falls by gravity.

ballistics *plural noun* (usually treated as *singular*) science of projectiles and firearms.

balloon /bəˈluːn/ ● *noun* small inflatable rubber toy or decoration; large inflatable flying bag, esp. one with basket below for passengers; outline containing words or thoughts in strip cartoon. ● *verb* (cause to) swell out like balloon. □ **balloonist** *noun*.

ballot /ˈbælət/ ● *noun* voting in writing and usually secret; votes recorded in ballot. ● *verb* (**-t-**) hold ballot; vote by ballot; take ballot of (voters). □ **ballot box** container for **ballot papers**, slips for marking votes.

ballroom /ˈbɔːlruːm/ *noun* large room for dancing. □ **ballroom dancing** formal social dancing for couples.

bally /ˈbælɪ/ *adjective & adverb slang* mild form of BLOODY.

ballyhoo /bælɪˈhuː/ *noun* loud noise, fuss; noisy publicity.

balm /bɑːm/ *noun* aromatic ointment; fragrant oil or resin exuded from some trees; thing that heals or soothes; aromatic herb.

balmy /ˈbɑːmɪ/ *adjective* (**-ier**, **-iest**) fragrant, mild, soothing; *slang* crazy.

balsa /ˈbɔːlsə/ *noun* lightweight tropical American wood used for making models.

balsam /ˈbɔːlsəm/ *noun* balm from trees; ointment; tree yielding balsam; any of several flowering plants.

baluster /ˈbæləstə/ *noun* short pillar supporting rail.

balustrade /bæləˈstreɪd/ *noun* railing supported by balusters, esp. on balcony.

bamboo /bæmˈbuː/ *noun* tropical giant woody grass; its hollow stem.

bamboozle /bæmˈbuːz(ə)l/ *verb* (**-ling**) *colloquial* cheat; mystify.

ban ● *verb* (**-nn-**) prohibit, esp. formally. ● *noun* formal prohibition.

banal /bəˈnɑːl/ *adjective* commonplace, trite. □ **banality** /-ˈnæl-/ *noun* (*plural* **-ies**).

banana /bəˈnɑːnə/ *noun* long curved yellow tropical fruit; treelike plant bearing it.

band ● *noun* flat strip or loop of thin material; stripe; group of musicians; organized group of criminals etc.; range of values, esp. frequencies or wavelengths. ● *verb* (usually + *together*) unite; put band on; mark with stripes. □ **bandbox** hatbox; **bandmaster** conductor of band; **bandsman** player in band; **bandstand** outdoor platform for musicians.

bandage /ˈbændɪdʒ/ ● *noun* strip of material for binding wound etc. ● *verb* (**-ging**) bind with bandage.

bandanna /bænˈdænə/ *noun* large patterned handkerchief.

bandeau /ˈbændəʊ/ *noun* (*plural* **-x** /-z/) narrow headband.

bandit /ˈbændɪt/ *noun* robber, esp. of travellers. □ **banditry** *noun*.

bandolier /bændəˈlɪə/ *noun* (also **bandoleer**) shoulder belt with loops or pockets for cartridges.

bandwagon *noun* □ **climb, jump on the bandwagon** join popular or successful cause.

bandy[1] /ˈbændɪ/ *adjective* (**-ier**, **-iest**) (of legs) curved wide apart at knees. □ **bandy-legged** *adjective*.

bandy[2] /ˈbændɪ/ *verb* (**-ies**, **-ied**) (often + *about*) pass (story etc.) to and fro, discuss disparagingly; (often + *with*) exchange (blows, insults, etc.).

bane *noun* cause of ruin or trouble.

bang ● *noun* loud short sound; sharp blow. ● *verb* strike or shut noisily; (cause to) make bang. ● *adverb* with bang; *colloquial* exactly. □ **bang on** *colloquial* exactly right.

banger *noun* firework making bang; *slang* sausage, noisy old car.

bangle /'bæŋg(ə)l/ *noun* rigid bracelet or anklet.

banian = BANYAN.

banish /'bænɪʃ/ *verb* condemn to exile; dismiss from one's mind. □ **banishment** *noun*.

banister /'bænɪstə/ *noun* (also **bannister**) (usually in *plural*) uprights and handrail beside staircase.

banjo /'bændʒəʊ/ *noun* (*plural* **-s** or **-es**) round-bodied guitar-like musical instrument. □ **banjoist** *noun*.

bank¹ ● *noun* sloping ground on each side of river; raised shelf of ground, esp. in sea; mass of cloud etc. ● *verb* (often + *up*) heap or rise into banks; pack (fire) tightly for slow burning; (cause to) travel round curve with one side higher than the other.

bank² ● *noun* establishment, usually a public company, where money is deposited, withdrawn, and borrowed; pool of money in gambling game; storage place. ● *verb* deposit (money) at bank; (often + *at*, *with*) keep money (at bank). □ **bank card** cheque card; **bank holiday** public holiday when banks are closed; **banknote** piece of paper money; **bank on** *colloquial* rely on.

bank³ *noun* row (of lights, switches, organ keys, etc.).

banker *noun* owner or manager of bank; keeper of bank in gambling game. □ **banker's card** cheque card.

bankrupt /'bæŋkrʌpt/ ● *adjective* insolvent; (often + *of*) drained (of emotion etc.). ● *noun* insolvent person. ● *verb* make bankrupt. □ **bankruptcy** *noun* (*plural* **-ies**).

banner /'bænə/ *noun* large portable cloth sign bearing slogan or design; flag.

bannister = BANISTER.

bannock /'bænək/ *noun* Scottish & Northern English round flat loaf, usually unleavened.

banns *plural noun* announcement of intended marriage read in church.

banquet /'bæŋkwɪt/ ● *noun* sumptuous esp. formal dinner. ● *verb* (**-t-**) give banquet for; attend banquet.

banquette /bæŋ'ket/ *noun* upholstered bench along wall.

banshee /bæn'ʃiː/ *noun* female spirit whose wail warns of death in a house.

bantam /'bæntəm/ *noun* kind of small domestic fowl; small but aggressive person. □ **bantamweight** boxing weight (51–54 kg).

banter /'bæntə/ ● *noun* good-humoured teasing. ● *verb* tease; exchange banter.

banyan /'bænjən/ *noun* (also **banian**) Indian fig tree with self-rooting branches.

baobab /'beɪəʊbæb/ *noun* African tree with massive trunk and edible fruit.

bap *noun* soft flattish bread roll.

baptism /'bæptɪz(ə)m/ *noun* symbolic admission to Christian Church, with immersing in or sprinkling with water and usually name-giving. □ **baptismal** /-'tɪz-/ *adjective*.

Baptist /'bæptɪst/ *noun* member of Church practising adult baptism by immersion.

baptize /bæp'taɪz/ *verb* (also **-ise**) (**-zing** or **-sing**) administer baptism to; give name to.

bar¹ ● *noun* long piece of rigid material, esp. used to confine or obstruct; (often + *of*) oblong piece (of chocolate, soap, etc.); band of colour or light; counter for serving alcoholic drinks etc., room or building containing it; counter for particular service; barrier; prisoner's enclosure in law court; section of music between vertical lines; heating element of electric fire; strip below clasp of medal as extra distinction; (**the Bar**) barristers, their profession. ● *verb* (**-rr-**) fasten with bar; (usually + *in*, *out*) keep in or out; obstruct, prevent; (usually + *from*) exclude. ● *preposition* except. □ **bar code** machine-readable striped code on packaging etc.; **barmaid**, **barman**, **bartender** woman, man, person serving in pub etc.

bar² *noun* unit of atmospheric pressure.

barathea /bærə'θiːə/ *noun* fine wool cloth.

barb ● *noun* backward-facing point on arrow, fish-hook, etc.; hurtful remark. ● *verb* fit with barb. □ **barbed wire** wire with spikes, used for fences.

barbarian /baːˈbeərɪən/ ● *noun* uncultured or primitive person. ● *adjective* uncultured; primitive.

barbaric /baːˈbærɪk/ *adjective* uncultured; cruel; primitive.

barbarism /ˈbaːbərɪz(ə)m/ *noun* barbaric state or act; non-standard word or expression.

barbarity /baːˈbærɪtɪ/ *noun* (*plural* -ies) savage cruelty; barbaric act.

barbarous /ˈbaːbərəs/ *adjective* uncultured; cruel.

barbecue /ˈbaːbɪkjuː/ ● *noun* meal cooked over charcoal etc. out of doors; party for this; grill etc. used for this. ● *verb* (-cues, -cued, -cuing) cook on barbecue.

barber /ˈbaːbə/ *noun* person who cuts men's hair.

barbican /ˈbaːbɪkən/ *noun* outer defence, esp. double tower over gate or bridge.

barbiturate /baːˈbɪtjʊrət/ *noun* sedative derived from **barbituric acid** /baːbɪˈtjʊərɪk/, an organic acid.

bard *noun* poet; *historical* Celtic minstrel; prizewinner at Eisteddfod. □ **bardic** *adjective*.

bare /beə/ ● *adjective* unclothed, uncovered; leafless; unadorned, plain; scanty, just sufficient. ● *verb* (-ring) uncover, reveal. □ **bareback** without saddle; **barefaced** shameless, impudent; **barefoot** with bare feet; **bareheaded** without hat.

barely *adverb* scarcely; scantily.

bargain /ˈbaːgɪn/ ● *noun* agreement on terms of sale etc.; cheap thing. ● *verb* discuss terms of sale etc. □ **bargain for** be prepared for; **into the bargain** moreover.

barge /baːdʒ/ ● *noun* large flat-bottomed cargo boat on canal or river; long ornamental pleasure boat. ● *verb* (-ging) (+ *into*) collide with. □ **barge in** interrupt.

bargee /baːˈdʒiː/ *noun* person in charge of barge.

baritone /ˈbærɪtəʊn/ *noun* adult male singing voice between tenor and bass; singer with this.

barium /ˈbeərɪəm/ *noun* white metallic element. □ **barium meal** mixture swallowed to reveal digestive tract on X-ray.

bark[1] ● *noun* sharp explosive cry of dog etc. ● *verb* give a bark; speak or utter sharply or brusquely.

bark[2] ● *noun* tough outer layer of tree. ● *verb* graze (shin etc.); strip bark from.

barker *noun* tout at auction or sideshow.

barley /ˈbaːlɪ/ *noun* cereal used as food and in spirits; (also **barleycorn**) its grain. □ **barley sugar** hard sweet made from sugar; **barley water** drink made from boiled barley.

barm *noun* froth on fermenting malt liquor.

bar mitzvah /baː ˈmɪtsvə/ *noun* religious initiation of Jewish boy at 13.

barmy /ˈbaːmɪ/ *adjective* (-ier, -iest) *slang* crazy.

barn *noun* building for storing grain etc. □ **barn dance** social gathering for country dancing; **barn owl** kind of owl frequenting barns.

barnacle /ˈbaːnək(ə)l/ *noun* small shellfish clinging to rocks, ships' bottoms, etc. □ **barnacle goose** kind of Arctic goose.

barney /ˈbaːnɪ/ *noun* (*plural* -s) *colloquial* noisy quarrel.

barometer /bəˈrɒmɪtə/ *noun* instrument measuring atmospheric pressure. □ **barometric** /bærəˈmetrɪk/ *adjective*.

baron /ˈbærən/ *noun* member of lowest order of British or foreign nobility; powerful businessman etc. □ **baronial** /bəˈrəʊnɪəl/ *adjective*.

baroness /ˈbærənɪs/ *noun* woman holding rank of baron; baron's wife or widow.

baronet /ˈbærənɪt/ *noun* member of lowest British hereditary titled order. □ **baronetcy** *noun* (*plural* -ies).

barony /ˈbærənɪ/ *noun* (*plural* -ies) rank or domain of baron.

baroque /bəˈrɒk/ ● *adjective* (esp. of 17th- & 18th-c. European architecture and music) ornate and extravagant in style. ● *noun* baroque style.

barque /baːk/ *noun* kind of sailing ship.

barrack[1] /ˈbærək/ *noun* (usually in *plural*, often treated as *singular*) housing for soldiers; large bleak building.

barrack[2] /ˈbærək/ *verb* shout or jeer (at).

barracuda /bærəˈkuːdə/ noun (plural same or **-s**) large voracious tropical sea fish.

barrage /ˈbærɑːʒ/ noun concentrated artillery bombardment; rapid succession of questions etc.; artificial barrier in river etc.

barrel /ˈbær(ə)l/ • noun cylindrical usually convex container; contents or capacity of this; tube forming part of thing, esp. gun or pen. • verb (**-ll-**; US **-l-**) put in barrels. □ **barrel organ** musical instrument with rotating pin-studded cylinder.

barren /ˈbærən/ adjective (**-er, -est**) unable to bear young; unable to produce fruit or vegetation; unprofitable; dull. □ **barrenness** noun.

barricade /ˈbærɪkeɪd/ • noun barrier, esp. improvised. • verb (**-ding**) block or defend with this.

barrier /ˈbærɪə/ noun fence etc. barring advance or access; obstacle to communication etc. □ **barrier cream** protective skin cream; **barrier reef** coral reef separated from land by channel.

barrister /ˈbærɪstə/ noun advocate practising in higher courts.

barrow[1] /ˈbærəʊ/ noun two-wheeled handcart; wheelbarrow.

barrow[2] /ˈbærəʊ/ noun ancient grave mound.

Bart. abbreviation Baronet.

barter /ˈbɑːtə/ • verb exchange goods, rights, etc., without using money. • noun trade by bartering.

basal /ˈbeɪs(ə)l/ adjective of, at, or forming base.

basalt /ˈbæsɔːlt/ noun dark volcanic rock. □ **basaltic** /bəˈsɔːltɪk/ adjective.

base[1] • noun what a thing rests or depends on, foundation; principle; starting point; headquarters; main ingredient; number in terms of which other numbers are expressed; substance combining with acid to form salt. • verb (**-sing**) (usually + **on, upon**) found, establish; station. □ **base rate** interest rate set by Bank of England and used as basis for other banks' rates.

base[2] adjective cowardly; despicable; menial; (of coin) alloyed; (of metal) low in value.

baseball noun game played esp. in US with bat and ball and circuit of 4 bases.

baseless adjective unfounded, groundless.

basement /ˈbeɪsmənt/ noun floor below ground level.

bases plural of BASE[1], BASIS.

bash • verb strike bluntly or heavily; (often + up) colloquial attack violently. • noun heavy blow; slang attempt, party.

bashful /ˈbæʃfʊl/ adjective shy; diffident.

BASIC /ˈbeɪsɪk/ noun computer programming language using familiar English words.

basic /ˈbeɪsɪk/ • adjective serving as base; fundamental; simplest; lowest in level. • noun (usually in plural) fundamental fact or principle. □ **basically** adverb.

basil /ˈbæz(ə)l/ noun aromatic herb.

basilica /bəˈzɪlɪkə/ noun ancient Roman hall with apse and colonnades; similar church.

basilisk /ˈbæzɪlɪsk/ noun mythical reptile with lethal breath and look; American crested lizard.

basin /ˈbeɪs(ə)n/ noun round vessel for liquids or preparing food in; washbasin; hollow depression; sheltered mooring area; round valley; area drained by river.

basis /ˈbeɪsɪs/ noun (plural **bases** /-siːz/) foundation; main ingredient or principle; starting point for discussion etc.

bask /bɑːsk/ verb relax in warmth and light; (+ in) revel in.

basket /ˈbɑːskɪt/ noun container made of woven canes, wire, etc.; amount held by this. □ **basketball** team game in which goals are scored by putting ball through high nets; **basketry**, **basketwork** art of weaving cane etc., work so produced.

bas-relief /ˈbæsrɪliːf/ noun carving or sculpture projecting slightly from background.

bass[1] /beɪs/ • noun lowest adult male voice; singer with this; colloquial double bass, bass guitar; low-frequency sound of radio, record player, etc. • adjective lowest in pitch; deep-sounding. □ **bass guitar** electric guitar playing low notes. □ **bassist** noun.

bass[2] /bæs/ noun (plural same or **-es**) common perch; other fish of perch family.

basset /'bæsɪt/ *noun* (in full **basset-hound**) short-legged hunting dog.

bassoon /bə'su:n/ *noun* bass instrument of oboe family. □ **bassoonist** *noun*.

bast /bæst/ *noun* fibre from inner bark of tree, esp. lime.

bastard /'bɑːstəd/ *often offensive* ● *noun* person born of parents not married to each other; *slang* person regarded with dislike or pity; difficult or awkward thing. ● *adjective* illegitimate by birth; hybrid. □ **bastardy** *noun*.

bastardize /'bɑːstədaɪz/ *verb* (also **-ise**) (**-zing** or **-sing**) corrupt, debase; declare illegitimate.

baste¹ /beɪst/ *verb* (**-ting**) moisten (roasting meat etc.) with fat etc.; beat, thrash.

baste² /beɪst/ *verb* (**-ting**) sew with long loose stitches, tack.

bastinado /bæstɪ'neɪdəʊ/ ● *noun* caning on soles of feet. ● *verb* (**-es**, **-ed**) punish with this.

bastion /'bæstɪən/ *noun* projecting part of fortification; thing regarded as protection.

bat¹ ● *noun* implement with handle for hitting ball in games; turn at using this; batsman. ● *verb* (**-tt-**) use bat; hit (as) with bat; take one's turn at batting. □ **batsman** person who bats, esp. at cricket.

bat² *noun* mouselike nocturnal flying mammal. □ **bats** *slang* crazy.

bat³ *verb* (**-tt-**) □ **not bat an eyelid** *colloquial* show no reaction.

batch ● *noun* group, collection, set; loaves baked at one time. ● *verb* arrange in batches.

bated /'beɪtɪd/ *adjective* □ **with bated breath** anxiously.

Bath /bɑːθ/ *noun* □ **Bath bun** round spiced bun with currants; **Bath chair** invalid's wheelchair.

bath /bɑːθ/ *noun* (*plural* **-s** /bɑːðz/) container for sitting in and washing the body; its contents; act of washing in it; (usually in *plural*) building for swimming or bathing. ● *verb* wash in bath. □ **bath cube** cube of **bath salts**, substance for scenting and softening bath water; **bathroom** room with bath, *US* room with lavatory.

bathe /beɪð/ ● *verb* (**-thing**) immerse oneself in water etc., esp. to swim or wash; immerse in or treat with liquid; (of sunlight etc.) envelop. ● *noun* swim. □ **bathing costume** garment worn for swimming.

bathos /'beɪθɒs/ *noun* lapse from sublime to trivial; anticlimax. □ **bathetic** /bə'θetɪk/ *adjective*.

bathyscaphe /'bæθɪskæf/, **bathysphere** /-sfɪə/ *nouns* vessel for deep-sea diving.

batik /bə'ti:k/ *noun* method of dyeing textiles by waxing parts to be left uncoloured.

batiste /bæ'ti:st/ *noun* fine cotton or linen fabric.

batman /'bætmən/ *noun* army officer's servant.

baton /'bæt(ə)n/ *noun* thin stick for conducting orchestra etc.; short stick carried in relay race; stick carried by drum major; staff of office.

batrachian /bə'treɪkɪən/ ● *noun* amphibian that discards gills and tail, esp. frog or toad. ● *adjective* of batrachians.

battalion /bə'tæljən/ *noun* army unit usually of 300–1000 men.

batten¹ /'bæt(ə)n/ ● *noun* long narrow piece of squared timber; strip for securing tarpaulin over ship's hatchway. ● *verb* strengthen or (often + *down*) fasten with battens.

batten² /'bæt(ə)n/ *verb* (often + *on*) thrive at the expense of.

batter /'bætə/ ● *verb* strike hard and repeatedly; (esp. as **battered** *adjective*) subject to long-term violence. ● *noun* mixture of flour and eggs beaten up with liquid for cooking. □ **battering ram** *historical* swinging beam for breaching walls.

battery /'bætərɪ/ *noun* (*plural* **-ies**) portable container of cell or cells for supplying electricity; series of cages etc. for poultry or cattle; set of connected or similar instruments etc.; emplacement for heavy guns; *Law* physical violence inflicted on person.

battle /'bæt(ə)l/ ● *noun* prolonged fight, esp. between armed forces; contest. ● *verb* (**-ling**) (often + *with, for*) struggle. □ **battleaxe** medieval weapon, *colloquial* domineering middle-aged woman;

battle-cruiser *historical* heavy-gunned ship of higher speed and lighter armour than battleship; **battledress** soldier's everyday uniform; **battlefield** scene of battle; **battleship** most heavily armed and armoured warship.

battlement /'bæt(ə)lmənt/ *noun* (usually in *plural*) parapet with gaps at intervals at top of wall.

batty /'bætɪ/ *adjective* (**-ier**, **-iest**) *slang* crazy.

batwing *adjective* (esp. of sleeve) shaped like a bat's wing.

bauble /'bɔːb(ə)l/ *noun* showy trinket.

baulk /bɔːlk/ (also **balk**) ● *verb* (often + *at*) jib, hesitate; thwart, hinder, disappoint. ● *noun* hindrance; stumbling block.

bauxite /'bɔːksaɪt/ *noun* claylike mineral, chief source of aluminium.

bawdy /'bɔːdɪ/ ● *adjective* (**-ier**, **-iest**) humorously indecent. ● *noun* bawdy talk or writing. □ **bawdy house** brothel.

bawl *verb* shout or weep noisily. □ **bawl out** reprimand severely.

bay[1] *noun* broad curving inlet of sea.

bay[2] *noun* laurel with deep green leaves; (in *plural*) victor's or poet's bay wreath, fame. □ **bay leaf** leaf of bay tree, used for flavouring.

bay[3] *noun* recess; alcove in wall; compartment; allotted area. □ **bay window** window projecting from line of wall.

bay[4] ● *adjective* reddish-brown (esp. of horse). ● *noun* bay horse.

bay[5] ● *verb* bark loudly. ● *noun* bark of large dog, esp. chorus of pursuing hounds. □ **at bay** unable to escape; **keep at bay** ward off.

bayonet /'beɪənɪt/ ● *noun* stabbing-blade attachable to rifle. ● *verb* (**-t-**) stab with bayonet. □ **bayonet fitting** connecting-part engaged by pushing and twisting.

bazaar /bə'zɑː/ *noun* orienta¹ market; sale of goods, esp. for charity.

bazooka /bə'zuːkə/ *noun* anti-tank rocket launcher.

BBC *abbreviation* British Broadcasting Corporation.

BC *abbreviation* before Christ; British Columbia.

BCG *abbreviation* Bacillus Calmette-Guérin, an anti-tuberculosis vaccine.

be /biː/ ● *verb* (*present singular 1st* **am**, *2nd* **are** /ɑː/, *3rd* **is** /ɪz/, *plural* **are** /ɑː/; *past singular 1st* **was** /wɒz/, *2nd* **were** /wɜː/, *3rd* **was** /wɒz/, *plural* **were** /wɜː/; *present participle* **being**; *past participle* **been**) exist, live; occur; remain, continue; have specified identity, state, or quality. ● *auxiliary verb with past participle to form passive, with present participle to form continuous tenses, with infinitive to express duty, intention, possibility, etc.* □ **be-all and end-all** *colloquial* whole being, essence.

beach ● *noun* sandy or pebbly shore of sea, lake, etc. ● *verb* run or haul (boat etc.) on shore. □ **beachcomber** person who searches beaches for articles of value; **beachhead** fortified position set up on beach by landing forces.

beacon /'biːkən/ *noun* signal-fire on hill or pole; signal; signal-station; Belisha beacon.

bead ● *noun* small ball of glass, stone, etc. pierced for threading with others; drop of liquid; small knob in front sight of gun. ● *verb* adorn with bead(s) or beading.

beading *noun* moulding with series of beads.

beadle /'biːd(ə)l/ *noun* ceremonial officer of church, college, etc.

beady *adjective* (**-ier**, **-iest**) (of eyes) small and bright. □ **beady-eyed** with beady eyes, observant.

beagle /'biːg(ə)l/ *noun* small hound used for hunting hares.

beak *noun* bird's horny projecting jaws; *slang* hooked nose; *historical* prow of warship; spout.

beaker /'biːkə/ *noun* tall cup for drinking; lipped glass vessel for scientific experiments.

beam ● *noun* long piece of squared timber or metal used in house-building etc.; ray of light or radiation; bright smile; series of radio or radar signals as guide to ship or aircraft; crossbar of balance; (in *plural*) horizontal cross-timbers of ship. ● *verb* emit (light, radio waves, etc.); shine; smile radiantly. □ **off beam** *colloquial* mistaken.

bean *noun* climbing plant with kidney-shaped seeds in long pods; seed of this or of coffee or other plant. □ **beanbag** small bag filled with dried beans and used as ball, large bag filled with polystyrene pieces and used as seat; **bean sprout** sprout of bean seed as food; **full of beans** *colloquial* lively, exuberant; **not a bean** *slang* no money.

beano /'biːnəʊ/ *noun* (*plural* -**s**) *slang* party, celebration.

bear¹ /beə/ *verb* (*past* **bore**; *past participle* **borne** or **born**) carry; show; produce, yield (fruit); give birth to; sustain; endure, tolerate.

bear² /beə/ *noun* heavy thick-furred mammal; rough surly person; person who sells shares for future delivery in hope of buying them more cheaply before then. □ **beargarden** noisy or rowdy scene; **bear-hug** powerful embrace; **bearskin** guardsman's tall furry cap.

bearable *adjective* endurable.

beard /biəd/ *noun* facial hair on chin etc.; part on animal (esp. goat) resembling beard. ● *verb* oppose, defy. □ **bearded** *adjective*.

bearer *noun* carrier of message, cheque, etc.; carrier of coffin, equipment, etc.

bearing *noun* outward behaviour, posture; (usually + *on*, *upon*) relation, relevance; part of machine supporting rotating part; direction relative to fixed point; (in *plural*) relative position; heraldic device or design.

beast *noun* animal, esp. wild mammal; brutal person; *colloquial* disliked person or thing.

beastly *adjective* (-**ier**, -**iest**) like a beast; *colloquial* unpleasant.

beat ● *verb* (*past* **beat**; *past participle* **beaten**) strike repeatedly or persistently; inflict blows on; overcome, surpass; exhaust, perplex; (often + *up*) whisk (eggs etc.) vigorously; (often + *out*) shape (metal etc.) by blows; pulsate; mark (time of music) with baton, foot, etc.; move or cause (wings) to move up and down. ● *noun* main accent in music or verse; strongly marked rhythm of popular music etc.; stroke on drum; movement of conductor's baton; throbbing; police officer's appointed course; one's habitual round.

● *adjective slang* exhausted, tired out. □ **beat about the bush** not come to the point; **beat down** cause (seller) to lower price by bargaining, (of sun, rain, etc.) shine or fall relentlessly; **beat it** *slang* go away; **beat up** beat with punches and kicks; **beat-up** *colloquial* dilapidated.

beater *noun* whisk; implement for beating carpet; person who rouses game at a shoot.

beatific /biːə'tɪfɪk/ *adjective* making blessed; *colloquial* blissful.

beatify /biː'ætɪfaɪ/ *verb* (-**ies**, -**ied**) *RC Church* declare to be blessed as first step to canonization; make happy. □ **beatification** *noun*.

beatitude /biː'ætɪtjuːd/ *noun* blessedness; (in *plural*) blessings in Matthew 5: 3–11.

beau /bəʊ/ *noun* (*plural* -**x** /-z/) boyfriend; dandy.

Beaufort scale /'bəʊfət/ *noun* scale of wind speeds.

Beaujolais /'bəʊʒəleɪ/ *noun* red or white wine from Beaujolais district of France.

beauteous /'bjuːtɪəs/ *adjective poetical* beautiful.

beautician /bjuː'tɪʃ(ə)n/ *noun* specialist in beauty treatment.

beautiful /'bjuːtɪful/ *adjective* having beauty; *colloquial* excellent. □ **beautifully** *adverb*.

beautify /'bjuːtɪfaɪ/ *verb* (-**ies**, -**ied**) make beautiful, adorn. □ **beautification** *noun*.

beauty /'bjuːtɪ/ *noun* (*plural* -**ies**) combination of qualities that delights the sight or other senses or the mind; person or thing having this. □ **beauty queen** woman judged most beautiful in contest; **beauty parlour**, **salon** establishment for cosmetic treatment; **beauty spot** beautiful locality.

beaver ● *noun* large amphibious broadtailed rodent; its fur; hat of this; (**Beaver**) member of most junior branch of Scout Association. ● *verb colloquial* (usually + *away*) work hard.

becalm /bɪ'kɑːm/ *verb* deprive (ship etc.) of wind.

became *past* of BECOME.

because /bɪˈkɒz/ *conjunction* for the reason that. □ **because of** by reason of.

beck[1] *noun* brook, mountain stream.

beck[2] *noun* □ **at (person's) beck and call** subject to his or her constant orders.

beckon /ˈbekən/ *verb* (often + *to*) summon by gesture; entice.

become /bɪˈkʌm/ *verb* (**-ming**; *past* **became**; *past participle* **become**) come to be, begin to be; suit, look well on. □ **become of** happen to.

becquerel /ˈbekərel/ *noun* SI unit of radioactivity.

bed •*noun* place to sleep or rest, esp. piece of furniture for sleeping on; garden plot for plants; bottom of sea, river, etc.; flat base on which thing rests; stratum. •*verb* (**-dd-**) (usually + *down*) put or go to bed; plant in bed; fix firmly; *colloquial* have sexual intercourse with. □ **bedclothes** sheets, blankets, etc.; **bedpan** pan for use as toilet by invalid in bed; **bedridden** confined to bed by infirmity; **bedrock** solid rock under alluvial deposits etc., basic principles; **bedroom** room for sleeping in; **bedsitting room**, **bedsitter** combined bedroom and sitting-room; **bedsore** sore developed by lying in bed; **bedspread** cloth for covering bed; **bedstead** framework of bed; **bedtime** hour for going to bed.

bedaub /bɪˈdɔːb/ *verb* smear with paint etc.

bedding *noun* mattress and bedclothes; litter for cattle etc. □ **bedding plant** annual flowering plant put in garden bed.

bedeck /bɪˈdek/ *verb* adorn, decorate.

bedevil /bɪˈdev(ə)l/ *verb* (**-ll-**; *US* **-l-**) torment, confuse, trouble. □ **bedevilment** *noun*.

bedlam /ˈbedləm/ *noun* scene of confusion or uproar.

Bedouin /ˈbeduːɪn/ *noun* (*plural* same) nomadic Arab of the desert.

bedraggled /bɪˈdræg(ə)ld/ *adjective* dishevelled, untidy.

bee *noun* 4-winged stinging insect, collecting nectar and pollen and producing wax and honey; busy worker; meeting for combined work or amusement. □ **beehive** hive; **beeline** straight line between two places; **beeswax** wax secreted by bees for honeycomb.

Beeb *noun* (**the Beeb**) *colloquial* the BBC.

beech *noun* smooth-barked glossy-leaved tree; its wood. □ **beechmast** fruit of beech.

beef •*noun* meat of ox, bull, or cow; (*plural* **beeves** or *US* **-s**) beef animal; (*plural* **-s**) *slang* protest. •*verb* *slang* complain. □ **beefburger** hamburger; **beefeater** warder in Tower of London; **beefsteak** thick slice of beef for grilling or frying; **beef tea** stewed beef extract for invalids; **beef tomato** large tomato.

beefy *adjective* (**-ier, -iest**) like beef; solid, muscular.

been *past participle* of BE.

beep •*noun* short high-pitched sound. •*verb* emit beep.

beer /bɪə/ *noun* alcoholic liquor made from fermented malt etc. flavoured esp. with hops. □ **beer garden** garden where beer is sold and drunk; **beer mat** small mat for beer glass.

beery *adjective* (**-ier, -iest**) showing influence of beer; like beer.

beeswing /ˈbiːzwɪŋ/ *noun* filmy crust on old port wine etc.

beet *noun* plant with succulent root used for salads etc. and sugar-making (see BEETROOT, SUGAR BEET).

beetle[1] /ˈbiːt(ə)l/ •*noun* insect with hard protective outer wings. •*verb* (**-ling**) *colloquial* (+ *about*, *off*, etc.) hurry, scurry.

beetle[2] /ˈbiːt(ə)l/ •*adjective* projecting, shaggy, scowling. •*verb* (usually as **beetling** *adjective*) overhang.

beetle[3] /ˈbiːt(ə)l/ *noun* heavy-headed tool for ramming, crushing, etc.

beetroot *noun* beet with dark red root used as vegetable.

befall /bɪˈfɔːl/ *verb* (*past* **befell**; *past participle* **befallen**) *poetical* happen; happen to.

befit /bɪˈfɪt/ *verb* (**-tt-**) be appropriate for.

befog /bɪˈfɒg/ *verb* (**-gg-**) obscure; envelop in fog.

before /bɪˈfɔː/ •*conjunction* sooner than; rather than. •*preposition* earlier than; in front of, ahead of; in presence of. •*adverb* ahead, in front; previously, already; in the past.

beforehand *adverb* in anticipation, in readiness, before time.

befriend /brɪˈfrend/ *verb* act as friend to; help.

befuddle /brɪˈfʌd(ə)l/ *verb* (**-ling**) make drunk; confuse.

beg *verb* (**-gg-**) ask for as gift; ask earnestly, entreat; live by begging; ask formally. □ **beg the question** assume truth of thing to be proved; **go begging** be unwanted.

■ **Usage** The expression *beg the question* is often used incorrectly to mean 'to invite the obvious question (that …)'.

began *past* of BEGIN.

begat *archaic past* of BEGET.

beget /brɪˈget/ *verb* (**-tt-**; *past* **begot**, *archaic* **begat**; *past participle* **begotten**) *literary* be the father of; give rise to.

beggar /ˈbegə/ ● *noun* person who begs or lives by begging; *colloquial* person. ● *verb* make poor; be too extraordinary for (belief, description, etc.).

beggarly *adjective* mean; poor, needy.

begin /brɪˈgɪn/ *verb* (**-nn-**; *past* **began**; *past participle* **begun**) perform first part of; come into being; (often + *to do*) start, take first step, (usually in negative) *colloquial* show any likelihood, be sufficient.

beginner *noun* learner.

beginning *noun* time at which thing begins; source, origin; first part.

begone /brɪˈgɒn/ *interjection poetical* go away at once!

begonia /brɪˈgəʊnɪə/ *noun* plant with ornamental foliage and bright flowers.

begot *past* of BEGET.

begotten *past participle* of BEGET.

begrudge /brɪˈgrʌdʒ/ *verb* (**-ging**) grudge; feel or show resentment at or envy of; be dissatisfied at.

beguile /brɪˈgaɪl/ *verb* charm, divert; delude, cheat. □ **beguilement** *noun*.

beguine /brɪˈgiːn/ *noun* W. Indian dance.

begum /ˈbeɪgəm/ *noun* (in India, Pakistan, and Bangladesh) Muslim woman of high rank; (**Begum**) *title of married Muslim woman.*

begun *past participle* of BEGIN.

behalf /brɪˈhɑːf/ *noun* □ **on behalf of, on (person's) behalf** in the interests of, as representative of.

behave /brɪˈheɪv/ *verb* (**-ving**) react or act in specified way; (often **behave oneself**) conduct oneself properly; work well (or in specified way).

behaviour /brɪˈheɪvjə/ *noun* (US **behavior**) manners, conduct, way of behaving. □ **behavioural** *adjective*.

behaviourism *noun* (US **behaviorism**) study of human actions by analysis of stimulus and response. □ **behaviourist** *noun*.

behead /brɪˈhed/ *verb* cut head from (person); execute thus.

beheld *past & past participle* of BEHOLD.

behest /brɪˈhest/ *noun literary* command, request.

behind /brɪˈhaɪnd/ ● *preposition* in or to rear of; hidden by, on farther side of; in past in relation to; inferior to; in support of. ● *adverb* in or to rear; on far side; remaining after others' departure; (usually + *with*) in arrears. ● *noun colloquial* buttocks. □ **behindhand** in arrears, behind time, too late; **behind time** unpunctual; **behind the times** old-fashioned, antiquated.

behold /brɪˈhəʊld/ *verb* (*past & past participle* **beheld**) *literary* look at; take notice, observe.

beholden /brɪˈhəʊld(ə)n/ *adjective* (usually + *to*) under obligation.

behove /brɪˈhəʊv/ *verb* (**-ving**) *formal* be incumbent on; befit.

beige /beɪʒ/ ● *noun* pale sandy fawn colour. ● *adjective* of this colour.

being /ˈbiːɪŋ/ *noun* existence; constitution, nature; existing person etc.

belabour /brɪˈleɪbə/ *verb* (US **belabor**) attack physically or verbally.

belated /brɪˈleɪtɪd/ *adjective* coming (too) late. □ **belatedly** *adverb*.

bel canto /bel ˈkæntəʊ/ *noun* singing marked by full rich tone.

belch ● *verb* emit wind from stomach through mouth; (of volcano, gun, etc.) emit (fire, smoke, etc.). ● *noun* act of belching.

beleaguer /brɪˈliːgə/ *verb* besiege; vex; harass.

belfry /ˈbelfrɪ/ *noun* (*plural* **-ies**) bell tower; space for bells in church tower.

belie /bɪˈlaɪ/ *verb* (**belying**) give false impression of; fail to confirm, fulfil, or justify.

belief /bɪˈliːf/ *noun* act of believing; what one believes; trust, confidence; acceptance as true.

believe /bɪˈliːv/ *verb* (**-ving**) accept as true; think; (+ *in*) have faith or confidence in; trust word of; have religious faith. □ **believable** *adjective*; **believer** *noun*.

Belisha beacon /bəˈliːʃə/ *noun* flashing orange ball on striped post, marking pedestrian crossing.

belittle /bɪˈlɪt(ə)l/ *verb* (**-ling**) disparage. □ **belittlement** *noun*.

bell *noun* hollow esp. cup-shaped metal body emitting musical sound when struck; sound of bell; bell-shaped thing. □ **bell-bottomed** (of trousers) widening below knee; **bell pull** cord pulled to sound bell; **bell push** button pressed to ring electric bell; **give (person) a bell** *colloquial* telephone him or her.

belladonna /beləˈdɒnə/ *noun* deadly nightshade; drug obtained from this.

belle /bel/ *noun* handsome woman; reigning beauty.

belles-lettres /bel ˈletr/ *plural noun* (also treated as *singular*) writings or studies of purely literary kind.

bellicose /ˈbelɪkəʊs/ *adjective* eager to fight.

belligerent /bɪˈlɪdʒərənt/ ● *adjective* engaged in war; given to constant fighting; pugnacious. ● *noun* belligerent person or nation. □ **belligerence** *noun*.

bellow /ˈbeləʊ/ ● *verb* emit deep loud roar. ● *noun* bellowing sound.

bellows /ˈbeləʊz/ *plural noun* (also treated as *singular*) device for driving air into fire, organ, etc.; expandable part of camera etc.

belly /ˈbelɪ/ ● *noun* (*plural* **-ies**) cavity of body containing stomach, bowels, etc.; stomach; front of body from waist to groin; underside of animal; cavity or bulging part of anything. ● *verb* (**-ies**, **-ied**) swell out. □ **bellyache** *noun colloquial* stomach pain, *verb slang* complain noisily or persistently; **belly button** *colloquial* navel; **belly dance** dance by woman (**belly dancer**) with voluptuous movements of belly; **belly laugh** loud unrestrained laugh.

bellyful *noun* enough to eat; *colloquial* more than one can tolerate.

belong /bɪˈlɒŋ/ *verb* (+ *to*) be property of, assigned to, or member of; fit socially; be rightly placed or classified.

belongings *plural noun* possessions, luggage.

beloved /bɪˈlʌvɪd/ ● *adjective* loved. ● *noun* beloved person.

below /bɪˈləʊ/ ● *preposition* under; lower than; less than; of lower rank or importance etc. than; unworthy of. ● *adverb* at or to lower point or level; further on in book etc.

belt ● *noun* strip of leather etc. worn round waist or across chest; continuous band in machinery; distinct strip of colour etc.; zone, district. ● *verb* put belt round; *slang* thrash; *slang* move rapidly. □ **below the belt** unfair(ly); **belt out** *slang* sing or play (music) loudly; **belt up** *slang* be quiet, *colloquial* put on seat belt; **tighten one's belt** economize; **under one's belt** securely acquired.

bemoan /bɪˈməʊn/ *verb* lament, complain about.

bemuse /bɪˈmjuːz/ *verb* (**-sing**) make (person) confused.

bench *noun* long seat of wood or stone; carpenter's or laboratory table; magistrate's or judge's seat; lawcourt. □ **benchmark** surveyor's mark at point in line of levels; standard, point of reference.

bend ● *verb* (*past & past participle* **bent** except in *bended knee*) force into curve or angle; be altered in this way; incline from vertical; bow, stoop; interpret or modify (rule) to suit oneself; (force to) submit. ● *noun* bending, curve; bent part of thing; (**the bends**) *colloquial* symptoms due to too rapid decompression under water. □ **round the bend** *colloquial* crazy, insane.

bender *noun slang* wild drinking spree.

beneath /bɪˈniːθ/ ● *preposition* below; under; unworthy of. ● *adverb* below, underneath.

Benedictine /benɪˈdɪktɪn/ ● *noun* monk or nun of Order of St Benedict; /-tiːn/ *proprietary term* kind of liqueur. ● *adjective* of St Benedict or his order.

benediction /benɪˈdɪkʃ(ə)n/ *noun* utterance of blessing. □ **benedictory** *adjective*.

benefaction /benɪ'fækʃ(ə)n/ noun charitable gift; doing good.

benefactor /'benɪfæktə/ noun (feminine **benefactress**) person who has given financial or other help.

benefice /'benɪfɪs/ noun living from a church office.

beneficent /bɪ'nefɪsənt/ adjective doing good; actively kind. □ **beneficence** noun.

beneficial /benɪ'fɪʃ(ə)l/ adjective advantageous. □ **beneficially** adverb.

beneficiary /benɪ'fɪʃərɪ/ noun (plural **-ies**) receiver of benefits; holder of church living.

benefit /'benɪfɪt/ ●noun advantage, profit; payment made under insurance or social security; performance or game etc. of which proceeds go to particular player or charity. ●verb (**-t-**; US **-tt-**) do good to; receive benefit. □ **benefit of the doubt** assumption of innocence rather than guilt.

benevolent /bɪ'nevələnt/ adjective wishing to do good; charitable; kind and helpful. □ **benevolence** noun.

Bengali /beŋ'gɔːlɪ/ ●noun (plural **-s**) native or language of Bengal. ●adjective of Bengal.

benighted /bɪ'naɪtɪd/ adjective intellectually or morally ignorant.

benign /bɪ'naɪn/ adjective kindly, gentle; favourable; salutary; Medicine mild, not malignant. □ **benignity** /bɪ'nɪgnɪtɪ/ noun.

benignant /bɪ'nɪgnənt/ adjective kindly; beneficial. □ **benignancy** noun.

bent ●past & past participle of BEND. ●adjective curved or having angle; slang dishonest, illicit; (+ on) set on doing or having. ●noun inclination, bias; (+ for) talent for.

benumb /bɪ'nʌm/ verb make numb; deaden; paralyse.

benzene /'benziːn/ noun chemical got from coal tar and used as solvent.

benzine /'benziːn/ noun spirit obtained from petroleum and used as cleaning agent.

benzoin /'benzəʊɪn/ noun fragrant resin of E. Asian tree. □ **benzoic** /-'zəʊɪk/ adjective.

bequeath /bɪ'kwiːð/ verb leave by will; transmit to posterity.

bequest /bɪ'kwest/ noun bequeathing; thing bequeathed.

berate /bɪ'reɪt/ verb (**-ting**) scold.

bereave /bɪ'riːv/ verb (**-ving**) (esp. as **bereaved** adjective) (often + of) deprive of relative, friend, etc., esp. by death. □ **bereavement** noun.

bereft /bɪ'reft/ adjective (+ of) deprived of.

beret /'bereɪ/ noun round flat brimless cap of felt etc.

berg noun iceberg.

bergamot /'bɜːgəmɒt/ noun perfume from fruit of a dwarf orange tree; an aromatic herb.

beriberi /berɪ'berɪ/ noun nervous disease caused by deficiency of vitamin B_1.

Bermuda shorts /bə'mjuːdə/ plural noun close-fitting knee-length shorts.

berry /'berɪ/ noun (plural **-ies**) any small round juicy stoneless fruit.

berserk /bə'zɜːk/ adjective (esp. after go) wild, frenzied.

berth ●noun sleeping place; ship's place at wharf; sea-room; colloquial situation, appointment. ●verb moor (ship) in berth; provide sleeping berth for.

beryl /'berɪl/ noun transparent (esp. green) precious stone; mineral species including this and emerald.

beryllium /bə'rɪlɪəm/ noun hard white metallic element.

beseech /bɪ'siːtʃ/ verb (past & past participle **besought** /-'sɔːt/ or **beseeched**) entreat; ask earnestly for.

beset /bɪ'set/ verb (**-tt-**; past & past participle **beset**) attack or harass persistently.

beside /bɪ'saɪd/ preposition at side of, close to; compared with; irrelevant to. □ **beside oneself** frantic with anger or worry etc.

besides ●preposition in addition to; apart from. ●adverb also, as well.

besiege /bɪ'siːdʒ/ verb (**-ging**) lay siege to; crowd round eagerly; assail with requests.

besmirch /bɪ'smɜːtʃ/ verb soil, dishonour.

besom /'biːz(ə)m/ noun broom made of twigs.

besotted /bɪ'sɒtɪd/ adjective infatuated; stupefied.

besought past & past participle of BESEECH.

bespatter /bɪˈspætə/ *verb* spatter all over; defame.

bespeak /bɪˈspiːk/ *verb* (*past* **bespoke**; *past participle* **bespoken**) engage beforehand; order (goods); be evidence of.

bespectacled /bɪˈspektək(ə)ld/ *adjective* wearing spectacles.

bespoke /bɪˈspəʊk/ *adjective* made to order.

best ● *adjective* (*superlative* of GOOD) most excellent. ● *adverb* (*superlative* of WELL¹) in the best way; to greatest degree. ● *noun* that which is best. ● *verb colloquial* defeat, outwit. □ **best man** bridegroom's chief attendant at wedding; **best-seller** book with large sale, author of such book; **do one's best** do all one can.

bestial /ˈbestɪəl/ *adjective* brutish; of or like beasts. □ **bestiality** /-ˈæl-/ *noun*.

bestiary /ˈbestɪərɪ/ *noun* (*plural* **-ies**) medieval treatise on beasts.

bestir /bɪˈstɜː/ *verb* (**-rr-**) (**bestir oneself**) exert or rouse oneself.

bestow /bɪˈstəʊ/ *verb* (+ *on, upon*) confer as gift. □ **bestowal** *noun*.

bestrew /bɪˈstruː/ *verb* (*past participle* **bestrewed** or **bestrewn**) strew; lie scattered over.

bestride /bɪˈstraɪd/ *verb* (**-ding**; *past* **bestrode**; *past participle* **bestridden**) sit astride on; stand astride over.

bet ● *verb* (**-tt-**; *past & past participle* **bet** or **betted**) risk one's money etc. against another's on result of event. ● *noun* such arrangement; sum of money bet.

beta /ˈbiːtə/ *noun* second letter of Greek alphabet (Β, β). □ **beta-blocker** drug used to prevent unwanted stimulation of the heart in angina etc.; **beta particle** fast-moving electron emitted by radioactive substance.

betake /bɪˈteɪk/ *verb* (**-king**; *past* **betook**; *past participle* **betaken**) (**betake oneself**) go.

betatron /ˈbiːtətrɒn/ *noun* apparatus for accelerating electrons.

betel /ˈbiːt(ə)l/ *noun* leaf chewed with betel-nut. □ **betel-nut** seed of tropical palm.

bête noire /beɪt ˈnwɑː/ *noun* (*plural* **bêtes noires** same pronunciation) particularly disliked person or thing. [French]

bethink /bɪˈθɪŋk/ *verb* (*past & past participle* **bethought** /-ˈθɔːt/) (**bethink oneself**)

formal reflect, stop to think; be reminded.

betide /bɪˈtaɪd/ *verb* □ **woe betide (person)** misfortune will befall him or her.

betimes /bɪˈtaɪmz/ *adverb literary* in good time, early.

betoken /bɪˈtəʊkən/ *verb* be sign of.

betook *past* of BETAKE.

betray /bɪˈtreɪ/ *verb* be disloyal to (a person, one's country, etc.); give up or reveal treacherously; reveal involuntarily; be evidence of. □ **betrayal** *noun*.

betroth /bɪˈtrəʊð/ *verb* (usually as **betrothed** *adjective*) bind with promise to marry. □ **betrothal** *noun*.

better /ˈbetə/ ● *adjective* (*comparative* of GOOD) more excellent; partly or fully recovered from illness. ● *adverb* (*comparative* of WELL¹) in better manner; to greater degree. ● *noun* better thing or person. ● *verb* improve (upon); surpass. □ **better off** in better (esp. financial) situation; **get the better of** defeat, outwit.

betterment *noun* improvement.

between /bɪˈtwiːn/ ● *preposition* in or into space or interval; separating; shared by; to and from; taking one or other of. ● *adverb* (also **in between**) between two or more points, between two extremes.

bevel /ˈbev(ə)l/ ● *noun* slope from horizontal or vertical in carpentry etc.; sloping edge or surface; tool for marking angles. ● *verb* (**-ll-**; *US* **-l-**) impart bevel to, slant.

beverage /ˈbevərɪdʒ/ *noun formal* drink.

bevvy /ˈbevɪ/ *slang* ● *noun* (*plural* **-ies**) ● *verb* (**-ies, -ied**) drink.

bevy /ˈbevɪ/ *noun* (*plural* **-ies**) company, flock.

bewail /bɪˈweɪl/ *verb* wail over; mourn for.

beware /bɪˈweə/ *verb* (only in *imperative* or *infinitive*) take heed; (+ *of*) be cautious of.

bewilder /bɪˈwɪldə/ *verb* perplex, confuse. □ **bewilderment** *noun*.

bewitch /bɪˈwɪtʃ/ *verb* enchant, greatly delight; cast spell on.

beyond /bɪˈjɒnd/ ● *preposition* at or to further side of; outside the range or understanding of; more than. ● *adverb* at or to further side, further on. ● *noun*

(the beyond) life after death. □ **back of beyond** very remote place.

bezel /'bez(ə)l/ *noun* sloped edge of chisel etc.; oblique face of cut gem; groove holding watch-glass or gem.

bezique /bɪ'zi:k/ *noun* card game for two.

biannual /baɪ'ænjʊəl/ *adjective* occurring etc. twice a year.

bias /'baɪəs/ • *noun* predisposition, prejudice; distortion of statistical results; edge cut obliquely across weave of fabric; *Sport* bowl's curved course due to its lopsided form. • *verb* (-s- or -ss-) give bias to; prejudice; (as **biased** *adjective*) influenced (usually unfairly). □ **bias binding** strip of fabric cut obliquely and used to bind edges.

biathlon /baɪ'æθlən/ *noun* athletic contest in skiing and shooting. □ **biathlete** *noun*.

bib *noun* cloth put under child's chin while eating; upper part of apron etc.

Bible /'baɪb(ə)l/ *noun* Christian scriptures; (**bible**) copy of these; (**bible**) *colloquial* any authoritative book. □ **biblical** /'bɪb-/ *adjective*.

bibliography /bɪblɪ'ɒgrəfɪ/ *noun* (*plural* **-ies**) list of books of any author, subject, etc.; history of books, their editions, etc. □ **bibliographer** *noun*; **bibliographical** /-ə'græf-/ *adjective*.

bibliophile /'bɪblɪəfaɪl/ *noun* collector of books, book-lover.

bibulous /'bɪbjʊləs/ *adjective* fond of or addicted to alcoholic drink.

bicameral /baɪ'kæm(ə)r(ə)l/ *adjective* having two legislative chambers.

bicarb /'baɪkɑːb/ *noun colloquial* bicarbonate of soda.

bicarbonate /baɪ'kɑːbənɪt/ *noun* any acid salt of carbonic acid; (in full **bicarbonate of soda**) compound used in cooking and as antacid.

bicentenary /baɪsen'tiːnərɪ/ *noun* (*plural* **-ies**) 200th anniversary.

bicentennial /baɪsen'tenɪəl/ • *noun* bicentenary. • *adjective* recurring every 200 years.

biceps /'baɪseps/ *noun* (*plural* same) muscle with double head or attachment, esp. that at front of upper arm.

bicker /'bɪkə/ *verb* quarrel, wrangle pettily.

bicuspid /baɪ'kʌspɪd/ • *adjective* having two cusps. • *noun* bicuspid premolar tooth.

bicycle /'baɪsɪk(ə)l/ • *noun* two-wheeled pedal-driven vehicle. • *verb* (-ling) ride bicycle.

bid • *verb* (-dd-; *past* **bid**, *archaic* **bade** /bæd, beɪd/; *past participle* **bid**, *archaic* **bidden**) make offer; command, invite; *literary* utter (greeting, farewell) to; *Cards* state before play number of tricks intended. • *noun* act of bidding; amount bid; *colloquial* attempt, effort.

biddable *adjective* obedient, docile.

bidding *noun* command, invitation.

bide *verb* (-ding) *archaic or dialect* stay, remain. □ **bide one's time** wait for good opportunity.

bidet /'biːdeɪ/ *noun* low basin that one can sit astride to wash crotch area.

biennial /baɪ'enɪəl/ • *adjective* lasting 2 years; recurring every 2 years. • *noun* plant that flowers, fruits, and dies in second year.

bier /bɪə/ *noun* movable stand on which coffin or corpse rests.

biff *slang* • *noun* smart blow. • *verb* strike.

bifid /'baɪfɪd/ *adjective* divided by cleft into two parts.

bifocal /baɪ'fəʊk(ə)l/ • *adjective* (of spectacle lenses) with two parts of different focal lengths. • *noun* (in *plural*) bifocal spectacles.

bifurcate /'baɪfəkeɪt/ *verb* (-ting) divide into two branches; fork. □ **bifurcation** *noun*.

big • *adjective* (-gg-) large; important; grown-up; boastful; (usually + *with*) advanced in pregnancy. • *adverb colloquial* in big manner; with great effect, impressively. □ **Big Apple** *US slang* New York City; **Big Brother** seemingly benevolent dictator; **big business** large-scale commerce; **big end** of connecting rod in engine, encircling crank-pin; **big-head** *colloquial* conceited person; **big-headed** conceited; **big-hearted** generous; **big shot** *colloquial* important person; **big time** *slang* highest rank among entertainers; **big top** main tent at circus; **bigwig** *colloquial* important person; **in a big way** *colloquial* with great enthusiasm. □ **biggish** *adjective*.

bigamy /ˈbɪgəmɪ/ noun (plural **-ies**) crime of making second marriage while first is still valid. □ **bigamist** noun; **bigamous** adjective.

bight /baɪt/ noun recess of coast, bay; loop of rope.

bigot /ˈbɪgət/ noun obstinate and intolerant adherent of creed or view. □ **bigoted** adjective; **bigotry** noun.

bijou /ˈbiːʒuː/ ● noun (plural **-x** same pronunciation) jewel, trinket. ● adjective (**bijou**) small and elegant. [French]

bike colloquial ● noun bicycle; motorcycle. ● verb (**-king**) ride a bike. □ **biker** noun.

bikini /bɪˈkiːnɪ/ noun (plural **-s**) woman's brief two-piece bathing suit.

bilateral /baɪˈlætər(ə)l/ adjective of, on, or with two sides; between two parties. □ **bilaterally** adverb.

bilberry /ˈbɪlbərɪ/ noun (plural **-ies**) N. European heathland shrub; its small dark blue edible berry.

bile noun bitter fluid secreted by liver to aid digestion; bad temper, peevishness.

bilge /bɪldʒ/ noun nearly flat part of ship's bottom; (in full **bilge-water**) foul water in bilge; slang nonsense, rubbish.

bilharzia /bɪlˈhɑːtsɪə/ noun disease caused by tropical parasitic flatworm.

biliary /ˈbɪlɪərɪ/ adjective of bile.

bilingual /baɪˈlɪŋgw(ə)l/ adjective of, in, or speaking two languages.

bilious /ˈbɪlɪəs/ adjective affected by disorder of the bile; bad-tempered.

bilk verb slang evade payment of, cheat.

bill[1] ● noun statement of charges for goods, work done, etc.; draft of proposed law; poster; programme of entertainment; US banknote. ● verb send statement of charges to; announce, put in programme; (+ as) advertise as. □ **bill of exchange** written order to pay sum on given date; **bill of fare** menu; **billposter**, **billsticker** person who pastes up advertisements on hoardings etc.

bill[2] ● noun beak (of bird); narrow promontory. ● verb (of doves etc.) stroke bill with bill. □ **bill and coo** exchange caresses.

bill[3] noun historical weapon with hook-shaped blade.

billabong /ˈbɪləbɒŋ/ noun Australian branch of river forming backwater.

billboard noun large outdoor board for advertisements.

billet[1] ● noun place where soldier etc. is lodged; colloquial appointment, job. ● verb (**-t-**) quarter (soldiers etc.).

billet[2] /ˈbɪlɪt/ noun thick piece of firewood; small metal bar.

billet-doux /ˈbɪlɪˈduː/ noun (plural **billets-doux** /-ˈduːz/) love letter.

billhook noun concave-edged pruning-instrument.

billiards /ˈbɪljədz/ noun game played with cues and 3 balls on cloth-covered table. □ **billiard ball, room, table**, etc., ones used for billiards.

billion /ˈbɪljən/ noun (plural same) thousand million; million million; (plural) colloquial very large number. □ **billionth** adjective & noun.

billow /ˈbɪləʊ/ ● noun wave; any large mass. ● verb rise or move in billows. □ **billowy** adjective.

billy[1] /ˈbɪlɪ/ noun (plural **-ies**) (in full **billycan**) Australian tin or enamel outdoor cooking pot.

billy[2] /ˈbɪlɪ/ noun (plural **-ies**) (in full **billy goat**) male goat.

bin noun large receptacle for rubbish or storage. □ **bin-liner** bag for lining rubbish bin; **binman** colloquial dustman.

binary /ˈbaɪnərɪ/ adjective of two parts, dual; of system using digits 0 and 1 to code information.

bind /baɪnd/ ● verb (past & past participle **bound** /baʊnd/) tie or fasten tightly; restrain; (cause to) cohere; compel, impose duty on; edge with braid etc.; fasten (pages of book) into cover. ● noun colloquial nuisance; restriction.

binder noun cover for loose papers; substance that binds things together; historical sheaf-binding machine; bookbinder.

bindery noun (plural **-ies**) bookbinder's workshop.

binding ● noun book cover; braid etc. for edging. ● adjective obligatory.

bindweed noun convolvulus.

binge /bɪndʒ/ slang ● noun bout of excessive eating, drinking, etc.; spree. ● verb (**-ging**) indulge in binge.

bingo /'bɪŋgəʊ/ *noun* gambling game in which each player marks off numbers on card as they are called.

binnacle /'bɪnək(ə)l/ *noun* case for ship's compass.

binocular /baɪ'nɒkjʊlə/ *adjective* for both eyes.

binoculars /bɪ'nɒkjʊləz/ *plural noun* instrument with lens for each eye, for viewing distant objects.

binomial /baɪ'nəʊmɪəl/ ● *noun* algebraic expression of sum or difference of two terms. ● *adjective* consisting of two terms.

bio- *combining form* biological; life.

biochemistry /baɪəʊ'kemɪstrɪ/ *noun* chemistry of living organisms. □ **biochemical** *adjective*; **biochemist** *noun*.

biodegradable /baɪəʊdɪ'greɪdəb(ə)l/ *adjective* able to be decomposed by bacteria or other living organisms.

biography /baɪ'ɒgrəfɪ/ *noun* (*plural* -**ies**) written life of person. □ **biographer** *noun*; **biographical** /-ə'græf-/ *adjective*.

biological /baɪə'lɒdʒɪk(ə)l/ *adjective* of biology; of living organisms. □ **biological warfare** use of bacteria etc. to spread disease among enemy. □ **biologically** *adverb*.

biology /baɪ'ɒlədʒɪ/ *noun* study of living organisms. □ **biologist** *noun*.

bionic /baɪ'ɒnɪk/ *adjective* having electronically operated body parts.

biorhythm /'baɪəʊrɪð(ə)m/ *noun* biological cycle thought to affect person's physical or mental state.

biosphere /'baɪəʊsfɪə/ *noun* earth's crust and atmosphere containing life.

bipartite /baɪ'pɑːtaɪt/ *adjective* of two parts; involving two parties.

biped /'baɪped/ ● *noun* two-footed animal. ● *adjective* two-footed.

biplane /'baɪpleɪn/ *noun* aeroplane with two pairs of wings, one above the other.

birch ● *noun* tree with thin peeling bark; bundle of birch twigs used for flogging. ● *verb* flog with birch.

bird *noun* feathered vertebrate with two wings and two feet; *slang* young woman. □ **a bird in the hand** something secured or certain; **birdlime** sticky stuff spread to catch birds; **bird of passage** migratory bird, person who travels habitually; **bird of prey** one hunting animals for food; **birdseed** seeds as food for caged birds; **bird's-eye view** general view from above; **birds of a feather** similar people; **bird table** platform on which food for wild birds is placed.

birdie /'bɜːdɪ/ *noun colloquial* little bird; *Golf* hole played in one under par.

biretta /bɪ'retə/ *noun* square cap of RC priest.

Biro /'baɪərəʊ/ *noun* (*plural* -**s**) *proprietary term* kind of ballpoint pen.

birth *noun* emergence of young from mother's body; origin, beginning; ancestry; inherited position. □ **birth control** prevention of undesired pregnancy; **birthday** anniversary of birth; **birthmark** unusual mark on body from birth; **birth rate** number of live births per thousand of population per year; **birthright** rights belonging to one by birth; **give birth to** produce (young).

biscuit /'bɪskɪt/ *noun* thin unleavened cake, usually crisp and sweet; fired unglazed pottery; light brown colour.

bisect /baɪ'sekt/ *verb* divide into two (usually equal) parts. □ **bisection** *noun*; **bisector** *noun*.

bisexual /baɪ'sekʃʊəl/ ● *adjective* feeling or involving sexual attraction to members of both sexes; hermaphrodite. ● *noun* bisexual person. □ **bisexuality** /-'æl-/ *noun*.

bishop /'bɪʃəp/ *noun* senior clergyman usually in charge of diocese; mitre-shaped chess piece.

bishopric /'bɪʃəprɪk/ *noun* office or diocese of bishop.

bismuth /'bɪzməθ/ *noun* reddish-white metallic element; compound of it used medicinally.

bison /'baɪs(ə)n/ *noun* (*plural* same) wild ox.

bisque[1] /bɪsk/ *noun* rich soup.

bisque[2] /bɪsk/ *noun* advantage of one free point or stroke in certain games.

bisque[3] /bɪsk/ *noun* fired unglazed pottery.

bistre /'bɪstə/ *noun* brown pigment made from soot.

bistro /'biːstrəʊ/ *noun* (*plural* -**s**) small informal restaurant.

bit¹ *noun* small piece or amount; short time or distance; mouthpiece of bridle; cutting part of tool etc. □ **bit by bit** gradually.

bit² *past of* BITE.

bit³ *noun Computing* unit of information expressed as choice between two possibilities.

bitch /bɪtʃ/ ● *noun* female dog, fox, or wolf; *offensive slang* spiteful woman. ● *verb colloquial* speak spitefully; grumble.

bitchy *adjective slang* spiteful. □ **bitchily** *adverb*; **bitchiness** *noun*.

bite ● *verb* (**-ting**; *past* **bit**; *past participle* **bitten**) nip or cut into or off with teeth; sting; penetrate, grip; accept bait; be harsh in effect, esp. intentionally. ● *noun* act of biting; wound so made; small amount to eat; pungency; incisiveness.

bitter /'bɪtə/ ● *adjective* having sharp pungent taste, not sweet; showing or feeling resentment; harsh, virulent; piercingly cold. ● *noun* bitter beer, strongly flavoured with hops; (in *plural*) liquor with bitter flavour, esp. of wormwood. □ **bitterly** *adverb*; **bitterness** *noun*.

bittern /'bɪt(ə)n/ *noun* wading bird of heron family.

bitty *adjective* (**-ier**, **-iest**) made up of bits.

bitumen /'bɪtjʊmɪn/ *noun* tarlike mixture of hydrocarbons derived from petroleum. □ **bituminous** /bɪˈtjuːmɪnəs/ *adjective*.

bivalve /'baɪvælv/ ● *noun* aquatic mollusc with hinged double shell. ● *adjective* with such a shell.

bivouac /'bɪvʊæk/ ● *noun* temporary encampment without tents. ● *verb* (**-ck-**) make, or camp in, bivouac.

bizarre /bɪˈzɑː/ *adjective* strange in appearance or effect; grotesque.

blab *verb* (**-bb-**) talk or tell foolishly or indiscreetly.

black ● *adjective* colourless from absence or complete absorption of light; very dark-coloured; of human group with dark skin, esp. African; heavily overcast; angry, gloomy, sinister, wicked; declared untouchable by workers in dispute. ● *noun* black colour, paint, clothes, etc.; (player using) darker pieces in chess etc.; (of tea or coffee) without milk; member of dark-skinned race, esp. African. ● *verb* make black; declare (goods etc.) 'black'. □ **black and blue** badly bruised; **black and white** not in colour, comprising only opposite extremes, (after *in*) in print; **black art** black magic; **blackball** exclude from club, society, etc.; **black beetle** common cockroach; **black belt** (holder of) highest grade of proficiency in judo, karate, etc.; **black box** flight recorder; **black comedy** comedy presenting tragedy in comic terms; **black eye** bruised skin round eye; **blackfly** kind of aphid; **Black Forest gateau** chocolate sponge with cherries and whipped cream; **blackhead** blacktopped pimple; **black hole** region of space from which matter and radiation cannot escape; **black ice** thin hard transparent ice; **blacklead** graphite; **blackleg** *derogatory* person refusing to join strike etc.; **black magic** magic supposed to invoke evil spirits; **Black Maria** *slang* police van; **black market** illicit traffic in rationed, prohibited, or scarce commodities; **Black Mass** travesty of Mass in worship of Satan; **black out** effect blackout on, undergo blackout; **blackout** temporary loss of consciousness or memory; loss of electric power, radio reception, etc.; compulsory darkness as precaution against air raids; **black pudding** sausage of blood, suet, etc.; **Black Rod** chief usher of House of Lords; **black sheep** disreputable member; **blackshirt** *historical* Fascist; **black spot** place of danger or trouble; **blackthorn** thorny shrub bearing white flowers and sloes; **black tie** man's formal evening dress; **black velvet** mixture of stout and champagne; **black widow** venomous spider of which female devours male; **in the black** in credit or surplus.

blackberry *noun* (*plural* **-ies**) dark edible fruit of bramble.

blackbird *noun* European songbird.

blackboard *noun* board for chalking on in classroom etc.

blackcurrant *noun* small black fruit; shrub on which it grows.

blacken *verb* make or become black; slander.

blackguard /'blægɑːd/ noun villain, scoundrel. □ **blackguardly** adjective.

blacking noun black polish for boots and shoes.

blacklist ● noun list of people etc. in disfavour. ● verb put on blacklist.

blackmail ● noun extortion of payment in return for silence; use of threats or pressure. ● verb extort money from (person) thus. □ **blackmailer** noun.

blacksmith noun smith working in iron.

bladder /'blædə/ noun sac in humans and other animals, esp. that holding urine.

blade noun cutting part of knife etc.; flat part of oar, spade, propeller, etc.; flat narrow leaf of grass and cereals; flat bone in shoulder.

blame ● verb (-ming) assign fault or responsibility to; (+ on) assign responsibility for (error etc.) to. ● noun responsibility for bad result; blaming, attributing of responsibility. □ **blameworthy** deserving blame. □ **blameless** adjective.

blanch /blɑːntʃ/ verb make or grow pale; peel (almonds etc.) by scalding; immerse briefly in boiling water; whiten (plant) by depriving of light.

blancmange /blə'mɒndʒ/ noun sweet opaque jelly of flavoured cornflour and milk.

bland adjective mild; insipid, tasteless; gentle, suave. □ **blandly** adverb.

blandishment /'blændɪʃmənt/ noun (usually in plural) flattering attention; cajolery.

blank ● adjective not written or printed on; (of form etc.) not filled in; (of space) empty; without interest, result, or expression. ● noun space to be filled up in form etc.; blank cartridge; empty surface; dash written in place of word. □ **blank cartridge** one without bullet; **blank cheque** one with amount left for payee to fill in; **blank verse** unrhymed verse, esp. iambic pentameters. □ **blankly** adverb.

blanket /'blæŋkɪt/ ● noun large esp. woollen sheet as bed-covering etc.; thick covering layer. ● adjective general, covering all cases or classes. ● verb (-t-) cover (as) with blanket. □ **blanket stitch** stitch used to finish edges of blanket etc.

blare ● verb (-ring) sound or utter loudly; make sound of trumpet. ● noun blaring sound.

blarney /'blɑːnɪ/ ● noun cajoling talk, flattery. ● verb (-eys, -eyed) flatter, use blarney.

blasé /'blɑːzeɪ/ adjective bored or indifferent, esp. through familiarity.

blaspheme /blæs'fiːm/ verb (-ming) treat religious name or subject irreverently; talk irreverently about.

blasphemy /'blæsfəmɪ/ noun (plural -ies) (instance of) blaspheming. □ **blasphemous** adjective.

blast /blɑːst/ ● noun strong gust; explosion; destructive wave of air from this; loud note from wind instrument, car horn, whistle, etc.; colloquial severe reprimand. ● verb blow up with explosive; blight; (cause to) make explosive sound. ● interjection damn. □ **blast furnace** one for smelting with compressed hot air driven in; **blast off** (of rocket) take off from launching site; **blast-off** noun.

blasted colloquial ● adjective annoying. ● adverb extremely.

blatant /'bleɪt(ə)nt/ adjective flagrant, unashamed. □ **blatantly** adverb.

blather /'blæðə/ ● noun (also **blether** /'bleðə/) foolish talk. ● verb talk foolishly.

blaze[1] ● noun bright flame or fire; violent outburst of passion; bright display or light. ● verb (-zing) burn or shine brightly or fiercely; burn with excitement etc. □ **blaze away** shoot continuously.

blaze[2] ● noun white mark on face of horse or chipped in bark of tree. ● verb (-zing) mark (tree, path) with blaze(s).

blazer noun jacket without matching trousers, esp. lightweight and part of uniform.

blazon /'bleɪz(ə)n/ verb proclaim; describe or paint (coat of arms). □ **blazonry** noun.

bleach ● verb whiten in sunlight or by chemical process. ● noun bleaching substance or process.

bleak adjective exposed, windswept; dreary, grim.

bleary /'blɪərɪ/ *adjective* (**-ier**, **-iest**) dim-sighted, blurred. □ **bleary-eyed** having dim sight.

bleat • *verb* utter cry of sheep, goat, etc.; speak plaintively. • *noun* bleating cry.

bleed *verb* (*past & past participle* **bled**) emit blood; draw blood from; *colloquial* extort money from.

bleep • *noun* intermittent high-pitched sound. • *verb* make bleep; summon by bleep.

bleeper *noun* small electronic device alerting person to message by bleeping.

blemish /'blemɪʃ/ • *noun* flaw, defect, stain. • *verb* spoil, mark, stain.

blench *verb* flinch, quail.

blend • *verb* mix (various sorts) into required sort; become one; mingle intimately. • *noun* mixture.

blender *noun* machine for liquidizing or chopping food.

blenny /'blenɪ/ *noun* (*plural* **-ies**) spiny-finned sea fish.

bless *verb* ask God to look favourably on; consecrate; glorify (God); thank; make happy.

blessed /'blesɪd/ *adjective* holy; *euphemistic* cursed; *RC Church* beatified.

blessing *noun* invocation of divine favour; grace said at meals; benefit, advantage.

blether = BLATHER.

blew *past* of BLOW¹.

blight /blaɪt/ • *noun* disease of plants caused esp. by insects; such insect; harmful or destructive force. • *verb* affect with blight; destroy; spoil.

blighter *noun colloquial* annoying person.

blimey /'blaɪmɪ/ *interjection slang: expressing surprise.*

blimp *noun* small non-rigid airship; (also (**Colonel**) **Blimp**) reactionary person.

blind /blaɪnd/ • *adjective* without sight; without adequate foresight, discernment, or information; (often + *to*) unwilling or unable to appreciate (a factor); not governed by purpose; reckless; concealed; closed at one end. • *verb* deprive of sight or judgement; deceive. • *noun* screen for window; thing used to hide truth; obstruction to sight or light. • *adverb* blindly. □ **blind date** *colloquial* date between two people who have not

met before; **blind man's buff** game in which blindfold player tries to catch others; **blind spot** spot on retina insensitive to light, area where vision or judgement fails; **blindworm** slow-worm. □ **blindly** *adverb*; **blindness** *noun*.

blindfold • *verb* cover eyes of (person) with tied cloth etc. • *noun* cloth etc. so used. • *adjective & adverb* with eyes covered; without due care.

blink • *verb* shut and open eyes quickly; (often + *back*) prevent (tears) by blinking; shine unsteadily, flicker. • *noun* act of blinking; momentary gleam. □ **blink at** ignore, shirk; **on the blink** *slang* (of machine etc.) out of order.

blinker • *noun* (usually in *plural*) either of screens on bridle preventing horse from seeing sideways. • *verb* obscure with blinkers; (as **blinkered** *adjective*) prejudiced, narrow-minded.

blinking *adjective & adverb slang: expressing mild annoyance.*

blip *noun* minor deviation or error; quick popping sound; small image on radar screen.

bliss *noun* perfect joy; being in heaven. □ **blissful** *adjective*; **blissfully** *adverb*.

blister /'blɪstə/ • *noun* small bubble on skin filled with watery fluid; any swelling resembling this. • *verb* become covered with blisters; raise blister on.

blithe /blaɪð/ *adjective* cheerful, happy; carefree, casual. □ **blithely** *adverb*.

blithering /'blɪðərɪŋ/ *adjective colloquial* utter, hopeless; contemptible.

blitz /blɪts/ *colloquial* • *noun* intensive (esp. aerial) attack. • *verb* inflict blitz on.

blizzard /'blɪzəd/ *noun* severe snowstorm.

bloat *verb* inflate, swell.

bloater *noun* herring cured by salting and smoking.

blob *noun* small drop or spot.

bloc *noun* group of governments etc. sharing some common purpose.

block • *noun* solid piece of hard material; large building, esp. when subdivided; group of buildings surrounded by streets; obstruction; large quantity as a unit; piece of wood or metal engraved for printing. • *verb* obstruct; restrict use of; stop (cricket ball) with bat.

□ **blockbuster** *slang* very successful film, book, etc.; **blockhead** stupid person; **block capitals, letters** separate capital letters; **block out** shut out (light, noise, view, etc.); **block up** shut in, fill (window etc.) in; **block vote** vote proportional in size to number of people voter represents; **mental block** mental inability due to subconscious factors.

blockade /blɒˈkeɪd/ • *noun* surrounding or blocking of place by enemy. • *verb* (**-ding**) subject to blockade.

blockage *noun* obstruction.

bloke *noun slang* man, fellow.

blond (of woman, usually **blonde**) • *adjective* light-coloured, fair-haired. • *noun* blond person.

blood /blʌd/ • *noun* fluid, usually red, circulating in arteries and veins of animals; killing, bloodshed; passion, temperament; race, descent; relationship. • *verb* give first taste of blood to (hound); initiate (person). □ **blood bank** store of blood for transfusion; **bloodbath** massacre; **blood count** number of corpuscles in blood; **blood-curdling** horrifying; **blood donor** giver of blood for transfusion; **blood group** any of types of human blood; **bloodhound** large keen-scented dog used for tracking; **bloodletting** surgical removal of blood; **blood orange** red-fleshed orange; **blood poisoning** diseased condition due to bacteria in blood; **blood pressure** pressure of blood in arteries; **blood relation** one related by birth; **bloodshed** killing; **bloodshot** (of eyeball) inflamed; **blood sport** one involving killing of animals; **bloodstream** circulating blood; **bloodsucker** leech, extortioner; **bloodthirsty** eager for bloodshed; **blood vessel** vein, artery, or capillary carrying blood.

bloodless *adjective* without blood or bloodshed; unemotional; pale.

bloody • *adjective* (**-ier, -iest**) of or like blood; running or stained with blood; involving bloodshed, cruel; *coarse slang* annoying, very great. • *adverb coarse slang* extremely. • *verb* (**-ies, -ied**) stain with blood. □ **bloody-minded** *colloquial* deliberately uncooperative.

bloom /bluːm/ • *noun* flower; flowering state; prime; freshness; fine powder on fruit etc. • *verb* bear flowers; be in flower; flourish.

bloomer[1] *noun slang* blunder.

bloomer[2] *noun* long loaf with diagonal marks.

bloomers *plural noun colloquial* woman's long loose knickers.

blooming • *adjective* flourishing, healthy; *slang* annoying, very great. • *adverb slang* extremely.

blossom /ˈblɒsəm/ • *noun* flower; mass of flowers on tree. • *verb* open into flower; flourish.

blot • *noun* spot of ink etc.; disgraceful act; blemish. • *verb* (**-tt-**) make blot on; stain; dry with blotting paper. □ **blot out** obliterate, obscure; **blotting paper** absorbent paper for drying wet ink.

blotch *noun* inflamed patch on skin; irregular patch of colour. □ **blotchy** *adjective* (**-ier, -iest**).

blotter *noun* device holding blotting paper.

blouse /blaʊz/ *noun* woman's shirtlike garment; type of military jacket.

blow[1] /bləʊ/ • *verb* (*past* **blew** /bluː/; *past participle* **blown**) send directed air-current esp. from mouth; drive or be driven by blowing; move as wind does; sound (wind instrument); (*past participle* **blowed**) *slang* curse, confound; clear (nose) by forceful breath; pant; make or shape by blowing; break or burst suddenly; (cause to) break electric circuit; *slang* squander. • *noun* blowing; short spell in fresh air. □ **blow-dry** arrange (hair) while using hand-held dryer; **blowfly** bluebottle; **blow in** send inwards by explosion, *colloquial* arrive unexpectedly; **blowlamp** device with flame for plumbing, burning off paint, etc.; **blow out** extinguish by blowing, send outwards by explosion; **blow-out** *colloquial* burst tyre, *slang* large meal; **blow over** fade away; **blowpipe** tube for blowing through, esp. one from which dart or arrow is projected; **blowtorch** *US* blowlamp; **blow up** explode, *colloquial* rebuke strongly, inflate, *colloquial* enlarge (photograph); **blow-up** *colloquial* enlargement of photograph.

blow[2] /bləʊ/ *noun* hard stroke with hand or weapon; disaster, shock.

blower /ˈbləʊə/ *noun* device for blowing; *colloquial* telephone.

blowy /ˈbləʊɪ/ *adjective* (**-ier, -iest**) windy.

blowzy /ˈblaʊzɪ/ *adjective* (**-ier, -iest**) coarse-looking, red-faced; dishevelled.

blub *verb* (**-bb-**) *slang* sob.

blubber /ˈblʌbə/ ● *noun* whale fat. ● *verb* sob noisily. □ **blubbery** *adjective*.

bludgeon /ˈblʌdʒ(ə)n/ ● *noun* heavy club. ● *verb* beat with bludgeon; coerce.

blue /bluː/ ● *adjective* (**-r, -st**) coloured like clear sky; sad, depressed; pornographic. ● *noun* blue colour, paint, clothes, etc.; person who represents Oxford or Cambridge University at sport; (in *plural*) type of melancholy music of American black origin, (**the blues**) depression. ● *verb* (**blues, blued, bluing** or **blueing**) *slang* squander. □ **blue baby** one with congenital heart defect; **bluebell** woodland plant with bell-shaped blue flowers; **blueberry** small edible blue or blackish fruit of various plants; **blue blood** noble birth; **bluebottle** large buzzing fly; **blue cheese** cheese with veins of blue mould; **blue-collar** manual, industrial; **blue-eyed boy** *colloquial* favourite; **bluegrass** type of country and western music; **Blue Peter** blue flag with central white square hoisted before sailing; **blueprint** photographic print of building plans etc. in white on blue paper, detailed plan; **bluestocking** *usually derogatory* intellectual woman; **blue tit** small blue and yellow bird; **blue whale** rorqual (largest known living mammal).

bluff[1] ● *verb* pretend to have strength, knowledge, etc. ● *noun* bluffing.

bluff[2] ● *adjective* blunt, frank, hearty; with steep or vertical broad front. ● *noun* bluff headland.

blunder /ˈblʌndə/ ● *noun* serious or foolish mistake. ● *verb* make blunder; move about clumsily.

blunderbuss /ˈblʌndəbʌs/ *noun historical* short large-bored gun.

blunt ● *adjective* without sharp edge or point; plain-spoken. ● *verb* make blunt. □ **bluntly** *adverb*; **bluntness** *noun*.

blur ● *verb* (**-rr-**) make or become less distinct; smear. ● *noun* indistinct object, sound, memory, etc.

blurb *noun* promotional description, esp. of book.

blurt *verb* (usually + *out*) utter abruptly or tactlessly.

blush ● *verb* be or become red (as) with shame or embarrassment; be ashamed. ● *noun* blushing; pink tinge.

blusher *noun* coloured cosmetic for cheeks.

bluster /ˈblʌstə/ ● *verb* behave pompously; storm boisterously. ● *noun* noisy pompous talk, empty threats. □ **blustery** *adjective*.

BMA *abbreviation* British Medical Association.

BMX *noun* organized bicycle racing on dirt track; bicycle used for this.

BO *abbreviation colloquial* body odour.

boa /ˈbəʊə/ *noun* large snake that kills its prey by crushing it; long stole of fur or feathers. □ **boa constrictor** species of boa.

boar *noun* male wild pig; uncastrated male pig.

board ● *noun* thin piece of sawn timber; material resembling this; slab of wood etc., e.g. ironing board, notice board; thick stiff card; provision of meals; directors of company; committee; (**the boards**) stage. ● *verb* go on board (ship etc.); receive or provide with, meals and usually lodging; (usually + *up*) cover with boards. □ **board game** game played on a board; **boarding house** unlicensed house providing board and lodging; **boarding school** one in which pupils live in term-time; **boardroom** room where board of directors meets; **on board** on or into ship, train, aircraft, etc.

boarder *noun* person who boards, esp. at boarding school.

boast ● *verb* declare one's achievements etc. with excessive pride; have (desirable thing). ● *noun* boasting; thing one is proud of. □ **boastful** *adjective*.

boat ● *noun* small vessel propelled by oars, sails, or engine; ship; long low jug for sauce etc. ● *verb* go in boat, esp. for pleasure. □ **boat-hook** long pole with hook for moving boats; **boathouse** shed at water's edge for boats; **boatman** person who hires out or provides transport by boats; **boat people**

refugees travelling by sea; **boat-train** train scheduled to connect with ship.

boater noun flat straw hat with straight brim.

boatswain /ˈbəʊs(ə)n/ noun (also **bosun**) ship's officer in charge of equipment and crew.

bob[1] ● verb (**-bb-**) move up and down; rebound; cut (hair) in bob; curtsy. ● noun bobbing movement; curtsy; hairstyle with hair hanging evenly above shoulders; weight on pendulum etc. □ **bobtail** docked tail, horse or dog with this.

bob[2] noun (plural same) historical slang shilling (= 5p).

bobbin /ˈbɒbɪn/ noun spool or reel for thread etc.

bobble /ˈbɒb(ə)l/ noun small woolly ball on hat etc.

bobby /ˈbɒbɪ/ noun (plural **-ies**) colloquial police officer.

bobsled noun US bobsleigh.

bobsleigh noun racing sledge steered and braked mechanically.

bod noun colloquial person.

bode verb (**-ding**) □ **bode well, ill** be good or bad sign.

bodge /bɒdʒ/ = BOTCH.

bodice /ˈbɒdɪs/ noun part of woman's dress above waist.

bodily /ˈbɒdɪlɪ/ ● adjective of the body. ● adverb as a whole (body); in person.

bodkin /ˈbɒdkɪn/ noun blunt thick needle for drawing tape etc. through hem.

body /ˈbɒdɪ/ noun (plural **-ies**) physical structure of person or animal, alive or dead; person's or animal's trunk; main part; group of people regarded as unit; quantity, mass; piece of matter; colloquial person; full or substantial quality of flavour etc.; body stocking. □ **body-building** exercises to enlarge and strengthen muscles; **bodyguard** escort or personal guard; **body politic** state, nation; **body shop** workshop where bodywork is repaired; **body stocking** woman's undergarment covering trunk; **bodywork** outer shell of vehicle.

Boer /ˈbɔː/ noun S. African of Dutch descent.

boffin /ˈbɒfɪn/ noun colloquial research scientist.

bog noun (area of) wet spongy ground; slang lavatory. □ **bogged down** unable to move or make progress. □ **boggy** adjective (**-ier, -iest**).

bogey[1] /ˈbəʊgɪ/ noun (plural **-s**) Golf score of one more than par for hole; (formerly) par.

bogey[2] /ˈbəʊgɪ/ noun (also **bogy**) (plural **-eys** or **-ies**) evil or mischievous spirit; awkward thing.

boggle /ˈbɒg(ə)l/ verb (**-ling**) colloquial be startled or baffled.

bogie /ˈbəʊgɪ/ noun wheeled undercarriage below locomotive etc.

bogus /ˈbəʊgəs/ adjective sham, spurious.

bogy = BOGEY[2].

Bohemian /bəʊˈhiːmɪən/ ● noun native of Bohemia; (also **bohemian**) socially unconventional person, esp. artist or writer. ● adjective of Bohemia; (also **bohemian**) socially unconventional. □ **bohemianism** noun.

boil[1] ● verb (of liquid or its vessel) bubble up with heat, reach temperature at which liquid turns to vapour; bring to boiling point; subject to heat of boiling water, cook thus; be agitated like boiling water. ● noun boiling; boiling point. □ **boiling** (**hot**) colloquial very hot; **boiling point** temperature at which a liquid boils; **boil over** spill over in boiling.

boil[2] noun inflamed pus-filled swelling under skin.

boiler noun apparatus for heating hot-water supply; tank for heating water or turning it into steam; vessel for boiling things in. □ **boiler suit** protective garment combining trousers and shirt.

boisterous /ˈbɔɪstərəs/ adjective noisily cheerful; violent, rough.

bold /bəʊld/ adjective confident; adventurous; impudent; distinct, vivid. □ **boldly** adverb; **boldness** noun.

bole noun trunk of tree.

bolero noun (plural **-s**) /bəˈleərəʊ/ Spanish dance; /ˈbɒlərəʊ/ woman's short jacket without fastenings.

boll /bəʊl/ noun round seed vessel of cotton, flax, etc.

bollard /ˈbɒlɑːd/ noun short thick post in street etc.; post on ship or quay for securing ropes to.

boloney /bəˈləʊnɪ/ noun slang nonsense.

bolshie /'bɒlʃɪ/ *adjective* (**-r, -st**) (also **Bolshie**) *slang* rebellious, uncooperative.

bolster /'bəʊlstə/ ● *noun* long cylindrical pillow. ● *verb* (usually + *up*) encourage, support, prop up.

bolt¹ /bəʊlt/ ● *noun* door-fastening of metal bar and socket; headed metal pin secured with rivet or nut; discharge of lightning; bolting. ● *verb* fasten with bolt; (+ *in, out*) keep in or out by bolting door; dart off, run away; (of horse) escape from control; gulp down unchewed; run to seed. □ **bolt-hole** means of escape; **bolt upright** erect.

bolt² /bəʊlt/ *verb* (also **boult**) sift.

bomb /bɒm/ ● *noun* container filled with explosive, incendiary material, etc., designed to explode and cause damage; (**the bomb**) the atomic bomb; *slang* large amount of money. ● *verb* attack with bombs; drop bombs on; *colloquial* travel fast. □ **bombshell** great surprise or disappointment.

bombard /bɒm'bɑːd/ *verb* attack with heavy guns etc.; question or abuse persistently; subject to stream of high-speed particles. □ **bombardment** *noun*.

bombardier /bɒmbə'dɪə/ *noun* artillery NCO below sergeant; *US* airman who releases bombs from aircraft.

bombast /'bɒmbæst/ *noun* pompous or extravagant language. □ **bombastic** /-'bæs-/ *adjective*.

Bombay duck /'bɒmbeɪ/ *noun* dried fish eaten as relish, esp. with curry.

bomber *noun* aircraft equipped for bombing; person who throws or plants bomb. □ **bomber jacket** one gathered at waist and cuffs.

bona fide /bəʊnə 'faɪdɪ/ *adjective & adverb* in good faith, genuine(ly).

bonanza /bə'nænzə/ *noun* source of great wealth; large output, esp. from mine.

bon-bon *noun* sweet.

bond ● *noun* thing or force that unites or (usually in *plural*) restrains; binding agreement; certificate issued by government or company promising to repay money at fixed rate of interest; adhesiveness; document binding person to pay or repay money; linkage of atoms in molecule. ● *verb* bind or connect together; put in bond. □ **bond**

paper high-quality writing paper; **in bond** stored by Customs until duty is paid.

bondage /'bɒndɪdʒ/ *noun* slavery; subjection to constraint.

bondsman /'bɒndzmən/ *noun* serf, slave.

bone ● *noun* any of separate parts of vertebrate skeleton; (in *plural*) skeleton, esp. as remains; substance of which bones consist. ● *verb* (**-ning**) remove bones from. □ **bone china** fine semitranslucent earthenware; **bone dry** completely dry; **bone idle** completely idle; **bone marrow** fatty substance in cavity of bones; **bonemeal** crushed bone as fertilizer; **boneshaker** jolting vehicle.

bonfire *noun* open-air fire.

bongo /'bɒŋgəʊ/ *noun* (*plural* **-s** or **-es**) either of pair of small drums played with fingers.

bonhomie /'bɒnɒmi:/ *noun* geniality.

bonkers /'bɒŋkəz/ *adjective slang* crazy.

bonnet /'bɒnɪt/ *noun* woman's or child's hat tied under chin; Scotsman's floppy beret; hinged cover over engine of vehicle.

bonny /'bɒnɪ/ *adjective* (**-ier, -iest**) *esp. Scottish & Northern English* healthy-looking, attractive.

bonsai /'bɒnsaɪ/ *noun* (*plural* same) dwarfed tree or shrub; art of growing these.

bonus /'bəʊnəs/ *noun* extra benefit or payment.

bon voyage /bɔ̃ vwaːˈjɑːʒ/ *interjection* have a good trip. [French]

bony /'bəʊnɪ/ *adjective* (**-ier, -iest**) thin with prominent bones; having many bones; of or like bone.

boo ● *interjection* expressing disapproval or contempt; sound intended to surprise. ● *noun* utterance of 'boo'. ● *verb* (**boos, booed**) utter boos (at).

boob ● *noun colloquial* silly mistake; *slang* woman's breast. ● *verb colloquial* make mistake.

booby /'buːbɪ/ *noun* (*plural* **-ies**) silly or awkward person. □ **booby prize** prize for coming last; **booby trap** practical joke in form of trap, disguised bomb etc. triggered by unknowing victim.

book /bʊk/ • *noun* written or printed work with pages bound along one side; work intended for publication; bound set of tickets, stamps, matches, cheques, etc.; (in *plural*) set of records or accounts; main division of literary work or Bible; telephone directory; *colloquial* magazine; libretto; record of bets made. • *verb* reserve (seat etc.) in advance; engage (entertainer etc.); take personal details of (offender); enter in book or list. □ **bookcase** cabinet of shelves for books; **bookend** prop to keep books upright; **bookkeeper** person who keeps accounts; **bookmaker** professional taker of bets; **bookmark** thing for marking place in book; **bookplate** decorative personalized label in book; **book token** voucher exchangeable for books; **bookworm** *colloquial* devoted reader, larva that eats through books.

bookie /ˈbʊkɪ/ *noun colloquial* bookmaker.

bookish *adjective* fond of reading; getting knowledge mainly from books.

booklet /ˈbʊklɪt/ *noun* small usually paper-covered book.

boom[1] /buːm/ • *noun* deep resonant sound. • *verb* make or speak with boom.

boom[2] /buːm/ • *noun* period of economic prosperity or activity. • *verb* be suddenly prosperous.

boom[3] /buːm/ *noun* pivoted spar to which sail is attached; long pole carrying camera, microphone, etc.; barrier across harbour etc.

boomerang /ˈbuːməræŋ/ • *noun* flat V-shaped Australian hardwood missile returning to thrower. • *verb* (of plan) backfire.

boon[1] /buːn/ *noun* advantage; blessing.

boon[2] /buːn/ *adjective* intimate, favourite.

boor /bʊə/ *noun* ill-mannered person. □ **boorish** *adjective*.

boost /buːst/ *colloquial* • *verb* promote, encourage; increase, assist; push from below. • *noun* boosting.

booster *noun* device for increasing power or voltage; auxiliary engine or rocket for initial speed; dose renewing effect of earlier one.

boot /buːt/ • *noun* outer foot-covering reaching above ankle; luggage compartment of car; *colloquial* firm kick, dismissal. • *verb* kick; (often + *out*) eject forcefully; (usually + *up*) make (computer) ready.

bootee /buːˈtiː/ *noun* baby's soft shoe.

booth /buːð/ *noun* temporary structure used esp. as market stall; enclosure for telephoning, voting, etc.

bootleg /ˈbuːtleg/ • *adjective* smuggled, illicit. • *verb* (-**gg**-) illicitly make or deal in. □ **bootlegger** *noun*.

bootstrap /ˈbuːtstræp/ *noun* □ **pull oneself up by one's bootstraps** better oneself by one's unaided effort.

booty /ˈbuːtɪ/ *noun* loot, spoils; *colloquial* prize.

booze *colloquial* • *noun* alcoholic drink. • *verb* (-**zing**) drink alcohol, esp. excessively. □ **boozy** *adjective* (-**ier**, -**iest**).

boozer *noun colloquial* habitual drinker; public house.

bop *colloquial* • *noun* spell of dancing, esp. to pop music; *colloquial* hit, blow. • *verb* (-**pp**-) dance, esp. to pop music; *colloquial* hit.

boracic /bəˈræsɪk/ *adjective* of borax. □ **boracic acid** boric acid.

borage /ˈbɒrɪdʒ/ *noun* plant with leaves used as flavouring.

borax /ˈbɔːræks/ *noun* salt of boric acid used as antiseptic.

border /ˈbɔːdə/ • *noun* edge, boundary, or part near it; line or region separating countries; distinct edging, esp. ornamental strip; long narrow flower-bed. • *verb* put or be border to; adjoin. □ **borderline** *noun* line marking boundary or dividing two conditions, *adjective* on borderline.

bore[1] • *verb* (-**ring**) make (hole), esp. with revolving tool; make hole in. • *noun* hollow of firearm barrel or cylinder; diameter of this; deep hole made to find water etc.

bore[2] • *noun* tiresome or dull person or thing. • *verb* (-**ring**) weary by tedious talk or dullness. □ **bored** *adjective*, **boring** *adjective*.

bore[3] *noun* very high tidal wave rushing up estuary.

bore[4] *past of* BEAR[1].

boredom *noun* being bored (BORE[2]).

boric acid /ˈbɔːrɪk/ *noun* acid used as antiseptic.

born *adjective* existing as a result of birth; being (specified thing) by nature; (usually + *to do*) destined.

borne *past participle* of BEAR¹.

boron /'bɔːrɒn/ *noun* non-metallic element.

borough /'bʌrə/ *noun* administrative area, esp. of Greater London; *historical* town with municipal corporation.

borrow /'bɒrəʊ/ *verb* get temporary use of (something to be returned); use another's (invention, idea, etc.). □ **borrower** *noun*.

Borstal /'bɔːst(ə)l/ *noun historical* residential institution for youth custody.

bosom /'bʊz(ə)m/ *noun* person's breasts; *colloquial* each of woman's breasts; enclosure formed by breast and arms; emotional centre. □ **bosom friend** intimate friend.

boss¹ *colloquial* ● *noun* employer, manager, or supervisor. ● *verb* (usually + *about, around*) give orders to.

boss² *noun* round knob or stud.

boss-eyed *adjective colloquial* cross-eyed; crooked.

bossy *adjective* (**-ier**, **-iest**) *colloquial* domineering. □ **bossiness** *noun*.

bosun = BOATSWAIN.

botany /'bɒtənɪ/ *noun* study of plants. □ **botanic(al)** /bə'tæn-/ *adjective*; **botanist** *noun*.

botch ● *verb* bungle; patch clumsily. ● *noun* bungled or spoilt work.

both /bəʊθ/ ● *adjective & pronoun* the two (not only one). ● *adverb* with equal truth in two cases.

bother /'bɒðə/ ● *verb* trouble, worry; take trouble. ● *noun* person or thing that bothers; nuisance; trouble, worry. ● *interjection of irritation*. □ **bothersome** /-səm/ *adjective*.

bottle /'bɒt(ə)l/ ● *noun* container, esp. glass or plastic, for storing liquid; liquid in bottle; *slang* courage. ● *verb* (**-ling**) put into bottles; preserve (fruit etc.) in jars; (+ *up*) restrain (feelings etc.). □ **bottle bank** place for depositing bottles for recycling; **bottle green** dark green; **bottleneck** narrow congested area esp. on road etc., thing that impedes; **bottle party** one to which guests bring bottles of drink.

bottom /'bɒtəm/ ● *noun* lowest point or part; buttocks; less honourable end of table, class, etc.; ground under water; basis; essential character. ● *adjective* lowest, last. ● *verb* find extent of; touch bottom (of); (usually + *out*) reach its lowest level. □ **bottom line** *colloquial* underlying truth, ultimate criterion.

bottomless *adjective* without bottom; inexhaustible.

botulism /'bɒtjʊlɪz(ə)m/ *noun* poisoning caused by bacillus in badly preserved food.

boudoir /'buːdwɑː/ *noun* woman's private room.

bougainvillaea /buːgən'vɪlɪə/ *noun* tropical plant with large coloured bracts.

bough /baʊ/ *noun* branch of tree.

bought *past & past participle* of BUY.

bouillon /'buːjɒn/ *noun* clear broth.

boulder /'bəʊldə/ *noun* large smooth rock.

boulevard /'buːləvɑːd/ *noun* broad tree-lined street.

boult = BOLT².

bounce /baʊns/ ● *verb* (**-cing**) (cause to) rebound; *slang* (of cheque) be returned to payee by bank when there are no funds to meet it; rush boisterously. ● *noun* rebound; *colloquial* swagger, self-confidence; *colloquial* liveliness. □ **bouncy** *adjective* (**-ier**, **-iest**).

bouncer *noun slang* doorman ejecting troublemakers from nightclub etc.

bouncing *adjective* big and healthy.

bound¹ /baʊnd/ ● *verb* spring, leap; (of ball etc.) bounce. ● *noun* springy leap; bounce.

bound² /baʊnd/ ● *noun* (usually in *plural*) limitation, restriction; border, boundary. ● *verb* limit; be boundary of. □ **out of bounds** outside permitted area.

bound³ /baʊnd/ *adjective* (usually + *for*) starting or having started.

bound⁴ /baʊnd/ *past & past participle* of BIND. □ **bound to** certain to; **bound up with** closely associated with.

boundary /'baʊndərɪ/ *noun* (*plural* **-ies**) line marking limits; *Cricket* hit crossing limit of field, runs scored for this.

boundless *adjective* unlimited.

bounteous /'baʊntɪəs/ *adjective poetical* bountiful.

bountiful /ˈbaʊntɪfʊl/ *adjective* generous; ample.

bounty /ˈbaʊntɪ/ *noun* (*plural* **-ies**) generosity; official reward; gift.

bouquet /buːˈkeɪ/ *noun* bunch of flowers; scent of wine; compliment. □ **bouquet garni** (/ˈɡɑːnɪ/) bunch or bag of herbs for flavouring.

bourbon /ˈbɜːbən/ *noun US* whisky from maize and rye.

bourgeois /ˈbʊəʒwɑː/ *often derogatory* ● *adjective* conventionally middle-class; materialist; capitalist. ● *noun* (*plural* same) bourgeois person.

bourgeoisie /bʊəʒwɑːˈziː/ *noun* bourgeois class.

bourn /bɔːn/ *noun* stream.

bourse /bʊəs/ *noun* money market, esp. (**Bourse**) Stock Exchange in Paris.

bout *noun* spell of work etc.; fit of illness; wrestling or boxing match.

boutique /buːˈtiːk/ *noun* small shop selling fashionable clothes etc.

bouzouki /buːˈzuːkɪ/ *noun* (*plural* **-s**) form of Greek mandolin.

bovine /ˈbəʊvaɪn/ *adjective* of cattle; dull, stupid.

bow¹ /bəʊ/ ● *noun* weapon for shooting arrows; rod with horsehair stretched from end to end for playing violin etc.; knot with two loops, ribbon etc. so tied; shallow curve or bend. ● *verb* use bow on (violin etc.). □ **bow-legged** having bandy legs; **bow tie** necktie in form of bow; **bow window** curved bay window.

bow² /baʊ/ ● *verb* incline head or body, esp. in greeting or acknowledgement; submit; incline (head etc.). ● *noun* bowing.

bow³ /baʊ/ *noun* (often in *plural*) front end of boat or ship; rower nearest bow.

bowdlerize /ˈbaʊdləraɪz/ *verb* (also **-ise**) (**-zing** or **-sing**) expurgate. □ **bowdlerization** *noun*.

bowel /ˈbaʊəl/ *noun* (often in *plural*) intestine; (in *plural*) innermost parts.

bower /ˈbaʊə/ *noun* arbour; summer house. □ **bowerbird** Australasian bird, the male of which constructs elaborate runs.

bowie knife /ˈbəʊɪ/ *noun* long hunting knife.

bowl¹ /bəʊl/ *noun* dish, esp. for food or liquid; hollow part of tobacco pipe, spoon, etc.

bowl² /bəʊl/ ● *noun* hard heavy ball made with bias to run in curve; (in *plural*; usually treated as *singular*) game with these on grass. ● *verb* roll (ball etc.); play bowls; *Cricket* deliver ball, (often + *out*) put (batsman) out by knocking off bails with bowled ball; (often + *along*) go along rapidly. □ **bowling alley** long enclosure for skittles or tenpin bowling; **bowling green** lawn for playing bowls.

bowler¹ /ˈbəʊlə/ *noun Cricket etc.* player who bowls.

bowler² /ˈbəʊlə/ *noun* hard round felt hat.

bowsprit /ˈbəʊsprɪt/ *noun* spar running forward from ship's bow.

box¹ /bɒks/ *noun* container, usually flat-sided and firm; amount contained in this; compartment in theatre, law court, etc.; telephone box; facility at newspaper office for replies to advertisement; (**the box**) *colloquial* television; enclosed area or space. ● *verb* put in or provide with box. □ **box girder** hollow girder with square cross-section; **box junction** yellow-striped road area which vehicle may enter only if exit is clear; **box office** ticket office at theatre etc.; **box pleat** two parallel pleats forming raised band.

box² /bɒks/ ● *verb* fight with fists as sport; slap (person's ears). ● *noun* slap on ear.

box³ *noun* evergreen shrub with small dark green leaves; its wood.

boxer *noun* person who boxes; short-haired dog with puglike face. □ **boxer shorts** man's loose underpants.

boxing *noun* fighting with fists, esp. as sport. □ **boxing glove** padded glove worn in this.

Boxing Day *noun* first weekday after Christmas Day.

boy ● *noun* male child, young man; son; male servant. ● *interjection* expressing pleasure, surprise, etc. ● **boyfriend** person's regular male companion; **boy scout** Scout. □ **boyhood** *noun*, **boyish** *adjective*.

boycott /ˈbɔɪkɒt/ ● *verb* refuse social or commercial relations with; refuse to handle (goods). ● *noun* such refusal.

bra /brɑː/ *noun* woman's undergarment supporting breasts.

brace ● *noun* device that clamps or fastens tightly; timber etc. strengthening framework; (in *plural*) straps supporting trousers from shoulders; wire device for straightening teeth; (*plural* same) pair. ● *verb* (**-cing**) make steady by supporting; fasten tightly; (esp. as **bracing** *adjective*) invigorate; (often **brace oneself**) prepare for difficulty, shock, etc.

bracelet /'breɪslɪt/ *noun* ornamental band or chain worn on wrist or arm; *slang* handcuff.

brachiosaurus /brækɪə'sɔːrəs/ *noun* (*plural* **-ruses**) huge long-necked plant-eating dinosaur.

bracken /'brækən/ *noun* large coarse fern; mass of these.

bracket /'brækɪt/ ● *noun* support projecting from vertical surface; shelf fixed to wall with this; punctuation mark used in pairs—( ), [ ]—enclosing words or figures (see panel); group classified as similar or falling between limits. ● *verb* (**-t-**) enclose in brackets; group in same category.

brackish /'brækɪʃ/ *adjective* (of water) slightly salty.

bract *noun* leaflike part of plant growing before flower.

brad *noun* thin flat nail.

bradawl /'brædɔːl/ *noun* small boring-tool.

brae /breɪ/ *noun Scottish* hillside.

brag ● *verb* (**-gg-**) talk boastfully. ● *noun* card game like poker; boastful statement or talk.

braggart /'brægət/ *noun* boastful person.

Brahma /'brɑːmə/ *noun* Hindu Creator; supreme Hindu reality.

Brahman /'brɑːmən/ *noun* (*plural* **-s**) (also **Brahmin**) member of Hindu priestly caste.

braid ● *noun* woven band as edging or trimming; *US* plait of hair. ● *verb US* plait; trim with braid.

Braille /breɪl/ *noun* system of writing and printing for the blind, with patterns of raised dots.

brain ● *noun* organ of soft nervous tissue in vertebrate's skull; centre of sensation or thought; (often in *plural*) intelligence, *colloquial* intelligent person. ● *verb* dash out brains of. □ **brainchild** *colloquial* person's clever idea or invention; **brain drain** *colloquial* emigration of

· ·

Brackets ( ) [ ]

Round brackets, also called parentheses, are used mainly to enclose:

1 explanations and extra information or comment, e.g.

> *Zimbabwe (formerly Rhodesia)*
> *He is (as he always was) a rebel.*
> *This is done using integrated circuits (see page 38).*

2 in this dictionary, optional words or parts of words, e.g.

> **crossword (puzzle)**   **king-size(d)**

and the type of word which can be used with the word being defined, e.g.

> **low** ... (of opinion) unfavourable
> **can** ... preserve (food etc.) in can

Square brackets are used mainly to enclose:

1 words added by someone other than the original writer or speaker, e.g.

> *Then the man said, 'He [the police officer] can't prove I did it.'*

2 various special types of information, such as stage directions, e.g.

> HEDLEY: Goodbye! [Exit].

· ·

skilled people; **brainstorm** mental disturbance; **brainstorming** pooling of spontaneous ideas about problem etc.; **brains trust** group of experts answering questions, usually impromptu; **brainwash** implant ideas or esp. ideology into (person) by repetition etc.; **brainwave** *colloquial* bright idea.

brainy *adjective* (**-ier, -iest**) intellectually clever.

braise /breɪz/ *verb* (**-sing**) stew slowly in closed container with little liquid.

brake ● *noun* device for stopping or slowing wheel or vehicle; thing that impedes. ● *verb* (**-king**) apply brake; slow or stop with brake.

bramble /'bræmb(ə)l/ *noun* wild thorny shrub, esp. blackberry.

bran *noun* husks separated from flour.

branch /brɑːntʃ/ ● *noun* limb or bough of tree; lateral extension or subdivision of river, railway, family, etc.; local office of business. ● *verb* (often + *off*) divide, diverge. □ **branch out** extend one's field of interest.

brand ● *noun* particular make of goods; trade mark, label, etc.; (usually + *of*) characteristic kind; identifying mark made with hot iron, iron stamp for this; piece of burning or charred wood; stigma; *poetical* torch. ● *verb* mark with hot iron; stigmatize; assign trade mark etc. to; impress unforgettably. □ **brand new** completely new.

brandish /'brændɪʃ/ *verb* wave or flourish.

brandy /'brændɪ/ *noun* (*plural* -**ies**) strong spirit distilled from wine or fermented fruit juice. □ **brandy snap** crisp rolled gingerbread wafer.

brash *adjective* vulgarly assertive; impudent. □ **brashly** *adverb*; **brashness** *noun*.

brass /brɑːs/ ● *noun* yellow alloy of copper and zinc; brass objects; brass wind instruments; *slang* money; brass memorial tablet; *colloquial* effrontery. ● *adjective* made of brass. □ **brass band** band of brass instruments; **brass rubbing** reproducing of design from engraved brass on paper by rubbing with heelball, impression obtained thus; **brass tacks** *slang* essential details.

brasserie /'bræsərɪ/ *noun* restaurant, originally one serving beer with food.

brassica /'bræsɪkə/ *noun* plant of cabbage family.

brassière /'bræzɪə/ *noun* bra.

brassy /'brɑːsɪ/ *adjective* (**-ier, -iest**) of or like brass; impudent; vulgarly showy; loud and blaring.

brat *noun* usually derogatory child.

bravado /brə'vɑːdəʊ/ *noun* show of boldness.

brave ● *adjective* (**-r, -st**) able to face and endure danger or pain; *formal* splendid, spectacular. ● *verb* (**-ving**) face bravely or defiantly. ● *noun* N. American Indian warrior. □ **bravely** *adverb*; **bravery** *noun*.

bravo /brɑː'vəʊ/ *interjection & noun* (*plural* -**s**) cry of approval.

bravura /brə'vjʊərə/ *noun* brilliance of execution; music requiring brilliant technique.

brawl ● *noun* noisy quarrel or fight. ● *verb* engage in brawl; (of stream) flow noisily.

brawn *noun* muscular strength; muscle, lean flesh; jellied meat made esp. from pig's head. □ **brawny** *adjective* (**-ier, -iest**).

bray ● *noun* cry of donkey; harsh sound. ● *verb* make a bray; utter harshly.

braze *verb* (**-zing**) solder with alloy of brass.

brazen /'breɪz(ə)n/ ● *adjective* shameless; of or like brass. ● *verb* (+ *out*) brazen or undergo defiantly. □ **brazenly** *adverb*.

brazier /'breɪzɪə/ *noun* pan or stand for holding burning coals.

Brazil nut /brə'zɪl/ *noun* large 3-sided S. American nut.

breach /briːtʃ/ ● *noun* breaking or neglect of rule, duty, promise, etc.; breaking off of relations, quarrel; gap. ● *verb* break through; make gap in; break (law etc.).

bread /bred/ *noun* baked dough of flour usually leavened with yeast; necessary food; *slang* money. □ **breadcrumb** small fragment of bread, esp. (in *plural*) for use in cooking; **breadline** subsistence level; **breadwinner** person whose work supports a family.

breadth /bredθ/ *noun* broadness, distance from side to side; freedom from mental limitations or prejudices.

break /breɪk/ ● *verb* (*past* **broke**; *past participle* **broken** /ˈbrəʊk(ə)n/) separate into pieces under blow or strain; shatter; make or become inoperative; break bone in (limb etc.); interrupt, pause; fail to observe or keep; make or become weak, destroy; weaken effect of (fall, blow, etc.); tame, subdue; surpass (record); reveal or be revealed; come, produce, change, etc., with suddenness or violence; (of waves) curl over and foam; (of voice) change in quality at manhood or with emotion; escape, emerge from. ● *noun* breaking; point where thing is broken; gap; pause in work etc.; sudden dash; a chance; *Cricket* deflection of ball on bouncing; points scored in one sequence at billiards etc. □ **break away** make or become free or separate; **break down** fail or collapse, demolish, analyse; **breakdown** mechanical failure, loss of (esp. mental) health, collapse, analysis; **break even** make neither profit nor loss; **break in** intrude forcibly esp. as thief, interrupt, accustom to habit; **breakneck** (of speed) dangerously fast; **break off** detach by breaking, bring to an end, cease talking etc.; **break open** open forcibly; **break out** escape by force, begin suddenly, (+ *in*) become covered in (rash etc.); **breakthrough** major advance in knowledge etc.; **break up** break into pieces, disband, part; **breakup** disintegration, collapse; **breakwater** barrier breaking force of waves; **break wind** release gas from anus.

breakable *adjective* easily broken.

breakage *noun* broken thing; breaking.

breaker *noun* heavy breaking wave.

breakfast /ˈbrekfəst/ ● *noun* first meal of day. ● *verb* have breakfast.

bream *noun* (*plural* same) yellowish freshwater fish; similar sea fish.

breast /brest/ ● *noun* either of two milk-secreting organs on woman's chest; chest; part of garment covering this; seat of emotions. ● *verb* contend with; reach top of (hill). □ **breastbone** bone connecting ribs in front; **breastfeed** feed (baby) from breast; **breastplate** armour covering chest; **breaststroke** stroke made while swimming on breast by extending arms forward and sweeping them back.

breath /breθ/ *noun* air drawn into or expelled from lungs; one respiration; breath as perceived by senses; slight movement of air. □ **breathtaking** astounding, awe-inspiring; **breath test** test with Breathalyser.

breathalyse *verb* give breath test to.

Breathalyser /ˈbreθəlaɪzə/ *noun* *proprietary term* instrument for measuring alcohol in breath.

breathe /briːð/ *verb* (*-thing*) take air into lungs and send it out again; live; utter or sound, esp. quietly; pause; send out or take in (as) with breathed air. □ **breathing-space** time to recover, pause.

breather /ˈbriːðə/ *noun* short rest period.

breathless /ˈbreθlɪs/ *adjective* panting, out of breath; still, windless. □ **breathlessly** *adverb*.

bred *past & past participle* of BREED.

breech /briːtʃ/ *noun* back part of gun or gun barrel; (in *plural*) short trousers fastened below knee. □ **breech birth** birth in which buttocks emerge first.

breed ● *verb* (*past & past participle* **bred**) produce offspring; propagate; raise (animals); yield, result in; arise, spread; train, bring up; create (fissile material) by nuclear reaction. ● *noun* stock of animals within species; race, lineage; sort, kind. □ **breeder reactor** nuclear reactor creating surplus fissile material. □ **breeder** *noun*.

breeding *noun* raising of offspring; social behaviour; ancestry.

breeze[1] ● *noun* gentle wind. ● *verb* (*-zing*) (+ *in*, *out*, *along*, etc.) *colloquial* saunter casually.

breeze[2] *noun* small cinders. □ **breeze-block** lightweight building block made from breeze.

breezy *adjective* (*-ier*, *-iest*) slightly windy.

Bren *noun* lightweight quick-firing machine-gun.

brent *noun* small migratory goose.

brethren see BROTHER.

Breton /ˈbret(ə)n/ ● *noun* native or language of Brittany. ● *adjective* of Brittany.

breve /briːv/ *noun* *Music* note equal to two semibreves; mark (˘) indicating short or unstressed vowel.

breviary /ˈbriːvɪərɪ/ *noun* (*plural* **-ies**) book containing RC daily office.

brevity /ˈbrevɪtɪ/ *noun* conciseness, shortness.

brew • *verb* make (beer etc.) by infusion, boiling, and fermenting; make (tea etc.) by infusion; undergo these processes; be forming. • *noun* amount brewed; liquor brewed. □ **brewer** *noun*.

brewery /ˈbruːərɪ/ *noun* (*plural* **-ies**) factory for brewing beer etc.

briar[1,2] = BRIER[1,2].

bribe • *verb* (**-bing**) persuade to act improperly by gift of money etc. • *noun* money or services offered in bribing. □ **bribery** *noun*.

bric-a-brac /ˈbrɪkəbræk/ *noun* cheap ornaments, trinkets, etc.

brick • *noun* small rectangular block of baked clay, used in building; toy building block; brick-shaped thing; *slang* generous or loyal person. • *verb* (+ *in*, *up*) close or block with brickwork. • *adjective* made of bricks. □ **brickbat** piece of brick, esp. as missile, insult; **bricklayer** person who builds with bricks; **brickwork** building or work in brick.

bridal /ˈbraɪd(ə)l/ *adjective* of bride or wedding.

bride *noun* woman on her wedding day and shortly before and after it. □ **bridegroom** man on his wedding day and shortly before and after it; **bridesmaid** woman or girl attending bride at wedding.

bridge[1] • *noun* structure providing way over road, railway, river, etc.; thing joining or connecting; superstructure from which ship is directed; upper bony part of nose; prop under strings of violin etc.; bridgework. • *verb* (**-ging**) be or make bridge over. □ **bridgehead** position held on enemy's side of river etc.; **bridgework** dental structure covering gap and joined to teeth on either side; **bridging loan** loan to cover interval between buying one house and selling another.

bridge[2] *noun* card game derived from whist.

bridle /ˈbraɪd(ə)l/ • *noun* headgear for controlling horse etc.; restraining thing. • *verb* (**-ling**) put bridle on, control, curb; express resentment, esp. by

throwing up head and drawing in chin. □ **bridle path** rough path for riders or walkers.

Brie /briː/ *noun* flat round soft creamy French cheese.

brief /briːf/ • *adjective* of short duration; concise; scanty. • *noun* (in *plural*) short pants; summary of case for guidance of barrister; instructions for a task. • *verb* instruct (barrister) by brief; inform or instruct in advance. □ **in brief** to sum up. □ **briefly** *adverb*.

briefcase /ˈbriːfkeɪs/ *noun* flat document case.

brier[1] /braɪə/ *noun* (also **briar**) wild-rose bush.

brier[2] /braɪə/ *noun* (also **briar**) white heath of S. Europe; tobacco pipe made from its root.

brig[1] *noun* two-masted square-rigged ship.

brig[2] *noun Scottish & Northern English* bridge.

brigade /brɪˈɡeɪd/ *noun* military unit forming part of division; organized band of workers etc.

brigadier /brɪɡəˈdɪə/ *noun* army officer next below major-general.

brigand /ˈbrɪɡənd/ *noun* member of robber gang.

bright /braɪt/ *adjective* emitting or reflecting much light, shining; vivid; clever; cheerful. □ **brighten** *verb*; **brightly** *adverb*; **brightness** *noun*.

brill[1] *noun* (*plural* same) flatfish resembling turbot.

brill[2] *adjective colloquial* excellent.

brilliant /ˈbrɪlɪənt/ • *adjective* bright, sparkling; highly talented; showy; *colloquial* excellent. • *noun* diamond of finest quality. □ **brilliance** *noun*; **brilliantly** *adverb*.

brilliantine /ˈbrɪlɪəntiːn/ *noun* cosmetic for making hair glossy.

brim • *noun* edge of vessel; projecting edge of hat. • *verb* (**-mm-**) fill or be full to brim.

brimstone /ˈbrɪmstəʊn/ *noun archaic* sulphur.

brindled /ˈbrɪnd(ə)ld/ *adjective* brown with streaks of other colour.

brine *noun* salt water; sea water.

bring *verb* (*past & past participle* **brought** /brɔːt/) come with, carry, convey;

cause, result in; be sold for; submit (criminal charge); initiate (legal action). □ **bring about** cause to happen; **bring down** cause to fall; **bring forward** move to earlier time, transfer from previous page or account, draw attention to; **bring in** introduce, produce as profit; **bring off** succeed in; **bring on** cause to happen, appear or progress; **bring out** emphasize, publish; **bring round** restore to consciousness, win over; **bring up** raise and educate, vomit, draw attention to.

brink noun edge of precipice etc.; furthest point before danger, discovery, etc. □ **brinkmanship** policy of pursuing dangerous course to brink of catastrophe.

briny /'braɪnɪ/ ● adjective (**-ier, -iest**) of brine or sea, salt. ● noun (**the briny**) slang the sea.

briquette /brɪ'ket/ noun block of compressed coal dust as fuel.

brisk adjective active, lively, quick. □ **briskly** adverb.

brisket /'brɪskɪt/ noun animal's breast, esp. as joint of meat.

brisling /'brɪzlɪŋ/ noun (plural same or **-s**) small herring or sprat.

bristle /'brɪs(ə)l/ ● noun short stiff hair, esp. one used in brushes etc. ● verb (**-ling**) (of hair etc.) stand up; cause to bristle; show irritation; (usually + with) be covered (with) or abundant (in). □ **bristly** adjective.

British /'brɪtɪʃ/ ● adjective of Britain. ● plural noun (**the British**) the British people. □ **British Summer Time** = SUMMER TIME.

Briton /'brɪt(ə)n/ noun inhabitant of S. Britain before Roman conquest; native of Great Britain.

brittle /'brɪt(ə)l/ adjective apt to break, fragile.

broach /brəʊtʃ/ verb raise for discussion; pierce (cask) to draw liquor; open and start using.

broad /brɔːd/ ● adjective large across, extensive; of specified breadth; full, clear; explicit; general; tolerant; coarse; (of accent) marked, strong. ● noun broad part; US slang woman; (**the Broads**) large areas of water in E. Anglia. □ **broad bean** bean with large flat seeds, one such seed; **broadloom** (carpet) woven in broad width; **broad-minded** tolerant, liberal; **broadsheet** large-sized newspaper. □ **broaden** verb; **broadly** adverb.

broadcast ● verb (past & past participle **-cast**) transmit by radio or television; take part in such transmission; scatter (seed) etc.; disseminate widely. ● noun radio or television programme or transmission. □ **broadcaster** noun; **broadcasting** noun.

broadside noun vigorous verbal attack; firing of all guns on one side of ship. □ **broadside on** sideways on.

brocade /brə'keɪd/ noun fabric woven with raised pattern.

broccoli /'brɒkəlɪ/ noun brassica with greenish flower heads.

brochure /'brəʊʃə/ noun booklet, pamphlet, esp. containing descriptive information.

broderie anglaise /brəʊdərɪ ɑ̃'gleɪz/ noun open embroidery on usually white cotton or linen.

brogue /brəʊg/ noun strong shoe with ornamental perforations; rough shoe of untanned leather; marked local, esp. Irish, accent.

broil verb grill (meat); make or be very hot.

broiler noun young chicken for broiling.

broke ● past of BREAK. ● adjective colloquial having no money, bankrupt.

broken /'brəʊkən/ ● past participle of BREAK. ● adjective that has been broken; reduced to despair; (of language) spoken imperfectly; interrupted. □ **broken-hearted** crushed by grief; **broken home** family disrupted by divorce or separation.

broker noun middleman, agent; stockbroker. □ **broking** noun.

brokerage noun broker's fee or commission.

brolly /'brɒlɪ/ noun (plural **-ies**) colloquial umbrella.

bromide /'brəʊmaɪd/ noun binary compound of bromine, esp. one used as sedative; trite remark.

bromine /'brəʊmiːn/ noun poisonous liquid non-metallic element with choking smell.

bronchial /ˈbrɒŋkɪəl/ *adjective* of two main divisions of windpipe or smaller tubes into which they divide.

bronchitis /brɒŋˈkaɪtɪs/ *noun* inflammation of bronchial mucous membrane.

bronco /ˈbrɒŋkəʊ/ *noun* (*plural* **-s**) wild or half-tamed horse of western US.

brontosaurus /brɒntəˈsɔːrəs/ *noun* (*plural* **-ruses**) = APATOSAURUS.

bronze /brɒnz/ ● *noun* brown alloy of copper and tin; its colour; work of art or medal in it. ● *adjective* made of or coloured like bronze. ● *verb* (**-zing**) make or grow brown; tan. □ **Bronze Age** period when tools were of bronze; **bronze medal** medal given usually as third prize.

brooch /brəʊtʃ/ *noun* ornamental hinged pin.

brood /ˈbruːd/ ● *noun* bird's or other animal's young produced at one hatch or birth; *colloquial* children of a family. ● *verb* worry or ponder, esp. resentfully; (of hen) sit on eggs.

broody *adjective* (**-ier**, **-iest**) (of hen) wanting to brood; sullenly thoughtful; *colloquial* (of woman) wanting pregnancy.

brook[1] /brʊk/ *noun* small stream.

brook[2] /brʊk/ *verb* tolerate; allow.

broom /bruːm/ *noun* long-handled brush for sweeping; chiefly yellow-flowered shrub. □ **broomstick** broom-handle.

Bros. *abbreviation* Brothers.

broth /brɒθ/ *noun* thin meat or fish soup.

brothel /ˈbrɒθ(ə)l/ *noun* premises for prostitution.

brother /ˈbrʌðə/ *noun* man or boy in relation to his siblings; close man friend; (*plural* also **brethren** /ˈbreðrɪn/) member of male religious order; (*plural* also **brethren**) fellow Christian etc.; fellow human being. □ **brother-in-law** (*plural* **brothers-in-law**) wife's or husband's brother, sister's husband. □ **brotherly** *adjective*.

brotherhood *noun* relationship (as) between brothers; (members of) association for mutual help etc.

brought *past & past participle* of BRING.

brow /braʊ/ *noun* forehead; (usually in *plural*) eyebrow; summit of hill; edge of cliff etc.

browbeat *verb* (*past* **-beat**, *past participle* **-beaten**) intimidate, bully.

brown /braʊn/ ● *adjective* of colour of dark wood or rich soil; dark-skinned; tanned. ● *noun* brown colour, paint, clothes, etc. ● *verb* make or become brown. □ **brown bread** bread made of wholemeal or wheatmeal flour; **browned off** *colloquial* bored, fed up; **Brown Owl** adult leader of Brownies; **brown rice** unpolished rice; **brown sugar** partially refined sugar. □ **brownish** *adjective*.

Brownie /ˈbraʊnɪ/ *noun* junior Guide; (**brownie**) small square of chocolate cake with nuts; (**brownie**) benevolent elf.

browse /braʊz/ ● *verb* (**-sing**) read or look around desultorily; feed on leaves and young shoots. ● *noun* browsing; twigs, shoots, etc. as fodder.

bruise /bruːz/ ● *noun* discoloration of skin caused by blow or pressure; similar damage on fruit etc. ● *verb* (**-sing**) inflict bruise on; be susceptible to bruises.

bruiser *noun colloquial* tough brutal person.

bruit /bruːt/ *verb* (often + *abroad*, *about*) spread (report or rumour).

brunch *noun* combination of breakfast and lunch.

brunette /bruːˈnet/ *noun* woman with dark hair.

brunt *noun* chief impact of attack etc.

brush ● *noun* cleaning or hairdressing or painting implement of bristles etc. set in holder; application of brush; short esp. unpleasant encounter; fox's tail; carbon or metal piece serving as electrical contact. ● *verb* use brush on; touch lightly, graze in passing. □ **brush off** dismiss abruptly; **brush-off** dismissal, rebuff; **brush up** clean up or smarten, revise (subject, skill); **brushwood** undergrowth, thicket, cut or broken twigs etc.; **brushwork** painter's way of using brush.

brusque /brʊsk/ *adjective* abrupt, offhand. □ **brusquely** *adverb*; **brusqueness** *noun*.

Brussels sprout /ˈbrʌs(ə)lz/ *noun* brassica with small cabbage-like buds on stem; such bud.

brutal /'bru:t(ə)l/ *adjective* savagely cruel; mercilessly frank. □ **brutality** /-'tæl-/ *noun* (*plural* **-ies**); **brutalize** *verb* (also **-ise**) (**-zing, -sing**).

brute /bru:t/ ● *noun* cruel person; *colloquial* unpleasant person; animal other than man. ● *adjective* unthinking; cruel, stupid. □ **brutish** *adjective*.

bryony /'braɪənɪ/ *noun* (*plural* **-ies**) climbing hedge plant.

B.Sc. *abbreviation* Bachelor of Science.

BST *abbreviation* British Summer Time.

Bt. *abbreviation* Baronet.

bubble /'bʌb(ə)l/ ● *noun* thin sphere of liquid enclosing air or gas; air-filled cavity in glass etc.; transparent domed cavity. ● *verb* (**-ling**) send up or rise in bubbles; make sound of boiling. □ **bubble and squeak** cooked potatoes and cabbage fried together; **bubble bath** additive to make bathwater bubbly; **bubblegum** chewing gum that can be blown into bubbles.

bubbly ● *adjective* (**-ier, -iest**) full of bubbles; exuberant. ● *noun* *colloquial* champagne.

bubonic /bju:'bɒnɪk/ *adjective* (of plague) marked by swellings esp. in groin and armpits.

buccaneer /bʌkə'nɪə/ *noun* pirate; adventurer. □ **buccaneering** *adjective & noun*.

buck¹ ● *noun* male deer, hare, or rabbit. ● *verb* (of horse) jump vertically with back arched, throw (rider) thus; (usually + *up*) *colloquial* cheer up, hurry up. □ **buckshot** coarse shot for gun; **buck-tooth** projecting upper tooth.

buck² *noun* US & Australian slang dollar.

buck³ *noun* slang small object placed before dealer at poker. □ **pass the buck** *colloquial* shift responsibility.

bucket /'bʌkɪt/ ● *noun* usually round open container with handle, for carrying or holding water etc.; amount contained in this; (in *plural*) *colloquial* large quantities; compartment or scoop in waterwheel, dredger, or grain elevator. ● *verb* (**-t-**) *colloquial* (often + *down*) (esp. of rain) pour heavily; (often + *along*) move jerkily or bumpily. □ **bucket seat** one with rounded back, for one person; **bucket shop** agency dealing in cheap airline tickets, unregistered broking agency.

buckle /'bʌk(ə)l/ ● *noun* clasp with usually hinged pin for securing strap or belt etc. ● *verb* (**-ling**) fasten with buckle; (cause to) crumple under pressure. □ **buckle down** make determined effort.

buckram /'bʌkrəm/ *noun* coarse linen etc. stiffened with paste etc.

buckshee /bʌk'ʃi:/ *adjective & adverb* slang free of charge.

buckwheat *noun* seed of plant related to rhubarb.

bucolic /bju:'kɒlɪk/ *adjective* of shepherds, rustic, pastoral.

bud ● *noun* projection from which branch, leaf, or flower develops; flower or leaf not fully open; asexual growth separating from organism as new animal. ● *verb* (**-dd-**) form buds; begin to grow or develop; graft bud of (plant) on another plant.

Buddhism /'bʊdɪz(ə)m/ *noun* Asian religion founded by Gautama Buddha. □ **Buddhist** *adjective & noun*.

buddleia /'bʌdlɪə/ *noun* shrub with flowers attractive to butterflies.

buddy /'bʌdɪ/ *noun* (*plural* **-ies**) *colloquial* friend; mate.

budge *verb* (**-ging**) move in slightest degree; (+ *up*) move to make room for another person.

budgerigar /'bʌdʒərɪ'gɑ:/ *noun* small parrot often kept as pet.

budget /'bʌdʒɪt/ ● *noun* amount of money needed or available; (**the Budget**) annual estimate of country's revenue and expenditure; similar estimate for person or group. ● *verb* (**-t-**) (often + *for*) allow or arrange for in budget. □ **budgetary** *adjective*.

budgie /'bʌdʒɪ/ *noun colloquial* budgerigar.

buff ● *adjective* of yellowish beige colour. ● *noun* this colour; *colloquial* enthusiast; velvety dull yellow leather. ● *verb* polish; make (leather) velvety. □ **in the buff** *colloquial* naked.

buffalo /'bʌfələʊ/ *noun* (*plural* same or **-es**) any of various kinds of ox; American bison.

buffer¹ *noun* apparatus for deadening impact esp. of railway vehicles. □ **buffer state** minor one between two larger ones, regarded as reducing friction.

buffer² *noun slang* old or incompetent fellow.

buffet¹ /'bʊfeɪ/ *noun* room or counter where refreshments are sold; self-service meal of several dishes set out at once; (also /'bʌfɪt/) sideboard. □ **buffet car** railway coach in which refreshments are served.

buffet² /'bʌfɪt/ ● *verb* (**-t-**) strike repeatedly. ● *noun* blow with hand; shock.

buffoon /bə'fuːn/ *noun* silly or ludicrous person; jester. □ **buffoonery** *noun*.

bug ● *noun* small insect; concealed microphone; *colloquial* error in computer program etc.; *slang* virus, infection; *slang* enthusiasm, obsession. ● *verb* (**-gg-**) conceal microphone in; *slang* annoy.

bugbear *noun* cause of annoyance; object of baseless fear.

buggy /'bʌgɪ/ *noun* (*plural* **-ies**) small sturdy motor vehicle; lightweight pushchair; light horse-drawn vehicle for one or two people.

bugle /'bjuːg(ə)l/ ● *noun* brass instrument like small trumpet. ● *verb* (**-ling**) sound bugle. □ **bugler** *noun*.

build /bɪld/ ● *verb* (*past & past participle* **built** /bɪlt/) construct or cause to be constructed; develop or establish. ● *noun* physical proportions; style of construction. □ **build in** incorporate; **build up** increase in size or strength, praise, gradually establish or be established; **build-up** favourable description in advance, gradual approach to climax, accumulation.

builder *noun* contractor who builds houses etc.

building *noun* house or other structure with roof and walls. □ **building society** financial organization (not public company) that pays interest on savings accounts, lends money esp. for mortgages, etc.

built /bɪlt/ *past & past participle* of BUILD. □ **built-in** integral; **built-up** covered with buildings.

bulb *noun* rounded base of stem of some plants; light bulb; bulb-shaped thing or part.

bulbous /'bʌlbəs/ *adjective* bulb-shaped; bulging.

bulge ● *noun* irregular swelling; *colloquial* temporary increase. ● *verb* (**-ging**) swell outwards. □ **bulgy** *adjective*.

bulimia /bjʊ'lɪmɪə/ *noun* (in full **bulimia nervosa** /nɜː'vəʊsə/) disorder in which overeating alternates with self-induced vomiting, fasting, etc.

bulk ● *noun* size, magnitude, esp. when great; (**the bulk**) the greater part; large quantity. ● *verb* seem (in size or importance); make thicker. □ **bulk buying** buying in quantity at discount; **bulkhead** upright partition in ship, aircraft, etc.

bulky /'bʌlkɪ/ *adjective* (**-ier**, **-iest**) large, unwieldy.

bull¹ /bʊl/ *noun* uncastrated male ox; male whale or elephant etc.; bull's-eye of target; person who buys shares in hope of selling at higher price later. □ **bulldog** short-haired heavy-jowled sturdy dog, tenacious and courageous person; **Bulldog clip** strong sprung clip for papers etc.; **bulldoze** clear with bulldozer, *colloquial* intimidate, *colloquial* make (one's way) forcibly; **bulldozer** powerful tractor with broad upright blade for clearing ground; **bullfight** public baiting, and usually killing, of bulls; **bullfinch** pink and black finch; **bullfrog** large American frog with booming croak; **bullring** arena for bullfight; **bull's-eye** centre of target, hard minty sweet; **bull terrier** cross between bulldog and terrier. □ **bullish** *adjective*.

bull² /bʊl/ *noun* papal edict.

bull³ /bʊl/ *noun slang* nonsense; *slang* unnecessary routine tasks; absurdly illogical statement.

bullet /'bʊlɪt/ *noun* small pointed missile fired from revolver etc. □ **bulletproof** resistant to bullets.

bulletin /'bʊlɪtɪn/ *noun* short official statement; short broadcast news report.

bullion /'bʊlɪən/ *noun* gold or silver in lump or valued by weight.

bullock /'bʊlək/ *noun* castrated bull.

bully¹ /'bʊlɪ/ ● *noun* (*plural* **-ies**) person coercing others by fear. ● *verb* (**-ies**, **-ied**) persecute or oppress by force or threats. ● *interjection* (+ *for*) very good.

bully² /'bʊlɪ/ (in full **bully off**) ● *noun* (*plural* **-ies**) putting ball into play in hockey. ●verb (-ies, -ied) start play thus.

bully³ /'bʊlɪ/ noun (in full **bully beef**) corned beef.

bulrush /'bʊlrʌʃ/ noun tall rush; *Biblical* papyrus.

bulwark /'bʊlwək/ noun defensive wall, esp. of earth; person or principle that protects; (usually in *plural*) ship's side above deck.

bum¹ noun *slang* buttocks. □ **bumbag** small pouch worn round waist.

bum² *US slang* ●noun loafer, dissolute person. ●verb (**-mm-**) (often + *around*) loaf, wander around; cadge. ●adjective of poor quality.

bumble /'bʌmb(ə)l/ verb (-ling) (+ *on*) speak ramblingly; be inept; blunder. □ **bumble-bee** large bee with loud hum.

bump ●noun dull-sounding blow or collision; swelling caused by it; uneven patch on road etc.; prominence on skull, thought to indicate mental faculty. ●verb come or strike with bump against; hurt thus; (usually + *along*) move along with jolts. □ **bump into** *colloquial* meet by chance; **bump off** *slang* murder; **bump up** *colloquial* increase. □ **bumpy** adjective (-ier, -iest).

bumper ●noun horizontal bar on motor vehicle to reduce damage in collisions; *Cricket* ball rising high after pitching; brim-full glass. ●adjective unusually large or abundant.

bumpkin /'bʌmpkɪn/ noun rustic or awkward person.

bumptious /'bʌmpʃəs/ adjective self-assertive, conceited.

bun noun small sweet cake or bread roll often with dried fruit; small coil of hair at back of head.

bunch ●noun cluster of things growing or fastened together; lot; *colloquial* gang, group. ●verb arrange in bunch(es); gather in folds; come, cling, or crowd together.

bundle /'bʌnd(ə)l/ ●noun collection of things tied or fastened together; set of nerve fibres etc.; *slang* large amount of money. ●verb (-ling) (usually + *up*) tie in bundle; (usually + *into*) throw or move carelessly; (usually + *out*, *off*, *away*, etc.) send away hurriedly.

bung ●noun stopper, esp. for cask. ●verb stop with bung; *slang* throw. □ **bunged up** blocked up.

bungalow /'bʌŋgələʊ/ noun one-storeyed house.

bungee /'bʌndʒɪ/ noun elasticated cord. □ **bungee jumping** sport of jumping from great height while secured by bungee.

bungle /'bʌŋg(ə)l/ ●verb (-ling) mismanage, fail to accomplish; work awkwardly. ●noun bungled work or attempt.

bunion /'bʌnjən/ noun swelling on foot, esp. on side of big toe.

bunk¹ noun shelflike bed against wall. □ **bunk bed** each of two or more bunks one above the other.

bunk² *slang* □ **do a bunk** run away.

bunk³ noun *slang* nonsense, humbug.

bunker noun container for fuel; reinforced underground shelter; sandy hollow in golf course.

bunkum /'bʌŋkəm/ noun nonsense, humbug.

bunny /'bʌnɪ/ noun (plural **-ies**) childish name for rabbit.

Bunsen burner /'bʌns(ə)n/ noun small adjustable gas burner used in laboratory.

bunting¹ /'bʌntɪŋ/ noun small bird related to finches.

bunting² /'bʌntɪŋ/ noun flags and other decorations; loosely woven fabric for these.

buoy /bɔɪ/ ●noun anchored float as navigational mark etc.; lifebuoy. ●verb (usually + *up*) keep afloat, encourage; (often + *out*) mark with buoy(s).

buoyant /'bɔɪənt/ adjective apt to float; resilient; exuberant. □ **buoyancy** noun.

bur noun (also **burr**) clinging seed vessel or flower head, plant producing burs; clinging person.

burble /'bɜːb(ə)l/ verb (-ling) talk ramblingly; make bubbling sound.

burden /'bɜːd(ə)n/ ●noun thing carried, load; oppressive duty, expense, emotion, etc.; refrain of song; theme. ●verb load, encumber, oppress. □ **burden of proof** obligation to prove one's case. □ **burdensome** adjective.

burdock /'bɜːdɒk/ *noun* plant with prickly flowers and docklike leaves.

bureau /'bjʊərəʊ/ *noun* (*plural* **-s** or **-x** /-z/) writing desk with drawers; *US* chest of drawers; office or department for specific business; government department.

bureaucracy /bjʊə'rɒkrəsɪ/ *noun* (*plural* **-ies**) government by central administration; government officials esp. regarded as oppressive and inflexible; conduct typical of these.

bureaucrat /'bjʊərəkræt/ *noun* official in bureaucracy. □ **bureaucratic** /-'krætɪk/ *adjective*.

burgeon /'bɜːdʒ(ə)n/ *verb* grow rapidly, flourish.

burger /'bɜːgə/ *noun colloquial* hamburger.

burgher /'bɜːgə/ *noun* citizen, esp. of foreign town.

burglar /'bɜːglə/ *noun* person who commits burglary.

burglary *noun* (*plural* **-ies**) illegal entry into building to commit theft or other crime.

burgle /'bɜːg(ə)l/ *verb* (**-ling**) commit burglary (on).

burgundy /'bɜːgəndɪ/ *noun* (*plural* **-ies**) red or white wine produced in Burgundy; dark red colour.

burial /'berɪəl/ *noun* burying, esp. of corpse; funeral.

burlesque /bɜː'lesk/ ● *noun* comic imitation, parody; *US* variety show, esp. with striptease. ● *adjective* of or using burlesque. ● *verb* (**-ques, -qued, -quing**) parody.

burly /'bɜːlɪ/ *adjective* (**-ier, -iest**) large and sturdy.

burn[1] ● *verb* (*past & past participle* **burnt** or **burned**) (cause to) be consumed by fire; blaze or glow with fire; (cause to) be injured or damaged by fire, sun, or great heat; use or be used as fuel; produce (hole etc.) by fire or heat; char in working; brand; give or feel sensation or pain (as) of heat. ● *noun* sore or mark made by burning. □ **burn out** be reduced to nothing by burning, (cause to) fail by burning, (usually **burn oneself out**) suffer exhaustion; **burnt offering** sacrifice offered by burning.

burn[2] *noun Scottish* brook.

burner *noun* part of lamp or cooker etc. that emits flame.

burnish /'bɜːnɪʃ/ *verb* polish by rubbing.

burnt *past & past participle* of BURN[1].

burp *verb & noun colloquial* belch.

burr[1] *noun* whirring sound; rough sounding of *r*; rough edge on metal etc.

burr[2] = BUR.

burrow /'bʌrəʊ/ ● *noun* hole dug by animal as dwelling. ● *verb* make burrow; make by digging; (+ *into*) investigate or search.

bursar /'bɜːsə/ *noun* treasurer of college etc.; holder of bursary.

bursary /'bɜːsərɪ/ *noun* (*plural* **-ies**) grant, esp. scholarship.

burst ● *verb* (*past & past participle* **burst**) fly violently apart or give way suddenly, explode; rush, move, speak, be spoken, etc. suddenly or violently. ● *noun* bursting, explosion, outbreak; spurt.

burton /'bɜːt(ə)n/ *noun* □ **go for a burton** *slang* be lost, destroyed, or killed.

bury /'berɪ/ *verb* (**-ies, -ied**) place (corpse) in ground, tomb, or sea; put underground, hide in earth; consign to obscurity; (**bury oneself** or in *passive*) involve (oneself) deeply. □ **bury the hatchet** cease to quarrel.

bus ● *noun* (*plural* **buses**, *US* **busses**) large public passenger vehicle usually plying on fixed route. ● *verb* (**buses** or **busses, bussed, bussing**) go by bus; *US* transport by bus (esp. to aid racial integration). □ **busman's holiday** leisure spent in same occupation as working hours; **bus shelter** shelter for people waiting for bus; **bus station** centre where buses depart and arrive; **bus stop** regular stopping place of bus.

busby /'bʌzbɪ/ *noun* (*plural* **-ies**) tall fur cap worn by hussars etc.

bush[1] /bʊʃ/ *noun* shrub, clump of shrubs; clump of hair or fur; *Australian etc.* uncultivated land, woodland. □ **bush-baby** small African lemur; **Bushman** member or language of a S. African aboriginal people; **bushman** dweller or traveller in Australian bush; **bush telegraph** rapid informal spreading of information etc.

bush[2] /bʊʃ/ *noun* metal lining of axle-hole etc.; electrically insulating sleeve.

bushel /'bʊʃ(ə)l/ noun measure of capacity for corn, fruit, etc. (8 gallons, 36.4 litres).

bushy adjective (-ier, -iest) growing thickly or like bush; having many bushes.

business /'bɪznɪs/ noun one's occupation or profession; one's own concern, task, duty; serious work; (difficult or unpleasant) matter or affair; thing(s) needing dealing with; buying and selling, trade; commercial firm. □ **businesslike** practical, systematic; **businessman**, **businesswoman** person engaged in trade or commerce.

busk verb perform esp. music in street etc. for tips. □ **busker** noun.

bust[1] noun human chest, esp. of woman; sculpture of head, shoulders, and chest.

bust[2] colloquial ● verb (past & past participle **bust** or **busted**) burst, break; raid, search; arrest. ● adjective burst, broken; bankrupt. □ **bust-up** quarrel, violent split or separation.

bustard /b'ʌstəd/ noun large swift-running bird.

bustle[1] /'bʌs(ə)l/ ● verb (-ling) (often + about) move busily and energetically; make (person) hurry; (as **bustling** adjective) active, lively. ● noun excited activity.

bustle[2] /'bʌs(ə)l/ noun historical padding worn under skirt to puff it out behind.

busy /'bɪzɪ/ ● adjective (-ier, -iest) occupied or engaged in work etc.; full of activity; fussy. ● verb (-ies, -ied) occupy, keep busy. □ **busybody** meddlesome person; **busy Lizzie** house plant with usually red, pink, or white flowers. □ **busily** adverb.

but ● conjunction however; on the other hand; otherwise than. ● preposition except, apart from. ● adverb only. □ **but for** without the help or hindrance etc. of; **but then** however.

butane /'bjuːteɪn/ noun hydrocarbon used in liquefied form as fuel.

butch /bʊtʃ/ adjective slang masculine, tough-looking.

butcher /'bʊtʃə/ ● noun person who sells meat; slaughterer of animals for food; brutal murderer. ● verb slaughter or cut up (animal); kill wantonly or cruelly; colloquial ruin through incompetence. □ **butchery** noun (plural **-ies**).

butler /'bʌtlə/ noun chief manservant of household.

butt[1] ● verb push with head; (cause to) meet end to end. ● noun push or blow with head or horns. □ **butt in** interrupt, meddle.

butt[2] noun (often + of) object of ridicule etc.; mound behind target; (in plural) shooting range.

butt[3] noun thicker end, esp. of tool or weapon; stub of cigarette etc.

butt[4] noun cask.

butter /'bʌtə/ ● noun yellow fatty substance made from cream, used as spread and in cooking; substance of similar texture. ● verb spread, cook, etc., with butter. □ **butter-bean** dried large flat white kind; **buttercup** plant with yellow flowers; **butter-fingers** colloquial person likely to drop things; **buttermilk** liquid left after butter-making; **butter muslin** thin loosely woven cloth; **butterscotch** sweet made of butter and sugar; **butter up** colloquial flatter.

butterfly /'bʌtəflaɪ/ noun (plural **-ies**) insect with 4 often showy wings; (in plural) nervous sensation in stomach. □ **butterfly nut** kind of wing-nut; **butterfly stroke** method of swimming with both arms lifted at same time.

buttery[1] adjective like or containing butter.

buttery[2] noun (plural **-ies**) food store or snack-bar, esp. in college.

buttock /'bʌtək/ noun either protuberance on lower rear part of human trunk; corresponding part of animal.

button /'bʌt(ə)n/ ● noun disc or knob sewn to garment etc. as fastening or for ornament; knob etc. pressed to operate electronic equipment. ● verb (often + up) fasten with buttons. □ **button mushroom** small unopened mushroom.

buttonhole ● noun slit in cloth for button; flower(s) worn in lapel buttonhole. ● verb (-ling) colloquial accost and detain (reluctant listener).

buttress /'bʌtrɪs/ ● noun support built against wall etc. ● verb support or strengthen.

buxom /ˈbʌksəm/ *adjective* plump and rosy, large and shapely.

buy /baɪ/ ● *verb* (**buys, buying**; *past & past participle* **bought** /bɔːt/) obtain in exchange for money etc.; procure by bribery, bribe; get by sacrifice etc.; *slang* accept, believe. ● *noun colloquial* purchase. □ **buy out** pay (a person) for ownership, an interest, etc.; **buyout** purchase of controlling share in company; **buy up** buy as much as possible of.

buyer *noun* person who buys, esp. stock for large shop. □ **buyer's market** time when goods are plentiful and cheap.

buzz ● *noun* hum of bee etc.; sound of buzzer; low murmur; hurried activity; *slang* telephone call; *slang* thrill. ● *verb* hum; summon with buzzer; (often + *about*) move busily; be filled with activity or excitement. □ **buzzword** *colloquial* fashionable technical word, catchword.

buzzard /ˈbʌzəd/ *noun* large bird of hawk family.

buzzer *noun* electrical buzzing device as signal.

by /baɪ/ ● *preposition* near, beside, along; through action, agency, or means of; not later than; past; via; during; to extent of; according to. ● *adverb* near; aside, in reserve; past. □ **by and by** before long; **by-election** parliamentary election between general elections;

by-product substance etc. produced incidentally in making of something else; **byroad** minor road; **by the by, by the way** incidentally; **byway** byroad or secluded path; **byword** person or thing as notable example, proverb.

bye[1] /baɪ/ *noun Cricket* run made from ball that passes batsman without being hit; (in tournament) position of competitor left without opponent in round.

bye[2] /baɪ/ *interjection* (also **bye-bye**) *colloquial* goodbye.

bygone *adjective* past, departed. □ **let bygones be bygones** forgive and forget past quarrels.

by-law *noun* regulation made by local authority etc.

byline *noun* line in newspaper etc. naming writer of article etc.

bypass ● *noun* main road round town or its centre. ● *verb* avoid.

byre /baɪə/ *noun* cowshed.

bystander *noun* person present but not taking part.

byte /baɪt/ *noun Computing* group of 8 binary digits, often representing one character.

Byzantine /bɪˈzæntaɪn/ *adjective* of Byzantium or E. Roman Empire; of architectural etc. style developed in Eastern Empire; complicated, underhand.

Cc

C¹ *noun* (also **c**) (Roman numeral) 100.

C² *abbreviation* Celsius; centigrade.

c.¹ *abbreviation* century; cent(s).

c.² *abbreviation* circa.

ca. *abbreviation* circa.

CAA *abbreviation* Civil Aviation Authority.

cab *noun* taxi; driver's compartment in lorry, train, crane, etc.

cabal /kə'bæl/ *noun* secret intrigue; political clique.

cabaret /'kæbəreɪ/ *noun* entertainment in restaurant etc.

cabbage /'kæbɪdʒ/ *noun* vegetable with green or purple leaves forming a round head; *colloquial* dull or inactive person. □ **cabbage white** kind of white butterfly.

cabby /'kæbɪ/ *noun* (*plural* **-ies**) *colloquial* taxi driver.

caber /'keɪbə/ *noun* tree trunk tossed as sport in Scotland.

cabin /'kæbɪn/ *noun* small shelter or house, esp. of wood; room or compartment in aircraft, ship, etc. □ **cabin boy** boy steward on ship; **cabin cruiser** large motor boat with accommodation.

cabinet /'kæbɪnɪt/ *noun* cupboard or case for storing or displaying things; casing of radio, television, etc.; (**Cabinet**) group of senior ministers in government. □ **cabinetmaker** skilled joiner.

cable /'keɪb(ə)l/ ● *noun* encased group of insulated wires for transmitting electricity etc.; thick rope of wire or hemp; cablegram. ● *verb* (**-ling**) send (message) or inform (person) by cable. □ **cable car** small cabin on loop of cable for carrying passengers up and down mountain etc.; **cablegram** message sent by undersea cable etc.; **cable stitch** knitting stitch resembling twisted rope; **cable television** transmission of television programmes by cable to subscribers.

caboodle /kə'bu:d(ə)l/ *noun*. □ **the whole caboodle** *slang* the whole lot.

caboose /kə'bu:s/ *noun* kitchen on ship's deck; *US* guard's van on train.

cabriolet /kæbrɪəʊ'leɪ/ *noun* car with folding top.

cacao /kə'kaʊ/ *noun* (*plural* **-s**) seed from which cocoa and chocolate are made; tree bearing it.

cache /kæʃ/ ● *noun* hiding place for treasure, supplies, etc.; things so hidden. ● *verb* (**-ching**) place in cache.

cachet /'kæʃeɪ/ *noun* prestige; distinguishing mark or seal; flat capsule for medicine.

cack-handed /kæk'hændɪd/ *adjective* *colloquial* clumsy, left-handed.

cackle /'kæk(ə)l/ ● *noun* clucking of hen; raucous laugh; noisy chatter. ● *verb* (**-ling**) emit cackle; chatter noisily.

cacophony /kə'kɒfənɪ/ *noun* (*plural* **-ies**) harsh discordant sound. □ **cacophonous** *adjective*.

cactus /'kæktəs/ *noun* (*plural* **-ti** /-taɪ/ or **-tuses**) plant with thick fleshy stem and usually spines but no leaves.

CAD *abbreviation* computer-aided design.

cad *noun* man who behaves dishonourably. □ **caddish** *adjective*.

cadaver /kə'dævə/ *noun* corpse. □ **cadaverous** *adjective*.

caddie /'kædɪ/ (also **caddy**) ● *noun* (*plural* **-ies**) golfer's attendant carrying clubs etc. ● *verb* (**caddying**) act as caddie.

caddis /'kædɪs/ *noun* □ **caddis-fly** small nocturnal insect living near water; **caddis-worm** larva of caddis-fly.

caddy¹ /'kædɪ/ *noun* (*plural* **-ies**) small container for tea.

caddy² = CADDIE.

cadence /'keɪd(ə)ns/ *noun* rhythm; fall in pitch of voice; tonal inflection; close of musical phrase.

cadenza /kə'denzə/ *noun* *Music* virtuoso passage for soloist during concerto.

cadet /kə'det/ *noun* young trainee in armed services or police force.

cadge *verb* (**-ging**) *colloquial* get or seek by begging.

cadi /'kɑːdɪ/ noun (plural **-s**) judge in Muslim country.

cadmium /'kædmɪəm/ noun soft bluish-white metallic element.

cadre /'kɑːdə/ noun basic unit, esp. of servicemen; group of esp. Communist activists.

caecum /'siːkəm/ noun (US **cecum**) (plural **-ca**) pouch between small and large intestines.

Caerphilly /keə'fɪlɪ/ noun kind of mild pale cheese.

Caesarean /sɪ'zeərɪən/ (US **Cesarean**, **Cesarian**) ● adjective (of birth) effected by Caesarean section. ● noun (in full **Caesarean section**) delivery of child by cutting into mother's abdomen.

caesura /sɪ'zjʊərə/ noun (plural **-s**) pause in line of verse.

café /'kæfeɪ/ noun coffee house, restaurant.

cafeteria /kæfɪ'tɪərɪə/ noun self-service restaurant.

cafetière /kæfə'tjeə/ noun coffee pot with plunger for pressing grounds to bottom.

caffeine /'kæfiːn/ noun alkaloid stimulant in tea leaves and coffee beans.

caftan /'kæftæn/ noun (also **kaftan**) long tunic worn by men in Near East; long loose dress.

cage ● noun structure of bars or wires, esp. for confining animals; open framework, esp. lift in mine etc. ● verb (**-ging**) confine in cage.

cagey /'keɪdʒɪ/ adjective (**-ier**, **-iest**) colloquial cautious and non-committal. □ **cagily** adverb.

cagoule /kə'guːl/ noun light hooded windproof jacket.

cahoots /kə'huːts/ plural noun □ **in cahoots** slang in collusion.

caiman = CAYMAN.

cairn /keən/ noun mound of stones. □ **cairn terrier** small shaggy short-legged terrier.

cairngorm /'keəngɔːm/ noun yellow or wine-coloured semiprecious stone.

caisson /'keɪs(ə)n/ noun watertight chamber for underwater construction work.

cajole /kə'dʒəʊl/ verb (**-ling**) persuade by flattery, deceit, etc. □ **cajolery** noun.

cake ● noun mixture of flour, butter, eggs, sugar, etc. baked in oven; flattish compact mass. ● verb (**-king**) form into compact mass; (usually + with) cover (with sticky mass).

calabash /'kæləbæʃ/ noun tropical American tree bearing gourds; bowl or pipe made from gourd.

calabrese /'kæləbriːs, kælə'breɪsɪ/ noun variety of broccoli.

calamine /'kæləmaɪn/ noun powdered zinc carbonate and ferric oxide used in skin lotion.

calamity /kə'læmɪtɪ/ noun (plural **-ies**) disaster. □ **calamitous** adjective.

calcareous /kæl'keərɪəs/ adjective of or containing calcium carbonate.

calceolaria /kælsɪə'leərɪə/ noun plant with slipper-shaped flowers.

calcify /'kælsɪfaɪ/ verb (**-ies**, **-ied**) harden by deposit of calcium salts. □ **calcification** noun.

calcine /'kælsaɪn/ verb (**-ning**) decompose or be decomposed by roasting or burning. □ **calcination** /-sɪn-/ noun.

calcium /'kælsɪəm/ noun soft grey metallic element.

calculate /'kælkjʊleɪt/ verb (**-ting**) ascertain or forecast by exact reckoning; plan deliberately. □ **calculable** adjective, **calculation** noun.

calculated adjective done with awareness of likely consequences; (+ to do) designed.

calculating adjective scheming, mercenary.

calculator noun device (esp. small electronic one) used for making calculations.

calculus /'kælkjʊləs/ noun (plural **-luses** or **-li** /-laɪ/) Mathematics particular method of calculation; stone in body.

Caledonian /kælɪ'dəʊnɪən/ literary ● adjective of Scotland. ● noun Scot.

calendar /'kælɪndə/ noun system fixing year's beginning, length, and subdivision; chart etc. showing such subdivisions; list of special dates or events. □ **calendar year** period from 1 Jan. to 31 Dec. inclusive.

calends /'kælendz/ plural noun (also **kalends**) first of month in ancient Roman calendar.

calf¹ /kɑːf/ noun (plural **calves** /kɑːvz/) young cow, bull, elephant, whale, etc.; calf leather. □ **calf-love** romantic adolescent love.

calf² /kɑːf/ noun (plural **calves** /kɑːvz/) fleshy hind part of human leg below knee.

calibrate /'kælɪbreɪt/ verb (**-ting**) mark (gauge) with scale of readings; correlate readings of (instrument) with standard; find calibre of (gun). □ **calibration** noun.

calibre /'kælɪbə/ noun (US **caliber**) internal diameter of gun or tube; diameter of bullet or shell; strength or quality of character; ability; importance.

calico /'kælɪkəʊ/ ● noun (plural **-es** or US **-s**) cotton cloth, esp. white or unbleached; US printed cotton cloth. ● adjective of calico; US multicoloured.

caliper = CALLIPER.

caliph /'keɪlɪf/ noun historical chief Muslim civil and religious ruler.

calk US = CAULK.

call /kɔːl/ ● verb (often + *out*) cry, shout, speak loudly; emit characteristic sound; communicate with by radio or telephone; summon; make brief visit; order to take place; name, describe, or regard as; rouse from sleep; (+ *for*) demand. ● noun shout; bird's cry; brief visit; telephone conversation; summons; need, demand. □ **call box** telephone box; **call-girl** prostitute accepting appointments by telephone; **call in** withdraw from circulation, seek advice or services of; **call off** cancel, order (pursuer) to desist; **call the shots, tune** colloquial be in control; **call up** verb telephone, recall, summon (esp. to do military service); **call-up** noun summons to do military service. □ **caller** noun.

calligraphy /kə'lɪgrəfɪ/ noun beautiful handwriting; art of this. □ **calligrapher** noun; **calligraphic** /kælɪ'græfɪk/ adjective.

calling noun profession, occupation; vocation.

calliper /'kælɪpə/ noun (also **caliper**) metal splint to support leg; (in plural) compasses for measuring diameters.

callisthenics /kælɪs'θenɪks/ plural noun exercises for fitness and grace. □ **callisthenic** adjective.

callosity /kə'lɒsɪtɪ/ noun (plural **-ies**) callus.

callous /'kæləs/ adjective unfeeling, unsympathetic; (also **calloused**) (of skin) hardened. □ **callously** adverb; **callousness** noun.

callow /'kæləʊ/ adjective inexperienced, immature.

callus /'kæləs/ noun (plural **calluses**) area of hard thick skin.

calm /kɑːm/ ● adjective tranquil, windless; not agitated. ● noun calm condition or period. ● verb (often + *down*) make or become calm. □ **calmly** adverb; **calmness** noun.

calomel /'kæləmel/ noun compound of mercury used as laxative.

Calor gas /'kælə/ noun proprietary term liquefied butane under pressure in containers for domestic use.

calorie /'kælərɪ/ noun unit of heat, amount required to raise temperature of one gram (**small calorie**) or one kilogram (**large calorie**) of water by 1°C.

calorific /kælə'rɪfɪk/ adjective producing heat.

calumny /'kæləmnɪ/ noun (plural **-ies**) slander; malicious misrepresentation. □ **calumnious** /kə'lʌm-/ adjective.

calvados /'kælvədɒs/ noun apple brandy.

calve /kɑːv/ verb (**-ving**) give birth to (calf).

calves plural of CALF¹,².

Calvinism /'kælvɪnɪz(ə)m/ noun Calvin's theology, stressing predestination. □ **Calvinist** noun & adjective; **Calvinistic** /-'nɪs-/ adjective.

calx noun (plural **calces** /'kælsiːz/) powdery residue left after heating of ore or mineral.

calypso /kə'lɪpsəʊ/ noun (plural **-s**) W. Indian song with improvised usually topical words.

calyx /'keɪlɪks/ noun (plural **calyces** /-lɪsiːz/ or **-es**) leaves forming protective case of flower in bud.

cam noun projection on wheel etc., shaped to convert circular into reciprocal or variable motion.

camaraderie /kæməˈrɑːdərɪ/ noun friendly comradeship.

camber /ˈkæmbə/ ● noun convex surface of road, deck, etc. ● verb construct with camber.

cambric /ˈkæmbrɪk/ noun fine linen or cotton cloth.

camcorder /ˈkæmkɔːdə/ noun combined portable video camera and recorder.

came past of COME.

camel /ˈkæm(ə)l/ noun long-legged ruminant with one hump (**Arabian camel**) or two humps (**Bactrian camel**); fawn colour.

camellia /kəˈmiːlɪə/ noun evergreen flowering shrub.

Camembert /ˈkæməmbeə/ noun kind of soft creamy cheese.

cameo /ˈkæmɪəʊ/ noun (plural -s) small piece of hard stone carved in relief; short literary sketch or acted scene; small part in play or film.

camera /ˈkæmrə/ noun apparatus for taking photographs or for making motion film or television pictures. □ **cameraman** operator of film or television camera; **in camera** in private.

camiknickers /ˈkæmɪnɪkəz/ plural noun woman's knickers and vest combined.

camisole /ˈkæmɪsəʊl/ noun woman's under-bodice.

camomile /ˈkæməmaɪl/ noun (also **chamomile**) aromatic herb with flowers used to make tea.

camouflage /ˈkæməflɑːʒ/ ● noun disguising of soldiers, tanks, etc., so that they blend into background; such disguise; animal's natural blending colouring. ● verb (**-ging**) hide by camouflage.

camp¹ ● noun place where troops are lodged or trained; temporary accommodation of tents, huts, etc., for detainees, holiday-makers, etc.; fortified site; party supporters regarded collectively. ● verb set up or live in camp. □ **camp bed** portable folding bed; **camp follower** civilian worker in military camp, disciple; **campsite** place for camping.

camp² colloquial ● adjective affected, theatrically exaggerated; effeminate; homosexual. ● noun camp manner. ● verb behave or do in camp way.

campaign /kæmˈpeɪn/ ● noun organized course of action, esp. to gain publicity; series of military operations. ● verb take part in campaign. □ **campaigner** noun.

campanile /kæmpəˈniːlɪ/ noun bell tower, usually free-standing.

campanology /kæmpəˈnɒlədʒɪ/ noun study of bells; bell-ringing. □ **campanologist** noun.

campanula /kæmˈpænjʊlə/ noun plant with bell-shaped flowers.

camper noun person who camps; motor vehicle with beds.

camphor /ˈkæmfə/ noun pungent crystalline substance used in medicine and formerly mothballs.

camphorate verb (**-ting**) impregnate with camphor.

campion /ˈkæmpɪən/ noun wild plant with usually pink or white notched flowers.

campus /ˈkæmpəs/ noun (plural -es) grounds of university or college.

camshaft noun shaft carrying cam(s).

can¹ auxiliary verb (3rd singular present **can**; past **could** /kʊd/) be able to; have the potential to; be permitted to.

can² ● noun metal vessel for liquid; sealed tin container for preservation of food or drink; (in plural) slang headphones; (**the can**) slang prison, US lavatory. ● verb (**-nn-**) preserve (food etc.) in can. □ **canned music** pre-recorded music; **carry the can** bear responsibility; **in the can** colloquial completed.

canal /kəˈnæl/ noun artificial inland waterway; tubular duct in plant or animal.

canalize /ˈkænəlaɪz/ verb (also **-ise**) (**-zing** or **-sing**) convert (river) into canal; provide (area) with canal(s); channel. □ **canalization** noun.

canapé /ˈkænəpeɪ/ noun small piece of bread or pastry with savoury topping.

canard /ˈkænɑːd/ noun unfounded rumour.

canary /kəˈneərɪ/ noun (plural **-ies**) small songbird with yellow feathers.

canasta /kəˈnæstə/ noun card game resembling rummy.

cancan /ˈkænkæn/ noun high-kicking dance.

cancel /'kæns(ə)l/ verb (**-ll-**; US **-l-**) revoke, discontinue (arrangement); delete; mark (ticket, stamp, etc.) to invalidate it; annul; (often + out) neutralize, counterbalance; Mathematics strike out (equal factor) on each side of equation etc. □ **cancellation** noun.

cancer /'kænsə/ noun malignant tumour, disease caused by this; corruption; (**Cancer**) fourth sign of zodiac. □ **cancerous** adjective.

candela /kæn'di:lə/ noun SI unit of luminous intensity.

candelabrum /kændɪ'lɑ:brəm/ noun (also **-bra**) (plural **-bra**, US **-brums**, **-bras**) large branched candlestick or lampholder.

candid /'kændɪd/ adjective frank; (of photograph) taken informally, usually without subject's knowledge. □ **candidly** adverb.

candidate /'kændɪdət/ noun person nominated for, seeking, or likely to gain, office, position, award, etc.; person entered for exam. □ **candidacy** noun; **candidature** noun.

candle /'kænd(ə)l/ noun (usually cylindrical) block of wax or tallow enclosing wick which gives light when burning. □ **candlelight** light from candle(s); **candlelit** lit by candle(s); **candlestick** holder for candle(s); **candlewick** thick soft yarn, tufted material made from this.

candour /'kændə/ noun (US **candor**) frankness.

candy /'kændɪ/ ● noun (plural **-ies**) (in full **sugar-candy**) sugar crystallized by repeated boiling and evaporation; US sweets, a sweet. ● verb (**-ies**, **-ied**) (usually as **candied** adjective) preserve (fruit etc.) in candy. □ **candyfloss** fluffy mass of spun sugar; **candy stripe** alternate white and esp. pink stripes.

candytuft /'kændɪtʌft/ noun plant with white, pink, or purple flowers in tufts.

cane ● noun hollow jointed stem of giant reed or grass, or solid stem of slender palm, used for wickerwork or as walking stick, plant support, instrument of punishment, etc.; sugar cane. ● verb (**-ning**) beat with cane; weave cane into (chair etc.).

canine /'keɪnaɪn/ ● adjective of a dog or dogs. ● noun dog; (in full **canine tooth**) tooth between incisors and molars.

canister /'kænɪstə/ noun small usually metal box for tea etc.; cylinder of shot, tear gas, etc.

canker /'kæŋkə/ ● noun disease of trees and plants; ulcerous ear disease of animals; corrupting influence. ● verb infect with canker; corrupt. □ **cankerous** adjective.

cannabis /'kænəbɪs/ noun hemp plant; parts of it used as narcotic.

cannelloni /kænə'ləʊnɪ/ plural noun tubes of pasta stuffed with savoury mixture.

cannibal /'kænɪb(ə)l/ noun person or animal that eats its own species. □ **cannibalism** noun; **cannibalistic** /-'lɪs-/ adjective.

cannibalize /'kænɪbəlaɪz/ verb (also **-ise**) (**-zing** or **-sing**) use (machine etc.) as source of spare parts.

cannon /'kænən/ ● noun automatic aircraft gun firing shells; historical (plural usually same) large gun; hitting of two balls successively by player's ball in billiards. ● verb (usually + against, into) collide. □ **cannon ball** historical large ball fired by cannon.

cannot /'kænɒt/ can not.

canny /'kænɪ/ adjective (**-ier**, **-iest**) shrewd; thrifty.

canoe /kə'nu:/ ● noun light narrow boat, usually paddled. ● verb (**-noes**, **-noed**, **-noeing**) travel in canoe. □ **canoeist** noun.

canon /'kænən/ noun general law, rule, principle, or criterion; church decree; member of cathedral chapter; set of (esp. sacred) writings accepted as genuine; part of RC Mass containing words of consecration; Music piece with different parts taking up same theme successively. □ **canon law** ecclesiastical law.

canonical /kə'nɒnɪk(ə)l/ ● adjective according to canon law; included in canon of Scripture; authoritative, accepted; of (member of) cathedral chapter. ● noun (in plural) canonical dress of clergy.

canonize /'kænənaɪz/ verb (also **-ise**) (**-zing** or **-sing**) declare officially to be saint. □ **canonization** noun.

canopy /'kænəpɪ/ • noun (plural **-ies**) suspended covering over throne, bed, etc.; sky; overhanging shelter; rooflike projection. • verb (**-ies**, **-ied**) supply or be canopy to.

cant[1] • noun insincere pious or moral talk; language peculiar to class, profession, etc.; jargon. • verb use cant.

cant[2] • noun slanting surface, bevel; oblique push or jerk; tilted position. • verb push or pitch out of level.

can't /kɑːnt/ can not.

cantabile /kæn'tɑːbɪleɪ/ Music • adverb & adjective in smooth flowing style. • noun cantabile passage or movement.

cantaloupe /'kæntəluːp/ noun (also **cantaloup**) small round ribbed melon.

cantankerous /kæn'tæŋkərəs/ adjective bad-tempered, quarrelsome. □ **cantankerously** adverb; **cantankerousness** noun.

cantata /kæn'tɑːtə/ noun composition for vocal soloists and usually chorus and orchestra.

canteen /kæn'tiːn/ noun restaurant for employees in office, factory, etc.; shop for provisions in barracks or camp; case of cutlery; soldier's or camper's water-flask.

canter /'kæntə/ • noun horse's pace between trot and gallop. • verb (cause to) go at a canter.

canticle /'kæntɪk(ə)l/ noun song or chant with biblical text.

cantilever /'kæntɪliːvə/ noun bracket, beam, etc. projecting from wall to support balcony etc.; beam or girder fixed at one end only. □ **cantilever bridge** bridge made of cantilevers projecting from piers and connected by girders. □ **cantilevered** adjective.

canto /'kæntəʊ/ noun (plural **-s**) division of long poem.

canton • noun /'kæntɒn/ subdivision of country, esp. Switzerland. • verb /kæn'tuːn/ put (troops) into quarters.

cantonment /kæn'tuːnmənt/ noun lodgings of troops.

cantor /'kæntɔː/ noun church choir leader; precentor in synagogue.

canvas /'kænvəs/ noun strong coarse cloth used for sails and tents etc. and for oil painting; a painting on canvas.

canvass /'kænvəs/ • verb solicit votes (from), ascertain opinions of; seek custom from; propose (idea etc.). • noun canvassing. □ **canvasser** noun.

canyon /'kænjən/ noun deep gorge.

CAP abbreviation Common Agricultural Policy (of EC).

cap • noun soft brimless hat, often with peak; head-covering of nurse etc.; cap as sign of membership of sports team; academic mortarboard; cover resembling cap, or designed to close, seal, or protect something; contraceptive diaphragm; percussion cap; dental crown. • verb (**-pp-**) put cap on; cover top or end of; limit; award sports cap to; form top of; surpass.

capable /'keɪpəb(ə)l/ adjective competent, able; (+ of) having ability, fitness, etc. for. □ **capability** noun (plural **-ies**); **capably** adverb.

capacious /kə'peɪʃəs/ adjective roomy. □ **capaciousness** noun.

capacitance /kə'pæsɪt(ə)ns/ noun ability to store electric charge.

capacitor /kə'pæsɪtə/ noun type of device for storing electric charge.

capacity /kə'pæsɪtɪ/ • noun (plural **-ies**) power to contain, receive, experience, or produce; maximum amount that can be contained etc.; mental power; position or function. • adjective fully occupying available space etc.

caparison /kə'pærɪs(ə)n/ literary • noun horse's trappings; finery. • verb adorn.

cape[1] noun short cloak.

cape[2] noun headland, promontory; (**the Cape**) Cape of Good Hope.

caper[1] /'keɪpə/ • verb jump playfully. • noun playful leap; prank; slang illicit activity.

caper[2] /'keɪpə/ noun bramble-like shrub; (in plural) its pickled buds.

capercaillie /kæpə'keɪlɪ/ noun (also **capercailzie** /-'keɪlzɪ/) large European grouse.

capillarity /kæpɪ'lærɪtɪ/ noun rise or depression of liquid in narrow tube.

capillary /kə'pɪlərɪ/ • adjective of hair; of narrow diameter. • noun (plural **-ies**) capillary tube or blood vessel. □ **capillary action** capillarity.

capital /'kæpɪt(ə)l/ • noun chief town or city of a country or region; money etc.

with which company starts in business; accumulated wealth; capital letter; head of column or pillar. • *adjective* involving punishment by death; most important; *colloquial* excellent. □ **capital gain** profit from sale of investments or property; **capital goods** machinery, plant, etc.; **capital letter** large kind, used to begin sentence or name; **capital transfer tax** *historical* tax levied on transfer of capital by gift or bequest etc.

capitalism *noun* economic and political system dependent on private capital and profit-making.

capitalist • *noun* person using or possessing capital; advocate of capitalism. • *adjective* of or favouring capitalism. □ **capitalistic** /-'lıs-/ *adjective*.

capitalize *verb* (also **-ise**) (**-zing** or **-sing**) convert into or provide with capital; write (letter of alphabet) as capital, begin (word) with capital letter; (+ *on*) use to one's advantage. □ **capitalization** *noun*.

capitulate /kə'pɪtjʊleɪt/ *verb* (**-ting**) surrender. □ **capitulation** *noun*.

capon /'keɪpən/ *noun* castrated cock.

cappuccino /kæpʊ'tʃiːnəʊ/ *noun* (*plural* **-s**) frothy milky coffee.

caprice /kə'priːs/ *noun* whim; lively or fanciful work of music etc.

capricious /kə'prɪʃəs/ *adjective* subject to whims, unpredictable. □ **capriciously** *adverb*; **capriciousness** *noun*.

Capricorn /'kæprɪkɔːn/ *noun* tenth sign of zodiac.

capsicum /'kæpsɪkəm/ *noun* plant with edible fruits; red, green, or yellow fruit of this.

capsize /kæp'saɪz/ *verb* (**-zing**) (of boat) be overturned; overturn (boat).

capstan /'kæpst(ə)n/ *noun* thick revolving cylinder for winding cable etc.; revolving spindle controlling speed of tape on tape recorder. □ **capstan lathe** lathe with revolving tool holder.

capsule /'kæpsjuːl/ *noun* small soluble case enclosing medicine; detachable compartment of spacecraft or nose-cone of rocket; enclosing membrane; dry fruit releasing seeds when ripe.

Capt. *abbreviation* Captain.

captain /'kæptɪn/ • *noun* chief, leader; leader of team; commander of ship; pilot of civil aircraft; army officer next above lieutenant. • *verb* be captain of. □ **captaincy** *noun* (*plural* **-ies**).

caption /'kæpʃ(ə)n/ • *noun* wording appended to illustration or cartoon; wording on cinema or television screen; heading of chapter, article etc. • *verb* provide with caption.

captious /'kæpʃəs/ *adjective* fault-finding.

captivate /'kæptɪveɪt/ *verb* (**-ting**) fascinate, charm. □ **captivation** *noun*.

captive /'kæptɪv/ • *noun* confined or imprisoned person or animal. • *adjective* taken prisoner; confined; unable to escape. □ **captivity** /-'tɪv-/ *noun*.

captor /'kæptə/ *noun* person who captures.

capture /'kæptʃə/ • *verb* (**-ring**) take prisoner; seize; portray in permanent form; record on film or for use in computer. • *noun* act of capturing; thing or person captured.

Capuchin /'kæpjʊtʃɪn/ *noun* friar of branch of Franciscans; (**capuchin**) monkey with hair like black hood.

car *noun* motor vehicle for driver and small number of passengers; railway carriage of specified type; *US* any railway carriage or van. □ **car bomb** terrorist bomb placed in or under parked car; **car boot sale** sale of goods from (tables stocked from) boots of cars; **car park** area for parking cars; **car phone** radio-telephone for use in car etc.; **carport** roofed open-sided shelter for car; **carsick** nauseous through car travel.

caracul = KARAKUL.

carafe /kə'ræf/ *noun* glass container for water or wine.

caramel /'kærəmel/ *noun* burnt sugar or syrup; kind of soft toffee. □ **caramelize** *verb*.

carapace /'kærəpeɪs/ *noun* upper shell of tortoise or crustacean.

carat /'kærət/ *noun* unit of weight for precious stones; measure of purity of gold.

caravan /'kærəvæn/ *noun* vehicle equipped for living in and usually towed by car; people travelling together, esp. across desert. □ **caravanner** noun.

caravanserai /kærə'vænsəraɪ/ noun Eastern inn with central courtyard.

caravel /'kærəvel/ noun historical small light fast ship.

caraway /'kærəweɪ/ noun plant with small aromatic fruit (**caraway seed**) used in cakes etc.

carbide /'kɑːbaɪd/ noun binary compound of carbon.

carbine /'kɑːbaɪn/ noun kind of short rifle.

carbohydrate /kɑːbə'haɪdreɪt/ noun energy-producing compound of carbon, hydrogen, and oxygen.

carbolic /kɑː'bɒlɪk/ noun (in full **carbolic acid**) kind of disinfectant and antiseptic. □ **carbolic soap** soap containing this.

carbon /'kɑːbən/ noun non-metallic element occurring as diamond, graphite, and charcoal, and in all organic compounds; carbon copy, carbon paper. □ **carbon copy** copy made with carbon paper; **carbon dating** determination of age of object from decay of carbon-14; **carbon dioxide** gas found in atmosphere and formed by respiration; **carbon fibre** thin filament of carbon used as strengthening material; **carbon-14** radioactive carbon isotope of mass 14; **carbon monoxide** poisonous gas formed by burning carbon incompletely; **carbon paper** thin carbon-coated paper for making copies; **carbon tax** tax on fuels producing greenhouse gases; **carbon-12** stable isotope of carbon used as a standard.

carbonate /'kɑːbəneɪt/ ● noun salt of carbonic acid. ● verb (**-ting**) fill with carbon dioxide.

carbonic /kɑː'bɒnɪk/ adjective containing carbon. □ **carbonic acid** weak acid formed from carbon dioxide in water.

carboniferous /kɑːbə'nɪfərəs/ adjective producing coal.

carbonize /'kɑːbənaɪz/ verb (also **-ise**) (**-zing** or **-sing**) reduce to charcoal or coke; convert to carbon; coat with carbon. □ **carbonization** noun.

carborundum /kɑːbə'rʌndəm/ noun compound of carbon and silicon used esp. as abrasive.

carboy /'kɑːbɔɪ/ noun large globular glass bottle.

carbuncle /'kɑːbʌŋk(ə)l/ noun severe skin abscess; bright red jewel.

carburettor /kɑːbə'retə/ noun apparatus mixing air with petrol vapour in internal-combustion engine.

carcass /'kɑːkəs/ noun (also **carcase**) dead body of animal or bird or (colloquial) person; framework; worthless remains.

carcinogen /kɑː'sɪnədʒ(ə)n/ noun substance producing cancer. □ **carcinogenic** /-'dʒen-/ adjective.

card¹ noun thick stiff paper or thin pasteboard; piece of this for writing or printing on, esp. to send greetings, to identify person, or to record information; small rectangular piece of plastic used to obtain credit etc.; playing card; (in plural) card-playing; (in plural) colloquial employee's tax etc. documents; programme of events at race meeting etc.; colloquial eccentric person. □ **card-carrying** registered as member (esp. of political party); **card index** index with separate card for each item; **cardphone** public telephone operated by card instead of money; **card-sharp** swindler at card games; **card vote** block vote.

card² ● noun wire brush etc. for raising nap on cloth etc. ● verb brush with card.

cardamom /'kɑːdəməm/ noun seeds of SE Asian aromatic plant used as spice.

cardboard noun pasteboard or stiff paper.

cardiac /'kɑːdɪæk/ adjective of the heart.

cardigan /'kɑːdɪgən/ noun knitted jacket.

cardinal /'kɑːdɪn(ə)l/ ● adjective chief, fundamental; deep scarlet. ● noun one of leading RC dignitaries who elect Pope. □ **cardinal number** number representing quantity (1, 2, 3, etc.); compare ORDINAL.

cardiogram /'kɑːdɪəʊgræm/ noun record of heart movements.

cardiograph /'kɑːdɪəʊgrɑːf/ noun instrument recording heart movements. □ **cardiographer** /-'ɒgrəfə/ noun; **cardiography** /-'ɒgrəfɪ/ noun.

cardiology /kɑːdɪ'ɒlədʒɪ/ noun branch of medicine concerned with heart. □ **cardiologist** noun.

cardiovascular /kɑːdɪəʊ'væskjʊlə/ adjective of heart and blood vessels.

care /keə/ ● noun (cause of) anxiety or concern; serious attention; caution; protection, charge; task. ● verb (-ring) (usually + about, for, whether) feel concern or interest or affection. □ **in care** (of child) under local authority supervision; **take care** be careful, (+ to do) not fail or neglect; **take care of** look after, deal with, dispose of.

careen /kə'riːn/ verb turn (ship) on side for repair; move or swerve wildly.

career /kə'rɪə/ ● noun professional etc. course through life; profession or occupation; swift course. ● adjective pursuing or wishing to pursue a career; working permanently in specified profession. ● verb move or swerve wildly.

careerist noun person predominantly concerned with personal advancement.

carefree adjective light-hearted, joyous.

careful adjective painstaking; cautious; taking care, not neglecting. □ **carefully** adverb; **carefulness** noun.

careless adjective lacking care or attention; unthinking, insensitive; light-hearted. □ **carelessly** adverb; **carelessness** noun.

carer noun person who cares for sick or elderly person, esp. at home.

caress /kə'res/ ● verb touch lovingly. ● noun loving touch.

caret /'kærət/ noun mark indicating insertion in text.

caretaker ● noun person in charge of maintenance of building. ● adjective taking temporary control.

careworn adjective showing effects of prolonged anxiety.

cargo /'kɑːgəʊ/ noun (plural -es or -s) goods carried by ship or aircraft.

Caribbean /kærə'biːən/ adjective of the West Indies.

caribou /'kærɪbuː/ noun (plural same) N. American reindeer.

caricature /'kærɪkətʃʊə/ ● noun grotesque usually comically exaggerated representation. ● verb (-ring) make or give caricature of. □ **caricaturist** noun.

caries /'keəriːz/ noun (plural same) decay of tooth or bone.

carillon /kə'rɪljən/ noun set of bells sounded from keyboard or mechanically; tune played on this.

Carmelite /'kɑːməlaɪt/ ● noun friar of Order of Our Lady of Mount Carmel; nun of similar order. ● adjective of Carmelites.

carminative /'kɑːmɪnətɪv/ ● adjective relieving flatulence. ● noun carminative drug.

carmine /'kɑːmaɪn/ ● adjective of vivid crimson colour. ● noun this colour; pigment from cochineal.

carnage /'kɑːnɪdʒ/ noun great slaughter.

carnal /'kɑːn(ə)l/ adjective worldly; sensual; sexual. □ **carnality** noun.

carnation /kɑː'neɪʃ(ə)n/ ● noun clove-scented pink; rosy-pink colour. ● adjective rosy-pink.

carnelian = CORNELIAN.

carnival /'kɑːnɪv(ə)l/ noun festivities or festival, esp. preceding Lent; merry-making.

carnivore /'kɑːnɪvɔː/ noun animal or plant that feeds on flesh. □ **carnivorous** /-'nɪvərəs-/ adjective.

carob /'kærəb/ noun seed pod of Mediterranean tree used as chocolate substitute.

carol /'kær(ə)l/ ● noun joyous song, esp. Christmas hymn. ● verb (-ll-; US -l-) sing carols; sing joyfully.

carotene /'kærətiːn/ noun orange-coloured pigment in carrots etc.

carotid /kə'rɒtɪd/ ● noun each of two main arteries carrying blood to head. ● adjective of these arteries.

carouse /kə'raʊz/ ● verb (-sing) have lively drinking party. ● noun such party. □ **carousal** noun; **carouser** noun.

carp[1] noun (plural same) freshwater fish often bred for food.

carp[2] verb find fault, complain. □ **carper** noun.

carpal /'kɑːp(ə)l/ ● adjective of the wrist-bones. ● noun wrist-bone.

carpel /'kɑːp(ə)l/ noun female reproductive organ of flower.

carpenter /'kɑːpɪntə/ ● noun person skilled in woodwork. ● verb do woodwork; make by woodwork. □ **carpentry** noun.

carpet /'kɑːpɪt/ ● *noun* thick fabric for covering floors etc.; piece of this; thing resembling this. ● *verb* (**-t-**) cover (as) with carpet; *colloquial* rebuke. □ **carpet-bag** travelling bag originally made of carpet-like material; **carpet-bagger** *colloquial* political candidate etc. without local connections; **carpet slipper** soft slipper; **carpet sweeper** implement for sweeping carpets.

carpeting *noun* material for carpets; carpets collectively.

carpus /'kɑːpəs/ *noun* (*plural* **-pi** /-paɪ/) group of small bones forming wrist.

carrageen /'kærəgiːn/ *noun* edible red seaweed.

carriage /'kærɪdʒ/ *noun* railway passenger vehicle; wheeled horse-drawn passenger vehicle; conveying of goods; cost of this; bearing, deportment; part of machine that carries other parts; gun carriage. □ **carriage clock** portable clock with handle; **carriageway** part of road used by vehicles.

carrier /'kærɪə/ *noun* person or thing that carries; transport or freight company; carrier bag; framework on bicycle for carrying luggage or passenger; person or animal that may transmit disease without suffering from it; aircraft carrier. □ **carrier bag** plastic or paper bag with handles; **carrier pigeon** pigeon trained to carry messages; **carrier wave** high-frequency electromagnetic wave used to convey signal.

carrion /'kærɪən/ *noun* dead flesh; filth. □ **carrion crow** crow feeding on carrion.

carrot /'kærət/ *noun* plant with edible tapering orange root; this root; incentive. □ **carroty** *adjective*.

carry /'kærɪ/ *verb* (**-ies, -ied**) support or hold up, esp. while moving; have with one; convey; (often + *to*) take (process etc.) to specified point; involve; transfer (figure) to column of higher value; hold in specified way; (of newspaper etc.) publish; (of radio or television station) broadcast; keep (goods) in stock; (of sound) be audible at a distance; win victory or acceptance for; win acceptance from; capture. □ **carry away** remove, inspire, deprive of self-control; **carrycot** portable cot for baby; **carry forward** transfer (figure) to new page or account; **carry it off** do well under difficulties; **carry off** remove (esp. by force), win, (esp. of disease) kill; **carry on** continue, *colloquial* behave excitedly, (often + *with*) *colloquial* flirt; **carry-on** *colloquial* fuss; **carry out** put into practice; **carry-out** takeaway; **carry over** carry forward, postpone; **carry through** complete, bring safely out of difficulties.

cart ● *noun* open usually horse-drawn vehicle for carrying loads; light vehicle for pulling by hand. ● *verb* carry in cart; *slang* carry with difficulty. □ **cart horse** horse of heavy build; **cartwheel** wheel of cart, sideways somersault with arms and legs extended.

carte blanche /kɑːt 'blɑ̃ʃ/ *noun* full discretionary power.

cartel /kɑː'tel/ *noun* union of suppliers etc. set up to control prices.

Cartesian coordinates /kɑː'tiːzɪən/ *plural noun* system of locating point by its distance from two perpendicular axes.

Carthusian /kɑː'θjuːzɪən/ ● *noun* monk of contemplative order founded by St Bruno. ● *adjective* of this order.

cartilage /'kɑːtɪlɪdʒ/ *noun* firm flexible connective tissue in vertebrates. □ **cartilaginous** /-'lædʒ-/ *adjective*.

cartography /kɑː'tɒgrəfɪ/ *noun* map-drawing. □ **cartographer** *noun*; **cartographic** /-tə'græf-/ *adjective*.

carton /'kɑːt(ə)n/ *noun* light esp. cardboard container.

cartoon /kɑː'tuːn/ *noun* humorous esp. topical drawing in newspaper etc.; sequence of drawings telling story; such sequence animated on film; full-size preliminary design for work of art. □ **cartoonist** *noun*.

cartouche /kɑː'tuːʃ/ *noun* scroll-like ornament; oval enclosing name and title of pharaoh.

cartridge /'kɑːtrɪdʒ/ *noun* case containing explosive charge or bullet; sealed container of film etc.; component carrying stylus on record player; ink-container for insertion in pen. □ **cartridge-belt** belt with pockets or loops for cartridges; **cartridge paper** thick paper for drawing etc.

carve *verb* (**-ving**) make or shape by cutting; cut pattern etc. in; (+ *into*) form pattern etc. from; cut (meat) into slices. □ **carve out** take from larger whole; **carve up** subdivide, drive aggressively into path of (another vehicle). □ **carver** *noun*.

carvery *noun* (*plural* **-ies**) restaurant etc. with joints displayed for carving.

carving *noun* carved object, esp. as work of art. □ **carving knife** knife for carving meat.

cascade /kæs'keɪd/ ● *noun* waterfall, esp. one in series. ● *verb* (**-ding**) fall in or like cascade.

case[1] /keɪs/ *noun* instance of something occurring; hypothetical or actual situation; person's illness, circumstances, etc. as regarded by doctor, social worker, etc.; such a person; crime etc. investigated by detective or police; suit at law; sum of arguments on one side; (valid) set of arguments; *Grammar* relation of word to others in sentence, form of word expressing this. □ **case law** law as established by decided cases; **casework** social work concerned with individual's background; **in any case** whatever the truth or possible outcome is; **in case** in the event that, lest, in provision against a possibility; **in case of** in the event of; **is** (**not**) **the case** is (not) so.

case[2] /keɪs/ ● *noun* container or cover enclosing something. ● *verb* (**-sing**) enclose in case; (+ *with*) surround with; *slang* inspect closely, esp. for criminal purpose. □ **case-harden** harden surface of (esp. steel), make callous.

casein /'keɪsɪɪn/ *noun* main protein in milk and cheese.

casement /'keɪsmənt/ *noun* (part of) window hinged to open like door.

cash ● *noun* money in coins or notes; full payment at time of purchase. ● *verb* give or obtain cash for. □ **cash and carry** (esp. wholesaling) system of cash payment for goods removed by buyer, store where this operates; **cashcard** plastic card for use in cash dispenser; **cash crop** crop produced for sale; **cash desk** counter etc. where goods are paid for; **cash dispenser** automatic machine for withdrawal of cash; **cash flow** movement of money into and out of a business; **cash in** obtain cash for, (usually + *on*) *colloquial* profit

(from); **cash register** till recording sales, totalling receipts, etc.; **cash up** count day's takings.

cashew /'kæʃuː/ *noun* evergreen tree bearing kidney-shaped edible nut; this nut.

cashier[1] /kæ'ʃɪə/ *noun* person dealing with cash transactions in bank etc.

cashier[2] /kæ'ʃɪə/ *verb* dismiss from service.

cashmere /kæʃ'mɪə/ *noun* fine soft (material of) wool, esp. of Kashmir goat.

casing *noun* enclosing material or cover.

casino /kə'siːnəʊ/ *noun* (*plural* **-s**) public room etc. for gambling.

cask /kɑːsk/ *noun* barrel, esp. for alcoholic liquor.

casket /'kɑːskɪt/ *noun* small box for holding valuables; *US* coffin.

cassava /kə'sɑːvə/ *noun* plant with starchy roots; starch or flour from these.

casserole /'kæsərəʊl/ ● *noun* covered dish for cooking food in oven; food cooked in this. ● *verb* (**-ling**) cook in casserole.

cassette /kə'set/ *noun* sealed case containing magnetic tape, film, etc., ready for insertion in tape recorder, camera, etc.

cassia /'kæsɪə/ *noun* tree whose leaves and pod yield senna.

cassis /kæ'siːs/ *noun* blackcurrant flavouring for drinks etc.

cassock /'kæsək/ *noun* long usually black or red clerical garment.

cassowary /'kæsəweərɪ/ *noun* (*plural* **-ies**) large flightless Australian bird.

cast /kɑːst/ ● *verb* (*past & past participle* **cast**) throw; direct, cause to fall; express (doubts etc.); let down (anchor etc.); shed or lose; register (vote); shape (molten metal etc.) in mould; make (product) thus; (usually + *as*) assign (actor) to role; allocate roles in (play, film, etc.); (+ *in, into*) arrange (facts etc.) in specified form. ● *noun* throwing of missile, dice, fishing line, etc.; thing made in mould; moulded mass of solidified material; actors in play etc.; form, type, or quality; tinge of colour; slight

squint; worm-cast. □ **cast about,
around** search; **cast aside** abandon;
casting vote deciding vote when votes
on two sides are equal; **cast iron** hard
but brittle iron alloy; **cast-iron** of cast
iron, very strong, unchallengeable;
cast off abandon, finish piece of knitting; **cast-off** abandoned or discarded
(thing, esp. garment); **cast on** make
first row of piece of knitting.

castanet /ˌkæstəˈnet/ noun (usually in
plural) each of pair of hand-held wooden
or ivory shells clicked together in time
with esp. Spanish dancing.

castaway /ˈkɑːstəweɪ/ • noun ship-
wrecked person. • adjective ship-
wrecked.

caste /kɑːst/ noun any of Hindu hereditary classes whose members have no
social contact with other classes;
exclusive social class.

castellated /ˈkæstəleɪtɪd/ adjective built
with battlements. □ **castellation** noun.

caster = CASTOR.

castigate /ˈkæstɪgeɪt/ verb (-ting) rebuke; punish. □ **castigation** noun.

castle /ˈkɑːs(ə)l/ • noun large fortified
residential building; Chess rook. • verb
(-ling) Chess make combined move of
king and rook.

castor /ˈkɑːstə/ noun (also **caster**) small
swivelled wheel enabling heavy furniture to be moved; container perforated
for sprinkling sugar etc. □ **castor
sugar** finely granulated white sugar.

castor oil noun vegetable oil used as
laxative and lubricant.

castrate /kæsˈtreɪt/ verb (-ting) remove
testicles of. □ **castration** noun.

casual /ˈkæʒʊəl/ • adjective chance; not
regular or permanent; unconcerned,
careless; (of clothes etc.) informal.
• noun casual worker; (usually in plural)
casual clothes or shoes. □ **casually**
adverb.

casualty /ˈkæʒʊəltɪ/ noun (plural -ies)
person killed or injured in war or
accident; thing lost or destroyed; casualty department; accident. □ **casualty
department** part of hospital for
treatment of casualties.

casuist /ˈkæʒʊɪst/ noun person who re-
solves cases of conscience etc., esp.
cleverly but falsely; sophist, quibbler.

□ **casuistic** adjective; **casuistry** /-ɪs-/
noun.

cat noun small furry domestic quadruped; wild animal of same family;
colloquial malicious or spiteful woman;
cat-o'-nine-tails. □ **cat burglar** burglar
who enters by climbing to upper storey;
catcall (make) shrill whistle of disapproval; **catfish** fish with whisker-like
filaments round mouth; **cat flap** small
flap allowing cat passage through
outer door; **catnap** (have) short
sleep; **cat-o'-nine-tails** historical whip
with nine knotted cords; **cat's cradle**
child's game with string; **cat's-eye**
proprietary term reflector stud set into
road; **cat's-paw** person used as tool
by another; **catsuit** close-fitting garment with trouser legs, covering
whole body; **catwalk** narrow walkway; **rain cats and dogs** rain hard.

catachresis /ˌkætəˈkriːsɪs/ noun (plural
-chreses /-siːz/) incorrect use of words.
□ **catachrestic** /-ˈkres-/ adjective.

cataclysm /ˈkætəklɪz(ə)m/ noun violent
upheaval. □ **cataclysmic** /-ˈklɪz-/ adjective.

catacomb /ˈkætəkuːm/ noun (often in
plural) underground cemetery.

catafalque /ˈkætəfælk/ noun decorated
bier, esp. for state funeral etc.

Catalan /ˈkætəlæn/ • noun native or language of Catalonia in Spain. • adjective of
Catalonia.

catalepsy /ˈkætəlepsɪ/ noun trance or
seizure with rigidity of body. □ **cataleptic** /-ˈlep-/ adjective & noun.

catalogue /ˈkætəlɒg/ (US **catalog**)
• noun complete or extensive list, usually in alphabetical or other systematic
order.   • verb (-logues, -logued,
-loguing; US -logs, -loged, -loging)
make catalogue of; enter in catalogue.

catalysis /kəˈtælɪsɪs/ noun (plural -lyses
/-siːz/) acceleration of chemical reaction by catalyst. □ **catalyse** verb (-sing)
(US -lyze; -zing).

catalyst /ˈkætəlɪst/ noun substance
speeding chemical reaction without itself permanently changing; person or
thing that precipitates change.

catalytic /ˌkætəˈlɪtɪk/ adjective involving
or causing catalysis. □ **catalytic con-
verter** device in vehicle for converting
pollutant gases into less harmful ones.

catamaran /ˌkætəmə'ræn/ *noun* boat or raft with two parallel hulls.

catapult /'kætəpʌlt/ ● *noun* forked stick with elastic for shooting stones; *historical* military machine for hurling stones etc.; device for launching glider etc. ● *verb* launch with catapult; fling forcibly; leap or be hurled forcibly.

cataract /'kætərækt/ *noun* waterfall, downpour; progressive opacity of eye lens.

catarrh /kə'tɑː/ *noun* inflammation of mucous membrane, air-passages, etc.; mucus in nose caused by this. □ **catarrhal** *adjective*.

catastrophe /kə'tæstrəfɪ/ *noun* great usually sudden disaster; denouement of drama. □ **catastrophic** /kætə'strɒf-/ *adjective*; **catastrophically** /kætə'strɒf-/ *adverb*.

catch /kætʃ/ ● *verb (past & past participle* **caught** /kɔːt/) capture in trap, hands, etc.; detect or surprise; intercept and hold (moving thing) in hand etc.; *Cricket* dismiss (batsman) by catching ball before it hits ground; contract (disease) by infection etc.; reach in time and board (train etc.); apprehend; check or be checked; become entangled; (of artist etc.) reproduce faithfully; reach or overtake. ● *noun* act of catching; *Cricket* chance or act of catching ball; amount of thing caught; thing or person caught or worth catching; question etc. intended to deceive etc.; unexpected difficulty or disadvantage; device for fastening door etc.; musical round. □ **catch fire** begin to burn; **catch on** *colloquial* become popular, understand what is meant; **catch out** detect in mistake etc., *Cricket* catch; **catchpenny** intended merely to sell quickly; **catchphrase** phrase in frequent use; **catch up** (often + *with*) reach (person etc. ahead), make up arrears, involve, fasten; **catchword** phrase or word in frequent use, word so placed as to draw attention.

catching *adjective* infectious.

catchment area *noun* area served by school, hospital, etc.; area from which rainfall flows into river etc.

catchy *adjective* (**-ier, -iest**) (of tune) easily remembered, attractive.

catechism /'kætɪkɪz(ə)m/ *noun* (book containing) principles of a religion in form of questions and answers; series of questions.

catechize /'kætɪkaɪz/ *verb* (also **-ise**) (**-zing** or **-sing**) instruct by question and answer. □ **catechist** *noun*.

catechumen /kætɪ'kjuːmən/ *noun* person being instructed before baptism.

categorical /kætɪ'gɒrɪk(ə)l/ *adjective* unconditional, absolute, explicit. □ **categorically** *adverb*.

categorize /'kætɪgəraɪz/ *verb* (also **-ise**) (**-zing** or **-sing**) place in category. □ **categorization** *noun*.

category /'kætɪgərɪ/ *noun* (*plural* **-ies**) class or division (of things, ideas, etc.).

cater /'keɪtə/ *verb* supply food; (+ *for*) provide what is required for. □ **caterer** *noun*.

caterpillar /'kætəpɪlə/ *noun* larva of butterfly or moth; (**Caterpillar**) (in full **Caterpillar track**) *proprietary term* articulated steel band passing round wheels of vehicle for travel on rough ground.

caterwaul /'kætəwɔːl/ *verb* howl like cat.

catgut *noun* thread made from intestines of sheep etc. used for strings of musical instruments etc.

catharsis /kə'θɑːsɪs/ *noun* (*plural* **catharses** /-siːz/) emotional release; emptying of bowels.

cathartic /kə'θɑːtɪk/ ● *adjective* effecting catharsis. ● *noun* laxative.

cathedral /kə'θiːdr(ə)l/ *noun* principal church of diocese.

Catherine wheel /'kæθrɪn/ *noun* rotating firework.

catheter /'kæθɪtə/ *noun* tube inserted into body cavity to introduce or drain fluid.

cathode /'kæθəʊd/ *noun* negative electrode of cell; positive terminal of battery. □ **cathode ray** beam of electrons from cathode of vacuum tube; **cathode ray tube** vacuum tube in which cathode rays produce luminous image on fluorescent screen.

catholic /'kæθlɪk/ ● *adjective* universal; broad-minded; all-embracing; (**Catholic**) Roman Catholic; (**Catholic**) including all Christians or all of Western Church. ● *noun* (**Catholic**) Roman Catholic. □ **Catholicism** /kə'θɒlɪs-/ *noun*; **catholicity** /-ə'lɪs-/ *noun*.

cation /'kætaɪən/ *noun* positively charged ion. □ **cationic** /-'ɒnɪk/ *adjective*.

catkin /'kætkɪn/ *noun* spike of usually hanging flowers of willow, hazel, etc.

catmint *noun* pungent plant attractive to cats.

catnip *noun* catmint.

cattery *noun* (*plural* **-ies**) place where cats are boarded.

cattle /'kæt(ə)l/ *plural noun* large ruminants, bred esp. for milk or meat. □ **cattle grid** grid over ditch, allowing vehicles to pass over but not livestock.

catty *adjective* (**-ier**, **-iest**) spiteful. □ **cattily** *adverb*; **cattiness** *noun*.

Caucasian /kɔ:'keɪʒ(ə)n/ ● *adjective* of the white or light-skinned race. ● *noun* Caucasian person.

caucus /'kɔ:kəs/ *noun* (*plural* **-es**) US meeting of party members to decide policy; *often derogatory* (meeting of) group within larger organization.

caudal /'kɔ:d(ə)l/ *adjective* of, like, or at tail.

caudate /'kɔ:deɪt/ *adjective* tailed.

caught *past & past participle of* CATCH.

caul /kɔ:l/ *noun* membrane enclosing foetus; part of this sometimes found on child's head at birth.

cauldron /'kɔ:ldrən/ *noun* large vessel for boiling things in.

cauliflower /'kɒlɪflaʊə/ *noun* cabbage with large white flower head.

caulk /kɔ:k/ *verb* (*US* **calk**) stop up (ship's seams); make watertight.

causal /'kɔ:z(ə)l/ *adjective* relating to cause (and effect). □ **causality** /-'zæl-/ *noun*.

causation /kɔ:'zeɪʃ(ə)n/ *noun* causing, causality.

cause /kɔ:z/ ● *noun* thing producing effect; reason or motive; justification; principle, belief, or purpose; matter to be settled, or case offered, at law. ● *verb* (**-sing**) be cause of; produce; (+ *to do*) make.

cause célèbre /kɔ:z se'lebr/ *noun* (*plural* **causes célèbres** *same pronunciation*) lawsuit that excites much interest. [French]

causeway /'kɔ:zweɪ/ *noun* raised road across low ground or water; raised path by road.

caustic /'kɔ:stɪk/ ● *adjective* corrosive, burning; sarcastic, biting. ● *noun* caustic substance. □ **caustic soda** sodium hydroxide. □ **causticity** /-'tɪs-/ *noun*.

cauterize /'kɔ:təraɪz/ *verb* (*also* **-ise**) (**-zing** or **-sing**) burn (tissue), esp. to stop bleeding.

caution /'kɔ:ʃ(ə)n/ ● *noun* attention to safety; warning; *colloquial* amusing or surprising person or thing. ● *verb* warn, admonish.

cautionary *adjective* warning.

cautious /'kɔ:ʃəs/ *adjective* having or showing caution. □ **cautiously** *adverb*; **cautiousness** *noun*.

cavalcade /kævəl'keɪd/ *noun* procession of riders, cars, etc.

cavalier /kævə'lɪə/ ● *noun* courtly gentleman; *archaic* horseman; (**Cavalier**) *historical* supporter of Charles I in English Civil War. ● *adjective* offhand, supercilious, curt.

cavalry /'kævəlrɪ/ *noun* (*plural* **-ies**) (usually treated as *plural*) soldiers on horseback or in armoured vehicles.

cave ● *noun* large hollow in side of cliff, hill, etc., or underground. ● *verb* (**-ving**) explore caves. □ **cave in** (cause to) subside or collapse, yield, submit.

caveat /'kævɪæt/ *noun* warning, proviso.

cavern /'kæv(ə)n/ *noun* cave, esp. large or dark one.

cavernous *adjective* full of caverns; huge or deep as cavern.

caviar /'kævɪɑ:/ *noun* (*also* **caviare**) pickled sturgeon-roe.

cavil /'kævɪl/ ● *verb* (**-ll-**; *US* **-l-**) (usually + *at, about*) make petty objections. ● *noun* petty objection.

cavity /'kævɪtɪ/ *noun* (*plural* **-ies**) hollow within solid body; decayed part of tooth. □ **cavity wall** two walls separated by narrow space.

cavort /kə'vɔ:t/ *verb* caper.

caw ● *noun* cry of rook etc. ● *verb* utter this cry.

cayenne /keɪ'en/ *noun* (in full **cayenne pepper**) powdered red pepper.

cayman /'keɪmən/ *noun* (*also* **caiman**) (*plural* **-s**) S. American alligator-like reptile.

CB *abbreviation* citizens' band; Commander of the Order of the Bath.

CBE *abbreviation* Commander of the Order of the British Empire.

CBI *abbreviation* Confederation of British Industry.

cc *abbreviation* cubic centimetre(s).

CD *abbreviation* compact disc; *Corps Diplomatique.*

CD-ROM *abbreviation* compact disc read-only memory.

cease /si:s/ *formal verb* (**-sing**) stop; bring or come to an end. □ **cease-fire** (order for) truce; **without cease** unending.

ceaseless *adjective* without end. □ **ceaselessly** *adverb.*

cedar /ˈsiːdə/ *noun* evergreen conifer; its durable fragrant wood.

cede /siːd/ *verb* (**-ding**) *formal* give up one's rights to or possession of.

cedilla /sɪˈdɪlə/ *noun* mark (ˌ) under *c* (in French, to show it is pronounced /s/, not /k/).

ceilidh /ˈkeɪli/ *noun* informal gathering for music, dancing, etc.

ceiling /ˈsiːlɪŋ/ *noun* upper interior surface of room; upper limit; maximum altitude of aircraft.

celandine /ˈselǝndaɪn/ *noun* yellow-flowered plant.

celebrant /ˈselɪbrǝnt/ *noun* person performing rite, esp. priest at Eucharist.

celebrate /ˈselɪbreɪt/ *verb* (**-ting**) mark with or engage in festivities; perform (rite or ceremony); praise publicly. □ **celebration** *noun,* **celebratory** /-ˈbreɪt-/ *adjective.*

celebrity /sɪˈlebrɪti/ *noun* (*plural* **-ies**) well-known person; fame.

celeriac /sɪˈlerɪæk/ *noun* variety of celery.

celery /ˈselǝri/ *noun* plant of which stalks are used as vegetable.

celesta /sɪˈlestə/ *noun* keyboard instrument with steel plates struck with hammers.

celestial /sɪˈlestɪǝl/ *adjective* of sky or heavenly bodies; heavenly, divinely good.

celibate /ˈselɪbǝt/ ● *adjective* unmarried, or abstaining from sexual relations, often for religious reasons. ● *noun* celibate person. □ **celibacy** *noun.*

cell /sel/ *noun* small room, esp. in prison or monastery; small compartment, e.g. in honeycomb; small active political group; unit of structure of organic matter; enclosed cavity in organism etc.; vessel containing electrodes for current-generation or electrolysis. □ **cellphone** portable radio-telephone.

cellar /ˈselə/ *noun* underground storage room; stock of wine in cellar.

cello /ˈtʃeləʊ/ *noun* (*plural* **-s**) bass instrument of violin family, held between legs of seated player. □ **cellist** *noun.*

Cellophane /ˈselǝfeɪn/ *noun proprietary term* thin transparent wrapping material.

cellular /ˈseljʊlə/ *adjective* consisting of cells; of open texture, porous. □ **cellularity** /-ˈlær-/ *noun.*

cellulite /ˈseljʊlaɪt/ *noun* lumpy fat, esp. on women's hips and thighs.

celluloid /ˈseljʊlɔɪd/ *noun* plastic made from camphor and cellulose nitrate; cinema film.

cellulose /ˈseljʊlǝʊs/ *noun* carbohydrate forming plant-cell walls; paint or lacquer consisting of cellulose acetate or nitrate in solution.

Celsius /ˈselsɪǝs/ *adjective* of scale of temperature on which water freezes at 0° and boils at 100°.

Celt /kelt/ *noun* (also **Kelt**) member of an ethnic group including inhabitants of Ireland, Wales, Scotland, Cornwall, and Brittany.

Celtic /ˈkeltɪk/ ● *adjective* of the Celts. ● *noun* group of Celtic languages.

cement /sɪˈment/ ● *noun* substance made from lime and clay, mixed with water, sand, etc. to form mortar or concrete; adhesive. ● *verb* unite firmly, strengthen; apply cement to.

cemetery /ˈsemɪtri/ *noun* (*plural* **-ies**) burial ground, esp. one not in churchyard.

cenotaph /ˈsenǝtɑːf/ *noun* tomblike monument to person(s) whose remains are elsewhere.

Cenozoic /siːnǝˈzǝʊɪk/ ● *adjective* of most recent geological era, marked by evolution of mammals etc. ● *noun* this era.

censer /ˈsensə/ *noun* incense-burning vessel.

censor /ˈsensə/ ●*noun* official with power to suppress or expurgate books, films, news, etc., on grounds of obscenity, threat to security, etc. ●*verb* act as censor of; make deletions or changes in. □ **censorial** /-ˈsɔːr-/ *adjective*; **censorship** *noun*.

■ **Usage** As a verb, *censor* is often confused with *censure*, which means 'to criticize harshly'.

censorious /senˈsɔːrɪəs/ *adjective* severely critical.

censure /ˈsenʃə/ ●*verb* (**-ring**) criticize harshly; reprove. ●*noun* hostile criticism; disapproval.

census /ˈsensəs/ *noun* (*plural* **-suses**) official count of population etc.

cent /sent/ *noun* one-hundredth of dollar or other decimal unit of currency.

cent. *abbreviation* century.

centaur /ˈsentɔː/ *noun* creature in Greek mythology with head, arms, and trunk of man joined to body and legs of horse.

centenarian /sentɪˈneərɪən/ ●*noun* person 100 or more years old. ●*adjective* 100 or more years old.

centenary /senˈtiːnərɪ/ ●*noun* (*plural* **-ies**) (celebration of) 100th anniversary. ●*adjective* of a centenary; recurring every 100 years.

centennial /senˈtenɪəl/ ●*adjective* lasting 100 years; recurring every 100 years. ●*noun US* centenary.

centi- *combining form* one-hundredth.

centigrade /ˈsentɪɡreɪd/ *adjective* Celsius.

■ **Usage** *Celsius* is the better term to use in technical contexts.

centilitre /ˈsentɪliːtə/ *noun* (*US* **centiliter**) one-hundredth of litre (0.018 pint).

centime /ˈsɑ̃tiːm/ *noun* one-hundredth of franc.

centimetre /ˈsentɪmiːtə/ *noun* (*US* **centimeter**) one-hundredth of metre (0.394 in.).

centipede /ˈsentɪpiːd/ *noun* arthropod with wormlike body and many legs.

central /ˈsentr(ə)l/ *adjective* of, forming, at, or from centre; essential, principal. □ **central bank** national bank issuing currency etc.; **central heating** heating of building from central source; **central processor**, **central processing unit** computer's main operating part. □ **centrality** *noun*; **centrally** *adverb*.

centralize *verb* (also **-ise**) (**-zing** or **-sing**) concentrate (administration etc.) at single centre; subject (state etc.) to this system. □ **centralization** *noun*.

centre /ˈsentə/ (*US* **center**) ●*noun* middle point; pivot; place or buildings forming a central point or main area for an activity; point of concentration or dispersion; political party holding moderate opinions; filling in chocolate etc. ●*verb* (**-ring**) (+ *in, on, round*) have as main centre; place in centre. □ **centrefold** centre spread that folds out, esp. with nude photographs; **centre forward**, **back** *Football etc.* middle player in forward or half-back line; **centre of gravity** point at which the mass of an object effectively acts; **centrepiece** ornament for middle of table, main item; **centre spread** two facing middle pages of magazine etc.

centrifugal /sentrɪˈfjuːɡ(ə)l/ *adjective* moving or tending to move from centre. □ **centrifugal force** apparent force acting outwards on body revolving round centre. □ **centrifugally** *adverb*.

centrifuge /ˈsentrɪfjuːdʒ/ *noun* rapidly rotating machine for separating e.g. cream from milk.

centripetal /senˈtrɪpɪt(ə)l/ *adjective* moving or tending to move towards centre. □ **centripetally** *adverb*.

centrist /ˈsentrɪst/ *noun often derogatory* person holding moderate views. □ **centrism** *noun*.

cents. *abbreviation* centuries.

centurion /senˈtjʊərɪən/ *noun* commander of century in ancient Roman army.

century /ˈsentʃərɪ/ *noun* (*plural* **-ies**) 100 years; *Cricket* score of 100 runs by one batsman; company in ancient Roman army.

■ **Usage** Strictly speaking, because the 1st century ran from the year 1 to the year 100, the first year of a century ends in 1. However, a century is commonly regarded as starting with a year ending in 00, the 20th century thus running from 1900 to 1999.

cephalic /sə'fælɪk/ *adjective* of or in head.

cephalopod /'sefələpɒd/ *noun* mollusc with tentacles on head, e.g. octopus.

ceramic /sɪ'ræmɪk/ ● *adjective* made of esp. baked clay; of ceramics. ● *noun* ceramic article.

ceramics *plural noun* ceramic products collectively; (usually treated as *singular*) ceramic art.

cereal /'sɪərɪəl/ ● *noun* edible grain; breakfast food made from cereal. ● *adjective* of edible grain.

cerebellum /serɪ'beləm/ *noun* (*plural* -s or -bella) part of brain at back of skull.

cerebral /'serɪbr(ə)l/ *adjective* of brain; intellectual. □ **cerebral palsy** paralysis resulting from brain damage before or at birth.

cerebration /serɪ'breɪʃ(ə)n/ *noun* working of brain.

cerebrospinal /serɪbrəʊ'spaɪn(ə)l/ *adjective* of brain and spine.

cerebrum /'serɪbrəm/ *noun* (*plural* -bra) principal part of brain, at front of skull.

ceremonial /serɪ'məʊnɪəl/ ● *adjective* of or with ceremony, formal. ● *noun* system of rites or ceremonies.

ceremonious /serɪ'məʊnɪəs/ *adjective* fond of or characterized by ceremony, formal. □ **ceremoniously** *adverb*.

ceremony /'serɪmənɪ/ *noun* (*plural* -ies) formal procedure; formalities, esp. ritualistic; excessively polite behaviour. □ **stand on ceremony** insist on formality.

cerise /sə'riːz/ *noun & adjective* light clear red.

cert /sɜːt/ *noun* (esp. **dead cert**) *slang* a certainty.

certain /'sɜːt(ə)n/ *adjective* convinced; indisputable; (often + *to do*) sure, destined; reliable; particular but not specified; some.

certainly *adverb* undoubtedly; (in answer) yes.

certainty *noun* (*plural* -ies) undoubted fact; absolute conviction; reliable thing or person.

certificate ● *noun* /sə'tɪfɪkət/ document formally attesting fact. ● *verb* /sə'tɪfɪkeɪt/ (-ting) (esp. as **certificated** *adjective*) provide with certificate; license or attest by certificate. □ **certification** /sɜː-/ *noun*.

certify /'sɜːtɪfaɪ/ *verb* (-ies, -ied) attest (to); declare by certificate; officially declare insane. □ **certifiable** *adjective*.

certitude /'sɜːtɪtjuːd/ *noun* feeling certain.

cerulean /sə'ruːlɪən/ *adjective* sky-blue.

cervical /sə'vaɪk(ə)l/ *adjective* of cervix or neck. □ **cervical smear** specimen from neck of womb for examination.

cervix /'sɜːvɪks/ *noun* (*plural* **cervices** /-siːz/) necklike structure, esp. neck of womb; neck.

Cesarean (also **Cesarian**) *US* = CAESAREAN.

cessation /se'seɪʃ(ə)n/ *noun* ceasing.

cession /'seʃ(ə)n/ *noun* ceding; territory ceded.

cesspit /'sespɪt/ *noun* pit for liquid waste or sewage.

cesspool /'sespuːl/ *noun* = cesspit.

cetacean /sɪ'teɪʃ(ə)n/ ● *noun* member of order of marine mammals including whales. ● *adjective* of cetaceans.

cf. *abbreviation* compare (Latin *confer*).

CFC *abbreviation* chlorofluorocarbon (compound used as refrigerant, aerosol propellant, etc.).

cg *abbreviation* centigram(s).

CH *abbreviation* Companion of Honour.

Chablis /'ʃæbliː/ *noun* (*plural* same /-liːz/) dry white wine from Chablis in France.

chaconne /ʃə'kɒn/ *noun* musical variations over ground bass; dance to this.

chafe /tʃeɪf/ ● *verb* (-fing) make or become sore or damaged by rubbing; irritate; show irritation, fret; rub (esp. skin) to warm. ● *noun* sore caused by rubbing.

chaff /tʃɑːf/ ● *noun* separated grainhusks; chopped hay or straw; good-humoured teasing; worthless stuff. ● *verb* tease, banter.

chaffinch /'tʃæfɪntʃ/ *noun* a common European finch.

chafing dish /'tʃeɪfɪŋ/ *noun* vessel in which food is cooked or kept warm at table.

chagrin /'ʃægrɪn/ ● *noun* acute vexation or disappointment. ● *verb* affect with this.

chain ● *noun* connected series of links, thing resembling this; (in *plural*) fetters, restraining force; sequence, series, or set; unit of length (66 ft). ● *verb* (often + *up*) secure with chain. □ **chain gang** *historical* convicts chained together at work etc.; **chain mail** armour made from interlaced rings; **chain reaction** reaction forming products which themselves cause further reactions, series of events each due to previous one; **chainsaw** motor-driven saw with teeth on loop of chain; **chain-smoke** smoke continuously, esp. by lighting next cigarette etc. from previous one; **chain store** one of series of shops owned by one firm.

chair ● *noun* seat usually with back for one person; (office of) chairperson; professorship; *US* electric chair. ● *verb* be chairperson of (meeting); carry aloft in triumph. □ **chairlift** series of chairs on loop of cable for carrying passengers up and down mountain etc.; **chairman, chairperson, chairwoman** person who presides over meeting, board, or committee.

chaise /ʃeɪz/ *noun* horse-drawn usually open carriage for one or two people.

chaise longue /ʃeɪz 'lɒŋ/ *noun* (*plural* **chaise longues** or **chaises longues** /'lɒŋ(z)/) sofa with one arm rest.

chalcedony /kæl'sedənɪ/ *noun* (*plural* **-ies**) type of quartz.

chalet /'ʃæleɪ/ *noun* Swiss hut or cottage; similar house; small cabin in holiday camp etc.

chalice /'tʃælɪs/ *noun* goblet; Eucharistic cup.

chalk /tʃɔ:k/ ● *noun* white soft limestone; (piece of) similar, sometimes coloured, substance for writing or drawing. ● *verb* rub, mark, draw, or write with chalk. □ **chalky** *adjective* (**-ier, -iest**).

challenge /'tʃælɪndʒ/ ● *noun* call to take part in contest etc. or to prove or justify something; demanding or difficult task; call to respond. ● *verb* (**-ging**) issue challenge to; dispute; (as **challenging** *adjective*) stimulatingly difficult. □ **challenger** *noun*.

chamber /'tʃeɪmbə/ *noun* hall used by legislative or judicial body; body that meets in it, esp. a house of a parliament; (in *plural*) set of rooms for barrister(s), esp. in Inns of Court; (in *plural*) judge's room for hearing cases not needing to be taken in court; *archaic* room, esp. bedroom; cavity or compartment in body, machinery, etc. (esp. part of gun that contains charge). □ **chambermaid** woman who cleans hotel bedrooms; **chamber music** music for small group of instruments; **Chamber of Commerce** association to promote local commercial interests; **chamber pot** vessel for urine etc., used in bedroom.

chamberlain /'tʃeɪmbəlɪn/ *noun* officer managing royal or noble household; treasurer of corporation etc.

chameleon /kə'mi:lɪən/ *noun* lizard able to change colour for camouflage.

chamfer /'tʃæmfə/ ● *verb* bevel symmetrically. ● *noun* bevelled surface.

chamois /'ʃæmwɑ:/ *noun* (*plural* same /-wɑ:z/) small mountain antelope; /'ʃæmɪ/ (piece of) soft leather from sheep, goats, etc.

chamomile = CAMOMILE.

champ[1] ● *verb* munch or bite noisily. ● *noun* chewing noise. □ **champ at the bit** show impatience.

champ[2] *noun slang* champion.

champagne /ʃæm'peɪn/ *noun* white sparkling wine from Champagne in France.

champion /'tʃæmpɪən/ ● *noun* person or thing that has defeated all rivals; person who fights for cause or another person. ● *verb* support cause of, defend. ● *adjective colloquial* splendid.

championship *noun* (often in *plural*) contest to decide champion in sport etc.; position of champion.

chance /tʃɑ:ns/ ● *noun* possibility; (often in *plural*) probability; unplanned occurrence; fate. ● *adjective* fortuitous. ● *verb* (**-cing**) *colloquial* risk; happen. □ **chance on** happen to find.

chancel /'tʃɑ:ns(ə)l/ *noun* part of church near altar.

chancellery /'tʃɑːnsələrɪ/ noun (plural -ies) chancellor's department, staff, or residence; US office attached to embassy.

chancellor /'tʃɑːnsələ/ noun state or legal official; head of government in some European countries; non-resident honorary head of university; (in full **Lord Chancellor**) highest officer of the Crown, presiding in House of Lords; (in full **Chancellor of the Exchequer**) UK finance minister.

Chancery /'tʃɑːnsərɪ/ noun Lord Chancellor's division of High Court of Justice.

chancy /'tʃɑːnsɪ/ adjective (-ier, -iest) uncertain; risky.

chandelier /ʃændə'lɪə/ noun branched hanging support for lights.

chandler /'tʃɑːndlə/ noun dealer in oil, candles, soap, paint, etc.

change /tʃeɪndʒ/ ● noun making or becoming different; low-value money in small coins; money returned as balance of that given in payment; new experience; substitution of one thing or person for another; (of different orders in which bells can be rung. ● verb (-ging) undergo, show, or subject to change; take or use another instead of; interchange; give or get money in exchange for; put fresh clothes or coverings on; (often + with) exchange. □ **change hands** be passed to different owner. □ **changeful** adjective; **changeless** adjective.

changeable adjective inconstant; able to change or be changed.

changeling noun child believed to be substitute for another.

channel /'tʃæn(ə)l/ ● noun piece of water connecting two seas; (**the Channel**) the English Channel; medium of communication, agency; band of frequencies used for radio and television transmission; course in which thing moves; hollow bed of water; navigable part of waterway; passage for liquid; lengthwise strip on recording tape etc. ● verb (-ll-; US -l-) guide, direct; form channel(s) in.

chant /tʃɑːnt/ ● noun spoken singsong phrase; melody for reciting unmetrical texts; song. ● verb talk or repeat monotonously; sing or intone (psalm etc.).

chanter noun melody-pipe of bagpipes.

chantry /'tʃɑːntrɪ/ noun (plural -ies) endowment for singing of masses; priests, chapel, etc., so endowed.

chaos /'keɪɒs/ noun utter confusion; formless matter supposed to have existed before universe's creation. □ **chaotic** /keɪ'ɒtɪk/ adjective.

chap[1] noun colloquial man, boy.

chap[2] ● verb (-pp-) (esp. of skin) develop cracks or soreness; (of wind etc.) cause this. ● noun (usually in plural) crack in skin etc.

chaparral /ʃæpə'ræl/ noun US dense tangled brushwood.

chapatti /tʃə'pɑːtɪ/ noun (also **chapatty**) (plural **chapattis** or **chupatties**) flat thin cake of unleavened bread.

chapel /'tʃæp(ə)l/ noun place for private worship in cathedral or church, with its own altar; place of worship attached to private house, institution, etc.; place or service of worship for Nonconformists; branch of printers' or journalists' trade union at a workplace.

chaperon /'ʃæpərəʊn/ ● noun person, esp. older woman, in charge of young unmarried woman on certain social occasions. ● verb act as chaperon to.

chaplain /'tʃæplɪn/ noun member of clergy attached to private chapel, institution, ship, regiment, etc. □ **chaplaincy** noun (plural -ies).

chaplet /'tʃæplɪt/ noun wreath or circlet for head; string of beads, short rosary.

chapter /'tʃæptə/ noun division of book; period of time; canons of cathedral etc.; meeting of these.

char[1] verb (-rr-) blacken with fire, scorch; burn to charcoal.

char[2] colloquial ● noun charwoman. ● verb (-rr-) work as charwoman. □ **charlady**, **charwoman** one employed to do housework.

char[3] noun slang tea.

char[4] noun (plural same) a kind of trout.

charabanc /'ʃærəbæŋ/ noun early form of motor coach.

character /'kærɪktə/ noun distinguishing qualities or characteristics; moral strength; reputation; person in novel, play, etc.; *colloquial* (esp. eccentric) person; letter, symbol; testimonial.

characteristic /kærɪktə'rɪstɪk/ ● *adjective* typical, distinctive. ● *noun* characteristic feature or quality. □ **characteristically** *adverb*.

characterize *verb* (also **-ise**) (**-zing** or **-sing**) describe character of; (+ *as*) describe as; be characteristic of. □ **characterization** *noun*.

charade /ʃə'rɑːd/ *noun* (usually in *plural*, treated as *singular*) game of guessing word(s) from acted clues; absurd pretence.

charcoal *noun* black residue of partly burnt wood etc.

charge ● *verb* (**-ging**) ask (amount) as price; ask (person) for amount as price; (+ *to*, *up to*) debit cost of to; (often + *with*) accuse (of offence); (+ *to do*) instruct or urge to do; (+ *with*) entrust with; make rushing attack (on); (often + *up*) give electric charge to, store energy in; (often + *with*) load, fill. ● *noun* price, financial liability; accusation; task; custody; person or thing entrusted; (signal for) impetuous attack, esp. in battle; appropriate amount of material to be put in mechanism at one time, esp. explosive in gun; cause of electrical phenomena in matter. □ **charge card** credit card, esp. used at particular shop; **in charge** having command. □ **chargeable** *adjective*.

chargé d'affaires /ʃɑːʒeɪ dæ'feə/ *noun* (*plural* **chargés d'affaires** same pronunciation) ambassador's deputy; envoy to minor country.

charger *noun* cavalry horse; apparatus for charging battery.

chariot /'tʃærɪət/ *noun historical* two-wheeled horse-drawn vehicle used in ancient warfare and racing.

charioteer /tʃærɪə'tɪə/ *noun* chariot driver.

charisma /kə'rɪzmə/ *noun* power to inspire or attract others; divinely conferred power or talent. □ **charismatic** /kʌrɪz'mætɪk/ *adjective*.

charitable /'tʃærɪtəb(ə)l/ *adjective* generous to those in need; of or connected with a charity; lenient in judging others. □ **charitably** *adverb*.

charity /'tʃærɪtɪ/ *noun* (*plural* **-ies**) giving voluntarily to those in need; organization for helping those in need; love of fellow men; lenience in judging others.

charlatan /'ʃɑːlət(ə)n/ *noun* person falsely claiming knowledge or skill. □ **charlatanism** *noun*.

charlotte /'ʃɑːlɒt/ *noun* pudding of stewed fruit under bread etc.

charm ● *noun* power of delighting, attracting, or influencing; trinket on bracelet etc.; object, act, or word(s) supposedly having magic power. ● *verb* delight, captivate; influence or protect (as) by magic; obtain or gain by charm. □ **charmer** *noun*.

charming *adjective* delightful. □ **charmingly** *adverb*.

charnel house /'tʃɑː n(ə)l/ *noun* place containing corpses or bones.

chart ● *noun* map esp. for sea or air navigation or showing weather conditions etc.; sheet of information in form of tables or diagrams; (usually in *plural*) *colloquial* list of currently best-selling pop records. ● *verb* make chart of.

charter ● *noun* written grant of rights, esp. by sovereign or legislature; written description of organization's functions etc. ● *verb* grant charter to; hire (aircraft etc.). □ **charter flight** flight by chartered aircraft.

chartered *adjective* qualified as member of professional body that has royal charter.

Chartism *noun* working-class reform movement of 1837–48. □ **Chartist** *noun*.

chartreuse /ʃɑː'trɜːz/ *noun* green or yellow brandy liqueur.

chary /'tʃeərɪ/ *adjective* (**-ier, -iest**) cautious; sparing.

chase[1] /tʃeɪs/ ● *verb* (**-sing**) pursue; (+ *from*, *out of*, *to*, etc.) drive; hurry; (usually + *up*) *colloquial* pursue (thing overdue); *colloquial* try to attain; court persistently. ● *noun* pursuit; unenclosed hunting-land.

chase[2] /tʃeɪs/ *verb* (**-sing**) emboss or engrave (metal).

chaser *noun* horse for steeplechasing; *colloquial* drink taken after another of different kind.

chasm /'kæz(ə)m/ *noun* deep cleft in earth, rock, etc.; wide difference in opinion etc.

chassis /'ʃæsɪ/ *noun* (*plural* same /-sɪz/) base frame of vehicle; frame for (radio etc.) components.

chaste /tʃeɪst/ *adjective* abstaining from extramarital or from all sexual intercourse; pure, virtuous; unadorned. □ **chastely** *adverb*; **chasteness** *noun*.

chasten /'tʃeɪs(ə)n/ *verb* (esp. as **chastening, chastened** *adjectives*) restrain; punish.

chastise /tʃæs'taɪz/ *verb* (**-sing**) rebuke severely; punish, beat. □ **chastisement** *noun*.

chastity /'tʃæstɪtɪ/ *noun* being chaste.

chasuble /'tʃæzjʊb(ə)l/ *noun* sleeveless outer vestment worn by celebrant of Eucharist.

chat ● *verb* (**-tt-**) talk in light familiar way. ● *noun* informal talk. □ **chatline** telephone service setting up conversations between groups of people on separate lines; **chat show** television or radio broadcast with informal celebrity interviews; **chat up** *colloquial* chat to, esp. flirtatiously.

chateau /'ʃætəʊ/ *noun* (*plural* **-x** /-z/) large French country house.

chatelaine /'ʃætəleɪn/ *noun* mistress of large house; *historical* appendage to woman's belt for carrying keys etc.

chattel /'tʃæt(ə)l/ *noun* (usually in *plural*) movable possession.

chatter /'tʃætə/ ● *verb* talk fast, incessantly, or foolishly. ● *noun* such talk.

chatty *adjective* (**-ier, -iest**) fond of or resembling chat.

chauffeur /'ʃəʊfə/ *noun* person employed to drive car. ● *verb* drive (car or person).

chauvinism /'ʃəʊvɪnɪz(ə)m/ *noun* exaggerated or aggressive patriotism; excessive or prejudiced support or loyalty for something. □ **chauvinist** *noun*; **chauvinistic** /-'nɪs-/ *adjective*.

cheap *adjective* low in price; charging low prices; of low quality or worth; easily got. □ **cheaply** *adverb*; **cheapness** *noun*.

cheapen *verb* make or become cheap; degrade.

cheapskate *noun* esp. *US colloquial* stingy person.

cheat ● *verb* (often + *into, out of*) deceive; (+ *of*) deprive of; gain unfair advantage. ● *noun* person who cheats; deception. □ **cheat on** *colloquial* be sexually unfaithful to.

check ● *verb* test, examine, verify; stop or slow motion of; *colloquial* rebuke; threaten opponent's king at chess; *US* agree on comparison; *US* deposit (luggage etc.). ● *noun* test for accuracy, quality, etc.; stopping or slowing of motion; rebuff; restraint; pattern of small squares; fabric so patterned; (also as *interjection*) exposure of chess king to attack; *US* restaurant bill; *US* cheque; *US* token of identification for left luggage etc.; *US* counter used in card games. □ **check in** register at hotel, airport, etc.; **check-in** act or place of checking in; **check out** leave hotel etc. with due formalities; **checkout** act of checking out, pay-desk in supermarket etc.; **check-up** thorough (esp. medical) examination.

checked *adjective* having a check pattern.

checker = CHEQUER.

checkmate ● *noun* (also as *interjection*) check at chess from which king cannot escape. ● *verb* (**-ting**) put into checkmate; frustrate.

Cheddar /'tʃedə/ *noun* kind of firm smooth cheese.

cheek ● *noun* side of face below eye; impertinence, impertinent speech; *slang* buttock. ● *verb* be impertinent to.

cheeky *adjective* (**-ier, -iest**) impertinent. □ **cheekily** *adverb*; **cheekiness** *noun*.

cheep ● *noun* shrill feeble note of young bird. ● *verb* make such cry.

cheer ● *noun* shout of encouragement or applause; mood, disposition; (as **cheers** *interjection*) *colloquial* *expressing good wishes or thanks*. ● *verb* applaud; (usually + *on*) urge with shouts; shout for joy; gladden, comfort. □ **cheer up** make or become less sad.

cheerful *adjective* in good spirits; bright, pleasant. □ **cheerfully** *adverb*; **cheerfulness** *noun*.

cheerless *adjective* gloomy, dreary.

cheery *adjective* (**-ier, -iest**) cheerful. □ **cheerily** *adverb*.

cheese /tʃiːz/ *noun* food made from milk curds; cake of this with rind; thick conserve of fruit. □ **cheeseburger** hamburger with cheese in or on it; **cheesecake** tart filled with sweetened curds, *slang* sexually stimulating display of women; **cheesecloth** thin loosely woven cloth; **cheesed** *slang* (often + *off*) bored, fed up; **cheese-paring** stingy; **cheese plant** climbing plant with holey leaves. □ **cheesy** *adjective*.

cheetah /tʃiːtə/ *noun* swift-running spotted feline resembling leopard.

chef /ʃef/ *noun* (esp. chief) cook in restaurant etc.

Chelsea /tʃelsɪ/ *noun* □ **Chelsea bun** kind of spiral-shaped currant bun; **Chelsea pensioner** inmate of Chelsea Royal Hospital for old or disabled soldiers.

chemical /kemɪk(ə)l/ • *adjective* of, made by, or employing chemistry. • *noun* substance obtained or used in chemistry. □ **chemical warfare** warfare using poison gas and other chemicals. □ **chemically** *adverb*.

chemise /ʃəmiːz/ *noun historical* woman's loose-fitting undergarment or dress.

chemist /kemɪst/ *noun* dealer in medicinal drugs etc.; expert in chemistry.

chemistry /kemɪstrɪ/ *noun* (*plural* **-ies**) science of elements and their laws of combination and change; *colloquial* sexual attraction.

chenille /ʃəniːl/ *noun* tufted velvety yarn; fabric made of this.

cheque /tʃek/ *noun* written order to bank to pay sum of money; printed form for this. □ **chequebook** book of forms for writing cheques; **cheque card** card issued by bank to guarantee honouring of cheques up to stated amount.

chequer /tʃekə/ (also **checker**) • *noun* (often in *plural*) pattern of squares often alternately coloured; (in *plural*; usually **checkers**) *US* game of draughts. • *verb* mark with chequers; variegate, break uniformity of; (as **chequered** *adjective*) with varied fortunes.

cherish /tʃerɪʃ/ *verb* tend lovingly; hold dear; cling to.

cheroot /ʃəruːt/ *noun* cigar with both ends open.

cherry /tʃerɪ/ • *noun* (*plural* **-ies**) small stone fruit, tree bearing it, wood of this; light red. • *adjective* of light red colour.

cherub /tʃerəb/ *noun* representation of winged child; beautiful child; (*plural* **-im**) angelic being. □ **cherubic** /tʃɪˈruːbɪk/ *adjective*.

chervil /tʃɜːvɪl/ *noun* herb with aniseed flavour.

chess *noun* game for two players with 16 **chessmen** each, on chequered **chessboard** of 64 squares.

chest *noun* large strong box; part of body enclosed by ribs, front surface of body from neck to bottom of ribs; small cabinet for medicines etc. □ **chest of drawers** piece of furniture with set of drawers in frame.

chesterfield /tʃestəfiːld/ *noun* sofa with arms and back of same height.

chestnut /tʃesnʌt/ • *noun* glossy hard brown edible nut; tree bearing it; horse chestnut; reddish-brown horse; *colloquial* stale joke etc.; reddish-brown. • *adjective* reddish-brown.

chesty *adjective* (**-ier, -iest**) *colloquial* inclined to or symptomatic of chest disease. □ **chestily** *adverb*; **chestiness** *noun*.

cheval glass /ʃəvæl/ *noun* tall mirror pivoting in upright frame.

chevalier /ʃevəˈlɪə/ *noun* member of certain orders of knighthood etc.

chevron /ˈʃevrən/ *noun* V-shaped line or stripe.

chew • *verb* work (food etc.) between teeth. • *noun* act of chewing; chewy sweet. □ **chewing gum** flavoured gum for chewing; **chew on** work continuously between teeth, think about; **chew over** discuss, think about.

chewy *adjective* (**-ier, -iest**) requiring or suitable for chewing.

chez /ʃeɪ/ *preposition* at the home of. [French]

Chianti /kɪˈæntɪ/ *noun* (*plural* **-s**) red wine from Chianti in Italy.

chiaroscuro /kɪɑːrəˈskʊərəʊ/ *noun* treatment of light and shade in painting; use of contrast in literature etc.

chic /ʃiːk/ • *adjective* (**chic-er, chic-est**) stylish, elegant. • *noun* stylishness, elegance.

chicane /ʃɪ'keɪn/ ● *noun* artificial barrier or obstacle on motor-racing course; chicanery. ● *verb* (**-ning**) *archaic* use chicanery; (usually + *into, out of,* etc.) cheat (person).

chicanery /ʃɪ'keɪnərɪ/ *noun* (*plural* **-ies**) clever but misleading talk; trickery, deception.

chick *noun* young bird; *slang* young woman.

chicken /'tʃɪkɪn/ ● *noun* domestic fowl; its flesh as food; young domestic fowl; youthful person. ● *adjective colloquial* cowardly. ● *verb* (+ *out*) *colloquial* withdraw through cowardice. □ **chicken feed** food for poultry, *colloquial* insignificant amount esp. of money; **chickenpox** infectious disease with rash of small blisters; **chicken wire** light wire netting.

chickpea *noun* pealike seed used as vegetable.

chickweed *noun* a small weed.

chicle /'tʃɪk(ə)l/ *noun* juice of tropical tree, used in chewing gum.

chicory /'tʃɪkərɪ/ *noun* (*plural* **-ies**) salad plant; its root, roasted and ground and used with or instead of coffee; endive.

chide *verb* (**-ding**; *past* **chided** or **chid**; *past participle* **chided** or **chidden**) *archaic* scold, rebuke.

chief /tʃiːf/ ● *noun* leader, ruler; head of tribe, clan, etc.; head of department etc. ● *adjective* first in position, importance, or influence; prominent, leading.

chiefly *adverb* above all; mainly but not exclusively.

chieftain /'tʃiːftən/ *noun* leader of tribe, clan, etc. □ **chieftaincy** *noun* (*plural* **-ies**).

chiffchaff /'tʃɪftʃæf/ *noun* small European warbler.

chiffon /'ʃɪfɒn/ *noun* diaphanous silky fabric.

chignon /'ʃiːnjɒ/ *noun* coil of hair at back of head.

chihuahua /tʃɪ'wɑːwə/ *noun* tiny smooth-coated dog.

chilblain /'tʃɪlbleɪn/ *noun* itching swelling on hand, foot, etc., caused by exposure to cold.

child /tʃaɪld/ *noun* (*plural* **children** /'tʃɪldrən/) young human being; one's son or daughter; (+ *of*) descendant, follower, or product of. □ **child benefit** regular state payment to parents of child up to certain age; **childbirth** giving birth to child; **child's play** easy task. □ **childless** *adjective*.

childhood *noun* state or period of being a child.

childish *adjective* of or like child; immature, silly. □ **childishly** *adverb*; **childishness** *noun*.

childlike *adjective* innocent, frank, etc., like child.

chili = CHILLI.

chill ● *noun* cold sensation; feverish cold; unpleasant coldness (of air etc.); depressing influence. ● *verb* make or become cold; depress, horrify; preserve (food or drink) by cooling. ● *adjective literary* chilly.

chilli /'tʃɪlɪ/ *noun* (also **chili**) (*plural* **-es**) hot-tasting dried red capsicum pod. □ **chilli con carne** /kɒn 'kɑːnɪ/ chilli-flavoured mince and beans.

chilly *adjective* (**-ier, -iest**) rather cold; sensitive to cold; unfriendly, unemotional.

chime ● *noun* set of attuned bells; sounds made by this. ● *verb* (**-ming**) (of bells) ring; show (time) by chiming; (usually + *together, with*) be in agreement. □ **chime in** *interject* remark, join in harmoniously.

chimera /kaɪ'mɪərə/ *noun* monster in Greek mythology with lion's head, goat's body, and serpent's tail; bogey; wild impossible scheme or fancy. □ **chimerical** /-'merɪk(ə)l/ *adjective*.

chimney /'tʃɪmnɪ/ *noun* (*plural* **-s**) channel conducting smoke etc. away from fire etc.; part of this above roof; glass tube protecting lamp-flame. □ **chimney breast** projecting wall round chimney; **chimney pot** pipe at top of chimney; **chimney sweep** person who clears chimneys of soot.

chimp *noun colloquial* chimpanzee.

chimpanzee /tʃɪmpən'zi:/ *noun* manlike African ape.

chin *noun* front of lower jaw. □ **chinless** *adjective* ineffectual person; **chinwag** *noun & verb slang* chat.

china /'tʃaɪnə/ ● *noun* fine white or translucent ceramic ware; things made of this. ● *adjective* made of china. □ **china clay** kaolin.

chinchilla /tʃɪnˈtʃɪlə/ *noun* S. American rodent; its soft grey fur; breed of cat or rabbit.

chine ● *noun* backbone; joint of meat containing this; ridge. ● *verb* (**-ning**) cut (meat) through backbone.

Chinese /tʃaɪˈniːz/ ● *adjective* of China. ● *noun* Chinese language; (*plural* same) native or national of China, person of Chinese descent. □ **Chinese lantern** collapsible paper lantern, plant with inflated orange-red calyx; **Chinese leaf** lettuce-like cabbage.

chink[1] *noun* narrow opening.

chink[2] ● *verb* (cause to) make sound of glasses or coins striking together. ● *noun* this sound.

chintz *noun* printed multicoloured usually glazed cotton cloth.

chip ● *noun* small piece cut or broken off; place where piece has been broken off; strip of potato usually fried; *US* potato crisp; counter used as money in some games; microchip. ● *verb* (**-pp-**) (often + *off*) cut or break (piece) from hard material; (often + *at, away at*) cut pieces off (hard material); be apt to break at edge; (usually as **chipped** *adjective*) make (potato) into chips. □ **chipboard** board made of compressed wood chips.

chipmunk /ˈtʃɪpmʌŋk/ *noun* N. American striped ground squirrel.

chipolata /tʃɪpəˈlɑːtə/ *noun* small thin sausage.

Chippendale /ˈtʃɪpəndeɪl/ *adjective* of an 18th-c. elegant style of furniture.

chiropody /kɪˈrɒpədɪ/ *noun* treatment of feet and their ailments. □ **chiropodist** *noun*.

chiropractic /kaɪərəʊˈpræktɪk/ *noun* treatment of disease by manipulation of spinal column. □ **chiropractor** /ˈkaɪə-/ *noun*.

chirp ● *verb* (of small bird etc.) utter short thin sharp note; speak merrily. ● *noun* chirping sound.

chirpy *adjective* (**-ier, -iest**) *colloquial* cheerful. □ **chirpily** *adverb*.

chirrup /ˈtʃɪrəp/ ● *verb* (**-p-**) chirp, esp. repeatedly. ● *noun* chirruping sound.

chisel /ˈtʃɪz(ə)l/ ● *noun* tool with bevelled blade for shaping wood, stone, or metal. ● *verb* (**-ll-**; *US* **-l-**) cut or shape with chisel; (as **chiselled** *adjective*) (of features) clear-cut; *slang* defraud.

chit[1] *noun* *derogatory or jocular* young small woman; young child.

chit[2] *noun* written note.

chit-chat *noun* *colloquial* light conversation, gossip.

chivalry /ˈʃɪvəlrɪ/ *noun* medieval knightly system; honour and courtesy, esp. to the weak. □ **chivalrous** *adjective*; **chivalrously** *adverb*.

chive *noun* herb related to onion.

chivvy /ˈtʃɪvɪ/ *verb* (**-ies, -ied**) urge persistently, nag.

chloral /ˈklɔːr(ə)l/ *noun* compound used in making DDT, sedatives, etc.

chloride /ˈklɔːraɪd/ *noun* compound of chlorine and another element or group.

chlorinate /ˈklɔːrɪneɪt/ *verb* (**-ting**) impregnate or treat with chlorine. □ **chlorination** *noun*.

chlorine /ˈklɔːriːn/ *noun* poisonous gas used for bleaching and disinfecting.

chlorofluorocarbon see CFC.

chloroform /ˈklɒrəfɔːm/ ● *noun* colourless volatile liquid formerly used as general anaesthetic. ● *verb* render unconscious with this.

chlorophyll /ˈklɒrəfɪl/ *noun* green pigment in most plants.

choc *noun* *colloquial* chocolate. □ **choc ice** bar of ice cream covered with chocolate.

chock ● *noun* block of wood, wedge. ● *verb* make fast with chock(s). □ **chock-a-block** (often + *with*) crammed together, full; **chock-full** (often + *of*) crammed full.

chocolate /ˈtʃɒklət/ ● *noun* food made as paste, powder, or solid block from ground cacao seeds; sweet made of or covered with this; drink containing chocolate; dark brown. ● *adjective* made from chocolate; dark brown.

choice ● *noun* act of choosing; thing or person chosen; range to choose from; power to choose. ● *adjective* of superior quality.

choir /kwaɪə/ *noun* regular group of singers; chancel in large church.

□ **choirboy**, **choirgirl** boy or girl singer in church choir.

choke • verb (**-king**) stop breathing of (person or animal); suffer such stoppage; block up; (as **choked** adjective) speechless from emotion, disgusted, disappointed. • noun valve in carburettor controlling inflow of air; device for smoothing variations of alternating electric current.

choker noun close-fitting necklace.

choler /'kɒlə/ noun historical bile; archaic anger, irascibility.

cholera /'kɒlərə/ noun infectious often fatal bacterial disease of small intestine.

choleric /'kɒlərɪk/ adjective easily angered.

cholesterol /kə'lestərɒl/ noun sterol present in human tissues including the blood.

choose /tʃuːz/ verb (**-sing**; past **chose** /tʃəʊz/; past participle **chosen**) select out of greater number; (usually + between, from) take one or another; (usually + to do) decide.

choosy /'tʃuːzɪ/ adjective (**-ier**, **-iest**) colloquial fussy; hard to please.

chop[1] • verb (**-pp-**) (usually + off, down, etc.) cut with axe etc.; (often + up) cut into small pieces; strike (ball) with heavy edgewise blow. • noun cutting blow; thick slice of meat usually including rib; (**the chop**) slang dismissal from job, killing, being killed.

chop[2] noun (usually in plural) jaw.

chop[3] verb (**-pp-**) □ **chop and change** vacillate.

chopper noun large-bladed short axe; cleaver; colloquial helicopter.

choppy adjective (**-ier**, **-iest**) (of sea etc.) fairly rough.

chopstick /'tʃɒpstɪk/ noun each of pair of sticks held in one hand as eating utensils by Chinese, Japanese, etc.

chop suey /tʃɒp'suːɪ/ noun (plural **-s**) Chinese-style dish of meat fried with vegetables.

choral /'kɔːr(ə)l/ adjective of, for, or sung by choir or chorus.

chorale /kə'rɑːl/ noun simple stately hymn tune; choir.

chord[1] /kɔːd/ noun combination of notes sounded together.

chord[2] /kɔːd/ noun straight line joining ends of arc; string of harp etc.

chore noun tedious or routine task, esp. domestic.

choreography /kɒrɪ'ɒɡrəfɪ/ noun design or arrangement of ballet etc. □ **choreograph** /'kɒrɪəɡrɑːf/ verb; **choreographer** noun; **choreographic** /-ə'ɡræf-/ adjective.

chorister /'kɒrɪstə/ noun member of choir, esp. choirboy.

chortle /'tʃɔːt(ə)l/ • noun gleeful chuckle. • verb (**-ling**) chuckle gleefully.

chorus /'kɔːrəs/ • noun (plural **-es**) group of singers, choir; music for choir; refrain of song; simultaneous utterance; group of singers and dancers performing together; group of performers commenting on action in ancient Greek play, any of its utterances. • verb (**-s-**) utter simultaneously.

chose past of CHOOSE.

chosen past participle of CHOOSE.

chough /tʃʌf/ noun red-legged crow.

choux pastry /ʃuː/ noun very light pastry made with eggs.

chow noun slang food; Chinese breed of dog.

chow mein /tʃaʊ 'meɪn/ noun Chinese-style dish of fried noodles usually with shredded meat and vegetables.

christen /'krɪs(ə)n/ verb baptize; name. □ **christening** noun.

Christendom /'krɪsəndəm/ noun Christians worldwide.

Christian /'krɪstʃ(ə)n/ • adjective of Christ's teaching; believing in or following Christian religion; charitable, kind. • noun adherent of Christianity. □ **Christian era** era counted from Christ's birth; **Christian name** forename, esp. given at christening; **Christian Science** system of belief including power of healing by prayer alone; **Christian Scientist** adherent of this.

Christianity /krɪstɪ'ænɪtɪ/ noun Christian religion, quality, or character.

Christmas /'krɪsməs/ noun (period around) festival of Christ's birth celebrated on 25 Dec. □ **Christmas box** present or tip given at Christmas; **Christmas Day** 25 Dec.; **Christmas**

Eve 24 Dec.; **Christmas pudding** rich boiled pudding with dried fruit; **Christmas rose** white-flowered hellebore flowering in winter; **Christmas tree** evergreen tree decorated at Christmas. □ **Christmassy** *adjective*.

chromatic /krə'mætɪk/ *adjective* of colour, in colours; *Music* of or having notes not belonging to prevailing key. □ **chromatic scale** scale that proceeds by semitones. □ **chromatically** *adverb*.

chrome /krəʊm/ *noun* chromium; yellow pigment got from a compound of chromium.

chromium /'krəʊmɪəm/ *noun* metallic element used as shiny decorative or protective coating.

chromosome /'krəʊməsəʊm/ *noun Biology* threadlike structure occurring in pairs in cell nucleus, carrying genes.

chronic /'krɒnɪk/ *adjective* (of disease) long-lasting; (of patient) having chronic illness; *colloquial* bad, intense, severe. □ **chronically** *adverb*.

chronicle /'krɒnɪk(ə)l/ • *noun* record of events in order of occurrence. • *verb* (-ling) record (events) thus.

chronological /krɒnə'lɒdʒɪk(ə)l/ *adjective* according to order of occurrence. □ **chronologically** *adverb*.

chronology /krə'nɒlədʒɪ/ *noun* (*plural* -ies) science of computing dates; (document displaying) arrangement of events etc. according to date.

chronometer /krə'nɒmɪtə/ *noun* time-measuring instrument, esp. one used in navigation.

chrysalis /'krɪsəlɪs/ *noun* (*plural* -lises) pupa of butterfly or moth; case enclosing it.

chrysanthemum /krɪ'sænθəməm/ *noun* garden plant flowering in autumn.

chub *noun* (*plural* same) thick-bodied river fish.

chubby *adjective* (-ier, -iest) plump, round.

chuck¹ • *verb colloquial* fling or throw carelessly; (often + *in*, *up*) give up; touch playfully, esp. under chin. • *noun* act of chucking; (**the chuck**) *slang* dismissal. □ **chuck out** *colloquial* expel, discard.

chuck² • *noun* cut of beef from neck to ribs; device for holding workpiece or bit. • *verb* fix in chuck.

chuckle /'tʃʌk(ə)l/ • *verb* (-ling) laugh quietly or inwardly. • *noun* quiet or suppressed laugh.

chuff *verb* (of engine etc.) work with regular sharp puffing sound.

chuffed *adjective slang* delighted.

chug *verb* (-gg-) make intermittent explosive sound; move with this.

chukker /'tʃʌkə/ *noun* period of play in polo.

chum *noun colloquial* close friend. □ **chum up** (-mm-) (often + *with*) become close friend (of). □ **chummy** *adjective* (-ier, -iest).

chump *noun colloquial* foolish person; thick end of loin of lamb or mutton; lump of wood.

chunk *noun* lump cut or broken off.

chunky *adjective* (-ier, -iest) consisting of or resembling chunks; small and sturdy.

chunter /'tʃʌntə/ *verb colloquial* mutter, grumble.

chupatty = CHAPATTI.

church *noun* building for public Christian worship; public worship; (**Church**) Christians collectively, clerical profession, organized Christian society. □ **churchgoer** person attending church regularly; **churchman** member of clergy or Church; **churchwarden** elected lay representative of Anglican parish; **churchyard** enclosed ground round church, esp. used for burials.

churl *noun* bad-mannered, surly, or stingy person. □ **churlish** *adjective*.

churn • *noun* large milk can; butter-making machine. • *verb* agitate (milk etc.) in churn; make (butter) in churn; (usually + *up*) upset, agitate. □ **churn out** produce in large quantities.

chute¹ /ʃuːt/ *noun* slide for taking things to lower level.

chute² /ʃuːt/ *noun colloquial* parachute.

chutney /'tʃʌtnɪ/ *noun* (*plural* -s) relish made of fruits, vinegar, spices, etc.

chyle /kaɪl/ *noun* milky fluid into which chyme is converted.

chyme /kaɪm/ *noun* pulp formed from partly-digested food.

CIA *abbreviation* (in *US*) Central Intelligence Agency.

ciabatta /tʃə'bɑːtə/ *noun* Italian bread made with olive oil.

ciao /tʃaʊ/ *interjection colloquial* goodbye; hello.

cicada /sɪ'kɑːdə/ *noun* winged chirping insect.

cicatrice /'sɪkətrɪs/ *noun* scar of healed wound.

cicely /'sɪsəlɪ/ *noun* (*plural* **-ies**) flowering plant related to parsley and chervil.

CID *abbreviation* Criminal Investigation Department.

cider /'saɪdə/ *noun* drink of fermented apple juice.

cigar /sɪ'gɑː/ *noun* roll of tobacco leaves for smoking.

cigarette /sɪgə'ret/ *noun* finely-cut tobacco rolled in paper for smoking.

cilium /'sɪlɪəm/ *noun* (*plural* **cilia**) hairlike structure on animal cells; eyelash. □ **ciliary** *adjective*.

cinch /sɪntʃ/ *noun colloquial* certainty; easy task.

cinchona /sɪŋ'kəʊnə/ *noun* S. American evergreen tree; (drug from) its bark which contains quinine.

cincture /'sɪŋktʃə/ *noun literary* girdle, belt, or border.

cinder /'sɪndə/ *noun* residue of coal etc. after burning.

Cinderella /sɪndə'relə/ *noun* person or thing of unrecognized merit.

cine- /sɪnɪ/ *combining form* cinematographic.

cinema /'sɪnɪmɑː/ *noun* theatre where films are shown; films collectively; art or industry of producing films. □ **cinematic** /-'mæt-/ *adjective*.

cinematography /sɪnɪmə'tɒgrəfɪ/ *noun* art of making films. □ **cinematographer** *noun*, **cinematographic** /-mætə'græfɪk/ *adjective*.

cineraria /sɪnə'reərɪə/ *noun* plant with bright flowers and downy leaves.

cinnabar /'sɪnəbɑː/ *noun* red mercuric sulphide; vermilion.

cinnamon /'sɪnəmən/ *noun* aromatic spice from bark of SE Asian tree; this tree; yellowish-brown.

cinquefoil /'sɪŋkfɔɪl/ *noun* plant with compound leaf of 5 leaflets.

Cinque Port /sɪŋk/ *noun* any of (originally 5) ports in SE England with ancient privileges.

cipher /'saɪfə/ (also **cypher**) ● *noun* secret or disguised writing, key to this; arithmetical symbol 0; person or thing of no importance. ● *verb* write in cipher.

circa /'sɜːkə/ *preposition* (usually before date) about. [Latin]

circle /'sɜːk(ə)l/ ● *noun* perfectly round plane figure; roundish enclosure or structure; curved upper tier of seats in theatre etc.; circular route; set or restricted group; people grouped round centre of interest. ● *verb* (**-ling**) (often + *round, about*) move in or form circle.

circlet /'sɜːklɪt/ *noun* small circle; circular band, esp. as ornament.

circuit /'sɜːkɪt/ *noun* line, course, or distance enclosing an area; path of electric current, apparatus through which current passes; judge's itinerary through district, such a district; chain of theatres, cinemas, etc. under single management; motor-racing track; sphere of operation; sequence of sporting events.

circuitous /sɜː'kjuːɪtəs/ *adjective* indirect, roundabout.

circuitry /'sɜːkɪtrɪ/ *noun* (*plural* **-ies**) system of electric circuits.

circular /'sɜːkjʊlə/ ● *adjective* having form of or moving in circle; (of reasoning) using point to be proved as argument for its own truth; (of letter etc.) distributed to several people. ● *noun* circular letter etc. □ **circular saw** power saw with rotating toothed disc. □ **circularity** /-'lærɪtɪ/ *noun*.

circularize *verb* (also **-ise**) (**-zing** or **-sing**) send circular to.

circulate /'sɜːkjʊleɪt/ *verb* (**-ting**) be or put in circulation; send circulars to; mingle among guests etc.

circulation *noun* movement from and back to starting point, esp. that of blood from and to heart; transmission, distribution; number of copies sold. □ **circulatory** *adjective*.

circumcise /'sɜːkəmsaɪz/ *verb* (**-sing**) cut off foreskin or clitoris of. □ **circumcision** /-'sɪʒ(ə)n/ *noun*.

circumference /sə'kʌmfərəns/ *noun* line enclosing circle; distance round.

circumflex /'sɜːkəmfleks/ *noun* (in full **circumflex accent**) mark (ˆ) over vowel indicating pronunciation.

circumlocution /sɜːkəmləˈkjuːʃ(ə)n/ *noun* roundabout expression; evasive speech; verbosity. □ **circumlocutory** /-ˈlɒkjʊt-/ *adjective*.

circumnavigate /sɜːkəmˈnævɪgeɪt/ *verb* (**-ting**) sail round. □ **circumnavigation** *noun*.

circumscribe /ˈsɜːkəmskraɪb/ *verb* (**-bing**) enclose or outline; lay down limits of; confine, restrict. □ **circumscription** /-ˈskrɪpʃ(ə)n/ *noun*.

circumspect /ˈsɜːkəmspekt/ *adjective* cautious, taking everything into account. □ **circumspection** /-ˈspekʃ(ə)n/ *noun*; **circumspectly** *adverb*.

circumstance /ˈsɜːkəmst(ə)ns/ *noun* fact, occurrence, or condition, esp. (in *plural*) connected with or affecting an event etc.; (in *plural*) financial condition; ceremony, fuss.

circumstantial /sɜːkəmˈstænʃ(ə)l/ *adjective* (of account, story) detailed; (of evidence) tending to establish a conclusion by reasonable inference.

circumvent /sɜːkəmˈvent/ *verb* evade, outwit.

circus /ˈsɜːkəs/ *noun* (*plural* **-es**) travelling show of performing acrobats, clowns, animals, etc.; *colloquial* scene of lively action, group of people in common activity; open space in town, where several streets converge; *historical* arena for sports and games.

cirrhosis /sɪˈrəʊsɪs/ *noun* chronic liver disease.

cirrus /ˈsɪrəs/ *noun* (*plural* **cirri** /-raɪ/) white wispy cloud.

cissy = SISSY.

Cistercian /sɪsˈtɜːʃ(ə)n/ ● *noun* monk or nun of strict Benedictine order. ● *adjective* of the Cistercians.

cistern /ˈsɪst(ə)n/ *noun* tank for storing water; underground reservoir.

citadel /ˈsɪtəd(ə)l/ *noun* fortress protecting or dominating city.

citation /saɪˈteɪʃ(ə)n/ *noun* citing or passage cited; description of reasons for award.

cite *verb* (**-ting**) mention as example; quote (book etc.) in support; mention in military dispatches; summon to law court.

citizen /ˈsɪtɪz(ə)n/ *noun* native or national of state; inhabitant of a city.

□ **citizen's band** system of local intercommunication by radio. □ **citizenship** *noun*.

citrate /ˈsɪtreɪt/ *noun* salt of citric acid.

citric /ˈsɪtrɪk/ *adjective* □ **citric acid** sharp-tasting acid in citrus fruits.

citron /ˈsɪtrən/ *noun* tree bearing large lemon-like fruits; this fruit.

citronella /sɪtrəˈnelə/ *noun* a fragrant oil; grass from S. Asia yielding it.

citrus /ˈsɪtrəs/ *noun* (*plural* **-es**) tree of group including orange, lemon, and grapefruit; (in full **citrus fruit**) fruit of such tree.

city /ˈsɪtɪ/ *noun* (*plural* **-ies**) large town; town created city by charter and containing cathedral; (**the City**) part of London governed by Lord Mayor and Corporation, business quarter of this, commercial circles.

civet /ˈsɪvɪt/ *noun* (in full **civet cat**) catlike animal of Central Africa; strong musky perfume got from this.

civic /ˈsɪvɪk/ *adjective* of city or citizenship.

civics *plural noun* (usually treated as *singular*) study of civic rights and duties.

civil /ˈsɪv(ə)l/ *adjective* of or belonging to citizens; non-military; polite, obliging; *Law* concerning private rights and not criminal offences. □ **civil defence** organization for protecting civilians in wartime; **civil engineer** person who designs or maintains roads, bridges, etc.; **civil list** annual allowance by Parliament for royal family's household expenses; **civil marriage** one solemnized without religious ceremony; **civil servant** member of civil service; **civil service** all non-military and non-judicial branches of state administration; **civil war** one between citizens of same country.

civilian /sɪˈvɪlɪən/ ● *noun* person not in armed forces. ● *adjective* of or for civilians.

civility /sɪˈvɪlɪtɪ/ *noun* (*plural* **-ies**) politeness; act of politeness.

civilization *noun* (also **-sation**) advanced stage of social development; peoples regarded as having achieved, or been instrumental in evolving, this.

civilize /'sɪvɪlaɪz/ verb (also **-ise**) (**-zing** or **-sing**) bring out of barbarism; enlighten, refine.

cl abbreviation centilitre(s).

clack ● verb make sharp sound as of boards struck together. ● noun such sound.

clad adjective clothed; provided with cladding.

cladding noun protective covering or coating.

claim ● verb assert; demand as one's due; represent oneself as having; (+ to do) profess. ● noun demand; (+ to, on) right or title; assertion; thing claimed.

claimant noun person making claim, esp. in lawsuit or for state benefit.

clairvoyance /kleə'vɔɪəns/ noun supposed faculty of perceiving the future or the unseen. □ **clairvoyant** noun & adjective.

clam ● noun edible bivalve mollusc. ● verb (**-mm-**) (+ up) colloquial refuse to talk.

clamber /'klæmbə/ verb climb using hands or with difficulty.

clammy /'klæmɪ/ adjective (**-ier, -iest**) damp and sticky.

clamour /'klæmə/ (US **clamor**) ● noun shouting, confused noise; protest, demand. ● verb make clamour, shout. □ **clamorous** adjective.

clamp[1] ● noun device, esp. brace or band of iron etc., for strengthening or holding things together; device for immobilizing illegally parked vehicles. ● verb strengthen or fasten with clamp; immobilize with clamp. □ **clamp down** (usually + on) become stricter (about).

clamp[2] noun heap of earth and straw over harvested potatoes etc.

clan noun group of families with common ancestor, esp. in Scotland; family holding together; group with common interest. □ **clannish** adjective; **clansman, clanswoman** noun.

clandestine /klæn'destɪn/ adjective surreptitious, secret.

clang ● noun loud resonant metallic sound. ● verb (cause) to make clang.

clangour /'klæŋgə/ noun (US **clangor**) continued clanging. □ **clangorous** adjective.

clank ● noun sound as of metal on metal. ● verb (cause) make clank.

clap ● verb (**-pp-**) strike palms of hands together, esp. as applause; put or place quickly or with determination; (+ on) give friendly slap on. ● noun act of clapping; explosive noise, esp. of thunder; slap. □ **clap eyes on** colloquial see.

clapper noun tongue or striker of bell. □ **clapperboard** device in film-making for making sharp noise to synchronize picture and sound.

claptrap noun insincere or pretentious talk; nonsense.

claque /klæk/ noun people hired to applaud.

claret /'klærət/ noun red Bordeaux wine.

clarify /'klærɪfaɪ/ verb (**-ies, -ied**) make or become clear; free from impurities; make transparent. □ **clarification** noun.

clarinet /klærɪ'net/ noun woodwind instrument with single reed. □ **clarinettist** noun.

clarion /'klærɪən/ noun rousing sound; historical war-trumpet.

clarity /'klærɪtɪ/ noun clearness.

clash ● noun loud jarring sound as of metal objects struck together; collision; conflict; discord of colours etc. ● verb (cause) to make clash; coincide awkwardly; (often + with) be discordant or at variance.

clasp /klɑːsp/ ● noun device with interlocking parts for fastening; embrace, handshake; bar on medal-ribbon. ● verb fasten (as) with clasp; grasp, embrace. □ **clasp-knife** large folding knife.

class /klɑːs/ ● noun any set of people or things grouped together or differentiated from others; division or order of society; colloquial high quality; set of students taught together; their time of meeting; their course of instruction. ● verb place in a class. □ **classmate** person in same class at school; **classroom** room where class of students is taught. □ **classless** adjective.

classic /'klæsɪk/ ● adjective first-class; of lasting importance; typical; of ancient Greek or Latin culture etc.; (of style) simple and harmonious; famous because long-established. ● noun classic writer, artist, work, or example; (in plural) study of ancient Greek and Latin.

classical *adjective* of ancient Greek or Latin literature etc.; (of language) having form used by standard authors; (of music) serious or conventional.

classicism /'klæsɪsɪz(ə)m/ *noun* following of classic style; classical scholarship. □ **classicist** *noun.*

classify /'klæsɪfaɪ/ *verb* (**-ies, -ied**) arrange in classes; class; designate as officially secret. □ **classification** *noun.*

classy /'klɑːsɪ/ *adjective* (**-ier, -iest**) *colloquial* superior. □ **classiness** *noun.*

clatter /'klætə/ ● *noun* sound as of hard objects struck together. ● *verb* (cause to) make clatter.

clause /klɔːz/ *noun* group of words including finite verb (see panel); single statement in treaty, law, contract, etc.

claustrophobia /klɔːstrə'fəʊbɪə/ *noun* abnormal fear of confined places. □ **claustrophobic** *adjective.*

clavichord /'klævɪkɔːd/ *noun* small keyboard instrument with very soft tone.

clavicle /'klævɪk(ə)l/ *noun* collar-bone.

claw ● *noun* pointed nail on animal's foot; foot armed with claws; pincers of shellfish; device for grappling, holding, etc. ● *verb* scratch, maul, or pull with claws or fingernails.

clay *noun* stiff sticky earth, used for bricks, pottery, etc. □ **clay pigeon** breakable disc thrown into air as target for shooting. □ **clayey** *adjective.*

claymore /'kleɪmɔː/ *noun historical* Scottish two-edged broad-bladed sword.

clean ● *adjective* free from dirt; clear; pristine; not obscene or indecent; attentive to cleanliness; clear-cut; without record of crime etc.; fair. ● *adverb* completely; simply; in a clean way.

● *verb* make or become clean. ● *noun* process of cleaning. □ **clean-cut** sharply outlined, (of person) clean and tidy; **clean out** clean thoroughly, *slang* empty or deprive (esp. of money); **clean-shaven** without beard or moustache; **clean up** make tidy or clean, *slang* acquire as or make profit. □ **cleaner** *noun*; **cleanness** *noun.*

cleanly[1] *adverb* in a clean way.

cleanly[2] /'klenlɪ/ *adjective* (**-ier, -iest**) habitually clean; attentive to cleanliness and hygiene. □ **cleanliness** *noun.*

cleanse /klenz/ *verb* (**-sing**) make clean or pure. □ **cleanser** *noun.*

clear ● *adjective* free from dirt or contamination; not clouded; transparent; readily perceived or understood; able to discern readily; convinced; (of conscience) guiltless; unobstructed; net; complete; (often + *of*) free, unhampered. ● *adverb* clearly; completely; apart. ● *verb* make or become clear; (often + *of*) free from obstruction etc.; (often + *of*) show (person) to be innocent; approve (person etc.) for special duty, access, etc.; pass through (customs); pass over or by without touching; make (sum) as net gain; pass (cheque) through clearing house. □ **clear-cut** sharply defined; **clear off** *colloquial* go away; **clear out** empty, remove, *colloquial* go away; **clear-out** tidying by emptying and sorting; **clear up** tidy, solve; **clearway** road where vehicles may not stop. □ **clearly** *adverb*; **clearness** *noun.*

clearance *noun* removal of obstructions etc.; space allowed for passing of two objects; special authorization; clearing for special duty, of cheque, etc.; clearing out.

Clause

A clause is a group of words that includes a finite verb. If it makes complete sense by itself, it is known as a main clause, e.g.

The sun came out.

Otherwise, although it makes some sense, it must be attached to a main clause; this is known as a subordinate clause, e.g.

when the sun came out
(as in *When the sun came out, we went outside.*)

clearing *noun* treeless area in forest. □ **clearing bank** member of clearing house; **clearing house** bankers' institution where cheques etc. are exchanged, agency for collecting and distributing information etc.

cleat *noun* device for fastening ropes to projection on gangway, sole, etc. to provide grip.

cleavage *noun* hollow between woman's breasts; division; line along which rocks etc. split.

cleave[1] *verb* (**-ving**; *past* **clove** /kləʊv/, **cleft**, or **cleaved**; *past participle* **cloven**, **cleft**, or **cleaved**) *literary* break or come apart; make one's way through.

cleave[2] *verb* (**-ving**) (+ *to*) *literary* adhere.

cleaver *noun* butcher's heavy chopping tool.

clef *noun Music* symbol at start of staff showing pitch of notes on it.

cleft[1] *adjective* split, partly divided. □ **cleft palate** congenital split in roof of mouth.

cleft[2] *noun* split, fissure.

clematis /ˈklemətɪs/ *noun* climbing flowering plant.

clement /ˈklemənt/ *adjective* mild; merciful. □ **clemency** *noun.*

clementine /ˈklemənti:n/ *noun* small tangerine-like fruit.

clench ● *verb* close tightly; grasp firmly. ● *noun* clenching action; clenched state.

clergy /ˈklɜ:dʒɪ/ *noun* (*plural* **-ies**) (usually treated as *plural*) those ordained for religious duties.

clergyman /ˈklɜ:dʒɪmən/ *noun* member of clergy.

cleric /ˈklerɪk/ *noun* member of clergy.

clerical *adjective* of clergy or clergymen; of or done by clerks.

clerihew /ˈklerɪhju:/ *noun* witty or comic 4-line biographical verse.

clerk /klɑ:k/ ● *noun* person employed to keep records, accounts, etc.; secretary or agent of local council, court, etc.; lay officer of church. ● *verb* work as clerk.

clever /ˈklevə/ *adjective* (**-er**, **-est**) skilful, talented, quick to understand and learn; adroit; ingenious. □ **cleverly** *adverb;* **cleverness** *noun.*

cliché /ˈkli:ʃeɪ/ *noun* hackneyed phrase or opinion.

clichéd *adjective* hackneyed, full of clichés.

click ● *noun* slight sharp sound. ● *verb* (cause to) make click; *colloquial* become clear, understood, or popular; (+ *with*) become friendly with.

client /ˈklaɪənt/ *noun* person using services of lawyer or other professional person; customer.

clientele /kli:ɒnˈtel/ *noun* clients collectively; customers.

cliff *noun* steep rock face, esp. on coast. □ **cliff-hanger** story etc. with strong element of suspense.

climacteric /klaɪˈmæktərɪk/ *noun* period of life when fertility and sexual activity are in decline.

climate /ˈklaɪmɪt/ *noun* prevailing weather conditions of an area; region with particular weather conditions; prevailing trend of opinion etc. □ **climatic** /-ˈmæt-/ *adjective;* **climatically** /-ˈmæt-/ *adverb.*

climax /ˈklaɪmæks/ ● *noun* event or point of greatest intensity or interest, culmination. ● *verb colloquial* reach or bring to a climax. □ **climactic** *adjective.*

climb /klaɪm/ ● *verb* (often + *up*) ascend, mount, go up; (of plant) grow up wall etc. by clinging etc.; rise, esp. in social rank. ● *noun* action of climbing; hill etc. (to be) climbed. □ **climber** *noun.*

clime *noun literary* region; climate.

clinch ● *verb* confirm or settle conclusively; (of boxers) become too closely engaged; secure (nail or rivet) by driving point sideways when through. ● *noun* clinching, resulting state; *colloquial* embrace.

cling *verb* (*past & past participle* **clung**) (often + *to*) adhere; (+ *to*) be emotionally dependent on or unwilling to give up; (often + *to*) maintain grasp. □ **cling film** thin transparent plastic covering for food. □ **clingy** *adjective* (**-ier**, **-iest**).

clinic /ˈklɪnɪk/ *noun* private or specialized hospital; place or occasion for giving medical treatment or specialist advice; teaching of medicine at hospital bedside.

clinical *adjective* of or for the treatment of patients; objective, coldly detached;

(of room etc.) bare, functional.
□ **clinically** *adverb*.

clink[1] • *noun* sharp ringing sound. • *verb* (cause to) make clink.

clink[2] *noun slang* prison.

clinker /'klɪŋkə/ *noun* mass of slag or lava; stony residue from burnt coal.

clinker-built *adjective* (of boat) with external planks overlapping downwards.

clip[1] • *noun* device for holding things together; piece of jewellery fastened by clip; set of attached cartridges for firearm. • *verb* (-**pp**-) fix with clip. □ **clipboard** board with spring clip for holding papers etc.

clip[2] • *verb* (-**pp**-) cut with shears or scissors; cut hair or wool of; *colloquial* hit sharply; omit (letter) from word; omit parts of (words uttered); punch hole in (ticket) to show it has been used; cut from newspaper etc. • *noun* clipping; *colloquial* sharp blow; extract from motion picture; yield of wool.

clipper *noun* (usually in *plural*) instrument for clipping; *historical* fast sailing ship.

clipping *noun* piece clipped, esp. from newspaper.

clique /kliːk/ *noun* exclusive group of people. □ **cliquey** *adjective* (**cliquier**, **cliquiest**); **cliquish** *adjective*.

clitoris /'klɪtərɪs/ *noun* small erectile part of female genitals.

Cllr. *abbreviation* Councillor.

cloak • *noun* loose usually sleeveless outdoor garment; covering. • *verb* cover with cloak; conceal, disguise. □ **cloakroom** room for outdoor clothes or luggage, *euphemistic* lavatory.

clobber[1] /'klɒbə/ *verb slang* hit (repeatedly); defeat; criticize severely.

clobber[2] /'klɒbə/ *noun slang* clothing, belongings.

cloche /klɒʃ/ *noun* small translucent cover for outdoor plants; woman's close-fitting bell-shaped hat.

clock[1] • *noun* instrument measuring and showing time; measuring device resembling this; *colloquial* speedometer, taximeter, or stopwatch; seed-head of dandelion. • *verb colloquial* (often + *up*) attain or register (distance etc.); time (race etc.) by stopwatch. □ **clock in** (or

on), or **out** (or **off**) register time of arrival, or departure, by automatic clock; **clockwise** (moving) in same direction as hands of clock; **clockwork** mechanism with coiled springs etc. on clock principle; **like clockwork** with mechanical precision.

clock[2] *noun* ornamental pattern on side of stocking or sock.

clod *noun* lump of earth or clay.

clog • *noun* wooden-soled shoe. • *verb* (-**gg**-) (often + *up*) (cause to) become obstructed, choke; impede.

cloister /'klɔɪstə/ • *noun* covered walk esp. in college or ecclesiastical building; monastic life, seclusion. • *verb* seclude.

clone • *noun* group of organisms produced asexually from one ancestor; one such organism; *colloquial* person or thing regarded as identical to another. • *verb* (-**ning**) propagate as clone.

close[1] /kləʊs/ • *adjective* (often + *to*) at short distance or interval; having strong or immediate relation; (almost) in contact; dense, compact; nearly equal; rigorous; concentrated; stifling; shut; secret; niggardly. • *adverb* at short distance or interval. • *noun* street closed at one end; precinct of cathedral. □ **close harmony** singing of parts within an octave; **close-knit** tightly interlocked, closely united; **close season** season when killing of game etc. is illegal; **close shave** *colloquial* narrow escape; **close-up** photograph etc. taken at short range. □ **closely** *adverb*; **closeness** *noun*.

close[2] /kləʊz/ • *verb* (-**sing**) shut; block up; bring or come to an end; end day's business; bring or come closer or into contact; make (electric circuit) continuous. • *noun* conclusion, end. □ **closed-circuit** (of television) transmitted by wires to restricted number of receivers; **closed shop** business etc. where employees must belong to specified trade union.

closet /'klɒzɪt/ • *noun* small room; cupboard; water-closet. • *adjective* secret. • *verb* (-**t**-) shut away, esp. in private consultation etc.

closure /'kləʊʒə/ *noun* closing, closed state; procedure for ending debate.

clot ●*noun* thick lump formed from liquid, esp. blood; *colloquial* foolish person. ●*verb* (**-tt-**) form into clots.

cloth /klɒθ/ *noun* woven or felted material; piece of this; (**the cloth**) the clergy.

clothe /kləʊð/ *verb* (**-thing**; *past & past participle* **clothed** or **clad**) put clothes on; provide with clothes; cover as with clothes.

clothes /kləʊðz/ *plural noun* things worn to cover body and limbs; bedclothes. □ **clothes-horse** frame for airing washed clothes.

clothier /'kləʊðɪə/ *noun* dealer in men's clothes.

clothing /'kləʊðɪŋ/ *noun* clothes.

cloud /klaʊd/ *noun* visible mass of condensed watery vapour floating in air; mass of smoke or dust; (+ *of*) great number of (birds, insects, etc.) moving together; state of gloom, trouble, or suspicion. ●*verb* cover or darken with cloud(s); (often + *over*, *up*) become overcast or gloomy; make unclear. □ **cloudburst** sudden violent rainstorm. □ **cloudless** *adjective*.

cloudy *adjective* (**-ier**, **-iest**) covered with clouds; not transparent, unclear. □ **cloudiness** *noun*.

clout /klaʊt/ ●*noun* heavy blow; *colloquial* influence, power of effective action; piece of cloth or clothing. ●*verb* hit hard.

clove[1] /kləʊv/ *noun* dried bud of tropical tree, used as spice.

clove[2] /kləʊv/ *noun* segment of compound bulb, esp. of garlic.

clove[3] *past of* CLEAVE[1].

clove hitch *noun* knot for fastening rope round pole etc.

cloven /'kləʊv(ə)n/ *adjective* split. □ **cloven hoof, foot** divided hoof, as of oxen, sheep, etc., or the Devil.

clover /'kləʊvə/ *noun* kind of trefoil used as fodder. □ **in clover** in ease and luxury.

clown /klaʊn/ ●*noun* comic entertainer, esp. in circus; foolish or playful person. ●*verb* (often + *about*, *around*) behave like clown.

cloy *verb* satiate or sicken by sweetness, richness, etc.

club ●*noun* heavy stick used as weapon; stick with head, used in golf; association of people for social, sporting, etc.

purposes; premises of this; playing card of suit marked with black trefoils; (in *plural*) this suit. ●*verb* (**-bb-**) strike (as) with club; (+ *together*) combine, esp. to make up sum of money. □ **club foot** congenitally deformed foot; **clubhouse** premises of club; **clubland** area with many nightclubs; **clubroot** disease of cabbages etc.; **club sandwich** sandwich with 2 layers of filling and 3 slices of bread or toast.

cluck ●*noun* chattering cry of hen. ●*verb* emit cluck(s).

clue ●*noun* guiding or suggestive fact; piece of evidence used in detection of crime; word(s) used to indicate word(s) for insertion in crossword. ●*verb* (**clues, clued, cluing** or **clueing**) provide clue to. □ **clue in, up** *slang* inform.

clump ●*noun* (+ *of*) cluster, esp. of trees. ●*verb* form clump; heap or plant together; tread heavily.

clumsy /'klʌmzɪ/ *adjective* (**-ier**, **-iest**) awkward in movement or shape; difficult to handle or use; tactless. □ **clumsily** *adverb*; **clumsiness** *noun*.

clung *past & past participle of* CLING.

cluster /'klʌstə/ ●*noun* close group or bunch of similar people or things. ●*verb* be in or form into cluster(s); (+ *round*, *around*) gather round.

clutch[1] ●*verb* seize eagerly; grasp tightly; (+ *at*) snatch at. ●*noun* tight or (in *plural*) cruel grasp; (in vehicle) device for connecting engine to transmission, pedal operating this. □ **clutch bag** handbag without handles.

clutch[2] *noun* set of eggs; brood of chickens.

clutter /'klʌtə/ ●*noun* crowded untidy collection of things. ●*verb* (often + *up*, *with*) crowd untidily, fill with clutter.

cm *abbreviation* centimetre(s).

Cmdr. *abbreviation* Commander.

CND *abbreviation* Campaign for Nuclear Disarmament.

CO *abbreviation* Commanding Officer.

Co. *abbreviation* company; county.

c/o *abbreviation* care of.

coach ●*noun* single-decker bus usually for longer journeys; railway carriage; closed horse-drawn carriage; sports trainer or private tutor. ●*verb* train or teach. □ **coachload** group of tourists etc. travelling by coach; **coachman** driver of horse-drawn carriage; **coachwork** bodywork of road or rail vehicle.

coagulate /kəʊˈægjʊleɪt/ verb (**-ting**) change from liquid to semi-solid; clot, curdle. □ **coagulant** noun; **coagulation** noun.

coal noun hard black mineral used as fuel etc.; piece of this. □ **coalface** exposed surface of coal in mine; **coalfield** area yielding coal; **coal gas** mixed gases formerly extracted from coal and used for heating, cooking, etc.; **coal mine** place where coal is dug; **coal miner** worker in coal mine; **coal scuttle** container for coal for domestic fire; **coal tar** tar extracted from coal; **coal tit** small bird with greyish plumage.

coalesce /kəʊəˈles/ verb (**-cing**) come together and form a whole. □ **coalescence** noun; **coalescent** adjective.

coalition /kəʊəˈlɪʃ(ə)n/ noun temporary alliance, esp. of political parties; fusion into one whole.

coaming /ˈkəʊmɪŋ/ noun raised border round ship's hatches etc.

coarse /kɔːs/ adjective rough or loose in texture; of large particles; lacking refinement; crude, obscene. □ **coarse fish** freshwater fish other than salmon and trout. □ **coarsely** adverb; **coarsen** verb; **coarseness** noun.

coast ● noun border of land near sea; seashore. ● verb ride or move (usually downhill) without use of power; make progress without exertion; sail along coast. □ **coastguard** (member of) group of people employed to keep watch on coasts, prevent smuggling, etc.; **coastline** line of seashore, esp. with regard to its shape. □ **coastal** adjective.

coaster noun ship that sails along coast; tray ● mat for bottle or glass.

coat ● noun sleeved outer garment, overcoat, jacket; animal's fur or hair; layer of paint etc. ● verb (usually + with, in) cover with coat or layer; form covering on. □ **coat of arms** heraldic bearings or shield; **coat-hanger** shaped piece of wood etc. for hanging clothes on.

coating noun layer of paint etc.; cloth for coats.

coax verb persuade gradually or by flattery; (+ out of) obtain (thing) from (person) thus; manipulate gently.

coaxial /kəʊˈæksɪəl/ adjective having common axis; (of electric cable etc.) transmitting by means of two concentric conductors separated by insulator.

cob noun roundish lump; domed loaf; corn cob; large hazelnut; sturdy short-legged riding-horse; male swan.

cobalt /ˈkəʊbɔːlt/ noun silvery-white metallic element; (colour of) deep blue pigment made from it.

cobber /ˈkɒbə/ noun Australian & NZ colloquial companion, friend.

cobble[1] /ˈkɒb(ə)l/ ● noun (in full **cobblestone**) rounded stone used for paving. ● verb (**-ling**) pave with cobbles.

cobble[2] /ˈkɒb(ə)l/ verb (**-ling**) mend or patch (esp. shoes); (often + together) assemble roughly.

cobbler noun mender of shoes; (in plural) slang nonsense.

COBOL /ˈkəʊbɒl/ noun computer language for use in business operations.

cobra /ˈkəʊbrə/ noun venomous hooded snake.

cobweb /ˈkɒbweb/ noun spider's network or thread. □ **cobwebby** adjective.

coca /ˈkəʊkə/ noun S. American shrub; its leaves chewed as stimulant.

cocaine /kəʊˈkeɪn/ noun drug from coca, used as local anaesthetic and as stimulant.

coccyx /ˈkɒksɪks/ noun (plural **coccyges** /-dʒiːz/) bone at base of spinal column.

cochineal /kɒtʃɪˈniːl/ noun scarlet dye; insects whose dried bodies yield this.

cock[1] ● noun male bird, esp. domestic fowl; slang (as form of address) friend, fellow; slang nonsense; firing lever in gun released by trigger; tap or valve controlling flow. ● verb raise or make upright; turn or move (eye or ear) attentively or knowingly; set (hat etc.) aslant; raise cock of (gun). □ **cock-a-hoop** exultant; **cock-a-leekie** Scottish soup of boiled fowl with leeks; **cockcrow** dawn; **cock-eyed** colloquial crooked, askew, absurd.

cock[2] noun conical heap of hay or straw.

cockade /kɒˈkeɪd/ noun rosette etc. worn in hat.

cockatoo /kɒkəˈtuː/ *noun* crested parrot.

cockchafer /ˈkɒktʃeɪfə/ *noun* large pale brown beetle.

cocker /ˈkɒkə/ *noun* (in full **cocker spaniel**) small spaniel.

cockerel /ˈkɒkər(ə)l/ *noun* young cock.

cockle /ˈkɒk(ə)l/ *noun* edible bivalve shellfish; its shell; (in full **cockleshell**) small shallow boat; pucker or wrinkle. □ **cockles of the heart** innermost feelings.

cockney /ˈkɒknɪ/ ● *noun* (*plural* -**s**) native of London, esp. East End; cockney dialect. ● *adjective* of cockneys.

cockpit *noun* place for pilot etc. in aircraft or spacecraft or for driver in racing car; arena of war etc.

cockroach /ˈkɒkrəʊtʃ/ *noun* dark brown insect infesting esp. kitchens.

cockscomb /ˈkɒkskəʊm/ *noun* cock's crest.

cocksure /kɒkˈʃɔː/ *adjective* arrogantly confident.

cocktail /ˈkɒkteɪl/ *noun* drink of spirits, fruit juices, etc.; appetizer containing shellfish etc.; any hybrid mixture. □ **cocktail stick** small pointed stick.

cocky *adjective* (-**ier**, -**iest**) *colloquial* conceited, arrogant. □ **cockiness** *noun*.

coco /ˈkəʊkəʊ/ *noun* (*plural* -**s**) coconut palm.

cocoa /ˈkəʊkəʊ/ *noun* powder of crushed cacao seeds; drink made from this.

coconut /ˈkəʊkənʌt/ *noun* large brown seed of coco, with edible white lining enclosing milky juice. □ **coconut matting** matting made from fibre of coconut husks; **coconut shy** fairground sideshow where balls are thrown to dislodge coconuts.

cocoon /kəˈkuːn/ ● *noun* silky case spun by larva to protect it as pupa; protective covering. ● *verb* wrap (as) in cocoon.

cocotte /kəˈkɒt/ *noun* small fireproof dish for cooking and serving food.

COD *abbreviation* cash (*US* collect) on delivery.

cod[1] *noun* (also **codfish**) (*plural* same) large sea fish. □ **cod liver oil** medicinal oil rich in vitamins.

cod[2] *noun* & *verb* (-**dd**-) *slang* hoax, parody.

coda /ˈkəʊdə/ *noun* final passage of piece of music.

coddle /ˈkɒd(ə)l/ *verb* (-**ling**) treat as an invalid, pamper; cook in water just below boiling point. □ **coddler** *noun*.

code ● *noun* system of signals or of symbols etc. used for secrecy, brevity, or computer processing of information; systematic set of laws etc.; standard of moral behaviour. ● *verb* (-**ding**) put into code.

codeine /ˈkəʊdiːn/ *noun* alkaloid derived from morphine, used as pain-killer.

codex /ˈkəʊdeks/ *noun* (*plural* **codices** /ˈkəʊdɪsiːz/) manuscript volume esp. of ancient texts.

codger /ˈkɒdʒə/ *noun* (usually in **old codger**) *colloquial* (strange) person.

codicil /ˈkəʊdɪsɪl/ *noun* addition to will.

codify /ˈkəʊdɪfaɪ/ *verb* (-**ies**, -**ied**) arrange (laws etc.) into code. □ **codification** *noun*.

codling[1] /ˈkɒdlɪŋ/ *noun* (also **codlin**) variety of apple; moth whose larva feeds on apples.

codling[2] *noun* (*plural* same) small cod.

co-education /kəʊedjuːˈkeɪʃ(ə)n/ *noun* education of both sexes together. □ **co-educational** *adjective*.

coefficient /kəʊɪˈfɪʃ(ə)nt/ *noun Mathematics* quantity or expression placed before and multiplying another; *Physics* multiplier or factor by which a property is measured.

coeliac disease /ˈsiːlɪæk/ *noun* intestinal disease whose symptoms include adverse reaction to gluten.

coequal /kəʊˈiːkw(ə)l/ *adjective* & *noun* equal.

coerce /kəʊˈɜːs/ *verb* (-**cing**) persuade or restrain by force. □ **coercion** /-ˈɜːʃ(ə)n/ *noun*; **coercive** *adjective*.

coeval /kəʊˈiːv(ə)l/ *formal* ● *adjective* of the same age; contemporary. ● *noun* coeval person or thing.

coexist /kəʊɪɡˈzɪst/ *verb* (often + *with*) exist together, esp. in mutual tolerance. □ **coexistence** *noun*; **coexistent** *adjective*.

coextensive /kəʊɪkˈstensɪv/ *adjective* extending over same space or time.

C. of E. *abbreviation* Church of England.

coffee /'kɒfɪ/ noun drink made from roasted and ground seeds of tropical shrub; cup of this; the shrub; the seeds; pale brown. □ **coffee bar** café selling coffee and light refreshments from bar; **coffee bean** seed of coffee; **coffee mill** small machine for grinding coffee beans; **coffee morning** morning gathering, esp. for charity, at which coffee is served; **coffee shop** small restaurant, esp. in hotel or store; **coffee table** small low table; **coffee-table book** large illustrated book.

coffer /'kɒfə/ noun large box for valuables; (in plural) funds, treasury; sunken panel in ceiling etc.

coffin /'kɒfɪn/ noun box in which corpse is buried or cremated.

cog noun each of series of projections on wheel etc. transferring motion by engaging with another series.

cogent /'kəʊdʒ(ə)nt/ adjective (of argument etc.) convincing, compelling. □ **cogency** noun; **cogently** adverb.

cogitate /'kɒdʒɪteɪt/ verb (-ting) ponder, meditate. □ **cogitation** noun.

cognac /'kɒnjæk/ noun French brandy.

cognate /'kɒɡneɪt/ • adjective descended from same ancestor or root. • noun cognate person or word.

cognition /kɒɡ'nɪʃ(ə)n/ noun knowing, perceiving, or conceiving, as distinct from emotion and volition. □ **cognitive** /'kɒɡ-/ adjective.

cognizance /'kɒɡnɪz(ə)ns/ noun formal knowledge or awareness.

cognizant /'kɒɡnɪz(ə)nt/ adjective formal (+ of) having knowledge or being aware of.

cognomen /kɒɡ'nəʊmen/ noun nickname; Roman History surname.

cohabit /kəʊ'hæbɪt/ verb (-t-) live together as husband and wife. □ **cohabitation** noun.

cohere /kəʊ'hɪə/ verb (-ring) stick together; (of reasoning) be logical or consistent.

coherent adjective intelligible; consistent, easily understood. □ **coherence** noun; **coherently** adverb.

cohesion /kəʊ'hi:ʒ(ə)n/ noun sticking together; tendency to cohere. □ **cohesive** /-sɪv/ adjective.

cohort /'kəʊhɔ:t/ noun one-tenth of Roman legion; people banded together.

coif /kɔɪf/ noun historical close-fitting cap.

coiffeur /kwa:'fɜ:/ noun (feminine **coiffeuse** /-'fɜ:z/) hairdresser.

coiffure /kwa:'fjʊə/ noun hairstyle.

coil • verb arrange or be arranged in concentric rings; move sinuously. • noun coiled arrangement (of rope, electrical conductor, etc.); single turn of something coiled; flexible contraceptive device in womb.

coin • noun stamped disc of metal as official money; metal money. • verb make (coins) by stamping; invent (word, phrase). □ **coin box** telephone operated by coins.

coinage noun coining; system of coins in use; invention of word, invented word.

coincide /kəʊɪn'saɪd/ verb (-ding) occur at same time; (often + with) agree or be identical.

coincidence /kəʊ'ɪnsɪd(ə)ns/ noun remarkable concurrence of events etc., apparently by chance. □ **coincident** adjective.

coincidental /kəʊɪnsɪ'dent(ə)l/ adjective in the nature of or resulting from coincidence. □ **coincidentally** adverb.

coir /'kɔɪə/ noun coconut fibre used for ropes, matting, etc.

coition /kəʊ'ɪʃ(ə)n/ noun coitus.

coitus /'kəʊɪtəs/ noun sexual intercourse. □ **coital** adjective.

coke¹ • noun solid left after gases have been extracted from coal. • verb (-king) convert (coal) into coke.

coke² noun slang cocaine.

Col. abbreviation Colonel.

col noun depression in summit-line of mountain chain.

cola /'kəʊlə/ noun W. African tree with seeds containing caffeine; carbonated drink flavoured with these.

colander /'kʌləndə/ noun perforated vessel used as strainer in cookery.

cold /kəʊld/ • adjective of or at low temperature; not heated; having lost heat; feeling cold; (of colour) suggesting cold; colloquial unconscious; lacking ardour or friendliness; dispiriting; (of hunting-scent) grown faint. ● *noun* prevalence of low temperature; cold weather; infection of nose or throat. ● *adverb* unrehearsed. □ **cold-blooded** having body temperature varying with that of environment, callous; **cold call** marketing call on person not previously interested in product; **cold cream** cleansing ointment; **cold feet** fear, reluctance; **cold fusion** nuclear fusion at room temperature; **cold shoulder** unfriendly treatment; **cold turkey** *slang* abrupt withdrawal from addictive drugs; **cold war** hostility between nations without actual fighting; **in cold blood** without emotion; **throw cold water on** discourage. □ **coldly** *adverb*; **coldness** *noun*.

coleslaw /'kəʊlslɔ:/ *noun* salad of sliced raw cabbage etc.

coley /'kəʊlɪ/ *noun* (*plural* **-s**) any of several edible fish, esp. rock-salmon.

colic /'kɒlɪk/ *noun* spasmodic abdominal pain. □ **colicky** *adjective*.

colitis /kə'laɪtɪs/ *noun* inflammation of colon.

collaborate /kə'læbəreɪt/ *verb* (**-ting**) (often + *with*) work jointly. □ **collaboration** *noun*; **collaborative** /-rətɪv/ *adjective*; **collaborator** *noun*.

collage /'kɒlɑ:ʒ/ *noun* picture made by gluing pieces of paper etc. on to backing.

collapse /kə'læps/ ● *noun* falling down of structure; sudden failure of plan etc.; physical or mental breakdown. ● *verb* (**-sing**) (cause to) undergo collapse; *colloquial* relax completely after effort. □ **collapsible** *adjective*.

collar /'kɒlə/ ● *noun* neckband, upright or turned over, of coat, shirt, dress, etc.; leather band round animal's neck; band, ring, or pipe in machinery. ● *verb* capture, seize, appropriate; *colloquial* accost. □ **collar-bone** bone joining breastbone and shoulder blade.

collate /kə'leɪt/ *verb* (**-ting**) collect and put in order. □ **collator** *noun*.

collateral /kə'lætər(ə)l/ ● *noun* security pledged as guarantee for repayment of loan. ● *adjective* side by side; additional but subordinate; descended from same ancestor but by different line. □ **collaterally** *adverb*.

collation *noun* collating; light meal.

colleague /'kɒli:g/ *noun* fellow worker, esp. in profession or business.

collect[1] /kə'lekt/ ● *verb* bring or come together; assemble, accumulate; seek and acquire (books, stamps, etc.); obtain (contributions, taxes, etc.) from people; call for, fetch; concentrate (one's thoughts etc.); (as **collected** *adjective*) not perturbed or distracted. ● *adjective & adverb US* (of telephone call, parcel, etc.) to be paid for by recipient.

collect[2] /'kɒlekt/ *noun* short prayer of Anglican or RC Church.

collectable /kə'lektɪb(ə)l/ *adjective* worth collecting.

collection /kə'lekʃ(ə)n/ *noun* collecting, being collected; things collected; money collected, esp. at church service etc.

collective /kə'lektɪv/ ● *adjective* of or relating to group or society as a whole; joint; shared. ● *noun* cooperative enterprise; its members. □ **collective bargaining** negotiation of wages etc. by organized group of employees; **collective noun** singular noun denoting group of individuals. □ **collectively** *adverb*; **collectivize** *verb* (also **-ise**) (**-zing** or **-sing**).

collectivism *noun* theory or practice of collective ownership of land and means of production. □ **collectivist** *noun & adjective*.

collector *noun* person collecting things of interest; person collecting taxes, rents, etc.

colleen /'kɒli:n/ *noun Irish* girl.

college /'kɒlɪdʒ/ *noun* establishment for further, higher, or professional education; teachers and students in a college; school; organized group of people with shared functions and privileges.

collegiate /kə'li:dʒɪət/ *adjective* of or constituted as college, corporate; (of university) consisting of different colleges.

collide /kə'laɪd/ *verb* (**-ding**) (often + *with*) come into collision or conflict.

collie /'kɒlɪ/ *noun* sheepdog originally of Scottish breed.

collier /'kɒlɪə/ *noun* coal miner; coal ship, member of its crew.

colliery /'kɒlɪərɪ/ *noun* (*plural* **-ies**) coal mine and its buildings.

collision /kəˈlɪʒ(ə)n/ *noun* violent impact of moving body against another or fixed object; clashing of interests etc.

collocate /ˈkɒləkeɪt/ *verb* (**-ting**) place (word etc.) next to another. □ **collocation** *noun*.

colloid /ˈkɒlɔɪd/ *noun* substance consisting of minute particles; mixture, esp. viscous solution, of this and another substance. □ **colloidal** *adjective*.

colloquial /kəˈləʊkwɪəl/ *adjective* of ordinary or familiar conversation, informal. □ **colloquially** *adverb*.

colloquialism /kəˈləʊkwɪəlɪz(ə)m/ *noun* colloquial word or phrase.

colloquy /ˈkɒləkwɪ/ *noun* (*plural* **-quies**) literary talk, dialogue.

collude /kəˈluːd/ *verb* (**-ding**) conspire. □ **collusion** /-ʒ(ə)n/ *noun*; **collusive** /-sɪv/ *adjective*.

collywobbles /ˈkɒlɪwɒb(ə)lz/ *plural noun colloquial* ache or rumbling in stomach; apprehensive feeling.

cologne /kəˈləʊn/ *noun* eau-de-Cologne or similar toilet water.

colon¹ /ˈkəʊlən/ *noun* punctuation mark (:) used between main clauses or before list or quotation (see panel).

colon² /ˈkəʊlən/ *noun* lower and greater part of large intestine.

colonel /ˈkɜːn(ə)l/ *noun* army officer commanding regiment, next in rank below brigadier. □ **colonelcy** *noun* (*plural* **-ies**).

colonial /kəˈləʊnɪəl/ ● *adjective* of a colony or colonies; of colonialism. ● *noun* inhabitant of colony.

colonialism *noun* policy of having colonies.

colonist /ˈkɒlənɪst/ *noun* settler in or inhabitant of colony.

colonize /ˈkɒlənaɪz/ *verb* (also **-ise**) (**-zing** or **-sing**) establish colony in; join colony. □ **colonization** *noun*.

colonnade /kɒləˈneɪd/ *noun* row of columns, esp. supporting roof. □ **colonnaded** *adjective*.

colony /ˈkɒlənɪ/ *noun* (*plural* **-ies**) settlement or settlers in new territory remaining subject to mother country; people of one nationality, occupation, etc. forming community in town etc.; group of animals that live close together.

colophon /ˈkɒləf(ə)n/ *noun* tailpiece in book.

color etc. *US* = COLOUR etc.

Colorado beetle /kɒləˈrɑːdəʊ/ *noun* small beetle destructive to potato.

coloration /kʌləˈreɪʃ(ə)n/ *noun* (also **colouration**) colouring, arrangement of colours.

coloratura /kɒlərəˈtʊərə/ *noun* elaborate passages in vocal music; singer of these, esp. soprano.

colossal /kəˈlɒs(ə)l/ *adjective* huge; *colloquial* splendid. □ **colossally** *adverb*.

colossus /kəˈlɒsəs/ *noun* (*plural* **-ssi** /-saɪ/ or **-ssuses**) statue much bigger than life size; gigantic or remarkable person etc.

colour /ˈkʌlə/ (*US* **color**) ● *noun* one, or any mixture, of the constituents into

---

Colon :

This is used:

1 between two main clauses of which the second explains, enlarges on, or follows from the first, e.g.

   It was not easy: to begin with I had to find the right house.

2 to introduce a list of items (a dash should not be added), and after expressions such as *namely, for example, to resume, to sum up,* and *the following,* e.g.

   You will need: a tent, a sleeping bag, cooking equipment, and a rucksack.

3 before a quotation, e.g.

   The poem begins: 'Earth has not anything to show more fair'.

which light is separated in rainbow
etc.; use of all colours as in photography; colouring substance, esp.
paint; skin pigmentation, esp. when
dark; ruddiness of face; appearance or
aspect; (in *plural*) flag of regiment or
ship etc.; coloured ribbon, rosette, etc.
worn as symbol of school, club, political party, etc. ● *verb* give colour to;
paint, stain, dye; blush; influence.
□ **colour-blind** unable to distinguish
certain colours; **colour-blindness**
noun; **colour scheme** arrangement of
colours; **colour supplement** magazine
with colour printing, sold with
newspaper.

coloured (*US* **colored**) ● *adjective* having
colour; wholly or partly of non-white
descent; *South African* of mixed white and
non-white descent. ● *noun* coloured
person.

colourful *adjective* (*US* **colorful**) full of
colour or interest. □ **colourfully** *adverb*.

colouring *noun* (*US* **coloring**) appearance as regards colour, esp. facial complexion; application of colour; substance giving colour.

colourless *adjective* (*US* **colorless**) without colour, lacking interest.

colt /kəʊlt/ *noun* young male horse; *Sport*
inexperienced player.

colter *US* = COULTER.

coltsfoot *noun* (*plural* **-s**) yellow wild
flower with large leaves.

columbine /ˈkɒləmbaɪn/ *noun* garden
plant with purple-blue flowers.

column /ˈkɒləm/ *noun* pillar, usually
round, with base and capital; column-
shaped thing; series of numbers, one
under the other; vertical division of
printed page; part of newspaper regularly devoted to particular subject or
written by one writer; long, narrow
arrangement of advancing troops, vehicles, etc.

columnist /ˈkɒləmnɪst/ *noun* journalist
contributing regularly to newspaper
etc.

coma /ˈkəʊmə/ *noun* (*plural* **-s**) prolonged
deep unconsciousness.

comatose /ˈkəʊmətəʊs/ *adjective* in
coma; sleepy.

comb /kəʊm/ ● *noun* toothed strip of
rigid material for arranging hair; thing

like comb, esp. for dressing wool etc.;
red fleshy crest of fowl, esp. cock etc.;
honeycomb. ● *verb* draw comb through
(hair), dress (wool etc.) with comb;
colloquial search (place) thoroughly.

combat /ˈkɒmbæt/ ● *noun* struggle,
fight. ● *verb* (**-t-**) do battle (with); strive
against, oppose.

combatant /ˈkɒmbət(ə)nt/ ● *noun*
fighter. ● *adjective* fighting.

combative /ˈkɒmbətɪv/ *adjective* pugnacious.

combe = COOMB.

combination /kɒmbɪˈneɪʃ(ə)n/ *noun*
combining, being combined; combined
state; combined set of things or people;
motorcycle with side-car; sequence of
numbers etc. used to open **combination lock**.

combine ● *verb* /kəmˈbaɪn/ (**-ning**) join
together; unite; form into chemical
compound. ● *noun* /ˈkɒmbaɪn/ combination of esp. businesses. □ **combine
harvester** /ˈkɒmbaɪn/ combined reaping and threshing machine.

combustible /kəmˈbʌstɪb(ə)l/ ● *adjective*
capable of or used for burning. ● *noun*
combustible substance. □ **combust-
ibility** *noun*.

combustion /kəmˈbʌstʃ(ə)n/ *noun* burning; development of light and heat from
combination of substance with oxygen.

come /kʌm/ *verb* (**-ming**; *past* **came**; *past
participle* **come**) move or be brought
towards or reach a place, time, situation, or result; be available; occur;
become; traverse; *colloquial* behave like.
□ **come about** happen; **come across**
meet or find by chance, give specified
impression, *colloquial* be effective or
understood; **come again** *colloquial* what
did you say?; **come along** make progress, hurry up; **come apart** disintegrate; **come at** attack; **comeback**
return to success, *slang* retort or retaliation; **come back (to)** recur to memory
(of); **come by** obtain; **come clean**
colloquial confess; **comedown** loss of
status; **come down** lose position, be
handed down, be reduced; **come forward** offer oneself for task etc.; **come
in** become fashionable or seasonable,
prove to be; **come in for** receive; **come
into** inherit; **come off** succeed, occur,
fare; **come off it** *colloquial* expression of

disbelief; **come on** make progress; **come out** emerge, become known, be published, go on strike, (of photograph or its subject) be (re)produced clearly, (of stain) be removed; **come out with** declare, disclose; **come over** come some distance to visit, (of feeling) affect, appear or sound in specified way; **come round** pay informal visit, recover consciousness, be converted to another's opinion; **come through** survive; **come to** recover consciousness, amount to; **come up** arise, be mentioned or discussed, attain position; **come up with** produce (idea etc.); **come up against** be faced with; **come upon** meet or find by chance.

comedian /kə'miːdɪən/ *noun* humorous performer; actor in comedy; *slang* buffoon.

comedienne /kəmiːdɪ'en/ *noun* female comedian.

comedy /'kɒmədɪ/ *noun* (*plural* **-ies**) play or film of amusing character; humorous kind of drama etc.; humour; amusing aspects. □ **comedic** /kə'miːdɪk/ *adjective*.

comely /'kʌmlɪ/ *adjective* (**-ier**, **-iest**) *literary* handsome, good-looking. □ **comeliness** *noun*.

comestibles /kə'mestɪb(ə)lz/ *plural noun* *formal* things to eat.

comet /'kɒmɪt/ *noun* hazy object with 'tail' moving in path round sun.

comeuppance /kʌm'ʌpəns/ *noun* *colloquial* deserved punishment.

comfort /'kʌmfət/ ● *noun* physical or mental well-being; consolation; person or thing bringing consolation; (usually in *plural*) things that make life comfortable. ● *verb* console. □ **comfortless** *adjective*.

comfortable /'kʌmfətəb(ə)l/ *adjective* giving ease; at ease; having adequate standard of living; appreciable. □ **comfortably** *adverb*.

comforter /'kʌmfətə/ *noun* person who comforts; baby's dummy; *archaic* woollen scarf.

comfrey /'kʌmfrɪ/ *noun* tall plant with bell-like flowers.

comfy /'kʌmfɪ/ *adjective* (**-ier**, **-iest**) *colloquial* comfortable.

comic /'kɒmɪk/ ● *adjective* of or like comedy; funny. ● *noun* comedian; periodical in form of comic strips. □ **comic strip** sequence of drawings telling comic story. □ **comical** *adjective*; **comically** *adverb*.

comma /'kɒmə/ *noun* punctuation mark (,) indicating pause or break between parts of sentence (see panel).

command /kə'mɑːnd/ ● *verb* give formal order to; have authority or control over; have at one's disposal; deserve and get; look down over, dominate. ● *noun* order, instruction; holding of authority, esp. in armed forces; mastery; troops or district under commander. □ **command module** control compartment in spacecraft; **command performance** one given at royal request.

commandant /'kɒmændænt/ *noun* commanding officer, esp. of military academy.

commandeer /kɒmən'dɪə/ *verb* seize (esp. goods) for military use; take possession of without permission.

commander *noun* person who commands, esp. naval officer next below captain. □ **commander-in-chief** (*plural* **commanders-in-chief**) supreme commander, esp. of nation's forces.

commanding *adjective* impressive; giving wide view; substantial.

commandment *noun* divine command.

commando /kə'mɑːndəʊ/ *noun* (*plural* **-s**) unit of shock troops; member of this.

commemorate /kə'meməreɪt/ *verb* (**-ting**) preserve in memory by celebration or ceremony; be memorial of. □ **commemoration** *noun*; **commemorative** /-rətɪv/ *adjective*.

commence /kə'mens/ *verb* (**-cing**) *formal* begin. □ **commencement** *noun*.

commend /kə'mend/ *verb* praise; recommend; entrust. □ **commendation** /kɒm-/ *noun*.

commendable *adjective* praiseworthy. □ **commendably** *adverb*.

commensurable /kə'menʃərəb(ə)l/ *adjective* (often + *with*, *to*) measurable by same standard; (+ *to*) proportionate to. □ **commensurability** *noun*.

commensurate /kə'menʃərət/ *adjective* (usually + *with*) extending over same space or time; (often + *to*, *with*) proportionate.

··

Comma ,

The comma marks a slight break between words, phrases, etc. In particular, it is used:

1 to separate items in a list, e.g.

> *red, white, and blue* or *red, white and blue*
> *We bought some shoes, socks, gloves, and handkerchiefs.*
> *potatoes, peas, or carrots* or *potatoes, peas or carrots*

2 to separate adjectives that describe something in the same way, e.g.

> *It is a hot, dry, dusty place.*

but not if they describe it in different ways, e.g.

> *a distinguished foreign author*

or if one adjective adds to or alters the meaning of another, e.g.

> *a bright red tie.*

3 to separate main clauses, e.g.

> *Cars will park here, and coaches will turn left.*

4 to separate a name or word used to address someone, e.g.

> *David, I'm here.*
> *Well, Mr Jones, we meet again.*
> *Have you seen this, my friend?*

5 to separate a phrase, e.g.

> *Having had lunch, we went back to work.*

especially in order to clarify meaning, e.g.

> *In the valley below, the village looked very small.*

6 after words that introduce direct speech, or after direct speech where there is no question mark or exclamation mark, e.g.

> *They answered, 'Here we are.'*
> *'Here we are,' they answered.*

7 after *Dear Sir, Dear Sarah,* etc., and *Yours faithfully, Yours sincerely,* etc. in letters.

8 to separate a word, phrase, or clause that is secondary or adds information or a comment, e.g.

> *I am sure, however, that it will not happen.*
> *Fred, who is bald, complained of the cold.*

but not with a relative clause (one usually beginning with *who, which,* or *that*) that restricts the meaning of the noun it follows, e.g.

> *Men who are bald should wear hats.*

No comma is needed between a month and a year in dates, e.g.

> *in December 1993*

or between a number and a road in addresses, e.g.

> *17 Devonshire Avenue*

··

comment /'kɒment/ ● *noun* brief critical or explanatory note or remark; opinion; commenting. ● *verb* (often + *on, that*) make comment(s). □ **no comment** *colloquial* I decline to answer your question.

commentary /'kɒməntəri/ *noun* (*plural* **-ies**) broadcast description of event happening; series of comments on book or performance etc.

commentate /'kɒmənteɪt/ *verb* (**-ting**) act as commentator.

commentator *noun* writer or speaker of commentary.

commerce /'kɒmɜːs/ *noun* buying and selling; trading.

commercial /kə'mɜːʃ(ə)l/ ● *adjective* of, in, or for commerce; done or run primarily for financial profit; (of broadcasting) financed by advertising. ● *noun* television or radio advertisement. □ **commercial broadcasting** broadcasting financed by advertising; **commercial traveller** firm's representative visiting shops etc. to get orders. □ **commercially** *adverb*.

commercialize *verb* (also **-ise**) (**-zing** or **-sing**) exploit or spoil for profit; make commercial. □ **commercialization** *noun*.

Commie /'kɒmi/ *noun slang derogatory* Communist.

commingle /kə'mɪŋg(ə)l/ *verb* (**-ling**) *literary* mix, unite.

commiserate /kə'mɪzəreɪt/ *verb* (**-ting**) (usually + *with*) have or express sympathy. □ **commiseration** *noun*.

commissar /'kɒmɪsɑː/ *noun historical* head of government department in USSR.

commissariat /kɒmɪ'seərɪət/ *noun* department responsible for supply of food etc. for army; food supplied.

commissary /'kɒmɪsəri/ *noun* (*plural* **-ies**) deputy, delegate.

commission /kə'mɪʃ(ə)n/ ● *noun* authority to perform task; person(s) given such authority; order for specially produced thing; warrant conferring officer rank in armed forces; rank so conferred; pay or percentage received by agent; committing. ● *verb* empower, give authority to; give (artist etc.) order for work; order (work) to be written

etc.; give (officer) command of ship; prepare (ship) for active service; bring (machine etc.) into operation. □ **in** or **out of commission** ready or not ready for active service.

commissionaire /kəmɪʃə'neə/ *noun* uniformed door attendant.

commissioner *noun* person commissioned to perform specific task; member of government commission; representative of government in district etc.

commit /kə'mɪt/ *verb* (**-tt-**) do or make (crime, blunder, etc.); (usually + *to*) entrust, consign; send (person) to prison; pledge or bind (esp. oneself) to policy or course of action; (as **committed** *adjective*) (often + *to*) dedicated, obliged.

commitment *noun* engagement, obligation; committing, being committed; dedication, committing oneself.

committal *noun* act of committing esp. to prison, grave, etc.

committee /kə'mɪti/ *noun* group of people appointed for special function by (and usually out of) larger body.

commode /kə'məʊd/ *noun* chamber pot in chair or box with cover; chest of drawers.

commodious /kə'məʊdɪəs/ *adjective* roomy.

commodity /kə'mɒdɪti/ *noun* (*plural* **-ies**) article of trade.

commodore /'kɒmədɔː/ *noun* naval officer next above captain; commander of squadron or other division of fleet; president of yacht club.

common /'kɒmən/ ● *adjective* (**-er, -est**) occurring often; ordinary, of the most familiar kind; shared by all; belonging to the whole community; *derogatory* inferior, vulgar; *Grammar* (of gender) referring to individuals of either sex. ● *noun* piece of open public land. □ **common ground** point or argument accepted by both sides; **common law** unwritten law based on custom and precedent; **common-law husband, wife** partner recognized by common law without formal marriage; **Common Market** European Community; **common or garden** *colloquial* ordinary; **common room** room for social use of students or teachers at college etc.; **common sense** good practical sense; **common time** *Music* 4 crotchets in a bar; **in common** shared, in joint use.

commonalty /'kɒmənəltɪ/ *noun* (*plural* **-ies**) general community, common people.

commoner *noun* person below rank of peer.

commonly *adverb* usually, frequently.

commonplace /'kɒmənpleɪs/ ● *adjective* lacking originality; ordinary. ● *noun* event, topic, etc. that is ordinary or usual; trite remark.

commons /'kɒmənz/ *plural noun* the common people; (**the Commons**) House of Commons.

commonwealth /'kɒmənwelθ/ *noun* independent state or community; (**the Commonwealth**) association of UK with states previously part of British Empire; republican government of Britain 1649–60.

commotion /kə'məʊʃ(ə)n/ *noun* noisy disturbance.

communal /'kɒmjʊn(ə)l/ *adjective* shared between members of group or community; (of conflict etc.) between communities. □ **communally** *adverb*.

commune[1] /'kɒmjuːn/ *noun* group of people sharing accommodation and goods; small administrative district in France etc.

commune[2] /kə'mjuːn/ *verb* (**-ning**) (usually + *with*) speak intimately; feel in close touch.

communicant /kə'mjuːnɪkənt/ *noun* receiver of Holy Communion.

communicate /kə'mjuːnɪkeɪt/ *verb* (**-ting**) impart, transmit (news, feelings, disease, ideas, etc.); (often + *with*) have social dealings. □ **communicator** *noun*.

communication *noun* communicating, being communicated; letter, message, etc.; connection or means of access; social dealings; (in *plural*) science and practice of transmitting information. □ **communication cord** cord or chain pulled to stop train in emergency; **communication(s) satellite** artificial satellite used to relay telephone calls, TV, radio, etc.

communicative /kə'mjuːnɪkətɪv/ *adjective* ready to talk and impart information.

communion /kə'mjuːnɪən/ *noun* sharing, esp. of thoughts, interests, etc.; fellowship; group of Christians of same denomination; (**Holy Communion**) Eucharist.

communiqué /kə'mjuːnɪkeɪ/ *noun* official communication, esp. news report.

communism /'kɒmjʊnɪz(ə)m/ *noun* social system based on public ownership of most property; political theory advocating this; (usually **Communism**) form of socialist society in Cuba, China, etc. □ **communist**, **Communist** *noun & adjective*; **communistic** /-'nɪstɪk/ *adjective*.

community /kə'mjuːnɪtɪ/ (*plural* **-ies**) *noun* group of people living in one place or having same religion, ethnic origin, profession, etc.; commune; joint ownership. □ **community centre** place providing social facilities for neighbourhood; **community charge** *historical* tax levied locally on every adult; **community home** institution housing young offenders; **community singing** singing by large group; **community spirit** feeling of belonging to community.

commute /kə'mjuːt/ *verb* (**-ting**) travel some distance to and from work; (usually + *to*) change (punishment) to one less severe.

commuter *noun* person who commutes to and from work.

compact[1] ● *adjective* /kəm'pækt/ closely packed together; economically designed; concise; (of person) small but well-proportioned. ● *verb* /kəm'pækt/ make compact. ● *noun* /'kɒmpækt/ small flat case for face powder etc. □ **compact disc** disc from which digital information or sound is reproduced by reflection of laser light. □ **compactly** *adverb*; **compactness** *noun*.

compact[2] /'kɒmpækt/ *noun* agreement, contract.

companion /kəm'pænjən/ *noun* person who accompanies or associates with another; person paid to live with another; handbook, reference book; thing that matches another; (**Companion**) member of some orders of knighthood. □ **companionway** staircase from ship's deck to cabins etc.

companionable *adjective* sociable, friendly. □ **companionably** *adverb*.

companionship *noun* friendship; being together.

company /'kʌmpənɪ/ *noun* (*plural* -**ies**) number of people assembled; guest(s); commercial business; actors etc. working together; subdivision of infantry battalion. □ **in company with** together with; **part company** (often + *with*) separate; **ship's company** entire crew.

comparable /'kɒmpərəb(ə)l/ *adjective* (often + *with*, *to*) able to be compared. □ **comparability** *noun*; **comparably** *adverb*.

■ **Usage** *Comparable* is often pronounced /kəm'pærəb(ə)l/ (with the stress on the -*par*-), but this is considered incorrect by some people.

comparative /kəm'pærətɪv/ ● *adjective* perceptible or estimated by comparison; relative; of or involving comparison; *Grammar* (of adjective or adverb) expressing higher degree of a quality. ● *noun Grammar* comparative expression or word. □ **comparatively** *adverb*.

compare /kəm'peə/ ● *verb* (-**ring**) (usually + *to*) express similarities in; (often + *to*, *with*) estimate similarity of; (often + *with*) bear comparison. ● *noun* comparison. □ **compare notes** exchange ideas or opinions.

comparison /kəm'pærɪs(ə)n/ *noun* comparing; example of similarity; (in full **degrees of comparison**) *Grammar* positive, comparative, and superlative forms of adjectives and adverbs. □ **bear comparison** (often + *with*) be able to be compared favourably.

compartment /kəm'pɑːtmənt/ *noun* space partitioned off within larger space.

compass /'kʌmpəs/ *noun* instrument showing direction of magnetic north and bearings from it; (usually in *plural*) V-shaped hinged instrument for drawing circles and taking measurements; scope, range.

compassion /kəm'pæʃ(ə)n/ *noun* pity.

compassionate /kəm'pæʃənət/ *adjective* showing compassion; sympathetic.

□ **compassionate leave** leave granted on grounds of bereavement etc. □ **compassionately** *adverb*.

compatible /kəm'pætɪb(ə)l/ *adjective* (often + *with*) able to coexist; (of equipment) able to be used in combination. □ **compatibility** *noun*.

compatriot /kəm'pætrɪət/ *noun* person from one's own country.

compel /kəm'pel/ *verb* (-**ll**-) force, constrain; arouse irresistibly; (as **compelling** *adjective*) arousing strong interest.

compendious /kəm'pendɪəs/ *adjective* comprehensive but brief.

compendium /kəm'pendɪəm/ *noun* (*plural* -**s** or -**dia**) abridgement, summary; collection of table games etc.

compensate /'kɒmpenseɪt/ *verb* (-**ting**) recompense, make amends; counterbalance.

compensation *noun* compensating, being compensated; money etc. given as recompense. □ **compensatory** /-'seɪt-/ *adjective*.

compère /'kɒmpeə/ ● *noun* person introducing variety show. ● *verb* (-**ring**) act as compère (to).

compete /kəm'piːt/ *verb* (-**ting**) take part in contest etc.; (often + *with* or *against* person, *for* thing) strive.

competence /'kɒmpɪt(ə)ns/ *noun* being competent; ability.

competent *adjective* adequately qualified or capable; effective. □ **competently** *adverb*.

competition /kɒmpə'tɪʃ(ə)n/ *noun* (often + *for*) competing; event in which people compete; other people competing; opposition.

competitive /kəm'petɪtɪv/ *adjective* of or involving competition; (of prices etc.) comparing well with those of rivals; having strong urge to win. □ **competitiveness** *noun*.

competitor /kəm'petɪtə/ *noun* person who competes; rival, esp. in business.

compile /kəm'paɪl/ *verb* (-**ling**) collect and arrange (material) into list, book, etc. □ **compilation** /kɒmpɪ'leɪʃ(ə)n/ *noun*.

complacent /kəm'pleɪs(ə)nt/ *adjective* smugly self-satisfied or contented. □ **complacency** *noun*.

complain /kəm'pleɪn/ *verb* express dissatisfaction; (+ *of*) say that one is suffering from (an ailment), state grievance concerning. □ **complainant** *noun*.

complaint *noun* complaining; grievance, cause of dissatisfaction; formal protest; ailment.

complaisant /kəm'pleɪz(ə)nt/ *adjective formal* deferential; willing to please; acquiescent. □ **complaisance** *noun*.

complement ● *noun* /'kɒmplɪmənt/ thing that completes; full number; word(s) added to verb to complete predicate of sentence; amount by which angle is less than 90°. ● *verb* /-ment/ complete; form complement to. □ **complementary** /-'men-/ *adjective*.

complete /kəm'pliːt/ ● *adjective* having all its parts; finished, total. ● *verb* (**-ting**) finish; make complete; fill in (form etc.). □ **completely** *adverb*; **completeness** *noun*, **completion** *noun*.

complex /'kɒmpleks/ ● *noun* buildings, rooms, etc. made up of related parts; group of usually repressed feelings or thoughts causing abnormal behaviour or mental state. ● *adjective* complicated; consisting of related parts. □ **complexity** /kəm'pleks-/ *noun* (*plural* **-ies**).

complexion /kəm'plekʃ(ə)n/ *noun* natural colour, texture, and appearance of skin, esp. of face; aspect.

compliance /kəm'plaɪəns/ *noun* obedience to request, command, etc.; capacity to yield.

compliant *adjective* obedient; yielding. □ **compliantly** *adverb*.

complicate /'kɒmplɪkeɪt/ *verb* (**-ting**) make difficult or complex; (as **complicated** *adjective*) complex, intricate.

complication *noun* involved or confused condition; complicating circumstance; difficulty; (often in *plural*) disease or condition arising out of another.

complicity /kəm'plɪsɪtɪ/ *noun* partnership in wrongdoing.

compliment ● *noun* /'kɒmplɪmənt/ polite expression of praise; (in *plural*) formal greetings accompanying gift etc. ● *verb* /-ment/ (often + *on*) congratulate; praise.

complimentary /kɒmplɪ'mentərɪ/ *adjective* expressing compliment; given free of charge.

comply /kəm'plaɪ/ *verb* (**-ies, -ied**) (often + *with*) act in accordance (with request or command).

component /kəm'pəʊnənt/ ● *adjective* being part of larger whole. ● *noun* component part.

comport /kəm'pɔːt/ *verb* (**comport oneself**) *literary* conduct oneself; behave. □ **comportment** *noun*.

compose /kəm'pəʊz/ *verb* (**-sing**) create in music or writing; make up, constitute; arrange artistically; set up (type); (as **composed** *adjective*) calm, self-possessed.

composer *noun* person who composes esp. music.

composite /'kɒmpəzɪt/ ● *adjective* made up of parts; (of plant) having head of many flowers forming one bloom. ● *noun* composite thing or plant.

composition /kɒmpə'zɪʃ(ə)n/ *noun* act of putting together; thing composed; school essay; arrangement of parts of picture etc.; constitution of substance; compound artificial substance.

compositor /kəm'pɒzɪtə/ *noun* person who sets up type for printing.

compost /'kɒmpɒst/ *noun* mixture of decayed organic matter used as fertilizer.

composure /kəm'pəʊʒə/ *noun* calm manner.

compote /'kɒmpəʊt/ *noun* fruit in syrup.

compound¹ /'kɒmpaʊnd/ ● *noun* mixture of two or more things; word made up of two or more existing words; substance formed from two or more elements chemically united. ● *adjective* made up of two or more ingredients or parts; combined, collective. ● *verb* /kəm'paʊnd/ mix or combine; increase (difficulties etc.); make up (whole); settle (matter) by mutual agreement. □ **compound fracture** one complicated by wound; **compound interest** interest paid on capital and accumulated interest.

compound² /'kɒmpaʊnd/ *noun* enclosure, fenced-in space.

comprehend /kɒmprɪ'hend/ *verb* understand; include.

comprehensible *adjective* that can be understood.

comprehension *noun* understanding; text set as test of understanding; inclusion.

comprehensive ● *adjective* including all or nearly all; (of motor insurance) providing protection against most risks. ● *noun* (in full **comprehensive school**) secondary school for children of all abilities. □ **comprehensively** *adverb*.

compress ● *verb* /kəm'pres/ squeeze together, bring into smaller space or shorter time. ● *noun* /'kɒmpres/ pad pressed on part of body to relieve inflammation, stop bleeding, etc. □ **compressible** *adjective*.

compression /kəm'preʃ(ə)n/ *noun* compressing; reduction in volume of fuel mixture in internal-combustion engine before ignition.

compressor *noun* machine for compressing air or other gas.

comprise /kəm'praɪz/ *verb* (-**sing**) include; consist of.

■ **Usage** It is a mistake to use *comprise* to mean 'to compose or make up'.

compromise /'kɒmprəmaɪz/ ● *noun* agreement reached by mutual concession; (often + *between*) intermediate state between conflicting opinions etc. ● *verb* (-**sing**) settle dispute by compromise; modify one's opinions, demands, etc.; bring into disrepute or danger by indiscretion.

comptroller /kən'trəʊlə/ *noun* controller.

compulsion /kəm'pʌlʃ(ə)n/ *noun* compelling, being compelled; irresistible urge.

compulsive *adjective* compelling; resulting or acting (as if) from compulsion; irresistible. □ **compulsively** *adverb*.

compulsory *adjective* required by law or rule. □ **compulsorily** *adverb*.

compunction /kəm'pʌŋkʃ(ə)n/ *noun* guilty feeling; slight regret.

compute /kəm'pjuːt/ *verb* (-**ting**) calculate; use computer. □ **computation** /kɒm-/ *noun*.

computer *noun* electronic device for storing and processing data, making calculations, or controlling machinery. □ **computer-literate** able to use computers; **computer science** study of computers; **computer virus** code maliciously introduced into program to destroy data etc.

computerize /kəm'pjuːtəraɪz/ *verb* (also **-ise**) (-**zing** or -**sing**) equip with or store, perform, or produce by computer. □ **computerization** *noun*.

comrade /'kɒmreɪd/ *noun* companion in some activity; fellow socialist or Communist. □ **comradeship** *noun*.

con¹ *slang* ● *noun* confidence trick. ● *verb* (-**nn**-) swindle, deceive.

con² *noun* (usually in *plural*) reason against.

con³ *verb* (*US* **conn**) (-**nn**-) direct steering of (ship).

concatenation /kɒnkætɪ'neɪʃ(ə)n/ *noun* series of linked things or events.

concave /kɒn'keɪv/ *adjective* curved like interior of circle or sphere. □ **concavity** /-'kæv-/ *noun*.

conceal /kən'siːl/ *verb* hide; keep secret. □ **concealment** *noun*.

concede /kən'siːd/ *verb* (-**ding**) admit to be true; admit defeat in; grant.

conceit /kən'siːt/ *noun* personal vanity; *literary* far-fetched comparison.

conceited *adjective* vain. □ **conceitedly** *adverb*.

conceive /kən'siːv/ *verb* (-**ving**) become pregnant (with); (often + *of*) imagine; (usually in *passive*) formulate (plan etc.). □ **conceivable** *adjective*; **conceivably** *adverb*.

concentrate /'kɒnsəntreɪt/ ● *verb* (-**ting**) (often + *on*) focus one's attention; bring together to one point; increase strength of (liquid etc.) by removing water etc.; (as **concentrated** *adjective*) strong. ● *noun* concentrated solution.

concentration *noun* concentrating, being concentrated; weight of substance in given amount of mixture; mental attention. □ **concentration camp** place for detention of political prisoners etc.

concentric /kən'sentrɪk/ *adjective* having common centre. □ **concentrically** *adverb*.

concept /'kɒnsept/ *noun* general notion; abstract idea.

conception /kən'sepʃ(ə)n/ *noun* conceiving, being conceived; idea; understanding.

conceptual /kən'septjʊəl/ *adjective* of mental concepts. □ **conceptually** *adverb*.

conceptualize *verb* (also **-ise**) (**-zing** or **-sing**) form concept or idea of. □ **conceptualization** *noun*.

concern /kən'sɜːn/ ● *verb* be relevant or important to; relate to; be about; worry, affect; (**concern oneself**; often + *with*, *about*, *in*) interest or involve oneself. ● *noun* anxiety, worry; matter of interest or importance to one; firm, business.

concerned *adjective* involved, interested; anxious, troubled.

concerning *preposition* about, regarding.

concert /'kɒnsət/ *noun* musical performance; agreement.

concerted /kən'sɜːtɪd/ *adjective* jointly planned.

concertina /kɒnsə'tiːnə/ ● *noun* portable musical instrument like accordion but smaller. ● *verb* (**-nas**, **-naed** /-nəd/ or **-na'd**, **-naing**) compress or collapse in folds like those of concertina.

concerto /kən'tʃeətəʊ/ *noun* (*plural* **-tos** or **-ti** /-tɪ/) composition for solo instrument(s) and orchestra.

concession /kən'seʃ(ə)n/ *noun* conceding, thing conceded; reduction in price for certain category of people; right to use land, sell goods, etc. □ **concessionary** *adjective*.

conch /kɒntʃ/ *noun* large spiral shell of various marine gastropod molluscs; such gastropod.

conchology /kɒŋ'kɒlədʒɪ/ *noun* study of shells.

conciliate /kən'sɪlɪeɪt/ *verb* (**-ting**) make calm; pacify; reconcile. □ **conciliation** *noun*; **conciliator** *noun*; **conciliatory** *adjective*.

concise /kən'saɪs/ *adjective* brief but comprehensive. □ **concisely** *adverb*; **conciseness** *noun*; **concision** *noun*.

conclave /'kɒnkleɪv/ *noun* private meeting; assembly or meeting-place of cardinals for election of pope.

conclude /kən'kluːd/ *verb* (**-ding**) bring or come to end; (often + *from*, *that*) infer; settle (treaty etc.).

conclusion /kən'kluːʒ(ə)n/ *noun* ending; judgement reached by reasoning; summing-up; settling of peace etc. □ **in conclusion** lastly.

conclusive /kən'kluːsɪv/ *adjective* decisive, convincing. □ **conclusively** *adverb*.

concoct /kən'kɒkt/ *verb* make by mixing ingredients; invent (story, lie, etc.). □ **concoction** *noun*.

concomitant /kən'kɒmɪt(ə)nt/ ● *adjective* (often + *with*) accompanying. ● *noun* accompanying thing. □ **concomitance** *noun*.

concord /'kɒŋkɔːd/ *noun* agreement, harmony. □ **concordant** /kən'kɔːd(ə)nt/ *adjective*.

concordance /kən'kɔːd(ə)ns/ *noun* agreement; index of words used in book or by author.

concordat /kən'kɔːdæt/ *noun* agreement, esp. between Church and state.

concourse /'kɒŋkɔːs/ *noun* crowd; large open area in railway station etc.

concrete /'kɒŋkriːt/ ● *adjective* existing in material form, real; definite. ● *noun* mixture of gravel, sand, cement, and water used for building. ● *verb* (**-ting**) cover with or embed in concrete.

concretion /kən'kriːʃ(ə)n/ *noun* hard solid mass; forming of this by coalescence.

concubine /'kɒŋkjʊbaɪn/ *ncun* literary mistress; (among polygamous peoples) secondary wife.

concupiscence /kən'kjuːpɪs(ə)ns/ *noun* formal lust. □ **concupiscent** *adjective*.

concur /kən'kɜː/ *verb* (**-rr-**) (often + *with*) agree; coincide.

concurrent /kən'kʌrənt/ *adjective* (often + *with*) existing or in operation at the same time. □ **concurrence** *noun*; **concurrently** *adverb*.

concuss /kən'kʌs/ *verb* subject to concussion.

concussion /kən'kʌʃ(ə)n/ *noun* temporary unconsciousness or incapacity due to head injury; violent shaking.

condemn /kən'dem/ *verb* express strong disapproval of; (usually + *to*) sentence (to punishment), doom (to something unpleasant); pronounce unfit for use. □ **condemnation** /kɒndem'neɪʃ(ə)n/ noun.

condensation /kɒnden'seɪʃ(ə)n/ noun condensing, being condensed; condensed liquid; abridgement.

condense /kən'dens/ verb (**-sing**) make denser or more concise; reduce or be reduced from gas to liquid.

condescend /kɒndɪ'send/ verb (+ to do) graciously consent to do a thing while showing one's superiority; (+ to) pretend to be on equal terms with (inferior); (as **condescending** adjective) patronizing. □ **condescendingly** adverb; **condescension** noun.

condiment /'kɒndɪmənt/ noun seasoning or relish for food.

condition /kən'dɪʃ(ə)n/ ●noun stipulation; thing on fulfilment of which something else depends; state of being or fitness of person or thing; ailment; (in plural) circumstances. ●verb bring into desired state; accustom; determine; be essential to.

conditional adjective (often + on) dependent, not absolute; Grammar (of clause, mood, etc.) expressing condition. □ **conditionally** adverb.

condole /kən'dəʊl/ verb (**-ling**) (+ with) express sympathy with (person) over loss etc.

■ **Usage** Condole is commonly confused with console, which means 'to comfort'.

condolence noun (often in plural) expression of sympathy.

condom /'kɒndɒm/ noun contraceptive sheath.

condominium /kɒndə'mɪnɪəm/ noun joint rule or sovereignty; US building containing individually owned flats.

condone /kən'dəʊn/ verb (**-ning**) forgive, overlook.

condor /'kɒndɔː/ noun large S. American vulture.

conducive /kən'djuːsɪv/ adjective (often + to) contributing or helping (towards something).

conduct ●noun /'kɒndʌkt/ behaviour; manner of conducting business, war,

etc. ●verb /kən'dʌkt/ lead, guide; control, manage; be conductor of (orchestra etc.); transmit by conduction; (**conduct oneself**) behave.

conduction /kən'dʌkʃ(ə)n/ noun transmission of heat, electricity, etc.

conductive /kən'dʌktɪv/ adjective transmitting heat, electricity, etc. □ **conductivity** /kɒndʌk'tɪv-/ noun.

conductor noun director of orchestra etc.; (feminine **conductress**) person who collects fares on bus etc.; conductive thing.

conduit /'kɒndɪt/ noun channel or pipe for conveying liquid or protecting insulated cable.

cone noun solid figure with usually circular base and tapering to a point; cone-shaped object; dry fruit of pine or fir; ice cream cornet.

coney = CONY.

confab /'kɒnfæb/ noun colloquial confabulation.

confabulate /kən'fæbjʊleɪt/ verb (**-ting**) talk together. □ **confabulation** noun.

confection /kən'fekʃ(ə)n/ noun sweet dish or delicacy.

confectioner noun dealer in sweets or pastries etc. □ **confectionery** noun.

confederacy /kən'fedərəsɪ/ noun (plural **-ies**) alliance or league, esp. of confederate states.

confederate /kən'fedərət/ ●adjective esp. Politics allied. ●noun ally; accomplice. ●verb /-reɪt/ (**-ting**) (often + with) bring or come into alliance. □ **Confederate States** those which seceded from US in 1860–1.

confederation /kənfedə'reɪʃ(ə)n/ noun union or alliance of states.

confer /kən'fɜː/ verb (**-rr-**) (often + on, upon) grant, bestow; (often + with) meet for discussion.

conference /'kɒnfər(ə)ns/ noun consultation; meeting for discussion.

conferment /kən'fɜːmənt/ noun conferring (of honour etc.).

confess /kən'fes/ verb acknowledge, admit; declare one's sins, esp. to priest; (of priest) hear confession of.

confessedly /kən'fesɪdlɪ/ adverb by one's own or general admission.

confession /kənˈfeʃ(ə)n/ noun act of confessing; thing confessed; statement of principles etc.

confessional ● noun enclosed place where priest hears confession. ● adjective of confession.

confessor noun priest who hears confession.

confetti /kənˈfeti/ noun small bits of coloured paper thrown by wedding guests at bride and groom.

confidant /ˈkɒnfɪdænt/ noun (feminine **confidante** same pronunciation) person trusted with knowledge of one's private affairs.

confide /kənˈfaɪd/ verb (-ding) (usually + to) tell (secret) or entrust (task). □ **confide in** talk confidentially to.

confidence /ˈkɒnfɪd(ə)ns/ noun firm trust; feeling of certainty; self-reliance; boldness; something told as a secret. □ **confidence trick** swindle in which victim is persuaded to trust swindler; **confidence trickster** person using confidence tricks; **in confidence** as a secret; **in (person's) confidence** trusted with his or her secrets.

confident adjective feeling or showing confidence. □ **confidently** adverb.

confidential /kɒnfɪˈden(t)ʃ(ə)l/ adjective spoken or written in confidence; entrusted with secrets; confiding. □ **confidentiality** /-ʃɪˈæl-/ noun; **confidentially** adjective.

configuration /kənfɪɡjʊˈreɪʃ(ə)n/ noun manner of arrangement; shape; outline. □ **configure** /-ˈfɪɡə/ verb.

confine ● verb /kənˈfaɪn/ (-ning) keep or restrict within certain limits; imprison. ● noun /ˈkɒnfaɪn/ (usually in plural) boundary. □ **be confined** be in childbirth.

confinement /kənˈfaɪnmənt/ noun confining, being confined; childbirth.

confirm /kənˈfɜːm/ verb provide support for truth or correctness of; establish more firmly; formally make definite; administer confirmation to.

confirmation /kɒnfəˈmeɪʃ(ə)n/ noun confirming circumstance or statement; rite confirming baptized person as member of Christian Church.

confirmed adjective firmly settled in habit or condition.

confiscate /ˈkɒnfɪskeɪt/ verb (-ting) take or seize by authority. □ **confiscation** noun.

conflagration /kɒnfləˈɡreɪʃ(ə)n/ noun large destructive fire.

conflate /kənˈfleɪt/ verb (-ting) fuse together, blend. □ **conflation** noun.

conflict ● noun /ˈkɒnflɪkt/ struggle, fight; opposition; (often + of) clashing of opposed interests etc. ● verb /kənˈflɪkt/ clash, be incompatible.

confluent /ˈkɒnfluənt/ ● adjective merging into one. ● noun stream joining another. □ **confluence** noun.

conform /kənˈfɔːm/ verb comply with rules or general custom; (+ to, with) be in accordance with.

conformable adjective (often + to) similar; (often + with) consistent.

conformation /kɒnfɔːˈmeɪʃ(ə)n/ noun thing's structure or shape.

conformist ● noun person who conforms to established practice. ● adjective conventional. □ **conformism** noun.

conformity noun conforming with established practice; suitability.

confound /kənˈfaʊnd/ ● verb baffle; confuse; archaic defeat. □ **confound (person, thing)!** interjection expressing annoyance.

confounded adjective colloquial damned.

confront /kənˈfrʌnt/ verb meet or stand facing, esp. in hostility or defiance; (of problem etc.) present itself to; (+ with) bring face to face with. □ **confrontation** /kɒn-/ noun; **confrontational** /kɒn-/ adjective.

confuse /kənˈfjuːz/ verb (-sing) bewilder; mix up; make obscure; (often as **confused** adjective) throw into disorder. □ **confusing** adjective; **confusion** noun.

confute /kənˈfjuːt/ verb (-ting) prove to be false or wrong. □ **confutation** /kɒn-/ noun.

conga /ˈkɒŋɡə/ noun Latin American dance, usually performed in single file; tall narrow drum beaten with hands.

congeal /kənˈdʒiːl/ verb make or become semi-solid by cooling; (of blood) coagulate.

congenial /kənˈdʒiːnɪəl/ adjective having sympathetic nature, similar interests, etc.; (often + to) suited or agreeable.

□ **congeniality** /-'æl-/ *noun*; **congeni-
ally** *adverb*.

congenital /kən'dʒenɪt(ə)l/ *adjective* existing or as such from birth. □ **congenitally** *adverb*.

conger /'kɒŋgə/ *noun* large sea eel.

congest /kən'dʒest/ *verb* (esp. as **congested** *adjective*) affect with congestion.

congestion *noun* abnormal accumulation or obstruction, esp. of traffic etc. or
of mucus in nose etc.

conglomerate /kən'glɒmərət/ ● *adjective*
gathered into rounded mass. ● *noun* heterogeneous mass; business etc. corporation of merged firms. ● *verb* /-reɪt/
(**-ting**) collect into coherent mass.
□ **conglomeration** *noun*.

congratulate /kən'grætʃʊleɪt/ *verb*
(**-ting**) (often + *on*) express pleasure at
happiness, excellence, or good fortune
of (person). □ **congratulatory** /-lətərɪ/
adjective.

congratulation *noun* congratulating,
(usually in *plural*) expression of this.

congregate /'kɒŋgrɪgeɪt/ *verb* (**-ting**)
collect or gather in crowd.

congregation *noun* assembly of people,
esp. for religious worship; group of
people regularly attending particular
church etc.

congregational *adjective* of a congregation; (**Congregational**) of or adhering to Congregationalism.

Congregationalism *noun* system in
which individual churches are self-
governing. □ **Congregationalist** *noun*.

congress /'kɒŋgres/ *noun* formal meeting of delegates for discussion; (**Congress**) national legislative body of US
etc. □ **congressman**, **congresswo-
man** member of US Congress. □ **con-
gressional** /kən'greʃ-/ *adjective*.

congruent /'kɒŋgrʊənt/ *adjective* (often
+ *with*) suitable, agreeing; *Geometry* (of
figures) coinciding exactly when superimposed. □ **congruence** *noun*.

conic /'kɒnɪk/ *adjective* of a cone.

conical *adjective* cone-shaped.

conifer /'kɒnɪfə/ *noun* cone-bearing tree.
□ **coniferous** /kə'nɪfərəs/ *adjective*.

conjectural /kən'dʒektʃər(ə)l/ *adjective*
involving conjecture.

conjecture /kən'dʒektʃə/ ● *noun* formation of opinion on incomplete information, guess. ● *verb* (**-ring**) guess.

conjoin /kən'dʒɔɪn/ *verb formal* join,
combine.

conjoint /kən'dʒɔɪnt/ *adjective formal* associated, conjoined.

conjugal /'kɒndʒʊg(ə)l/ *adjective* of marriage; between husband and wife.

conjugate ● *verb* /'kɒndʒʊgeɪt/ (**-ting**)
give the different forms of (verb); unite,
become fused. ● *adjective* /-gət/ joined
together.

conjugation *noun Grammar* system of
verbal inflection.

conjunct /kən'dʒʌŋkt/ *adjective* joined;
combined; associated.

conjunction *noun* joining, connection;
word used to connect sentences,
clauses, or words (see panel); combination of events or circumstances.
□ **conjunctive** *adjective*.

conjunctiva /kɒndʒʌŋk'taɪvə/ *noun*
(*plural* **-s**) mucous membrane covering
front of eye and inside of eyelid.

conjunctivitis /kəndʒʌŋktɪ'vaɪtɪs/ *noun*
inflammation of conjunctiva.

conjure /'kʌndʒə/ *verb* (**-ring**) perform
seemingly magical tricks, esp. by
movement of hands. □ **conjure up**
produce as if by magic, evoke.

conjuror *noun* (also **conjurer**) performer of conjuring tricks.

conk[1] *verb colloquial* (usually + *out*)
break down; become exhausted; faint;
fall asleep.

conk[2] *slang* ● *noun* (punch on) nose or
head. ● *verb* hit on nose or head.

conker /'kɒŋkə/ *noun* horse chestnut
fruit; (in *plural*) children's game played
with conkers on strings.

con man *noun* confidence trickster.

connect /kə'nekt/ *verb* (often + *to*, *with*)
join, be joined; associate mentally or
practically; (+ *with*) (of train etc.) arrive in time for passengers to transfer
to another; put into communication by
telephone; (usually in *passive*, as + *with*)
unite or associate with (others) in relationship etc. □ **connecting rod** rod
between piston and crankpin etc. in
engine. □ **connector** *noun*.

connection *noun* (also **connexion**)
connecting, being connected; point at
which things are connected; association of ideas; link, esp. by telephone;

(often in *plural*) (esp. influential) relative or associate; connecting train etc.

connective *adjective* connecting. □ **connective tissue** body tissue forming tendons and ligaments, supporting organs, etc.

conning tower /'kɒnɪŋ/ *noun* raised structure of submarine containing periscope; wheelhouse of warship.

connive /kə'naɪv/ *verb* (**-ving**) (+ *at*) tacitly consent to (wrongdoing); conspire. □ **connivance** *noun*.

connoisseur /kɒnə'sɜ:/ *noun* (often + *of*, *in*) person with good taste and judgement.

connote /kə'nəʊt/ *verb* (**-ting**) imply in addition to literal meaning; mean. □ **connotation** /kɒnə-/ *noun*; **connotative** /'kɒnəteɪtɪv/ *adjective*.

connubial /kə'nju:bɪəl/ *adjective* conjugal.

conquer /'kɒŋkə/ *verb* overcome, defeat; be victorious; subjugate. □ **conqueror** *noun*.

conquest /'kɒŋkwest/ *noun* conquering; something won; person whose affections have been won.

consanguineous /kɒnsæŋ'gwɪnɪəs/ *adjective* descended from same ancestor; akin. □ **consanguinity** *noun*.

conscience /'kɒnʃ(ə)ns/ *noun* moral sense of right and wrong, esp. as affecting behaviour. □ **conscience money** money paid to relieve conscience,

esp. in respect of evaded payment etc.; **conscience-stricken** made uneasy by bad conscience.

conscientious /kɒnʃɪ'enʃəs/ *adjective* diligent and scrupulous. □ **conscientious objector** person who refuses to do military service on grounds of conscience. □ **conscientiously** *adverb*; **conscientiousness** *noun*.

conscious /'kɒnʃəs/ *adjective* awake and aware of one's surroundings etc.; (usually + *of*, *that*) aware, knowing; intentional. □ **consciously** *adverb*; **consciousness** *noun*.

conscript ● *verb* /kən'skrɪpt/ summon for compulsory state (esp. military) service. ● *noun* /'kɒnskrɪpt/ conscripted person. □ **conscription** *noun*.

consecrate /'kɒnsɪkreɪt/ *verb* (**-ting**) make or declare sacred; dedicate formally to religious purpose; (+ *to*) devote to (a purpose). □ **consecration** *noun*.

consecutive /kən'sekjʊtɪv/ *adjective* following continuously; in unbroken or logical order. □ **consecutively** *adverb*.

consensus /kən'sensəs/ *noun* (often + *of*) general agreement or opinion.

consent /kən'sent/ ● *verb* (often + *to*) express willingness, give assent; agree. ● *noun* agreement; permission.

consequence /'kɒnsɪkwəns/ *noun* result of what has gone before; importance.

··

Conjunction

A conjunction is used to join parts of sentences which usually, but not always, contain their own verbs, e.g.

> *He found it difficult but I helped him.*
> *They made lunch for Alice and Mary.*
> *I waited until you came.*

The most common conjunctions are:

after	*for*	*since*	*unless*
although	*if*	*so*	*until*
and	*in order that*	*so that*	*when*
as	*like*	*than*	*where*
because	*now*	*that*	*whether*
before	*once*	*though*	*while*
but	*or*	*till*	

··

consequent /'kɒnsɪkwənt/ *adjective* that results; (often + *on*, *upon*) following as consequence. □ **consequently** *adverb*.

consequential /ˌkɒnsɪ'kwenʃ(ə)l/ *adjective* resulting, esp. indirectly; important.

conservancy /kən'sɜːvənsɪ/ *noun* (*plural* **-ies**) body controlling river, port, etc. or concerned with conservation; official environmental conservation.

conservation /ˌkɒnsə'veɪʃ(ə)n/ *noun* preservation, esp. of natural environment. □ **conservationist** *noun*.

conservative /kən'sɜːvətɪv/ ● *adjective* averse to rapid change; (of estimate) purposely low; (usually **Conservative**) of Conservative Party. ● *noun* conservative person; (usually **Conservative**) member or supporter of Conservative Party. □ **Conservative Party** political party promoting free enterprise. □ **conservatism** *noun*.

conservatoire /kən'sɜːvətwɑː/ *noun* (usually European) school of music or other arts.

conservatory /kən'sɜːvətərɪ/ *noun* (*plural* **-ies**) greenhouse for tender plants; esp. *US* conservatoire.

conserve ● *verb* /kən'sɜːv/ (**-ving**) preserve, keep from harm or damage. ● *noun* /'kɒnsɜːv/ fruit etc. preserved in sugar; fruit jam, esp. fresh.

consider /kən'sɪdə/ *verb* contemplate; deliberate thoughtfully; make allowance for, take into account; (+ *that*) have the opinion that; show consideration for; regard as; (as **considered** *adjective*) (esp. of an opinion) formed after careful thought.

considerable *adjective* a lot of; notable, important. □ **considerably** *adverb*.

considerate /kən'sɪdərət/ *adjective* giving thought to feelings or rights of others. □ **considerately** *adverb*.

consideration /kənsɪdə'reɪʃ(ə)n/ *noun* careful thought; being considerate; fact or thing taken into account; compensation, payment. □ **take into consideration** make allowance for.

considering *preposition* in view of.

consign /kən'saɪn/ *verb* (often + *to*) commit, deliver; send (goods etc.). □ **consignee** /kɒnsaɪ'niː/ *noun*, **consignor** *noun*.

consignment *noun* consigning; goods consigned.

consist /kən'sɪst/ *verb* (+ *of*) be composed of; (+ *in*, *of*) have its essential features in.

consistency *noun* (*plural* **-ies**) degree of density or firmness, esp. of thick liquids; being consistent.

consistent *adjective* constant to same principles; (usually + *with*) compatible. □ **consistently** *adverb*.

consistory *noun* (*plural* **-ies**) *RC Church* council of cardinals.

consolation /kɒnsə'leɪʃ(ə)n/ *noun* alleviation of grief or disappointment; consoling person or thing. □ **consolation prize** one given to competitor just failing to win main prize. □ **consolatory** /kən'sɒl-/ *adjective*.

console[1] /kən'səʊl/ *verb* (**-ling**) bring consolation to.

■ *Usage* Console is often confused with *condole*. To condole with someone is to express sympathy with them.

console[2] /'kɒnsəʊl/ *noun* panel for switches, controls, etc.; cabinet for television etc.; cabinet with keys and stops of organ; bracket supporting shelf etc.

consolidate /kən'sɒlɪdeɪt/ *verb* (**-ting**) make or become strong or secure; combine (territories, companies, debts, etc.) into one whole. □ **consolidation** *noun*.

consommé /kən'sɒmeɪ/ *noun* clear meat soup.

consonance /'kɒnsənəns/ *noun* agreement, harmony.

consonant ● *noun* speech sound that forms syllable only in combination with vowel; letter(s) representing this. ● *adjective* (+ *with*, *to*) consistent with; in agreement or harmony. □ **consonantal** /-'næn-/ *adjective*.

consort[1] ● *noun* /'kɒnsɔːt/ wife or husband, esp. of royalty. ● *verb* /kən'sɔːt/ (usually + *with*, *together*) keep company; harmonize.

consort[2] /'kɒnsɔːt/ *noun* *Music* group of players or instruments.

consortium /kən'sɔːtɪəm/ *noun* (*plural* **-tia** or **-s**) association, esp. of several business companies.

conspicuous /kən'spɪkjʊəs/ *adjective* clearly visible; attracting attention. □ **conspicuously** *adverb*.

conspiracy /kən'spɪrəsɪ/ noun (plural **-ies**) act of conspiring; plot.

conspirator /kən'spɪrətə/ noun person who takes part in conspiracy. □ **conspiratorial** /-'tɔː-/ adjective.

conspire /kən'spaɪə/ verb (**-ring**) combine secretly for unlawful or harmful purpose; (of events) seemingly work together.

constable /'kʌnstəb(ə)l/ noun (also **police constable**) police officer of lowest rank; governor of royal castle. □ **Chief Constable** head of police force of county etc.

constabulary /kən'stæbjʊlərɪ/ noun (plural **-ies**) police force.

constancy /'kɒnstənsɪ/ noun dependability; faithfulness.

constant ●adjective continuous; frequently occurring; having constancy. ●noun Mathematics & Physics unvarying quantity. □ **constantly** adverb.

constellation /kɒnstə'leɪʃ(ə)n/ noun group of fixed stars.

consternation /kɒnstə'neɪʃ(ə)n/ noun amazement, dismay.

constipate /'kɒnstɪpeɪt/ verb (**-ting**) (esp. as **constipated** adjective) affect with constipation.

constipation noun difficulty in emptying bowels.

constituency /kən'stɪtjʊənsɪ/ noun (plural **-ies**) body electing representative; area represented.

constituent /kən'stɪtjʊənt/ ●adjective making part of whole; appointing, electing. ●noun member of constituency; component part.

constitute /'kɒnstɪtjuːt/ verb (**-ting**) be essence or components of; amount to; establish.

constitution /kɒnstɪ'tjuːʃ(ə)n/ noun composition; set of principles by which state etc. is governed; person's inherent state of health, strength, etc.

constitutional ●adjective of or in line with the constitution; inherent. ●noun walk taken as exercise. □ **constitutionally** adverb.

constitutive /'kɒnstɪtjuːtɪv/ adjective able to form or appoint; constituent.

constrain /kən'streɪn/ verb compel; confine; (as **constrained** adjective) forced, embarrassed.

constraint noun compulsion; restriction; self-control.

constrict /kən'strɪkt/ verb make narrow or tight; compress. □ **constriction** noun; **constrictive** adjective.

constrictor noun snake that kills by compressing; muscle that contracts a part.

construct ●verb /kən'strʌkt/ fit together, build; Geometry draw. ●noun /'kɒnstrʌkt/ thing constructed, esp. by the mind. □ **constructor** /kən'strʌktə/ noun.

construction /kən'strʌkʃ(ə)n/ noun constructing; thing constructed; syntactical arrangement; interpretation. □ **constructional** adjective.

constructive /kən'strʌktɪv/ adjective positive, helpful. □ **constructively** adverb.

construe /kən'struː/ verb (**-strues**, **-strued**, **struing**) interpret; (often + with) combine (words) grammatically; translate literally.

consubstantiation /kɒnsəbstænʃɪ'eɪʃ(ə)n/ noun presence of Christ's body and blood together with bread and wine in Eucharist.

consul /'kɒns(ə)l/ noun official appointed by state to protect its interests and citizens in foreign city; historical either of two annually-elected magistrates in ancient Rome. □ **consular** /-sjʊlə/ adjective.

consulate /'kɒnsjʊlət/ noun offices or position of consul.

consult /kən'sʌlt/ verb seek information or advice from; (often + with) refer to; take into consideration.

consultant /kən'sʌlt(ə)nt/ noun person who gives professional advice; senior medical specialist. □ **consultancy** noun.

consultation /kɒnsəl'teɪʃ(ə)n/ noun (meeting for) consulting.

consultative /kən'sʌltətɪv/ adjective of or for consultation.

consume /kən'sjuːm/ verb (**-ming**) eat or drink; use up; destroy. □ **consumable** adjective.

consumer noun user of product or service. □ **consumer goods** goods for consumers, not for producing other goods.

consumerism *noun* protection or promotion of consumers' interests; *often derogatory* continual increase in consumption. □ **consumerist** *adjective*.

consummate ● *verb* /ˈkɒnsəmeɪt/ **(-ting)** complete (esp. marriage by sexual intercourse). ● *adjective* /kənˈsʌmɪt/ complete, perfect; fully skilled. □ **consummation** /kɒnsə-/ *noun*.

consumption /kənˈsʌmpʃ(ə)n/ *noun* consuming, being consumed; purchase and use of goods etc.; *archaic* tuberculosis of lungs.

consumptive /kənˈsʌmptɪv/ *archaic* ● *adjective* suffering or tending to suffer from tuberculosis. ● *noun* consumptive person.

cont. *abbreviation* continued.

contact /ˈkɒntækt/ ● *noun* condition or state of touching, meeting, or communicating; person who is, or may be, contacted for information etc.; person likely to carry contagious disease through being near infected person; connection for passage of electric current. ● *verb* get in touch with. □ **contact lens** small lens placed on eyeball to correct vision.

contagion /kənˈteɪdʒ(ə)n/ *noun* spreading of disease by contact; moral corruption. □ **contagious** *adjective*.

contain /kənˈteɪn/ *verb* hold or be capable of holding within itself; include; comprise; prevent from moving or extending; control, restrain.

container *noun* box etc. for holding things; large metal box for transporting goods.

containment /kənˈteɪnmənt/ *noun* action or policy of preventing expansion of hostile country or influence.

contaminate /kənˈtæmɪneɪt/ *verb* **(-ting)** pollute; infect. □ **contaminant** *noun*; **contamination** *noun*.

contemplate /ˈkɒntəmpleɪt/ *verb* **(-ting)** survey with eyes or mind; regard as possible; intend. □ **contemplation** *noun*.

contemplative /kənˈtemplətɪv/ *adjective* of or given to (esp. religious) contemplation.

contemporaneous /kəntempəˈreɪnɪəs/ *adjective* (usually + *with*) existing or occurring at same time.

contemporary /kənˈtempərərɪ/ ● *adjective* belonging to same time; of same age; modern in style or design. ● *noun* (*plural* **-ies**) contemporary person or thing.

contempt /kənˈtempt/ *noun* feeling that person or thing deserves scorn or reproach; condition of being held in contempt; (in full **contempt of court**) disobedience to or disrespect for court of law. □ **contemptible** *adjective*.

contemptuous *adjective* feeling or showing contempt. □ **contemptuously** *adverb*.

contend /kənˈtend/ *verb* compete; (usually + *with*) argue; (+ *that*) maintain that. □ **contender** *noun*.

content¹ /kənˈtent/ ● *adjective* satisfied; (+ *to do*) willing. ● *verb* make content; satisfy. ● *noun* contented state; satisfaction. □ **contented** *adjective*; **contentment** *noun*.

content² /ˈkɒntent/ *noun* (usually in *plural*) what is contained, esp. in vessel, house, or book; amount contained; substance of book etc. as opposed to form; capacity, volume.

contention /kənˈtenʃ(ə)n/ *noun* dispute, rivalry; point contended for in argument.

contentious /kənˈtenʃəs/ *adjective* quarrelsome; likely to cause argument.

contest ● *noun* /ˈkɒntest/ contending; a competition. ● *verb* /kənˈtest/ dispute; contend or compete for; compete in.

contestant /kənˈtest(ə)nt/ *noun* person taking part in contest.

context /ˈkɒntekst/ *noun* what precedes and follows word or passage; relevant circumstances. □ **contextual** /kənˈtekstjʊəl/ *adjective*.

contiguous /kənˈtɪɡjʊəs/ *adjective* (usually + *with*, *to*) touching; in contact.

continent¹ /ˈkɒntɪnənt/ *noun* any of the earth's main continuous bodies of land; (**the Continent**) the mainland of Europe.

continent² /ˈkɒntɪnənt/ *adjective* able to control bowels and bladder; exercising esp. sexual self-restraint. □ **continence** *noun*.

continental /kɒntrɪˈnent(ə)l/ *adjective* of or characteristic of a continent or (**Continental**) the Continent. □ **continental breakfast** light breakfast of coffee, rolls, etc.; **continental quilt** duvet; **continental shelf** shallow sea-bed bordering continent.

contingency /kən'tɪndʒənsɪ/ *noun* (*plural* **-ies**) event that may or may not occur; something dependent on another uncertain event.

contingent ● *adjective* (usually + *on, upon*) conditional, dependent; that may or may not occur; fortuitous. ● *noun* group (of troops, ships, etc.) forming part of larger group; people sharing interest, origin, etc.

continual /kən'tɪnjʊəl/ *adjective* frequently recurring; always happening. □ **continually** *adverb*.

continuance /kən'tɪnjʊəns/ *noun* continuing in existence or operation; duration.

continuation /kəntɪnjʊ'eɪʃ(ə)n/ *noun* continuing, being continued; thing that continues something else.

continue /kən'tɪnjuː/ *verb* (**-ues, -ued, -uing**) maintain; resume; prolong; remain.

continuity /kɒntɪ'njuːɪtɪ/ *noun* (*plural* **-ies**) being continuous; logical sequence; detailed scenario of film; linkage of broadcast items.

continuo /kən'tɪnjʊəʊ/ *noun* (*plural* **-s**) *Music* bass accompaniment played usually on keyboard instrument.

continuous /kən'tɪnjʊəs/ *adjective* connected without break; uninterrupted. □ **continuously** *adverb*.

continuum /kən'tɪnjʊəm/ *noun* (*plural* **-nua**) thing with continuous structure.

contort /kən'tɔːt/ *verb* twist or force out of normal shape. □ **contortion** *noun*.

contortionist *noun* entertainer who adopts contorted postures.

contour /'kɒntʊə/ *noun* outline; (in full **contour line**) line on map joining points at same altitude.

contraband /'kɒntrəbænd/ ● *noun* smuggled goods. ● *adjective* forbidden to be imported or exported.

contraception /kɒntrə'sepʃ(ə)n/ *noun* use of contraceptives.

contraceptive /kɒntrə'septɪv/ ● *adjective* preventing pregnancy. ● *noun* contraceptive device or drug.

contract ● *noun* /'kɒntrækt/ written or spoken agreement, esp. one enforceable by law; document recording it.

● *verb* /kən'trækt/ make or become smaller; (usually + *with*) make contract; (often + *out*) arrange (work) to be done by contract; become affected by (a disease); incur (debt); draw together; shorten. □ **contract bridge** type of bridge in which only tricks bid and won count towards game; **contract in** (or **out**) elect (not) to enter scheme etc.

contraction /kən'trækʃ(ə)n/ *noun* contracting; shortening of uterine muscles during childbirth; shrinking; diminution; shortened word.

contractor /kən'træktə/ *noun* person who undertakes contract, esp. in building, engineering, etc.

contractual /kən'træktjʊəl/ *adjective* of or in the nature of a contract.

contradict /kɒntrə'dɪkt/ *verb* deny; oppose verbally; be at variance with. □ **contradiction** *noun*; **contradictory** *adjective*.

contradistinction /kɒntrədɪs'tɪŋkʃ(ə)n/ *noun* distinction made by contrasting.

contraflow /'kɒntrəfləʊ/ *noun* transfer of traffic from usual half of road to lane(s) of other half.

contralto /kən'træltəʊ/ *noun* (*plural* **-s**) lowest female singing voice; singer with this voice.

contraption /kən'træpʃ(ə)n/ *noun* machine or device, esp. strange one.

contrapuntal /kɒntrə'pʌnt(ə)l/ *adjective* *Music* of or in counterpoint.

contrariwise /kən'treərɪwaɪz/ *adverb* on the other hand; in the opposite way.

contrary /'kɒntrərɪ/ ● *adjective* (usually + *to*) opposed in nature, tendency, or direction; /kən'treərɪ/ perverse, self-willed. ● *noun* (**the contrary**) the opposite. ● *adverb* (+ *to*) in opposition. □ **on the contrary** the opposite is true.

contrast ● *noun* /'kɒntrɑːst/ comparison showing differences; difference so revealed; (often + *to*) thing or person having different qualities; degree of difference between tones in photograph or television picture. ● *verb* /kən'trɑːst/ (often + *with*) compare to reveal contrast; show contrast.

contravene /kɒntrə'viːn/ *verb* (**-ning**) infringe; conflict with. □ **contravention** /-'ven-/ *noun*.

contretemps /'kɒntrətã/ noun (plural same /-tãz/) unlucky accident; unfortunate occurrence.

contribute /kən'trɪbjuːt/ verb (**-ting**) (often + to) give jointly with others to common purpose; supply (article etc.) for publication with others; (+ to) help to bring about. □ **contribution** /kɒntrɪ'bjuːʃ(ə)n/ noun; **contributor** noun; **contributory** adjective.

■ **Usage** Contribute is often pronounced /'kɒntrɪbjuːt/ (with the stress on the con-), but this is considered incorrect by some people.

contrite /kən'traɪt/ adjective penitent, feeling guilt. □ **contrition** /-'trɪʃ-/ noun.

contrivance noun something contrived, esp. device or plan; act of contriving.

contrive /kən'traɪv/ verb (**-ving**) devise, plan; (often + to do) manage.

contrived adjective artificial, forced.

control /kən'trəʊl/ ● noun power of directing or restraining; self-restraint; means of restraining or regulating; (usually in plural) device to operate machine, vehicle, etc.; place where something is controlled or verified; standard of comparison for checking results of experiment. ● verb (**-ll-**) have control of; regulate; hold in check; verify. □ **in control** (often + of) in charge; **out of control** no longer manageable.

controller noun person or thing that controls; person controlling expenditure.

controversial /kɒntrə'vɜːʃ(ə)l/ adjective causing or subject to controversy.

controversy /'kɒntrəvɜːsɪ/ noun (plural **-ies**) dispute, argument.

■ **Usage** Controversy is often pronounced /kən'trɒvəsɪ/ (with the stress on the -trov-), but this is considered incorrect by some people.

controvert /kɒntrə'vɜːt/ verb dispute, deny.

contuse /kən'tjuːz/ verb (**-sing**) bruise. □ **contusion** noun.

conundrum /kə'nʌndrəm/ noun riddle; hard question.

conurbation /kɒnɜː'beɪʃ(ə)n/ noun group of towns united by expansion.

convalesce /kɒnvə'les/ verb (**-cing**) recover health after illness.

convalescent /kɒnvə'les(ə)nt/ ● adjective recovering from illness. ● noun convalescent person. □ **convalescence** noun.

convection /kən'vekʃ(ə)n/ noun heat transfer by upward movement of heated medium.

convector /kən'vektə/ noun heating appliance that circulates warm air by convection.

convene /kən'viːn/ verb (**-ning**) summon; assemble. □ **convener, convenor** noun.

convenience /kən'viːnɪəns/ noun state of being convenient; suitability; advantage; useful thing; public lavatory. □ **convenience food** food needing little preparation.

convenient adjective serving one's comfort or interests; suitable; available or occurring at suitable time or place; well situated. □ **conveniently** adverb.

convent /'kɒnv(ə)nt/ noun religious community, esp. of nuns; its house.

convention /kən'venʃ(ə)n/ noun general agreement on social behaviour etc. by implicit consent of majority; customary practice; assembly, conference; agreement, treaty.

conventional adjective depending on or according with convention; bound by social conventions; not spontaneous or sincere; (of weapons etc.) non-nuclear. □ **conventionally** adverb.

converge /kən'vɜːdʒ/ verb (**-ging**) come together or towards same point; (+ on, upon) approach from different directions. □ **convergence** noun, **convergent** adjective.

conversant /kən'vɜːs(ə)nt/ adjective (+ with) well acquainted with.

conversation /kɒnvə'seɪʃ(ə)n/ noun informal spoken communication; instance of this.

conversational adjective of or in conversation; colloquial. □ **conversationally** adverb.

conversationalist noun person fond of or good at conversation.

converse¹ /kən'vɜːs/ verb (**-sing**) (often + with) talk.

converse[2] /'kɒnvɜːs/ ● *adjective* opposite, contrary, reversed. ● *noun* converse statement or proposition. □ **conversely** *adverb*.

conversion /kən'vɜːʃ(ə)n/ *noun* converting, being converted; converted (part of) building.

convert ● *verb* /kən'vɜːt/ (usually + *into*) change; cause (person) to change belief etc.; change (money etc.) into different form or currency etc.; alter (building) for new purpose; *Rugby* kick goal after (try). ● *noun* /'kɒnvɜːt/ person converted, esp. to religious faith.

convertible /kən'vɜːtɪb(ə)l/ ● *adjective* able to be converted. ● *noun* car with folding or detachable roof.

convex /'kɒnveks/ *adjective* curved like outside of sphere or circle.

convey /kən'veɪ/ *verb* transport; carry; communicate (meaning etc.); transfer by legal process; transmit (sound etc.).

conveyance *noun* conveying, being conveyed; vehicle; legal transfer of property, document effecting this.

conveyancing *noun* branch of law dealing with transfer of property. □ **conveyancer** *noun*.

conveyor *noun* person or thing that conveys. □ **conveyor belt** endless moving belt conveying articles in factory etc.

convict ● *verb* /kən'vɪkt/ (often + *of*) prove or declare guilty. ● *noun* /'kɒnvɪkt/ *esp. historical* sentenced criminal.

conviction /kən'vɪkʃ(ə)n/ *noun* convicting, being convicted; being convinced; firm belief.

convince /kən'vɪns/ *verb* (-**cing**) firmly persuade. □ **convincing** *adjective*; **convincingly** *adverb*.

convivial /kən'vɪvɪəl/ *adjective* fond of company; sociable, lively. □ **conviviality** /-'æl-/ *noun*.

convocation /kɒnvə'keɪʃ(ə)n/ *noun* convoking; large formal gathering.

convoke /kən'vəʊk/ *verb* (-**king**) call together; summon to assemble.

convoluted /ˈkɒnvəˈluːtɪd/ *adjective* coiled, twisted; complex.

convolution /kɒnvə'luːʃ(ə)n/ *noun* coiling; coil, twist; complexity.

convolvulus /kən'vɒlvjʊləs/ *noun* (*plural* -**es**) twining plant, esp. bindweed.

convoy /'kɒnvɔɪ/ *noun* group of ships, vehicles, etc. travelling together. □ **in convoy** as a group.

convulse /kən'vʌls/ *verb* (-**sing**) affect with convulsions.

convulsion *noun* (usually in *plural*) violent irregular motion of limbs or body caused by involuntary contraction of muscles; violent disturbance; (in *plural*) uncontrollable laughter. □ **convulsive** *adjective*; **convulsively** *adverb*.

cony /'kəʊnɪ/ *noun* (*plural* -**ies**) (also **coney**) rabbit; its fur.

coo ● *noun* soft murmuring sound as of doves. ● *verb* (**coos**, **cooed**) emit coo.

cooee /'kuːiː/ *interjection used to attract attention*.

cook /kʊk/ ● *verb* prepare (food) by heating; undergo cooking; *colloquial* falsify (accounts etc.). ● *noun* person who cooks. □ **cookbook** US cookery book; **cooking apple** one suitable for eating cooked.

cooker *noun* appliance or vessel for cooking food; fruit (esp. apple) suitable for cooking.

cookery *noun* art of cooking. □ **cookery book** book containing recipes.

cookie /'kʊkɪ/ *noun* US sweet biscuit.

cool /kuːl/ ● *adjective* of or at fairly low temperature; suggesting or achieving coolness; calm; lacking enthusiasm; unfriendly; *slang esp. US* marvellous. ● *noun* coolness; cool place; *slang* composure. ● *verb* (often + *down*, *off*) make or become cool. □ **coolly** /'kuːllɪ/ *adverb*; **coolness** *noun*.

coolant *noun* cooling agent, esp. fluid.

cooler *noun* vessel in which thing is cooled; *slang* prison cell.

coomb /kuːm/ *noun* (also **combe**) valley on side of hill; short valley running up from coast.

coon /kuːn/ *noun* US racoon.

coop /kuːp/ ● *noun* cage for keeping poultry. ● *verb* (often + *up*, *in*) confine.

co-op /'kəʊɒp/ *noun colloquial* cooperative society or shop.

cooper *noun* maker or repairer of casks and barrels.

cooperate /kəʊ'ɒpəreɪt/ *verb* (also **co-operate**) (-**ting**) (often + *with*) work or act together. □ **cooperation** noun.

cooperative /kəʊˈɒpərətɪv/ (also **co-operative**) ● adjective willing to cooperate; (of business etc.) jointly owned and run by members, with profits shared. ● noun cooperative society or enterprise.

co-opt /kəʊˈɒpt/ verb appoint to committee etc. by invitation of existing members. □ **co-option** noun; **co-optive** adjective.

coordinate (also **co-ordinate**) ● verb /kəʊˈɔːdɪneɪt/ (**-ting**) cause to work together efficiently; work or act together effectively. ● adjective /-nət/ equal in status. ● noun /-nət/ Mathematics each of set of quantities used to fix position of point, line, or plane; (in plural) matching items of clothing. □ **coordination** noun; **coordinator** noun.

coot /kuːt/ noun black waterfowl with white horny plate on head; colloquial stupid person.

cop slang ● noun police officer; capture. ● verb (**-pp-**) catch. □ **cop-out** cowardly evasion; **not much cop** of little value or use.

copal /ˈkəʊp(ə)l/ noun kind of resin used for varnish.

copartner /kəʊˈpɑːtnə/ noun partner, associate. □ **copartnership** noun.

cope[1] verb (**-ping**) deal effectively or contend; (often + with) manage.

cope[2] noun priest's long cloaklike vestment.

copeck /ˈkəʊpek/ noun (also **kopek**, **kopeck**) hundredth of rouble.

copier /ˈkɒpɪə/ noun machine that copies (esp. documents).

copilot /ˈkəʊpaɪlət/ noun second pilot in aircraft.

coping /ˈkəʊpɪŋ/ noun top (usually sloping) course of masonry in wall. □ **coping stone** stone used in coping.

copious /ˈkəʊpɪəs/ adjective abundant; producing much. □ **copiously** adverb.

copper[1] /ˈkɒpə/ ● noun red-brown metal; bronze coin; large metal vessel for boiling laundry. ● adjective made of or coloured like copper. □ **copperplate** copper plate for engraving or etching, print taken from it, ornate sloping handwriting.

copper[2] /ˈkɒpə/ noun slang police officer.

coppice /ˈkɒpɪs/ noun area of undergrowth and small trees.

copulate /ˈkɒpjʊleɪt/ verb (**-ting**) (often + with) (esp. of animals) have sexual intercourse. □ **copulation** noun.

copy /ˈkɒpɪ/ ● noun (plural **-ies**) thing made to look like another; specimen of book etc.; material to be printed, esp. regarded as good etc. reading matter. ● verb (**-ies**, **-ied**) make copy of; imitate. □ **copy-typist** typist working from document or recording; **copywriter** writer of copy, esp. for advertisements.

copyist /ˈkɒpɪɪst/ noun person who makes copies.

copyright ● noun exclusive right to print, publish, perform, etc., material. ● adjective protected by copyright. ● verb secure copyright for (material).

coquette /kəˈket/ noun woman who flirts. □ **coquettish** adjective; **coquetry** /ˈkɒkɪtrɪ/ noun (plural **-ies**).

coracle /ˈkɒrək(ə)l/ noun small boat of wickerwork covered with waterproof material.

coral /ˈkɒr(ə)l/ ● noun hard substance built up by marine polyps. ● adjective of (red or pink colour of) coral. □ **coral island**, **reef** one formed by growth of coral.

cor anglais /kɔːr ˈɒŋɡleɪ/ noun (plural **cors anglais** /kɔːz/) woodwind instrument like oboe but lower in pitch.

corbel /ˈkɔːb(ə)l/ noun stone or timber projection from wall, acting as supporting bracket.

cord ● noun thick string; piece of this; similar structure in body; ribbed cloth, esp. corduroy; (in plural) corduroy trousers; electric flex. ● verb secure with cords.

cordial /ˈkɔːdɪəl/ ● adjective heartfelt; friendly. ● noun fruit-flavoured drink. □ **cordiality** /-ˈæl-/ noun; **cordially** adverb.

cordite /ˈkɔːdaɪt/ noun smokeless explosive.

cordless adjective (of handheld electric device) battery-powered.

cordon /ˈkɔːd(ə)n/ ● noun line or circle of police etc.; ornamental cord or braid; fruit tree trained to grow as single stem. ● verb (often + off) enclose or separate with cordon of police etc.

cordon bleu /kɔːdɒn 'blɜː/ *adjective* (of cooking) first-class.

corduroy /'kɔːdərɔɪ/ *noun* fabric with velvety ribs.

core ● *noun* horny central part of certain fruits, containing seeds; centre or most important part; part of nuclear reactor containing fissile material; inner strand of electric cable; piece of soft iron forming centre of magnet etc. ● *verb* (**-ring**) remove core from.

co-respondent /kəʊrɪ'spɒnd(ə)nt/ *noun* person cited in divorce case as having committed adultery with respondent.

corgi /'kɔːgɪ/ *noun* (*plural* **-s**) short-legged breed of dog.

coriander /kɒrɪ'ændə/ *noun* aromatic plant; its seed, used as flavouring.

cork ● *noun* thick light bark of S. European oak; bottle-stopper made of cork etc. ● *verb* (often + *up*) stop, confine; restrain (feelings etc.).

corkage *noun* charge made by restaurant etc. for serving customer's own wine etc.

corked *adjective* (of wine) spoilt by defective cork.

corkscrew ● *noun* spiral steel device for extracting corks from bottles. ● *verb* move spirally.

corm *noun* swollen underground stem in certain plants, e.g. crocus.

cormorant /'kɔːmərənt/ *noun* diving seabird with black plumage.

corn[1] *noun* cereal before or after harvesting, esp. chief crop of a region; grain or seed of cereal plant; *colloquial* something corny. □ **corn cob** cylindrical centre of maize ear; **corncrake** ground-nesting bird with harsh cry; **corn dolly** plaited straw figure; **cornflakes** breakfast cereal of toasted maize flakes; **cornflour** fine-ground maize flour; **cornflower** blue-flowered plant originally growing in cornfields; **corn on the cob** maize eaten from the corn cob.

corn[2] *noun* small tender hard area of skin, esp. on toe.

cornea /'kɔːnɪə/ *noun* transparent circular part of front of eyeball.

corned *adjective* preserved in salt or brine.

cornelian /kɔː'niːlɪən/ *noun* (also **carnelian** /kɑː-/) dull red variety of chalcedony.

corner /'kɔːnə/ ● *noun* place where converging sides, edges, streets, etc. meet; recess formed by meeting of two internal sides of room, box, etc.; difficult or inescapable position; remote or secluded place; action or result of buying whole available stock of a commodity; *Football & Hockey* free kick or hit from corner of pitch. ● *verb* force into difficult or inescapable position; buy whole available stock of (commodity); dominate (market) in this way; go round corner. □ **cornerstone** stone in projecting angle of wall, indispensable part or basis.

cornet /'kɔːnɪt/ *noun* brass instrument resembling trumpet; conical wafer for holding ice cream.

cornice /'kɔːnɪs/ *noun* ornamental moulding, esp. along top of internal wall.

Cornish /'kɔːnɪʃ/ ● *adjective* of Cornwall. ● *noun* Celtic language of Cornwall. □ **Cornish pasty** pastry envelope containing meat and vegetables.

cornucopia /kɔːnjʊ'kəʊpɪə/ *noun* horn overflowing with flowers, fruit, etc., as symbol of plenty.

corny *adjective* (**-ier**, **-iest**) *colloquial* banal; feebly humorous; sentimental.

corolla /kə'rɒlə/ *noun* whorl of petals forming inner envelope of flower.

corollary /kə'rɒlərɪ/ *noun* (*plural* **-ies**) proposition that follows from one proved; (often + *of*) natural consequence.

corona /kə'rəʊnə/ *noun* (*plural* **-nae** /-niː/) halo round sun or moon, esp. that seen in total eclipse of sun.

coronary /'kɒrənərɪ/ *noun* (*plural* **-ies**) coronary thrombosis. □ **coronary artery** artery supplying blood to heart; **coronary thrombosis** blockage of coronary artery by blood clot.

coronation /kɒrə'neɪʃ(ə)n/ *noun* ceremony of crowning sovereign.

coroner /'kɒrənə/ *noun* official holding inquest on deaths thought to be violent or accidental.

coronet /'kɒrənɪt/ *noun* small crown.

corpora *plural* of CORPUS.

corporal[1] /'kɔ:pr(ə)l/ *noun* army or air-force NCO next below sergeant.

corporal[2] /'kɔ:pər(ə)l/ *adjective* of human body. □ **corporal punishment** physical punishment.

corporate /'kɔ:pərət/ *adjective* of, being, or belonging to a corporation or group.

corporation /kɔ:pə'reɪʃ(ə)n/ *noun* group of people authorized to act as individual, esp. in business; civic authorities.

corporative /'kɔ:pərətɪv/ *adjective* of corporation; governed by or organized in corporations.

corporeal /kɔ:'pɔ:rɪəl/ *adjective* bodily, physical, material.

corps /kɔ:/ *noun* (*plural* same /kɔ:z/) military unit with particular function; organized group of people.

corpse /kɔ:ps/ *noun* dead body.

corpulent /'kɔ:pjʊlənt/ *adjective* fleshy, bulky. □ **corpulence** *noun*.

corpus /'kɔ:pəs/ *noun* (*plural* **-pora** /-pərə/) body or collection of writings, texts, etc.

corpuscle /'kɔ:pʌs(ə)l/ *noun* minute body or cell in organism, esp. (in *plural*) red or white cells in blood of vertebrates. □ **corpuscular** /-'pʌskjʊlə/ *adjective*.

corral /kə'rɑ:l/ ● *noun* US pen for horses, cattle, etc.; enclosure for capturing wild animals. ● *verb* (**-ll-**) put or keep in corral.

correct /kə'rekt/ ● *adjective* true, accurate; proper, in accordance with taste, standards, etc. ● *verb* set right; mark errors in; admonish; counteract. □ **correctly** *adverb*; **correctness** *noun*.

correction *noun* correcting, being corrected; thing substituted for what is wrong.

correctitude /kə'rektɪtju:d/ *noun* consciously correct behaviour.

corrective ● *adjective* serving to correct or counteract. ● *noun* corrective measure or thing.

correlate /'kɒrəleɪt/ ● *verb* (**-ting**) (usually + *with, to*) have or bring into mutual relation. ● *noun* either of two related or complementary things. □ **correlation** *noun*.

correlative /kə'relətɪv/ ● *adjective* (often + *with, to*) having a mutual relation; (of words) corresponding and regularly used together. ● *noun* correlative thing or word.

correspond /kɒrɪ'spɒnd/ *verb* (usually + *to*) be similar or equivalent; (usually + *to, with*) agree; (usually + *with*) exchange letters.

correspondence *noun* agreement or similarity; (exchange of) letters. □ **correspondence course** course of study conducted by post.

correspondent *noun* person who writes letter(s); person employed to write or report for newspaper or broadcasting.

corridor /'kɒrɪdɔ:/ *noun* passage giving access into rooms; passage in train giving access into compartments; strip of territory of one state running through that of another; route for aircraft over foreign country.

corrigendum /kɒrɪ'dʒendəm/ *noun* (*plural* **-da**) error to be corrected.

corrigible /'kɒrɪdʒɪb(ə)l/ *adjective* able to be corrected.

corroborate /kə'rɒbəreɪt/ *verb* (**-ting**) give support to, confirm. □ **corroboration** *noun*; **corroborative** /-rətɪv/ *adjective*; **corroboratory** /-rət(ə)rɪ/ *adjective*.

corrode /kə'rəʊd/ *verb* (**-ding**) wear away, esp. by chemical action; destroy gradually; decay.

corrosion /kə'rəʊʒ(ə)n/ *noun* corroding, being corroded; corroded area. □ **corrosive** /-sɪv/ *adjective & noun*.

corrugate /'kɒrəgeɪt/ *verb* (**-ting**) (esp. as **corrugated** *adjective*) bend into wavy ridges. □ **corrugation** *noun*.

corrupt /kə'rʌpt/ ● *adjective* influenced by or using bribery; immoral, wicked. ● *verb* make or become corrupt. □ **corruptible** *adjective*; **corruption** *noun*; **corruptly** *adverb*.

corsage /kɔ:'sɑ:ʒ/ *noun* small bouquet worn by woman.

corsair /'kɔ:seə/ *noun* pirate ship; pirate.

corset /'kɔ:sɪt/ *noun* tight-fitting supporting undergarment worn esp. by women. □ **corsetry** *noun*.

cortège /kɔ:'teɪʒ/ *noun* procession, esp. for funeral.

cortex /'kɔ:teks/ *noun* (*plural* **-tices** /-tɪsi:z/) outer part of organ, esp. brain. □ **cortical** *adjective*.

cortisone /'kɔːtɪzəʊn/ *noun* hormone used in treating inflammation and allergy.

corvette /kɔː'vet/ *noun* small naval escort-vessel.

cos¹ /kɒs/ *noun* crisp long-leaved lettuce.

cos² /kɒz/ *abbreviation* cosine.

cosh *colloquial* ●*noun* heavy blunt weapon. ●*verb* hit with cosh.

cosine /'kəʊsaɪn/ *noun* ratio of side adjacent to acute angle (in right-angled triangle) to hypotenuse.

cosmetic /kɒz'metɪk/ ●*adjective* beautifying, enhancing; superficially improving; (of surgery etc.) restoring or enhancing normal appearance. ●*noun* cosmetic preparation. □ **cosmetically** *adverb*.

cosmic /'kɒzmɪk/ *adjective* of the cosmos; of or for space travel. □ **cosmic rays** high-energy radiations from outer space.

cosmogony /kɒz'mɒgənɪ/ *noun* (*plural* **-ies**) (theory about) origin of universe.

cosmology /kɒz'mɒlədʒɪ/ *noun* science or theory of universe. □ **cosmological** /-mə'lɒdʒ-/ *adjective*; **cosmologist** *noun*.

cosmonaut /'kɒzmənɔːt/ *noun* Russian astronaut.

cosmopolitan /kɒzmə'pɒlɪt(ə)n/ ●*adjective* of or knowing all parts of world; free from national limitations. ●*noun* cosmopolitan person. □ **cosmopolitanism** *noun*.

cosmos /'kɒzmɒs/ *noun* universe as a well-ordered whole.

Cossack /'kɒsæk/ *noun* member of S. Russian people famous as horsemen.

cosset /'kɒsɪt/ *verb* (**-t-**) pamper.

cost ●*verb* (*past & past participle* **cost**) have as price; involve as loss or sacrifice; (*past & past participle* **costed**) fix or estimate cost of. ●*noun* price; loss, sacrifice; (in *plural*) legal expenses. □ **cost-effective** effective in relation to cost; **cost of living** cost of basic necessities of life; **cost price** price paid for thing by person who later sells it.

costal /'kɒst(ə)l/ *adjective* of ribs.

costermonger /'kɒstəmʌŋgə/ *noun* person who sells fruit etc. from barrow.

costive /'kɒstɪv/ *adjective* constipated.

costly *adjective* (**-ier**, **-iest**) costing much, expensive. □ **costliness** *noun*.

costume /'kɒstjuːm/ ●*noun* style of dress, esp. of particular place or period; set of clothes; clothing for particular activity; actor's clothes for part. ●*verb* provide with costume. □ **costume jewellery** artificial jewellery.

costumier /kɒs'tjuːmɪə/ *noun* person who deals in or makes costumes.

cosy /'kəʊzɪ/ (*US* **cozy**) ●*adjective* (**-ier**, **-iest**) snug, comfortable. ●*noun* (*plural* **-ies**) cover to keep teapot etc. hot. □ **cosily** *adverb*; **cosiness** *noun*.

cot *noun* small high-sided bed for child etc.; small light bed. □ **cot death** unexplained death of sleeping baby.

cote *noun* shelter for birds or animals.

coterie /'kəʊtərɪ/ *noun* exclusive group of people sharing interests.

cotoneaster /kətəʊnɪ'æstə/ *noun* shrub bearing red or orange berries.

cottage /'kɒtɪdʒ/ *noun* small house, esp. in the country. □ **cottage cheese** soft white lumpy cheese; **cottage industry** small business carried on at home; **cottage pie** shepherd's pie.

cottager *noun* person who lives in cottage.

cotter /'kɒtə/ *noun* (also **cotter pin**) wedge or pin for securing machine part such as bicycle pedal crank.

cotton /'kɒt(ə)n/ *noun* soft white fibrous substance covering seeds of certain plants; such a plant; thread or cloth from this. □ **cotton on** (often + *to*) *colloquial* begin to understand; **cotton wool** wadding originally made from raw cotton.

cotyledon /kɒtɪ'liːd(ə)n/ *noun* first leaf produced by plant embryo.

couch¹ /kaʊtʃ/ ●*noun* upholstered piece of furniture for several people; sofa. ●*verb* (+ *in*) express in (language of specified kind). □ **couch potato** *US slang* person who likes lazing at home.

couch² /kuːtʃ/ *noun* (in full **couch grass**) kind of grass with long creeping roots.

couchette /kuː'ʃet/ *noun* railway carriage with seats convertible into sleeping berths; berth in this.

cougar /'kuːgə/ *noun* *US* puma.

cough /kɒf/ ● *verb* expel air from lungs with sudden sharp sound. ● *noun* (sound of) coughing; condition of respiratory organs causing coughing. □ **cough mixture** medicine to relieve cough; **cough up** eject with coughs, *slang* give (money, information, etc.) reluctantly.

could *past of* CAN¹.

couldn't /'kʊd(ə)nt/ could not.

coulomb /'ku:lɒm/ *noun* SI unit of electrical charge.

coulter /'kəʊltə/ *noun* (*US* **colter**) vertical blade in front of ploughshare.

council /'kaʊns(ə)l/ *noun* (meeting of) advisory, deliberative, or administrative body; local administrative body of county, city, town, etc. □ **council flat, house** one owned and let by local council; **council tax** local tax based on value of property and number of residents.

councillor *noun* member of (esp. local) council.

counsel /'kaʊns(ə)l/ ● *noun* advice, esp. formal; consultation; (*plural* same) legal adviser, esp. barrister; group of these. ● *verb* (**-ll-**; *US* **-l-**) advise, esp. on personal problems. □ **counsellor** (*US* **counselor**) *noun*.

count¹ ● *verb* find number of, esp. by assigning successive numerals; repeat numbers in order; (+ *in*) include or be included in reckoning; consider to be. ● *noun* counting; reckoning; total; *Law* each charge in an indictment. □ **countdown** counting numbers backwards to zero, esp. before launching rocket etc.; **count on** rely on; **count out** exclude, disregard.

count² *noun* foreign noble corresponding to earl.

countenance /'kaʊntɪnəns/ ● *noun* face or its expression; composure; moral support. ● *verb* (**-cing**) support, approve.

counter¹ *noun* flat-topped fitment in shop etc. across which business is conducted; small disc used for playing or scoring in board games, cards, etc.; device for counting things.

counter² ● *verb* oppose, contradict; meet by countermove. ● *adverb* in opposite direction. ● *adjective* opposite. ● *noun* parry, countermove.

counteract /kaʊntə'rækt/ *verb* neutralize or hinder by contrary action. □ **counteraction** *noun*.

counter-attack *verb* & *noun* attack in reply to enemy's attack.

counterbalance ● *noun* weight or influence balancing another. ● *verb* (**-cing**) act as counterbalance to.

counter-clockwise *adverb* & *adjective US* anticlockwise.

counter-espionage *noun* action taken against enemy spying.

counterfeit /'kaʊntəfɪt/ ● *adjective* imitation; forged; not genuine. ● *noun* forgery, imitation. ● *verb* imitate fraudulently; forge.

counterfoil *noun* part of cheque, receipt, etc. retained as record.

counter-intelligence *noun* counterespionage.

countermand /kaʊntə'mɑːnd/ *verb* revoke, recall by contrary order.

countermeasure *noun* action taken to counteract danger, threat, etc.

countermove *noun* move or action in opposition to another.

counterpane *noun* bedspread.

counterpart *noun* person or thing equivalent or complementary to another; duplicate.

counterpoint *noun* harmonious combination of melodies in music; melody combined with another; contrasting argument, plot, literary theme, etc.

counterpoise ● *noun* counterbalance; state of equilibrium. ● *verb* (**-sing**) counterbalance.

counter-productive *adjective* having opposite of desired effect.

counter-revolution *noun* revolution opposing former one or reversing its results.

countersign ● *verb* add confirming signature to. ● *noun* password spoken to person on guard.

countersink *verb* (*past & past participle* **-sunk**) shape (screw-hole) so that screw-head lies level with surface; provide (screw) with countersunk hole.

counter-tenor *noun* male alto singing voice; singer with this.

countervailing /'kaʊntəveɪlɪŋ/ *adjective* (of influence etc.) counterbalancing.

counterweight *noun* counterbalancing weight.

countess /ˈkaʊntɪs/ *noun* earl's or count's wife or widow; woman with rank of earl or count.

countless *adjective* too many to count.

countrified /ˈkʌntrɪfaɪd/ *adjective* rustic.

country /ˈkʌntrɪ/ *noun* (*plural* **-ies**) nation's territory, state; land of person's birth or citizenship; rural districts, as opposed to towns; region with regard to its aspect, associations, etc.; national population, esp. as voters. □ **country and western** type of folk music originated by southern US whites; **country dance** traditional dance; **countryman**, **countrywoman** person of one's own country or district; person living in rural area; **countryside** rural areas.

county /ˈkaʊntɪ/ *noun* (*plural* **-ies**) territorial division of country, forming chief unit of local administration; *US* political and administrative division of State; people, esp. gentry, of county. □ **county council** elected governing body of county; **county court** law court for civil cases; **county town** administrative capital of county.

coup /kuː/ *noun* (*plural* **-s** /kuːz/) successful stroke or move; *coup d'état.*

coup de grâce /kuː də ˈɡrɑːs/ *noun* finishing stroke. [French]

coup d'état /kuː deɪˈtɑː/ *noun* (*plural* **coups d'état** same pronunciation) sudden overthrow of government, esp. by force. [French]

coupé /ˈkuːpeɪ/ *noun* (*US* **coupe** /kuːp/) two-door car with hard roof and sloping back.

couple /ˈkʌp(ə)l/ ● *noun* (about) two; two people who are married or in a sexual relationship; pair of partners in a dance etc. ● *verb* (**-ling**) link, fasten, or associate together; copulate.

couplet /ˈkʌplɪt/ *noun* two successive lines of rhyming verse.

coupling /ˈkʌplɪŋ/ *noun* link connecting railway carriages or parts of machinery.

coupon /ˈkuːpɒn/ *noun* ticket or form entitling holder to something.

courage /ˈkʌrɪdʒ/ *noun* ability to disregard fear; bravery. □ **courageous** /kəˈreɪdʒəs/ *adjective*; **courageously** *adverb.*

courgette /kʊəˈʒet/ *noun* small vegetable marrow.

courier /ˈkʊrɪə/ *noun* person employed to guide and assist group of tourists; special messenger.

course /kɔːs/ ● *noun* onward movement or progression; direction taken; line of conduct; series of lectures, lessons, etc.; each successive part of meal; golf course, race-course, etc.; sequence of medical treatment etc.; continuous line of masonry or bricks at one level of building; channel in which water flows. ● *verb* (**-sing**) use hounds to hunt (esp. hares); move or flow freely. □ **in the course of** during; **of course** naturally, as expected, admittedly.

court /kɔːt/ ● *noun* number of houses enclosing a yard; courtyard; rectangular area for a game; (in full **court of law**) judicial body hearing legal cases; courtroom; sovereign's establishment and retinue. ● *verb* pay amorous attention to, seek to win favour of; try to win (fame etc.); unwisely invite. □ **court card** playing card that is king, queen, or jack; **court house** building in which judicial court is held, *US* county administrative offices; **court martial** (*plural* **courts martial**) judicial court of military officers; **court-martial** (**-ll-**; *US* **-l-**) try by court martial; **courtroom** room in which court of law sits; **court shoe** woman's light shoe with low-cut upper; **courtyard** space enclosed by walls or buildings.

courteous /ˈkɜːtɪəs/ *adjective* polite, considerate. □ **courteously** *adverb*; **courteousness** *noun.*

courtesan /kɔːtɪˈzæn/ *noun* prostitute, esp. one with wealthy or upper-class clients.

courtesy /ˈkɜːtəsɪ/ *noun* (*plural* **-ies**) courteous behaviour or act. □ **by courtesy of** with formal permission of; **courtesy light** light in car switched on when door is opened.

courtier /ˈkɔːtɪə/ *noun* person who attends sovereign's court.

courtly *adjective* (**-ier**, **-iest**) dignified; refined in manners. □ **courtliness** *noun.*

courtship *noun* courting, wooing.

couscous /'ku:sku:s/ *noun* N. African dish of cracked wheat steamed over broth.

cousin /'kʌz(ə)n/ *noun* (also **first cousin**) child of one's uncle or aunt.

couture /ku:'tjʊə/ *noun* design and making of fashionable garments.

couturier /ku:'tjʊərɪeɪ/ *noun* fashion designer.

cove /kəʊv/ *noun* small bay or inlet; sheltered recess.

coven /'kʌv(ə)n/ *noun* assembly of witches.

covenant /'kʌvənənt/ ● *noun* agreement; *Law* sealed contract. ● *verb* agree, esp. by legal covenant.

Coventry /'kɒvəntrɪ/ *noun* □ **send to Coventry** refuse to associate with or speak to.

cover /'kʌvə/ ● *verb* (often + *with*) protect or conceal with cloth, lid, etc.; extend over; protect; clothe; include; (of sum) be large enough to meet (expense); protect by insurance; report on for newspaper, television, etc.; travel (specified distance); aim gun etc. at; protect by aiming gun. ● *noun* thing that covers, esp. lid, wrapper, etc.; shelter, protection; funds to meet liability or contingent loss; place-setting at table. □ **cover charge** service charge per person in restaurant; **cover note** temporary certificate of insurance; **cover up** *verb* cover completely, conceal; **cover-up** *noun* concealing of facts; **take cover** find shelter.

coverage *noun* area or amount covered; reporting of events in newspaper etc.

covering letter *noun* explanatory letter with other documents.

coverlet /'kʌvəlɪt/ *noun* bedspread.

covert /'kʌvət/ ● *adjective* secret, disguised. ● *noun* shelter, esp. thicket hiding game. □ **covertly** *adverb*.

covet /'kʌvɪt/ *verb* (**-t-**) desire greatly (esp. thing belonging to another person). □ **covetous** *adjective*.

covey /'kʌvɪ/ *noun* (*plural* **-s**) brood of partridges; family, set.

coving /'kəʊvɪŋ/ *noun* curved surface at junction of wall and ceiling.

cow[1] /kaʊ/ *noun* fully-grown female of esp. domestic bovine animal; female of elephant, rhinoceros, whale, seal, etc. □ **cowboy**, **cowgirl** person who tends cattle, esp. in western US, *colloquial* unscrupulous or incompetent business person; **cowherd** person who tends cattle; **cowhide** (leather made from) cow's hide; **cow-pat** round flat piece of cow-dung; **cowpox** disease of cows, source of smallpox vaccine.

cow[2] /kaʊ/ *verb* intimidate.

coward /'kaʊəd/ *noun* person easily frightened. □ **cowardly** *adjective*.

cowardice /'kaʊədɪs/ *noun* lack of bravery.

cower /'kaʊə/ *verb* crouch or shrink back in fear.

cowl /kaʊl/ *noun* (hood of) monk's cloak; (also **cowling**) hood-shaped covering of chimney or shaft. □ **cowl neck** wide loose roll neck on garment.

cowrie /'kaʊrɪ/ *noun* tropical mollusc with bright shell; its shell as money in parts of Asia etc.

cowslip /'kaʊslɪp/ *noun* yellow-flowered primula growing in pastures etc.

cox ● *noun* coxswain. ● *verb* act as cox (of).

coxcomb /'kɒkskəʊm/ *noun* conceited showy person.

coxswain /'kɒks(ə)n/ *noun* person who steers person's rowing boat.

coy *adjective* affectedly shy; irritatingly reticent. □ **coyly** *adverb*.

coyote /kɔɪ'əʊtɪ/ *noun* (*plural* same or **-s**) N. American wild dog.

coypu /'kɔɪpu:/ *noun* (*plural* **-s**) amphibious rodent like small beaver, originally from S. America.

cozen /'kʌz(ə)n/ *verb* *literary* cheat, defraud; beguile.

cozy *US* = cosy.

crab ● *noun* shellfish with 10 legs; this as food; (in full **crab-louse**) (often in *plural*) parasite infesting human body. ● *verb* (**-bb-**) *colloquial* criticize, grumble; spoil. □ **catch a crab** (in rowing) get oar jammed under water, miss water; **crab-apple** wild apple tree, its sour fruit.

crabbed /kræbɪd/ *adjective* crabby; (of handwriting) ill-formed, illegible.

crabby *adjective* (**-ier**, **-iest**) morose, irritable. □ **crabbily** *adverb*.

crack ● *noun* sudden sharp noise; sharp blow; narrow opening; break or split; *colloquial* joke, malicious remark; sudden change in vocal pitch; *slang* crystalline cocaine. ● *verb* (cause to) make crack; suffer crack or partial break; (of voice) change pitch sharply; tell (joke); open (bottle of wine etc.); break into (safe); find solution to (problem); give way, yield; hit sharply; (as **cracked** *adjective*) crazy, (of wheat) coarsely broken. □ **crack-brained** crazy; **crack-down** *colloquial* severe measures (esp. against law-breakers); **crack down on** *colloquial* take severe measures against; **crack of dawn** daybreak; **crackpot** *colloquial* eccentric or impractical person; **crack up** *colloquial* collapse under strain.

cracker *noun* small paper cylinder containing paper hat, joke, etc., exploding with crack when ends are pulled; explosive firework; thin crisp savoury biscuit.

crackers *adjective slang* crazy.

crackle /ˈkræk(ə)l/ ● *verb* (**-ling**) make repeated light cracking sound. ● *noun* such a sound. □ **crackly** *adjective*.

crackling *noun* crisp skin of roast pork.

cracknel /ˈkræknəl/ *noun* light crisp biscuit.

cradle /ˈkreɪd(ə)l/ ● *noun* baby's bed, esp. on rockers; place regarded as origin of something; supporting framework or structure. ● *verb* (**-ling**) contain or shelter as in cradle.

craft /krɑːft/ *noun* special skill or technique; occupation needing this; (*plural* same) boat, vessel, aircraft, or spacecraft; cunning.

craftsman /ˈkrɑːftsmən/ *noun* (*feminine* **-woman**) person who practises a craft. □ **craftsmanship** *noun*.

crafty *adjective* (**-ier**, **-iest**) cunning, artful. □ **craftily** *adverb*.

crag *noun* steep rugged rock.

craggy *adjective* (**-ier**, **-iest**) rugged; rough-textured.

cram *verb* (**-mm-**) fill to bursting; (often + *in*, *into*) force; study or teach intensively for exam.

crammer *noun* institution that crams pupils for exam.

cramp ● *noun* painful involuntary contraction of muscles. ● *verb* affect with cramp; restrict, confine.

cramped *adjective* (of space) small; (of handwriting) small and with the letters close together.

crampon /ˈkræmpɒn/ *noun* spiked iron plate fixed to boot for climbing on ice.

cranberry /ˈkrænbəri/ *noun* (*plural* **-ies**) (shrub bearing) small red acid berry.

crane ● *noun* machine with projecting arm for moving heavy weights; large long-legged wading bird. ● *verb* (**-ning**) stretch (one's neck) in order to see something. □ **crane-fly** two-winged long-legged fly; **cranesbill** kind of wild geranium.

cranium /ˈkreɪnɪəm/ *noun* (*plural* **-s** or **-nia**) bones enclosing brain, skull. □ **cranial** *adjective*.

crank ● *noun* part of axle or shaft bent at right angles for converting rotary into reciprocal motion or vice versa; eccentric person. ● *verb* turn with crank. □ **crankpin** pin attaching connecting rod to crank; **crankshaft** shaft driven by crank; **crank up** start (engine) by turning crank.

cranky *adjective* (**-ier**, **-iest**) eccentric; shaky; *esp. US* crotchety.

cranny /ˈkrænɪ/ *noun* (*plural* **-ies**) chink, crevice.

crape *noun* crêpe, usually of black silk, formerly used for mourning.

craps *plural noun* (also **crap game**) *US* gambling game played with dice.

crapulent /ˈkræpjʊlənt/ *adjective* suffering the effects of drunkenness. □ **crapulence** *noun*; **crapulous** *adjective*.

crash ● *verb* (cause to) make loud smashing noise; (often + *into*) (cause to) collide or fall violently; fail, esp. financially; *colloquial* gatecrash; (of computer, system, etc.) fail suddenly; (often + *out*) *slang* fall asleep, sleep. ● *noun* sudden violent noise; violent fall or impact, esp. of vehicle; ruin, esp. financial; sudden collapse, esp. of computer, system, etc. ● *adjective* done rapidly or urgently. □ **crash barrier** barrier to prevent car leaving road; **crash-dive** *verb* (of submarine) dive hastily and steeply, (of aircraft) dive and crash, *noun* such a dive; **crash-helmet** helmet worn to protect head; **crash-land** land or cause (aircraft etc.) to land with crash; **crash landing** instance of crash-landing.

crass *adjective* grossly stupid; insensitive. □ **crassly** *adverb*; **crassness** *noun*.

crate ●*noun* slatted wooden case; *slang* old aircraft, car, etc. ●*verb* (**-ting**) pack in crate.

crater /'kreɪtə/ *noun* mouth of volcano; bowl-shaped cavity, esp. hollow on surface of moon etc.

cravat /krə'væt/ *noun* man's scarf worn inside open-necked shirt.

crave *verb* (**-ving**) (often + *for*) long or beg for.

craven /'kreɪv(ə)n/ *adjective* cowardly, abject.

craving *noun* strong desire, longing.

craw *noun* crop of bird or insect.

crawfish *noun* (*plural* same) large spiny sea-lobster.

crawl ●*verb* move slowly, esp. on hands and knees or with body close to ground; *colloquial* behave obsequiously; (often + *with*) be filled with moving people or things; (esp. of skin) creep. ●*noun* crawling motion; slow rate of motion; fast swimming stroke.

crayfish /'kreɪfɪʃ/ *noun* (*plural* same) lobster-like freshwater crustacean; crawfish.

crayon /'kreɪən/ ●*noun* stick or pencil of coloured wax, chalk, etc. ●*verb* draw or colour with crayons.

craze ●*verb* (**-zing**) (usually as **crazed** *adjective*) make insane; produce fine surface cracks on, develop such cracks. ●*noun* usually temporary enthusiasm; object of this.

crazy *adjective* (**-ier**, **-iest**) insane, mad; foolish; (usually + *about*) *colloquial* extremely enthusiastic. □ **crazy paving** paving made of irregular pieces. □ **crazily** *adverb*.

creak *noun* harsh scraping or squeaking sound. ●*verb* emit creak; move stiffly. □ **creaky** *adjective* (**-ier**, **-iest**).

cream ●*noun* fatty part of milk; its yellowish-white colour; food or drink like or made with cream; creamlike cosmetic etc.; (usually + *the*) best part or pick of something. ●*verb* take cream

from; make creamy; form cream or scum. ●*adjective* yellowish-white. □ **cream cheese** soft rich cheese made of cream and unskimmed milk; **cream cracker** crisp unsweetened biscuit; **cream off** remove best part of; **cream of tartar** purified cream, used in medicine, baking powder, etc.; **cream tea** afternoon tea with scones, jam, and cream. □ **creamy** *adjective* (**-ier**, **-iest**).

creamer *noun* cream substitute for coffee; jug for cream.

creamery *noun* (*plural* **-ies**) factory producing dairy products; dairy.

crease /kriːs/ ●*noun* line made by folding or crushing; *Cricket* line defining position of bowler or batsman. ●*verb* (**-sing**) make creases in, develop creases.

create /kriː'eɪt/ *verb* (**-ting**) bring into existence; originate; invest with rank; *slang* make fuss.

creation /kriː'eɪʃ(ə)n/ *noun* creating, being created; (usually **the Creation**) God's creating of the universe; (usually **Creation**) all created things; product of imaginative work.

creative /kriː'eɪtɪv/ *adjective* inventive, imaginative. □ **creatively** *adverb*; **creativity** /-'tɪv-/ *noun*.

creator /kriː'eɪtə/ *noun* person who creates; (**the Creator**) God.

creature /'kriːtʃə/ *noun* living being, esp. animal; person, esp. one in subservient position; anything created.

crèche /kreʃ/ *noun* day nursery.

credence /'kriːd(ə)ns/ *noun* belief.

credentials /krɪ'denʃ(ə)lz/ *plural noun* documents attesting to person's education, character, etc.

credible /'kredɪb(ə)l/ *adjective* believable; worthy of belief. □ **credibility** *noun*.

■ **Usage** *Credible* is sometimes confused with *credulous*, which means 'gullible'.

credit /'kredɪt/ ●*noun* belief, trust; good reputation; person's financial standing; power to obtain goods before payment; acknowledgement of payment by entry in account, sum entered; acknowledgement of merit or (usually in *plural*) of contributor's services to film, book, etc.; grade above pass in exam; educational course counting towards degree. ● *verb* (**-t-**) believe; (usually + *to, with*) enter on credit side of account. □ **credit card** card authorizing purchase of goods on credit; **credit** (**person**) **with** ascribe to him or her; **credit rating** estimate of person's suitability for commercial credit; **creditworthy** suitable to receive credit; **on credit** with arrangement to pay later; **to one's credit** in one's favour.

creditable *adjective* praiseworthy. □ **creditably** *adverb*.

creditor *noun* person to whom debt is owing.

credo /'kriːdəʊ/ *noun* (*plural* **-s**) creed.

credulous /'kredjʊləs/ *adjective* too ready to believe; gullible. □ **credulity** /krɪ'djuː-/ *noun*.

■ **Usage** *Credulous* is sometimes confused with *credible*, which means 'believable'.

creed *noun* set of beliefs; system of beliefs; (often **the Creed**) formal summary of Christian doctrine.

creek *noun* inlet on sea-coast; arm of river; stream.

creel *noun* fisherman's wicker basket.

creep ● *verb* (*past & past participle* **crept**) crawl; move stealthily, timidly, or slowly; (of plant) grow along ground or up wall etc.; advance or develop gradually; (of flesh) shudder with horror etc. ● *noun* act of creeping; (**the creeps**) *colloquial* feeling of revulsion or fear; *slang* unpleasant person; gradual change in shape of metal under stress.

creeper *noun* creeping or climbing plant.

creepy *adjective* (**-ier, -iest**) *colloquial* feeling or causing horror or fear. □ **creepy-crawly** (*plural* **-crawlies**) small crawling insect etc. □ **creepily** *adverb*.

cremate /krɪ'meɪt/ *verb* (**-ting**) burn (corpse) to ashes. □ **cremation** *noun*.

crematorium /kremə'tɔːrɪəm/ *noun* (*plural* **-ria** or **-s**) place where corpses are cremated.

crenellated /'krenəleɪtɪd/ *adjective* having battlements. □ **crenellation** *noun*.

Creole /'kriːəʊl/ ● *noun* descendant of European settlers in W. Indies or Central or S. America, or of French settlers in southern US; person of mixed European and black descent; language formed from a European and African language. ● *adjective* of Creoles; (usually **creole**) of Creole origin etc.

creosote /'kriːəsəʊt/ ● *noun* oily wood-preservative distilled from coal tar. ● *verb* (**-ting**) treat with creosote.

crêpe /kreɪp/ *noun* fine crinkled fabric; thin pancake with savoury or sweet filling; wrinkled sheet rubber used for shoe-soles etc. □ **crêpe de Chine** /də 'ʃiːn/ fine silk crêpe; **crêpe paper** thin crinkled paper.

crept *past & past participle* of CREEP.

crepuscular /krɪ'pʌskjʊlə/ *adjective* of twilight; (of animal) active etc. at twilight.

crescendo /krɪ'ʃendəʊ/ *Music* ● *noun* (*plural* **-s**) gradual increase in loudness. ● *adjective & adverb* increasing in loudness.

■ **Usage** *Crescendo* is sometimes wrongly used to mean a climax rather than the progress towards it.

crescent /'kres(ə)nt/ ● *noun* sickle shape, as of waxing or waning moon; thing with this shape, esp. curved street. ● *adjective* crescent-shaped.

cress *noun* plant with pungent edible leaves.

crest ● *noun* comb or tuft on animal's head; plume of helmet; top of mountain, wave, etc.; *Heraldry* device above shield or on writing paper etc. ● *verb* reach crest of; crown; serve as crest to; form crest. □ **crestfallen** dejected. □ **crested** *adjective*.

cretaceous /krɪ'teɪʃəs/ *adjective* chalky.

cretin /'kretɪn/ *noun* person with deformity and mental retardation caused by thyroid deficiency; *colloquial* stupid person. □ **cretinism** *noun*; **cretinous** *adjective*.

cretonne /kre'tɒn/ *noun* heavy cotton usually floral upholstery fabric.

crevasse /krə'væs/ *noun* deep open crack in glacier.

crevice /'krevɪs/ *noun* narrow opening or fissure, esp. in rock.

crew¹ /kruː/ ● *noun* group of people working together, esp. manning ship, aircraft, spacecraft, etc.; these, other than the officers. ● *verb* supply or act as crew (member) for; act as crew. □ **crew cut** close-cropped hairstyle; **crew neck** round close-fitting neckline.

crew² *archaic past* of CROW.

crewel /ˈkruːəl/ *noun* thin worsted yarn for embroidery.

crib ● *noun* baby's small bed or cot; model of Nativity with manger; *colloquial* plagiarism; translation; *colloquial* cribbage. ● *verb* (**-bb-**) copy unfairly; confine in small space.

cribbage /ˈkrɪbɪdʒ/ *noun* a card game.

crick ● *noun* sudden painful stiffness, esp. in neck. ● *verb* cause crick in.

cricket¹ /ˈkrɪkɪt/ *noun* team game, played on grass pitch, in which ball is bowled at wicket defended with bat by player of other team. □ **not cricket** *colloquial* unfair behaviour. □ **cricketer** *noun*.

cricket² /ˈkrɪkɪt/ *noun* jumping chirping insect.

cried *past & past participle* of CRY.

crier /ˈkraɪə/ *noun* (also **cryer**) official making public announcements in law court or street.

crikey /ˈkraɪkɪ/ *interjection slang: expressing astonishment.*

crime *noun* act punishable by law; such acts collectively; evil act; *colloquial* shameful act.

criminal /ˈkrɪmɪn(ə)l/ ● *noun* person guilty of crime. ● *adjective* of, involving, or concerning crime; *colloquial* deplorable. □ **criminality** /-ˈnæl-/ *noun*; **criminally** *adverb*.

criminology /krɪmɪˈnɒlədʒɪ/ *noun* study of crime. □ **criminologist** *noun*.

crimp *verb* press into small folds or waves; corrugate.

Crimplene /ˈkrɪmpliːn/ *noun* proprietary term synthetic crease-resistant fabric.

crimson /ˈkrɪmz(ə)n/ *adjective & noun* rich deep red.

cringe *verb* (**-ging**) cower; (often + *to*) behave obsequiously.

crinkle /ˈkrɪŋk(ə)l/ ● *noun* wrinkle, crease. ● *verb* (**-ling**) form crinkles (in). □ **crinkly** *adjective*.

crinoline /ˈkrɪnəlɪn/ *noun* hooped petticoat.

cripple /ˈkrɪp(ə)l/ ● *noun* lame person. ● *verb* (**-ling**) lame, disable; damage seriously.

crisis /ˈkraɪsɪs/ *noun* (*plural* **crises** /-siːz/) time of acute danger or difficulty; decisive moment.

crisp ● *adjective* hard but brittle; bracing; brisk, decisive; clear-cut; crackling; curly. ● *noun* (in full **potato crisp**) very thin fried slice of potato. ● *verb* make or become crisp. □ **crispbread** thin crisp biscuit. □ **crisply** *adverb*; **crispness** *noun*.

crispy *adjective* (**-ier**, **-iest**) crisp.

criss-cross ● *noun* pattern of crossing lines. ● *adjective* crossing; in crossing lines. ● *adverb* crosswise. ● *verb* intersect repeatedly; mark with criss-cross lines.

criterion /kraɪˈtɪərɪən/ *noun* (*plural* **-ria**) principle or standard of judgement.

■ **Usage** It is a mistake to use the plural form *criteria* when only one criterion is meant.

critic /ˈkrɪtɪk/ *noun* person who criticizes; reviewer of literary, artistic, etc. works.

critical *adjective* fault-finding; expressing criticism; providing textual criticism; of the nature of a crisis, decisive; marking transition from one state to another. □ **critically** *adverb*.

criticism /ˈkrɪtɪsɪz(ə)m/ *noun* finding fault, censure; work of critic; critical article, remark, etc.

criticize /ˈkrɪtɪsaɪz/ *verb* (also **-ise**) (**-zing** or **-sing**) find fault with; discuss critically.

critique /krɪˈtiːk/ *noun* critical analysis.

croak ● *noun* deep hoarse sound, esp. of frog. ● *verb* utter or speak with croak; *slang* die. □ **croaky** *adjective* (**-ier**, **-iest**); **croakily** *adverb*.

Croat /ˈkrəʊæt/ (also **Croatian** /krəʊˈeɪʃ(ə)n/) ● *noun* native of Croatia; person of Croatian descent; Slavonic dialect of Croats. ● *adjective* of Croats or their dialect.

crochet /ˈkrəʊʃeɪ/ ● *noun* needlework of hooked yarn producing lacy patterned fabric. ● *verb* (**crocheted** /-ʃeɪd/; **crocheting** /-ʃeɪɪŋ/) make by crochet.

crock[1] *noun colloquial* old or worn-out person or vehicle.

crock[2] *noun* earthenware jar; broken piece of this.

crockery *noun* earthenware or china dishes, plates, etc.

crocodile /'krɒkədaɪl/ *noun* large amphibious reptile; *colloquial* line of school children etc. walking in pairs. □ **crocodile tears** insincere grief.

crocus /'krəʊkəs/ *noun* (*plural* **-es**) small plant with corm and yellow, purple, or white flowers.

croft ● *noun* small piece of arable land; small rented farm in Scotland or N. England. ● *verb* farm croft.

crofter *noun* person who farms croft.

Crohn's disease /krəʊnz/ *noun* inflammatory disease of alimentary tract.

croissant /'krwʌsɑ̃/ *noun* rich crescent-shaped roll.

cromlech /'krɒmlek/ *noun* dolmen; prehistoric stone circle.

crone *noun* withered old woman.

crony /'krəʊnɪ/ *noun* (*plural* **-ies**) friend; companion.

crook /krʊk/ ● *noun* hooked staff of shepherd or bishop; bend, curve; *colloquial* swindler, criminal. ● *verb* bend, curve.

crooked /'krʊkɪd/ *adjective* (**-er**, **-est**) not straight, bent; *colloquial* dishonest. □ **crookedly** *adverb*; **crookedness** *noun*.

croon /kruːn/ ● *verb* hum or sing in low voice. ● *noun* such singing. □ **crooner** *noun*.

crop ● *noun* produce of any cultivated plant or of land; group or amount produced at one time; handle of whip; very short haircut; pouch in bird's gullet where food is prepared for digestion. ● *verb* (**-pp-**) cut off; bite off, eat down; cut (hair) short; raise crop on (land); bear crop. □ **crop circle** circle of crops inexplicably flattened; **crop up** occur unexpectedly.

cropper *noun slang* □ **come a cropper** fall heavily, fail badly.

croquet /'krəʊkeɪ/ ● *noun* lawn game with hoops, wooden balls, and mallets; croqueting. ● *verb* (**croqueted** /-keɪd/; **croqueting** /-keɪɪŋ/) drive away (opponent's ball) by striking one's own ball placed in contact with it.

croquette /krə'ket/ *noun* fried breaded ball of meat, potato, etc.

crosier /'krəʊzɪə/ *noun* (also **crozier**) bishop's ceremonial hooked staff.

cross ● *noun* upright stake with transverse bar, used in antiquity for crucifixion; representation of this as emblem of Christianity; cross-shaped thing or mark, esp. two short intersecting lines (+ or ×); cross-shaped military etc. decoration; intermixture of breeds, hybrid; (+ *between*) mixture of two things; trial, affliction. ● *verb* (often + *over*) go across; place crosswise; draw line(s) across; make sign of cross on or over; meet and pass; thwart; (cause) to interbreed; cross-fertilize (plants). ● *adjective* (often + *with*) peevish, angry; transverse; reaching from side to side; intersecting; reciprocal. □ **at cross purposes** misunderstanding each other; **crossbar** horizontal bar, esp. between uprights; **cross-bench** bench in House of Lords for non-party members; **crossbones** SEE SKULL AND CROSSBONES; **crossbow** bow fixed across wooden stock with mechanism working string; **cross-breed** (produce) hybrid animal or plant; **cross-check** check by alternative method; **cross-country** across fields etc., not following roads, *noun* such a race; **cross-examine** question (esp. opposing witness in law court); **cross-examination** such questioning; **cross-eyed** having one or both eyes turned inwards; **cross-fertilize** fertilize (animal or plant) from another of same species; **crossfire** firing of guns in two crossing directions; **cross-grained** (of wood) with grain running irregularly, (of person) perverse or intractable; **cross-hatch** shade with crossing parallel lines; **cross-legged** (sitting) with legs folded across each other; **cross off**, **out** cancel, expunge; **crossover** point or process of crossing; **crosspatch** *colloquial* bad-tempered person; **cross-ply** (of tyre) having crosswise layers of cords; **cross-question** cross-examine, quiz; **cross-reference** reference to another passage in same book; **crossroad** (usually in *plural*) intersection of roads; **cross-section** drawing etc. of thing as if cut through, representative sample; **cross stitch** cross-shaped stitch; **crosswise** intersecting, diagonally; **crossword (puzzle)** puzzle in which words crossing each other vertically and horizontally have to be filled in from clues; **on the cross** diagonally. □ **crossly** *adverb;* **crossness** *noun.*

crossing *noun* place where things (esp. roads) meet; place for crossing street; journey across water.

crotch *noun* fork, esp. between legs (of person, trousers, etc.).

crotchet /ˈkrɒtʃɪt/ *noun Music* black-headed note with stem, equal to quarter of semibreve and usually one beat.

crotchety *adjective* peevish.

crouch ● *verb* stand, squat, etc. with legs bent close to body. ● *noun* this position.

croup[1] /kruːp/ *noun* laryngitis in children, with sharp cough.

croup[2] /kruːp/ *noun* rump, esp. of horse.

croupier /ˈkruːpɪə/ *noun* person in charge of gaming table.

croûton /ˈkruːtɒn/ *noun* small piece of fried or toasted bread served esp. with soup.

crow /krəʊ/ ● *noun* any of various kinds of large black-plumaged bird; cry of cock or baby. ● *verb* (*past* **crowed** or *archaic* **crew** /kruː/) (of cock) utter loud cry; (of baby) utter happy sounds; exult. □ **crow's-foot** wrinkle at outer corner of eye; **crow's-nest** shelter for look-out man at ship's masthead.

crowbar *noun* iron bar used as lever.

crowd /kraʊd/ ● *noun* large gathering of people; *colloquial* particular set of people. ● *verb* (cause to) collect in crowd; (+ *with*) cram with; (+ *into, through,* etc.) force way into, through, etc.; *colloquial* come aggressively close to. □ **crowd out** exclude by crowding.

crown /kraʊn/ ● *noun* monarch's jewelled headdress; (**the Crown**) monarch as head of state, his or her authority; wreath for head as emblem of victory; top part of head, hat, etc.; visible part of tooth, artificial replacement for this; coin worth 5 shillings or 25 pence. ● *verb* put crown on; make king or queen; (often as **crowning** *adjective*) be consummation, reward, or finishing touch to;

slang hit on head. □ **Crown colony** British colony controlled by the Crown; **Crown Court** court of criminal jurisdiction in England and Wales; **crown jewels** sovereign's regalia; **crown prince** male heir to throne; **crown princess** wife of crown prince, female heir to throne.

crozier = CROSIER.

CRT *abbreviation* cathode ray tube.

cruces *plural of* CRUX.

crucial /ˈkruːʃ(ə)l/ *adjective* decisive, critical; very important; *slang* excellent. □ **crucially** *adverb.*

crucible /ˈkruːsɪb(ə)l/ *noun* melting pot for metals.

cruciferous /kruːˈsɪfərəs/ *adjective* with 4 equal petals arranged crosswise.

crucifix /ˈkruːsɪfɪks/ *noun* image of Christ on Cross.

crucifixion /kruːsɪˈfɪkʃ(ə)n/ *noun* crucifying, esp. of Christ.

cruciform /ˈkruːsɪfɔːm/ *adjective* cross-shaped.

crucify /ˈkruːsɪfaɪ/ *verb* (**-ies, -ied**) put to death by fastening to cross; persecute, torment.

crude ● *adjective* in natural or raw state; lacking finish, unpolished; rude, blunt; indecent. ● *noun* natural mineral oil. □ **crudely** *adverb;* **crudeness** *noun;* **crudity** *noun.*

crudités /kruːdɪˈteɪ/ *plural noun* hors d'oeuvre of mixed raw vegetables. [French]

cruel /ˈkruːəl/ *adjective* (**-ll-** or **-l-**) causing pain or suffering, esp. deliberately; harsh, severe. □ **cruelly** *adverb;* **cruelty** *noun* (*plural* **-ies**).

cruet /ˈkruːɪt/ *noun* set of small salt, pepper, etc. containers for use at table.

cruise /kruːz/ ● *verb* (**-sing**) sail about, esp. travel by sea for pleasure, calling at ports; travel at relaxed or economical speed; achieve objective with ease. ● *noun* cruising voyage. □ **cruise missile** one able to fly low and guide itself.

cruiser *noun* high-speed warship; cabin cruiser. □ **cruiserweight** light heavyweight.

crumb /krʌm/ ● *noun* small fragment esp. of bread; soft inner part of loaf;

(**crumbs** *interjection*) *slang*: expressing dismay. ● *verb* coat with breadcrumbs; crumble (bread). □ **crumby** *adjective*.

crumble /ˈkrʌmb(ə)l/ ● *verb* (**-ling**) break or fall into fragments, disintegrate. ● *noun* dish of cooked fruit with crumbly topping. □ **crumbly** *adjective* (**-ier**, **-iest**).

crumhorn = KRUMMHORN.

crummy /ˈkrʌmi/ *adjective* (**-ier**, **-iest**) *slang* squalid, inferior.

crumpet /ˈkrʌmpɪt/ *noun* flat soft yeasty cake eaten toasted.

crumple /ˈkrʌmp(ə)l/ *verb* (**-ling**) (often + *up*) crush or become crushed into creases; give way, collapse.

crunch ● *verb* crush noisily with teeth; make or emit crunch. ● *noun* crunching sound; *colloquial* decisive event. □ **crunchy** *adjective* (**-ier**, **-iest**).

crupper /ˈkrʌpə/ *noun* strap looped under horse's tail to hold harness back.

crusade /kruːˈseɪd/ ● *noun historical* medieval Christian military expedition to recover Holy Land from Muslims; vigorous campaign for cause. ● *verb* (**-ding**) take part in crusade. □ **crusader** *noun*.

cruse /kruːz/ *noun archaic* earthenware jar.

crush ● *verb* compress violently so as to break, bruise, etc.; crease, crumple; defeat or subdue completely. ● *noun* act of crushing; crowded mass of people; drink made from juice of crushed fruit; (usually + *on*) *colloquial* infatuation.

crust ● *noun* hard outer part of bread etc.; pastry covering pie; rocky outer part of the earth; deposit, esp. on sides of wine bottle. ● *verb* cover with, form into, or become covered with crust.

crustacean /krʌˈsteɪʃ(ə)n/ ● *noun* hard-shelled usually aquatic animals, e.g. crab or lobster. ● *adjective* of crustaceans.

crusty *adjective* (**-ier**, **-iest**) having a crisp crust; irritable, curt.

crutch *noun* support for lame person, usually with cross-piece fitting under armpit; support; crotch.

crux *noun* (*plural* **-es** or **cruces** /ˈkruːsiːz/) decisive point at issue.

cry /kraɪ/ ● *verb* (**cries**, **cried**) (often + *out*) make loud or shrill sound, esp.

to express pain, grief, joy, etc.; weep; (often + *out*) utter loudly, exclaim; (+ *for*) appeal for. ● *noun* (*plural* **cries**) loud shout of grief, fear, joy, etc.; loud excited utterance; urgent appeal; fit of weeping; call of animal. □ **cry-baby** person who weeps frequently; **cry down** disparage; **cry off** withdraw from undertaking; **cry out for** need badly; **cry wolf** see WOLF; **a far cry** a long way.

cryer = CRIER.

crying *adjective* (of injustice etc.) flagrant, demanding redress.

cryogenics /kraɪəʊˈdʒɛnɪks/ *noun* branch of physics dealing with very low temperatures. □ **cryogenic** *adjective*.

crypt /krɪpt/ *noun* vault, esp. below church, usually used as burial place.

cryptic *adjective* obscure in meaning; secret, mysterious. □ **cryptically** *adverb*.

cryptogam /ˈkrɪptəgæm/ *noun* plant with no true flowers or seeds; e.g. fern or fungus. □ **cryptogamic** /-ˈgæm-/ *adjective*.

cryptogram /ˈkrɪptəgræm/ *noun* text written in cipher.

crystal /ˈkrɪst(ə)l/ ● *noun* (piece of) transparent colourless mineral; (articles of) highly transparent glass; substance solidified in definite geometrical form. ● *adjective* of or as clear as crystal. □ **crystal ball** glass globe supposedly used in foretelling the future.

crystalline /ˈkrɪstəlaɪn/ *adjective* of or as clear as crystal.

crystallize /ˈkrɪstəlaɪz/ *verb* (also **-ise**) (**-zing** or **-sing**) form into crystals; make or become definite; preserve or be preserved in sugar. □ **crystallization** *noun*.

CS gas *noun* tear gas used to control riots.

cu. *abbreviation* cubic.

cub ● *noun* young of fox, bear, lion, etc.; **Cub** (**Scout**) junior Scout; *colloquial* young newspaper reporter. ● *verb* give birth to (cubs).

cubby-hole /ˈkʌbɪhəʊl/ *noun* very small room; snug space.

cube /kjuːb/ ● *noun* solid contained by 6 equal squares; cube-shaped block; product of a number multiplied by its square. ● *verb* (**-bing**) find cube of; cut into small cubes. □ **cube root** number which produces given number when cubed.

cubic /ˈkjuːbɪk/ *adjective* of 3 dimensions; involving cube of a quantity. □ **cubic metre** etc., volume of cube whose edge is one metre etc. □ **cubical** *adjective*.

cubicle /ˈkjuːbɪk(ə)l/ *noun* small screened space, esp. sleeping compartment.

cubism /ˈkjuːbɪz(ə)m/ *noun* art style in which objects are represented geometrically. □ **cubist** *adjective & noun*.

cubit /ˈkjuːbɪt/ *noun* ancient measure of length, approximately length of forearm.

cuboid /ˈkjuːbɔɪd/ ● *adjective* like a cube; cube-shaped. ● *noun* solid with 6 rectangular faces.

cuckold /ˈkʌkəʊld/ ● *noun* husband of adulteress. ● *verb* make cuckold of.

cuckoo /ˈkʊkuː/ ● *noun* bird with characteristic cry and laying eggs in nests of small birds. ● *adjective slang* crazy. □ **cuckoo clock** clock with figure of cuckoo emerging to make call on the hour; **cuckoo-pint** wild arum; **cuckoo-spit** froth exuded by larvae of certain insects.

cucumber /ˈkjuːkʌmbə/ *noun* long green fleshy fruit used in salads.

cud *noun* half-digested food chewed by ruminant.

cuddle /ˈkʌd(ə)l/ ● *verb* (**-ling**) hug; lie close and snug; nestle. ● *noun* prolonged hug.

cuddly *adjective* (**-ier, -iest**) soft and yielding.

cudgel /ˈkʌdʒ(ə)l/ ● *noun* thick stick used as weapon. ● *verb* (**-ll-**; *US* **-l-**) beat with cudgel.

cue[1] /kjuː/ ● *noun* last words of actor's speech as signal for another to begin; signal, hint. ● *verb* (**cues, cued, cueing** or **cuing**) give cue to. □ **cue in** insert cue for; **on cue** at correct moment.

cue[2] /kjuː/ ● *noun* long rod for striking ball in billiards etc. ● *verb* (**cues, cued, cueing** or **cuing**) strike with cue. □ **cue ball** ball to be struck with cue.

cuff[1] *noun* end part of sleeve; trouser turn-up; (in *plural*) *colloquial* handcuffs.

□ **cuff link** either of pair of fasteners for shirt cuffs; **off the cuff** extempore, without preparation.

cuff[2] ● *verb* strike with open hand. ● *noun* such a blow.

cuisine /kwɪˈziːn/ *noun* style of cooking.

cul-de-sac /ˈkʌldəsæk/ *noun* (*plural* **culs-de-sac** same pronunciation, or **cul-de-sacs** /-sæks/) road etc. closed at one end.

culinary /ˈkʌlɪnərɪ/ *adjective* of or for cooking.

cull ● *verb* select, gather; pick (flowers); select and kill (surplus animals). ● *noun* culling; animal(s) culled.

culminate /ˈkʌlmɪneɪt/ *verb* (**-ting**) (usually + *in*) reach highest or final point. □ **culmination** *noun*.

culottes /kjuːˈlɒts/ *plural noun* woman's trousers cut like skirt.

culpable /ˈkʌlpəb(ə)l/ *adjective* deserving blame. □ **culpability** *noun*.

culprit /ˈkʌlprɪt/ *noun* guilty person.

cult *noun* religious system, sect, etc.; devotion or homage to person or thing.

cultivar /ˈkʌltɪvɑː/ *noun* plant variety produced by cultivation.

cultivate /ˈkʌltɪveɪt/ *verb* (**-ting**) prepare and use (soil) for crops; raise (plant etc.); (often as **cultivated** *adjective*) improve (manners etc.); nurture (friendship etc.). □ **cultivation** *noun*.

cultivator *noun* agricultural implement for breaking up ground etc.

culture /ˈkʌltʃə/ ● *noun* intellectual and artistic achievement or expression; refined appreciation of arts etc.; customs and civilization of a particular time or people; improvement through mental or physical training; cultivation of plants, rearing of bees etc.; quantity of bacteria grown for study. ● *verb* (**-ring**) grow (bacteria) for study. □ **culture shock** disorientation felt by person subjected to unfamiliar way of life. □ **cultural** *adjective*.

cultured *adjective* having refined tastes etc. □ **cultured pearl** one formed by oyster after insertion of foreign body into its shell.

culvert /ˈkʌlvət/ *noun* underground channel carrying water under road etc.

cumbersome /ˈkʌmbəsəm/ *adjective* (also **cumbrous** /ˈkʌmbrəs/) inconveniently bulky, unwieldy.

cumin /ˈkʌmɪn/ *noun* (also **cummin**) plant with aromatic seeds; these as flavouring.

cummerbund /ˈkʌməbʌnd/ *noun* waist sash.

cumulative /ˈkjuːmjʊlətɪv/ *adjective* increasing in force etc. by successive additions. □ **cumulatively** *adverb*.

cumulus /ˈkjuːmjʊləs/ *noun* (*plural* **-li** /-laɪ/) cloud formation of heaped-up rounded masses.

cuneiform /ˈkjuːnɪfɔːm/ ● *noun* writing made up of wedge shapes. ● *adjective* of or using cuneiform.

cunning /ˈkʌnɪŋ/ ● *adjective* (**-er**, **-est**) deceitful, crafty; ingenious. ● *noun* ingenuity; craft. □ **cunningly** *adverb*.

cup ● *noun* small bowl-shaped drinking vessel; cupful; cup-shaped thing; flavoured usually chilled wine, cider, etc.; cup-shaped trophy as prize. ● *verb* (**-pp-**) make cup-shaped; hold as in cup. □ **Cup Final** final match in (esp. football) competition; **cup-tie** match in such competition. □ **cupful** *noun*.

■ **Usage** A *cupful* is a measure, and so *three cupfuls* is a quantity of something; *three cups full* means the actual cups and their contents, as in *He brought us three cups full of water*.

cupboard /ˈkʌbəd/ *noun* recess or piece of furniture with door and usually shelves.

Cupid /ˈkjuːpɪd/ *noun* Roman god of love, pictured as winged boy with bow.

cupidity /kjuːˈpɪdɪtɪ/ *noun* greed, avarice.

cupola /ˈkjuːpələ/ *noun* small dome; revolving gun-turret on ship or in fort.

cuppa /ˈkʌpə/ *noun colloquial* cup of (tea).

cur *noun* mangy bad-tempered dog; contemptible person.

curable /ˈkjʊərəb(ə)l/ *adjective* able to be cured.

curaçao /ˈkjʊərəsəʊ/ *noun* (*plural* **-s**) orange-flavoured liqueur.

curacy /ˈkjʊərəsɪ/ *noun* (*plural* **-ies**) curate's office or position.

curare /kjʊəˈrɑːrɪ/ *noun* vegetable poison used on arrows by S. American Indians.

curate /ˈkjʊərət/ *noun* assistant to parish priest. □ **curate's egg** thing good in parts.

curative /ˈkjʊərətɪv/ ● *adjective* tending to cure. ● *noun* curative agent.

curator /kjʊəˈreɪtə/ *noun* custodian of museum etc.

curb ● *noun* check, restraint; (bit with) chain etc. passing under horse's lower jaw; kerb. ● *verb* restrain; put curb on.

curd *noun* (often in *plural*) coagulated acidic milk product, made into cheese or eaten as food.

curdle /ˈkɜːd(ə)l/ *verb* (**-ling**) coagulate. □ **make (person's) blood curdle** horrify.

cure /kjʊə/ ● *verb* (often + *of*) restore to health, relieve; eliminate (evil etc.); preserve (meat etc.) by salting etc. ● *noun* restoration to health; thing that cures; course of treatment.

curé /ˈkjʊəreɪ/ *noun* parish priest in France etc. [French]

curette /kjʊəˈret/ ● *noun* surgeon's scraping-instrument. ● *verb* (**-tting**) scrape with this. □ **curettage** *noun*.

curfew /ˈkɜːfjuː/ *noun* signal or time after which people must remain indoors.

curie /ˈkjʊərɪ/ *noun* unit of radioactivity.

curio /ˈkjʊərɪəʊ/ *noun* (*plural* **-s**) rare or unusual object.

curiosity /kjʊərɪˈɒsɪtɪ/ *noun* (*plural* **-ies**) desire to know; inquisitiveness; rare or strange thing.

curious /ˈkjʊərɪəs/ *adjective* eager to learn; inquisitive; strange, surprising. □ **curiously** *adverb*.

curl ● *verb* (often + *up*) bend or coil into spiral; move in curve; (of upper lip) be raised in contempt; play curling. ● *noun* curled lock of hair; anything spiral or curved inwards. □ **curly** *adjective* (**-ier**, **-iest**).

curler *noun* pin, roller, etc. for curling hair.

curlew /ˈkɜːljuː/ *noun* long-billed wading bird with musical cry.

curling *noun* game like bowls played on ice with round flat stones.

curmudgeon /kəˈmʌdʒ(ə)n/ *noun* bad-tempered or miserly person. □ **curmudgeonly** *adjective*.

currant /ˈkʌrənt/ *noun* small seedless dried grape; (fruit of) any of various shrubs producing red, black, or white berries.

currency /'kʌrənsi/ *noun* (*plural* **-ies**) money in use in a country; being current; prevalence (of ideas etc.).

current ●*adjective* belonging to present time; happening now; in general circulation or use. ●*noun* body of moving water, air, etc., passing through still water etc.; movement of electrically charged particles; general tendency or course. □ **current account** bank account that may be drawn on by cheque without notice. □ **currently** *adverb*.

curriculum /kə'rɪkjʊləm/ *noun* (*plural* **-la**) course of study. □ **curriculum vitae** /'viːtaɪ/ brief account of one's education, career, etc.

curry[1] /'kʌrɪ/ ●*noun* (*plural* **-ies**) meat, vegetables, etc. cooked in spicy sauce, usually served with rice. ●*verb* (**-ies**, **-ied**) make into or flavour like curry. □ **curry powder** mixture of spices for making curry.

curry[2] /'kʌrɪ/ *verb* (**-ies**, **-ied**) groom (horse etc.) with curry-comb; dress (leather). □ **curry-comb** metal device for grooming horses etc.; **curry favour** ingratiate oneself.

curse /kɜːs/ ●*noun* invocation of destruction or punishment; violent or profane exclamation; thing causing evil. ●*verb* (**-sing**) utter curse against; (usually in *passive*, + *with*) afflict with; swear. □ **cursed** /'kɜːsɪd/ *adjective*.

cursive /'kɜːsɪv/ ●*adjective* (of writing) having joined characters. ●*noun* cursive writing.

cursor /'kɜːsə/ *noun* indicator on VDU screen showing particular position in displayed matter.

cursory /'kɜːsərɪ/ *adjective* hasty, hurried. □ **cursorily** *adverb*.

curt *adjective* noticeably or rudely brief. □ **curtly** *adverb*; **curtness** *noun*.

curtail /kɜː'teɪl/ *verb* cut short, reduce. □ **curtailment** *noun*.

curtain /'kɜːt(ə)n/ ●*noun* piece of cloth etc. hung up as screen, esp. at window; rise or fall of stage curtain; curtain-call; (in *plural*) *slang* the end. ●*verb* provide or (+ *off*) shut off with curtains. □ **curtain-call** audience's applause summoning actors to take bow; **curtain-raiser** short opening play etc., preliminary event.

curtsy /'kɜːtsɪ/ (also **curtsey**) ●*noun* (*plural* **-ies** or **-eys**) woman's or girl's acknowledgement or greeting made by bending knees. ●*verb* (**-ies**, **-ied** or **-eys**, **-eyed**) make curtsy.

curvaceous /kɜː'veɪʃəs/ *adjective* *colloquial* (esp. of woman) shapely.

curvature /'kɜːvətʃə/ *noun* curving; curved form; deviation of curve from plane.

curve ●*noun* line or surface of which no part is straight; curved line on graph. ●*verb* (**-ving**) bend or shape so as to form curve. □ **curvy** *adjective* (**-ier**, **-iest**).

curvet /kɜː'vet/ ●*noun* horse's frisky leap. ●*verb* (**-tt-** or **-t-**) perform curvet.

curvilinear /kɜːvɪ'lɪnɪə/ *adjective* contained by or consisting of curved lines.

cushion /'kʊʃ(ə)n/ ●*noun* bag stuffed with soft material for sitting on etc.; protection against shock; padded rim of billiard table; air supporting hovercraft. ●*verb* provide or protect with cushions; mitigate effects of.

cushy /'kʊʃɪ/ *adjective* (**-ier**, **-iest**) *colloquial* (of job etc.) easy, pleasant.

cusp *noun* point at which two curves meet, e.g. horn of crescent moon.

cuss *colloquial* ●*noun* curse; awkward person. ●*verb* curse.

cussed /'kʌsɪd/ *adjective colloquial* awkward, stubborn.

custard /'kʌstəd/ *noun* pudding or sweet sauce of eggs or flavoured cornflour and milk.

custodian /kʌs'təʊdɪən/ *noun* guardian, keeper.

custody /'kʌstədɪ/ *noun* guardianship; imprisonment. □ **custodial** /-'stəʊ-/ *adjective*.

custom /'kʌstəm/ *noun* usual behaviour; established custom; business dealings, customers; (in *plural*; also treated as *singular*) duty on imports, government department or (part of) building at port etc. dealing with this. □ **custom house** customs office at frontier etc.; **custom-built, -made** made to customer's order.

customary /'kʌstəmərɪ/ *adjective* in accordance with custom; usual. □ **customarily** *adverb*.

customer *noun* person who buys goods or services; *colloquial* person of specified (esp. awkward) kind.

customize *verb* (also **-ise**) (**-zing** or **-sing**) make or modify to order; personalize.

cut ● *verb* (**-tt-**; *past & past participle* **cut**) divide, wound, or penetrate with edged instrument; detach, trim, etc. by cutting; (+ *loose, open,* etc.) loosen by cutting; (esp. as **cutting** *adjective*) cause pain to; reduce (prices, wages, services, etc.); make by cutting or removing material; cross, intersect; divide (pack of cards); edit (film), stop cameras; end acquaintance or ignore presence of; *US* deliberately miss (class etc.); chop (ball); switch off (engine etc.); (+ *across, through,* etc.) pass through as shorter route. ● *noun* act of cutting; division or wound made by cutting; stroke with knife, sword, whip, etc.; reduction (in price, wages, services, etc.); cessation (of power supply etc.); removal of part of play, film, etc.; *slang* commission, share of profits, etc.; style in which hair, clothing, etc. is cut; particular piece of meat; cutting of ball; deliberate ignoring of person. □ **a cut above** noticeably superior to; **cut and dried** completely decided, inflexible; **cut back** reduce (expenditure), prune; **cut-back** reduction in expenditure; **cut both ways** serve both sides; **cut corners** do task perfunctorily; **cut glass** glass with patterns cut on it; **cut in** interrupt, pull in too closely in front of another vehicle; **cut one's losses** abandon an unprofitable scheme; **cut no ice** *slang* have no influence; **cut off** *verb* remove by cutting, bring to abrupt end, interrupt, disconnect, *adjective* isolated; **cut out** shape by cutting, (cause to) cease functioning, stop doing or using; **cut-out** device for automatic disconnection; **cutthroat** *noun* murderer, *adjective* murderous, (of competition) intense and merciless; **cutthroat razor** one with long unguarded blade set in handle; **cut a tooth** have it appear through gum; **cut up** cut in pieces, (usually in *passive*) greatly distress; **cut up rough** show resentment.

cutaneous /kjuːˈteɪnɪəs/ *adjective* of the skin.

cute /kjuːt/ *adjective colloquial esp. US* attractive, sweet; clever, ingenious. □ **cutely** *adverb*; **cuteness** *noun*.

cuticle /ˈkjuːtɪk(ə)l/ *noun* skin at base of fingernail or toenail.

cutlass /ˈkʌtləs/ *noun historical* short broad-bladed curved sword.

cutlery /ˈkʌtlərɪ/ *noun* knives, forks, and spoons for use at table.

cutlet /ˈkʌtlɪt/ *noun* neck-chop of mutton or lamb; small piece of veal etc. for frying; flat cake of minced meat etc.

cutter *noun* person or thing that cuts; (in *plural*) cutting tool; small fast sailing ship; small boat carried by large ship.

cutting ● *noun* piece cut from newspaper etc.; piece cut from plant for replanting; excavated channel in hillside etc. for railway or road. ● *adjective* that cuts; hurtful. □ **cuttingly** *adverb*.

cuttlefish /ˈkʌt(ə)lfɪʃ/ *noun* (*plural* same or **-es**) 10-armed sea mollusc ejecting black fluid when pursued.

cutwater *noun* forward edge of ship's prow; wedge-shaped projection from pier of bridge.

C.V. *abbreviation* (also **CV**) curriculum vitae.

cwm /kuːm/ *noun* (in Wales) coomb.

cwt *abbreviation* hundredweight.

cyanide /ˈsaɪənaɪd/ *noun* highly poisonous substance used in extraction of gold and silver.

cyanosis /saɪəˈnəʊsɪs/ *noun* bluish skin due to oxygen-deficient blood.

cybernetics /saɪbəˈnetɪks/ *plural noun* (usually treated as *singular*) science of control systems and communications in animals and machines. □ **cybernetic** *adjective*.

cyclamen /ˈsɪkləmən/ *noun* plant with pink, red, or white flowers with backward-turned petals.

cycle /ˈsaɪk(ə)l/ ● *noun* recurrent round or period (of events, phenomena, etc.); series of related poems etc.; bicycle, tricycle, etc. ● *verb* (**-ling**) ride bicycle etc.; move in cycles. □ **cycle lane** part of road reserved for bicycles; **cycle track**, **cycleway** path for bicycles.

cyclic /ˈsaɪklɪk/ *adjective* (also **cyclical** /ˈsɪklɪk(ə)l/) recurring in cycles; belonging to chronological cycle. □ **cyclically** *adverb*.

cyclist /ˈsaɪklɪst/ *noun* rider of bicycle.

cyclone /ˈsaɪkləʊn/ *noun* winds rotating around low-pressure region; violent destructive form of this. □ **cyclonic** /-ˈklɒn-/ *adjective*.

cyclotron /ˈsaɪklətrɒn/ *noun* apparatus for acceleration of charged atomic particles revolving in magnetic field.

cygnet /ˈsɪgnɪt/ *noun* young swan.

cylinder /ˈsɪlɪndə/ *noun* solid or hollow roller-shaped body; container for liquefied gas etc.; piston-chamber in engine. □ **cylindrical** /-ˈlɪn-/ *adjective*.

cymbal /ˈsɪmb(ə)l/ *noun* concave disc struck usually with another to make ringing sound.

cynic /ˈsɪnɪk/ *noun* person with pessimistic view of human nature. □ **cynical** *adjective*; **cynically** *adverb*; **cynicism** /-sɪz(ə)m/ *noun*.

cynosure /ˈsaɪnəzjʊə/ *noun* centre of attention or admiration.

cypher = CIPHER.

cypress /ˈsaɪprəs/ *noun* conifer with dark foliage.

Cypriot /ˈsɪprɪət/ (also **Cypriote** /-əʊt/) ● *noun* native or national of Cyprus. ● *adjective* of Cyprus.

Cyrillic /sɪˈrɪlɪk/ ● *adjective* of alphabet used esp. for Russian and Bulgarian. ● *noun* this alphabet.

cyst /sɪst/ *noun* sac formed in body, containing liquid matter.

cystic *adjective* of the bladder; like a cyst. □ **cystic fibrosis** hereditary disease usually with respiratory infections.

cystitis /sɪˈstaɪtɪs/ *noun* inflammation of the bladder.

czar = TSAR.

czarina = TSARINA.

Czech /tʃek/ ● *noun* native or national of Czech Republic, or *historical* Czechoslovakia; language of Czech people. ● *adjective* of Czechs or their language; of Czech Republic.

Czechoslovak /ˌtʃekəˈsləʊvæk/ (also **Czechoslovakian** /-sləˈvækɪən/) *historical* ● *noun* native or national of Czechoslovakia. ● *adjective* of Czechoslovaks or Czechoslovakia.

Dd

D *noun* (also **d**) (Roman numeral) 500. □ **D-Day** day of Allied invasion of France (6 June 1944), important or decisive day.

d. *abbreviation* died; (pre-decimal) penny.

dab[1] ● *verb* (**-bb-**) (often + *at*) press briefly and repeatedly with cloth etc.; (+ *on*) apply by dabbing; (often + *at*) aim feeble blow; strike lightly. ● *noun* dabbing; small amount (of paint etc.) dabbed on; light blow.

dab[2] *noun* (*plural* same) kind of marine flatfish.

dabble /ˈdæb(ə)l/ *verb* (**-ling**) (usually + *in, at*) engage (in an activity etc.) superficially; move about in shallow water etc. □ **dabbler** *noun*.

dabchick *noun* little grebe.

dab hand *noun* (usually + *at*) expert.

da capo /dɑː ˈkɑːpəʊ/ *adverb Music* repeat from beginning.

dace *noun* (*plural* same) small freshwater fish.

dacha /ˈdætʃə/ *noun* Russian country cottage.

dachshund /ˈdækshʊnd/ *noun* short-legged long-bodied dog.

dactyl /ˈdæktɪl/ *noun* metrical foot of one long followed by two short syllables. □ **dactylic** /-ˈtɪl-/ *adjective*.

dad *noun colloquial* father.

daddy /ˈdædɪ/ *noun* (*plural* **-ies**) *colloquial* father. □ **daddy-long-legs** crane-fly.

dado /ˈdeɪdəʊ/ *noun* (*plural* **-s**) lower, differently decorated, part of interior wall.

daffodil /ˈdæfədɪl/ *noun* spring bulb with trumpet-shaped yellow flowers.

daft /dɑːft/ *adjective* (**-er, -est**) foolish, silly, crazy.

dagger /'dægə/ *noun* short knifelike weapon; obelus.

daguerreotype /də'gerəʊtaɪp/ *noun* early photograph using silvered plate.

dahlia /'deɪlɪə/ *noun* garden plant with large showy flowers.

Dáil (Eireann) /dɔɪl 'eɪrən/ *noun* lower house of Parliament in Republic of Ireland.

daily /'deɪlɪ/ ● *adjective* done, produced, or occurring every (week)day. ● *adverb* every day; constantly. ● *noun* (*plural* **-ies**) *colloquial* daily newspaper; cleaning woman.

dainty /'deɪntɪ/ ● *adjective* (**-ier, -iest**) delicately pretty or small; choice; fastidious. ● *noun* (*plural* **-ies**) delicacy. □ **daintily** *adverb*; **daintiness** *noun*.

daiquiri /'dækərɪ/ *noun* (*plural* **-s**) cocktail of rum, lime juice, etc.

dairy /'deərɪ/ ● *noun* (*plural* **-ies**) place for processing, distributing, or selling milk and milk products. ● *adjective* of, containing, or used for milk and milk products. □ **dairymaid** woman employed in dairy; **dairyman** man looking after cows.

dais /'deɪs/ *noun* low platform, esp. at upper end of hall.

daisy /'deɪzɪ/ *noun* (*plural* **-ies**) flowering plant with white radiating petals. □ **daisy chain** string of field daisies threaded together; **daisy wheel** spoked disc bearing printing characters, used in word processors and typewriters.

dale *noun* valley.

dally /'dælɪ/ *verb* (**-ies, -ied**) delay; waste time; (often + *with*) flirt. □ **dalliance** *noun*.

Dalmatian /dæl'meɪʃ(ə)n/ *noun* large white dog with dark spots.

dam[1] ● *noun* barrier across river etc., usually forming reservoir or preventing flooding. ● *verb* (**-mm-**) provide or confine with dam; (often + *up*) block up, obstruct.

dam[2] *noun* mother (of animal).

damage /'dæmɪdʒ/ ● *noun* harm; injury; (in *plural*) financial compensation for loss or injury; (**the damage**) *slang* cost. ● *verb* (**-ging**) inflict damage on.

damask /'dæməsk/ ● *noun* fabric with woven design made visible by reflection of light. ● *adjective* made of damask; velvety pink. □ **damask rose** old sweet-scented rose.

dame *noun* (**Dame**) (title of) woman who has been knighted; comic female pantomime character played by man; *US slang* woman.

damn /dæm/ ● *verb* (often as *interjection*) curse; censure; condemn to hell; (often as **damning** *adjective*) show or prove to be guilty. ● *noun* uttered curse. ● *adjective* & *adverb* damned. □ **damn all** *slang* nothing.

damnable /'dæmnəb(ə)l/ *adjective* hateful; annoying.

damnation /dæm'neɪʃ(ə)n/ ● *noun* eternal punishment in hell. ● *interjection* expressing anger.

damned /dæmd/ ● *adjective* damnable. ● *adverb* extremely.

damp ● *adjective* slightly wet. ● *noun* slight diffused or condensed moisture. ● *verb* make damp; (often + *down*) discourage, make burn less strongly; *Music* stop vibration of (string etc.). □ **damp course** layer of damp-proof material in wall to keep damp from rising. □ **dampness** *noun*.

dampen *verb* make or become damp; discourage.

damper *noun* device that reduces shock, vibration, or noise; discouraging person or thing; metal plate in flue to control draught.

damsel /'dæmz(ə)l/ *noun archaic* young unmarried woman.

damson /'dæmz(ə)n/ *noun* small dark purple plum.

dance /dɑːns/ ● *verb* (**-cing**) move rhythmically, usually to music; perform (dance role etc.); jump or bob about. ● *noun* dancing as art; style or form of this; social gathering for dancing; lively motion. □ **dance attendance (on)** serve obsequiously. □ **dancer** *noun*.

dandelion /'dændɪlaɪən/ *noun* yellow-flowered wild plant.

dander *noun* □ **get one's dander up** *colloquial* become angry.

dandle /'dænd(ə)l/ *verb* (**-ling**) bounce (child) on one's knees etc.

dandruff /'dændrʌf/ noun flakes of dead skin in hair.

dandy /'dændɪ/ ● noun (plural **-ies**) man excessively devoted to style and fashion. ● adjective (**-ier, -iest**) colloquial splendid. □ **dandy-brush** stiff brush for grooming horses.

Dane noun native or national of Denmark; historical Viking invader of England.

danger /'deɪndʒə/ noun liability or exposure to harm; thing causing harm. □ **danger list** list of those dangerously ill; **danger money** extra payment for dangerous work.

dangerous adjective involving or causing danger. □ **dangerously** adverb.

dangle /'dæŋɡ(ə)l/ verb (**-ling**) hang loosely; hold or carry swaying loosely; hold out (temptation etc.).

Danish /'deɪnɪʃ/ ● adjective of Denmark. ● noun Danish language; (**the Danish**) the Danish people. □ **Danish blue** white blue-veined cheese; **Danish pastry** yeast cake with icing, nuts, fruit, etc.

dank adjective damp and cold.

daphne /'dæfnɪ/ noun a flowering shrub.

dapper adjective neat and precise, esp. in dress; sprightly.

dapple /'dæp(ə)l/ verb (**-ling**) mark with spots of colour or shade; mottle. □ **dapple-grey** (of horse) grey with darker spots; **dapple grey** such a horse.

Darby and Joan noun devoted old married couple. □ **Darby and Joan club** social club for pensioners.

dare /deə/ ● verb (**-ring**) 3rd singular present often **dare** (+ (to) do) have the courage or impudence (to); (usually + to do) defy, challenge. ● noun challenge. □ **daredevil** reckless (person); **I dare say** very likely, I grant that.

daring ● noun adventurous courage. ● adjective bold, prepared to take risks. □ **daringly** adverb.

dariole /'dærɪəʊl/ noun dish cooked and served in a small mould.

dark ● adjective with little or no light; of deep or sombre colour; (of a person) with dark colouring; gloomy; sinister; angry; secret, mysterious. ● noun absence of light or knowledge; unlit place. □ **after dark** after nightfall'.; **Dark Ages** 5th–10th-c., unenlightened period; **dark horse** little-known person who is unexpectedly successful; **darkroom** darkened room for photographic work; **in the dark** without information or light. □ **darken** verb; **darkly** adverb; **darkness** noun.

darling /'dɑːlɪŋ/ ● noun beloved or endearing person or animal. ● adjective beloved, lovable; colloquial charming.

darn¹ ● verb mend by interweaving wool etc. across hole. ● noun darned area.

darn² verb, interjection, adjective, & adverb colloquial mild form of DAMN.

darnel /'dɑːn(ə)l/ noun grass growing in cereal crops.

dart ● noun small pointed missile; (in plural treated as singular) indoor game of throwing darts at a dartboard; sudden rapid movement; tapering tuck in garment. ● verb (often + out, in, past, etc.) move, send, or go suddenly or rapidly. □ **dartboard** circular target in game of darts.

Darwinian /dɑːˈwɪnɪən/ ● adjective of Darwin's theory of evolution. ● noun adherent of this. □ **Darwinism** /'dɑː-/ noun, **Darwinist** /'dɑː-/ noun.

dash ● verb rush; strike or fling forcefully so as to shatter; frustrate, dispirit; colloquial (as interjection) damn. ● noun rush, onset; punctuation mark (—) used to indicate break in sense (see panel); longer signal of two in Morse code; slight admixture; (capacity for) impetuous vigour. □ **dashboard** instrument panel of vehicle or aircraft; **dash off** write hurriedly.

dashing adjective spirited; showy.

dastardly /'dæstədlɪ/ adjective cowardly, despicable.

data /'deɪtə/ plural noun (also treated as singular) known facts used for inference or reckoning; quantities or characters operated on by computer. □ **data bank** store or source of data; **database** structured set of data held in computer; **data processing** series of operations on data by computer.

■ **Usage** In scientific, philosophical, and general use, *data* is usually considered to mean a number of items and is treated as plural, with *datum* as its singular. In computing and allied subjects (and sometimes in general use), it is treated as singular, as in *Much useful data has been collected.* However, *data* is not singular, and it is wrong to say *a data* or *every data* or to make the plural form *datas*.

date[1] ● *noun* day of month; historical day or year; day, month, and year of writing etc. at head of document etc.; period to which work of art etc. belongs; time when an event takes place; *colloquial* social appointment, esp. with person of opposite sex; *US colloquial* person to be met at this. ● *verb* (**-ting**) mark with date; assign date to; (+ *to*) assign to a particular time, period, etc.; (often + *from*, *back to*, etc.) have origin at a particular time; expose as or appear old-fashioned; *US colloquial* make date with, go out together as sexual partners. □ **date line** line partly along meridian 180° from Greenwich, to the east of which date is a day earlier than to the west; date and place of writing at head of newspaper article etc.; **out of date** (**out-of-date** before noun) old-fashioned, obsolete; **to date** until now; **up to date** (**up-to-date** before noun) fashionable, current.

date[2] *noun* oval stone fruit; (in full **date-palm**) tree bearing this.

dative /'deɪtɪv/ *Grammar* ● *noun* case expressing indirect object or recipient. ● *adjective* of or in the dative.

datum /'deɪtəm/ *singular* of DATA.

daub /dɔːb/ ● *verb* paint or spread (paint etc.) crudely or unskilfully; smear (surface) with paint etc. ● *noun* paint etc. daubed on a surface; crude painting; clay etc. coating wattles to form wall.

daughter /'dɔːtə/ *noun* female child in relation to her parents; female descendant or member of family etc. □ **daughter-in-law** (*plural* **daughters-in-law**) son's wife.

daunt /dɔːnt/ *verb* discourage, intimidate. □ **daunting** *adjective*.

dauntless *adjective* intrepid, persevering.

dauphin /'dɔːfɪn/ *noun historical* eldest son of King of France.

Davenport /'dævənpɔːt/ *noun* kind of writing desk; *US* large sofa.

davit /'dævɪt/ *noun* small crane on ship for holding lifeboat.

daw *noun* jackdaw.

dawdle /'dɔːd(ə)l/ *verb* (**-ling**) walk slowly and idly; waste time, procrastinate.

dawn ● *noun* daybreak; beginning. ● *verb* (of day) begin, grow light; (often + *on*, *upon*) become evident (to). □ **dawn chorus** birdsong at daybreak.

day *noun* time between sunrise and sunset; 24 hours as a unit of time; daylight; time during which work is normally

---

Dash –

This is used:

1 to mark the beginning and end of an interruption in the structure of a sentence:
   My son—where has he gone?—would like to meet you.

2 to show faltering speech in conversation:
   Yes—well—I would—only you see—it's not easy.

3 to show other kinds of break in a sentence, where a comma, semicolon, or colon would traditionally be used, e.g.
   Come tomorrow—if you can.
   The most important thing is this—don't rush the work.

A dash is not used in this way in formal writing.

done; (also *plural*) historical period; (**the day**) present time; period of prosperity. □ **daybreak** first light in morning; **day centre** place for care of elderly or handicapped during day; **daydream** (indulge in) fantasy etc. while awake; **day off** day's holiday; **day release** part-time education for employees; **day return** reduced fare or ticket for a return journey in one day; **day school** school for pupils living at home; **daytime** part of day when there is natural light; **day-to-day** mundane, routine; **day-trip** trip completed in one day.

daylight *noun* light of day; dawn; visible gap between things; (usually in *plural*) *slang* life. □ **daylight robbery** blatantly excessive charge; **daylight saving** longer summer evening daylight, achieved by putting clocks forward.

daze ● *verb* (**-zing**) stupefy, bewilder. ● *noun* dazed state.

dazzle /'dæz(ə)l/ ● *verb* (**-ling**) blind or confuse temporarily with sudden bright light; impress or overpower with knowledge, ability, etc. ● *noun* bright confusing light. □ **dazzling** *adjective*.

dB *abbreviation* decibel(s).

DC *abbreviation* direct current; District of Columbia; da capo.

DDT *abbreviation* colourless chlorinated hydrocarbon used as insecticide.

deacon /'di:kən/ *noun* (in episcopal churches) minister below priest; (*feminine* **deaconess** /-'nes/) (in Nonconformist churches) lay officer.

deactivate /di:'æktɪveɪt/ *verb* (**-ting**) make inactive or less reactive.

dead /ded/ ● *adjective* no longer alive; numb; *colloquial* extremely tired or unwell; (+ *to*) insensitive to; not effective; extinct; extinguished; inanimate; lacking vigour; not resonant; quiet; not transmitting sounds; out of play; abrupt; complete. ● *adverb* absolutely, completely; *colloquial* very. ● *noun* time of silence or inactivity. □ **dead beat** utterly exhausted; **dead-beat** tramp; **dead duck** useless person or thing; **dead end** closed end of road etc.; **dead-end** having no prospects; **dead heat** race in which competitors tie; **dead letter** law etc. no longer observed; **deadline** time limit; **deadlock**

noun state of unresolved conflict, *verb* bring or come to a standstill; **dead loss** useless person or thing; **dead man's handle** handle on electric train etc. disconnecting power supply if released; **dead march** funeral march; **dead on** exactly right; **deadpan** lacking expression or emotion; **dead reckoning** estimation of ship's position from log, compass, etc., when visibility is bad; **dead shot** unerring marksman; **dead weight** inert mass, heavy burden; **dead wood** *colloquial* useless person(s) or thing(s).

deaden *verb* deprive of or lose vitality, force, etc.; (+ *to*) make insensitive.

deadly ● *adjective* (**-ier, -iest**) causing fatal injury or serious damage; intense; accurate; deathlike; dreary. ● *adverb* as if dead; extremely. □ **deadly nightshade** plant with poisonous black berries.

deaf /def/ *adjective* wholly or partly unable to hear; (+ *to*) refusing to listen or comply. □ **deaf-aid** hearing aid; **deaf-and-dumb alphabet, language** sign language; **deaf mute** deaf and dumb person. □ **deafness** *noun*.

deafen *verb* (often as **deafening** *adjective*) overpower or make deaf with noise, esp. temporarily. □ **deafeningly** *adverb*.

deal[1] ● *verb* (*past & past participle* **dealt** /delt/) (+ *with*) take measures to resolve, placate, etc., do business or associate with, treat (subject); (often + *by, with*) behave in specified way; (+ *in*) sell; (often + *out, round*) distribute; administer. ● *noun* (usually a **good** or **great deal**) large amount, considerably; business arrangement etc.; specified treatment; dealing of cards, player's turn to deal.

deal[2] *noun* fir or pine timber, esp. as boards.

dealer *noun* trader; player dealing at cards.

dealings *plural noun* conduct or transactions.

dean *noun* head of ecclesiastical chapter; (usually **rural dean**) clergyman supervising parochial clergy; college or university official with disciplinary functions; head of university faculty.

deanery *noun* (*plural* **-ies**) dean's house or position; parishes presided over by rural dean.

dear ● *adjective* beloved; *used before person's name, esp. at beginning of letter*; (+ *to*) precious; expensive. ● *noun* dear person. ● *adverb* at great cost. ● *interjection* (usually **oh dear!** or **dear me!**) *expressing surprise, dismay, etc.* □ **dearly** *adverb*.

dearth /dɜːθ/ *noun* scarcity, lack.

death /deθ/ *noun* dying, end of life; being dead; cause of death; destruction. □ **deathblow** blow etc. causing death, or action, event, etc. ending something; **death-mask** cast of dead person's face; **death penalty** capital punishment; **death rate** yearly deaths per 1000 of population; **death-rattle** gurgling in throat at death; **death row** part of prison for those sentenced to death; **death squad** paramilitary group; **death-trap** unsafe place, vehicle, etc.; **death-warrant** order of execution; **death-watch beetle** beetle that bores into wood and makes ticking sound. □ **deathlike** *adjective*.

deathly ● *adjective* (**-ier**, **-iest**) like death. ● *adverb* in deathly manner.

deb *noun colloquial* débutante.

débâcle /deɪˈbɑːk(ə)l/ *noun* utter collapse; confused rush.

debar /dɪˈbɑː/ *verb* (**-rr-**) (+ *from*) exclude. □ **debarment** *noun*.

debase /dɪˈbeɪs/ *verb* (**-sing**) lower in character, quality, or value; depreciate (coin) by alloying etc. □ **debasement** *noun*.

debatable /dɪˈbeɪtəb(ə)l/ *adjective* questionable.

debate /dɪˈbeɪt/ ● *verb* (**-ting**) discuss or dispute, esp. formally; consider, ponder. ● *noun* discussion, esp. formal.

debauch /dɪˈbɔːtʃ/ ● *verb* corrupt, deprave, debase; (as **debauched** *adjective*) dissolute. ● *noun* bout of debauchery.

debauchee /dɪbɔːˈtʃiː/ *noun* debauched person.

debauchery *noun* excessive sensual indulgence.

debenture /dɪˈbentʃə/ *noun* company bond providing for payment of interest.

debilitate /dɪˈbɪlɪteɪt/ *verb* (**-ting**) enfeeble. □ **debilitation** *noun*.

debility *noun* feebleness, esp. of health.

debit /ˈdebɪt/ ● *noun* entry in account recording sum owed. ● *verb* (**-t-**) (+ *against, to*) enter on debit side of account.

debonair /debəˈneə/ *adjective* self-assured; pleasant.

debouch /dɪˈbaʊtʃ/ *verb* come out into open ground; (often + *into*) (of river etc.) merge. □ **debouchment** *noun*.

debrief /diːˈbriːf/ *verb* question (diplomat etc.) about completed mission. □ **debriefing** *noun*.

debris /ˈdebriː/ *noun* scattered fragments; wreckage.

debt /det/ *noun* money etc. owing; obligation; state of owing.

debtor *noun* person owing money etc.

debug /diːˈbʌg/ *verb* (**-gg-**) remove hidden microphones from; remove defects from.

debunk /diːˈbʌŋk/ *verb colloquial* expose as spurious or false.

début /ˈdeɪbjuː/ *noun* first public appearance.

débutante /ˈdebjʊtɑːnt/ *noun* young woman making her social début.

Dec. *abbreviation* December.

deca- *combining form* ten.

decade /ˈdekeɪd/ *noun* 10 years; set or series of 10.

decadence /ˈdekəd(ə)ns/ *noun* moral or cultural decline; immoral behaviour. □ **decadent** *adjective*.

decaffeinated /diːˈkæfɪneɪtɪd/ *adjective* with caffeine removed.

decagon /ˈdekəgən/ *noun* plane figure with 10 sides and angles. □ **decagonal** /-ˈkæg-/ *adjective*.

decahedron /dekəˈhiːdrən/ *noun* solid figure with 10 faces. □ **decahedral** *adjective*.

decamp /dɪˈkæmp/ *verb* depart suddenly; break up or leave camp.

decant /dɪˈkænt/ *verb* pour off (wine etc.) leaving sediment behind.

decanter *noun* stoppered glass container for decanted wine or spirit.

decapitate /dɪˈkæpɪteɪt/ *verb* (**-ting**) behead. □ **decapitation** *noun*.

decarbonize /diːˈkɑːbənaɪz/ *verb* (also **-ise**) (**-zing** or **-sing**) remove carbon etc. from (engine of car etc.). □ **decarbonization** *noun*.

decathlon /dɪˈkæθlən/ *noun* athletic contest of 10 events. □ **decathlete** *noun*.

decay /dɪˈkeɪ/ ● *verb* (cause to) rot or decompose; decline in quality, power, etc. ● *noun* rotten state; decline.

decease /dɪˈsiːs/ *noun formal esp. Law* death.

deceased *formal* ● *adjective* dead. ● *noun* (**the deceased**) person who has died.

deceit /dɪˈsiːt/ *noun* deception; trick. □ **deceitful** *adjective*.

deceive /dɪˈsiːv/ *verb* (**-ving**) make (person) believe what is false; (**deceive oneself**) persist in mistaken belief; mislead; be unfaithful to.

decelerate /diːˈseləreɪt/ *verb* (**-ting**) (cause to) reduce speed. □ **deceleration** *noun*.

December /dɪˈsembə/ *noun* twelfth month of year.

decency /ˈdiːsənsɪ/ *noun* (*plural* -**ies**) correct, honourable, or decent behaviour; (in *plural*) proprieties, manners.

decennial /dɪˈsenɪəl/ *adjective* lasting 10 years; recurring every 10 years.

decent /ˈdiːs(ə)nt/ *adjective* conforming with standards of decency; not obscene; respectable; acceptable; kind. □ **decently** *adverb*.

decentralize /diːˈsentrəlaɪz/ *verb* (also -**ise**) (**-zing** or -**sing**) transfer (power etc.) from central to local authority. □ **decentralization** *noun*.

deception /dɪˈsepʃ(ə)n/ *noun* deceiving, being deceived; thing that deceives.

deceptive /dɪˈseptɪv/ *adjective* likely to mislead.

deci- *combining form* one-tenth.

decibel /ˈdesɪbel/ *noun* unit used in comparison of sound etc. levels.

decide /dɪˈsaɪd/ *verb* (**-ding**) (usually + *to do, that, on, about*) resolve after consideration; settle (issue etc.); (usually + *between, for, against, in favour of, that*) give judgement.

decided *adjective* definite, unquestionable; positive, resolute. □ **decidedly** *adverb*.

deciduous /dɪˈsɪdjʊəs/ *adjective* (of tree) shedding leaves annually; (of leaves etc.) shed periodically.

decimal /ˈdesɪm(ə)l/ ● *adjective* (of system of numbers, weights, measures, etc.)

based on 10; of tenths or 10; proceeding by tens. ● *noun* decimal fraction. □ **decimal fraction** fraction expressed in tenths, hundredths, etc., esp. by units to right of decimal point; **decimal point** dot placed before fraction in decimal fraction.

decimalize *verb* (also -**ise**) (**-zing** or -**sing**) express as decimal; convert to decimal system. □ **decimalization** *noun*.

decimate /ˈdesɪmeɪt/ *verb* (**-ting**) destroy large proportion of. □ **decimation** *noun*.

■ **Usage** *Decimate* should not be used to mean 'defeat utterly'.

decipher /dɪˈsaɪfə/ *verb* convert (coded information) into intelligible language; determine the meaning of. □ **decipherable** *adjective*.

decision /dɪˈsɪʒ(ə)n/ *noun* deciding; resolution after consideration; settlement; resoluteness.

decisive /dɪˈsaɪsɪv/ *adjective* conclusive, settling an issue; quick to decide. □ **decisively** *adverb*; **decisiveness** *noun*.

deck ● *noun* platform in a ship serving as a floor; floor of bus etc.; section for playing discs or tapes etc. in sound system; *US* pack of cards. ● *verb* (often + *out*) decorate. □ **deck-chair** outdoor folding chair.

declaim /dɪˈkleɪm/ *verb* speak, recite, etc. as if addressing audience. □ **declamation** *noun*; **declamatory** /-ˈklæm-/ *adjective*.

declaration /dekləˈreɪʃ(ə)n/ *noun* declaring; emphatic, deliberate, or formal statement.

declare /dɪˈkleə/ *verb* (**-ring**) announce openly or formally; pronounce; (usually + *that*) assert emphatically; acknowledge possession of (dutiable goods, income, etc.); *Cricket* close (innings) voluntarily before team is out; *Cards* name trump suit. □ **declaratory** /-ˈklær-/ *adjective*.

declassify /diːˈklæsɪfaɪ/ *verb* (**-ies**, -**ied**) declare (information etc.) to be no longer secret. □ **declassification** *noun*.

declension /dɪˈklenʃ(ə)n/ *noun Grammar* variation of form of noun etc., to show grammatical case; class of nouns with same inflections; deterioration.

declination /deklɪˈneɪʃ(ə)n/ noun downward bend; angular distance north or south of celestial equator; deviation of compass needle from true north.

decline /dɪˈklaɪn/ ● verb (-ning) deteriorate, lose strength or vigour; decrease; refuse; slope or bend downwards; *Grammar* state case forms of (noun etc.). ● noun deterioration.

declivity /dɪˈklɪvɪtɪ/ noun (*plural* -ies) downward slope.

declutch /diːˈklʌtʃ/ verb disengage clutch of motor vehicle.

decode /diːˈkəʊd/ verb (-ding) decipher. □ **decoder** noun.

decoke /diːˈkəʊk/ verb (-king) *colloquial* decarbonize.

décolletage /deɪkɒlˈtɑːʒ/ noun low neckline of woman's dress. [French]

décolleté /deɪˈkɒlteɪ/ adjective (also **décolletée**) having low neckline. [French]

decompose /diːkəmˈpəʊz/ verb (-sing) rot; separate into elements. □ **decomposition** /diːkɒmpəˈzɪʃ(ə)n/ noun.

decompress /diːkəmˈpres/ verb subject to decompression.

decompression /diːkəmˈpreʃ(ə)n/ noun release from compression; reduction of pressure on deep-sea diver etc. □ **decompression chamber** enclosed space for decompression.

decongestant /diːkənˈdʒest(ə)nt/ noun medicine etc. that relieves nasal congestion.

decontaminate /diːkənˈtæmɪneɪt/ verb (-ting) remove contamination from. □ **decontamination** noun.

décor /ˈdeɪkɔː/ noun furnishings and decoration of room, stage, etc.

decorate /ˈdekəreɪt/ verb (-ting) adorn; paint, wallpaper, etc. (room etc.); give medal or award to.

decoration noun decorating; thing that decorates; medal etc.; (in *plural*) flags etc. put up on festive occasion.

decorative /ˈdekərətɪv/ adjective pleasing in appearance. □ **decoratively** adverb.

decorator noun person who decorates for a living.

decorous /ˈdekərəs/ adjective having or showing decorum. □ **decorously** adverb.

decorum /dɪˈkɔːrəm/ noun polite dignified behaviour.

decoy ● noun /ˈdiːkɔɪ/ thing or person used as lure; bait, enticement. ● verb /dɪˈkɔɪ/ lure by decoy.

decrease ● verb /dɪˈkriːs/ (-sing) make or become smaller or fewer. ● noun /ˈdiːkriːs/ decreasing; amount of this.

decree /dɪˈkriː/ ● noun official legal order; legal decision. ● verb (-ees, -eed) ordain by decree. □ **decree absolute** final order for completion of divorce; **decree nisi** /ˈnaɪsaɪ/ provisional order for divorce.

decrepit /dɪˈkrepɪt/ adjective weakened by age or infirmity; dilapidated. □ **decrepitude** noun.

decry /dɪˈkraɪ/ verb (-ies, -ied) disparage.

dedicate /ˈdedɪkeɪt/ verb (-ting) (often + to) devote (oneself) to a purpose etc.; address (book etc.) to friend or patron etc.; devote (building etc.) to saint etc.; (as **dedicated** adjective) having single-minded loyalty. □ **dedicatory** adjective.

dedication noun dedicating; words with which book is dedicated.

deduce /dɪˈdjuːs/ verb (-cing) (often + from) infer logically. □ **deducible** adjective.

deduct /dɪˈdʌkt/ verb (often + from) subtract; take away; withhold.

deductible adjective that may be deducted esp. from tax or taxable income.

deduction /dɪˈdʌkʃ(ə)n/ noun deducting; amount deducted; inference from general to particular.

deductive adjective of or reasoning by deduction.

deed noun thing done; action; legal document. □ **deed of covenant** agreement to pay regular sum, esp. to charity; **deed poll** deed made by one party only, esp. to change one's name.

deem verb *formal* consider, judge.

deep ● adjective extending far down or in; to or at specified depth; low-pitched; intense; profound; (+ in) fully absorbed, overwhelmed. ● adverb deeply; far down or in. ● noun deep state; (**the deep**) *poetical* the sea. □ **deep-freeze** noun freezer, verb freeze or store in freezer; **deep-fry** fry with fat covering food. □ **deepen** verb; **deeply** adverb.

deer *noun* (*plural* same) 4-hoofed grazing animal, male usually with antlers. □ **deerstalker** cloth peaked cap with ear-flaps.

deface /dɪˈfeɪs/ *verb* (**-cing**) disfigure. □ **defacement** *noun.*

de facto /deɪ ˈfæktəʊ/ ● *adjective* existing in fact, whether by right or not. ● *adverb* in fact.

defame /dɪˈfeɪm/ *verb* (**-ming**) attack good name of. □ **defamation** /defəˈmeɪʃ(ə)n/ *noun*; **defamatory** /-ˈfæm-/ *adjective.*

default /dɪˈfɔːlt/ ● *noun* failure to act, appear, or pay; option selected by computer program etc. unless given alternative instruction. ● *verb* fail to fulfil obligations. □ **by default** because of lack of an alternative etc. □ **defaulter** *noun.*

defeat /dɪˈfiːt/ ● *verb* overcome in battle, contest, etc.; frustrate, baffle. ● *noun* defeating, being defeated.

defeatism *noun* readiness to accept defeat. □ **defeatist** *noun & adjective.*

defecate /ˈdiːfɪkeɪt/ *verb* (**-ting**) evacuate the bowels. □ **defecation** *noun.*

defect ● *noun* /ˈdiːfekt/ shortcoming; fault. ● *verb* /dɪˈfekt/ desert one's country, cause, etc., for another. □ **defection** *noun*; **defector** *noun.*

defective /dɪˈfektɪv/ *adjective* faulty; imperfect. □ **defectiveness** *noun.*

defence /dɪˈfens/ *noun* (*US* **defense**) (means of) defending; justification; defendant's case or counsel; players in defending position; (in *plural*) fortifications. □ **defenceless** *adjective.*

defend /dɪˈfend/ *verb* (often + *against*, *from*) resist attack made on; protect; uphold by argument; *Law* conduct defence (of); compete to retain (title). □ **defender** *noun.*

defendant *noun* person accused or sued in court of law.

defense *US* = DEFENCE.

defensible /dɪˈfensɪb(ə)l/ *adjective* able to be defended or justified.

defensive /dɪˈfensɪv/ *adjective* done or intended for defence; over-reacting to criticism. □ **on the defensive** expecting criticism, ready to defend. □ **defensively** *adverb*; **defensiveness** *noun.*

defer[1] /dɪˈfɜː/ *verb* (**-rr-**) postpone. □ **deferment** *noun.*

defer[2] /dɪˈfɜː/ *verb* (**-rr-**) (+ *to*) yield or make concessions.

deference /ˈdefərəns/ *noun* respectful conduct; compliance with another's wishes. □ **in deference to** out of respect for.

deferential /defəˈrenʃ(ə)l/ *adjective* respectful. □ **deferentially** *adverb.*

defiance /dɪˈfaɪəns/ *noun* open disobedience; bold resistance. □ **defiant** *adjective*; **defiantly** *adverb.*

deficiency /dɪˈfɪʃənsɪ/ *noun* (*plural* **-ies**) being deficient; (usually + *of*) lack or shortage; thing lacking; deficit. □ **deficiency disease** disease caused by lack of essential element in diet.

deficient /dɪˈfɪʃ(ə)nt/ *adjective* (often + *in*) incomplete or insufficient.

deficit /ˈdefɪsɪt/ *noun* amount by which total falls short; excess of liabilities over assets.

defile[1] /dɪˈfaɪl/ *verb* (**-ling**) make dirty; pollute; profane. □ **defilement** *noun.*

defile[2] /dɪˈfaɪl/ ● *noun* narrow gorge or pass. ● *verb* (**-ling**) march in file.

define /dɪˈfaɪn/ *verb* (**-ning**) give meaning of; describe scope of; outline; mark out the boundary of. □ **definable** *adjective.*

definite /ˈdefɪnɪt/ *adjective* certain; clearly defined; precise. □ **definite article** the word (*the* in English) placed before a noun and implying a specific object, person, or idea. □ **definitely** *adverb.*

definition /defɪˈnɪʃ(ə)n/ *noun* defining; statement of meaning of word etc.; distinctness in outline.

definitive /dɪˈfɪnɪtɪv/ *adjective* decisive, unconditional, final; most authoritative.

deflate /dɪˈfleɪt/ *verb* (**-ting**) let air out of (tyre etc.); (cause to) lose confidence; subject (economy) to deflation.

deflation *noun* deflating; reduction of money in circulation to combat inflation. □ **deflationary** *adjective.*

deflect /dɪˈflekt/ *verb* bend or turn aside from purpose or course; (often + *from*) (cause to) deviate. □ **deflection** *noun.*

deflower /diːˈflaʊə/ *verb* deprive of virginity; ravage.

defoliate /diːˈfəʊlɪeɪt/ verb (-ting) destroy leaves of. □ **defoliant** noun; **defoliation** noun.

deforest /diːˈfɒrɪst/ verb clear of forests. □ **deforestation** noun.

deform /dɪˈfɔːm/ verb (often as **deformed** adjective) make ugly or misshapen, disfigure. □ **deformation** /diː-/ noun.

deformity /dɪˈfɔːmɪtɪ/ noun (plural **-ies**) being deformed; malformation.

defraud /dɪˈfrɔːd/ verb (often + of) cheat by fraud.

defray /dɪˈfreɪ/ verb provide money for (cost). □ **defrayal** noun.

defrock /diːˈfrɒk/ verb deprive (esp. priest) of office.

defrost /diːˈfrɒst/ verb remove frost or ice from; unfreeze; become unfrozen.

deft adjective dexterous, skilful. □ **deftly** adverb; **deftness** noun.

defunct /dɪˈfʌŋkt/ adjective no longer existing or in use; dead.

defuse /diːˈfjuːz/ verb (-sing) remove fuse from (bomb etc.); reduce tension in (crisis etc.).

defy /dɪˈfaɪ/ verb (-ies, -ied) resist openly; present insuperable obstacles to; (+ to do) challenge to do or prove something.

degenerate /dɪˈdʒenərət/ ● adjective having lost usual or good qualities; immoral. ● noun degenerate person etc. ● verb /-reɪt/ (-ting) become degenerate; get worse. □ **degeneracy** noun; **degeneration** noun.

degrade /dɪˈɡreɪd/ verb (-ding) (often as **degrading** adjective) humiliate; dishonour; reduce to lower rank. □ **degradation** /deɡrəˈdeɪʃ(ə)n/ noun.

degree /dɪˈɡriː/ noun stage in scale, series, or process; unit of measurement of angle or temperature; extent of burns; academic rank conferred by university etc.

dehumanize /diːˈhjuːmənaɪz/ verb (also **-ise**) (-zing or -sing) remove human qualities from; make impersonal. □ **dehumanization** noun.

dehydrate /diːhaɪˈdreɪt/ verb (-ting) remove water from; make dry; (often as **dehydrated** adjective) deprive of fluids, make very thirsty. □ **dehydration** noun.

de-ice /diːˈaɪs/ verb (-cing) remove ice from; prevent formation of ice on. □ **de-icer** noun.

deify /ˈdiːɪfaɪ/ verb (-ies, -ied) make god or idol of. □ **deification** noun.

deign /deɪn/ verb (+ to do) condescend.

deism /ˈdiːɪz(ə)m/ noun reasoned belief in existence of a god. □ **deist** noun; **deistic** /-ˈɪstɪk/ adjective.

deity /ˈdeɪɪtɪ/ noun (plural **-ies**) god or goddess; divine status or nature.

déjà vu /deɪʒɑː ˈvuː/ noun illusion of having already experienced present situation. [French]

dejected /dɪˈdʒektɪd/ adjective sad, depressed. □ **dejectedly** adverb; **dejection** noun.

delay /dɪˈleɪ/ ● verb postpone; make or be late. ● noun delaying, being delayed; time lost by this.

delectable /dɪˈlektəb(ə)l/ adjective delightful.

delectation /diːlekˈteɪʃ(ə)n/ noun enjoyment.

delegate ● noun /ˈdelɪɡət/ elected representative sent to conference; member of delegation etc. ● verb /ˈdelɪɡeɪt/ (-ting) (often + to) commit (power etc.) to deputy etc.; entrust (task) to another; send or authorize as representative.

delegation /delɪˈɡeɪʃ(ə)n/ noun group representing others; delegating, being delegated.

delete /dɪˈliːt/ verb (-ting) strike out (word etc.). □ **deletion** noun.

deleterious /delɪˈtɪərɪəs/ adjective harmful.

delft noun (also **delftware**) type of glazed earthenware.

deli /ˈdelɪ/ noun (plural -s) colloquial delicatessen.

deliberate ● adjective /dɪˈlɪbərət/ intentional, considered; unhurried. ● verb /dɪˈlɪbəreɪt/ (-ting) think carefully; discuss. □ **deliberately** adverb.

deliberation /dɪlɪbəˈreɪʃ(ə)n/ noun careful consideration or slowness.

deliberative /dɪˈlɪbərətɪv/ adjective (esp. of assembly etc.) of or for deliberation.

delicacy /ˈdelɪkəsɪ/ noun (plural **-ies**) being delicate; choice food.

delicate /ˈdelɪkət/ adjective fine in texture, quality, etc.; subtle, hard to discern; susceptible, tender; requiring tact. □ **delicately** adverb.

delicatessen /delɪkə'tes(ə)n/ *noun* shop selling esp. exotic cooked meats, cheeses, etc.

delicious /dɪ'lɪʃəs/ *adjective* highly enjoyable esp. to taste or smell. □ **deliciously** *adverb*.

delight /dɪ'laɪt/ ● *verb* (often as **delighted** *adjective*) please greatly; (+ *in*) take great pleasure in. ● *noun* great pleasure; thing that delights. □ **delightful** *adjective*, **delightfully** *adverb*.

delimit /dɪ'lɪmɪt/ *verb* (**-t-**) fix limits or boundary of. □ **delimitation** *noun*.

delineate /dɪ'lɪnɪeɪt/ *verb* (**-ting**) portray by drawing or in words. □ **delineation** *noun*.

delinquent /dɪ'lɪŋkwənt/ ● *noun* offender. ● *adjective* guilty of misdeed; failing in a duty. □ **delinquency** *noun*.

deliquesce /delɪ'kwes/ *verb* (**-cing**) become liquid; dissolve in moisture from the air. □ **deliquescence** *noun*, **deliquescent** *adjective*.

delirious /dɪ'lɪrɪəs/ *adjective* affected with delirium; wildly excited. □ **deliriously** *adverb*.

delirium /dɪ'lɪrɪəm/ *noun* disordered state of mind, with incoherent speech etc.; wildly excited mood. □ **delirium tremens** /'tri:menz/ psychosis of chronic alcoholism with tremors and hallucinations.

deliver /dɪ'lɪvə/ *verb* convey (letters, goods) to destination; (often + *to*) hand over; (often + *from*) save, rescue, set free; assist in giving birth or at birth of; utter (speech); launch or aim (blow etc.); (in full **deliver the goods**) *colloquial* provide or carry out what is required.

deliverance *noun* rescuing.

delivery /dɪ'lɪvərɪ/ *noun* (*plural* **-ies**) delivering; distribution of letters etc.; thing delivered; childbirth; manner of delivering.

dell *noun* small wooded valley.

delouse /di:'laʊs/ *verb* (**-sing**) rid of lice.

delphinium /del'fɪnɪəm/ *noun* (*plural* **-s**) garden plant with spikes of usually blue flowers.

delta /'deltə/ *noun* triangular alluvial tract at mouth of river; fourth letter of Greek alphabet (Δ, δ); fourth-class mark for work etc. □ **delta wing** triangular swept-back wing of aircraft.

delude /dɪ'lu:d/ *verb* (**-ding**) deceive, mislead.

deluge /'delju:dʒ/ ● *noun* flood; downpour of rain; overwhelming rush. ● *verb* (**-ging**) flood, inundate.

delusion /dɪ'lu:ʒ(ə)n/ *noun* false belief or hope. □ **delusive** *adjective*, **delusory** *adjective*.

de luxe /də 'lʌks/ *adjective* luxurious; superior; sumptuous.

delve *verb* (**-ving**) (often + *in*, *into*) research, search deeply; *poetical* dig.

demagogue /'deməgɒg/ *noun* political agitator appealing to emotion. □ **demagogic** /-'gɒgɪk/ *adjective*, **demagogy** /-gɒgɪ/ *noun*.

demand /dɪ'mɑ:nd/ ● *noun* insistent and peremptory request; desire for commodity; urgent claim. ● *verb* (often + *of*, *from*, *to do*, *that*) ask for insistently; require; (as **demanding** *adjective*) requiring effort, attention, etc. □ **demand feeding** feeding baby whenever it cries.

demarcation /di:mɑ:'keɪʃ(ə)n/ *noun* marking of boundary or limits; trade union practice of restricting job to one union. □ **demarcate** /'di:-/ *verb* (**-ting**).

demean /dɪ'mi:n/ *verb* (usually **demean oneself**) lower dignity of.

demeanour /dɪ'mi:nə/ *noun* (*US* **demeanor**) bearing; outward behaviour.

demented /dɪ'mentɪd/ *adjective* mad.

dementia /dɪ'menʃə/ *noun* chronic insanity. □ **dementia praecox** /'pri:kɒks/ schizophrenia.

demerara /demə'reərə/ *noun* light brown cane sugar.

demerit /di:'merɪt/ *noun* fault, defect.

demesne /dɪ'mi:n/ *noun* landed property, estate; possession (of land) as one's own.

demigod /'demɪgɒd/ *noun* partly divine being; *colloquial* godlike person.

demijohn /'demɪdʒɒn/ *noun* large wicker-cased bottle.

demilitarize /di:'mɪlɪtəraɪz/ *verb* (also **-ise**) (**-zing** or **-sing**) remove army etc. from (zone etc.).

demi-monde /'demɪmɒnd/ *noun* class of women of doubtful morality; semi-respectable group. [French]

demise /dɪˈmaɪz/ *noun* death; termination.

demisemiquaver /ˌdemɪˈsemɪkweɪvə/ *noun Music* note equal to half semiquaver.

demist /diːˈmɪst/ *verb* clear mist from (windscreen etc.). □ **demister** *noun*.

demo /ˈdeməʊ/ *noun* (*plural* **-s**) *colloquial* demonstration, esp. political.

demobilize /diːˈməʊbɪlaɪz/ *verb* (also **-ise**) (**-zing** or **-sing**) disband (troops etc.). □ **demobilization** *noun*.

democracy /dɪˈmɒkrəsɪ/ *noun* (*plural* **-ies**) government by the whole population, usually through elected representatives; state so governed.

democrat /ˈdeməkræt/ *noun* advocate of democracy; (**Democrat**) member of US Democratic Party.

democratic /deməˈkrætɪk/ *adjective* of, like, or practising democracy; favouring social equality. □ **democratically** *adverb*; **democratize** /dɪˈmɒkrətaɪz/ *verb* (also **-ise**) (**-zing** or **-sing**); **democratization** *noun*.

demography /dɪˈmɒgrəfɪ/ *noun* study of statistics of birth, deaths, disease, etc. □ **demographic** /deməˈgræfɪk/ *adjective*.

demolish /dɪˈmɒlɪʃ/ *verb* pull down (building); destroy; refute; eat up voraciously. □ **demolition** /deməˈlɪʃ(ə)n/ *noun*.

demon /ˈdiːmən/ *noun* devil; evil spirit; forceful or skilful performer. □ **demonic** /dɪˈmɒnɪk/ *adjective*.

demoniac /dɪˈməʊnɪæk/ ● *adjective* frenzied; supposedly possessed by evil spirit; of or like demons. ● *noun* demoniac person. □ **demoniacal** /diːməˈnaɪək(ə)l/ *adjective*.

demonology /diːməˈnɒlədʒɪ/ *noun* study of demons.

demonstrable /ˈdemənstrəb(ə)l/ *adjective* able to be shown or proved. □ **demonstrably** *adverb*.

demonstrate /ˈdemənstreɪt/ *verb* (**-ting**) show (feelings etc.); describe and explain by experiment etc.; prove truth or existence of; take part in public demonstration.

demonstration *noun* demonstrating; (+ *of*) show of feeling etc.; political public march, meeting, etc.; proof by logic, argument, etc.

demonstrative /dɪˈmɒnstrətɪv/ *adjective* showing feelings readily; affectionate; *Grammar* indicating person or thing referred to. □ **demonstratively** *adverb*; **demonstrativeness** *noun*.

demonstrator /ˈdemənstreɪtə/ *noun* person making or taking part in demonstration.

demoralize /dɪˈmɒrəlaɪz/ *verb* (also **-ise**) (**-zing** or **-sing**) destroy morale of. □ **demoralization** *noun*.

demote /diːˈməʊt/ *verb* (**-ting**) reduce to lower rank or class. □ **demotion** /-ˈməʊʃ(ə)n/ *noun*.

demotic /dɪˈmɒtɪk/ ● *noun* colloquial form of a language. ● *adjective* colloquial, vulgar.

demotivate /diːˈməʊtɪveɪt/ *verb* (**-ting**) cause to lose motivation. □ **demotivation** *noun*.

demur /dɪˈmɜː/ ● *verb* (**-rr-**) (often + *to*, *at*) raise objections. ● *noun* (usually in negative) objection, objecting.

demure /dɪˈmjʊə/ *adjective* (**-r**, **-st**) quiet, modest; coy. □ **demurely** *adverb*.

demystify /diːˈmɪstɪfaɪ/ *verb* (**-ies**, **-ied**) remove mystery from.

den *noun* wild animal's lair; place of crime or vice; small private room.

denarius /dɪˈneərɪəs/ *noun* (*plural* **-rii** /-rɪaɪ/) ancient Roman silver coin.

denationalize /diːˈnæʃənəlaɪz/ *verb* (also **-ise**) (**-zing** or **-sing**) transfer (industry etc.) from national to private ownership. □ **denationalization** *noun*.

denature /diːˈneɪtʃə/ *verb* (**-ring**) change properties of; make (alcohol) unfit for drinking.

dendrology /denˈdrɒlədʒɪ/ *noun* study of trees. □ **dendrologist** *noun*.

denial /dɪˈnaɪəl/ *noun* denying or refusing.

denier /ˈdenjə/ *noun* unit of weight measuring fineness of silk, nylon, etc.

denigrate /ˈdenɪgreɪt/ *verb* (**-ting**) sully reputation of. □ **denigration** *noun*; **denigratory** /-ˈgreɪt-/ *adjective*.

denim /ˈdenɪm/ *noun* twilled cotton fabric; (in *plural*) jeans etc. made of this.

denizen /ˈdenɪz(ə)n/ *noun* (usually + *of*) inhabitant or occupant.

denominate /dɪˈnɒmɪneɪt/ *verb* (**-ting**) give name to, describe as, call.

denomination *noun* Church or religious sect; class of measurement or money; name, esp. for classification. □ **denominational** *adjective*.

denominator *noun* number below line in vulgar fraction; divisor.

denote /dɪˈnəʊt/ *verb* (**-ting**) (often + *that*) be sign of; indicate; be name for, signify. □ **denotation** /diːnəˈteɪʃ(ə)n/ *noun*.

denouement /deɪˈnuːmɑ̃/ *noun* final resolution in play, novel, etc.

denounce /dɪˈnaʊns/ *verb* (**-cing**) accuse publicly; inform against.

dense /dens/ *adjective* closely compacted; crowded together; stupid. □ **densely** *adverb*; **denseness** *noun*.

density /ˈdensɪtɪ/ *noun* (*plural* **-ies**) denseness; quantity of mass per unit volume; opacity of photographic image.

dent ● *noun* depression in surface; noticeable adverse effect. ● *verb* make dent in.

dental /ˈdent(ə)l/ *adjective* of teeth or dentistry; (of sound) made with tongue-tip against front teeth. □ **dental floss** thread used to clean between teeth; **dental surgeon** dentist.

dentate /ˈdenteɪt/ *adjective* toothed, notched.

dentifrice /ˈdentɪfrɪs/ *noun* tooth powder or toothpaste.

dentine /ˈdentiːn/ *noun* hard dense tissue forming most of tooth.

dentist /ˈdentɪst/ *noun* person qualified to treat, extract, etc., teeth. □ **dentistry** *noun*.

denture /ˈdentʃə/ *noun* (usually in *plural*) removable artificial teeth.

denude /dɪˈnjuːd/ *verb* (**-ding**) make naked or bare; (+ *of*) strip of (covering etc.). □ **denudation** /diː-/ *noun*.

denunciation /dɪnʌnsɪˈeɪʃ(ə)n/ *noun* denouncing.

deny /dɪˈnaɪ/ *verb* (**-ies**, **-ied**) declare untrue or non-existent; repudiate; (often + *to*) withhold from; (**deny oneself**) be abstinent.

deodorant /diːˈəʊdərənt/ *noun* substance applied to body or sprayed into air to conceal smells.

deodorize /diːˈəʊdəraɪz/ *verb* (also **-ise**) (**-zing** or **-sing**) remove smell of. □ **deodorization** *noun*.

deoxyribonucleic acid /diːˌɒksɪraɪˈbəʊnjuːˈkleɪɪk/ see DNA.

dep. *abbreviation* departs; deputy.

depart /dɪˈpɑːt/ *verb* (often + *from*) go away, leave; (usually + *for*) set out; (usually + *from*) deviate. □ **depart this life** *formal* die.

departed ● *adjective* bygone. ● *noun* (**the departed**) *euphemistic* dead person or people.

department *noun* separate part of complex whole, esp. branch of administration; division of school etc.; section of large store; area of expertise; French administrative district. □ **department store** shop with many departments. □ **departmental** /diːpɑːtˈment(ə)l/ *adjective*.

departure /dɪˈpɑːtʃə/ *noun* departing; new course of action etc.

depend /dɪˈpend/ *verb* (often + *on, upon*) be controlled or determined by; (+ *on, upon*) need, rely on.

dependable *adjective* reliable. □ **dependability** *noun*.

dependant *noun* person supported, esp. financially, by another.

dependence *noun* depending, being dependent; reliance.

dependency *noun* (*plural* **-ies**) country etc. controlled by another; dependence (on drugs etc.).

dependent *adjective* (usually + *on*) depending; unable to do without (esp. drug); maintained at another's cost; (of clause etc.) subordinate to word etc.

depict /dɪˈpɪkt/ *verb* represent in painting etc.; describe. □ **depiction** *noun*.

depilate /ˈdepɪleɪt/ *verb* (**-ting**) remove hair from. □ **depilation** *noun*; **depilator** *noun*.

depilatory /dɪˈpɪlətərɪ/ ● *adjective* that removes unwanted hair. ● *noun* (*plural* **-ies**) depilatory substance.

deplete /dɪˈpliːt/ *verb* (**-ting**) (esp. as **depleted** *adjective*) reduce in numbers, quantity, etc.; exhaust. □ **depletion** *noun*.

deplorable /dɪˈplɔːrəb(ə)l/ *adjective* exceedingly bad. □ **deplorably** *adverb*.

deplore /dɪˈplɔː/ *verb* (**-ring**) find deplorable; regret.

deploy /dɪˈplɔɪ/ *verb* spread out (troops) into line for action; use (arguments etc.) effectively. □ **deployment** *noun*.

deponent /dɪ'pəʊnənt/ *noun* person making deposition under oath.

depopulate /di:'pɒpjʊleɪt/ *verb* (**-ting**) reduce population of. □ **depopulation** *noun*.

deport /dɪ'pɔːt/ *verb* remove forcibly or exile to another country; (**deport oneself**) behave (well, badly, etc.). □ **deportation** /di:-/ *noun*.

deportee /di:pɔː'tiː/ *noun* deported person.

deportment *noun* bearing, demeanour.

depose /dɪ'pəʊz/ *verb* (**-sing**) remove from office; dethrone; (usually + *to, that*) testify on oath.

deposit /dɪ'pɒzɪt/ ● *noun* money in bank account; thing stored for safe keeping; payment as pledge or first instalment; returnable sum paid on hire of item; layer of accumulated matter. ● *verb* (**-t-**) entrust for keeping; pay or leave as deposit; put or lay down. □ **deposit account** bank account that pays interest but is not usually immediately accessible.

depositary /dɪ'pɒzɪtərɪ/ *noun* (*plural* **-ies**) person to whom thing is entrusted.

deposition /depə'zɪʃ(ə)n/ *noun* deposing; sworn evidence; giving of this; depositing.

depositor /dɪ'pɒzɪtər/ *noun* person who deposits money, property, etc.

depository /dɪ'pɒzɪtərɪ/ *noun* (*plural* **-ies**) storehouse; store (of wisdom etc.); depositary.

depot /'depəʊ/ *noun* military storehouse or headquarters; place where vehicles, e.g. buses, are kept; goods yard.

deprave /dɪ'preɪv/ *verb* (**-ving**) corrupt morally.

depravity /dɪ'prævɪtɪ/ *noun* (*plural* **-ies**) moral corruption; wickedness.

deprecate /'deprɪkeɪt/ *verb* (**-ting**) express disapproval of. □ **deprecation** *noun*; **deprecatory** /-'keɪtərɪ/ *adjective*.

■ **Usage** *Deprecate* is often confused with *depreciate*.

depreciate /dɪ'priːʃɪeɪt/ *verb* (**-ting**) diminish in value; belittle. □ **depreciatory** /-ʃətərɪ/ *adjective*.

■ **Usage** *Depreciate* is often confused with *deprecate*.

depreciation *noun* depreciating; decline in value.

depredation /deprɪ'deɪʃ(ə)n/ *noun* (usually in *plural*) despoiling, ravaging.

depress /dɪ'pres/ *verb* make dispirited; lower; push down; reduce activity of (esp. trade); (as **depressed** *adjective*) suffering from depression. □ **depressing** *adjective*; **depressingly** *adverb*.

depressant ● *adjective* reducing activity, esp. of body function. ● *noun* depressant substance.

depression /dɪ'preʃ(ə)n/ *noun* extreme dejection; long slump; lowering of atmospheric pressure; hollow on a surface.

depressive /dɪ'presɪv/ ● *adjective* tending towards depression; tending to depress. ● *noun* chronically depressed person.

deprivation /deprɪ'veɪʃ(ə)n/ *noun* depriving, being deprived.

deprive /dɪ'praɪv/ *verb* (**-ving**) (usually + *of*) prevent from having or enjoying; (as **deprived** *adjective*) lacking what is needed, underprivileged.

Dept. *abbreviation* Department.

depth *noun* deepness; measure of this; wisdom; intensity; (usually in *plural*) deep, lowest, or inmost part, middle (of winter etc.), abyss, depressed state. □ **depth-charge** bomb exploding under water; **in depth** thoroughly.

deputation /depjʊ'teɪʃ(ə)n/ *noun* delegation.

depute /dɪ'pjuːt/ *verb* (**-ting**) (often + *to*) delegate (task, authority); authorize as representative.

deputize /'depjʊtaɪz/ *verb* (also **-ise**) (**-zing** or **-sing**) (usually + *for*) act as deputy.

deputy /'depjʊtɪ/ *noun* (*plural* **-ies**) person appointed to act for another; parliamentary representative in some countries.

derail /di:'reɪl/ *verb* cause (train etc.) to leave rails. □ **derailment** *noun*.

derange /dɪ'reɪndʒ/ *verb* (**-ging**) (usually as **deranged** *adjective*) make insane. □ **derangement** *noun*.

Derby /'dɑːbɪ/ *noun* (*plural* **-ies**) annual horse race at Epsom; similar race or sporting event.

derelict /ˈderɪlɪkt/ ● *adjective* dilapidated; abandoned. ● *noun* vagrant; abandoned property.

dereliction /derɪˈlɪkʃ(ə)n/ *noun* (usually + *of*) neglect (of duty etc.).

deride /dɪˈraɪd/ *verb* (**-ding**) mock. □ **derision** /-ˈrɪʒ-/ *noun*.

de rigueur /də rɪˈɡɜː/ *adjective* required by fashion or etiquette.

derisive /dɪˈraɪsɪv/ *adjective* scoffing, ironical. □ **derisively** *adverb*.

derisory /dɪˈraɪsərɪ/ *adjective* (of sum offered etc.) ridiculously small; derisive.

derivation /derɪˈveɪʃ(ə)n/ *noun* deriving, being derived; origin or formation of word; tracing of this.

derivative /dɪˈrɪvətɪv/ ● *adjective* derived, not original. ● *noun* derived word or thing.

derive /dɪˈraɪv/ *verb* (**-ving**) (usually + *from*) get or trace from a source; (+ *from*) arise from; (usually + *from*) assert origin and formation of (word etc.).

dermatitis /dɜːməˈtaɪtɪs/ *noun* inflammation of skin.

dermatology /dɜːməˈtɒlədʒɪ/ *noun* study of skin diseases. □ **dermatological** /-təˈlɒdʒ-/ *adjective*; **dermatologist** *noun*.

derogatory /dɪˈrɒɡətərɪ/ *adjective* disparaging; insulting.

derrick /ˈderɪk/ *noun* crane; framework over oil well etc. for drilling machinery.

derris /ˈderɪs/ *noun* insecticide made from powdered root of tropical plant.

derv *noun* diesel fuel for road vehicles.

dervish /ˈdɜːvɪʃ/ *noun* member of Muslim fraternity vowed to poverty and austerity.

DES *abbreviation historical* Department of Education and Science.

descale /diːˈskeɪl/ *verb* (**-ling**) remove scale from.

descant /ˈdeskænt/ *noun* harmonizing treble melody above basic hymn tune etc.

descend /dɪˈsend/ *verb* come, go, or slope down; sink; (usually + *on*) make sudden attack or visit; (+ *to*) stoop (to unworthy act); be passed on by inheritance. □ **be descended from** have as an ancestor.

descendant /dɪˈsend(ə)nt/ *noun* person etc. descended from another.

descent /dɪˈsent/ *noun* act or way of descending; downward slope; lineage; decline, fall; sudden attack.

describe /dɪˈskraɪb/ *verb* (**-bing**) state appearance, characteristics, etc. of; (+ *as*) assert to be; draw or move in (curve etc.).

description /dɪˈskrɪpʃ(ə)n/ *noun* describing, being described; sort, kind.

descriptive /dɪˈskrɪptɪv/ *adjective* describing, esp. vividly.

descry /dɪˈskraɪ/ *verb* (**-ies**, **-ied**) catch sight of; discern.

desecrate /ˈdesɪkreɪt/ *verb* (**-ting**) violate sanctity of. □ **desecration** *noun*; **desecrator** *noun*.

desegregate /diːˈseɡrɪɡeɪt/ *verb* (**-ting**) abolish racial segregation in. □ **desegregation** *noun*.

deselect /diːsɪˈlekt/ *verb* reject (esp. sitting MP) in favour of another. □ **deselection** *noun*.

desensitize /diːˈsensɪtaɪz/ *verb* (also **-ise**) (**-zing** or **-sing**) reduce or destroy sensitivity of. □ **desensitization** *noun*.

desert[1] /dɪˈzɜːt/ *verb* leave without intending to return; (esp. as **deserted** *adjective*) forsake, abandon; run away from military service. □ **deserter** *noun Military*; **desertion** *noun*.

desert[2] /ˈdezət/ *noun* dry barren, esp. sandy, tract. □ **desert island** (usually tropical) uninhabited island.

desertification /dɪzɜːtɪfɪˈkeɪʃ(ə)n/ *noun* making or becoming a desert.

deserts /dɪˈzɜːts/ *plural noun* deserved reward or punishment.

deserve /dɪˈzɜːv/ *verb* (**-ving**) (often + *to do*) be worthy of (reward, punishment); (as **deserving** *adjective*) (often + *of*) worthy (esp. of help, praise, etc.). □ **deservedly** /-vɪdlɪ/ *adverb*.

desiccate /ˈdesɪkeɪt/ *verb* (**-ting**) remove moisture from, dry out. □ **desiccation** *noun*.

desideratum /dɪzɪdəˈrɑːtəm/ *noun* (*plural* **-ta**) something lacking but desirable.

design /dɪˈzaɪn/ ● *noun* (art of producing) sketch or plan for product; lines or shapes as decoration; layout; established form of product; mental plan;

purpose. ● *verb* produce design for; be designer; intend; (as **designing** *adjective*) crafty, scheming. □ **have designs on** plan to take, seduce, etc.

designate ● *verb* /'dezigneit/ (**-ting**) (often + *as*) appoint to office or function; specify; (often + *as*) describe as. ● *adjective* /'dezignət/ (after noun) appointed but not yet installed.

designation /dezig'neiʃ(ə)n/ *noun* name or title; designating.

designedly /di'zainidli/ *adverb* intentionally.

designer ● *noun* person who designs e.g. clothing, machines, theatre sets; draughtsman. ● *adjective* bearing label of famous fashion designer; prestigious. □ **designer drug** synthetic equivalent of illegal drug.

desirable /di'zaiərəb(ə)l/ *adjective* worth having or doing; sexually attractive. □ **desirability** *noun*.

desire /di'zaiə/ ● *noun* unsatisfied longing; expression of this; request; thing desired; sexual appetite. ● *verb* (**-ring**) (often + *to do, that*) long for; request.

desirous *adjective* (usually + *of*) desiring, wanting; hoping.

desist /di'zist/ *verb* (often + *from*) cease.

desk *noun* piece of furniture with writing surface, and often drawers; counter in hotel, bank, etc.; section of newspaper office.

desktop *noun* working surface of desk; computer for use on ordinary desk. □ **desktop publishing** printing with desktop computer and high-quality printer.

desolate ● *adjective* /'desələt/ left alone; uninhabited; dreary, forlorn. ● *verb* /'desəleit/ (**-ting**) depopulate; devastate; (esp. as **desolated** *adjective*) make wretched. □ **desolately** /-lətli/ *adverb*; **desolation** *noun*.

despair /di'speə/ ● *noun* loss or absence of hope; cause of this. ● *verb* (often + *of*) lose all hope.

despatch = DISPATCH.

desperado /despə'rɑːdəʊ/ *noun* (*plural* **-es** or US **-s**) desperate or reckless criminal etc.

desperate /'despərət/ *adjective* reckless from despair; violent and lawless; extremely dangerous or serious; (usually

+ *for*) needing or desiring very much. □ **desperately** *adverb*; **desperation** *noun*.

despicable /'despikəb(ə)l, di'spik-/ *adjective* contemptible. □ **despicably** *adverb*.

despise /di'spaiz/ *verb* (**-sing**) regard as inferior or contemptible.

despite /di'spait/ *preposition* in spite of.

despoil /di'spɔil/ *verb* (often + *of*) plunder, rob. □ **despoliation** /-spəʊli-/ *noun*.

despondent /di'spɒnd(ə)nt/ *adjective* in low spirits, dejected. □ **despondence** *noun*; **despondency** *noun*; **despondently** *adverb*.

despot /'despɒt/ *noun* absolute ruler; tyrant. □ **despotic** /-'spɒt-/ *adjective*.

despotism /'despətiz(ə)m/ *noun* rule by despot.

dessert /di'zɜːt/ *noun* sweet course of a meal. □ **dessertspoon** medium-sized spoon for dessert, also (**dessertspoonful**) amount held by this.

destabilize /diː'steibilaiz/ *verb* (also **-ise**) (**-zing** or **-sing**) make unstable; subvert (esp. foreign government). □ **destabilization** *noun*.

destination /desti'neiʃ(ə)n/ *noun* place to which person or thing is going.

destine /'destin/ *verb* (**-ning**) (often + *to, for, to do*) appoint; preordain; intend. □ **be destined to** be fated to.

destiny /'destini/ *noun* (*plural* **-ies**) fate; this as power.

destitute /'destitjuːt/ *adjective* without food or shelter etc.; (usually + *of*) lacking. □ **destitution** /-'tjuː-/ *noun*.

destroy /di'strɔi/ *verb* pull or break down; kill; make useless; ruin financially; defeat.

destroyer /di'strɔiə/ *noun* fast medium-sized warship; person or thing that destroys.

destruct /di'strʌkt/ *verb* destroy or be destroyed deliberately. □ **destructible** *adjective*.

destruction *noun* destroying, being destroyed.

destructive *adjective* destroying or tending to destroy; negatively critical.

desuetude /di'sjuːitjuːd/ *noun* formal state of disuse.

desultory /ˈdezəltərɪ/ adjective constantly turning from one subject to another; unmethodical.

detach /dɪˈtætʃ/ verb (often + from) unfasten and remove; send (troops) on separate mission; (as **detached** adjective) impartial, unemotional, (of house) standing separate. □ **detachable** adjective.

detachment noun indifference; impartiality; detaching, being detached; troops etc. detached for special duty.

detail /ˈdiːteɪl/ ● noun small separate item or particular; these collectively; minor or intricate decoration; small part of picture etc. shown alone; small military detachment. ● verb give particulars of, relate in detail; (as **detailed** adjective) containing many details, itemized; assign for special duty. □ **in detail** item by item, minutely.

detain /dɪˈteɪn/ verb keep waiting, delay; keep in custody. □ **detainment** noun.

detainee /diːteɪˈniː/ noun person kept in custody, esp. for political reasons.

detect /dɪˈtekt/ verb discover; perceive. □ **detectable** adjective; **detection** noun; **detector** noun.

detective /dɪˈtektɪv/ noun person, usually police officer, investigating crime etc.

détente /deɪˈtɒt/ noun relaxing of strained international relations. [French]

detention /dɪˈtenʃ(ə)n/ noun detaining, being detained. □ **detention centre** short-term prison for young offenders.

deter /dɪˈtɜː/ verb (**-rr-**) (often + from) discourage or prevent, esp. through fear.

detergent /dɪˈtɜːdʒ(ə)nt/ ● noun synthetic cleansing agent used with water. ● adjective cleansing.

deteriorate /dɪˈtɪərɪəreɪt/ verb (**-ting**) become worse. □ **deterioration** noun.

determinant /dɪˈtɜːmɪnənt/ noun decisive factor.

determinate /dɪˈtɜːmɪnət/ adjective limited; of definite scope or nature.

determination /dɪtɜːmɪˈneɪʃ(ə)n/ noun resolute purpose; deciding, determining.

determine /dɪˈtɜːmɪn/ verb (**-ning**) find out precisely; settle, decide; (+ to do) resolve; be decisive factor in.

determined adjective resolute. □ **be determined** (usually + to do) be resolved. □ **determinedly** adverb.

determinism /dɪˈtɜːmɪnɪz(ə)m/ noun theory that action is determined by forces independent of will. □ **determinist** noun & adjective; **deterministic** /-ˈnɪs-/ adjective.

deterrent /dɪˈterənt/ ● adjective deterring. ● noun thing that deters (esp. nuclear weapon).

detest /dɪˈtest/ verb hate, loathe. □ **detestation** /diːtesˈteɪʃ(ə)n/ noun.

detestable /dɪˈtestəb(ə)l/ adjective hated, loathed.

dethrone /diːˈθrəʊn/ verb(**-ning**) remove from throne or high regard. □ **dethronement** noun.

detonate /ˈdetəneɪt/ verb (**-ting**) set off (explosive charge); be set off. □ **detonation** noun.

detonator noun device for detonating.

detour /ˈdiːtʊə/ noun divergence from usual route; roundabout course.

detoxify /diːˈtɒksɪfaɪ/ verb (**-ies, -ied**) remove poison or harmful substances from. □ **detoxification** noun.

detract /dɪˈtrækt/ verb (+ from) diminish. □ **detraction** noun.

detractor noun person who criticizes unfairly.

detriment /ˈdetrɪmənt/ noun damage, harm; cause of this. □ **detrimental** /-ˈmen-/ adjective.

detritus /dɪˈtraɪtəs/ noun gravel, rock, etc. produced by erosion; debris.

de trop /də ˈtrəʊ/ adjective superfluous; in the way. [French]

deuce[1] /djuːs/ noun two on dice or cards; Tennis score of 40 all.

deuce[2] /djuːs/ noun (**the deuce**) (in exclamations) the Devil.

deuterium /djuːˈtɪərɪəm/ noun stable isotope of hydrogen with mass about twice that of the usual isotope.

Deutschmark /ˈdɔɪtʃmɑːk/ noun chief monetary unit of Germany.

devalue /diːˈvæljuː/ verb (**-ues, -ued, -uing**) reduce value of, esp. currency relative to others or to gold. □ **devaluation** noun.

devastate /ˈdevəsteɪt/ verb (**-ting**) lay waste; cause great destruction to; (often as **devastated** adjective) overwhelm with shock or grief. □ **devastation** noun.

devastating adjective crushingly effective; overwhelming; colloquial stunningly beautiful. □ **devastatingly** adverb.

develop /dɪ'veləp/ verb (**-p-**) make or become fuller, bigger, or more elaborate, etc.; bring or come to active, visible, or mature state; begin to exhibit or suffer from; build on (land); convert (land) to new use; treat (photographic film) to make image visible. □ **developing country** poor or primitive country. □ **developer** noun.

development noun developing, being developed; stage of growth or advancement; newly developed thing, event, etc.; area of developed land, esp. with buildings. □ **developmental** /-'ment(ə)l/ adjective.

deviant /'di:vɪənt/ ● adjective deviating from normal, esp. sexual, behaviour. ● noun deviant person or thing. □ **deviance** noun; **deviancy** noun (plural **-ies**).

deviate /'di:vɪeɪt/ verb (**-ting**) (often + from) turn aside; diverge. □ **deviation** noun.

device /dɪ'vaɪs/ noun thing made or adapted for particular purpose; scheme, trick; heraldic design. □ **leave (person) to his** or **her own devices** leave (person) to do as he or she wishes.

devil /'dev(ə)l/ ● noun (usually **the Devil**) Satan; supreme spirit of evil; personified evil; mischievously clever person. ● verb (**-ll-**; US **-l-**) (usually as **devilled** adjective) cook with hot spices. □ **devil-may-care** cheerful and reckless; **devil's advocate** person who tests proposition by arguing against it.

devilish ● adjective of or like a devil; mischievous. ● adverb colloquial very. □ **devilishly** adverb.

devilment noun mischief; wild spirits.

devilry /'devəlrɪ/ noun (plural **-ies**) wickedness; reckless mischief; black magic.

devious /'di:vɪəs/ adjective not straightforward, underhand; winding, circuitous. □ **deviously** adverb; **deviousness** noun.

devise /dɪ'vaɪz/ verb (**-sing**) plan or invent; Law leave (real estate) by will.

devoid /dɪ'vɔɪd/ adjective (+ of) lacking, free from.

devolution /di:və'lu:ʃ(ə)n/ noun delegation of power esp. to local or regional administration. □ **devolutionist** noun & adjective.

devolve /dɪ'vɒlv/ verb (**-ving**) (+ on, upon, etc.) (of duties etc.) pass or be passed to another; (+ on, to, upon) (of property) descend to.

devote /dɪ'vəʊt/ verb (**-ting**) (+ to) apply or give over to (particular activity etc.).

devoted adjective loving, loyal. □ **devotedly** adverb.

devotee /devəʊ'ti:/ noun (usually + of) enthusiast, supporter; pious person.

devotion /dɪ'vəʊʃ(ə)n/ noun (usually + to) great love or loyalty; worship; (in plural) prayers. □ **devotional** adjective.

devour /dɪ'vaʊə/ verb eat voraciously; (of fire etc.) engulf, destroy; take in greedily (with eyes or ears).

devout /dɪ'vaʊt/ adjective earnestly religious or sincere. □ **devoutly** adverb; **devoutness** noun.

dew noun condensed water vapour forming on cool surfaces at night; similar glistening moisture. □ **dewberry** fruit like blackberry; **dew-claw** rudimentary inner toe on some dogs; **dewdrop** drop of dew; **dew point** temperature at which dew forms. □ **dewy** adjective (**-ier**, **-iest**).

Dewey Decimal system /'dju:ɪ/ noun system of library classification.

dewlap noun fold of loose skin hanging from throat esp. in cattle.

dexter /'dekstə/ adjective on or of the right-hand side (observer's left) of a heraldic shield etc.

dexterous /'dekstrəs/ adjective (also **dextrous**) skilful at handling. □ **dexterity** /-'ter-/ noun; **dexterously** adverb.

dhal /dɑ:l/ noun (also **dal**) kind of split pulse from India; dish made with this.

dharma /'dɑ:mə/ noun right behaviour; Buddhist truth; Hindu moral law.

dhoti /'dəʊtɪ/ noun (plural **-s**) loincloth worn by male Hindus.

dia. abbreviation diameter.

diabetes /daɪə'bi:ti:z/ noun disease in which sugar and starch are not properly absorbed by the body.

diabetic /daɪəˈbetɪk/ ● *adjective* of or having diabetes; for diabetics. ● *noun* diabetic person.

diabolical /daɪəˈbɒlɪk(ə)l/ *adjective* (also **diabolic**) of the Devil; inhumanly cruel or wicked; extremely bad. □ **diabolically** *adverb*.

diabolism /daɪˈæbəlɪz(ə)m/ *noun* worship of the Devil; sorcery.

diaconate /daɪˈækənət/ *noun* office of deacon; deacons collectively.

diacritic /daɪəˈkrɪtɪk/ *noun* sign (e.g. accent) indicating sound or value of letter.

diacritical *adjective* distinguishing.

diadem /ˈdaɪədem/ *noun* crown.

diaeresis /daɪˈɪərəsɪs/ *noun* (*plural* **-reses** /-siːz/) (*US* **dieresis**) mark (¨) over vowel to show it is sounded separately.

diagnose /ˈdaɪəgnəʊz/ *verb* (**-sing**) make diagnosis of.

diagnosis /daɪəgˈnəʊsɪs/ *noun* (*plural* **-noses** /-siːz/) identification of disease or fault from symptoms etc.

diagnostic /daɪəgˈnɒstɪk/ ● *adjective* of or assisting diagnosis. ● *noun* symptom.

diagnostics *noun* (treated as *plural*) programs etc. used to identify faults in computing; (treated as *singular*) science of diagnosing disease.

diagonal /daɪˈægən(ə)l/ ● *adjective* crossing a straight-sided figure from corner to corner, oblique. ● *noun* straight line joining two opposite corners. □ **diagonally** *adverb*.

diagram /ˈdaɪəgræm/ *noun* outline drawing, plan, etc. of thing or process. □ **diagrammatic** /-grəˈmætɪk/ *adjective*.

dial /ˈdaɪəl/ ● *noun* plate with scale and pointer for measuring; numbered disc on telephone for making connection; face of clock or watch; disc on television etc. for selecting channel etc. ● *verb* (**-ll-**; *US* **-l-**) select (telephone number) with dial. □ **dialling tone** sound indicating that telephone caller may dial.

dialect /ˈdaɪəlekt/ *noun* regional form of language (see panel).

dialectic /daɪəˈlektɪk/ *noun* process or situation involving contradictions or conflict of opposites and their resolution; = DIALECTICS.

dialectical *adjective* of dialectic. □ **dialectical materialism** Marxist theory that historical events arise from conflicting economic (and therefore social) conditions. □ **dialectically** *adverb*.

dialectics *noun* (treated as *singular* or *plural*) art of investigating truth by discussion and logic.

dialogue /ˈdaɪəlɒg/ *noun* (*US* **dialog**) conversation, esp. in a play, novel, etc.; discussion between people of different opinions.

dialysis /daɪˈæləsɪs/ *noun* (*plural* **-lyses** /-siːz/) separation of particles in liquid by differences in their ability to pass through membrane; purification of blood by this technique.

diamanté /dɪəˈmɒteɪ/ *adjective* decorated with synthetic diamonds etc.

diameter /daɪˈæmɪtə/ *noun* straight line passing through centre of circle or sphere to its edges; transverse measurement.

diametrical /daɪəˈmetrɪk(ə)l/ *adjective* (also **diametric**) of or along diameter; (of opposites) absolute. □ **diametrically** *adverb*.

diamond /ˈdaɪəmənd/ *noun* transparent very hard precious stone; rhombus;

Dialect

Everyone speaks a particular dialect: that is, a particular type of English distinguished by its vocabulary and its grammar. Different parts of the world and different groups of people speak different dialects: for example, Australians may say *arvo* while others say *afternoon*, and a London Cockney may say *I done it* while most other people say *I did it*. A dialect is not the same thing as an accent, which is the way a person pronounces words.

See also the panel at STANDARD ENGLISH.

playing card of suit marked with red rhombuses. □ **diamond jubilee, wedding** 60th (or 75th) anniversary of reign or wedding.

diapason /daɪəˈpeɪz(ə)n/ *noun* compass of musical instrument or voice; either of two main organ stops.

diaper /ˈdaɪəpə/ *noun US* baby's nappy.

diaphanous /daɪˈæfənəs/ *adjective* (of fabric etc.) light and almost transparent.

diaphragm /ˈdaɪəfræm/ *noun* muscular partititon between thorax and abdomen in mammals; = DUTCH CAP; vibrating disc in microphone, telephone, loudspeaker, etc.; device for varying aperture of camera lens.

diapositive /daɪəˈpɒzɪtɪv/ *noun* positive photographic transparency.

diarist /ˈdaɪərɪst/ *noun* person famous for keeping diary.

diarrhoea /daɪəˈriːə/ *noun* (*US* **diarrhea**) condition of excessively loose and frequent bowel movements.

diary /ˈdaɪərɪ/ *noun* (*plural* **-ies**) daily record of events etc.; book for this or for noting future engagements.

Diaspora /daɪˈæspərə/ *noun* dispersion of the Jews; the dispersed Jews.

diatonic /daɪəˈtɒnɪk/ *adjective Music* (of scale etc.) involving only notes of prevailing key.

diatribe /ˈdaɪətraɪb/ *noun* forceful verbal criticism.

diazepam /daɪˈæzɪpæm/ *noun* tranquilizing drug.

dibble /ˈdɪb(ə)l/ ● *noun* (also **dibber** /ˈdɪbə/) tool for making small holes for planting. ● *verb* (**-ling**) plant with dibble.

dice ● *noun* (*plural* same) small cube marked on each face with 1-6 spots, used in games or gambling; game played with dice. ● *verb* (**-cing**) gamble, take risks; cut into small cubes.

dicey /ˈdaɪsɪ/ *adjective* (**dicier, diciest**) *slang* risky, unreliable.

dichotomy /daɪˈkɒtəmɪ/ *noun* (*plural* **-ies**) division into two.

dichromatic /daɪkrəʊˈmætɪk/ *adjective* of two colours.

dick¹ *noun colloquial* (esp. in **clever dick**) person.

dick² *noun slang* detective.

dickens /ˈdɪkɪnz/ *noun* (**the dickens**) (usually after *how, what, why,* etc.) *colloquial* the Devil.

dicky /ˈdɪkɪ/ ● *noun* (*plural* **-ies**) *colloquial* false shirt-front. ● *adjective* (**-ier, -iest**) *slang* unsound.

dicotyledon /daɪkɒtɪˈliːd(ə)n/ *noun* flowering plant with two cotyledons. □ **dicotyledonous** *adjective.*

Dictaphone /ˈdɪktəfəʊn/ *noun proprietary term* machine for recording and playing back dictation for typing.

dictate ● *verb* /dɪkˈteɪt/ (**-ting**) say or read aloud (material to be recorded etc.); state authoritatively; order peremptorily. ● *noun* /ˈdɪkt-/ (usually in *plural*) authoritative requirement of conscience etc. □ **dictation** *noun.*

dictator *noun* usually unelected absolute ruler; omnipotent or domineering person. □ **dictatorship** *noun.*

dictatorial /dɪktəˈtɔːrɪəl/ *adjective* of or like a dictator; overbearing. □ **dictatorially** *adverb.*

diction /ˈdɪkʃ(ə)n/ *noun* manner of enunciation.

dictionary /ˈdɪkʃənərɪ/ *noun* (*plural* **-ies**) book listing (usually alphabetically) and explaining words of a language, or giving corresponding words in another language; similar book of terms for reference.

dictum /ˈdɪktəm/ *noun* (*plural* **dicta** or **-s**) formal expression of opinion; a saying.

did *past of* DO¹.

didactic /dɪˈdæktɪk/ *adjective* meant to instruct; (of person) tediously pedantic. □ **didactically** *adverb;* **didacticism** /-sɪz(ə)m/ *noun.*

diddle /ˈdɪd(ə)l/ *verb* (**-ling**) *colloquial* swindle.

didgeridoo /dɪdʒərɪˈduː/ *noun* long tubular Australian Aboriginal musical instrument.

didn't /ˈdɪd(ə)nt/ did not.

die¹ /daɪ/ *verb* (**dying** /ˈdaɪɪŋ/) cease to live or exist; fade away; (of fire) go out; (+ *on*) cease to function while in the presence or charge of (person); (+ *of, from, with*) be exhausted or tormented. □ **be dying for, to** desire greatly; **die down** become less loud or strong; **die hard** (of habits etc.) die reluctantly; **die-hard** conservative or stubborn person; **die off** die one after another; **die out** become extinct, cease to exist.

die² /daɪ/ noun engraved device for stamping coins etc.; (plural **dice**) a dice. □ **die-casting** process or product of casting from metal moulds.

dielectric /daɪˈlektrɪk/ ● adjective not conducting electricity. ● noun dielectric substance.

dierisis US = DIAERESIS.

diesel /ˈdiːz(ə)l/ noun (in full **diesel engine**) internal-combustion engine in which heat produced by compression of air in the cylinder ignites the fuel; vehicle driven by or fuel for diesel engine. □ **diesel-electric** driven by electric current from diesel-engined generator; **diesel oil** petroleum fraction used in diesel engines.

diet¹ /ˈdaɪət/ ● noun habitual food; prescribed food. ● verb (**-t-**) keep to special diet, esp. to slim. □ **dietary** adjective; **dieter** noun.

diet² /ˈdaɪət/ noun legislative assembly; historical congress.

dietetic /daɪəˈtetɪk/ adjective of diet and nutrition.

dietetics plural noun (usually treated as singular) study of diet and nutrition.

dietitian /daɪəˈtɪʃ(ə)n/ noun (also **dietician**) expert in dietetics.

differ /ˈdɪfə/ verb (often + from) be unlike or distinguishable; (often + with) disagree.

difference /ˈdɪfrəns/ noun being different or unlike; degree of this; way in which things differ; remainder after subtraction; disagreement. □ **make a** (or **all the, no,** etc.) **difference** have significant (or very significant, no, etc.) effect; **with a difference** having new or unusual feature.

different /ˈdɪfrənt/ adjective (often + from, to) unlike, of another nature; separate, unusual. □ **differently** adverb.

■ Usage It is safer to use *different from*, but *different to* is common in informal use.

differential /dɪfəˈrenʃ(ə)l/ ● adjective constituting or relating to specific difference; of, exhibiting, or depending on a difference; Mathematics relating to infinitesimal differences. ● noun difference, esp. between rates of interest or wage-rates. □ **differential calculus** method of calculating rates of change, maximum or minimum values, etc.; **differential gear** gear enabling wheels to revolve at different speeds on corners.

differentiate /dɪfəˈrenʃɪeɪt/ verb (**-ting**) constitute difference between or in; distinguish; become different. □ **differentiation** noun.

difficult /ˈdɪfɪk(ə)lt/ adjective hard to do, deal with, or understand; troublesome.

difficulty /ˈdɪfɪkəltɪ/ noun (plural **-ies**) being difficult; difficult thing; hindrance; (often in plural) distress, esp. financial.

diffident /ˈdɪfɪd(ə)nt/ adjective lacking self-confidence. □ **diffidence** noun; **diffidently** adverb.

diffract /dɪˈfrækt/ verb break up (beam of light) into series of dark and light bands or coloured spectra. □ **diffraction** noun; **diffractive** adjective.

diffuse ● verb /dɪˈfjuːz/ (**-sing**) spread widely or thinly; intermingle. ● adjective /dɪˈfjuːs/ spread out; not concentrated; not concise. □ **diffusible** adjective; **diffusive** adjective; **diffusion** noun.

dig ● verb (**-gg-**; past & past participle **dug**) (often + up) break up and turn over (ground etc.); make (hole etc.) by digging; (+ up, out) obtain by digging, find, discover; excavate; slang like, understand; (+ in, into) thrust, prod. ● noun piece of digging; thrust, poke; colloquial pointed remark; archaeological excavation; (in plural) lodgings. □ **dig in** colloquial begin eating; **dig oneself in** prepare defensive position.

digest ● verb /daɪˈdʒest/ assimilate (food, information, etc.). ● noun /ˈdaɪdʒest/ periodical synopsis of current news etc.; summary, esp. of laws. □ **digestible** adjective.

digestion noun digesting; capacity to digest food.

digestive ● adjective of or aiding digestion. ● noun (in full **digestive biscuit**) wholemeal biscuit.

digger /ˈdɪgə/ noun person or machine that digs; colloquial Australian, New Zealander.

digit /ˈdɪdʒɪt/ noun any numeral from 0 to 9; finger or toe.

digital /'dɪdʒɪt(ə)l/ *adjective* of digits; (of clock, etc.) giving a reading by displayed digits; (of computer) operating on data represented by digits; (of recording) sound-information represented by digits for more reliable transmission. □ **digitally** *adverb*.

digitalis /dɪdʒɪ'teɪlɪs/ *noun* heart stimulant made from foxgloves.

digitize *verb* (also **ise**) (**-zing** or **-sing**) convert (computer data etc.) into digital form.

dignified /'dɪgnɪfaɪd/ *adjective* having or showing dignity.

dignify /'dɪgnɪfaɪ/ *verb* (**ies**, **-ied**) give dignity to.

dignitary /'dɪgnɪtərɪ/ *noun* (*plural* **-ies**) person of high rank or office.

dignity /'dɪgnɪtɪ/ *noun* (*plural* **-ies**) composed and serious manner; being worthy of respect; high rank or position.

digraph /'daɪgrɑːf/ *noun* two letters representing one sound, e.g. *sh* in *show*, or *ey* in *key*.

■ **Usage** *Digraph* is sometimes confused with *ligature*, which means 'two or more letters joined'.

digress /daɪ'gres/ *verb* depart from main subject. □ **digression** *noun*.

dike = DYKE.

dilapidated /dɪ'læpɪdeɪtɪd/ *adjective* in disrepair. □ **dilapidation** *noun*.

dilate /daɪ'leɪt/ *verb* (**-ting**) widen or expand; speak or write at length. □ **dilatation** *noun*; **dilation** *noun*.

dilatory /'dɪlətərɪ/ *adjective* given to or causing delay.

dilemma /daɪ'lemə/ *noun* situation in which difficult choice has to be made.

■ **Usage** *Dilemma* is sometimes also used to mean 'a difficult situation or predicament', but this is considered incorrect by some people.

dilettante /dɪlɪ'tæntɪ/ *noun* (*plural* **dilettanti** /-tɪ/ or **-s**) dabbler in a subject. □ **dilettantism** *noun*.

diligent /'dɪlɪdʒ(ə)nt/ *adjective* hardworking; showing care and effort. □ **diligence** *noun*; **diligently** *adverb*.

dill *noun* herb with aromatic leaves and seeds.

dilly-dally /dɪlɪ'dælɪ/ *verb* (**-ies**, **-ied**) *colloquial* dawdle, vacillate.

dilute /daɪ'ljuːt/ ● *verb* (**-ting**) reduce strength (of fluid) by adding water etc.; weaken in effect. ● *adjective* diluted. □ **dilution** *noun*.

diluvial /daɪ'luːvɪəl/ *adjective* of flood, esp. Flood in Genesis.

dim ● *adjective* (**-mm-**) not bright; faintly luminous or visible; indistinctly perceived or remembered; (of eyes) not seeing clearly; *colloquial* stupid. ● *verb* (**-mm-**) make or become dim. □ **dimly** *adverb*; **dimness** *noun*.

dime *noun US* 10-cent coin.

dimension /daɪ'men(ʃ)(ə)n/ *noun* any measurable extent; (in *plural*) size; aspect. □ **dimensional** *adjective*.

diminish /dɪ'mɪnɪʃ/ *verb* make or become smaller or less; (often as **diminished** *adjective*) lessen reputation of (person), humiliate.

diminuendo /dɪmɪnjʊ'endəʊ/ *Music* ● *noun* (*plural* **-s**) gradual decrease in loudness. ● *adverb* & *adjective* decreasing in loudness.

diminution /dɪmɪ'njuːʃ(ə)n/ *noun* diminishing.

diminutive /dɪ'mɪnjʊtɪv/ ● *adjective* tiny; (of word or suffix) implying smallness or affection. ● *noun* diminutive word or suffix.

dimmer *noun* (in full **dimmer switch**) device for varying brightness of electric light.

dimple /'dɪmp(ə)l/ ● *noun* small hollow, esp. in cheek or chin. ● *verb* (**-ling**) produce dimples (in).

din ● *noun* prolonged loud confused noise. ● *verb* (**-nn-**) (+ *into*) force (information) into person by repetition; make din.

dinar /'diːnɑː/ *noun* chief monetary unit of (former) Yugoslavia and several Middle Eastern and N. African countries.

dine *verb* (**-ning**) eat dinner; (+ *on*, *upon*) eat for dinner; (esp. in **wine and dine**) entertain with food. □ **dining-car** restaurant on train; **dining-room** room in which meals are eaten.

diner *noun* person who dines; small dining-room; dining-car; *US* restaurant.

ding-dong /'dɪŋdɒŋ/ noun sound of chimes; colloquial heated argument.

dinghy /'dɪŋɡɪ/ noun (plural **-ies**) small, often inflatable, boat.

dingle /'dɪŋɡ(ə)l/ noun deep wooded valley.

dingo /'dɪŋɡəʊ/ noun (plural **-es**) wild Australian dog.

dingy /'dɪndʒɪ/ adjective (**-ier, -iest**) drab; dirty-looking. □ **dinginess** noun.

dinkum /'dɪŋkəm/ adjective & adverb (in full **fair dinkum**) Australian & NZ colloquial genuine(ly), honest(ly).

dinky /'dɪŋkɪ/ adjective (**-ier, -iest**) colloquial pretty, small and neat.

dinner /'dɪnə/ noun main meal, at midday or in the evening. □ **dinner-dance** formal dinner followed by dancing; **dinner jacket** man's formal evening jacket; **dinner lady** woman who supervises school dinners; **dinner service** set of matching crockery for dinner.

dinosaur /'daɪnəsɔː/ noun extinct usually large reptile.

dint ● noun dent. ● verb mark with dints. □ **by dint of** by force or means of.

diocese /'daɪəsɪs/ noun district under bishop's pastoral care. □ **diocesan** /daɪ'ɒsɪs(ə)n/ adjective.

diode /'daɪəʊd/ noun semiconductor allowing current in one direction and having two terminals; thermionic valve with two electrodes.

dioxide /daɪ'ɒksaɪd/ noun oxide with two atoms of oxygen.

Dip. abbreviation Diploma.

dip ● verb (**-pp-**) put or lower briefly into liquid etc.; immerse; go below a surface or level; decline slightly or briefly; slope or extend downwards; go briefly under water; (+ *into*) look cursorily into (book, subject, etc.); (+ *into*) put (hand etc.) into (container) to take something out, use part of (resources); lower or be lowered, esp. in salute; lower beam of (headlights). ● noun dipping, being dipped; liquid for dipping; brief bathe in sea etc.; downward slope or hollow; sauce into which food is dipped. □ **dip-switch** switch for dipping vehicle's headlights.

diphtheria /dɪf'θɪərɪə/ noun infectious disease with inflammation of mucous membrane esp. of throat.

diphthong /'dɪfθɒŋ/ noun union of two vowels in one syllable.

diplodocus /dɪ'plɒdəkəs/ noun (plural **-cuses**) huge long-necked plant-eating dinosaur.

diploma /dɪ'pləʊmə/ noun certificate of educational qualification; document conferring honour, privilege, etc.

diplomacy /dɪ'pləʊməsɪ/ noun management of international relations; tact.

diplomat /'dɪpləmæt/ noun member of diplomatic service; tactful person.

diplomatic /dɪplə'mætɪk/ adjective of or involved in diplomacy; tactful. □ **diplomatic bag** container for dispatching embassy mail; **diplomatic immunity** exemption of foreign diplomatic staff from arrest, taxation, etc.; **diplomatic service** branch of civil service concerned with representing a country abroad. □ **diplomatically** adverb.

diplomatist /dɪ'pləʊmətɪst/ noun diplomat.

dipper /'dɪpə/ noun diving bird; ladle.

dippy /'dɪpɪ/ adjective (**-ier, -iest**) slang crazy, silly.

dipsomania /dɪpsə'meɪnɪə/ noun alcoholism. □ **dipsomaniac** noun.

dipstick noun rod for measuring depth, esp. of oil in vehicle's engine.

dipterous /'dɪptərəs/ adjective two-winged.

diptych /'dɪptɪk/ noun painted altarpiece on two hinged panels.

dire adjective dreadful; ominous; colloquial very bad; urgent.

direct /daɪ'rekt/ ● adjective extending or moving in straight line or by shortest route, not crooked or circuitous; straightforward, frank; without intermediaries; complete, greatest possible. ● adverb in a direct way; by direct route. ● verb control; guide; (+ *to do, that*) order; (+ *to*) tell way to (place); address (letter etc.); (+ *at, to, towards*) point, aim, or turn; supervise acting etc. of (film, play, etc.). □ **direct current** electric current flowing in one direction only; **direct debit** regular debiting of bank account at request of payee; **direct-grant school** school funded by government, not local authority; **direct object** primary object of verbal action (see panel at OBJECT); **direct**

speech words actually spoken, not reported (see panel); **direct tax** tax on income, paid directly to government. □ **directness** noun.

direction /daɪˈrekʃ(ə)n/ noun directing; (usually in plural) orders, instructions; point to, from, or along which person or thing moves or looks.

directional adjective of or indicating direction; sending or receiving radio or sound waves in one direction only.

directive /daɪˈrektɪv/ noun order from an authority.

directly ● adverb at once, without delay; presently, shortly; exactly; in a direct way. ● conjunction colloquial as soon as.

director noun person who directs, esp. for stage etc. or as member of board of company. □ **director-general** chief executive. □ **directorial** /-ˈtɔː-/ adjective; **directorship** noun.

directorate /daɪˈrektərət/ noun board of directors; office of director.

directory /daɪˈrektərɪ/ noun (plural **-ies**) book with list of telephone subscribers, inhabitants of town etc., members of profession, etc. □ **directory enquiries** telephone service providing subscriber's number on request.

dirge noun lament for the dead; dreary piece of music.

dirham /ˈdɪrəm/ noun monetary unit of Morocco and United Arab Emirates.

dirigible /ˈdɪrɪdʒɪb(ə)l/ ● adjective that can be steered. ● noun dirigible balloon or airship.

dirk noun short dagger.

dirndl /ˈdɜːnd(ə)l/ noun dress with close-fitting bodice and full skirt; gathered full skirt with tight waistband.

dirt noun unclean matter that soils; earth; foul or malicious talk; excrement. □ **dirt cheap** colloquial extremely cheap; **dirt track** racing track with surface of earth or cinders etc.

dirty /ˈdɜːtɪ/ ● adjective (**-ier, -iest**) soiled, unclean; sordid, obscene; unfair; (of weather) rough; muddy-looking. ● adverb slang very; in a dirty or obscene way. ● verb (**-ies, -ied**) make or become dirty. □ **dirty look** colloquial look of disapproval or disgust. □ **dirtiness** noun.

disability /dɪsəˈbɪlɪtɪ/ noun (plural **-ies**) permanent physical or mental incapacity; lack of some capacity, preventing action.

disable /dɪˈseɪb(ə)l/ verb (**-ling**) deprive of an ability; (often as **disabled** adjective) physically incapacitate. □ **disablement** noun.

....

Direct Speech

Direct speech is the actual words of a speaker quoted in writing.

1 In a novel etc., speech punctuation is used for direct speech:
  a The words spoken are usually put in quotation marks.
  b Each new piece of speech begins with a capital letter.
  c Each paragraph within one person's piece of speech begins with quotation marks, but only the last paragraph ends with them.

2 In a script (the written words of a play, a film, or a radio or television programme):
  a The names of speakers are written in the margin in capital letters.
  b Each name is followed by a colon.
  c Quotation marks are not needed.
  d Any instructions about the way the words are spoken or about the scenery or the actions of the speakers (stage directions) are written in the present tense in brackets or italics.

For example:

  CHRISTOPHER: [Looks into box.] There's nothing in here.

....

disabuse /dɪsə'bjuːz/ verb (-sing) (usually + of) free from mistaken idea; disillusion.

disadvantage /dɪsəd'vɑːntɪdʒ/ ● noun unfavourable condition or circumstance; loss; damage. ● verb (-ging) cause disadvantage to. □ **at a disadvantage** in an unfavourable position. □ **disadvantageous** /ˌdɪsædvən'teɪdʒəs/ adjective.

disadvantaged adjective lacking normal opportunities through poverty, disability, etc.

disaffected /dɪsə'fektɪd/ adjective discontented, alienated (esp. politically). □ **disaffection** noun.

disagree /dɪsə'griː/ verb (-ees, -eed) (often + with) hold different opinion; not correspond; upset. □ **disagreement** noun.

disagreeable adjective unpleasant; bad-tempered. □ **disagreeably** adverb.

disallow /dɪsə'laʊ/ verb refuse to allow or accept; prohibit.

disappear /dɪsə'pɪə/ verb cease to be visible or in existence or circulation etc.; go missing. □ **disappearance** noun.

disappoint /dɪsə'pɔɪnt/ verb fail to fulfil desire or expectation of; frustrate. □ **disappointing** adjective; **disappointment** noun.

disapprobation /dɪsæprə'beɪʃ(ə)n/ noun disapproval.

disapprove /dɪsə'pruːv/ verb (-ving) (usually + of) have or express unfavourable opinion. □ **disapproval** noun.

disarm /dɪs'ɑːm/ verb deprive of weapons; abandon or reduce one's own weapons; (often as **disarming** adjective) make less hostile, charm, win over. □ **disarmament** noun; **disarmingly** adverb.

disarrange /dɪsə'reɪndʒ/ verb (-ging) put into disorder.

disarray /dɪsə'reɪ/ noun disorder.

disassociate /dɪsə'səʊʃɪeɪt/ verb (-ting) dissociate. □ **disassociation** noun.

disaster /dɪ'zɑːstə/ noun sudden or great misfortune; colloquial complete failure. □ **disastrous** adjective; **disastrously** adverb.

disavow /dɪsə'vaʊ/ verb disclaim knowledge or approval of or responsibility for. □ **disavowal** noun.

disband /dɪs'bænd/ verb break up, disperse.

disbar /dɪs'bɑː/ verb (-rr-) deprive of status of barrister. □ **disbarment** noun.

disbelieve /dɪsbɪ'liːv/ verb (-ving) refuse to believe; not believe; be sceptical. □ **disbelief** noun; **disbelievingly** adverb.

disburse /dɪs'bɜːs/ verb (-sing) pay out (money). □ **disbursement** noun.

disc noun flat thinnish circular object; round flat or apparently flat surface or mark; layer of cartilage between vertebrae; gramophone record; Computing = DISK. □ **disc brake** one using friction of pads against a disc; **disc jockey** presenter of recorded popular music.

discard /dɪs'kɑːd/ verb reject as unwanted; remove or put aside.

discern /dɪ'sɜːn/ verb perceive clearly with mind or senses; make out. □ **discernible** adjective.

discerning adjective having good judgement or insight. □ **discernment** noun.

discharge ● verb /dɪs'tʃɑːdʒ/ (-ging) release, let go; dismiss from office or employment; fire (gun etc.); throw; eject; emit, pour out; pay or perform (debt, duty); relieve (bankrupt) of residual liability; release an electrical charge from; relieve of cargo; unload. ● noun /'dɪstʃɑːdʒ/ discharging, being discharged; matter or thing discharged; release of electric charge, esp. with spark.

disciple /dɪ'saɪp(ə)l/ noun follower of a teacher or leader, esp. of Christ.

disciplinarian /dɪsɪplɪ'neərɪən/ noun enforcer of or believer in strict discipline.

disciplinary /dɪsɪ'plɪnərɪ/ adjective of or enforcing discipline.

discipline /'dɪsɪplɪn/ ● noun control or order exercised over people or animals; system of rules for this; training or way of life aimed at self-control or conformity; branch of learning; punishment. ● verb (-ning) punish; control by training in obedience.

disclaim /dɪs'kleɪm/ verb disown, deny; renounce legal claim to.

disclaimer noun statement disclaiming something.

disclose /dɪs'kləʊz/ verb (-sing) expose, make known, reveal. □ **disclosure** noun.

disco /ˈdɪskəʊ/ *noun* (*plural* **-s**) *colloquial* discothèque.

discolour /dɪsˈkʌlə/ *verb* (*US* **discolor**) cause to change from its usual colour; stain or become stained. □ **discoloration** *noun*.

discomfit /dɪsˈkʌmfɪt/ *verb* (**-t-**) disconcert; baffle; frustrate. □ **discomfiture** *noun*.

■ **Usage** *Discomfit* is sometimes confused with *discomfort*.

discomfort /dɪsˈkʌmfət/ *noun* lack of comfort; uneasiness of body or mind.

■ **Usage** As a verb, *discomfort* is sometimes confused with *discomfit*.

discompose /dɪskəmˈpəʊz/ *verb* (**-sing**) disturb composure of. □ **discomposure** *noun*.

disconcert /dɪskənˈsɜːt/ *verb* disturb composure of; fluster.

disconnect /dɪskəˈnekt/ *verb* break connection of or between; put (apparatus) out of action by disconnecting parts. □ **disconnection** *noun*.

disconnected *adjective* incoherent and illogical.

disconsolate /dɪsˈkɒnsələt/ *adjective* forlorn, unhappy; disappointed. □ **disconsolately** *adverb*.

discontent /dɪskənˈtent/ ● *noun* dissatisfaction; lack of contentment. ● *verb* (esp. as **discontented** *adjective*) make dissatisfied.

discontinue /dɪskənˈtɪnjuː/ *verb* (**-ues**, **-ued**, **-uing**) (cause to) cease; not go on with (activity).

discontinuous /dɪskənˈtɪnjʊəs/ *adjective* lacking continuity; intermittent. □ **discontinuity** /-kɒntɪˈnjuːɪtɪ/ *noun*.

discord /ˈdɪskɔːd/ *noun* disagreement, strife; harsh noise, clashing sounds; lack of harmony. □ **discordant** /-ˈkɔːdənt/ *adjective*.

discothèque /ˈdɪskətek/ *noun* nightclub etc. where pop records are played for dancing.

discount ● *noun* /ˈdɪskaʊnt/ amount deducted from normal price. ● *verb* /dɪsˈkaʊnt/ disregard as unreliable or unimportant; deduct amount from (price etc.); give or get present value of (investment certificate which has yet to mature). □ **at a discount** below nominal or usual price.

discountenance /dɪsˈkaʊntɪmæns/ *verb* (**-cing**) disconcert; refuse to approve of.

discourage /dɪsˈkʌrɪdʒ/ *verb* (**-ging**) reduce confidence or spirits of; dissuade, deter; show disapproval of. □ **discouragement** *noun*.

discourse ● *noun* /ˈdɪskɔːs/ conversation; lengthy treatment of theme; lecture, speech. ● *verb* /dɪsˈkɔːs/ (**-sing**) converse; speak or write at length.

discourteous /dɪsˈkɜːtɪəs/ *adjective* rude, uncivil. □ **discourteously** *adverb*; **discourtesy** *noun* (*plural* **-ies**).

discover /dɪsˈkʌvə/ *verb* find or find out, by effort or chance; be first to find or find out in particular case; find and promote (little-known performer).

discovery *noun* (*plural* **-ies**) discovering, being discovered; person or thing discovered.

discredit /dɪsˈkredɪt/ ● *verb* (**-t-**) cause to be disbelieved; harm good reputation of; refuse to believe. ● *noun* harm to reputation; cause of this; lack of credibility.

discreditable *adjective* bringing discredit, shameful.

discreet /dɪsˈkriːt/ *adjective* (**-er**, **-est**) tactful, prudent; cautious in speech or action; unobtrusive. □ **discreetly** *adverb*; **discreetness** *noun*.

discrepancy /dɪsˈkrepənsɪ/ *noun* (*plural* **-ies**) difference; inconsistency.

discrete /dɪsˈkriːt/ *adjective* separate; distinct.

discretion /dɪsˈkreʃ(ə)n/ *noun* being discreet; prudence, judgement; freedom or authority to act as one thinks fit. □ **discretionary** *adjective*.

discriminate /dɪsˈkrɪmɪneɪt/ *verb* (**-ting**) (often + *between*) make or see a distinction; (usually + *against*, *in favour of*) treat badly or well, esp. on the basis of race, gender, etc. □ **discriminating** *adjective*; **discrimination** *noun*; **discriminatory** /-nətərɪ/ *adjective*.

discursive /dɪsˈkɜːsɪv/ *adjective* rambling, tending to digress.

discus /ˈdɪskəs/ *noun* (*plural* **-cuses**) heavy disc thrown in athletic events.

discuss /dɪsˈkʌs/ *verb* talk about; talk or write about (subject) in detail. □ **discussion** *noun*.

disdain /dɪsˈdeɪn/ ●noun scorn, contempt. ●verb regard with disdain; refrain or refuse out of disdain. □ **disdainful** adjective.

disease /dɪˈziːz/ noun unhealthy condition of organism or part of organism; (specific) disorder or illness. □ **diseased** adjective.

disembark /dɪsɪmˈbɑːk/ verb put or go ashore; get off aircraft, bus, etc. □ **disembarkation** /-embɑː-/ noun.

disembarrass /dɪsɪmˈbærəs/ verb (usually + of) rid or relieve (of a load etc.); free from embarrassment. □ **disembarrassment** noun.

disembodied /dɪsɪmˈbɒdɪd/ adjective (of soul etc.) separated from body or concrete form; without a body.

disembowel /dɪsɪmˈbaʊəl/ verb (-ll-; US -l-) remove entrails of. □ **disembowelment** noun.

disenchant /dɪsɪnˈtʃɑːnt/ verb disillusion. □ **disenchantment** noun.

disencumber /dɪsɪnˈkʌmbə/ verb free from encumbrance.

disenfranchise /dɪsɪnˈfræntʃaɪz/ verb (-sing) deprive of right to vote, or of citizen's rights, or of franchise held. □ **disenfranchisement** noun.

disengage /dɪsɪnˈɡeɪdʒ/ verb (-ging) detach; loosen; release; remove (troops) from battle etc.; become detached; (as **disengaged** adjective) at leisure, uncommitted. □ **disengagement** noun.

disentangle /dɪsɪnˈtæŋɡ(ə)l/ verb (-ling) free or become free of tangles or complications. □ **disentanglement** noun.

disestablish /dɪsɪˈstæblɪʃ/ verb deprive (Church) of state support; end the establishment of. □ **disestablishment** noun.

disfavour /dɪsˈfeɪvə/ noun (US **disfavor**) dislike; disapproval; being disliked.

disfigure /dɪsˈfɪɡə/ verb (-ring) spoil appearance of. □ **disfigurement** noun.

disgorge /dɪsˈɡɔːdʒ/ verb (-ging) eject from throat; pour forth (food, fluid, etc.).

disgrace /dɪsˈɡreɪs/ ●noun shame, ignominy; shameful or very bad person or thing. ●verb (-cing) bring shame or discredit on; dismiss from position of honour or favour.

disgraceful adjective causing disgrace; shameful. □ **disgracefully** adverb.

disgruntled /dɪsˈɡrʌnt(ə)ld/ adjective discontented; sulky.

disguise /dɪsˈɡaɪz/ ●verb (-sing) conceal identity of, make unrecognizable; conceal. ●noun costume, make-up, etc. used to disguise; action, manner, etc. used to deceive; disguised condition.

disgust /dɪsˈɡʌst/ ●noun strong aversion; repugnance. ●verb cause disgust in. □ **disgusting** adjective; **disgustingly** adverb.

dish ●noun shallow flat-bottomed container for food; food served in dish; particular kind of food; (in plural) crockery etc. to be washed after a meal; dish-shaped object or cavity; colloquial sexually attractive person. ●verb make dish-shaped; colloquial outmanoeuvre, frustrate. □ **dish out** colloquial distribute, allocate; **dish up** (prepare to) serve meal.

disharmony /dɪsˈhɑːmənɪ/ noun lack of harmony, discord.

dishearten /dɪsˈhɑːt(ə)n/ verb cause to lose courage or confidence.

dishevelled /dɪˈʃev(ə)ld/ adjective (US **disheveled**) ruffled, untidy.

dishonest /dɪsˈɒnɪst/ adjective fraudulent; insincere. □ **dishonestly** adverb; **dishonesty** noun.

dishonour /dɪsˈɒnə/ (US **dishonor**) ●noun loss of honour, disgrace; cause of this. ●verb disgrace (person, family, etc.); refuse to pay (cheque etc.).

dishonourable adjective (US **dishonorable**) causing disgrace; ignominious; unprincipled. □ **dishonourably** adverb.

dishy adjective (-ier, -iest) colloquial sexually attractive.

disillusion /dɪsɪˈluːʒ(ə)n/ ●verb free from illusion or mistaken belief, esp. disappointingly. ●noun disillusioned state. □ **disillusionment** noun.

disincentive /dɪsɪnˈsentɪv/ noun thing that discourages, esp. from a particular line of action.

disincline /dɪsɪnˈklaɪn/ verb (-ning) (usually as **disinclined** adjective) make unwilling. □ **disinclination** /-klɪˈneɪ-/ noun.

disinfect /dɪsɪnˈfekt/ verb cleanse of infection. □ **disinfection** noun.

disinfectant ● *noun* substance that destroys germs etc. ● *adjective* disinfecting.

disinformation /dɪsɪnfə'meɪʃ(ə)n/ *noun* false information, propaganda.

disingenuous /dɪsɪn'dʒenjuəs/ *adjective* insincere; not candid. □ **disingenuously** *adverb*; **disingenuousness** *noun*.

disinherit /dɪsɪn'herɪt/ *verb* (**-t-**) deprive of right to inherit; reject as one's heir. □ **disinheritance** *noun*.

disintegrate /dɪ'sɪntɪgreɪt/ *verb* (**-ting**) separate into component parts; break up; *colloquial* break down, esp. mentally. □ **disintegration** *noun*.

disinter /dɪsɪn'tɜː/ *verb* (**-rr-**) dig up (esp. corpse). □ **disinterment** *noun*.

disinterested /dɪ'sɪntrɪstɪd/ *adjective* impartial; uninterested. □ **disinterest** *noun*; **disinterestedly** *adverb*.

■ **Usage** The use of *disinterested* to mean 'uninterested' is common in informal use but is widely considered incorrect. The use of the noun *disinterest* to mean 'lack of interest' is also objected to, but it is rarely used in any other sense and the alternative *uninterest* is rare.

disjointed /dɪs'dʒɔɪntɪd/ *adjective* disconnected, incoherent.

disjunction /dɪs'dʒʌŋkʃ(ə)n/ *noun* separation.

disjunctive /dɪs'dʒʌŋktɪv/ *adjective* involving separation; (of a conjunction) expressing alternative.

disk *noun* flat circular computer storage device. □ **disk drive** mechanism for rotating disk and reading or writing data from or to it.

dislike /dɪs'laɪk/ ● *verb* (**-king**) have aversion to, not like. ● *noun* feeling of repugnance or not liking; object of this.

dislocate /'dɪsləkeɪt/ *verb* (**-ting**) disturb normal connection of (esp. a joint in the body); disrupt. □ **dislocation** *noun*.

dislodge /dɪs'lɒdʒ/ *verb* (**-ging**) disturb or move. □ **dislodgement** *noun*.

disloyal /dɪs'lɔɪəl/ *adjective* unfaithful; lacking loyalty. □ **disloyalty** *noun*.

dismal /'dɪzm(ə)l/ *adjective* gloomy; miserable; dreary; *colloquial* feeble, inept. □ **dismally** *adverb*.

dismantle /dɪs'mænt(ə)l/ *verb* (**-ling**) pull down, take to pieces; deprive of defences, equipment, etc.

dismay /dɪs'meɪ/ ● *noun* feeling of intense disappointment and discouragement. ● *verb* affect with dismay.

dismember /dɪs'membə/ *verb* remove limbs from; partition (country etc.). □ **dismemberment** *noun*.

dismiss /dɪs'mɪs/ *verb* send away; disband; allow to go; terminate employment of, esp. dishonourably; put out of one's thoughts; *Law* refuse further hearing to; *Cricket* put (batsman, side) out. □ **dismissal** *noun*.

dismissive *adjective* dismissing rudely or casually; disdainful. □ **dismissively** *adverb*.

dismount /dɪs'maʊnt/ *verb* get off or down from cycle or horseback etc.; remove (thing) from mounting.

disobedient /dɪsə'biːdɪənt/ *adjective* disobeying; rebellious. □ **disobedience** *noun*; **disobediently** *adverb*.

disobey /dɪsə'beɪ/ *verb* fail or refuse to obey.

disoblige /dɪsə'blaɪdʒ/ *verb* (**-ging**) refuse to help or cooperate with (person).

disorder /dɪs'ɔːdə/ *noun* confusion; tumult, riot; bodily or mental ailment. □ **disordered** *adjective*.

disorderly *adjective* untidy; confused; riotous.

disorganize /dɪs'ɔːgənaɪz/ *verb* (also **-ise**) (**-zing** or **-sing**) throw into confusion or disorder; (as **disorganized** *adjective*) badly organized, untidy. □ **disorganization** *noun*.

disorientate /dɪs'ɔːrɪənteɪt/ *verb* (also **disorient**) (**-ting**) confuse (person) as to his or her bearings. □ **disorientation** *noun*.

disown /dɪs'əʊn/ *verb* deny or give up any connection with; repudiate.

disparage /dɪ'spærɪdʒ/ *verb* (**-ging**) criticize; belittle. □ **disparagement** *noun*.

disparate /'dɪspərət/ *adjective* essentially different, unrelated.

disparity /dɪ'spærɪtɪ/ *noun* (*plural* **-ies**) inequality, difference; incongruity.

dispassionate /dɪ'spæʃənət/ *adjective* free from emotion; impartial. □ **dispassionately** *adverb*.

dispatch /dɪs'pætʃ/ (also **despatch**) ● *verb* send off; perform (task etc.) promptly; kill; *colloquial* eat (food) quickly. ● *noun* dispatching, being dispatched; official written message, esp. military or political; promptness, efficiency. □ **dispatch box** case for esp. parliamentary documents; **dispatch rider** motorcyclist etc. carrying messages.

dispel /dɪˈspel/ *verb* (**-ll-**) drive away (esp. unwanted ideas or feelings); scatter.

dispensable /dɪˈspensəb(ə)l/ *adjective* that can be dispensed with.

dispensary /dɪˈspensərɪ/ *noun* (*plural* **-ies**) place where medicines etc. are dispensed.

dispensation /dɪspenˈseɪʃ(ə)n/ *noun* distributing, dispensing; exemption from penalty, rule, etc.; ordering or management, esp. of world by Providence.

dispense /dɪˈspens/ *verb* (**-sing**) distribute; administer; make up and give out (medicine); (+ *with*) do without, make unnecessary.

dispenser *noun* person who dispenses something; device that dispenses selected amount at a time.

disperse /dɪˈspɜːs/ *verb* (**-sing**) go or send widely or in different directions, scatter; station at different points; disseminate; separate (light) into coloured constituents. □ **dispersal** *noun*; **dispersion** *noun*.

dispirit /dɪˈspɪrɪt/ *verb* (esp. as **dispiriting, dispirited** *adjectives*) make despondent.

displace /dɪsˈpleɪs/ *verb* (**-cing**) move from its place; remove from office; oust, take the place of. □ **displaced person** refugee in war etc. or from persecution.

displacement *noun* displacing, being displaced; amount of fluid displaced by object floating or immersed in it.

display /dɪˈspleɪ/ ● *verb* show; exhibit. ● *noun* displaying; exhibition; ostentation; image shown on a visual display unit etc.

displease /dɪsˈpliːz/ *verb* (**-sing**) offend; make angry or upset. □ **displeasure** /-ˈpleʒə/ *noun*.

disport /dɪsˈpɔːt/ *verb* (also **disport oneself**) frolic, enjoy oneself.

disposable *adjective* that can be disposed of; designed to be discarded after one use.

disposal *noun* disposing of. □ **at one's disposal** available.

dispose /dɪˈspəʊz/ *verb* (**-sing**) (usually + *to*, *to do*) (usually in *passive*) incline, make willing; (in *passive*) tend; arrange suitably; (as **disposed** *adjective*) having a specified inclination; determine events. □ **dispose of** get rid of, deal with, finish.

disposition /dɪspəˈzɪʃ(ə)n/ *noun* natural tendency; temperament; arrangement (of parts etc.).

dispossess /dɪspəˈzes/ *verb* (usually + *of*) (esp. as **dispossessed** *adjective*) deprive; oust, dislodge. □ **dispossession** *noun*.

disproof /dɪsˈpruːf/ *noun* refutation.

disproportion /dɪsprəˈpɔːʃ(ə)n/ *noun* lack of proportion.

disproportionate *adjective* out of proportion; relatively too large or too small. □ **disproportionately** *adverb*.

disprove /dɪsˈpruːv/ *verb* (**-ving**) prove (theory etc.) false.

disputable *adjective* open to question.

disputant *noun* person in dispute.

disputation /dɪspjuˈteɪʃ(ə)n/ *noun* debate, esp. formal; argument, controversy.

disputatious /dɪspjuˈteɪʃəs/ *adjective* argumentative.

dispute /dɪˈspjuːt/ ● *verb* (**-ting**) hold debate; quarrel; question truth or validity of; contend for; resist. ● *noun* controversy, debate; quarrel; disagreement leading to industrial action.

disqualify /dɪsˈkwɒlɪfaɪ/ *verb* (**-ies**, **-ied**) make or pronounce (competitor, applicant, etc.) unfit or ineligible. □ **disqualification** *noun*.

disquiet /dɪsˈkwaɪət/ ● *verb* make anxious. ● *noun* uneasiness, anxiety. □ **disquietude** *noun*.

disquisition /dɪskwɪˈzɪʃ(ə)n/ *noun* discursive treatise or discourse.

disregard /dɪsrɪˈɡɑːd/ ● *verb* ignore, treat as unimportant. ● *noun* indifference, neglect.

disrepair /dɪsrɪˈpeə/ *noun* bad condition due to lack of repairs.

disreputable /dɪsˈrepjʊtəb(ə)l/ *adjective* having a bad reputation; not respectable. □ **disreputably** *adverb*.

disrepute /ˌdɪsrɪˈpjuːt/ noun lack of good reputation; discredit.

disrespect /ˌdɪsrɪˈspekt/ noun lack of respect. □ **disrespectful** adjective.

disrobe /dɪsˈrəʊb/ verb (**-bing**) literary undress.

disrupt /dɪsˈrʌpt/ verb interrupt continuity of; bring disorder to; break (thing) apart. □ **disruption** noun; **disruptive** adjective.

dissatisfy /dɪsˈsætɪsfaɪ/ verb (**-ies**, **-ied**) (usually as **dissatisfied** adjective; often + with) fail to satisfy; make discontented. □ **dissatisfaction** /-ˈfæk-/ noun.

dissect /dɪˈsekt/ verb cut in pieces, esp. for examination or post-mortem; analyse or criticize in detail. □ **dissection** noun.

■ **Usage** Dissect is often wrongly pronounced /daɪˈsekt/ (and sometimes written with only one s) because of confusion with bisect.

dissemble /dɪˈsemb(ə)l/ verb (**-ling**) be hypocritical or insincere; conceal or disguise (a feeling, intention, etc.).

disseminate /dɪˈsemɪneɪt/ verb (**-ting**) scatter about, spread (esp. ideas) widely. □ **dissemination** noun.

dissension /dɪˈsenʃ(ə)n/ noun angry disagreement.

dissent /dɪˈsent/ ● verb (often + from) disagree, esp. openly; differ, esp. from established or official opinion. ● noun such difference; expression of this.

dissenter noun person who dissents; (**Dissenter**) Protestant dissenting from Church of England.

dissentient /dɪˈsenʃ(ə)nt/ ● adjective disagreeing with the established or official view. ● noun person who dissents.

dissertation /ˌdɪsəˈteɪʃ(ə)n/ noun detailed discourse, esp. as submitted for academic degree.

disservice /dɪsˈsɜːvɪs/ noun harmful action.

dissident /ˈdɪsɪd(ə)nt/ ● adjective disagreeing, esp. with established government. ● noun dissident person.

dissimilar /dɪˈsɪmɪlə/ adjective not similar. □ **dissimilarity** /-ˈlærɪtɪ/ noun (plural **-ies**).

dissimulate /dɪˈsɪmjʊleɪt/ verb (**-ting**) dissemble. □ **dissimulation** noun.

dissipate /ˈdɪsɪpeɪt/ verb (**-ting**) dispel, disperse; squander; (as **dissipated** adjective) dissolute.

dissipation noun dissolute way of life; dissipating, being dissipated.

dissociate /dɪˈsəʊʃɪeɪt/ verb (**-ting**) disconnect or separate; become disconnected; (**dissociate oneself from**) declare oneself unconnected with. □ **dissociation** noun.

dissolute /ˈdɪsəluːt/ adjective lax in morals, licentious.

dissolution /ˌdɪsəˈluːʃ(ə)n/ noun dissolving, being dissolved; dismissal or dispersal of assembly, esp. parliament; breaking up, abolition (of institution); death.

dissolve /dɪˈzɒlv/ verb (**-ving**) make or become liquid, esp. by immersion or dispersion in liquid; (cause to) disappear gradually; dismiss (assembly); put an end to, annul; (often + in, into) be overcome (by tears, laughter, etc.).

dissonant /ˈdɪsənənt/ adjective discordant, harsh-toned; incongruous. □ **dissonance** noun.

dissuade /dɪˈsweɪd/ verb (**-ding**) (often + from) discourage, persuade against. □ **dissuasion** /-ˈsweɪʒ(ə)n/ noun.

distaff /ˈdɪstɑːf/ noun cleft stick holding wool etc. for spinning by hand. □ **distaff side** female branch of family.

distance /ˈdɪst(ə)ns/ ● noun being far off; remoteness; space between two points; distant point; aloofness, reserve; remoter field of vision. ● verb (**-cing**) place or cause to seem far off; leave behind in race etc. □ **at a distance** far off; **keep one's distance** remain aloof.

distant adjective at specified distance; remote in space, time, relationship, etc.; aloof; abstracted; faint. □ **distantly** adverb.

distaste /dɪsˈteɪst/ noun (usually + for) dislike; aversion. □ **distasteful** adjective.

distemper[1] /dɪˈstempə/ ● noun paint for walls, using glue etc. as base. ● verb paint with distemper.

distemper[2] /dɪˈstempə/ noun catarrhal disease of dogs etc.

distend /dɪˈstend/ verb swell out by pressure from within. □ **distension** /-ˈsten-/ noun.

distich /ˈdɪstɪk/ noun verse couplet.

distil | dither

distil /dɪˈstɪl/ *verb* (*US* **distill**) (**-ll-**) purify or extract essence from (substance) by vaporizing and condensing it and collecting remaining liquid; extract gist of (idea etc.); make (whisky, essence, etc.) by distilling. □ **distillation** *noun*.

distiller *noun* person who distils, esp. alcoholic liquor.

distillery *noun* (*plural* **-ies**) factory etc. for distilling alcoholic liquor.

distinct /dɪˈstɪŋkt/ *adjective* (often + *from*) separate, different in quality or kind; clearly perceptible; definite, decided. □ **distinctly** *adverb*.

distinction /dɪˈstɪŋkʃ(ə)n/ *noun* discriminating, distinguishing; difference between things; thing that differentiates; special consideration or honour; excellence; mark of honour.

distinctive *adjective* distinguishing, characteristic. □ **distinctively** *adverb*; **distinctiveness** *noun*.

distingué /dɪˈstæŋgeɪ/ *adjective* having distinguished air, manners, etc. [French]

distinguish /dɪˈstɪŋgwɪʃ/ *verb* (often + *from*, *between*) see or draw distinctions; characterize; make out by listening or looking etc.; (usually **distinguish oneself**; often + *by*) make prominent. □ **distinguishable** *adjective*.

distinguished *adjective* eminent, famous; dignified.

distort /dɪˈstɔːt/ *verb* pull or twist out of shape; misrepresent (facts etc.); transmit (sound) inaccurately. □ **distortion** *noun*.

distract /dɪˈstrækt/ *verb* (often + *from*) draw away attention of; bewilder; (as **distracted** *adjective*) confused, mad, or angry; amuse, esp. to divert from pain etc.

distraction /dɪˈstrækʃ(ə)n/ *noun* distracting, being distracted; thing which distracts; amusement, relaxation; mental confusion; frenzy, madness.

distrain /dɪˈstreɪn/ *verb* (usually + *upon*) impose distraint (on person, goods, etc.).

distraint /dɪˈstreɪnt/ *noun* seizure of goods to enforce payment.

distrait /dɪˈstreɪ/ *adjective* inattentive; distraught. [French]

distraught /dɪˈstrɔːt/ *adjective* distracted with worry, fear, etc.; very agitated.

distress /dɪˈstres/ ● *noun* suffering caused by pain, grief, anxiety, etc.; poverty; *Law* distraint. ● *verb* cause distress to; make unhappy. □ **distressed** *adjective*; **distressing** *adjective*.

distribute /dɪˈstrɪbjuːt/ *verb* (**-ting**) give shares or; deal out; spread about; put at different points; arrange, classify. □ **distribution** /-ˈbjuː-/ *noun*; **distributive** *adjective*.

■ **Usage** *Distribute* is often pronounced /ˈdɪstrɪbjuːt/ (with the stress on the *dis-*), but this is considered incorrect by some people.

distributor *noun* agent who supplies goods; device in internal-combustion engine for passing current to each spark plug in turn.

district /ˈdɪstrɪkt/ *noun* region; administrative division. □ **district attorney** (in the US) public prosecutor of district; **district nurse** nurse who makes home visits in an area.

distrust /dɪsˈtrʌst/ ● *noun* lack of trust; suspicion. ● *verb* have no confidence in. □ **distrustful** *adjective*.

disturb /dɪsˈtɜːb/ *verb* break rest or quiet of; worry; disorganize; (as **disturbed** *adjective*) emotionally or mentally unstable.

disturbance *noun* disturbing, being disturbed; tumult, disorder, agitation.

disunion /dɪsˈjuːnɪən/ *noun* separation; lack of union.

disunite /dɪsjuːˈnaɪt/ *verb* (**-ting**) separate; divide. □ **disunity** /-ˈjuː-/ *noun*.

disuse /dɪsˈjuːs/ *noun* state of no longer being used.

disused /dɪsˈjuːzd/ *adjective* no longer in use.

disyllable /daɪˈsɪləb(ə)l/ *noun* word or metrical foot of two syllables. □ **disyllabic** /-ˈlæb-/ *adjective*.

ditch ● *noun* long narrow excavation esp. for drainage or as boundary. ● *verb* make or repair ditches; *slang* abandon, discard.

dither /ˈdɪðə/ ● *verb* hesitate; be indecisive; tremble, quiver. ● *noun colloquial* state of agitation or hesitation. □ **ditherer** *noun*; **dithery** *adjective*.

dithyramb /ˈdɪθɪræm/ *noun* ancient Greek wild choral hymn; passionate or inflated poem etc. □ **dithyrambic** /-ˈræmbɪk/ *adjective*.

ditto /ˈdɪtəʊ/ *noun* (*plural* **-s**) the aforesaid, the same (in accounts, lists, etc., or *colloquial* in speech).

ditty /ˈdɪtɪ/ *noun* (*plural* **-ies**) short simple song.

diuretic /daɪjʊˈretɪk/ ● *adjective* causing increased output of urine. ● *noun* diuretic drug.

diurnal /daɪˈɜːn(ə)l/ *adjective* in or of day; daily; occupying one day.

diva /ˈdiːvə/ *noun* (*plural* **-s**) great woman opera singer.

divan /dɪˈvæn/ *noun* low couch or bed without back or ends.

dive ● *verb* (**-ving**) plunge head foremost into water; (of aircraft) descend fast and steeply; (of submarine or diver) submerge; go deeper; (+ *into*) *colloquial* put one's hand into. ● *noun* act of diving; plunge; *colloquial* disreputable nightclub, bar, etc. □ **dive-bomb** bomb (target) from diving aircraft; **diving board** elevated board for diving from.

diver *noun* person who dives, esp. one who works under water; diving bird.

diverge /daɪˈvɜːdʒ/ *verb* (**-ging**) (often + *from*) depart from set course; (of opinions etc.) differ; take different courses; spread outward from central point. □ **divergence** *noun*; **divergent** *adjective*.

divers /ˈdaɪvɜːz/ *adjective archaic* various, several.

diverse /daɪˈvɜːs/ *adjective* varied.

diversify /daɪˈvɜːsɪfaɪ/ *verb* (**-ies**, **-ied**) make diverse; vary; spread (investment) over several enterprises; (often + *into*) expand range of products. □ **diversification** *noun*.

diversion /daɪˈvɜːʃ(ə)n/ *noun* diverting, being diverted; recreation, pastime; alternative route when road is temporarily closed; stratagem for diverting attention. □ **diversionary** *adjective*.

diversity /daɪˈvɜːsɪtɪ/ *noun* variety.

divert /daɪˈvɜːt/ *verb* turn aside; deflect; distract (attention); (often as **diverting** *adjective*) entertain, amuse.

divest /daɪˈvest/ *verb* (usually + *of*) unclothe, strip; deprive, rid.

divide /dɪˈvaɪd/ ● *verb* (**-ding**) (often + *in*, *into*) separate into parts; split or break up; (often + *out*) distribute, deal, share; separate (one thing) from another; classify into parts or groups; cause to disagree; (+ *by*) find how many times number contains another; (+ *into*) be contained exact number of times; (of parliament) vote (by members entering either of two lobbies). ● *noun* dividing line; watershed.

dividend /ˈdɪvɪdend/ *noun* share of profits paid to shareholders, football pools winners, etc.; number to be divided.

divider *noun* screen etc. dividing room; (in *plural*) measuring compasses.

divination /dɪvɪˈneɪʃ(ə)n/ *noun* supposed foreseeing of the future, using special technique.

divine /dɪˈvaɪn/ ● *adjective* (**-r**, **-st**) of, from, or like God or a god; sacred; *colloquial* excellent. ● *verb* (**-ning**) discover by intuition or guessing; foresee; practise divination. ● *noun* theologian. □ **divining-rod** dowser's forked twig. □ **divinely** *adverb*.

diviner *noun* practitioner of divination; dowser.

divinity /dɪˈvɪnɪtɪ/ *noun* (*plural* **-ies**) being divine; god; theology.

divisible /dɪˈvɪzɪb(ə)l/ *adjective* capable of being divided. □ **divisibility** *noun*.

division /dɪˈvɪʒ(ə)n/ *noun* dividing, being divided; dividing one number by another; disagreement; one of parts into which thing is divided; administrative unit, esp. group of army units or of teams in sporting league. □ **divisional** *adjective*.

divisive /dɪˈvaɪsɪv/ *adjective* causing disagreement. □ **divisively** *adverb*; **divisiveness** *noun*.

divisor /dɪˈvaɪzə/ *noun* number by which another is to be divided.

divorce /dɪˈvɔːs/ ● *noun* legal dissolution of marriage; separation. ● *verb* (**-cing**) (usually as **divorced** *adjective*) (often + *from*) legally dissolve marriage of; separate by divorce; end marriage with by divorce; separate.

divorcee /dɪvɔːˈsiː/ *noun* divorced person.

divot /ˈdɪvət/ *noun* piece of turf dislodged by head of golf club.

divulge /dar'vʌldʒ/ *verb* (**-ging**) disclose (secret).

divvy /'dɪvɪ/ *colloquial* ● *noun* (*plural* **-ies**) dividend. ● *verb* (**-ies, -ied**) (often + *up*) share out.

Dixie /'dɪksɪ/ *noun* Southern States of US. □ **Dixieland** Dixie, kind of jazz.

dixie /'dɪksɪ/ *noun* large iron cooking pot.

DIY *abbreviation* do-it-yourself.

dizzy /'dɪzɪ/ ● *adjective* (**-ier, -iest**) giddy; dazed; causing dizziness. ● *verb* (**-ies, -ied**) make dizzy; bewilder. □ **dizzily** *adverb*; **dizziness** *noun*.

DJ *abbreviation* disc jockey; dinner jacket.

dl *abbreviation* decilitre(s).

D.Litt. *abbreviation* Doctor of Letters.

DM *abbreviation* Deutschmark.

dm *abbreviation* decimetre(s).

DNA *abbreviation* deoxyribonucleic acid (substance carrying genetic information in chromosomes).

do[1] /du:/ ● *verb* (*3rd singular present* **does** /dʌz/; *past* **did**; *past participle* **done** /dʌn/; *present participle* **doing**) perform, carry out; produce, make; impart; act, proceed; work at; be suitable, satisfy; attend to, deal with; fare; solve; *colloquial* finish; (as **done** *adjective*) finished, completely cooked; *colloquial* exhaust, defeat, kill; *colloquial* cater for; *slang* rob, swindle, prosecute, convict. ● *auxiliary verb used in questions and negative or emphatic statements and commands; as verbal substitute to avoid repetition.* ● *noun* (*plural* **dos** or **do's**) *colloquial* elaborate party or other undertaking. □ **do away with** *colloquial* abolish; kill; **do down** *colloquial* swindle, overcome; **do for** be sufficient for, *colloquial* (esp. as **done for** *adjective*) destroy or ruin or kill, *colloquial* do housework for; **do in** *slang* kill, *colloquial* exhaust; **do-it-yourself** (to be) done or made by householder etc.; **do up** fasten, *colloquial* restore, repair, dress up; **do with** (after *could*) would appreciate, would profit by; **do without** forgo, manage without.

do[2] = DOH.

do. *abbreviation* ditto.

docile /'dəʊsaɪl/ *adjective* submissive, easily managed. □ **docility** /-'sɪl-/ *noun*.

dock[1] ● *noun* enclosed harbour for loading, unloading, and repair of ships;

(usually in *plural*) range of docks with wharves, warehouses, etc. ● *verb* bring or come into dock; join (spacecraft) together in space, be thus joined. □ **dockyard** area with docks and equipment for building and repairing ships.

dock[2] *noun* enclosure in criminal court for accused.

dock[3] *noun* weed with broad leaves.

dock[4] *verb* cut short (tail); reduce or deduct (money etc.).

docker *noun* person employed to load and unload ships.

docket /'dɒkɪt/ ● *noun* document listing goods delivered, jobs done, contents of package, etc. ● *verb* (**-t-**) label with or enter on docket.

doctor /'dɒktə/ ● *noun* qualified medical practitioner; holder of doctorate. ● *verb* *colloquial* tamper with, adulterate; castrate, spay.

doctoral *adjective* of the degree of doctor.

doctorate /'dɒktərət/ *noun* highest university degree in any faculty.

doctrinaire /ˌdɒktrɪ'neə/ *adjective* applying theory or doctrine dogmatically.

doctrine /'dɒktrɪn/ *noun* what is taught; principle or set of principles of religious or political etc. belief. □ **doctrinal** /-'traɪn(ə)l/ *adjective*.

document ● *noun* /'dɒkjʊmənt/ something written etc. that provides record or evidence of events, circumstances, etc. ● *verb* /'dɒkjʊment/ prove by or support with documents. □ **documentation** *noun*.

documentary /ˌdɒkjʊ'mentərɪ/ ● *adjective* consisting of documents; factual, based on real events. ● *noun* (*plural* **-ies**) documentary film etc.

dodder /'dɒdə/ *verb* tremble, totter, be feeble. □ **dodderer** *noun*; **doddery** *adjective*.

doddle /'dɒd(ə)l/ *noun* *colloquial* easy task.

dodecagon /dəʊ'dekəgən/ *noun* plane figure with 12 sides.

dodecahedron /ˌdəʊdekə'hi:drən/ *noun* solid figure with 12 faces.

dodge ● *verb* (**-ging**) move quickly to elude pursuer, blow, etc.; evade by cunning or trickery. ● *noun* quick evasive movement; trick, clever expedient.

dodgem /'dɒdʒəm/ *noun* small electrically powered car at funfair, bumped into others in enclosure.

dodgy *adjective* (**-ier**, **-iest**) *colloquial* unreliable, risky.

dodo /'dəʊdəʊ/ *noun* (*plural* **-s**) large extinct flightless bird.

DoE *abbreviation* Department of the Environment.

doe *noun* (*plural* same or **-s**) female fallow deer, reindeer, hare, or rabbit.

does *3rd singular present of* DO¹.

doesn't /'dʌz(ə)nt/ does not.

doff *verb* take off (hat etc.).

dog ● *noun* 4-legged flesh-eating animal of many breeds akin to wolf etc.; male of this or of fox or wolf; *colloquial* despicable person; (**the dogs**) *colloquial* greyhound racing; mechanical device for gripping. ● *verb* (**-gg-**) follow closely; pursue, track. □ **dogcart** two-wheeled driving-cart with cross seats back to back; **dog-collar** *colloquial* clergyman's stiff collar; **dog days** hottest period of year; **dog-eared** (of book-page etc.) with worn corners; **dog-end** *slang* cigarette-end; **dogfight** fight between aircraft, rough fight; **dogfish** small shark; **doghouse** *US & Australian* kennel (**in the doghouse** *slang* in disgrace); **dog rose** wild hedge-rose; **dogsbody** *colloquial* drudge; **dog-star** Sirius; **dog-tired** tired out.

doge /dəʊdʒ/ *noun historical* chief magistrate of Venice or Genoa.

dogged /'dɒɡɪd/ *adjective* tenacious. □ **doggedly** *adverb*.

doggerel /'dɒɡər(ə)l/ *noun* poor or trivial verse.

doggo /'dɒɡəʊ/ *adverb slang* □ **lie doggo** wait motionless or hidden.

doggy *adjective* of or like dogs; devoted to dogs. □ **doggy bag** bag for restaurant customer to take home leftovers; **doggy-paddle** elementary swimming stroke.

dogma /'dɒɡmə/ *noun* principle, tenet; doctrinal system.

dogmatic /dɒɡ'mætɪk/ *adjective* imposing personal opinions; authoritative, arrogant. □ **dogmatically** *adverb*; **dogmatism** /'dɒɡmətɪz(ə)m/ *noun*.

doh /dəʊ/ *noun* (also **do**) *Music* first note of scale in tonic sol-fa.

doily /'dɔɪlɪ/ *noun* (*plural* **-ies**) small lacy paper mat placed on plate for cakes etc.

doings /'duːɪŋz/ *plural noun* actions, exploits; *slang* thing(s) needed.

Dolby /'dɒlbɪ/ *noun proprietary term* system used esp. in tape-recording to reduce hiss.

doldrums /'dɒldrəmz/ *plural noun* (usually **the doldrums**) low spirits; period of inactivity; equatorial ocean region of calms.

dole ● *noun* unemployment benefit; charitable (esp. niggardly) gift or distribution. ● *verb* (**-ling**) (usually + *out*) distribute sparingly. □ **on the dole** *colloquial* receiving unemployment benefit.

doleful /'dəʊlfʊl/ *adjective* mournful; dreary, dismal. □ **dolefully** *adverb*.

doll ● *noun* model of esp. infant human figure as child's toy; *colloquial* attractive young woman; ventriloquist's dummy. ● *verb* (+ *up*) *colloquial* dress smartly.

dollar /'dɒlə/ *noun* chief monetary unit in US, Australia, etc.

dollop /'dɒləp/ *noun* shapeless lump of food etc.

dolly *noun* (*plural* **-ies**) *child's word for* doll; movable platform for cine-camera etc.

dolman sleeve /'dɒlmən/ *noun* loose sleeve cut in one piece with bodice.

dolmen /'dɒlmən/ *noun* megalithic tomb with large flat stone laid on upright ones.

dolomite /'dɒləmaɪt/ *noun* mineral or rock of calcium magnesium carbonate.

dolphin /'dɒlfɪn/ *noun* large porpoise-like sea mammal.

dolt /dəʊlt/ *noun* stupid person. □ **doltish** *adjective*.

Dom *noun*: title prefixed to names of some RC dignitaries and Carthusian and Benedictine monks.

domain /də'meɪn/ *noun* area ruled over; realm; estate etc. under one's control; sphere of authority.

dome ● *noun* rounded vault as roof; dome-shaped thing. ● *verb* (**-ming**) (usually as **domed** *adjective*) cover with or shape as dome.

domestic /də'mestɪk/ ● *adjective* of home, household, or family affairs; of one's own country; (of animal) tamed; fond of home life. ● *noun* household servant.

domesticate /dəˈmestɪkeɪt/ *verb* (**-ting**) tame (animal) to live with humans; accustom to housework etc. □ **domestication** *noun*.

domesticity /dɒməˈstɪsɪtɪ/ *noun* being domestic; home life.

domicile /ˈdɒmɪsaɪl/ ● *noun* dwelling place; place of permanent residence. ● *verb* (**-ling**) (usually as **domiciled** *adjective*) (usually + *at, in*) settle in a place.

domiciliary /dɒmɪˈsɪlɪərɪ/ *adjective formal* (esp. of doctor's etc. visit) to or at person's home.

dominant /ˈdɒmɪnənt/ ● *adjective* dominating, prevailing. ● *noun Music* 5th note of diatonic scale. □ **dominance** *noun*.

dominate /ˈdɒmɪneɪt/ *verb* (**-ting**) command, control; be most influential or obvious; (of place) overlook. □ **domination** *noun*.

domineer /dɒmɪˈnɪə/ *verb* (often as **domineering** *adjective*) behave overbearingly.

Dominican /dəˈmɪnɪkən/ ● *noun* friar or nun of order founded by St Dominic. ● *adjective* of this order.

dominion /dəˈmɪnjən/ *noun* sovereignty; realm; domain; *historical* self-governing territory of British Commonwealth.

domino /ˈdɒmɪnəʊ/ *noun* (*plural* **-es**) any of 28 small oblong pieces marked with 0–6 pips in each half; (in *plural*) game played with these; loose cloak worn with half-mask.

don[1] *noun* university teacher, esp. senior member of college at Oxford or Cambridge; (**Don**) *Spanish title prefixed to man's name.*

don[2] *verb* (**-nn-**) put on (garment).

donate /dəʊˈneɪt/ *verb* (**-ting**) give (money etc.), esp. to charity.

donation *noun* donating, being donated; thing (esp. money) donated.

done /dʌn/ ● *past participle* of DO[1]. ● *adjective* completed; cooked; *colloquial* socially acceptable; (often + *in*) *colloquial* tired out; (esp. as *interjection* in response to offer etc.) accepted. □ **be done with** have or be finished with; **done for** *colloquial* in serious trouble.

doner kebab /ˈdɒnə kɪˈbæb/ *noun* spiced lamb cooked on spit and served in slices, often with pitta bread.

donkey /ˈdɒŋkɪ/ *noun* (*plural* **-s**) domestic ass; *colloquial* stupid person. □ **donkey jacket** thick weatherproof jacket; **donkey's years** *colloquial* very long time; **donkey-work** drudgery.

Donna /ˈdɒnə/ *noun*: title of Italian, Spanish, or Portuguese lady.

donnish *adjective* like a college don; pedantic.

donor /ˈdəʊnə/ *noun* person who donates; person who provides blood for transfusion, organ for transplantation, etc.

don't /dəʊnt/ ● *verb* do not. ● *noun* prohibition.

doodle /ˈduːd(ə)l/ ● *verb* (**-ling**) scribble or draw absent-mindedly. ● *noun* such scribble or drawing.

doom /duːm/ ● *noun* terrible fate or destiny; ruin, death. ● *verb* (usually + *to*) condemn or destine; (esp. as **doomed** *adjective*) consign to ruin, destruction, etc. □ **doomsday** day of Last Judgement.

door /dɔː/ *noun* hinged or sliding barrier closing entrance to building, room, cupboard, etc.; doorway. □ **doormat** mat for wiping shoes on, *colloquial* subservient person; **doorstep** step or area immediately outside esp. outer door, *slang* thick slice of bread; **doorstop** device for keeping door open or to keep it from striking wall; **door-to-door** (of selling etc.) done at each house in turn; **doorway** opening filled by door; **out of doors** in(to) open air.

dope ● *noun slang* drug, esp. narcotic; thick liquid used as lubricant etc.; varnish; *slang* stupid person; *slang* information. ● *verb* (**-ping**) give or add drug to; apply dope to.

dopey *adjective* (also **dopy**) (**dopier**, **dopiest**) *colloquial* half asleep, stupefied; stupid.

doppelganger /ˈdɒp(ə)lgæŋə/ *noun* (also **doppelgänger** /-geŋə/) apparition or double of living person.

Doppler effect /ˈdɒplə/ *noun* change in frequency of esp. sound waves when source and observer are moving closer or apart.

dormant /ˈdɔːmənt/ *adjective* lying inactive; sleeping; inactive. □ **dormancy** *noun*.

dormer /ˈdɔːmə/ *noun* (in full **dormer window**) upright window in sloping roof.

dormitory /ˈdɔːmɪtərɪ/ *noun* (*plural* -ies) sleeping-room with several beds; (in full **dormitory town** etc.) commuter town or suburb.

dormouse /ˈdɔːmaʊs/ *noun* (*plural* -mice) small mouselike hibernating rodent.

dorsal /ˈdɔːs(ə)l/ *adjective* of or on back.

dory /ˈdɔːrɪ/ *noun* (*plural* same or -ies) edible sea fish.

dosage *noun* size of dose; giving of dose.

dose /dəʊs/ ● *noun* single portion of medicine; amount of radiation received. ● *verb* (-sing) give medicine to; (+ *with*) treat with.

doss *verb* (often + *down*) *slang* sleep on makeshift bed or in doss-house. □ **doss-house** cheap lodging house. □ **dosser** *noun*.

dossier /ˈdɒsɪeɪ/ *noun* file containing information about person, event, etc.

dot *noun* small spot, esp. as decimal point, part of *i* or *j* etc.; shorter signal of the two in Morse code. ● *verb* (-tt-) mark or scatter with dot(s); (often + *about*) scatter like dots; place dot over (letter); partly cover as with dots; *slang* hit. □ **dotted line** line of dots for signature etc. on document; **on the dot** exactly on time.

dotage /ˈdəʊtɪdʒ/ *noun* feeble-minded senility.

dote *verb* (-ting) (usually + *on* or as **doting** *adjective*) be excessively fond of.

dotterel /ˈdɒtər(ə)l/ *noun* small plover.

dotty *adjective* (-ier, -iest) *colloquial* eccentric, silly, crazy; (+ *about*) infatuated with.

double /ˈdʌb(ə)l/ ● *adjective* consisting of two things; multiplied by two; twice as much or many etc.; twice the usual size, quantity, strength, etc.; having some part double; (of flower) with two or more circles of petals; ambiguous; deceitful. ● *adverb* at or to twice the amount; two together. ● *noun* double quantity (of spirits etc.) or thing; twice the amount or quantity; person or thing looking exactly like

another; (in *plural*) game between two pairs of players; pair of victories; bet in which winnings and stake from first bet are transferred to second. ● *verb* (-ling) make or become double; increase twofold; amount to twice as much as; fold over upon itself; become folded; play (two parts) in same play etc.; (usually + *as*) play twofold role; turn sharply; *Nautical* get round (headland). □ **at the double** running; **double agent** spy working for two rival countries etc.; **double-barrelled** (of gun) having two barrels, (of surname) hyphenated; **double-bass** largest instrument of violin family; **double-book** mistakenly reserve (seat, room, etc.) for two people at once; **double-breasted** (of garment) overlapping across body; **double chin** chin with fold of flesh below it; **double cream** thick cream with high fat-content; **double-cross** deceive or betray; **double-dealing** (practising) deceit, esp. in business; **double-decker** bus etc. with two decks, *colloquial* sandwich with two layers of filling; **double Dutch** *colloquial* gibberish; **double eagle** figure of eagle with two heads; **double-edged** presenting both a danger and an advantage; **double figures** numbers from 10 to 99; **double glazing** two layers of glass in window; **double negative** *Grammar* negative statement (incorrectly) containing two negative elements (see note below); **double pneumonia** pneumonia of both lungs; **double standard** rule or principle not impartially applied; **double take** delayed reaction to unexpected element of situation; **double-talk** (usually deliberately) ambiguous or misleading speech.

■ **Usage** Double negatives like *He didn't do nothing* and *I'm never going nowhere like that* are mistakes in standard English because one negative element is redundant. However, two negatives are perfectly acceptable in, for instance, *a not ungenerous sum* (meaning 'quite a generous sum').

double entendre /duːˈb(ə)l ɑːnˈtɑːndrə/ *noun* phrase capable of two meanings, one usually indecent. [French]

doublet /ˈdʌblɪt/ noun historical man's close-fitting jacket; one of pair of similar things.

doubloon /dʌˈbluːn/ noun historical Spanish gold coin.

doubt /daʊt/ ● noun uncertainty; undecided state of mind; cynicism; uncertain state. ● verb feel uncertain or undecided about; hesitate to believe; call in question. □ **in doubt** open to question; **no doubt** certainly, admittedly.

doubtful adjective feeling or causing doubt; unreliable. □ **doubtfully** adverb.

doubtless adverb certainly; probably.

douche /duːʃ/ ● noun jet of liquid applied to part of body for cleansing or medicinal purposes; device for producing this. ● verb (**-ching**) treat with douche; use douche.

dough /dəʊ/ noun thick paste of flour mixed with liquid for baking; slang money. □ **doughnut** (US **donut**) small fried cake of sweetened dough. □ **doughy** adjective (**-ier**, **-iest**).

doughty /ˈdaʊtɪ/ adjective (**-ier**, **-iest**) archaic valiant. □ **doughtily** adverb.

dour /dʊə/ adjective stern, grim, obstinate.

douse /daʊs/ verb (also **dowse**) (**-sing**) throw water over; plunge into water; extinguish (light).

dove /dʌv/ noun bird with short legs and full breast; advocate of peaceful policies; gentle or innocent person. □ **dovecot(e)** pigeon house.

dovetail ● noun mortise-and-tenon joint shaped like dove's spread tail. ● verb fit together, combine neatly; join with dovetails.

dowager /ˈdaʊədʒə/ noun woman with title or property from her late husband.

dowdy /ˈdaʊdɪ/ adjective (**-ier**, **-iest**) (of clothes) unattractively dull; dressed dowdily. □ **dowdily** adverb; **dowdiness** noun.

dowel /ˈdaʊəl/ noun cylindrical peg for holding parts of structure together.

dowelling noun rods for cutting into dowels.

dower /ˈdaʊə/ noun widow's share for life of husband's estate.

down¹ /daʊn/ ● adverb towards or into lower place, esp. to ground; in lower place or position; to or in place regarded as lower, esp. southwards or away from major city or university; in or into low or weaker position or condition; losing by; (of a computer system) out of action; from earlier to later time; in written or recorded form. ● preposition downwards along, through, or into; from top to bottom of; along; at lower part of. ● adjective directed downwards. ● verb colloquial knock or bring etc. down; swallow. ● noun reverse of fortune; colloquial period of depression. □ **be down to** be the responsibility of, have nothing left but; **down and out** destitute; **down-and-out** destitute person; **downcast** dejected, (of eyes) looking down; **downfall** fall from prosperity or power, cause of this; **downgrade** reduce in rank etc.; **downhearted** despondent; **downhill** adverb in descending direction, on a decline, adjective sloping down, declining; **down in the mouth** looking unhappy; **down-market** of or to cheaper sector of market; **downpour** heavy fall of rain; **downside** negative aspect, drawback; **downstairs** adverb down the stairs, to or on lower floor, adjective situated downstairs; **downstream** in direction of flow of stream etc.; **down-to-earth** practical, realistic; **downtown** US (of) lower or central part of town or city; **downtrodden** oppressed; **downturn** decline, esp. in economic activity; **down under** colloquial in Australia or NZ; **downwind** in direction in which wind is blowing; **down with** expressing rejection of person or thing; **have a down on** colloquial be hostile to. □ **downward** adjective & adverb; **downwards** adverb.

down² /daʊn/ noun baby birds' fluffy covering; bird's under-plumage; fine soft feathers or hairs.

down³ /daʊn/ noun open rolling land; (in plural) chalk uplands of S. England etc.

downright ● adjective plain, straightforward; utter. ● adverb thoroughly.

Down's syndrome noun congenital disorder with mental retardation and physical abnormalities.

downy adjective (**-ier**, **-iest**) of, like, or covered with down.

dowry /ˈdaʊərɪ/ noun (plural **-ies**) property brought by bride to her husband.

dowse[1] /dauz/ *verb* (**-sing**) search for underground water or minerals by holding stick or rod which dips abruptly when over right spot. □ **dowser** *noun*.

dowse[2] = DOUSE.

doxology /dɒkˈsɒlədʒɪ/ *noun* (*plural* **-ies**) liturgical hymn etc. of praise to God.

doyen /ˈdɔɪən/ *noun* (*feminine* **doyenne** /dɔɪˈen/) senior member of group.

doz. *abbreviation* dozen.

doze ● *verb* (**-zing**) sleep lightly, be half asleep. ● *noun* short light sleep. □ **doze off** fall lightly asleep.

dozen /ˈdʌz(ə)n/ *noun* (*plural* same (after numeral) or **-s**) set of twelve; (**dozens**, usually + *of*) *colloquial* very many.

D.Phil. *abbreviation* Doctor of Philosophy.

Dr *abbreviation* Doctor.

drab *adjective* (**-bb-**) dull, uninteresting; of dull brownish colour. □ **drabness** *noun*.

drachm /dræm/ *noun* weight formerly used by apothecaries, = $\frac{1}{8}$ ounce.

drachma /ˈdrækmə/ *noun* (*plural* **-s**) chief monetary unit of Greece.

Draconian /drəˈkəʊnɪən/ *adjective* (of laws) harsh, cruel.

draft /drɑːft/ ● *noun* preliminary written outline of scheme or version of speech, document, etc.; written order for payment of money by bank; drawing of money on this; detachment from larger group; selection of this; *US* conscription; *US* draught. ● *verb* prepare draft of; select for special duty or purpose; *US* conscript.

draftsman /ˈdrɑːftsmən/ *noun* person who drafts documents; person who makes drawings.

drafty *US* = DRAUGHTY.

drag ● *verb* (**-gg-**) pull along with effort; (allow to) trail; (of time etc.) pass tediously or slowly; search bottom of (river etc.) with grapnels, nets, etc. ● *noun* obstruction to progress, retarding force; *colloquial* boring or tiresome task, person, etc.; lure before hounds as substitute for fox; apparatus for dredging; *colloquial* pull at cigarette; *slang* women's clothes worn by men. □ **drag out** protract.

draggle /ˈdræg(ə)l/ *verb* (**-ling**) make dirty and wet by trailing; hang trailing.

dragon /ˈdrægən/ *noun* mythical monster like reptile, usually with wings and able to breathe fire; fierce woman.

dragonfly *noun* (*plural* **-ies**) large long-bodied gauzy-winged insect.

dragoon /drəˈguːn/ ● *noun* cavalryman; fierce fellow. ● *verb* (+ *into*) coerce or bully into.

drain ● *verb* draw off liquid from; draw off (liquid); flow or trickle away; dry or become dry; exhaust; drink to the dregs; empty (glass etc.) by drinking. ● *noun* channel or pipe carrying off liquid, sewage, etc.; constant outflow or expenditure. □ **draining board** sloping grooved surface beside sink for draining dishes; **drainpipe** pipe for carrying off water etc.

drainage *noun* draining; system of drains; what is drained off.

drake *noun* male duck.

dram *noun* small drink of spirits etc.; drachm.

drama /ˈdrɑːmə/ *noun* play for stage or broadcasting; art of writing, acting, or presenting plays; dramatic event or quality.

dramatic /drəˈmætɪk/ *adjective* of drama; unexpected and exciting; striking; theatrical. □ **dramatically** *adverb*.

dramatics *plural noun* (often treated as *singular*) performance of plays; exaggerated behaviour.

dramatis personae /ˈdræmətɪs pɜːˈsəʊnaɪ/ *plural noun* characters in a play.

dramatist /ˈdræmətɪst/ *noun* writer of plays.

dramatize /ˈdræmətaɪz/ *verb* (also **-ise**) (**-zing** or **-sing**) convert into play; make dramatic; behave dramatically. □ **dramatization** *noun*.

drank *past of* DRINK.

drape ● *verb* (**-ping**) cover or hang or adorn with cloth etc.; arrange in graceful folds. ● *noun* (in *plural*) *US* curtains.

draper *noun* retailer of textile fabrics.

drapery *noun* (*plural* **-ies**) clothing or hangings arranged in folds; draper's trade or fabrics.

drastic /ˈdræstɪk/ *adjective* far-reaching in effect; severe. □ **drastically** *adverb*.

drat *colloquial* ● *verb* (**-tt-**) (usually as *interjection*) curse. ● *interjection* expressing annoyance.

draught /drɑːft/ *noun* (*US* **draft**) current of air indoors; traction; depth of water needed to float ship; drawing of liquor from cask etc.; single act of drinking or inhaling; amount so drunk; (in *plural*) game for two with 12 pieces each, on **draughtboard** (like chessboard). □ **draught beer** beer drawn from cask, not bottled.

draughtsman /ˈdrɑːftsmən/ *noun* person who makes drawings; piece in game of draughts.

draughty *adjective* (*US* **drafty**) (**-ier, -iest**) (of a room etc.) letting in sharp currents of air.

draw ● *verb* (*past* **drew** /druː/; *past participle* **drawn**) pull or cause to move towards or after one; pull (thing) up, over, or across; attract; pull (curtains) open or shut; take in; (+ *at, on*) inhale from; extract; take from or out; make (line, mark, or outline); make (picture) in this way; represent (thing) in this way; finish (game etc.) with equal scores; proceed to specified position; infer; elicit, evoke; induce; haul up (water) from well; bring out (liquid from tap, wound, etc.); draw lots; obtain by lot; (of tea) infuse; (of chimney, pipe, etc.) promote or allow draught; write out (bill, cheque); search (cover) for game etc.; (as **drawn** *adjective*) looking strained and tense. ● *noun* act of drawing; person or thing that draws custom or attention; drawing of lots; raffle; drawn game etc. □ **draw back** withdraw; **drawback** disadvantage; **drawbridge** hinged retractable bridge; **draw in** (of days etc.) become shorter, (of train etc.) arrive at station; **draw out** prolong, induce to talk, (of days etc.) become longer; **drawstring** string or cord threaded through waistband, bag opening, etc.; **draw up** draft (document etc.), bring into order, come to a halt, (**draw oneself up**) make oneself erect.

drawer /ˈdrɔːə/ *noun* person who draws; (also /drɔː/) receptacle sliding in and out of frame (**chest of drawers**) or of table etc.; (in *plural*) knickers, underpants.

drawing *noun* art of representing by line with pencil etc.; picture etc. made thus. □ **drawing-board** board on which paper is fixed for drawing on;

drawing-pin flat-headed pin for fastening paper to a surface.

drawing-room *noun* room in private house for sitting or entertaining in.

drawl ● *verb* speak with drawn-out vowel sounds. ● *noun* drawling utterance or way of speaking.

dray *noun* low cart without sides for heavy loads, esp. beer barrels.

dread /dred/ ● *verb* fear greatly, esp. in advance. ● *noun* great fear or apprehension. ● *adjective* dreaded; *archaic* awe-inspiring.

dreadful *adjective* terrible; *colloquial* very annoying, very bad. □ **dreadfully** *adverb*.

dream ● *noun* series of scenes in mind of sleeping person; daydream or fantasy; ideal; aspiration. ● *verb* (*past & past participle* **dreamt** /dremt/ or **dreamed**) experience dream; imagine as in dream; (esp. in negative; + *of, that*) consider possible or acceptable; be inactive or unrealistic. □ **dreamer** *noun*.

dreamy *adjective* (**-ier, -iest**) given to daydreaming; dreamlike; vague; *colloquial* delightful. □ **dreamily** *adverb*.

dreary /ˈdrɪərɪ/ *adjective* (**-ier, -iest**) dismal, gloomy, dull. □ **drearily** *adverb*; **dreariness** *noun*.

dredge[1] ● *noun* apparatus used to collect oysters etc., or to clear mud etc., from bottom of sea etc. ● *verb* (**-ging**) bring up or clear (mud etc.) with dredge; (+ *up*) bring up (something forgotten); clean with or use dredge.

dredge[2] *verb* (**-ging**) sprinkle with flour etc.

dredger[1] *noun* boat with dredge; dredge.

dredger[2] *noun* container with perforated lid for sprinkling flour etc.

dregs *plural noun* sediment, grounds; worst part.

drench ● *verb* wet thoroughly; force (animal) to take medicine. ● *noun* dose of medicine for animal.

dress ● *verb* put clothes on; have and wear clothes; put on evening dress; arrange or adorn; put dressing on (wound etc.); prepare (poultry, crab, etc.) for cooking or eating; apply manure to. ● *noun* woman's one-piece garment of bodice and skirt; clothing, esp.

whole outfit. □ **dress circle** first gallery in theatre; **dressmaker** person who makes women's clothes, esp. for a living; **dress rehearsal** (esp. final) rehearsal in costume; **dress up** put on special clothes, make (person, thing) more attractive or interesting.

dressage /'dresɑːʒ/ *noun* training of horse in obedience and deportment.

dresser[1] /'dresə/ *noun* tall kitchen sideboard with shelves.

dresser[2] *noun* person who helps actors or actresses to dress for stage.

dressing *noun* putting one's clothes on; sauce, esp. of oil, vinegar, etc., for salads; bandage, ointment, etc. for wound; compost etc. spread over land. □ **dressing down** *colloquial* scolding; **dressing gown** loose robe worn while one is not fully dressed; **dressing table** table with mirror etc. for use while dressing, applying make-up, etc.

dressy *adjective* (**-ier, -iest**) *colloquial* (of clothes or person) smart, elegant.

drew *past of* DRAW.

drey /dreɪ/ *noun* squirrel's nest.

dribble /'drɪb(ə)l/ ● *verb* (**-ling**) allow saliva to flow from the mouth; flow or allow to flow in drops; *Football etc.* move (ball) forward with slight touches of feet etc. ● *noun* act of dribbling; dribbling flow.

driblet /'drɪblɪt/ *noun* small quantity (of liquid etc.).

dribs and drabs *plural noun colloquial* small scattered amounts.

dried *past & past participle of* DRY.

drier[1] *comparative of* DRY.

drier[2] /'draɪə/ *noun* (also **dryer**) machine for drying hair, laundry, etc.

driest *superlative of* DRY.

drift ● *noun* slow movement or variation; this caused by current; intention, meaning, etc. of what is said etc.; mass of snow etc. heaped up by wind; state of inaction; deviation of craft etc. due to current, wind, etc. ● *verb* be carried by or as if by current of air or water; progress casually or aimlessly; (of current) carry; heap or be heaped into drifts. □ **drift-net** net for sea fishing, which is allowed to drift; **driftwood** wood floating on moving water or washed ashore.

drifter *noun* aimless person; fishing boat with drift-net.

drill[1] ● *noun* tool or machine for boring holes; instruction in military exercises; routine procedure in emergency; thorough training, esp. by repetition; *colloquial* recognized procedure. ● *verb* make hole in or through with drill; make (hole) with drill; train or be trained by drill.

drill[2] ● *noun* machine for making furrows, sowing, and covering seed; small furrow for sowing seed in; row of seeds sown by drill. ● *verb* plant in drills.

drill[3] *noun* coarse twilled cotton or linen fabric.

drill[4] *noun* W. African baboon related to mandrill.

drily *adverb* (also **dryly**) in a dry way.

drink ● *verb* (*past* **drank**; *past participle* **drunk**) swallow (liquid); take alcohol, esp. to excess; (of plant etc.) absorb (moisture). ● *noun* liquid for drinking; draught or specified amount of this; alcoholic liquor; glass, portion, etc., of this; (**the drink**) *colloquial* the sea. □ **drink-driver** *colloquial* person driving with excess alcohol in the blood; **drink in** listen eagerly to; **drink to** toast, wish success to; **drink up** drink all or remainder of. □ **drinker** *noun*.

drip ● *verb* (**-pp-**) fall or let fall in drops; (often + *with*) be so wet as to shed drops. ● *noun* liquid falling in drops; drop of liquid; sound of dripping; *colloquial* dull or ineffectual person.

drip-dry ● *verb* dry or leave to dry crease-free when hung up. ● *adjective* able to be drip-dried.

drip-feed ● *verb* feed intravenously in drops. ● *noun* feeding thus; apparatus for doing this.

dripping *noun* fat melted from roasting meat.

drive ● *verb* (**-ving**; *past* **drove** /drəʊv/; *past participle* **driven** /'drɪv(ə)n/) urge forward, esp. forcibly; compel; force into specified state; operate and direct (vehicle etc.); carry or be carried in vehicle; strike golf ball from tee; (of wind etc.) carry along, propel. ● *noun* excursion in vehicle; driveway; street, road; motivation and energy; inner urge; forcible stroke of bat etc.; organized group effort; transmission of power to machinery or wheels of motor vehicle etc.; organized whist, bingo, etc. competition. □ **drive at** seek, intend, mean; **drive-in** (bank, cinema, etc.) used while one sits in one's car; **driveway** private road through garden to house; **driving licence** licence permitting person to drive vehicle; **driving test** official test of competence to drive; **driving wheel** wheel transmitting power of vehicle to ground.

drivel /ˈdrɪv(ə)l/ • *noun* silly nonsense. • *verb* (**-ll-**; *US* **-l-**) talk drivel; run at mouth or nose.

driver *noun* person who drives; golf club for driving from tee.

drizzle /ˈdrɪz(ə)l/ • *noun* very fine rain. • *verb* (**-ling**) fall in very fine drops.

droll /drəʊl/ *adjective* quaintly amusing, strange, odd. □ **drollery** *noun* (*plural* **-ies**).

dromedary /ˈdrɒmɪdərɪ/ *noun* (*plural* **-ies**) one-humped (esp. Arabian) camel bred for riding.

drone • *noun* non-working male of honey-bee; idler; deep humming sound; monotonous speaking tone; bass-pipe of bagpipes or its continuous note. • *verb* (**-ning**) make deep humming sound; speak or utter monotonously.

drool *verb* slobber, dribble; (often + *over*) admire extravagantly.

droop /druːp/ • *verb* bend or hang down, esp. from fatigue or lack of food, drink, etc.; flag. • *noun* drooping position; loss of spirit. □ **droopy** *adjective*.

drop • *noun* globule of liquid that falls, hangs, or adheres to surface; very small amount of liquid; abrupt fall or slope; amount of this; act of dropping; fall in prices, temperature, etc.; drop-shaped thing, esp. pendant or sweet; (in *plural*) liquid medicine swallowed in drops. • *verb* (**-pp-**) fall, allow to fall; let go; fall, let fall, or shed in drops; sink down from exhaustion or injury; cease, lapse; abandon; *colloquial* cease to associate with or discuss; set down (passenger etc.); utter or be uttered casually; fall or let fall in direction, amount, degree, pitch, etc.; (of person) jump down lightly; let oneself fall; omit; give birth to (lamb); deliver from the air by parachute etc.; *Football* send (ball) or score (goal) by

drop-kick. □ **drop back**, **behind** fall back, get left behind; **drop in**, **by** *colloquial* visit casually; **drop-kick** kick at football made by dropping ball and kicking it as it touches ground; **drop off** fall asleep, drop (passenger); **drop out** (often + *of*) *colloquial* cease to participate (in); **drop-out** *colloquial* person who has dropped out of esp. course of study or conventional society; **drop scone** scone made by dropping spoonful of mixture into pan etc.; **drop-shot** tennis shot dropping abruptly after clearing net. □ **droplet** *noun*.

dropper *noun* device for releasing liquid in drops.

droppings *plural noun* dung; thing that falls or has fallen in drops.

dropsy /ˈdrɒpsɪ/ *noun* oedema. □ **dropsical** *adjective*.

dross *noun* rubbish; scum of molten metal; impurities.

drought /draʊt/ *noun* prolonged absence of rain.

drove[1] *past of* DRIVE.

drove[2] /drəʊv/ *noun* moving crowd; (in *plural*) *colloquial* great number; herd or flock moving together.

drover *noun* herder of cattle.

drown /draʊn/ *verb* kill or die by submersion; submerge; flood; drench; deaden (grief etc.) by drinking; (often + *out*) overpower (sound) with louder sound.

drowse /draʊz/ *verb* (**-sing**) be lightly asleep.

drowsy /ˈdraʊzɪ/ *adjective* (**-ier**, **-iest**) very sleepy, almost asleep. □ **drowsily** *adverb*; **drowsiness** *noun*.

drub *verb* (**-bb-**) thrash, beat; defeat thoroughly. □ **drubbing** *noun*.

drudge • *noun* person who does dull, laborious, or menial work. • *verb* (**-ging**) work hard or laboriously. □ **drudgery** *noun*.

drug • *noun* medicinal substance; (esp. addictive) hallucinogen, stimulant, narcotic, etc. • *verb* (**-gg-**) add drug to (drink, food, etc.); administer drug to; stupefy. □ **drugstore** *US* combined chemist's shop and café.

drugget /ˈdrʌɡɪt/ *noun* coarse woven fabric used for floor coverings etc.

druggist *noun* pharmacist.

Druid /'dru:ɪd/ noun ancient Celtic priest; member of a modern Druidic order, esp. the Gorsedd. □ **Druidic** /-'ɪdɪk/ adjective; **Druidism** noun.

drum ● noun hollow esp. cylindrical percussion instrument covered at one or both ends with plastic, skin, etc.; sound of this; cylindrical structure or object; cylinder used for storage etc.; eardrum. ● verb (**-mm-**) play drum; beat or tap continuously with fingers etc.; (of bird etc.) make loud noise with wings. □ **drumbeat** stroke or sound of stroke on drum; **drum brake** kind in which shoes on vehicle press against drum on wheel; **drum into** drive (facts etc.) into (person) by persistence; **drum machine** electronic device that simulates percussion; **drum major** leader of marching band; **drum majorette** female baton-twirling member of parading group; **drum out** dismiss with ignominy; **drumstick** stick for beating drum, lower leg of fowl for eating; **drum up** summon or get by vigorous effort.

drummer noun player of drum.

drunk /drʌŋk/ ● past participle of DRINK. ● adjective lacking control from drinking alcohol; (often + with) overcome with joy, success, power, etc. ● noun person who is drunk, esp. habitually.

drunkard /'drʌŋkəd/ noun person habitually drunk.

drunken /'drʌŋkən/ adjective drunk; caused by or involving drunkenness; often drunk. □ **drunkenly** adverb; **drunkenness** noun.

drupe /dru:p/ noun fleshy stone fruit.

dry ● adjective (**drier**, **driest**) free from moisture, esp. with moisture having evaporated, drained away, etc; (of eyes) free from tears; (of climate) not rainy; (of river, well, etc.) dried up; (of wine etc.) not sweet; plain, unelaborated, uninteresting; (of sense of humour) ironic, understated; prohibiting sale of alcohol; (of bread) without butter etc.; (of provisions etc.) solid, not liquid; colloquial thirsty. ● verb (**dries**, **dried**) make or become dry; (usually as **dried** adjective) preserve (food) by removing moisture. □ **dry-clean** clean (clothes etc.) with solvents without water; **dry-fly** (of fishing) with floating artificial fly; **dry ice** solid carbon dioxide;

dry out make or become fully dry, treat or be treated for alcoholism; **dry rot** decay in wood not exposed to air, fungi causing this; **dry run** colloquial rehearsal; **dry-shod** without wetting one's shoes; **dry up** make or become completely dry, dry dishes. □ **dryness** noun.

dryad /'draɪæd/ noun wood nymph.

dryer = DRIER[2].

dryly = DRILY.

D.Sc. abbreviation Doctor of Science.

DSC, DSM, DSO abbreviations Distinguished Service Cross, Medal, Order.

DSS abbreviation Department of Social Security (formerly DHSS).

DT abbreviation (also **DT's** /di:'ti:z/) delirium tremens.

DTI abbreviation Department of Trade and Industry.

dual /'dju:əl/ ● adjective in two parts; twofold; double. ● noun Grammar dual number or form. □ **dual carriageway** road with dividing strip between traffic flowing in opposite directions; **dual control** two linked sets of controls, esp. of vehicle used for teaching driving etc., enabling operation by either of two people. □ **duality** /-'æl-/ noun.

dub[1] verb (**-bb-**) make (person) into knight; give name or nickname to.

dub[2] verb (**-bb-**) provide (film etc.) with alternative, esp. translated, soundtrack; add (sound effects, music) to film or broadcast.

dubbin /'dʌbɪn/ noun (also **dubbing**) grease for softening and waterproofing leather.

dubiety /dju:'baɪətɪ/ noun literary doubt.

dubious /'dju:bɪəs/ adjective doubtful; questionable; unreliable. □ **dubiously** adverb; **dubiousness** noun.

ducal /'dju:k(ə)l/ adjective of or like duke.

ducat /'dʌkət/ noun gold coin formerly current in most European countries.

duchess /'dʌtʃɪs/ noun duke's wife or widow; woman holding rank of duke.

duchy /'dʌtʃɪ/ noun (plural **-ies**) duke's or duchess's territory.

duck ● noun (plural same or **-s**) swimming bird, esp. domesticated form of mallard or wild duck; female of this; its flesh as food; *Cricket* batsman's score of 0; (also **ducks**) *colloquial* (esp. as form of address) darling. ● *verb* bob down, esp. to avoid being seen or hit; dip head briefly under water; plunge (person) briefly in water. □ **duckweed** any of various plants that grow on surface of still water.

duckling *noun* young duck.

duct *noun* channel, tube; tube in body carrying secretions etc.

ductile /ˈdʌktaɪl/ *adjective* (of metal) capable of being drawn into wire; pliable; easily moulded; docile. □ **ductility** /-ˈtɪl-/ *noun*.

ductless *adjective* (of gland) secreting directly into bloodstream.

dud *slang* ● *noun* useless or broken thing; counterfeit article; (in *plural*) clothes, rags. ● *adjective* defective, useless.

dude /duːd/ *noun slang* fellow; *US* dandy; *US* city man staying on ranch.

dudgeon /ˈdʌdʒ(ə)n/ *noun* resentment; indignation.

due ● *adjective* owing, payable; merited, appropriate; (often + *to do*) expected or under obligation to do something or arrive at certain time. ● *noun* what one owes or is owed; (usually in *plural*) fee or amount payable. ● *adverb* (of compass point) exactly, directly. □ **due to** because of, caused by.

■ **Usage** Many people believe that *due to*, meaning 'because of', should only be used after the verb *to be*, as in *The mistake was due to ignorance*, and not as in *All trains may be delayed due to a signal failure*. Instead, *owing to a signal failure* could be used.

duel /ˈdjuːəl/ ● *noun* armed contest between two people, usually to the death; two-sided contest. ● *verb* (**-ll-**; *US* **-l-**) fight duel. □ **duellist** *noun*.

duenna /djuːˈenə/ *noun* older woman acting as chaperon to girls, esp. in Spain.

duet /djuːˈet/ *noun* musical composition for two performers.

duff ● *noun* boiled pudding. ● *adjective slang* worthless, useless, counterfeit.

duffer /ˈdʌfə/ *noun colloquial* inefficient or stupid person.

duffle /ˈdʌf(ə)l/ *noun* (also **duffel**) coarse woollen cloth. □ **duffle bag** cylindrical

canvas bag closed by drawstring; **duffle-coat** hooded overcoat of duffle with toggle fastenings.

dug[1] *past & past participle* of DIG.

dug[2] *noun* udder, teat.

dugong /ˈduːgɒŋ/ *noun* (*plural* same or **-s**) Asian sea mammal.

dugout *noun* roofed shelter, esp. for troops in trenches; underground shelter; canoe made from tree trunk.

duke /djuːk/ *noun* person holding highest hereditary title of the nobility; sovereign prince ruling duchy or small state. □ **dukedom** *noun*.

dulcet /ˈdʌlsɪt/ *adjective* sweet-sounding.

dulcimer /ˈdʌlsɪmə/ *noun* metal-stringed instrument struck with two hand-held hammers.

dull ● *adjective* tedious; not interesting; (of weather) overcast; (of colour, light, sound, etc.) not bright, vivid, or clear; slow-witted; stupid; (of knife-edge etc.) blunt; listless, depressed. ● *verb* make or become dull. □ **dullard** *noun*; **dullness** *noun*; **dully** /ˈdʌlɪ/ *adverb*.

duly /ˈdjuːlɪ/ *adverb* in due time or manner; rightly, properly.

dumb /dʌm/ *adjective* unable to speak; silent, taciturn; *colloquial* stupid, ignorant. □ **dumb-bell** short bar with weight at each end, for muscle-building etc.; **dumbstruck** speechless with surprise.

dumbfound /dʌmˈfaʊnd/ *verb* nonplus; make speechless with surprise.

dumdum /ˈdʌmdʌm/ *noun* (in full **dumdum bullet**) soft-nosed bullet that expands on impact.

dummy /ˈdʌmɪ/ ● *noun* (*plural* **-ies**) model of human figure, esp. as used to display clothes or by ventriloquist or as target; imitation object used to replace real or normal one; baby's rubber teat; *colloquial* stupid person; imaginary player in bridge etc., whose cards are exposed and played by partner. ● *adjective* sham, imitation. ● *verb* (**-ies**, **-ied**) make pretended pass etc. in football. □ **dummy run** trial attempt.

dump ● *noun* place for depositing rubbish; *colloquial* unpleasant or dreary place; temporary store of ammunition etc. ● *verb* put down firmly or clumsily; deposit as rubbish; *colloquial* abandon; sell (surplus goods) to foreign market at low price; copy (contents of computer memory etc.) as diagnostic aid or for security.

dumpling /'dʌmplɪŋ/ noun ball of dough boiled in stew or containing apple etc.

dumps plural noun (usually in **down in the dumps**) colloquial low spirits.

dumpy /'dʌmpɪ/ adjective (**-ier, -iest**) short and stout.

dun ● adjective greyish-brown. ● noun dun colour; dun horse.

dunce noun person slow at learning.

dunderhead /'dʌndəhed/ noun stupid person.

dune /djuːn/ noun drift of sand etc. formed by wind.

dung ● noun excrement of animals; manure. ● verb apply dung to (land). □ **dunghill** heap of dung or refuse.

dungarees /dʌŋgə'riːz/ plural noun trousers with bib attached.

dungeon /'dʌndʒ(ə)n/ noun underground prison cell.

dunk verb dip food into liquid before eating it.

dunlin /'dʌnlɪn/ noun red-backed sandpiper.

dunnock /'dʌnək/ noun hedge sparrow.

duo /'djuːəʊ/ noun (plural **-s**) pair of performers; duet.

duodecimal /djuːəʊ'desɪm(ə)l/ adjective of twelfths or 12; proceeding by twelves.

duodenum /djuːəʊ'diːnəm/ noun (plural **-s**) part of small intestine next to stomach. □ **duodenal** adjective.

duologue /'djuːəlɒg/ noun dialogue between two people.

dupe /djuːp/ ● noun victim of deception. ● verb (**-ping**) deceive, trick.

duple /'djuːp(ə)l/ adjective of two parts. □ **duple time** Music rhythm with two beats to bar.

duplex /'djuːpleks/ ● noun US flat on two floors, house subdivided for two families. ● adjective having two elements; twofold.

duplicate ● adjective /'djuːplɪkət/ identical; doubled. ● noun /-kət/ identical thing, esp. copy. ● verb /-keɪt/ (**-ting**) double; make or be exact copy of; repeat (an action etc.), esp. unnecessarily. □ **in duplicate** in two exact copies. □ **duplication** noun.

duplicator noun machine for producing multiple copies of texts.

duplicity /djuː'plɪsɪtɪ/ noun doubledealing; deceitfulness. □ **duplicitous** adjective.

durable /'djʊərəb(ə)l/ adjective lasting; hard-wearing. □ **durability** noun.

duration /djʊə'reɪʃ(ə)n/ noun time taken by event. □ **for the duration** until end of event, for very long time.

duress /djʊə'res/ noun compulsion, esp. illegal use of force or threats.

Durex /'djʊəreks/ noun proprietary term condom.

during /'djʊərɪŋ/ preposition throughout; at some point in.

dusk noun darker stage of twilight.

dusky adjective (**-ier, -iest**) shadowy, dim; dark-coloured.

dust ● noun finely powdered earth or other material etc.; dead person's remains. ● verb wipe the dust from (furniture etc.); sprinkle with powder, sugar, etc. □ **dustbin** container for household refuse; **dust bowl** desert made by drought or erosion; **dustcover** dustsheet, dust-jacket; **dust-jacket** paper cover on hardback book; **dustman** man employed to collect household refuse; **dustpan** pan into which dust is brushed from floor etc.; **dust-sheet** protective cloth over furniture; **dust-up** colloquial fight, disturbance.

duster noun cloth etc. for dusting furniture etc.

dusty adjective (**-ier, -iest**) covered with or full of or like dust.

Dutch ● adjective of the Netherlands or its people or language. ● noun Dutch language; (**the Dutch**) (treated as plural) the people of the Netherlands. □ **Dutch auction** one in which price is progressively reduced; **Dutch barn** roof on poles over hay etc.; **Dutch cap** dome-shaped contraceptive device fitting over cervix; **Dutch courage** courage induced by alcohol; **Dutchman**, **Dutchwoman** native or national of the Netherlands; **Dutch treat** party, outing, etc. at which people pay for themselves; **go Dutch** share expenses on outing.

dutiable /'djuːtɪəb(ə)l/ adjective requiring payment of duty.

dutiful /'djuːtɪfʊl/ *adjective* doing one's duty; obedient. □ **dutifully** *adverb*.

duty /'djuːtɪ/ *noun* (*plural* **-ies**) moral or legal obligation; responsibility; tax on certain goods, imports, etc.; job or function arising from a business or office. □ **duty-free** (of goods) on which duty is not payable; **on**, **off duty** working or not working.

duvet /'duːveɪ/ *noun* thick soft quilt used instead of sheets and blankets.

dwarf /dwɔːf/ ● *noun* (*plural* **-s** or **dwarves** /dwɔːvz/) person, animal, or plant much below normal size, esp. with normal-sized head and body but short limbs; small mythological being with magical powers. ● *verb* stunt in growth; make look small by contrast.

dwell *verb* (*past & past participle* **dwelt** or **dwelled**) reside, live. □ **dwell on** think, write, or speak at length on. □ **dweller** *noun*.

dwelling *noun* house, residence.

dwindle /'dwɪnd(ə)l/ *verb* (**-ling**) become gradually less or smaller; lose importance.

dye /daɪ/ ● *noun* substance used to change colour of fabric, wood, hair, etc.; colour produced by this. ● *verb* (**dyeing**, **dyed**) colour with dye; dye a specified colour. □ **dyer** *noun*.

dying /'daɪɪŋ/ ● *present participle* of DIE[1]. ● *adjective* of, or at the time of, death.

dyke /daɪk/ (also **dike**) ● *noun* embankment built to prevent flooding; low wall. ● *verb* (**-king**) provide or protect with dyke(s).

dynamic /daɪ'næmɪk/ *adjective* energetic, active; of motive force; of force in operation; of dynamics. □ **dynamically** *adverb*.

dynamics *plural noun* (usually treated as *singular*) mathematical study of motion and forces causing it.

dynamism /'daɪnəmɪz(ə)m/ *noun* energy; dynamic power.

dynamite /'daɪnəmaɪt/ ● *noun* highly explosive mixture containing nitroglycerine. ● *verb* (**-ting**) charge or blow up with this.

dynamo /'daɪnəməʊ/ *noun* (*plural* **-s**) machine converting mechanical into electrical energy; *colloquial* energetic person.

dynast /'dɪnəst/ *noun* ruler; member of dynasty.

dynasty /'dɪnəstɪ/ *noun* (*plural* **-ies**) line of hereditary rulers. □ **dynastic** /-'næs-/ *adjective*.

dyne *noun Physics* force required to give a mass of one gram an acceleration of one centimetre per second per second.

dysentery /'dɪsəntrɪ/ *noun* inflammation of bowels, causing severe diarrhoea.

dysfunction /dɪs'fʌŋkʃ(ə)n/ *noun* abnormality or impairment of functioning.

dyslexia /dɪs'leksɪə/ *noun* abnormal difficulty in reading and spelling. □ **dyslectic** /-'lektɪk/ *adjective & noun*; **dyslexic** *adjective & noun*.

dyspepsia /dɪs'pepsɪə/ *noun* indigestion. □ **dyspeptic** *adjective & noun*.

dystrophy /'dɪstrəfɪ/ *noun* defective nutrition.

Ee

E *abbreviation* (also **E.**) east(ern).
□ **E-number** number prefixed by letter E identifying food additive.

each ● *adjective* every one of two or more, regarded separately. ● *pronoun* each person or thing. □ **each way** (of bet) backing horse etc. to win or come second or third.

eager /'iːgə/ *adjective* keen, enthusiastic. □ **eagerly** *adverb*; **eagerness** *noun*.

eagle /'iːg(ə)l/ *noun* large bird of prey; *Golf* score of two under par for hole. □ **eagle eye** keen sight, watchfulness; **eagle-eyed** *adjective*.

eaglet /'iːglɪt/ *noun* young eagle.

ear[1] /ɪə/ *noun* organ of hearing, esp. external part; faculty of discriminating sound; attention. □ **all ears** listening attentively; **earache** pain in inner ear; **eardrum** membrane of middle ear; **earphone** (usually in *plural*) device worn on ear to listen to recording, radio, etc.; **earplug** device worn in ear as protection from water, noise, etc.; **earring** jewellery worn on ear; **earshot** hearing-range; **ear-trumpet** trumpet-shaped tube formerly used as hearing aid.

ear[2] /ɪə/ *noun* seed-bearing head of cereal plant.

earl /ɜːl/ *noun* British nobleman ranking between marquess and viscount. □ **earldom** *noun*.

early /'ɜːlɪ/ *adjective & adverb* (**-ier**, **-iest**) before due, usual, or expected time; not far on in day or night or in development etc. □ **early bird** *colloquial* person who arrives, gets up, etc. early; **early days** too soon to expect results etc.

earmark *verb* set aside for special purpose.

earn /ɜːn/ *verb* obtain as reward for work or merit; bring as income or interest. □ **earner** *noun*.

earnest /'ɜːnɪst/ *adjective* intensely serious. □ **in earnest** serious(ly). □ **earnestly** *adverb*; **earnestness** *noun*.

earnings /'ɜːnɪŋz/ *plural noun* money earned.

earth /ɜːθ/ ● *noun* planet we live on (also **Earth**); land and sea as opposed to sky; ground; soil, mould; this world as opposed to heaven or hell; *Electricity* connection to earth as completion of circuit; hole of fox etc. ● *verb Electricity* connect to earth; cover (roots) with earth. □ **earthwork** bank of earth in fortification; **earthworm** worm living in earth; **run to earth** find after long search.

earthen *adjective* made of earth or baked clay. □ **earthenware** pottery made of fired clay.

earthly *adjective* of earth, terrestrial; *colloquial* (usually with negative) remotely possible. □ **not an earthly** *colloquial* no chance or idea whatever.

earthquake *noun* violent shaking of earth's surface.

earthy *adjective* (**-ier**, **-iest**) of or like earth or soil; coarse, crude.

earwig *noun* insect with pincers at rear end.

ease /iːz/ ● *noun* facility, effortlessness; freedom from pain, trouble, or constraint. ● *verb* (**-sing**) relieve from pain etc.; (often + *off*, *up*) become less burdensome or severe; relax, slacken; move or be moved by gentle force.

easel /'iːz(ə)l/ *noun* stand for painting, blackboard, etc.

easement *noun Law* right of way over another's property.

easily /'iːzɪlɪ/ *adverb* without difficulty; by far; very probably.

east ● *noun* point of horizon where sun rises at equinoxes; corresponding compass point; (usually **the East**) eastern part of world, country, town, etc. ● *adjective* towards, at, near, or facing east; (of wind) from east. ● *adverb* towards, at, or near east; (+ *of*) further east than. □ **eastbound** travelling or leading east; **East End** part of London east of City; **east-north-east**, **east-south-east** point midway between east and north-east or south-east. □ **eastward** *adjective, adverb, & noun*; **eastwards** *adverb*.

Easter /ˈiːstə/ *noun* festival of Christ's resurrection. □ **Easter egg** artificial usually chocolate egg given at Easter; **Easter Saturday** day before Easter, (properly) Saturday after Easter.

easterly /ˈiːstəlɪ/ *adjective & adverb* in eastern position or direction; (of wind) from east.

eastern /ˈiːst(ə)n/ *adjective* of or in east. □ **Eastern Church** Orthodox Church. □ **easternmost** *adjective*.

easterner *noun* native or inhabitant of east.

easy /ˈiːzɪ/ ● *adjective* (**-ier, -iest**) not difficult; free from pain, trouble, or anxiety; relaxed and pleasant; compliant. ● *adverb* with ease, in an effortless or relaxed way. □ **easy chair** large comfortable armchair; **easygoing** placid and tolerant; **go easy** (usually + *on, with*) be sparing or cautious; **take it easy** proceed gently, relax.

eat *verb* (*past* **ate** /et, eɪt/; *past participle* **eaten**) chew and swallow (food); consume food, have meal; destroy, consume. □ **eating apple** one suitable for eating raw; **eat out** have meal away from home, esp. in restaurant; **eat up** eat completely.

eatable ● *adjective* fit to be eaten. ● *noun* (usually in *plural*) food.

eater *noun* person who eats; eating apple.

eau-de-Cologne /əʊdəkəˈləʊn/ *noun* toilet water originally from Cologne.

eaves /iːvz/ *plural noun* underside of projecting roof.

eavesdrop *verb* (**-pp-**) listen to private conversation. □ **eavesdropper** *noun*.

ebb ● *noun* outflow of tide. ● *verb* flow back; decline.

ebony /ˈebənɪ/ ● *noun* hard heavy black tropical wood. ● *adjective* made of or black as ebony.

ebullient /ɪˈbʌlɪənt/ *adjective* exuberant. □ **ebullience** *noun*, **ebulliently** *adverb*.

EC *abbreviation* European Community; East Central.

eccentric /ɪkˈsentrɪk/ ● *adjective* odd or capricious in behaviour or appearance; not placed centrally, not having axis etc. placed centrally; not concentric; not circular. ● *noun* eccentric person. □ **eccentrically** *adverb*, **eccentricity** /eksen'trɪs-/ *noun* (*plural* **-ies**).

ecclesiastic /ɪkliːzɪˈæstɪk/ *noun* clergyman.

ecclesiastical *adjective* of the Church or clergy.

ECG *abbreviation* electrocardiogram.

echelon /ˈeʃəlɒn/ *noun* level in organization, society, etc.; wedge-shaped formation of troops, aircraft, etc.

echidna /ɪˈkɪdnə/ *noun* Australian egg-laying spiny mammal.

echo /ˈekəʊ/ ● *noun* (*plural* **-es**) repetition of sound by reflection of sound waves; reflected radio or radar beam; close imitation; circumstance or event reminiscent of earlier one. ● *verb* (**-es, -ed**) resound with echo; repeat, imitate; be repeated.

éclair /eɪˈkleə/ *noun* finger-shaped iced cake of choux pastry filled with cream.

éclat /eɪˈklɑː/ *noun* brilliant display; conspicuous success; prestige.

eclectic /ɪˈklektɪk/ ● *adjective* selecting ideas, style, etc. from various sources. ● *noun* eclectic person. □ **eclecticism** /-tɪs-/ *noun*.

eclipse /ɪˈklɪps/ ● *noun* obscuring of light of sun by moon (**solar eclipse**) or of moon by earth (**lunar eclipse**); loss of light or importance. ● *verb* (**-sing**) cause eclipse of; intercept (light); outshine, surpass.

eclogue /ˈeklɒg/ *noun* short pastoral poem.

ecology /ɪˈkɒlədʒɪ/ *noun* study of relations of organisms to one another and their surroundings. □ **ecological** /iːkəˈlɒdʒ-/ *adjective*; **ecologically** /iːkəˈlɒdʒ-/ *adverb*; **ecologist** *noun*.

economic /iːkəˈnɒmɪk/ *adjective* of economics; profitable; connected with trade and industry. □ **economically** *adverb*.

economical /iːkəˈnɒmɪk(ə)l/ *adjective* sparing; avoiding waste. □ **economically** *adverb*.

economics /iːkəˈnɒmɪks/ *plural noun* (treated as *singular*) science of production and distribution of wealth; application of this to particular subject. □ **economist** /ɪˈkɒnəmɪst/ *noun*.

economize /ɪˈkɒnəmaɪz/ *verb* (also **-ise**) (**-zing** or **-sing**) make economies; reduce expenditure.

economy /ɪˈkɒnəmɪ/ noun (plural **-ies**) community's system of wealth creation; frugality, instance of this; sparing use.

ecosystem /ˈiːkəʊsɪstəm/ noun biological community of interacting organisms and their physical environment.

ecru /ˈeɪkruː/ noun light fawn colour.

ecstasy /ˈekstəsɪ/ noun (plural **-ies**) overwhelming joy or rapture; slang type of hallucinogenic drug. □ **ecstatic** /ɪkˈstætɪk/ adjective.

ECT abbreviation electroconvulsive therapy.

ectoplasm /ˈektəʊplæz(ə)m/ noun supposed substance exuding from body of spiritualistic medium during trance.

ecu /ˈeɪkjuː/ noun (also **Ecu**) (plural **-s**) European Currency Unit.

ecumenical /iːkjuˈmenɪk(ə)l/ adjective of or representing whole Christian world; seeking worldwide Christian unity. □ **ecumenism** /iːˈkjuːmən-/ noun.

eczema /ˈeksɪmə/ noun kind of inflammation of skin.

ed. abbreviation edited by; edition; editor.

Edam /ˈiːdæm/ noun round Dutch cheese with red rind.

eddy /ˈedɪ/ ● noun (plural **-ies**) circular movement of water, smoke, etc. ● verb (**-ies, -ied**) move in eddies.

edelweiss /ˈeɪd(ə)lvaɪs/ noun Alpine plant with woolly white bracts.

edema US = OEDEMA.

Eden /ˈiːd(ə)n/ noun (in full **Garden of Eden**) home of Adam and Eve; delightful place or state.

edge ● noun boundary-line or margin of area or surface; narrow surface of thin object; meeting-line of surfaces; sharpness; sharpened side of blade; brink of precipice; crest of ridge; effectiveness. ● verb (**-ging**) advance gradually or furtively; give or form border to; sharpen. □ **edgeways, edgewise** with edge foremost or uppermost; **have the edge on, over** have slight advantage over; **on edge** excited or irritable; **set (person's) teeth on edge** cause unpleasant nervous sensation in.

edging noun thing forming edge or border.

edgy adjective (**-ier, -iest**) irritable; anxious.

edible /ˈedɪb(ə)l/ adjective fit to be eaten.

edict /ˈiːdɪkt/ noun order proclaimed by authority.

edifice /ˈedɪfɪs/ noun building, esp. imposing one.

edify /ˈedɪfaɪ/ verb (**-ies, -ied**) improve morally. □ **edification** noun.

edit /ˈedɪt/ verb (**-t-**) prepare for publication or broadcast; be editor of; cut and collate (films etc.) to make unified sequence; reword, modify; (+ out) remove (part) from text, recording, etc.

edition /ɪˈdɪʃ(ə)n/ noun edited or published form of book etc.; copies of book or newspaper etc. issued at one time; instance of regular broadcast.

editor /ˈedɪtə/ noun person who edits; person who directs writing of newspaper or news programme or section of one; person who selects material for publication. □ **editorship** noun.

editorial /edɪˈtɔːrɪəl/ ● adjective of editing or an editor. ● noun article giving newspaper's views on current topic.

educate /ˈedjʊkeɪt/ verb (**-ting**) train or instruct mentally and morally; provide systematic instruction for. □ **educable** adjective; **education** noun; **educational** adjective; **educator** noun.

educationist noun (also **educationalist**) expert in educational methods.

Edwardian /edˈwɔːdɪən/ ● adjective of or characteristic of reign (1901–10) of Edward VII. ● noun person of this period.

EEC abbreviation European Economic Community.

EEG abbreviation electroencephalogram.

eel noun snakelike fish.

eerie /ˈɪərɪ/ adjective (**-r, -st**) strange; weird. □ **eerily** adverb.

efface /ɪˈfeɪs/ verb (**-cing**) rub or wipe out; surpass, eclipse; (**efface oneself**) treat oneself as unimportant. □ **effacement** noun.

effect /ɪˈfekt/ ● noun result, consequence; efficacy; impression; (in plural) possessions; (in plural) lighting, sound, etc. giving realism to play etc.; physical phenomenon. ● verb bring about.

■ **Usage** As a verb, *effect* should not be confused with *affect*. *He effected an entrance* means 'He got in (somehow)', but *This won't affect me* means 'My life won't be changed by this'.

effective *adjective* operative; impressive; actual; producing intended result. □ **effectively** *adverb*; **effectiveness** *noun*.

effectual /ɪˈfektʃʊəl/ *adjective* producing required effect; valid.

effeminate /ɪˈfemɪnət/ *adjective* (of a man) unmanly, womanish. □ **effeminacy** *noun*.

effervesce /efəˈves/ *verb* (-**cing**) give off bubbles of gas. □ **effervescence** *noun*; **effervescent** *adjective*.

effete /ɪˈfiːt/ *adjective* feeble; effeminate.

efficacious /efɪˈkeɪʃəs/ *adjective* producing desired effect. □ **efficacy** /ˈefɪkəsɪ/ *noun*.

efficient /ɪˈfɪʃ(ə)nt/ *adjective* productive with minimum waste of effort; competent, capable. □ **efficiency** *noun*; **efficiently** *adverb*.

effigy /ˈefɪdʒɪ/ *noun* (*plural* -**ies**) sculpture or model of person.

effloresce /eflɔːˈres/ *verb* (-**cing**) burst into flower. □ **efflorescence** *noun*.

effluence /ˈeflʊəns/ *noun* flowing out (of light, electricity, etc.); what flows out.

effluent /ˈeflʊənt/ • *adjective* flowing out. • *noun* sewage or industrial waste discharged into river etc.; stream flowing from lake etc.

effluvium /ɪˈfluːvɪəm/ *noun* (*plural* -**via**) unpleasant or harmful outflow.

effort /ˈefət/ *noun* exertion; determined attempt; force exerted; *colloquial* something accomplished. □ **effortless** *adjective*; **effortlessly** *adverb*.

effrontery /ɪˈfrʌntərɪ/ *noun* impudence.

effuse /ɪˈfjuːz/ *verb* (-**sing**) pour forth.

effusion /ɪˈfjuːʒ(ə)n/ *noun* outpouring.

effusive /ɪˈfjuːsɪv/ *adjective* demonstrative; gushing. □ **effusively** *adverb*; **effusiveness** *noun*.

EFL *abbreviation* English as a foreign language.

Efta /ˈeftə/ *noun* (also **EFTA**) European Free Trade Association.

e.g. *abbreviation* for example.

egalitarian /ɪɡælɪˈteərɪən/ • *adjective* of or advocating equal rights for all. • *noun* egalitarian person. □ **egalitarianism** *noun*.

egg[1] *noun* body produced by female of birds, insects, etc., capable of developing into new individual; edible egg of domestic hen; ovum. □ **eggcup** cup for holding boiled egg; **egghead** *colloquial* intellectual; **eggplant** aubergine; **egg white** white or clear part round yolk of egg.

egg[2] *verb* (+ *on*) urge.

eglantine /ˈeɡləntaɪn/ *noun* sweet-brier.

ego /ˈiːɡəʊ/ *noun* (*plural* -**s**) the self; part of mind that has sense of individuality; self-esteem.

egocentric /iːɡəʊˈsentrɪk/ *adjective* self-centred.

egoism /ˈiːɡəʊɪz(ə)m/ *noun* self-interest as moral basis of behaviour; systematic selfishness; egotism. □ **egoist** *noun*; **egoistic** /-ˈɪs-/ *adjective*.

egotism /ˈiːɡətɪz(ə)m/ *noun* self-conceit; selfishness. □ **egotist** *noun*; **egotistic(al)** /-ˈtɪs-/ *adjective*.

egregious /ɪˈɡriːdʒəs/ *adjective* extremely bad; *archaic* remarkable.

egress /ˈiːɡres/ *noun* going out; way out.

egret /ˈiːɡrɪt/ *noun* kind of white heron.

Egyptian /ɪˈdʒɪpʃ(ə)n/ • *adjective* of Egypt. • *noun* native or national of Egypt; language of ancient Egyptians.

Egyptology /iːdʒɪpˈtɒlədʒɪ/ *noun* study of ancient Egypt. □ **Egyptologist** *noun*.

eh /eɪ/ *interjection colloquial*: expressing inquiry, surprise, etc.

eider /ˈaɪdə/ *noun* northern species of duck. □ **eiderdown** quilt stuffed with soft material, esp. down.

eight /eɪt/ *adjective & noun* one more than seven; 8-oared boat, its crew. □ **eightsome reel** lively Scottish dance for 8 people. □ **eighth** /eɪtθ/ *adjective & noun*.

eighteen /eɪˈtiːn/ *adjective & noun* one more than seventeen. □ **eighteenth** *adjective & noun*.

eighty /ˈeɪtɪ/ *adjective & noun* (*plural* -**ies**) eight times ten. □ **eightieth** *adjective & noun*.

eisteddfod /aɪˈstedfəd/ *noun* congress of Welsh poets and musicians gathering for musical and literary competition.

either /ˈaɪðə, ˈiːðə/ • *adjective & pronoun* one or other of two; each of two. • *adverb* (with negative) any more than the other. □ **either ... or ...** as one possibility ... and as the other ...

ejaculate /ɪˈdʒækjʊleɪt/ verb (-ting) emit (semen) in orgasm; exclaim. □ **ejaculation** noun.

eject /ɪˈdʒekt/ verb throw out, expel; (of pilot etc.) cause oneself to be propelled from aircraft in emergency; emit. □ **ejection** noun.

ejector seat noun device in aircraft for emergency ejection of pilot etc.

eke verb (**eking**) □ **eke out** supplement (income etc.), make (living) or support (existence) with difficulty.

elaborate ● adjective /ɪˈlæbərət/ minutely worked out; complicated. ● verb /ɪˈlæbəreɪt/ (**-ting**) work out or explain in detail. □ **elaborately** adverb; **elaboration** noun.

élan /eɪˈlɑ̃/ noun vivacity, dash. [French]

eland /ˈiːlənd/ noun (plural same or **-s**) large African antelope.

elapse /ɪˈlæps/ verb (**-sing**) (of time) pass by.

elastic /ɪˈlæstɪk/ ● adjective able to resume normal bulk or shape after being stretched or squeezed; springy; flexible. ● noun elastic cord or fabric, usually woven with strips of rubber. □ **elastic band** rubber band. □ **elasticity** /iːlæˈstɪs-/ noun.

elasticated /ɪˈlæstɪkeɪtɪd/ adjective (of fabric) made elastic by weaving with rubber thread.

elate /ɪˈleɪt/ verb (**-ting**) (esp. as **elated** adjective) make delighted or proud. □ **elation** noun.

elbow /ˈelbəʊ/ ● noun joint between forearm and upper arm; part of sleeve covering elbow; elbow-shaped thing. ● verb thrust or jostle (person); make (one's) way thus. □ **elbow-grease** jocular vigorous polishing, hard work; **elbow-room** sufficient space to move or work in.

elder[1] /ˈeldə/ ● adjective older; senior. ● noun older person; official in early Christian and some modern Churches.

elder[2] /ˈeldə/ noun tree with white flowers and black **elderberries**.

elderly /ˈeldəlɪ/ adjective rather old.

eldest /ˈeldɪst/ adjective first-born; oldest surviving.

eldorado /eldəˈrɑːdəʊ/ noun (plural **-s**) imaginary land of great wealth.

elect /ɪˈlekt/ ● verb choose by voting; choose, decide. ● adjective chosen; select, choice; (after noun) chosen but not yet in office.

election /ɪˈlekʃ(ə)n/ noun electing, being elected; occasion for this.

electioneer /ɪlekʃəˈnɪə/ verb take part in election campaign.

elective /ɪˈlektɪv/ adjective chosen by or derived from election; entitled to elect; optional.

elector /ɪˈlektə/ noun person entitled to vote in election. □ **electoral** adjective.

electorate /ɪˈlektərət/ noun group of electors.

electric /ɪˈlektrɪk/ adjective of, worked by, or charged with electricity; causing or charged with excitement. □ **electric blanket** one heated by internal wires; **electric chair** chair used for electrocution of criminals; **electric eel** eel-like fish able to give electric shock; **electric fire** portable electric heater; **electric shock** effect of sudden discharge of electricity through body of person etc. □ **electrically** adverb.

electrical adjective of or worked by electricity. □ **electrically** adverb.

electrician /ɪlekˈtrɪʃ(ə)n/ noun person who installs or maintains electrical equipment.

electricity /ɪlekˈtrɪsɪtɪ/ noun form of energy present in protons and electrons; science of electricity; supply of electricity.

electrify /ɪˈlektrɪfaɪ/ verb (**-ies, -ied**) charge with electricity; convert to electric working; startle, excite. □ **electrification** noun.

electro- combining form of or caused by electricity.

electrocardiogram /ɪlektrəʊˈkɑːdɪəgræm/ noun record of electric currents generated by heartbeat. □ **electrocardiograph** instrument for recording such currents.

electroconvulsive /ɪlektrəʊkənˈvʌlsɪv/ adjective (of therapy) using convulsive response to electric shocks.

electrocute /ɪˈlektrəkjuːt/ verb (**-ting**) kill by electric shock. □ **electrocution** /-ˈkjuːʃ(ə)n/ noun.

electrode /ɪˈlektrəʊd/ noun conductor through which electricity enters or leaves electrolyte, gas, vacuum, etc.

electroencephalogram /ɪlektrəʊnˈsefələɡræm/ noun record of electrical activity of brain. □ **electroencephalograph** instrument for recording such activity.

electrolysis /ɪlekˈtrɒlɪsɪs/ noun chemical decomposition by electric action; breaking up of tumours, hair-roots, etc. thus.

electrolyte /ɪˈlektrəlaɪt/ noun solution that can conduct electricity; substance that can dissolve to produce this. □ **electrolytic** /-trəʊˈlɪt-/ adjective.

electromagnet /ɪlektrəʊˈmæɡnɪt/ noun soft metal core made into magnet by electric current through coil surrounding it.

electromagnetism /ɪlektrəʊˈmæɡnɪtɪz(ə)m/ noun magnetic forces produced by electricity; study of these.

electron /ɪˈlektrɒn/ noun stable elementary particle with charge of negative electricity, found in all atoms and acting as primary carrier of electricity in solids. □ **electron microscope** one with high magnification, using electron beam instead of light.

electronic /ɪlekˈtrɒnɪk/ adjective of electrons or electronics; (of music) produced electronically. □ **electronic mail** messages distributed by a computer system. □ **electronically** adverb.

electronics plural noun (treated as singular) science of movement of electrons in vacuum, gas, semiconductor, etc.

electroplate /ɪˈlektrəʊpleɪt/ ● verb (-ting) coat with chromium, silver, etc. by electrolysis. ● noun electroplated articles.

elegant /ˈelɪɡənt/ adjective graceful, tasteful, refined; ingeniously simple. □ **elegance** noun, **elegantly** adverb.

elegy /ˈelɪdʒɪ/ noun (plural **-ies**) sorrowful song or poem, esp. for the dead. □ **elegiac** /-ˈdʒaɪək/ adjective.

element /ˈelɪmənt/ noun component part; substance which cannot be resolved by chemical means into simpler substances; (any of **the four elements** (earth, water, air, fire) formerly supposed to make up all matter; wire that gives out heat in electric heater, cooker, etc.; (in plural) atmospheric agencies; (in plural) rudiments, first principles; (in plural) bread and wine of Eucharist. □ **in one's element** in one's preferred situation.

elemental /elɪˈment(ə)l/ adjective of or like the elements or the forces of nature; basic, essential.

elementary /elɪˈmentərɪ/ adjective dealing with simplest facts of subject; unanalysable. □ **elementary particle** Physics subatomic particle, esp. one not known to consist of simpler ones.

elephant /ˈelɪf(ə)nt/ noun (plural same or **-s**) largest living land animal, with trunk and ivory tusks.

elephantiasis /elɪfənˈtaɪəsɪs/ noun skin disease causing gross enlargement of limbs etc.

elephantine /elɪˈfæntaɪn/ adjective of elephants; huge; clumsy.

elevate /ˈelɪveɪt/ verb (**-ting**) lift up, raise; exalt in rank etc.; (usually as **elevated** adjective) raise morally or intellectually.

elevation noun elevating, being elevated; angle above horizontal; height above given level; drawing showing one side of building.

elevator noun US lift; movable part of tailplane for changing aircraft's altitude; hoisting machine.

eleven /ɪˈlev(ə)n/ adjective & noun one more than ten; team of 11 people in cricket etc. □ **eleventh hour** last possible moment. □ **eleventh** adjective & noun.

elevenses /ɪˈlevənzɪz/ noun colloquial light mid-morning refreshment.

elf noun (plural **elves** /elvz/) mythological being, esp. small and mischievous one. □ **elfish** adjective.

elfin /ˈelfɪn/ adjective of elves; elflike.

elicit /ɪˈlɪsɪt/ verb (**-t-**) draw out (facts, response, etc.).

elide /ɪˈlaɪd/ verb (**-ding**) omit in pronunciation.

eligible /ˈelɪdʒɪb(ə)l/ adjective (often + for) fit or entitled to be chosen; desirable or suitable, esp. for marriage. □ **eligibility** noun.

eliminate /ɪˈlɪmɪneɪt/ verb (**-ting**) remove, get rid of; exclude. □ **elimination** noun, **eliminator** noun.

elision /ɪˈlɪʒ(ə)n/ noun omission of vowel or syllable in pronunciation.

élite /eɪˈliːt/ noun select group or class; (**the élite**) the best (of a group).

élitism noun advocacy of or reliance on dominance by select group. □ **élitist** noun & adjective.

elixir /ɪˈlɪksɪə/ noun alchemist's preparation supposedly able to change metal into gold or prolong life indefinitely; aromatic medicine.

Elizabethan /ɪlɪzəˈbiːθ(ə)n/ ● adjective of time of Elizabeth I or II. ● noun person of this time.

elk noun (plural same or **-s**) large type of deer.

ellipse /ɪˈlɪps/ noun regular oval.

ellipsis /ɪˈlɪpsɪs/ noun (plural **ellipses** /-siːz/) omission of words needed to complete construction or sense.

elliptical /ɪˈlɪptɪk(ə)l/ adjective of or like an ellipse; (of language) confusingly concise.

elm noun tree with rough serrated leaves; its wood.

elocution /elə'kjuːʃ(ə)n/ noun art of clear and expressive speaking.

elongate /ˈiːlɒŋɡeɪt/ verb (**-ting**) extend, lengthen. □ **elongation** noun.

elope /ɪˈləʊp/ verb (**-ping**) run away to marry secretly. □ **elopement** noun.

eloquence /ˈeləkwəns/ noun fluent and effective use of language. □ **eloquent** adjective, **eloquently** adverb.

else /els/ adverb besides; instead; otherwise, if not. □ **elsewhere** in or to some other place.

elucidate /ɪˈluːsɪdeɪt/ verb (**-ting**) throw light on, explain. □ **elucidation** noun.

elude /ɪˈluːd/ verb (**-ding**) escape adroitly from; avoid; baffle.

elusive /ɪˈluːsɪv/ adjective difficult to find, catch, or remember; avoiding the point raised. □ **elusiveness** noun.

elver /ˈelvə/ noun young eel.

elves plural of ELF.

Elysium /ɪˈlɪzɪəm/ noun Greek Mythology home of the blessed after death; place of ideal happiness. □ **Elysian** adjective.

em noun Printing unit of measurement approximately equal to width of M.

emaciate /ɪˈmeɪsɪeɪt/ verb (**-ting**) (esp. as **emaciated** adjective) make thin or feeble. □ **emaciation** noun.

emanate /ˈeməneɪt/ verb (**-ting**) (usually + from) issue or originate (from source). □ **emanation** noun.

emancipate /ɪˈmænsɪpeɪt/ verb (**-ting**) free from social, political, or moral restraint. □ **emancipation** noun.

emasculate ● verb /ɪˈmæskjʊleɪt/ (**-ting**) enfeeble; castrate. ● adjective /ɪˈmæskjʊlət/ enfeebled; castrated; effeminate. □ **emasculation** noun.

embalm /ɪmˈbɑːm/ verb preserve (corpse) from decay; preserve from oblivion; make fragrant.

embankment /ɪmˈbæŋkmənt/ noun bank constructed to confine water or carry road or railway.

embargo /ɪmˈbɑːɡəʊ/ ● noun (plural **-es**) order forbidding ships to enter or leave port; suspension of commerce or other activity. ● verb (**-es**, **-ed**) place under embargo.

embark /ɪmˈbɑːk/ verb put or go on board ship; (+ on, in) begin (enterprise).

embarkation /embɑːˈkeɪʃ(ə)n/ noun embarking on ship.

embarrass /ɪmˈbarəs/ verb make (person) feel awkward or ashamed; encumber; (as **embarrassed** adjective) encumbered with debts. □ **embarrassment** noun.

embassy /ˈembəsɪ/ noun (plural **-ies**) ambassador's residence or offices; deputation to foreign government.

embattled /ɪmˈbæt(ə)ld/ adjective prepared or arrayed for battle; fortified with battlements; under heavy attack, in trying circumstances.

embed /ɪmˈbed/ verb (also **imbed**) (**-dd-**) (esp. as **embedded** adjective) fix in surrounding mass.

embellish /ɪmˈbelɪʃ/ verb beautify, adorn; make fictitious additions to. □ **embellishment** noun.

ember /ˈembə/ noun (usually in plural) small piece of glowing coal etc. in dying fire. □ **ember days** days of fasting and prayer in Christian Church, associated with ordinations.

embezzle /ɪmˈbez(ə)l/ verb (**-ling**) divert (money) fraudulently to own use. □ **embezzlement** noun; **embezzler** noun.

embitter /ɪmˈbɪtə/ verb arouse bitter feelings in. □ **embitterment** noun.

emblazon /ɪmˈbleɪz(ə)n/ *verb* portray or adorn conspicuously.

emblem /ˈembləm/ *noun* symbol; (+ *of*) type, embodiment; distinctive badge. □ **emblematic** /-ˈmæt-/ *adjective*.

embody /ɪmˈbɒdɪ/ *verb* (**-ies, -ied**) give concrete form to; be expression of; include, comprise. □ **embodiment** *noun*.

embolden /ɪmˈbəʊld(ə)n/ *verb* encourage.

embolism /ˈembəlɪz(ə)m/ *noun* obstruction of artery by blood clot etc.

emboss /ɪmˈbɒs/ *verb* carve or decorate with design in relief.

embrace /ɪmˈbreɪs/ ● *verb* (**-cing**) hold closely in arms; enclose; accept, adopt; include. ● *noun* act of embracing, clasp.

embrasure /ɪmˈbreɪʒə/ *noun* bevelling of wall at sides of window etc.; opening in parapet for gun.

embrocation /embrəˈkeɪʃ(ə)n/ *noun* liquid for rubbing on body to relieve muscular pain.

embroider /ɪmˈbrɔɪdə/ *verb* decorate with needlework; embellish. □ **embroidery** *noun*.

embroil /ɪmˈbrɔɪl/ *verb* (often + *in*) involve (in conflict or difficulties).

embryo /ˈembrɪəʊ/ *noun* (*plural* **-s**) unborn or unhatched offspring; thing in rudimentary stage. □ **embryonic** /-ˈɒn-/ *adjective*.

emend /iˈmend/ *verb* correct, remove errors from (text etc.). □ **emendation** /iː-/ *noun*.

emerald /ˈemər(ə)ld/ ● *noun* bright green gem; colour of this. ● *adjective* bright green.

emerge /iˈmɜːdʒ/ *verb* (**-ging**) come up or out into view or notice. □ **emergence** *noun*; **emergent** *adjective*.

emergency /iˈmɜːdʒənsɪ/ *noun* (*plural* **-ies**) sudden state of danger etc., requiring immediate action.

emeritus /iˈmerɪtəs/ *adjective* retired and holding honorary title.

emery /ˈemərɪ/ *noun* coarse corundum for polishing metal etc. □ **emery board** emery-coated nail-file.

emetic /iˈmetɪk/ ● *adjective* that causes vomiting. ● *noun* emetic medicine.

emigrate /ˈemɪɡreɪt/ *verb* (**-ting**) leave own country to settle in another. □ **emigrant** *noun & adjective*; **emigration** *noun*.

émigré /ˈemɪɡreɪ/ *noun* emigrant, esp. political exile.

eminence /ˈemɪnəns/ *noun* recognized superiority; high ground; (**His, Your Eminence**) *title used of or to cardinal*.

eminent /ˈemɪnənt/ *adjective* distinguished, notable. □ **eminently** *adverb*.

emir /eˈmɪə/ *noun* (also **amir** /əˈmɪə/) *title of various Muslim rulers*.

emirate /ˈemɪrət/ *noun* position, reign, or domain of emir.

emissary /ˈemɪsərɪ/ *noun* (*plural* **-ies**) person sent on diplomatic mission.

emit /iˈmɪt/ *verb* (**-tt-**) give or send out; discharge. □ **emission** /iˈmɪʃ(ə)n/ *noun*.

emollient /iˈmɒlɪənt/ ● *adjective* softening; soothing. ● *noun* emollient substance.

emolument /iˈmɒljʊmənt/ *noun* fee from employment, salary.

emotion /iˈməʊʃ(ə)n/ *noun* strong instinctive feeling such as love or fear; emotional intensity or sensibility.

emotional *adjective* of or expressing emotion(s); especially liable to emotion; arousing emotion. □ **emotionalism** *noun*; **emotionally** *adverb*.

■ **Usage** See note at EMOTIVE.

emotive /iˈməʊtɪv/ *adjective* of or arousing emotion.

■ **Usage** Although the senses of *emotive* and *emotional* overlap, *emotive* is more common in the sense 'arousing emotion', as in *an emotive issue*, and only *emotional* can mean 'especially liable to emotion', as in *a highly emotional person*.

empanel /ɪmˈpæn(ə)l/ *verb* (also **impanel**) (**-ll-**; *US* **-l-**) enter (jury) on panel.

empathize /ˈempəθaɪz/ *verb* (also **-ise**) (**-zing** or **-sing**) (usually + *with*) exercise empathy.

empathy /ˈempəθɪ/ *noun* ability to identify with person or object.

emperor /ˈempərə/ *noun* ruler of empire.

emphasis /ˈemfəsɪs/ *noun* (*plural* **emphases** /-siːz/) importance attached to something; significant stress on word(s); vigour of expression etc.

emphasize /ˈemfəsaɪz/ verb (also -**ise**) (-**zing** or -**sing**) lay stress on.

emphatic /ɪmˈfætɪk/ adjective forcibly expressive; (of word) bearing emphasis (e.g. *myself* in *I did it myself*). □ **emphatically** adverb.

emphysema /emfɪˈsiːmə/ noun disease of lungs causing breathlessness.

empire /ˈempaɪə/ noun large group of states under single authority; supreme dominion; large commercial organization etc. owned or directed by one person.

empirical /ɪmˈpɪrɪk(ə)l/ adjective based on observation or experiment, not on theory. □ **empiricism** /-rɪs-/ noun; **empiricist** /-rɪs-/ noun.

emplacement /ɪmˈpleɪsmənt/ noun platform for gun(s); putting in position.

employ /ɪmˈplɔɪ/ verb use services of (person) in return for payment; use (thing, time, energy, etc.); keep (person) occupied. □ **in the employ of** employed by. □ **employer** noun.

employee /emplɔɪˈiː/ noun person employed for wages.

employment noun employing, being employed; person's trade or profession. □ **employment office** government office finding work for the unemployed.

emporium /emˈpɔːrɪəm/ noun large shop; centre of commerce.

empower /ɪmˈpaʊə/ verb give power to.

empress /ˈemprɪs/ noun wife or widow of emperor; woman emperor.

empty /ˈemptɪ/ ● adjective (-**ier**, -**iest**) containing nothing; vacant, unoccupied; hollow, insincere; without purpose; colloquial hungry; vacuous, foolish. ● verb (-**ies**, -**ied**) remove contents of; transfer (contents); become empty; (of river) discharge itself. ● noun (plural -**ies**) colloquial emptied bottle etc. □ **empty-handed** bringing or taking nothing. □ **emptiness** noun.

EMS abbreviation European Monetary System.

emu /ˈiːmjuː/ noun (plural -**s**) large flightless Australian bird.

emulate /ˈemjʊleɪt/ verb (-**ting**) try to equal or excel; imitate. □ **emulation** noun; **emulator** noun.

emulsify /ɪˈmʌlsɪfaɪ/ verb (-**ies**, -**ied**) make emulsion of. □ **emulsifier** noun.

emulsion /ɪˈmʌlʃ(ə)n/ noun fine dispersion of one liquid in another, esp. as paint, medicine, etc.

en noun Printing unit of measurement equal to half em.

enable /ɪˈneɪb(ə)l/ verb (-**ling**) (+ *to do*) supply with means or authority; make possible.

enact /ɪˈnækt/ verb ordain, decree; make (bill etc.) law; play (part). □ **enactment** noun.

enamel /ɪˈnæm(ə)l/ ● noun glasslike opaque coating on metal; any hard smooth coating; kind of hard gloss paint; hard coating of teeth. ● verb (-**ll**-; US -**l**-) coat with enamel.

enamour /ɪˈnæmə/ verb (US **enamor**) (usually in *passive*; + *of*) inspire with love or delight.

en bloc /ɑ̃ ˈblɒk/ adverb in a block, all at same time. [French]

encamp /ɪnˈkæmp/ verb settle in (esp. military) camp. □ **encampment** noun.

encapsulate /ɪnˈkæpsjʊleɪt/ verb (-**ting**) enclose (as) in capsule; summarize.

encase /ɪnˈkeɪs/ verb (-**sing**) confine (as) in a case.

encash /ɪnˈkæʃ/ verb convert into cash. □ **encashment** noun.

encephalitis /ensefəˈlaɪtɪs/ noun inflammation of brain.

enchant /ɪnˈtʃɑːnt/ verb delight; bewitch. □ **enchanting** adjective; **enchantment** noun.

enchanter noun (feminine **enchantress**) person who enchants, esp. by magic.

encircle /ɪnˈsɜːk(ə)l/ verb (-**ling**) surround. □ **encirclement** noun.

enclave /ˈenkleɪv/ noun part of territory of one state surrounded by that of another; group of people distinct from those surrounding them, esp. ethnically.

enclose /ɪnˈkləʊz/ verb (-**sing**) surround with wall, fence, etc.; shut in; put in receptacle (esp. in envelope besides letter); (as **enclosed** adjective) (of religious community) secluded from outside world.

enclosure /ɪnˈkləʊʒə/ noun enclosing; enclosed space or area; thing enclosed.

encode /ɪnˈkəʊd/ *verb* (**-ding**) put into code.

encomium /ɪnˈkəʊmɪəm/ *noun* (*plural* **-s**) formal praise.

encompass /ɪnˈkʌmpəs/ *verb* contain, include; surround.

encore /ˈɒŋkɔː/ ● *noun* audience's call for repetition of item, or for further item; such item. ● *verb* (**-ring**) call for repetition of or by. ● *interjection* again.

encounter /ɪnˈkaʊntə/ ● *verb* meet by chance; meet as adversary. ● *noun* meeting by chance or in conflict.

encourage /ɪnˈkʌrɪdʒ/ *verb* (**-ging**) give courage to; urge; promote. □ **encouragement** *noun*.

encroach /ɪnˈkrəʊtʃ/ *verb* (usually + *on*, *upon*) intrude on other's territory etc. □ **encroachment** *noun*.

encrust /ɪnˈkrʌst/ *verb* cover with or form crust; coat with hard casing or deposit.

encumber /ɪnˈkʌmbə/ *verb* be burden to; hamper.

encumbrance /ɪnˈkʌmbrəns/ *noun* burden; impediment.

encyclical /ɪnˈsɪklɪk(ə)l/ *noun* papal letter to all RC bishops.

encyclopedia /ɪnsaɪkləˈpiːdɪə/ *noun* (also **-paedia**) book of information on many subjects or on many aspects of one subject.

encyclopedic *adjective* (also **-paedic**) (of knowledge or information) comprehensive.

end ● *noun* limit; farthest point; extreme point or part; conclusion; latter part; destruction; death; result; goal, object; remnant. ● *verb* bring or come to end. □ **endpaper** blank leaf of paper at beginning or end of book; **end-product** final product of manufacture etc.; **end up** be or become eventually, arrive; **in the end** finally; **make ends meet** live within one's income; **no end** *colloquial* to a great extent.

endanger /ɪnˈdeɪndʒə/ *verb* place in danger. □ **endangered species** one in danger of extinction.

endear /ɪnˈdɪə/ *verb* (usually + *to*) make dear. □ **endearing** *adjective*.

endearment *noun* expression of affection.

endeavour /ɪnˈdevə/ (*US* **endeavor**) ● *verb* try, strive. ● *noun* attempt, effort.

endemic /enˈdemɪk/ *adjective* (often + *to*) regularly found among particular people or in particular area. □ **endemically** *adverb*.

ending *noun* end of word or story.

endive /ˈendaɪv/ *noun* curly-leaved plant used in salads.

endless *adjective* infinite; continual. □ **endlessly** *adverb*.

endocrine /ˈendəʊkraɪn/ *adjective* (of gland) secreting directly into blood.

endogenous /enˈdɒdʒɪnəs/ *adjective* growing or originating from within.

endorse /ɪnˈdɔːs/ *verb* (**-sing**) approve; write on (document), esp. sign (cheque); enter details of offence on (driving licence). □ **endorsement** *noun*.

endoskeleton /ˈendəʊskelɪtən/ *noun* internal skeleton.

endow /ɪnˈdaʊ/ *verb* give permanent income to; (esp. as **endowed** *adjective*) provide with talent or ability.

endowment *noun* endowing; money with which person or thing is endowed. □ **endowment mortgage** one in which borrower pays only premiums until policy repays mortgage capital; **endowment policy** life insurance policy paying out on set date or earlier death.

endue /ɪnˈdjuː/ *verb* (**-dues**, **-dued**, **-duing**) (+ *with*) provide (person) with (quality etc.).

endurance *noun* power of enduring.

endure /ɪnˈdjʊə/ *verb* (**-ring**) undergo; bear; last.

endways *adverb* with an end facing forwards.

ENE *abbreviation* east-north-east.

enema /ˈenɪmə/ *noun* injection of liquid etc. into rectum, esp. to expel its contents; liquid used for this.

enemy /ˈenəmɪ/ ● *noun* (*plural* **-ies**) person actively hostile to another; hostile army or nation; member of this; adversary, opponent. ● *adjective* of or belonging to enemy.

energetic /enəˈdʒetɪk/ *adjective* full of energy. □ **energetically** *adverb*.

energize /ˈenədʒaɪz/ *verb* (also **-ise**) (**-zing** or **-sing**) give energy to.

energy /'enədʒɪ/ noun (plural **-ies**) force, vigour, activity; ability of matter or radiation to do work.

enervate /'enəveɪt/ verb (**-ting**) deprive of vigour. □ **enervation** noun.

en famille /ɑ̃ fæ'miː/ adverb in or with one's family. [French]

enfant terrible /ɑ̃fɑ̃ te'riːbl/ noun (plural **enfants terribles** same pronunciation) indiscreet or unruly person. [French]

enfeeble /ɪn'fiːb(ə)l/ verb (**-ling**) make feeble. □ **enfeeblement** noun.

enfilade /enfɪ'leɪd/ ● noun gunfire directed down length of enemy position. ● verb (**-ding**) direct enfilade at.

enfold /ɪn'fəʊld/ verb wrap; embrace.

enforce /ɪn'fɔːs/ verb (**-cing**) compel observance of; impose. □ **enforceable** adjective; **enforcement** noun.

enfranchise /ɪn'fræntʃaɪz/ verb (**-sing**) give (person) right to vote. □ **enfranchisement** /-tʃɪz-/ noun.

engage /ɪn'geɪdʒ/ verb (**-ging**) employ, hire; (as **engaged** adjective) occupied, busy, having promised to marry; hold (person's attention); cause parts of (gear) to interlock; fit, interlock; bring into battle; come into battle with (enemy); (usually + in) take part in; (+ that, to do) undertake. □ **engagement** noun.

engender /ɪn'dʒendə/ verb give rise to.

engine /'endʒɪn/ noun mechanical contrivance of parts working together, esp. as source of power; railway locomotive.

engineer /endʒɪ'nɪə/ ● noun person skilled in a branch of engineering; person who makes or is in charge of engines etc.; person who designs and constructs military works; mechanic, technician. ● verb contrive, bring about; act as engineer; construct or manage as engineer.

engineering noun application of science to design, building, and use of machines etc.

English /'ɪŋglɪʃ/ ● adjective of England. ● noun language of England, now used in UK, US, and most Commonwealth countries; (**the English**) (treated as plural) the people of England. □ **Englishman**, **Englishwoman** native of England.

engraft /ɪn'grɑːft/ verb (usually + into, on) graft, implant, incorporate.

engrave /ɪn'greɪv/ verb (**-ving**) inscribe or cut (design) on hard surface; inscribe (surface) thus; (often + on) impress deeply (on memory etc.). □ **engraver** noun.

engraving noun print made from engraved plate.

engross /ɪn'grəʊs/ verb (usually as **engrossed** adjective + in) fully occupy.

engulf /ɪn'gʌlf/ verb flow over and swamp, overwhelm.

enhance /ɪn'hɑːns/ verb (**-cing**) intensify; improve. □ **enhancement** noun.

enigma /ɪ'nɪgmə/ noun puzzling person or thing; riddle. □ **enigmatic** /enɪg'mætɪk/ adjective.

enjoin /ɪn'dʒɔɪn/ verb command, order.

enjoy /ɪn'dʒɔɪ/ verb find pleasure in; (**enjoy oneself**) find pleasure in; have use or benefit of; experience. □ **enjoyable** adjective; **enjoyably** adverb; **enjoyment** noun.

enlarge /ɪn'lɑːdʒ/ verb (**-ging**) make or become larger; (often + on, upon) describe in greater detail; reproduce on larger scale. □ **enlargement** noun.

enlarger noun apparatus for enlarging photographs.

enlighten /ɪn'laɪt(ə)n/ verb inform; (as **enlightened** adjective) progressive. □ **enlightenment** noun.

enlist /ɪn'lɪst/ verb enrol in armed services; secure as means of help or support. □ **enlistment** noun.

enliven /ɪn'laɪv(ə)n/ verb make lively or cheerful. □ **enlivenment** noun.

en masse /ɑ̃ 'mæs/ adverb all together. [French]

enmesh /ɪn'meʃ/ verb entangle (as) in net.

enmity /'enmɪtɪ/ noun (plural **-ies**) hostility; state of being an enemy.

ennoble /ɪ'nəʊb(ə)l/ verb (**-ling**) make noble. □ **ennoblement** noun.

ennui /ɒ'nwiː/ noun boredom.

enormity /ɪ'nɔːmɪtɪ/ noun (plural **-ies**) great wickedness; monstrous crime; great size.

■ **Usage** Many people believe it is wrong to use *enormity* to mean 'great size'.

enormous /ɪˈnɔːməs/ *adjective* huge. □ **enormously** *adverb*.

enough /ɪˈnʌf/ ● *adjective* as much or as many as required. ● *noun* sufficient amount or quantity. ● *adverb* to required degree; fairly; very, quite.

enquire /ɪnˈkwaɪə/ *verb* (**-ring**) seek information; ask question; inquire.

enquiry *noun* (*plural* **-ies**) asking; inquiry.

enrage /ɪnˈreɪdʒ/ *verb* (**-ging**) make furious.

enrapture /ɪnˈræptʃə/ *verb* (**-ring**) delight intensely.

enrich /ɪnˈrɪtʃ/ *verb* make rich(er). □ **enrichment** *noun*.

enrol /ɪnˈrəʊl/ *verb* (*US* **enroll**) (**-ll-**) (cause to) join society, course, etc.; write name of (person) on list. □ **enrolment** *noun*.

en route /ɑ̃ ˈruːt/ *adverb* on the way. [French]

ensconce /ɪnˈskɒns/ *verb* (**-cing**) (usually **ensconce oneself** or in *passive*) settle comfortably.

ensemble /ɒnˈsɒmb(ə)l/ *noun* thing viewed as whole; set of clothes worn together; group of performers working together; *Music* passage for ensemble.

enshrine /ɪnˈʃraɪn/ *verb* (**-ning**) enclose in shrine; protect, make inviolable.

ensign /ˈensaɪn/ *noun* banner, flag, esp. military or naval flag of nation; standard-bearer; *historical* lowest commissioned infantry officer; *US* lowest commissioned naval officer.

enslave /ɪnˈsleɪv/ *verb* (**-ving**) make slave of. □ **enslavement** *noun*.

ensnare /ɪnˈsneə/ *verb* (**-ring**) entrap.

ensue /ɪnˈsjuː/ *verb* (**-sues, -sued, -suing**) happen later or as a result.

en suite /ɑ̃ ˈswiːt/ ● *adverb* forming single unit. ● *adjective* (of bathroom) attached to bedroom; (of bedroom) with bathroom attached.

ensure /ɪnˈʃʊə/ *verb* (**-ring**) make certain or safe.

ENT *abbreviation* ear, nose, and throat.

entail /ɪnˈteɪl/ ● *verb* necessitate or involve unavoidably; *Law* bequeath (estate) to specified line of beneficiaries. ● *noun* entailed estate.

entangle /ɪnˈtæŋɡ(ə)l/ *verb* (**-ling**) catch or hold fast in snare etc.; involve in difficulties; complicate. □ **entanglement** *noun*.

entente /ɒnˈtɒnt/ *noun* friendly understanding between states. □ **entente cordiale** entente, esp. between Britain and France since 1904.

enter /ˈentə/ *verb* go or come in or into; come on stage; penetrate; put (name, fact, etc.) into list or record etc.; (usually + *for*) name, or name oneself, as competitor; become member of. □ **enter into** engage in, bind oneself by, form part of, sympathize with; **enter (up)on** begin, begin to deal with, assume possession of.

enteric /enˈterɪk/ *adjective* of intestines.

enteritis /entəˈraɪtɪs/ *noun* inflammation of intestines.

enterprise /ˈentəpraɪz/ *noun* bold undertaking; readiness to engage in this; business firm or venture.

enterprising *adjective* showing enterprise.

entertain /entəˈteɪn/ *verb* amuse; receive as guest; harbour (feelings); consider (idea). □ **entertainer** *noun*; **entertaining** *adjective*.

entertainment *noun* entertaining; thing that entertains, performance.

enthral /ɪnˈθrɔːl/ *verb* (*US* **enthrall**) (**-ll-**) captivate; please greatly. □ **enthralment** *noun*.

enthrone /ɪnˈθrəʊn/ *verb* (**-ning**) place on throne. □ **enthronement** *noun*.

enthuse /ɪnˈθjuːz/ *verb* (**-sing**) *colloquial* be or make enthusiastic.

enthusiasm /ɪnˈθjuːzɪæz(ə)m/ *noun* great eagerness or admiration; object of this. □ **enthusiast** *noun*; **enthusiastic** /-ˈæst-/ *adjective*; **enthusiastically** *adverb*.

entice /ɪnˈtaɪs/ *verb* (**-cing**) attract by offer of pleasure or reward. □ **enticement** *noun*; **enticing** *adjective*; **enticingly** *adverb*.

entire /ɪnˈtaɪə/ *adjective* complete; unbroken; absolute; in one piece.

entirely *adverb* wholly.

entirety /ɪnˈtaɪərətɪ/ *noun* (*plural* **-ies**) completeness; sum total. □ **in its entirety** in its complete form.

entitle /ɪn'taɪt(ə)l/ verb (-ling) (usually + to) give (person) right or claim; give title to. □ **entitlement** noun.

entity /'entɪtɪ/ noun (plural -ies) thing with distinct existence; thing's existence.

entomb /ɪn'tuːm/ verb place in tomb; serve as tomb for. □ **entombment** noun.

entomology /entə'mɒlədʒɪ/ noun study of insects. □ **entomological** /-mə'lɒdʒɪ-/ adjective; **entomologist** noun.

entourage /'ɒntʊrɑːʒ/ noun people attending important person.

entr'acte /'ɒntrækt/ noun (music or dance performed in) interval in play.

entrails /'entreɪlz/ plural noun intestines; inner parts.

entrance[1] /'entrəns/ noun place for entering; coming or going in; right of admission.

entrance[2] /ɪn'trɑːns/ verb (-cing) enchant, delight; put into trance.

entrant /'entrənt/ noun person who enters exam, profession, etc.

entrap /ɪn'træp/ verb (-pp-) catch (as) in trap.

entreat /ɪn'triːt/ verb ask earnestly, beg.

entreaty noun (plural -ies) earnest request.

entrecôte /'ɒntrəkəʊt/ noun boned steak cut off sirloin.

entrée /'ɒntreɪ/ noun main dish of meal; dish served between fish and meat courses; right of admission.

entrench /ɪn'trentʃ/ verb establish firmly; (as **entrenched** adjective) (of attitude etc.) not easily modified; surround or fortify with trench. □ **entrenchment** noun.

entrepreneur /ɒntrəprə'nɜː/ noun person who undertakes commercial venture. □ **entrepreneurial** adjective.

entropy /'entrəpɪ/ noun measure of disorganization of universe; measure of unavailability of system's thermal energy for conversion into mechanical work.

entrust /ɪn'trʌst/ verb (+ to) give (person, thing) into care of; (+ with) assign responsibility for (person, thing) to.

entry /'entrɪ/ noun (plural -ies) coming or going in; entering; item entered; place of entrance; alley.

entwine /ɪn'twaɪn/ verb (-ning) twine round, interweave.

enumerate /ɪ'njuːməreɪt/ verb (-ting) specify (items); count. □ **enumeration** noun.

enunciate /ɪ'nʌnsɪeɪt/ verb (-ting) pronounce (words) clearly; state definitely. □ **enunciation** noun.

envelop /ɪn'veləp/ verb (-p-) wrap up, cover; surround. □ **envelopment** noun.

envelope /'envələʊp/ noun folded paper cover for letter etc.; wrapper, covering.

enviable /'envɪəb(ə)l/ adjective likely to excite envy. □ **enviably** adverb.

envious /'envɪəs/ adjective feeling or showing envy.

environment /ɪn'vaɪərənmənt/ noun surroundings; circumstances affecting person's life. □ **environmental** /-'men-/ adjective; **environmentally** /-'men-/ adverb.

environmentalist /ɪnvaɪərən'mentəlɪst/ noun person concerned with protection of natural environment.

environs /ɪn'vaɪərənz/ plural noun district round town etc.

envisage /ɪn'vɪzɪdʒ/ verb (-ging) visualize, imagine, contemplate.

envoy /'envɔɪ/ noun messenger, representative; diplomat ranking below ambassador.

envy /'envɪ/ ● noun (plural -ies) discontent aroused by another's better fortune etc.; object or cause of this. ● verb (-ies, -ied) feel envy of.

enzyme /'enzaɪm/ noun protein catalyst of specific biochemical reaction.

eolian harp US = AEOLIAN HARP.

eon = AEON.

EP abbreviation extended-play (record).

epaulette /'epəlet/ noun (US **epaulet**) ornamental shoulder-piece, esp. on uniform.

ephedrine /'efədrɪn/ noun alkaloid drug used to relieve asthma etc.

ephemera /ɪ'femərə/ plural noun things of only short-lived relevance.

ephemeral adjective short-lived, transitory.

epic /'epɪk/ ● noun long poem narrating adventures of heroic figure etc.; book or film based on this. ● adjective like an epic; grand, heroic.

epicene /'epɪsiːn/ *adjective* of or for both sexes; having characteristics of both sexes or of neither sex.

epicentre /'epɪsentə/ *noun* (*US* **epicenter**) point at which earthquake reaches earth's surface.

epicure /'epɪkjʊə/ *noun* person with refined taste in food and drink. □ **epicurism** *noun*.

epicurean /epɪkjʊə'riːən/ ● *noun* person fond of pleasure and luxury. ● *adjective* characteristics of an epicurean. □ **epicureanism** *noun*.

epidemic /epɪ'demɪk/ ● *noun* widespread occurrence of particular disease in community at particular time. ● *adjective* in the nature of an epidemic.

epidemiology /epɪdiːmɪ'ɒlədʒɪ/ *noun* study of epidemics and their control.

epidermis /epɪ'dɜːmɪs/ *noun* outer layer of skin.

epidiascope /epɪ'daɪəskəʊp/ *noun* optical projector giving images of both opaque and transparent objects.

epidural /epɪ'djʊər(ə)l/ ● *adjective* (of anaesthetic) injected close to spinal cord. ● *noun* epidural injection.

epiglottis /epɪ'glɒtɪs/ *noun* flap of cartilage at root of tongue that covers windpipe during swallowing. □ **epiglottal** *adjective*.

epigram /'epɪgræm/ *noun* short poem with witty ending; pointed saying. □ **epigrammatic** /-grə'mæt-/ *adjective*.

epigraph /'epɪgrɑːf/ *noun* inscription.

epilepsy /'epɪlepsɪ/ *noun* nervous disorder with convulsions and often loss of consciousness. □ **epileptic** /-'lep-/ *adjective & noun*.

epilogue /'epɪlɒg/ *noun* short piece ending literary work; short speech at end of play etc.

Epiphany /ɪ'pɪfənɪ/ *noun* (festival on 6 Jan. commemorating) visit of Magi to Christ.

episcopacy /ɪ'pɪskəpəsɪ/ *noun* (*plural* **-ies**) government by bishops; bishops collectively.

episcopal /ɪ'pɪskəp(ə)l/ *adjective* of bishop or bishops; (of church) governed by bishops. □ **Episcopal Church** Anglican Church in Scotland and US.

Episcopalian /ɪpɪskə'peɪlɪən/ ● *adjective* of the Episcopal Church or (**episcopalian**) an episcopal church. ● *noun* member of the Episcopal Church.

episcopate /ɪ'pɪskəpət/ *noun* office or tenure of bishop; bishops collectively.

episode /'epɪsəʊd/ *noun* event as part of sequence; part of serial story; incident in narrative. □ **episodic** /-'sɒd-/ *adjective*.

epistemology /ɪpɪstɪ'mɒlədʒɪ/ *noun* philosophy of knowledge. □ **epistemological** /-ə'lɒdʒ-/ *adjective*.

epistle /ɪ'pɪs(ə)l/ *noun* letter; poem etc. in form of letter.

epistolary /ɪ'pɪstələrɪ/ *adjective* of or in form of letters.

epitaph /'epɪtɑːf/ *noun* words in memory of dead person, esp. on tomb.

epithelium /epɪ'θiːlɪəm/ *noun* (*plural* **-s** or **-lia**) *Biology* tissue forming outer layer of body and lining many hollow structures. □ **epithelial** *adjective*.

epithet /'epɪθet/ *noun* adjective etc. expressing quality or attribute.

epitome /ɪ'pɪtəmɪ/ *noun* person or thing embodying a quality etc.

epitomize *verb* (also **-ise**) (**-zing** or **-sing**) make or be perfect example of (a quality etc.).

EPNS *abbreviation* electroplated nickel silver.

epoch /'iːpɒk/ *noun* period marked by special events; beginning of era. □ **epoch-making** notable, significant.

eponym /'epənɪm/ *noun* word derived from person's name; person whose name is used in this way. □ **eponymous** /ɪ'pɒnɪməs/ *adjective*.

epoxy resin /ɪ'pɒksɪ/ *noun* synthetic thermosetting resin, used esp. as glue.

Epsom salts /'epsəm/ *noun* magnesium sulphate used as purgative.

equable /'ekwəb(ə)l/ *adjective* not varying; moderate; not easily disturbed. □ **equably** *adverb*.

equal /'iːkw(ə)l/ ● *adjective* same in number, size, merit, etc.; evenly matched; having same rights or status. ● *noun* person etc. equal to another. ● *verb* (**-ll-**; *US* **-l-**) be equal to; achieve something equal to. □ **equal opportunity** (often in *plural*) opportunity to compete equally for jobs regardless of race, sex, etc. □ **equally** adverb.

■ **Usage** It is a mistake to say *equally as*, as in *She was equally as guilty*. The correct version is *She was equally guilty* or possibly, for example, *She was as guilty as he was*.

equality /ɪˈkwɒlɪtɪ/ noun being equal.

equalize verb (also **-ise**) (**-zing** or **-sing**) make or become equal; (in games) reach opponent's score. □ **equalization** noun.

equalizer noun (also **-iser**) equalizing goal etc.

equanimity /ekwəˈnɪmɪtɪ/ noun composure, calm.

equate /ɪˈkweɪt/ verb (**-ting**) (usually + *to, with*) regard as equal or equivalent; (+ *with*) be equal or equivalent to.

equation /ɪˈkweɪʒ(ə)n/ noun making or being equal; *Mathematics* statement that two expressions are equal; *Chemistry* symbolic representation of reaction.

equator /ɪˈkweɪtə/ noun imaginary line round the earth or other body, equidistant from poles.

equatorial /ekwəˈtɔːrɪəl/ adjective of or near equator.

equerry /ˈekwərɪ/ noun (plural **-ies**) officer attending British royal family.

equestrian /ɪˈkwestrɪən/ adjective of horse-riding; on horseback. □ **equestrianism** noun.

equiangular /iːkwɪˈæŋɡjʊlə/ adjective having equal angles.

equidistant /iːkwɪˈdɪst(ə)nt/ adjective at equal distances.

equilateral /iːkwɪˈlætər(ə)l/ adjective having all sides equal.

equilibrium /iːkwɪˈlɪbrɪəm/ noun state of balance; composure.

equine /ˈekwaɪn/ adjective of or like horse.

equinox /ˈiːkwɪnɒks/ noun time or date at which sun crosses equator and day and night are of equal length.

equip /ɪˈkwɪp/ verb (**-pp-**) supply with what is needed.

equipment noun necessary tools, clothing, etc.; equipping, being equipped.

equipoise /ˈekwɪpɔɪz/ noun equilibrium; counterbalancing thing.

equitable /ˈekwɪtəb(ə)l/ adjective fair, just; *Law* valid in equity. □ **equitably** adverb.

equitation /ekwɪˈteɪʃ(ə)n/ noun horsemanship; horse-riding.

equity /ˈekwɪtɪ/ noun (plural **-ies**) fairness; principles of justice supplementing law; value of shares issued by company; (in plural) stocks and shares not bearing fixed interest.

equivalent /ɪˈkwɪvələnt/ ● adjective (often + *to*) equal in value, meaning, etc.; corresponding. ● noun equivalent amount etc. □ **equivalence** noun.

equivocal /ɪˈkwɪvək(ə)l/ adjective of double or doubtful meaning; of uncertain nature; (of person etc.) questionable. □ **equivocally** adverb.

equivocate /ɪˈkwɪvəkeɪt/ verb (**-ting**) use words ambiguously to conceal truth. □ **equivocation** noun.

ER abbreviation Queen Elizabeth (*Elizabetha Regina*).

era /ˈɪərə/ noun system of chronology starting from particular point; historical or other period.

eradicate /ɪˈrædɪkeɪt/ verb (**-ting**) root out, destroy. □ **eradication** noun.

erase /ɪˈreɪz/ verb (**-sing**) rub out; obliterate; remove recording from (magnetic tape etc.).

eraser noun piece of rubber etc. for removing esp. pencil marks.

erasure /ɪˈreɪʒə/ noun erasing; erased word etc.

ere /eə/ preposition & conjunction poetical or archaic before.

erect /ɪˈrekt/ ● adjective upright, vertical; (of part of body) enlarged and rigid, esp. from sexual excitement. ● verb raise, set upright; build; establish. □ **erection** noun.

erectile /ɪˈrektaɪl/ adjective that can become erect.

erg noun unit of work or energy.

ergo /ˈɜːɡəʊ/ adverb therefore. [Latin]

ergonomics /ɜːɡəˈnɒmɪks/ plural noun (treated as *singular*) study of relationship between people and their working environment. □ **ergonomic** adjective.

ergot /ˈɜːɡət/ noun disease of rye etc. caused by fungus.

ERM *abbreviation* Exchange Rate Mechanism.

ermine /'ɜ:mɪn/ *noun* (*plural* same or **-s**) stoat, esp. in its white winter fur; this fur.

Ernie /'ɜ:nɪ/ *noun* device for drawing prize-winning numbers of Premium Bonds.

erode /ɪ'rəʊd/ *verb* (**-ding**) wear away, gradually destroy. □ **erosion** *noun*; **erosive** *adjective*.

erogenous /ɪ'rɒdʒɪnəs/ *adjective* (of part of body) sexually sensitive.

erotic /ɪ'rɒtɪk/ *adjective* arousing sexual desire or excitement. □ **erotically** *adverb*; **eroticism** /-sɪz-/ *noun*.

erotica *plural noun* erotic literature or art.

err /ɜ:/ *verb* be mistaken or incorrect; sin.

errand /'erənd/ *noun* short journey, esp. on another's behalf, to take message etc.; object of journey.

errant /'erənt/ *adjective* erring; *literary* travelling in search of adventure.

erratic /ɪ'rætɪk/ *adjective* inconsistent or uncertain in movement or conduct etc. □ **erratically** *adverb*.

erratum /ɪ'rɑːtəm/ *noun* (*plural* **-ta**) error in printing etc.

erroneous /ɪ'rəʊnɪəs/ *adjective* incorrect. □ **erroneously** *adverb*.

error /'erə/ *noun* mistake; condition of being morally wrong; degree of inaccuracy in calculation or measurement.

ersatz /'eəzæts/ *adjective & noun* substitute; imitation.

erstwhile /'ɜ:stwaɪl/ *adjective* former.

eructation /iːrʌk'teɪʃ(ə)n/ *noun formal* belching.

erudite /'eruːdaɪt/ *adjective* learned. □ **erudition** /-'dɪʃ-/ *noun*.

erupt /ɪ'rʌpt/ *verb* break out; (of volcano) shoot out lava etc.; (of rash) appear on skin. □ **eruption** *noun*.

erysipelas /erɪ'sɪpɪləs/ *noun* disease causing deep red inflammation of skin.

escalate /'eskəleɪt/ *verb* (**-ting**) increase or develop by stages. □ **escalation** *noun*.

escalator *noun* moving staircase.

escalope /'eskələʊp/ *noun* thin slice of meat, esp. veal.

escapade /'eskəpeɪd/ *noun* piece of reckless behaviour.

escape /ɪs'keɪp/ ● *verb* (**-ping**) get free; leak; avoid punishment etc.; get free of; elude, avoid. ● *noun* escaping; means of escaping; leakage. □ **escape clause** clause releasing contracting party from obligation in specified circumstances.

escapee /ɪskeɪ'piː/ *noun* person who has escaped.

escapism *noun* pursuit of distraction and relief from reality. □ **escapist** *adjective & noun*.

escapology /eskə'pɒlədʒɪ/ *noun* techniques of escaping from confinement, esp. as entertainment. □ **escapologist** *noun*.

escarpment /ɪs'kɑːpmənt/ *noun* long steep slope at edge of plateau etc.

eschatology /eskə'tɒlədʒɪ/ *noun* doctrine of death and final destiny. □ **eschatological** /-tə'lɒdʒ-/ *adjective*.

escheat /ɪs'tʃiːt/ ● *noun* lapse of property to the state etc.; property so lapsing. ● *verb* hand over as escheat, confiscate; revert by escheat.

eschew /ɪs'tʃuː/ *verb formal* abstain from.

escort ● *noun* /'eskɔːt/ person(s) etc. accompanying another for protection or as courtesy; person accompanying another of opposite sex socially. ● *verb* /ɪ'skɔːt/ act as escort to.

escritoire /eskrɪ'twɑː/ *noun* writing desk with drawers etc.

escutcheon /ɪ'skʌtʃ(ə)n/ *noun* shield bearing coat of arms.

ESE *abbreviation* east-south-east.

Eskimo /'eskɪməʊ/ ● *noun* (*plural* same or **-s**) member of people inhabiting N. Canada, Alaska, Greenland, and E. Siberia; their language. ● *adjective* of Eskimos or their language.

■ **Usage** The Eskimos of N. America prefer the name *Inuit*.

ESN *abbreviation* educationally subnormal.

esophagus *US* = OESOPHAGUS.

esoteric /esə'terɪk, iːsə'terɪk/ *adjective* intelligible only to those with special knowledge.

ESP *abbreviation* extrasensory perception.

esp. *abbreviation* especially.

espadrille /ˈespəˈdrɪl/ *noun* light canvas shoe with plaited fibre sole.

espalier /ɪˈspælɪə/ *noun* framework for training tree etc.; tree trained on this.

esparto /eˈspɑːtəʊ/ *noun* kind of grass used to make paper.

especial /ɪˈspeʃ(ə)l/ *adjective* special, notable.

especially *adverb* in particular; more than in other cases; particularly.

Esperanto /espəˈræntəʊ/ *noun* artificial universal language.

espionage /ˈespɪənɑːʒ/ *noun* spying or using spies.

esplanade /espləˈneɪd/ *noun* level space, esp. used as public promenade.

espousal /ɪˈspaʊz(ə)l/ *noun* espousing; *archaic* marriage, betrothal.

espouse /ɪˈspaʊz/ *verb* (**-sing**) support (cause); *archaic* marry.

espresso /eˈspresəʊ/ *noun* (*plural* **-s**) coffee made under steam pressure.

esprit de corps /espriː də ˈkɔː/ *noun* devotion to and pride in one's group. [French]

espy /ɪˈspaɪ/ *verb* (**-ies, -ied**) catch sight of.

Esq. *abbreviation* Esquire.

esquire /ɪˈskwaɪə/ *noun: title placed after man's name in writing.*

essay ● *noun* /ˈeseɪ/ short piece of writing, esp. on given subject; *formal* attempt. ● *verb* /eˈseɪ/ attempt.

essayist *noun* writer of essays.

essence /ˈes(ə)ns/ *noun* fundamental nature, inherent characteristics; extract obtained by distillation etc.; perfume. □ **in essence** fundamentally.

essential /ɪˈsenʃ(ə)l/ ● *adjective* necessary, indispensable; of or constituting a thing's essence. ● *noun* (esp. in *plural*) indispensable element or thing. □ **essential oil** volatile oil with characteristic odour. □ **essentially** *adverb*.

establish /ɪˈstæblɪʃ/ *verb* set up; settle; (esp. as **established** *adjective*) achieve permanent acceptance for; place beyond dispute. □ **Established Church** Church recognized by state.

establishment *noun* establishing, being established; public institution; place of business; staff, household, etc.; Church system established by law;

(the Establishment) social group with authority or influence and resisting change.

estate /ɪˈsteɪt/ *noun* landed property; area of homes or businesses planned as a whole; dead person's collective assets and liabilities. □ **estate agent** person whose business is sale and lease of buildings and land on behalf of others; **estate car** car with continuous area for rear passengers and luggage.

esteem /ɪˈstiːm/ ● *verb* (usually in *passive*) think highly of; *formal* consider. ● *noun* high regard.

ester /ˈestə/ *noun* compound formed by replacing the hydrogen of an acid by an organic radical.

estimable /ˈestɪməb(ə)l/ *adjective* worthy of esteem.

estimate ● *noun* /ˈestɪmət/ approximate judgement of cost, value, etc.; approximate price stated in advance for work. ● *verb* /ˈestɪmeɪt/ (**-ting**) form estimate of; (+ *that*) make rough calculation; (+ *at*) put (sum etc.) at by estimating.

estimation /estɪˈmeɪʃ(ə)n/ *noun* estimating; judgement of worth.

estrange /ɪˈstreɪndʒ/ *verb* (**-ging**) (usually in *passive*; often + *from*) alienate, make hostile or indifferent; (as **estranged** *adjective*) no longer living with spouse. □ **estrangement** *noun*.

estrogen *US* = OESTROGEN.

estuary /ˈestjʊərɪ/ *noun* (*plural* **-ies**) tidal mouth of river.

ETA *abbreviation* estimated time of arrival.

et al. *abbreviation* and others (*et alii*).

etc. *abbreviation* et cetera.

et cetera /et ˈsetrə/ *adverb* (also **etcetera**) and the rest; and so on. □ **etceteras** *plural noun* the usual extras.

etch *verb* reproduce (picture etc.) by engraving metal plate with acid, esp. to print copies; engrave (plate) thus; practise this craft; (usually + *on, upon*) impress deeply.

etching *noun* print made from etched plate.

eternal /ɪˈtɜːn(ə)l/ *adjective* existing always; without end or beginning; unchanging; *colloquial* constant, too frequent. □ **eternally** *adverb*.

eternity /ɪˈtɜːnɪtɪ/ noun infinite time; endless life after death; (**an eternity**) colloquial a very long time.

ethane /ˈiːθeɪn/ noun hydrocarbon gas present in petroleum and natural gas.

ethanol /ˈeθənɒl/ noun alcohol.

ether /ˈiːθə/ noun volatile liquid used as anaesthetic or solvent; clear sky, upper air.

ethereal /ɪˈθɪərɪəl/ adjective light, airy; delicate, esp. in appearance; heavenly.

ethic /ˈeθɪk/ noun set of moral principles.

ethical adjective relating to morals or ethics; morally correct; (of drug etc.) available only on prescription. □ **ethically** adverb.

ethics plural noun (also treated as singular) moral philosophy; (set of) moral principles.

Ethiopian /iːθɪˈəʊpɪən/ ● noun native or national of Ethiopia. ● adjective of Ethiopia.

ethnic /ˈeθnɪk/ adjective (of social) group having common national or cultural tradition; (of clothes etc.) resembling those of an exotic people; (of person) having specified origin by birth or descent rather than nationality. □ **ethnic cleansing** euphemistic expulsion or murder of people of ethnic or religious group in certain area. □ **ethnically** adverb.

ethnology /eθˈnɒlədʒɪ/ noun comparative study of peoples. □ **ethnological** /-nəˈlɒdʒ-/ adjective.

ethos /ˈiːθɒs/ noun characteristic spirit of community, people, or system.

ethylene /ˈeθɪliːn/ noun flammable hydrocarbon gas.

etiolate /ˈiːtɪəleɪt/ verb (-ting) make pale by excluding light; give sickly colour to. □ **etiolation** noun.

etiology US = AETIOLOGY.

etiquette /ˈetɪket/ noun conventional rules of social behaviour or professional conduct.

étude /eɪˈtjuːd/ noun musical composition designed to develop player's skill.

etymology /etɪˈmɒlədʒɪ/ noun (plural **-ies**) origin and sense-development of word; account of these. □ **etymological** /-məˈlɒdʒ-/ adjective.

eucalyptus /juːkəˈlɪptəs/ noun (plural **-tuses** or **-ti** /-taɪ/) tall evergreen tree; its oil, used as antiseptic etc.

Eucharist /ˈjuːkərɪst/ noun Christian sacrament in which bread and wine are consecrated and consumed; consecrated elements, esp. bread. □ **Eucharistic** /-ˈrɪs-/ adjective.

eugenics /juːˈdʒenɪks/ plural noun (also treated as singular) improvement of qualities of race by control of inherited characteristics. □ **eugenic** adjective; **eugenically** adverb.

eulogize /ˈjuːlədʒaɪz/ verb (also **-ise**) (**-zing** or **-sing**) extol; praise.

eulogy /ˈjuːlədʒɪ/ noun (plural **-ies**) speech or writing in praise or commendation. □ **eulogistic** /-ˈdʒɪs-/ adjective.

eunuch /ˈjuːnək/ noun castrated man.

euphemism /ˈjuːfɪmɪz(ə)m/ noun mild expression substituted for blunt one. □ **euphemistic** /-ˈmɪs-/ adjective; **euphemistically** /-ˈmɪs-/ adverb.

euphonium /juːˈfəʊnɪəm/ noun brass instrument of tuba family.

euphony /ˈjuːfənɪ/ noun pleasantness of sound, esp. in words. □ **euphonious** /-ˈfəʊ-/ adjective.

euphoria /juːˈfɔːrɪə/ noun intense sense of well-being and excitement. □ **euphoric** /-ˈfɒr-/ adjective.

Eurasian /jʊəˈreɪʒ(ə)n/ ● adjective of mixed European and Asian parentage; of Europe and Asia. ● noun Eurasian person.

eureka /jʊəˈriːkə/ interjection I have found it!

Eurodollar /ˈjʊərəʊdɒlə/ noun dollar held in bank in Europe etc.

European /jʊərəˈpɪən/ ● adjective of, in, or extending over Europe. ● noun native or inhabitant of Europe; descendant of one.

Eustachian tube /juːˈsteɪʃ(ə)n/ noun passage between middle ear and back of throat.

euthanasia /juːθəˈneɪzɪə/ noun killing person painlessly, esp. one who has incurable painful disease.

evacuate /ɪˈvækjʊeɪt/ verb (**-ting**) remove (people) from place of danger; make empty, clear; withdraw from (place); empty (bowels). □ **evacuation** noun.

evacuee /ɪvækjuˈiː/ noun person evacuated.

evade /ɪ'veɪd/ verb (**-ding**) escape from, avoid; avoid doing or answering directly; avoid paying (tax) illegally.

evaluate /ɪ'væljʊeɪt/ verb (**-ting**) assess, appraise; find or state number or amount of. □ **evaluation** noun.

evanesce /evə'nes/ verb (**-cing**) literary fade from sight. □ **evanescence** noun; **evanescent** adjective.

evangelical /iːvæn'dʒelɪk(ə)l/ ● adjective of or according to gospel teaching; of Protestant groups maintaining doctrine of salvation by faith. ● noun member of evangelical group. □ **evangelicalism** noun.

evangelist /ɪ'vændʒəlɪst/ noun writer of one of the 4 Gospels; preacher of gospel. □ **evangelism** noun; **evangelistic** /-'lɪs-/ adjective.

evangelize verb (also **-ise**) (**-zing** or **-sing**) preach gospel to. □ **evangelization** noun.

evaporate /ɪ'væpəreɪt/ verb (**-ting**) turn into vapour; (cause to) lose moisture as vapour; (cause to) disappear. □ **evaporation** noun.

evasion /ɪ'veɪʒ(ə)n/ noun evading; evasive answer.

evasive /ɪ'veɪsɪv/ adjective seeking to evade.

eve noun evening or day before festival etc.; time just before event; archaic evening.

even /'iːv(ə)n/ ● adjective (**-er, -est**) level, smooth; uniform; equal; equable, calm; divisible by two. ● adverb still, yet; (with negative) so much as. ● verb (often + up) make or become even. □ **even if** in spite of the fact that, no matter whether; **even out** become level or regular, spread (thing) over period or among group. □ **evenly** adverb.

evening /'iːvnɪŋ/ noun end part of day, esp. from about 6 p.m. to bedtime. □ **evening class** adult education class held in evening; **evening dress** formal clothes for evening wear; **evening star** planet, esp. Venus, conspicuous in west after sunset.

evensong noun evening service in Church of England.

event /ɪ'vent/ noun thing that happens; fact of thing occurring; item in (esp. sports) programme. □ **in any event, at**

all events whatever happens; **in the event** as it turns or turned out; **in the event of** if (thing) happens.

eventful adjective marked by noteworthy events.

eventual /ɪ'ventʃʊəl/ adjective occurring in due course. □ **eventually** adverb.

eventuality /ɪventʃʊ'ælɪtɪ/ noun (plural **-ies**) possible event.

ever /'evə/ adverb at all times; always; at any time. □ **ever since** throughout period since (then); **ever so** colloquial very; **ever such a(n)** colloquial a very.

evergreen ● adjective retaining green leaves throughout year. ● noun evergreen plant.

everlasting adjective lasting for ever or a long time; (of flower) retaining shape and colour when dried.

evermore adverb for ever; always.

every /'evrɪ/ adjective each; all. □ **everybody** every person; **everyday** occurring every day, ordinary; **Everyman** ordinary or typical human being; **every now and again** or **then** occasionally; **everyone** everybody; **every other** each alternate; **everything** all things, the most important thing; **everywhere** in every place.

evict /ɪ'vɪkt/ verb expel (tenant) by legal process. □ **eviction** noun.

evidence /'evɪd(ə)ns/ ● noun (often + for, of) indication, sign; information given to establish fact etc.; statement etc. admissible in court of law. ● verb (**-cing**) be evidence of.

evident adjective obvious, manifest.

evidential /evɪ'denʃ(ə)l/ adjective of or providing evidence.

evidently adverb seemingly; as shown by evidence.

evil /'iːv(ə)l/ ● adjective wicked; harmful. ● noun evil thing; wickedness. □ **evil eye** gaze believed to cause harm. □ **evilly** adverb.

evince /ɪ'vɪns/ verb (**-cing**) show, indicate.

eviscerate /ɪ'vɪsəreɪt/ verb (**-ting**) disembowel. □ **evisceration** noun.

evocative /ɪ'vɒkətɪv/ adjective evoking (feelings etc.).

evoke /ɪ'vəʊk/ verb (**-king**) call up (feeling etc.). □ **evocation** /evə-/ noun.

evolution /iːvəˈluːʃ(ə)n/ *noun* evolving; development of species from earlier forms; unfolding of events etc.; change in disposition of troops or ships. □ **evolutionary** *adjective*.

evolutionist *noun* person who regards evolution as explaining origin of species.

evolve /ɪˈvɒlv/ *verb* (**-ving**) develop gradually and naturally; devise; unfold, open out.

ewe /juː/ *noun* female sheep.

ewer /ˈjuːə/ *noun* water-jug with wide mouth.

ex¹ *preposition* (of goods) sold from (warehouse etc.).

ex² *noun colloquial* former husband or wife.

ex- *prefix* formerly.

exacerbate /ekˈsæsəbeɪt/ *verb* (**-ting**) make worse; irritate. □ **exacerbation** *noun*.

exact /ɪgˈzækt/ ● *adjective* accurate; correct in all details. ● *verb* demand and enforce payment of (fees etc.); demand, insist on. □ **exactness** *noun*.

exaction *noun* exacting, being exacted; illegal or exorbitant demand.

exactitude *noun* exactness.

exactly *adverb* precisely; I agree.

exaggerate /ɪgˈzædʒəreɪt/ *verb* (**-ting**) make seem larger or greater than it really is; increase beyond normal or due proportions. □ **exaggeration** *noun*.

exalt /ɪgˈzɔːlt/ *verb* raise in rank, power, etc.; praise, extol; (usually as **exalted** *adjective*) make lofty or noble. □ **exaltation** /eg-/ *noun*.

exam /ɪgˈzæm/ *noun* examination, test.

examination /ɪgzæmɪˈneɪʃ(ə)n/ *noun* examining, being examined; detailed inspection; testing of knowledge or ability by questions; formal questioning of witness etc. in court.

examine /ɪgˈzæmɪn/ *verb* (**-ning**) inquire into; look closely at; test knowledge or ability of; check health of; question formally. □ **examinee** /-ˈniː/ *noun*, **examiner** *noun*.

example /ɪgˈzɑːmp(ə)l/ *noun* thing illustrating general rule; model, pattern; specimen; precedent; warning to others. □ **for example** by way of illustration.

exasperate /ɪgˈzæːspəreɪt/ *verb* (**-ting**) irritate intensely. □ **exasperation** *noun*.

ex cathedra /eks kəˈθiːdrə/ *adjective & adverb* with full authority (esp. of papal pronouncement). [Latin]

excavate /ˈekskəveɪt/ *verb* (**-ting**) make (hole etc.) by digging; dig out material from (ground); reveal or extract by digging; dig systematically to explore (archaeological site). □ **excavation** *noun*, **excavator** *noun*.

exceed /ɪkˈsiːd/ *verb* be more or greater than; go beyond, do more than is warranted by; surpass.

exceedingly *adverb* very.

excel /ɪkˈsel/ *verb* (**-ll-**) surpass; be pre-eminent.

excellence /ˈeksələns/ *noun* great merit.

Excellency *noun* (*plural* **-ies**) (**His, Her, Your Excellency**) *title used of or to ambassador, governor, etc.*

excellent *adjective* extremely good.

except /ɪkˈsept/ ● *verb* exclude from general statement etc. ● *preposition* (often + *for*) not including, other than.

excepting *preposition* except.

exception /ɪkˈsepʃ(ə)n/ *noun* excepting; thing or case excepted. □ **take exception** (often + *to*) object.

exceptionable *adjective* open to objection.

■ **Usage** *Exceptionable* is sometimes confused with *exceptional*.

exceptional *adjective* forming exception; unusual. □ **exceptionally** *adverb*.

■ **Usage** *Exceptional* is sometimes confused with *exceptionable*.

excerpt ● *noun* /ˈeksɜːpt/ short extract from book, film, etc. ● *verb* /ɪkˈsɜːpt/ take excerpts from. □ **excerption** /ɪkˈsɜːpʃ(ə)n/ *noun*.

excess ● *noun* /ɪkˈses/ exceeding; amount by which thing exceeds; intemperance in eating or drinking. ● *adjective* /ˈekses/ that exceeds limit or given amount. □ **in, to excess** exceeding proper amount or degree; **in excess of** more than.

excessive /ɪkˈsesɪv/ *adjective* too much; too great. □ **excessively** *adverb*.

exchange /ɪksˈtʃeɪndʒ/ ● *noun* giving one thing and receiving another in its place; exchanging of money for equivalent, esp. in other currency; centre where telephone connections are made; place where merchants, stockbrokers, etc. transact business; employment office; short conversation. ● *verb* (**-ging**) give or receive in exchange; interchange. □ **exchange rate** price of one currency expressed in another. □ **exchangeable** *adjective*.

exchequer /ɪksˈtʃekə/ *noun* former government department in charge of national revenue; royal or national treasury.

excise[1] /ˈeksaɪz/ *noun* tax levied on goods produced or sold within the country; tax on certain licences.

excise[2] /ɪkˈsaɪz/ *verb* (**-sing**) cut out or away. □ **excision** /-ˈsɪʒ-/ *noun*.

excitable *adjective* easily excited. □ **excitability** *noun*.

excite /ɪkˈsaɪt/ *verb* (**-ting**) move to strong emotion; arouse (feelings etc.); provoke (action etc.); stimulate to activity. □ **excitement** *noun*; **exciting** *adjective*.

exclaim /ɪkˈskleɪm/ *verb* cry out suddenly; utter or say thus.

exclamation /ekskləˈmeɪʃ(ə)n/ *noun* exclaiming; word(s) etc. exclaimed. □ **exclamation mark** punctuation mark (!) indicating exclamation (see panel). □ **exclamatory** /ɪkˈsklæmətərɪ/ *adjective*.

exclude /ɪkˈskluːd/ *verb* (**-ding**) shut out, leave out; make impossible, preclude. □ **exclusion** *noun*.

exclusive /ɪkˈskluːsɪv/ ● *adjective* excluding other things; (+ *of*) not including; (of society etc.) tending to exclude outsiders; high-class; not obtainable or published elsewhere. ● *noun* exclusive item of news, film, etc. □ **exclusively** *adverb*; **exclusiveness** *noun*, **exclusivity** /eksklu:ˈsɪvɪtɪ/ *noun*.

excommunicate /ekskəˈmju:nɪkeɪt/ *verb* (**-ting**) deprive (person) of membership and sacraments of Church. □ **excommunication** *noun*.

excoriate /eksˈkɔ:rɪeɪt/ *verb* (**-ting**) remove part of skin of by abrasion; remove (skin); censure severely. □ **excoriation** *noun*.

excrement /ˈekskrɪmənt/ *noun* faeces.

excrescence /ɪkˈskres(ə)ns/ *noun* abnormal or morbid outgrowth. □ **excrescent** *adjective*.

excreta /ɪkˈskri:tə/ *plural noun* faeces and urine.

excrete /ɪkˈskri:t/ *verb* (**-ting**) (of animal or plant) expel (waste). □ **excretion** *noun*; **excretory** *adjective*.

excruciating /ɪkˈskru:ʃɪeɪtɪŋ/ *adjective* acutely painful. □ **excruciatingly** *adverb*.

exculpate /ˈekskʌlpeɪt/ *verb* (**-ting**) *formal* free from blame. □ **exculpation** *noun*.

excursion /ɪkˈskɜ:ʃ(ə)n/ *noun* journey to place and back, made for pleasure.

excursive /ɪkˈskɜ:sɪv/ *adjective literary* digressive.

excuse ● *verb* /ɪkˈskju:z/ (**-sing**) try to lessen blame attaching to; serve as reason to judge (person, act) less severely; (often + *from*) grant exemption to; forgive. ● *noun* /ɪkˈskju:s/ reason put forward to mitigate or justify offence; apology. □ **be excused** be allowed not to do something or to leave or be absent; **excuse me** *polite request to*

Exclamation mark **!**

This is used instead of a full stop at the end of a sentence to show that the speaker or writer is very angry, enthusiastic, insistent, disappointed, hurt, surprised, etc., e.g.

I am not pleased at all!   *I wish I could have gone!*
I just love sweets!   *Ow!*
Go away!   *He didn't even say goodbye!*

be allowed to pass, polite apology for interrupting or disagreeing. □ **excusable** /-'skju:z-/ *adjective.*

ex-directory *adjective* not listed in telephone directory, at subscriber's wish.

execrable /'eksɪkrəb(ə)l/ *adjective* abominable.

execrate /'eksɪkreɪt/ *verb* (**-ting**) express or feel abhorrence for; curse. □ **execration** *noun.*

execute /'eksɪkju:t/ *verb* (**-ting**) carry out, perform; put to death.

execution /eksɪ'kju:ʃ(ə)n/ *noun* carrying out, performance; capital punishment.

executioner *noun* person carrying out death sentence.

executive /ɪg'zekjʊtɪv/ *noun* person or body with managerial or administrative responsibility; branch of government etc. concerned with executing laws, agreements, etc. ● *adjective* concerned with executing laws, agreements, etc. or with administration etc.

executor /ɪg'zekjʊtə/ *noun* (*feminine* **executrix** /-trɪks/) person appointed by testator to carry out terms of will. □ **executorial** /-'tɔ:rɪəl/ *adjective.*

exegesis /eksɪ'dʒi:sɪs/ *noun* explanation, esp. of Scripture. □ **exegetic** /-'dʒetɪk/ *adjective.*

exemplar /ɪg'zemplə/ *noun* model; typical instance.

exemplary *adjective* outstandingly good; serving as example or warning.

exemplify /ɪg'zemplɪfaɪ/ *verb* (**-ies**, **-ied**) give or be example of. □ **exemplification** *noun.*

exempt /ɪg'zempt/ ● *adjective* (often + *from*) free from obligation or liability imposed on others. ● *verb* (+ *from*) make exempt from. □ **exemption** *noun.*

exercise /'eksəsaɪz/ ● *noun* use of muscles etc., esp. for health; task set for physical or other training; use or application of faculties etc.; practice; (often in *plural*) military drill or manoeuvres. ● *verb* (**-sing**) use; perform (function); take exercise; give exercise to; tax powers of; perplex, worry.

exert /ɪg'zɜ:t/ *verb* use; bring to bear; (**exert oneself**) make effort. □ **exertion** *noun.*

exfoliate /eks'fəʊlɪeɪt/ *verb* (**-ting**) come off in scales or layers. □ **exfoliation** *noun.*

ex gratia /eks 'greɪʃə/ ● *adverb* as favour and not under (esp. legal) compulsion. ● *adjective* granted on this basis. [Latin]

exhale /eks'heɪl/ *verb* (**-ling**) breathe out; give off or be given off in vapour. □ **exhalation** /-hə-/ *noun.*

exhaust /ɪg'zɔ:st/ ● *verb* (often as **exhausted** *adjective* or **exhausting** *adjective*) consume, use up; tire out; study or expound completely; empty of contents. ● *noun* waste gases etc. expelled from engine after combustion; pipe or system through which they are expelled. □ **exhaustible** *adjective*; **exhaustion** *noun.*

exhaustive *adjective* complete, comprehensive. □ **exhaustively** *adverb.*

exhibit /ɪg'zɪbɪt/ ● *verb* (**-t-**) show, esp. publicly; display. ● *noun* thing exhibited. □ **exhibitor** *noun.*

exhibition /eksɪ'bɪʃ(ə)n/ *noun* display, public show; exhibiting, being exhibited; scholarship, esp. from funds of college etc.

exhibitioner *noun* student receiving exhibition.

exhibitionism *noun* tendency towards attention-seeking behaviour; compulsion to expose genitals in public. □ **exhibitionist** *noun.*

exhilarate /ɪg'zɪləreɪt/ *verb* (**-ting**) (often as **exhilarating** *adjective* or **exhilarated** *adjective*) enliven, gladden. □ **exhilaration** *noun.*

exhort /ɪg'zɔ:t/ *verb* (often + *to do*) urge strongly or earnestly. □ **exhortation** /eg-/ *noun*; **exhortative** *adjective*; **exhortatory** *adjective.*

exhume /eks'hju:m/ *verb* (**-ming**) dig up. □ **exhumation** *noun.*

exigency /'eksɪdʒənsɪ/ *noun* (*plural* **-ies**) (also **exigence**) urgent need; emergency. □ **exigent** *adjective.*

exiguous /eg'zɪgjʊəs/ *adjective* scanty, small. □ **exiguity** /-'gju:ɪtɪ/ *noun.*

exile /'eksaɪl/ ● *noun* expulsion or long absence from one's country etc.; person in exile. ● *verb* (**-ling**) send into or condemn to exile.

exist /ɪg'zɪst/ *verb* be, have being; occur, be found; live with no pleasure; live.

existence noun fact or manner of existing; all that exists. □ **existent** adjective.

existential /egzɪ'stenʃ(ə)l/ adjective of or relating to existence.

existentialism noun philosophical theory emphasizing existence of individual as free and self-determining agent. □ **existentialist** adjective & noun.

exit /'eksɪt/ ● noun way out; going out; place where vehicles leave motorway etc.; departure. ● verb (-t-) make one's exit.

exodus /'eksədəs/ noun mass departure; (**Exodus**) that of Israelites from Egypt.

ex officio /eks ə'fɪʃɪəʊ/ adverb & adjective by virtue of one's office.

exonerate /ɪg'zɒnəreɪt/ verb (-ting) free or declare free from blame. □ **exoneration** noun.

exorbitant /ɪg'zɔːbɪt(ə)nt/ adjective grossly excessive.

exorcize /'eksɔːsaɪz/ verb (also **-ise**) (**-zing** or **-sing**) drive out (evil spirit) by prayers etc.; free (person, place) thus. □ **exorcism** noun; **exorcist** noun.

exoskeleton /'eksəʊskelɪtən/ noun external skeleton.

exotic /ɪg'zɒtɪk/ ● adjective introduced from abroad; strange, unusual. ● noun exotic plant etc. □ **exotically** adverb.

expand /ɪk'spænd/ verb increase in size or importance; (often + on) give fuller account; become more genial; write out in full; spread out flat. □ **expandable** adjective; **expansion** noun.

expanse /ɪk'spæns/ noun wide area or extent of land, space, etc.

expansionism noun advocacy of expansion, esp. of state's territory. □ **expansionist** noun & adjective.

expansive adjective able or tending to expand; extensive; genial.

expatiate /ɪk'speɪʃɪeɪt/ verb (-ting) (usually + on, upon) speak or write at length. □ **expatiation** noun.

expatriate ● adjective /eks'pætrɪət/ living abroad; exiled. ● noun /eks'pætrɪət/ expatriate person. ● verb /eks'pætrɪeɪt/ (**-ting**) expel from native country.

expect /ɪk'spekt/ verb regard as likely; look for as one's due; colloquial suppose. □ **be expecting** colloquial be pregnant.

expectant adjective expecting; expecting to become; pregnant. □ **expectancy** noun; **expectantly** adverb.

expectation /ekspek'teɪʃ(ə)n/ noun expecting, anticipation; what one expects; probability; (in plural) prospects of inheritance.

expectorant /ek'spektərənt/ ● adjective causing expectoration. ● noun expectorant medicine.

expectorate /ek'spektəreɪt/ verb (-ting) cough or spit out from chest or lungs; spit. □ **expectoration** noun.

expedient /ɪk'spiːdɪənt/ ● adjective advantageous; advisable on practical rather than moral grounds. ● noun means of achieving an end; resource. □ **expediency** noun.

expedite /'ekspɪdaɪt/ verb (-ting) assist progress of; accomplish quickly.

expedition /ekspɪ'dɪʃ(ə)n/ noun journey or voyage for particular purpose; people etc. undertaking this; speed.

expeditionary adjective of or used on expedition.

expeditious /ekspɪ'dɪʃəs/ adjective acting or done with speed and efficiency.

expel /ɪk'spel/ verb (**-ll-**) deprive of membership; force out; eject.

expend /ɪk'spend/ verb spend (money, time, etc.); use up.

expendable adjective that may be sacrificed or dispensed with.

expenditure /ɪk'spendɪtʃə/ noun expending; amount expended.

expense /ɪk'spens/ noun cost, charge; (in plural) costs incurred in doing job etc., reimbursement of this.

expensive adjective costing or charging much. □ **expensively** adverb.

experience /ɪk'spɪərɪəns/ ● noun personal observation or contact; knowledge or skill based on this; event that affects one. ● verb (**-cing**) have experience of; undergo; feel. □ **experiential** /-'en-/ adjective.

experienced adjective having had much experience; skilful through experience.

experiment /ɪk'sperɪmənt/ ● noun procedure adopted to test hypothesis or demonstrate known fact. ● verb (also /-ment/) make experiment(s). □ **experimentation** /-men-/ noun; **experimenter** noun.

experimental /ɪksperɪ'ment(ə)l/ adjective based on or done by way of experiment. □ **experimentally** adverb.

expert /ˈekspɜːt/ (often + *at, in*) ● *adjective* well informed or skilful in a subject. ● *noun* expert person. □ **expertly** *adverb*.

expertise /ekspɜːˈtiːz/ *noun* special skill or knowledge.

expiate /ˈekspɪeɪt/ *verb* (**-ting**) pay penalty or make amends for (wrong). □ **expiation** *noun*.

expire /ɪkˈspaɪə/ *verb* (**-ring**) come to an end; cease to be valid; die; breathe out. □ **expiration** /ekspɪ-/ *noun*.

expiry *noun* end of validity or duration.

explain /ɪksˈpleɪn/ *verb* make intelligible; make known; say by way of explanation; account for. □ **explanation** /eksplə-/ *noun*.

explanatory /ɪksˈplænətərɪ/ *adjective* serving to explain.

expletive /ɪksˈpliːtɪv/ *noun* swear-word or exclamation.

explicable /ɪksˈplɪkəb(ə)l/ *adjective* explainable.

explicit /ɪksˈplɪsɪt/ *adjective* expressly stated; stated in detail; definite; outspoken. □ **explicitly** *adverb*; **explicitness** *noun*.

explode /ɪksˈpləʊd/ (**-ding**) *verb* expand violently with loud noise; cause (bomb etc.) to do this; give vent suddenly to emotion, esp. anger; (of population etc.) increase suddenly; discredit.

exploit ● *noun* /ˈeksplɔɪt/ daring feat. ● *verb* /ɪksˈplɔɪt/ use or develop for one's own ends; take advantage of (esp. person). □ **exploitation** /eksplɔɪ-/ *noun*; **exploitative** /-ˈsplɔɪt-/ *adjective*.

explore /ɪksˈplɔː/ *verb* (**-ring**) travel through (country etc.) to learn about it; inquire into; examine (part of body), probe (wound). □ **exploration** /eksplə-/ *noun*; **exploratory** /-ˈsplɒr-/ *adjective*; **explorer** *noun*.

explosion /ɪksˈpləʊʒ(ə)n/ *noun* exploding; loud noise caused by this; outbreak; sudden increase.

explosive /ɪksˈpləʊsɪv/ ● *adjective* tending to explode; likely to cause violent outburst etc. ● *noun* explosive substance.

exponent /ɪksˈpəʊnənt/ *noun* person promoting idea etc.; practitioner of activity, profession, etc.; person who explains or interprets; type, representative; *Mathematics* raised number or symbol showing how many of a number are

to be multiplied together, e.g. ^{3} in $2^3 = 2 \times 2 \times 2$.

exponential /ekspəˈnenʃ(ə)l/ *adjective* (of increase) more and more rapid. □ **exponentially** *adverb*.

export /ɪkˈspɔːt/ ● *verb* sell or send (goods or services) to another country. ● *noun* /ˈekspɔːt/ exporting; exported article or service; (in *plural*) amount exported. □ **exportation** *noun*; **exporter** /ɪkˈspɔːtə/ *noun*.

expose /ɪkˈspəʊz/ *verb* (**-sing**) leave unprotected, esp. from weather; (+ *to*) put at risk of, subject to (influence etc.); *Photography* subject (film etc.) to light; reveal, disclose; exhibit, display; (**expose oneself**) display one's genitals indecently in public.

exposé /ekˈspəʊzeɪ/ *noun* orderly statement of facts; disclosure of discreditable thing.

exposition /ekspəˈzɪʃ(ə)n/ *noun* expounding, explanation; *Music* part of movement in which principal themes are presented; exhibition.

ex post facto /eks pəʊst ˈfæktəʊ/ *adjective & adverb* retrospective(ly). [Latin]

expostulate /ɪkˈspɒstjʊleɪt/ *verb* (**-ting**) make protest, remonstrate. □ **expostulation** *noun*.

exposure /ɪkˈspəʊʒə/ *noun* exposing, being exposed; physical condition resulting from being exposed to elements; *Photography* length of time film etc. is exposed, section of film etc. exposed at one time.

expound /ɪkˈspaʊnd/ *verb* set out in detail; explain, interpret.

express /ɪkˈspres/ ● *verb* represent by symbols etc. or in language; put into words; squeeze out (juice, milk, etc.); (**express oneself**) communicate what one thinks, feels, or means. ● *adjective* operating at high speed; definitely stated; delivered by specially fast service. ● *adverb* with speed; by express messenger or train. ● *noun* express train etc. □ **expressible** *adjective*.

expression /ɪkˈspreʃ(ə)n/ *noun* expressing, being expressed; wording, word, phrase; conveying or depiction of feeling; appearance (of face), intonation (of voice); *Mathematics* collection of symbols expressing quantity. □ **expressionless** *adjective*.

expressionism noun style of painting etc. seeking to express emotion rather than depict external world. □ **expressionist** noun & adjective.

expressive adjective full of expression; (+ of) serving to express. □ **expressiveness** noun.

expressly adverb explicitly.

expropriate /ɪks'prəʊprɪeɪt/ verb (-ting) take away (property); dispossess. □ **expropriation** noun; **expropriator** noun.

expulsion /ɪk'spʌlʃ(ə)n/ noun expelling, being expelled.

expunge /ɪk'spʌndʒ/ verb (-ging) erase, remove.

expurgate /'ekspəgeɪt/ verb (-ting) remove matter considered objectionable from (book etc.); clear away (such matter). □ **expurgation** noun; **expurgator** noun.

exquisite /'ekskwɪzɪt, ek'skwɪzɪt/ adjective extremely beautiful or delicate; acute, keen. □ **exquisitely** adverb.

ex-serviceman /eks'sɜːvɪsmən/ noun man formerly member of armed forces.

extant /ek'stænt/ adjective still existing.

extempore /ɪk'stempərɪ/ adverb & adjective without preparation.

extemporize /ɪk'stempəraɪz/ verb (also **-ise**) (**-zing** or **-sing**) improvise. □ **extemporization** noun.

extend /ɪk'stend/ verb lengthen in space or time; lay out at full length; reach or be or make continuous over certain area; (+ to) have certain scope; offer or accord (feeling, invitation, etc.); tax powers of. □ **extendible** adjective; **extensible** adjective.

extension /ɪk'stenʃ(ə)n/ noun extending; enlargement, additional part; subsidiary telephone on same line as main one; additional period of time.

extensive /ɪk'stensɪv/ adjective large, far-reaching. □ **extensively** adverb.

extent /ɪk'stent/ noun space covered; width of application, scope.

extenuate /ɪk'stenjʊeɪt/ verb (-ting) (often as **extenuating** adjective) make (guilt etc.) seem less serious by partial excuse. □ **extenuation** noun.

exterior /ɪk'stɪərɪə/ ● adjective outer; coming from outside. ● noun exterior aspect or surface; outward demeanour.

exterminate /ɪk'stɜːmɪneɪt/ verb (-ting) destroy utterly. □ **extermination** noun; **exterminator** noun.

external /ɪk'stɜːn(ə)l/ ● adjective of or on the outside; coming from outside; relating to a country's foreign affairs; (of medicine) for use on outside of body. ● noun (in plural) external features or circumstances. □ **externality** /eksts:-'nælɪtɪ/ noun; **externally** adverb.

externalize verb (also **-ise**) (**-zing** or **-sing**) give or attribute external existence to.

extinct /ɪk'stɪŋkt/ adjective no longer existing; no longer burning; (of volcano) that no longer erupts; obsolete.

extinction noun making or becoming extinct; extinguishing, being extinguished.

extinguish /ɪk'stɪŋgwɪʃ/ verb put out (flame, light, etc.); terminate, destroy; wipe out (debt).

extinguisher noun = FIRE EXTINGUISHER.

extirpate /'ekstəpeɪt/ verb (-ting) destroy; root out. □ **extirpation** noun.

extol /ɪk'stəʊl/ verb (-ll-) praise enthusiastically.

extort /ɪk'stɔːt/ verb get by coercion.

extortion noun extorting, esp. of money; illegal exaction.

extortionate /ɪk'stɔːʃənət/ adjective exorbitant.

extra /'ekstrə/ ● adjective additional; more than usual or necessary. ● adverb more than usually; additionally. ● noun extra thing; thing for which one is charged extra; person playing one of crowd etc. in film; special edition of newspaper; Cricket run not scored from hit with bat.

extra- combining form outside, beyond scope of.

extract ● verb /ɪk'strækt/ take out; obtain against person's will; obtain from earth; copy out, quote; obtain (juice etc.) by pressure, distillation, etc.; derive (pleasure etc.); Mathematics find (root of number). ● noun /'ekstrækt/ passage from book etc.; preparation containing concentrated constituent of substance.

extraction /ɪkˈstrækʃ(ə)n/ *noun* extracting; removal of tooth; lineage.

extractor /ɪkˈstræktə/ *noun* machine that extracts. □ **extractor fan** one that extracts bad air etc.

extracurricular /ekstrəkəˈrɪkjʊlə/ *adjective* outside normal curriculum.

extraditable *adjective* liable to extradition; (of crime) warranting extradition.

extradite /ˈekstrədaɪt/ *verb* (**-ting**) hand over (person accused of crime) to state where crime was committed. □ **extradition** /-ˈdɪʃ/- *noun*.

extramarital /ekstrəˈmærɪt(ə)l/ *adjective* (of sexual relationship) outside marriage.

extramural /ekstrəˈmjʊər(ə)l/ *adjective* additional to ordinary teaching or studies.

extraneous /ɪkˈstreɪnɪəs/ *adjective* of external origin; (often + *to*) separate, irrelevant, unrelated.

extraordinary /ɪkˈstrɔːdɪnəri/ *adjective* unusual, remarkable; unusually great; (of meeting etc.) additional. □ **extraordinarily** *adverb*.

extrapolate /ɪkˈstræpəleɪt/ *verb* (**-ting**) estimate (unknown facts or values) from known data. □ **extrapolation** *noun*.

extrasensory /ekstrəˈsensəri/ *adjective* derived by means other than known senses.

extraterrestrial /ekstrətɪˈrestrɪəl/ ● *adjective* outside the earth or its atmosphere. ● *noun* fictional being from outer space.

extravagant /ɪkˈstrævəgənt/ *adjective* spending (esp. money) excessively; excessive; absurd; costing much. □ **extravagance** *noun*; **extravagantly** *adverb*.

extravaganza /ɪkstrævəˈgænzə/ *noun* spectacular theatrical or television production; fanciful composition.

extreme /ɪkˈstriːm/ ● *adjective* reaching high or highest degree; severe, not moderate; outermost; utmost. ● *noun* either of two things as remote or different as possible; thing at either end; highest degree. □ **extreme unction** anointing by priest of dying person. □ **extremely** *adverb*.

extremis see IN EXTREMIS.

extremism *noun* advocacy of extreme measures. □ **extremist** *adjective* & *noun*.

extremity /ɪkˈstremɪti/ *noun* (*plural* **-ies**) extreme point, end; (in *plural*) hands and feet; condition of extreme adversity.

extricate /ˈekstrɪkeɪt/ *verb* (**-ting**) disentangle, release. □ **extrication** *noun*.

extrinsic /ekˈstrɪnsɪk/ *adjective* not inherent or intrinsic; (often + *to*) extraneous. □ **extrinsically** *adverb*.

extrovert /ˈekstrəvɜːt/ ● *noun* sociable or unreserved person; person mainly concerned with external things. ● *adjective* typical or having nature of extrovert. □ **extroversion** /-ˈvɜː-/ *noun*.

extrude /ɪkˈstruːd/ *verb* (**-ding**) thrust or squeeze out; shape by forcing through nozzle. □ **extrusion** *noun*.

exuberant /ɪgˈzjuːbərənt/ *adjective* high-spirited, lively; luxuriant, prolific; (of feelings etc.) abounding. □ **exuberance** *noun*.

exude /ɪgˈzjuːd/ *verb* (**-ding**) ooze out; give off; display (emotion) freely. □ **exudation** *noun*.

exult /ɪgˈzʌlt/ *verb* rejoice. □ **exultant** *adjective*; **exultation** /eg-/ *noun*.

eye /aɪ/ ● *noun* organ or faculty of sight; iris of eye; region round eye; gaze; perception; eyelike thing; leaf bud of potato; centre of hurricane; spot, hole, loop. ● *verb* (**eyes**, **eyed**, **eyeing** or **eying**) (often + *up*) observe, watch suspiciously or closely. □ **all eyes** watching intently; **eyeball** ball of eye within lids and socket; **eyebath** vessel for applying lotion to eye; **eye-brow** hair growing on ridge over eye; **eye-catching** *colloquial* striking; **eyeglass** lens for defective eye; **eyehole** hole to look through; **eyelash** any of hairs on edge of eyelid; **eyelid** fold of skin that can cover eye; **eyeliner** cosmetic applied as line round eye; **eye-opener** *colloquial* enlightening experience, unexpected revelation; **eyepiece** lens(es) to which eye is applied at end of optical instrument; **eye-shade** device to protect eyes from strong light; **eye-shadow** cosmetic for eyelids; **eyesight** faculty or power of sight; **eyesore** ugly thing; **eye-tooth** canine tooth in upper jaw; **eyewash** lotion for eyes, *slang* nonsense; **eyewitness** person who saw thing happen and can tell of it; **have one's eye on** wish or plan to obtain; **keep an eye on** watch, look after; **see eye to eye** (often + *with*) agree; **set eyes on** see.

eyeful *noun* (*plural* -**s**) *colloquial* good look; visually striking person or thing.

eyelet /ˈaɪlɪt/ *noun* small hole for passing cord etc. through.

eyrie /ˈɪərɪ/ *noun* nest of bird of prey, esp. eagle, built high up.

Ff

F *abbreviation* Fahrenheit.

f *abbreviation* (also **f.**) female; feminine; Music forte.

FA *abbreviation* Football Association.

fa = FAH.

fable /ˈfeɪb(ə)l/ *noun* fictional tale, esp. legendary, or moral tale, often with animal characters.

fabled *adjective* celebrated; legendary.

fabric /ˈfæbrɪk/ *noun* woven material; walls, floor, and roof of building; structure.

fabricate /ˈfæbrɪkeɪt/ *verb* (-**ting**) construct, esp. from components; invent (fact), forge (document). □ **fabrication** *noun*.

fabulous /ˈfæbjʊləs/ *adjective colloquial* marvellous; legendary. □ **fabulously** *adverb*.

façade /fəˈsɑːd/ *noun* face or front of building; outward, esp. deceptive, appearance.

face ● *noun* front of head; facial expression; surface; façade of building; side of mountain; dial of clock etc.; functional side of tool, bat, etc.; effrontery; aspect, feature. ● *verb* (-**cing**) look or be positioned towards; be opposite; meet resolutely, confront; put facing on (garment, wall, etc.). □ **face-lift** cosmetic surgery to remove wrinkles etc., improvement in appearance; **face up to** accept bravely; **face value** nominal value, superficial appearance; **lose face** be humiliated; **on the face of it** apparently; **pull a face** distort features; **save face** avoid humiliation.

faceless *adjective* without identity; not identifiable.

facet /ˈfæsɪt/ *noun* aspect; side of cut gem etc.

facetious /fəˈsiːʃəs/ *adjective* intended to be amusing, esp. inappropriately. □ **facetiously** *adverb*; **facetiousness** *noun*.

facia = FASCIA.

facial /ˈfeɪʃ(ə)l/ ● *adjective* of or for the face. ● *noun* beauty treatment for the face. □ **facially** *adverb*.

facile /ˈfæsaɪl/ *adjective* easily achieved but of little value; glib.

facilitate /fəˈsɪlɪteɪt/ *verb* (-**ting**) ease (process etc.). □ **facilitation** *noun*.

facility /fəˈsɪlɪtɪ/ *noun* (*plural* -**ies**) ease, absence of difficulty; dexterity; (esp. in *plural*) opportunity or equipment for doing something.

facing *noun* material over part of garment etc. for contrast or strength; outer covering on wall etc.

facsimile /fækˈsɪmɪlɪ/ *noun* exact copy of writing, picture, etc.

fact *noun* thing known to exist or be true; reality. □ **factsheet** information leaflet; **in fact** in reality, in short; **the facts of life** information on sexual functions etc.

faction /ˈfækʃ(ə)n/ *noun* small dissenting group within larger one, esp. in politics; such dissension. □ **factional** *adjective*.

factious /ˈfækʃəs/ *adjective* of or inclined to faction.

factitious /fækˈtɪʃəs/ *adjective* specially contrived; artificial.

factor /ˈfæktə/ *noun* thing contributing to result; whole number etc. that when multiplied produces given number (e.g. 2, 3, 4, and 6 are the factors of 12).

factorial /fæk'tɔːrɪəl/ *noun* the product of a number and all whole numbers below it.

factory /'fæktərɪ/ *noun* (*plural* **-ies**) building(s) for manufacture of goods. □ **factory farming** using intensive or industrial methods of rearing livestock.

factotum /fæk'təʊtəm/ *noun* (*plural* **-s**) employee doing all kinds of work.

factual /'fæktjʊəl/ *adjective* based on or concerned with fact. □ **factually** *adverb*.

faculty /'fækəltɪ/ *noun* (*plural* **-ies**) aptitude for particular activity; physical or mental power; group of related university departments; *US* teaching staff of university etc.

fad *noun* craze; peculiar notion.

faddy *adjective* (**-ier**, **-iest**) having petty likes and dislikes.

fade ● *verb* (**-ding**) (cause to) lose colour, light, or sound; slowly diminish; lose freshness or strength. ● *noun* action of fading. □ **fade away** die away, disappear, *colloquial* languish, grow thin.

faeces /'fiːsiːz/ *plural noun* (*US* **feces**) waste matter from bowels. □ **faecal** /-k(ə)l/ *adjective*.

fag ● *noun colloquial* tedious task; *slang* cigarette; (at public schools) junior boy who runs errands for a senior. ● *verb* (**-gg-**) (often + *out*) *colloquial* exhaust; act as fag. □ **fag-end** *slang* cigarette-end.

faggot /'fægət/ *noun* (*US* **fagot**) baked or fried ball of seasoned chopped liver etc.; bundle of sticks etc.

fah /fɑː/ *noun* (also **fa**) *Music* fourth note of scale in tonic sol-fa.

Fahrenheit /'færənhaɪt/ *adjective* of scale of temperature on which water freezes at 32° and boils at 212°.

faience /'faɪɑ̃s/ *noun* decorated and glazed earthenware and porcelain.

fail ● *verb* not succeed; be or judge to be unsuccessful in (exam etc.); (+ *to do*) be unable, neglect; disappoint; be absent or insufficient; become weaker; cease functioning. ● *noun* failure in exam. □ **fail-safe** reverting to safe condition when faulty; **without fail** for certain, whatever happens.

failed *adjective* unsuccessful; bankrupt.

failing ● *noun* fault; weakness. ● *preposition* in default of.

failure /'feɪljə/ *noun* lack of success; unsuccessful person or thing; nonperformance; breaking down, ceasing to function; running short of supply etc.

fain *archaic* ● *adjective* (+ *to do*) willing, obliged. ● *adverb* gladly.

faint ● *adjective* dim, pale; weak, giddy; slight; timid. ● *verb* lose consciousness; become faint. ● *noun* act or state of fainting. □ **faint-hearted** cowardly, timid. □ **faintly** *adverb*; **faintness** *noun*.

fair[1] *adjective* just, equitable; blond, not dark; moderate in quality or amount; (of weather) fine; (of wind) favourable; *archaic* beautiful. ● *adverb* in a fair or just manner; exactly, completely. □ **fair and square** exactly, straightforwardly; **fair copy** transcript free from corrections; **fair game** legitimate target or object; **fair play** just treatment or behaviour; **fair-weather friend** friend or ally who deserts in crisis. □ **fairness** *noun*.

fair[2] *noun* stalls, amusements, etc. for public entertainment; periodic market, often with entertainments; trade exhibition. □ **fairground** outdoor site for fair.

Fair Isle *noun* multicoloured knitwear design characteristic of Fair Isle in the Shetlands.

fairly *adverb* in a fair way; moderately; to a noticeable degree.

fairway *noun* navigable channel; mown grass between golf tee and green.

fairy /'feərɪ/ *noun* (*plural* **-ies**) small winged legendary being. □ **fairy cake** small iced sponge cake; **fairy godmother** benefactress; **fairyland** home of fairies, enchanted region; **fairy lights** small coloured lights for decoration; **fairy ring** ring of darker grass caused by fungi; **fairy story**, **tale** tale about fairies, unbelievable story, lie.

fait accompli /feɪt ə'kɒmpliː/ *noun* thing done and past arguing about. [French]

faith /feɪθ/ *noun* trust; religious belief; creed; loyalty, trustworthiness. □ **faith-healer** person who practises **faith-healing**, healing dependent on faith rather than treatment.

faithful *adjective* showing faith; (often + *to*) loyal, trustworthy; accurate.

faithfully adverb in a faithful way. □ **Yours faithfully** written before signature at end of business letter.

faithless adjective disloyal; without religious faith.

fake ● noun thing or person that is not genuine. ● adjective counterfeit, not genuine. ● verb (**-king**) make fake or imitation of; feign.

fakir /ˈfeɪkɪə/ noun Muslim or Hindu religious beggar or ascetic.

falcon /ˈfɔːlkən/ noun small hawk trained to hunt.

falconry noun breeding and training of hawks.

fall /fɔːl/ ● verb (past **fell**; past participle **fallen**) go or come down freely; descend; (often + over) lose balance and come suddenly to ground; slope or hang down; sink lower, decline in power, status, etc.; subside; occur; become; (of face) show dismay etc.; be defeated; die. ● noun falling; amount or thing that falls; overthrow; (esp. in plural) waterfall; US autumn. □ **fall back on** have recourse to; **fall behind** be outstripped, be in arrears; **fall down (on)** colloquial fail (in); **fall for** be captivated or deceived by; **fall foul of** come into conflict with; **fall guy** slang easy victim, scapegoat; **fall in** Military take place in parade; **fall in with** meet by chance, agree or coincide with; **falling star** meteor; **fall off** decrease, deteriorate; **fall out** verb quarrel, (of hair, teeth, etc.) become detached, result, occur, Military come out of formation; **fallout** noun radioactive nuclear debris; **fall short of** fail to reach or obtain; **fall through** fail; **fall to** start eating, working, etc.

fallacy /ˈfæləsɪ/ noun (plural **-ies**) mistaken belief; faulty reasoning; misleading argument. □ **fallacious** /fəˈleɪʃəs/ adjective.

fallible /ˈfælɪb(ə)l/ adjective capable of making mistakes. □ **fallibility** noun.

Fallopian tube /fəˈləʊpɪən/ noun either of two tubes along which ova travel from ovaries to womb.

fallow /ˈfæləʊ/ ● adjective (of land) ploughed but left unsown; uncultivated. ● noun fallow land.

fallow deer noun small deer with white-spotted reddish-brown summer coat.

false /fɔːls/ adjective wrong, incorrect; sham, artificial; (+ to) deceitful, treacherous, unfaithful; deceptive. □ **false alarm** alarm given needlessly; **false pretences** misrepresentations meant to deceive. □ **falsely** adverb; **falsity** noun; **falseness** noun.

falsehood noun untrue thing; lying, lie.

falsetto /fɔːlˈsetəʊ/ noun male voice above normal range.

falsify /ˈfɔːlsɪfaɪ/ verb (**-ies**, **-ied**) fraudulently alter; misrepresent. □ **falsification** noun.

falter /ˈfɔːltə/ verb stumble; go unsteadily; lose courage; speak hesitatingly.

fame noun renown, being famous; archaic reputation.

famed adjective (+ for) much spoken of or famous because of.

familial /fəˈmɪlɪəl/ adjective of a family or its members.

familiar /fəˈmɪlɪə/ ● adjective (often + to) well known, often encountered; (+ with) knowing (a thing) well; (excessively) informal. ● noun intimate friend; supposed attendant of witch etc. □ **familiarity** /-ˈær-/ noun (plural **-ies**); **familiarly** adverb.

familiarize /fəˈmɪlɪəraɪz/ verb (also **-ise**) (**-zing** or **-sing**) (usually + with) make (person etc.) conversant. □ **familiarization** noun.

family /ˈfæmɪlɪ/ noun (plural **-ies**) set of relations, esp. parents and children; person's children; household; all the descendants of common ancestor; group of similar things, people, etc.; group of related genera of animals or plants. □ **family credit** regular state payment to low-income family; **family planning** birth control; **family tree** genealogical chart.

famine /ˈfæmɪn/ noun extreme scarcity, esp. of food.

famish /ˈfæmɪʃ/ verb (usually as **famished** adjective colloquial) make or become extremely hungry.

famous /ˈfeɪməs/ adjective (often + for) well-known; celebrated; colloquial excellent. □ **famously** adverb.

fan[1] ● noun apparatus, usually with rotating blades, for ventilation etc.; device, semicircular and folding, waved to cool oneself; fan-shaped thing. ● verb

(**-nn-**) blow air on, (as) with fan; (usually + *out*) spread out like fan. □ **fan belt** belt driving fan to cool radiator in vehicle; **fanlight** small, originally semicircular, window over door etc.; **fantail** pigeon with broad tail.

fan² *noun* devotee. □ **fan club** (club of) devotees; **fan mail** letters from fans.

fanatic /fəˈnætɪk/ ● *noun* person obsessively devoted to a belief, activity, etc. ● *adjective* excessively enthusiastic. □ **fanatical** *adjective*; **fanatically** *adverb*; **fanaticism** /-tɪsɪz(ə)m/ *noun*.

fancier /ˈfænsɪə/ *noun* connoisseur, enthusiast; breeder, esp. of pigeons.

fanciful /ˈfænsɪfʊl/ *adjective* imaginary; indulging in fancies. □ **fancifully** *adverb*.

fancy /ˈfænsɪ/ ● *noun* (*plural* **-ies**) inclination, whim; supposition; imagination. ● *adjective* (**-ier**, **-iest**) extravagant; ornamental. ● *verb* (**-ies**, **-ied**) (+ *that*) imagine; suppose; *colloquial* find attractive, desire; have unduly high opinion of. □ **fancy dress** costume for masquerading; **fancy-free** without (emotional) commitments; **fancy man, woman** woman's or man's lover. □ **fancily** *adverb*.

fandango /fænˈdæŋɡəʊ/ *noun* (*plural* **-es** or **-s**) lively Spanish dance.

fanfare /ˈfænfeə/ *noun* short showy sounding of trumpets etc.

fang *noun* canine tooth, esp. of dog or wolf; tooth of venomous snake; (prong of) root of tooth.

fantasia /fænˈteɪzɪə/ *noun* free or improvisatory musical etc. composition.

fantasize /ˈfæntəsaɪz/ *verb* (also **-ise**) (**-zing** or **-sing**) daydream; imagine; create fantasy about.

fantastic /fænˈtæstɪk/ *adjective* extravagantly fanciful; grotesque, quaint; *colloquial* excellent, extraordinary. □ **fantastically** *adverb*.

fantasy /ˈfæntəsɪ/ *noun* (*plural* **-ies**) imagination, esp. when unrelated to reality; mental image, daydream; fantastic invention or composition.

fanzine /ˈfænziːn/ *noun* magazine for fans of science fiction, a football team, etc.

far (**further, furthest** or **farther, farthest**) ● *adverb* at, to, or by a great distance in space or time; by much. ● *ad-*

jective distant; remote; extreme. □ **far and wide** over large area; **far-away** remote, dreamy, distant; **the Far East** countries of E. Asia; **far-fetched** unconvincing, exaggerated, fanciful; **far-flung** widely scattered, remote; **far from** almost the opposite of; **far gone** very ill, drunk, etc.; **far-off** remote; **far-out** *slang* unconventional, excellent; **far-reaching** widely influential or applicable; **far-seeing** showing foresight; **far-sighted** having foresight, *esp. US* long-sighted.

farad /ˈfærəd/ *noun* SI unit of electrical capacitance.

farce /fɑːs/ *noun* comedy with ludicrously improbable plot; absurdly futile proceedings; pretence. □ **farcical** *adjective*.

fare ● *noun* price of journey on public transport; passenger; food. ● *verb* (**-ring**) progress; get on. □ **fare-stage** section of bus route for which fixed fare is charged; stop marking this.

farewell /feəˈwel/ ● *interjection* goodbye. ● *noun* leave-taking.

farina /fəˈriːnə/ *noun* flour of corn, nuts, or starchy roots. □ **farinaceous** /færɪˈneɪʃəs/ *adjective*.

farm ● *noun* land and its buildings used for growing crops, rearing animals, etc.; farmhouse. ● *verb* use (land) thus; be farmer; breed (fish etc.) commercially; (+ *out*) delegate or subcontract (work). □ **farm-hand** worker on farm; **farmhouse** house attached to farm; **farmyard** yard adjacent to farmhouse. □ **farming** *noun*.

farmer *noun* owner or manager of farm.

faro /ˈfeərəʊ/ *noun* gambling card-game.

farrago /fəˈrɑːɡəʊ/ *noun* (*plural* **-s** or *US* **-es**) medley, hotchpotch.

farrier /ˈfærɪə/ *noun* smith who shoes horses.

farrow /ˈfærəʊ/ ● *verb* give birth to (piglets). ● *noun* litter of pigs.

Farsi /ˈfɑːsɪ/ *noun* modern Persian language.

farther = FURTHER.

farthest = FURTHEST.

farthing /ˈfɑːðɪŋ/ *noun* *historical* coin worth quarter of old penny.

farthingale /ˈfɑːðɪŋɡeɪl/ *noun* *historical* hooped petticoat.

fascia /'feɪʃə/ noun (also **facia**) (plural **-s**) instrument panel of vehicle; similar panel etc. for operating machinery; long flat surface of wood or stone.

fascicle /'fæsɪk(ə)l/ noun instalment of book.

fascinate /'fæsɪneɪt/ verb (**-ting**) (often as **fascinating** adjective) capture interest of; attract. □ **fascination** noun.

Fascism /'fæʃɪz(ə)m/ noun extreme right-wing totalitarian nationalist movement in Italy (1922–43); (also **fascism**) any similar movement. □ **Fascist**, **fascist** noun & adjective; **Fascistic**, **fascistic** /-'ʃɪs-/ adjective.

fashion /'fæʃ(ə)n/ ● noun current popular custom or style, esp. in dress; manner of doing something. ● verb (often + into) form, make. □ **in fashion** fashionable; **out of fashion** not fashionable.

fashionable adjective of or conforming to current fashion; of or favoured by high society. □ **fashionably** adverb.

fast[1] /fɑːst/ ● adjective rapid; capable of or intended for high speed; (of clock) ahead of correct time; firm, fixed; (of colour) not fading; pleasure-seeking. ● adverb quickly; firmly; soundly, completely. □ **fastback** car with sloping rear; **fast breeder** (**reactor**) reactor using neutrons with high kinetic energy; **fast food** restaurant food that is produced quickly; **pull a fast one** colloquial try to deceive someone.

fast[2] /fɑːst/ ● verb abstain from food. ● noun act or period of fasting.

fasten /'fɑːs(ə)n/ verb make or become fixed or secure; (+ in, up) shut in, lock securely; (+ on) direct (attention) towards; (+ off) fix with knot or stitches.

fastener noun (also **fastening**) device that fastens.

fastidious /fæ'stɪdɪəs/ adjective fussy; easily disgusted, squeamish.

fastness /'fɑːstnɪs/ noun stronghold.

fat ● noun oily substance, esp. in animal bodies; part of meat etc. containing this. ● adjective (**-tt-**) plump; containing much fat; thick, substantial. ● verb (**-tt-**) (esp. as **fatted** adjective) make or become fat. □ **fat-head** colloquial stupid person; **fat-headed** stupid; **a fat lot** colloquial very little. □ **fatless** adjective; **fatten** verb.

fatal /'feɪt(ə)l/ adjective causing or ending in death or ruin. □ **fatally** adverb.

fatalism noun belief in predetermination; submissive acceptance. □ **fatalist** noun; **fatalistic** /-'lɪs-/ adjective.

fatality /fə'tælɪtɪ/ noun (plural **-ies**) death by accident, in war, etc.

fate ● noun supposed power predetermining events; destiny; death, destruction. ● verb (**-ting**) preordain; (as **fated** adjective) doomed, (+ to do) preordained.

fateful adjective decisive; important; controlled by fate.

father /'fɑːðə/ ● noun male parent; (usually in plural) forefather; originator; early leader; (also **Father**) priest; (**the Father**) God; (in plural) elders. ● verb be father of; originate. □ **father-in-law** (plural **fathers-in-law**) wife's or husband's father; **fatherland** native country. □ **fatherhood** noun; **fatherless** adjective.

fatherly adjective of or like a father.

fathom /'fæð(ə)m/ ● noun measure of 6ft, esp. in soundings. ● verb comprehend; measure depth of (water). □ **fathomable** adjective.

fathomless adjective too deep to fathom.

fatigue /fə'tiːg/ ● noun extreme tiredness; weakness in metals etc. from repeated stress; non-military army duty, (in plural) clothing for this. ● verb (**-gues**, **-gued**, **-guing**) cause fatigue in.

fatty ● adjective (**-ier**, **-iest**) like or containing fat. ● noun (plural **-ies**) colloquial fat person. □ **fatty acid** type of organic compound.

fatuous /'fætjʊəs/ adjective vacantly silly; purposeless. □ **fatuity** /fə'tjuːɪtɪ/ noun (plural **-ies**); **fatuously** adverb; **fatuousness** noun.

fatwa /'fætwɑː/ noun legal ruling by Islamic religious leader.

faucet /'fɔːsɪt/ noun esp. US tap.

fault /fɔːlt/ ● noun defect, imperfection; responsibility for wrongdoing, error, etc.; break in electric circuit; Tennis etc. incorrect service; break in rock strata. ● verb find fault with. □ **find fault** (often + with) criticize or complain (about); **to a fault** excessively. □ **faultless** adjective; **faultlessly** adverb.

faulty adjective (**-ier**, **-iest**) having faults. □ **faultily** adverb.

faun /fɔ:n/ *noun* Latin rural deity with goat's horns, legs, and tail.

fauna /'fɔ:nə/ *noun* (*plural* **-s**) animal life of a region or period.

faux pas /fəʊ 'pɑ:/ *noun* (*plural* same /'pɑ:z/) tactless mistake. [French]

favour /'feɪvə/ (*US* **favor**) ● *noun* kind act; approval, goodwill; partiality; badge, ribbon, etc. as emblem of support. ● *verb* regard or treat with favour; support, facilitate; tend to confirm (idea etc.); (+ *with*) oblige; (as **favoured** *adjective*) having special advantages. □ **in favour** approved of, (+ *of*) in support of or to the advantage of; **out of favour** disapproved of.

favourable *adjective* (*US* **favorable**) well-disposed; approving; promising; helpful, suitable. □ **favourably** *adverb*.

favourite /'feɪvərɪt/ (*US* **favorite**) ● *adjective* preferred to all others. ● *noun* favourite person or thing; competitor thought most likely to win.

favouritism *noun* (*US* **favoritism**) unfair favouring of one person etc.

fawn[1] ● *noun* deer in first year; light yellowish brown. ● *adjective* fawn-coloured. ● *verb* give birth to fawn.

fawn[2] *verb* (often + *on, upon*) behave servilely; (of dog) show extreme affection.

fax ● *noun* electronic transmission of exact copy of document etc.; such copy; (in full **fax machine**) apparatus used for this. ● *verb* transmit in this way.

faze *verb* (**-zing**) (often as **fazed** *adjective*) *colloquial* disconcert.

FBI *abbreviation* Federal Bureau of Investigation.

FC *abbreviation* Football Club.

FCO *abbreviation* Foreign and Commonwealth Office.

FE *abbreviation* further education.

fealty /'fi:əltɪ/ *noun* (*plural* **-ies**) fidelity to feudal lord; allegiance.

fear ● *noun* panic etc. caused by impending danger, pain, etc.; cause of this; alarm, dread. ● *verb* be afraid of; (+ *for*) feel anxiety about; dread; shrink from; revere (God).

fearful *adjective* afraid; terrible, awful; extremely unpleasant. □ **fearfully** *adverb*; **fearfulness** *noun*.

fearless *adjective* not afraid; brave. □ **fearlessly** *adverb*; **fearlessness** *noun*.

fearsome *adjective* frightening. □ **fearsomely** *adverb*.

feasible /'fi:zɪb(ə)l/ *adjective* practicable, possible. □ **feasibility** *noun*; **feasibly** *adverb*.

■ *Usage Feasible* should not be used to mean 'likely'. *Possible* or *probable* should be used instead.

feast ● *noun* sumptuous meal; religious festival; sensual or mental pleasure. ● *verb* (often + *on*) have feast, eat and drink sumptuously; regale.

feat *noun* remarkable act or achievement.

feather /'feðə/ ● *noun* one of structures forming bird's plumage, with fringed horny shaft; these as material. ● *verb* cover or line with feathers; turn (oar) through air edgeways. □ **feather bed** *noun* bed with feather-stuffed mattress; **feather-bed** *verb* cushion, esp. financially; **feather-brained, -headed** silly; **featherweight** amateur boxing weight (54–57 kg). □ **feathery** *adjective*.

feature /'fi:tʃə/ ● *noun* characteristic or distinctive part; (usually in *plural*) part of face; specialized article in newspaper etc.; (in full **feature film**) main film in cinema programme. ● *verb* (**-ring**) make or be special feature of; emphasize; take part in. □ **featureless** *adjective*.

Feb. *abbreviation* February.

febrile /'fi:braɪl/ *adjective* of fever.

February /'februərɪ/ *noun* (*plural* **-ies**) second month of year.

fecal *US* = FAECAL.

feces *US* = FAECES.

feckless /'feklɪs/ *adjective* feeble, ineffectual; irresponsible.

fecund /'fekənd/ *adjective* fertile. □ **fecundity** /fɪ'kʌndɪtɪ/ *noun*.

fecundate /'fekəndeɪt/ *verb* (**-ting**) make fruitful; fertilize. □ **fecundation** *noun*.

fed *past & past participle of* FEED. □ **fed up** (often + *with*) discontented, bored.

federal /'fedər(ə)l/ *adjective* of system of government in which self-governing states unite for certain functions; of such a federation; (**Federal**) US of Northern States in Civil War. □ **federalism** noun; **federalist** noun; **federalize** verb (also **-ise**) (**-zing** or **-sing**); **federalization** noun; **federally** adverb.

federate ● verb /'fedəreɪt/ (**-ting**) unite on federal basis. ● adjective /'fedərət/ federally organized. □ **federative** /-rətɪv/ adjective.

federation /fedə'reɪʃ(ə)n/ noun federal group; act of federating.

fee noun payment for professional advice or services; (often in plural) payment for admission, membership, licence, education, exam, etc.; money paid for transfer of footballer etc. □ **fee-paying** paying fee(s), (of school) charging fees.

feeble /'fiːb(ə)l/ adjective (**-r, -st**) weak; lacking energy, strength, or effectiveness. □ **feebly** adverb.

feed ● verb (past & past participle **fed**) supply with food; put food in mouth of; eat; graze; keep supplied with; (+ into) supply (material) to machine etc.; (often + on) nourish, be nourished by. ● noun food, esp. for animals or infants; feeding; colloquial meal. □ **feedback** information about result of experiment, response, Electronics return of part of output signal to input.

feeder noun person or thing that feeds in specified way; baby's feeding bottle; bib; tributary; branch road or railway line; electricity main supplying distribution point; feeding apparatus in machine.

feel ● verb (past & past participle **felt**) examine, search, or perceive by touch; experience; be affected by; (+ that) have impression; consider, think; seem; be consciously; (+ for, with) have sympathy or pity for. ● noun feeling; sense of touch; sensation characterizing something. □ **feel like** have wish or inclination for; **feel up to** be ready to face or deal with.

feeler noun organ in certain animals for touching, foraging, etc. □ **put out feelers** make tentative proposal.

feeling ● noun capacity to feel; sense of touch; physical sensation; emotion; (in

plural) susceptibilities; sensitivity; notion, opinion. ● adjective sensitive; sympathetic. □ **feelingly** adverb.

feet plural of FOOT.

feign /feɪn/ verb simulate; pretend.

feint /feɪnt/ ● noun sham attack or diversionary blow; pretence. ● verb make a feint. ● adjective (of paper etc.) having faintly ruled lines.

feldspar /'feldspɑː/ noun (also **felspar** /'felspɑː/) common aluminium silicate.

felicitation /fəlɪsɪ'teɪʃ(ə)n/ noun (usually in plural) congratulation.

felicitous /fə'lɪsɪtəs/ adjective apt; well-chosen.

felicity /fə'lɪsɪtɪ/ noun (plural **-ies**) formal great happiness; capacity for apt expression.

feline /'fiːlaɪn/ ● adjective of cat family; catlike. ● noun animal of cat family.

fell¹ past of FALL.

fell² verb cut down (tree); strike down.

fell³ noun hill or stretch of hills in N. England.

fell⁴ adjective □ **at, in one fell swoop** in a single (originally deadly) action.

fell⁵ noun animal's hide or skin with hair.

fellow /'feləʊ/ ● noun comrade, associate; counterpart, equal; colloquial man, boy; incorporated senior member of college; member of learned society. ● adjective of same group etc. □ **fellow-feeling** sympathy; **fellow-traveller** person who travels with another, sympathizer with Communist party.

fellowship /'feləʊʃɪp/ noun friendly association, companionship; group of associates; position or income of college fellow.

felon /'felən/ noun person who has committed felony.

felony /'felənɪ/ noun (plural **-ies**) serious usually violent crime. □ **felonious** /fɪ'ləʊ-/ adjective.

felspar = FELDSPAR.

felt¹ ● noun fabric of matted and pressed fibres of wool etc. ● verb make into or cover with felt; become matted. □ **felt tip** or **pen, felt-tip(ped) pen** pen with fibre point.

felt² past & past participle of FEEL.

female /'fi:meɪl/ ● *adjective* of the sex that can give birth or produce eggs; (of plants) fruit-bearing; of female people, animals, or plants; (of screw, socket, etc.) hollow to receive inserted part. ● *noun* female person, animal, or plant.

feminine /'femɪnɪn/ *adjective* of women; womanly; *Grammar* (of noun) belonging to gender including words for most female people and animals. □ **femininity** /-'nɪn-/ *noun*.

feminism /'femɪnɪz(ə)m/ *noun* advocacy of women's rights and sexual equality. □ **feminist** *noun & adjective*.

femme fatale /fæm fæ'tɑːl/ *noun* (*plural* **femmes fatales** same pronunciation) dangerously seductive woman. [French]

femur /'fi:mə/ *noun* (*plural* **-s** or **femora** /'femərə/) thigh-bone. □ **femoral** /'femər(ə)l/ *adjective*.

fen *noun* low marshy land.

fence ● *noun* barrier or railing enclosing field, garden, etc.; jump for horses; *slang* receiver of stolen goods. ● *verb* (**-cing**) surround (as) with fence; practise sword play; be evasive; deal in (stolen goods). □ **fencer** *noun*.

fencing *noun* fences, material for fences; sword-fighting, esp. as sport.

fend *verb* (+ *off*) ward off; (+ *for*) look after (esp. oneself).

fender *noun* low frame round fireplace; matting etc. to protect side of ship; *US* bumper of vehicle.

fennel /'fen(ə)l/ *noun* fragrant plant with edible leaf-stalks and seeds.

fenugreek /'fenju:gri:k/ *noun* leguminous plant with aromatic seeds used for flavouring.

feral /'fer(ə)l/ *adjective* wild; (of animal) escaped and living wild.

ferial /'fɪərɪəl/ *adjective* (of day) not a church festival or fast.

ferment ● *noun* /'fɜ:ment/ excitement; fermentation; fermenting agent. ● *verb* /fə'ment/ undergo or subject to fermentation; excite.

fermentation /fɜ:men'teɪʃ(ə)n/ *noun* breakdown of substance by yeasts, bacteria, etc.; excitement.

fern *noun* flowerless plant usually with feathery fronds.

ferocious /fə'rəʊʃəs/ *adjective* fierce. □ **ferociously** *adverb*; **ferocity** /-'rɒs-/ *noun*.

ferret /'ferɪt/ ● *noun* small polecat used in catching rabbits, rats, etc. ● *verb* (**-t-**) hunt with ferrets; (often + *out*, *about*, etc.) rummage; (+ *out*) search out.

ferric /'ferɪk/ *adjective* of iron; containing iron in trivalent form.

Ferris wheel /'ferɪs/ *noun* tall revolving vertical wheel with passenger cars in fairgrounds etc.

ferroconcrete /ferəʊ'kɒnkri:t/ *noun* reinforced concrete.

ferrous /'ferəs/ *adjective* containing iron, esp. in divalent form.

ferrule /'feru:l/ *noun* ring or cap on end of stick etc.

ferry ● *noun* (*plural* **-ies**) boat etc. for esp. regular transport across water; ferrying place or service. ● *verb* (**-ies**, **-ied**) take or go in ferry; transport from place to place, esp. regularly. □ **ferryman** *noun*.

fertile /'fɜ:taɪl/ *adjective* (of soil) abundantly productive; fruitful; (of seed, egg, etc.) capable of growth; inventive; (of animal or plant) able to reproduce. □ **fertility** /-'tɪl-/ *noun*.

fertilize /'fɜ:tɪlaɪz/ *verb* (also **-ise**) (**-zing** or **-sing**) make fertile; cause (egg, female animal, etc.) to develop new individual. □ **fertilization** *noun*.

fertilizer *noun* (also **-iser**) substance added to soil to make it more fertile.

fervent /'fɜ:v(ə)nt/ *adjective* ardent, intense. □ **fervency** *noun*; **fervently** *adverb*.

fervid /'fɜ:vɪd/ *adjective* fervent. □ **fervidly** *adverb*.

fervour /'fɜ:və/ *noun* (*US* **fervor**) passion, zeal.

fescue /'feskju:/ *noun* pasture and fodder grass.

fester /'festə/ *verb* make or become septic; cause continuing bitterness; rot; stagnate.

festival /'festɪv(ə)l/ *noun* day or period of celebration; series of cultural events in town etc.

festive /'festɪv/ *adjective* of or characteristic of festival; joyous.

festivity /fe'stɪvɪtɪ/ *noun* (*plural* **-ies**) gaiety, (in *plural*) celebration; party.

festoon /fe'stu:n/ ● *noun* curved hanging chain of flowers, ribbons, etc. ● *verb* (often + *with*) adorn with or form into festoons.

feta /'fetə/ *noun* salty white Greek cheese made from ewe's or goat's milk.

fetal *US* = FOETAL.

fetch *verb* go for and bring back; be sold for; draw forth; deal (blow). □ **fetch up** *colloquial* arrive, come to rest.

fetching *adjective* attractive. □ **fetchingly** *adverb*.

fête /feɪt/ ● *noun* outdoor fund-raising event. ● *verb* (**-ting**) honour or entertain lavishly.

fetid /'fetɪd/ *adjective* (also **foetid**) stinking.

fetish /'fetɪʃ/ *noun* abnormal object of sexual desire; object worshipped by primitive peoples; object of obsessive concern. □ **fetishism** *noun*; **fetishist** *noun*; **fetishistic** /-'ʃɪs-/ *adjective*.

fetlock /'fetlɒk/ *noun* back of horse's leg where tuft of hair grows above hoof.

fetter /'fetə/ ● *noun* shackle for ankles; (in *plural*) captivity; restraint. ● *verb* put into fetters, restrict.

fettle /'fet(ə)l/ *noun* condition, trim.

fetus *US* = FOETUS.

feud /fju:d/ ● *noun* prolonged hostility, esp. between families, tribes, etc. ● *verb* conduct feud.

feudal /'fju:d(ə)l/ *adjective* of, like, or according to feudal system; reactionary. □ **feudal system** medieval system in which vassal held land in exchange for allegiance and service to landowner. □ **feudalism** *noun*; **feudalistic** /-'lɪs-/ *adjective*.

fever /'fi:və/ ● *noun* abnormally high body temperature; disease characterized by this; nervous agitation. ● *verb* (esp. as **fevered** *adjective*) affect with fever or excitement. □ **fever pitch** state of extreme excitement.

feverfew /'fi:vəfju:/ *noun* aromatic plant, used formerly to reduce fever, now to treat migraine.

feverish *adjective* having symptoms of fever; excited, restless. □ **feverishly** *adverb*.

few ● *adjective* not many. ● *noun* (treated as *plural*) not many; (**a few**) some but not many. □ **a good few** a considerable number (of); **quite a few** *colloquial* a fairly large number (of); **very few** a very small number (of).

fey /feɪ/ *adjective* strange, other-worldly; whimsical.

fez *noun* (*plural* **fezzes**) man's flat-topped conical red cap, worn by some Muslims.

ff *abbreviation Music* fortissimo.

ff. *abbreviation* following pages etc.

fiancé /fɪ'ɒnseɪ/ *noun* (*feminine* **-cée** same pronunciation) person one is engaged to.

fiasco /fɪ'æskəʊ/ *noun* (*plural* **-s**) ludicrous or humiliating failure.

fiat /'faɪæt/ *noun* authorization; decree.

fib ● *noun* trivial lie. ● *verb* (**-bb-**) tell fib. □ **fibber** *noun*.

fibre /'faɪbə/ *noun* (*US* **fiber**) thread or filament forming tissue or textile; piece of threadlike glass; substance formed of fibres; moral character; roughage. □ **fibreboard** board made of compressed wood etc. fibres; **fibreglass** fabric made from woven glass fibres, plastic reinforced with glass fibres; **fibre optics** optics using glass fibres, usually to carry signals. □ **fibrous** *adjective*.

fibril /'faɪbrɪl/ *noun* small fibre.

fibroid /'faɪbrɔɪd/ ● *adjective* of, like, or containing fibrous tissue or fibres. ● *noun* benign fibrous tumour, esp. in womb.

fibrosis /faɪ'brəʊsɪs/ *noun* thickening and scarring of connective tissue.

fibrositis /faɪbrə'saɪtɪs/ *noun* rheumatic inflammation of fibrous tissue.

fibula /'fɪbjʊlə/ *noun* (*plural* **-lae** /-li:/ or **-s**) bone on outer side of lower leg.

fiche /fi:ʃ/ *noun* microfiche.

fickle /'fɪk(ə)l/ *adjective* inconstant, changeable. □ **fickleness** *noun*.

fiction /'fɪkʃ(ə)n/ *noun* non-factual literature, esp. novels; invented idea, thing, etc.; generally accepted falsehood. □ **fictional** *adjective*.

fictitious /fɪk'tɪʃəs/ *adjective* imaginary, unreal; not genuine.

fiddle /'fɪd(ə)l/ ● *noun colloquial* violin; *colloquial* cheat, fraud; fiddly task. ● *verb* (**-ling**) (often + *with*, *at*) play restlessly;

(often + *about*) move aimlessly; (usually + *with*) tamper, tinker; *slang* falsify, swindle, get by cheating; **play fiddle**. □ **fiddler** *noun*.

fiddling *adjective* petty, trivial; *colloquial* fiddly.

fiddly *adjective* (**-ier, -iest**) *colloquial* awkward to do or use.

fidelity /fɪˈdelɪti/ *noun* faithfulness, loyalty; accuracy; precision in sound reproduction.

fidget /ˈfɪdʒɪt/ ● *verb* (**-t-**) move restlessly; be or make uneasy. ● *noun* person who fidgets; (**the fidgets**) restless state or mood. □ **fidgety** *adjective*.

fiduciary /fɪˈdjuːʃərɪ/ ● *adjective* of a trust, trustee, etc.; held or given in trust; (of currency) dependent on public confidence. ● *noun* (*plural* **-ies**) trustee.

fief /fiːf/ *noun* land held under feudal system.

field /fiːld/ ● *noun* area of esp. cultivated enclosed land; area rich in some natural product; competitors; expanse of sea, snow, etc.; battlefield; area of activity or study; *Computing* part of record, representing item of data. ● *verb* *Cricket etc.* act as fielder(s), stop and return (ball); select (player, candidate, etc.); deal with (questions etc.). □ **field-day** exciting or successful time, military exercise or review; **field events** athletic events other than races; **field-glasses** outdoor binoculars; **Field Marshal** army officer of highest rank; **fieldmouse** small long-tailed rodent; **fieldsman** = FIELDER; **field sports** outdoor sports, esp. hunting, shooting, and fishing; **fieldwork** practical surveying, science, sociology, etc. conducted in natural environment; **fieldworker** person doing fieldwork.

fielder *noun* *Cricket etc.* member (other than bowler) of fielding side.

fieldfare *noun* grey thrush.

fiend /fiːnd/ *noun* evil spirit; wicked or cruel person; mischievous or annoying person; *slang* devotee; difficult or unpleasant thing. □ **fiendish** *adjective*; **fiendishly** *adverb*.

fierce *adjective* (**-r, -st**) violently aggressive or frightening; eager; intense. □ **fiercely** *adverb*; **fierceness** *noun*.

fiery /ˈfaɪərɪ/ *adjective* (**-ier, -iest**) consisting of or flaming with fire; bright red; burning hot; spirited.

fiesta /fɪˈesta/ *noun* festival, holiday.

FIFA /ˈfiːfə/ *abbreviation* International Football Federation (*Fédération Internationale de Football Association*).

fife /faɪf/ *noun* small shrill flute.

fifteen /fɪfˈtiːn/ *adjective & noun* one more than fourteen; *Rugby* team of fifteen players. □ **fifteenth** *adjective & noun*.

fifth ● *adjective & noun* next after fourth; any of 5 equal parts of thing. □ **fifth column** group working for enemy within country at war.

fifty /ˈfɪftɪ/ *adjective & noun* (*plural* **-ies**) five times ten. □ **fifty-fifty** half and half, equal(ly). □ **fiftieth** *adjective & noun*.

fig *noun* soft fruit with many seeds; tree bearing it. □ **fig leaf** device concealing genitals.

fig. *abbreviation* figure.

fight /faɪt/ ● *verb* (*past & past participle* **fought** /fɔːt/) (often + *against, with*) contend with in war, combat, etc.; engage in (battle etc.); (+ *for*) strive to secure or on behalf of; contest (election); strive to overcome; (as **fighting** *adjective*) able and eager or trained to fight. ● *noun* combat; boxing match; battle; struggle; power or inclination to fight. □ **fight back** counter-attack, suppress (tears etc.); **fighting chance** chance of success if effort is made; **fighting fit** extremely fit; **fight off** repel with effort; **fight shy of** avoid; **put up a fight** offer resistance.

fighter *noun* person who fights; aircraft designed for attacking other aircraft.

figment /ˈfɪgmənt/ *noun* imaginary thing.

figurative /ˈfɪgərətɪv/ *adjective* metaphorical; (of art) not abstract, representational. □ **figuratively** *adverb*.

figure /ˈfɪgə/ ● *noun* external form, bodily shape; person of specified kind; representation of human form; image; numerical symbol or number, esp. 0–9; value, amount; (in *plural*) arithmetical calculations; diagram, illustration; dance etc. movement or sequence; (in full **figure of speech**) metaphor, hyperbole, etc. ● *verb* (**-ring**) appear, be mentioned; (usually as **figured** *adjective*) embellish with pattern; calculate; *esp. US colloquial* understand, consider, make sense. □ **figurehead** nominal leader, carved image etc. over ship's prow; **figure on** *esp. US colloquial* count on, expect; **figure out** work out by arithmetic or logic; **figure-skating** skating in prescribed patterns.

figurine /ˈfɪɡəˈriːn/ *noun* statuette.

filament /ˈfɪləmənt/ *noun* threadlike strand or fibre; conducting wire or thread in electric bulb.

filbert /ˈfɪlbət/ *noun* (nut of) cultivated hazel.

filch *verb* steal, pilfer.

file[1] ● *noun* folder, box, etc. for holding loose papers; paper kept in this; collection of related computer data; row of people or things one behind another. ● *verb* (**-ling**) place in file or among records; submit (petition for divorce etc.); walk in line. □ **filing cabinet** cabinet with drawers for storing files.

file[2] ● *noun* tool with rough surface for smoothing wood, fingernails, etc. ● *verb* (**-ling**) smooth or shape with file.

filial /ˈfɪlɪəl/ *adjective* of or due from son or daughter.

filibuster /ˈfɪlɪbʌstə/ ● *noun* obstruction of progress in legislative assembly; *esp. US* person who engages in this. ● *verb* act as filibuster.

filigree /ˈfɪlɪɡriː/ *noun* fine ornamental work in gold etc. wire; similar delicate work.

filings *plural noun* particles rubbed off by file.

Filipino /ˈfɪlɪˈpiːnəʊ/ ● *noun* (*plural* **-s**) native or national of Philippines. ● *adjective* of Philippines or Filipinos.

fill ● *verb* (often + *with*) make or become full; occupy completely; spread over or through; block up (hole, tooth, etc.); appoint to or hold (office etc.); (as **filling** *adjective*) (of food) satisfying. ● *noun* enough to satisfy or fill. □ **fill in** complete (form etc.), fill completely, (often + *for*) act as substitute, *colloquial* inform more fully; **fill out** enlarge or become enlarged, esp. to proper size, fill in (form etc.); **fill up** fill completely, fill petrol tank (of).

filler *noun* material used to fill cavity or increase bulk.

fillet /ˈfɪlɪt/ ● *noun* boneless piece of fish or meat; (in full **fillet steak**) undercut of sirloin; ribbon etc. binding hair; narrow flat band between mouldings. ● *verb* (**-t-**) remove bones from (fish etc.) or divide into fillets; bind or provide with fillet(s).

filling *noun* material used to fill tooth, sandwich, pie, etc. □ **filling-station** garage selling petrol etc.

fillip /ˈfɪlɪp/ *noun* stimulus, incentive.

filly /ˈfɪlɪ/ *noun* (*plural* **-ies**) young female horse.

film ● *noun* thin coating or layer; strip or sheet of plastic etc. coated with light-sensitive emulsion for exposure in camera; story etc. on film; (in *plural*) cinema industry; slight veil, haze, etc. ● *verb* make photographic film of; (often + *over*) cover or become covered (as) with film. □ **film star** well-known film actor or actress. □ **filmy** *adjective* (**-ier**, **-iest**).

filmsetting *noun* typesetting by projecting characters on to photographic film. □ **filmset** *verb*; **filmsetter** *noun*.

Filofax /ˈfaɪləʊfæks/ *noun* proprietary term personal organizer.

filo pastry /ˈfiːləʊ/ *noun* pastry in very thin sheets.

filter /ˈfɪltə/ ● *noun* porous esp. paper device for removing impurities from liquid or gas or making coffee; screen for absorbing or modifying light; device for suppressing unwanted electrical or sound waves; arrangement for filtering traffic. ● *verb* pass through filter; (usually as **filtered** *adjective*) make (coffee) by dripping hot water through ground beans; (+ *through*, *into*, etc.) make way gradually through, into, etc.; (of traffic) be allowed to turn left or right at junction when other traffic is held up. □ **filter tip** (cigarette with) filter for removing some impurities.

filth *noun* disgusting dirt; obscenity.

filthy ● *adjective* (**-ier**, **-iest**) disgustingly dirty; obscene; (of weather) very unpleasant. ● *adverb colloquial* extremely. □ **filthy lucre** dishonourable gain; money.

filtrate /ˈfɪltreɪt/ ● *verb* (**-ting**) filter. ● *noun* filtered liquid. □ **filtration** *noun*.

fin *noun* organ, esp. of fish, for propelling and steering; similar projection for stabilizing aircraft etc.

finagle /fɪˈneɪg(ə)l/ *verb* (**-ling**) *colloquial* act or obtain dishonestly.

final /ˈfaɪn(ə)l/ ● *adjective* at the end, coming last; conclusive, decisive. ● *noun* last or deciding heat or game; last edition of day's newspaper; (usually in *plural*) exams at end of degree course. □ **finality** /-ˈnæl-/ *noun*, **finally** *adverb*.

finale /fɪˈnɑːlɪ/ *noun* last movement or section of drama, piece of music, etc.

finalist *noun* competitor in final.

finalize *verb* (also **-ise**) (**-zing** or **-sing**) put in final form; complete. □ **finalization** *noun*.

finance /ˈfaɪnæns/ ● *noun* management of money; monetary support for enterprise; (in *plural*) money resources. ● *verb* (**-cing**) provide capital for. □ **financial** /-ˈnæn-/ *adjective*; **financially** /-ˈnæn-/ *adverb*.

financier /faɪˈnænsɪə/ *noun* capitalist; entrepreneur.

finch *noun* small seed-eating bird.

find /faɪnd/ ● *verb* (past & past participle **found**) discover, get by chance or after search; become aware of; obtain, provide; summon up; perceive, experience; consider to be; (often in *passive*) discover to be present; reach; *Law* judge and declare. ● *noun* discovery of treasure etc.; valued thing or person newly discovered. □ **all found** (of wages) with board and lodging provided free; **find out** (often + *about*) discover, detect. □ **finder** *noun*.

finding *noun* (often in *plural*) conclusion reached by inquiry.

fine[1] ● *adjective* of high quality; excellent; good, satisfactory; pure, refined; imposing; bright and clear; small or thin, in small particles; smart, showy; flattering. ● *adverb* finely; very well. □ **fine arts** poetry, music, painting, sculpture, architecture, etc.; **fine-spun** delicate, too subtle; **fine-tune** make small adjustments to. □ **finely** *adverb*.

fine[2] ● *noun* money paid as penalty. ● *verb* (**-ning**) punish by fine.

finery /ˈfaɪnərɪ/ *noun* showy dress or decoration.

finesse /fɪˈnes/ ● *noun* refinement; subtlety; artfulness; *Cards* attempt to win trick with card that is not the highest held. ● *verb* (**-ssing**) use or manage by finesse; *Cards* make finesse.

finger /ˈfɪŋgə/ ● *noun* any of terminal projections of hand (usually excluding thumb); part of glove for finger; fingerlike object. ● *verb* touch, turn about, or play with fingers. □ **finger-bowl** bowl for rinsing fingers during meal; **finger-dry** dry and style hair by running fingers through it; **fingernail** nail on each finger; **fingerprint** impression made on surface by fingers, used in detecting crime; **finger-stall** protective cover for injured finger; **fingertip** tip of finger.

fingering *noun* manner of using fingers in music; indication of this in score.

finial /ˈfɪnɪəl/ *noun* ornamental top to gable, canopy, etc.

finicky /ˈfɪnɪkɪ/ *adjective* (also **finical**, **finicking**) over-particular; fastidious; detailed; fiddly.

finis /ˈfɪnɪs/ *noun* end, esp. of book.

finish /ˈfɪnɪʃ/ ● *verb* (often + *off*) bring or come to end or end of; complete; (often + *off*, *up*) complete consuming; treat surface of. ● *noun* last stage, completion; end of race etc.; method etc. of surface treatment.

finite /ˈfaɪnaɪt/ *adjective* limited, not infinite; (of verb) having specific number and person.

Finn *noun* native or national of Finland.

finnan /ˈfɪnən/ *noun* (in full **finnan haddock**) smoke-cured haddock.

Finnish ● *adjective* of Finland. ● *noun* language of Finland.

fiord /fjɔːd/ *noun* (also **fjord**) narrow inlet of sea as in Norway.

fir *noun* evergreen conifer with needles growing singly on the stems; its wood. □ **fir-cone** its fruit.

fire ● *noun* state of combustion of substance with oxygen, giving out light and heat; flame, glow; destructive burning; burning fuel in grate etc.; electric or gas heater; firing of guns; fervour, spirit; burning heat. ● *verb* (**-ring**) shoot (gun etc. or missile from it); shoot gun or missile; produce (salute etc.) by shooting; (of gun) be discharged; deliver or utter rapidly; detonate; dismiss (employee); set fire to;

supply with fuel; stimulate, enthuse; undergo ignition; bake or dry (pottery, bricks, etc.). □ **fire-alarm** bell etc. warning of fire; **firearm** gun, esp. pistol or rifle; **fire-ball** large meteor, ball of flame; **fire-bomb** incendiary bomb; **firebrand** piece of burning wood, trouble-maker; **fire-break** obstacle preventing spread of fire in forest etc.; **fire-brick** fireproof brick in grate; **fire brigade** group of firefighters; **firedog** support for logs in hearth; **fire door** fire-resistant door; **fire-drill** rehearsal of procedure in case of fire; **fire-engine** vehicle carrying hoses, firefighters, etc.; **fire-escape** emergency staircase etc. for use in fire; **fire extinguisher** apparatus discharging water, foam, etc. to extinguish fire; **firefighter** person who extinguishes fires; **firefly** insect emitting phosphorescent light, e.g. glow-worm; **fire-irons** tongs, poker, and shovel for domestic fire; **fireman** male firefighter, person who tends steam engine or steamship furnace; **fireplace** place in wall for domestic fire; **fire-power** destructive capacity of guns etc.; **fire-practice** fire-drill; **fire-raiser** arsonist; **fireside** area round fireplace; **fire-screen** ornamental screen for fireplace, screen against direct heat of fire; **fire station** headquarters of local fire brigade; **fire-trap** building without fire-escapes etc.; **firework** device producing flashes, bangs, etc. from burning chemicals, (in *plural*) outburst of anger etc.; **on fire** burning, excited; **under fire** being shot at or criticized.

firing *noun* discharge of guns. □ **firing line** front line in battle, centre of criticism etc.; **firing squad** soldiers ordered to shoot condemned person.

firm[1] ● *adjective* solid; fixed, steady; resolute; steadfast; (of offer etc.) definite. ● *verb* (often + *up*) make or become firm or secure. □ **firmly** *adverb*; **firmness** *noun*.

firm[2] *noun* business concern, its members.

firmament /ˈfɜːməmənt/ *noun* sky regarded as vault.

first ● *adjective* foremost in time, order, or importance. ● *noun* (**the first**) first person or thing; beginning; first occurrence of something notable; first-class

degree; first gear; first place in race. ● *adverb* before all or something else; for the first time. □ **at first hand** directly from original source; **first aid** emergency medical treatment; **first class** *noun* best category or accommodation, mail given priority, highest division in exam; **first-class** *adjective & adverb* of or by first class, excellent(ly); **first floor** (US **second floor**) floor above ground floor; **first-footing** first crossing of threshold in New Year; **firsthand** direct, original; **first mate** (on merchant ship) second in command; **first name** personal or Christian name; **first night** first public performance of play etc.; **first-rate** excellent; **first thing** before anything else, very early. □ **firstly** *adverb*.

firth /fɜːθ/ *noun* inlet, estuary.

fiscal /ˈfɪsk(ə)l/ ● *adjective* of public revenue. ● *noun* Scottish procurator fiscal. □ **fiscal year** financial year.

fish[1] ● *noun* (*plural* same or **-es**) vertebrate cold-blooded animal living in water; its flesh as food; person of specified kind. ● *verb* try to catch fish (in); (+ *for*) search for; seek indirectly; (+ *up*, *out*) retrieve with effort. □ **fish cake** fried cake of fish and mashed potato; **fish-eye lens** wide-angled lens; **fish farm** place where fish are bred for food; **fish finger** small oblong piece of fish in breadcrumbs; **fish-hook** barbed hook for catching fish; **fish-kettle** oval pan for boiling fish; **fish-knife** knife for eating or serving fish; **fish-meal** ground dried fish as fertilizer etc.; **fishmonger** dealer in fish; **fishnet** open-meshed fabric; **fish-slice** slotted cooking utensil; **fishwife** coarse or noisy woman, woman selling fish.

fish[2] *noun* piece of wood or iron for strengthening mast etc. □ **fish-plate** flat plate of iron etc. holding rails together.

fisherman /ˈfɪʃəmən/ *noun* man who catches fish as occupation or sport.

fishery *noun* (*plural* **-ies**) place where fish are caught or reared; industry of fishing or breeding fish.

fishing *noun* occupation or sport of trying to catch fish. □ **fishing-rod** tapering rod for fishing.

fishy *adjective* (**-ier**, **-iest**) of or like fish; *slang* dubious, suspect.

fissile /ˈfɪsaɪl/ ● *adjective* capable of undergoing nuclear fission; tending to split.

fission /ˈfɪʃ(ə)n/ ● *noun* splitting of atomic nucleus; division of cell as mode of reproduction. ● *verb* (cause to) undergo fission.

fissure /ˈfɪʃə/ ● *noun* narrow crack or split. ● *verb* (**-ring**) split.

fist *noun* clenched hand. □ **fisticuffs** fighting with the fists. □ **fistful** *noun* (*plural* **-s**).

fistula /ˈfɪstjʊlə/ *noun* (*plural* **-s** or **fistulae** /-liː/) abnormal or artificial passage in body. □ **fistular** *adjective*; **fistulous** *adjective*.

fit[1] ● *adjective* (**-tt-**) well suited; qualified, competent; in good health or condition; (+ *for*) good enough, right; ready. ● *verb* (**-tt-**) be of right size and shape; find room for; (often + *in*, *into*) be correctly positioned; (+ *on*, *together*) fix in place; (+ *with*) supply; befit. ● *noun* way thing fits. □ **fit in** (often + *with*) be compatible, accommodate, make room or time for; **fit out**, **up** equip. □ **fitness** *noun*.

fit[2] *noun* sudden esp. epileptic seizure; sudden brief bout or burst.

fitful *adjective* spasmodic, intermittent. □ **fitfully** *adverb*.

fitment *noun* (usually in *plural*) fixed item of furniture.

fitted *adjective* made to fit closely; with built-in fittings; built-in.

fitter *noun* mechanic who fits together and adjusts machinery etc.; supervisor of cutting, fitting, etc. of garments.

fitting ● *noun* action of fitting on a garment; (usually in *plural*) fixture, fitment. ● *adjective* proper, befitting. □ **fittingly** *adverb*.

five *adjective & noun* one more than four. □ **five o'clock shadow** beard growth visible in latter part of day; **five-star** of highest class; **fivestones** jacks played with five pieces of metal etc. and usually no ball.

fiver *noun colloquial* five-pound note.

fives *noun* game in which ball is struck with gloved hand or bat against walls of court.

fix ● *verb* make firm, stable, or permanent; fasten, secure; settle, specify; mend, repair; (+ *on*, *upon*) direct (eyes etc.) steadily on; attract and hold (attention etc.); identify, locate; *US colloquial* prepare (food, drink); *colloquial* kill, deal with (person); arrange result fraudulently. ● *noun* dilemma, predicament; position determined by bearings etc.; *slang* dose of addictive drug; *colloquial* fraudulently arranged result. □ **fix up** arrange, (often + *with*) provide (person). □ **fixer** *noun*.

fixate /fɪkˈseɪt/ *verb* (**-ting**) *Psychology* (usually in *passive*, often + *on*, *upon*) cause to become abnormally attached to person or thing.

fixation /fɪkˈseɪʃ(ə)n/ *noun* fixating, being fixated; obsession.

fixative /ˈfɪksətɪv/ ● *adjective* tending to fix (colours etc.). ● *noun* fixative substance.

fixedly /ˈfɪksɪdlɪ/ *adverb* intently.

fixity *noun* fixed state; stability, permanence.

fixture /ˈfɪkstʃə/ *noun* thing fixed in position; (date fixed for) sporting event; (in *plural*) articles belonging to land or house.

fizz ● *verb* make hissing or spluttering sound; effervesce. ● *noun* fizzing sound; effervescence; *colloquial* effervescent drink. □ **fizzy** *adjective* (**-ier**, **-iest**).

fizzle /ˈfɪz(ə)l/ ● *verb* (**-ling**) hiss or splutter feebly. ● *noun* fizzling sound. □ **fizzle out** end feebly.

fjord = FIORD.

fl. *abbreviation* fluid; floruit.

flab *noun colloquial* fat, flabbiness.

flabbergast /ˈflæbəɡɑːst/ *verb* (esp. as **flabbergasted** *adjective*) *colloquial* astonish; dumbfound.

flabby /ˈflæbɪ/ *adjective* (**-ier**, **-iest**) (of flesh) limp, not firm; feeble. □ **flabbiness** *noun*.

flaccid /ˈflæksɪd/ *adjective* flabby. □ **flaccidity** /-ˈsɪd-/ *noun*.

flag[1] ● *noun* piece of cloth attached by one edge to pole or rope as country's emblem, standard, or signal. ● *verb* (**-gg-**) grow tired; lag; droop; mark out with flags. □ **flag-day** day when charity collects money and gives stickers to contributors; **flag down** signal to stop; **flag-officer** admiral or vice or rear admiral; **flag-pole** flagstaff; **flagship** ship with admiral on board, leading example of thing; **flagstaff** pole on which flag is hung; **flag-waving** noun populist agitation, chauvinism, adjective chauvinistic.

flag² noun (also **flagstone**) flat paving stone. ● verb (**-gg-**) pave with flags.

flag³ noun plant with bladed leaf, esp. iris.

flagellant /ˈflædʒələnt/ ● noun person who flagellates himself, herself, or others. ● adjective of flagellation.

flagellate /ˈflædʒəleɪt/ verb (**-ting**) whip or flog, esp. as religious discipline or sexual stimulus. □ **flagellation** noun.

flageolet /flædʒəˈlet/ noun small flute blown at end.

flagon /ˈflægən/ noun quart bottle or other vessel for wine etc.

flagrant /ˈfleɪgrənt/ adjective blatant; scandalous. □ **flagrancy** noun; **flagrantly** adverb.

flagrante see IN FLAGRANTE DELICTO.

flail ● verb (often + about) wave or swing wildly; beat (as) with flail. ● noun staff with heavy stick swinging from it, used for threshing.

flair noun natural talent; style, finesse.

flak noun anti-aircraft fire; criticism; abuse.

flake ● noun thin light piece of snow etc.; thin broad piece peeled or split off. ● verb (**-king**) (often + away, off) take or come away in flakes; fall in or sprinkle with flakes. □ **flake out** fall asleep or drop from exhaustion, faint.

flaky adjective (**-ier, -iest**) of, like, or in flakes. □ **flaky pastry** lighter version of puff pastry.

flambé /ˈflɒmbeɪ/ adjective (of food) covered with alcohol and set alight briefly.

flamboyant /flæmˈbɔɪənt/ adjective ostentatious, showy; florid. ● **flamboyance** noun; **flamboyantly** adverb.

flame ● noun ignited gas; portion of this; bright light; brilliant orange colour; passion, esp. love; colloquial sweetheart. ● verb (**-ming**) (often + out, up) burn; blaze; (of passion) break out; become angry; shine or glow like flame.

flamenco /fləˈmeŋkəʊ/ noun (plural **-s**) Spanish Gypsy guitar music with singing and dancing.

flaming adjective emitting flames; very hot; passionate; brightly coloured; colloquial expressing annoyance.

flamingo /fləˈmɪŋgəʊ/ noun (plural **-s** or **-es**) tall long-necked wading bird with usually pink plumage.

flammable /ˈflæməb(ə)l/ adjective inflammable.

■ **Usage** Flammable is often used because inflammable could be taken to mean 'not flammable'. The negative of flammable is non-flammable.

flan noun pastry case with savoury or sweet filling; sponge base with sweet topping.

flange /flændʒ/ noun projecting flat rim, for strengthening etc.

flank ● noun side of body between ribs and hip; side of mountain, army, etc. ● verb (often as **flanked** adjective) be at or move along side of.

flannel /ˈflæn(ə)l/ ● noun woven woollen usually napless fabric; (in plural) flannel trousers; face-cloth; slang nonsense, flattery. ● verb (**-ll-**; US **-l-**) slang flatter; wash with flannel.

flannelette /flænəˈlet/ noun napped cotton fabric like flannel.

flap ● verb (**-pp-**) move or be moved loosely up and down; beat; flutter; colloquial be agitated or panicky; colloquial (of ears) listen intently. ● noun piece of cloth, wood, etc. attached by one side, esp. to cover gap; flapping; colloquial agitation; aileron. □ **flapjack** sweet oatcake, esp. US small pancake.

flapper noun person apt to panic; slang (in 1920s) young unconventional woman.

flare ● verb (**-ring**) blaze with bright unsteady flame; (usually as **flared** adjective) widen gradually; burst out, esp. angrily. ● noun bright unsteady flame, outburst of this; flame or bright light as signal etc.; gradual widening; (in plural) wide-bottomed trousers. □ **flare-path** line of lights on runway to guide aircraft; **flare up** verb burst into blaze, anger, activity, etc.; **flare-up** noun outburst.

flash ● verb (cause to) emit brief or sudden light; gleam; send or reflect like sudden flame; burst suddenly into view etc.; move swiftly; send (news etc.) by radio etc.; signal (to) with vehicle lights; show ostentatiously; *slang* indecently expose oneself. • *noun* sudden bright light or flame; an instant; sudden brief feeling or display; *Photography* flashlight. • *adjective* colloquial gaudy, showy; vulgar. □ **flashback** scene set in earlier time than main action; **flash bulb** *Photography* bulb for flashlight; **flash-gun** device operating camera flashlight; **flash in the pan** promising start followed by failure; **flash-lamp** portable flashing electric lamp; **flashlight** *Photography* light giving intense flash, *US* electric torch; **flashpoint** temperature at which vapour from oil etc. will ignite in air, point at which anger is expressed.

flasher *noun slang* man who indecently exposes himself; automatic device for switching lights rapidly on and off.

flashing *noun* (usually metal) strip to prevent water penetration at roof joint etc.

flashy *adjective* (**-ier, -iest**) showy; cheaply attractive. □ **flashily** *adverb.*

flask /flɑːsk/ *noun* narrow-necked bulbous bottle; hip-flask; vacuum flask.

flat[1] • *adjective* (**-tt-**) horizontally level; smooth, even; level and shallow; downright; dull; dejected; having lost its effervescence; (of battery) having exhausted its charge; (of tyre etc.) deflated; *Music* below correct or normal pitch, having flats in key signature. • *adverb* spread out; completely, exactly; flatly. • *noun* flat part; level esp. marshy ground; *Music* note lowered by semitone, sign (♭) indicating this; flat theatre scenery on frame; punctured tyre; (**the flat**) flat racing, its season. □ **flatfish** fish with flattened body, e.g. sole, plaice; **flat foot** foot with flattened arch; **flat-footed** having flat feet, *colloquial* uninspired; **flat out** at top speed, using all one's strength etc.; **flat race** horse race over level ground without jumps; **flat rate** unvarying rate or charge; **flat spin** aircraft's nearly horizontal spin, *colloquial* state of panic; **flatworm** worm with flattened body, e.g. fluke. □ **flatly** *adverb;* **flatness** *noun;* **flattish** *adjective.*

flat[2] *noun* set of rooms, usually on one floor, as residence. □ **flatmate** person sharing flat. □ **flatlet** *noun.*

flatten *verb* make or become flat; *colloquial* humiliate; knock down.

flatter /'flætə/ *verb* compliment unduly; enhance appearance of; (usually **flatter oneself**; usually + *that*) congratulate or delude (oneself etc.). □ **flatterer** *noun;* **flattering** *adjective;* **flatteringly** *adverb;* **flattery** *noun.*

flatulent /'flætjʊlənt/ *adjective* causing, caused by, or troubled with, intestinal wind; inflated, pretentious. □ **flatulence** *noun.*

flaunt /flɔːnt/ *verb* display proudly; show off, parade.

■ **Usage** *Flaunt* is often confused with *flout*, which means 'to disobey contemptuously'.

flautist /'flɔːtɪst/ *noun* flute-player.

flavour /'fleɪvə/ (*US* **flavor**) • *noun* mixed sensation of smell and taste; distinctive taste, characteristic quality. • *verb* give flavour to, season. □ **flavour of the month** temporary trend or fashion. □ **flavourless** *adjective;* **flavoursome** *adjective.*

flavouring *noun* (*US* **flavoring**) substance used to flavour food or drink.

flaw • *noun* imperfection; blemish; crack; invalidating defect. • *verb* damage; spoil; (as **flawed** *adjective*) morally etc. defective. □ **flawless** *adjective.*

flax *noun* blue-flowered plant grown for its oily seeds (linseed) and for making into linen.

flaxen *adjective* of flax; (of hair) pale yellow.

flay *verb* strip skin or hide off; criticize severely; peel off.

flea *noun* small wingless jumping parasitic insect. □ **flea market** street market selling second-hand goods etc.

fleck • *noun* small patch of colour or light; speck. • *verb* mark with flecks.

flection *US* = FLEXION.

fled past & past participle of FLEE.

fledgling /'fledʒlɪŋ/ (also **fledgeling**) • *noun* young bird. • *adjective* new, inexperienced.

flee *verb* (**flees**; past & past participle **fled**) run away (from); leave hurriedly.

fleece • *noun* woolly coat of sheep etc.; this shorn from sheep; fleecy lining etc. • *verb* (**-cing**) (often + *of*) strip of money etc., swindle; shear; (as **fleeced** *adjective*) cover as with fleece. □ **fleecy** *adjective* (**-ier, -iest**).

fleet • *noun* warships under one commander-in-chief; (**the fleet**) navy; vehicles in one company etc. • *adjective* swift, nimble.

fleeting *adjective* transitory; brief. □ **fleetingly** *adverb*.

Fleming /ˈflemɪŋ/ *noun* native of medieval Flanders; member of Flemish-speaking people of N. and W. Belgium.

Flemish /ˈflemɪʃ/ • *adjective* of Flanders. • *noun* language of the Flemings.

flesh *noun* soft substance between skin and bones; plumpness, fat; body, esp. as sinful; pulpy substance of fruit etc.; (also **flesh-colour**) yellowish pink colour. □ **flesh and blood** human body, human nature, esp. as fallible, humankind, near relations; **flesh out** make or become substantial; **fleshpots** luxurious living; **flesh-wound** superficial wound; **in the flesh** in person. □ **fleshy** *adjective* (**-ier, -iest**).

fleshly /ˈfleʃlɪ/ *adjective* worldly; carnal.

fleur-de-lis /flɜːdəˈliː/ *noun* (also **fleur-de-lys**) (*plural* **fleurs-** same pronunciation) iris flower; *Heraldry* lily of 3 petals; former royal arms of France.

flew *past of* FLY[1].

flews *plural noun* hanging lips of bloodhound etc.

flex[1] *verb* bend (joint, limb); move (muscle) to bend joint.

flex[2] *noun* flexible insulated cable.

flexible /ˈfleksɪb(ə)l/ *adjective* able to bend without breaking; pliable; adaptable. □ **flexibility** *noun*; **flexibly** *adverb*.

flexion /ˈflekʃ(ə)n/ *noun* (*US* **flection**) bending; bent part.

flexitime /ˈfleksɪtaɪm/ *noun* system of flexible working hours.

flibbertigibbet /ˈflɪbətɪdʒɪbɪt/ *noun* gossiping, frivolous, or restless person.

flick • *noun* light sharp blow; sudden release of bent finger etc. to propel thing; jerk; *colloquial* cinema film; (**the flicks**) the cinema. • *verb* (often + *away, off*) strike or move with flick.

□ **flick-knife** knife with blade that springs out; **flick through** glance at or through by turning over (pages etc.) rapidly.

flicker /ˈflɪkə/ • *verb* shine or burn unsteadily; flutter; waver. • *noun* flickering light or motion; brief feeling (of hope etc.); slightest reaction or degree. □ **flicker out** die away.

flier = FLYER.

flight[1] /flaɪt/ *noun* act or manner of flying; movement, passage, or journey through air or space; timetabled airline journey; flock of birds etc.; (usually + *of*) series of stairs etc.; imaginative excursion; volley; tail of dart. □ **flight bag** small zipped shoulder bag for air travel; **flight-deck** cockpit of large aircraft, deck of aircraft carrier; **flight lieutenant** RAF officer next below squadron leader; **flight path** planned course of aircraft etc.; **flight recorder** device in aircraft recording technical details of flight; **flight sergeant** RAF rank next above sergeant.

flight[2] /flaɪt/ *noun* fleeing; hasty retreat.

flightless *adjective* (of bird etc.) unable to fly.

flighty *adjective* (**-ier, -iest**) frivolous; fickle.

flimsy /ˈflɪmzɪ/ *adjective* (**-ier, -iest**) insubstantial, rickety; unconvincing; (of clothing) thin. □ **flimsily** *adverb*.

flinch *verb* draw back in fear etc.; shrink; wince.

fling • *verb* (*past & past participle* **flung**) throw, hurl; rush, esp. angrily; discard rashly. • *noun* flinging; throw; bout of wild behaviour; whirling Scottish dance.

flint *noun* hard grey stone; piece of this, esp. as tool or weapon; piece of hard alloy used to produce spark. □ **flintlock** old type of gun fired by spark from flint. □ **flinty** *adjective* (**-ier, -iest**).

flip • *verb* (**-pp-**) toss (coin etc.) so that it spins in air; turn or flick (small object) over; *slang* flip one's lid. • *noun* act of flipping. • *adjective* glib; flippant. □ **flip chart** large pad of paper on stand; **flip-flop** sandal with thong between toes; **flip one's lid** *slang* lose self-control, go mad; **flip side** reverse side of gramophone record etc.; **flip through** flick through.

flippant /'flɪpənt/ adjective frivolous; disrespectful. □ **flippancy** noun; **flippantly** adverb.

flipper noun limb of turtle, penguin, etc., used in swimming; rubber attachment to foot for underwater swimming.

flirt ● verb try to attract sexually but without serious intent; (usually + with) superficially engage in, trifle. ● noun person who flirts. □ **flirtation** noun; **flirtatious** adjective; **flirtatiously** adverb; **flirtatiousness** noun.

flit ● verb (-tt-) pass lightly or rapidly; make short flights; disappear secretly, esp. to escape creditors. ● noun act of flitting.

flitch noun side of bacon.

flitter verb flit about.

float ● verb (cause to) rest or drift on surface of liquid; move or be suspended freely in liquid or gas; launch (company, scheme); offer (stocks, shares, etc.) on stock market; (cause or allow to) have fluctuating exchange rate; circulate or cause (rumour, idea) to circulate. ● noun device or structure that floats; electrically powered vehicle or cart; decorated platform or tableau on lorry in procession etc.; supply of loose change, petty cash.

floating adjective not settled; variable; not committed. □ **floating rib** lower rib not attached to breastbone.

floaty adjective (-ier, -iest) (of fabric) light and airy.

flocculent /'flɒkjʊlənt/ adjective like tufts of wool.

flock¹ ● noun animals, esp. birds or sheep, as group or unit; large crowd of people; people in care of priest, teacher, etc. ● verb (often + to, in, out, together) congregate; mass; troop.

flock² noun shredded wool, cotton, etc. used as stuffing; powdered wool used to make pattern on wallpaper.

floe noun sheet of floating ice.

flog verb (-gg-) beat with whip, stick, etc.; (often + off) slang sell.

flood /flʌd/ ● noun overflowing or influx of water, esp. over land; outburst, outpouring; inflow of tide; (**the Flood**) the flood described in Genesis. ● verb overflow; cover or be covered with flood; irrigate; deluge; come in great quantities; overfill (carburettor) with petrol. □ **floodgate** gate for admitting or excluding water, (usually in plural) last restraint against tear, anger, etc.; **floodlight** (illuminate with) large powerful light; **floodlit** lit thus.

floor /flɔː/ ● noun lower surface of room; bottom of sea, cave, etc.; storey; part of legislative chamber where members sit and speak; right to speak in debate; minimum of prices, wages, etc. ● verb provide with floor; knock down; baffle; overcome. □ **floor manager** stage manager of television production; **floor plan** diagram of rooms etc. on one storey; **floor show** cabaret.

flop ● verb (-pp-) sway about heavily or loosely; (often + down, on, into) move, fall, sit, etc. awkwardly or suddenly; slang collapse, fail; make dull soft thud or splash. ● noun flopping motion or sound; slang failure. ● adverb with a flop.

floppy ● adjective (-ier, -iest) tending to flop; flaccid. ● noun (plural -ies) (in full **floppy disk**) flexible disc for storage of computer data.

flora /'flɔːrə/ noun (plural -s or -rae /-riː/) plant life of region or period.

floral adjective of or decorated with flowers.

floret /'flɒrɪt/ noun each of small flowers of composite flower head; each stem of head of cauliflower, broccoli, etc.

florid /'flɒrɪd/ adjective ruddy; ornate; showy.

florin /'flɒrɪn/ noun historical gold or silver coin, esp. British two-shilling coin.

florist /'flɒrɪst/ noun person who deals in or grows flowers.

floruit /'flɒrʊɪt/ verb (of painter, writer, etc.) lived and worked.

floss ● noun rough silk of silkworm's cocoon; dental floss. ● verb clean (teeth) with dental floss. □ **flossy** adjective (-ier, -iest).

flotation /fləʊ'teɪʃ(ə)n/ noun launching of commercial enterprise etc.

flotilla /flə'tɪlə/ noun small fleet; fleet of small ships.

flotsam /'flɒtsəm/ noun floating wreckage. □ **flotsam and jetsam** odds and ends, vagrants.

flounce[1] /flaʊns/ ● verb (**-cing**) (often + off, out, etc.) go or move angrily or impatiently. ● noun flouncing movement.

flounce[2] /flaʊns/ ● noun frill on dress, skirt, etc. ● verb (**-cing**) (usually as **flounced** adjective) trim with flounces.

flounder[1] /'flaʊndə/ verb struggle helplessly; do task clumsily.

flounder[2] /'flaʊndə/ noun (plural same) small flatfish.

flour /flaʊə/ ● noun meal or powder from ground wheat etc. ● verb sprinkle with flour. □ **floury** adjective (**-ier, -iest**).

flourish /'flʌrɪʃ/ ● verb grow vigorously; thrive, prosper; wave, brandish. ● noun showy gesture; ornamental curve in writing; Music ornate passage; fanfare.

flout verb disobey (law etc.) contemptuously.

■ **Usage** Flout is often confused with flaunt, which means 'to display proudly or show off'.

flow /fləʊ/ ● verb glide along, move smoothly; gush out; circulate; be plentiful or in flood; (often + from) result. ● noun flowing movement or liquid; stream; rise of tide. □ **flow chart, diagram, sheet** diagram of movement or action in complex activity.

flower /'flaʊə/ ● noun part of plant from which seed or fruit develops; plant bearing blossom. ● verb bloom; reach peak. □ **flower-bed** garden bed for flowers; **the flower of** the best of; **flowerpot** pot for growing plant in; **in flower** blooming. □ **flowered** adjective.

flowery adjective florally decorated; (of speech etc.) high-flown; full of flowers.

flowing adjective fluent; smoothly continuous; (of hair etc.) unconfined.

flown past participle of FLY[1].

flu noun colloquial influenza.

fluctuate /'flʌktʃʊeɪt/ verb (**-ting**) vary, rise and fall. □ **fluctuation** noun.

flue noun smoke duct in chimney; channel for conveying heat.

fluent /'fluːənt/ adjective expressing oneself easily and naturally, esp. in foreign language. □ **fluency** noun; **fluently** adverb.

fluff ● noun soft fur, feathers, fabric particles, etc.; slang mistake in performance etc. ● verb (often + up) shake into

or become soft mass; slang make mistake in performance etc. □ **fluffy** adjective (**-ier, -iest**).

flugelhorn /'fluːg(ə)lhɔːn/ noun brass instrument like cornet.

fluid /'fluːɪd/ ● noun substance, esp. gas or liquid, capable of flowing freely; liquid secretion. ● adjective able to flow freely; constantly changing. □ **fluid ounce** twentieth or US sixteenth of pint. □ **fluidity** /-'ɪdɪtɪ/ noun.

fluke[1] /fluːk/ noun lucky accident. □ **fluky** adjective (**-ier, -iest**).

fluke[2] /fluːk/ noun parasitic flatworm.

flummery /'flʌmərɪ/ noun (plural **-ies**) nonsense; flattery; sweet milk dish.

flummox /'flʌməks/ verb colloquial bewilder.

flung past & past participle of FLING.

flunk verb US colloquial fail (esp. exam).

flunkey /'flʌŋkɪ/ noun (also **flunky**) (plural **-eys** or **-ies**) usually derogatory footman.

fluorescence /flʊə'res(ə)ns/ noun light radiation from certain substances; property of absorbing invisible light and emitting visible light. □ **fluoresce** verb (**-scing**); **fluorescent** adjective.

fluoridate /'flʊərɪdeɪt/ verb (**-ting**) add fluoride to (water). □ **fluoridation** noun.

fluoride /'flʊəraɪd/ noun compound of fluorine with metal, esp. used to prevent tooth decay.

fluorinate /'flʊərɪneɪt/ verb (**-ting**) fluoridate; introduce fluorine into (compound). □ **fluorination** noun.

fluorine /'flʊəriːn/ noun poisonous pale yellow gaseous element.

flurry /'flʌrɪ/ ● noun (plural **-ies**) gust, squall; burst of activity, excitement, etc. ● verb (**-ies, -ied**) agitate, confuse.

flush[1] ● verb redden as **flushed** adjective + with) (cause to) glow or blush (with pride etc.); cleanse (drain, lavatory, etc.) by flow of water; (often + away, down) dispose of thus. ● noun glow, blush; rush of water; cleansing (of lavatory etc.) thus; rush of esp. elation or triumph; freshness, vigour; (also **hot flush**) sudden hot feeling during menopause; feverish redness or temperature etc. ● adjective level, in same plane; colloquial having plenty of money.

flush[2] noun hand of cards all of one suit.

flush³ verb (cause to) fly up suddenly. □ **flush out** reveal, drive out.

fluster /'flʌstə/ ● verb confuse, make nervous. ● noun confused or agitated state.

flute /fluːt/ ● noun high-pitched woodwind instrument held sideways; vertical groove in pillar etc. ● verb (**-ting**) (often as **fluted** adjective) make grooves in; play on flute. □ **fluting** noun.

flutter /'flʌtə/ ● verb flap (wings) in flying or trying to fly; fall quiveringly; wave or flap quickly; move about restlessly; (of pulse etc.) beat feebly or irregularly. ● noun fluttering; tremulous excitement; slang small bet on horse etc.; abnormally rapid heartbeat; rapid variation of pitch, esp. of recorded sound.

fluvial /'fluːvɪəl/ adjective of or found in rivers.

flux noun flowing, flowing out; discharge; continuous change; substance mixed with metal etc. to assist fusion.

fly¹ /flaɪ/ ● verb (**flies**; past **flew** /fluː/; past participle **flown** /fləʊn/) move or travel through air with wings or in aircraft; control flight of (aircraft); cause to fly or remain aloft; wave; move swiftly; be driven forcefully; flee (from); (+ at, upon) attack or criticize fiercely. ● noun (plural **-ies**) (usually in plural) flap to cover front fastening on trousers, this fastening; flap at entrance of tent; (in plural) space over stage, for scenery and lighting; act of flying. □ **fly-by-night** unreliable; **fly-half** Rugby stand-off half; **flyleaf** blank leaf at beginning or end of book; **flyover** bridge carrying road etc. over another; **fly-past** ceremonial flight of aircraft; **fly-post** fix (posters etc.) illegally; **flysheet** canvas cover over tent for extra protection, short tract or circular; **fly-tip** illegally dump (waste); **flywheel** heavy wheel regulating machinery or accumulating power.

fly² /flaɪ/ (plural **flies**) noun two-winged insect; disease caused by flies; (esp. artificial) fly used as bait in fishing. □ **fly-blown** tainted by flies; **flycatcher** bird that catches flies in flight; **fly-fish** verb fish with fly; **fly in the ointment** minor irritation or setback; **fly on the wall** unnoticed observer; **fly-paper** sticky treated paper for catching flies; **fly-trap** plant that catches flies; **flyweight** amateur boxing weight (48–51 kg).

fly³ /flaɪ/ adjective slang knowing, clever.

flyer noun (also **flier**) airman, airwoman; thing or person that flies in specified way; small handbill.

flying ● adjective that flies; hasty. ● noun flight. □ **flying boat** boatlike seaplane; **flying buttress** (usually arched) buttress running from upper part of wall to outer support; **flying doctor** doctor who uses aircraft to visit patients; **flying fish** fish gliding through air with winglike fins; **flying fox** fruit-eating bat; **flying officer** RAF officer next below flight lieutenant; **flying saucer** supposed alien spaceship; **flying squad** rapidly mobile police detachment, midwifery unit, etc.; **flying start** start (of race) at full speed, vigorous start.

FM abbreviation Field Marshal; frequency modulation.

FO abbreviation Flying Officer.

foal ● noun young of horse or related animal. ● verb give birth to (foal).

foam ● noun froth formed in liquid; froth of saliva or sweat; spongy rubber or plastic. ● verb emit foam; froth. □ **foam at the mouth** be very angry. □ **foamy** adjective (**-ier, -iest**).

fob¹ noun (attachment to) watch-chain; small pocket for watch etc.

fob² verb (**-bb-**) □ **fob off** (often + with) deceive into accepting something inferior, (often + on, on to) offload (unwanted thing on person).

focal /'fəʊk(ə)l/ adjective of or at a focus. □ **focal distance, length** distance between centre of lens etc. and its focus; **focal point** focus, centre of interest or activity.

fo'c's'le = FORECASTLE.

focus /'fəʊkəs/ ● noun (plural **focuses** or **foci** /'fəʊsaɪ/) point at which rays etc. meet after reflection or refraction or from which rays etc. seem to come; point at which object must be situated to give clearly defined image; adjustment of eye or lens to produce clear image; state of clear definition; centre of interest or activity. ● verb (**-s-** or **-ss-**) bring into focus; adjust focus of (lens, eye); concentrate or be concentrated on; (cause to) converge to focus.

fodder /ˈfɒdə/ noun hay, straw, etc. as animal food.

foe noun enemy.

foetid = FETID.

foetus /ˈfiːtəs/ noun (US **fetus**) (plural **-tuses**) unborn mammalian offspring, esp. human embryo of 8 weeks or more. □ **foetal** adjective.

fog ● noun thick cloud of water droplets or smoke suspended at or near earth's surface; thick mist; cloudiness on photographic negative; confused state. ● verb (**-gg-**) envelop (as) in fog; perplex. □ **fog-bank** mass of fog at sea; **foghorn** horn warning ships in fog, colloquial penetrating voice.

fogey /ˈfəʊgɪ/ noun (also **fogy**) (plural **-ies** or **-eys**) (esp. **old fogey**) dull old-fashioned person.

foggy adjective (**-ier, -iest**) full of fog; of or like fog; vague. □ **not the foggiest** colloquial no idea.

foible /ˈfɔɪb(ə)l/ noun minor weakness or idiosyncrasy.

foil[1] verb frustrate, defeat.

foil[2] noun thin sheet of metal; person or thing setting off another to advantage.

foil[3] noun blunt fencing sword.

foist verb (+ on) force (thing, oneself) on to (unwilling person).

fold[1] /fəʊld/ ● verb double (flexible thing) over on itself; bend portion of; become or be able to be folded; (+ away, up) make compact by folding; (often + up) colloquial collapse, cease to function; enfold; clasp; (+ in) mix in gently. ● noun folding; line made by folding; hollow among hills.

fold[2] /fəʊld/ noun sheepfold; religious group or congregation.

folder noun folding cover or holder for loose papers.

foliaceous /fəʊlɪˈeɪʃəs/ adjective of or like leaves; laminated.

foliage /ˈfəʊlɪɪdʒ/ noun leaves, leafage.

foliar /ˈfəʊlɪə/ adjective of leaves. □ **foliar feed** fertilizer supplied to leaves.

foliate ● adjective /ˈfəʊlɪət/ leaflike; having leaves. ● verb /ˈfəʊlɪeɪt/ (**-ting**) split into thin layers. □ **foliation** noun.

folio /ˈfəʊlɪəʊ/ ● noun (plural **-s**) leaf of paper etc. numbered only on front; sheet of paper folded once; book of such sheets. ● adjective (of book) made of folios.

folk /fəʊk/ ● noun (plural same or **-s**) (treated as plural) people in general or of specified class; (in plural, usually **folks**) one's relatives; (treated as singular) a people or nation; (in full **folk-music**) (treated as singular) traditional, esp. working-class, music, or music in style of this. ● adjective of popular origin. □ **folklore** traditional beliefs etc., study of these; **folkweave** rough loosely woven fabric.

folksy /ˈfəʊksɪ/ adjective (**-ier, -iest**) of or like folk art; in deliberately popular style.

follicle /ˈfɒlɪk(ə)l/ noun small sac or vesicle, esp. for hair-root. □ **follicular** /fəˈlɪkjʊlə/ adjective.

follow /ˈfɒləʊ/ verb go or come after; go along; come next in order or time; practise; understand; take as guide; take interest in; (+ with) provide with (sequel etc.); (+ from) result from; be necessary inference. □ **follow on** verb continue, (of cricket team) bat twice in succession; **follow-on** noun instance of this; **follow suit** play card of suit led, conform to another's actions; **follow through** verb continue to conclusion, continue movement of stroke after hitting the ball; **follow-through** noun instance of this; **follow up** verb act or investigate further; **follow-up** noun subsequent action.

follower noun supporter, devotee; person who follows.

following ● preposition after in time; as sequel to. ● noun group of supporters. ● adjective that follows. □ **the following** what follows, now to be mentioned.

folly /ˈfɒlɪ/ noun (plural **-ies**) foolishness; foolish act, idea, etc.; building for display only.

foment /fəˈment/ verb instigate, stir up (trouble etc.). □ **fomentation** /fəʊmenˈteɪʃ(ə)n/ noun.

fond adjective (+ of) liking; affectionate; doting; foolishly optimistic. □ **fondly** adverb; **fondness** noun.

fondant /ˈfɒnd(ə)nt/ noun soft sugary sweet.

fondle /ˈfɒnd(ə)l/ verb (**-ling**) caress.

fondue /ˈfɒndjuː/ noun dish of melted cheese.

font[1] *noun* receptacle for baptismal water.

font[2] = FOUNT[2].

fontanelle /fɒntə'nel/ *noun* (*US* **fontanel**) space in infant's skull, which later closes up.

food /fuːd/ *noun* substance taken in to maintain life and growth; solid food; mental stimulus. □ **food-chain** series of organisms each dependent on next for food; **food poisoning** illness due to bacteria etc. in food; **food processor** machine for chopping and mixing food; **foodstuff** substance used as food.

foodie /'fuːdɪ/ *noun colloquial* person who makes a cult of food.

fool[1] ● *noun* unwise or stupid person; *historical* jester, clown. ● *verb* deceive; trick; cheat; joke; tease; (+ *around*, *about*) play, trifle. □ **act**, **play the fool** behave in silly way; **foolproof** incapable of misuse or mistake; **fool's paradise** illusory happiness; **make a fool of** make (person) look foolish, trick.

fool[2] *noun* dessert of fruit purée with cream or custard.

foolery *noun* foolish behaviour.

foolhardy *adjective* (**-ier**, **-iest**) foolishly bold; reckless. □ **foolhardily** *adverb*; **foolhardiness** *noun*.

foolish *adjective* lacking good sense or judgement. □ **foolishly** *adverb*; **foolishness** *noun*.

foolscap /'fuːlskæp/ *noun* large size of paper, about 330 mm x 200 (or 400) mm.

foot /fʊt/ ● *noun* (*plural* **feet**) part of leg below ankle; lower part or end; (*plural* same or **feet**) linear measure of 12 in. (30.48 cm); metrical unit of verse forming part of line; *historical* infantry. ● *verb* pay (bill); (usually as **foot it**) go on foot. □ **foot-and-mouth** (**disease**) contagious viral disease of cattle etc.; **footfall** sound of footstep; **foot-fault** (in tennis) serving with foot over baseline; **foothill** low hill lying at base of mountain or range; **foothold** secure place for feet in climbing, secure initial position; **footlights** row of floor-level lights along front of stage; **footloose** free to act as one pleases; **footman** liveried servant; **footmark** footprint; **footnote** note at foot of page; **footpath**

path for pedestrians only; **footplate** platform for crew in locomotive; **footprint** impression left by foot or shoe; **footsore** having sore feet, esp. from walking; **footstep** (sound of) step taken in walking; **footstool** stool for resting feet on when sitting; **on foot** walking. □ **footless** *adjective*.

footage *noun* a length of TV or cinema film etc.; length in feet.

football *noun* large inflated usually leather ball; team game played with this. □ **football pool(s)** organized gambling on results of football matches. □ **footballer** *noun*.

footing *noun* foothold; secure position; operational basis; relative position or status; (often in *plural*) foundations of wall.

footling /'fuːtlɪŋ/ *adjective colloquial* trivial, silly.

Footsie /'fʊtsɪ/ *noun* FT-SE.

footsie /'fʊtsɪ/ *noun colloquial* amorous play with feet.

fop *noun* dandy. □ **foppery** *noun*; **foppish** *adjective*.

for /fə, fɔː/ ● *preposition* in interest, defence, or favour of; appropriate to; regarding; representing; at the price of; as consequence or on account of; in order to get or reach; so as to start promptly at; notwithstanding. ● *conjunction* because, since. □ **be for it** be liable or about to be punished.

forage /'fɒrɪdʒ/ ● *noun* food for horses and cattle; searching for food. ● *verb* (**-ging**) (often + *for*) search for food; rummage; collect food from. □ **forage cap** infantry undress cap.

foray /'fɒreɪ/ ● *noun* sudden attack, raid. ● *verb* make foray.

forbade (also **forbad**) *past* of FORBID.

forbear[1] /fɔː'beə/ *verb* (*past* **forbore**; *past participle* **forborne**) *formal* abstain or refrain from.

forbear[2] = FOREBEAR.

forbearance *noun* patient self-control; tolerance.

forbid /fə'bɪd/ *verb* (**forbidding**; *past* **forbade** /-bæd/ or **forbad**; *past participle* **forbidden**) (+ *to do*) order not; not allow; refuse entry to. □ **forbidden fruit** thing desired esp. because not allowed.

forbidding adjective stern, threatening. □ **forbiddingly** adverb.

forbore past of FORBEAR[1].

forborne past participle of FORBEAR[1].

force ● noun strength, power, intense effort; group of soldiers, police, etc.; coercion, compulsion; influence (person etc.) with moral power. ● verb (-cing) compel, coerce; make way, break into or open by force; drive, propel; (+ on, upon) impose or press on (person); cause or produce by effort; strain; artificially hasten maturity of; accelerate. □ **forced landing** emergency landing of aircraft; **forced march** lengthy and vigorous march, esp. by troops; **force-feed** feed (prisoner etc.) against his or her will; **force (person's) hand** make him or her act prematurely or unwillingly.

forceful adjective powerful; impressive. □ **forcefully** adverb; **forcefulness** noun.

force majeure /fɔːs mæˈʒɜː/ noun irresistible force; unforeseeable circumstances. [French]

forcemeat /ˈfɔːsmiːt/ noun minced seasoned meat for stuffing etc.

forceps /ˈfɔːseps/ noun (plural same) surgical pincers.

forcible /ˈfɔːsɪb(ə)l/ adjective done by or involving force; forceful. □ **forcibly** adverb.

ford ● noun shallow place where river etc. may be crossed. ● verb cross (water) at ford. □ **fordable** adjective.

fore ● adjective situated in front. ● noun front part; bow of ship. ● interjection (in golf) warning to person in path of ball. □ **fore-and-aft** (of sails or rigging) lengthwise, at bow and stern; **to the fore** conspicuous.

forearm[1] /ˈfɔːrɑːm/ noun arm from elbow to wrist or fingertips.

forearm[2] /fɔːˈrɑːm/ verb arm beforehand, prepare.

forebear /ˈfɔːbeə/ noun (also **forbear**) (usually in plural) ancestor.

forebode /fɔːˈbəʊd/ verb (-ding) be advance sign of; portend.

foreboding noun expectation of trouble.

forecast ● verb (past & past participle -cast or -casted) predict; estimate beforehand. ● noun prediction, esp. of weather. □ **forecaster** noun.

forecastle /ˈfəʊks(ə)l/ noun (also **fo'c's'le**) forward part of ship, formerly living quarters.

foreclose /fɔːˈkləʊz/ verb (-sing) stop (mortgage) from being redeemable; repossess mortgaged property of (person) when loan is not duly repaid; exclude, prevent. □ **foreclosure** noun.

forecourt noun part of filling-station with petrol pumps; enclosed space in front of building.

forefather noun (usually in plural) ancestor.

forefinger noun finger next to thumb.

forefoot noun front foot of animal.

forefront noun leading position; foremost part.

forego = FORGO.

foregoing /fɔːˈgəʊɪŋ/ adjective preceding; previously mentioned.

foregone conclusion /ˈfɔːɡɒn/ noun easily foreseeable result.

foreground noun part of view nearest observer.

forehand Tennis etc. ● adjective (of stroke) played with palm of hand facing forward. ● noun forehand stroke.

forehead /ˈfɒrɪd, ˈfɔːhed/ noun part of face above eyebrows.

foreign /ˈfɒrən/ adjective of, from, in, or characteristic of country or language other than one's own; dealing with other countries; of another district, society, etc.; (often + to) unfamiliar, alien; coming from outside. □ **foreign legion** group of foreign volunteers in (esp. French) army. □ **foreignness** noun.

foreigner noun person born in or coming from another country.

foreknowledge /fɔːˈnɒlɪdʒ/ noun knowledge in advance of (an event etc.).

foreleg noun animal's front leg.

forelock noun lock of hair just above forehead. □ **touch one's forelock** defer to person of higher social rank.

foreman /ˈfɔːmən/ noun (feminine **forewoman**) worker supervising others; spokesman of jury.

foremast noun mast nearest bow of ship.

foremost ● adjective most notable, best; first, front. ● adverb most importantly.

forename noun first or Christian name.

forensic /fə'rensɪk/ *adjective* of or used in courts of law; of or involving application of science to legal problems.

foreplay *noun* stimulation preceding sexual intercourse.

forerunner *noun* predecessor.

foresail /'fɔ:seɪl/ *noun* principal sail on foremast.

foresee /fɔ:'si:/ *verb* (*past* **-saw**; *past participle* **-seen**) see or be aware of beforehand. □ **foreseeable** *adjective*.

foreshadow /fɔ:'ʃædəʊ/ *verb* be warning or indication of (future event).

foreshore *noun* shore between high and low water marks.

foreshorten /fɔ:'ʃɔ:t(ə)n/ *verb* portray (object) with apparent shortening due to perspective.

foresight *noun* care or provision for future; foreseeing.

foreskin *noun* fold of skin covering end of penis.

forest /'fɒrɪst/ ● *noun* large area of trees; large number, dense mass. ● *verb* plant with trees; convert into forest.

forestall /fɔ:'stɔ:l/ *verb* prevent by advance action; deal with beforehand.

forester *noun* manager of forest; expert in forestry; dweller in forest.

forestry *noun* science or management of forests.

foretaste *noun* small preliminary experience of something.

foretell /fɔ:'tel/ *verb* (*past & past participle* **-told**) predict, prophesy; indicate approach of.

forethought *noun* care or provision for future; deliberate intention.

forever /fə'revə/ *adverb* always, constantly.

forewarn /fɔ:'wɔ:n/ *verb* warn beforehand.

foreword *noun* introductory remarks in book, often not by author.

forfeit /'fɔ:fɪt/ ● *noun* (thing surrendered as) penalty. ● *adjective* lost or surrendered as penalty. ● *verb* (**-t-**) lose right to, surrender as penalty. □ **forfeiture** *noun*.

forgather /fɔ:'gæðə/ *verb* assemble; associate.

forgave *past* of FORGIVE.

forge[1] ● *verb* (**-ging**) make or write in fraudulent imitation; shape by heating and hammering. ● *noun* furnace etc. for melting or refining metal; blacksmith's workshop. □ **forger** *noun*.

forge[2] *verb* (**-ging**) advance gradually. □ **forge ahead** take lead, progress rapidly.

forgery /'fɔ:dʒərɪ/ *noun* (*plural* **-ies**) (making of) forged document etc.

forget /fə'get/ *verb* (**forgetting**; *past* **forgot**; *past participle* **forgotten** or *US* **forgot**) lose remembrance of; neglect, overlook; cease to think of; (**forget oneself**) act without dignity. □ **forget-me-not** plant with small blue flowers. □ **forgettable** *adjective*.

forgetful *adjective* apt to forget; (often + *of*) neglectful. □ **forgetfully** *adverb*; **forgetfulness** *noun*.

forgive /fə'gɪv/ *verb* (**-ving**; *past* **forgave**; *past participle* **forgiven**) cease to resent; pardon; remit (debt). □ **forgivable** *adjective*; **forgiveness** *noun*; **forgiving** *adjective*.

forgo /fɔ:'gəʊ/ *verb* (also **forego**) (**-goes**; *past* **-went**; *past participle* **-gone**) go without, relinquish.

forgot *past* of FORGET.

forgotten *past participle* of FORGET.

fork ● *noun* pronged item of cutlery; similar large tool for digging etc.; forked part, esp. of bicycle frame; (place of) divergence of road etc. ● *verb* form fork or branch; take one road at fork; dig with fork. □ **fork-lift truck** vehicle with fork for lifting and carrying; **fork out** *slang* pay, esp. reluctantly.

forlorn /fə'lɔ:n/ *adjective* sad and abandoned; pitiful. □ **forlorn hope** faint remaining hope or chance. □ **forlornly** *adverb*.

form ● *noun* shape, arrangement of parts, visible aspect; person or animal as visible or tangible; mode in which thing exists or manifests itself; kind, variety; document with blanks to be filled in; class in school; (often as **the form**) customary or correct behaviour or method; set order of words; (of athlete, horse, etc.) condition of health and training; disposition; bench. ● *verb* make, be made; constitute; develop or establish as concept, practice, etc.; (+

into) organize; (of troops etc.) bring or move into formation; mould, fashion.

formal /'fɔːm(ə)l/ *adjective* in accordance with rules, convention, or ceremony; (of garden etc.) symmetrical; prim, stiff; perfunctory; drawn up correctly; concerned with outward form. □ **formally** *adverb*.

formaldehyde /fɔː'mældɪhaɪd/ *noun* colourless gas used as preservative and disinfectant.

formalin /'fɔːməlɪn/ *noun* solution of formaldehyde in water.

formalism *noun* strict adherence to external form, esp. in art. □ **formalist** *noun*.

formality /fɔː'mælɪtɪ/ *noun* (*plural* **-ies**) formal, esp. meaningless, regulation or act; rigid observance of rules or convention.

formalize *verb* (also **-ise**) (**-zing** or **-sing**) give definite (esp. legal) form to; make formal. □ **formalization** *noun*.

format /'fɔːmæt/ ● *noun* shape and size (of book etc.); style or manner of procedure etc.; arrangement of computer data etc. ● *verb* (**-tt-**) arrange in format; prepare (storage medium) to receive computer data.

formation /fɔː'meɪʃ(ə)n/ *noun* forming; thing formed; particular arrangement (e.g. of troops); rocks or strata with common characteristic.

formative /'fɔːmətɪv/ *adjective* serving to form; of formation.

former /'fɔːmə/ *adjective* of the past, earlier, previous; (**the former**) the first or first-named of two.

formerly *adverb* in former times; previously.

Formica /fɔː'maɪkə/ *noun* proprietary term hard plastic laminate for surfaces.

formic acid /'fɔːmɪk/ *noun* colourless irritant volatile acid contained in fluid emitted by ants.

formidable /'fɔːmɪdəb(ə)l/ *adjective* inspiring awe, respect, or dread; difficult to deal with. □ **formidably** *adverb*.

■ **Usage** *Formidable* is also pronounced /fə'mɪdəb(ə)l/ (with the stress on the *-mid-*), but this is considered incorrect by some people.

formless *adjective* without definite or regular form. □ **formlessness** *noun*.

formula /'fɔːmjʊlə/ *noun* (*plural* **-s** or **-lae** /-liː/) chemical symbols showing constituents of substance; mathematical rule expressed in symbols; fixed form of words; list of ingredients; classification of racing car, esp. by engine capacity. □ **formulaic** /-'leɪɪk/ *adjective*.

formulate /'fɔːmjʊleɪt/ *verb* express in formula; express clearly and precisely. □ **formulation** *noun*.

fornicate /'fɔːnɪkeɪt/ *verb* (**-ting**) usually *jocular* have extramarital sexual intercourse. □ **fornication** *noun*; **fornicator** *noun*.

forsake /fə'seɪk/ *verb* (**-king**; *past* **forsook** /-'sʊk/; *past participle* **forsaken**) *literary* give up, renounce; desert, abandon.

forswear /fɔː'sweə/ *verb* (*past* **forswore**; *past participle* **forsworn**) abjure, renounce; (**forswear oneself**) perjure oneself; (as **forsworn** *adjective*) perjured.

forsythia /fɔː'saɪθɪə/ *noun* shrub with bright yellow flowers.

fort *noun* fortified building or position. □ **hold the fort** act as temporary substitute.

forte[1] /'fɔːteɪ/ *noun* thing in which one excels or specializes.

forte[2] /'fɔːteɪ/ *Music* ● *adjective* loud. ● *adverb* loudly. ● *noun* loud playing, singing, or passage.

forth /fɔːθ/ *adverb* forward(s); out; onwards in time. □ **forthcoming** /fɔː'θkʌmɪŋ/ coming or available soon, produced when wanted, informative, responsive.

forthright *adjective* straightforward, outspoken, decisive.

forthwith /fɔː'θwɪθ/ *adverb* immediately, without delay.

fortification /fɔːtɪfɪ'keɪʃ(ə)n/ *noun* fortifying; (usually in *plural*) defensive works.

fortify /'fɔːtɪfaɪ/ *verb* (**-ies**, **-ied**) provide with fortifications; strengthen; (usually as **fortified** *adjective*) strengthen (wine etc.) with alcohol, increase nutritive value of (food, esp. with vitamins).

fortissimo /fɔː'tɪsɪməʊ/ *Music* ● *adjective* very loud. ● *adverb* very loudly. ● *noun* (*plural* **-mos** or **-mi** /-miː/) very loud playing, singing, or passage.

fortitude /'fɔːtɪtjuːd/ *noun* courage in pain or adversity.

fortnight /'fɔːtnaɪt/ *noun* two weeks.

fortnightly ●*adjective* done, produced, or occurring once a fortnight. ●*adverb* every fortnight. ●*noun* (*plural* **-ies**) fortnightly magazine etc.

Fortran /'fɔːtræn/ *noun* (also **FORTRAN**) computer language used esp. for scientific calculations.

fortress /'fɔːtrɪs/ *noun* fortified building or town.

fortuitous /fɔː'tjuːɪtəs/ *adjective* happening by chance. □ **fortuitously** *adverb*; **fortuitousness** *noun*; **fortuity** *noun* (*plural* **-ies**).

fortunate /'fɔːtʃənət/ *adjective* lucky, auspicious. □ **fortunately** *adverb*.

fortune /'fɔːtʃ(ə)n/ *noun* chance or luck in human affairs; person's destiny; prosperity, wealth; *colloquial* large sum of money. □ **fortune-teller** person claiming to foretell one's destiny.

forty /'fɔːtɪ/ *adjective & noun* (*plural* **-ies**) four times ten. □ **forty winks** *colloquial* short sleep. □ **fortieth** *adjective & noun*.

forum /'fɔːrəm/ *noun* place of or meeting for public discussion; court, tribunal.

forward /'fɔːwəd/ ●*adjective* onward, towards front; bold, precocious, presumptuous; relating to the future; well-advanced. ●*noun* attacking player in football etc. ●*adverb* to front; into prominence; so as to make progress; towards future; forwards. ●*verb* send (letter etc.) on; dispatch; help to advance, promote.

forwards *adverb* in direction one is facing.

forwent *past of* FORGO.

fossil /'fɒs(ə)l/ ●*noun* remains or impression of (usually prehistoric) plant or animal hardened in rock; *colloquial* antiquated or unchanging person or thing. ●*adjective* of or like fossil. □ **fossil fuel** natural fuel extracted from ground. □ **fossilize** *verb* (also **-ise**) (**-zing** or **-sing**); **fossilization** *noun*.

foster /'fɒstə/ ●*verb* promote growth of; encourage or harbour (feeling); bring up (another's child); assign as foster-child. ●*adjective* related by or concerned with fostering.

fought *past & past participle of* FIGHT.

foul /faʊl/ ●*adjective* offensive, loathsome, stinking; dirty, soiled; *colloquial* awful; noxious; obscene; unfair, against rules; (of weather) rough; entangled. ●*noun* foul blow or play; entanglement. ●*adverb* unfairly. ●*verb* make or become foul; commit foul on (player); (often + *up*) (cause to) become entangled or blocked. □ **foul-mouthed** using obscene or offensive language; **foul play** unfair play, treacherous or violent act, esp. murder. □ **foully** /'faʊlɪ/ *adverb*; **foulness** *noun*.

found[1] *past & past participle of* FIND.

found[2] /faʊnd/ *verb* establish, originate; lay base of; base. □ **founder** *noun*.

found[3] /faʊnd/ *verb* melt and mould (metal), fuse (materials for glass); make thus. □ **founder** *noun*.

foundation /faʊn'deɪʃ(ə)n/ *noun* solid ground or base under building; (usually in *plural*) lowest part of building, usually below ground; basis; underlying principle; establishing (esp. endowed institution); base for cosmetics; (in full **foundation garment**) woman's supporting undergarment. □ **foundation-stone** one laid ceremonially at founding of building, basis.

founder /'faʊndə/ *verb* (of ship) fill with water and sink; (of plan) fail; (of horse) stumble, fall lame.

foundling /'faʊndlɪŋ/ *noun* abandoned infant of unknown parentage.

foundry /'faʊndrɪ/ *noun* (*plural* **-ies**) workshop for casting metal.

fount[1] /faʊnt/ *noun* *poetical* source, spring, fountain.

fount[2] /fɒnt/ *noun* (also **font**) set of printing type of same size and face.

fountain /'faʊntɪn/ *noun* jet(s) of water as ornament or for drinking; spring; (often + *of*) source. □ **fountain-head** source; **fountain pen** pen with reservoir or cartridge for ink.

four /fɔː/ *adjective & noun* one more than three; 4-oared boat, its crew. □ **four-letter word** short obscene word; **four-poster** bed with 4 posts supporting canopy; **four-square** *adjective* solidly based, steady, *adverb* resolutely; **four-stroke** (of internal-combustion engine) having power cycle completed in two up-and-down movements of piston; **four-wheel drive** drive acting on all 4 wheels of vehicle.

fourfold *adjective & adverb* four times as much or many.

foursome *noun* group of 4 people; golf match between two pairs.

fourteen /fɔː'tiːn/ *adjective & noun* one more than thirteen. □ **fourteenth** *adjective & noun.*

fourth /fɔːθ/ *adjective & noun* next after third; any of four equal parts of thing. □ **fourthly** *adverb.*

fowl /faʊl/ *noun* (*plural* same or -s) chicken kept for eggs and meat; poultry as food.

fox ●*noun* wild canine animal with red or grey fur and bushy tail; its fur; crafty person. ●*verb* deceive; puzzle. □ **foxglove** tall plant with purple or white flowers; **foxhole** hole in ground as shelter etc. in battle; **foxhound** hound bred to hunt foxes; **fox-hunting** hunting foxes with hounds; **fox-terrier** small short-haired terrier; **foxtrot** ballroom dance with slow and quick steps. □ **foxlike** *adjective.*

foxy *adjective* (-ier, -iest) foxlike; sly, cunning; reddish-brown. □ **foxily** *adverb.*

foyer /'fɔɪeɪ/ *noun* entrance hall in hotel, theatre, etc.

FPA *abbreviation* Family Planning Association.

Fr. *abbreviation* Father; French.

fr. *abbreviation* franc(s).

fracas /'frækɑː/ *noun* (*plural* same /-kɑːz/) noisy quarrel.

fraction /'frækʃ(ə)n/ *noun* part of whole number; small part, amount, etc.; portion of mixture obtainable by distillation etc. □ **fractional** *adjective;* **fractionally** *adverb.*

fractious /'frækʃəs/ *adjective* irritable, peevish.

fracture /'fræktʃə/ ●*noun* breakage, esp. of bone. ●*verb* (-ring) cause fracture in, suffer fracture.

fragile /'frædʒaɪl/ *adjective* easily broken; delicate. □ **fragility** /frə'dʒɪl-/ *noun.*

fragment ●*noun* /'frægmənt/ part broken off; remains or unfinished portion of book etc. ●*verb* /fræg'ment/ break into fragments. □ **fragmental** /-'men-/

adjective; **fragmentary** *adjective;* **fragmentation** *noun.*

fragrance /'freɪgrəns/ *noun* sweetness of smell; sweet scent.

fragrant *adjective* sweet-smelling.

frail *adjective* fragile, delicate; morally weak. □ **frailly** /'freɪllɪ/ *adverb;* **frailness** *noun.*

frailty *noun* (*plural* **-ies**) frail quality; weakness, foible.

frame ●*noun* case or border enclosing picture etc.; supporting structure; (in *plural*) structure of spectacles holding lenses; build of person or animal; framework; construction; (in **frame of mind**) temporary state; single picture on photographic film; (in snooker etc.) triangular structure for positioning balls, round of play; glazed structure to protect plants. ●*verb* (-ming) set in frame; serve as frame for; construct, devise; (+ to, into) adapt, fit; *slang* concoct false charge etc. against; articulate (words). □ **frame-up** *slang* conspiracy to convict innocent person; **framework** essential supporting structure, basic system.

franc *noun* French, Belgian, Swiss, etc. unit of currency.

franchise /'fræntʃaɪz/ ●*noun* right to vote; citizenship; authorization to sell company's goods etc. in particular area; right granted to person or corporation. ●*verb* (-sing) grant franchise to.

Franciscan /fræn'sɪskən/ ●*adjective* of (order of) St Francis. ●*noun* Franciscan friar or nun.

franglais /'frɒ̃gleɪ/ *noun* French with many English words and idioms. [French]

Frank *noun* member of Germanic people that conquered Gaul in 6th c. □ **Frankish** *adjective.*

frank ●*adjective* candid, outspoken; undisguised; open. ●*verb* mark (letter etc.) to record payment of postage. ●*noun* franking signature or mark. □ **frankly** *adverb;* **frankness** *noun.*

frankfurter /'fræŋkfɜːtə/ *noun* seasoned smoked sausage.

frankincense /'fræŋkɪnsens/ *noun* aromatic gum resin burnt as incense.

frantic /'fræntɪk/ *adjective* wildly excited; frenzied; hurried, anxious; desperate;

violent; *colloquial* extreme. □ **frantically** *adverb*.

fraternal /frə'tɜːn(ə)l/ *adjective* of brothers, brotherly; comradely. □ **fraternally** *adverb*.

fraternity /frə'tɜːnɪtɪ/ *noun* (*plural* **-ies**) religious brotherhood; group with common interests or of same professional class; *US* male students' society; brotherliness.

fraternize /'frætənaɪz/ *verb* (also **-ise**) (**-zing** or **-sing**) (often + *with*) associate, make friends, esp. with enemy etc. □ **fraternization** *noun*.

fratricide /'frætrɪsaɪd/ *noun* killing of one's brother or sister; person who does this. □ **fratricidal** /-'saɪd(ə)l/ *adjective*.

Frau /frau/ *noun* (*plural* **Frauen** /'frauən/) title used of or to married or widowed German-speaking woman.

fraud /frɔːd/ *noun* criminal deception; dishonest trick; impostor.

fraudulent /'frɔːdjʊlənt/ *adjective* of, involving, or guilty of fraud. □ **fraudulence** *noun*; **fraudulently** *adverb*.

fraught /frɔːt/ *adjective* (+ *with*) filled or attended with (danger etc.); *colloquial* distressing; tense.

Fräulein /'frɔɪlaɪn/ *noun*: title used of or to unmarried German-speaking woman.

fray[1] *verb* wear or become worn; unravel at edge; (esp. as **frayed** *adjective*) (of nerves) become strained.

fray[2] *noun* fight, conflict; brawl.

frazzle /'fræz(ə)l/ *colloquial* ● *noun* worn, exhausted, or shrivelled state. ● *verb* (**-ling**) (usually as **frazzled** *adjective*) wear out; exhaust.

freak ● *noun* monstrosity; abnormal person or thing; *colloquial* unconventional person, fanatic of specified kind. ● *verb* (often + *out*) *colloquial* make or become very angry; (cause to) undergo esp. drug-induced etc. hallucinations or strong emotional experience. □ **freakish** *adjective*; **freaky** *adjective* (**-ier**, **-iest**).

freckle /'frek(ə)l/ ● *noun* light brown spot on skin. ● *verb* (**-ling**) (usually as **freckled** *adjective*) spot or be spotted with freckles. □ **freckly** *adjective* (**-ier**, **-iest**).

free ● *adjective* (**freer** /'friːə/, **freest** /'friːɪst/) not a slave; having personal rights and social and political liberty; autonomous; democratic; unrestricted, not confined; (+ *of*, *from* or in combination) exempt from, not containing or subject to; (+ *to do*) permitted, at liberty; costing nothing; available; spontaneous; lavish, unreserved; (of translation) not literal. ● *adverb* freely; without cost. ● *verb* (**frees**, **freed**) make free, liberate; disentangle. □ **for free** *colloquial* gratis; **freebooter** pirate; **freeboard** part of ship's side between waterline and deck; **Free Church** Nonconformist Church; **free enterprise** freedom of private business from state control; **free fall** movement under force of gravity only; **free hand** *noun* liberty to act at one's own discretion; **freehand** *adjective* (of drawing) done without ruler, compasses, etc., *adverb* in a freehand way; **free house** pub not controlled by brewery; **freeloader** *slang* sponger; **freeman** holder of freedom of city etc.; **free port** port without customs duties, or open to all traders; **free-range** (of hens etc.) roaming freely, (of eggs) produced by such hens; **free spirit** independent or uninhibited person; **free-standing** not supported by another structure; **freestyle** swimming race in which any stroke may be used, wrestling allowing almost any hold; **freethinker** /-'θɪŋkə/ person who rejects dogma, esp. in religious belief; **free trade** trade without import restrictions etc.; **freeway** *US* motorway; **freewheel** ride bicycle with pedals at rest, act without constraint; **free will** power of acting independently of fate or without coercion.

freebie /'friːbɪ/ *noun colloquial* thing given free of charge.

freedom *noun* being free; personal or civil liberty; liberty of action; (+ *from*) exemption from; (+ *of*) honorary membership or citizenship of, unrestricted use of (house etc.).

freehold *noun* complete ownership of property for unlimited period; such property. □ **freeholder** *noun*.

freelance ● *noun* person working for no fixed employer. ● *verb* work as freelance. ● *adverb* as freelance.

Freemason /ˈfriːmeɪs(ə)n/ *noun* member of fraternity for mutual help with secret rituals. □ **Freemasonry** *noun*.

freesia /ˈfriːzjə/ *noun* fragrant flowering African bulb.

freeze ● *verb* (**-zing**; *past* **froze**; *past participle* **frozen** /ˈfrəʊz(ə)n/) turn into ice or other solid by cold; make or become rigid from cold; be or feel very cold; cover or be covered with ice; refrigerate below freezing point; make or become motionless; (as **frozen** *adjective*) devoid of emotion; make (assets etc.) unrealizable; fix (prices etc.) at certain level; stop (movement in film). ● *noun* period or state of frost; price-fixing etc.; (in full **freeze-frame**) still film-shot. □ **freeze-dry** preserve (food) by freezing and then drying in vacuum; **freeze up** *verb* obstruct or be obstructed by ice; **freeze-up** *noun* period of extreme cold; **freezing point** temperature at which liquid freezes.

freezer *noun* refrigerated cabinet for preserving food in frozen state.

freight /freɪt/ *noun* transport of goods; goods transported; charge for transport of goods.

freighter *noun* ship or aircraft for carrying freight.

French ● *adjective* of France or its people or language. ● *noun* French language; (**the French**) (*plural*) the French people. □ **French bean** kidney or haricot bean as unripe pods or as ripe seeds; **French bread** long crisp loaf; **French dressing** salad dressing of oil and vinegar; **French fried potatoes, French fries** chips; **French horn** coiled brass wind instrument; **French letter** *colloquial* condom; **Frenchman, Frenchwoman** native or national of France; **French polish** *noun* shellac polish for wood; **French-polish** *verb*; **French window** glazed door in outside wall.

frenetic /frəˈnetɪk/ *adjective* frantic, frenzied. □ **frenetically** *adverb*.

frenzy /ˈfrenzɪ/ ● *noun* (*plural* **-ies**) wild excitement or fury. ● *verb* (**-ies, -ied**) (usually as **frenzied** *adjective*) drive to frenzy. □ **frenziedly** *adverb*.

frequency /ˈfriːkwənsɪ/ *noun* (*plural* **-ies**) commonness of occurrence; frequent occurrence; rate of recurrence (of vibration etc.). □ **frequency modulation** Electronics modulation by varying carrier-wave frequency.

frequent ● *adjective* /ˈfriːkwənt/ occurring often or in close succession; habitual. ● *verb* /frɪˈkwent/ go to habitually. □ **frequently** /ˈfriːkwəntlɪ/ *adverb*.

fresco /ˈfreskəʊ/ *noun* (*plural* **-s**) painting in water-colour on fresh plaster.

fresh ● *adjective* newly made or obtained; other, different; new; additional; (+ *from*) lately arrived from; not stale or faded; (of food) not preserved; (of water) not salty; pure; refreshing; (of wind) brisk; *colloquial* cheeky, amorously impudent; inexperienced. ● *adverb* newly, recently. □ **freshwater** (of fish etc.) not of the sea. □ **freshly** *adverb*; **freshness** *noun*.

freshen *verb* make or become fresh; (+ *up*) wash, tidy oneself, etc.; revive.

fresher *noun* *colloquial* first-year student at university or (*US*) high school.

freshet /ˈfreʃɪt/ *noun* rush of fresh water into sea; river flood.

freshman /ˈfreʃmən/ *noun* fresher.

fret[1] ● *verb* (**-tt-**) be worried or distressed. ● *noun* worry, vexation. □ **fretful** *adjective*; **fretfully** *adverb*.

fret[2] ● *noun* ornamental pattern of straight lines joined usually at right angles. ● *verb* (**-tt-**) adorn with fret etc. □ **fretsaw** narrow saw on frame for cutting thin wood in patterns; **fretwork** work done with fretsaw.

fret[3] *noun* bar or ridge on finger-board of guitar etc.

Freudian /ˈfrɔɪdɪən/ ● *adjective* of Freud's theories or method of psychoanalysis. ● *noun* follower of Freud. □ **Freudian slip** unintentional verbal error revealing subconscious feelings.

Fri. *abbreviation* Friday.

friable /ˈfraɪəb(ə)l/ *adjective* easily crumbled. □ **friability** *noun*.

friar /ˈfraɪə/ *noun* member of male non-enclosed religious order. □ **friar's balsam** type of inhalant.

friary /ˈfraɪərɪ/ *noun* (*plural* **-ies**) monastery for friars.

fricassee /ˈfrɪkəseɪ/ ● *noun* pieces of meat in thick sauce. ● *verb* (**fricassees, fricasseed**) make fricassee of.

fricative /ˈfrɪkətɪv/ ● *adjective* sounded by friction of breath in narrow opening. ● *noun* such consonant (e.g. *f, th*).

friction /ˈfrɪkʃ(ə)n/ *noun* rubbing of one object against another; resistance so encountered; clash of wills, opinions, etc. □ **frictional** *adjective*.

Friday /ˈfraɪdeɪ/ *noun* day of week following Thursday.

fridge *noun colloquial* refrigerator. □ **fridge-freezer** combined refrigerator and freezer.

friend /frend/ *noun* supportive and respected associate, esp. one for whom affection is felt; ally; kind person; person already mentioned; **(Friend)** Quaker.

friendly ● *adjective* (**-ier, -iest**) outgoing, kindly; (often + *with*) on amicable terms; not hostile; user-friendly. ● *noun* (*plural* **-ies**) friendly match. □ **-friendly** not harming, helping; **friendly match** match played for enjoyment rather than competition; **Friendly Society** society for insurance against sickness etc. □ **friendliness** *noun*.

friendship *noun* friendly relationship or feeling.

frier = FRYER.

Friesian /ˈfriːzɪən/ ● *noun* one of breed of black and white dairy cattle. ● *adjective* of Friesians.

frieze /friːz/ *noun* part of entablature, often filled with sculpture, between architrave and cornice; band of decoration, esp. at top of wall.

frigate /ˈfrɪgɪt/ *noun* naval escort-vessel.

fright /fraɪt/ *noun* (instance of) sudden or extreme fear; grotesque-looking person or thing. □ **take fright** become frightened.

frighten *verb* fill with fright; (+ *away, off, out of, into*) drive by fright. □ **frightening** *adjective*; **frighteningly** *adverb*.

frightful *adjective* dreadful, shocking; ugly; *colloquial* extremely bad; *colloquial* extreme. □ **frightfully** *adverb*.

frigid /ˈfrɪdʒɪd/ *adjective* unfriendly, cold; (of woman) sexually unresponsive; cold. □ **frigidity** /-ˈdʒɪd-/ *noun*.

frill ● *noun* ornamental edging of gathered or pleated material; (in *plural*) unnecessary embellishments. ● *verb* (usually as **frilled** *adjective*) decorate with frill. □ **frilly** *adjective* (**-ier, -iest**).

fringe ● *noun* border of tassels or loose threads; front hair cut to hang over forehead; outer limit; unimportant area or part. ● *verb* (**-ging**) adorn with fringe; serve as fringe to. □ **fringe benefit** employee's benefit additional to salary.

frippery /ˈfrɪpərɪ/ *noun* (*plural* **-ies**) showy finery; empty display; (usually in *plural*) knick-knacks.

frisk ● *verb* leap or skip playfully; *slang* search (person). ● *noun* playful leap or skip.

frisky *adjective* (**-ier, -iest**) lively, playful.

frisson /ˈfriːsɒn/ *noun* emotional thrill. [French]

fritillary /frɪˈtɪlərɪ/ *noun* (*plural* **-ies**) plant with bell-like flowers; butterfly with red and black chequered wings.

fritter[1] /ˈfrɪtə/ *verb* (usually + *away*) waste triflingly.

fritter[2] /ˈfrɪtə/ *noun* fruit, meat, etc. coated in batter and fried.

frivolous /ˈfrɪvələs/ *adjective* not serious, shallow, silly; trifling. □ **frivolity** /-ˈvɒl-/ *noun* (*plural* **-ies**).

frizz ● *verb* form (hair) into tight curls. ● *noun* frizzed hair or state. □ **frizzy** *adjective* (**-ier, -iest**).

frizzle[1] /ˈfrɪz(ə)l/ *verb* (**-ling**) fry or cook with sizzling noise; (often + *up*) burn, shrivel.

frizzle[2] /ˈfrɪz(ə)l/ *verb* (**-ling**) & *noun* frizz.

frock *noun* woman's or girl's dress; monk's or priest's gown. □ **frock-coat** man's long-skirted coat.

frog *noun* tailless leaping amphibian. □ **frog in one's throat** *colloquial* phlegm in throat that hinders speech; **frogman** underwater swimmer equipped with rubber suit and flippers; **frogmarch** hustle forward with arms pinned behind; **frog-spawn** frog's eggs.

frolic /ˈfrɒlɪk/ ● *verb* (**-ck-**) play about merrily. ● *noun* merrymaking.

frolicsome *adjective* playful.

from /frəm/ *preposition expressing separation or origin*.

fromage frais /frɒmɑːʒ ˈfreɪ/ *noun* type of soft cheese.

frond *noun* leaflike part of fern or palm.

front /frʌnt/ ● *noun* side or part most prominent or important, or nearer spectator or direction of motion; line of battle; scene of actual fighting; organized political group; demeanour; pretext, bluff; person etc. as cover for subversive or illegal activities; land along edge of sea or lake, esp. in town; forward edge of advancing cold or warm air; auditorium; breast of garment. ● *adjective* of or at front. ● *verb* (+ *on, to, towards*, etc.) have front facing or directed towards; (+ *for*) *slang* act as front for; (usually as **fronted** *adjective* + *with*) provide with or have front; lead (band, organization, etc.). □ **front bench** seats in Parliament for leading members of government and opposition; **front line** foremost part of army or group under attack; **front runner** favourite in race etc.

frontage *noun* front of building; land next to street, water, etc.; extent of front.

frontal *adjective* of or on front; of forehead.

frontier /ˈfrʌntɪə/ *noun* border between countries, district on each side of this; limits of attainment or knowledge in subject; *esp. US historical* border between settled and unsettled country. □ **frontiersman** *noun*.

frontispiece /ˈfrʌntɪspiːs/ *noun* illustration facing title-page of book.

frost ● *noun* frozen dew or vapour; temperature below freezing point. ● *verb* (usually + *over, up*) become covered with frost; cover (as) with frost; (usually as **frosted** *adjective*) roughen surface of (glass) to make opaque. □ **frostbite** injury to body tissue due to freezing; **frostbitten** *adjective*.

frosting *noun* icing for cakes.

frosty *adjective* (**-ier, -iest**) cold or covered with frost; unfriendly.

froth ● *noun* foam; idle talk. ● *verb* emit or gather froth. □ **frothy** *adjective* (**-ier, -iest**).

frown ● *verb* wrinkle brows, esp. in displeasure or concentration; (+ *at, on*) disapprove of. ● *noun* act of frowning, frowning look.

frowsty /ˈfraʊstɪ/ *adjective* (**-ier, -iest**) fusty; stuffy.

frowzy /ˈfraʊzɪ/ *adjective* (also **frowsy**) (**-ier, -iest**) fusty; slatternly, dingy.

froze *past* of FREEZE.

frozen *past participle* of FREEZE.

FRS *abbreviation* Fellow of the Royal Society.

fructify /ˈfrʌktɪfaɪ/ *verb* (**-ies, -ied**) bear fruit; make fruitful.

fructose /ˈfrʌktəʊz/ *noun* sugar in fruits, honey, etc.

frugal /ˈfruːg(ə)l/ *adjective* sparing; meagre. □ **frugality** /-ˈgæl-/ *noun*; **frugally** *adverb*.

fruit /fruːt/ ● *noun* seed-bearing part of plant or tree; this as food; (usually in *plural*) products, profits, rewards. ● *verb* bear fruit. □ **fruit cake** cake containing dried fruit; **fruit cocktail** diced fruit salad; **fruit machine** gambling machine operated by coins; **fruit salad** dessert of mixed fruit; **fruit sugar** fructose.

fruiterer /ˈfruːtərə/ *noun* dealer in fruit.

fruitful *adjective* productive; successful. □ **fruitfully** *adverb*.

fruition /fruːˈɪʃ(ə)n/ *noun* realization of aims or hopes.

fruitless *adjective* not bearing fruit; useless, unsuccessful. □ **fruitlessly** *adverb*.

fruity *adjective* (**-ier, -iest**) of or resembling fruit; (of voice) deep and rich; *colloquial* slightly indecent.

frump *noun* dowdy woman. □ **frumpish** *adjective*; **frumpy** *adjective* (**-ier, -iest**).

frustrate /frʌsˈtreɪt/ *verb* (**-ting**) make (efforts) ineffective; prevent from achieving purpose; (as **frustrated** *adjective*) discontented, unfulfilled. □ **frustrating** *adjective*; **frustratingly** *adverb*; **frustration** *noun*.

fry[1] ● *verb* (**fries, fried**) cook in hot fat. ● *noun* fried food, esp. (usually **fries**) chips. □ **frying-pan** shallow long-handled pan for frying; **fry-up** *colloquial* fried bacon, eggs, etc.

fry[2] *plural noun* young or freshly hatched fishes.

fryer *noun* (also **frier**) person who fries; vessel for frying esp. fish.

ft *abbreviation* foot, feet.

FT-SE *abbreviation* Financial Times Stock Exchange (100 share index).

fuchsia /ˈfjuːʃə/ *noun* shrub with drooping flowers.

fuddle /ˈfʌd(ə)l/ ● *verb* (**-ling**) confuse, esp. with alcohol. ● *noun* confusion; intoxication.

fuddy-duddy /ˈfʌdɪdʌdɪ/ *slang* ● *adjective* fussy, old-fashioned. ● *noun* (*plural* **-ies**) such person.

fudge ● *noun* soft toffee-like sweet; faking. ● *verb* (**-ging**) make or do clumsily or dishonestly; fake.

fuel /ˈfjuːəl/ ● *noun* material for burning or as source of heat, power, or nuclear energy; thing that sustains or inflames passion etc. ● *verb* (**-ll-**; *US* **-l-**) supply with fuel; inflame (feeling).

fug *noun colloquial* stuffy atmosphere. □ **fuggy** *adjective* (**-ier**, **-iest**).

fugitive /ˈfjuːdʒɪtɪv/ ● *noun* (often + *from*) person who flees. ● *adjective* fleeing; transient, fleeting.

fugue /fjuːg/ *noun* piece of music in which short melody or phrase is introduced by one part and developed by others. □ **fugal** *adjective*.

fulcrum /ˈfʌlkrəm/ *noun* (*plural* **-s** or **-cra**) point on which lever is supported.

fulfil /fʊlˈfɪl/ *verb* (*US* **fulfill**) (**-ll-**) carry out; satisfy; (as **fulfilled** *adjective*) completely happy; (**fulfil oneself**) realize one's potential. □ **fulfilment** *noun*.

full /fʊl/ ● *adjective* holding all it can; replete; abundant; satisfying; (+ *of*) having abundance of, engrossed in; complete, perfect; resonant; plump; ample. ● *adverb* quite, exactly. □ **full back** defensive player near goal in football etc.; **full-blooded** vigorous, sensual, not hybrid; **full-blown** fully developed; **full board** provision of bed and all meals; **full-bodied** rich in quality, tone, etc.; **full frontal** (of nude) fully exposed at front, explicit; **full house** maximum attendance at theatre etc., hand in poker with 3 of a kind and a pair; **full-length** of normal length, not shortened, (of portrait) showing whole figure; **full moon** moon with whole disc illuminated; **full stop** punctuation mark (.) at end of sentence etc. (see panel), complete cessation; **full term**

••

Full stop .

This is used:

1 at the end of a sentence, e.g.

    I am going to the cinema tonight.
    The film begins at seven.

The full stop is replaced by a question mark at the end of a question, and by an exclamation mark at the end of an exclamation.

2 after an abbreviation, e.g.

    H. G. Wells   *p. 19* (= *page 19*)   *Sun.* (= *Sunday*)
    Ex. 6 (= *Exercise 6*).

Full stops are **not** used with:

    a numerical abbreviations, e.g. *1st, 2nd, 15th, 23rd*
    b acronyms, e.g. *FIFA, NATO*
    c abbreviations that are used as ordinary words, e.g. *con, demo, recap*
    d chemical symbols, e.g. Fe, K, H_2O

Full stops are not essential for:

    a abbreviations consisting entirely of capitals, e.g. *BBC, AD, BC, PLC*
    b *C* (= *Celsius*), *F* (= *Fahrenheit*)
    c measures of length, weight, time, etc., except for *in.* (= *inch*), *st.* (= *stone*)
    d *Dr, Revd* (but note *Rev.*), *Mr, Mrs, Ms, Mme, Mlle, St* (= *Saint*), *Hants, Northants, p* (= *penny* or *pence*).

••

completion of normal pregnancy; **full-time** *adjective* for or during whole of working week, *adverb* on full-time basis. □ **fullness** *noun*.

fully *adverb* completely; at least.

fulmar /'fʊlmə/ *noun* kind of petrel.

fulminate /'fʊlmɪneɪt/ *verb* (**-ting**) criticize loudly and forcibly; explode, flash. □ **fulmination** *noun*.

fulsome /'fʊlsəm/ *adjective* excessive, cloying; insincere. □ **fulsomely** *adverb*.

■ **Usage** Fulsome is sometimes wrongly used to mean 'generous', as in *fulsome praise*, or 'generous with praise', as in *a fulsome tribute*.

fumble /'fʌmb(ə)l/ ● *verb* (**-ling**) grope about; handle clumsily or nervously. ● *noun* act of fumbling.

fume ● *noun* (usually in *plural*) exuded smoke, gas, or vapour. ● *verb* (**-ming**) emit fumes; be very angry; subject (oak etc.) to fumes to darken.

fumigate /'fju:mɪgeɪt/ *verb* (**-ting**) disinfect or purify with fumes. □ **fumigation** *noun*; **fumigator** *noun*.

fun *noun* playful amusement; source of this; mockery. □ **funfair** fair consisting of amusements and sideshows; **fun run** *colloquial* sponsored run for charity; **make fun of, poke fun at** ridicule.

function /'fʌŋkʃ(ə)n/ ● *noun* proper role etc.; official duty; public or social occasion; *Mathematics* quantity whose value depends on varying values of others. ● *verb* fulfil function; operate.

functional *adjective* of or serving a function; practical rather than attractive. □ **functionally** *adverb*.

functionalism *noun* belief that function should determine design. □ **functionalist** *noun* & *adjective*.

functionary *noun* (*plural* **-ies**) official.

fund ● *noun* permanently available stock; money set apart for purpose; (in *plural*) money resources. ● *verb* provide with money; make (debt) permanent at fixed interest. □ **fund-raising** raising money for charity etc.; **fund-raiser** *noun*.

fundamental /fʌndə'ment(ə)l/ ● *adjective* of or serving as base or foundation; essential, primary. ● *noun* fundamental principle. □ **fundamentally** *adverb*.

fundamentalism *noun* strict adherence to traditional religious beliefs. □ **fundamentalist** *noun* & *adjective*.

funeral /'fju:nər(ə)l/ ● *noun* ceremonial burial or cremation of dead. ● *adjective* of or used at funerals. □ **funeral director** undertaker; **funeral parlour** establishment where corpses are prepared for funerals.

funerary /'fju:nərərɪ/ *adjective* of or used at funerals.

funereal /fju:'nɪərɪəl/ *adjective* of or appropriate to funeral; dismal, dark.

fungicide /'fʌndʒɪsaɪd/ *noun* substance that kills fungus. □ **fungicidal** /-'saɪd(ə)l/ *adjective*.

fungus /'fʌŋgəs/ *noun* (*plural* **-gi** /-gaɪ/ or **-guses**) mushroom, toadstool, or allied plant; spongy morbid growth. ● **fungal** *adjective*; **fungoid** *adjective*; **fungous** *adjective*.

funicular /fju:'nɪkjʊlə/ *noun* (in full **funicular railway**) cable railway with ascending and descending cars counterbalanced.

funk *slang* ● *noun* fear, panic. ● *verb* evade through fear.

funky *adjective* (**-ier, -iest**) *slang* (esp. of jazz etc.) with heavy rhythm.

funnel /'fʌn(ə)l/ ● *noun* tube widening at top, for pouring liquid etc. into small opening; chimney of steam engine or ship. ● *verb* (**-ll-**; *US* **-l-**) (cause to) move (as) through funnel.

funny /'fʌnɪ/ *adjective* (**-ier, -iest**) amusing, comical; strange. ● **funny bone** part of elbow over which very sensitive nerve passes. □ **funnily** *adverb*.

fur ● *noun* short fine animal hair; hide with fur on it; garment of or lined with this; coating inside kettle etc. ● *verb* (**-rr-**) (esp. as **furred** *adjective*) line or trim with fur; (often + *up*) (of kettle etc.) become coated with fur.

furbelow /'fɜ:bɪləʊ/ *noun* (in *plural*) showy ornaments.

furbish /'fɜ:bɪʃ/ *verb* (often + *up*) refurbish.

furcate /'fɜ:keɪt/ ● *adjective* forked, branched. ● *verb* (**-ting**) fork, divide. □ **furcation** *noun*.

furious /'fjʊərɪəs/ *adjective* very angry, raging, frantic. □ **furiously** *adverb*.

furl *verb* roll up (sail, umbrella); become furled.

furlong /ˈfɜːlɒŋ/ *noun* eighth of mile.

furlough /ˈfɜːləʊ/ *noun* leave of absence.

furnace /ˈfɜːnɪs/ *noun* chamber for intense heating by fire; very hot place.

furnish /ˈfɜːnɪʃ/ *verb* provide with furniture; (often + *with*) supply; (as **furnished** *adjective*) let with furniture. □ **furnishings** *plural noun*.

furniture /ˈfɜːnɪtʃə/ *noun* movable contents of building or room; ship's equipment; accessories, e.g. handles and locks.

furore /fjʊəˈrɔːri/ *noun* (*US* **furor** /ˈfjʊərɔː/) uproar; enthusiasm.

furrier /ˈfʌrɪə/ *noun* dealer in or dresser of furs.

furrow /ˈfʌrəʊ/ ● *noun* narrow trench made by plough; rut; wrinkle. ● *verb* plough; make furrows in.

furry /ˈfɜːrɪ/ *adjective* (**-ier**, **-iest**) like or covered with fur.

further /ˈfɜːðə/ ● *adverb* (also **farther** /ˈfɑːðə/) more distant in space or time; more, to greater extent; in addition. ● *adjective* (also **farther** /ˈfɑːðə/) more distant or advanced; more, additional. ● *verb* promote, favour. □ **further education** education for people above school age; **furthermore** in addition, besides.

furtherance *noun* furthering of scheme etc.

furthest /ˈfɜːðɪst/ (also **farthest** /ˈfɑːðɪst/) ● *adjective* most distant. ● *adverb* to or at the greatest distance.

furtive /ˈfɜːtɪv/ *adjective* sly, stealthy. □ **furtively** *adverb*.

fury /ˈfjʊərɪ/ *noun* (*plural* **-ies**) wild and passionate anger; violence (of storm etc.); (**Fury**) (usually in *plural*) avenging goddess; angry woman.

furze *noun* gorse. □ **furzy** *adjective* (**-ier**, **-iest**).

fuse[1] /fjuːz/ ● *verb* (**-sing**) melt with intense heat; blend by melting; supply with fuse; fail due to melting of fuse; cause fuse(s) of to melt. ● *noun* easily melted wire in circuit, designed to melt when circuit is overloaded.

fuse[2] /fjuːz/ ● *noun* combustible device for igniting bomb etc. ● *verb* (**-sing**) fit fuse to.

fuselage /ˈfjuːzəlɑːʒ/ *noun* body of aircraft.

fusible /ˈfjuːzɪb(ə)l/ *adjective* that can be melted. □ **fusibility** *noun*.

fusilier /fjuːzɪˈlɪə/ *noun* soldier of any of several regiments formerly armed with light muskets.

fusillade /fjuːzɪˈleɪd/ *noun* continuous discharge of firearms or outburst of criticism etc.

fusion /ˈfjuːʒ(ə)n/ *noun* fusing; blending; coalition; nuclear fusion.

fuss ● *noun* excited commotion; bustle; excessive concern about trivial thing; sustained protest. ● *verb* behave with nervous concern; agitate, worry. □ **fusspot** *colloquial* person given to fussing; **make a fuss** complain vigorously; **make a fuss of**, **over** treat affectionately.

fussy *adjective* (**-ier**, **-iest**) inclined to fuss; over-elaborate; fastidious.

fustian /ˈfʌstɪən/ *noun* thick usually dark twilled cotton cloth; bombast.

fusty /ˈfʌstɪ/ *adjective* (**-ier**, **-iest**) musty, stuffy; antiquated.

futile /ˈfjuːtaɪl/ *adjective* useless, ineffectual. □ **futility** /-ˈtɪl-/ *noun*.

futon /ˈfuːtɒn/ *noun* Japanese mattress used as bed; this with frame, convertible into couch.

future /ˈfjuːtʃə/ ● *adjective* about to happen, be, or become; of time to come; *Grammar* (of tense) describing event yet to happen. ● *noun* time to come; future condition or events etc.; prospect of success etc.; *Grammar* future tense; (in *plural*) (on stock exchange) goods etc. sold for future delivery. □ **future perfect** *Grammar* tense giving sense 'will have done'.

futurism *noun* 20th-c. artistic movement celebrating technology etc. □ **futurist** *adjective & noun*.

futuristic /fjuːtʃəˈrɪstɪk/ *adjective* suitable for the future; ultra-modern; of futurism.

futurity /fjuːˈtjʊərɪtɪ/ *noun* (*plural* **-ies**) *literary* future time, events, etc.

fuzz *noun* fluff; fluffy or frizzy hair; (**the fuzz**) *slang* police (officer).

fuzzy /ˈfʌzɪ/ *adjective* (**-ier**, **-iest**) fluffy; blurred, indistinct.

Gg

G □ **G-man** *US colloquial* FBI special agent; **G-string** narrow strip of cloth etc. attached to string round waist for covering genitals.

g *abbreviation* (also **g.**) gram(s).

gab *noun colloquial* talk, chatter.

gabardine /ɡæbə'diːn/ *noun* a strong twilled cloth; raincoat etc. of this.

gabble /ˈɡæb(ə)l/ ● *verb* (**-ling**) talk or utter unintelligibly or too fast. ● *noun* rapid talk.

gaberdine = GABARDINE.

gable /ˈɡeɪb(ə)l/ *noun* triangular part of wall at end of ridged roof. □ **gabled** *adjective*.

gad *verb* (**-dd-**) (+ *about*) go about idly or in search of pleasure. □ **gadabout** person who gads about.

gadfly /ˈɡædflaɪ/ *noun* (*plural* **-ies**) fly that bites cattle.

gadget /ˈɡædʒɪt/ *noun* small mechanical device or tool. □ **gadgetry** *noun*.

Gael /ɡeɪl/ *noun* Scottish or Gaelic-speaking Celt.

Gaelic /ˈɡeɪlɪk/ ● *noun* Celtic language of Scots (also /ˈɡælɪk/) or Irish. ● *adjective* of Gaelic or Gaelic-speaking people.

gaff [1] ● *noun* stick with hook for landing fish; barbed fishing-spear. ● *verb* seize (fish) with gaff.

gaff [2] *noun slang* □ **blow the gaff** let out secret.

gaffe /ɡæf/ *noun* blunder, tactless mistake.

gaffer /ˈɡæfə/ *noun* old man; *colloquial* foreman, boss; chief electrician in film unit.

gag ● *noun* thing thrust into or tied across mouth to prevent speech etc.; joke or comic scene. ● *verb* (**-gg-**) apply gag to; silence; choke, retch; make jokes.

gaga /ˈɡɑːɡɑː/ *adjective slang* senile; crazy.

gage [1] *noun* pledge, security; challenge.

gage [2] *US* = GAUGE.

gaggle /ˈɡæɡ(ə)l/ *noun* flock (of geese); *colloquial* disorganized group.

gaiety /ˈɡeɪətɪ/ *noun* (*US* **gayety**) being gay, mirth; merrymaking; bright appearance.

gaily /ˈɡeɪlɪ/ *adverb* in a gay way.

gain ● *verb* obtain, win; acquire, earn; (often + *in*) increase, improve; benefit; (of clock etc.) become fast (by); reach; (often + *on*, *upon*) get closer to (person or thing one is following). ● *noun* increase (of wealth), profit; (in *plural*) money made in trade etc.

gainful /ˈɡeɪnfʊl/ *adjective* paid, lucrative. □ **gainfully** *adverb*.

gainsay /ɡeɪn'seɪ/ *verb* deny, contradict.

gait *noun* manner of walking or proceeding.

gaiter /ˈɡeɪtə/ *noun* covering of leather etc. for lower leg.

gal. *abbreviation* gallon(s).

gala /ˈɡɑːlə/ *noun* festive occasion or gathering.

galactic /ɡə'læktɪk/ *adjective* of galaxy.

galantine /ˈɡæləntiːn/ *noun* cold dish of meat boned, spiced, and covered in jelly.

galaxy /ˈɡæləksɪ/ *noun* (*plural* **-ies**) independent system of stars etc. in space; (**the Galaxy**) Milky Way; (+ *of*) gathering of beautiful or famous people.

gale *noun* strong wind; outburst, esp. of laughter.

gall [1] /ɡɔːl/ *noun colloquial* impudence; rancour; bile. □ **gall bladder** bodily organ containing bile; **gallstone** small hard mass that forms in gall bladder.

gall [2] /ɡɔːl/ ● *noun* sore made by chafing; (cause of) vexation; place rubbed bare. ● *verb* rub sore; vex, humiliate.

gall [3] /ɡɔːl/ *noun* growth produced on tree etc. by insect etc.

gallant /ˈɡælənt/ ● *adjective* brave; fine, stately; (/ɡə'lænt/) attentive to women. ● *noun* (/ɡə'lænt/) ladies' man. □ **gallantly** *adverb*.

gallantry /ˈɡæləntrɪ/ *noun* (*plural* **-ies**) bravery; courteousness to women; polite act or speech.

galleon /'gælɪən/ *noun historical* (usually Spanish) warship.

galleria /gælə'riːə/ *noun* group of small shops, cafés, etc. under one roof.

gallery /'gælərɪ/ *noun* (*plural* **-ies**) room etc. for showing works of art; balcony, esp. in church, hall, etc.; highest balcony in theatre; covered walk, colonnade; passage, corridor.

galley /'gælɪ/ *noun* (*plural* **-s**) *historical* long flat one-decked vessel usually rowed by slaves or criminals; ship's or aircraft's kitchen; (in full **galley proof**) printer's proof before division into pages.

Gallic /'gælɪk/ *adjective* (typically) French; of Gaul or Gauls.

Gallicism /'gælɪsɪz(ə)m/ *noun* French idiom.

gallimimus /gælɪ'maɪməs/ *noun* (*plural* **-muses**) medium-sized dinosaur that ran fast on two legs.

gallinaceous /gælɪ'neɪʃəs/ *adjective* of order of birds including domestic poultry.

gallivant /'gælɪvænt/ *verb colloquial* gad about.

gallon /'gælən/ *noun* measure of capacity (4.546 litres).

gallop /'gæləp/ • *noun* horse's fastest pace; ride at this pace. • *verb* (**-p-**) (cause to) go at gallop; talk etc. fast; progress rapidly.

gallows /'gæləʊz/ *plural noun* (usually treated as *singular*) structure for hanging criminals.

Gallup poll /'gæləp/ *noun* kind of opinion poll.

galore /gə'lɔː/ *adverb* in plenty.

galosh /gə'lɒʃ/ *noun* waterproof overshoe.

galumph /gə'lʌmf/ *verb colloquial* (esp. as **galumphing** *adjective*) move noisily or clumsily.

galvanic /gæl'vænɪk/ *adjective* producing an electric current by chemical action; (of electric current) produced thus; stimulating, full of energy.

galvanize /'gælvənaɪz/ *verb* (also **-ise**) (**-zing** or **-sing**) (often + *into*) rouse by shock; stimulate (as) by electricity; coat (iron, steel) with zinc to protect from rust.

galvanometer /gælvə'nɒmɪtə/ *noun* instrument for measuring electric currents.

gambit /'gæmbɪt/ *noun Chess* opening with sacrifice of pawn etc.; trick, device.

gamble /'gæmb(ə)l/ • *verb* (**-ling**) play games of chance for money; bet (sum of money); (often + *away*) lose by gambling. • *noun* risky undertaking; spell of gambling. □ **gambler** *noun*.

gambol /'gæmb(ə)l/ • *verb* (**-ll-**; *US* **-l-**) jump about playfully. • *noun* caper.

game[1] • *noun* form or period of play or sport, esp. competitive one organized with rules; portion of play forming scoring unit; (in *plural*) athletic contests; piece of fun, (in *plural*) tricks; *colloquial* scheme, activity; wild animals or birds etc. hunted for sport or food; their flesh as food. • *adjective* spirited, eager. • *verb* (**-ming**) gamble for money. □ **gamekeeper** person employed to breed and protect game; **gamesmanship** art of winning games by psychological means. □ **gamely** *adverb*.

game[2] *adjective colloquial* (of leg etc.) crippled.

gamete /'gæmiːt/ *noun* mature germ cell uniting with another in sexual reproduction.

gamin /'gæmɪn/ *noun* street urchin; impudent child.

gamine /gæ'miːn/ *noun* girl gamin; attractively mischievous or boyish girl.

gamma /'gæmə/ *noun* third letter of Greek alphabet (Γ, γ). □ **gamma rays** very short X-rays emitted by radioactive substances.

gammon /'gæmən/ *noun* back end of side of bacon, including leg.

gammy /'gæmɪ/ *adjective* (**-ier, -iest**) *slang* (of leg etc.) crippled.

gamut /'gæmət/ *noun* entire range or scope. □ **run the gamut of** experience or perform complete range of.

gamy /'geɪmɪ/ *adjective* (**-ier, -iest**) smelling or tasting like high game.

gander /'gændə/ *noun* male goose.

gang • *noun* set of associates, esp. for criminal purposes; set of workers, slaves, or prisoners. • *verb colloquial* (+ *up with*) act together with; (+ *up on*) combine against.

ganger /'gæŋə/ *noun* foreman of gang of workers.

gangling /'gæŋglɪŋ/ *adjective* (of person) tall and thin, lanky.

ganglion /'gæŋglɪən/ *noun* (*plural* **ganglia** or **-s**) knot on nerve containing assemblage of nerve cells.

gangly *adjective* (**-ier**, **-iest**) gangling.

gangplank /'gæŋplæŋk/ *noun* plank for walking on to or off boat etc.

gangrene /'gæŋgriːn/ *noun* death of body tissue, usually caused by obstruction of circulation. □ **gangrenous** *adjective*.

gangster /'gæŋstə/ *noun* member of gang of violent criminals.

gangue /gæŋ/ *noun* valueless part of ore deposit.

gangway *noun* passage, esp. between rows of seats; opening in ship's bulwarks; bridge.

gannet /'gænɪt/ *noun* large seabird; *slang* greedy person.

gantry /'gæntrɪ/ *noun* (*plural* **-ies**) structure supporting travelling crane, railway or road signals, rocket-launching equipment, etc.

gaol etc. = JAIL etc.

gap *noun* empty space, interval; deficiency; breach in hedge, wall, etc.; wide divergence.

gape ● *verb* (**-ping**) open mouth wide; be or become wide open; (+ *at*) stare at. ● *noun* open-mouthed stare; opening.

garage /'gærɑːdʒ/ *noun* building for keeping vehicle(s) in; establishment selling petrol etc. or repairing and selling vehicles. ● *verb* (**-ging**) put or keep in garage.

garb ● *noun* clothing, esp. of distinctive kind. ● *verb* dress.

garbage /'gɑːbɪdʒ/ *noun* US refuse; *colloquial* nonsense.

garble /'gɑːb(ə)l/ *verb* (**-ling**) (esp. as **garbled** *adjective*) distort or confuse (facts, statements, etc.).

garden /'gɑːd(ə)n/ ● *noun* piece of ground for growing flowers, fruit, or vegetables, or for recreation; (esp. in *plural*) public pleasure-grounds. ● *verb* cultivate or tend garden. □ **garden centre** place selling plants and garden equipment. □ **gardener** *noun*; **gardening** *noun*.

gardenia /gɑːˈdiːnɪə/ *noun* tree or shrub with fragrant flowers.

gargantuan /gɑːˈgæntjuən/ *adjective* gigantic.

gargle /'gɑːg(ə)l/ ● *verb* (**-ling**) rinse (throat) with liquid kept in motion by breath. ● *noun* liquid so used.

gargoyle /'gɑːgɔɪl/ *noun* grotesque carved spout projecting from gutter of building.

garish /'geərɪʃ/ *adjective* obtrusively bright, gaudy. □ **garishly** *adverb*; **garishness** *noun*.

garland /'gɑːlənd/ ● *noun* wreath of flowers etc. as decoration. ● *verb* adorn or crown with garland(s).

garlic /'gɑːlɪk/ *noun* plant with pungent bulb used in cookery. □ **garlicky** *adjective* *colloquial*.

garment /'gɑːmənt/ *noun* article of dress.

garner /'gɑːnə/ ● *verb* collect, store. ● *noun* storehouse for corn etc.

garnet /'gɑːnɪt/ *noun* glassy mineral, esp. red kind used as gem.

garnish /'gɑːnɪʃ/ ● *verb* decorate (esp. food). ● *noun* decoration, esp. to food.

garret /'gærɪt/ *noun* room, esp. small, cold, etc. immediately under roof.

garrison /'gærɪs(ə)n/ ● *noun* troops stationed in town. ● *verb* (**-n-**) provide with or occupy as garrison.

garrotte /gəˈrɒt/ (also **garotte**, US **garrote**) ● *verb* (**garrotting**, US **garroting**) execute by strangulation, esp. with wire collar. ● *noun* device for this.

garrulous /'gærələs/ *adjective* talkative. □ **garrulity** /gəˈruːlɪtɪ/ *noun*; **garrulousness** *noun*.

garter /'gɑːtə/ *noun* band to keep sock or stocking up; (**the Garter**) (badge of) highest order of English knighthood. □ **garter stitch** plain knitting stitch.

gas /gæs/ ● *noun* (*plural* **-es**) any airlike substance (i.e. not liquid or solid); such substance (esp. coal gas or natural gas) used as fuel; gas used as anaesthetic; poisonous gas used in war; US *colloquial* petrol; *slang* empty talk, boasting; *slang* amusing thing or person. ● *verb* (**gases**, **gassed**, **gassing**) expose to gas, esp. to kill; *colloquial* talk emptily or boastfully. □ **gasbag** *slang* empty talker; **gas**

chamber room filled with poisonous gas to kill people or animals; **gasholder** gasometer; **gas mask** respirator for protection against harmful gases; **gas ring** ring pierced with gas jet(s) for cooking etc.; **gasworks** place where gas is manufactured.

gaseous /ˈɡæsɪəs/ adjective of or as gas.

gash • noun long deep cut or wound. • verb make gash in.

gasify /ˈɡæsɪfaɪ/ verb (**-ies, -ied**) convert into gas. □ **gasification** noun.

gasket /ˈɡæskɪt/ noun sheet or ring of rubber etc. to seal joint between metal surfaces.

gasoline /ˈɡæsəliːn/ noun (also **gasolene**) US petrol.

gasometer /ɡæˈsɒmɪtə/ noun large tank from which gas is distributed.

gasp /ɡɑːsp/ • verb catch breath with open mouth; utter with gasps. • noun convulsive catching of breath.

gassy /ˈɡæsɪ/ adjective (**-ier, -iest**) of, like, or full of gas; colloquial verbose.

gastric /ˈɡæstrɪk/ adjective of stomach. □ **gastric flu** colloquial intestinal disorder of unknown cause; **gastric juice** digestive fluid secreted by stomach glands.

gastritis /ɡæˈstraɪtɪs/ noun inflammation of stomach.

gastroenteritis /ˌɡæstrəʊentəˈraɪtɪs/ noun inflammation of stomach and intestines.

gastronome /ˈɡæstrənəʊm/ noun gourmet. □ **gastronomic** /-ˈnɒm-/ adjective; **gastronomical** /-ˈnɒm-/ adjective; **gastronomically** /-ˈnɒm-/ adverb; **gastronomy** /-ˈstrɒn-/ noun.

gastropod /ˈɡæstrəpɒd/ noun mollusc that moves using underside of abdomen, e.g. snail.

gate noun barrier, usually hinged, used to close opening in wall, fence, etc.; such opening; means of entrance or exit; numbered place of access to aircraft at airport; device regulating passage of water in lock etc.; number of people paying to enter stadium etc., money thus taken. □ **gateleg (table)** table with legs in gateleg frame for supporting folding flaps; **gatepost** post at either side of gate; **gateway**

opening closed by gate, means of access.

gateau /ˈɡætəʊ/ noun (plural **-s** or **-x** /-z/) large rich elaborate cake.

gatecrash verb attend (party etc.) uninvited. □ **gatecrasher** noun.

gather /ˈɡæðə/ • verb bring or come together; collect (harvest, dust, etc.); infer, deduce; increase (speed); summon up (energy etc.); draw together in folds or wrinkles; (of boil etc.) come to a head. • noun fold or pleat.

gathering noun assembly; pus-filled swelling.

GATT /ɡæt/ abbreviation General Agreement on Tariffs and Trade.

gauche /ɡəʊʃ/ adjective socially awkward, tactless. □ **gauchely** adverb; **gaucheness** noun.

gaucho /ˈɡaʊtʃəʊ/ noun (plural **-s**) cowboy in S. American pampas.

gaudy /ˈɡɔːdɪ/ adjective (**-ier, -iest**) tastelessly showy. □ **gaudily** adverb; **gaudiness** noun.

gauge /ɡeɪdʒ/ (US **gage**) • noun standard measure; instrument for measuring; distance between rails or opposite wheels; capacity, extent; criterion, test. • verb (**-ging**) measure exactly; measure contents of; estimate.

Gaul /ɡɔːl/ noun inhabitant of ancient Gaul. □ **Gaulish** adjective & noun.

gaunt /ɡɔːnt/ adjective lean, haggard; grim. □ **gauntness** noun.

gauntlet[1] /ˈɡɔːntlɪt/ noun glove with long loose wrist; historical armoured glove.

gauntlet[2] /ˈɡɔːntlɪt/ noun □ **run the gauntlet** undergo criticism, pass between two rows of people wielding sticks etc., as punishment.

gauze /ɡɔːz/ noun thin transparent fabric; fine mesh of wire etc. □ **gauzy** adjective (**-ier, -iest**).

gave past of GIVE.

gavel /ˈɡæv(ə)l/ noun auctioneer's, chairman's, or judge's hammer.

gavotte /ɡəˈvɒt/ noun 18th-c. French dance; music for this.

gawk • verb colloquial gawp. • noun awkward or bashful person. □ **gawky** adjective (**-ier, -iest**).

gawp verb colloquial stare stupidly.

gay ● *adjective* light-hearted, cheerful; showy; homosexual; *colloquial* carefree. ● *noun* (esp. male) homosexual.

gayety *US* = GAIETY.

gaze ● *verb* (**-zing**) (+ *at, into, on,* etc.) look fixedly. ● *noun* intent look.

gazebo /gə'zi:bəʊ/ *noun* (*plural* **-s**) summer house etc. giving view.

gazelle /gə'zel/ *noun* (*plural* same or **-s**) small graceful antelope.

gazette /gə'zet/ ● *noun* newspaper; official publication. ● *verb* (**-tting**) publish in official gazette.

gazetteer /gæzɪ'tɪə/ *noun* geographical index.

gazump /gə'zʌmp/ *verb colloquial* raise price after accepting offer from (buyer); swindle.

gazunder /gə'zʌndə/ *verb colloquial* lower an offer made to (seller) just before exchange of contracts.

GB *abbreviation* Great Britain.

GBH *abbreviation* grievous bodily harm.

GC *abbreviation* George Cross.

GCE *abbreviation* General Certificate of Education.

GCSE *abbreviation* General Certificate of Secondary Education.

GDR *abbreviation historical* German Democratic Republic.

gear /gɪə/ ● *noun* (often in *plural*) set of toothed wheels working together, esp. those connecting engine to road wheels; particular setting of these; equipment; *colloquial* clothing. ● *verb* (+ *to*) adjust or adapt to; (often + *up*) equip with gears; (+ *up*) make ready. □ **gearbox** (case enclosing) gears of machine or vehicle; **gear lever** lever moved to engage or change gear; **in gear** with gear engaged.

gecko /'gekəʊ/ *noun* (*plural* **-s**) tropical house-lizard.

gee /dʒi:/ *interjection expressing surprise* etc.

geese *plural* of GOOSE.

geezer /'gi:zə/ *noun slang* man, esp. old one.

Geiger counter /'gaɪgə/ *noun* instrument for measuring radioactivity.

geisha /'geɪʃə/ *noun* (*plural* same or **-s**) Japanese professional hostess and entertainer.

gel /dʒel/ ● *noun* semi-solid jelly-like colloid; jelly-like substance for hair. ● *verb* (**-ll-**) form gel; jell.

gelatin /'dʒelətɪn/ *noun* (also **gelatine** /-ti:n/) transparent tasteless substance used in cookery, photography, etc. □ **gelatinous** /dʒɪ'læt-/ *adjective*.

geld /geld/ *verb* castrate.

gelding /'geldɪŋ/ *noun* castrated horse etc.

gelignite /'dʒelɪgnaɪt/ *noun* nitroglycerine explosive.

gem /dʒem/ ● *noun* precious stone; thing or person of great beauty or worth. ● *verb* (**-mm-**) adorn (as) with gems.

Gemini /'dʒemɪnaɪ/ *noun* third sign of zodiac.

Gen. *abbreviation* General.

gen /dʒen/ *slang* ● *noun* information. ● *verb* (**-nn-**) (+ *up*) gain or give information.

gendarme /'ʒɒndɑ:m/ *noun* police officer in France etc.

gender /'dʒendə/ *noun* (grammatical) classification roughly corresponding to the two sexes and sexlessness; one of these classes; person's sex.

gene /dʒi:n/ *noun* unit in chromosome, controlling particular inherited characteristic.

genealogy /dʒi:nɪ'ælədʒɪ/ *noun* (*plural* **-ies**) descent traced continuously from ancestor, pedigree; study of pedigrees. □ **genealogical** /-ə'lɒdʒ-/ *adjective*; **genealogically** /-ə'lɒdʒ-/ *adverb*; **genealogist** *noun*.

genera *plural* of GENUS.

general /'dʒenər(ə)l/ ● *adjective* including, affecting, or applicable to (nearly) all; prevalent, usual; vague; not partial or particular; lacking detail; chief, head. ● *noun* army officer next below Field Marshal; commander of army. □ **general anaesthetic** one affecting whole body; **general election** national election of representatives to parliament; **general practice** work of **general practitioner**, doctor treating cases of all kinds; **general strike** simultaneous strike of workers in all or most trades; **in general** as a rule, usually.

generalissimo /dʒenərə'lɪsɪməʊ/ *noun* (*plural* **-s**) commander of combined forces.

generality /dʒenəˈrælɪtɪ/ noun (plural **-ies**) general statement; general applicability; indefiniteness; (+ *of*) majority of.

generalize /ˈdʒenərəlaɪz/ verb (also **-ise**) (**-zing** or **-sing**) speak in general or indefinite terms, form general notion(s); reduce to general statement; infer (rule etc.) from particular cases; bring into general use. □ **generalization** noun.

generally /ˈdʒenərəlɪ/ adverb usually; in most respects; in general sense; in most cases.

generate /ˈdʒenəreɪt/ verb (**-ting**) bring into existence, produce.

generation noun all people born about same time; stage in family history or in (esp. technological) development; period of about 30 years; production, esp. of electricity; procreation.

generative /ˈdʒenərətɪv/ adjective of procreation; productive.

generator noun dynamo; apparatus for producing gas, steam, etc.

generic /dʒɪˈnerɪk/ adjective characteristic of or relating to class or genus; not specific or special; (of esp. drug) with no brand name. □ **generically** adverb.

generous /ˈdʒenərəs/ adjective giving or given freely; magnanimous; abundant. □ **generosity** /-ˈrɒs-/ noun; **generously** adverb.

genesis /ˈdʒenɪsɪs/ noun origin, mode of formation; (**Genesis**) first book of Old Testament.

genetic /dʒɪˈnetɪk/ adjective of genetics; of or in origin. □ **genetic engineering** manipulation of DNA to modify hereditary features; **genetic fingerprinting** identification of individuals by DNA patterns. □ **genetically** adverb.

genetics plural noun (treated as *singular*) study of heredity and variation among animals and plants. □ **geneticist** /-sɪst/ noun.

genial /ˈdʒiːnɪəl/ adjective sociable, kindly; mild, warm; cheering. □ **geniality** /-ˈæl-/ noun; **genially** adverb.

genie /ˈdʒiːnɪ/ noun (plural **genii** /-nɪaɪ/) sprite or goblin of Arabian tales.

genital /ˈdʒenɪt(ə)l/ ● adjective of animal reproduction or reproductive organs.

● noun (in *plural*; also **genitalia**) external reproductive organs.

genitive /ˈdʒenɪtɪv/ Grammar ● noun case expressing possession, origin, etc., corresponding to *of*, *from*, etc. ● adjective of or in this case.

genius /ˈdʒiːnɪəs/ noun (plural **-es**) exceptional natural ability; person having this; guardian spirit.

genocide /ˈdʒenəsaɪd/ noun mass murder, esp. among particular race or nation.

genre /ˈʒɑːrə/ noun kind or style of art etc.; portrayal of scenes from ordinary life.

gent /dʒent/ noun colloquial gentleman; (**the Gents**) colloquial men's public lavatory.

genteel /dʒenˈtiːl/ adjective affectedly refined; upper-class.

gentian /ˈdʒenʃ(ə)n/ noun mountain plant with usually blue flowers. □ **gentian violet** violet dye used as antiseptic.

Gentile /ˈdʒentaɪl/ ● adjective not Jewish; heathen. ● noun non-Jewish person.

gentility /dʒenˈtɪlɪtɪ/ noun social superiority; genteel habits.

gentle /ˈdʒent(ə)l/ adjective (**-r**, **-st**) not rough or severe; mild, kind; well-born; quiet. □ **gentleness** noun; **gently** adverb.

gentlefolk /ˈdʒentəlfəʊk/ noun people of good family.

gentleman /ˈdʒentəlmən/ noun man; chivalrous well-bred man; man of good social position. □ **gentlemanly** adjective.

gentlewoman noun archaic woman of good birth or breeding.

gentrification /dʒentrɪfɪˈkeɪʃ(ə)n/ noun upgrading of working-class urban area by arrival of affluent residents. □ **gentrify** verb (**-ies**, **-ied**).

gentry /ˈdʒentrɪ/ plural noun people next below nobility; derogatory people.

genuflect /ˈdʒenjuːflekt/ verb bend knee, esp. in worship. □ **genuflection**, **genuflexion** /-ˈflekʃ(ə)n/ noun.

genuine /ˈdʒenjuːɪn/ adjective really coming from its reputed source; properly so called; not sham. □ **genuinely** adverb; **genuineness** noun.

genus /ˈdʒiːnəs/ noun (plural **genera** /ˈdʒenərə/) group of animals or plants

with common structural characteristics, usually containing several species; kind, class.

geocentric /dʒiːə'sentrɪk/ adjective considered as viewed from earth's centre;
having earth as centre.

geode /'dʒiːəʊd/ noun cavity lined with
crystals; rock containing this.

geodesic /dʒiːəʊ'diːzɪk/ adjective (also
geodetic /-'det-/) of geodesy.
□ **geodesic line** shortest possible line
on surface between two points.

geodesy /dʒiː'ɒdɪsɪ/ noun study of shape
and area of the earth.

geography /dʒɪ'ɒɡrəfɪ/ noun science of
earth's physical features, resources,
etc.; features of place. □ **geographer**
noun; **geographic(al)** /-ə'ɡræf-/ adjective;
geographically /-ə'ɡræf-/ adverb.

geology /dʒɪ'ɒlədʒɪ/ noun science of
earth's crust, strata, etc. □ **geological**
/-ə'lɒdʒ-/ adjective; **geologist** noun.

geometry /dʒɪ'ɒmətrɪ/ noun science of
properties and relations of lines, surfaces, and solids. □ **geometric(al)**
/-ə'met-/ adjective; **geometrician** /-'trɪ-
ʃ(ə)n/ noun.

Geordie /'dʒɔːdɪ/ noun native of Tyneside.

georgette /dʒɔː'dʒet/ noun kind of fine
dress material.

Georgian /'dʒɔːdʒ(ə)n/ adjective of time of
George I–IV or George V and VI.

geranium /dʒə'reɪnɪəm/ noun (plural **-s**)
cultivated pelargonium; herb or shrub
with fruit shaped like crane's bill.

gerbil /'dʒɜːbɪl/ noun mouselike desert
rodent with long hind legs.

geriatric /dʒerɪ'ætrɪk/ ● adjective of geriatrics or old people; derogatory old. ● noun
often derogatory old person.

geriatrics /dʒerɪ'ætrɪks/ plural noun (usually treated as singular) branch of medicine dealing with health and care of old
people. □ **geriatrician** /-ə'trɪʃ(ə)n/ noun.

germ /dʒɜːm/ noun microbe; portion of
organism capable of developing into
new one; thing that may develop; rudiment, elementary principle.

German /'dʒɜːmən/ ● noun (plural **-s**) native, national, or language of Germany.
● adjective of Germany. □ **German
measles** disease like mild measles;
German shepherd (dog) Alsatian.

german /'dʒɜːmən/ adjective (placed after
brother, sister, or cousin) having same
two parents or grandparents.

germander /dʒɜː'mændə/ noun plant of
mint family.

Germanic /dʒɜː'mænɪk/ ● adjective having
German characteristics. ● noun group of
languages including English, German,
Dutch, and Scandinavian languages.

germicide /'dʒɜːmɪsaɪd/ noun substance
that destroys germs. □ **germicidal**
/-'saɪd(ə)l/ adjective.

germinal /'dʒɜːmɪn(ə)l/ adjective of germs;
in earliest stage of development.

germinate /'dʒɜːmɪneɪt/ verb (**-ting**)
(cause to) sprout or bud. □ **germination**
noun.

gerontology /dʒerɒn'tɒlədʒɪ/ noun study
of old age and ageing.

gerrymander /dʒerɪ'mændə/ verb manipulate boundaries of (constituency
etc.) to gain unfair electoral advantage.

gerund /'dʒerənd/ noun verbal noun, in
English ending in -ing.

Gestapo /ge'stɑːpəʊ/ noun historical Nazi
secret police.

gestation /dʒe'steɪʃ(ə)n/ noun carrying
or being carried in womb between conception and birth; this period; development of plan etc. □ **gestate** verb (**-ting**).

gesticulate /dʒe'stɪkjʊleɪt/ verb (**-ting**)
use gestures instead of or with speech.
□ **gesticulation** noun.

gesture /'dʒestʃə/ ● noun meaningful
movement of limb or body; action performed as courtesy or to indicate intention. ● verb (**-ring**) gesticulate.

get /get/ verb (**getting**; past **got**; past
participle **got** or US **gotten**) obtain, earn;
fetch; procure; go to reach or catch;
prepare (meal); (cause to) reach some
state or become; obtain from calculation; contract (disease); contact; have
(punishment) inflicted on one; succeed in bringing, placing, etc.; (cause
to) succeed in coming or going; colloquial understand, annoy, harm, attract;
archaic beget. □ **get about** go from
place to place; **get across** communicate; **get along** (often + with) live
harmoniously; **get around** = GET ABOUT;
get at reach, get hold of, colloquial im-

ply, *colloquial* nag; **get away** escape; **getaway** *noun*; **get by** *colloquial* cope; **get in** obtain place at college etc., win election; **get off** alight (from), *colloquial* escape with little or no punishment, start, depart, (+ *with*) *colloquial* start sexual relationship with; **get on** make progress, manage, advance, enter (bus etc.), (often + *with*) live harmoniously, (usually as **be getting on**) age; **get out of** avoid, escape; **get over** recover from, surmount; **get round** coax or cajole (person), evade (law etc.), (+ *to*) deal with (task) in due course; **get through** pass (exam etc.), use up (resources), make contact by telephone, (+ *to*) succeed in making (person) understand; **get-together** *colloquial* social assembly; **get up** rise esp. from bed, (of wind etc.) strengthen, organize, stimulate, arrange appearance of; **get-up** *colloquial* style of dress etc.; **have got** possess, (+ *to do*) must.

geyser /ˈgiːzə/ *noun* hot spring; apparatus for heating water.

ghastly /ˈgɑːstlɪ/ *adjective* (**-ier, -iest**) horrible, frightful; deathlike, pallid.

ghee /giː/ *noun* Indian clarified butter.

gherkin /ˈgɜːkɪn/ *noun* small cucumber for pickling.

ghetto /ˈgetəʊ/ *noun* (*plural* **-s**) part of city occupied by minority group; *historical* Jews' quarter in city; segregated group or area. □ **ghetto-blaster** large portable radio or cassette player.

ghost /gəʊst/ ● *noun* apparition of dead person etc., disembodied spirit; (+ *of*) semblance; secondary image in defective telescope or television picture. ● *verb* (often + *for*) act as ghost-writer of (book etc.). □ **ghost-writer** writer doing work for which another takes credit. □ **ghostly** *adjective* (**-ier, -iest**).

ghoul /guːl/ *noun* person morbidly interested in death etc.; evil spirit; (in Arabic mythology) spirit preying on corpses. □ **ghoulish** *adjective*.

GHQ *abbreviation* General Headquarters.

ghyll = GILL³.

GI /dʒiːˈaɪ/ *noun* soldier in US army.

giant /ˈdʒaɪənt/ ● *noun* mythical being of human form but superhuman size; person, animal, or thing of extraordinary size, ability, etc. ● *adjective* gigantic.

gibber /ˈdʒɪbə/ *verb* chatter inarticulately.

gibberish /ˈdʒɪbərɪʃ/ *noun* unintelligible or meaningless speech or sounds.

gibbet /ˈdʒɪbɪt/ *noun historical* gallows; post with arm from which executed criminal was hung after execution.

gibbon /ˈgɪbən/ *noun* long-armed ape.

gibbous /ˈgɪbəs/ *adjective* convex; (of moon etc.) with bright part greater than semicircle.

gibe /dʒaɪb/ (also **jibe**) ● *verb* (**-bing**) (often + *at*) jeer, mock. ● *noun* jeering remark, taunt.

giblets /ˈdʒɪblɪts/ *plural noun* liver, gizzard, etc. of bird removed and usually cooked separately.

giddy /ˈgɪdɪ/ *adjective* (**-ier, -iest**) dizzy, tending to fall or stagger; mentally intoxicated; excitable, flighty; making dizzy. □ **giddiness** *noun*.

gift /gɪft/ *noun* thing given, present; talent; *colloquial* easy task.

gifted *adjective* talented.

gig¹ /gɪg/ *noun* light two-wheeled one-horse carriage; light boat on ship; rowing boat, esp. for racing.

gig² /gɪg/ ● *noun* engagement to play music, usually on one occasion. ● *verb* (**-gg-**) perform gig.

giga- /ˈgɪgə/ *combining form* one thousand million.

gigantic /dʒaɪˈgæntɪk/ *adjective* huge, giant-like.

giggle /ˈgɪg(ə)l/ ● *verb* (**-ling**) laugh in half-suppressed spasms. ● *noun* such laugh; *colloquial* amusing person or thing. □ **giggly** *adjective* (**-ier, -iest**).

gigolo /ˈdʒɪgələʊ/ *noun* (*plural* **-s**) young man paid by older woman to be escort or lover.

gild¹ /gɪld/ *verb* (*past participle* **gilded** or as *adjective* **gilt**) cover thinly with gold; tinge with golden colour.

gild² = GUILD.

gill¹ /gɪl/ *noun* (usually in *plural*) respiratory organ of fish etc.; vertical radial plate on underside of mushroom etc.; flesh below person's jaws and ears.

gill² /dʒɪl/ *noun* quarter-pint measure.

gill³ /gɪl/ *noun* (also **ghyll**) deep wooded ravine; narrow mountain torrent.

gillie /ˈɡɪlɪ/ *noun Scottish* man or boy attending hunter or angler.

gillyflower /ˈdʒɪlɪflaʊə/ *noun* clove-scented flower; e.g. wallflower.

gilt¹ /ɡɪlt/ ● *adjective* overlaid (as) with gold. ● *noun* gilding. □ **gilt-edged** (of securities etc.) having high degree of reliability.

gilt² /ɡɪlt/ *noun* young sow.

gimbals /ˈdʒɪmb(ə)lz/ *plural noun* contrivance of rings etc. for keeping things horizontal in ship, aircraft, etc.

gimcrack /ˈdʒɪmkræk/ ● *adjective* flimsy, tawdry. ● *noun* showy ornament etc.

gimlet /ˈɡɪmlɪt/ *noun* small boring-tool.

gimmick /ˈɡɪmɪk/ *noun* trick or device, esp. to attract attention. □ **gimmickry** *noun*; **gimmicky** *adjective*.

gimp /ɡɪmp/ *noun* twist of silk etc. with cord or wire running through.

gin¹ /dʒɪn/ *noun* spirit distilled from grain or malt and flavoured with juniper berries.

gin² /dʒɪn/ ● *noun* snare, trap; machine separating cotton from seeds; kind of crane or windlass. ● *verb* (**-nn-**) treat (cotton) in gin; trap.

ginger /ˈdʒɪndʒə/ ● *noun* hot spicy root used in cooking; plant having this root; light reddish-yellow. ● *adjective* of ginger colour. ● *verb* flavour with ginger; (+ *up*) enliven. □ **ginger ale**, **beer** ginger-flavoured fizzy drinks; **gingerbread** ginger-flavoured treacle cake; **ginger group** group urging party or movement to stronger action; **ginger-nut** kind of ginger-flavoured biscuit. □ **gingery** *adjective*.

gingerly /ˈdʒɪndʒəlɪ/ ● *adverb* in a careful or cautious way. ● *adjective* showing extreme care or caution.

gingham /ˈɡɪŋəm/ *noun* plain-woven usually checked cotton cloth.

gingivitis /dʒɪndʒɪˈvaɪtɪs/ *noun* inflammation of the gums.

ginkgo /ˈɡɪŋkəʊ/ *noun* (*plural* **-s**) tree with fan-shaped leaves and yellow flowers.

ginseng /ˈdʒɪnseŋ/ *noun* plant found in E. Asia and N. America; medicinal root of this.

Gipsy = GYPSY.

giraffe /dʒɪˈrɑːf/ *noun* (*plural* same or **-s**) tall 4-legged African animal with long neck.

gird /ɡɜːd/ (*past & past participle* **girded** or **girt**) encircle or fasten (on) with waistbelt etc. □ **gird (up) one's loins** prepare for action.

girder /ˈɡɜːdə/ *noun* iron or steel beam or compound structure used for bridges etc.

girdle¹ /ˈɡɜːd(ə)l/ ● *noun* belt or cord worn round waist; corset; thing that surrounds; bony support for limbs. ● *verb* (**-ling**) surround with girdle.

girdle² /ˈɡɜːd(ə)l/ *noun Scottish & Northern English* = GRIDDLE.

girl /ɡɜːl/ *noun* female child; *colloquial* young woman; *colloquial* girlfriend; female servant. □ **girlfriend** person's regular female companion; **girl guide** Guide; **girl scout** female Scout. □ **girlhood** *noun*; **girlish** *adjective*; **girly** *adjective*.

giro /ˈdʒaɪrəʊ/ ● *noun* (*plural* **-s**) system of credit transfer between banks, Post Offices, etc.; cheque or payment by giro. ● *verb* (**-es**, **-ed**) pay by giro.

girt *past & past participle of* GIRD.

girth /ɡɜːθ/ *noun* distance round a thing; band round body of horse securing saddle.

gist /dʒɪst/ *noun* substance or essence of a matter.

gîte /ʒiːt/ *noun* furnished holiday house in French countryside. [French]

give /ɡɪv/ ● *verb* (**-ving**; *past* **gave**; *past participle* **given**) transfer possession of freely; provide with; administer; deliver; (often + *for*) make over in exchange or payment; confer; accord; pledge; perform (action etc.); utter, declare; yield to pressure; collapse; yield as product; consign; devote; present, offer (one's hand, arm, etc.); impart; be source of; concede; assume, grant, specify. ● *noun* capacity to comply; elasticity. □ **give and take** exchange of talk or ideas, ability to compromise; **give away** transfer as gift, hand over (bride) to bridegroom, betray or expose; **give-away** *colloquial* unintentional disclosure, free or inexpensive thing; **give in** yield, hand in; **give off** emit, send out; **give out** announce, emit, distribute, be exhausted, run short; **give over** *colloquial* desist, hand over, devote; **give up** resign, surrender, part with, renounce hope (of), cease (activity). □ **giver** *noun*.

given ● *past participle* of GIVE. ● *adjective* (+ *to*) disposed or prone to; assumed as basis of reasoning etc.; fixed, specified.

gizmo /ˈgɪzməʊ/ *noun* (*plural* **-s**) gadget.

gizzard /ˈgɪzəd/ *noun* bird's second stomach, for grinding food.

glacé /ˈglæseɪ/ *adjective* (of fruit) preserved in sugar; (of cloth etc.) smooth, polished.

glacial /ˈgleɪʃ(ə)l/ *adjective* of ice or glaciers.

glaciated /ˈgleɪsɪeɪtɪd/ *adjective* marked or polished by moving ice; covered with glaciers. □ **glaciation** *noun*.

glacier /ˈglæsɪə/ *noun* slowly moving mass of ice on land.

glad *adjective* (**-dd-**) pleased; joyful, cheerful. □ **glad rags** *colloquial* best clothes. □ **gladden** *verb*; **gladly** *adverb*; **gladness** *noun*.

glade *noun* clear space in forest.

gladiator /ˈglædɪeɪtə/ *noun historical* trained fighter in ancient Roman shows. □ **gladiatorial** /-əˈtɔːrɪəl/ *adjective*.

gladiolus /glædɪˈəʊləs/ *noun* (*plural* **-li** /-laɪ/) plant of lily family with bright flower-spikes.

gladsome *adjective poetical* cheerful, joyful.

Gladstone bag /ˈglædst(ə)n/ *noun* kind of light portmanteau.

glair *noun* white of egg; similar or derivative viscous substance.

glamour /ˈglæmə/ *noun* (*US* **glamor**) physical, esp. cosmetic, attractiveness; alluring or exciting beauty or charm. □ **glamorize** *verb* (also **-ise**) (**-zing** or **-sing**); **glamorous** *adjective*; **glamorously** *adverb*.

glance /glɑːns/ ● *verb* (**-cing**) (often + *down, up, over*, etc.) look or refer briefly; (often + *off*) hit at fine angle and bounce off. ● *noun* brief look; flash, gleam; swift oblique stroke in cricket. □ **at a glance** immediately on looking.

gland *noun* organ etc. secreting substances for use in body; similar organ in plant.

glanders /ˈglændəz/ *plural noun* contagious horse disease.

glandular /ˈglændjʊlə/ *adjective* of gland(s). □ **glandular fever** infectious disease with swelling of lymph glands.

glare /gleə/ ● *verb* (**-ring**) look fiercely; shine oppressively; (esp. as **glaring** *adjective*) be very evident. ● *noun* oppressive light or public attention; fierce look; tawdry brilliance. □ **glaringly** *adverb*.

glasnost /ˈglæznɒst/ *noun* (in former USSR) policy of more open government.

glass /glɑːs/ ● *noun* hard, brittle, usually transparent substance made by fusing sand with soda and lime etc.; glass objects collectively; glass drinking vessel, its contents; glazed frame for plants; barometer; covering of watch-face; lens; (in *plural*) spectacles, binoculars; mirror. ● *verb* (usually as **glassed** *adjective*) fit with glass. □ **glass-blowing** blowing of semi-molten glass to make glass objects; **glass fibre** glass filaments made into fabric or reinforcing plastic; **glasshouse** greenhouse, *slang* military prison; **glass-paper** paper covered with powdered glass, for smoothing etc.; **glass wool** fine glass fibres for packing and insulation. □ **glassful** *noun* (*plural* **-s**).

glassy /ˈglɑːsɪ/ *adjective* (**-ier, -iest**) like glass; (of eye etc.) dull, fixed.

glaucoma /glɔːˈkəʊmə/ *noun* eye disease with pressure in eyeball and gradual loss of sight.

glaze ● *verb* (**-zing**) fit with glass or windows; cover (pottery etc.) with vitreous substance or (surface) with smooth shiny coating; (often + *over*) (of eyes) become glassy. ● *noun* substance used for or surface produced by glazing.

glazier /ˈgleɪzɪə/ *noun* person who glazes windows etc.

gleam ● *noun* faint or brief light or show. ● *verb* emit gleam(s).

glean *verb* gather (facts etc.); gather (corn left by reapers). □ **gleanings** *plural noun*.

glebe *noun* piece of land yielding revenue to benefice.

glee *noun* mirth, delight; musical composition for several voices. □ **gleeful** *adjective*; **gleefully** *adverb*.

glen *noun* narrow valley.

glengarry /glenˈgærɪ/ *noun* (*plural* **-ies**) kind of Highland cap.

glib *adjective* (**-bb-**) speaking or spoken fluently but insincerely. □ **glibly** *adverb*; **glibness** *noun*.

glide ● *verb* (**-ding**) move smoothly or continuously; (of aircraft) fly without engine-power; go stealthily. ● *noun* gliding motion.

glider /'glaɪdə/ *noun* light aircraft without engine.

glimmer /'glɪmə/ ● *verb* shine faintly or intermittently. ● *noun* faint or wavering light; (also **glimmering**) (usually + *of*) small sign.

glimpse /glɪmps/ ● *noun* (often + *of, at*) brief view; faint transient appearance. ● *verb* (**-sing**) have brief view of.

glint *verb & noun* flash, glitter.

glissade /glɪ'sɑːd/ ● *noun* controlled slide down snow slope; gliding. ● *verb* (**-ding**) perform glissade.

glissando /glɪ'sændəʊ/ *noun* (*plural* **-di** /-dɪ/ or **-s**) *Music* continuous slide of adjacent notes.

glisten /'glɪs(ə)n/ ● *verb* shine like wet or polished surface. ● *noun* glitter.

glitch *noun* *colloquial* irregularity, malfunction.

glitter /'glɪtə/ ● *verb* shine with brilliant reflected light, sparkle; (often + *with*) be showy. ● *noun* sparkle; showiness; tiny pieces of glittering material.

glitz *noun* *slang* showy glamour. □ **glitzy** *adjective* (**-ier, -iest**).

gloaming /'gləʊmɪŋ/ *noun* twilight.

gloat *verb* (often + *over* etc.) look or ponder with greedy or malicious pleasure.

global /'gləʊb(ə)l/ *adjective* worldwide; all-embracing. □ **global warming** increase in temperature of earth's atmosphere. □ **globally** *adverb*.

globe *noun* spherical object; spherical map of earth; (**the globe**) the earth. □ **globe artichoke** partly edible head of artichoke plant; **globe-trotter** person travelling widely.

globular /'glɒbjʊlə/ *adjective* globe-shaped; composed of globules.

globule /'glɒbjuːl/ *noun* small globe, round particle, or drop.

glockenspiel /'glɒkənspiːl/ *noun* musical instrument of bells or metal bars played with hammers.

gloom /gluːm/ *noun* darkness; melancholy, depression.

gloomy /'gluːmɪ/ *adjective* (**-ier, -iest**) dark; depressed, depressing.

glorify /'glɔːrɪfaɪ/ *verb* (**-ies, -ied**) make glorious; make seem more splendid than is the case; (as **glorified** *adjective*) treated as more important etc. than it is; extol. □ **glorification** *noun*.

glorious /'glɔːrɪəs/ *adjective* possessing or conferring glory; *colloquial* splendid, excellent. □ **gloriously** *adverb*.

glory /'glɔːrɪ/ ● *noun* (*plural* **-ies**) (thing bringing) renown, honourable fame, etc.; adoring praise; resplendent majesty, beauty, etc.; halo of saint. ● *verb* (**-ies, -ied**) (often + *in*) take pride.

gloss[1] ● *noun* surface lustre; deceptively attractive appearance; (in full *gloss paint*) paint giving glossy finish. ● *verb* make glossy. □ **gloss over** seek to conceal.

gloss[2] ● *noun* explanatory comment added to text; interpretation. ● *verb* add gloss to.

glossary /'glɒsərɪ/ *noun* (*plural* **-ies**) dictionary of technical or special words, esp. as appendix.

glossy ● *adjective* (**-ier, -iest**) smooth and shiny; printed on such paper. ● *noun* (*plural* **-ies**) *colloquial* glossy magazine or photograph.

glottal /'glɒt(ə)l/ *adjective* of the glottis. □ **glottal stop** sound produced by sudden opening or shutting of glottis.

glottis /'glɒtɪs/ *noun* opening at upper end of windpipe between vocal cords.

glove /glʌv/ ● *noun* hand-covering for protection, warmth, etc.; boxing glove. ● *verb* (**-ving**) cover or provide with gloves. □ **glove compartment** recess for small articles in car dashboard; **glove puppet** small puppet fitted on hand.

glow /gləʊ/ ● *verb* emit flameless light and heat; (often + *with*) feel bodily heat or strong emotion; show warm colour; (as **glowing** *adjective*) expressing pride or satisfaction. ● *noun* glowing state, appearance, or feeling. □ **glow-worm** beetle that emits green light.

glower /'glaʊə/ *verb* (often + *at*) scowl.

glucose /'gluːkəʊs/ *noun* kind of sugar found in blood, fruits, etc.

glue ● *noun* substance used as adhesive. ● *verb* (**glues, glued, gluing** or **glueing**) attach (as) with glue; hold closely. □ **glue ear** blocking of (esp. child's) Eustachian tube; **glue-sniffing** inhalation of fumes from adhesives as intoxicant. ● **gluey** adjective (**gluier, gluiest**).

glum adjective (**-mm-**) dejected, sullen. □ **glumly** adverb; **glumness** noun.

glut ● verb (**-tt-**) feed or indulge to the full, satiate; overstock. ● noun excessive supply; surfeit.

gluten /'glu:t(ə)n/ noun sticky part of wheat flour.

glutinous /'glu:tɪnəs/ adjective sticky, gluelike.

glutton /'glʌt(ə)n/ noun excessive eater; (often + for) colloquial insatiably eager person; voracious animal of weasel family. □ **gluttonous** adjective; **gluttonously** adverb; **gluttony** noun.

glycerine /'glɪsəri:n/ noun (also **glycerol**, US **glycerin**) colourless sweet viscous liquid used in medicines, explosives, etc.

gm abbreviation gram(s).

GMT abbreviation Greenwich Mean Time.

gnarled /nɑ:ld/ adjective knobbly, twisted, rugged.

gnash /næʃ/ verb grind (one's teeth); (of teeth) strike together.

gnat /næt/ noun small biting fly.

gnaw /nɔ:/ verb (usually + away etc.) wear away by biting; (often + at, into) bite persistently; corrode; torment.

gneiss /naɪs/ noun coarse-grained rock of feldspar, quartz, and mica.

gnome /nəʊm/ noun dwarf, goblin; (esp. in plural) colloquial person with sinister influence, esp. financial.

gnomic /'nəʊmɪk/ adjective of aphorisms; sententious.

gnomon /'nəʊmɒn/ noun rod etc. on sundial, showing time by its shadow.

gnostic /'nɒstɪk/ ● adjective of knowledge; having special mystic knowledge. ● noun (**Gnostic**) early Christian heretic claiming mystical knowledge. □ **Gnosticism** /-sɪz(ə)m/ noun.

GNP abbreviation gross national product.

gnu /nu:/ noun (plural same or **-s**) oxlike antelope.

go[1] ● verb (3rd singular present **goes** /gəʊz/; past **went**; past participle **gone** /gɒn/) walk, travel, proceed; participate in (doing something); extend in a certain direction; depart; move, function; make specified movement or sound, colloquial say; be, become; elapse, be traversed; (of song etc.) have specified wording etc.; match; be regularly kept, fit; be successful; be sold, (of money) be spent; be relinquished; fail, decline, collapse; be acceptable or accepted; (often + by, with, on, upon) be guided by; attend regularly; (+ to, towards) contribute to; (+ for) apply to. ● noun (plural **goes**) animation; vigorous activity; success; turn, attempt. □ **go-ahead** adjective enterprising, noun permission to proceed; **go-between** intermediary; **go down** descend, become less, decrease (in price), subside, sink, (of sun) set, deteriorate, cease to function, be recorded, be swallowed, (+ with) find acceptance with, colloquial leave university, colloquial be sent to prison, (+ with) become ill with; **go for** go to fetch, prefer, choose, pass or be accounted as, colloquial attack, colloquial strive to attain; **go-getter** colloquial pushily enterprising person; **go in for** compete or engage in; **go-kart, -cart** miniature racing car with skeleton body; **go off** explode, deteriorate, fall asleep, begin to dislike; **go off well, badly** succeed, fail; **go on** continue, proceed, colloquial talk at great length, (+ at) colloquial nag, use as evidence; **go out** leave room or house, be extinguished, be broadcast, cease to be fashionable, (often + with) have romantic or sexual relationship, (usually + to) sympathize; **go over** inspect details of, rehearse; **go round** spin, revolve, suffice for all; **go slow** work slowly as industrial protest; **go under** sink, succumb, fail; **go up** rise, increase (in price), be consumed (in flames etc.), explode, colloquial enter university; **go without** manage without or forgo (something); **have a go at** attack, attempt; **on the go** colloquial active.

go[2] noun Japanese board game.

goad ● verb urge with goad; (usually + on, into) irritate, stimulate. ● noun spiked stick for urging cattle; thing that torments or incites.

goal noun object of effort; destination; structure into or through which ball is to be driven in certain games; point(s) so won; point where race ends.

goalkeeper player protecting goal;
goalpost either post supporting cross-bar of goal.

goalie noun colloquial goalkeeper.

goat noun small domesticated mammal with horns and (in male) beard; lascivious man; colloquial fool. □ **get (person's) goat** colloquial irritate him or her.

goatee /gəʊˈtiː/ noun small pointed beard.

gob¹ noun slang mouth. □ **gobsmacked** slang flabbergasted; **gob-stopper** large hard sweet.

gob² slang ● noun clot of slimy matter. ● verb spit.

gobbet /ˈgɒbɪt/ noun lump of flesh, food, etc.; extract from text set for translation or comment.

gobble¹ /ˈgɒb(ə)l/ verb (**-ling**) eat hurriedly and noisily.

gobble² /ˈgɒb(ə)l/ verb (**-ling**) (of turkey-cock) make guttural sound; speak thus.

gobbledegook /ˈgɒbəldɪɡuːk/ noun (also **gobbledeygook**) colloquial pompous or unintelligible jargon.

goblet /ˈgɒblɪt/ noun drinking vessel with foot and stem.

goblin /ˈgɒblɪn/ noun mischievous demon.

goby /ˈgəʊbɪ/ noun (plural **-ies**) small fish with sucker on underside.

god noun superhuman being worshipped as possessing power over nature, human fortunes, etc.; (**God**) creator and ruler of universe; idol; adored person; (**the gods**) (occupants of gallery in theatre. □ **godchild** person in relation to godparent; **god-daughter** female godchild; **godfather** male godparent; **God-fearing** religious; **God-forsaken** dismal; **godmother** female godparent; **godparent** person who responds on behalf of candidate at baptism; **godsend** unexpected welcome event or acquisition; **godson** male godchild. □ **godlike** adjective.

goddess /ˈgɒdɪs/ noun female deity; adored woman.

godhead noun divine nature; deity.

godless adjective impious, wicked; not believing in God. □ **godlessness** noun.

godly /ˈgɒdlɪ/ adjective (**-ier**, **-iest**) pious, devout. □ **godliness** noun.

goer /ˈgəʊə/ noun person or thing that goes; colloquial lively or sexually promiscuous person. □ **-goer** regular attender.

goggle /ˈgɒg(ə)l/ ● verb (**-ling**) (often + at) look with wide-open eyes; (of eyes) be rolled, project; roll (eyes). ● adjective (of eyes) protuberant, rolling. ● noun (in plural) spectacles for protecting eyes. □ **goggle-box** colloquial television set.

going /ˈgəʊɪŋ/ ● noun condition of ground as affecting riding etc. ● adjective in action; existing, available; current, prevalent. □ **going concern** thriving business; **going-over** (plural **goings-over**) colloquial inspection or overhaul, slang thrashing; **goings-on** strange conduct.

goitre /ˈgɔɪtə/ noun (US **goiter**) abnormal enlargement of thyroid gland.

gold /gəʊld/ ● noun precious yellow metal; colour of this; coins or articles of gold. ● adjective of or coloured like gold. □ **gold-digger** slang woman who goes after men for their money; **gold field** area with naturally occurring gold; **goldfinch** brightly coloured songbird; **goldfish** small golden-red Chinese carp; **gold leaf** gold beaten into thin sheet; **gold medal** medal given usually as first prize; **gold plate** vessels of gold, material plated with gold; **gold-plate** plate with gold; **gold-rush** rush to newly discovered gold field; **goldsmith** worker in gold; **gold standard** financial system in which value of money is based on gold.

golden /ˈgəʊld(ə)n/ adjective of gold; coloured or shining like gold; precious, excellent. □ **golden handshake** colloquial gratuity as compensation for redundancy or compulsory retirement; **golden jubilee** 50th anniversary of reign; **golden mean** principle of moderation; **golden retriever** retriever with gold-coloured coat; **golden wedding** 50th anniversary of wedding.

golf ● noun game in which small hard ball is struck with clubs over ground into series of small holes. ● verb play golf. □ **golf ball** ball used in golf, spherical unit carrying type in some electric typewriters; **golf course** area of land on which golf is played; **golf club** club used in golf, (premises of) association for playing golf. □ **golfer** noun.

golliwog /'gɒlɪwɒg/ noun black-faced soft doll with fuzzy hair.

gonad /'gəʊnæd/ noun animal organ producing gametes, e.g. testis or ovary.

gondola /'gɒndələ/ noun light Venetian canal-boat; car suspended from airship.

gondolier /gɒndə'lɪə/ noun oarsman of gondola.

gone /gɒn/ ● past participle of GO¹. ● adjective (of time) past; lost, hopeless, dead; colloquial pregnant for specified time.

goner /'gɒnə/ noun slang person or thing that is doomed or irrevocably lost.

gong noun metal disc giving resonant note when struck; saucer-shaped bell; slang medal.

gonorrhoea /gɒnə'rɪːə/ noun (US **gonorrhea**) a venereal disease.

goo noun colloquial sticky or slimy substance; sickly sentiment. □ **gooey** adjective (**gooier, gooiest**).

good /gʊd/ ● adjective (**better, best**) having right qualities, adequate; competent, effective; kind, morally excellent, virtuous; well-behaved; agreeable; considerable; not less than; beneficial; valid. ● noun (only in singular) good quality or circumstance; (in plural) movable property, merchandise. □ **good-for-nothing** worthless (person); **good humour** genial mood; **good-looking** handsome; **good nature** kindly disposition; **goodwill** kindly feeling, established value-enhancing reputation of a business.

goodbye /gʊd'baɪ/ (US **goodby**) ● interjection expressing good wishes at parting. ● noun (plural **-byes** or US **-bys**) parting, farewell.

goodly /'gʊdlɪ/ adjective (**-ier, -iest**) handsome; of imposing size etc.

goodness /'gʊdnɪs/ noun virtue; excellence; kindness; nutriment.

goody /'gʊdɪ/ ● noun (plural **-ies**) colloquial good person; (usually in plural) something good or attractive, esp. to eat. ● interjection expressing childish delight. □ **goody-goody** colloquial (person who is) smugly or obtrusively virtuous.

goof /guːf/ slang ● noun foolish or stupid person or mistake. ● verb bungle, blunder. □ **goofy** adjective (**-ier, -iest**).

googly /'guːglɪ/ noun (plural **-ies**) Cricket ball bowled so as to bounce in unexpected direction.

goon /guːn/ noun slang stupid person; esp. US hired ruffian.

goose /guːs/ noun (plural **geese** /giːs/) large web-footed bird; female of this; colloquial simpleton. □ **goose-flesh, -pimples** (US **-bumps**) bristling state of skin due to cold or fright; **goose-step** stiff-legged marching step.

gooseberry /'gʊzbərɪ/ noun (plural **-ies**) small green usually sour berry; thorny shrub bearing this.

gopher /'gəʊfə/ noun American burrowing rodent.

gore¹ noun clotted blood.

gore² verb (**-ring**) pierce with horn, tusk, etc.

gore³ ● noun wedge-shaped piece in garment; triangular or tapering piece in umbrella etc. ● verb (**-ring**) shape with gore.

gorge ● noun narrow opening between hills; surfeit; contents of stomach. ● verb (**-ging**) feed greedily; satiate.

gorgeous /'gɔːdʒəs/ adjective richly coloured; colloquial splendid; colloquial strikingly beautiful. □ **gorgeously** adverb.

gorgon /'gɔːgən/ noun (in Greek mythology) any of 3 snake-haired sisters able to turn people to stone; frightening or repulsive woman.

Gorgonzola /gɔːgən'zəʊlə/ noun rich blue-veined Italian cheese.

gorilla /gə'rɪlə/ noun largest anthropoid ape.

gormless /'gɔːmlɪs/ adjective colloquial foolish, lacking sense. □ **gormlessly** adverb.

gorse /gɔːs/ noun prickly shrub with yellow flowers.

Gorsedd /'gɔːseð/ noun Druidic order meeting before eisteddfod.

gory /'gɔːrɪ/ adjective (**-ier, -iest**) involving bloodshed; bloodstained.

gosh interjection expressing surprise.

goshawk /'gɒshɔːk/ noun large short-winged hawk.

gosling /'gɒzlɪŋ/ noun young goose.

gospel /'gɒsp(ə)l/ noun teaching or revelation of Christ; (**Gospel**) (each of 4 books giving) account of Christ's life in

New Testament; portion of this read at church service; thing regarded as absolutely true. □ **gospel music** black American religious singing.

gossamer /'gɒsəmə/ ●noun filmy substance of small spiders' webs; delicate filmy material. ●adjective light and flimsy as gossamer.

gossip /'gɒsɪp/ ●noun unconstrained talk or writing, esp. about people; idle talk; person indulging in gossip. ●verb (-p-) talk or write gossip. □ **gossip column** regular newspaper column of gossip. □ **gossipy** adjective.

got past & past participle of GET.

Goth noun member of Germanic tribe that invaded Roman Empire in 3rd–5th c.

Gothic adjective of Goths; Architecture in the pointed-arch style prevalent in W. Europe in 12th–16th c.; (of novel etc.) in a style popular in 18th & 19th c., with supernatural or horrifying events.

gotten US past participle of GET.

gouache /gu:'ɑːʃ/ noun painting with opaque water-colour; pigments used for this.

Gouda /'gaʊdə/ noun flat round Dutch cheese.

gouge /gaʊdʒ/ ●noun concave-bladed chisel. ●verb (-ging) cut or (+ out) force out (as) with gouge.

goulash /'gu:læʃ/ noun stew of meat and vegetables seasoned with paprika.

gourd /ɡʊəd/ noun fleshy fruit of trailing or climbing cucumber-like plant; this plant; dried rind of this fruit used as bottle etc.

gourmand /'ɡʊəmənd/ noun glutton; gourmet.

■ **Usage** The use of *gourmand* to mean a 'gourmet' is considered incorrect by some people.

gourmet /'ɡʊəmeɪ/ noun connoisseur of good food.

gout /gaʊt/ noun disease with inflammation of small joints. □ **gouty** adjective.

govern /'ɡʌv(ə)n/ verb rule with authority; conduct policy and affairs of; influence or determine; curb, control.

governance noun act, manner, or function of governing.

governess /'ɡʌvənɪs/ noun woman employed to teach children in private household.

government noun manner or system of governing; group of people governing state. □ **governmental** /-'men-/ adjective.

governor noun ruler; official governing a province, town, etc.; executive head of each State of US; member of governing body of institution; slang one's employer or father; automatic regulator controlling speed of engine etc. □ **Governor-General** representative of Crown in Commonwealth country regarding Queen as head of state. □ **governorship** noun.

gown /gaʊn/ noun woman's, esp. formal or elegant, long dress; official robe of alderman, judge, cleric, academic, etc.; surgeon's overall.

goy noun (plural **-im** or **-s**) Jewish name for non-Jew.

GP abbreviation general practitioner.

GPO abbreviation General Post Office.

gr abbreviation (also **gr.**) gram(s); grain(s); gross.

grab ●verb (-bb-) seize suddenly; take greedily; slang impress; (+ at) snatch at. ●noun sudden clutch or attempt to seize; device for clutching.

grace ●noun elegance of proportions, manner, or movement; courteous good will; attractive feature; unmerited favour of God; goodwill; delay granted; thanksgiving at meals; (**His**, **Her**, **Your Grace**) title used of or to duke, duchess, or archbishop. ●verb (-cing) (often + with) add grace to; bestow honour on. □ **grace note** Music note embellishing melody.

graceful adjective full of grace or elegance. □ **gracefully** adverb.

graceless adjective lacking grace or charm.

gracious /'ɡreɪʃəs/ adjective kindly, esp. to inferiors; merciful. □ **gracious living** elegant way of life. □ **graciously** adverb; **graciousness** noun.

gradate /ɡrə'deɪt/ verb (-ting) (cause to) pass gradually from one shade to another; arrange in steps or grades.

gradation noun (usually in plural) stage of transition or advance; degree in rank, intensity, etc.; arrangement in grades. □ **gradational** *adjective.*

grade ●*noun* degree in rank, merit, etc.; mark indicating quality of student's work; slope; *US* class in school. ●*verb* (**-ding**) arrange in grades; (+ *up, down, off, into*, etc.) pass between grades; give grade to; reduce to easy gradients. □ **make the grade** succeed.

gradient /ˈɡreɪdɪənt/ *noun* sloping road etc.; amount of such slope.

gradual /ˈɡrædʒʊəl/ *adjective* happening by degrees; not steep or abrupt. □ **gradually** *adverb.*

graduate ●*noun* /ˈɡrædʒʊət/ holder of academic degree. ●*verb* /-eɪt/ (**-ting**) obtain academic degree; (+ *to*) move up to; mark in degrees or portions; arrange in gradations; apportion (tax etc.) according to scale. □ **graduation** *noun.*

graffiti /ɡrəˈfiːtɪ/ *plural noun* (*singular* **graffito**) writing or drawing on wall etc.

■ **Usage** *Graffiti* should be used with plural verbs, as in *Graffiti have appeared* everywhere.

graft[1] /ɡrɑːft/ ●*noun* shoot or scion planted in slit in another stock; piece of transplanted living tissue; *slang* hard work. ●*verb* (often + *in, on, together,* etc.) insert (graft); transplant (living tissue); (+ *in, on*) insert or fix (thing) permanently to another; *slang* work hard.

graft[2] /ɡrɑːft/ *colloquial* ●*noun* practices for securing illicit gains in politics or business; such gains. ●*verb* seek or make graft.

Grail *noun* (in full **Holy Grail**) legendary cup or platter used by Christ at Last Supper.

grain ●*noun* fruit or seed of cereal; wheat or allied food-grass; corn; particle of sand, salt, etc.; unit of weight (0.065 g); least possible amount; texture in skin, wood, stone, etc.; arrangement of lines of fibre in wood. ●*verb* paint in imitation of grain of wood; form into grains.

gram *noun* (also **gramme**) metric unit of weight.

grammar /ˈɡræmə/ *noun* study or rules of relations between words in (a) language; application of such rules; book

on grammar. □ **grammar school** *esp. historical* secondary school with academic curriculum.

grammarian /ɡrəˈmeərɪən/ *noun* expert in grammar.

grammatical /ɡrəˈmætɪk(ə)l/ *adjective* of or according to grammar.

gramophone /ˈɡræməfəʊn/ *noun* record player.

grampus /ˈɡræmpəs/ *noun* (*plural* **-es**) sea mammal of dolphin family.

gran *noun colloquial* grandmother.

granary /ˈɡrænərɪ/ *noun* (*plural* **-ies**) storehouse for grain; region producing much corn.

grand ●*adjective* splendid, imposing; chief, of chief importance; (**Grand**) of highest rank; *colloquial* excellent. ●*noun* grand piano; (*plural* same) (usually in *plural*) *slang* 1,000 dollars or pounds. □ **grand jury** jury to examine validity of accusation before trial; **grand piano** piano with horizontal strings; **grand slam** winning of all of group of matches; **grand total** sum of other totals. □ **grandly** *adverb;* **grandness** *noun.*

grandad *noun* (also **grand-dad**) *colloquial* grandfather.

grandchild *noun* child of one's son or daughter.

granddaughter *noun* one's child's daughter.

grandee /ɡrænˈdiː/ *noun* Spanish or Portuguese noble of highest rank; great personage.

grandeur /ˈɡrændʒə/ *noun* majesty, splendour, dignity; high rank, eminence.

grandfather *noun* one's parent's father. □ **grandfather clock** clock in tall wooden case.

grandiloquent /ɡrænˈdɪləkwənt/ *adjective* pompous or inflated in language. □ **grandiloquence** *noun.*

grandiose /ˈɡrændɪəʊs/ *adjective* imposing; planned on large scale. □ **grandiosity** /-ˈɒsɪtɪ/ *noun.*

grandma *noun colloquial* grandmother.

grandmother *noun* one's parent's mother.

grandparent *noun* one's parent's parent.

Grand Prix /grã 'pri:/ *noun* any of several international motor-racing events.

grandson *noun* one's child's son.

grandstand *noun* main stand for spectators at racecourse etc.

grange /greɪndʒ/ *noun* country house with farm buildings.

granite /'grænɪt/ *noun* granular crystalline rock of quartz, mica, etc.

granny /'grænɪ/ *noun* (also **grannie**) (*plural* **-ies**) *colloquial* grandmother; (in full **granny knot**) reef-knot crossed wrong way.

grant /grɑːnt/ • *verb* consent to fulfil; allow to have; give formally, transfer legally; (often + *that*) admit, concede. • *noun* granting; thing, esp. money, granted. □ **take for granted** assume to be true, cease to appreciate through familiarity. □ **grantor** /grɑːn'tɔː/ *noun*.

granular /'grænjʊlə/ *adjective* of or like grains or granules.

granulate /'grænjʊleɪt/ *verb* (**-ting**) form into grains; roughen surface of. □ **granulation** *noun*.

granule /'grænjuːl/ *noun* small grain.

grape *noun* usually green or purple berry growing in clusters on vine. □ **grapeshot** *historical* small balls as scattering charge for cannon etc.; **grapevine** vine, means of transmission of rumour.

grapefruit /'greɪpfruːt/ *noun* (*plural* same) large round usually yellow citrus fruit.

graph /grɑːf/ • *noun* symbolic diagram representing relation between two or more variables. • *verb* plot on graph.

graphic /'græfɪk/ *adjective* of writing, drawing, etc.; vividly descriptive. □ **graphic arts** visual and technical arts involving design or lettering. □ **graphically** *adverb*.

graphics *plural noun* (usually treated as *singular*) products of graphic arts; use of diagrams in calculation and design.

graphite /'græfaɪt/ *noun* crystalline form of carbon used as lubricant, in pencils, etc.

graphology /grə'fɒlədʒɪ/ *noun* study of handwriting. □ **graphologist** *noun*.

grapnel /'græpn(ə)l/ *noun* iron-clawed instrument for dragging or grasping; small many-fluked anchor.

grapple /'græp(ə)l/ • *verb* (**-ling**) (often + *with*) fight at close quarters; (+ *with*) try to manage (problem etc.); grip with hands, come to close quarters with; seize. • *noun* hold (as) of wrestler; contest at close quarters; clutching-instrument. □ **grappling-iron**, **-hook** grapnel.

grasp /grɑːsp/ • *verb* clutch at, seize greedily; hold firmly; understand, realize. • *noun* firm hold, grip; (+ *of*) mastery, mental hold.

grasping *adjective* avaricious.

grass /grɑːs/ • *noun* (any of several) plants with bladelike leaves eaten by ruminants; pasture land; grass-covered ground; grazing; *slang* marijuana; *slang* informer. • *verb* cover with turf; *US* pasture; *slang* betray, inform police. □ **grass roots** fundamental level or source, rank and file; **grass snake** small non-poisonous snake; **grass widow, widower** person whose husband or wife is temporarily absent. □ **grassy** *adjective* (**-ier, -iest**).

grasshopper /'grɑːshɒpə/ *noun* jumping and chirping insect.

grate[1] *verb* (**-ting**) reduce to small particles by rubbing on rough surface; (often + *against, on*) rub with, utter with, or make harsh sound, have irritating effect; grind, creak. □ **grater** *noun*.

grate[2] *noun* (metal) frame holding fuel in fireplace etc.

grateful /'greɪtfʊl/ *adjective* thankful; feeling or showing gratitude. □ **gratefully** *adverb*.

gratify /'grætɪfaɪ/ *verb* (**-ies, -ied**) please, delight; indulge. □ **gratification** *noun*.

grating /'greɪtɪŋ/ *noun* framework of parallel or crossed metal bars.

gratis /'grɑːtɪs/ *adverb & adjective* free, without charge.

gratitude /'grætɪtjuːd/ *noun* being thankful.

gratuitous /grə'tjuːɪtəs/ *adjective* given or done gratis; uncalled-for, motiveless. □ **gratuitously** *adverb*; **gratuitousness** *noun*.

gratuity /grə'tjuːɪtɪ/ *noun* (*plural* **-ies**) money given for good service.

grave[1] /greɪv/ *noun* hole dug for burial of corpse; mound or monument over this; (**the grave**) death. □ **gravestone**

(usually inscribed) stone over grave; **graveyard** burial ground.

grave² /greɪv/ adjective weighty, serious; dignified, solemn; threatening. □ **gravely** adverb.

grave³ /greɪv/ verb (-ving; past participle **graven** or **graved**) (+ in, on) fix indelibly on (memory etc.); archaic engrave, carve. □ **graven image** idol.

grave⁴ /grɑːv/ noun (in full **grave accent**) mark (`) over letter indicating pronunciation.

gravel /ˈgræv(ə)l/ • noun coarse sand and small stones; formation of crystals in bladder. • verb (-ll-; US -l-) lay with gravel.

gravelly /ˈgrævəlɪ/ adjective of or like gravel; (of voice) deep and roughsounding.

gravid /ˈgrævɪd/ adjective pregnant.

gravitate /ˈgrævɪteɪt/ verb (-ting) (+ to, towards) move, be attracted, or tend by force of gravity to(wards); sink (as) by gravity.

gravitation noun attraction between each particle of matter and every other; effect of this, esp. falling of bodies to earth. □ **gravitational** adjective.

gravity /ˈgrævɪtɪ/ noun force that attracts body to centre of earth etc.; intensity of this; weight; importance, seriousness; solemnity.

gravy /ˈgreɪvɪ/ noun (plural -ies) (sauce made from) juices exuding from meat in and after cooking. □ **gravy-boat** long shallow jug for gravy; **gravy train** slang source of easy financial benefit.

gray US = GREY.

grayling noun (plural same) silver-grey freshwater fish.

graze¹ verb (-zing) feed on growing grass; pasture cattle.

graze² • verb (-zing) rub or scrape (part of body); (+ against, along, etc.) touch lightly in passing, move with such contact. • noun abrasion.

grazier /ˈgreɪzɪə/ noun person who feeds cattle for market.

grazing noun grassland suitable for pasturage.

grease /griːs/ • noun oily or fatty matter, esp. as lubricant; melted fat of dead animal. • verb (-sing) smear or lubricate with grease. □ **greasepaint** actor's make-up; **greaseproof** impervious to grease.

greasy /ˈgriːsɪ/ adjective (-ier, -iest) of, like, smeared with, or having too much grease; (of person, manner) unctuous. □ **greasiness** noun.

great /greɪt/ • adjective above average in bulk, number, extent, or intensity; important, pre-eminent; imposing, distinguished; of remarkable ability etc.; (+ at, on) competent, well-informed; colloquial very satisfactory. • noun great person or thing. □ **greatcoat** heavy overcoat; **Great Dane** dog of large short-haired breed. □ **greatness** noun.

great- /greɪt/ combining form (of family relationships) one degree more remote (great-grandfather, great-niece, etc.).

greatly adverb much.

grebe noun a diving bird.

Grecian /ˈgriːʃ(ə)n/ adjective Greek.

greed noun excessive desire, esp. for food or wealth.

greedy /ˈgriːdɪ/ adjective (-ier, -iest) showing greed; (+ for, to do) eager. □ **greedily** adverb.

Greek • noun native, national, or language of Greece. • adjective of Greece.

green • adjective coloured like grass; unripe, unseasoned; not dried, smoked, or tanned; inexperienced; jealous; (also **Green**) concerned with protection of environment, not harmful to environment. • noun green colour, paint, clothes, etc.; piece of grassy public land; grassy area for special purpose; (in plural) green vegetables; (also **Green**) supporter of protection of environment. □ **green belt** area of open land for preservation round city; **green card** motorist's international insurance document; **greenfinch** bird with greenish plumage; **green fingers** colloquial skill in gardening; **greenfly** green aphid; **greengage** round green plum; **greenhorn** novice; **green light** signal or permission to proceed; **green pound** the agreed value of the pound for payments to agricultural producers in EC; **green-room** room in theatre for actors when off stage; **greensward** grassy turf.

greenery noun green foliage.

greengrocer /ˈgriːnɡrəʊsə/ noun retailer of fruit and vegetables. □ **greengrocery** noun (plural **-ies**).

greenhouse noun structure with sides and roof mainly of glass, for rearing plants. □ **greenhouse effect** trapping of sun's warmth in earth's lower atmosphere; **greenhouse gas** gas contributing to greenhouse effect, esp. carbon dioxide.

greet verb address on meeting or arrival; receive or acknowledge in specified way; become apparent to (eye, ear, etc.).

greeting noun act or words used to greet. □ **greetings card** decorative card carrying goodwill message etc.

gregarious /grɪˈgeərɪəs/ adjective fond of company; living in flocks etc. □ **gregariousness** noun.

Gregorian calendar /grɪˈgɔːrɪən/ noun calendar introduced in 1582 by Pope Gregory XIII.

Gregorian chant /grɪˈgɔːrɪən/ noun form of plainsong named after Pope Gregory I.

gremlin /ˈgremlɪn/ noun colloquial mischievous sprite said to cause mechanical faults etc.

grenade /grɪˈneɪd/ noun small bomb thrown by hand or shot from rifle.

grenadier /grenəˈdɪə/ noun (**Grenadier**) member of first regiment of royal household infantry; historical soldier armed with grenades.

grew past of GROW.

grey /greɪ/ (US **gray**) ● adjective of colour between black and white; clouded, dull; (of hair) turning white, (of person) having grey hair; anonymous, unidentifiable; undistinguished, boring. ● noun grey colour, paint, clothes, etc.; grey horse. ● verb make or become grey. □ **grey area** indefinite situation or topic; **Grey Friar** Franciscan friar; **grey matter** darker tissues of brain, colloquial intelligence.

greyhound noun slender swift dog used in racing.

greylag noun European wild goose.

grid noun grating; system of numbered squares for map references; network of lines, electric power connections, etc.;

pattern of lines marking starting-place on motor-racing track.

griddle /ˈgrɪd(ə)l/ noun iron plate placed over heat for baking etc.

gridiron /ˈgrɪdaɪən/ noun barred metal frame for broiling or grilling; American football field.

grief /griːf/ noun (cause of) intense sorrow. □ **come to grief** meet with disaster.

grievance noun real or imagined cause for complaint.

grieve /griːv/ verb (**-ving**) (cause to) feel grief.

grievous /ˈgriːvəs/ adjective severe; causing grief; injurious; flagrant, heinous. □ **grievously** adverb.

griffin /ˈgrɪfɪn/ noun (also **gryphon** /-f(ə)n/) mythical creature with eagle's head and wings and lion's body.

griffon /ˈgrɪf(ə)n/ noun small coarsehaired terrier-like dog; large vulture; griffin.

grill ● noun device on cooker for radiating heat downwards; gridiron; grilled food; (in full **grill room**) restaurant specializing in grills. ● verb cook under grill or on gridiron; subject to or experience extreme heat; subject to severe questioning.

grille /grɪl/ noun (also **grill**) grating, latticed screen; metal grid protecting vehicle radiator.

grilse /grɪls/ noun (plural same or **-s**) young salmon that has been to the sea only once.

grim adjective (**-mm-**) of stern appearance; harsh, merciless; ghastly, joyless; unpleasant. □ **grimly** adverb; **grimness** noun.

grimace /ˈgrɪməs/ ● noun distortion of face made in disgust etc. or to amuse. ● verb (**-cing**) make grimace.

grime ● noun deeply ingrained dirt. ● verb (**-ming**) blacken, befoul. □ **grimy** adjective (**-ier**, **-iest**).

grin ● verb (**-nn-**) smile broadly. ● noun broad smile.

grind /graɪnd/ ● verb (past & past participle **ground** /graʊnd/) crush to small particles; sharpen; rub gratingly; (often + down) oppress; (often + away) work or study hard. ● noun grinding; colloquial hard dull work. □ **grindstone** thick revolving abrasive disc for grinding, sharpening, etc. □ **grinder** noun.

grip ● verb (**-pp-**) grasp tightly; take firm hold; compel attention of. ● noun firm hold, grasp; way of holding; power of holding attention; intellectual mastery; control of one's behaviour; part of machine that grips; part of weapon etc. that is gripped; hairgrip; travelling bag.

gripe ● verb (**-ping**) colloquial complain; affect with colic. ● noun (usually in plural) colic; colloquial complaint. □ **Gripe Water** proprietary term medicine to relieve colic in babies.

grisly /'grɪzlɪ/ adjective (**-ier, -iest**) causing horror, disgust, or fear.

grist noun corn for grinding. □ **grist to the mill** source of profit or advantage.

gristle /'grɪs(ə)l/ noun tough flexible tissue; cartilage. □ **gristly** adjective.

grit ● noun small particles of sand etc.; coarse sandstone; colloquial pluck, endurance. ● verb (**-tt-**) spread grit on (icy roads etc.); clench (teeth); make grating sound. □ **gritty** adjective (**-ier, -iest**).

grits plural noun coarse oatmeal; unground husked oats.

grizzle /'grɪz(ə)l/ verb (**-ling**) colloquial cry fretfully. □ **grizzly** adjective (**-ier, -iest**).

grizzled adjective grey-haired.

grizzly /'grɪzlɪ/ adjective (**-ier, -iest**) grey-haired. ● noun (plural **-ies**) (in full **grizzly bear**) large fierce N. American bear.

groan ● verb make deep sound expressing pain, grief, or disapproval; (usually + under, beneath, with) be loaded or oppressed. ● noun sound made in groaning.

groat noun historical silver coin worth 4 old pence.

groats plural noun hulled or crushed grain, esp. oats.

grocer /'grəʊsə/ noun dealer in food and household provisions.

grocery /'grəʊsərɪ/ noun (plural **-ies**) grocer's trade, shop, or (in plural) goods.

grog noun drink of spirit (originally rum) and water.

groggy /'grɒgɪ/ adjective (**-ier, -iest**) incapable, unsteady. □ **groggily** adverb.

groin¹ ● noun depression between belly and thigh; edge formed by intersecting vaults. ● verb build with groins.

groin² US = GROYNE.

grommet /'grɒmɪt/ noun eyelet placed in hole to protect or insulate rope or cable passed through it; tube passed through eardrum to middle ear.

groom /gruːm/ ● noun person employed to tend horses; bridegroom. ● verb tend (horse); give neat or attractive appearance to; prepare (person) for office or occasion etc.

groove ● noun channel, elongated hollow; spiral cut in gramophone record for needle. ● verb (**-ving**) make groove(s) in.

groovy /'gruːvɪ/ adjective (**-ier, -iest**) slang excellent; of or like a groove.

grope ● verb (**-ping**) (usually + for) feel about or search blindly; (+ for, after) search mentally; fondle clumsily for sexual pleasure; feel (one's way). ● noun act of groping.

grosgrain /'grəʊgreɪn/ noun corded fabric of silk etc.

gross /grəʊs/ ● adjective overfed, bloated; coarse, indecent; flagrant; total, not net. ● verb produce as gross profit. ● noun (plural same) 12 dozen. □ **grossly** adverb.

grotesque /grəʊ'tesk/ ● adjective comically or repulsively distorted; incongruous, absurd. ● noun decoration interweaving human and animal features; comically distorted figure or design. □ **grotesquely** adverb.

grotto /'grɒtəʊ/ noun (plural **-es** or **-s**) picturesque cave; structure imitating cave.

grotty /'grɒtɪ/ adjective (**-ier, -iest**) slang unpleasant, dirty, ugly.

grouch /graʊtʃ/ colloquial ● verb grumble. ● noun grumbler; complaint; sulky grumbling mood. □ **grouchy** adjective (**-ier, -iest**).

ground¹ /graʊnd/ ● noun surface of earth; extent of subject; (often in plural) foundation, motive; area of special kind; (in plural) enclosed land attached to house etc.; area or basis for agreement etc.; surface worked on in painting; (in plural) dregs; bottom of sea; floor of room etc. ● verb prevent from taking off or flying; run aground, strand; (+

in) instruct thoroughly; (often as **grounded** *adjective*) (+ *on*) base cause or principle on. □ **ground control** personnel directing landing etc. of aircraft etc.; **ground cover** low-growing plants; **ground floor** storey at ground level; **ground frost** frost on surface of ground; **groundnut** peanut; **ground-rent** rent for land leased for building; **groundsman** person who maintains sports ground; **ground speed** aircraft's speed relative to ground; **ground swell** heavy sea due to distant or past storm etc.; **groundwork** preliminary or basic work.

ground² *past & past participle of* GRIND.

grounding *noun* basic instruction.

groundless *adjective* without motive or foundation.

groundsel /ˈɡraʊnds(ə)l/ *noun* yellow-flowered weed.

group /ɡruːp/ ● *noun* number of people or things near, classed, or working together; number of companies under common ownership; pop group; division of air force. ● *verb* form into group; place in group(s). □ **group captain** RAF officer next below air commodore.

groupie *noun slang* ardent follower of touring pop group(s).

grouse¹ /ɡraʊs/ *noun* (*plural* same) game bird with feathered feet.

grouse² /ɡraʊs/ *verb* (**-sing**) & *noun colloquial* grumble.

grout /ɡraʊt/ ● *noun* thin fluid mortar. ● *verb* apply grout to.

grove /ɡrəʊv/ *noun* small wood; group of trees.

grovel /ˈɡrɒv(ə)l/ *verb* (**-ll-**; *US* **-l-**) behave obsequiously; lie prone.

grow /ɡrəʊ/ *verb* (*past* **grew**; *past participle* **grown**) increase in size, height, amount, etc.; develop or exist as living plant or natural product; produce by cultivation; become gradually; (+ *on*) become more favoured by; (in *passive*; + *over*) be covered with growth. □ **grown-up** adult; **grow up** mature. □ **grower** *noun*.

growl /ɡraʊl/ ● *verb* (often + *at*) make low guttural sound, usually of anger; rumble. ● *noun* growling sound; angry murmur.

grown *past participle of* GROW.

growth /ɡrəʊθ/ *noun* process of growing; increase; what has grown or is growing; tumour. □ **growth industry** one that is developing rapidly.

groyne /ɡrɔɪn/ *noun* (*US* **groin**) wall built out into sea to stop beach erosion.

grub ● *noun* larva of insect; *colloquial* food. ● *verb* (**-bb-**) dig superficially; (+ *up*, *out*) extract by digging.

grubby /ˈɡrʌbɪ/ *adjective* (**-ier**, **-iest**) dirty.

grudge ● *noun* persistent resentment or ill will. ● *verb* (**-ging**) be unwilling to give or allow, feel resentful about (doing something).

gruel /ˈɡruːəl/ *noun* liquid food of oatmeal etc. boiled in milk or water.

gruelling (*US* **grueling**) *adjective* exhausting, punishing.

gruesome /ˈɡruːsəm/ *adjective* grisly, disgusting.

gruff *adjective* rough-voiced; surly. □ **gruffly** *adverb*.

grumble /ˈɡrʌmb(ə)l/ ● *verb* (**-ling**) complain peevishly; rumble. ● *noun* complaint; rumble. □ **grumbler** *noun*.

grumpy /ˈɡrʌmpɪ/ *adjective* (**-ier**, **-iest**) ill-tempered.

grunt ● *noun* low guttural sound characteristic of pig. ● *verb* utter (with) grunt.

Gruyère /ˈɡruːjeə/ *noun* kind of Swiss cheese with holes in.

gryphon = GRIFFIN.

guano /ˈɡwɑːnəʊ/ *noun* (*plural* **-s**) excrement of seabirds, used as manure.

guarantee /ɡærənˈtiː/ ● *noun* formal promise or assurance; guaranty; giver of guaranty or security. ● *verb* (**-tees**, **-teed**) give or serve as guarantee for; promise; secure. □ **guarantor** *noun*.

guaranty /ˈɡærəntɪ/ *noun* (*plural* **-ies**) written or other undertaking to answer for performance of obligation; thing serving as security.

guard /ɡɑːd/ ● *verb* (often + *from*, *against*) defend, protect; keep watch, prevent from escaping; keep in check; (+ *against*) take precautions against. ● *noun* vigilant state; protector; soldiers etc. protecting place or person; official in charge of train; (in *plural* (usually **Guards**) household troops of monarch; device to prevent injury or accident;

defensive posture. □ **guardhouse**, **guardroom** building or room for accommodating military guard or for detaining prisoners; **guardsman** soldier in guards or Guards.

guarded /ˈguarded/ *adjective* (of remark etc.) cautious. □ **guardedly** *adverb*.

guardian /ˈgɑːdɪən/ *noun* protector, keeper; person having custody of another, esp. minor. □ **guardianship** *noun*.

guava /ˈgwɑːvə/ *noun* edible orange acid fruit; tropical tree bearing this.

gubernatorial /gjuːbənəˈtɔːrɪəl/ *adjective* US of governor.

gudgeon[1] /ˈgʌdʒ(ə)n/ *noun* small freshwater fish.

gudgeon[2] /ˈgʌdʒ(ə)n/ *noun* kind of pivot or pin; tubular part of hinge; socket for rudder.

guelder rose /ˈgeldə/ *noun* shrub with round bunches of white flowers.

Guernsey /ˈgɜːnzɪ/ *noun* (*plural* **-s**) one of breed of cattle from Guernsey; (**guernsey**) type of thick knitted woollen jersey.

guerrilla /gəˈrɪlə/ *noun* (also **guerilla**) member of one of several independent groups fighting against regular forces.

guess /ges/ ● *verb* estimate without calculation or measurement; conjecture, think likely; conjecture rightly. ● *noun* estimate, conjecture. □ **guesswork** guessing.

guest /gest/ *noun* person invited to visit another's house or have meal etc. at another's expense, or lodging at hotel etc. □ **guest house** superior boarding house.

guestimate /ˈgestɪmət/ *noun* (also **guesstimate**) estimate based on guesswork and calculation.

guffaw /gʌˈfɔː/ ● *noun* boisterous laugh. ● *verb* utter guffaw.

guidance /ˈgaɪd(ə)ns/ *noun* advice; guiding.

guide /gaɪd/ ● *noun* person who shows the way; conductor of tours; adviser; directing principle; guidebook; (**Guide**) member of girls' organization similar to Scouts. ● *verb* (**-ding**) act as guide to; lead, direct. □ **guidebook** book of information about place etc.; **guided missile** missile under remote control or directed by equipment within itself; **guide-dog** dog trained to lead blind person; **guideline** principle directing action.

Guider /ˈgaɪdə/ *noun* adult leader of Guides.

guild /gɪld/ *noun* (also **gild**) society for mutual aid or with common object; medieval association of craftsmen. □ **guildhall** meeting-place of medieval guild, town hall.

guilder /ˈgɪldə/ *noun* monetary unit of Netherlands.

guile /gaɪl/ *noun* sly behaviour; treachery, deceit. □ **guileless** *adjective*.

guillemot /ˈgɪlɪmɒt/ *noun* kind of auk.

guillotine /ˈgɪlətiːn/ ● *noun* beheading machine; machine for cutting paper; method of shortening debate in parliament by fixing time of vote. ● *verb* (**-ning**) use guillotine on.

guilt /gɪlt/ *noun* fact of having committed offence; (feeling of) culpability.

guiltless *adjective* (often + *of*) innocent.

guilty *adjective* (**-ier, -iest**) having, feeling, or causing feeling of guilt. □ **guiltily** *adverb*.

guinea /ˈgɪnɪ/ *noun* (*historical* coin worth) £1.05. □ **guinea fowl** domestic fowl with white-spotted grey plumage; **guinea pig** domesticated S. American rodent, person used in experiment.

guipure /ˈgiːpjʊə/ *noun* heavy lace of patterned pieces joined by stitches.

guise /gaɪz/ *noun* external, esp. assumed, appearance; pretence.

guitar /gɪˈtɑː/ *noun* usually 6-stringed musical instrument played with fingers or plectrum. □ **guitarist** *noun*.

gulch *noun* US ravine, gully.

gulf *noun* large area of sea with narrow-mouthed inlet; deep hollow, chasm; wide difference of opinion etc. □ **Gulf Stream** warm current from Gulf of Mexico to Europe.

gull[1] *noun* long-winged web-footed seabird.

gull[2] *verb* dupe, fool.

gullet /ˈgʌlɪt/ *noun* food-passage from mouth to stomach.

gullible /ˈgʌlɪb(ə)l/ *adjective* easily persuaded or deceived. □ **gullibility** *noun*.

gully /ˈgʌlɪ/ *noun* (*plural* **-ies**) water-worn ravine; gutter, drain; *Cricket* fielding position between point and slips.

gulp ● verb (often + *down*) swallow hastily or with effort; choke; (+ *down*, *back*) suppress. ● noun act of gulping; large mouthful.

gum¹ ● noun sticky secretion of some trees and shrubs, used as glue etc.; chewing gum; (also **gumdrop**) hard jelly sweet. ● verb (**-mm-**) (usually + *down*, *together*, etc.) fasten with gum; apply gum to. □ **gum arabic** gum exuded by some kinds of acacia; **gumboot** rubber boot; **gum tree** tree exuding gum, esp. eucalyptus; **gum up** *colloquial* interfere with, spoil.

gum² noun (usually in *plural*) firm flesh around roots of teeth. □ **gumboil** small abscess on gum.

gummy¹ /'gʌmɪ/ adjective (**-ier**, **-iest**) sticky; exuding gum.

gummy² /'gʌmɪ/ adjective (**-ier**, **-iest**) toothless.

gumption /'gʌmpʃ(ə)n/ noun *colloquial* resourcefulness, enterprise; common sense.

gun ● noun metal tube for throwing missiles with explosive propellant; starting pistol; device for discharging grease, electrons, etc., in desired direction; member of shooting party. ● verb (**-nn-**) (usually + *down*) shoot with gun; (+ *for*) seek out determinedly to attack or rebuke. □ **gunboat** small warship with heavy guns; **gun carriage** wheeled support for gun; **gun cotton** cotton steeped in acids, used as explosive; **gun dog** dog trained to retrieve game; **gunfire** firing of guns; **gunman** armed lawbreaker; **gun metal** bluish-grey colour, alloy of copper, tin, and usually zinc; **gunpowder** explosive of saltpetre, sulphur, and charcoal; **gunrunner** person selling or bringing guns into country illegally; **gunshot** shot from gun, the range of a gun; **gunslinger** *esp. US* gunman; **gunsmith** maker and repairer of small firearms.

gunge /gʌndʒ/ *colloquial* ● noun sticky substance. ● verb (**-ging**) (usually + *up*) clog with gunge. □ **gungy** adjective.

gung-ho /gʌŋ'həʊ/ adjective (arrogantly) eager.

gunner /'gʌnə/ noun artillery soldier; *Nautical* warrant officer in charge of battery, magazine, etc.; airman who operates gun.

gunnery /'gʌnərɪ/ noun construction and management, or firing, of large guns.

gunny /'gʌnɪ/ noun (*plural* **-ies**) coarse sacking usually of jute fibre; sack made of this.

gunwale /'gʌn(ə)l/ noun upper edge of ship's or boat's side.

guppy /'gʌpɪ/ noun (*plural* **-ies**) very small brightly coloured tropical freshwater fish.

gurgle /'gɜːg(ə)l/ ● verb (**-ling**) make bubbling sound as of water; utter with such sound. ● noun bubbling sound.

gurnard /'gɜːnəd/ noun (*plural* same or **-s**) sea fish with large spiny head.

guru /'goruː/ noun (*plural* **-s**) Hindu spiritual teacher; influential or revered teacher.

gush ● verb flow in sudden or copious stream; speak or behave effusively. ● noun sudden or copious stream; effusiveness.

gusher /'gʌʃə/ noun oil well emitting unpumped oil; effusive person.

gusset /'gʌsɪt/ noun piece let into garment etc. to strengthen or enlarge it.

gust ● noun sudden violent rush of wind; burst of rain, smoke, anger, etc. ● verb blow in gusts. □ **gusty** adjective (**-ier**, **-iest**).

gusto /'gʌstəʊ/ noun zest, enjoyment.

gut ● noun intestine; (in *plural*) bowels, entrails; (in *plural*) *colloquial* courage and determination; *slang* stomach; (in *plural*) contents, essence; material for violin etc. strings or for fishing line; instinctive, fundamental. ● verb (**-tt-**) remove or destroy internal fittings of (buildings); remove guts of. □ **gutless** adjective.

gutsy /'gʌtsɪ/ adjective (**-ier**, **-est**) *colloquial* courageous; greedy.

gutta-percha /gʌtə'pɜːtʃə/ noun tough plastic substance made from latex.

gutted adjective *slang* bitterly disappointed.

gutter /'gʌtə/ ● noun shallow trough below eaves, or channel at side of street, for carrying off rainwater; (**the gutter**) poor or degraded environment; channel, groove. ● verb (of candle) burn unsteadily and melt away.

guttering noun (material for) gutters.

guttersnipe noun street urchin.

guttural /'gʌtər(ə)l/ ● adjective throaty, harsh-sounding; (of sound) produced in throat. ● noun guttural consonant.

guy[1] /gaɪ/ ● noun colloquial man; effigy of Guy Fawkes burnt on 5 Nov. ● verb ridicule.

guy[2] /gaɪ/ ● noun rope or chain to secure tent or steady crane-load etc. ● verb secure with guy(s).

guzzle /'gʌz(ə)l/ verb (-ling) eat or drink greedily.

gybe /dʒaɪb/ verb (US **jibe**) (-bing) (of fore-and-aft sail or boom) swing across boat, momentarily pointing into wind; cause (sail) to do this; (of boat etc.) change course thus.

gym /dʒɪm/ noun colloquial gymnasium; gymnastics. □ **gymslip**, **gym tunic** schoolgirl's sleeveless dress.

gymkhana /dʒɪm'kɑːnə/ noun horse-riding competition.

gymnasium /dʒɪm'neɪzɪəm/ noun (plural -siums or -sia) room etc. equipped for gymnastics.

gymnast /'dʒɪmnæst/ noun expert in gymnastics.

gymnastic /dʒɪm'næstɪk/ adjective of gymnastics. □ **gymnastically** adverb.

gymnastics plural noun (also treated as singular) exercises to develop or demonstrate physical (or mental) agility.

gynaecology /gaɪnɪ'kɒlədʒɪ/ noun (US **gynecology**) science of physiological functions and diseases of women. □ **gynaecological** /-kə'lɒdʒ-/ adjective; **gynaecologist** noun.

gypsum /'dʒɪpsəm/ noun mineral used esp. to make plaster of Paris.

Gypsy /'dʒɪpsɪ/ noun (also **Gipsy**) (plural -ies) member of nomadic dark-skinned people of Europe.

gyrate /dʒaɪə'reɪt/ verb (-ting) move in circle or spiral. □ **gyration** noun; **gyratory** adjective.

gyro /'dʒaɪərəʊ/ noun (plural -s) colloquial gyroscope.

gyroscope /'dʒaɪərəskəʊp/ noun rotating wheel whose axis is free to turn but maintains fixed direction unless perturbed, esp. used for stabilization.

Hh

H abbreviation hard (pencil lead); (water) hydrant; slang heroin. □ **H-bomb** hydrogen bomb.

h. abbreviation (also **h**) hour(s); (also **h**) height; hot. □ **h. & c.** hot and cold (water).

ha[1] /hɑː/ (also **hah**) interjection expressing surprise, triumph, etc.

ha[2] abbreviation hectare(s).

habeas corpus /heɪbɪəs 'kɔːpəs/ noun writ requiring person to be brought before judge etc., esp. to investigate lawfulness of his or her detention.

haberdasher /'hæbədæʃə/ noun dealer in dress accessories and sewing goods. □ **haberdashery** noun (plural -ies).

habit /'hæbɪt/ noun settled tendency or practice; practice that is hard to give up; mental constitution or attitude; clothes, esp. of religious order.

habitable /'hæbɪtəb(ə)l/ adjective suitable for living in. □ **habitability** noun.

habitat /'hæbɪtæt/ noun natural home of plant or animal.

habitation /hæbɪ'teɪʃ(ə)n/ noun inhabiting; house, home.

habitual /hə'bɪtʃʊəl/ adjective done as a habit; usual; given to a habit. □ **habitually** adverb.

habituate /hə'bɪtʃʊeɪt/ verb (-ting) (often + to) accustom. □ **habituation** noun.

habitué /hə'bɪtʃʊeɪ/ noun (often + of) frequent visitor or resident. [French]

háček /'hætʃek/ noun mark used (ˇ) over letter to modify its sound in some languages. [Czech]

hacienda /hæsɪ'endə/ noun (in Spanish-speaking countries) plantation etc. with dwelling house.

hack[1] ● *verb* cut or chop roughly; kick shin of; (often + *at*) deal cutting blows; cut (one's way) through; *colloquial* gain unauthorized access to (computer data); *slang* manage, tolerate. ● *noun* kick with toe of boot, wound from this. □ **hacksaw** saw for cutting metal.

hack[2] ● *noun* horse for ordinary riding; hired horse; person hired to do dull routine work, esp. as writer. ● *adjective* used as hack; commonplace. ● *verb* ride on horseback on road at ordinary pace.

hacker *noun colloquial* computer enthusiast; person who gains unauthorized access to computer network.

hacking *adjective* (of cough) short, dry, and frequent.

hackle /'hæk(ə)l/ *noun* (in *plural*) hairs on animal's neck which rise when it is angry or alarmed; long feather(s) on neck of domestic cock etc.; steel flax-comb. □ **make (person's) hackles rise** arouse anger or indignation.

hackney /'hækni/ *noun* (*plural* **-s**) horse for ordinary riding. □ **hackney carriage** taxi.

hackneyed /'hæknid/ *adjective* over-used, trite.

had *past & past participle* of HAVE.

haddock /'hædək/ *noun* (*plural* same) common edible sea fish.

Hades /'heidi:z/ *noun* (in Greek mythology) the underworld.

hadj = HAJJ.

hadji = HAJJI.

hadn't /'hæd(ə)nt/ had not.

haematite /'hi:mətait/ *noun* (*US* **hem-**) red or brown iron ore.

haematology /hi:mə'tɒlədʒi/ *noun* (*US* **hem-**) study of the blood. □ **haematologist** *noun*.

haemoglobin /hi:mə'gləʊbin/ *noun* (*US* **hem-**) oxygen-carrying substance in red blood cells.

haemophilia /hi:mə'filiə/ *noun* (*US* **hem-**) hereditary tendency to severe bleeding from even a slight injury through failure of blood to clot. □ **haemophiliac** *noun*.

haemorrhage /'heməridʒ/ (*US* **hem-**) ● *noun* profuse bleeding. ● *verb* (**-ging**) suffer haemorrhage.

haemorrhoids /'heməroidz/ *plural noun* (*US* **hem-**) swollen veins near anus, piles.

haft /hɑ:ft/ *noun* handle of knife etc.

hag *noun* ugly old woman; witch. □ **hagridden** afflicted by nightmares or fears.

haggard /'hægəd/ *adjective* looking exhausted and distraught.

haggis /'hægis/ *noun* Scottish dish of offal boiled in bag with oatmeal etc.

haggle /'hæg(ə)l/ ● *verb* (**-ling**) (often + *over*, *about*) bargain persistently. ● *noun* haggling.

hagiography /hægi'ɒgrəfi/ *noun* writing about saints' lives. □ **hagiographer** *noun*.

hah = HA[1].

ha ha /hɑ:'hɑ:/ *interjection representing laughter*.

ha-ha /'hɑ:hɑ:/ *noun* ditch with wall in it bounding park or garden.

haiku /'haiku:/ *noun* (*plural* same) Japanese 3-line poem of usually 17 syllables.

hail[1] ● *noun* pellets of frozen rain; (+ *of*) barrage, onslaught. ● *verb* (after *it*) hail falls; pour down as or like hail. □ **hailstone** pellet of hail; **hailstorm** period of heavy hail.

hail[2] ● *verb* signal (taxi etc.) to stop; greet enthusiastically; (+ *from*) originate. ● *interjection archaic or jocular: expressing greeting*. ● *noun* act of hailing.

hair *noun* any or all of fine filaments growing from skin of mammals, esp. of human head; hairlike thing. □ **haircut** (style of) cutting hair; **hairdo** style of or act of styling hair; **hairdresser** person who cuts and styles hair; **hairdressing** *noun*; **hair-drier**, **-dryer** device for drying hair with warm air; **hairgrip** flat hairpin with ends close together; **hairline** edge of person's hair on forehead, very narrow crack or line; **hairnet** piece of netting for confining hair; **hair of the dog** further alcoholic drink taken to cure effects of previous drinking; **hairpiece** false hair augmenting person's natural hair; **hairpin** U-shaped pin for fastening the hair; **hairpin bend** U-shaped bend in road; **hair-raising** terrifying; **hair's breadth** minute distance; **hair shirt** ascetic's or penitent's shirt made of hair; **hair-**

slide clip for keeping hair in position; **hair-splitting** quibbling; **hairspray** liquid sprayed on hair to keep it in place; **hairspring** fine spring regulating balance-wheel of watch; **hairstyle** particular way of arranging hair; **hairstylist** *noun*; **hair-trigger** trigger acting on very slight pressure. □ **hairless** *adjective*; **hairy** *adjective* (**-ier, -iest**).

hajj /hædʒ/ *noun* (also **hadj**) Islamic pilgrimage to Mecca.

hajji /ˈhædʒɪ/ *noun* (also **hadji**) (*plural* **-s**) Muslim who has made pilgrimage to Mecca.

haka /ˈhɑːkə/ *noun NZ* Maori ceremonial war dance; similar dance by sports team before match.

hake *noun* (*plural* same) codlike sea fish.

halal /hɑːˈlɑːl/ *noun* (also **hallal**) meat from animal killed according to Muslim law.

halberd /ˈhælbəd/ *noun historical* combined spear and battleaxe.

halcyon /ˈhælsɪən/ *adjective* calm, peaceful, happy.

hale *adjective* strong and healthy (esp. in **hale and hearty**).

half /hɑːf/ ● *noun* (*plural* **halves** /hɑːvz/) either of two (esp. equal) parts into which a thing is divided; *colloquial* half pint, esp. of beer; *Sport* either of two equal periods of play, half-back; half-price (esp. child's) ticket. ● *adjective* forming a half. ● *adverb* partly. □ **half and half** being half one thing and half another; **half-back** player between forwards and full back(s) in football etc.; **half-baked** not thoroughly thought out; **half board** provision of bed, breakfast, and one main meal; **half-brother, -sister** one having only one parent in common; **half-crown** *historical* coin worth 2 shillings and 6 pence (= 12½p); **half-dozen** (about) six; **half-hearted** lacking courage or zeal; **halfheartedly** *adverb*; **half holiday** half day as holiday; **half-hour, half an hour** 30 minutes, point of time 30 minutes after any hour o'clock; **half-hourly** *adjective & adverb*; **half-life** time after which radioactivity etc. is half its original value; **half-mast** position of flag halfway down mast as symbol of mourning; **half measures** unsatisfactory com-

promise etc.; **half-moon** (shape of) moon with disc half illuminated; **half nelson** see NELSON; **half-term** short holiday halfway through school term; **half-timbered** having walls with timber frame and brick or plaster filling; **half-time** (short break at) mid-point of game or contest; **halftone** photograph representing tones by large or small dots; **half-truth** statement that conveys only part of truth; **half-volley** playing of ball as soon as it bounces off ground; **halfwit** stupid person; **halfwitted** *adjective*.

halfpenny /ˈheɪpnɪ/ *noun* (*plural* **-pennies** or **-pence** /ˈheɪpəns/) *historical* coin worth half penny (withdrawn in 1984).

halfway ● *adverb* at a point midway between two others; to some extent. ● *adjective* situated halfway. □ **halfway house** compromise, halfway point, rehabilitation centre, inn etc. between two towns.

halibut /ˈhælɪbət/ *noun* (*plural* same) large flatfish.

halitosis /hælɪˈtəʊsɪs/ *noun* bad breath.

hall /hɔːl/ *noun* entrance area of house; large room or building for meetings, concerts, etc.; large country house or estate; (in full **hall of residence**) residence for students; college dining-room; large public room; *esp. US* corridor. □ **hallmark** mark used to show standard of gold, silver, and platinum, distinctive feature; **hallway** entrance hall or corridor.

hallal = HALAL.

hallelujah = ALLELUIA.

hallo = HELLO.

hallow /ˈhæləʊ/ *verb* (usually as **hallowed** *adjective*) make or honour as holy.

Hallowe'en /hæləʊˈiːn/ *noun* eve of All Saints' Day, 31 Oct.

hallucinate /həˈluːsɪneɪt/ *verb* (**-ting**) experience hallucinations.

hallucination *noun* illusion of seeing or hearing something not actually present. □ **hallucinatory** /həˈluːsɪnətərɪ/ *adjective*.

hallucinogen /həˈluːsɪnədʒ(ə)n/ *noun* drug causing hallucinations. □ **hallucinogenic** /-ˈdʒen-/ *adjective*.

halm = HAULM.

halo /ˈheɪləʊ/ ● *noun* (*plural* **-es**) disc of light shown round head of sacred person; glory associated with idealized person; circle of light round sun or moon etc. ● *verb* (**-es**, **-ed**) surround with halo.

halogen /ˈhælədʒ(ə)n/ *noun* any of the non-metallic elements (fluorine, chlorine, etc.) which form a salt when combined with a metal.

halon /ˈheɪlon/ *noun* gaseous halogen compound used to extinguish fires.

halt¹ /hɔːlt/ ● *noun* stop (usually temporary); minor stopping place on local railway line. ● *verb* (cause to) make a halt.

halt² /hɔːlt/ ● *verb* (esp. as **halting** *adjective*) proceed hesitantly. □ **haltingly** *adverb*.

halter /ˈhɔːltə/ *noun* rope with headstall for leading or tying up horses etc.; strap passing round back of neck holding dress etc. up, (also **halterneck**) dress etc. held by this.

halva /ˈhælvə/ *noun* confection of sesame flour, honey, etc.

halve /hɑːv/ *verb* (**-ving**) divide into halves; reduce to half.

halves *plural* of HALF.

halyard /ˈhæljəd/ *noun* rope or tackle for raising and lowering sail etc.

ham ● *noun* upper part of pig's leg cured for food; back of thigh; thigh and buttock; *colloquial* inexpert or unsubtle performer or actor; *colloquial* operator of amateur radio station. ● *verb* (**-mm-**) (usually in **ham it up**) *colloquial* overact. □ **ham-fisted**, **-handed** *colloquial* clumsy.

hamburger /ˈhæmbɜːgə/ *noun* cake of minced beef, usually eaten in soft bread roll.

hamlet /ˈhæmlɪt/ *noun* small village, esp. without church.

hammer /ˈhæmə/ ● *noun* tool with heavy metal head at right angles to handle, used for driving nails etc.; similar device, as for exploding charge in gun, striking strings of piano, etc.; auctioneer's mallet; metal ball attached to a wire for throwing as athletic contest. ● *verb* strike or drive (as) with hammer; *colloquial* defeat utterly. □ **hammer and tongs** *colloquial* with great energy;

hammerhead shark with flattened hammer-shaped head; **hammerlock** wrestling hold in which twisted arm is bent behind back; **hammer-toe** toe bent permanently downwards. □ **hammering** *noun*.

hammock /ˈhæmək/ *noun* bed of canvas or netting suspended by cords at ends.

hamper¹ /ˈhæmpə/ *noun* large basket, usually with hinged lid and containing food.

hamper² /ˈhæmpə/ *verb* obstruct movement of; hinder.

hamster /ˈhæmstə/ *noun* short-tailed mouselike rodent often kept as pet.

hamstring ● *noun* any of 5 tendons at back of human knee; (in quadruped) tendon at back of hock. ● *verb* (*past & past participle* **-strung** or **-stringed**) cripple by cutting hamstrings; impair efficiency of.

hand ● *noun* end part of human arm beyond wrist; similar member of monkey; (often in *plural*) control, disposal, agency; share in action, active support; handlike thing, esp. pointer of clock etc.; right or left side, direction, etc.; skill or style, esp. of writing; person who does or makes something; person etc. as source; manual worker in factory etc.; pledge of marriage; playing cards dealt to player, round or game of cards; *colloquial* round of applause; measure of horse's height, = 4 in. (10.16 cm). ● *verb* (+ *in, to, over, round,* etc.) deliver or transfer (as) with hand. □ **at hand** close by; **by hand** by person not machine, not by post; **handbag** small bag carried esp. by woman; **handball** game with ball thrown by hand, *Football* foul touching of ball; **handbell** small bell for ringing by hand; **handbook** short manual or guidebook; **handbrake** brake operated by hand; **handcuff** secure (prisoner) with **handcuffs**, pair of lockable metal rings joined by short chain; **handgun** small firearm held in one hand; **handhold** something for hand to grip; **hand in glove** in collusion; **handmade** made by hand (rather than machine); **hand-me-down** article passed on from another person; **handout** thing given to needy person, information etc. distributed to press etc., notes given out in class; **handover** act of handing over; **hand-over-fist** *colloquial* with rapid progress; **hand-picked** carefully chosen; **handrail** rail along edge of stairs etc.; **hands down** without effort; **handset** part of telephone held in hand; **handshake** clasping of person's hand, esp. as greeting etc.; **hands-on** practical rather than theoretical; **handstand** act of supporting oneself vertically on one's hands; **hand-to-hand** (of fighting) at close quarters; **handwriting** (style of) writing by hand; **take in hand** start doing or dealing with, undertake control or reform of; **to hand** within reach.

handful *noun* (*plural* -**s**) enough to fill the hand; small number or quantity; *colloquial* troublesome person or task.

handicap /ˈhændɪkæp/ ● *noun* physical or mental disability; thing that makes progress difficult; disadvantage imposed on superior competitor to equalize chances; race etc. in which this is imposed. ● *verb* (-**pp-**) impose handicap on; place at disadvantage.

handicapped *adjective* suffering from physical or mental disability.

handicraft /ˈhændɪkrɑːft/ *noun* work requiring manual and artistic skill.

handiwork /ˈhændɪwɜːk/ *noun* work done or thing made by hand, or by particular person.

handkerchief /ˈhæŋkətʃɪf/ *noun* (*plural* -**s** or -**chieves** /-tʃiːvz/) square of cloth used to wipe nose etc.

handle /ˈhænd(ə)l/ ● *noun* part by which thing is held. ● *verb* (-**ling**) touch, feel, operate, etc. with hands; manage, deal with; deal in (goods etc.). □ **handlebar** (usually in *plural*) steering-bar of bicycle etc.

handler *noun* person in charge of trained dog etc.

handsome /ˈhænsəm/ *adjective* (-**r**, -**st**) good-looking; imposing; generous; considerable. □ **handsomely** *adverb*.

handy *adjective* (-**ier**, -**iest**) convenient to handle; ready to hand; clever with hands. □ **handyman** person able to do odd jobs.

hang ● *verb* (*past & past participle* **hung** except as below) (cause to) be supported from above; attach by suspending from top; set up on hinges etc.; place (picture) on wall or in exhibition; attach (wallpaper); (*past & past participle* **hanged**) suspend or be suspended by neck, esp. as capital punishment; let droop; remain or be hung. ● *noun* way thing hangs. □ **get the hang of** *colloquial* get knack of, understand; **hang about, around** loiter, not move away; **hangdog** shamefaced; **hang fire** delay acting; **hang-glider** fabric wing on light frame from which pilot is suspended; **hang-gliding** *noun*; **hangman** executioner by hanging; **hangnail** agnail; **hang on** (often + *to*) continue to hold, retain, wait for short time, not ring off during pause in telephoning; **hangover** after-effects of excess of alcohol; **hang up** *verb* hang from hook etc., end telephone conversation; **hang-up** *noun* *slang* emotional inhibition.

hangar /ˈhæŋə/ *noun* building for housing aircraft etc.

hanger *noun* person or thing that hangs; (in full **coat-hanger**) shaped piece of wood etc. for hanging clothes on. □ **hanger-on** (*plural* **hangers-on**) follower, dependant.

hanging *noun* execution by suspending by neck; (usually in *plural*) drapery for walls etc.

hank *noun* coil of yarn etc.

hanker /ˈhæŋkə/ *verb* (+ *for, after, to do*) crave, long for. □ **hankering** *noun*.

hanky /ˈhæŋkɪ/ *noun* (also **hankie**) (*plural* -**ies**) *colloquial* handkerchief.

hanky-panky /ˈhæŋkɪˈpæŋkɪ/ *noun* *slang* misbehaviour; trickery.

Hansard /ˈhænsɑːd/ *noun* verbatim record of parliamentary debates.

hansom /ˈhænsəm/ *noun* (in full **hansom cab**) *historical* two-wheeled horse-drawn cab.

haphazard /hæpˈhæzəd/ *adjective* casual, random. □ **haphazardly** *adverb*.

hapless /ˈhæplɪs/ *adjective* unlucky.

happen /ˈhæpən/ *verb* occur; (+ *to do*) have the (good or bad) fortune; (+ *to*) be fate or experience of; (+ *on*) come by chance on. □ **happening** *noun*.

happy /ˈhæpɪ/ *adjective* (-**ier**, -**iest**) feeling or showing pleasure or contentment; fortunate; apt, pleasing. □ **happy-go-lucky** taking things cheerfully as they happen; **happy hour** time of day when drinks are sold at reduced prices; **happy medium** compromise. □ **happily** *adverb*; **happiness** *noun*.

hara-kiri /hærə'kırı/ *noun historical* Japanese suicide by ritual disembowelling.

harangue /hə'ræŋ/ ●*noun* lengthy and earnest speech. ●*verb* (**-guing**) make harangue to.

harass /'hærəs/ *verb* trouble, annoy; attack repeatedly. □ **harassment** *noun*.

■ Usage *Harass* is often pronounced /hə'ræs/ (with the stress on the *-rass*), but this is considered incorrect by some people.

harbinger /'hɑːbɪndʒə/ *noun* person or thing announcing another's approach, forerunner.

harbour /'hɑːbə/ (*US* **harbor**) ●*noun* place of shelter for ships; shelter. ●*verb* give shelter to; entertain (thoughts etc.).

hard ●*adjective* firm, solid; difficult to bear, do, or understand; unfeeling, harsh, severe; strenuous, enthusiastic; *Politics* extreme, radical; (of drinks) strongly alcoholic; (of drug) potent and addictive; (of water) difficult to lather; (of currency etc.) not likely to fall in value; not disputable. ●*adverb* strenuously, severely, intensely. □ **hard and fast** (of rule etc.) strict; **hardback** (book) bound in stiff covers; **hardbitten** *colloquial* tough, cynical; **hardboard** stiff board of compressed wood pulp; **hard-boiled** (of eggs) boiled until yolk and white are solid, (of person) tough, shrewd; **hard cash** coins and banknotes, not cheques etc.; **hard copy** printed material produced by computer; **hardcore** stones, rubble, etc. as foundation; **hard core** central or most enduring part; **hard disk** *Computing* rigid storage disk, esp. fixed in computer; **hard-done-by** unfairly treated; **hard-headed** practical, not sentimental; **hard-hearted** unfeeling; **hard line** firm adherence to policy; **hardliner** *noun*; **hard-nosed** *colloquial* realistic, uncompromising; **hard of hearing** somewhat deaf; **hard-pressed** closely pursued, burdened with urgent business; **hard sell** aggressive salesmanship; **hard shoulder** strip at side of motorway for emergency stops; **hard up** short of money; **hardware** tools,

weapons, machinery, etc., mechanical and electronic components of computer; **hardwood** wood of deciduous tree. □ **hardness** *noun*.

harden *verb* make or become hard or unyielding.

hardihood /'hɑːdɪhʊd/ *noun* boldness.

hardly *adverb* scarcely; with difficulty.

hardship *noun* severe suffering or privation.

hardy /'hɑːdɪ/ *adjective* (**-ier, -iest**) robust; capable of endurance; (of plant) able to grow in the open all year. □ **hardiness** *noun*.

hare /heə/ ●*noun* mammal like large rabbit, with long ears, short tail, and long hind legs. ●*verb* (**-ring**) run rapidly. □ **hare-brained** rash, wild.

harebell *noun* plant with pale blue bell-shaped flowers.

harem /'hɑːriːm/ *noun* women of Muslim household; their quarters.

haricot /'hærɪkəʊ/ *noun* (in full **haricot bean**) French bean with small white seeds; these as vegetable.

hark *verb* (usually in *imperative*) *archaic* listen. □ **hark back** revert to earlier topic.

Harlequin /'hɑːlɪkwɪn/ ●*noun* masked pantomime character in diamond-patterned costume. ●*adjective* (**harlequin**) in varied colours.

harlot /'hɑːlət/ *noun archaic* prostitute.

harm *noun & verb* damage, hurt.

harmful *adjective* causing or likely to cause harm. □ **harmfully** *adverb*.

harmless *adjective* not able or likely to harm. □ **harmlessly** *adverb*.

harmonic /hɑː'mɒnɪk/ ●*adjective* of or relating to harmony; harmonious. ●*noun Music* overtone accompanying (and forming a note with) a fundamental at a fixed interval.

harmonica /hɑː'mɒnɪkə/ *noun* small rectangular instrument played by blowing and sucking air through it.

harmonious /hɑː'məʊnɪəs/ *adjective* sweet-sounding, tuneful; forming a pleasant or consistent whole; free from dissent. □ **harmoniously** *adverb*.

harmonium /hɑː'məʊnɪəm/ *noun* keyboard instrument with bellows and metal reeds.

harmonize /ˈhɑːmənaɪz/ *verb* (also **-ise**) (**-zing** or **-sing**) add notes to (melody) to produce harmony; bring into or be in harmony. □ **harmonization** *noun*.

harmony /ˈhɑːmənɪ/ *noun* (*plural* **-ies**) combination of notes to form chords; melodious sound; agreement, concord.

harness /ˈhɑːnɪs/ ● *noun* straps etc. by which horse is fastened to cart etc. and controlled; similar arrangement for fastening thing to person. ● *verb* put harness on; utilize (natural forces), esp. to produce energy.

harp ● *noun* large upright stringed instrument plucked with fingers. ● *verb* (+ *on*, *on about*) dwell on tediously. □ **harpist** *noun*.

harpoon /hɑːˈpuːn/ ● *noun* spearlike missile for shooting whales etc. ● *verb* spear with harpoon.

harpsichord /ˈhɑːpsɪkɔːd/ *noun* keyboard instrument with strings plucked mechanically. □ **harpsichordist** *noun*.

harpy /ˈhɑːpɪ/ *noun* (*plural* **-ies**) mythological monster with woman's face and bird's wings and claws; grasping unscrupulous person.

harridan /ˈhærɪd(ə)n/ *noun* bad-tempered old woman.

harrier /ˈhærɪə/ *noun* hound used in hunting hares; kind of falcon.

harrow /ˈhærəʊ/ ● *noun* frame with metal teeth or discs for breaking clods of earth. ● *verb* draw harrow over; (usually as **harrowing** *adjective*) distress greatly.

harry /ˈhærɪ/ *verb* (**-ies**, **-ied**) ravage, despoil; harass.

harsh *adjective* rough to hear, taste, etc.; severe, cruel. □ **harshly** *adverb*; **harshness** *noun*.

hart *noun* (*plural* same or **-s**) male of (esp. red) deer.

hartebeest /ˈhɑːtɪbiːst/ *noun* large African antelope with curved horns.

harum-scarum /ˌheərəmˈskeərəm/ *adjective colloquial* reckless, wild.

harvest /ˈhɑːvɪst/ ● *noun* gathering in of crops etc.; season for this; season's yield; product of any action. ● *verb* reap and gather in.

harvester *noun* reaper, reaping machine.

has *3rd singular present* of HAVE.

hash[1] ● *noun* dish of reheated pieces of cooked meat; mixture, jumble; recycled material. ● *verb* (often + *up*) recycle (old material). □ **make a hash of** *colloquial* make a mess of, bungle.

hash[2] *noun colloquial* hashish.

hashish /ˈhæʃɪʃ/ *noun* narcotic drug got from hemp.

hasn't /ˈhæz(ə)nt/ has not.

hasp /hɑːsp/ *noun* hinged metal clasp passing over staple and secured by padlock.

hassle /ˈhæs(ə)l/ *colloquial* ● *noun* trouble, problem; argument. ● *verb* (**-ling**) harass.

hassock /ˈhæsək/ *noun* kneeling-cushion.

haste /heɪst/ *noun* urgency of movement; hurry. □ **make haste** be quick.

hasten /ˈheɪs(ə)n/ *verb* (cause to) proceed or go quickly.

hasty /ˈheɪstɪ/ *adjective* (**-ier**, **-iest**) hurried; said, made, or done too quickly. □ **hastily** *adverb*; **hastiness** *noun*.

hat *noun* (esp. outdoor) head-covering. □ **hat trick** *Cricket* taking 3 wickets with successive balls, *Football* scoring of 3 goals in one match by same player, 3 consecutive successes.

hatch[1] *noun* opening in wall between kitchen and dining-room for serving food; opening or door in aircraft etc.; (cover for) hatchway. □ **hatchback** car with rear door hinged at top; **hatchway** opening in ship's deck for lowering cargo.

hatch[2] ● *verb* (often + *out*) emerge from egg; (of egg) produce young animal; incubate; (also + *up*) devise (plot). ● *noun* hatching; brood hatched.

hatch[3] *verb* mark with parallel lines. □ **hatching** *noun*.

hatchet /ˈhætʃɪt/ *noun* light short axe.

hate ● *verb* (**-ting**) dislike intensely. ● *noun* hatred.

hateful *adjective* arousing hatred.

hatred /ˈheɪtrɪd/ *noun* intense dislike; ill will.

hatter *noun* maker or seller of hats.

haughty /ˈhɔːtɪ/ *adjective* (**-ier**, **-iest**) proud, arrogant. □ **haughtily** *adverb*; **haughtiness** *noun*.

haul /hɔːl/ ● *verb* pull or drag forcibly; transport by lorry, cart, etc. ● *noun* hauling; amount gained or acquired; distance to be traversed.

haulage *noun* (charge for) commercial transport of goods.

haulier /ˈhɔːlɪə/ *noun* person or firm engaged in transport of goods.

haulm /hɔːm/ *noun* (also **halm**) stalk or stem; stalks of beans, peas, potatoes, etc. collectively.

haunch /hɔːntʃ/ *noun* fleshy part of buttock and thigh; leg and loin of deer etc. as food.

haunt /hɔːnt/ ● *verb* (of ghost etc.) visit regularly; frequent (place); linger in mind of. ● *noun* place frequented by person.

haunting *adjective* (of memory, melody, etc.) lingering; poignant, evocative.

haute couture /əʊt kuːˈtjʊə/ *noun* (world of) high fashion.

hauteur /əʊˈtɜː/ *noun* haughtiness.

have /hæv/ ● *verb* (**having;** *3rd singular present* **has** /hæz/; *past & past participle* **had**) *used as auxiliary verb with past participle to form past tenses;* hold in possession or relationship, be provided with; contain as part or quality; experience; (come to) be subjected to a specified state; engage in; tolerate, permit to; give birth to; receive; obtain or know (qualification, language, etc.); *colloquial* get the better of, (usually in *passive*) cheat. ● *noun* (usually in *plural*) *colloquial* wealthy person; *slang* swindle. □ **have on** wear (clothes), have (engagement), *colloquial* hoax; **have-not** (usually in *plural*) person lacking wealth; **have to** be obliged to, must.

haven /ˈheɪv(ə)n/ *noun* refuge; harbour.

haven't /ˈhæv(ə)nt/ have not.

haver /ˈheɪvə/ *verb* hesitate; talk foolishly.

haversack /ˈhævəsæk/ *noun* canvas bag carried on back or over shoulder.

havoc /ˈhævək/ *noun* devastation, confusion.

haw *noun* hawthorn berry.

hawk[1] ● *noun* bird of prey with rounded wings; *Politics* person who advocates aggressive policy. ● *verb* hunt with hawk.

hawk[2] *verb* carry (goods) about for sale.

hawk[3] *verb* clear throat noisily; (+ *up*) bring (phlegm etc.) up thus.

hawker *noun* person who hawks goods.

hawser /ˈhɔːzə/ *noun* thick rope or cable for mooring ship.

hawthorn *noun* thorny shrub with red berries.

hay *noun* grass mown and dried for fodder. □ **haycock** conical heap of hay; **hay fever** allergic irritation of nose, throat, etc. caused by pollen, dust, etc.; **haymaking** mowing grass and spreading it to dry; **hayrick**, **haystack** packed pile of hay; **haywire** *colloquial* badly disorganized, out of control.

hazard /ˈhæzəd/ ● *noun* danger, risk; obstacle on golf course. ● *verb* venture on (guess etc.); risk.

hazardous *adjective* risky.

haze *noun* slight mist; mental obscurity, confusion.

hazel /ˈheɪz(ə)l/ *noun* nut-bearing hedgerow shrub; greenish-brown. □ **hazelnut** nut of hazel.

hazy *adjective* (**-ier, -iest**) misty; vague; confused. □ **hazily** *adverb*; **haziness** *noun*.

HB *abbreviation* hard black (pencil lead).

HE *abbreviation* His or Her Excellency; high explosive.

he /hiː/ *pronoun* (as subject of verb) the male person or animal in question; person of unspecified sex. □ **he-man** masterful or virile man.

head /hed/ ● *noun* uppermost part of human body, or foremost part of body of animal, containing brain, sense organs, etc.; seat of intellect; thing like head in form or position; top, front, or upper end; person in charge, esp. of school; position of command; individual as unit; side of coin bearing image of head, (in *plural*) this as call when tossing coin; signal-converting device on tape recorder etc.; foam on top of beer etc.; confined body of water or steam, pressure exerted by this; (usually in **come to a head**) climax, crisis. ● *verb* be at front or in charge of; (often + *for*) move or send in specified direction; provide with heading; *Football* strike (ball) with head. □ **headache** continuous pain in head, *colloquial* troublesome problem; **headachy** *adjective*; **headband** band worn round head as decoration or to confine hair; **headboard** upright panel at head of bed; **headcount** (counting of) total number of people; **headdress** (esp. ornamental) covering for head; **headhunting** collecting of enemies' heads as trophies, seeking of staff by approaching people employed elsewhere; **headlamp**, **headlight** (main) light at front of vehicle; **headline** heading at top of page, newspaper article, etc., (in *plural*) summary of broadcast news; **headlock** wrestling hold round opponent's head; **headlong** with head foremost, in a rush; **headman** tribal chief; **headmaster**, **headmistress** head teacher; **head-on** (of collision etc.) with front foremost; **headphones** pair of earphones fitting over head; **headquarters** (treated as *singular* or *plural*) organization's administrative centre; **headroom** overhead space; **headset** headphones, often with microphone; **headshrinker** *slang* psychiatrist; **headstall** part of bridle or halter fitting round horse's head; **head start** advantage granted or gained at early stage; **headstone** stone set up at head of grave; **headstrong** self-willed; **head teacher** teacher in charge of school; **headway** progress; **head wind** one blowing from directly in front.

header *noun* Football act of heading ball; *colloquial* headlong dive or plunge.

heading *noun* title at head of page etc.

heady *adjective* (**-ier, -iest**) (of liquor etc.) potent; exciting, intoxicating; impetuous; headachy.

heal *verb* (often + *up*) become healthy again; cure; put right (differences). □ **healer** *noun*.

health /helθ/ *noun* state of being well in body or mind; mental or physical condition. □ **health centre** building containing local medical services; **health food** natural food, thought to promote good health; **health service** public medical service; **health visitor** nurse who visits mothers and babies, the elderly, etc. at home.

healthy *adjective* (**-ier, -iest**) having, conducive to, or indicative of, good health. □ **healthily** *adverb*; **healthiness** *noun*.

heap ● *noun* disorderly pile; (esp. in *plural*) *colloquial* large number or amount; *slang* dilapidated vehicle. ● *verb* (+ *up, together*, etc.) pile or collect in heap; (+ *with*) load copiously with; (+ *on, upon*) offer copiously.

hear *verb* (*past & past participle* **heard** /hɜːd/) perceive with ear; listen to; listen judicially to; be informed; (+ *from*) receive message etc. from. □ **hearsay** rumour, gossip. □ **hearer** *noun*.

hearing *noun* faculty of perceiving sounds; range within which sounds may be heard; opportunity to state one's case; trial of case before court. □ **hearing-aid** small sound-amplifier worn by partially deaf person.

hearse /hɜːs/ *noun* vehicle for carrying coffin.

heart /hɑːt/ *noun* organ in body keeping up circulation of blood by contraction and dilation; region of heart, breast; seat of thought, feeling, or emotion (esp. love); courage; mood; central or innermost part, essence; tender inner part of vegetable etc.; (conventionally) heart-shaped thing; playing card of suit marked with red hearts. □ **at heart** in inmost feelings; **by heart** from memory; **have the heart** (usually in negative, + *to do*) be hard-hearted enough; **heartache** mental anguish; **heart attack** sudden heart failure; **heartbeat** pulsation of heart; **heartbreak** overwhelming distress; **heartbreaking** *adjective*; **heartbroken** *adjective*; **heartburn** burning sensation in chest from indigestion; **heartfelt** sincere; **heart-rending** very distressing; **heartsick** despondent; **heartstrings** deepest affections or pity; **heartthrob** *colloquial* object of (esp. immature) romantic feelings; **heart-to-heart** frank (talk); **heart-warming** emotionally moving and encouraging; **take to heart** be much affected by.

hearten *verb* make or become more cheerful. □ **heartening** *adjective*.

hearth /hɑːθ/ *noun* floor of fireplace. □ **hearthrug** rug laid before fireplace.

heartless *adjective* unfeeling, pitiless. □ **heartlessly** *adverb*.

hearty *adjective* (**-ier, -iest**) strong, vigorous; (of meal or appetite) large; warm, friendly. □ **heartily** *adverb*; **heartiness** *noun*.

heat ● *noun* condition or sensation of being hot; energy arising from motion of molecules; hot weather; warmth of feeling; anger; most intense part or period of activity; preliminary contest, winner(s) of which compete in final. ● *verb* make or become hot; inflame. □ **heatproof** able to resist great heat; **heatwave** period of very hot weather; **on heat** (of female animals) sexually receptive.

heated *adjective* angry, impassioned. □ **heatedly** *adverb*.

heater *noun* device for heating room, water, etc.

heath /hi:θ/ *noun* flattish tract of uncultivated land with low shrubs; plant growing on heath, esp. heather.

heathen /'hi:ð(ə)n/ ● *noun* person not belonging to predominant religion. ● *adjective* of heathens; having no religion.

heather /'heðə/ *noun* purple-flowered plant of moors and heaths.

heating *noun* equipment used to heat building.

heave ● *verb* (**-ving**; *past & past participle* **heaved** or *esp. Nautical* **hove** /həʊv/) lift, haul, or utter with effort; *colloquial* throw; rise and fall periodically; *Nautical* haul by rope; retch. ● *noun* heaving. □ **heave in sight** come into view; **heave to** bring vessel to standstill.

heaven /'hev(ə)n/ *noun* home of God and of blessed after death; place or state of bliss, delightful thing; (**the heavens**) sky as seen from earth. □ **heavenly** *adjective*.

heavy /'hevɪ/ ● *adjective* (**-ier**, **-iest**) of great weight, difficult to lift; of great density; abundant; severe, extensive; striking or falling with force; (of machinery etc.) very large of its kind; needing much physical effort; hard to digest; hard to read or understand; (of ground) difficult to travel over; dull, tedious, oppressive; coarse, ungraceful. ● *noun* (*plural* **-ies**) *colloquial* thug (esp. hired); villain. □ **heavy-duty** designed to withstand hard use; **heavy-handed** clumsy, oppressive; **heavy hydrogen** deuterium; **heavy industry** that concerned with production of metal and machines etc.; **heavy metal** *colloquial* loud rock music with pounding rhythm; **heavy water** water composed of deuterium and oxygen; **heavyweight** amateur boxing weight (over 81 kg). □ **heavily** *adverb*; **heaviness** *noun*.

Hebraic /hi:'breɪɪk/ *adjective* of Hebrew or the Hebrews.

Hebrew /'hi:bru:/ ● *noun* member of a Semitic people in ancient Palestine; their language; modern form of this, used esp. in Israel. ● *adjective* of or in Hebrew; of the Jews.

heckle /'hek(ə)l/ ● *verb* (**-ling**) interrupt or harass (speaker). ● *noun* act of heckling. □ **heckler** *noun*.

hectare /'hekteə/ *noun* metric unit of square measure (2.471 acres).

hectic /'hektɪk/ *adjective* busy and confused; excited; feverish. □ **hectically** *adverb*.

hecto- /'hektəʊ/ *combining form* one hundred.

hector /'hektə/ *verb* bluster, bully. □ **hectoring** *adjective*.

he'd /hi:d/ he had; he would.

hedge ● *noun* fence of bushes or low trees; protection against possible loss. ● *verb* (**-ging**) surround with hedge; (+ *in*) enclose; secure oneself against loss on (bet etc.); avoid committing oneself. □ **hedgehog** small spiny insect-eating mammal; **hedge-hop** fly at low altitude; **hedgerow** row of bushes forming hedge; **hedge sparrow** common brown-backed bird.

hedonism /'hi:dənɪz(ə)m/ *noun* (behaviour based on) belief in pleasure as humankind's proper aim. □ **hedonist** *noun*; **hedonistic** /-'nɪs-/ *adjective*.

heed ● *verb* attend to; take notice of. ● *noun* care, attention. □ **heedless** *adjective*; **heedlessly** *adverb*.

hee-haw /'hi:hɔ:/ *noun & verb* bray.

heel[1] ● *noun* back of foot below ankle; part of sock etc. covering this, or of shoe etc. supporting it; crust end of loaf; *colloquial* scoundrel; (as *interjection* command to dog to walk near owner's heel. ● *verb* fit or renew heel on (shoe); touch ground with heel; (+ *out*) *Rugby* pass ball with heel. □ **cool, kick one's heels** be kept waiting; **heelball** shoemaker's polishing mixture of wax etc., esp. used in brass rubbing.

heel[2] • *verb* (often + *over*) (of ship etc.) lean over; cause (ship) to do this. • *noun* heeling.

hefty /'heftı/ *adjective* (**-ier**, **-iest**) (of person) big, strong; (of thing) heavy, powerful.

hegemony /hɪ'gemənɪ/ *noun* leadership.

heifer /'hefə/ *noun* young cow, esp. one that has not had more than one calf.

height /haɪt/ *noun* measurement from base to top; elevation above ground or other level; high point; top; extreme example.

heighten *verb* make or become higher or more intense.

heinous /'heɪnəs/ *adjective* atrocious.

heir /eə/ *noun* (*feminine* **heiress**) person entitled to property or rank as legal successor of former holder. □ **heir apparent** one whose claim cannot be superseded by birth of nearer heir; **heirloom** piece of property that has been in family for generations; **heir presumptive** one whose claim may be superseded by birth of nearer heir.

held *past & past participle of* HOLD[1].

helical /'helɪk(ə)l/ *adjective* spiral.

helices *plural of* HELIX.

helicopter /'helɪkɒptə/ *noun* wingless aircraft lifted and propelled by overhead blades revolving horizontally.

heliograph /'hi:lɪəgrɑ:f/ • *noun* signalling apparatus reflecting flashes of sunlight. • *verb* send (message) thus.

heliotrope /'hi:lɪətrəʊp/ *noun* plant with fragrant purple flowers.

heliport /'helɪpɔ:t/ *noun* place where helicopters take off and land.

helium /'hi:lɪəm/ *noun* light nonflammable gaseous element.

helix /'hi:lɪks/ *noun* (*plural* **helices** /'hi:lɪsi:z/) spiral or coiled curve.

hell *noun* home of the damned after death; place or state of misery. □ **hellish** *adjective*; **hellishly** *adverb*.

he'll /hi:l/ he will; he shall.

hellebore /'helɪbɔ:/ *noun* evergreen plant of kind including Christmas rose.

Hellene /'heli:n/ *noun* Greek. □ **Hellenic** /-'len-/ *adjective*; **Hellenism** /-lɪn-/ *noun*; **Hellenist** /-lɪn-/ *noun*.

Hellenistic /helɪ'nɪstɪk/ *adjective* of Greek history, language, and culture of late 4th to late 1st c. BC.

hello /hə'ləʊ/ (*also* **hallo**, **hullo**) • *interjection* expressing informal greeting or surprise, or calling attention. • *noun* (*plural* **-s**) cry of 'hello'.

helm *noun* tiller or wheel for managing rudder. □ **at the helm** in control; **helmsman** person who steers ship.

helmet /'helmɪt/ *noun* protective headcover of policeman, motorcyclist, etc.

help • *verb* provide with means to what is needed or sought, be useful to; (usually in negative) prevent, refrain from; (**help oneself**) (often + *to*) serve oneself, take without permission. • *noun* act of helping; person or thing that helps; *colloquial* domestic assistant or assistance; remedy etc. □ **helpline** telephone service providing help with problems. □ **helper** *noun*.

helpful *adjective* giving help, useful. □ **helpfully** *adverb*; **helpfulness** *noun*.

helping *noun* portion of food.

helpless *adjective* lacking help, defenceless; unable to act without help. □ **helplessly** *adverb*; **helplessness** *noun*.

helter-skelter /heltə'skeltə/ • *adverb & adjective* in disorderly haste. • *noun* spiral slide at funfair.

hem[1] • *noun* border of cloth where edge is turned under and sewn down. • *verb* (**-mm-**) sew edge thus. □ **hem in** confine, restrict; **hemline** lower edge of skirt etc.; **hemstitch** (make hem with) ornamental stitch.

hem[2] *interjection* expressing hesitation or calling attention by slight cough.

hemisphere /'hemɪsfɪə/ *noun* half sphere; half earth, esp. as divided by equator or by line passing through poles; each half of brain. □ **hemispherical** /-'sfer-/ *adjective*.

hemlock /'hemlɒk/ *noun* poisonous plant with small white flowers; poison made from it.

hemp *noun* (in full **Indian hemp**) Asian herbaceous plant; its fibre used for rope etc.; narcotic drug made from it. □ **hempen** *adjective* made of hemp.

hen *noun* female bird, esp. of domestic fowl. □ **henbane** poisonous hairy plant; **hen-party** *colloquial* party of women only; **henpecked** (of husband) domineered over by his wife.

hence *adverb* from now; for this reason. □ **henceforth**, **henceforward** from this time onwards.

henchman /'hentʃmən/ *noun* usually *derogatory* trusted supporter.

henge *noun* prehistoric circle of wood or stone uprights, as at *Stonehenge*.

henna /'henə/ ● *noun* tropical shrub; reddish dye made from it and used esp. to colour hair. ● *verb* (**hennaed**, **hennaing**) dye with henna.

henry /'henrɪ/ *noun* (plural -**s**, -**ies**) SI unit of inductance.

hep = HIP[4].

hepatitis /hepə'taɪtɪs/ *noun* inflammation of the liver.

hepta- *combining form* seven.

heptagon /'heptəgən/ *noun* plane figure with 7 sides and angles. □ **heptagonal** /-'tæg-/ *adjective*.

her ● *pronoun* (as object of verb) the female person or thing in question; *colloquial* she. ● *adjective* of or belonging to her.

herald /'her(ə)ld/ ● *noun* messenger; forerunner; official. ● *verb* proclaim approach of; usher in. □ **heraldic** /-'ræld-/ *adjective*.

heraldry /'herəldrɪ/ *noun* (science or art of) armorial bearings.

herb *noun* non-woody seed-bearing plant; plant with leaves, seeds, or flowers used for flavouring, medicine, etc.

herbaceous /hɜː'beɪʃəs/ *adjective* of or like herbs. □ **herbaceous border** border in garden etc. containing flowering plants.

herbage *noun* vegetation collectively, esp. pasturage.

herbal ● *adjective* of herbs. ● *noun* book about herbs.

herbalist *noun* dealer in medicinal herbs; writer on herbs.

herbarium /hɜː'beərɪəm/ *noun* (plural -**ria**) collection of dried plants.

herbicide /'hɜːbɪsaɪd/ *noun* poison used to destroy unwanted vegetation.

herbivore /'hɜːbɪvɔː/ *noun* plant-eating animal. □ **herbivorous** /-'bɪvərəs/ *adjective*.

Herculean /hɜːkjʊ'liːən/ *adjective* having or requiring great strength or effort.

herd ● *noun* number of cattle etc. feeding or travelling together; (**the herd**) *derogatory* large number of people. ● *verb* (cause to) go in herd; tend. □ **herdsman** keeper of herds.

here ● *adverb* in or to this place; *indicating a person or thing*; at this point. ● *noun* this place. □ **hereabout(s)** somewhere near here; **hereafter** (in) future, (in) next world; **hereby** by this means; **herein** *formal* in this place, book, etc.; **hereinafter** *formal* from this point on, below (in document); **hereof** *formal* of this; **hereto** *formal* to this; **heretofore** *formal* formerly; **hereupon** after or in consequence of this; **herewith** with this.

hereditary /hɪ'redɪtərɪ/ *adjective* transmitted genetically from one generation to another; descending by inheritance; holding position by inheritance.

heredity /hɪ'redɪtɪ/ *noun* genetic transmission of physical or mental characteristics; these characteristics; genetic constitution.

heresy /'herəsɪ/ *noun* (plural -**ies**) esp. RC *Church* religious belief contrary to orthodox doctrine; opinion contrary to what is normally accepted.

heretic /'herətɪk/ *noun* believer in heresy. □ **heretical** /hɪ'ret-/ *adjective*.

heritable /'herɪtəb(ə)l/ *adjective* that can be inherited.

heritage /'herɪtɪdʒ/ *noun* what is or may be inherited; inherited circumstances, benefits, etc.; nation's historic buildings, countryside, etc.

hermaphrodite /hɜː'mæfrədaɪt/ ● *noun* person, animal, or plant with organs of both sexes. ● *adjective* combining both sexes. □ **hermaphroditic** /-'dɪt-/ *adjective*.

hermetic /hɜː'metɪk/ *adjective* with an airtight seal. □ **hermetically** *adverb*.

hermit /'hɜːmɪt/ *noun* person living in solitude. □ **hermit-crab** crab which lives in mollusc's cast-off shell.

hermitage *noun* hermit's dwelling; secluded residence.

hernia /'hɜːnɪə/ *noun* protrusion of part of organ through wall of cavity containing it.

hero /'hɪərəʊ/ *noun* (plural -**es**) person admired for courage, outstanding achievements, etc.; chief male character in play, story, etc. □ **hero-worship** idealization of admired person.

heroic /hɪˈrəʊɪk/ ● *adjective* fit for, or like, a hero; very brave. ● *noun* (in *plural*) overdramatic talk or behaviour. □ **heroically** *adverb*.

heroin /ˈherəʊɪn/ *noun* sedative addictive drug prepared from morphine.

heroine /ˈherəʊɪn/ *noun* female hero; chief female character in play, story, etc.

heroism /ˈherəʊɪz(ə)m/ *noun* heroic conduct.

heron /ˈher(ə)n/ *noun* long-necked long-legged wading bird.

herpes /ˈhɜːpiːz/ *noun* virus disease causing blisters.

Herr /heə/ *noun* (*plural* **Herren** /ˈherən/) *title of German man*.

herring /ˈherɪŋ/ *noun* (*plural* same or **-s**) N. Atlantic edible fish. □ **herring-bone** stitch or weave of small 'V' shapes making zigzag pattern.

hers /hɜːz/ *pronoun* the one(s) belonging to her.

herself /həˈself/ *pronoun: emphatic form of* SHE *or* HER; *reflexive form of* HER.

hertz *noun* (*plural* same) SI unit of frequency (one cycle per second).

he's /hiːz/ he is; he has.

hesitant /ˈhezɪt(ə)nt/ *adjective* hesitating. □ **hesitance** *noun*; **hesitancy** *noun*; **hesitantly** *adverb*.

hesitate /ˈhezɪteɪt/ *verb* (**-ting**) feel or show indecision; pause; (often + *to do*) be reluctant. □ **hesitation** *noun*.

hessian /ˈhesɪən/ *noun* strong coarse hemp or jute sacking.

heterodox /ˈhetərəʊdɒks/ *adjective* not orthodox. □ **heterodoxy** *noun*.

heterogeneous /hetərəˈdʒiːnɪəs/ *adjective* diverse; varied in content. □ **heterogeneity** /-dʒɪˈniːɪtɪ/ *noun*.

heteromorphic /hetərəʊˈmɔːfɪk/ *adjective* (also **heteromorphous** /-ˈmɔːfəs/) *Biology* of dissimilar forms.

heterosexual /hetərəʊˈsekʃʊəl/ ● *adjective* feeling or involving sexual attraction to opposite sex. ● *noun* heterosexual person. □ **heterosexuality** /-ˈæl-/ *noun*.

het up *adjective colloquial* overwrought.

heuristic /hjʊəˈrɪstɪk/ *adjective* serving to discover; using trial and error.

hew *verb* (*past participle* **hewn** /hjuːn/ or **hewed**) chop or cut with axe, sword, etc.; cut into shape.

hex ● *verb* practise witchcraft; bewitch. ● *noun* magic spell.

hexa- *combining form* six.

hexagon /ˈheksəgən/ *noun* plane figure with 6 sides and angles. □ **hexagonal** /-ˈsæg-/ *adjective*.

hexagram /ˈheksəgræm/ *noun* 6-pointed star formed by two intersecting equilateral triangles.

hexameter /hekˈsæmɪtə/ *noun* verse line of 6 metrical feet.

hey /heɪ/ *interjection* calling attention or expressing surprise, inquiry, etc. □ **hey presto!** *conjuror's phrase on completing trick*.

heyday /ˈheɪdeɪ/ *noun* time of greatest success, prime.

HF *abbreviation* high frequency.

HGV *abbreviation* heavy goods vehicle.

HH *abbreviation* Her or His Highness; His Holiness; double-hard (pencil lead).

hi /haɪ/ *interjection* calling attention or as greeting.

hiatus /haɪˈeɪtəs/ *noun* (*plural* **-tuses**) gap in series etc.; break between two vowels coming together but not in same syllable.

hibernate /ˈhaɪbəneɪt/ *verb* (**-ting**) (of animal) spend winter in dormant state. □ **hibernation** *noun*.

Hibernian /haɪˈbɜːnɪən/ *archaic poetical* ● *adjective* of Ireland. ● *noun* native of Ireland.

hibiscus /hɪˈbɪskəs/ *noun* (*plural* **-cuses**) cultivated shrub with large brightly coloured flowers.

hiccup /ˈhɪkʌp/ (also **hiccough**) ● *noun* involuntary audible spasm of respiratory organs; temporary or minor stoppage or difficulty. ● *verb* (**-p-**) make hiccup.

hick *noun esp. US colloquial* yokel.

hickory /ˈhɪkərɪ/ *noun* (*plural* **-ies**) N. American tree related to walnut; its wood.

hid *past of* HIDE[1].

hidden *past participle of* HIDE[1]. □ **hidden agenda** secret motivation behind policy etc., ulterior motive.

hide[1] ● *verb* (**-ding**; *past* **hid**; *past participle* **hidden** /ˈhɪd(ə)n/) put or keep out of sight; conceal oneself; (usually + *from*) conceal (fact). ● *noun* camouflaged shelter for observing wildlife. □ **hide-and-seek** game in which players hide and another searches for them; **hideaway** hiding place, retreat; **hide-out** *colloquial* hiding place.

hide[2] *noun* animal's skin, esp. tanned; *colloquial* human skin. □ **hidebound** rigidly conventional.

hideous /ˈhɪdɪəs/ *adjective* repulsive, revolting. □ **hideously** *adverb*.

hiding *noun colloquial* thrashing.

hierarchy /ˈhaɪərɑːkɪ/ *noun* (*plural* **-ies**) system of grades of authority ranked one above another. □ **hierarchical** /-ˈrɑːk-/ *adjective*.

hieroglyph /ˈhaɪərəɡlɪf/ *noun* picture representing word or syllable, esp. in ancient Egyptian. □ **hieroglyphic** /-ˈɡlɪf-/ *adjective*; **hieroglyphics** /-ˈɡlɪf-/ *plural noun*.

hi-fi /ˈhaɪfaɪ/ *colloquial* ● *adjective* of high fidelity. ● *noun* (*plural* **-s**) equipment for such sound reproduction.

higgledy-piggledy /hɪɡəldɪˈpɪɡəldɪ/ *adverb & adjective* in disorder.

high /haɪ/ ● *adjective* of great or specified upward extent; far above ground or sea level; coming above normal level; of exalted rank or position, of superior quality; extreme, intense; (often + *on*) *colloquial* intoxicated by alcohol or drugs; (of sound) shrill; (of period etc.) at its peak; (of meat etc.) beginning to go bad. ● *noun* high or highest level or number; area of high barometric pressure; *slang* euphoric state, esp. drug-induced. ● *adverb* far up, aloft; in or to high degree; at high price; (of sound) at high pitch. □ **high altar** chief altar in church; **highball** *US* drink of spirits and soda etc.; **highbrow** *colloquial* (person) of superior intellect or culture; **high chair** child's chair with long legs and meal-tray; **High Church** section of Church of England emphasizing ritual, priestly authority, and sacraments; **high command** army commander-in-chief and associated staff; **High Commission** embassy from one Commonwealth country to another; **High Court** supreme court of justice for civil cases;

highfalutin(g) *colloquial* pompous, pretentious; **high fidelity** high-quality sound reproduction; **high-flown** extravagant, bombastic; **high-flyer**, **-flier** person of great potential or ambition; **high frequency** *Radio* 3–30 megahertz; **high heels** woman's shoes with high heels; **high jump** athletic event consisting of jumping over high bar, *colloquial* drastic punishment; **high-level** conducted by people of high rank, (of computer language) close to ordinary language; **high-minded** of firm moral principles; **high-mindedness** *noun*; **high pressure** high degree of activity, atmospheric condition with pressure above average; **high priest** chief priest, head of cult; **high-rise** (of building) having many storeys; **high road** main road; **high school** secondary school; **high sea(s)** seas outside territorial waters; **high-spirited** cheerful; **high street** principal shopping street of town; **high tea** early evening meal of tea and cooked food; **high-tech** employing, requiring, or involved in high technology, imitating its style; **high technology** advanced (esp. electronic) technology; **high tension**, **voltage** electrical potential large enough to injure or damage; **high tide**, **water time** or level of tide at its peak; **high water mark** level reached at high water.

highland /ˈhaɪlənd/ ● *noun* (usually in *plural*) mountainous country, esp. (**the Highlands**) of N. Scotland. ● *adjective* of highland or Highlands. □ **highlander**, **Highlander** *noun*.

highlight ● *noun* moment or detail of vivid interest; bright part of picture; bleached streak in hair. ● *verb* bring into prominence; mark with highlighter.

highlighter *noun* coloured marker pen for emphasizing printed word.

highly *adverb* in high degree, favourably. □ **highly-strung** sensitive, nervous.

highness *noun* state of being high; (**His**, **Her**, **Your Highness**) *title of prince, princess, etc.*

highway *noun* public road, main route. □ **Highway Code** official handbook for road-users; **highwayman** *historical* (usually mounted) robber of stagecoaches.

hijack /'haɪdʒæk/ ● *verb* seize control of (vehicle, aircraft, etc.), esp. to force it to different destination; steal (goods) in transit. ● *noun* hijacking. □ **hijacker** *noun*.

hike ● *noun* long walk, esp. in country for pleasure; rise in prices etc. ● *verb* (**-king**) go on hike. □ **hiker** *noun*.

hilarious /hɪ'leərɪəs/ *adjective* extremely funny; boisterously merry. □ **hilariously** *adverb*; **hilarity** /-'lær-/ *noun*.

hill *noun* natural elevation of ground, lower than mountain; heap, mound. □ **hill-billy** *US colloquial often derogatory* person from remote rural area. □ **hilly** *adjective* (**-ier**, **-iest**).

hillock /'hɪlək/ *noun* small hill, mound.

hilt *noun* handle of sword, dagger, etc.

him *pronoun* (as object of verb) the male person or animal in question, person of unspecified sex; *colloquial* he.

himself /hɪm'self/ *pronoun: emphatic form of* HE *or* HIM; *reflexive form of* HIM.

hind[1] /haɪnd/ *adjective* at back. □ **hindquarters** rump and hind legs of quadruped; **hindsight** wisdom after event. □ **hindmost** *adjective*.

hind[2] /haɪnd/ *noun* female (esp. red) deer.

hinder[1] /'hɪndə/ *verb* impede; delay.

hinder[2] /'haɪndə/ *adjective* rear, hind.

Hindi /'hɪndɪ/ *noun* group of spoken languages in N. India; one of official languages of India, literary form of Hindustani.

hindrance /'hɪndrəns/ *noun* obstruction.

Hindu /'hɪnduː/ ● *noun* (*plural* **-s**) follower of Hinduism. ● *adjective* of Hindus or Hinduism.

Hinduism /'hɪnduːɪz(ə)m/ *noun* main religious and social system of India, including belief in reincarnation and worship of several gods.

Hindustani /hɪnduː'stɑːnɪ/ *noun* language based on Hindi, used in much of India.

hinge ● *noun* movable joint on which door, lid, etc. swings; principle on which all depends. ● *verb* (**-ging**) (+ *on*) depend on (event etc.); attach or be attached with hinge.

hinny /'hɪnɪ/ *noun* (*plural* **-ies**) offspring of female donkey and male horse.

hint ● *noun* indirect suggestion; slight indication; small piece of practical information; faint trace. ● *verb* suggest indirectly. □ **hint at** refer indirectly to.

hinterland /'hɪntəlænd/ *noun* district behind that lying along coast etc.

hip[1] *noun* projection of pelvis and upper part of thigh-bone. □ **hip-flask** small flask for spirits.

hip[2] *noun* fruit of rose.

hip[3] *interjection used to introduce* cheer.

hip[4] *adjective* (also **hep**) (**-pp-**) *slang* trendy, stylish. □ **hip hop, hip-hop** subculture combining rap music, graffiti art, and break-dancing.

hippie /'hɪpɪ/ *noun* (also **hippy**) (*plural* **-ies**) *colloquial* person (esp. in 1960s) rejecting convention, typically with long hair, jeans, etc.

hippo /'hɪpəʊ/ *noun* (*plural* **-s**) *colloquial* hippopotamus.

Hippocratic oath /hɪpə'krætɪk/ *noun* statement of ethics of medical profession.

hippodrome /'hɪpədrəʊm/ *noun* music-hall, dance hall, etc.; *historical* course for chariot races etc.

hippopotamus /hɪpə'pɒtəməs/ *noun* (*plural* **-muses** or **-mi** /-maɪ/) large African mammal with short legs and thick skin, living by rivers etc.

hippy = HIPPIE.

hipster[1] /'hɪpstə/ ● *adjective* (of garment) hanging from hips rather than waist. ● *noun* (in *plural*) such trousers.

hipster[2] /'hɪpstə/ *noun slang* hip person.

hire ● *verb* (**-ring**) obtain use of (thing) or services of (person) for payment. ● *noun* hiring, being hired; payment for this. □ **hire out** grant temporary use of (thing) for payment; **hire purchase** system of purchase by paying in instalments. □ **hirer** *noun*.

hireling /'haɪəlɪŋ/ *noun usually derogatory* person who works for hire.

hirsute /'hɜːsjuːt/ *adjective* hairy.

his /hɪz/ ● *adjective* of or belonging to him. ● *pronoun* the one(s) belonging to him.

Hispanic /hɪ'spænɪk/ ● *adjective* of Spain or Spain and Portugal; of Spain and other Spanish-speaking countries.

• *noun* Spanish-speaking person living in US.

hiss /hɪs/ • *verb* make sharp sibilant sound, as of letter *s*; express disapproval of thus; whisper urgently or angrily. • *noun* sharp sibilant sound.

histamine /'hɪstəmiːn/ *noun* chemical compound in body tissues associated with allergic reactions.

histology /hɪ'stɒlədʒɪ/ *noun* study of tissue structure.

historian /hɪ'stɔːrɪən/ *noun* writer of history; person learned in history.

historic /hɪ'stɒrɪk/ *adjective* famous in history or potentially so; *Grammar* (of tense) used to narrate past events.

historical *adjective* of history; belonging to or dealing with the past; not legendary; studying development over period of time. □ **historically** *adverb*.

historicity /hɪstə'rɪsɪtɪ/ *noun* historical genuineness or accuracy.

historiography /hɪstɔːrɪ'ɒɡrəfɪ/ *noun* writing of history; study of this. □ **historiographer** *noun*.

history /'hɪstərɪ/ *noun* (*plural* **-ies**) continuous record of (esp. public) events; study of past events; total accumulation of these; (esp. eventful) past or record.

histrionic /hɪstrɪ'ɒnɪk/ • *adjective* (of behaviour) theatrical, dramatic. • *noun* (in *plural*) insincere and dramatic behaviour designed to impress.

hit • *verb* (**-tt-**; *past & past participle* **hit**) strike with blow or missile; (of moving body) strike with force; affect adversely; (often + *at*) aim blow; propel (ball etc.) with bat etc.; achieve, reach; *colloquial* encounter, arrive at. • *noun* blow; shot that hits target; *colloquial* popular success. □ **hit it off** (often + *with*, *together*) get on well; **hit-and-run** (of person) causing damage or injury and leaving immediately, (of accident etc.) caused by such person(s); **hit-or-miss** random.

hitch • *verb* fasten with loop etc.; move (thing) with jerk; *colloquial* hitchhike; obtain (lift). • *noun* temporary difficulty, snag; jerk; kind of noose or knot; *colloquial* free ride in vehicle. □ **hitchhike** travel by means of free

lifts in passing vehicles; **hitchhiker** *noun*.

hi-tech /'haɪtek/ *adjective* high-tech.

hither /'hɪðə/ *adverb formal* to this place. □ **hitherto** up to now.

HIV *abbreviation* human immunodeficiency virus, either of two viruses causing Aids.

hive *noun* beehive. □ **hive off** (**-ving**) separate from larger group.

hives /haɪvz/ *plural noun* skin eruption, esp. nettle-rash.

HM *abbreviation* Her or His Majesty('s).

HMG *abbreviation* Her or His Majesty's Government.

HMI *abbreviation* Her or His Majesty's Inspector (of Schools).

HMS *abbreviation* Her or His Majesty's Ship.

HMSO *abbreviation* Her or His Majesty's Stationery Office.

HNC, HND *abbreviations* Higher National Certificate, Diploma.

ho /həʊ/ *interjection expressing triumph, derision, etc., or calling attention etc.*

hoard /hɔːd/ • *noun* store (esp. of money or food). • *verb* amass and store. □ **hoarder** *noun*.

hoarding /'hɔːdɪŋ/ *noun* structure erected to carry advertisements; temporary fence round building site etc.

hoar-frost /'hɔːfrɒst/ *noun* frozen water vapour on lawns.

hoarse /hɔːs/ *adjective* (of voice) rough, husky; having hoarse voice. □ **hoarsely** *adverb*; **hoarseness** *noun*.

hoary /'hɔːrɪ/ *adjective* (**-ier**, **-iest**) white or grey with age; aged; old and trite.

hoax • *noun* humorous or malicious deception. • *verb* deceive with hoax.

hob *noun* hotplates etc. on cooker or as separate unit; flat metal shelf at side of fire for heating pans etc. □ **hobnail** heavy-headed nail for boot-sole.

hobble /'hɒb(ə)l/ • *verb* (**-ling**) walk lamely, limp; tie together legs of (horse etc.) to keep it from straying. • *noun* limping gait; rope etc. used to hobble horse.

hobby /'hɒbɪ/ *noun* (*plural* **-ies**) leisure-time activity pursued for pleasure. □ **hobby-horse** stick with horse's head, used as toy, favourite subject or idea.

hobgoblin /ˈhɒbgɒblɪn/ *noun* mischievous imp; bogy.

hobnob /ˈhɒbnɒb/ *verb* (**-bb-**) (usually + *with*) mix socially or informally.

hobo /ˈhəʊbəʊ/ *noun* (*plural* **-es** or **-s**) *US* wandering worker; tramp.

hock[1] *noun* joint of quadruped's hind leg between knee and fetlock.

hock[2] *noun* German white wine.

hock[3] *verb* esp. *US* colloquial pawn. □ **in hock** in pawn, in debt, in prison.

hockey /ˈhɒkɪ/ *noun* team game played with ball and hooked sticks.

hocus-pocus /həʊkəsˈpəʊkəs/ *noun* trickery.

hod *noun* trough on pole for carrying bricks etc.; portable container for coal.

hodgepodge = HOTCHPOTCH.

hoe ● *noun* long-handled tool for weeding etc. ● *verb* (**hoes, hoed, hoeing**) weed (crops), loosen (soil), or dig up etc. with hoe.

hog ● *noun* castrated male pig; *colloquial* greedy person. ● *verb* (**-gg-**) *colloquial* take greedily; monopolize. □ **go the whole hog** *colloquial* do thing thoroughly; **hogwash** *colloquial* nonsense.

hogmanay /ˈhɒgmǝneɪ/ *noun* Scottish New Year's Eve.

hogshead /ˈhɒgzhed/ *noun* large cask; liquid or dry measure (about 50 gals.).

ho-ho /həʊˈhəʊ/ *interjection* representing deep jolly laugh or expressing surprise, triumph, or derision.

hoick *verb* colloquial (often + *out*) lift or jerk.

hoi polloi /hɔɪ pǝˈlɔɪ/ *noun* the masses; ordinary people. [Greek]

hoist ● *verb* raise or haul up; raise with ropes and pulleys etc. ● *noun* act of hoisting; apparatus for hoisting. □ **hoist with one's own petard** caught by one's own trick etc.

hoity-toity /hɔɪtɪˈtɔɪtɪ/ *adjective* haughty.

hokum /ˈhəʊkǝm/ *noun* esp. *US* slang sentimental or unreal material in film etc.; bunkum; rubbish.

hold[1] ● *verb* (*past & past participle* **held**) keep fast; grasp; keep in particular position; contain, have capacity for; possess, have (property, qualifications, job, etc.); conduct, celebrate; detain; think, believe; not give way; reserve. ● *noun* (+ *on*, *over*) power over; grasp; manner or means of holding. □ **holdall** large soft travelling bag; **hold back** impede, keep for oneself, (often + *from*) refrain; **hold down** repress, *colloquial* be competent enough to keep (job); **hold forth** speak at length or tediously; **hold on** maintain grasp, wait, not ring off; **hold one's tongue** *colloquial* remain silent; **hold out** stretch forth (hand etc.), offer (inducement etc.), maintain resistance, (+ *for*) continue to demand; **hold over** postpone; **hold up** *verb* sustain, display, obstruct, stop and rob by force; **hold-up** *noun* stoppage, delay, robbery by force; **hold with** (usually in negative) *colloquial* approve of.

hold[2] /həʊld/ *noun* cavity in lower part of ship or aircraft for cargo.

holder *noun* device for holding something; possessor of title, shares, etc.; occupant of office etc.

holding *noun* tenure of land; stocks, property, etc. held. □ **holding company** one formed to hold shares of other companies.

hole *noun* empty space in solid body; opening in or through something; burrow; *colloquial* small or gloomy place; *colloquial* awkward situation; (in games) cavity or receptacle for ball, *Golf* section of course from tee to hole. □ **hole up** (**-ling**) *US* colloquial hide oneself. □ **holey** *adjective*.

holiday /ˈhɒlɪdeɪ/ ● *noun* (often in *plural*) extended period of recreation, esp. spent away from home; break from work or school. ● *verb* spend holiday.

holiness /ˈhəʊlɪnɪs/ *noun* being holy or sacred; (**His, Your Holiness**) *title of* Pope.

holism /ˈhəʊlɪz(ǝ)m/ *noun* (also **wholism**) theory that certain wholes are greater than sum of their parts; *Medicine* treating of whole person rather than symptoms of disease. □ **holistic** /-ˈlɪst-/ *adjective*.

hollandaise sauce /hɒlǝnˈdeɪz/ *noun* creamy sauce of butter, egg yolks, vinegar, etc.

holler /ˈhɒlǝ/ *verb & noun* US colloquial shout.

hollow /ˈhɒlǝʊ/ ● *adjective* having cavity; not solid; sunken; echoing; empty;

hungry; meaningless; insincere. ● *noun* hollow place; hole; valley. ● *verb* (often + *out*) make hollow, excavate. ● *adverb colloquial* completely.

holly /'hɒlɪ/ *noun* (*plural* **-ies**) evergreen prickly-leaved shrub with red berries.

hollyhock /'hɒlɪhɒk/ *noun* tall plant with showy flowers.

holm /həʊm/ *noun* (in full **holm-oak**) evergreen oak.

holocaust /'hɒləkɔ:st/ *noun* wholesale destruction; (**the Holocaust**) mass murder of Jews by Nazis 1939–45.

hologram /'hɒləgræm/ *noun* photographic pattern having 3-dimensional effect.

holograph /'hɒləgrɑ:f/ ● *adjective* wholly in handwriting of person named as author. ● *noun* such document.

holography /həˈlɒgrəfɪ/ *noun* study or production of holograms.

holster /'həʊlstə/ *noun* leather case for pistol or revolver on belt etc.

holy /'həʊlɪ/ *adjective* (**-ier, -iest**) morally and spiritually excellent; belonging or devoted to God. □ **Holy Ghost** Holy Spirit; **Holy Land** area between River Jordan and Mediterranean; **holy of holies** inner chamber of Jewish temple, thing regarded as most sacred; **holy orders** those of bishop, priest, and deacon; **Holy Saturday** day before Easter; **Holy See** papacy, papal court; **Holy Spirit** Third Person of Trinity; **Holy Week** week before Easter; **Holy Writ** Bible.

homage /'hɒmɪdʒ/ *noun* tribute, expression of reverence.

Homburg /'hɒmbɜ:g/ *noun* man's felt hat with narrow curled brim and lengthwise dent in crown.

home ● *noun* place where one lives; residence; (esp. good or bad) family circumstances; native land; institution caring for people or animals; place where thing originates, is kept, is most common, etc.; (in games) finishing line in race, goal, home match or win etc. ● *adjective* of or connected with home; carried on or done at home; not foreign; played etc. on team's own ground. ● *adverb* to or at home; to point aimed at. ● *verb* (**-ming**) (of pigeon) return home; (often + *on, in on*) (of missile etc.) be

guided to destination. □ **at home** *adjective* in one's house or native land, at ease, well-informed, available to callers; **at-home** *noun* social reception in person's home; **home-brew** beer etc. brewed at home; **Home Counties** those lying round London; **home economics** study of household management; **homeland** native land, any of several areas reserved for black South Africans; **Home Office** British government department concerned with immigration, law and order, etc.; **home rule** self-government; **Home Secretary** minister in charge of Home Office; **homesick** depressed by absence from home; **homesickness** such depression; **homestead** house with outbuildings, farm; **homework** lessons to be done by schoolchild at home. □ **homeless** *adjective*; **homeward** *adjective* & *adverb*; **homewards** *adverb*.

homely *adjective* (**-ier, -iest**) plain; unpretentious; *US* unattractive; cosy. □ **homeliness** *noun*.

homeopathy etc. *US* = HOMOEOPATHY etc.

Homeric /həʊ'merɪk/ *adjective* of or in style of the ancient Greek poet Homer; of Bronze Age Greece.

homey *adjective* (**-mier, -miest**) suggesting home; cosy.

homicide /'hɒmɪsaɪd/ *noun* killing of person by another; person who kills another. □ **homicidal** /-'saɪd-/ *adjective*.

homily /'hɒmɪlɪ/ *noun* (*plural* **-ies**) short sermon; moralizing lecture. □ **homiletic** /-'let-/ *adjective*.

homing *adjective* (of pigeon) trained to fly home; (of device) for guiding to target etc.

hominid /'hɒmɪnɪd/ ● *adjective* of mammal family of existing and fossil man. ● *noun* member of this.

hominoid /'hɒmɪnɔɪd/ ● *adjective* like a human. ● *noun* animal resembling human.

homoeopathy /ˌhəʊmɪ'ɒpəθɪ/ *noun* (*US* **homeopathy**) treatment of disease by drugs that in healthy person would produce symptoms of the disease. □ **homoeopath** /'həʊmɪəʊpæθ/ *noun*; **homoeopathic** /-'pæθ-/ *adjective*.

homogeneous /ˌhɒmə'dʒi:nɪəs/ *adjective* (having parts) of same kind or nature;

uniform. □ **homogeneity** /-dʒɪˈniːɪtɪ/ noun; **homogeneously** adverb.

■ **Usage** *Homogeneous* is often confused with *homogenous* (and pronounced /həˈmɒdʒənəs/, with the stress on the *-mog-*), but that is a term in biology meaning 'similar owing to common descent'.

homogenize /həˈmɒdʒɪnaɪz/ verb (also **-ise**) (**-zing** or **-sing**) make homogeneous; treat (milk) so that cream does not separate.

homologous /həˈmɒləgəs/ adjective having same relation, relative position, etc.; corresponding.

homology /həˈmɒlədʒɪ/ noun homologous relation, correspondence.

homonym /ˈhɒmənɪm/ noun word spelt or pronounced like another but of different meaning.

homophobia /hɒməˈfəʊbɪə/ noun hatred or fear of homosexuals. □ **homophobe** /ˈhɒm-/ noun; **homophobic** adjective.

homophone /ˈhɒməfəʊn/ noun word pronounced like another but having different meaning, e.g. *beach, beech*.

Homo sapiens /həʊməʊ ˈsæpɪenz/ noun modern humans regarded as a species. [Latin]

homosexual /hɒməˈsekʃʊəl/ ● adjective feeling or involving sexual attraction to people of same sex. ● noun homosexual person. □ **homosexuality** /-ˈæl-/ noun.

Hon. abbreviation Honorary; Honourable.

hone ● noun whetstone, esp. for razors. ● verb (**-ning**) sharpen (as) on hone.

honest /ˈɒnɪst/ ● adjective not lying, cheating, or stealing; sincere; fairly earned. ● adverb colloquial genuinely, really. □ **honestly** adverb.

honesty /ˈɒnɪstɪ/ noun being honest, truthfulness; plant with purple or white flowers and flat round pods.

honey /ˈhʌnɪ/ noun (plural **-s**) sweet sticky yellowish fluid made by bees from nectar; colour of this; sweetness; darling.

honeycomb ● noun beeswax structure of hexagonal cells for honey and eggs; pattern arranged hexagonally. ● verb fill with cavities; mark with honeycomb pattern.

honeydew noun sweet substance excreted by aphids; variety of melon.

honeyed adjective sweet, sweetsounding.

honeymoon ● noun holiday of newly married couple; initial period of enthusiasm or goodwill. ● verb spend honeymoon.

honeysuckle noun climbing shrub with fragrant flowers.

honk ● noun sound of car horn; cry of wild goose. ● verb (cause to) make honk.

honky-tonk /ˈhɒŋkɪtɒŋk/ noun colloquial ragtime piano music.

honor US = HONOUR.

honorable US = HONOURABLE.

honorarium /ɒnəˈreərɪəm/ noun (plural **-s** or **-ria**) voluntary payment for professional services.

honorary /ˈɒnərərɪ/ adjective conferred as honour; unpaid.

honorific /ɒnəˈrɪfɪk/ adjective conferring honour; implying respect.

honour /ˈɒnə/ (US **honor**) ● noun high respect, public regard; adherence to what is right; nobleness of mind; thing conferred as distinction (esp. official award for bravery or achievement); privilege; (**His, Her, Your Honour**) title of judge etc.; person or thing that brings honour; chastity, reputation for this; (in plural) specialized degree course or special distinction in exam; (in plural) (in card games) 4 or 5 highest-ranking cards; Golf right of driving off first. ● verb respect highly; confer honour on; accept or pay (bill, cheque) when due. □ **do the honours** perform duties of host etc.

honourable adjective (US **honorable**) deserving, bringing, or showing honour; (**Honourable**) courtesy title of MPs, certain officials, and children of certain ranks of the nobility. □ **honourably** adverb.

hooch /huːtʃ/ noun US colloquial alcoholic spirits, esp. inferior or illicit.

hood¹ /hʊd/ ● noun covering for head and neck, esp. as part of garment; separate hoodlike garment; folding top of car etc.; US bonnet of car etc.; protective cover. ● verb cover with hood. □ **hooded** adjective.

hood² /hʊd/ *noun US slang* gangster, gun-man.

hoodlum /'huːdləm/ *noun* hooligan; gangster.

hoodoo /'huːduː/ *noun US* bad luck; thing or person that brings this.

hoodwink *verb* deceive, delude.

hoof /huːf/ *noun* (*plural* **-s** or **hooves** /huːvz/) horny part of foot of horse etc. □ **hoof it** *slang* go on foot.

hook /hʊk/ ● *noun* bent piece of metal etc. for catching hold or for hanging things on; curved cutting instrument; hook-shaped thing; hooking stroke; *Boxing* short swinging blow. ● *verb* grasp, se-cure, fasten, or catch with hook; (in sports) send (ball) in curving or deviat-ing path; *Rugby* secure (ball) in scrum with foot. □ **hook and eye** small hook and loop as fastener; **hook, line, and sinker** completely; **hook-up** connec-tion, esp. of broadcasting equipment; **hookworm** worm infesting intestines of humans and animals.

hookah /'hʊkə/ *noun* tobacco pipe with long tube passing through water to cool smoke.

hooked *adjective* hook-shaped; (often + **on**) *slang* addicted or captivated.

hooker *noun Rugby* player in front row of scrum who tries to hook ball; *slang* prostitute.

hooligan /'huːlɪɡən/ *noun* young ruffian. □ **hooliganism** *noun*.

hoop /huːp/ ● *noun* circular band of metal, wood, etc., esp. as part of frame-work; wooden etc. circle bowled by child or used by circus performer etc.; arch through which balls are hit in croquet. ● *verb* bind with hoop(s). □ **hoop-la** game with rings thrown to encircle prizes.

hoopoe /'huːpuː/ *noun* bird with varie-gated plumage and fanlike crest.

hooray = HURRAH.

hoot /huːt/ ● *noun* owl's cry; sound of car's horn etc.; shout of derision etc.; *colloquial* (cause of) laughter; (also **two hoots**) *slang* anything, in the slightest. ● *verb* utter hoot(s); greet or drive away with hoots; sound (horn).

hooter *noun* thing that hoots, esp. car's horn or siren; *slang* nose.

Hoover /'huːvə/ ● *noun* proprietary term va-cuum cleaner. ● *verb* (**hoover**) clean or (+ *up*) suck up with vacuum cleaner.

hooves *plural of* HOOF.

hop¹ ● *verb* (**-pp-**) (of bird, frog, etc.) spring with all feet at once; (of person) jump on one foot; move or go quickly, leap. ● *noun* hopping movement; *colloquial* dance; short journey, esp. flight. □ **hop in**, **out** *colloquial* get into or out of car etc.; **hopscotch** child's game of hop-ping over squares marked on ground.

hop² *noun* climbing plant with bitter cones used to flavour beer etc.; (in *plural*) these cones.

hope ● *noun* expectation and desire; per-son or thing giving cause for hope; what is hoped for. ● *verb* (**-ping**) feel hope; expect and desire.

hopeful *adjective* feeling or inspiring hope, promising.

hopefully *adverb* in a hopeful way; it is to be hoped.

■ **Usage** The use of *hopefully* to mean 'it is to be hoped' is common, but it is considered incorrect by some people.

hopeless *adjective* feeling or admitting no hope; inadequate, incompetent. □ **hopelessly** *adverb*; **hopelessness** *noun*.

hopper *noun* funnel-like device for feed-ing grain into mill etc.; hopping insect.

horde *noun usually derogatory* large group, gang.

horehound /'hɔːhaʊnd/ *noun* herb with aromatic bitter juice.

horizon /hə'raɪz(ə)n/ *noun* line at which earth and sky appear to meet; limit of mental perception, interest, etc.

horizontal /hɒrɪ'zɒnt(ə)l/ ● *adjective* par-allel to plane of horizon; level, flat. ● *noun* horizontal line, plane, etc. □ **horizontally** *adverb*.

hormone /'hɔːməʊn/ *noun* substance produced by body and transported in tissue fluids to stimulate cells or tis-sues to growth etc.; similar synthetic substance. □ **hormone replacement therapy** treatment with hormones to relieve menopausal symptoms. □ **hor-monal** /-'məʊn-/ *adjective*.

horn *noun* hard outgrowth, often curved and pointed, on head of animal; horn-like projection; substance of horns;

brass wind instrument; instrument giving warning. □ **hornbeam** tough-wooded hedgerow tree; **hornbill** bird with hornlike excrescence on bill; **horn of plenty** cornucopia; **horn-rimmed** (of spectacles) having rims of horn or similar substance. □ **horned** *adjective.*

hornblende /'hɔ:nblend/ *noun* dark brown etc. mineral constituent of granite etc.

hornet /'hɔ:nɪt/ *noun* large species of wasp.

hornpipe *noun* (music for) lively dance associated esp. with sailors.

horny *adjective* (**-ier, -iest**) of or like horn; hard; *slang* sexually excited. □ **horniness** *noun.*

horology /hə'rɒlədʒɪ/ *noun* clock-making. □ **horological** /hɒrə'lɒdʒ-/ *adjective.*

horoscope /'hɒrəskəʊp/ *noun* prediction of person's future based on position of planets at his or her birth.

horrendous /hə'rendəs/ *adjective* horrifying. □ **horrendously** *adverb.*

horrible /'hɒrɪb(ə)l/ *adjective* causing horror; *colloquial* unpleasant. □ **horribly** *adverb.*

horrid /'hɒrɪd/ *adjective* horrible; *colloquial* unpleasant.

horrific /hə'rɪfɪk/ *adjective* horrifying. □ **horrifically** *adverb.*

horrify /'hɒrɪfaɪ/ *verb* (**-ies, -ied**) arouse horror in; shock. □ **horrifying** *adjective.*

horror /'hɒrə/ ● *noun* intense loathing or fear; (often + *of*) deep dislike; *colloquial* intense dismay; horrifying thing. ● *adjective* (of films etc.) designed to arouse feelings of horror.

hors d'oeuvre /ɔ: 'dɜ:vr/ *noun* appetizer served at start of meal.

horse ● *noun* large 4-legged hoofed mammal with mane, used for riding etc.; adult male horse; vaulting-block; supporting frame. ● *verb* (**-sing**) (+ *around*) fool about. □ **horsebox** closed vehicle for transporting horse(s); **horse brass** brass ornament originally for horse's harness; **horse chestnut** tree with conical clusters of flowers, its dark brown fruit; **horse-drawn** pulled by horse(s); **horsefly** biting insect troublesome to horses; **Horse Guards** cavalry brigade of British household

troops; **horsehair** (padding etc. of) hair from mane or tail of horse; **horseman** (skilled) rider on horseback; **horsemanship** skill in riding; **horseplay** boisterous play; **horsepower** (*plural* same) unit of rate of doing work; **horse race** race between horses with riders; **horse racing** sport of racing horses; **horseradish** plant with pungent root used to make sauce; **horse sense** *colloquial* plain common sense; **horseshoe** U-shaped iron shoe for horse, thing of this shape; **horsetail** (plant resembling) horse's tail; **horsewhip** *noun* whip for horse, *verb* beat (person) with this; **horsewoman** (skilled) woman rider on horseback.

horsy *adjective* (**-ier, -iest**) of or like horse; concerned with horses.

horticulture /'hɔ:tɪkʌltʃə/ *noun* art of gardening. □ **horticultural** /-'kʌlt-/ *adjective*, **horticulturist** /-'kʌlt-/ *noun.*

hosanna /həʊ'zænə/ *noun & interjection* cry of adoration.

hose /həʊz/ ● *noun* (also **hose-pipe**) flexible tube for conveying liquids; ((treated as *plural*) stockings and socks collectively; *historical* breeches. ● *verb* (**-sing**) (often + *down*) water, spray, or drench with hose.

hosier /'həʊzɪə/ *noun* dealer in stockings and socks. □ **hosiery** *noun.*

hospice /'hɒspɪs/ *noun* home for (esp. terminally) ill or destitute people; travellers' lodging kept by religious order etc.

hospitable /hɒs'pɪtəb(ə)l/ *adjective* giving hospitality. □ **hospitably** *adverb.*

hospital /'hɒspɪt(ə)l/ *noun* institution providing medical and surgical treatment and nursing for ill and injured people; *historical* hospice.

hospitality /hɒspɪ'tælɪtɪ/ *noun* friendly and generous reception of guests or strangers.

hospitalize /'hɒspɪtəlaɪz/ *verb* (also **-ise**) (**-zing** or **-sing**) send or admit to hospital. □ **hospitalization** *noun.*

host[1] /həʊst/ *noun* (usually + *of*) large number of people or things.

host[2] /həʊst/ ● *noun* person who entertains another as guest; compère; animal or plant having parasite; recipient of transplanted organ; landlord of inn. ● *verb* be host to (person) or of (event).

host³ /həʊst/ *noun* (usually **the Host**) bread consecrated in Eucharist.

hostage /ˈhɒstɪdʒ/ *noun* person seized or held as security for fulfilment of a condition.

hostel /ˈhɒst(ə)l/ *noun* house of residence for students etc.; youth hostel.

hostelling *noun* (*US* **hosteling**) practice of staying in youth hostels. □ **hosteller** *noun*.

hostelry *noun* (*plural* **-ies**) *archaic* inn.

hostess /ˈhəʊstɪs/ *noun* woman who entertains guests, or customers at nightclub.

hostile /ˈhɒstaɪl/ *adjective* of enemy; (often + *to*) unfriendly, opposed.

hostility /hɒˈstɪlɪtɪ/ *noun* (*plural* **-ies**) being hostile; enmity; warfare; (in *plural*) acts of war.

hot ● *adjective* (**-tt-**) having high temperature, very warm; causing sensation of or feeling heat; pungent; excited; (often + *on, for*) eager; (of news) fresh; skilful, formidable; (+ *on*) knowledgeable about; *slang* (of stolen goods) difficult to dispose of. ● *verb* (**-tt-**) (usually + *up*) *colloquial* make or become hot; become more active, exciting, or dangerous. □ **hot air** *slang* empty or boastful talk; **hot-air balloon** balloon containing air heated by burners, causing it to rise; **hotbed** (+ *of*) environment conducive to (vice etc.), bed of earth heated by fermenting manure; **hot cross bun** bun marked with cross, eaten on Good Friday; **hot dog** *colloquial* hot sausage in bread roll; **hotfoot** in eager haste; **hothead** impetuous person; **hotheaded** impetuous; **hothouse** heated (mainly glass) building for growing plants, environment conducive to rapid growth; **hotline** direct telephone line; **hotplate** heated metal plate for cooking food or keeping it hot; **hotpot** dish of stewed meat and vegetables; **hot rod** vehicle modified for extra power and speed; **hot seat** *slang* awkward or responsible position, electric chair; **hot water** *colloquial* difficulty, trouble; **hot-water bottle** container filled with hot water to warm bed etc. □ **hotly** *adverb*.

hotchpotch /ˈhɒtʃpɒtʃ/ *noun* (also **hodgepodge** /ˈhɒdʒpɒdʒ/) confused mixture, jumble, esp. of ideas.

hotel /həʊˈtel/ *noun* (usually licensed) place providing meals and accommodation for payment.

hotelier /həʊˈtelɪə/ *noun* hotel-keeper.

houmous = HUMMUS.

hound /haʊnd/ ● *noun* dog used in hunting; *colloquial* despicable man. ● *verb* harass or pursue.

hour /aʊə/ *noun* twenty-fourth part of day and night, 60 minutes; time of day, point in time; (in *plural* after numerals in form 18.00, 20.30, etc.) this number of hours and minutes past midnight on the 24-hour clock; period set aside for some purpose; (in *plural*) working or open period; short time; time for action etc.; (**the hour**) each time o'clock of a whole number of hours. □ **hourglass** two connected glass bulbs containing sand that takes an hour to pass from upper to lower bulb. □ **hourly** *adjective* & *adverb*.

houri /ˈhʊərɪ/ *noun* (*plural* **-s**) beautiful young woman in Muslim paradise.

house ● *noun* /haʊs/ (*plural* /ˈhaʊzɪz/) building for human habitation; building for special purpose or for keeping animals or goods; (buildings of) religious community; section of boarding school etc.; division of school for games etc.; royal family, dynasty; (premises of) firm or institution; (building for) legislative etc. assembly; audience or performance in theatre etc. ● *verb* /haʊz/ (**-sing**) provide house for; store; enclose or encase (part etc.); fix in socket etc. □ **house arrest** detention in one's own house; **houseboat** boat equipped for living in; **housebound** confined to one's house through illness etc.; **housebreaker** burglar; **housebreaking** burglary; **housefly** common fly; **house-husband** man who does wife's traditional duties; **housekeeper** woman managing affairs of house; **housekeeping** management of house, money for this, record-keeping etc.; **houseman** resident junior doctor of hospital; **house-martin** bird which builds nests on house walls etc.; **housemaster, housemistress** teacher in charge of house in boarding school; **house music** pop music with synthesized drums and bass and fast beat; **House of Commons** elected chamber of Parliament; **House of Lords** chamber of Parliament that is mainly hereditary; **house plant** one grown indoors; **house-proud** attentive to care etc. of home; **house-trained** (of domestic animal) trained to be clean in house; **house-warming** party celebrating move to new house; **housewife** woman whose chief occupation is managing household; **housewifely** *adjective*; **housework** regular cleaning and cooking etc. in home.

household *noun* occupants of house; house and its affairs. □ **household name** well-known name; **household troops** those nominally guarding sovereign; **household word** well-known saying or name.

householder *noun* person who owns or rents house; head of household.

housing /ˈhaʊzɪŋ/ *noun* (provision of) houses; protective casing. □ **housing estate** residential area planned as a unit.

hove *past* of HEAVE.

hovel /ˈhɒv(ə)l/ *noun* small miserable dwelling.

hover /ˈhɒvə/ *verb* (of bird etc.) remain in one place in air; (often + *about, round*) linger.

hovercraft *noun* (*plural* same) vehicle moving on air-cushion provided by downward blast.

hoverport *noun* terminal for hovercraft.

how /haʊ/ *interrogative & relative adverb* by what means, in what way; in what condition; to what extent. □ **however** nevertheless, in whatever way, to whatever extent.

howdah /ˈhaʊdə/ *noun* (usually canopied) seat for riding elephant or camel.

howitzer /ˈhaʊɪtsə/ *noun* short gun firing shells at high elevation.

howl /haʊl/ ● *noun* long doleful cry of dog etc.; prolonged wailing noise; loud cry of pain, rage, derision, or laughter. ● *verb* make howl; weep loudly; utter with howl.

howler *noun colloquial* glaring mistake.

hoy *interjection* used to call attention.

hoyden /ˈhɔɪd(ə)n/ *noun* boisterous girl.

HP *abbreviation* hire purchase; (also **hp**) horsepower.

HQ *abbreviation* headquarters.

hr. *abbreviation* hour.

HRH *abbreviation* Her or His Royal Highness.

HRT *abbreviation* hormone replacement therapy.

HT *abbreviation* high tension.

hub *noun* central part of wheel, rotating on or with axle; centre of interest, activity, etc.

hubble-bubble /ˈhʌb(ə)lbʌb(ə)l/ *noun* simple hookah; confused sound or talk.

hubbub /ˈhʌbʌb/ *noun* confused noise of talking; disturbance.

hubby /ˈhʌbɪ/ *noun* (*plural* **-ies**) *colloquial* husband.

hubris /ˈhjuːbrɪs/ *noun* arrogant pride, presumption.

huckleberry /ˈhʌk(ə)lbərɪ/ *noun* (*plural* **-ies**) low N. American shrub; its fruit.

huckster /ˈhʌkstə/ ● *noun* hawker; aggressive salesman. ● *verb* haggle; hawk (goods).

huddle /ˈhʌd(ə)l/ ● *verb* (**-ling**) (often + *up*) crowd together; nestle closely; (often + *up*) curl one's body up. ● *noun* confused mass; *colloquial* secret conference.

hue *noun* colour, tint.

hue and cry *noun* loud outcry.

huff ● *noun colloquial* fit of petulance. ● *verb* blow air, steam, etc.; (esp. **huff and puff**) bluster; remove (opponent's man) as forfeit in draughts. □ **huffy** *adjective* (**-ier**, **-iest**).

hug ● *verb* (**-gg-**) squeeze tightly in one's arms, esp. with affection; keep close to, fit tightly around. ● *noun* close clasp.

huge /hjuːdʒ/ *adjective* very large or great.

hugely *adverb* extremely, very much.

hugger-mugger /ˈhʌgəmʌgə/ *adjective & adverb* in secret; in confusion.

Huguenot /ˈhjuːgənəʊ/ *noun historical* French Protestant.

hula /ˈhuːlə/ *noun* (also **hula-hula**) Polynesian women's dance. □ **hula hoop** large hoop spun round the body.

hulk *noun* body of dismantled ship; *colloquial* large clumsy-looking person or thing.

hulking *adjective colloquial* bulky, clumsy.

hull¹ *noun* body of ship etc.

hull² ● *noun* outer covering of fruit. ● *verb* remove hulls of.

hullabaloo /ˌhʌləbəˈluː/ *noun* uproar.

hullo = HELLO.

hum ● *verb* (**-mm-**) make low continuous sound like bee; sing with closed lips; make slight inarticulate sound; *colloquial* be active; *colloquial* smell unpleasantly. ● *noun* humming sound. □ **hummingbird** small tropical bird whose wings hum.

human /ˈhjuːmən/ ● *adjective* of or belonging to species *Homo sapiens*; consisting of human beings; having characteristics of humankind, as being weak, fallible, sympathetic, etc. ● *noun* (*plural* **-s**) human being. □ **human being** man, woman, or child; **human chain** line of people for passing things along etc.; **humankind** human beings collectively; **human rights** those held to belong to all people; **human shield** person(s) placed in line of fire to discourage attack.

humane /hjuːˈmeɪn/ *adjective* benevolent, compassionate; inflicting minimum pain; (of studies) tending to civilize. □ **humanely** *adverb*.

humanism /ˈhjuːmənɪz(ə)m/ *noun* nonreligious philosophy based on liberal human values; (often **Humanism**) literary culture, esp. in Renaissance. □ **humanist** *noun*; **humanistic** /-ˈnɪst-/ *adjective*.

humanitarian /hjuːˌmænɪˈteərɪən/ ● *noun* person who seeks to promote human welfare. ● *adjective* of humanitarians. □ **humanitarianism** *noun*.

humanity /hjuːˈmænɪtɪ/ *noun* (*plural* **-ies**) human race; human nature; humaneness, benevolence; (usually in *plural*) subjects concerned with human culture.

humanize *verb* (also **-ise**) (**-zing** or **-sing**) make human or humane. □ **humanization** *noun*.

humanly *adverb* within human capabilities; in a human way.

humble /ˈhʌmb(ə)l/ ● *adjective* (**-r**, **-st**) having or showing low self-esteem; lowly, modest. ● *verb* (**-ling**) make humble; lower rank of. □ **eat humble pie** apologize humbly, accept humiliation. □ **humbly** *adverb*.

humbug /ˈhʌmbʌg/ ● *noun* deception, hypocrisy; impostor; striped peppermint-flavoured boiled sweet. ● *verb* (**-gg-**) be impostor; hoax.

humdinger /ˈhʌmdɪŋə/ *noun slang* remarkable person or thing.

humdrum /ˈhʌmdrʌm/ *adjective* dull, commonplace.

humerus /ˈhjuːmərəs/ *noun* (*plural* **-ri** /-raɪ/) bone of upper arm.

humid /ˈhjuːmɪd/ *adjective* warm and damp.

humidifier /hjuːˈmɪdɪfaɪə/ *noun* device for keeping atmosphere moist.

humidify /hjuːˈmɪdɪfaɪ/ *verb* (**-ies**, **-ied**) make (air etc.) humid.

humidity /hjuːˈmɪdɪtɪ/ *noun* (*plural* **-ies**) dampness; degree of moisture, esp. in atmosphere.

humiliate /hjuːˈmɪlɪeɪt/ *verb* (**-ting**) injure dignity or self-respect of. □ **humiliating** *adjective*; **humiliation** *noun*.

humility /hjuːˈmɪlɪtɪ/ *noun* humbleness, meekness.

hummock /ˈhʌmək/ *noun* hillock, hump.

hummus /ˈhʊməs/ *noun* (also **houmous**) dip of chickpeas, sesame paste, lemon juice, and garlic.

humor *US* = HUMOUR.

humorist /ˈhjuːmərɪst/ *noun* humorous writer, talker, or actor.

humorous /ˈhjuːmərəs/ *adjective* showing humour, comic. □ **humorously** *adverb*.

humour /ˈhjuːmə/ (*US* **humor**) ● *noun* quality of being amusing; expression of humour in literature etc.; (in full **sense of humour**) ability to perceive or express humour; state of mind, mood; each of 4 fluids formerly held to determine physical and mental qualities. ● *verb* gratify or indulge (person, taste, etc.). □ **humourless** *adjective*.

hump ● *noun* rounded lump, esp. on back; rounded raised mass of earth etc.; (**the hump**) *slang* fit of depression or annoyance. ● *verb* (often + *about*) *colloquial* lift or carry with difficulty; make hump-shaped. □ **humpback** (**whale**) whale with dorsal fin; **humpback bridge** one with steep approach to top; **over the hump** past the most difficult stage.

humph /hʌmf/ *interjection & noun* inarticulate sound of dissatisfaction etc.

humus /'hjuːməs/ *noun* organic constituent of soil formed by decomposition of plants.

hunch ● *verb* bend or arch into a hump. ● *noun* intuitive feeling; hump.

hundred /'hʌndrəd/ *adjective & noun* (*plural* same in first sense) ten times ten; *historical* subdivision of county; (**hundreds**) *colloquial* large number. □ **hundreds and thousands** tiny coloured sweets; **hundredweight** (*plural* same or **-s**) 112 lb (50.80 kg), *US* 100 lb. (45.4 kg) □ **hundredth** *adjective & noun*.

hundredfold *adjective & adverb* a hundred times as much or many.

hung *past & past participle* of HANG. □ **hung-over** suffering from hangover; **hung parliament** parliament in which no party has clear majority.

Hungarian /hʌŋ'geərɪən/ ● *noun* native, national, or language of Hungary. ● *adjective* of Hungary or its people or language.

hunger /'hʌŋgə/ ● *noun* lack of food; discomfort or exhaustion caused by this; (often + *for*, *after*) strong desire. ● *verb* (often + *for*, *after*) crave, desire; feel hunger. □ **hunger strike** refusal of food as protest.

hungry /'hʌŋgrɪ/ *adjective* (**-ier**, **-iest**) feeling, showing, or inducing hunger; craving. □ **hungrily** *adverb*.

hunk *noun* large piece cut off; *colloquial* sexually attractive man.

hunt ● *verb* pursue wild animals for food or sport; (of animal) pursue prey; (+ *after*, *for*) search; (as **hunted** *adjective*) (of look) frightened. ● *noun* hunting; hunting area or society. □ **huntsman** hunter, person in charge of hounds. □ **hunting** *noun*.

hunter *noun* (*feminine* **huntress**) person who hunts; horse ridden for hunting.

hurdle /'hɜːd(ə)l/ ● *noun* frame to be jumped over by athlete in race; (in *plural*) hurdle race; obstacle; portable rectangular frame used as temporary fence. ● *verb* (**-ling**) run in hurdle race. □ **hurdler** *noun*.

hurdy-gurdy /hɜːdɪ'gɜːdɪ/ *noun* (*plural* **-ies**) droning musical instrument played by turning handle; *colloquial* barrel organ.

hurl ● *verb* throw violently. ● *noun* violent throw.

hurley /'hɜːlɪ/ *noun* (also **hurling**) (stick used in) Irish game resembling hockey.

hurly-burly /hɜːlɪ'bɜːlɪ/ *noun* boisterous activity; commotion.

hurrah /hʊˈrɑː/ (also **hurray** /hʊˈreɪ/) ● *interjection* expressing joy or approval. ● *noun* utterance of 'hurrah'.

hurricane /'hʌrɪkən/ *noun* storm with violent wind, esp. W. Indian cyclone. □ **hurricane lamp** lamp with flame protected from wind.

hurry /'hʌrɪ/ ● *noun* great haste; eagerness; (with negative or in questions) need for haste. ● *verb* (**-ies**, **-ied**) (cause to) move or act hastily; (as **hurried** *adjective*) hasty, done rapidly. □ **hurriedly** *adverb*.

hurt ● *verb* (*past & past participle* **hurt**) cause pain, injury, or distress to; suffer pain. ● *noun* injury; harm. □ **hurtful** *adjective*; **hurtfully** *adverb*.

hurtle /'hɜːt(ə)l/ *verb* (**-ling**) move or hurl rapidly or noisily, come with crash.

husband /'hʌzbənd/ ● *noun* married man in relation to his wife. ● *verb* use (resources) economically.

husbandry *noun* farming; management of resources.

hush ● *verb* make, become, or be silent. ● *interjection* calling for silence. ● *noun* silence. □ **hush-hush** *colloquial* highly secret; **hush money** *slang* sum paid to ensure discretion; **hush up** suppress (fact).

husk ● *noun* dry outer covering of fruit or seed. ● *verb* remove husk from.

husky[1] /'hʌskɪ/ *adjective* (**-ier**, **-iest**) dry in the throat, hoarse; strong, hefty. □ **huskily** *adverb*.

husky[2] /'hʌskɪ/ *noun* (*plural* **-ies**) powerful dog used for pulling sledges.

hussar /hʊˈzɑː/ *noun* light-cavalry soldier.

hussy /'hʌsɪ/ *noun* (*plural* **-ies**) pert girl; promiscuous woman.

hustings /'hʌstɪŋz/ *noun* election proceedings.

hustle /'hʌs(ə)l/ ● *verb* (**-ling**) jostle; (+ *into*, *out of*, etc.) force, hurry; *slang* solicit business. ● *noun* act or instance of hustling. □ **hustler** *noun*.

hut *noun* small simple or crude house or shelter.

hutch *noun* box or cage for rabbits etc.

hyacinth /ˈhaɪəsɪnθ/ *noun* bulbous plant with bell-shaped flowers.

hybrid /ˈhaɪbrɪd/ ● *noun* offspring of two animals or plants of different species etc.; thing of mixed origins. ● *adjective* bred as hybrid; heterogeneous. □ **hybridism** *noun*; **hybridization** *noun*; **hybridize** *verb* (also **-ise**) (**-zing** or **-sing**).

hydra /ˈhaɪdrə/ *noun* freshwater polyp; something hard to destroy.

hydrangea /haɪˈdreɪndʒə/ *noun* shrub with globular clusters of white, blue, or pink flowers.

hydrant /ˈhaɪdrənt/ *noun* outlet for drawing water from main.

hydrate /ˈhaɪdreɪt/ ● *noun* chemical compound of water with another compound etc. ● *verb* (**-ting**) (cause to) combine with water. □ **hydration** *noun*.

hydraulic /haɪˈdrɔːlɪk/ *adjective* (of water etc.) conveyed through pipes etc.; operated by movement of liquid. □ **hydraulically** *adverb*.

hydraulics *plural noun* (usually treated as *singular*) science of conveyance of liquids through pipes etc., esp. as motive power.

hydro /ˈhaɪdrəʊ/ *noun* (*plural* **-s**) *colloquial* hotel etc. originally providing hydropathic treatment; hydroelectric powerplant.

hydro- *combining form* water; combined with hydrogen.

hydrocarbon /haɪdrəʊˈkɑːbən/ *noun* compound of hydrogen and carbon.

hydrocephalus /haɪdrəˈsefələs/ *noun* accumulated fluid in brain, esp. in young children. □ **hydrocephalic** /-sɪˈfælɪk/ *adjective*.

hydrochloric acid /haɪdrəˈklɒrɪk/ *noun* solution of hydrogen chloride in water.

hydrodynamics /haɪdrəʊdaɪˈnæmɪks/ *plural noun* (usually treated as *singular*) science of forces acting on or exerted by liquids.

hydroelectric /haɪdrəʊɪˈlektrɪk/ *adjective* generating electricity by water-power; (of electricity) so generated. □ **hydroelectricity** /-ˈtrɪs-/ *noun*.

hydrofoil /ˈhaɪdrəfɔɪl/ *noun* boat fitted with planes for raising hull out of water at speed; such a plane.

hydrogen /ˈhaɪdrədʒ(ə)n/ *noun* light colourless odourless gas combining with oxygen to form water. □ **hydrogen bomb** immensely powerful bomb utilizing explosive fusion of hydrogen nuclei; **hydrogen peroxide** see PEROXIDE.

hydrogenate /haɪˈdrɒdʒɪneɪt/ *verb* (**-ting**) charge with or cause to combine with hydrogen. □ **hydrogenation** *noun*.

hydrography /haɪˈdrɒɡrəfɪ/ *noun* science of surveying and charting seas, lakes, rivers, etc. □ **hydrographer** *noun*; **hydrographic** /-drəˈɡræf-/ *adjective*.

hydrology /haɪˈdrɒlədʒɪ/ *noun* science of relationship between water and land.

hydrolyse /ˈhaɪdrəlaɪz/ *verb* (**-sing**) (*US* **-lyze**; **-zing**) decompose by hydrolysis.

hydrolysis /haɪˈdrɒlɪsɪs/ *noun* decomposition by chemical reaction with water.

hydrometer /haɪˈdrɒmɪtə/ *noun* instrument for measuring density of liquids.

hydropathy /haɪˈdrɒpəθɪ/ *noun* (medically unorthodox) treatment of disease by water. □ **hydropathic** /-drəˈpæθ-/ *adjective*.

hydrophobia /haɪdrəˈfəʊbɪə/ *noun* aversion to water, esp. as symptom of rabies in humans; rabies. □ **hydrophobic** *adjective*.

hydroplane /ˈhaɪdrəpleɪn/ *noun* light fast motor boat; finlike device enabling submarine to rise or fall.

hydroponics /haɪdrəˈpɒnɪks/ *noun* growing plants without soil, in sand, water, etc. with added nutrients.

hydrostatic /haɪdrəˈstætɪk/ *adjective* of the equilibrium of liquids and the pressure exerted by liquids at rest.

hydrostatics *plural noun* (usually treated as *singular*) study of hydrostatic properties of liquids.

hydrotherapy /haɪdrəˈθerəpɪ/ *noun* use of water, esp. swimming, in treatment of disease.

hydrous /ˈhaɪdrəs/ *adjective* containing water.

hyena /haɪˈiːnə/ *noun* doglike flesh-eating mammal.

hygiene /ˈhaɪdʒiːn/ *noun* conditions or practices conducive to maintaining health; cleanliness; sanitary science. □ **hygienic** /-ˈdʒiːn-/ *adjective*; **hygienically** /-ˈdʒiːn-/ *adverb*; **hygienist** *noun*.

hygrometer /haɪˈgrɒmɪtə/ *noun* instrument for measuring humidity of air etc.

hygroscopic /haɪgrəˈskɒpɪk/ *adjective* tending to absorb moisture from air.

hymen /ˈhaɪmen/ *noun* membrane at opening of vagina, usually broken at first sexual intercourse.

hymenopterous /haɪməˈnɒptərəs/ *adjective* of order of insects with 4 membranous wings, including bees and wasps.

hymn /hɪm/ ● *noun* song of esp. Christian praise. ● *verb* praise or celebrate in hymns.

hymnal /ˈhɪmn(ə)l/ *noun* book of hymns.

hymnology /hɪmˈnɒlədʒɪ/ *noun* composition or study of hymns. □ **hymnologist** *noun*.

hyoscine /ˈhaɪəsiːn/ *noun* alkaloid used to prevent motion sickness etc.

hype /haɪp/ *slang* ● *noun* intensive promotion of product etc. ● *verb* (**-ping**) promote with hype. □ **hyped up** excited.

hyper /ˈhaɪpə/ *adjective slang* hyperactive.

hyper- /ˈhaɪpə/ *prefix* over, above; too.

hyperbola /haɪˈpɜːbələ/ *noun* (*plural* **-s** or **-lae** /-liː/) curve produced when cone is cut by plane making larger angle with base than side of cone makes. □ **hyperbolic** /-pəˈbɒl-/ *adjective*.

hyperbole /haɪˈpɜːbəlɪ/ *noun* exaggeration, esp. for effect. □ **hyperbolical** /-ˈbɒl-/ *adjective*.

hyperglycaemia /haɪpəglaɪˈsiːmɪə/ *noun* (*US* **hyperglycemia**) excess of glucose in bloodstream.

hypermarket /ˈhaɪpəmɑːkɪt/ *noun* very large supermarket.

hypermedia /ˈhaɪpəmiːdɪə/ *noun* provision of several media (audio, video, etc.) on one computer system.

hypersensitive /haɪpəˈsensɪtɪv/ *adjective* excessively sensitive. □ **hypersensitivity** /-ˈtɪv-/ *noun*.

hypersonic /haɪpəˈsɒnɪk/ *adjective* of speeds more than 5 times that of sound.

hypertension /haɪpəˈtenʃ(ə)n/ *noun* abnormally high blood pressure; extreme tension.

hypertext /ˈhaɪpətekst/ *noun* provision of several texts on one computer system.

hyperthermia /haɪpəˈθɜːmɪə/ *noun* abnormally high body-temperature.

hyperthyroidism /haɪpəˈθaɪrɔɪdɪz(ə)m/ *noun* overactivity of thyroid gland.

hyperventilation /haɪpəventɪˈleɪʃ(ə)n/ *noun* abnormally rapid breathing. □ **hyperventilate** *verb* (**-ting**).

hyphen /ˈhaɪf(ə)n/ ● *noun* punctuation mark (-) used to join or divide words (see panel). ● *verb* hyphenate.

hyphenate /ˈhaɪfəneɪt/ *verb* (**-ting**) join or divide with hyphen. □ **hyphenation** *noun*.

hypnosis /hɪpˈnəʊsɪs/ *noun* state like sleep in which subject acts only on external suggestion; artificially induced sleep.

hypnotherapy /hɪpnəʊˈθerəpɪ/ *noun* treatment of mental disorders by hypnosis.

hypnotic /hɪpˈnɒtɪk/ ● *adjective* of or causing hypnosis; sleep-inducing. ● *noun* hypnotic drug or influence. □ **hypnotically** *adverb*.

hypnotism /ˈhɪpnətɪz(ə)m/ *noun* study or practice of hypnosis. □ **hypnotist** *noun*.

hypnotize /ˈhɪpnətaɪz/ *verb* (also **-ise**) (**-zing** or **-sing**) produce hypnosis in; fascinate.

hypo /ˈhaɪpəʊ/ *noun* sodium thiosulphate, used as photographic fixer.

hypo- /ˈhaɪpəʊ/ *prefix* under; below normal; slightly.

hypochondria /haɪpəˈkɒndrɪə/ *noun* abnormal anxiety about one's health.

hypochondriac /haɪpəˈkɒndrɪæk/ ● *noun* person given to hypochondria. ● *adjective* of hypochondria.

hypocrisy /hɪˈpɒkrɪsɪ/ *noun* (*plural* **-ies**) simulation of virtue; insincerity.

hypocrite /ˈhɪpəkrɪt/ *noun* person guilty of hypocrisy. □ **hypocritical** /-ˈkrɪt-/ *adjective*; **hypocritically** /-ˈkrɪt-/ *adverb*.

hypodermic /haɪpəˈdɜːmɪk/ ● *adjective* (of drug, syringe, etc.) introduced under the skin. ● *noun* hypodermic injection or syringe.

hypotension /haɪpəʊˈtenʃ(ə)n/ *noun* abnormally low blood pressure.

hypotenuse /haɪˈpɒtənjuːz/ *noun* side opposite right angle of right-angled triangle.

hypothalamus /haɪpəˈθæləməs/ *noun* (*plural* **-mi** /-maɪ/) region of brain controlling body temperature, thirst, hunger, etc.

hypothermia /haɪpəˈθɜːmɪə/ *noun* abnormally low body-temperature.

hypothesis /haɪˈpɒθɪsɪs/ *noun* (*plural* **-theses** /-siːz/) supposition made as basis for reasoning etc. □ **hypothesize** *verb* (also **-ise**) (**-zing** or **-sing**).

hypothetical /haɪpəˈθetɪk(ə)l/ *adjective* of or resting on hypothesis. □ **hypothetically** *adverb*.

hypothyroidism /haɪpəʊˈθaɪrɔɪdɪz(ə)m/ *noun* subnormal activity of the thyroid gland.

hypoventilation /haɪpəʊventɪˈleɪʃ(ə)n/ *noun* abnormally slow breathing.

hyssop /ˈhɪsəp/ *noun* small bushy aromatic herb.

hysterectomy /hɪstəˈrektəmɪ/ *noun* (*plural* **-ies**) surgical removal of womb.

••

Hyphen -

This is used:

1 to join two or more words so as to form a compound or single expression, e.g.

mother-in-law, non-stick, dressing-table

This use is growing less common; often you can do without such hyphens:

nonstick, treelike, dressing table

2 to join words in an attributive compound (one put before a noun, like an adjective), e.g.

a well-known man (but *the man is well known*)
an out-of-date list (but *the list is out of date*)

3 to join a prefix etc. to a proper name, e.g.

anti-Darwinian; half-Italian; non-British

4 to make a meaning clear by linking words, e.g.

twenty-odd people/twenty odd people

or by separating a prefix, e.g.

re-cover/recover; re-present/represent; re-sign/resign

5 to separate two identical letters in adjacent parts of a word, e.g.

pre-exist, Ross-shire

6 to represent a common second element in the items of a list, e.g.

two-, three-, or fourfold.

7 to divide a word if there is no room to complete it at the end of the line, e.g.

... diction-
ary ...

The hyphen comes at the end of the line, not at the beginning of the next line. In general, words should be divided at the end of a syllable: *dicti-onary* would be quite wrong. In handwriting, typing, and word-processing, it is safest (and often neatest) not to divide words at all.

••

hysteria /hɪˈstɪərɪə/ *noun* uncontrollable emotion or excitement; functional disturbance of nervous system.

hysteric /hɪˈstɛrɪk/ *noun* (in *plural*) fit of hysteria, *colloquial* overwhelming laughter; hysterical person. □ **hysterical** *adjective*; **hysterically** *adverb*.

Hz *abbreviation* hertz.

I i

I[1] *noun* (also **i**) (Roman numeral) 1.

I[2] /aɪ/ *pronoun used by speaker or writer to refer to himself or herself as subject of verb.*

I[3] *abbreviation* (also **I.**) Island(s); Isle(s).

iambic /aɪˈæmbɪk/ ● *adjective* of or using iambuses. ● *noun* (usually in *plural*) iambic verse.

iambus /aɪˈæmbəs/ *noun* (*plural* **-buses** or **-bi** /-baɪ/) metrical foot of one short followed by one long syllable.

IBA *abbreviation* Independent Broadcasting Authority.

ibex /ˈaɪbɛks/ *noun* (*plural* **-es**) wild mountain goat with large backward-curving ridged horns.

ibid. /ˈɪbɪd/ *abbreviation* in same book or passage etc. (*ibidem*).

ibis /ˈaɪbɪs/ *noun* (*plural* **-es**) storklike bird with long curved bill.

ice ● *noun* frozen water; portion of ice cream etc. ● *verb* (**icing**) mix with or cool in ice; (often + *over, up*) cover or become covered (as) with ice; freeze; cover (a cake etc.) with icing. □ **ice age** glacial period; **icebox** compartment in refrigerator for making or storing ice, *US* refrigerator; **ice-breaker** boat designed to break through ice; **icecap** mass of thick ice permanently covering polar region etc.; **ice cream** sweet creamy frozen food; **ice field** extensive sheet of floating ice; **ice hockey** form of hockey played on ice with flat disc instead of ball; **ice lolly** flavoured ice on stick; **ice rink** area of ice for skating etc.; **ice-skate** *noun* boot with blade attached for gliding over ice, *verb* move on ice-skates; **on ice** performed by ice-skaters, *colloquial* in reserve.

iceberg /ˈaɪsbɜːg/ *noun* mass of floating ice at sea. □ **tip of the iceberg** small perceptible part of something very large or complex.

Icelander /ˈaɪsləndə/ *noun* native of Iceland.

Icelandic /aɪsˈlændɪk/ ● *adjective* of Iceland. ● *noun* language of Iceland.

ichneumon /ɪkˈnjuːmən/ *noun* (in full **ichneumon fly**) wasplike insect parasitic on other insects; mongoose of N. Africa etc.

ichthyology /ɪkθɪˈɒlədʒɪ/ *noun* study of fishes. □ **ichthyological** /-əˈlɒdʒɪk(ə)l/ *adjective*; **ichthyologist** *noun*.

ichthyosaur /ˈɪkθɪəsɔː/ *noun* large extinct reptile like dolphin.

icicle /ˈaɪsɪk(ə)l/ *noun* tapering hanging spike of ice, formed from dripping water.

icing *noun* sugar etc. coating for cake etc.; formation of ice on ship or aircraft. □ **icing sugar** finely powdered sugar.

icon /ˈaɪkɒn/ *noun* (also **ikon**) sacred painting, mosaic, etc.; image, statue. □ **iconic** /-ˈkɒn-/ *adjective*.

iconoclast /aɪˈkɒnəklæst/ *noun* person who attacks cherished beliefs; *historical* breaker of religious images. □ **iconoclasm** *noun*; **iconoclastic** /-ˈklæstɪk/ *adjective*.

iconography /aɪkəˈnɒgrəfɪ/ *noun* illustration of subject by drawings etc.; study of portraits, esp. of one person, or of artistic images or symbols.

icy /ˈaɪsɪ/ *adjective* (**-ier, -iest**) very cold; covered with or abounding in ice; (of manner) unfriendly.

ID *abbreviation* identification, identity.

I'd /aɪd/ I had; I should; I would.

id *noun Psychology* part of mind comprising instinctive impulses of individual etc.

idea /aɪˈdɪə/ *noun* plan etc. formed by mental effort; mental impression or concept; vague belief or fancy; purpose, intention. □ **have no idea** *colloquial* not know at all, be completely incompetent.

ideal /aɪˈdiːəl/ ● *adjective* perfect; existing only in idea; visionary. ● *noun* perfect type, thing, principle, etc. as standard for imitation.

idealism *noun* forming or pursuing ideals; representation of things in ideal form; philosophy in which objects are held to be dependent on mind. □ **idealist** *noun*; **idealistic** /-ˈlɪst-/ *adjective*.

idealize *verb* (also **-ise**) (**-zing** or **-sing**) regard or represent as ideal. □ **idealization** *noun*.

identical /aɪˈdentɪk(ə)l/ *adjective* (often + *with*) absolutely alike; same; (of twins) developed from single ovum and very similar in appearance. □ **identically** *adverb*.

identify /aɪˈdentɪfaɪ/ *verb* (**-ies**, **-ied**) establish identity of; select, discover; (+ *with*) closely associate with; (+ *with*) regard oneself as sharing basic characteristics with; (often + *with*) treat as identical. □ **identification** *noun*.

identity /aɪˈdentɪtɪ/ *noun* (*plural* **-ies**) being specified person or thing; individuality; identification or the result of it; absolute sameness.

ideogram /ˈɪdɪəɡræm/ *noun* (also **ideograph** /-ɡrɑːf/) symbol representing thing or idea without indicating sounds in its name (e.g. Chinese character, or '=' for 'equals').

ideology /aɪdɪˈɒlədʒɪ/ *noun* (*plural* **-ies**) scheme of ideas at basis of political etc. theory or system; characteristic thinking of class etc. □ **ideological** /-əˈlɒdʒ-/ *adjective*.

idiocy /ˈɪdɪəsɪ/ *noun* (*plural* **-ies**) utter foolishness; foolish act; mental condition of idiot.

idiom /ˈɪdɪəm/ *noun* phrase etc. established by usage and not immediately comprehensible from the words used; form of expression peculiar to a language; language; characteristic mode of expression. □ **idiomatic** /-ˈmæt-/ *adjective*.

idiosyncrasy /ɪdɪəʊˈsɪŋkrəsɪ/ *noun* (*plural* **-ies**) attitude or form of behaviour peculiar to person. □ **idiosyncratic** /-ˈkræt-/ *adjective*.

idiot /ˈɪdɪət/ *noun* stupid person; person too deficient in mind to be capable of rational conduct. □ **idiotic** /-ˈɒt-/ *adjective*.

idle /ˈaɪd(ə)l/ ● *adjective* (**-r**, **-st**) lazy, indolent; not in use; unoccupied; useless, purposeless. ● *verb* (**-ling**) be idle; (of engine) run slowly without doing any work; pass (time) in idleness. □ **idleness** *noun*; **idler** *noun*; **idly** *adverb*.

idol /ˈaɪd(ə)l/ *noun* image as object of worship; object of devotion.

idolater /aɪˈdɒlətə/ *noun* worshipper of idols; devout admirer. □ **idolatrous** *adjective*; **idolatry** *noun*.

idolize *verb* (also **-ise**) (**-zing** or **-sing**) venerate or love to excess; treat as idol. □ **idolization** *noun*.

idyll /ˈɪdɪl/ *noun* account of picturesque scene or incident etc.; such scene etc. □ **idyllic** /ɪˈdɪlɪk/ *adjective*.

i.e. *abbreviation* that is to say (*id est*).

if *conjunction* on condition or supposition that; (*with past tense*) implying that the condition is not fulfilled; even though; whenever; whether; *expressing wish, request, or* (*with negative*) *surprise*. □ **if only** even if for no other reason than, I wish that.

igloo /ˈɪɡluː/ *noun* dome-shaped snow house.

igneous /ˈɪɡnɪəs/ *adjective* of fire; (esp. of rocks) produced by volcanic action.

ignite /ɪɡˈnaɪt/ *verb* (**-ting**) set fire to; catch fire; provoke or excite (feelings etc.).

ignition /ɪɡˈnɪʃ(ə)n/ *noun* mechanism for starting combustion in cylinder of motor engine; igniting.

ignoble /ɪɡˈnəʊb(ə)l/ *adjective* (**-r**, **-st**) dishonourable; of low birth or position.

ignominious /ɪɡnəˈmɪnɪəs/ *adjective* humiliating. □ **ignominiously** *adverb*.

ignominy /ˈɪɡnəmɪnɪ/ *noun* dishonour, infamy.

ignoramus /ɪɡnəˈreɪməs/ *noun* (*plural* **-muses**) ignorant person.

ignorant /ˈɪɡnərənt/ *adjective* lacking knowledge; (+ *of*) uninformed; *colloquial* uncouth. □ **ignorance** *noun*.

ignore /ɪgˈnɔː/ *verb* (**-ring**) refuse to take notice of.

iguana /ɪgˈwɑːnə/ *noun* large Central and S. American tree lizard.

iguanodon /ɪgˈwɑːnədɒn/ *noun* large plant-eating dinosaur.

ikebana /ɪkɪˈbɑːnə/ *noun* Japanese art of flower arrangement.

ikon = ICON.

ilex /ˈaɪleks/ *noun* (*plural* **-es**) plant of genus including holly; holm-oak.

iliac /ˈɪlɪæk/ *adjective* of flank or hip-bone.

ilk *noun* colloquial sort, kind. □ **of that ilk** *Scottish* of ancestral estate of same name as family.

I'll /aɪl/ I shall; I will.

ill ● *adjective* in bad health, sick; harmful, unfavourable; hostile, unkind; faulty, deficient. ● *adverb* badly, unfavourably; scarcely. ● *noun* harm; evil. □ **ill-advised** unwise; **ill-bred** rude; **ill-favoured** unattractive; **ill-gotten** gained unlawfully or wickedly; **ill health** poor physical condition; **ill-mannered** rude; **ill-natured** churlish; **ill-tempered** morose, irritable; **ill-timed** done or occurring at unsuitable time; **ill-treat**, **-use** treat badly.

illegal /ɪˈliːg(ə)l/ *adjective* contrary to law. □ **illegality** /-ˈgæl-/ *noun* (*plural* **-ies**); **illegally** *adverb*.

illegible /ɪˈledʒɪb(ə)l/ *adjective* not legible, unreadable. □ **illegibility** *noun*; **illegibly** *adverb*.

illegitimate /ɪlɪˈdʒɪtɪmət/ *adjective* born of parents not married to each other; unlawful; improper; wrongly inferred. □ **illegitimacy** *noun*.

illiberal /ɪˈlɪbər(ə)l/ *adjective* narrow-minded; stingy. □ **illiberality** /-ˈræl-/ *noun*.

illicit /ɪˈlɪsɪt/ *adjective* unlawful; forbidden. □ **illicitly** *adverb*.

illiterate /ɪˈlɪtərət/ ● *adjective* unable to read; uneducated. ● *noun* illiterate person. □ **illiteracy** *noun*.

illness *noun* disease; ill health.

illogical /ɪˈlɒdʒɪk(ə)l/ *adjective* devoid of or contrary to logic. □ **illogicality** /-ˈkæl-/ *noun* (*plural* **-ies**); **illogically** *adverb*.

illuminate /ɪˈluːmɪneɪt/ *verb* (**-ting**) light up; decorate with lights; decorate (manuscript etc.) with gold, colour, etc.; help to explain (subject etc.); enlighten spiritually or intellectually. □ **illuminating** *adjective*; **illumination** *noun*.

illumine /ɪˈljuːmɪn/ *verb* (**-ning**) *literary* light up; enlighten.

illusion /ɪˈluːʒ(ə)n/ *noun* false belief; deceptive appearance. □ **be under the illusion** (+ *that*) believe mistakenly. □ **illusive** *adjective*; **illusory** *adjective*.

illusionist *noun* conjuror.

illustrate /ˈɪləstreɪt/ *verb* (**-ting**) provide with pictures; make clear, esp. by examples or drawings; serve as example of. □ **illustrator** *noun*.

illustration *noun* drawing etc. in book; explanatory example; illustrating.

illustrative /ˈɪləstrətɪv/ *adjective* (often + *of*) explanatory.

illustrious /ɪˈlʌstrɪəs/ *adjective* distinguished, renowned.

I'm /aɪm/ I am.

image /ˈɪmɪdʒ/ ● *noun* representation of object, esp. figure of saint or divinity; reputation or persona of person, company, etc.; appearance as seen in mirror or through lens; idea, conception; simile, metaphor. ● *verb* (**-ging**) make image of; mirror; picture.

imagery /ˈɪmɪdʒəri/ *noun* figurative illustration; use of images in literature etc.; images, statuary; mental images collectively.

imaginary /ɪˈmædʒɪnəri/ *adjective* existing only in imagination.

imagination /ɪmædʒɪˈneɪʃ(ə)n/ *noun* mental faculty of forming images of objects not present to senses; creative faculty of mind.

imaginative /ɪˈmædʒɪnətɪv/ *adjective* having or showing high degree of imagination. □ **imaginatively** *adverb*.

imagine /ɪˈmædʒɪn/ *verb* (**-ning**) form mental image of, conceive; suppose, think.

imago /ɪˈmeɪgəʊ/ *noun* (*plural* **-s** or **imagines** /ɪˈmædʒɪniːz/) fully developed stage of insect.

imam /ɪˈmɑːm/ *noun* prayer-leader of mosque; *title of some Muslim leaders.*

imbalance /ɪmˈbæləns/ *noun* lack of balance; disproportion.

imbecile /'ɪmbɪsiːl/ ● noun colloquial stupid person; adult with mental age of about 5. ● adjective mentally weak, stupid. □ **imbecilic** /-'sɪlɪk/ adjective; **imbecility** /-'sɪlɪtɪ/ noun (plural -ies).

imbed = EMBED.

imbibe /ɪm'baɪb/ verb (-bing) drink; drink in; absorb; inhale.

imbroglio /ɪm'brəʊlɪəʊ/ noun (plural -s) confused or complicated situation.

imbue /ɪm'bjuː/ verb (-bues, -bued, -buing) (often + with) inspire; saturate, dye.

imitate /'ɪmɪteɪt/ verb (-ting) follow example of; mimic; make copy of; be like. □ **imitable** adjective; **imitative** /-tətɪv/ adjective; **imitator** noun.

imitation noun imitating, being imitated; copy; counterfeit.

immaculate /ɪ'mækjʊlət/ adjective perfectly clean, spotless; faultless; innocent, sinless. □ **immaculately** adverb; **immaculateness** noun.

immanent /'ɪmənənt/ adjective inherent; (of God) omnipresent. □ **immanence** noun.

immaterial /ɪmə'tɪərɪəl/ adjective unimportant; irrelevant; not material. □ **immateriality** /-'æl-/ noun.

immature /ɪmə'tjʊə/ adjective not mature; undeveloped, esp. emotionally. □ **immaturity** noun.

immeasurable /ɪ'meʒərəb(ə)l/ adjective not measurable, immense. □ **immeasurably** adverb.

immediate /ɪ'miːdɪət/ adjective occurring at once; direct; nearest; having priority. □ **immediacy** noun; **immediately** adverb.

immemorial /ɪmɪ'mɔːrɪəl/ adjective ancient beyond memory.

immense /ɪ'mens/ adjective vast, huge. □ **immensity** noun.

immensely adverb colloquial vastly, very much.

immerse /ɪ'mɜːs/ verb (-sing) (often + in) dip, plunge; put under water; (often **immerse oneself** or in passive; often + in) involve deeply, embed.

immersion /ɪ'mɜːʃ(ə)n/ noun immersing, being immersed. □ **immersion heater** electric heater designed to be immersed in liquid to be heated.

immigrant /'ɪmɪgrənt/ ● noun person who immigrates. ● adjective immigrating; of immigrants.

immigrate /'ɪmɪgreɪt/ verb (-ting) enter a country to settle permanently. □ **immigration** noun.

imminent /'ɪmɪnənt/ adjective soon to happen. □ **imminence** noun; **imminently** adverb.

immobile /ɪ'məʊbaɪl/ adjective motionless; immovable. □ **immobility** noun.

immobilize /ɪ'məʊbɪlaɪz/ verb (also -ise) (-zing or -sing) prevent from being moved. □ **immobilization** noun.

immoderate /ɪ'mɒdərət/ adjective excessive. □ **immoderately** adverb.

immodest /ɪ'mɒdɪst/ adjective conceited; indecent. □ **immodesty** noun.

immolate /'ɪməleɪt/ verb (-ting) kill as sacrifice. □ **immolation** noun.

immoral /ɪ'mɒr(ə)l/ adjective opposed to, or not conforming to, (esp. sexual) morality; dissolute. □ **immorality** /ɪmə'rælɪtɪ/ noun.

immortal /ɪ'mɔːt(ə)l/ ● adjective living for ever; unfading; divine; famous for all time. ● noun immortal being, esp. (in plural) gods of antiquity. □ **immortality** /-'tæl-/ noun; **immortalize** verb (also -ise) (-zing or -sing).

immovable /ɪ'muːvəb(ə)l/ adjective not movable; unyielding. □ **immovability** noun.

immune /ɪ'mjuːn/ adjective having immunity; relating to immunity; exempt.

immunity noun (plural -ies) living organism's power of resisting and overcoming infection; (often + from) freedom, exemption.

immunize /'ɪmjʊnaɪz/ verb (also -ise) (-zing or -sing) make immune. □ **immunization** noun.

immure /ɪ'mjʊə/ verb (-ring) imprison.

immutable /ɪ'mjuːtəb(ə)l/ adjective unchangeable. □ **immutability** noun.

imp noun mischievous child; little devil.

impact ● noun /'ɪmpækt/ collision, striking; (immediate) effect or influence. ● verb /ɪm'pækt/ drive or wedge together; (as **impacted** adjective) (of tooth) wedged between another tooth and jaw. □ **impaction** /ɪm'pækʃ(ə)n/ noun.

impair /ɪm'peə/ verb damage, weaken. □ **impairment** noun.

impala /ɪmˈpɑːlə/ noun (plural same or **-s**) small African antelope.

impale /ɪmˈpeɪl/ verb (**-ling**) transfix on stake. □ **impalement** noun.

impalpable /ɪmˈpælpəb(ə)l/ adjective not easily grasped; imperceptible to touch.

impart /ɪmˈpɑːt/ verb communicate (news etc.); give share of.

impartial /ɪmˈpɑːʃ(ə)l/ adjective fair, not partial. □ **impartiality** /-ʃɪˈæl-/ noun; **impartially** adverb.

impassable /ɪmˈpɑːsəb(ə)l/ adjective that cannot be traversed. □ **impassability** noun.

impasse /ˈæmpæs/ noun deadlock.

impassioned /ɪmˈpæʃ(ə)nd/ adjective filled with passion, ardent.

impassive /ɪmˈpæsɪv/ adjective not feeling or showing emotion. □ **impassively** adverb; **impassivity** /-ˈsɪv-/ noun.

impasto /ɪmˈpæstəʊ/ noun technique of laying on paint thickly.

impatiens /ɪmˈpeɪʃɪenz/ noun any of several plants including busy Lizzie.

impatient /ɪmˈpeɪʃ(ə)nt/ adjective not patient; intolerant; restlessly eager. □ **impatience** noun; **impatiently** adverb.

impeach /ɪmˈpiːtʃ/ verb accuse, esp. of treason etc.; call in question; disparage. □ **impeachment** noun.

impeccable /ɪmˈpekəb(ə)l/ adjective faultless; exemplary. □ **impeccability** noun; **impeccably** adverb.

impecunious /ˌɪmpɪˈkjuːnɪəs/ adjective having little or no money.

impedance /ɪmˈpiːd(ə)ns/ noun total effective resistance of electric circuit etc. to alternating current.

impede /ɪmˈpiːd/ verb (**-ding**) obstruct; hinder.

impediment /ɪmˈpedɪmənt/ noun hindrance; defect in speech, esp. lisp or stammer.

impedimenta /ɪmpedɪˈmentə/ plural noun encumbrances; baggage, esp. of army.

impel /ɪmˈpel/ verb (**-ll-**) drive, force; propel.

impend /ɪmˈpend/ verb be imminent; hang. □ **impending** adjective.

impenetrable /ɪmˈpenɪtrəb(ə)l/ adjective not penetrable; inscrutable; inaccessible to influences etc. □ **impenetrability** noun.

impenitent /ɪmˈpenɪt(ə)nt/ adjective not penitent. □ **impenitence** noun.

imperative /ɪmˈperətɪv/ ● adjective urgent, obligatory; peremptory; Grammar (of mood) expressing command. ● noun Grammar imperative mood; command; essential or urgent thing.

imperceptible /ˌɪmpəˈseptɪb(ə)l/ adjective not perceptible; very slight or gradual. □ **imperceptibility** noun; **imperceptibly** adverb.

imperfect /ɪmˈpɜːfɪkt/ ● adjective not perfect; incomplete; faulty; Grammar (of past tense) implying action going on but not completed. ● noun imperfect tense. □ **imperfectly** adverb.

imperfection /ˌɪmpəˈfekʃ(ə)n/ noun imperfectness; fault, blemish.

imperial /ɪmˈpɪərɪəl/ adjective of empire or sovereign state ranking with this; of emperor; majestic; (of non-metric weights and measures) used by statute in UK.

imperialism noun imperial system of government etc.; usually derogatory policy of dominating other nations by acquisition of dependencies or through trade etc. □ **imperialist** noun & adjective.

imperil /ɪmˈperɪl/ verb (**-ll-**; US **-l-**) endanger.

imperious /ɪmˈpɪərɪəs/ adjective overbearing, domineering. □ **imperiously** adverb.

imperishable /ɪmˈperɪʃəb(ə)l/ adjective that cannot perish.

impermanent /ɪmˈpɜːmənənt/ adjective not permanent. □ **impermanence** noun.

impermeable /ɪmˈpɜːmɪəb(ə)l/ adjective not permeable. □ **impermeability** noun.

impersonal /ɪmˈpɜːsən(ə)l/ adjective having no personality or personal feeling or reference; impartial; unfeeling; Grammar (of verb) used esp. with it as subject. □ **impersonality** /-ˈnæl-/ noun.

impersonate /ɪmˈpɜːsəneɪt/ verb (**-ting**) pretend to be, play part of. □ **impersonation** noun; **impersonator** noun.

impertinent /ɪmˈpɜːtɪnənt/ adjective insolent, saucy; irrelevant. □ **impertinence** noun; **impertinently** adverb.

imperturbable /ˌɪmpəˈtɜːbəb(ə)l/ adjective not excitable; calm. □ **imperturbability** noun; **imperturbably** adverb.

impervious /ɪmˈpɜːvɪəs/ adjective (usually + to) impermeable; not responsive.

impetigo /ɪmpɪˈtaɪgəʊ/ noun contagious skin disease.

impetuous /ɪmˈpetjʊəs/ adjective acting or done rashly or suddenly; moving violently or fast. □ **impetuosity** /-ˈɒs-/ noun; **impetuously** adverb.

impetus /ˈɪmpɪtəs/ noun moving force; momentum; impulse.

impiety /ɪmˈpaɪətɪ/ noun (plural -ies) lack of piety; act showing this.

impinge /ɪmˈpɪndʒ/ verb (-ging) (usually + on) make impact; (usually + upon) encroach.

impious /ˈɪmpɪəs/ adjective not pious; wicked.

impish adjective of or like imp, mischievous. □ **impishly** adverb.

implacable /ɪmˈplækəb(ə)l/ adjective not appeasable. □ **implacability** noun; **implacably** adverb.

implant ● verb /ɪmˈplɑːnt/ insert, fix; instil; plant; (in passive) (of fertilized ovum) become attached to wall of womb. ● noun /ˈɪmplɑːnt/ thing implanted. □ **implantation** noun.

implausible /ɪmˈplɔːzɪb(ə)l/ adjective not plausible. □ **implausibly** adverb.

implement ● noun /ˈɪmplɪmənt/ tool, utensil. ● verb /ˈɪmplɪment/ carry into effect. □ **implementation** noun.

implicate /ˈɪmplɪkeɪt/ verb (-ting) (often + in) show (person) to be involved (in crime etc.); imply.

implication noun thing implied; implying; implicating.

implicit /ɪmˈplɪsɪt/ adjective implied though not expressed; unquestioning. □ **implicitly** adverb.

implode /ɪmˈpləʊd/ verb (-ding) (cause to) burst inwards. □ **implosion** /ɪmˈpləʊʒ(ə)n/ noun.

implore /ɪmˈplɔː/ verb (-ring) beg earnestly.

imply /ɪmˈplaɪ/ verb (-ies, -ied) (often + that) insinuate, hint; mean.

impolite /ɪmpəˈlaɪt/ adjective uncivil, rude. □ **impolitely** adverb; **impoliteness** noun.

impolitic /ɪmˈpɒlɪtɪk/ adjective inexpedient, not advisable. □ **impoliticly** adverb.

imponderable /ɪmˈpɒndərəb(ə)l/ ● adjective that cannot be estimated; very light. ● noun (usually in plural) imponderable thing. □ **imponderability** noun; **imponderably** adverb.

import ● verb /ɪmˈpɔːt/ bring in (esp. foreign goods) from abroad; imply, mean. ● noun /ˈɪmpɔːt/ article or (in plural) amount imported; importing; meaning, implication; importance. □ **importation** noun; **importer** /-ˈpɔːtə/ noun.

important /ɪmˈpɔːt(ə)nt/ adjective (often + to) of great consequence; momentous; (of person) having position of authority or rank; pompous. □ **importance** noun; **importantly** adverb.

importunate /ɪmˈpɔːtjʊnət/ adjective making persistent or pressing requests. □ **importunity** /-ˈtjuːn-/ noun.

importune /ɪmpəˈtjuːn/ verb (-ning) pester (person) with requests; solicit as prostitute.

impose /ɪmˈpəʊz/ verb (-sing) enforce compliance with; (often + on) inflict, lay (tax etc.); (+ on, upon) take advantage of.

imposing adjective impressive, esp. in appearance.

imposition /ɪmpəˈzɪʃ(ə)n/ noun imposing, being imposed; unfair demand or burden; tax, duty.

impossible /ɪmˈpɒsɪb(ə)l/ adjective not possible; not easy or convenient; colloquial outrageous, intolerable. □ **impossibility** noun; **impossibly** adverb.

impost /ˈɪmpəʊst/ noun tax, duty.

impostor /ɪmˈpɒstə/ noun (also **imposter**) person who assumes false character; swindler.

imposture /ɪmˈpɒstʃə/ noun fraudulent deception.

impotent /ˈɪmpət(ə)nt/ adjective powerless; (of male) unable to achieve erection of penis or have sexual intercourse. □ **impotence** noun.

impound /ɪmˈpaʊnd/ verb confiscate; shut up in pound.

impoverish /ɪmˈpɒvərɪʃ/ verb make poor. □ **impoverishment** noun.

impracticable /ɪmˈpræktɪkəb(ə)l/ adjective impossible in practice. □ **impracticability** noun; **impracticably** adverb.

impractical /ɪmˈpræktɪk(ə)l/ *adjective* not practical; *esp. US* not practicable. □ **impracticality** /-ˈkæl-/ *noun*.

imprecation /ɪmprɪˈkeɪʃ(ə)n/ *noun formal* curse.

imprecise /ɪmprɪˈsaɪs/ *adjective* not precise.

impregnable /ɪmˈpregnəb(ə)l/ *adjective* safe against attack. □ **impregnability** *noun*.

impregnate /ˈɪmpregneɪt/ *verb* (**-ting**) fill, saturate; make pregnant. □ **impregnation** *noun*.

impresario /ɪmprɪˈsɑːrɪəʊ/ *noun* (*plural* **-s**) organizer of public entertainments.

impress *verb* /ɪmˈpres/ affect or influence deeply; arouse admiration or respect in; (often + *on*) emphasize; imprint, stamp. ● *noun* /ˈɪmpres/ mark impressed; characteristic quality.

impression /ɪmˈpreʃ(ə)n/ *noun* effect produced on mind; belief; imitation of person or sound, esp. done to entertain; impressing, mark impressed; unaltered reprint of book etc.; issue of book or newspaper etc.; print from type or engraving.

impressionable *adjective* easily influenced.

impressionism *noun* school of painting concerned with conveying effect of natural light on objects; style of music or writing seeking to convey esp. fleeting feelings or experience. □ **impressionist** *noun*, **impressionistic** /-ˈnɪs-/ *adjective*.

impressive /ɪmˈpresɪv/ *adjective* arousing respect, approval, or admiration. □ **impressively** *adverb*.

imprimatur /ɪmprɪˈmɑːtə/ *noun* licence to print; official approval.

imprint ● *verb* /ɪmˈprɪnt/ (often + *on*) impress firmly, esp. on mind; make impression of (figure etc.) on thing; make impression on with stamp etc. ● *noun* /ˈɪmprɪnt/ impression; printer's or publisher's name in book etc.

imprison /ɪmˈprɪz(ə)n/ *verb* (**-n-**) put into prison; confine. □ **imprisonment** *noun*.

improbable /ɪmˈprɒbəb(ə)l/ *adjective* not likely, difficult to believe. □ **improbability** *noun*, **improbably** *adverb*.

improbity /ɪmˈprəʊbɪtɪ/ *noun* (*plural* **-ies**) wickedness; dishonesty; wicked or dishonest act.

impromptu /ɪmˈprɒmptjuː/ ● *adverb & adjective* unrehearsed. ● *noun* (*plural* **-s**) impromptu performance or speech; short, usually solo, musical piece, often improvisatory in style.

improper /ɪmˈprɒpə/ *adjective* unseemly, indecent; inaccurate, wrong. □ **improperly** *adverb*.

impropriety /ɪmprəˈpraɪətɪ/ *noun* (*plural* **-ies**) indecency; instance of this; incorrectness, unfitness.

improve /ɪmˈpruːv/ *verb* (**-ving**) make or become better; (+ *on*) produce something better than; (as **improving** *adjective*) giving moral benefit. □ **improvement** *noun*.

improvident /ɪmˈprɒvɪd(ə)nt/ *adjective* lacking foresight; wasteful. □ **improvidence** *noun*, **improvidently** *adverb*.

improvise /ˈɪmprəvaɪz/ *verb* (**-sing**) compose extempore; provide or construct from materials etc. not intended for the purpose. □ **improvisation** *noun*, **improvisational** *adjective*, **improvisatory** /-ˈzeɪtərɪ/ *adjective*.

imprudent /ɪmˈpruːd(ə)nt/ *adjective* rash, indiscreet. □ **imprudence** *noun*, **imprudently** *adverb*.

impudent /ˈɪmpjʊd(ə)nt/ *adjective* impertinent. □ **impudence** *noun*, **impudently** *adverb*.

impugn /ɪmˈpjuːn/ *verb* challenge; call in question.

impulse /ˈɪmpʌls/ *noun* sudden urge; tendency to follow such urges; impelling; impetus.

impulsive /ɪmˈpʌlsɪv/ *adjective* apt to act on impulse; done on impulse; tending to impel. □ **impulsively** *adverb*, **impulsiveness** *noun*.

impunity /ɪmˈpjuːnɪtɪ/ *noun* exemption from punishment or injurious consequences. □ **with impunity** without punishment etc.

impure /ɪmˈpjʊə/ *adjective* adulterated; dirty; unchaste.

impurity *noun* (*plural* **-ies**) being impure; impure thing or part.

impute /ɪmˈpjuːt/ *verb* (**-ting**) (+ *to*) ascribe (fault etc.) to. □ **imputation** *noun*.

in ● *preposition expressing inclusion or position within limits of space, time, circumstance, etc.*; after (specified period of time); with respect to; as proportionate part of; with form or arrangement of; as member of; involved with; within ability of; having the condition of; affected by; having as aim; by means of; meaning; into (with verb of motion or change). ● *adverb expressing position bounded by certain limits, or movement to point enclosed by them*; into room etc.; at home etc.; so as to be enclosed; as part of a publication; in fashion, season, or office; (of player etc.) having turn or right to play; (of transport) at platform etc.; (of season, harvest, ordered goods, etc.) having arrived or been received; (of fire etc.) burning; (of tide) at highest point. ● *adjective* internal, living etc. inside; fashionable; (of joke etc.) confined to small group. □ **in-between** *colloquial* intermediate; **in-house** within an institution, company, etc.; **ins and outs** (often + *of*) details; **in so far as** to the extent that; **in that** because, in so far as; **in-tray** tray for incoming documents etc.; **in with** on good terms with.

in. *abbreviation* inch(es).

inability /ɪnəˈbɪlɪtɪ/ *noun* being unable.

inaccessible /ɪnəkˈsesɪb(ə)l/ *adjective* not accessible; unapproachable. □ **inaccessibility** *noun*.

inaccurate /ɪnˈækjʊrət/ *adjective* not accurate. □ **inaccuracy** *noun* (*plural* **-ies**); **inaccurately** *adverb*.

inaction /ɪnˈækʃ(ə)n/ *noun* absence of action.

inactive /ɪnˈæktɪv/ *adjective* not active; not operating. □ **inactivity** /-ˈtɪv-/ *noun*.

inadequate /ɪnˈædɪkwət/ *adjective* insufficient; incompetent. □ **inadequacy** *noun* (*plural* **-ies**); **inadequately** *adverb*.

inadmissible /ɪnədˈmɪsɪb(ə)l/ *adjective* not allowable. □ **inadmissibility** *noun*; **inadmissibly** *adverb*.

inadvertent /ɪnədˈvɜːt(ə)nt/ *adjective* unintentional; inattentive. □ **inadvertence** *noun*; **inadvertently** *adverb*.

inadvisable /ɪnədˈvaɪzəb(ə)l/ *adjective* not advisable. □ **inadvisability** *noun*.

inalienable /ɪnˈeɪlɪənəb(ə)l/ *adjective* that cannot be transferred to another or taken away.

inane /ɪˈneɪn/ *adjective* silly, senseless; empty. □ **inanity** /-ˈnæn-/ *noun* (*plural* **-ies**).

inanimate /ɪnˈænɪmət/ *adjective* not endowed with animal life; spiritless, dull.

inapplicable /ɪnəˈplɪkəb(ə)l/ *adjective* not applicable; irrelevant. □ **inapplicability** *noun*.

inapposite /ɪnˈæpəzɪt/ *adjective* not apposite.

inappropriate /ɪnəˈprəʊprɪət/ *adjective* not appropriate. □ **inappropriately** *adverb*; **inappropriateness** *noun*.

inapt /ɪnˈæpt/ *adjective* not suitable; unskilful. □ **inaptitude** *noun*.

inarticulate /ɪnɑːˈtɪkjʊlət/ *adjective* unable to express oneself clearly; not articulate, indistinct; dumb; not jointed. □ **inarticulately** *adverb*.

inasmuch /ɪnəzˈmʌtʃ/ *adverb* (+ *as*) since, because; to the extent that.

inattentive /ɪnəˈtentɪv/ *adjective* not paying attention; neglecting to show courtesy. □ **inattention** *noun*; **inattentively** *adverb*.

inaudible /ɪnˈɔːdɪb(ə)l/ *adjective* that cannot be heard. □ **inaudibly** *adverb*.

inaugural /ɪnˈɔːgjʊr(ə)l/ ● *adjective* of inauguration. ● *noun* inaugural speech or lecture.

inaugurate /ɪnˈɔːgjʊreɪt/ *verb* (**-ting**) admit (person) to office; initiate use of or begin with ceremony; begin, introduce. □ **inauguration** *noun*.

inauspicious /ɪnɔːˈspɪʃəs/ *adjective* not of good omen; unlucky.

inborn /ˈɪnbɔːn/ *adjective* existing from birth; innate.

inbred /ɪnˈbred/ *adjective* inborn; produced by inbreeding.

inbreeding /ɪnˈbriːdɪŋ/ *noun* breeding from closely related animals or people.

Inc. *abbreviation US* Incorporated.

incalculable /ɪnˈkælkjʊləb(ə)l/ *adjective* too great for calculation; not calculable beforehand; uncertain. □ **incalculability** *noun*; **incalculably** *adverb*.

incandesce /ɪnkænˈdes/ *verb* (**-cing**) (cause to) glow with heat.

incandescent *adjective* glowing with heat, shining; (of artificial light) produced by glowing filament etc. □ **incandescence** *noun*.

incantation /ɪnkænˈteɪʃ(ə)n/ *noun* spell, charm. □ **incantational** *adjective*.

incapable /ɪnˈkeɪpəb(ə)l/ *adjective* not capable; too honest, kind, etc. to do something; not capable of rational conduct. □ **incapability** *noun*.

incapacitate /ɪnkəˈpæsɪteɪt/ *verb* (**-ting**) make incapable or unfit.

incapacity /ɪnkəˈpæsɪti/ *noun* inability; legal disqualification.

incarcerate /ɪnˈkɑːsəreɪt/ *verb* (**-ting**) imprison. □ **incarceration** *noun*.

incarnate /ɪnˈkɑːnət/ *adjective* in esp. human form.

incarnation /ɪnkɑːˈneɪʃ(ə)n/ *noun* embodiment in flesh; (**the Incarnation**) embodiment of God in Christ; (often + *of*) living type (of a quality etc.).

incautious /ɪnˈkɔːʃəs/ *adjective* rash. □ **incautiously** *adverb*.

incendiary /ɪnˈsendɪəri/ ● *adjective* (of bomb) filled with material for causing fires; of arson; guilty of arson; inflammatory. ● *noun* (*plural* **-ies**) incendiary person or bomb.

incense[1] /ˈɪnsens/ *noun* gum or spice giving sweet smell when burned; smoke of this, esp. in religious ceremonial.

incense[2] /ɪnˈsens/ *verb* (**-sing**) make angry.

incentive /ɪnˈsentɪv/ ● *noun* motive, incitement; payment etc. encouraging effort in work. ● *adjective* serving to motivate or incite.

inception /ɪnˈsepʃ(ə)n/ *noun* beginning.

incessant /ɪnˈses(ə)nt/ *adjective* unceasing, continual; repeated. □ **incessantly** *adverb*.

incest /ˈɪnsest/ *noun* crime of sexual intercourse between people prohibited from marrying because of closeness of their blood relationship.

incestuous /ɪnˈsestjʊəs/ *adjective* of or guilty of incest; having relationships restricted to a particular group etc.

inch ● *noun* twelfth of (linear) foot (2.54 cm); this as unit of map-scale (e.g. 1 inch to 1 mile) or as unit of rainfall (= 1 inch depth of water). ● *verb* move gradually. □ **every inch** entirely; **within an inch of one's life** almost to death.

inchoate /ˈɪnkəʊeɪt/ *adjective* just begun; undeveloped. □ **inchoation** *noun*.

incidence /ˈɪnsɪd(ə)ns/ *noun* range, scope, extent, manner, or rate of occurrence; falling of line, ray, particles, etc.

on surface; coming into contact with thing.

incident /ˈɪnsɪd(ə)nt/ ● *noun* event, occurrence; violent episode, civil or military; episode in play, film, etc. ● *adjective* (often + *to*) apt to occur, naturally attaching; (often + *on*, *upon*) (of light etc.) falling.

incidental /ɪnsɪˈdent(ə)l/ *adjective* (often + *to*) minor, supplementary; not essential. □ **incidental music** music played during or between scenes of play, film, etc.

incidentally *adverb* by the way; in an incidental way.

incinerate /ɪnˈsɪnəreɪt/ *verb* (**-ting**) burn to ashes. □ **incineration** *noun*.

incinerator *noun* furnace or device for incineration.

incipient /ɪnˈsɪpɪənt/ *adjective* beginning, in early stage.

incise /ɪnˈsaɪz/ *verb* (**-sing**) make cut in; engrave.

incision /ɪnˈsɪʒ(ə)n/ *noun* cutting, esp. by surgeon; cut.

incisive /ɪnˈsaɪsɪv/ *adjective* sharp; clear and effective.

incisor /ɪnˈsaɪzə/ *noun* cutting-tooth, esp. at front of mouth.

incite /ɪnˈsaɪt/ *verb* (**-ting**) (often + *to*) urge on, stir up. □ **incitement** *noun*.

incivility /ɪnsɪˈvɪlɪti/ *noun* (*plural* **-ies**) rudeness; impolite act.

inclement /ɪnˈklemənt/ *adjective* (of weather) severe, stormy. □ **inclemency** *noun*.

inclination /ɪnklɪˈneɪʃ(ə)n/ *noun* propensity; liking, affection; slope, slant.

incline ● *verb* /ɪnˈklaɪn/ (**-ning**) (usually in *passive*) dispose, influence; have specified tendency; be disposed, tend; (cause to) lean or bend. ● *noun* /ˈɪnklaɪn/ slope.

include /ɪnˈkluːd/ *verb* (**-ding**) comprise, regard or treat as part of whole. □ **inclusion** /-ʒ(ə)n/ *noun*.

inclusive /ɪnˈkluːsɪv/ *adjective* (often + *of*) including; including the limits stated; comprehensive; including all accessory payments. □ **inclusively** *adverb*; **inclusiveness** *noun*.

incognito /ɪnkɒgˈniːtəʊ/ ● *adjective* & *adverb* with one's name or identity concealed. ● *noun* (*plural* **-s**) person who is incognito; pretended identity.

incoherent /ɪnkəʊˈhɪərənt/ adjective unintelligible; lacking logic or consistency; not clear. □ **incoherence** noun; **incoherently** adverb.

incombustible /ɪnkəmˈbʌstɪb(ə)l/ adjective that cannot be burnt.

income /ˈɪnkʌm/ noun money received, esp. periodically, from work, investments, etc. □ **income tax** tax levied on income.

incoming adjective coming in; succeeding another.

incommensurable /ɪnkəˈmenʃərəb(ə)l/ adjective (often + with) not comparable in size, value, etc.; having no common factor. □ **incommensurability** noun.

incommensurate /ɪnkəˈmenʃərət/ adjective (often + with, to) out of proportion; inadequate; incommensurable.

incommode /ɪnkəˈməʊd/ verb (-ding) formal inconvenience; trouble, annoy.

incommodious /ɪnkəˈməʊdɪəs/ adjective formal too small for comfort; inconvenient.

incommunicable /ɪnkəˈmjuːnɪkəb(ə)l/ adjective that cannot be shared or communicated.

incommunicado /ɪnkəmjuːnɪˈkɑːdəʊ/ adjective without means of communication, in solitary confinement in prison etc.

incomparable /ɪnˈkɒmpərəb(ə)l/ adjective without an equal; matchless. □ **incomparability** noun; **incomparably** adverb.

incompatible /ɪnkəmˈpætɪb(ə)l/ adjective not compatible. □ **incompatibility** noun.

incompetent /ɪnˈkɒmpɪt(ə)nt/ adjective inept; (often + to) lacking the necessary skill, not legally qualified. □ **incompetence** noun.

incomplete /ɪnkəmˈpliːt/ adjective not complete.

incomprehensible /ɪnkɒmprɪˈhensɪb(ə)l/ adjective that cannot be understood.

incomprehension /ɪnkɒmprɪˈhenʃ(ə)n/ noun failure to understand.

inconceivable /ɪnkənˈsiːvəb(ə)l/ adjective that cannot be imagined. □ **inconceivably** adverb.

inconclusive /ɪnkənˈkluːsɪv/ adjective (of argument etc.) not convincing or decisive.

incongruous /ɪnˈkɒŋɡrʊəs/ adjective out of place; absurd; (often + with) out of keeping. □ **incongruity** /-ˈɡruːɪtɪ/ noun (plural -ies); **incongruously** adverb.

inconsequent /ɪnˈkɒnsɪkwənt/ adjective irrelevant; not following logically; disconnected. □ **inconsequence** noun.

inconsequential /ɪnkɒnsɪˈkwenʃ(ə)l/ adjective unimportant; inconsequent. □ **inconsequentially** adverb.

inconsiderable /ɪnkənˈsɪdərəb(ə)l/ adjective of small size, value, etc.; not worth considering. □ **inconsiderably** adverb.

inconsiderate /ɪnkənˈsɪdərət/ adjective not considerate of others; thoughtless. □ **inconsiderately** adverb; **inconsiderateness** noun.

inconsistent /ɪnkənˈsɪst(ə)nt/ adjective not consistent. □ **inconsistency** noun (plural -ies); **inconsistently** adverb.

inconsolable /ɪnkənˈsəʊləb(ə)l/ adjective that cannot be consoled. □ **inconsolably** adverb.

inconspicuous /ɪnkənˈspɪkjʊəs/ adjective not conspicuous; not easily noticed. □ **inconspicuously** adverb; **inconspicuousness** noun.

inconstant /ɪnˈkɒnst(ə)nt/ adjective fickle; variable. □ **inconstancy** noun (plural -ies).

incontestable /ɪnkənˈtestəb(ə)l/ adjective that cannot be disputed. □ **incontestably** adverb.

incontinent /ɪnˈkɒntɪnənt/ adjective unable to control bowels or bladder; lacking self-restraint. □ **incontinence** noun.

incontrovertible /ɪnkɒntrəˈvɜːtɪb(ə)l/ adjective indisputable. □ **incontrovertibly** adverb.

inconvenience /ɪnkənˈviːnɪəns/ • noun lack of ease or comfort; trouble; cause or instance of this. • verb (-cing) cause inconvenience to.

inconvenient adjective causing trouble, difficulty, or discomfort; awkward. □ **inconveniently** adverb.

incorporate • verb /ɪnˈkɔːpəreɪt/ (-ting) include as part or ingredient; (often + in, with) unite (in one body); admit as member of company etc.; (esp. as **incorporated** adjective) constitute as legal corporation. ● *adjective* /ɪnˈkɔːpərət/ incorporated. □ **incorporation** *noun*.

incorporeal /ɪnkɔːˈpɔːrɪəl/ *adjective* without substance or material existence. □ **incorporeally** *adverb*.

incorrect /ɪnkəˈrekt/ *adjective* untrue, inaccurate; improper, unsuitable. □ **incorrectly** *adverb*.

incorrigible /ɪnˈkɒrɪdʒɪb(ə)l/ *adjective* that cannot be corrected or improved. □ **incorrigibility** *noun*, **incorrigibly** *adverb*.

incorruptible /ɪnkəˈrʌptɪb(ə)l/ *adjective* that cannot decay or be corrupted. □ **incorruptibility** *noun*, **incorruptibly** *adverb*.

increase ● *verb* /ɪnˈkriːs/ (-sing) become or make greater or more numerous. ● *noun* /ˈɪnkriːs/ growth, enlargement; (of people, animals, or plants) multiplication; increased amount. □ **on the increase** increasing.

increasingly /ɪnˈkriːsɪŋlɪ/ *adverb* more and more.

incredible /ɪnˈkredɪb(ə)l/ *adjective* that cannot be believed; *colloquial* surprising, extremely good. □ **incredibility** *noun*, **incredibly** *adverb*.

incredulous /ɪnˈkredjʊləs/ *adjective* unwilling to believe; showing disbelief. □ **incredulity** /ɪnkrɪˈdjuːlɪtɪ/ *noun*, **incredulously** *adverb*.

increment /ˈɪnkrɪmənt/ *noun* amount of increase; added amount. □ **incremental** /-ˈment(ə)l/ *adjective*.

incriminate /ɪnˈkrɪmɪneɪt/ *verb* (-ting) indicate as guilty; charge with crime. □ **incrimination** *noun*, **incriminatory** *adjective*.

incrustation /ɪnkrʌsˈteɪʃ(ə)n/ *noun* encrusting, being encrusted; crust, hard coating; deposit on surface.

incubate /ˈɪnkjʊbeɪt/ *verb* (-ting) hatch (eggs) by sitting on them or by artificial heat; cause (bacteria etc.) to develop; develop slowly.

incubation *noun* incubating, being incubated; period between infection and appearance of first symptoms.

incubator *noun* apparatus providing warmth for hatching eggs, rearing premature babies, or developing bacteria.

incubus /ˈɪnkjʊbəs/ *noun* (*plural* **-buses** or **-bi** /-baɪ/) demon or male spirit formerly believed to have sexual intercourse with sleeping women; nightmare; oppressive person or thing.

inculcate /ˈɪnkʌlkeɪt/ *verb* (-ting) (often + *upon*, *in*) urge, impress persistently. □ **inculcation** *noun*.

incumbency /ɪnˈkʌmbənsɪ/ *noun* (*plural* **-ies**) office or tenure of incumbent.

incumbent /ɪnˈkʌmbənt/ ● *adjective* lying, pressing; currently holding office. ● *noun* holder of office, esp. benefice. □ **it is incumbent on a person** (+ *to do*) it is a person's duty.

incur /ɪnˈkɜː/ *verb* (-rr-) bring on oneself.

incurable /ɪnˈkjʊərəb(ə)l/ ● *adjective* that cannot be cured. ● *noun* incurable person. □ **incurability** *noun*, **incurably** *adverb*.

incurious /ɪnˈkjʊərɪəs/ *adjective* lacking curiosity.

incursion /ɪnˈkɜːʃ(ə)n/ *noun* invasion; sudden attack. □ **incursive** *adjective*.

indebted /ɪnˈdetɪd/ *adjective* (usually + *to*) owing money or gratitude. □ **indebtedness** *noun*.

indecent /ɪnˈdiːs(ə)nt/ *adjective* offending against decency; unbecoming; unsuitable. □ **indecent assault** sexual attack not involving rape. □ **indecency** *noun*, **indecently** *adverb*.

indecipherable /ɪndɪˈsaɪfərəb(ə)l/ *adjective* that cannot be deciphered.

indecision /ɪndɪˈsɪʒ(ə)n/ *noun* inability to decide; hesitation.

indecisive /ɪndɪˈsaɪsɪv/ *adjective* not decisive; irresolute; not conclusive. □ **indecisively** *adverb*, **indecisiveness** *noun*.

indecorous /ɪnˈdekərəs/ *adjective* improper, undignified; in bad taste. □ **indecorously** *adverb*.

indeed /ɪnˈdiːd/ ● *adverb* in truth; really; admittedly. ● *interjection* expressing irony, incredulity, etc.

indefatigable /ɪndɪˈfætɪɡəb(ə)l/ *adjective* unwearying, unremitting. □ **indefatigably** *adverb*.

indefeasible /ɪndɪˈfiːzɪb(ə)l/ *adjective* literary (esp. of claim, rights, etc.) that cannot be forfeited or annulled.

indefensible /ɪndɪˈfensɪb(ə)l/ *adjective* that cannot be defended. □ **indefensibility** *noun*, **indefensibly** *adverb*.

indefinable /ɪndɪˈfaɪnəb(ə)l/ *adjective* that cannot be defined; mysterious. □ **indefinably** *adverb*.

indefinite /ɪnˈdefɪnɪt/ *adjective* vague, undefined; unlimited; (of adjectives, adverbs, and pronouns) not determining the person etc. referred to. □ **indefinite article** word (*a, an* in English) placed before noun and meaning 'one, some, any'.

indefinitely *adverb* for an unlimited time; in an indefinite manner.

indelible /ɪnˈdelɪb(ə)l/ *adjective* that cannot be rubbed out; permanent. □ **indelibly** *adverb*.

indelicate /ɪnˈdelɪkət/ *adjective* coarse, unrefined; tactless. □ **indelicacy** *noun* (*plural* **-ies**); **indelicately** *adverb*.

indemnify /ɪnˈdemnɪfaɪ/ *verb* (**-ies, -ied**) (often + *against, from*) secure against loss or legal responsibility; (often + *for*) exempt from penalty; compensate. □ **indemnification** *noun*.

indemnity /ɪnˈdemnɪtɪ/ *noun* (*plural* **-ies**) compensation for damage; sum exacted by victor in war; security against damage or loss; exemption from penalties.

indent ● *verb* /ɪnˈdent/ make or impress notches, dents, or recesses in; set back (beginning of line) inwards from margin; draw up (legal document) in duplicate; (often + *for*) make requisition. ● *noun* /ˈɪndent/ order (esp. from abroad) for goods; official requisition for stores; indented line; indentation; indenture.

indentation /ɪndenˈteɪʃ(ə)n/ *noun* indenting, being indented; notch.

indenture /ɪnˈdentʃə/ ● *noun* (usually in *plural*) sealed agreement; formal list, certificate, etc. ● *verb* *historical* bind by indentures, esp. as apprentice.

independent /ɪndɪˈpend(ə)nt/ ● *adjective* (often + *of*) not depending on authority; self-governing; not depending on another person for one's livelihood or opinions; (of income) making it unnecessary to earn one's livelihood; unwilling to be under obligation to others; not depending on something else for validity etc.; (of institution) not supported by public funds. ● *noun* politician etc. independent of any political party. □ **independence** *noun*; **independently** *adverb*.

indescribable /ɪndɪˈskraɪbəb(ə)l/ *adjective* beyond description; that cannot be described. □ **indescribably** *adverb*.

indestructible /ɪndɪˈstrʌktɪb(ə)l/ *adjective* that cannot be destroyed. □ **indestructibility** *noun*; **indestructibly** *adverb*.

indeterminable /ɪndɪˈtɜːmɪnəb(ə)l/ *adjective* that cannot be ascertained or settled.

indeterminate /ɪndɪˈtɜːmɪnət/ *adjective* not fixed in extent, character, etc.; vague. □ **indeterminacy** *noun*.

index /ˈɪndeks/ ● *noun* (*plural* **-es** or **indices** /ˈɪndɪsiːz/) alphabetical list of subjects etc. with references, usually at end of book; card index; measure of prices or wages compared with a previous month, year, etc.; *Mathematics* exponent. ● *verb* furnish (book) with index, enter in index; relate (wages, investment income, etc.) to a price index. □ **index finger** finger next to thumb; **index-linked** related to value of price index.

Indian /ˈɪndɪən/ ● *noun* native or national of India; person of Indian descent; (in full **American Indian**) original inhabitant of America. ● *adjective* of India; of the subcontinent comprising India, Pakistan, and Bangladesh; of the original inhabitants of America. □ **Indian corn** maize; **Indian file** single file; **Indian ink** black pigment, ink made from this; **Indian summer** period of calm dry warm weather in late autumn, happy tranquil period late in life.

indiarubber *noun* rubber, esp. for rubbing out pencil marks etc.

indicate /ˈɪndɪkeɪt/ *verb* (**-ting**) point out, make known; show; be sign of; require, call for; state briefly; give as reading or measurement; point by hand; use a vehicle's indicator. □ **indication** *noun*.

indicative /ɪnˈdɪkətɪv/ ● *adjective* (+ *of*) suggestive, giving indications; *Grammar* (of mood) stating thing as fact. ● *noun* *Grammar* indicative mood; verb in this mood.

indicator *noun* flashing light on vehicle showing direction in which it is about to turn; person or thing that indicates; device indicating condition of machine etc.; recording instrument; board giving current information.

indices *plural of* INDEX.

indict /ɪn'daɪt/ *verb* accuse formally by legal process.

indictable *adjective* (of an offence) rendering person liable to be indicted; so liable.

indictment *noun* indicting, accusation; document containing this; thing that serves to condemn or censure.

indifference /ɪn'dɪfrəns/ *noun* lack of interest or attention; unimportance.

indifferent *adjective* (+ *to*) showing indifference; neither good nor bad; of poor quality or ability. □ **indifferently** *adverb*.

indigenous /ɪn'dɪdʒɪnəs/ *adjective* (often + *to*) native or belonging naturally to a place.

indigent /'ɪndɪdʒ(ə)nt/ *adjective formal* needy, poor. □ **indigence** *noun*.

indigestible /ɪndɪ'dʒestɪb(ə)l/ *adjective* difficult or impossible to digest.

indigestion /ɪndɪ'dʒestʃ(ə)n/ *noun* difficulty in digesting food; pain caused by this.

indignant /ɪn'dɪgnənt/ *adjective* feeling or showing indignation. □ **indignantly** *adverb*.

indignation /ɪndɪg'neɪʃ(ə)n/ *noun* anger at supposed injustice etc.

indignity /ɪn'dɪgnɪtɪ/ *noun* (*plural* -**ies**) humiliating treatment; insult.

indigo /'ɪndɪgəʊ/ *noun* (*plural* -**s**) deep violet-blue; dye of this colour.

indirect /ɪndɪ'rekt/ *adjective* not going straight to the point; (of route etc.) not straight. □ **indirect object** word or phrase representing person or thing affected by action of verb but not acted on (see panel at OBJECT); **indirect speech** reported speech; **indirect tax** tax on goods and services, not income. □ **indirectly** *adverb*.

indiscernible /ɪndɪ'sɜːnɪb(ə)l/ *adjective* that cannot be discerned.

indiscipline /ɪn'dɪsɪplɪn/ *noun* lack of discipline.

indiscreet /ɪndɪ'skriːt/ *adjective* not discreet; injudicious, unwary. □ **indiscreetly** *adverb*.

indiscretion /ɪndɪ'skreʃ(ə)n/ *noun* indiscreet conduct or action.

indiscriminate /ɪndɪ'skrɪmɪnət/ *adjective* making no distinctions; done or acting at random. □ **indiscriminately** *adverb*.

indispensable /ɪndɪ'spensəb(ə)l/ *adjective* that cannot be dispensed with; necessary. □ **indispensably** *adverb*.

indisposed /ɪndɪ'spəʊzd/ *adjective* slightly unwell; averse, unwilling. □ **indisposition** /-spə'zɪʃ(ə)n/ *noun*.

indisputable /ɪndɪ'spjuːtəb(ə)l/ *adjective* that cannot be disputed. □ **indisputably** *adverb*.

indissoluble /ɪndɪ'sɒljʊb(ə)l/ *adjective* that cannot be dissolved; lasting, stable. □ **indissolubly** *adverb*.

indistinct /ɪndɪ'stɪŋkt/ *adjective* not distinct; confused, obscure. □ **indistinctly** *adverb*.

indistinguishable /ɪndɪ'stɪŋgwɪʃəb(ə)l/ *adjective* (often + *from*) not distinguishable.

indite /ɪn'daɪt/ *verb* (**-ting**) *formal or jocular* put into words; write (letter etc.).

individual /ɪndɪ'vɪdʒʊəl/ ● *adjective* of, for, or characteristic of single person or thing; having distinct character; designed for use by one person; single; particular. ● *noun* single member of class, group, etc.; single human being; *colloquial* person; distinctive person.

individualism *noun* social theory favouring free action by individuals; being independent or different. □ **individualist** *noun*; **individualistic** /-'lɪs-/ *adjective*.

individuality /ɪndɪvɪdʒʊ'ælɪtɪ/ *noun* individual character, esp. when strongly marked; separate existence.

individualize *verb* (also **-ise**) (**-zing** or **-sing**) give individual character to; (esp. as **individualized** *adjective*) personalize.

individually *adverb* one by one; personally; distinctively.

indivisible /ɪndɪ'vɪzɪb(ə)l/ *adjective* not divisible.

indoctrinate /ɪn'dɒktrɪneɪt/ *verb* (**-ting**) teach to accept a particular belief uncritically. □ **indoctrination** *noun*.

Indo-European /ɪndəʊjʊərə'pɪən/ ● *adjective* of family of languages spoken over most of Europe and Asia as far as N. India; of hypothetical parent language of this family. ● *noun* Indo-European family of languages; hypothetical parent language of these.

indolent /ˈɪndələnt/ *adjective* lazy; averse to exertion. □ **indolence** *noun;* **indolently** *adverb.*

indomitable /ɪnˈdɒmɪtəb(ə)l/ *adjective* unconquerable; unyielding. □ **indomitably** *adverb.*

indoor /ˈɪndɔː/ *adjective* done etc. in building or under cover.

indoors /ɪnˈdɔːz/ *adverb* in(to) a building.

indubitable /ɪnˈdjuːbɪtəb(ə)l/ *adjective* that cannot be doubted. □ **indubitably** *adverb.*

induce /ɪnˈdjuːs/ *verb* (**-cing**) prevail on, persuade; bring about; bring on (labour) artificially; bring on labour in (mother); speed up birth of (baby); produce by induction; infer. □ **inducible** *adjective.*

inducement *noun* attractive offer; incentive; bribe.

induct /ɪnˈdʌkt/ *verb* install into office etc.

inductance *noun* property of electric circuit in which variation in current produces electromotive force.

induction /ɪnˈdʌkʃ(ə)n/ *noun* inducting, inducing; act of bringing on (esp. labour) artificially; general inference from particular instances; formal introduction to new job etc.; production of electric or magnetic state by proximity to electric circuit or magnetic field.

inductive /ɪnˈdʌktɪv/ *adjective* (of reasoning etc.) based on induction; of electric or magnetic induction.

indulge /ɪnˈdʌldʒ/ *verb* (**-ging**) (often + *in*) take one's pleasure freely; yield freely to (desire etc.); gratify by compliance with wishes.

indulgence *noun* indulging; thing indulged in; *RC Church* remission of punishment still due after absolution; privilege granted.

indulgent *adjective* lenient; willing to overlook faults; indulging. □ **indulgently** *adverb.*

industrial /ɪnˈdʌstrɪəl/ *adjective* of, engaged in, for use in, or serving the needs of, industry; having highly developed industries. □ **industrial action** strike or disruptive action by workers as protest; **industrial estate** area of land zoned for factories etc. □ **industrially** *adverb.*

industrialism *noun* system in which manufacturing industries predominate.

industrialist *noun* owner or manager in industry.

industrialize *verb* (also **-ise**) (**-zing** or **-sing**) make (nation etc.) industrial. □ **industrialization** *noun.*

industrious /ɪnˈdʌstrɪəs/ *adjective* hardworking. □ **industriously** *adverb.*

industry /ˈɪndəstrɪ/ *noun* (*plural* **-ies**) branch of trade or manufacture; commercial enterprise; trade or manufacture collectively; concerted activity; diligence.

inebriate ● *verb* /ɪˈniːbrɪeɪt/ (**-ting**) make drunk; excite. ● *adjective* /ɪˈniːbrɪət/ drunken. ● *noun* /ɪˈniːbrɪət/ drunkard. □ **inebriation** *noun.*

inedible /ɪnˈedɪb(ə)l/ *adjective* not suitable for eating.

ineducable /ɪnˈedjʊkəb(ə)l/ *adjective* incapable of being educated.

ineffable /ɪnˈefəb(ə)l/ *adjective* too great for description in words; that must not be uttered. □ **ineffability** *noun;* **ineffably** *adverb.*

ineffective /ɪnɪˈfektɪv/ *adjective* not achieving desired effect or results. □ **ineffectively** *adverb;* **ineffectiveness** *noun.*

ineffectual /ɪnɪˈfektʃʊəl/ *adjective* ineffective, feeble. □ **ineffectually** *adverb.*

inefficient /ɪnɪˈfɪʃ(ə)nt/ *adjective* not efficient or fully capable; (of machine etc.) wasteful. □ **inefficiency** *noun;* **inefficiently** *adverb.*

inelegant /ɪnˈelɪɡənt/ *adjective* ungraceful, unrefined. □ **inelegance** *noun;* **inelegantly** *adverb.*

ineligible /ɪnˈelɪdʒɪb(ə)l/ *adjective* not eligible or qualified. □ **ineligibility** *noun.*

ineluctable /ɪnɪˈlʌktəb(ə)l/ *adjective* inescapable, unavoidable.

inept /ɪˈnept/ *adjective* unskilful; absurd; silly; out of place. □ **ineptitude** *noun;* **ineptly** *adverb.*

inequality /ˌɪnɪˈkwɒlɪtɪ/ noun (plural **-ies**) lack of equality; variability; unevenness.

inequitable /ɪnˈekwɪtəb(ə)l/ adjective unfair, unjust.

inequity /ɪnˈekwɪtɪ/ noun (plural **-ies**) unfairness, injustice.

ineradicable /ˌɪnɪˈrædɪkəb(ə)l/ adjective that cannot be rooted out.

inert /ɪˈnɜːt/ adjective without inherent power of action etc.; chemically inactive; sluggish, slow; lifeless.

inertia /ɪˈnɜːʃə/ noun property by which matter continues in existing state of rest or motion unless acted on by external force; inertness; tendency to remain unchanged. □ **inertia reel** reel allowing seat belt to unwind freely but locking on impact; **inertia selling** sending of unsolicited goods in hope of making a sale.

inescapable /ˌɪnɪˈskeɪpəb(ə)l/ adjective that cannot be escaped or avoided. □ **inescapably** adverb.

inessential /ˌɪnɪˈsenʃ(ə)l/ ● adjective not necessary; dispensable. ● noun inessential thing.

inestimable /ɪnˈestɪməb(ə)l/ adjective too great etc. to be estimated. □ **inestimably** adverb.

inevitable /ɪnˈevɪtəb(ə)l/ adjective unavoidable; bound to happen or appear; colloquial tiresomely familiar. □ **inevitability** noun; **inevitably** adverb.

inexact /ˌɪnɪɡˈzækt/ adjective not exact. □ **inexactitude** noun.

inexcusable /ˌɪnɪkˈskjuːzəb(ə)l/ adjective that cannot be justified. □ **inexcusably** adverb.

inexhaustible /ˌɪnɪɡˈzɔːstɪb(ə)l/ adjective that cannot be used up.

inexorable /ɪnˈeksərəb(ə)l/ adjective relentless. □ **inexorably** adverb.

inexpedient /ˌɪnɪkˈspiːdɪənt/ adjective not expedient.

inexpensive /ˌɪnɪkˈspensɪv/ adjective not expensive.

inexperience /ˌɪnɪkˈspɪərɪəns/ noun lack of experience. □ **inexperienced** adjective.

inexpert /ɪnˈekspɜːt/ adjective unskilful.

inexpiable /ɪnˈekspɪəb(ə)l/ adjective that cannot be expiated.

inexplicable /ˌɪnɪkˈsplɪkəb(ə)l/ adjective that cannot be explained. □ **inexplicably** adverb.

inexpressible /ˌɪnɪkˈspresɪb(ə)l/ adjective that cannot be expressed. □ **inexpressibly** adverb.

in extremis /ɪn ɪkˈstriːmɪs/ adjective at point of death; in great difficulties. [Latin]

inextricable /ˌɪnɪkˈstrɪkəb(ə)l/ adjective that cannot be separated, loosened, or resolved; inescapable. □ **inextricably** adverb.

infallible /ɪnˈfælɪb(ə)l/ adjective incapable of error; unfailing, sure. □ **infallibility** noun; **infallibly** adverb.

infamous /ˈɪnfəməs/ adjective notoriously vile, evil; abominable. □ **infamously** adverb; **infamy** noun (plural **-ies**).

infant /ˈɪnf(ə)nt/ noun child during earliest period of life; thing in early stage of development; Law person under 18. □ **infancy** noun.

infanta /ɪnˈfæntə/ noun historical daughter of Spanish or Portuguese king.

infanticide /ɪnˈfæntɪsaɪd/ noun killing of infant, esp. soon after birth; person guilty of this.

infantile /ˈɪnfəntaɪl/ adjective of or like infants. □ **infantile paralysis** poliomyelitis.

infantry /ˈɪnfəntrɪ/ noun (plural **-ies**) (group of) foot-soldiers. □ **infantryman** soldier of infantry regiment.

infatuate /ɪnˈfætjʊeɪt/ verb (**-ting**) (usually as **infatuated** adjective) inspire with intense fondness. □ **infatuation** noun.

infect /ɪnˈfekt/ verb affect or contaminate with germ, virus, or disease; imbue, taint.

infection /ɪnˈfekʃ(ə)n/ noun infecting; being infected; disease; communication of disease.

infectious adjective infecting; transmissible by infection; apt to spread. □ **infectiously** adverb.

infelicity /ˌɪnfɪˈlɪsɪtɪ/ noun (plural **-ies**) inapt expression; unhappiness. □ **infelicitous** adjective.

infer /ɪnˈfɜː/ verb (**-rr-**) deduce, conclude.

■ **Usage** It is a mistake to use *infer* to mean 'imply', as in *Are you inferring that I'm a liar?*

inference /'ɪnfərəns/ *noun* act of inferring; thing inferred. □ **inferential** /-'ren(ə)l/ *adjective*.

inferior /ɪn'fɪərɪə/ ● *adjective* lower in rank etc.; of poor quality; situated below. ● *noun* inferior person.

inferiority /ɪnfɪərɪ'ɒrɪtɪ/ *noun* being inferior. □ **inferiority complex** feeling of inadequacy, sometimes marked by compensating aggressive behaviour.

infernal /ɪn'fɜːn(ə)l/ *adjective* of hell; hellish; *colloquial* detestable, tiresome. □ **infernally** *adverb*.

inferno /ɪn'fɜːnəʊ/ *noun* (*plural* **-s**) raging fire; scene of horror or distress; hell.

infertile /ɪn'fɜːtaɪl/ *adjective* not fertile. □ **infertility** /-fə'tɪl-/ *noun*.

infest /ɪn'fest/ *verb* overrun in large numbers. □ **infestation** *noun*.

infidel /'ɪnfɪd(ə)l/ ● *noun* disbeliever in esp. the supposed true religion. ● *adjective* of infidels; unbelieving.

infidelity /ɪnfɪ'delɪtɪ/ *noun* (*plural* **-ies**) being unfaithful.

infighting *noun* conflict or competitiveness in organization; boxing within arm's length.

infiltrate /'ɪnfɪltreɪt/ *verb* (**-ting**) enter (territory, political party, etc.) gradually and imperceptibly; cause to do this; permeate by filtration; (often + *into*, *through*) introduce (fluid) by filtration. □ **infiltration** *noun*; **infiltrator** *noun*.

infinite /'ɪnfɪnɪt/ *adjective* boundless; endless; very great or many. □ **infinitely** *adverb*.

infinitesimal /ɪnfɪnɪ'tesɪm(ə)l/ *adjective* infinitely or very small. □ **infinitesimally** *adverb*.

infinitive /ɪn'fɪnɪtɪv/ ● *noun* verb-form expressing verbal notion without particular subject, tense, etc. ● *adjective* having this form.

infinitude /ɪn'fɪnɪtjuːd/ *noun literary* infinite number etc.; being infinite.

infinity /ɪn'fɪnɪtɪ/ *noun* (*plural* **-ies**) infinite number or extent; being infinite; boundlessness; infinite distance; *Mathematics* infinite quantity.

infirm /ɪn'fɜːm/ *adjective* weak.

infirmary /ɪn'fɜːmərɪ/ *noun* (*plural* **-ies**) hospital; sickbay in school etc.

infirmity *noun* (*plural* **-ies**) being infirm; particular physical weakness.

in flagrante delicto /ɪn flə'græntɪ dɪ'lɪktəʊ/ *adverb* in act of committing offence. [Latin]

inflame /ɪn'fleɪm/ *verb* (**-ming**) provoke to strong feeling; cause inflammation in; aggravate; make hot; (cause to) catch fire.

inflammable /ɪn'flæməb(ə)l/ *adjective* easily set on fire or excited. □ **inflammability** *noun*.

◼ **Usage** Because *inflammable* could be thought to mean 'not easily set on fire', *flammable* is often used instead. The negative of *inflammable* is *non-inflammable*.

inflammation /ɪnflə'meɪʃ(ə)n/ *noun* inflaming; disordered bodily condition marked by heat, swelling, redness, and usually pain.

inflammatory /ɪn'flæmətərɪ/ *adjective* tending to inflame; of inflammation.

inflatable ● *adjective* that can be inflated. ● *noun* inflatable object.

inflate /ɪn'fleɪt/ *verb* (**-ting**) distend with air or gas; (usually + *with*; usually in *passive*) puff up (with pride etc.); resort to inflation of (currency); raise (prices) artificially; (as **inflated** *adjective*) (esp. of language, opinions, etc.) bombastic, exaggerated.

inflation *noun* inflating, being inflated; general rise in prices, increase in supply of money regarded as cause of such rise. □ **inflationary** *adjective*.

inflect /ɪn'flekt/ *verb* change or vary pitch of (voice); modify (word) to express grammatical relation; undergo such modification.

inflection /ɪn'flekʃ(ə)n/ *noun* (also **inflexion**) inflecting, being inflected; inflected form; inflecting suffix etc.; modulation of voice. □ **inflectional** *adjective*.

inflexible /ɪn'fleksɪb(ə)l/ *adjective* unbendable; unhending; unyielding. □ **inflexibility** *noun*; **inflexibly** *adverb*.

inflexion = INFLECTION.

inflict /ɪn'flɪkt/ *verb* deal (blow etc.); impose. □ **infliction** *noun*.

inflight *adjective* occurring or provided during a flight.

inflorescence /ˌɪnfləˈres(ə)ns/ *noun* collective flower head of plant; arrangement of flowers on plant; flowering.

inflow *noun* flowing in; that which flows in.

influence /ˈɪnflʊəns/ ● *noun* (usually + *on*) effect a person or thing has on another; (usually + *over*, *with*) ascendancy, moral power; thing or person exercising this. ● *verb* (-cing) exert influence on; affect. □ **under the influence** *colloquial* drunk.

influential /ɪnflʊˈenʃ(ə)l/ *adjective* having great influence.

influenza /ɪnflʊˈenzə/ *noun* infectious viral disease with fever, severe aching, and catarrh.

influx /ˈɪnflʌks/ *noun* flowing in.

inform /ɪnˈfɔːm/ *verb* tell; (usually + *against*, *on*) give incriminating information about person to authorities.

informal /ɪnˈfɔːm(ə)l/ *adjective* without formality; not formal. □ **informality** /-ˈmæl-/ *noun* (*plural* **-ies**); **informally** *adverb*.

informant *noun* giver of information.

information /ɪnfəˈmeɪʃ(ə)n/ *noun* what is told; knowledge; news; formal charge or accusation. □ **information retrieval** tracing of information stored in books, computers, etc.; **information technology** study or use of processes (esp. computers etc.) for storing, retrieving, and sending information.

informative /ɪnˈfɔːmətɪv/ *adjective* giving information, instructive.

informed *adjective* knowing the facts; having some knowledge.

informer *noun* person who informs, esp. against others.

infraction /ɪnˈfrækʃ(ə)n/ *noun* infringement.

infra dig /ɪnfrə ˈdɪg/ *adjective colloquial* beneath one's dignity.

infrared /ɪnfrəˈred/ *adjective* of or using radiation just beyond red end of spectrum.

infrastructure /ˈɪnfrəstrʌktʃə/ *noun* structural foundations of a society or enterprise; roads, bridges, sewers, etc., regarded as country's economic foundation; permanent installations as basis for military etc. operations.

infrequent /ɪnˈfriːkwənt/ *adjective* not frequent. □ **infrequently** *adverb*.

infringe /ɪnˈfrɪndʒ/ *verb* (-ging) break or violate (law, another's rights, etc.); (usually + *on*) encroach, trespass. □ **infringement** *noun*.

infuriate /ɪnˈfjʊərieɪt/ *verb* (-ting) enrage; irritate greatly. □ **infuriating** *adjective*.

infuse /ɪnˈfjuːz/ *verb* (-sing) (usually + *with*) fill (with a quality); steep or be steeped in liquid to extract properties; (usually + *into*) instil (life etc.).

infusible /ɪnˈfjuːzɪb(ə)l/ *adjective* that cannot be melted. □ **infusibility** *noun*.

infusion /ɪnˈfjuːʒ(ə)n/ *noun* infusing; liquid extract so obtained; infused element.

ingenious /ɪnˈdʒiːnɪəs/ *adjective* clever at contriving; cleverly contrived. □ **ingeniously** *adverb*.

■ **Usage** *Ingenious* is sometimes confused with *ingenuous*.

ingénue /ˈæʒeɪˈnjuː/ *noun* artless young woman, esp. as stage type. [French]

ingenuity /ɪndʒɪˈnjuːɪtɪ/ *noun* inventiveness, cleverness.

ingenuous /ɪnˈdʒenjʊəs/ *adjective* artless; frank. □ **ingenuously** *adverb*.

■ **Usage** *Ingenuous* is sometimes confused with *ingenious*.

ingest /ɪnˈdʒest/ *verb* take in (food etc.); absorb (knowledge etc.). □ **ingestion** *noun*.

inglenook /ˈɪŋgəlnʊk/ *noun* space within opening either side of old-fashioned wide fireplace.

inglorious /ɪnˈglɔːrɪəs/ *adjective* shameful; not famous.

ingoing *adjective* going in.

ingot /ˈɪŋgət/ *noun* (usually oblong) mass of cast metal, esp. gold, silver, or steel.

ingrained /ɪnˈgreɪnd/ *adjective* deeply rooted, inveterate; (of dirt etc.) deeply embedded.

ingratiate /ɪnˈgreɪʃieɪt/ *verb* (-ting) (**ingratiate oneself**; usually + *with*) bring oneself into favour. □ **ingratiating** *adjective*.

ingratitude /ɪnˈgrætɪtjuːd/ *noun* lack of due gratitude.

ingredient /ɪn'gri:dɪənt/ noun component part in mixture.

ingress /'ɪngres/ noun going in; right to go in.

ingrowing adjective (of nail) growing into the flesh.

inhabit /ɪn'hæbɪt/ verb (-t-) dwell in, occupy. □ **inhabitable** adjective; **inhabitant** noun.

inhalant /ɪn'heɪlənt/ noun medicinal substance to be inhaled.

inhale /ɪn'heɪl/ verb (-ling) breathe in. □ **inhalation** /-hə'leɪʃ(ə)n/ noun.

inhaler noun device for administering inhalant, esp. to relieve asthma.

inhere /ɪn'hɪə/ verb (-ring) be inherent.

inherent /ɪn'herənt/ adjective (often + in) existing in something as essential or permanent attribute. □ **inherently** adverb.

inherit /ɪn'herɪt/ verb (-t-) receive as heir; derive (characteristic) from ancestors; derive or take over (situation) from predecessor. □ **inheritor** noun.

inheritance noun what is inherited; inheriting.

inhibit /ɪn'hɪbɪt/ verb (-t-) hinder, restrain, prevent; (as **inhibited** adjective) suffering from inhibition; (usually + from) prohibit.

inhibition /ɪnhɪ'bɪʃ(ə)n/ noun restraint of direct expression of instinct; colloquial emotional resistance to thought or action; inhibiting, being inhibited.

inhospitable /ɪnhɒs'pɪtəb(ə)l/ adjective not hospitable; affording no shelter.

inhuman /ɪn'hju:mən/ adjective brutal, unfeeling, barbarous. □ **inhumanity** /-'mæn-/ noun (plural **-ies**); **inhumanly** adverb.

inhumane /ɪnhju:'meɪn/ adjective not humane, callous.

inimical /ɪ'nɪmɪk(ə)l/ adjective hostile; harmful.

inimitable /ɪ'nɪmɪtəb(ə)l/ adjective that cannot be imitated. □ **inimitably** adverb.

iniquity /ɪ'nɪkwɪtɪ/ noun (plural **-ies**) wickedness; gross injustice. □ **iniquitous** adjective.

initial /ɪ'nɪʃ(ə)l/ ● adjective of or at beginning. ● noun first letter, esp. of person's name. ● verb (**-ll-**; US **-l-**) mark or sign with one's initials. □ **initially** adverb.

initiate ● verb /ɪ'nɪʃɪeɪt/ (**-ting**) originate, set going; admit into society, office, etc., esp. with ritual; (+ into) instruct in subject. ● noun /ɪ'nɪʃɪət/ initiated person. □ **initiation** noun; **initiatory** /ɪ'nɪʃɪətərɪ/ adjective.

initiative /ɪ'nɪʃɪətɪv/ noun ability to initiate, enterprise; first step; (**the initiative**) power or right to begin.

inject /ɪn'dʒekt/ verb (usually + into) force (medicine etc.) (as) by syringe; administer medicine etc. to (person) by injection; place (quality etc.) where needed in something. □ **injection** noun.

injudicious /ɪndʒu:'dɪʃəs/ adjective unwise, ill-judged.

injunction /ɪn'dʒʌŋkʃ(ə)n/ noun authoritative order; judicial order restraining from specified act or compelling restitution etc.

injure /'ɪndʒə/ verb (-ring) hurt, harm, impair; do wrong to.

injurious /ɪn'dʒʊərɪəs/ adjective hurtful; defamatory; wrongful.

injury /'ɪndʒərɪ/ noun (plural **-ies**) physical damage, harm; offence to feelings etc.; esp. Law wrongful treatment. □ **injury time** extra time at football match etc. to compensate for that lost in dealing with injuries.

injustice /ɪn'dʒʌstɪs/ noun unfairness; unjust act.

ink ● noun coloured fluid or paste for writing or printing; black liquid ejected by cuttlefish etc. ● verb mark, cover, or smear with ink. □ **ink-jet printer** printing machine firing tiny jets of ink at paper; **inkwell** pot for ink, esp. in hole in desk. □ **inky** adjective (**-ier, -iest**).

inkling /'ɪŋklɪŋ/ noun (often + of) hint, slight knowledge or suspicion.

inland ● adjective /'ɪnlənd/ remote from sea or border within a country; carried on within country. ● adverb /ɪn'lænd/ in or towards interior of country. □ **Inland Revenue** government department assessing and collecting taxes.

in-laws /'ɪnlɔ:z/ plural noun relatives by marriage.

inlay ● verb /ɪn'leɪ/ (past & past participle **inlaid** /ɪn'leɪd/) embed (thing in another); decorate (thing) thus. ● noun

/'ɪnleɪ/ inlaid material or work; filling shaped to fit tooth-cavity.

inlet /'ɪnlɛt/ *noun* small arm of sea etc.; piece inserted; way of admission.

inmate /'ɪnmeɪt/ *noun* occupant of house, hospital, prison, etc.

in memoriam /ɪn mɪ'mɔːrɪæm/ *preposition* in memory of.

inmost /'ɪnməʊst/ *adjective* most inward.

inn *noun* pub, sometimes with accommodation; *historical* house providing lodging etc. for payment, esp. for travellers. □ **innkeeper** keeper of inn; **Inns of Court** 4 legal societies admitting people to English bar.

innards /'ɪnədz/ *plural noun* colloquial entrails.

innate /ɪ'neɪt/ *adjective* inborn; natural. □ **innately** *adverb*.

inner /'ɪnə/ ● *adjective* interior, internal. ● *noun* circle nearest bull's-eye of target. □ **inner city** central area of city, esp. regarded as having social problems; **inner tube** separate inflatable tube in pneumatic tyre. □ **innermost** *adjective*.

innings /'ɪnɪŋz/ *noun* (*plural* same) esp. *Cricket* batsman's or side's turn at batting; term of office etc. when person, party, etc. can achieve something.

innocent /'ɪnəs(ə)nt/ ● *adjective* free from moral wrong; not guilty; guileless; harmless. ● *noun* innocent person, esp. young child. □ **innocence** *noun*; **innocently** *adverb*.

innocuous /ɪ'nɒkjʊəs/ *adjective* harmless.

innovate /'ɪnəveɪt/ *verb* (**-ting**) bring in new ideas etc.; make changes. □ **innovation** *noun*; **innovative** /-vətɪv/ *adjective*; **innovator** *noun*.

innuendo /ɪnjʊ'endəʊ/ *noun* (*plural* **-es** or **-s**) allusive (usually depreciatory or sexually suggestive) remark.

innumerable /ɪ'njuːmərəb(ə)l/ *adjective* countless.

innumerate /ɪ'njuːmərət/ *adjective* not knowing basic mathematics. □ **innumeracy** *noun*.

inoculate /ɪ'nɒkjʊleɪt/ *verb* (**-ting**) treat with vaccine or serum to promote immunity against a disease. □ **inoculation** *noun*.

inoffensive /ɪnə'fensɪv/ *adjective* not objectionable; harmless.

inoperable /ɪ'nɒpərəb(ə)l/ *adjective* that cannot be cured by surgical operation.

inoperative /ɪ'nɒpərətɪv/ *adjective* not working or taking effect.

inopportune /ɪ'nɒpətjuːn/ *adjective* not appropriate, esp. as regards time.

inordinate /ɪ'nɔːdɪnət/ *adjective* excessive. □ **inordinately** *adverb*.

inorganic /ɪnɔː'gænɪk/ *adjective* Chemistry not organic; without organized physical structure; extraneous.

input /'ɪnpʊt/ ● *noun* what is put in; place of entry of energy, information, etc.; action of putting in or feeding in; contribution of information etc. ● *verb* (**inputting**; *past & past participle* **input** or **inputted**) put in; supply (data, programs, etc.) to computer.

inquest /'ɪŋkwest/ *noun* inquiry held by coroner into cause of death.

inquietude /ɪn'kwaɪɪtjuːd/ *noun* uneasiness.

inquire /ɪn'kwaɪə/ *verb* (**-ring**) seek information formally; make inquiry; ask question.

inquiry /ɪn'kwaɪərɪ/ *noun* (*plural* **-ies**) investigation, esp. official; asking; question.

inquisition /ɪnkwɪ'zɪʃ(ə)n/ *noun* investigation; official inquiry; (**the Inquisition**) *RC Church History* ecclesiastical tribunal for suppression of heresy. □ **inquisitional** *adjective*.

inquisitive /ɪn'kwɪzɪtɪv/ *adjective* curious, prying; seeking knowledge. □ **inquisitively** *adverb*; **inquisitiveness** *noun*.

inquisitor /ɪn'kwɪzɪtə/ *noun* investigator; *historical* officer of Inquisition.

inquisitorial /ɪnkwɪzɪ'tɔːrɪəl/ *adjective* inquisitor-like; prying.

inroad *noun* (often in *plural*) encroachment; using up of resources etc.; hostile incursion.

inrush *noun* rapid influx.

insalubrious /ɪnsə'luːbrɪəs/ *adjective* (of climate or place) unhealthy.

insane /ɪn'seɪn/ *adjective* mad; *colloquial* extremely foolish. □ **insanely** *adverb*; **insanity** /ɪn'sænɪtɪ/ *noun* (*plural* **-ies**).

insanitary /ɪn'sænɪtərɪ/ *adjective* not sanitary.

insatiable /ɪnˈseɪʃəb(ə)l/ *adjective* that cannot be satisfied; extremely greedy. □ **insatiability** *noun*; **insatiably** *adverb*.

insatiate /ɪnˈseɪʃɪət/ *adjective* never satisfied.

inscribe /ɪnˈskraɪb/ *verb* (**-bing**) (usually + *in, on*) write or carve (words etc.) on surface; mark (surface) with characters; (usually + *to*) write informal dedication in or on (book etc.); enter on list; *Geometry* draw (figure) within another so that some points of their boundaries coincide.

inscription /ɪnˈskrɪpʃ(ə)n/ *noun* words inscribed; inscribing.

inscrutable /ɪnˈskruːtəb(ə)l/ *adjective* mysterious, impenetrable. □ **inscrutability** *noun*; **inscrutably** *adverb*.

insect /ˈɪnsekt/ *noun* small invertebrate animal with segmented body, 6 legs, and usually wings.

insecticide /ɪnˈsektɪsaɪd/ *noun* preparation used for killing insects.

insectivore /ɪnˈsektɪvɔː/ *noun* animal or plant that feeds on insects. □ **insectivorous** /-ˈtɪvərəs/ *adjective*.

insecure /ɪnsɪˈkjʊə/ *adjective* not secure or safe; not feeling safe. □ **insecurity** /-ˈkjʊr-/ *noun*.

inseminate /ɪnˈsemɪneɪt/ *verb* (**-ting**) introduce semen into; sow (seed etc.). □ **insemination** *noun*.

insensate /ɪnˈsenseɪt/ *adjective* without esp. physical sensibility; stupid.

insensible /ɪnˈsensɪb(ə)l/ *adjective* unconscious; unaware; callous; imperceptible. □ **insensibility** *noun*; **insensibly** *adverb*.

insensitive /ɪnˈsensɪtɪv/ *adjective* not sensitive. □ **insensitively** *adverb*; **insensitiveness** *noun*; **insensitivity** /-ˈtɪv-/ *noun*.

insentient /ɪnˈsenʃ(ə)nt/ *adjective* inanimate.

inseparable /ɪnˈsepərəb(ə)l/ *adjective* that cannot be separated. □ **inseparability** *noun*; **inseparably** *adverb*.

insert • *verb* /ɪnˈsɜːt/ place or put (thing into another). • *noun* /ˈɪnsɜːt/ thing inserted.

insertion /ɪnˈsɜːʃ(ə)n/ *noun* inserting; thing inserted.

inset • *noun* /ˈɪnset/ extra piece inserted in book, garment, etc.; small map etc.

within border of larger. • *verb* /ɪnˈset/ (**insetting**; *past & past participle* **inset** or **insetted**) put in as inset; decorate with inset.

inshore /ɪnˈʃɔː/ *adverb & adjective* at sea but close to shore.

inside • *noun* /ɪnˈsaɪd/ inner side or part; interior; side of path away from road; (usually in *plural*) *colloquial* stomach and bowels. • *adjective* /ˈɪnsaɪd/ of, on, or in the inside; nearer to centre of games field. • *adverb* /ɪnˈsaɪd/ on, in, or to the inside; *slang* in prison. • *preposition* /ɪnˈsaɪd/ within, on the inside of; in less than. □ **inside out** with inner side turned outwards; **know inside out** know thoroughly.

insider /ɪnˈsaɪdə/ *noun* person within organization etc.; person privy to secret.

insidious /ɪnˈsɪdɪəs/ *adjective* proceeding inconspicuously but harmfully. □ **insidiously** *adverb*.

insight *noun* capacity for understanding hidden truths etc.; instance of this.

insignia /ɪnˈsɪɡnɪə/ *plural noun* badges or marks of office etc.

insignificant /ɪnsɪɡˈnɪfɪkənt/ *adjective* unimportant; trivial. □ **insignificance** *noun*.

insincere /ɪnsɪnˈsɪə/ *adjective* not sincere. □ **insincerely** *adverb*; **insincerity** /-ˈser-/ *noun*.

insinuate /ɪnˈsɪnjʊeɪt/ *verb* (**-ting**) hint obliquely; (usually + *into*) introduce subtly or deviously. □ **insinuation** *noun*.

insipid /ɪnˈsɪpɪd/ *adjective* dull, lifeless; flavourless. □ **insipidity** /-ˈpɪd-/ *noun*; **insipidly** *adverb*.

insist /ɪnˈsɪst/ *verb* demand or maintain emphatically. □ **insistence** *noun*; **insistent** *adjective*; **insistently** *adverb*.

in situ /ɪn ˈsɪtjuː/ *adverb* in its original place. [Latin]

insobriety /ɪnsəˈbraɪətɪ/ *noun* intemperance, esp. in drinking.

insole *noun* removable inner sole for use in shoe.

insolent /ˈɪnsələnt/ *adjective* impertinently insulting. □ **insolence** *noun*; **insolently** *adverb*.

insoluble /ɪnˈsɒljʊb(ə)l/ *adjective* that cannot be solved or dissolved. □ **insolubility** *noun*; **insolubly** *adverb*.

insolvent /ɪnˈsɒlv(ə)nt/ ● *adjective* unable to pay debts. ● *noun* insolvent debtor. □ **insolvency** *noun*.

insomnia /ɪnˈsɒmnɪə/ *noun* sleeplessness.

insomniac /ɪnˈsɒmnɪæk/ *noun* person suffering from insomnia.

insouciant /ɪnˈsuːsɪənt/ *adjective* carefree, unconcerned. □ **insouciance** *noun*.

inspect /ɪnˈspekt/ *verb* look closely at; examine officially. □ **inspection** *noun*.

inspector *noun* official employed to inspect or supervise; police officer next above sergeant in rank. □ **inspectorate** *noun*.

inspiration /ɪnspəˈreɪʃ(ə)n/ *noun* creative force or influence; person etc. stimulating creativity etc.; sudden brilliant idea; divine influence, esp. on writing of Scripture.

inspire /ɪnˈspaɪə/ *verb* (**-ring**) stimulate (person) to esp. creative activity; animate; instil thought or feeling into; prompt, give rise to; (as **inspired** *adjective*) characterized by inspiration. □ **inspiring** *adjective*.

inspirit /ɪnˈspɪrɪt/ *verb* (**-t-**) put life into, animate; encourage.

inst. *abbreviation* instant, of current month.

instability /ɪnstəˈbɪlɪtɪ/ *noun* lack of stability.

install /ɪnˈstɔːl/ *verb* place (equipment etc.) in position ready for use; place (person) in office with ceremony. □ **installation** /-stəˈleɪ-/ *noun*.

instalment *noun* (*US* **installment**) any of several usually equal payments for something; any of several parts, esp. of broadcast or published story.

instance /ˈɪnst(ə)ns/ ● *noun* example; particular case. ● *verb* (**-cing**) cite as instance.

instant /ˈɪnst(ə)nt/ ● *adjective* occurring immediately; (of food etc.) processed for quick preparation; urgent, pressing; of current month. ● *noun* precise moment; short space of time.

instantaneous /ɪnstənˈteɪnɪəs/ *adjective* occurring or done in an instant. □ **instantaneously** *adverb*.

instantly *adverb* immediately.

instead /ɪnˈsted/ *adverb* (+ *of*) in place of; as substitute or alternative.

instep /ˈɪnstep/ *noun* inner arch of foot between toes and ankle; part of shoe etc. fitting this.

instigate /ˈɪnstɪgeɪt/ *verb* (**-ting**) bring about by persuasion; incite. □ **instigation** *noun*; **instigator** *noun*.

instil /ɪnˈstɪl/ *verb* (*US* **instill**) (**-ll-**) (often + *into*) put (ideas etc. into mind etc.) gradually; put in by drops. □ **instillation** *noun*; **instilment** *noun*.

instinct /ˈɪnstɪŋkt/ *noun* inborn pattern of behaviour; innate impulse; intuition. □ **instinctive** /-ˈstɪŋktɪv/ *adjective*; **instinctively** /-ˈstɪŋktɪvlɪ/ *adverb*; **instinctual** /-ˈstɪŋktjʊəl/ *adjective*.

institute /ˈɪnstɪtjuːt/ ● *noun* organized body for promotion of science, education, etc. ● *verb* (**-ting**) establish; initiate (inquiry etc.); (usually + *to, into*) appoint (person) as cleric in church etc.

institution /ɪnstɪˈtjuːʃ(ə)n/ *noun* (esp. charitable) organization or society; established law or custom; *colloquial* well-known person; instituting, being instituted.

institutional *adjective* of or like an institution; typical of institutions.

institutionalize *verb* (also **-ise**) (**-zing** or **-sing**) (as **institutionalized** *adjective*) made dependent by long period in institution; place or keep in institution; make institutional.

instruct /ɪnˈstrʌkt/ *verb* teach; (usually + *to do*) direct, command; employ (lawyer); inform. □ **instructor** *noun*.

instruction /ɪnˈstrʌkʃ(ə)n/ *noun* (often in *plural*) order, direction (as to how thing works etc.); teaching. □ **instructional** *adjective*.

instructive /ɪnˈstrʌktɪv/ *adjective* tending to instruct; enlightening.

instrument /ˈɪnstrəmənt/ *noun* tool, implement; (in full **musical instrument**) contrivance for producing musical sounds; thing used in performing action; person made use of; measuring device, esp. in aircraft; formal (esp. legal) document.

instrumental /ɪnstrəˈment(ə)l/ *adjective* serving as instrument or means; (of music) performed on instruments.

instrumentalist *noun* performer on musical instrument.

instrumentality /ɪnstrəmen'tælɪtɪ/ noun agency, means.

instrumentation /ɪnstrəmen'teɪʃ(ə)n/ noun provision or use of instruments; arrangement of music for instruments; particular instruments used in piece.

insubordinate /ɪnsəb'bɔːdɪnət/ adjective disobedient; unruly. □ **insubordination** noun.

insubstantial /ɪnsəb'stænʃ(ə)l/ adjective lacking solidity or substance; not real.

insufferable /ɪn'sʌfərəb(ə)l/ adjective unbearable; unbearably conceited etc. □ **insufferably** adverb.

insufficient /ɪnsə'fɪʃ(ə)nt/ adjective not enough, inadequate. □ **insufficiency** noun, **insufficiently** adverb.

insular /'ɪnsjʊlə/ adjective of or like an island; separated, remote; narrow-minded. □ **insularity** /-'lær-/ noun.

insulate /'ɪnsjʊleɪt/ verb (-ting) isolate, esp. by non-conductor of electricity, heat, sound, etc. □ **insulation** noun, **insulator** noun.

insulin /'ɪnsjʊlɪn/ noun hormone regulating the amount of glucose in the blood, the lack of which causes diabetes.

insult ● verb /ɪn'sʌlt/ abuse scornfully; offend self-respect etc. of. ● noun /'ɪnsʌlt/ insulting remark or action. □ **insulting** adjective, **insultingly** adverb.

insuperable /ɪn'suːpərəb(ə)l/ adjective impossible to surmount; impossible to overcome. □ **insuperability** noun, **insuperably** adverb.

insupportable /ɪnsə'pɔːtəb(ə)l/ adjective unbearable; unjustifiable.

insurance /ɪn'ʃʊərəns/ noun procedure or contract securing compensation for loss, damage, injury, or death on payment of premium; sum paid to effect insurance.

insure /ɪn'ʃʊə/ verb (-ring) (often + against) effect insurance with respect to.

insurgent /ɪn'sɜːdʒ(ə)nt/ ● adjective in revolt; rebellious. ● noun rebel. □ **insurgence** noun.

insurmountable /ɪnsə'maʊntəb(ə)l/ adjective insuperable.

insurrection /ɪnsə'rekʃ(ə)n/ noun rising in resistance to authority; incipient rebellion. □ **insurrectionist** noun.

intact /ɪn'tækt/ adjective unimpaired; entire; untouched.

intaglio /ɪn'tɑːlɪəʊ/ noun (plural -s) gem with incised design; engraved design.

intake noun action of taking in; people, things, or quantity taken in; place where water is taken into pipe, or fuel or air into engine.

intangible /ɪn'tændʒɪb(ə)l/ adjective that cannot be touched or mentally grasped. □ **intangibility** noun, **intangibly** adverb.

integer /'ɪntɪdʒə/ noun whole number.

integral /'ɪntɪgr(ə)l/ adjective of or essential to a whole; complete; of or denoted by an integer.

■ **Usage** *Integral* is often pronounced /ɪn'tegr(ə)l/ (with the stress on the -teg-), but this is considered incorrect by some people.

integrate /'ɪntɪgreɪt/ verb (-ting) combine (parts) into whole; complete by adding parts; bring or come into equal membership of society; desegregate (school etc.), esp. racially. □ **integrated circuit** small piece of material replacing electrical circuit of many components. □ **integration** noun.

integrity /ɪn'tegrɪtɪ/ noun honesty; wholeness; soundness.

integument /ɪn'tegjʊmənt/ noun skin, husk, or other (natural) covering.

intellect /'ɪntəlekt/ noun faculty of knowing and reasoning; understanding.

intellectual /ɪntə'lektʃʊəl/ ● adjective of, requiring, or using intellect; having highly developed intellect. ● noun intellectual person. □ **intellectualize** verb (also -ise) (-zing or -sing); **intellectually** adverb.

intelligence /ɪn'telɪdʒ(ə)ns/ noun intellect; quickness of understanding; collecting of information, esp. secretly for military or political purposes; information so collected; people employed in this. □ **intelligence quotient** number denoting ratio of person's intelligence to the average.

intelligent adjective having or showing good intelligence, clever. □ **intelligently** adverb.

intelligentsia /ɪntelɪ'dʒentsɪə/ noun class of intellectuals regarded as cultured and politically enterprising.

intelligible /ɪnˈtelɪdʒɪb(ə)l/ *adjective* that can be understood. □ **intelligibility** *noun*; **intelligibly** *adverb*.

intemperate /ɪnˈtempərət/ *adjective* immoderate; excessive in consumption of alcohol, or in general indulgence of appetite. □ **intemperance** *noun*.

intend /ɪnˈtend/ *verb* have as one's purpose; (usually + *for, as, to do*) design, destine.

intended ● *adjective* done on purpose. ● *noun colloquial* fiancé(e).

intense /ɪnˈtens/ *adjective* (**-r, -st**) existing in high degree; vehement; violent, forceful; extreme; very emotional. □ **intensity** *noun* (*plural* **-ies**); **intensely** *adverb*.

■ *Usage Intense* is sometimes confused with *intensive*, and wrongly used to describe a course of study etc.

intensify *verb* (**-ies, -ied**) make or become (more) intense. □ **intensification** *noun*.

intensive /ɪnˈtensɪv/ *adjective* thorough, vigorous; concentrated; of or relating to intensity; increasing production relative to cost. □ **-intensive** making much use of; **intensive care** medical treatment with constant supervision of dangerously ill patient. □ **intensively** *adverb*.

intent /ɪnˈtent/ ● *noun* intention; purpose. ● *adjective* (usually + *on*) resolved, bent; attentively occupied; eager. □ **to all intents and purposes** practically. □ **intently** *adverb*.

intention /ɪnˈtenʃ(ə)n/ *noun* purpose, aim; intending.

intentional *adjective* done on purpose. □ **intentionally** *adverb*.

inter /ɪnˈtɜː/ *verb* (**-rr-**) bury (corpse etc.).

inter- *combining form* among, between; mutually, reciprocally.

interact /ɪntəˈrækt/ *verb* act on each other. □ **interaction** *noun*.

interactive *adjective* reciprocally active; (of computer etc.) allowing two-way flow of information between itself and user. □ **interactively** *adverb*.

interbreed /ɪntəˈbriːd/ *verb* (*past & past participle* **-bred**) (cause to) produce hybrid individual.

intercalary /ɪnˈtɜːkələri/ *adjective* inserted to harmonize calendar with solar year; having such addition; interpolated.

intercede /ɪntəˈsiːd/ *verb* (**-ding**) intervene on behalf of another; plead.

intercept /ɪntəˈsept/ *verb* seize, catch, stop, etc. in transit; cut off. □ **interception** *noun*; **interceptor** *noun*.

intercession /ɪntəˈseʃ(ə)n/ *noun* interceding. □ **intercessor** *noun*.

interchange ● *verb* /ɪntəˈtʃeɪndʒ/ (**-ging**) (of two people) exchange (things) with each other; make exchange of (two things); alternate. ● *noun* /ˈɪntətʃeɪndʒ/ reciprocal exchange; alternation; road junction where traffic streams do not cross. □ **interchangeable** *adjective*.

inter-city /ɪntəˈsɪti/ *adjective* existing or travelling between cities.

intercom /ˈɪntəkɒm/ *noun colloquial* system of intercommunication by telephone or radio.

intercommunicate /ɪntəkəˈmjuːnɪkeɪt/ *verb* (**-ting**) have communication with each other; (of rooms etc.) open into each other. □ **intercommunication** *noun*.

intercommunion /ɪntəkəˈmjuːnɪən/ *noun* mutual communion, esp. between religious bodies.

interconnect /ɪntəkəˈnekt/ *verb* connect with each other. □ **interconnection** *noun*.

intercontinental /ɪntəkɒntɪˈnent(ə)l/ *adjective* connecting or travelling between continents.

intercourse /ˈɪntəkɔːs/ *noun* social, international, etc. communication or dealings; sexual intercourse.

interdenominational /ɪntədɪnɒmɪˈneɪʃən(ə)l/ *adjective* of or involving more than one Christian denomination.

interdependent /ɪntədɪˈpend(ə)nt/ *adjective* mutually dependent. □ **interdependence** *noun*.

interdict ● *noun* /ˈɪntədɪkt/ formal prohibition; *RC Church* sentence debarring person, or esp. place, from ecclesiastical functions and privileges. ● *verb* /ɪntəˈdɪkt/ prohibit (action); forbid use of; (usually + *from*) restrain (person).

□ **interdiction** /-'dɪk-/ *noun*; **interdictory** /-'dɪk-/ *adjective*.

interdisciplinary /ɪntədɪsɪ'plɪnərɪ/ *adjective* of or involving different branches of learning.

interest /'ɪntrəst/ ● *noun* concern; curiosity; quality causing this; subject, hobby, etc., towards which one feels it; advantage; money paid for use of money borrowed etc.; thing in which one has stake or concern; financial stake; legal concern, title, or right. ● *verb* arouse interest of; (usually + *in*) cause to take interest; (as **interested** *adjective*) having private interest, not impartial.

interesting *adjective* causing curiosity; holding the attention. □ **interestingly** *adverb*.

interface /'ɪntəfeɪs/ ● *noun* surface forming common boundary of two regions; place where interaction occurs between two systems etc.; apparatus for connecting two pieces of esp. computing equipment so they can be operated jointly. ● *verb* (**-cing**) connect by means of interface; interact.

interfere /ɪntə'fɪə/ *verb* (**-ring**) (often + *with*) meddle; be an obstacle; intervene; (+ *with*) molest sexually.

interference *noun* interfering; fading of received radio signals.

interferon /ɪntə'fɪərɒn/ *noun* protein inhibiting development of virus in cell.

interfuse /ɪntə'fjuːz/ *verb* (**-sing**) mix, blend. □ **interfusion** *noun*.

interim /'ɪntərɪm/ ● *noun* intervening time. ● *adjective* provisional, temporary.

interior /ɪn'tɪərɪə/ ● *adjective* inner; inland; internal, domestic. ● *noun* inner part; inside; inland region; home affairs of country; representation of inside of room etc.

interject /ɪntə'dʒekt/ *verb* make (remark etc.) abruptly or parenthetically; interrupt.

interjection /ɪntə'dʒekʃ(ə)n/ *noun* exclamation.

interlace /ɪntə'leɪs/ *verb* (**-cing**) bind intricately together; interweave.

interlard /ɪntə'lɑːd/ *verb* mix (speech etc.) with unusual words or phrases.

interleave /ɪntə'liːv/ *verb* (**-ving**) insert (usually blank) leaves between leaves of (book).

interline /ɪntə'laɪn/ *verb* (**-ning**) put extra layer of material between fabric of (garment) and its lining.

interlink /ɪntə'lɪŋk/ *verb* link together.

interlock /ɪntə'lɒk/ ● *verb* engage with each other by overlapping etc.; lock together. ● *noun* machine-knitted fabric with fine stitches.

interlocutor /ɪntə'lɒkjʊtə/ *noun formal* person who takes part in conversation. □ **interlocutory** *adjective*.

interloper /'ɪntələʊpə/ *noun* intruder; person who thrusts himself or herself into others' affairs.

interlude /'ɪntəluːd/ *noun* interval between parts of play etc., performance filling this; contrasting time, event, etc. in middle of something.

intermarry /ɪntə'mærɪ/ *verb* (**-ies, -ied**) (+ *with*) (of races, castes, families, etc.) become connected by marriage. □ **intermarriage** /-rɪdʒ/ *noun*.

intermediary /ɪntə'miːdɪərɪ/ ● *noun* (*plural* **-ies**) mediator. ● *adjective* acting as mediator; intermediate.

intermediate /ɪntə'miːdɪət/ ● *adjective* coming between in time, place, order, etc. ● *noun* intermediate thing.

interment /ɪn'tɜːmənt/ *noun* burial.

intermezzo /ɪntə'metsəʊ/ *noun* (*plural* **-mezzi** /-sɪ/ or **-s**) *Music* short connecting movement or composition.

interminable /ɪn'tɜːmɪnəb(ə)l/ *adjective* endless; tediously long. □ **interminably** *adverb*.

intermingle /ɪntə'mɪŋɡ(ə)l/ *verb* (**-ling**) mix together, mingle.

intermission /ɪntə'mɪʃ(ə)n/ *noun* pause, cessation; interval in cinema etc.

intermittent /ɪntə'mɪt(ə)nt/ *adjective* occurring at intervals, not continuous or steady. □ **intermittently** *adverb*.

intermix /ɪntə'mɪks/ *verb* mix together.

intern ● *noun* /'ɪntɜːn/ *US* resident junior doctor in hospital. ● *verb* /ɪn'tɜːn/ confine within prescribed limits. □ **internee** /-'niː/ *noun*; **internment** *noun*.

internal /ɪn'tɜːn(ə)l/ *adjective* of or in the inside of thing; relating to inside of the body; of domestic affairs of country; (of students) attending a university as well as taking its exams; used or applying within an organization; intrinsic; of mind or soul. □ **internal-combustion engine** engine in which motive power comes from explosion of gas or vapour with air in cylinder. □ **internally** adverb.

international /ɪntəˈnæʃən(ə)l/ ● adjective existing or carried on between nations; agreed on by many nations. ● noun contest (usually in sports) between representatives of different nations; such representative; (**International**) any of 4 successive associations for socialist or Communist action. □ **internationality** /-ˈnæl-/ noun; **internationally** adverb.

internationalism noun advocacy of community of interests among nations. □ **internationalist** noun.

internationalize verb (also **-ise**) (**-zing** or **-sing**) make international; bring under joint protection etc. of different nations.

internecine /ɪntəˈniːsaɪn/ adjective mutually destructive.

interpenetrate /ɪntəˈpenɪtreɪt/ verb (**-ting**) penetrate each other; pervade. □ **interpenetration** noun.

interpersonal /ɪntəˈpɜːsən(ə)l/ adjective between people.

interplanetary /ɪntəˈplænɪtərɪ/ adjective between planets.

interplay /ˈɪntəpleɪ/ noun reciprocal action.

Interpol /ˈɪntəpɒl/ noun International Criminal Police Organization.

interpolate /ɪnˈtɜːpəleɪt/ verb (**-ting**) insert or introduce between other things; make (esp. misleading) insertions in. □ **interpolation** noun.

interpose /ɪntəˈpəʊz/ verb (**-sing**) insert (thing between others); introduce, use, say, etc. as interruption or interference; interrupt; advance (objection etc.) so as to interfere; intervene. □ **interposition** /-pəˈzɪʃ(ə)n/ noun.

interpret /ɪnˈtɜːprɪt/ verb (**-t-**) explain the meaning of (esp. words); render, represent; act as interpreter. □ **interpretation** noun.

interpreter noun person who translates orally.

interracial /ɪntəˈreɪʃ(ə)l/ adjective between or affecting different races.

interregnum /ɪntəˈregnəm/ noun (plural **-s**) interval with suspension of normal

government between successive reigns or regimes; interval, pause.

interrelated /ɪntərɪˈleɪtɪd/ adjective related to each other. □ **interrelation** noun; **interrelationship** noun.

interrogate /ɪnˈterəgeɪt/ verb (**-ting**) question closely or formally. □ **interrogation** noun; **interrogator** noun.

interrogative /ɪntəˈrɒgətɪv/ ● adjective of, like, or used in questions. ● noun interrogative word.

interrogatory /ɪntəˈrɒgətərɪ/ ● adjective questioning. ● noun (plural **-ies**) set of questions.

interrupt /ɪntəˈrʌpt/ verb break continuity of (action, speech, etc.); obstruct (view etc.). □ **interruption** noun.

intersect /ɪntəˈsekt/ verb divide by passing or lying across; cross or cut each other.

intersection /ɪntəˈsekʃ(ə)n/ noun intersecting; place where two roads intersect; point or line common to lines or planes that intersect.

intersperse /ɪntəˈspɜːs/ verb (**-sing**) (usually + between, among) scatter; (+ with) vary (thing) by scattering others among it.

interstate /ˈɪntəsteɪt/ adjective existing etc. between states, esp. of US.

interstellar /ɪntəˈstelə/ adjective between stars.

interstice /ɪnˈtɜːstɪs/ noun gap, chink, crevice.

interstitial /ɪntəˈstɪʃ(ə)l/ adjective forming or in interstices.

intertwine /ɪntəˈtwaɪn/ verb (**-ning**) (often + with) twine closely together.

interval /ˈɪntəv(ə)l/ noun intervening time or space; pause; break; Music difference of pitch between two sounds. □ **at intervals** here and there, now and then.

intervene /ɪntəˈviːn/ verb (**-ning**) occur in meantime; interfere; prevent or modify events; come between people or things; mediate.

intervention /ɪntəˈvenʃ(ə)n/ noun intervening; interference; mediation.

interview /ˈɪntəvjuː/ ● noun oral examination of applicant; conversation with reporter, for broadcast or publication; meeting of people, esp. for discussion.

● *verb* hold interview with. □ **interviewee** /-vju:'i:/ *noun*; **interviewer** *noun*.

interweave /ɪntə'wi:v/ *verb* (**-ving**; *past* **-wove**; *past participle* **-woven**) weave together; blend intimately.

intestate /ɪn'testeɪt/ ● *adjective* not having made a will before death. ● *noun* person who has died intestate. □ **intestacy** /-təsɪ/ *noun*.

intestine /ɪn'testɪn/ *noun* (in *singular* or *plural*) lower part of alimentary canal. □ **intestinal** *adjective*.

intimate[1] ● *adjective* /'ɪntɪmət/ closely acquainted; familiar; closely personal; (usually + *with*) having sexual relations; (of knowledge) thorough; close. ● *noun* intimate friend. □ **intimacy** /-məsɪ/ *noun*; **intimately** *adverb*.

intimate[2] /'ɪntɪmeɪt/ *verb* (**-ting**) state or make known; imply. □ **intimation** *noun*.

intimidate /ɪn'tɪmɪdeɪt/ *verb* (**-ting**) frighten, esp. in order to influence conduct. □ **intimidation** *noun*.

into /'ɪntu, 'ɪntə/ *preposition expressing motion or direction to point within, direction of attention, or change of state*; after the beginning of; *colloquial* interested in.

intolerable /ɪn'tɒlərəb(ə)l/ *adjective* that cannot be endured. □ **intolerably** *adverb*.

intolerant /ɪn'tɒlərənt/ *adjective* not tolerant. □ **intolerance** *noun*.

intonation /ɪntə'neɪʃ(ə)n/ *noun* modulation of voice, accent; intoning.

intone /ɪn'təʊn/ *verb* (**-ning**) recite with prolonged sounds, esp. in monotone.

in toto /ɪn 'təʊtəʊ/ *adverb* entirely. [Latin]

intoxicant /ɪn'tɒksɪkənt/ ● *adjective* intoxicating. ● *noun* intoxicating substance.

intoxicate /ɪn'tɒksɪkeɪt/ *verb* (**-ting**) make drunk; excite or elate beyond self-control. □ **intoxication** *noun*.

intractable /ɪn'træktəb(ə)l/ *adjective* not easily dealt with; stubborn. □ **intractability** *noun*.

intramural /ɪntrə'mjʊər(ə)l/ *adjective* situated or done within walls of institution etc.

intransigent /ɪn'trænsɪdʒ(ə)nt/ ● *adjective* uncompromising. ● *noun* such person. □ **intransigence** *noun*.

intransitive /ɪn'trænsɪtɪv/ *adjective* (of verb) not taking direct object.

intrauterine /ɪntrə'ju:təraɪn/ *adjective* within the womb.

intravenous /ɪntrə'vi:nəs/ *adjective* in(to) vein(s). □ **intravenously** *adverb*.

intrepid /ɪn'trepɪd/ *adjective* fearless; brave.

intricate /'ɪntrɪkət/ *adjective* complicated; perplexingly detailed. □ **intricacy** /-kəsɪ/ *noun* (*plural* **-ies**); **intricately** *adverb*.

intrigue ● *verb* /ɪn'tri:g/ (**-gues**, **-gued**, **-guing**) carry on underhand plot; use secret influence; rouse curiosity of. ● *noun* /'ɪntri:g/ underhand plotting or plot; secret arrangement, esp. with romantic associations. □ **intriguing** *adjective*; **intriguingly** *adverb*.

intrinsic /ɪn'trɪnzɪk/ *adjective* inherent; essential. □ **intrinsically** *adverb*.

intro /'ɪntrəʊ/ *noun* (*plural* **-s**) *colloquial* introduction.

introduce /ɪntrə'dju:s/ *verb* (**-cing**) make (person) known by name to another; announce or present to audience; bring (custom etc.) into use; bring (bill etc.) before Parliament; (+ *to*) initiate (person) in subject; insert; bring in; usher in, bring forward. □ **introducible** *adjective*.

introduction /ɪntrə'dʌkʃ(ə)n/ *noun* introducing, being introduced; formal presentation; preliminary matter in book; introductory treatise. □ **introductory** *adjective*.

introspection /ɪntrə'spekʃ(ə)n/ *noun* examination of one's own thoughts. □ **introspective** *adjective*.

introvert ● *noun* person chiefly concerned with his or her own thoughts; shy thoughtful person. ● *adjective* (also **introverted**) characteristic of an introvert. □ **introversion** /-'vɜ:ʃ(ə)n/ *noun*.

intrude /ɪn'tru:d/ *verb* (**-ding**) (+ *on, upon, into*) come uninvited or unwanted; force on a person. □ **intruder** *noun*; **intrusion** /-ʒ(ə)n/ *noun*; **intrusive** /-sɪv/ *adjective*.

intuition /ɪntju:'ɪʃ(ə)n/ *noun* immediate apprehension by mind without reasoning; immediate insight. □ **intuit** /ɪn'tju:ɪt/ *verb*; **intuitional** *adjective*.

intuitive /ɪnˈtjuːɪtɪv/ *adjective* of, having, or perceived by intuition. □ **intuitively** *adverb*; **intuitiveness** *noun*.

Inuit /ˈɪnjuːɪt/ ● *noun* (*plural* same or **-s**) N. American Eskimo; language of Inuit. ● *adjective* of Inuit or their language.

inundate /ˈɪnʌndeɪt/ *verb* (**-ting**) (often + *with*) flood, overwhelm. □ **inundation** *noun*.

inure /ɪˈnjʊə/ *verb* (**-ring**) habituate, accustom. □ **inurement** *noun*.

invade /ɪnˈveɪd/ *verb* (**-ding**) enter (country etc.) with arms to control or subdue it; swarm into; (of disease etc.) attack; encroach on. □ **invader** *noun*.

invalid[1] /ˈɪnvəlɪd, -liːd/ ● *noun* person enfeebled or disabled by illness or injury. ● *adjective* of or for invalids; sick, disabled. ● *verb* (**-d-**) (often + *out* etc.) remove from active service; disable (person) by illness. □ **invalidism** *noun*; **invalidity** /-ˈlɪd-/ *noun*.

invalid[2] /ɪnˈvælɪd/ *adjective* not valid. □ **invalidity** /-vəˈlɪd-/ *noun*.

invalidate /ɪnˈvælɪdeɪt/ *verb* (**-ting**) make invalid. □ **invalidation** *noun*.

invaluable /ɪnˈvæljʊəb(ə)l/ *adjective* beyond price, very valuable.

invariable /ɪnˈveərɪəb(ə)l/ *adjective* unchangeable; always the same. □ **invariably** *adverb*.

invasion /ɪnˈveɪʒ(ə)n/ *noun* invading, being invaded. □ **invasive** /-sɪv/ *adjective*.

invective /ɪnˈvektɪv/ *noun* violent attack in words.

inveigh /ɪnˈveɪ/ *verb* (+ *against*) speak or write with strong hostility against.

inveigle /ɪnˈveɪg(ə)l/ *verb* (**-ling**) (+ *into*, *to do*) entice, persuade by guile. □ **inveiglement** *noun*.

invent /ɪnˈvent/ *verb* create by thought; originate; fabricate. □ **inventor** *noun*.

invention /ɪnˈvenʃ(ə)n/ *noun* inventing; being invented; thing invented; inventiveness.

inventive *adjective* able to invent; imaginative. □ **inventively** *adverb*; **inventiveness** *noun*.

inventory /ˈɪnvəntərɪ/ ● *noun* (*plural* **-ies**) list of goods etc. ● *verb* (**-ies**, **-ied**) make inventory of; enter in inventory.

inverse /ɪnˈvɜːs/ ● *adjective* inverted in position, order, or relation. ● *noun* inverted state; (often + *of*) direct opposite. □ **inverse proportion**, **ratio** relation between two quantities such that one increases in proportion as the other decreases.

inversion /ɪnˈvɜːʃ(ə)n/ *noun* inverting, esp. reversal of normal order of words.

invert /ɪnˈvɜːt/ *verb* turn upside down; reverse position, order, or relation of. □ **inverted commas** quotation marks.

invertebrate /ɪnˈvɜːtɪbrət/ ● *adjective* without backbone. ● *noun* invertebrate animal.

invest /ɪnˈvest/ *verb* (often + *in*) apply or use (money) for profit; devote (time etc.) to an enterprise; (+ *in*) buy (something useful or otherwise rewarding); (+ *with*) endue with qualities etc.; (often + *with*, *in*) clothe with insignia of office. □ **investor** *noun*.

investigate /ɪnˈvestɪɡeɪt/ *verb* (**-ting**) inquire into, examine. □ **investigation** *noun*; **investigative** /-ɡətɪv/ *adjective*; **investigator** *noun*.

investiture /ɪnˈvestɪtʃə/ *noun* formal investing of person with honours and rank.

investment *noun* investing; money invested; property etc. in which money is invested.

inveterate /ɪnˈvetərət/ *adjective* (of person) confirmed in (usually undesirable) habit etc.; (of habit etc.) long-established. □ **inveteracy** *noun*.

invidious /ɪnˈvɪdɪəs/ *adjective* likely to excite ill-will against performer, possessor, etc.

invigilate /ɪnˈvɪdʒɪleɪt/ *verb* (**-ting**) supervise examinees. □ **invigilation** *noun*; **invigilator** *noun*.

invigorate /ɪnˈvɪɡəreɪt/ *verb* (**-ting**) give vigour to. □ **invigorating** *adjective*.

invincible /ɪnˈvɪnsɪb(ə)l/ *adjective* unconquerable. □ **invincibility** *noun*; **invincibly** *adverb*.

inviolable /ɪnˈvaɪələb(ə)l/ *adjective* not to be violated. □ **inviolability** *noun*.

inviolate /ɪnˈvaɪələt/ *adjective* not violated; safe (from harm). □ **inviolacy** *noun*.

invisible /ɪnˈvɪzɪb(ə)l/ *adjective* that cannot be seen. □ **invisible exports**, **imports** items for which payment is made by or to another country but which are not goods. □ **invisibility** *noun*; **invisibly** *adverb*.

invite ● *verb* /ɪnˈvaɪt/ **(-ting)** request courteously to come, to do, etc.; solicit courteously; tend to evoke unintentionally; attract. ● *noun* /ˈɪnvaɪt/ *colloquial* invitation. □ **invitation** /ɪnvɪˈteɪʃ(ə)n/ *noun*.

inviting *adjective* attractive. □ **invitingly** *adverb*.

in vitro /ɪn ˈviːtrəʊ/ *adverb* (of biological processes) taking place in test-tube or other laboratory environment. [Latin]

invocation /ɪnvəˈkeɪʃ(ə)n/ *noun* invoking; calling on, esp. in prayer or for inspiration etc. □ **invocatory** /ɪnˈvɒkətərɪ/ *adjective*.

invoice /ˈɪnvɔɪs/ ● *noun* bill for usually itemized goods etc. ● *verb* **(-cing)** send invoice to; make invoice of.

invoke /ɪnˈvəʊk/ *verb* **(-king)** call on in prayer or as witness; appeal to (law, authority, etc.); summon (spirit) by charms; ask earnestly for (vengeance, justice, etc.).

involuntary /ɪnˈvɒləntərɪ/ *adjective* done etc. without exercise of will; not controlled by will. □ **involuntarily** *adverb*.

involute /ˈɪnvəluːt/ *adjective* intricate; curled spirally.

involution /ɪnvəˈluːʃ(ə)n/ *noun* involving; intricacy; curling inwards, part so curled.

involve /ɪnˈvɒlv/ *verb* **(-ving)** (often + *in*) cause (person, thing) to share experience or effect; imply, make necessary; (often + *in*) implicate (person) in charge, crime, etc.; include or affect in its operation; (as **involved** *adjective*) complicated. □ **involvement** *noun*.

invulnerable /ɪnˈvʌlnərəb(ə)l/ *adjective* that cannot be wounded. □ **invulnerability** *noun*.

inward /ˈɪnwəd/ ● *adjective* directed towards inside; going in; situated within; mental, spiritual. ● *adverb* (also **inwards**) towards inside; in mind or soul.

inwardly *adverb* on the inside; in mind or spirit; not aloud.

inwrought /ɪnˈrɔːt/ *adjective* (often + *with*) decorated (with pattern); (often + *in*, *on*) (of pattern) wrought (in or on fabric).

iodine /ˈaɪədiːn/ *noun* black solid halogen element forming violet vapour; solution of this used as antiseptic.

IOM *abbreviation* Isle of Man.

ion /ˈaɪən/ *noun* atom or group of atoms that has lost or gained one or more electrons.

ionic /aɪˈɒnɪk/ *adjective* of or using ions.

ionize *verb* (also **-ise**) **(-zing** or **-sing)** convert or be converted into ion(s). □ **ionization** *noun*.

ionosphere /aɪˈɒnəsfɪə/ *noun* ionized region in upper atmosphere. □ **ionospheric** /-ˈsfer-/ *adjective*.

iota /aɪˈəʊtə/ *noun* ninth letter of Greek alphabet (I, ι); (usually with negative) a jot.

IOU /aɪəʊˈjuː/ *noun* (*plural* **-s**) signed document acknowledging debt.

IOW *abbreviation* Isle of Wight.

IPA *abbreviation* International Phonetic Alphabet.

ipecacuanha /ɪpɪkækjʊˈɑːnə/ *noun* root of S. American plant used as emetic etc.

ipso facto /ɪpsəʊ ˈfæktəʊ/ *adverb* by that very fact. [Latin]

IQ *abbreviation* intelligence quotient.

IRA *abbreviation* Irish Republican Army.

Iranian /ɪˈreɪnɪən/ ● *adjective* of Iran (formerly Persia); of group of languages including Persian. ● *noun* native or national of Iran.

Iraqi /ɪˈrɑːkɪ/ ● *adjective* of Iraq. ● *noun* (*plural* **-s**) native or national of Iraq.

irascible /ɪˈræsɪb(ə)l/ *adjective* irritable; hot-tempered. □ **irascibility** *noun*.

irate /aɪˈreɪt/ *adjective* angry, enraged.

ire /ˈaɪə/ *noun* *literary* anger.

iridescent /ɪrɪˈdes(ə)nt/ *adjective* showing rainbow-like glowing colours; changing colour with position. □ **iridescence** *noun*.

iris /ˈaɪrɪs/ *noun* circular coloured membrane surrounding pupil of eye; bulbous or tuberous plant with sword-shaped leaves and showy flowers.

Irish /ˈaɪərɪʃ/ ● *adjective* of Ireland. ● *noun* Celtic language of Ireland; **(the Irish;** treated as *plural*) the Irish people. □ **Irish coffee** coffee with dash of whiskey and a little sugar, topped with cream; **Irishman**, **Irishwoman** native of Ireland; **Irish stew** dish of stewed mutton, onions, and potatoes.

irk *verb* irritate, annoy.

irksome *adjective* annoying, tiresome.

iron /'aɪən/ ● *noun* common strong grey metallic element; this as symbol of strength or firmness; tool etc. of iron; implement heated to smooth clothes etc.; golf club with iron or steel head; (in *plural*) fetters; (in *plural*) stirrups; (often in *plural*) leg-support to rectify malformations. ● *adjective* of iron; robust; unyielding. ● *verb* smooth (clothes etc.) with heated iron. □ **Iron Age** era characterized by use of iron weapons etc.; **Iron Curtain** *historical* notional barrier to passage of people and information between Soviet bloc and West; **ironing board** narrow folding table etc. for ironing clothes on; **iron lung** rigid case over patient's body for administering prolonged artificial respiration; **ironmonger** dealer in **ironmongery**, household and building hardware; **iron rations** small emergency supply of food; **ironstone** hard iron ore, kind of hard white pottery.

ironic /aɪ'rɒnɪk/ *adjective* (also **ironical**) using or displaying irony. □ **ironically** *adverb*.

irony /'aɪrənɪ/ *noun* (*plural* **-ies**) expression of meaning, usually humorous or sarcastic, by use of words normally conveying opposite meaning; apparent perversity of fate or circumstances.

irradiate /ɪ'reɪdɪeɪt/ *verb* (**-ting**) subject to radiation; shine on; throw light on; light up. □ **irradiation** *noun*.

irrational /ɪ'ræʃən(ə)l/ *adjective* unreasonable, illogical; not endowed with reason; *Mathematics* not expressible as an ordinary fraction. □ **irrationality** /-'næl-/ *noun*; **irrationally** *adverb*.

irreconcilable /ɪ'rekənsaɪləb(ə)l/ *adjective* implacably hostile; (of ideas etc.) incompatible. □ **irreconcilably** *adverb*.

irrecoverable /ɪrɪ'kʌvərəb(ə)l/ *adjective* that cannot be recovered or remedied.

irredeemable /ɪrɪ'diːməb(ə)l/ *adjective* that cannot be redeemed, hopeless. □ **irredeemably** *adverb*.

irreducible /ɪrɪ'djuːsɪb(ə)l/ *adjective* not able to be reduced or simplified.

irrefutable /ɪrɪ'fjuːtəb(ə)l/ *adjective* that cannot be refuted. □ **irrefutably** *adverb*.

irregular /ɪ'regjʊlə/ ● *adjective* not regular; unsymmetrical, uneven; varying in form; not occurring at regular intervals; contrary to rule; (of troops) not in regular army; (of verb, noun, etc.) not inflected according to usual rules. ● *noun* (in *plural*) irregular troops. □ **irregularity** /-'lær-/ *noun* (*plural* **-ies**); **irregularly** *adverb*.

irrelevant /ɪ'relɪv(ə)nt/ *adjective* not relevant. □ **irrelevance** *noun*; **irrelevancy** *noun* (*plural* **-ies**).

irreligious /ɪrɪ'lɪdʒəs/ *adjective* lacking or hostile to religion; irreverent.

irremediable /ɪrɪ'miːdɪəb(ə)l/ *adjective* that cannot be remedied. □ **irremediably** *adverb*.

irremovable /ɪrɪ'muːvəb(ə)l/ *adjective* not removable. □ **irremovably** *adverb*.

irreparable /ɪ'repərəb(ə)l/ *adjective* that cannot be rectified or made good. □ **irreparably** *adverb*.

irreplaceable /ɪrɪ'pleɪsəb(ə)l/ *adjective* that cannot be replaced.

irrepressible /ɪrɪ'presɪb(ə)l/ *adjective* that cannot be repressed. □ **irrepressibly** *adverb*.

irreproachable /ɪrɪ'prəʊtʃəb(ə)l/ *adjective* faultless, blameless. □ **irreproachably** *adverb*.

irresistible /ɪrɪ'zɪstɪb(ə)l/ *adjective* too strong, convincing, charming, etc. to be resisted. □ **irresistibly** *adverb*.

irresolute /ɪ'rezəluːt/ *adjective* hesitating; lacking in resolution. □ **irresoluteness** *noun*; **irresolution** /-'luːʃ(ə)n/ *noun*.

irrespective /ɪrɪ'spektɪv/ *adjective* (+ *of*) not taking into account, regardless of.

irresponsible /ɪrɪ'spɒnsɪb(ə)l/ *adjective* acting or done without due sense of responsibility; not responsible. □ **irresponsibility** *noun*; **irresponsibly** *adverb*.

irretrievable /ɪrɪ'triːvəb(ə)l/ *adjective* that cannot be retrieved or restored. □ **irretrievably** *adverb*.

irreverent /ɪ'revərənt/ *adjective* lacking in reverence. □ **irreverence** *noun*; **irreverently** *adverb*.

irreversible /ɪrɪ'vɜːsɪb(ə)l/ *adjective* that cannot be reversed or altered. □ **irreversibly** *adverb*.

irrevocable /ɪ'revəkəb(ə)l/ *adjective* unalterable; gone beyond recall. □ **irrevocably** *adverb*.

irrigate /'ɪrɪgeɪt/ *verb* (**-ting**) water (land) by system of artificial channels; (of stream etc.) supply (land) with water; *Medicine* moisten (wound etc.) with constant flow of liquid. □ **irrigable** *adjective*, **irrigation** *noun*; **irrigator** *noun*.

irritable /'ɪrɪtəb(ə)l/ *adjective* easily annoyed; very sensitive to contact. □ **irritability** *noun*; **irritably** *adverb*.

irritant /'ɪrɪt(ə)nt/ • *adjective* causing irritation. • *noun* irritant substance or agent.

irritate /'ɪrɪteɪt/ *verb* (**-ting**) excite to anger, annoy; stimulate discomfort in (part of body). □ **irritating** *adjective*; **irritation** *noun*.

Is. *abbreviation* Island(s); Isle(s).

is *3rd singular present of* BE.

isinglass /'aɪzɪŋglɑːs/ *noun* kind of gelatin obtained from sturgeon etc.

Islam /'ɪzlɑːm/ *noun* religion of Muslims, proclaimed by Prophet Muhammad; the Muslim world. □ **Islamic** /-'læm-/ *adjective*.

island /'aɪlənd/ *noun* piece of land surrounded by water; traffic island; detached or isolated thing.

islander *noun* native or inhabitant of island.

isle /aɪl/ *noun literary* (usually small) island.

islet /'aɪlɪt/ *noun* small island.

isn't /'ɪz(ə)nt/ is not.

isobar /'aɪsəbɑː/ *noun* line on map connecting places with same atmospheric pressure. □ **isobaric** /-'bær-/ *adjective*.

isolate /'aɪsəleɪt/ *verb* (**-ting**) place apart or alone; separate (esp. infectious patient from others); insulate (electrical apparatus), esp. by gap; disconnect. □ **isolation** *noun*.

isolationism *noun* policy of holding aloof from affairs of other countries or groups. □ **isolationist** *noun*.

isomer /'aɪsəmə/ *noun* one of two or more compounds with same molecular formula but different arrangement of atoms. □ **isomeric** /-'mer-/ *adjective*; **isomerism** /aɪ'sɒmərɪz(ə)m/ *noun*.

isosceles /aɪ'sɒsɪliːz/ *adjective* (of triangle) having two sides equal.

isotherm /'aɪsəθɜːm/ *noun* line on map connecting places with same temperature. □ **isothermal** /-'θɜːm(ə)l/ *adjective*.

isotope /'aɪsətəʊp/ *noun* any of two or more forms of chemical element with different relative atomic mass and different nuclear but not chemical properties. □ **isotopic** /-'tɒp-/ *adjective*.

Israeli /ɪz'reɪlɪ/ • *adjective* of modern state of Israel. • *noun* (*plural* **-s**) native or national of Israel.

issue /'ɪʃuː/ • *noun* giving out or circulation of shares, notes, stamps, etc.; copies of journal etc. circulated at one time; each of regular series of magazine etc.; outgoing, outflow; point in question, essential subject of dispute; result, outcome; offspring. • *verb* (**issues**, **issued**, **issuing**) go or come out; give or send out; publish, circulate; supply, (+ *with*) supply with equipment etc.; (+ *from*) be derived, result; (+ *from*) emerge.

isthmus /'ɪsməs/ *noun* (*plural* **-es**) neck of land connecting two larger land masses.

IT *abbreviation* information technology.

it *pronoun* the thing in question; indefinite, undefined, or impersonal subject, action, condition, object, etc.; substitute for deferred subject or object; exactly what is needed; perfection; *slang* sexual intercourse, sex appeal. □ **that's it** *colloquial* that is what is required, that is the difficulty, that is the end, enough.

Italian /ɪ'tæljən/ • *noun* native, national, or language of Italy. • *adjective* of Italy.

italic /ɪ'tælɪk/ • *adjective* (of type etc.) of sloping kind; (of handwriting) neat and pointed; (**Italic**) of ancient Italy. • *noun* (usually in *plural*) italic type.

italicize /ɪ'tælɪsaɪz/ *verb* (also **-ise**) (**-zing** or **-sing**) print in italics.

itch • *noun* irritation in skin; restless desire; disease with itch. • *verb* feel irritation or restless desire.

itchy *adjective* (**-ier**, **-iest**) having or causing itch. □ **have itchy feet** *colloquial* be restless, have urge to travel.

it'd /ɪtəd/ it had; it would.

item /ˈaɪtəm/ noun any one of enumerated things; separate or distinct piece of news etc.

itemize verb (also **-ise**) (**-zing** or **-sing**) state by items. □ **itemization** noun.

iterate /ˈɪtəreɪt/ verb (**-ting**) repeat; state repeatedly. □ **iteration** noun; **iterative** /-rətɪv/ adjective.

itinerant /aɪˈtɪnərənt/ ● adjective travelling from place to place. ● noun itinerant person.

itinerary /aɪˈtɪnərərɪ/ noun (plural **-ies**) route; record of travel; guidebook.

it'll /ˈɪt(ə)l/ it will; it shall.

its adjective of or belonging to it.

it's /ɪts/ it is; it has.

■ **Usage** Because it has an apostrophe, *it's* is easily confused with *its*. Both are correctly used in *Where's the dog?—It's in its kennel, and it's eaten its food* (= *It is in its kennel, and it has eaten its food.*)

itself /ɪtˈself/ pronoun: emphatic & reflexive form of IT.

ITV abbreviation Independent Television.

IUD abbreviation intrauterine (contraceptive) device.

I've /aɪv/ I have.

ivory /ˈaɪvərɪ/ noun (plural **-ies**) white substance of tusks of elephant etc.; colour of this; (in plural) slang things made of or resembling ivory, esp. dice, piano keys, or teeth. □ **ivory tower** seclusion from harsh realities of life.

ivy /ˈaɪvɪ/ noun (plural **-ies**) climbing evergreen with shiny 5-angled leaves.

Jj

jab ● verb (**-bb-**) poke roughly; stab; (+ *into*) thrust (thing) hard or abruptly. ● noun abrupt blow or thrust; colloquial hypodermic injection.

jabber ● verb chatter volubly; utter fast and indistinctly. ● noun chatter, gabble.

jabot /ˈʒæbəʊ/ noun frill on front of shirt or blouse.

jacaranda /dʒækəˈrændə/ noun tropical American tree with blue flowers or one with hard scented wood.

jacinth /ˈdʒæsɪnθ/ noun reddish-orange zircon used as gem.

jack ● noun device for lifting heavy objects, esp. vehicles; lowest-ranking court card; ship's flag, esp. showing nationality; device using single-pronged plug to connect electrical equipment; small white target ball in bowls; (in plural) game played with jackstones. ● verb (usually + *up*) raise (as) with jack. □ **jackboot** boot reaching above knee; **jack in** slang abandon (attempt etc.); **jack-in-the-box** toy figure that springs out of box; **jack of all trades** person with many skills; **jack plug** electrical plug with single prong; **jackstone** metal etc. piece used in tossing games.

jackal /ˈdʒæk(ə)l/ noun African or Asian wild animal of dog family.

jackass noun male ass; stupid person.

jackdaw noun grey-headed bird of crow family.

jacket /ˈdʒækɪt/ noun short coat with sleeves; covering round boiler etc.; outside wrapper of book; skin of potato. □ **jacket potato** one baked in its skin.

jackknife ● noun large clasp-knife. ● verb (**-fing**) (of articulated vehicle) fold against itself in accident.

jackpot noun large prize, esp. accumulated in game, lottery, etc.

Jacobean /dʒækəˈbiːən/ adjective of reign of James I.

Jacobite /ˈdʒækəbaɪt/ noun historical supporter of James II in exile, or of Stuarts.

Jacuzzi /dʒə'kuːzɪ/ noun (plural **-s**) proprietary term large bath with massaging underwater jets.

jade¹ noun hard usually green stone for ornaments; green colour of jade.

jade² noun inferior or worn-out horse.

jaded adjective tired out, surfeited.

jag ● noun sharp projection of rock etc. ● verb (**-gg-**) cut or tear unevenly; make indentations in.

jagged /'dʒægɪd/ adjective unevenly cut or torn. □ **jaggedly** adverb; **jaggedness** noun.

jaguar /'dʒægjʊə/ noun large American spotted animal of cat family.

jail /dʒeɪl/ (also **gaol**) ● noun place for detention of prisoners; confinement in jail. ● verb put in jail. □ **jailbird** prisoner, habitual criminal. □ **jailer** noun.

jalap /'dʒæləp/ noun purgative drug.

jalopy /dʒə'lɒpɪ/ noun (plural **-ies**) colloquial dilapidated old motor vehicle.

jalousie /'ʒæluːzɪ/ noun slatted blind or shutter.

jam¹ ● verb (**-mm-**) (usually + into, together, etc.) squeeze or cram into space; become wedged; cause (machinery) to become wedged and so unworkable, become wedged in this way; block (exit, road, etc.) by crowding; (usually + on) apply (brakes) suddenly; make (radio transmission) unintelligible with interference. ● noun squeeze; stoppage; crowded mass, esp. of traffic; colloquial predicament. □ **jam session** (in jazz etc.) improvised ensemble playing.

jam² noun conserve of boiled fruit and sugar; colloquial easy or pleasant thing.

jamb /dʒæm/ noun side post or side face of doorway or window frame.

jamboree /dʒæmbə'riː/ noun celebration; large rally of Scouts.

jammy adjective (**-ier, -iest**) covered with jam; colloquial lucky, profitable.

Jan. abbreviation January.

jangle /'dʒæŋg(ə)l/ ● verb (**-ling**) (cause to) make harsh metallic sound. ● noun such sound.

janitor /'dʒænɪtə/ noun doorkeeper; caretaker.

January /'dʒænjʊərɪ/ noun (plural **-ies**) first month of year.

japan /dʒə'pæn/ ● noun hard usually black varnish. ● verb (**-nn-**) make black and glossy (as) with japan.

Japanese /dʒæpə'niːz/ ● noun (plural same) native, national, or language of Japan. ● adjective of Japan or its people or language.

jape noun practical joke.

japonica /dʒə'pɒnɪkə/ noun flowering shrub with red flowers and edible fruits.

jar¹ noun container, usually of glass and cylindrical.

jar² ● verb (**-rr-**) (often + on) (of sound, manner, etc.) strike discordantly, grate; (often + against, on) (cause to) strike (esp. part of body) with vibration or shock; (often + with) be at variance. ● noun jarring sound, shock, or vibration.

jardinière /ʒɑːdɪ'njeə/ noun ornamental pot or stand for plants.

jargon /'dʒɑːgən/ noun words used by particular group or profession; debased or pretentious language.

jasmine /'dʒæzmɪn/ noun shrub with white or yellow flowers.

jasper /'dʒæspə/ noun red, yellow, or brown opaque quartz.

jaundice /'dʒɔːndɪs/ ● noun yellowing of skin caused by liver disease, bile disorder, etc. ● verb (as **jaundiced** adjective) affected with jaundice; envious, resentful.

jaunt /dʒɔːnt/ ● noun pleasure trip. ● verb take a jaunt.

jaunty adjective (**-ier, -iest**) cheerful and self-confident; sprightly. □ **jauntily** adverb; **jauntiness** noun.

javelin /'dʒævəlɪn/ noun light spear thrown in sport or, formerly, as weapon.

jaw ● noun bony structure containing teeth; (in plural) mouth, gripping parts of tool etc.; colloquial tedious talk. ● verb slang speak at tedious length. □ **jawbone** lower jaw in most mammals.

jay noun noisy European bird of crow family with vivid plumage. □ **jaywalk** walk across road carelessly or dangerously; **jaywalker** person who does this.

jazz noun rhythmic syncopated esp. improvised music of American black origin. □ **and all that jazz** colloquial and other related things; **jazz up** enliven.

jazzy *adjective* (**-ier**, **-iest**) of or like jazz; vivid.

jealous /ˈdʒeləs/ *adjective* resentful of rivalry in love; (often + *of*) envious (of person etc.), protective (of rights etc.). □ **jealously** *adverb*; **jealousy** *noun* (*plural* **-ies**).

jeans /dʒiːnz/ *plural noun* casual esp. denim trousers.

Jeep *noun* proprietary term small sturdy esp. military vehicle with 4-wheel drive.

jeer ● *verb* (often + *at*) scoff, deride. ● *noun* taunt.

Jehovah /dʒɪˈhəʊvə/ *noun* (in Old Testament) God. □ **Jehovah's Witness** member of unorthodox Christian sect.

jejune /dʒɪˈdʒuːn/ *adjective* (of ideas, writing, etc.) shallow, naïve, or dry and uninteresting.

jell *verb colloquial* set as jelly; (of ideas etc.) take definite form; cohere.

jellied /ˈdʒelɪd/ *adjective* (of food etc.) set as or in jelly.

jelly /ˈdʒelɪ/ *noun* (*plural* **-ies**) (usually fruit-flavoured) semi-transparent dessert set with gelatin; similar preparation as jam or condiment; *slang* gelignite. □ **jelly baby** jelly-like baby-shaped sweet; **jellyfish** (*plural* same or **-es**) marine animal with jelly-like body and stinging tentacles.

jemmy /ˈdʒemɪ/ *noun* (*plural* **-ies**) burglar's crowbar.

jeopardize *verb* (also **-ise**) (**-zing** or **-sing**) endanger.

jeopardy /ˈdʒepədɪ/ *noun* danger, esp. severe.

jerboa /dʒɜːˈbəʊə/ *noun* small jumping desert rodent.

Jeremiah /dʒerɪˈmaɪə/ *noun* dismal prophet.

jerk[1] ● *noun* sharp sudden pull, twist, etc.; spasmodic muscular twitch; *slang* fool. ● *verb* move, pull, throw, etc. with jerk. □ **jerky** *adjective* (**-ier**, **-iest**); **jerkily** *adverb*; **jerkiness** *noun*.

jerk[2] *verb* cure (beef) by cutting in long slices and drying in the sun.

jerkin /ˈdʒɜːkɪn/ *noun* sleeveless jacket.

jeroboam /dʒerəˈbəʊəm/ *noun* wine bottle of 4–12 times ordinary size.

jerry-building *noun* building of shoddy houses with bad materials. □ **jerry-builder** *noun*; **jerry-built** *adjective*.

jerrycan *noun* kind of petrol- or water-can.

jersey /ˈdʒɜːzɪ/ *noun* (*plural* **-s**) knitted usually woollen pullover; knitted fabric; (**Jersey**) dairy cow from Jersey.

Jerusalem artichoke /dʒəˈruːsələm/ *noun* kind of sunflower with edible tubers; this tuber as vegetable.

jest ● *noun* joke; fun; banter; object of derision. ● *verb* joke; fool about. □ **in jest** in fun.

jester *noun historical* professional clown at medieval court etc.

Jesuit /ˈdʒezjʊɪt/ *noun* member of RC Society of Jesus. □ **Jesuitical** /-ˈɪt-/ *adjective*.

jet[1] ● *noun* stream of water, steam, gas, flame, etc. shot esp. from small opening; spout or nozzle for this purpose; jet engine or plane. ● *verb* (**-tt-**) spurt out in jet(s); *colloquial* send or travel by jet plane. □ **jet engine** one using jet propulsion; **jet lag** exhaustion felt after long flight across time zones; **jet plane** one with jet engine; **jet-propelled** having jet propulsion, very fast; **jet propulsion** propulsion by backward ejection of high-speed jet of gas etc.; **jet set** wealthy people who travel widely, esp. for pleasure; **jet-setter** such a person.

jet[2] *noun* hard black lignite, often carved and highly polished. □ **jet black** deep glossy black.

jetsam /ˈdʒetsəm/ *noun* objects washed ashore, esp. jettisoned from ship.

jettison /ˈdʒetɪs(ə)n/ *verb* throw (cargo, fuel, etc.) from ship or aircraft to lighten it; abandon; get rid of.

jetty /ˈdʒetɪ/ *noun* (*plural* **-ies**) pier or breakwater protecting or defending harbour etc.; landing-pier.

Jew /dʒuː/ *noun* person of Hebrew descent or whose religion is Judaism.

jewel /ˈdʒuːəl/ ● *noun* precious stone; this used in watchmaking; jewelled personal ornament; precious person or thing. ● *verb* (**-ll-**; *US* **-l-**) (esp. as **jewelled** *adjective*) adorn or set with jewels.

jeweller *noun* (*US* **jeweler**) maker of or dealer in jewels or jewellery.

jewellery /ˈdʒuːəlrɪ/ noun (also **jewelry**) rings, brooches, necklaces, etc. collectively.

Jewish adjective of Jews or Judaism. □ **Jewishness** noun.

Jewry /ˈdʒʊərɪ/ noun Jews collectively.

Jezebel /ˈdʒezəbəl/ noun shameless or immoral woman.

jib ● noun projecting arm of crane; triangular staysail. ● verb (**-bb-**) (esp. of horse) stop and refuse to go on; (+ at) show aversion to.

jibe¹ = GIBE.

jibe² US = GYBE.

jiffy /ˈdʒɪfɪ/ noun (plural **-ies**) (also **jiff**) colloquial short time, moment. □ **Jiffy bag** proprietary term padded envelope.

jig ● noun lively dance; music for this; device that holds piece of work and guides tools operating on it. ● verb (**-gg-**) dance jig; (often + about) move quickly up and down; fidget.

jigger /ˈdʒɪgə/ noun small glass for measure of spirits.

jiggery-pokery /dʒɪgərɪˈpəʊkərɪ/ noun colloquial trickery; swindling.

jiggle /ˈdʒɪg(ə)l/ ● verb (**-ling**) (often + about) rock or jerk lightly; fidget. ● noun light shake.

jigsaw noun (in full **jigsaw puzzle**) picture on board etc. cut into irregular interlocking pieces to be reassembled as pastime; mechanical fine-bladed fret saw.

jihad /dʒɪˈhæd/ noun Muslim holy war against unbelievers.

jilt verb abruptly reject or abandon (esp. lover).

jingle /ˈdʒɪŋg(ə)l/ ● noun mixed ringing or clinking noise; repetition of sounds in phrase; short catchy verse in advertising etc. ● verb (**-ling**) (cause to) make jingling sound.

jingo /ˈdʒɪŋgəʊ/ noun (plural **-es**) blustering patriot. □ **jingoism** noun; **jingoist** noun; **jingoistic** /-ˈɪs-/ adjective.

jink ● verb move elusively; elude by dodging. ● noun jinking. □ **high jinks** boisterous fun.

jinnee /ˈdʒiniː/ noun (also **jinn**, **djinn** /dʒɪn/) (plural **jinn** or **djinn**) (in Muslim mythology) spirit of supernatural power in human or animal form.

jinx colloquial ● noun person or thing that seems to bring bad luck. ● verb (esp. as **jinxed** adjective) subject to bad luck.

jitter /ˈdʒɪtə/ colloquial ● noun (**the jitters**) extreme nervousness. ● verb be nervous; act nervously. □ **jittery** adjective.

jive ● noun lively dance of 1950s; music for this. ● verb (**-ving**) dance to or play jive music. □ **jiver** noun.

Jnr. abbreviation Junior.

job ● noun piece of work (to be) done; paid employment; colloquial difficult task; slang a crime, esp. a robbery. ● verb (**-bb-**) do jobs; do piece-work; buy and sell (stocks etc.); deal corruptly with (matter). □ **jobcentre** local government office advertising available jobs; **job-hunt** colloquial seek employment; **job lot** mixed lot bought at auction etc.

jobber /ˈdʒɒbə/ noun person who jobs; historical principal or wholesaler on Stock Exchange.

jobbery noun corrupt dealing.

jobless adjective unemployed. □ **joblessness** noun.

job-sharing noun sharing of full-time job by two or more people. □ **job-share** noun & verb.

jockey /ˈdʒɒkɪ/ ● noun rider in horse races. ● verb (**-eys**, **-eyed**) cheat, trick. □ **jockey for position** manoeuvre for advantage.

jockstrap /ˈdʒɒkstræp/ noun support or protection for male genitals worn esp. in sport.

jocose /dʒəˈkəʊs/ adjective playful; jocular. □ **jocosely** adverb; **jocosity** /-ˈkɒs-/ noun (plural **-ies**).

jocular /ˈdʒɒkjʊlə/ adjective fond of joking; humorous. □ **jocularity** /-ˈlær-/ noun (plural **-ies**); **jocularly** adverb.

jocund /ˈdʒɒkənd/ adjective literary merry, cheerful. □ **jocundity** /dʒəˈkʌn-/ noun (plural **-ies**); **jocundly** adverb.

jodhpurs /ˈdʒɒdpəz/ plural noun riding breeches tight below knee.

jog ● verb (**-gg-**) run slowly, esp. as exercise; push, jerk; nudge, esp. to alert; stimulate (person's memory). ● noun spell of jogging; slow walk or trot; push, jerk; nudge. □ **jogtrot** slow regular trot. □ **jogger** noun.

joggle /ˈdʒɒg(ə)l/ ● verb (**-ling**) move in jerks. ● noun slight shake.

joie de vivre /ʒwɑː də 'viːvrə/ noun exuberance; high spirits. [French]

join ● verb (often + *to*, *together*) put together, fasten, unite; connect (points) by line etc.; become member of (club etc.); take one's place with (person, group, etc.); (+ *in*, *for*, etc.) take part with (others) in activity etc.; (often + *with*, *to*) come together, be united; (of river etc.) become connected or continuous with. ● noun point, line, or surface of junction. □ **join in** take part in (activity); **join up** enlist for military service.

joiner noun maker of furniture and light woodwork. □ **joinery** noun.

joint ● noun place at which two or more things are joined; device for doing this; point at which two bones fit together; division of animal carcass as meat; *slang* restaurant, bar, etc.; *slang* marijuana cigarette. ● adjective held by, done by, or belonging to two or more people etc.; sharing with another. ● verb connect by joint(s); divide at joint or into joints. □ **joint stock** capital held jointly.

jointure /'dʒɔɪntʃə/ noun estate settled on wife by husband for use after his death.

joist noun supporting beam in floor, ceiling, etc.

jojoba /həʊ'həʊbə/ noun plant with seeds yielding oil used in cosmetics etc.

joke ● noun thing said or done to cause laughter; witticism; ridiculous person or thing. ● verb (**-king**) make jokes. □ **jokily** adverb; **jokiness** noun; **jokingly** adverb; **jokey**, **joky** adjective.

joker noun person who jokes; playing card used in some games.

jollification /dʒɒlɪfɪ'keɪʃ(ə)n/ noun merrymaking.

jolly /'dʒɒlɪ/ ● adjective (**-ier**, **-iest**) cheerful; festive, jovial; *colloquial* pleasant, delightful. ● adverb *colloquial* very. ● verb (**-ies**, **-ied**) (usually + *along*) *colloquial* coax, humour. □ **jollity** noun (*plural* **-ies**).

jolt /dʒəʊlt/ ● verb shake (esp. in vehicle) with jerk; shock, perturb; move along jerkily. ● noun jerk; surprise, shock.

jonquil /'dʒɒŋkwɪl/ noun narcissus with white or yellow fragrant flowers.

josh *slang* ● verb tease, make fun of. ● noun good-natured joke.

joss noun Chinese idol. □ **joss-stick** incense stick for burning.

jostle /'dʒɒs(ə)l/ ● verb (**-ling**) (often + *against*) knock; elbow; (+ *with*) struggle. ● noun jostling.

jot ● verb (**-tt-**) (usually + *down*) write briefly or hastily. ● noun very small amount.

jotter noun small pad or notebook.

joule /dʒuːl/ noun SI unit of work and energy.

journal /'dʒɜːn(ə)l/ noun newspaper, periodical; daily record of events; diary; account book; part of shaft or axle resting on bearings.

journalese /dʒɜːnə'liːz/ noun hackneyed style of writing characteristic of newspapers.

journalism /'dʒɜːnəlɪz(ə)m/ noun work of journalist.

journalist /'dʒɜːnəlɪst/ noun person writing for or editing newspapers etc. □ **journalistic** /-'lɪs-/ adjective.

journey /'dʒɜːnɪ/ ● noun (*plural* **-s**) act of going from one place to another; distance travelled, time taken. ● verb (**-s**, **-ed**) make journey, travel. □ **journeyman** qualified mechanic or artisan working for another.

joust /dʒaʊst/ *historical* ● noun combat with lances between two mounted knights. ● verb engage in joust. □ **jouster** noun.

jovial /'dʒəʊvɪəl/ adjective merry, convivial, hearty. □ **joviality** /-'æl-/ noun; **jovially** adverb.

jowl /dʒaʊl/ noun jaw, jawbone; cheek; loose skin on throat.

joy noun gladness, pleasure; thing causing joy; *colloquial* satisfaction. □ **joyride** *colloquial* (go for) pleasure ride in esp. stolen car; **joystick** control column of aircraft, lever for moving image on VDU screen. □ **joyful** adjective; **joyfully** adverb; **joyfulness** noun; **joyless** adjective; **joyous** adjective; **joyously** adverb.

JP abbreviation Justice of the Peace.

Jr. abbreviation Junior.

jubilant /'dʒuːbɪlənt/ adjective exultant, rejoicing. □ **jubilantly** adverb; **jubilation** noun.

jubilee /'dʒuːbɪliː/ noun anniversary (esp. 25th or 50th); time of rejoicing.

Judaic /dʒuːˈdeɪɪk/ *adjective* of or characteristic of Jews.

Judaism /ˈdʒuːdeɪɪz(ə)m/ *noun* religion of Jews.

Judas /ˈdʒuːdəs/ *noun* traitor.

judder /ˈdʒʌdə/ ● *verb* shake noisily or violently. ● *noun* juddering.

judge /dʒʌdʒ/ ● *noun* public official appointed to hear and try legal cases; person appointed to decide dispute or contest; person who decides question; person having judgement of specified type. ● *verb* (**-ging**) form opinion (about); estimate; act as judge (of); try legal case; (often + *to do, that*) conclude, consider.

judgement *noun* (also **judgment**) critical faculty, discernment, good sense; opinion; sentence of court of justice; *often jocular* deserved misfortune. □ **Judgement Day** day on which God will judge humankind. □ **judgemental** /-ˈmen-/ *adjective*.

judicature /ˈdʒuːdɪkətʃə/ *noun* administration of justice; judge's position; judges collectively.

judicial /dʒuːˈdɪʃ(ə)l/ *adjective* of, done by, or proper to court of law; of or proper to a judge; having function of judge; impartial. □ **judicially** *adverb*.

judiciary /dʒuːˈdɪʃərɪ/ *noun* (*plural* **-ies**) judges collectively.

judicious /dʒuːˈdɪʃəs/ *adjective* sensible, prudent. □ **judiciously** *adverb*.

judo /ˈdʒuːdəʊ/ *noun* sport derived from ju-jitsu.

jug ● *noun* deep vessel for liquids, with handle and lip; contents of this; *slang* prison. ● *verb* (**-gg-**) (usually as **jugged** *adjective*) stew (hare) in casserole. □ **jugful** *noun* (*plural* **-s**).

juggernaut /ˈdʒʌgənɔːt/ *noun* large heavy lorry; overwhelming force or object.

juggle /ˈdʒʌg(ə)l/ ● *verb* (**-ling**) (often + *with*) keep several objects in the air at once by throwing and catching; manipulate or rearrange (facts). ● *noun* juggling; fraud. □ **juggler** *noun*.

jugular /ˈdʒʌgjʊlə/ ● *adjective* of neck or throat. ● *noun* jugular vein. □ **jugular vein** any of large veins in neck carrying blood from head.

juice /dʒuːs/ *noun* liquid part of vegetable, fruit, or meat; animal fluid, esp. secretion; *colloquial* petrol, electricity.

juicy /ˈdʒuːsɪ/ *adjective* (**-ier**, **-iest**) full of juice; *colloquial* interesting, scandalous; *colloquial* profitable. □ **juicily** *adverb*.

ju-jitsu /dʒuːˈdʒɪtsuː/ *noun* Japanese system of unarmed combat.

ju-ju /ˈdʒuːdʒuː/ *noun* (*plural* **-s**) charm or fetish of some W. African peoples; supernatural power attributed to this.

jujube /ˈdʒuːdʒuːb/ *noun* flavoured jelly-like lozenge.

jukebox /ˈdʒuːkbɒks/ *noun* coin-operated machine playing records or compact discs.

Jul. *abbreviation* July.

julep /ˈdʒuːlep/ *noun* sweet drink, esp. medicated; *US* spirits and water iced and flavoured.

julienne /dʒuːlɪˈen/ ● *noun* vegetables cut into thin strips. ● *adjective* cut into thin strips.

Juliet cap /ˈdʒuːlɪət/ *noun* small close-fitting cap worn by brides etc.

July /dʒuːˈlaɪ/ *noun* (*plural* **Julys**) seventh month of year.

jumble /ˈdʒʌmb(ə)l/ ● *verb* (**-ling**) (often + *up*) mix; confuse; muddle. ● *noun* confused heap etc.; muddle; articles in jumble sale. □ **jumble sale** sale of second-hand articles, esp. for charity.

jumbo /ˈdʒʌmbəʊ/ *noun* (*plural* **-s**) big animal (esp. elephant), person, or thing. □ **jumbo jet** large airliner for several hundred passengers, esp. Boeing 747.

jump ● *verb* spring from ground etc.; (often + *up, from, in, out,* etc.) rise or move suddenly; jerk from shock or excitement; pass over (obstacle) by jumping; (+ *to, at*) reach (conclusion) hastily; (of train etc.) leave (rails); pass (red traffic light); get on or off (train etc.) quickly, esp. illegally; attack (person) unexpectedly. ● *noun* act of jumping; sudden movement caused by shock etc.; abrupt rise in price, status, etc.; obstacle to be jumped; death by horse; gap in series etc. □ **jump at** accept eagerly; **jumped-up** *adjective colloquial* upstart; **jump the gun** start prematurely; **jump-jet** vertical take-off jet plane; **jump-lead** cable for carrying current from one battery to another; **jump-off** deciding round in show-jumping; **jump the queue** take unfair precedence; **jump ship** (of seaman) desert; **jump suit** one-piece garment for whole body; **jump to it** *colloquial* act promptly and energetically.

jumper /'dʒʌmpə/ *noun* knitted pullover; loose outer jacket worn by sailors; *US* pinafore dress.

jumpy *adjective* (**-ier**, **-iest**) nervous, easily startled. □ **jumpiness** *noun*.

Jun. *abbreviation* June; Junior.

junction /'dʒʌŋkʃ(ə)n/ *noun* joining-point; place where railway lines or roads meet. □ **junction box** box containing junction of electric cables etc.

juncture /'dʒʌŋktʃə/ *noun* point in time, esp. critical one; joining-point.

June *noun* sixth month of year.

jungle /'dʒʌŋg(ə)l/ *noun* land overgrown with tangled vegetation, esp. in tropics; tangled mass; place of bewildering complexity or struggle.

junior /'dʒuːnɪə/ *adjective* (often + *to*) lower in rank, standing, or position; the younger (esp. after name); (of school) for younger pupils. ●*noun* junior person.

juniper /'dʒuːnɪpə/ *noun* prickly evergreen shrub or tree with purple berry-like cones.

junk [1] ●*noun* discarded articles, rubbish; anything regarded as of little value; *slang* narcotic drug, esp. heroin. ●*verb* discard as junk. □ **junk food** food which is not nutritious; **junk mail** unsolicited advertising sent by post.

junk [2] *noun* flat-bottomed sailing vessel in China seas.

junket /'dʒʌŋkɪt/ ●*noun* pleasure outing; official's tour at public expense; sweetened and flavoured milk curds; feast. ●*verb* (**-t-**) feast, picnic.

junkie /'dʒʌŋkɪ/ *noun slang* drug addict.

junta /'dʒʌntə/ *noun* (usually *military*) clique taking power after *coup d'état*.

juridical /dʒʊə'rɪdɪk(ə)l/ *adjective* of judicial proceedings, relating to the law.

jurisdiction /dʒʊərɪs'dɪkʃ(ə)n/ *noun* (often + *over*) administration of justice; legal or other authority; extent of this.

jurisprudence /dʒʊərɪs'pruːd(ə)ns/ *noun* science or philosophy of law.

jurist /'dʒʊərɪst/ *noun* expert in law. □ **juristic** /-'rɪs-/ *adjective*.

juror /'dʒʊərə/ *noun* member of jury.

jury /'dʒʊərɪ/ *noun* (*plural* **-ies**) group of people giving verdict in court of justice; judges of competition. □ **jury-box** enclosure in court for jury.

just ●*adjective* morally right, fair; deserved; well-grounded; justified. ●*adverb* exactly; very recently; barely; quite; *colloquial* simply, merely, positively. □ **just now** at this moment, a little time ago. □ **justly** *adverb*.

justice /'dʒʌstɪs/ *noun* fairness; authority exercised in maintenance of right; judicial proceedings; magistrate, judge. □ **do justice to** treat fairly, appreciate properly; **Justice of the Peace** lay magistrate.

justify /'dʒʌstɪfaɪ/ *verb* (**-ies**, **-ied**) show justice or truth of; (esp. in *passive*) be adequate grounds for, vindicate; *Printing* adjust (line of type) to fill space evenly; (as **justified** *adjective*) just, right. □ **justifiable** *adjective*; **justification** *noun*.

jut ●*verb* (**-tt-**) (often + *out*) protrude. ●*noun* projection.

jute /dʒuːt/ *noun* fibre from bark of E. Indian plant, used for sacking, mats, etc.; plant yielding this.

juvenile /'dʒuːvənaɪl/ ●*adjective* youthful; of or for young people; *often derogatory* immature. ●*noun* young person; actor playing juvenile part. □ **juvenile delinquency** offences committed by people below age of legal responsibility; **juvenile delinquent** such offender.

juvenilia /dʒuːvə'nɪlɪə/ *plural noun* youthful works of author or artist.

juxtapose /dʒʌkstə'pəʊz/ *verb* (**-sing**) put side by side; (+ *with*) put (thing) beside another. □ **juxtaposition** /-pə'zɪʃ(ə)n/ *noun*.

K *abbreviation* (also **K.**) kelvin(s); Köchel (list of Mozart's works); (also **k**) 1,000.

k *abbreviation* kilo-; knot(s).

kaftan = CAFTAN.

kaiser /'kaɪzə/ *noun historical* emperor, esp. of Germany or Austria.

kale *noun* variety of cabbage, esp. with wrinkled leaves.

kaleidoscope /kə'laɪdəskəup/ *noun* tube containing angled mirrors and pieces of coloured glass producing reflected patterns when shaken; constantly changing scene, group, etc. □ **kaleidoscopic** /-'skɒp-/ *adjective*.

kalends = CALENDS.

kamikaze /kæmɪ'kɑːzɪ/ *noun historical* explosive-laden Japanese aircraft deliberately crashed on to target in 1939–45 war; pilot of this. *adjective* reckless, esp. suicidal.

kangaroo /kæŋgə'ruː/ *noun* (*plural* **-s**) Australian marsupial with strong hind legs for jumping. □ **kangaroo court** illegal court held by strikers, mutineers, etc.

kaolin /'keɪəlɪn/ *noun* fine white clay used esp. for porcelain and in medicines.

kapok /'keɪpɒk/ *noun* fine cotton-like material from tropical tree, used to stuff cushions etc.

kaput /kə'put/ *adjective slang* broken, ruined.

karabiner /kærə'biːnə/ *noun* coupling link used by mountaineers.

karakul /'kærəkʌl/ *noun* (also **caracul**) Asian sheep whose lambs have dark curled fleece; fur of this.

karaoke /kærɪ'əʊkɪ/ *noun* entertainment in nightclubs etc. with customers singing to backing music.

karate /kə'rɑːtɪ/ *noun* Japanese system of unarmed combat.

karma /'kɑːmə/ *noun Buddhism & Hinduism* person's actions in one life, believed to decide fate in next; destiny.

kauri /kaʊ'rɪ/ *noun* (*plural* **-s**) coniferous NZ timber tree.

kayak /'kaɪæk/ *noun* Eskimo one-man canoe.

kazoo /kə'zuː/ *noun* toy musical instrument into which player sings wordlessly.

KBE *abbreviation* Knight Commander of the Order of the British Empire.

kea /'kiːə/ *noun* green and red NZ parrot.

kebab /kɪ'bæb/ *noun* pieces of meat and sometimes vegetables grilled on skewer.

kedge *verb* (**-ging**) move (ship) with hawser attached to small anchor. *noun* (in full **kedge-anchor**) small anchor for this purpose.

kedgeree /kedʒə'riː/ *noun* dish of fish, rice, hard-boiled eggs, etc.

keel *noun* main lengthwise member of base of ship etc. *verb* (often + *over*) (cause to) fall down or over; turn keel upwards. □ **keelhaul** drag (person) under keel as punishment; **on an even keel** steady, balanced.

keen¹ *adjective* enthusiastic, eager; (often + *on*) enthusiastic about, fond of; intellectually acute; (of knife) sharp; (of price) competitive. □ **keenly** *adverb*; **keenness** *noun*.

keen² *noun* Irish wailing funeral song. *verb* (often + *over*, *for*) wail mournfully, esp. at funeral.

keep *verb* (*past & past participle* **kept**) have charge of; retain possession of; (+ *for*) retain or reserve (for future); maintain or remain in good or specified condition; restrain; detain; observe or respect (law, secret, etc.); own and look after (animal); clothe, feed, etc. (person); carry on (a business); maintain, guard, protect. *noun* maintenance, food; *historical* tower, stronghold. □ **for keeps** *colloquial* permanently; **keep at** (cause to) persist with; **keep away** (often + *from*) avoid, prevent from being near; **keep-fit** regular physical exercises; **keep off** (cause to) stay away from, abstain from, avoid; **keep**

on continue, (+ *at*) nag; **keep out** (cause to) stay outside; **keep up** maintain, prevent from going to bed, (often + *with*) not fall behind; **keep up with the Joneses** compete socially with neighbours.

keeper *noun* person who looks after or is in charge of an animal, person, or thing; custodian of museum, forest, etc.; wicket-keeper, goalkeeper; ring holding another on finger.

keeping *noun* custody, charge; (esp. in **in** or **out of keeping with**) agreement, harmony.

keepsake *noun* souvenir, esp. of person.

keg *noun* small barrel. □ **keg beer** beer kept in pressurized metal keg.

kelp *noun* large seaweed suitable for manure.

kelpie /ˈkelpɪ/ *noun Scottish* malevolent water-spirit; Australian sheepdog.

Kelt = CELT.

kelter = KILTER.

kelvin /ˈkelvɪn/ *noun* SI unit of temperature.

ken ● *noun* range of knowledge or sight. ● *verb* (**-nn-**; *past & past participle* **kenned** or **kent**) *Scottish & Northern English* recognize, know.

kendo /ˈkendəʊ/ *noun* Japanese fencing with bamboo swords.

kennel /ˈken(ə)l/ ● *noun* small shelter for dog; (in *plural*) breeding or boarding place for dogs. ● *verb* (**-ll-**; *US* **-l-**) put or keep in kennel.

Kenyan /ˈkenjən/ ● *adjective* of Kenya. ● *noun* native or national of Kenya.

kept *past & past participle* of KEEP.

keratin /ˈkerətɪn/ *noun* fibrous protein in hair, hooves, claws, etc.

kerb *noun* stone etc. edging to pavement etc. □ **kerb-crawling** *colloquial* driving slowly to pick up prostitute; **kerb drill** rules taught to children about crossing roads.

kerfuffle /kəˈfʌf(ə)l/ *noun colloquial* fuss, commotion.

kermes /ˈkɜːmɪz/ *noun* female of insect with berry-like appearance that feeds on **kermes o k**, evergreen oak; red dye made from these insects.

kernel /ˈkɜːn(ə)l/ *noun* (usually soft) edible centre within hard shell of nut, fruit stone, seed, etc.; central or essential part.

kerosene /ˈkerəsiːn/ *noun esp. US* fuel oil distilled from petroleum etc.; paraffin oil.

kestrel /ˈkestr(ə)l/ *noun* small hovering falcon.

ketch *noun* kind of two-masted sailing boat.

ketchup /ˈketʃəp/ *noun* (*US* **catsup** /ˈkætsəp/) spicy sauce made esp. from tomatoes.

kettle /ˈket(ə)l/ *noun* vessel for boiling water in. □ **kettledrum** large bowl-shaped drum.

key /kiː/ ● *noun* (*plural* **-s**) instrument for moving bolt of lock, operating switch, etc.; instrument for winding clock etc. or grasping screw, nut, etc.; finger-operated button or lever on typewriter, piano, computer terminal, etc.; explanation, word, or system for understanding list of symbols, code, etc.; *Music* system of related notes based on particular note; roughness of surface helping adhesion of plaster etc. ● *verb* fasten with pin, wedge, bolt, etc.; (often + *in*) enter (data) by means of (computer) keyboard; roughen (surface) to help adhesion of plaster etc. □ **keyed up** tense, excited; **keyhole** hole by which key is put into lock; **keynote** prevailing tone or idea, *Music* note on which key is based; **keypad** miniature keyboard etc. for telephone, portable computer, etc.; **keyring** ring for keeping keys on; **keystone** central principle of policy, system, etc., central stone of arch.

keyboard ● *noun* set of keys on typewriter, computer, piano, etc. ● *verb* enter (data) by means of keyboard. □ **keyboarder** *noun Computing*.

KG *abbreviation* Knight of the Order of the Garter.

kg *abbreviation* kilogram(s).

KGB *noun historical* secret police of USSR.

khaki /ˈkɑːkɪ/ ● *adjective* dull brownish-yellow. ● *noun* (*plural* **-s**) khaki colour, cloth, or uniform.

khan /kɑːn/ *noun: title of ruler or official in Central Asia.* □ **khanate** *noun.*

kHz *abbreviation* kilohertz.

kibbutz /kɪˈbʊts/ *noun* (*plural* **-im** /-iːm/) communal esp. farming settlement in Israel.

kibosh /ˈkaɪbɒʃ/ *noun slang* nonsense. □ **put the kibosh on** put an end to.

kick ● *verb* strike, strike out, or propel forcibly with foot or hoof; (often + *at*, *against*) protest, rebel; *slang* give up (habit); (often + *out*) expel, dismiss; (**kick oneself**, **could kick oneself**) be annoyed with oneself; score (goal) by kicking. ● *noun* kicking action or blow; recoil of gun; *colloquial* temporary enthusiasm, sharp stimulant effect; (often in *plural*) thrill. □ **kick about** drift idly, discuss informally; **kickback** recoil, payment esp. for illegal help; **kick the bucket** *slang* die; **kick off** *verb* begin football game, remove (shoes etc.) by kicking, *colloquial* start; **kick-off** *noun* start, esp. of football game; **kick-start(er)** (pedal on) device to start engine of motorcycle etc.; **kick up a fuss** *colloquial* create disturbance, object; **kick upstairs** get rid of by promotion.

kid¹ ● *noun* young goat; leather from this; *colloquial* child. ● *verb* (**-dd-**) (of goat) give birth to kid.

kid² *verb* (**-dd-**) *colloquial* deceive, tease. □ **no kidding** *slang* that is the truth.

kidnap /ˈkɪdnæp/ *verb* (**-pp-**; *US* **-p-**) carry off (person) illegally, esp. to obtain ransom. □ **kidnapper** *noun*.

kidney /ˈkɪdnɪ/ *noun* (*plural* **-s**) either of two organs serving to excrete urine; animal's kidney as food. ● **kidney bean** red-skinned kidney-shaped bean; **kidney machine** apparatus able to perform function of damaged kidney; **kidney-shaped** having one side concave and the other convex.

kill ● *verb* deprive of life or vitality; end; (**kill oneself**) *colloquial* overexert oneself, laugh heartily; *colloquial* overwhelm with amusement; switch off; pass (time) while waiting; *Computing* delete; *Sport* stop (ball) dead. ● *noun* (esp. in hunting) act of killing, animal(s) killed. □ **killjoy** depressing person; **kill off** destroy completely, bring about death of (fictional character).

killer *noun* person or thing that kills; murderer. □ **killer whale** dolphin with prominent dorsal fin.

killing ● *noun* causing death; *colloquial* great financial success. ● *adjective colloquial* very funny; exhausting.

kiln *noun* oven for burning, baking, or drying esp. pottery.

kilo /ˈkiːləʊ/ *noun* (*plural* **-s**) kilogram.

kilo- *combining form* one thousand.

kilobyte /ˈkɪləbaɪt/ *noun Computing* 1,024 bytes as measure of memory size etc.

kilocalorie /ˈkɪləkælərɪ/ *noun* large calorie (see CALORIE).

kilocycle /ˈkɪləsaɪk(ə)l/ *noun historical* kilohertz.

kilogram /ˈkɪləgræm/ *noun* SI unit of mass (2.205 lb).

kilohertz /ˈkɪləhɜːts/ *noun* 1,000 hertz.

kilolitre /ˈkɪləliːtə/ *noun* (*US* **-liter**) 1,000 litres.

kilometre /ˈkɪləmiːtə/ *noun* (*US* **-meter**) 1,000 metres (0.6214 mile).

■ **Usage** *Kilometre* is often pronounced /kɪˈlɒmɪtə/ (with the stress on the *-lom-*), but this is considered incorrect by some people.

kiloton /ˈkɪlətʌn/ *noun* (also **kilotonne**) unit of explosive power equal to that of 1,000 tons of TNT.

kilovolt /ˈkɪləvəʊlt/ *noun* 1,000 volts.

kilowatt /ˈkɪləwɒt/ *noun* 1,000 watts. □ **kilowatt-hour** electrical energy equal to 1 kilowatt used for 1 hour.

kilt ● *noun* pleated skirt usually of tartan, traditionally worn by Highland man. ● *verb* tuck up (skirts) round body; (esp. as **kilted** *adjective*) gather in vertical pleats.

kilter /ˈkɪltə/ *noun* (also **kelter** /ˈkeltə/) good working order.

kimono /kɪˈməʊnəʊ/ *noun* (*plural* **-s**) wide-sleeved Japanese robe; similar dressing gown.

kin ● *noun* one's relatives or family. ● *adjective* related.

kind /kaɪnd/ ● *noun* species, natural group of animals, plants, etc.; class, type, variety. ● *adjective* (often + *to*) friendly, benevolent. □ **in kind** in same form, (of payment) in goods etc. instead of money.

kindergarten /ˈkɪndəgɑːt(ə)n/ *noun* class or school for young children.

kind-hearted *adjective* of kind disposition. □ **kind-heartedly** *adverb*; **kind-heartedness** *noun*.

kindle /ˈkɪnd(ə)l/ *verb* (**-ling**) set on fire, light; inspire; become aroused or animated.

kindling /ˈkɪndlɪŋ/ *noun* small sticks etc. for lighting fires.

kindly /ˈkaɪndlɪ/ ● *adverb* in a kind way; please. ● *adjective* (**-ier, -iest**) kind; (of climate etc.) pleasant, mild.

kindred /ˈkɪndrɪd/ ● *adjective* related, allied, similar. ● *noun* blood relationship; one's relations.

kinetic /kɪˈnetɪk/ *adjective* of or due to motion. □ **kinetic energy** energy of motion. □ **kinetically** *adverb*.

king *noun* (as title usually **King**) male sovereign, esp. hereditary; outstanding man or thing in specified field; largest kind of a thing; chess piece which must be checkmated for a win; crowned piece in draughts; court card depicting king; (**the King**) national anthem when sovereign is male. □ **King Charles spaniel** small black and tan kind; **kingcup** marsh marigold; **kingpin** main or large bolt, essential person or thing; **king-size(d)** large. □ **kingly** *adjective*; **kingship** *noun*.

kingdom *noun* state or territory ruled by king or queen; spiritual reign of God; domain; division of natural world. □ **kingdom come** *colloquial* the next world.

kingfisher *noun* small river bird with brilliant blue plumage, which dives for fish.

kink ● *noun* twist or bend in wire etc.; tight wave in hair; mental peculiarity. ● *verb* (cause to) form kink.

kinky *adjective* (**-ier, -iest**) *colloquial* sexually perverted or unconventional; (of clothing) bizarre and sexually provocative. □ **kinkily** *adverb*.

kinship *noun* blood relationship; similarity.

kinsman /ˈkɪnzmən/ *noun* (*feminine* **kinswoman**) blood relation.

kiosk /ˈkiːɒsk/ *noun* open-fronted booth selling newspapers, food, etc.; telephone box.

kip *slang* ● *noun* sleep, bed. ● *verb* (**-pp-**) (often + *down*) sleep.

kipper /ˈkɪpə/ ● *noun* fish, esp. herring, split, salted, dried, and usually smoked. ● *verb* treat (herring etc.) this way.

kir /kɪə/ *noun* dry white wine with blackcurrant liqueur.

kirk *noun* *Scottish & Northern English* church. □ **Kirk-session** lowest court in Church of Scotland.

kirsch /kɪəʃ/ *noun* spirit distilled from cherries.

kismet /ˈkɪzmet/ *noun* destiny.

kiss ● *verb* touch with lips, esp. as sign of love, reverence, etc.; touch lightly. ● *noun* touch of lips; light touch. □ **kiss-curl** small curl of hair on forehead or nape of neck; **kiss of life** mouth-to-mouth resuscitation.

kisser *noun* *slang* mouth; face.

kissogram *noun* novelty greeting delivered with kiss.

kit ● *noun* equipment, clothing, etc. for particular purpose; specialized, esp. sports, clothing or uniform; set of parts needed to assemble furniture, model, etc. ● *verb* (**-tt-**) supply; (often + *out*) equip with kit. □ **kitbag** usually cylindrical canvas etc. bag for carrying soldier's etc. kit.

kitchen /ˈkɪtʃɪn/ *noun* place where food is cooked; kitchen fitments. □ **kitchen garden** garden for growing fruit and vegetables.

kitchenette /kɪtʃɪˈnet/ *noun* small kitchen or cooking area.

kite *noun* light framework with thin covering flown on long string in wind; soaring bird of prey.

kith /kɪθ/ *noun* □ **kith and kin** friends and relations.

kitsch /kɪtʃ/ *noun* vulgar, pretentious, or worthless art.

kitten /ˈkɪt(ə)n/ ● *noun* young cat, ferret, etc. ● *verb* give birth to (kittens).

kittenish *adjective* playful; flirtatious.

kittiwake /ˈkɪtɪweɪk/ *noun* kind of small seagull.

kitty[1] /ˈkɪtɪ/ *noun* (*plural* **-ies**) joint fund; pool in some card games.

kitty[2] /ˈkɪtɪ/ *noun* (*plural* **-ies**) *childish name* for kitten or cat.

kiwi /ˈkiːwiː/ *noun* flightless NZ bird; (**Kiwi**) *colloquial* New Zealander. □ **kiwi fruit** green-fleshed fruit.

Klaxon /'klæks(ə)n/ *noun proprietary term* horn, warning hooter.

Kleenex /'kli:neks/ *noun (plural same or -es) proprietary term* disposable paper handkerchief.

kleptomania /kleptə'meɪnɪə/ *noun* irresistible urge to steal. □ **kleptomaniac** /-nɪæk/ *adjective & noun.*

km *abbreviation* kilometre(s).

knack /næk/ *noun* acquired faculty of doing something skilfully; habit of action, speech, etc.

knacker /'nækə/ ● *noun* buyer of useless horses for slaughter. ● *verb slang* (esp. as **knackered** *adjective*) exhaust, wear out.

knapsack /'næpsæk/ *noun* soldier's or hiker's bag carried on back.

knapweed /'næpwi:d/ *noun* plant with thistle-like flower.

knave /neɪv/ *noun* rogue, scoundrel; jack (in playing cards). □ **knavery** *noun;* **knavish** *adjective.*

knead /ni:d/ *verb* work into dough, paste, etc., esp. by hand; make (bread, pottery) thus; massage.

knee /ni:/ ● *noun* joint between thigh and lower leg; lap of sitting person; part of garment covering knee. ● *verb* (**knees, kneed, kneeing**) touch or strike with knee. □ **kneecap** convex bone in front of knee; **knees-up** *colloquial* lively party or gathering.

kneel /ni:l/ *verb* (*past & past participle* **knelt**) rest or lower oneself on knee(s).

kneeler *noun* cushion for kneeling on.

knell /nel/ *noun* sound of bell, esp. for death or funeral; event etc. seen as bad omen.

knelt *past & past participle* of KNEEL.

knew *past* of KNOW.

knickerbockers /'nɪkəbɒkəz/ *plural noun* loose-fitting breeches gathered in at knee. □ **Knickerbocker Glory** ice cream and fruit in tall glass.

knickers /'nɪkəz/ *plural noun* woman's or girl's undergarment for lower torso.

knick-knack /'nɪknæk/ *noun* (also **nick-nack**) trinket, small ornament.

knife /naɪf/ ● *noun* (*plural* **knives**) cutting blade or weapon with long sharpened edge fixed in handle; cutting-blade in machine; **(the knife)** *colloquial* surgery. ● *verb* (**-fing**) cut or stab with knife. □ **knife-edge** edge of knife, position of extreme uncertainty; **knife-pleat** overlapping narrow flat pleat.

knight /naɪt/ ● *noun* man awarded non-hereditary title (*Sir*) by sovereign; *historical* man raised to honourable military rank; *historical* lady's champion in tournament etc.; chess piece usually in shape of horse's head. ● *verb* confer knighthood on. □ **knighthood** *noun;* **knightly** *adjective.*

knit /nɪt/ *verb* (**-tt-**; *past & past participle* **knitted** or **knit**) make (garment etc.) by interlocking loops of esp. wool with knitting-needles or knitting machine; make (plain stitch) in knitting; wrinkle (brow); (often + *together*) make or become close, (of broken bone) become joined. □ **knitwear** knitted garments.

knitting *noun* work being knitted. □ **knitting-needle** thin pointed rod used usually in pairs for knitting.

knob /nɒb/ *noun* rounded protuberance, e.g. door handle, radio control, etc.; small lump (of butter, coal, etc.). □ **knobby** *adjective.*

knobbly /'nɒblɪ/ *adjective* (**-ier, -iest**) hard and lumpy.

knock /nɒk/ ● *verb* strike with audible sharp blow; (often + *at*) strike (door etc.) for admittance; (usually + *in, off,* etc.) drive by striking; make (hole) by knocking; (of engine) make thumping etc. noise; *slang* criticize. ● *noun* audible sharp blow; rap, esp. at door. □ **knock about, around** treat roughly, wander about aimlessly, (usually + *with*) associate socially; **knock back** *slang* eat or drink, esp. quickly; **knock down** *verb* strike (esp. person) to ground, demolish, (usually + *to*) (at auction) sell to bidder, *colloquial* lower price of; **knock-down** *adjective* (of price) very low; **knock knees** legs curved inward at the knee; **knock-kneed** with knock knees; **knock off** strike off with blow, *colloquial* finish work, do or make rapidly, (often + *from*) deduct (amount) from price, *slang* steal, kill; **knock on the head** put end to (scheme etc.);

knock on wood US touch wood; **knock out** verb make unconscious by blow to head, defeat (boxer) by knocking down for count of 10, defeat in knockout competition, colloquial tire out; **knock-out** noun blow that knocks boxer out, competition in which loser of each match is eliminated, slang outstanding person or thing; **knock together** construct hurriedly; **knock up** verb make hastily, arouse by knock at door, practise tennis etc. before formal game begins, US slang make pregnant; **knock-up** noun practice at tennis etc.

knocker noun hinged metal device on door for knocking with.

knoll /nəʊl/ noun small hill, mound.

knot /nɒt/ ● noun intertwining of rope, string, etc. so as to fasten; set method of this; tangle in hair, knitting, etc.; unit of ship's or aircraft's speed equal to one nautical mile per hour; hard mass formed in tree trunk where branch grows out; round cross-grained piece in board caused by this; (usually + of) cluster. ● verb (-tt-) tie in knot; entangle. □ **knotgrass** wild plant with creeping stems and pink flowers; **knot-hole** hole in timber where knot has fallen out.

knotty adjective (-ier, -iest) full of knots; puzzling.

know /nəʊ/ verb (past **knew** /njuː/; past participle **known**) (often + that, how, what, etc.) have in the mind, have learnt; be acquainted with; recognize, identify; (often + from) be able to distinguish; (as **known** adjective) publicly acknowledged. □ **in the know** having inside information; **know-how** practical knowledge or skill.

knowing adjective cunning; showing knowledge, shrewd.

knowingly adverb in a knowing way; consciously, intentionally.

knowledge /ˈnɒlɪdʒ/ noun (usually + of) awareness, familiarity, person's range of information, understanding (of subject); sum of what is known.

knowledgeable adjective (also **knowledgable**) well-informed, intelligent. □ **knowledgeably** adverb.

known past participle of KNOW.

knuckle /ˈnʌk(ə)l/ ● noun bone at finger-joint; knee- or ankle-joint of quadruped; this as joint of meat. ● verb (-ling) strike, rub, etc. with knuckles. □ **knuckle down** (often + to) apply oneself earnestly; **knuckleduster** metal guard worn over knuckles in fighting, esp. to inflict greater damage; **knuckle under** give in, submit.

KO abbreviation knockout.

koala /kəʊˈɑːlə/ noun (also **koala bear**) small Australian bearlike marsupial with thick grey fur.

kohl /kəʊl/ noun black powder used as eye make-up, esp. in Eastern countries.

kohlrabi /kəʊlˈrɑːbɪ/ noun (plural **-bies**) cabbage with edible turnip-like stem.

kookaburra /ˈkʊkəbʌrə/ noun Australian kingfisher with strange laughing cry.

Koran /kɔːˈrɑːn/ noun Islamic sacred book.

Korean /kəˈriːən/ ● noun native or national of N. or S. Korea; language of Korea. ● adjective of Korea or its people or language.

kosher /ˈkəʊʃə/ ● adjective (of food or food-shop) fulfilling requirements of Jewish law; colloquial correct, genuine. ● noun kosher food or shop.

kowtow /kaʊˈtaʊ/ ● noun historical Chinese custom of touching ground with forehead, esp. in submission. ● verb (usually + to) act obsequiously; perform kowtow.

k.p.h. abbreviation kilometres per hour.

kraal /krɑːl/ noun South African village of huts enclosed by fence; enclosure for cattle etc.

kremlin /ˈkremlɪn/ noun citadel within Russian town; (**the Kremlin**) that in Moscow, Russian government.

krill noun tiny plankton crustaceans eaten by whales etc.

krugerrand /ˈkruːgərænd/ noun S. African gold coin.

krummhorn /ˈkrʌmhɔːn/ noun (also **crumhorn**) medieval wind instrument.

krypton /ˈkrɪptɒn/ noun gaseous element used in lamps etc.

Kt. *abbreviation* Knight.

kts. *abbreviation* knots.

kudos /'kjuːdɒs/ *noun colloquial* glory, renown.

kumquat /'kʌmkwɒt/ *noun* (also **cumquat**) small orange-like fruit.

kung fu /kʌŋ 'fuː/ *noun* Chinese form of karate.

kV *abbreviation* kilovolt(s).

kW *abbreviation* kilowatt(s).

kWh *abbreviation* kilowatt-hour(s).

L¹ *noun* (also **l**) (Roman numeral) 50.

L² *abbreviation* Lake. □ **L-plate** sign bearing letter L, attached to vehicle to show that driver is learner.

l *abbreviation* left; line; litre(s).

LA *abbreviation* Los Angeles.

la = LAH.

Lab. *abbreviation* Labour.

lab *noun colloquial* laboratory.

label /'leɪb(ə)l/ ● *noun* piece of paper attached to object to give information about it; classifying phrase etc.; logo, title, or trademark of company. ● *verb* (**-ll-**; *US* **-l-**) attach label to; (usually + *as*) assign to category.

labial /'leɪbɪəl/ ● *adjective* of lips; *Phonetics* pronounced with (closed) lips. ● *noun Phonetics* labial sound.

labium /'leɪbɪəm/ *noun* (*plural* **labia**) each fold of skin of pairs enclosing vulva.

labor etc. *US & Australian* = LABOUR etc.

laboratory /lə'bɒrətərɪ/ *noun* (*plural* **-ies**) place used for scientific experiments and research.

laborious /lə'bɔːrɪəs/ *adjective* needing hard work; (esp. of literary style) showing signs of effort. □ **laboriously** *adverb*.

labour /'leɪbə/ (*US & Australian* **labor**) ● *noun* physical or mental work, exertion; workers, esp. as political force; (**Labour**) the Labour Party; process of giving birth; task. ● *verb* work hard, exert oneself; elaborate needlessly; proceed with difficulty; (as **laboured** *adjective*) done with great effort; (+ *under*) suffer because of. □ **labour**

camp prison camp enforcing hard labour; **Labour Exchange** *colloquial or historical* jobcentre; **Labour Party** political party formed to represent workers' interests; **labour-saving** designed to reduce or eliminate work.

labourer *noun* (*US* **laborer**) person doing unskilled paid manual work.

Labrador /'læbrədɔː/ *noun* dog of retriever breed with black or golden coat.

laburnum /lə'bɜːnəm/ *noun* tree with drooping golden flowers and poisonous seeds.

labyrinth /'læbərɪnθ/ *noun* complicated network of passages; intricate or tangled arrangement. □ **labyrinthine** /-'rɪnθaɪn/ *adjective*.

lac *noun* resinous substance from SE Asian insect, used to make varnish and shellac.

lace ● *noun* open patterned fabric or trimming made by twisting, knotting, or looping threads; cord etc. passed through eyelets or hooks for fastening shoes etc. ● *verb* (**-cing**) (usually + *up*) fasten or tighten with lace(s); add spirits to (drink); (+ *through*) pass (shoelace etc.) through. □ **lace-up** shoe fastened with lace.

lacerate /'læsəreɪt/ *verb* (**-ting**) tear (esp. flesh etc.) roughly; wound (feelings etc.). □ **laceration** *noun*.

lachrymal /'lækrɪm(ə)l/ *adjective* (also **lacrimal**) of tears.

lachrymose /'lækrɪməʊs/ *adjective formal* often weeping; tearful.

lack ● *noun* (usually + *of*) deficiency, want. ● *verb* be without or deficient in.

☐ **lacklustre** (*US* **lackluster**) dull, lacking in vitality etc.

lackadaisical /lækə'deɪzɪk(ə)l/ *adjective* languid; unenthusiastic.

lackey /'lækɪ/ *noun* (*plural* **-s**) servile follower; footman, manservant.

lacking *adjective* undesirably absent; (+ *in*) deficient in.

laconic /lə'kɒnɪk/ *adjective* using few words. ☐ **laconically** *adverb*.

lacquer /'lækə/ ● *noun* hard shiny shellac or synthetic varnish; substance sprayed on hair to keep it in place. ● *verb* coat with lacquer.

lacrimal = LACHRYMAL.

lacrosse /lə'krɒs/ *noun* hockey-like game played with ball carried in net at end of stick.

lactate /læk'teɪt/ *verb* (**-ting**) (of mammals) secrete milk. ☐ **lactation** *noun*.

lactic /'læktɪk/ *adjective* of milk.

lactose /'læktəʊs/ *noun* sugar present in milk.

lacuna /lə'kju:nə/ *noun* (*plural* **-s** or **-nae** /-ni:/) missing part, esp. in manuscript; gap.

lacy /'leɪsɪ/ *adjective* (**-ier, -iest**) like lace fabric.

lad *noun* boy, youth; *colloquial* man.

ladder /'lædə/ ● *noun* set of horizontal bars fixed at intervals between two uprights for climbing up and down; unravelled stitching in stocking etc.; means of advancement in career etc. ● *verb* cause or develop ladder in (stocking etc.).

lade *verb* (**-ding**; *past participle* **laden**) load (ship); ship (goods); (as **laden** *adjective*) (usually + *with*) loaded, burdened.

la-di-da /lɑ:dɪ'dɑ:/ *adjective colloquial* pretentious or affected, esp. in manner or speech.

ladle /'leɪd(ə)l/ ● *noun* deep long-handled spoon for serving liquids. ● *verb* (**-ling**) (often + *out*) transfer with ladle.

lady /'leɪdɪ/ *noun* (*plural* **-ies**) woman regarded as having superior status or refined manners; *polite form of address for woman*; *colloquial* wife, girlfriend; (**Lady**) *title used before name of peeresses, peers' female relatives, wives and widows of knights, etc.*; (**Ladies**) women's public lavatory. ☐ **ladybird**

small beetle, usually red with black spots; **Lady chapel** chapel dedicated to Virgin Mary; **Lady Day** Feast of the Annunciation, 25 Mar.; **ladylike** like or appropriate to lady.

Ladyship *noun* ☐ **Her** or **Your Ladyship** *title used of or to* Lady.

lag[1] ● *verb* (**-gg-**) fall behind; not keep pace. ● *noun* delay.

lag[2] *verb* (**-gg-**) enclose (boiler etc.) with heat-insulating material.

lag[3] *noun slang* habitual convict.

lager /'lɑ:gə/ *noun* kind of light beer. ☐ **lager lout** *colloquial* youth behaving violently through drinking too much.

laggard /'lægəd/ *noun* person lagging behind.

lagging *noun* insulating material for boiler etc.

lagoon /lə'gu:n/ *noun* salt-water lake separated from sea by sandbank, reef, etc.

lah *noun* (also **la**) *Music* sixth note of scale in tonic sol-fa.

laid *past & past participle* of LAY[1]. ☐ **laid-back** relaxed, easy-going.

lain *past participle* of LIE[1].

lair *noun* wild animal's home; person's hiding place.

laird /leəd/ *noun Scottish* landed proprietor.

laissez-faire /leɪseɪ'feə/ *noun* (also **laisser-faire**) policy of not interfering. [French]

laity /'leɪɪtɪ/ *noun* lay people, as distinct from clergy.

lake[1] *noun* large body of water surrounded by land. ☐ **Lake District** region of lakes in Cumbria.

lake[2] *noun* reddish pigment originally made from lac.

lam *verb* (**-mm-**) *slang* hit hard, thrash.

lama /'lɑ:mə/ *noun* Tibetan or Mongolian Buddhist monk.

lamasery /'lɑ:məsərɪ/ *noun* (*plural* **-ies**) lama monastery.

lamb /læm/ ● *noun* young sheep; its flesh as food; gentle, innocent, or weak person. ● *verb* (of sheep) give birth.

lambaste /læm'beɪst/ *verb* (**-ting**) (also **lambast** /-'bæst/) *colloquial* thrash, beat.

lambent /'læmbənt/ *adjective* (of flame etc.) playing on a surface; (of eyes, wit, etc.) gently brilliant. □ **lambency** *noun*.

lambswool *noun* soft fine wool from young sheep.

lame ● *adjective* disabled in foot or leg; (of excuse etc.) unconvincing; (of verse etc.) halting. ● *verb* (**-ming**) make lame, disable. □ **lame duck** helpless person or firm. □ **lamely** *adverb*; **lameness** *noun*.

lamé /'lɑːmeɪ/ *noun* fabric with gold or silver thread woven in.

lament /lə'ment/ ● *noun* passionate expression of grief; song etc. of mourning. ● *verb* express or feel grief for or about; utter lament; (as **lamented** *adjective*) recently dead. □ **lamentation** /læmən-/ *noun*.

lamentable /'læməntəb(ə)l/ *adjective* deplorable, regrettable. □ **lamentably** *adverb*.

lamina /'læmɪnə/ *noun* (*plural* **-nae** /-niː/) thin plate or layer. □ **laminar** *adjective*.

laminate ● *verb* /'læmɪneɪt/ (**-ting**) beat or roll into thin plates; overlay with plastic layer etc.; split into layers. ● *noun* /'læmɪnət/ laminated structure, esp. of layers fixed together. □ **lamination** *noun*.

lamp *noun* device for giving light from electricity, gas, oil, etc.; apparatus producing esp. ultraviolet or infrared radiation. □ **lamppost** post supporting street light; **lampshade** usually partial cover for lamp.

lampoon /læm'puːn/ ● *noun* satirical attack on person etc. ● *verb* satirize. □ **lampoonist** *noun*.

lamprey /'læmprɪ/ *noun* (*plural* **-s**) eel-like fish with sucker mouth.

Lancastrian /læŋ'kæstrɪən/ ● *noun* native of Lancashire or Lancaster. ● *adjective* of Lancashire or Lancaster; of House of Lancaster in Wars of Roses.

lance /lɑːns/ ● *noun* long spear, esp. one used by horseman. ● *verb* (**-cing**) prick or open with lancet. □ **lance-corporal** army NCO below corporal.

lanceolate /'lɑːnsɪələt/ *adjective* shaped like spearhead, tapering to each end.

lancer /'lɑːnsə/ *noun historical* soldier of cavalry regiment originally armed with lances; (in *plural*) quadrille.

lancet /'lɑːnsɪt/ *noun* small broad two-edged surgical knife with sharp point.

land ● *noun* solid part of earth's surface; ground, soil, expanse of country; nation, state; landed property; (in *plural*) estates. ● *verb* set or go ashore; bring (aircraft) down; alight on ground etc.; bring (fish) to land; (often + *up*) bring to or arrive at certain situation or place; *colloquial* deal (person etc. a blow etc.); (+ *with*) present (person) with (problem etc.); *colloquial* win (prize, appointment, etc.). □ **landfall** approach to land after sea or air journey; **landfill** waste material used to landscape or reclaim land, disposing of waste in this way; **landlady** woman owning rented property or keeping pub, guest-house, etc.; **landlocked** (almost) enclosed by land; **landlord** man owning rented property or keeping pub, guest-house, etc.; **landlubber** person unfamiliar with sea and ships; **landmark** conspicuous object, notable event; **land-mine** explosive mine laid in or on ground; **landslide** sliding down of mass of land from cliff or mountain, overwhelming majority in election.

landau /'lændɔː/ *noun* (*plural* **-s**) 4-wheeled enclosed carriage with divided top.

landed *adjective* owning or consisting of land.

landing /'lændɪŋ/ *noun* platform or passage at top of or part way up stairs. □ **landing-craft** craft used for putting troops and equipment ashore; **landing-gear** undercarriage of aircraft; **landing-stage** platform for disembarking passengers and goods.

landscape /'lændskeɪp/ ● *noun* scenery in area of land; picture of it. ● *verb* (**-ping**) improve (piece of land) by **landscape gardening**, laying out of grounds to resemble natural scenery.

lane *noun* narrow road; division of road for one line of traffic; strip of track or water for competitor in race; regular course followed by ship or aircraft.

language /'læŋgwɪdʒ/ *noun* use of words in agreed way as means of human communication; system of words of particular community, country, etc.; faculty of speech; style of expression;

system of symbols and rules for computer programs. □ **language laboratory** room with tape recorders etc. for learning foreign language.

languid /ˈlæŋgwɪd/ *adjective* lacking vigour; idle. □ **languidly** *adverb*.

languish /ˈlæŋgwɪʃ/ *verb* lose or lack vitality. □ **languish for** long for; **languish under** live under (depression etc.).

languor /ˈlæŋgə/ *noun* lack of energy; idleness; soft or tender mood or effect. □ **languorous** *adjective*.

lank *adjective* (of grass, hair, etc.) long and limp; thin and tall.

lanky *adjective* (**-ier, -iest**) ungracefully thin and long or tall.

lanolin /ˈlænəlɪn/ *noun* fat from sheep's wool used in cosmetics, ointments, etc.

lantern /ˈlænt(ə)n/ *noun* lamp with transparent case protecting flame etc.; glazed structure on top of dome or room; light-chamber of lighthouse. □ **lantern jaws** long thin jaws.

lanyard /ˈlænjəd/ *noun* cord round neck or shoulder for holding knife etc.; *Nautical* short rope.

lap[1] *noun* front of sitting person's body from waist to knees; clothing covering this. □ **lap-dog** small pet dog; **laptop** (microcomputer) suitable for use while travelling.

lap[2] ● *noun* one circuit of racetrack etc.; section of journey etc.; amount of overlap. ● *verb* (**-pp-**) overtake (competitor in race who is a lap behind); (often + *about, around*) fold or wrap (garment etc.).

lap[3] ● *verb* (**-pp-**) (esp. of animal) drink by scooping with tongue; (usually + *up, down*) drink greedily; (usually + *up*) receive (gossip, praise, etc.) eagerly; (of waves etc.) ripple; make lapping sound against (shore). ● *noun* act or sound of lapping.

lapel /ləˈpel/ *noun* part of coat-front folded back.

lapidary /ˈlæpɪdərɪ/ ● *adjective* concerned with stones; engraved on stone; concise, well-expressed. ● *noun* (*plural* **-ies**) cutter, polisher, or engraver of gems.

lapis lazuli /ˌlæpɪs ˈlæzjʊlɪ/ *noun* bright blue gem; its colour.

lapse /læps/ ● *noun* slight error; slip of memory etc.; weak or careless decline into inferior state. ● *verb* (**-sing**) fail to maintain position or standard; (+ *into*) fall back into (inferior or previous state); (of right etc.) become invalid.

lapwing /ˈlæpwɪŋ/ *noun* plover with shrill cry.

larceny /ˈlɑːsənɪ/ *noun* (*plural* **-ies**) theft of personal property. □ **larcenous** *adjective*.

larch *noun* deciduous coniferous tree with bright foliage; its wood.

lard ● *noun* pig fat used in cooking etc. ● *verb* insert strips of bacon in (meat etc.) before cooking; (+ *with*) embellish (talk etc.) with (strange terms etc.).

larder *noun* room or cupboard for storing food.

lardy-cake *noun* cake made with lard, currants, etc.

large *adjective* of relatively great size or extent; of larger kind; comprehensive. □ **at large** at liberty, as a body or whole; **large as life** in person, esp. prominently. □ **largeness** *noun*, **largish** *adjective*.

largely *adverb* to a great extent.

largesse /lɑːˈʒes/ *noun* (also **largess**) money or gifts freely given.

largo /ˈlɑːgəʊ/ *Music* ● *adverb & adjective* in slow time and dignified style. ● *noun* (*plural* **-s**) largo movement or passage.

lariat /ˈlærɪət/ *noun* lasso; rope for tethering animal.

lark[1] *noun* small bird with tuneful song, esp. skylark.

lark[2] *colloquial* ● *noun* frolic; amusing incident; type of activity. ● *verb* (+ *about*) play tricks.

larkspur *noun* plant with spur-shaped calyx.

larva /ˈlɑːvə/ *noun* (*plural* **-vae** /-viː/) insect in stage between egg and pupa. □ **larval** *adjective*.

laryngeal /ləˈrɪndʒɪəl/ *adjective* of the larynx.

laryngitis /ˌlærɪnˈdʒaɪtɪs/ *noun* inflammation of larynx.

larynx /ˈlærɪŋks/ *noun* (*plural* **larynges** /ləˈrɪndʒiːz/ or **-xes**) cavity in throat holding vocal cords.

lasagne /ləˈsænjə/ *noun* pasta sheets.

lascivious /ləˈsɪvɪəs/ adjective lustful.
□ **lasciviously** adverb.

laser /ˈleɪzə/ noun device producing intense beam of special kind of light.
□ **laser printer** printing machine using laser to produce image.

lash ● verb make sudden whiplike movement; beat with whip; (often + against, down) (of rain etc.) beat, strike; criticize harshly; rouse, incite; (often + together, down) fasten with rope etc. ● noun sharp blow with whip etc.; flexible part of whip; eyelash.
□ **lash out** speak or hit out angrily, colloquial spend money extravagantly.

lashings plural noun colloquial (often + of) plenty.

lass noun esp. Scottish & Northern English or poetical girl.

lassitude /ˈlæsɪtjuːd/ noun languor; disinclination to exert oneself.

lasso /læˈsuː/ ● noun (plural -s or -es) rope with running noose used esp. for catching cattle. ● verb (-es, -ed) catch with lasso.

last¹ /lɑːst/ ● adjective after all others; coming at end; most recent; only remaining. ● adverb after all others; on most recent occasion. ● noun last, last-mentioned, or most recent person or thing; last mention, sight, etc.; end; death. □ **at (long) last** in the end, after much delay; **the last straw** slight addition to task etc. making it unbearable.

last² /lɑːst/ verb remain unexhausted, adequate, or alive for specified or long time. □ **last out** be sufficient for whole of given period.

last³ /lɑːst/ noun shoemaker's model for shaping shoe etc. □ **stick to one's last** keep to what one understands.

lasting adjective permanent, durable.

lastly adverb finally.

lat. abbreviation latitude.

latch ● noun bar with catch as fastening of gate etc.; spring-lock as fastening of outer door. ● verb fasten with latch.
□ **latchkey** key of outer door; **latch on to** colloquial attach oneself to, understand.

late ● adjective after due or usual time; far on in day, night, period, etc.; flowering, ripening, etc. towards end of season; no longer alive or having specified

status; of recent date. ● adverb after due or usual time; far on in time; at or till late hour; at late stage of development; formerly but not now. □ **late in the day** at late stage of proceedings etc.
□ **lateness** noun.

lateen sail /ləˈtiːn/ noun triangular sail on long yard at angle of 45° to mast.

lately adverb not long ago; recently.

latent /ˈleɪt(ə)nt/ adjective existing but not developed or manifest; concealed, dormant. □ **latency** noun.

lateral /ˈlætər(ə)l/ ● adjective of, at, towards, or from side(s). ● noun lateral shoot or branch. □ **lateral thinking** method of solving problems by indirect or illogical methods. □ **laterally** adverb.

latex /ˈleɪteks/ noun milky fluid of esp. rubber tree; synthetic substance like this.

lath /lɑːθ/ noun thin flat strip of wood.

lathe /leɪð/ noun machine for shaping wood, metal, etc. by rotating article against cutting tools.

lather /ˈlɑːðə/ ● noun froth made by agitating soap etc. and water; frothy sweat; state of agitation. ● verb (of soap) form lather; cover with lather; colloquial thrash.

Latin /ˈlætɪn/ ● noun language of ancient Rome. ● adjective of or in Latin; of countries or peoples speaking languages developed from Latin; of RC Church.
□ **Latin America** parts of Central and S. America where Spanish or Portuguese is main language.

Latinate /ˈlætɪneɪt/ adjective having character of Latin.

latitude /ˈlætɪtjuːd/ noun angular distance N. or S. of equator; (usually in plural) regions, climes; freedom from restriction in action or opinion.

latrine /ləˈtriːn/ noun communal lavatory, esp. in camp.

latter /ˈlætə/ ● adjective second-mentioned of two; nearer the end. ● noun (**the latter**) the latter thing or person.
□ **latter-day** modern, contemporary.

latterly adverb recently; in latter part of life or period.

lattice /ˈlætɪs/ noun structure of crossed laths or bars with spaces between, used as fence, screen, etc.; arrangement resembling this. □ **lattice window** one with small panes set in lead. □ **latticed** adjective.

Latvian /ˈlætvɪən/ ● noun native, national, or language of Latvia. ● adjective of Latvia.

laud /lɔːd/ verb praise, extol.

laudable adjective praiseworthy. □ **laudably** adverb.

laudanum /ˈlɔːdənəm/ noun solution prepared from opium.

laudatory /ˈlɔːdətərɪ/ adjective praising.

laugh /lɑːf/ ● verb make sounds etc. usual in expressing amusement, scorn, etc.; express by laughing; (+ at) make fun of, ridicule. ● noun sound or act of laughing; colloquial comical person or thing. □ **laugh off** shrug off (embarrassment etc.) by joking.

laughable adjective amusing; ridiculous. □ **laughably** adverb.

laughing noun laughter. □ **laughing gas** nitrous oxide as anaesthetic; **laughing jackass** kookaburra; **laughing stock** object of general derision. □ **laughingly** adverb.

laughter /ˈlɑːftə/ noun act or sound of laughing.

launch[1] /lɔːntʃ/ ● verb set (vessel) afloat; hurl or send forth (rocket etc.); start or set in motion (enterprise, person, etc.); formally introduce (new product) with publicity; (+ into) make start on; (+ out) make start on new enterprise. ● noun launching. □ **launch pad** platform with structure for launching rockets from.

launch[2] /lɔːntʃ/ noun large motor boat.

launder /ˈlɔːndə/ verb wash and iron etc. (clothes etc.); colloquial transfer (money) to conceal its origin.

launderette /lɔːnˈdret/ noun (also **laundrette**) establishment with coin-operated washing machines and driers for public use.

laundress /ˈlɔːndrɪs/ noun woman who launders.

laundry /ˈlɔːndrɪ/ noun (plural **-ies**) place where clothes etc. are laundered; clothes etc. that need to be or have been laundered.

laurel /ˈlɒr(ə)l/ noun any of various kinds of shrub with dark green glossy leaves; (in singular or plural) wreath of bay-leaves as emblem of victory or poetic merit. □ **look to one's laurels** beware of losing one's pre-eminence; **rest on one's laurels** stop seeking further success.

lava /ˈlɑːvə/ noun matter flowing from volcano and solidifying as it cools.

lavatorial /lævəˈtɔːrɪəl/ adjective of or like lavatories; (esp. of humour) relating to excretion.

lavatory /ˈlævətərɪ/ noun (plural **-ies**) receptacle for urine and faeces, usually with means of disposal; room etc. containing this.

lave verb (**-ving**) literary wash, bathe; wash against; flow along.

lavender /ˈlævɪndə/ noun evergreen fragrant-flowered shrub; its dried flowers used to scent linen; pale purplish colour. □ **lavender-water** light perfume.

laver /ˈleɪvə/ noun kind of edible seaweed.

lavish /ˈlævɪʃ/ ● adjective profuse; abundant; generous. ● verb (often + on) bestow or spend (money, praise, etc.) abundantly. □ **lavishly** adverb.

law noun rule or set of rules established in a community, demanding or prohibiting certain actions; such rules as social system or branch of study; binding force; (**the law**) legal profession, colloquial police; law courts, legal remedy; science or philosophy of law; statement of regularity of natural occurrences. □ **law-abiding** obedient to the laws; **law court** court of law; **Law Lord** member of House of Lords qualified to perform its legal work; **lawsuit** bringing of claim etc. before law court; **lay down the law** give dogmatic opinions; **take the law into one's own hands** get one's rights without help of the law.

lawful adjective permitted, appointed, or recognized by law; not illegal. □ **lawfully** adverb; **lawfulness** noun.

lawless adjective having no laws; disregarding laws. □ **lawlessness** noun.

lawn[1] noun piece of close-mown grass in garden etc. □ **lawnmower** machine for cutting lawns; **lawn tennis** tennis played with soft ball on grass or hard court.

lawn[2] noun kind of fine linen or cotton.

lawyer /ˈlɔːjə/ noun person practising law, esp. solicitor.

lax *adjective* lacking care or precision; not strict. □ **laxity** *noun*; **laxly** *adverb*; **laxness** *noun*.

laxative /ˈlæksətɪv/ ● *adjective* helping evacuation of bowels. ● *noun* laxative medicine.

lay¹ ● *verb* (*past & past participle* **laid**) place on surface, esp. horizontally; put or bring into required position or state; make by laying; (of bird) produce (egg); cause to subside or lie flat; (usually + *on*) attribute (blame etc.); make ready (trap, plan); prepare (table) for meal; put fuel ready to light (fire); put down as bet. ● *noun* way, position, or direction in which something lies. □ **lay bare** expose, reveal; **lay-by** extra strip beside road where vehicles may park; **lay claim to** claim as one's own; **lay down** relinquish, make (rule), store (wine) in cellar, sacrifice (one's life); **lay in** provide oneself with stock of; **lay into** *colloquial* attack violently with blows or verbally; **lay it on thick** or **with a trowel** *colloquial* flatter, exaggerate grossly; **lay off** discharge (workers) temporarily, *colloquial* desist; **lay on** provide, spread on; **lay out** spread, expose to view, prepare (body) for burial, *colloquial* knock unconscious, expend (money); **layout** way in which land, building, printed matter, etc., is arranged or set out; **lay up** store, save (money), (as **laid up** *adjective*) confined to bed or the house; **lay waste** ravage, destroy.

■ **Usage** It is incorrect in standard English to use *lay* to mean 'lie', as in *She was laying on the floor.*

lay² *adjective* not ordained into the clergy; not professionally qualified; of or done by such people. □ **layman**, **laywoman** person not in holy orders, one without professional or special knowledge; **lay reader** lay person licensed to conduct some religious services.

lay³ *noun* short poem meant to be sung; song.

lay⁴ *past of* LIE¹.

layer ● *noun* thickness of matter, esp. one of several, covering surface; hen that lays eggs. ● *verb* arrange in layers; propagate (plant) by fastening shoot down to take root.

layette /leɪˈet/ *noun* clothes etc. prepared for newborn child.

lay figure *noun* artist's jointed wooden model of human figure; unrealistic character in novel etc.

laze ● *verb* (**-zing**) spend time idly. ● *noun* spell of lazing.

lazy *adjective* (**-ier, -iest**) disinclined to work, doing little work; of or inducing idleness. □ **lazybones** *colloquial* lazy person. □ **lazily** *adverb*; **laziness** *noun*.

lb *abbreviation* pound(s) weight.

■ **Usage** It is a common mistake to write *lbs* as an abbreviation for *pounds*. *28 lb* is correct.

l.b.w. *abbreviation* leg before wicket.

l.c. *abbreviation* loc. cit.; lower case.

LCD *abbreviation* liquid crystal display.

L/Cpl *abbreviation* Lance-Corporal.

LEA *abbreviation* Local Education Authority.

lea *noun poetical* meadow, field.

leach *verb* make (liquid) percolate through some material; subject (bark, ore, ash, soil) to this; (usually + *away, out*) remove (soluble matter) or be removed in this way.

lead¹ /liːd/ ● *verb* (*past & past participle* **led**) conduct, esp. by going in front; direct actions or opinions of; (often + *to*) guide by persuasion; provide access to; pass or spend (life etc.); have first place in; go or be first; play (card) as first player in trick; (+ *to*) result in; (+ *with*) (of newspapers or broadcast) have as main story. ● *noun* guidance, example; leader's place; amount by which competitor is ahead of others; clue; strap etc. for leading dog etc.; *Electricity* conductor carrying current to place of use; chief part in play etc.; *Cards* act or right of playing first. □ **lead by the nose** make (someone) do all one wishes them to; **lead-in** introduction, opening; **lead on** entice dishonestly; **lead up the garden path** *colloquial* mislead; **lead up to** form preparation for, direct conversation towards.

lead² /led/ ● *noun* heavy soft grey metal; graphite used in pencils; lump of lead used in sounding; blank space between lines of print. ● *verb* cover, frame, or space with lead(s). □ **lead-free** (of petrol) without added lead compounds.

leaded /'ledɪd/ *adjective* (of petrol) with added lead compounds; (of window pane) framed with lead.

leaden /'led(ə)n/ *adjective* of or like lead; heavy, slow; lead-coloured.

leader /'liːdə/ *noun* person or thing that leads; leading performer in orchestra, quartet, etc.; leading article. □ **leadership** *noun*.

leading /'liːdɪŋ/ *adjective* chief, most important. □ **leading aircraftman** one ranking just below NCO in RAF; **leading article** newspaper article giving editorial opinion; **leading light** prominent influential person; **leading note** Music seventh note of ascending scale; **leading question** one prompting the answer wanted.

■ **Usage** *Leading question* does not mean a 'principal' or 'loaded' or 'searching' question.

leaf ● *noun* (*plural* **leaves**) flat usually green part of plant growing usually on stem; foliage; single thickness of paper, esp. in book; very thin sheet of metal etc.; hinged part, extra section, or flap of table etc. ● *verb* (of plants etc.) begin to grow leaves; (+ *through*) turn over pages of (book etc.). □ **leaf-mould** soil composed chiefly of decaying leaves. □ **leafage** *noun*; **leafy** *adjective* (**-ier**, **-iest**).

leaflet /'liːflɪt/ *noun* sheet of paper, pamphlet, etc., giving information; young leaf.

league¹ /liːg/ ● *noun* people, countries, etc., joining together for particular purpose; group of sports clubs who contend for championship; class of contestants. ● *verb* (**-gues**, **-gued**, **-guing**) (often + *together*) join in league. □ **in league** allied, conspiring; **league table** list in order of success.

league² /liːg/ *noun* archaic measure of travelling distance, usually about 3 miles.

leak ● *noun* hole through which liquid etc. passes accidentally in or out; liquid etc. thus passing through; similar escape of electric charge; disclosure of secret information. ● *verb* (let) pass out or in through leak; disclose (secret); (often + *out*) become known. □ **leaky** *adjective* (**-ier**, **-iest**).

leakage *noun* action or result of leaking.

lean¹ ● *verb* (*past & past participle* **leaned** or **leant** /lent/) (often + *across*, *back*, *over*, etc.) be or place in sloping position; (usually + *against*, *on*) rest for support against; (usually + *on*, *upon*) rely, depend; (usually + *to*, *towards*) be inclined or partial. ● *noun* inclination, slope. □ **lean on** *colloquial* put pressure on (person) to act in certain way; **lean-to** building with roof resting against larger building or wall.

lean² ● *adjective* (of person etc.) having no superfluous fat; (of meat) containing little fat; meagre. ● *noun* lean part of meat. □ **lean years** time of scarcity. □ **leanness** *noun*.

leaning *noun* tendency or inclination.

leap ● *verb* (*past & past participle* **leaped** or **leapt** /lept/) jump, spring forcefully. ● *noun* forceful jump. □ **by leaps and bounds** with very rapid progress; **leap-frog** game in which player vaults with parted legs over another bending down; **leap year** year with 29 Feb. as extra day.

learn /lɜːn/ *verb* (*past & past participle* **learned** /lɜːnt, lɜːnd/ or **learnt**) get knowledge of or skill in by study, experience, or being taught; commit to memory; (usually + *of*, *about*) be told about, find out.

learned /'lɜːnɪd/ *adjective* having much knowledge from studying; showing or requiring learning.

learner *noun* person learning, beginner; (in full **learner driver**) person who is learning to drive but has not yet passed driving test.

learning *noun* knowledge got by study.

lease /liːs/ ● *noun* contract by which owner of land or building allows another to use it for specified time, usually for rent. ● *verb* (**-sing**) grant or take on lease. □ **leasehold** holding of property by lease; **leaseholder** *noun*; **new lease of** (US **on**) **life** improved prospect of living, or of use after repair.

leash /liːʃ/ ● *noun* strap for holding dog(s). ● *verb* put leash on; restrain. □ **straining at the leash** eager to begin.

least • *adjective* smallest, slightest. • *noun* least amount. • *adverb* in the least degree. □ **at least** at any rate; **to say the least** putting the case moderately.

leather /'leðə/ • *noun* material made from skin of animal by tanning etc.; piece of leather for cleaning esp. windows; *slang* cricket ball, football. • *verb* beat, thrash; cover or polish with leather. □ **leather-jacket** larva of crane-fly.

leatherette /leðə'ret/ *noun* imitation leather.

leathery *adjective* like leather; tough.

leave[1] *verb* (**-ving**; *past & past participle* **left**) go away (from); cause or allow to remain; depart without taking; cease to reside at, belong to, work for, etc.; abandon; (usually + *to*) commit to another person; bequeath; deposit or entrust (object, message, etc.) to be dealt with in one's absence; not consume or make an end, stop; **leave out** omit. □ **leave off** come to or make an end, stop; **leave out** omit.

leave[2] *noun* permission; (in full **leave of absence**) permission to be absent from duty; period for which this lasts. □ **on leave** absent thus; **take one's leave of** say goodbye to.

leaven /'lev(ə)n/ • *noun* substance used to make dough ferment and rise; transforming influence. • *verb* ferment (dough) with leaven; permeate, transform.

leavings *plural noun* what is left.

Lebanese /lebə'ni:z/ • *adjective* of Lebanon. • *noun* (*plural* same) native or national of Lebanon.

lecher /'letʃə/ *noun* lecherous man.

lecherous *adjective* lustful. □ **lecherously** *adverb*; **lechery** *noun*.

lectern /'lekt(ə)n/ *noun* stand for holding Bible etc. in church; similar stand for lecturer etc.

lecture /'lektʃə/ • *noun* talk giving information to class etc.; admonition, reprimand. • *verb* (**-ring**) (often + *on*) deliver lecture(s); admonish, reprimand.

lecturer *noun* person who lectures, esp. as teacher in higher education.

lectureship *noun* university post as lecturer.

led *past & past participle* of LEAD[1].

ledge *noun* narrow shelf or projection from vertical surface.

ledger /'ledʒə/ *noun* book in which firm's accounts are kept.

lee *noun* shelter given by neighbouring object; side of thing away from the wind. □ **leeway** allowable deviation, drift of ship to leeward.

leech *noun* bloodsucking worm formerly used medicinally for bleeding; person who sponges on others.

leek *noun* vegetable of onion family with long cylindrical white bulb.

leer • *verb* look slyly, lasciviously, or maliciously. • *noun* leering look.

leery *adjective* (**-ier, -iest**) *slang* knowing, sly; (usually + *of*) wary.

lees /li:z/ *plural noun* sediment of wine etc.; dregs.

leeward /'li:wəd, *Nautical* 'lu:əd/ • *adjective & adverb* on or towards sheltered side. • *noun* this direction.

left[1] • *adjective* on or towards west side of person or thing facing north; (also **Left**) *Politics* of the Left. • *adverb* on or to left side. • *noun* left part, region, or direction; *Boxing* left hand, blow with this; (often **Left**) *Politics* group favouring socialism, radicals collectively. □ **left-hand** on left side; **left-handed** naturally using left hand for writing etc., made by or for left hand, turning to left, (of screw) turned anti-clockwise to tighten, awkward, clumsy, (of compliment etc.) ambiguous; **left-handedness** *noun*; **left-hander** left-handed person or blow; **left wing** more radical section of political party, left side of army, football team, etc.; **left-wing** socialist, radical; **left-winger** member of left wing. □ **leftward** *adjective & adverb*; **leftwards** *adverb*.

left[2] *past & past participle* of LEAVE[1].

leg *noun* each of limbs on which person or animal walks and stands; leg of animal as food; part of garment covering leg; support of chair, table, etc.; section of journey, race, competition, etc.; *Cricket* half of field behind batsman's back. □ **leg before wicket** *Cricket* (of batsman) declared out for illegal obstruction of ball that would have hit wicket; **leg it** (**-gg-**) *colloquial* walk or run hard; **leg warmer** either of pair of tubular knitted garments covering leg from ankle to thigh; **pull (person's) leg** deceive playfully. □ **legged** adjective.

legacy /ˈlegəsɪ/ noun (plural **-ies**) gift left by will; anything handed down by predecessor.

legal /ˈliːg(ə)l/ adjective of, based on, or concerned with law; appointed, required, or permitted by law. □ **legal aid** state help with cost of legal advice; **legal tender** currency that cannot legally be refused in payment of debt. □ **legality** /lɪˈgælɪtɪ/ noun; **legally** adverb.

legalize /ˈliːgəlaɪz/ verb (also **-ise**) (**-zing** or **-sing**) make lawful; bring into harmony with law. □ **legalization** noun.

legate /ˈlegət/ noun papal ambassador.

legatee /legəˈtiː/ noun recipient of legacy.

legation /lɪˈgeɪʃ(ə)n/ noun diplomatic minister and his or her staff; this minister's official residence.

legato /lɪˈgɑːtəʊ/ Music ● adverb & adjective in smooth flowing manner. ● noun (plural **-s**) legato passage.

legend /ˈledʒ(ə)nd/ noun traditional story, myth; colloquial famous or remarkable person or event; inscription; explanation on map etc. of symbols used.

legendary adjective existing in legend; colloquial remarkable.

legerdemain /ledʒədəˈmeɪn/ noun sleight of hand; trickery, sophistry.

leger line /ˈledʒə/ noun Music short line added for notes above or below range of staff.

legging noun (usually in plural) close-fitting trousers for women or children; outer covering of leather etc. for lower leg.

leggy adjective (**-ier**, **-iest**) long-legged; long-stemmed and weak.

legible /ˈledʒɪb(ə)l/ adjective easily read. □ **legibility** noun; **legibly** adverb.

legion /ˈliːdʒ(ə)n/ ● noun division of 3,000–6,000 men in ancient Roman army; other large organized body. ● adjective great in number.

legionary ● adjective of legions. ● noun (plural **-ies**) member of legion.

legionnaire /liːdʒəˈneə/ noun member of foreign legion. □ **legionnaires' disease** form of bacterial pneumonia.

legislate /ˈledʒɪsleɪt/ verb (**-ting**) make laws. □ **legislator** noun.

legislation noun making laws; laws made.

legislative /ˈledʒɪslətɪv/ adjective of or empowered to make legislation.

legislature /ˈledʒɪsleɪtʃə/ noun legislative body of a state.

legitimate /lɪˈdʒɪtɪmət/ adjective (of child) born of parents married to one another; lawful, proper, regular; logically admissible. ● **legitimacy** noun; **legitimately** adverb.

legitimize /lɪˈdʒɪtɪmaɪz/ verb (also **-ise**) (**-zing** or **-sing**) make legitimate; serve as justification for. □ **legitimization** noun.

legume /ˈlegjuːm/ noun leguminous plant; edible part of this.

leguminous /lɪˈgjuːmɪnəs/ adjective of the family of plants with seeds in pods, e.g. peas and beans.

lei /ˈleɪ/ noun Polynesian garland of flowers.

leisure /ˈleʒə/ noun free time, time at one's own disposal. □ **at leisure** not occupied, in an unhurried way; **at one's leisure** when one has time; **leisure centre** public building with sports facilities etc.; **leisurewear** informal clothes, esp. sportswear.

leisured adjective having ample leisure.

leisurely ● adjective relaxed, unhurried. ● adverb without hurry.

leitmotif /ˈlaɪtməʊtiːf/ noun (also **leitmotiv**) recurring theme in musical etc. composition representing particular person, idea, etc.

lemming /ˈlemɪŋ/ noun Arctic rodent reputed to rush, during migration, in large numbers into sea and drown.

lemon /ˈlemən/ noun acid yellow citrus fruit; tree bearing it; pale yellow colour. □ **lemon cheese**, **curd** thick creamy lemon spread. □ **lemony** adjective.

lemonade /leməˈneɪd/ noun drink made from lemons; synthetic substitute for this, often fizzy.

lemon sole /ˈlemən/ noun (plural same or **-s**) fish of plaice family.

lemur /ˈliːmə/ noun tree-dwelling primate of Madagascar.

lend *verb* (*past & past participle* **lent**) grant temporary use of (thing); allow use of (money) in return for interest; bestow, contribute; (**lend itself to**) be suitable for. □ **lend an ear** listen. □ **lender** *noun*.

length *noun* measurement from end to end; extent in or of time; length of horse, boat, etc. as measure of lead in race; long stretch or extent; degree of thoroughness in action. □ **at length** in detail, after a long time. □ **lengthways** *adverb*; **lengthwise** *adverb & adjective*.

lengthen *verb* make or become longer.

lengthy *adjective* (**-ier, -iest**) of unusual length, prolix, tedious.

lenient /ˈliːnɪənt/ *adjective* merciful, not severe, mild. □ **lenience** *noun*; **leniency** *noun*; **leniently** *adverb*.

lens /lenz/ *noun* piece of transparent substance with one or both sides curved, used in spectacles, telescopes, cameras, etc.; combination of lenses used in photography.

Lent *noun* religious period of fasting and penitence from Ash Wednesday to Easter Eve. □ **Lenten** *adjective*.

lent *past & past participle* of LEND.

lentil /ˈlentɪl/ *noun* edible seed of leguminous plant; this plant.

lento /ˈlentəʊ/ *Music* ● *adjective* slow. ● *adverb* slowly. ● *noun* lento movement or passage.

Leo /ˈliːəʊ/ *noun* fifth sign of zodiac.

leonine /ˈliːənaɪn/ *adjective* lionlike; of lions.

leopard /ˈlepəd/ *noun* large animal of cat family with dark-spotted fawn or all black coat, panther.

leotard /ˈliːətɑːd/ *noun* close-fitting one-piece garment worn by dancers etc.

leper /ˈlepə/ *noun* person with leprosy.

leprechaun /ˈleprəkɔːn/ *noun* small mischievous sprite in Irish folklore.

leprosy /ˈleprəsɪ/ *noun* contagious disease of skin and nerves. □ **leprous** *adjective*.

lesbian /ˈlezbɪən/ ● *noun* homosexual woman. ● *adjective* of homosexuality in women. □ **lesbianism** *noun*.

lesion /ˈliːʒ(ə)n/ *noun* damage; injury; change in part of body due to injury or disease.

less ● *adjective* smaller; of smaller quantity; not so much. ● *adverb* to smaller extent, in lower degree. ● *noun* smaller amount, quantity, or number. ● *preposition* minus, deducting.

■ **Usage** The use of *less* to mean 'fewer', as in *There are less people than yesterday*, is incorrect in standard English.

lessee /leˈsiː/ *noun* (often + *of*) person holding property by lease.

lessen /ˈles(ə)n/ *verb* diminish.

lesser *adjective* not so great as the other(s).

lesson /ˈles(ə)n/ *noun* period of teaching; (in *plural*, usually + *in*) systematic instruction; thing learnt by pupil; experience that serves to warn or encourage; passage from Bible read aloud during church service.

lessor /leˈsɔː/ *noun* person who lets property by lease.

lest *conjunction* in order that not, for fear that.

let[1] ● *verb* (**-tt-**; *past & past participle* **let**) allow, enable, or cause to; grant use of (rooms, land, etc.) for rent or hire. ● *auxiliary verb in exhortations, commands, assumptions, etc.* ● *noun* act of letting. □ **let alone** not to mention; **let be** not interfere with; **let down** *verb* lower, fail to support or satisfy, disappoint; **let-down** *noun* disappointment; **let go** release, lose hold of; **let in** allow to enter, (usually + *for*) involve (person, often oneself) in loss, problem, etc., (usually + *on*) allow (person) to share secret etc.; **let off** fire (gun), cause (steam etc.) to escape, not punish or compel; **let on** *colloquial* reveal secret; **let out** *verb* release, reveal (secret etc.), slacken, put out to rent; **let-out** *noun* *colloquial* opportunity to escape; **let up** *verb* *colloquial* become less severe, diminish; **let-up** *noun* *colloquial* relaxation of effort, diminution.

let[2] *noun* obstruction of ball or player in tennis etc. after which ball must be served again. □ **without let or hindrance** unimpeded.

lethal /ˈliːθ(ə)l/ *adjective* causing or sufficient to cause death. □ **lethally** *adverb*.

lethargy /ˈleθədʒɪ/ *noun* lack of energy; unnatural sleepiness. □ **lethargic** /lɪˈθɑːdʒɪk/ *adjective*; **lethargically** /lɪˈθɑːdʒɪkəlɪ/ *adverb*.

letter /ˈletə/ ● *noun* character representing one or more of sounds used in speech; written or printed communication, usually sent in envelope by post; precise terms of statement; (in *plural*) literature. ● *verb* inscribe letters on; classify with letters. □ **letter bomb** terrorist explosive device sent by post; **letter box** box for delivery or posting of letters, slit in door for delivery of letters; **letterhead** printed heading on stationery; **letterpress** printed words in illustrated book, printing from raised type; **to the letter** keeping to every detail.

lettuce /ˈletɪs/ *noun* plant with crisp leaves used in salad.

leucocyte /ˈluːkəsaɪt/ *noun* white blood cell.

leukaemia /luːˈkiːmɪə/ *noun* (*US* **leukemia**) malignant progressive disease in which too many white blood cells are produced.

Levant /lɪˈvænt/ *noun* (**the Levant**) *archaic* East-Mediterranean region.

Levantine /ˈlevəntaɪn/ ● *adjective* of or trading to the Levant. ● *noun* native or inhabitant of the Levant.

levee /ˈlevɪ/ *noun US* embankment against river floods.

level /ˈlev(ə)l/ ● *noun* horizontal line or plane; height or value reached; position on real or imaginary scale; social, moral, or intellectual standard; plane of rank or authority; instrument giving line parallel to plane of horizon; level surface, flat country. ● *adjective* flat, not bumpy; horizontal; (often + *with*) on same horizontal plane as something else, having equality with something else; even, uniform, well-balanced. ● *verb* (**-ll-**; *US* **-l-**) make level; raze, completely destroy; (usually + *at*) aim (gun etc.); (usually + *at*, *against*) direct (accusation etc.). □ **do one's level best** *colloquial* do one's utmost; **find one's level** reach right social, intellectual, etc., position; **level crossing** crossing of road and railway etc. at same level; **level-headed** mentally well-balanced, cool; **level pegging** equality of scores etc.; **on the level** *colloquial* truthfully, honestly.

lever /ˈliːvə/ ● *noun* bar pivoted about fulcrum to transfer force; bar used on pivot to prise or lift; projecting handle used to operate mechanism; means of exerting moral pressure. ● *verb* use lever; lift, move, etc. (as) with lever.

leverage *noun* action or power of lever; means of accomplishing a purpose.

leveret /ˈlevərɪt/ *noun* young hare.

leviathan /lɪˈvaɪəθ(ə)n/ *noun Biblical* sea monster; very large or powerful thing.

Levis /ˈliːvaɪz/ *plural noun proprietary term* type of (originally blue) denim jeans.

levitate /ˈlevɪteɪt/ *verb* (**-ting**) (cause to) rise and float in air. □ **levitation** *noun*.

levity /ˈlevɪtɪ/ *noun* lack of serious thought; frivolity.

levy /ˈlevɪ/ ● *verb* (**-ies**, **-ied**) impose or collect (payment etc.) compulsorily; enrol (troops etc.). ● *noun* (*plural* **-ies**) levying; payment etc. or (in *plural*) troops levied.

lewd /ljuːd/ *adjective* lascivious, indecent.

lexical /ˈleksɪk(ə)l/ *adjective* of the words of a language; (as) of a lexicon.

lexicography /leksɪˈkɒɡrəfɪ/ *noun* compiling of dictionaries. □ **lexicographer** *noun*.

lexicon /ˈleksɪkən/ *noun* dictionary.

Leyden jar /ˈlaɪd(ə)n/ *noun* early kind of capacitor.

LF *abbreviation* low frequency.

liability /laɪəˈbɪlɪtɪ/ *noun* (*plural* **-ies**) being liable; troublesome person or thing; handicap; (in *plural*) debts for which one is liable.

liable /ˈlaɪəb(ə)l/ *adjective* legally bound; (+ *to*) subject to; (+ *to do*) under an obligation; (+ *to*) exposed or open to (something undesirable); (+ *for*) answerable for.

■ *Usage Liable* is often used to mean 'likely', as in *It is liable to rain*, but this is considered incorrect by some people.

liaise /lɪˈeɪz/ *verb* (**-sing**) (usually + *with*, *between*) *colloquial* establish co-operation, act as link.

liaison /lɪˈeɪzɒn/ *noun* communication, cooperation; illicit sexual relationship.

liana /lɪˈɑːnə/ *noun* climbing plant in tropical forests.

liar /ˈlaɪə/ *noun* person who tells lies.

Lib. *abbreviation* Liberal.

lib *noun colloquial* liberation.

libation /laɪˈbeɪʃ(ə)n/ *noun* (pouring out of) drink-offering to a god.

libel /ˈlaɪb(ə)l/ • *noun Law* published false statement damaging to person's reputation, publishing of this; false defamatory statement. • *verb* (**-ll-**; *US* **-l-**) *Law* publish libel against. □ **libellous** *adjective*.

liberal /ˈlɪbər(ə)l/ • *adjective* abundant; giving freely; generous; open-minded; not rigorous; (of studies) for general broadening of mind; *Politics* favouring moderate reforms. • *noun* person of liberal views, esp. (**Liberal**) member of a Liberal Party. □ **Liberal Democrat** member of **Liberal Democrats**, UK political party. □ **liberalism** *noun*; **liberality** /-ˈræl-/ *noun*; **liberally** *adverb*.

liberalize *verb* (also **-ise**) (**-zing** or **-sing**) make or become more liberal or less strict. □ **liberalization** *noun*.

liberate /ˈlɪbəreɪt/ *verb* (**-ting**) (often + *from*) set free; free (country etc.) from aggressor; (as **liberated** *adjective*) (of person etc.) freed from oppressive social conventions. □ **liberation** *noun*; **liberator** *noun*.

libertine /ˈlɪbətiːn/ *noun* licentious person.

liberty /ˈlɪbətɪ/ *noun* (*plural* **-ies**) being free, freedom; right or power to do as one pleases; (in *plural*) privileges granted by authority. □ **at liberty** free, (+ *to do*) permitted; **take liberties** (often + *with*) behave in unacceptably familiar way.

libidinous /lɪˈbɪdɪnəs/ *adjective* lustful.

libido /lɪˈbiːdəʊ/ *noun* (*plural* **-s**) psychic impulse or drive, esp. that associated with sex instinct. □ **libidinal** /lɪˈbɪdɪn(ə)l/ *adjective*.

Libra /ˈliːbrə/ *noun* seventh sign of zodiac.

librarian /laɪˈbreərɪən/ *noun* person in charge of or assistant in library. □ **librarianship** *noun*.

library /ˈlaɪbrərɪ/ *noun* (*plural* **-ies**) a collection of books, films, records, etc.; room or building etc. where these are kept; series of books issued in similar bindings.

libretto /lɪˈbretəʊ/ *noun* (*plural* **-ti** /-tɪ/ or **-s**) text of opera etc. □ **librettist** *noun*.

lice *plural of* LOUSE.

licence /ˈlaɪs(ə)ns/ *noun* (*US* **license**) official permit to own, use, or do, something, or carry on trade; permission; excessive liberty of action; writer's etc. deliberate deviation from fact.

license /ˈlaɪs(ə)ns/ • *verb* (**-sing**) grant licence to; authorize use of (premises) for certain purpose. • *noun US =* LICENCE.

licensee /laɪsənˈsiː/ *noun* holder of licence, esp. to sell alcoholic liquor.

licentiate /laɪˈsenʃɪət/ *noun* holder of certificate of professional competence.

licentious /laɪˈsenʃəs/ *adjective* sexually promiscuous.

lichee = LYCHEE.

lichen /ˈlaɪkən/ *noun* plant composed of fungus and alga in association, growing on rocks, trees, etc.

lich-gate /ˈlɪtʃgeɪt/ *noun* (also **lychgate**) roofed gateway of churchyard.

licit /ˈlɪsɪt/ *adjective formal* lawful, permitted.

lick • *verb* pass tongue over; bring into specified condition by licking; (of flame etc.) play lightly over; *colloquial* thrash, defeat. • *noun* act of licking with tongue; *colloquial* pace, speed; smart blow. □ **lick one's lips**, **chops** look forward with great pleasure.

licorice = LIQUORICE.

lid *noun* hinged or removable cover, esp. at top of container; eyelid. □ **put the lid on** *colloquial* be the culmination of, put stop to. □ **lidded** *adjective*.

lido /ˈliːdəʊ/ *noun* (*plural* **-s**) public open-air swimming pool or bathing beach.

lie[1] /laɪ/ • *verb* (**lying**; *past* **lay**; *past participle* **lain**) be in or assume horizontal position on supporting surface; (of thing) rest on flat surface; remain undisturbed or undiscussed; be kept, remain, or be in specified place etc.; (of abstract things) be situated or spread out to view etc.; be situated or spread out to view etc. • *noun* way, position, or direction in which something lies. □ **lie in** stay in bed late in morning; **lie-in** noun; **lie low** keep quiet or unseen; **lie of the land** state of affairs.

■ **Usage** It is incorrect in standard English to use lie to mean 'lay', as in lie her on the bed.

lie² /laɪ/ ● noun intentional false statement; something that deceives. ● verb (**lies, lied, lying**) tell lie(s); (of thing) be deceptive. □ **give the lie to** show the falsity of.

lied /liːd/ noun (plural **lieder**) German song of Romantic period for voice and piano.

liege /liːdʒ/ historical ● adjective entitled to receive, or bound to give, feudal service or allegiance. ● noun (in full **liege lord**) feudal superior; (usually in plural) vassal, subject.

lien /ˈliːən/ noun Law right to hold another's property till debt on it is paid.

lieu /ljuː/ noun □ **in lieu** instead; (+ of) in place of.

Lieut. abbreviation Lieutenant.

lieutenant /lefˈtenənt/ noun army officer next below captain; naval officer next below lieutenant commander; deputy. □ **lieutenant colonel, commander, general** officers ranking next below colonel etc. □ **lieutenancy** noun (plural **-ies**).

life noun (plural **lives**) capacity for growth, functional activity, and continual change until death; living things and their activity; period during which life lasts; period from birth to present time or from present time to death; duration of thing's existence or ability to function; person's state of existence; living person; business and pleasures of the world; energy, liveliness; biography; colloquial imprisonment for life. □ **life assurance** life insurance; **lifebelt** buoyant ring to keep person afloat; **lifeblood** blood as necessary to life, vital factor or influence; **lifeboat** boat for rescues at sea, ship's boat for emergency use; **lifebuoy** buoyant support to keep person afloat; **life cycle** series of changes in life of organism; **lifeguard** expert swimmer employed to rescue bathers from drowning; **Life Guards** regiment of royal household cavalry; **life insurance**

insurance which makes payment on death of insured person; **life-jacket** buoyant jacket to keep person afloat; **lifeline** rope etc. used for life-saving, sole means of communication or transport; **life peer** peer whose title lapses on death; **life sentence** imprisonment for life; **life-size(d)** of same size as person or thing represented; **lifestyle** way of life; **life-support machine** respirator; **lifetime** duration of person's life.

lifeless adjective dead; unconscious; lacking movement or vitality. □ **lifelessly** adverb.

lifelike adjective closely resembling life or person or thing represented.

lifer noun slang person serving life sentence.

lift ● verb (often + up, of, etc.) raise to higher position, go up, be raised; yield to upward force; give upward direction to (eyes etc.); add interest to; (of fog etc.) rise, disperse; remove (barrier etc.); transport supplies, troops, etc. by air; colloquial steal, plagiarize. ● noun lifting; ride in another person's vehicle; apparatus for raising and lowering people or things to different floors of building, or for carrying people up or down mountain etc.; transport by air; upward pressure on aerofoil; supporting or elevating influence; elated feeling. □ **lift-off** vertical take-off of spacecraft or rocket.

ligament /ˈlɪgəmənt/ noun band of tough fibrous tissue linking bones.

ligature /ˈlɪgətʃə/ noun tie, bandage; Music slur, tie; Printing two or more letters joined, e.g. æ.

■ **Usage** Ligature, in the Printing sense, is sometimes confused with digraph, which means 'two letters representing one sound'.

light¹ /laɪt/ ● noun electromagnetic radiation that stimulates sight and makes things visible; appearance of brightness; source of light; (often in plural) traffic light; flame, spark, or device for igniting; aspect in which thing is regarded; mental or spiritual illumination; vivacity, esp. in person's eyes. ● verb (past **lit**; past participle **lit** or **lighted**) set burning, begin to burn; (often +

up) give light to; make prominent by light; show (person) way etc. with light; (usually + *up)* (of face or eyes) brighten with pleasure etc. ● *adjective* well-provided with light, not dark; (of colour) pale. □ **bring** or **come to light** reveal or be revealed; **in the light of** taking account of; **light bulb** glass bulb containing metal filament giving light when current is passed through it; **lighthouse** tower with beacon light to warn or guide ships at sea; **lightship** anchored ship with beacon light; **light year** distance light travels in one year.

light² /laɪt/ ● *adjective* not heavy; relatively low in weight, amount, density, or intensity; (of railway) suitable for small loads; carrying only light arms; (of food) easy to digest; (of music etc.) intended only as entertainment; not profound; (of sleep or sleeper) easily disturbed; easily done; nimble; cheerful. ● *adverb* lightly; with light load. ● *verb* (*past & past participle* **lit** or **lighted**) (+ *on, upon*) come upon or find by chance. □ **light-fingered** given to stealing; **light flyweight** amateur boxing weight (up to 48 kg); **light-headed** giddy, delirious; **light-hearted** cheerful; **light heavyweight** amateur boxing weight (75–81 kg); **light industry** manufacture of small or light articles; **light middleweight** amateur boxing weight (67–71 kg); **lightweight** *adjective* below average weight, of little importance, *noun* lightweight person or thing, amateur boxing weight (57–60kg); **light welterweight** amateur boxing weight (60–63.5 kg). □ **lightly** *adverb*; **lightness** *noun*.

lighten¹ *verb* make or become lighter in weight; reduce weight or load of.

lighten² *verb* shed light on, make or grow bright.

lighter¹ *noun* device for lighting cigarettes etc.

lighter² *noun* boat for transporting goods between ship and wharf etc.

lightning /ˈlaɪtnɪŋ/ *noun* flash of light produced by electric discharge between clouds or between clouds and ground. □ **lightning-conductor** metal rod or wire fixed to building or mast to divert lightning to earth or sea.

lights *plural noun* lungs of sheep, pigs, etc. as food, esp. for pets.

ligneous /ˈlɪgnɪəs/ *adjective* of the nature of wood.

lignite /ˈlɪgnaɪt/ *noun* brown coal of woody texture.

lignum vitae /lɪgnəm ˈvaɪtɪ/ *noun* a hard-wooded tree.

like¹ ● *adjective* (**more like, most like**) similar to another, each other, or original; resembling; such as; characteristic of; in suitable state or mood for. ● *preposition* in manner of, to same degree as. ● *adverb slang* so to speak; *colloquial* probably. ● *conjunction colloquial* as, as if (see note below). ● *noun* counterpart, equal; similar person or thing.

■ **Usage** It is incorrect in standard English to use *like* as a conjunction, as in *Tell it like it is* or *He's spending money like it was going out of fashion.*

like² ● *verb* (**-king**) find agreeable or enjoyable; feel attracted by, choose to have, prefer. ● *noun* (in *plural*) things one likes or prefers.

likeable *adjective* (also **likable**) pleasant, easy to like. □ **likeably** *adverb*.

likelihood /ˈlaɪklɪhʊd/ *noun* probability.

likely /ˈlaɪklɪ/ ● *adjective* (**-ier, -iest**) probable; such as may well happen or be true; to be expected; promising, apparently suitable. ● *adverb* probably. □ **not likely!** *colloquial* certainly not.

liken *verb* (+ *to*) point out resemblance between (person, thing) and (another).

likeness *noun* (usually + *between, to*) resemblance; (+ *of*) semblance, guise; portrait, representation.

likewise *adverb* also, moreover, similarly.

liking *noun* what one likes; one's taste; (+ *for*) fondness, taste, fancy.

lilac /ˈlaɪlək/ ● *noun* shrub with fragrant pinkish-violet or white flowers; pale pinkish-violet colour. ● *adjective* of this colour.

liliaceous /lɪlɪˈeɪʃəs/ *adjective* of the lily family.

lilliputian /lɪlɪˈpjuːʃ(ə)n/ ● *noun* diminutive person or thing. ● *adjective* diminutive.

lilt ● *noun* light springing rhythm; tune with this. ● *verb* (esp. as **lilting** *adjective*) speak etc. with lilt.

lily /'lɪlɪ/ noun (plural **-ies**) tall bulbous plant with large trumpet-shaped flowers; heraldic fleur-de-lis. □ **lily of the valley** plant with fragrant white bell-shaped flowers.

limb[1] /lɪm/ noun leg, arm, wing; large branch of tree; branch of cross. □ **out on a limb** isolated.

limb[2] /lɪm/ noun specified edge of sun moon, etc.

limber[1] /'lɪmbə/ ● adjective lithe, flexible; agile. ● verb (usually + up) make one-self supple; warm up for athletic etc. activity.

limber[2] /'lɪmbə/ ● noun detachable front of gun-carriage. ● verb attach limber to.

limbo[1] /'lɪmbəʊ/ noun (plural **-s**) supposed abode of souls of unbaptized infants, and of the just who died before Christ; intermediate state or condition of awaiting decision.

limbo[2] /'lɪmbəʊ/ noun (plural **-s**) W. Indian dance in which dancer bends backwards to pass under progressively lowered horizontal bar.

lime[1] ● noun white caustic substance got by heating limestone. ● verb (**-ming**) treat with lime. □ **limekiln** kiln for heating limestone. □ **limy** adjective (**-ier**, **-iest**).

lime[2] noun round green acid fruit; tree producing this fruit. □ **lime-green** yellowish-green colour.

lime[3] noun (in full **lime tree**) tree with heart-shaped leaves and fragrant creamy blossom.

limelight noun intense white light used formerly in theatres; glare of publicity.

limerick /'lɪmərɪk/ noun humorous 5-line verse.

limestone noun rock composed mainly of calcium carbonate.

limit /'lɪmɪt/ ● noun point, line, or level beyond which something does not or may not extend or pass; greatest or smallest amount permitted. ● verb (**-t-**) set or serve as limit to; (+ to) restrict to. □ **limitless** adjective.

limitation /lɪmɪ'teɪʃ(ə)n/ noun limiting, being limited; limit of ability; limiting circumstance.

limn /lɪm/ verb archaic paint.

limousine /lɪmʊ'ziːn/ noun large luxurious car.

limp[1] ● verb walk or proceed lamely or awkwardly. ● noun lame walk.

limp[2] adjective not stiff or firm; without will or energy. □ **limply** adverb; **limpness** noun.

limpet /'lɪmpɪt/ noun mollusc with conical shell sticking tightly to rocks.

limpid /'lɪmpɪd/ adjective clear, transparent. □ **limpidity** /-'pɪd-/ noun.

linage /'laɪnɪdʒ/ noun number of lines in printed or written page etc.; payment by the line.

linchpin /'lɪntʃpɪn/ noun pin passed through axle-end to keep wheel on; person or thing vital to organization etc.

linctus /'lɪŋktəs/ noun syrupy medicine, esp. soothing cough mixture.

linden /'lɪnd(ə)n/ noun = LIME TREE.

line[1] ● noun continuous mark made on surface; furrow, wrinkle; use of lines in art; straight or curved track of moving point; outline; limit, boundary; row of persons or things; US queue; mark defining area of play or start or finish of race; row of printed or written words; portion of verse written in line; (in plural) piece of poetry, words of actor's part; length of cord, rope, etc. serving specified purpose; wire or cable for telephone or telegraph; connection by means of this; single track or branch of railway; regular succession of buses, ships, aircraft, etc., plying between certain places, company conducting this; several generations (of family); stock; manner of procedure, conduct, thought, etc.; channel; department of activity, branch of business; type of product; connected series of military field works, arrangement of soldiers or ships side by side; each of very narrow horizontal sections forming television picture. ● verb (**-ning**) mark with lines; position or stand at intervals along. □ **line printer** machine that prints computer output a line at a time; **linesman** umpire's or referee's assistant who decides whether ball has fallen within playing area or not; **line up** verb arrange or be arranged in lines, have ready; **line-up** noun line of people for inspection, arrangement of team, band, etc.

line[2] verb (**-ning**) apply layer of usually different material to cover inside of (garment, box, etc.); serve as lining for; *colloquial* fill (purse etc.).

lineage /'lɪnɪɪdʒ/ *noun* lineal descent, ancestry.

lineal /'lɪnɪəl/ *adjective* in direct line of descent or ancestry; linear. □ **lineally** *adverb*.

lineament /'lɪnɪəmənt/ *noun* (usually in *plural*) distinctive feature or characteristic, esp. of face.

linear /'lɪnɪə/ *adjective* of or in lines; long and narrow and of uniform breadth.

linen /'lɪnɪn/ ● *noun* cloth woven from flax; articles made or originally made of linen, as sheets, shirts, underwear, etc. ● *adjective* made of linen.

liner[1] *noun* ship or aircraft carrying passengers on regular line.

liner[2] *noun* removable lining.

ling[1] *noun* (*plural* same) long slender marine fish.

ling[2] *noun* kind of heather.

linger /'lɪŋgə/ *verb* stay about; (+ *over, on*, etc.) dally; be protracted; (often + *on*) die slowly.

lingerie /'læʒərɪ/ *noun* women's underwear and nightclothes.

lingo /'lɪŋgəʊ/ *noun* (*plural* **-s** or **-es**) *colloquial* foreign language.

lingual /'lɪŋgw(ə)l/ *adjective* of tongue; of speech or languages.

linguist /'lɪŋgwɪst/ *noun* person skilled in languages or linguistics.

linguistic /lɪŋ'gwɪstɪk/ *adjective* of language or the study of languages. □ **linguistically** *adverb*.

linguistics *noun* study of language and its structure.

liniment /'lɪnɪmənt/ *noun* embrocation.

lining *noun* material used to line surface.

link ● *noun* one loop or ring of chain etc.; one in series; means of connection. ● *verb* (+ *together, to, with*) connect, join; clasp or intertwine (hands etc.).

linkage *noun* linking or being linked.

links *noun* (treated as *singular* or *plural*) golf course.

Linnaean /lɪ'niːən/ *adjective* of Linnaeus or his system of classifying plants and animals.

linnet /'lɪnɪt/ *noun* brown-grey finch.

lino /'laɪnəʊ/ *noun* (*plural* **-s**) linoleum. □ **linocut** design carved in relief on block of linoleum, print made from this.

linoleum /lɪ'nəʊlɪəm/ *noun* canvas-backed material coated with linseed oil, cork, etc.

linseed /'lɪnsiːd/ *noun* seed of flax.

lint *noun* linen or cotton with one side made fluffy, used for dressing wounds; fluff.

lintel /'lɪnt(ə)l/ *noun* horizontal timber, stone, etc. over door or window.

lion /'laɪən/ *noun* (*feminine* **lioness**) large tawny flesh-eating wild cat of Africa and S. Asia; brave or celebrated person.

lionize *verb* (also **-ise**) (**-zing** or **-sing**) treat as celebrity.

lip *noun* either edge of opening of mouth; edge of cup, vessel, cavity, etc., esp. part shaped for pouring from; *colloquial* impudent talk. □ **lip-read** understand (speech) by observing speaker's lip-movements; **lip-service** insincere expression of support; **lipstick** stick of cosmetic for colouring lips.

liquefy /'lɪkwɪfaɪ/ *verb* (**-ies, -ied**) make or become liquid. □ **liquefaction** /-'fækʃ(ə)n/ *noun*.

liqueur /lɪ'kjʊə/ *noun* any of several strong sweet alcoholic spirits.

liquid /'lɪkwɪd/ ● *adjective* having consistency like that of water or oil, flowing freely but of constant volume; having appearance of water; (of sounds) clear, pure; (of assets) easily convertible into cash. ● *noun* liquid substance; *Phonetics* sound of *l* or *r*. □ **liquid crystal** liquid in state approaching that of crystalline solid; **liquid crystal display** visual display in some electronic devices.

liquidate /'lɪkwɪdeɪt/ *verb* (**-ting**) wind up affairs of (firm etc.); pay off (debt); wipe out; kill. □ **liquidator** *noun*.

liquidation /lɪkwɪ'deɪʃ(ə)n/ *noun* liquidating, esp. of firm. □ **go into liquidation** be wound up and have assets apportioned.

liquidity /lɪ'kwɪdɪtɪ/ *noun* (*plural* **-ies**) state of being liquid; having liquid assets.

liquidize *verb* (also **-ise**) (**-zing** or **-sing**) reduce to liquid state.

liquidizer *noun* (also **-iser**) machine for liquidizing foods.

liquor /'lıkə/ *noun* alcoholic (esp. distilled) drink; other liquid, esp. that produced in cooking.

liquorice /'lıkərıs/ *noun* (also **licorice**) black root extract used as sweet and in medicine; plant from which it is obtained.

lira /'lıərə/ *noun* chief monetary unit of Italy (*plural* **lire** /-rı/) and Turkey (*plural* **-s**).

lisle /laıl/ *noun* fine cotton thread for stockings etc.

lisp • *noun* speech defect in which *s* is pronounced like *th* in *thick* and *z* like *th* in *this*. • *verb* speak or utter with lisp.

lissom /'lısəm/ *adjective* lithe, agile.

list[1] • *noun* number of items, names, etc. written or printed together as record; (in *plural*) palisades enclosing tournament area. • *verb* arrange as or enter in list; (as **listed** *adjective*) approved for Stock Exchange dealings, (of a building) of historical importance and officially protected. □ **enter the lists** issue or accept challenge.

list[2] • *verb* (of ship etc.) lean over to one side. • *noun* listing position, tilt.

listen /'lıs(ə)n/ *verb* make effort to hear something, attentively hear person speaking; (+ *to*) give attention with ear to, take notice of. □ **listen in** tap telephonic communication, use radio receiving set. □ **listener** *noun*.

listless /'lıstlıs/ *adjective* lacking energy or enthusiasm. □ **listlessly** *adverb*; **listlessness** *noun*.

lit *past & past participle* of LIGHT[1,2].

litany /'lıtənı/ *noun* (*plural* **-ies**) series of supplications to God used in church services; (**the Litany**) that in Book of Common Prayer.

litchi = LYCHEE.

liter *US* = LITRE.

literacy /'lıtərəsı/ *noun* ability to read and write.

literal /'lıtər(ə)l/ *adjective* taking words in their basic sense without metaphor etc.; corresponding exactly to original words; prosaic; matter-of-fact. □ **literalism** *noun*; **literally** *adverb*.

literary /'lıtərərı/ *adjective* of or concerned with or interested in literature.

literate /'lıtərət/ • *adjective* able to read and write. • *noun* literate person.

literati /lıtə'rɑ:tı/ *plural noun* the class of learned people.

literature /'lıtərətʃə/ *noun* written works, esp. those valued for form and style; writings of country or period or on particular subject; *colloquial* printed matter, leaflets, etc.

lithe /laıð/ *adjective* flexible, supple.

litho /'laıθəʊ/ *colloquial* • *noun* lithography. • *verb* (**-oes**, **-oed**) lithograph.

lithograph /'lıθəgrɑ:f/ • *noun* lithographic print. • *verb* print by lithography.

lithography /lı'θɒgrəfı/ *noun* process of printing from plate so treated that ink sticks only to design to be printed. □ **lithographer** *noun*; **lithographic** /lıθə'græfık/ *adjective*.

Lithuanian /lıθju:'eınıən/ • *noun* native, national, or language of Lithuania. • *adjective* of Lithuania.

litigant /'lıtıgənt/ • *noun* party to lawsuit. • *adjective* engaged in lawsuit.

litigate /'lıtıgeıt/ *verb* (**-ting**) go to law; contest (point) at law. □ **litigation** *noun*; **litigator** *noun*.

litigious /lı'tıdʒəs/ *adjective* fond of litigation; contentious.

litmus /'lıtməs/ *noun* dye turned red by acid and blue by alkali.

litre /'li:tə/ *noun* (*US* **liter**) metric unit of capacity (1.76 pints).

litter /'lıtə/ • *noun* refuse, esp. paper, discarded in public place, odds and ends lying about; young animals brought forth at one birth; vehicle containing couch and carried on men's shoulders or by animals; kind of stretcher for sick and wounded; straw etc. as bedding for animals; material for animal's, esp. cat's, indoor toilet. • *verb* make (place) untidy; give birth to (puppies etc.); provide (horse etc.) with bedding.

little /'lıt(ə)l/ • *adjective* (**-r**, **-st**; **less** or **lesser**, **least**) small in size, amount, degree, etc.; short in stature; of short distance or duration; (**a little**) certain but small amount of; trivial; only small amount; operating on small scale; humble, ordinary; young, younger. • *noun* not much, only small amount;

short time or distance. ● *adverb* (**less, least**) to small extent only; not at all. □ **little by little** by degrees, gradually; **the little people** fairies.

littoral /'lɪtəd(ə)l/ ● *adjective* of or on the shore. ● *noun* region lying along shore.

liturgy /'lɪtədʒɪ/ *noun* (*plural* **-ies**) fixed form of public worship; (**the Liturgy**) the Book of Common Prayer. □ **liturgical** /-'tɜːdʒ-/ *adjective*.

live[1] /lɪv/ *verb* (**-ving**) have life; be or remain alive; have one's home; (+ *on, off*) subsist or feed on; keep one's position; pass, spend; conduct oneself in specified way; enjoy life to the full. □ **live down** cause (scandal etc.) to be forgotten through blameless behaviour thereafter; **live it up** *colloquial* live exuberantly and extravagantly.

live[2] /laɪv/ ● *adjective* that is alive, living; (of broadcast, performance, etc.) heard or seen while happening or with audience present; of current interest; glowing, burning; (of match, bomb, etc.) not yet kindled or exploded; charged with electricity. ● *adverb* as live performance. □ **livestock** (usually treated as *plural*) animals kept on farm for use or profit; **live wire** spirited person.

liveable /'lɪvəb(ə)l/ *adjective* (also **livable**) *colloquial* (usually **liveable-in**) (of house etc.) fit to live in; (of life) worth living; *colloquial* (usually **liveable-with**) (of person) easy to live with.

livelihood /'laɪvlɪhʊd/ *noun* means of living; job, income.

livelong /'lɪvlɒŋ/ *adjective* in its entire length.

lively /'laɪvlɪ/ *adjective* (**-ier, -iest**) full of life, energetic; (of imagination) vivid; cheerful; *jocular* exciting, dangerous. □ **liveliness** *noun*.

liven /'laɪv(ə)n/ *verb* (often + *up*) make or become lively, cheer up.

liver[1] /'lɪvə/ *noun* large glandular organ in abdomen of vertebrates; liver of some animals as food.

liver[2] /'lɪvə/ *noun* person who lives in specified way.

liverish /'lɪvərɪʃ/ *adjective* suffering from liver disorder; peevish, glum.

liverwort *noun* mosslike plant sometimes lobed like liver.

livery /'lɪvərɪ/ *noun* (*plural* **-ies**) distinctive uniform of member of City Company or servant; distinctive guise or marking; distinctive colour scheme for company's vehicles etc. □ **at livery** (of horse) kept for owner at fixed charge; **livery stable** stable where horses are kept at livery or let out for hire.

lives *plural* of LIFE.

livid /'lɪvɪd/ *adjective colloquial* furious; of bluish leaden colour.

living /'lɪvɪŋ/ ● *noun* being alive; livelihood; position held by clergyman, providing income. ● *adjective* contemporary; now alive; (of likeness) exact; (of language) still in vernacular use. □ **living-room** room for general day use; **living wage** wage on which one can live without privation; **within living memory** within memory of living people.

lizard /'lɪzəd/ *noun* reptile with usually long body and tail, 4 legs, and scaly hide.

llama /'lɑːmə/ *noun* S. American ruminant kept as beast of burden and for woolly fleece.

Lloyd's /lɔɪdz/ *noun* incorporated society of underwriters in London. □ **Lloyd's Register** annual classified list of all ships.

lo *interjection archaic* look.

loach *noun* (*plural* same or **-es**) small freshwater fish.

load ● *noun* what is (to be) carried; amount usually or actually carried; burden of work, responsibility, care, etc.; (in *plural*; often + *of*) plenty; (**a load of**) a quantity of; amount of power carried by electrical circuit or supplied by generating station. ● *verb* put load on or aboard; place (load) aboard ship or on vehicle etc.; (often + *up*) (of vehicle or person) take load aboard; (often + *with*) burden, strain, overwhelm; put ammunition in (gun), film in (camera), cassette in (tape recorder), program in (computer), etc. □ **load line** Plimsoll line.

loaded *adjective slang* rich, drunk, *US* drugged; (of dice etc.) weighted; (of question or statement) carrying hidden implication.

loadstone = LODESTONE.

loaf[1] noun (plural **loaves**) unit of baked bread, usually of standard size or shape; other cooked food in loaf shape; slang head.

loaf[2] verb (often + about) spend time idly, hang about.

loam noun rich soil of clay, sand, and humus. □ **loamy** adjective.

loan noun thing lent, esp. money; lending, being lent. ● verb lend (money, works of art, etc.). □ **on loan** being lent.

loath adjective (also **loth**) disinclined, reluctant.

loathe /ləʊð/ verb (**-thing**) detest, hate. □ **loathing** noun.

loathsome /ˈləʊðsəm/ adjective arousing hatred or disgust; repulsive.

loaves plural of LOAF[1].

lob ● verb (**-bb-**) hit or throw (ball etc.) slowly or in high arc. ● noun such ball.

lobar /ˈləʊbə/ adjective of a lobe, esp. of lung.

lobate /ˈləʊbeɪt/ adjective having lobe(s).

lobby /ˈlɒbɪ/ ● noun (plural **-ies**) porch, ante-room, entrance hall, corridor; (in House of Commons) large hall used esp. for interviews between MPs and the public; (also **division lobby**) each of two corridors to which MPs retire to vote; group of lobbyists. ● verb (**-ies**, **-ied**) solicit support of (influential person); inform (legislators etc.) in order to influence them. □ **lobby correspondent** journalist who receives unattributable briefings from government.

lobbyist noun person who lobbies MP etc.

lobe noun lower soft pendulous part of outer ear; similar part of other organs. □ **lobed** adjective.

lobelia /ləˈbiːlɪə/ noun plant with bright, esp. blue, flowers.

lobotomy /ləˈbɒtəmɪ/ noun (plural **-ies**) incision into frontal lobe of brain to relieve mental disorder.

lobster /ˈlɒbstə/ noun marine crustacean with two pincer-like claws; its flesh as food. □ **lobster pot** basket for trapping lobsters.

lobworm noun large earthworm used as fishing bait.

local /ˈləʊk(ə)l/ ● adjective belonging to, existing in, or peculiar to particular place; of the neighbourhood; of or affecting a part and not the whole; (of telephone call) to nearby place and at lower charge. ● noun inhabitant of particular place; (often **the local**) colloquial local public house. □ **local authority** administrative body in local government; **local colour** touches of detail in story etc. designed to provide realistic background; **local government** system of administration of county, district, parish, etc. by elected representatives of those who live there. □ **locally** adverb.

locale /ləʊˈkɑːl/ noun scene or locality of event or occurrence.

locality /ləʊˈkælɪtɪ/ noun (plural **-ies**) district; thing's site or scene; thing's position.

localize /ˈləʊkəlaɪz/ verb (also **-ise**) (**-zing** or **-sing**) restrict or assign to particular place; invest with characteristics of place; decentralize.

locate /ləʊˈkeɪt/ verb (**-ting**) discover exact place of; establish in a place, situate; state locality of.

■ **Usage** In standard English, it is incorrect to use locate to mean merely 'find' as in I can't locate my key.

location noun particular place; locating; natural, not studio, setting for film etc.

loc. cit. abbreviation in the passage cited (loco citato).

loch /lɒx, lɒk/ noun Scottish lake or narrow inlet of the sea.

lock[1] ● noun mechanism for fastening door etc. with bolt requiring key of particular shape; section of canal or river confined within sluice-gates for moving boats from one level to another; turning of vehicle's front wheels; interlocked or jammed state; wrestling hold. ● verb fasten with lock; (+ up) shut (house etc.) thus; (of door etc.) be lockable; (+ up, in, into) enclose (person, thing) by locking; (often + up, away) store inaccessibly; make or become rigidly fixed; (cause to) jam or catch. □ **lockjaw** form of tetanus in which jaws become rigidly closed; **lock-keeper** keeper of river or canal lock; **lock on to** (of missile etc.) automatically find and then track (target);

lock out verb keep out by locking door, (of employer) subject (employees) to lockout; **lockout** noun employer's exclusion of employees from workplace until certain terms are accepted; **locksmith** maker and mender of locks; **lock-up** house or room for temporary detention of prisoners; premises that can be locked up. □ **lockable** adjective.

lock² noun portion of hair that hangs together; (in plural) the hair.

locker noun (usually lockable) cupboard, esp. for public use.

locket /ˈlɒkɪt/ noun small ornamental case for portrait etc., usually on chain round neck.

locomotion /ləʊkəˈməʊʃ(ə)n/ noun motion or power of motion from place to place.

locomotive /ləʊkəˈməʊtɪv/ ● noun engine for pulling trains. ● adjective of, having, or bringing about locomotion.

locum tenens /ləʊkəm ˈtiːnenz/ noun (plural **locum tenentes** /tɪˈnentiːz/) (also colloquial **locum**) deputy acting esp. for doctor or member of clergy.

locus /ˈləʊkəs/ noun (plural **loci** /-saɪ/) position, place; line or curve etc. made by all points satisfying certain conditions or by defined motion of point, line, or surface.

locust /ˈləʊkəst/ noun African or Asian grasshopper migrating in swarms and consuming all vegetation.

locution /ləˈkjuːʃ(ə)n/ noun phrase, word, or idiom; style of speech.

lode noun vein of metal ore. □ **lodestar** star used as guide in navigation, esp. pole star; **lodestone, loadstone** magnetic oxide of iron, piece of this as magnet.

lodge ● noun small house, esp. one for gatekeeper at entrance to park or grounds of large house; porter's room etc.; members or meeting-place of branch of society such as Freemasons; beaver's or otter's lair. ● verb (-ging) reside, esp. as lodger; provide with sleeping quarters; submit (complaint etc.); become fixed or caught; deposit for security; settle, place.

lodger noun person paying for accommodation in another's house.

lodging noun temporary accommodation; (in plural) room(s) rented for lodging in.

loft ● noun attic; room over stable; gallery in church or hall; pigeon house. ● verb send (ball etc.) high up.

lofty adjective (-ier, -iest) of imposing height; haughty, aloof; exalted, noble. □ **loftily** adverb; **loftiness** noun.

log¹ ● noun unhewn piece of felled tree; any large rough piece of wood; historical floating device for ascertaining ship's speed; record of ship's or aircraft's voyage; any systematic record of experiences etc. ● verb (-gg-) enter (ship's speed or other transport details) in logbook; enter (data etc.) in regular record; cut into logs. □ **logbook** book containing record or log, vehicle registration document; **log on** or **off, log in** or **out** begin or end operations at terminal of esp. multi-access computer.

log² noun logarithm.

logan /ˈləʊgən/ noun (in full **logan-stone**) poised heavy stone rocking at a touch.

loganberry /ˈləʊgənbəri/ noun (plural **-ies**) dark red fruit, hybrid of blackberry and raspberry.

logarithm /ˈlɒgərɪð(ə)m/ noun an arithmetic exponent used in computation. □ **logarithmic** /-ˈrɪðmɪk/ adjective.

loggerhead /ˈlɒgəhed/ noun □ **at loggerheads** (often + with) disagreeing or disputing.

loggia /ˈləʊdʒə/ noun open-sided gallery or arcade.

logging noun work of cutting and preparing forest timber.

logic /ˈlɒdʒɪk/ noun science of reasoning; chain of reasoning; use of or ability in argument; inexorable force; principles used in designing computer etc.; circuits based on these. □ **logician** /ləˈdʒɪʃ(ə)n/ noun.

logical adjective of or according to logic; correctly reasoned, consistent; capable of correct reasoning. □ **logicality** /-ˈkæl-/ noun; **logically** adverb.

logistics /ləˈdʒɪstɪks/ plural noun organization of (originally military) services and supplies. □ **logistic** adjective; **logistical** adjective; **logistically** adverb.

logo /ˈləʊgəʊ/ noun (plural **-s**) organization's emblem used in display material.

loin noun (in plural) side and back of body between ribs and hip-bones; joint of meat from this part of animal. □ **loincloth** cloth worn round hips, esp. as sole garment.

loiter /ˈlɔɪtə/ verb stand about idly; linger. □ **loiter with intent** linger to commit felony.

loll verb stand, sit, or recline in lazy attitude; hang loosely.

lollipop /ˈlɒlɪpɒp/ noun hard sweet on stick. □ **lollipop man, lady** colloquial warden using circular sign on pole to stop traffic for children to cross road.

lollop /ˈlɒləp/ verb (**-p-**) colloquial flop about; move in ungainly bounds.

lolly /ˈlɒlɪ/ noun (plural **-ies**) colloquial lollipop; ice lolly; slang money.

lone adjective solitary; without companions; isolated; unmarried. □ **lone hand** hand played or player playing against the rest at cards, person or action without allies; **lone wolf** loner.

lonely /ˈləʊnlɪ/ adjective (**-ier, -iest**) without companions; sad because of this; isolated; uninhabited. □ **loneliness** noun.

loner noun person or animal preferring to be alone.

lonesome adjective esp. US lonely; causing loneliness.

long[1] ● adjective (**longer** /ˈlɒŋgə/, **longest** /ˈlɒŋgɪst/) measuring much from end to end in space or time; (following measurement) in length or duration; consisting of many items; tedious; of elongated shape; reaching far back or forward in time; involving great interval or difference. ● noun long interval or period. ● adverb (**longer** /ˈlɒŋgə/, **longest** /ˈlɒŋgɪst/) by or for a long time; (following nouns of duration) throughout specified time; (in comparative) after implied point of time. □ **as, so long as** provided that; **before long** soon; **in the long run** eventually; **longboat** sailing ship's largest boat; **longbow** one drawn by hand and shooting long arrow; **long-distance** travelling or operating between distant places; **long face** dismal expression; **longhand** ordinary handwriting; **long johns** colloquial long underpants; **long jump** athletic contest of jumping along ground in one leap;

long-life (of milk etc.) treated to prolong shelf-life; **long odds** chances with low probability; **long-playing** (of gramophone record) playing for about 20–30 minutes on each side; **long-range** having a long range, relating to period of time far into future; **longshore** existing on or frequenting the shore; **long shot** wild guess or venture; **long sight** ability to see clearly only what is comparatively distant; **long-sighted** having long sight, far-sighted; **long-suffering** bearing provocation patiently; **long-term** of or for long period of time; **long-winded** (of speech or writing) tediously lengthy.

long[2] verb (+ for, to do) have strong wish or desire for. □ **longing** noun & adjective; **longingly** adverb.

long. abbreviation longitude.

longevity /lɒnˈdʒevɪtɪ/ noun formal long life.

longitude /ˈlɒŋgɪtjuːd/ noun angular distance E. or W. of (esp. Greenwich) meridian.

longitudinal /lɒŋgɪˈtjuːdɪn(ə)l/ adjective of or in length; running lengthwise; of longitude. □ **longitudinally** adverb.

longways adverb (also **longwise**) in direction parallel with thing's length.

loo noun colloquial lavatory.

loofah /ˈluːfə/ noun rough bath-sponge made from dried pod of type of gourd.

look /lʊk/ ● verb (often + at, down, up, etc.) use or direct one's eyes; examine; make visual or mental search; (+ at) consider; (+ for) seek; have specified appearance, seem; (+ into) investigate; (of thing) face some direction; indicate (emotion) by looks; (+ to do) expect. ● noun act of looking; gaze, glance; appearance of face, expression; (in plural) personal appearance. □ **look after** attend to; **look back** (+ on, to) turn one's thoughts to (something past); **look down (up)on** regard with contempt; **look forward to** await (expected event) eagerly or with specified feelings; **look in** verb make short visit; **look-in** noun colloquial chance of participation or success; **looking-glass** mirror; **look on** be spectator; **look out** verb (often + for) be vigilant or prepared; **lookout** noun watch, observation-post, person etc. stationed to keep watch, prospect, *colloquial* person's own concern; **look up** search for (esp. information in book), *colloquial* visit (person), improve in prospect; **look up to** respect.

loom[1] /luːm/ *noun* apparatus for weaving.

loom[2] /luːm/ *verb* appear dimly, esp. as vague often threatening shape.

loon /luːn/ *noun* kind of diving bird; *colloquial* crazy person.

loony /'luːnɪ/ *slang* ● *noun* (*plural* **-ies**) lunatic. ● *adjective* (**-ier, -iest**) crazy.

loop /luːp/ ● *noun* figure produced by curve or doubled thread etc. crossing itself; thing, path, etc. forming this figure; similarly shaped attachment used as fastening; contraceptive coil; endless band of tape or film allowing continuous repetition; repeated sequence of computer operations. ● *verb* form or bend into loop; fasten with loop(s); form loop. □ **loop line** railway or telegraph line that diverges from main line and joins it again.

loophole *noun* means of evading rule etc. without infringing it; narrow vertical slit in wall of fort etc.

loopy *adjective* (**-ier, -iest**) *slang* crazy.

loose /luːs/ ● *adjective* not tightly held; free from bonds or restraint; not held together; not compact or dense; inexact; morally lax. ● *verb* (**-sing**) free; untie, detach; release; relax (hold etc.). □ **at a loose end** unoccupied; **let loose** release; **loose cover** removable cover for armchair etc.; **loose-leaf** (of notebook etc.) with pages that can be removed and replaced; **on the loose** escaped from captivity, enjoying oneself freely. □ **loosely** *adverb*.

loosen *verb* make or become loose or looser. □ **loosen up** relax.

loot /luːt/ ● *noun* spoil, booty; *slang* money. ● *verb* rob or steal, esp. after rioting etc.; plunder.

lop *verb* (**-pp-**) (often + *off*) cut or remove (part or parts) from whole, esp. branches from tree; prune (tree).

lope ● *verb* (**-ping**) run with long bounding stride. ● *noun* such stride.

lop-eared *adjective* having drooping ears.

lopsided *adjective* unevenly balanced.

loquacious /lə'kweɪʃəs/ *adjective* talkative. □ **loquacity** /-'kwæsɪtɪ/ *noun*.

lord ● *noun* master, ruler; *historical* feudal superior, esp. of manor; peer of realm, person with title **Lord**; (**Lord**) (often **the Lord**) God, Christ; (**Lord**) *title used before name of certain male peers and officials*; (**the Lords**) House of Lords. ● *interjection* expressing surprise, dismay, etc. □ **lord it over** domineer; **Lord Mayor** *title of mayor in some large cities*; **Lord's Day** Sunday; **Lord's Prayer** the Our Father; **Lord's Supper** Eucharist.

lordly *adjective* (**-ier, -iest**) haughty, imperious; suitable for a lord.

Lordship *noun* □ **His, Your Lordship** *title used of or to man with rank of Lord*.

lore *noun* body of tradition and information on a subject or held by particular group.

lorgnette /lɔː'njet/ *noun* pair of eyeglasses or opera-glasses on long handle.

lorn *adjective archaic* desolate, forlorn.

lorry /'lɒrɪ/ *noun* (*plural* **-ies**) large vehicle for transporting goods etc.

lose /luːz/ *verb* (**-sing**; *past & past participle* **lost**) be deprived of; cease to have, esp. by negligence; be deprived of (person) by death; become unable to find, follow, or understand; let pass from one's control; be defeated in; get rid of; forfeit (right to something); suffer loss or detriment; cause (person) the loss of; (of clock etc.) become slow; (in *passive*) disappear, perish. □ **be lost without** be dependent on.

loser *noun* person or thing that loses esp. contest; *colloquial* person who regularly fails.

loss *noun* losing, being lost; what is lost; detriment resulting from losing. □ **at a loss** (sold etc.) for less than was paid for it; **be at a loss** be puzzled or uncertain; **loss-leader** item sold at a loss to attract customers.

lost *past & past participle of* LOSE.

lot *noun colloquial* (**a lot**, or **lots**) large number or amount; each of set of objects used to make chance selection; this method of deciding, share or responsibility resulting from it; destiny, fortune, condition; *esp. US* plot, allotment; article or set of articles for sale at auction etc.; group of associated people or things. □ **draw**, **cast lots** decide by lots; **the (whole) lot** total number or quantity.

■ *Usage* A lot of, as in a lot of people, is fairly informal, though acceptable in serious writing, but lots of people is not acceptable.

loth = LOATH.

lotion /ˈləʊʃ(ə)n/ noun medical or cosmetic liquid preparation applied externally.

lottery /ˈlɒtərɪ/ noun (plural -ies) means of raising money by selling numbered tickets and giving prizes to holders of numbers drawn at random.

lotto /ˈlɒtəʊ/ noun game of chance like bingo.

lotus /ˈləʊtəs/ noun legendary plant inducing luxurious langour when eaten; kind of water lily. □ **lotus position** cross-legged position of meditation.

loud ● adjective strongly audible; noisy; (of colours etc.) gaudy, obtrusive. ● adverb loudly. □ **loudspeaker** apparatus that converts electrical signals into sounds. □ **loudly** adverb; **loudness** noun.

lough /lɒk, lɒx/ noun Irish lake, sea inlet.

lounge ● verb (-ging) recline comfortably; loll; stand or move idly. ● noun place for lounging, esp. sitting-room in house; public room (in hotel etc.); place in airport etc. with seats for waiting passengers; spell of lounging. □ **lounge suit** man's suit for ordinary day wear.

lour /laʊə/ verb (also **lower** /laʊə/) frown, look sullen; (of sky etc.) look dark and threatening.

louse /laʊs/ ● noun (plural **lice**) parasitic insect; (plural **louses**) slang contemptible person. ● verb (-sing) delouse.

lousy /ˈlaʊzɪ/ adjective (-ier, -iest) colloquial very bad, disgusting, ill; (often + with) colloquial well supplied; infested with lice etc.

lout noun rough-mannered person. □ **loutish** adjective.

louvre /ˈluːvə/ noun (also **louver**) each of set of overlapping slats designed to admit air and some light and exclude rain; domed structure on roof with side openings for ventilation etc.

lovable /ˈlʌvəb(ə)l/ adjective (also **loveable**) inspiring affection.

lovage /ˈlʌvɪdʒ/ noun herb used for flavouring etc.

love /lʌv/ ● noun deep affection or fondness; sexual passion; sexual relations; beloved one; sweetheart; colloquial form of address regardless of affection; colloquial person of whom one is fond; affectionate greetings; (in games) no score, nil. ● verb (-ving) feel love for; delight in, admire; colloquial like very much. □ **fall in love** (often + with) suddenly begin to love; **in love** (often + with) enamoured (of); **love affair** romantic or sexual relationship between two people; **love-bird** kind of parakeet; **love-in-a-mist** blue-flowered cultivated plant; **lovelorn** pining from unrequited love; **lovesick** languishing with love; **make love** (often + to) have sexual intercourse (with), pay amorous attention (to).

loveable = LOVABLE.

loveless adjective unloving or unloved or both.

lovely adjective (-ier, -iest) colloquial pleasing, delightful; beautiful. □ **loveliness** noun.

lover noun person in love with another, or having sexual relations with another; (in plural) unmarried couple in love or having sexual relations; person who enjoys specified thing.

loving adjective feeling or showing love, affectionate. ● noun affection. □ **loving cup** two-handled drinking cup passed round at banquets. □ **lovingly** adverb.

low[1] /ləʊ/ ● adjective not high or tall; not elevated in position; (of sun) near horizon; of humble rank; of small or less than normal amount, extent, or intensity; dejected; lacking vigour; (of sound) not shrill or loud; commonplace; (of opinion) unfavourable; mean, vulgar. ● noun low or lowest level or number; area of low pressure. ● adverb in or to low position; in low tone, at low pitch. □ **lowbrow** colloquial not intellectual or cultured; **Low Church** section of Church of England attaching little importance to ritual, priestly authority, and sacraments; **Low Countries** Netherlands, Belgium, and Luxembourg; **low-down** adjective mean, dishonourable, noun colloquial (**the lowdown**; usually + on) relevant information; **lower case** small letters, not capitals; **low frequency** *Radio* 30–300 kilohertz; **low pressure** low degree of activity, atmospheric condition with pressure below average; **Low Sunday** Sunday after Easter; **low tide, water** time or level of tide at its ebb; **low water mark** level reached at low water.

low² /ləʊ/ ● *noun* sound made by cattle; moo. ● *verb* make this sound.

lower¹ *verb* let or haul down; make or become lower; degrade.

lower² = LOWER.

lowland /'ləʊlənd/ ● *noun* (usually in *plural*) low-lying country. ● *adjective* of or in lowland. □ **lowlander** *noun*.

lowly *adjective* (**-ier, -iest**) humble; unpretentious. □ **lowliness** *noun*.

loyal /'lɔɪəl/ *adjective* (often + *to*) faithful; steadfast in allegiance etc. □ **loyally** *adverb*; **loyalty** *noun* (*plural* **-ies**).

loyalist *noun* person remaining loyal to legitimate sovereign etc.; (**Loyalist**) supporter of union between Great Britain and Northern Ireland. □ **loyalism** *noun*.

lozenge /'lɒzɪndʒ/ *noun* rhombus; small sweet or medicinal tablet to be dissolved in mouth; lozenge-shaped object.

LP *abbreviation* long-playing (record).

LSD *abbreviation* lysergic acid diethylamide, a powerful hallucinogenic drug.

Lt. *abbreviation* Lieutenant; light.

Ltd. *abbreviation* Limited.

lubber /'lʌbə/ *noun* clumsy fellow, lout.

lubricant /'lu:brɪkənt/ *noun* substance used to reduce friction.

lubricate /'lu:brɪkeɪt/ *verb* (**-ting**) apply oil, grease, etc. to; make slippery. □ **lubrication** *noun*.

lubricious /lu:'brɪʃəs/ *adjective* slippery, evasive; lewd. □ **lubricity** *noun*.

lucerne /lu:'sɜːn/ *noun* alfalfa.

lucid /'lu:sɪd/ *adjective* expressing or expressed clearly; sane. □ **lucidity** /-'sɪd-/ *noun*; **lucidly** *adverb*.

luck *noun* good or bad fortune; circumstances brought by this; success due to chance.

luckless *adjective* unlucky; ending in failure.

lucky *adjective* (**-ier, -iest**) having or resulting from good luck; bringing good luck. □ **lucky dip** tub containing articles from which one chooses at random. □ **luckily** *adverb*.

lucrative /'lu:krətɪv/ *adjective* profitable. □ **lucratively** *adverb*.

lucre /'lu:kə/ *noun derogatory* financial gain.

ludicrous /'lu:dɪkrəs/ *adjective* absurd, ridiculous, laughable. □ **ludicrously** *adverb*; **ludicrousness** *noun*.

ludo /'lu:dəʊ/ *noun* board game played with dice and counters.

lug ● *verb* (**-gg-**) drag or carry with effort; pull hard. ● *noun* hard or rough pull; *cc!loquial* ear; projection on object by which it may be carried, fixed in place, etc.

luggage /'lʌgɪdʒ/ *noun* suitcases, bags, etc., for traveller's belongings.

lugger /'lʌgə/ *noun* small ship with 4-cornered sails (**lugsails**).

lugubrious /lʊ'gu:brɪəs/ *adjective* doleful. □ **lugubriously** *adverb*; **lugubriousness** *noun*.

lukewarm /lu:k'wɔːm/ *adjective* moderately warm, tepid; unenthusiastic.

lull ● *verb* soothe, send to sleep; (usually + *into*) deceive (person) into undue confidence; allay (suspicions etc.); (of noise, storm, etc.) lessen, fall quiet. ● *noun* temporary quiet period.

lullaby /'lʌləbaɪ/ *noun* (*plural* **-ies**) soothing song to send child to sleep.

lumbago /lʌm'beɪgəʊ/ *noun* rheumatic pain in muscles of lower back.

lumbar /'lʌmbə/ *adjective* of lower back. □ **lumbar puncture** withdrawal of spinal fluid from lower back for diagnosis.

lumber /'lʌmbə/ ● *noun* disused and cumbersome articles; partly prepared timber. ● *verb* (usually + *with*) encumber (person); move in slow clumsy way; cut and prepare forest timber for transporting. □ **lumberjack** person who fells and transports lumber; **lumber-room** room where things in disuse are kept.

lumen /'lu:men/ *noun* SI unit of luminous flux.

luminary /'lu:mɪnərɪ/ *noun* (*plural* **-ies**) *literary* natural light-giving body; wise person; celebrated member of group.

luminescence /luːmɪˈnes(ə)ns/ *noun* emission of light without heat. □ **luminescent** *adjective*.

luminous /ˈluːmɪnəs/ *adjective* shedding light; phosphorescent, visible in darkness. □ **luminosity** /-ˈnɒs-/ *noun*.

lump[1] ● *noun* compact shapeless mass; tumour; swelling, bruise; heavy ungainly person etc. ● *verb* (usually + *together* etc.) class, mass. □ **lump sugar** sugar in small lumps or cubes; **lump sum** sum including number of items or paid down all at once.

lump[2] *verb colloquial* (in contrast with *like*) put up with ungraciously.

lumpish *adjective* heavy, clumsy; stupid.

lumpy *adjective* (**-ier, -iest**) full of or covered with lumps. □ **lumpily** *adverb*; **lumpiness** *noun*.

lunacy /ˈluːnəsɪ/ *noun* (*plural* **-ies**) insanity; great folly.

lunar /ˈluːnə/ *adjective* of, like, concerned with, or determined by the moon. □ **lunar module** craft for travelling between moon and orbiting spacecraft; **lunar month** period of moon's revolution, (in general use) 4 weeks.

lunate /ˈluːneɪt/ *adjective* crescent-shaped.

lunatic /ˈluːnətɪk/ ● *noun* insane person; wildly foolish person. ● *adjective* insane; very reckless or foolish.

lunation /luːˈneɪʃ(ə)n/ *noun* interval between new moons, about 29½ days.

lunch ● *noun* midday meal. ● *verb* take lunch; provide lunch for.

luncheon /ˈlʌntʃ(ə)n/ *noun formal* lunch. □ **luncheon voucher** voucher issued to employees and exchangeable for food at restaurant etc.

lung *noun* either of pair of respiratory organs in humans and many other vertebrates.

lunge ● *noun* sudden movement forward; attacking move in fencing. ● *verb* (**-ging**) (usually + *at*) deliver or make lunge.

lupin /ˈluːpɪn/ *noun* cultivated plant with long tapering spikes of flowers.

lupine /ˈluːpaɪn/ *adjective* of or like wolves.

lupus /ˈluːpəs/ *noun* inflammatory skin disease.

lurch[1] ● *noun* stagger; sudden unsteady movement or tilt. ● *verb* stagger, move unsteadily.

lurch[2] *noun* □ **leave in the lurch** desert (friend etc.) in difficulties.

lurcher /ˈlɜːtʃə/ *noun* crossbred dog, usually working dog crossed with greyhound.

lure ● *verb* (**-ring**) (usually + *away, into*) entice; recall with lure. ● *noun* thing used to entice, enticing quality (of chase etc.); falconer's apparatus for recalling hawk.

lurid /ˈljʊərɪd/ *adjective* bright and glaring in colour; sensational, shocking; ghastly, wan. □ **luridly** *adverb*.

lurk *verb* linger furtively; lie in ambush; (usually + *in, about*, etc.) hide, esp. for sinister purpose; (as **lurking** *adjective*) latent.

luscious /ˈlʌʃəs/ *adjective* richly sweet in taste or smell; voluptuously attractive.

lush[1] *adjective* luxuriant and succulent.

lush[2] *noun slang* alcoholic, drunkard.

lust ● *noun* strong sexual desire; (usually + *for, of*) passionate desire for or enjoyment of; sensuous appetite (as sinful. ● *verb* (usually + *after, for*) have strong or excessive (esp. sexual) desire. □ **lustful** *adjective*; **lustfully** *adverb*.

lustre /ˈlʌstə/ *noun* (*US* **luster**) gloss, shining surface; brilliance, splendour; iridescent glaze on pottery and porcelain. □ **lustrous** *adjective*.

lusty *adjective* (**-ier, -iest**) healthy and strong; vigorous, lively. □ **lustily** *adverb*.

lute[1] /luːt/ *noun* guitar-like instrument with long neck and pear-shaped body.

lute[2] /luːt/ ● *noun* clay or cement for making joints airtight. ● *verb* (**-ting**) apply lute to.

lutenist /ˈluːtənɪst/ *noun* lute-player.

Lutheran /ˈluːθərən/ ● *noun* follower of Martin Luther; member of Lutheran Church. ● *adjective* of Luther, the doctrines associated with him, or the Protestant Reformation. □ **Lutheranism** *noun*.

lux /lʌks/ *noun* (*plural* same) SI unit of illumination.

luxuriant /lʌgˈzjʊərɪənt/ *adjective* growing profusely; exuberant, florid. □ **luxuriance** *noun*; **luxuriantly** *adverb*.

■ **Usage** *Luxuriant* is sometimes confused with *luxurious*.

luxuriate /lʌg'zjʊərɪeɪt/ *verb* (**-ting**) (+ *in*) take self-indulgent delight in, enjoy as luxury.

luxurious /lʌg'zjʊərɪəs/ *adjective* supplied with luxuries; very comfortable; fond of luxury. □ **luxuriously** *adverb*.

■ **Usage** *Luxurious* is sometimes confused with *luxuriant*.

luxury /'lʌkʃərɪ/ ● *noun* (*plural* **-ies**) choice or costly surroundings, possessions, etc.; thing giving comfort or enjoyment but inessential. ● *adjective* comfortable, expensive, etc.

LV *abbreviation* luncheon voucher.

lychee /'laɪtʃɪ/ *noun* (also **litchi**, **lichee**) sweet white juicy brown-skinned fruit; tree bearing this.

lych-gate = LICH-GATE.

Lycra /'laɪkrə/ *noun proprietary term* elastic polyurethane fabric.

lye /laɪ/ *noun* water made alkaline with wood ashes; any alkaline solution for washing.

lying *present participle of* LIE[1,2].

lymph /lɪmf/ *noun* colourless fluid from tissues of body, containing white blood cells; this fluid as vaccine.

lymphatic /lɪm'fætɪk/ *adjective* of, secreting, or carrying lymph; (of person) pale, flabby. □ **lymphatic system** vessels carrying lymph.

lynch /lɪntʃ/ *verb* put (person) to death by mob action without legal trial. □ **lynching** *noun*.

lynx /lɪŋks/ *noun* (*plural* same or **-es**) wild cat with short tail, spotted fur, and proverbially keen sight.

lyre /laɪə/ *noun* ancient U-shaped stringed instrument.

lyric /'lɪrɪk/ ● *adjective* (of poetry) expressing writer's emotion, usually briefly; (of poet) writing in this way; songlike. ● *noun* lyric poem; (in *plural*) words of song.

lyrical *adjective* lyric; resembling, or using language appropriate to, lyric poetry; *colloquial* highly enthusiastic. □ **lyrically** *adverb*.

lyricism /'lɪrɪsɪz(ə)m/ *noun* quality of being lyrical.

lyricist /'lɪrɪsɪst/ *noun* writer of lyrics.

Mm

M[1] *noun* (also **m**) (Roman numeral) 1,000.

M[2] *abbreviation* (also **M.**) Master; *Monsieur*; motorway; mega-.

m *abbreviation* (also **m.**) male; masculine; married; mile(s); metre(s); million(s); minute(s); milli-.

MA *abbreviation* Master of Arts.

ma /mɑː/ *noun colloquial* mother.

ma'am /mæm/ *noun* madam (esp. used in addressing royal lady).

mac *noun* (also **mack**) *colloquial* mackintosh.

macabre /mə'kɑːbr/ *adjective* gruesome, grim.

macadam /mə'kædəm/ *noun* broken stone as material for road-making; tar-macadam. □ **macadamize** *verb* (also **-ise**) (**-zing** or **-sing**).

macaroni /mækə'rəʊnɪ/ *noun* pasta tubes.

macaroon /mækə'ruːn/ *noun* biscuit made of ground almonds etc.

macaw /mə'kɔː/ *noun* kind of parrot.

mace[1] *noun* staff of office, esp. symbol of Speaker's authority in House of Commons.

mace[2] *noun* dried outer covering of nutmeg as spice.

macédoine /'mæsɪdwɑːn/ *noun* mixture of fruits or vegetables, esp. cut up small.

macerate /'mæsəreɪt/ *verb* (**-ting**) soften by soaking. □ **maceration** *noun*.

machete /mə'ʃetɪ/ *noun* broad heavy knife used in Central America and W. Indies.

machiavellian /mækɪə'velɪən/ *adjective* unscrupulous, cunning.

machination /mækɪ'neɪʃ(ə)n/ *noun* (usually in *plural*) intrigue, plot.

machine /mə'ʃiːn/ ● *noun* apparatus for applying mechanical power, having several interrelated parts; bicycle, motorcycle, etc.; aircraft; computer; controlling system of an organization. ● *verb* (-ning) make or operate on with machine. □ **machine-gun** automatic gun that gives continuous fire; **machine-readable** in form that computer can process; **machine tool** mechanically operated tool.

machinery *noun* (*plural* -ies) machines; mechanism; organized system; means arranged.

machinist *noun* person who works machine.

machismo /mə'kɪzməʊ/ *noun* being macho; masculine pride.

macho /'mætʃəʊ/ *adjective* aggressively masculine.

macintosh = MACKINTOSH.

mack = MAC.

mackerel /'mækr(ə)l/ *noun* (*plural* same or -s) edible sea fish. □ **mackerel sky** sky dappled with rows of small fleecy white clouds.

mackintosh /'mækɪntɒʃ/ *noun* (also **macintosh**) waterproof coat or cloak; cloth waterproofed with rubber.

macramé /mə'krɑːmɪ/ *noun* art of knotting cord or string in patterns; work so made.

macrobiotic /mækrəʊbaɪ'ɒtɪk/ *adjective* of diet intended to prolong life, esp. consisting of wholefoods.

macrocosm /'mækrəʊkɒz(ə)m/ *noun* universe; whole of a complex structure.

mad *adjective* (-dd-) insane; frenzied; wildly foolish; infatuated; *colloquial* annoyed. □ **madcap** *adjective* wildly impulsive, *noun* reckless person; **madhouse** *colloquial* confused uproar, *archaic* mental home or hospital; **madman, madwoman** mad person. □ **madly** *adverb*; **madness** *noun*.

madam /'mædəm/ *noun* polite formal address to woman; *colloquial* conceited or precocious girl or young woman; woman brothel-keeper.

Madame /mə'dɑːm/ *noun* (*plural* **Mesdames** /meɪ'dɑːm/) title used of or to French-speaking woman.

madden *verb* make mad; irritate. □ **maddening** *adjective*.

madder /'mædə/ *noun* herbaceous climbing plant; red dye from its root; synthetic substitute for this dye.

made past & past participle of MAKE.

Madeira /mə'dɪərə/ *noun* fortified wine from Madeira; (in full **Madeira cake**) kind of sponge cake.

Mademoiselle /mædəmwə'zel/ *noun* (*plural* **Mesdemoiselles** /meɪdm-/) title used of or to unmarried French-speaking woman.

Madonna /mə'dɒnə/ *noun* (**the Madonna**) the Virgin Mary; (**madonna**) picture or statue of her.

madrigal /'mædrɪg(ə)l/ *noun* part-song for several voices, usually unaccompanied.

maelstrom /'meɪlstrəm/ *noun* great whirlpool.

maestro /'maɪstrəʊ/ *noun* (*plural* **maestri** /-strɪ/ or -s) eminent musician, esp. teacher or conductor.

Mafia /'mæfɪə/ *noun* organized international group of criminals.

Mafioso /mæfɪ'əʊsəʊ/ *noun* (*plural* **Mafiosi** /-sɪ/) member of the Mafia.

mag *noun colloquial* magazine.

magazine /mægə'ziːn/ *noun* periodical publication containing contributions by various writers; chamber containing cartridges fed automatically to breech of gun; similar device in slide projector etc.; store for explosives, arms, or military provisions.

magenta /mə'dʒentə/ *noun* shade of crimson; aniline dye of this colour.

maggot /'mægət/ *noun* larva, esp. of bluebottle. □ **maggoty** *adjective*.

Magi /'meɪdʒaɪ/ *plural noun* (**the Magi**) the 'wise men from the East' in the Gospel.

magic /'mædʒɪk/ ● *noun* art of influencing events supernaturally; conjuring tricks; inexplicable influence. ● *adjective* of magic. □ **magic lantern** simple form of slide projector.

magical *adjective* of magic; resembling, or produced as if by, magic; wonderful, enchanting. □ **magically** *adverb*.

magician /məˈdʒɪʃ(ə)n/ *noun* person skilled in magic; conjuror.

magisterial /mædʒɪˈstɪərɪəl/ *adjective* imperious; authoritative; of a magistrate.

magistracy /ˈmædʒɪstrəsɪ/ *noun* (*plural* **-ies**) magisterial office; magistrates.

magistrate /ˈmædʒɪstreɪt/ *noun* civil officer administering law, esp. one trying minor offences etc.

magnanimous /mægˈnænɪməs/ *adjective* nobly generous, not petty in feelings or conduct. □ **magnanimity** /-nəˈnɪm-/ *noun.*

magnate /ˈmægneɪt/ *noun* person of wealth, authority, etc.

magnesia /mægˈniːʃə/ *noun* magnesium oxide; hydrated magnesium carbonate, used as antacid and laxative.

magnesium /mægˈniːzɪəm/ *noun* silvery metallic element.

magnet /ˈmægnɪt/ *noun* piece of iron, steel, etc., having properties of attracting iron and of pointing approximately north when suspended; lodestone; person or thing that attracts.

magnetic /mægˈnetɪk/ *adjective* having properties of magnet; produced or acting by magnetism; capable of being attracted by or acquiring properties of magnet; very attractive. □ **magnetic field** area of influence of magnet; **magnetic north** point indicated by north end of compass needle; **magnetic storm** disturbance of earth's magnetic field; **magnetic tape** coated plastic strip for recording sound or pictures.

magnetism /ˈmægnɪtɪz(ə)m/ *noun* magnetic phenomena; science of these; personal charm.

magnetize /ˈmægnɪtaɪz/ *verb* (also **-ise**) (**-zing** or **-sing**) make into magnet; attract like magnet. □ **magnetization** *noun.*

magneto /mægˈniːtəʊ/ *noun* (*plural* **-s**) electric generator using permanent magnets (esp. for ignition in internal-combustion engine).

magnificent /mægˈnɪfɪs(ə)nt/ *adjective* splendid; imposing; *colloquial* excellent. □ **magnificence** *noun;* **magnificently** *adverb.*

magnify /ˈmægnɪfaɪ/ *verb* (**-ies, -ied**) make (thing) appear larger than it is, as with lens (**magnifying glass**) etc.; exaggerate; intensify; *archaic* extol. □ **magnification** *noun.*

magnitude /ˈmægnɪtjuːd/ *noun* largeness, size; importance.

magnolia /mægˈnəʊlɪə/ *noun* kind of flowering tree; very pale pinkish colour of its flowers.

magnum /ˈmægnəm/ *noun* (*plural* **-s**) wine bottle twice normal size.

magpie /ˈmægpaɪ/ *noun* crow with long tail and black and white plumage; chatterer; indiscriminate collector.

Magyar /ˈmægjɑː/ • *noun* member of the chief ethnic group in Hungary; their language. • *adjective* of this people.

maharaja /mɑːhəˈrɑːdʒə/ *noun* (also **maharajah**) *historical* title of some Indian princes.

maharanee /mɑːhəˈrɑːniː/ *noun* (also **maharani**) (*plural* **-s**) *historical* maharaja's wife or widow.

maharishi /mɑːhəˈrɪʃɪ/ *noun* (*plural* **-s**) great Hindu sage.

mahatma /məˈhɑːtmə/ *noun* (in India etc.) revered person.

mah-jong /mɑːˈdʒɒŋ/ *noun* (also **-jongg**) originally Chinese game played with 136 or 144 pieces.

mahogany /məˈhɒɡənɪ/ *noun* (*plural* **-ies**) reddish-brown wood used for furniture etc.; colour of this.

mahout /məˈhaʊt/ *noun* elephant driver.

maid *noun* female servant; *archaic* girl, young woman. □ **maidservant** female servant.

maiden /ˈmeɪd(ə)n/ • *noun archaic* girl, young unmarried woman; *Cricket* maiden over. • *adjective* unmarried; (of voyage, speech by MP, etc.) first. □ **maidenhair** delicate kind of fern; **maiden name** woman's surname before marriage; **maiden over** *Cricket* over in which no runs are scored. □ **maidenly** *adjective.*

mail[1] • *noun* letters etc. conveyed by post; the post. • *verb* send by mail. □ **mail order** purchase of goods by post.

mail[2] *noun* armour of metal rings or plates.

maim *verb* cripple, mutilate.

main • *adjective* chief, principal. • *noun* principal channel for water, gas, etc., or (usually in *plural*) electricity; (in *plural*) domestic electricity supply as distinct from batteries; *archaic* high seas. □ **in the main** mostly, on the whole; **mainframe** central processing unit of large computer, large computer system; **mainland** continuous extent of land excluding nearby islands etc.; **mainmast** principal mast; **mainsail** lowest sail or sail set on after part of mainmast; **mainspring** principal spring of watch or clock, chief motive power etc.; **mainstay** chief support; **mainstream** prevailing trend of opinion, fashion, etc.

mainly *adverb* mostly; chiefly.

maintain /meɪnˈteɪn/ *verb* keep up; keep going; support; assert as true; keep in repair.

maintenance /ˈmeɪntənəns/ *noun* maintaining, being maintained; provision of enough to support life; alimony.

maiolica /məˈjɒlɪkə/ *noun* (also **majolica**) kind of decorated Italian earthenware.

maisonette /meɪzəˈnet/ *noun* flat on more than one floor; small house.

maize *noun* N. American cereal plant; cobs or grain of this.

Maj. *abbreviation* Major.

majestic /məˈdʒestɪk/ *adjective* stately and dignified; imposing. □ **majestically** *adverb*.

majesty /ˈmædʒɪstɪ/ *noun* (*plural* **-ies**) stateliness of aspect, language, etc.; sovereign power; (**His**, **Her**, **Your Majesty**) *title used of or to sovereign or sovereign's wife or widow*.

majolica = MAIOLICA.

major /ˈmeɪdʒə/ ● *adjective* greater or relatively great in size etc.; unusually serious or significant; *Music* of or based on scale having semitone next above third and seventh notes; of full legal age. ● *noun* army officer next below lieutenant colonel; person of full legal age; *US* student's main subject or course, student of this. ● *verb* (+ *in*) *US* study or qualify in as a major. □ **major-domo** /-ˈdəʊməʊ/ (*plural* **-s**) house-steward; **major-general** army officer next below lieutenant general.

majority /məˈdʒɒrɪtɪ/ *noun* (*plural* **-ies**) (usually + *of*) greater number or part;

number by which winning vote exceeds next; full legal age.

■ **Usage** *Majority* should strictly be used of a number of people or things, as in *the majority of people*, and not of a quantity of something, as in *the majority of the work*.

make ● *verb* (**-king**; *past & past participle* **made**) construct, frame, create, esp. from parts or other substance; compel; bring about, give rise to; cause to become or seem; write, compose; constitute, amount to; undertake; perform; gain, acquire, obtain as result; prepare for consumption or use; proceed; *colloquial* arrive at or in time for, manage to attend; *colloquial* achieve place in; establish, enact; consider to be, estimate as; secure success or advancement of; accomplish; become; represent as; form in the mind. ● *noun* origin of manufactured goods, brand; way thing is made. □ **make believe** *verb* pretend; **make-believe** *noun* pretence, *adjective* pretended; **make do** (often + *with*) manage (with substitute etc.); **make for** tend to result in, proceed towards; **make good** compensate for, repair, succeed in an undertaking; **make off** depart hastily; **make out** discern, understand, assert, pretend, *colloquial* progress, write out, fill in; **makeshift** (serving as) temporary substitute or device; **make up** *verb* act to overcome (deficiency), complete, (+ *for*) compensate for, be reconciled, put together, prepare, invent (story), apply cosmetics (to); **make-up** *noun* cosmetics, similar preparation used as disguise by actor, person's temperament etc., composition; **makeweight** small quantity added to make full weight; **on the make** *colloquial* intent on gain.

maker *noun* person who makes, esp. (**Maker**) God.

making *noun* (in *plural*) earnings, profit; essential qualities for becoming. □ **be the making of** ensure success of; **in the making** in the course of being made.

malachite /ˈmæləkaɪt/ *noun* green mineral used for ornament.

maladjusted /mæləˈdʒʌstɪd/ *adjective* (of person) unable to cope with demands of social environment. □ **maladjustment** noun.

maladminister /mæləd'mɪnɪstə/ verb manage badly or improperly. □ **maladministration** noun.

maladroit /mælə'drɔɪt/ adjective bungling, clumsy.

malady /'mælədɪ/ noun (plural -ies) ailment, disease.

malaise /mə'leɪz/ noun feeling of illness or uneasiness.

malapropism /'mæləprɒpɪz(ə)m/ noun comical confusion between words.

malaria /mə'leərɪə/ noun fever transmitted by mosquitoes. □ **malarial** adjective.

Malay /mə'leɪ/ ● noun member of a people predominating in Malaysia and Indonesia; their language. ● adjective of this people or language.

malcontent /'mælkəntent/ ● noun discontented person. ● adjective discontented.

male ● adjective of the sex that can beget offspring by fertilizing; (of plants or flowers) containing stamens but no pistil; (of parts of machinery) designed to enter or fill corresponding hollow part. ● noun male person or animal.

malediction /mælɪ'dɪkʃ(ə)n/ noun curse. □ **maledictory** adjective.

malefactor /'mælɪfæktə/ noun criminal; evil-doer. □ **malefaction** /-'fækʃ(ə)n/ noun.

malevolent /mə'levələnt/ adjective wishing evil to others. □ **malevolence** noun.

malformation /mælfɔː'meɪʃ(ə)n/ noun faulty formation. □ **malformed** /-'fɔːmd/ adjective.

malfunction /mæl'fʌŋkʃ(ə)n/ ● noun failure to function normally. ● verb function faultily.

malice /'mælɪs/ noun ill-will; desire to do harm.

malicious /mə'lɪʃəs/ adjective given to or arising from malice. □ **maliciously** adverb.

malign /mə'laɪn/ ● adjective injurious; malignant; malevolent. ● verb speak ill of; slander. □ **malignity** /mə'lɪgnɪtɪ/ noun.

malignant /mə'lɪgnənt/ adjective (of disease) very virulent; (of tumour) spreading, recurring, cancerous; feeling or showing intense ill-will. □ **malignancy** noun.

malinger /mə'lɪŋgə/ verb pretend to be ill, esp. to escape duty.

mall /mæl, mɔːl/ noun sheltered walk; shopping precinct.

mallard /'mælɑːd/ noun (plural same) kind of wild duck.

malleable /'mælɪəb(ə)l/ adjective that can be shaped by hammering; pliable. □ **malleability** noun.

mallet /'mælɪt/ noun hammer, usually of wood; implement for striking croquet or polo ball.

mallow /'mæləʊ/ noun flowering plant with hairy stems and leaves.

malmsey /'mɑːmzɪ/ noun a strong sweet wine.

malnutrition /mælnjuː'trɪʃ(ə)n/ noun lack of foods necessary for health.

malodorous /mæl'əʊdərəs/ adjective evil-smelling.

malpractice /mæl'præktɪs/ noun improper, negligent, or criminal professional conduct.

malt /mɔːlt/ ● noun barley or other grain prepared for brewing etc.; colloquial malt whisky. ● verb convert (grain) into malt. □ **malted milk** drink made from dried milk and extract of malt; **malt whisky** whisky made from malted barley.

Maltese /mɔːl'tiːz/ ● noun native, national, or language of Malta. ● adjective of Malta. □ **Maltese cross** one with equal arms broadened at ends.

maltreat /mæl'triːt/ verb ill-treat. □ **maltreatment** noun.

mama /mə'mɑː/ noun (also **mamma**) archaic mother.

mamba /'mæmbə/ noun venomous African snake.

mamma = MAMA.

mammal /'mæm(ə)l/ noun animal of class secreting milk to feed young. □ **mammalian** /-'meɪlɪən/ adjective.

mammary /'mæmərɪ/ adjective of breasts.

Mammon /'mæmən/ noun wealth regarded as god or evil influence.

mammoth /'mæməθ/ ● noun large extinct elephant. ● adjective huge.

man ● noun (plural **men**) adult human male; human being, person; the human race; employee, workman; (usually in *plural*) soldier, sailor, etc.; suitable or appropriate person; husband; *colloquial* boyfriend; human being of specified type; piece in chess, draughts, etc. ● *verb* (**-nn-**) supply with person(s) for work or defence. □ **manhole** opening giving person access to sewer, conduit, etc.; **man-hour** work done by one person in one hour; **man in the street** ordinary person; **man-of-war** warship; **manpower** people available for work or military service; **manservant** (*plural* **menservants**) male servant; **mantrap** trap set to catch esp. trespassers.

manacle /ˈmænək(ə)l/ ● *noun* (usually in *plural*) handcuff. ● *verb* (**-ling**) put manacles on.

manage /ˈmænɪdʒ/ *verb* (**-ging**) organize, regulate; succeed in achieving, contrive; succeed with limited resources, cope; succeed in controlling; cope with. □ **managing director** director with executive control or authority. □ **manageable** *adjective*.

management *noun* managing, being managed; administration; people managing a business.

manager *noun* person controlling or administering business etc.; person controlling activities of person, team, etc.; person who manages money etc. in specified way. □ **managerial** /-ˈdʒɪərɪəl/ *adjective*.

manageress /mænɪdʒəˈres/ *noun* woman manager, esp. of shop, hotel, etc.

mañana /mænˈjɑːnə/ *adverb & noun* some time in the future. [Spanish]

manatee /mænəˈtiː/ *noun* large aquatic plant-eating mammal.

Mancunian /mænˈkjuːnɪən/ ● *noun* native of Manchester. ● *adjective* of Manchester.

mandarin /ˈmændərɪn/ *noun* (**Mandarin**) official language of China; *historical* Chinese official; influential person, esp. bureaucrat; (in full **mandarin orange**) tangerine.

mandate /ˈmændeɪt/ ● *noun* official command; authority given by electors to government etc.; authority to act for another. ● *verb* (**-ting**) instruct (delegate) how to act or vote.

mandatory /ˈmændətərɪ/ *adjective* compulsory; of or conveying a command.

mandible /ˈmændɪb(ə)l/ *noun* jaw, esp. lower one; either part of bird's beak; either half of crushing organ in mouthparts of insect etc.

mandolin /mændəˈlɪn/ *noun* kind of lute with paired metal strings plucked with a plectrum.

mandrake /ˈmændreɪk/ *noun* narcotic plant with forked root.

mandrill /ˈmændrɪl/ *noun* large W. African baboon.

mane *noun* long hair on horse's or lion's neck; *colloquial* person's long hair.

manège /mæˈneɪʒ/ *noun* riding-school; movements of trained horse; horsemanship.

maneuver *US* = MANOEUVRE.

manful *adjective* brave, resolute. □ **manfully** *adverb*.

manganese /ˈmæŋɡəniːz/ *noun* grey brittle metallic element; black oxide of this.

mange /meɪndʒ/ *noun* skin disease of dogs etc.

mangel-wurzel /ˈmæŋɡ(ə)l wɜːz(ə)l/ *noun* large beet used as cattle food.

manger /ˈmeɪndʒə/ *noun* eating-trough in stable.

mangle[1] /ˈmæŋɡ(ə)l/ *verb* (**-ling**) hack, cut about; mutilate, spoil.

mangle[2] /ˈmæŋɡ(ə)l/ ● *noun* machine with rollers for pressing water out of washed clothes. ● *verb* (**-ling**) put through mangle.

mango /ˈmæŋɡəʊ/ *noun* (*plural* **-es** or **-s**) tropical fruit with yellowish flesh; tree bearing it.

mangold /ˈmæŋɡ(ə)ld/ *noun* mangelwurzel.

mangrove /ˈmæŋɡrəʊv/ *noun* tropical seashore tree with many tangled roots above ground.

mangy /ˈmeɪndʒɪ/ *adjective* (**-ier**, **-iest**) having mange; squalid, shabby.

manhandle *verb* (**-ling**) *colloquial* handle roughly; move by human effort.

manhood *noun* state of being a man; manliness; a man's sexual potency; men of a country.

mania /ˈmeɪnɪə/ *noun* mental illness marked by excitement and violence;

(often + *for*) excessive enthusiasm, obsession.

maniac /ˈmeɪniæk/ ● *noun colloquial* person behaving wildly; *colloquial* obsessive enthusiast; person suffering from mania. ● *adjective* of or behaving like maniac. □ **maniacal** /məˈnaɪək(ə)l/ *adjective*.

manic /ˈmænɪk/ *adjective* of or affected by mania. □ **manic-depressive** *adjective* relating to mental disorder with alternating periods of elation and depression, *noun* person having such disorder.

manicure /ˈmænɪkjʊə/ ● *noun* cosmetic treatment of the hands. ● *verb* (**-ring**) give manicure to. □ **manicurist** *noun*.

manifest /ˈmænɪfest/ ● *adjective* clear to sight or mind; indubitable. ● *verb* make manifest; (**manifest itself**) reveal itself. ● *noun* cargo or passenger list. □ **manifestation** *noun*; **manifestly** *adverb*.

manifesto /mænɪˈfestəʊ/ *noun* (*plural* **-s**) declaration of policies.

manifold /ˈmænɪfəʊld/ ● *adjective* many and various; having various forms, applications, parts, etc. ● *noun* manifold thing; pipe etc. with several outlets.

manikin /ˈmænɪkɪn/ *noun* little man, dwarf.

Manila /məˈnɪlə/ *noun* strong fibre of Philippine tree; (also **manila**) strong brown paper made of this.

manipulate /məˈnɪpjʊleɪt/ *verb* (**-ting**) handle, esp. with skill; manage to one's own advantage, esp. unfairly. □ **manipulation** *noun*; **manipulator** *noun*.

manipulative /məˈnɪpjʊlətɪv/ *adjective* tending to exploit a situation, person, etc., for one's own ends.

mankind *noun* human species.

manly *adjective* (**-ier, -iest**) having qualities associated with or befitting a man. □ **manliness** *noun*.

manna /ˈmænə/ *noun* food miraculously supplied to Israelites in wilderness.

mannequin /ˈmænɪkɪn/ *noun* fashion model; dummy for display of clothes.

manner /ˈmænə/ *noun* way thing is done or happens; (in *plural*) social behaviour; style; (in *plural*) polite behaviour; outward bearing, way of speaking, etc.; kind, sort.

mannered *adjective* behaving in specified way; showing mannerisms.

mannerism *noun* distinctive gesture or feature of style; excessive use of these in art etc.

mannerly *adjective* well-behaved, polite.

mannish *adjective* (of woman) masculine in appearance or manner; characteristic of man as opposed to woman.

manoeuvre /məˈnuːvə/ (*US* **maneuver**) ● *noun* planned movement of vehicle or troops; (in *plural*) large-scale exercise of troops etc.; agile or skilful movement; artful plan. ● *verb* (**-ring**) move (thing, esp. vehicle) carefully; perform or cause to perform manoeuvres; manipulate by scheming or adroitness; use artifice. □ **manoeuvrable** *adjective*.

manor /ˈmænə/ *noun* large country house with lands; *historical* feudal lordship over lands. □ **manorial** /məˈnɔːrɪəl/ *adjective*.

mansard /ˈmænsɑːd/ *noun* roof with 4 sloping sides, each of which becomes steeper halfway down.

manse /mæns/ *noun* (esp. Scottish Presbyterian) minister's house.

mansion /ˈmænʃ(ə)n/ *noun* large grand house; (in *plural*) block of flats.

manslaughter *noun* unintentional but not accidental unlawful killing of human being.

mantel /ˈmænt(ə)l/ *noun* mantelpiece, mantelshelf. □ **mantelpiece** structure above and around fireplace, mantelshelf; **mantelshelf** shelf above fireplace.

mantilla /mænˈtɪlə/ *noun* Spanish woman's lace scarf worn over head and shoulders.

mantis /ˈmæntɪs/ *noun* (*plural* same or **mantises**) kind of predatory insect.

mantle /ˈmænt(ə)l/ ● *noun* loose sleeveless cloak; covering; fragile tube round gas jet to give incandescent light. ● *verb* (**-ling**) clothe; conceal, envelop.

manual /ˈmænjʊəl/ ● *adjective* of or done with hands. ● *noun* reference book; organ keyboard played with hands, not feet. □ **manually** *adverb*.

manufacture /mænjʊˈfæktʃə/ ● *noun* making of articles, esp. in factory etc.; branch of industry. ● *verb* (**-ring**) make, esp. on industrial scale; invent, fabricate. □ **manufacturer** noun.

manure /məˈnjʊə/ ● noun fertilizer, esp. dung. ● verb (**-ring**) treat with manure.

manuscript /ˈmænjʊskrɪpt/ ● noun book or document written by hand or typed, not printed. ● adjective written by hand.

Manx ● adjective of Isle of Man. ● noun Celtic language of Isle of Man. □ **Manx cat** tailless variety.

many /ˈmenɪ/ ● adjective (**more, most**) numerous, great in number. ● noun (treated as plural) many people or things; (**the many**) the majority of people.

Maori /ˈmaʊrɪ/ ● noun (plural same or **-s**) member of aboriginal NZ race; their language. ● adjective of this people.

map ● noun flat representation of (part of) earth's surface, or of sky; diagram. ● verb (**-pp-**) represent on map. □ **map out** plan in detail.

maple /ˈmeɪp(ə)l/ noun kind of tree. □ **maple leaf** emblem of Canada; **maple sugar** sugar got by evaporating sap of some kinds of maple; **maple syrup** syrup got from maple sap or maple sugar.

maquette /mæˈket/ noun preliminary model or sketch.

Mar. abbreviation March.

mar verb (**-rr-**) spoil; disfigure.

marabou /ˈmærəbuː/ noun (plural **-s**) large W. African stork; its down as trimming etc.

maraca /məˈrækə/ noun clublike bean-filled gourd etc., shaken as percussion instrument.

maraschino /mærəˈskiːnəʊ/ noun (plural **-s**) liqueur made from cherries. □ **maraschino cherry** one preserved in maraschino.

marathon /ˈmærəθ(ə)n/ noun long-distance foot race; long-lasting, esp. difficult, undertaking.

maraud /məˈrɔːd/ verb make raid; pillage. □ **marauder** noun.

marble /ˈmɑːb(ə)l/ ● noun kind of limestone used in sculpture and architecture; anything of or like marble; small ball of glass etc. as toy; (in plural, treated as singular) game played with these; (in plural) slang one's mental faculties; (in

plural) collection of sculptures. ● verb (**-ling**) (esp. as **marbled** adjective) give veined or mottled appearance to (esp. paper).

marcasite /ˈmɑːkəsaɪt/ noun crystalline iron sulphide; crystals of this used in jewellery.

March noun third month of year. □ **March hare** hare in breeding season.

march[1] ● verb walk in military manner or with regular paces; proceed steadily; cause to march or walk. ● noun act of marching; uniform military step; long difficult walk; procession as demonstration; progress; piece of music suitable for marching to. □ **march past** ceremonial march of troops past saluting point. □ **marcher** noun.

march[2] noun historical boundary (often in plural); tract of (often disputed) land between countries etc.

marchioness /mɑːʃəˈnes/ noun marquess's wife or widow; woman holding rank of marquess.

mare /meə/ noun female equine animal, esp. horse. □ **mare's nest** illusory discovery.

margarine /mɑːdʒəˈriːn/ noun butter substitute made from edible oils etc.

marge /mɑːdʒ/ noun colloquial margarine.

margin /ˈmɑːdʒɪn/ noun edge or border of surface; plain space round printed page etc.; amount by which thing exceeds, falls short, etc. □ **margin of error** allowance for miscalculation or mischance.

marginal adjective written in margin; of or at edge; (of constituency) having elected MP with small majority; close to limit, esp. of profitability; insignificant; barely adequate. □ **marginally** adverb.

marginalize verb (also **-ise**) (**-zing** or **-sing**) make or treat as insignificant. □ **marginalization** noun.

marguerite /mɑːɡəˈriːt/ noun ox-eye daisy.

marigold /ˈmærɪɡəʊld/ noun plant with golden or bright yellow flowers.

marijuana /mærɪˈhwɑːnə/ noun dried leaves etc. of hemp smoked as drug.

marimba /məˈrɪmbə/ noun African and Central American xylophone; orchestral instrument developed from this.

marina /məˈriːnə/ *noun* harbour for pleasure boats.

marinade /ˌmærɪˈneɪd/ ● *noun* mixture of wine, vinegar, oil, spices, etc., for soaking fish or meat. ● *verb* (**-ding**) soak in marinade.

marinate /ˈmærɪneɪt/ *verb* (**-ting**) marinade.

marine /məˈriːn/ ● *adjective* of, found in, or produced by, the sea; of shipping; for use at sea. ● *noun* member of corps trained to fight on land or sea; country's shipping, fleet, or navy.

mariner /ˈmærɪnə/ *noun* seaman.

marionette /ˌmærɪəˈnet/ *noun* puppet worked with strings.

marital /ˈmærɪt(ə)l/ *adjective* of or between husband and wife; of marriage.

maritime /ˈmærɪtaɪm/ *adjective* connected with the sea or seafaring; living or found near the sea.

marjoram /ˈmɑːdʒərəm/ *noun* aromatic herb used in cookery.

mark[1] ● *noun* visible sign left by person or thing; stain, scar, etc; written or printed symbol; number or letter denoting conduct or proficiency; (often + *of*) sign, indication; lasting effect; target, thing aimed at; line etc. serving to indicate position; (followed by numeral) particular design of piece of equipment. ● *verb* make mark on; distinguish with mark; correct and assess (student's work etc.); attach prize to; notice, observe; characterize; acknowledge, celebrate; indicate on map etc.; keep close to (opposing player) in games; (in *passive*) have natural marks. □ **mark down** reduce price of; **mark off** separate by boundary; **mark out** plan (course), destine, trace out (boundaries etc.); **mark time** march on spot without moving forward, await opportunity to advance; **mark-up** *verb* increase price of; **mark-up** *noun* amount added to price by retailer for profit.

mark[2] *noun* Deutschmark.

marked /mɑːkt/ *adjective* having a visible mark; clearly noticeable. □ **markedly** /-kɪdlɪ/ *adverb*.

marker *noun* thing that marks a position; person or thing that marks; pen with broad felt tip; scorer, esp. at billiards.

market /ˈmɑːkɪt/ ● *noun* gathering for sale of commodities, livestock, etc.; space for this; (often + *for*) demand for commodity etc.; place or group providing such demand; conditions for buying and selling; stock market. ● *verb* (**-t-**) offer for sale; *archaic* buy or sell goods in market. □ **market garden** place where vegetables are grown for market; **market-place** open space for market, commercial world; **market research** surveying of consumers' needs and preferences; **market town** town where market is held; **market value** value as saleable thing; **on the market** offered for sale. □ **marketing** *noun*.

marketable *adjective* able or fit to be sold.

marking *noun* (usually in *plural*) identification mark; colouring of fur, feathers, etc.

marksman /ˈmɑːksmən/ *noun* skilled shot, esp. with rifle. □ **marksmanship** *noun*.

marl *noun* soil composed of clay and lime, used as fertilizer.

marlinspike /ˈmɑːlɪnspaɪk/ *noun* pointed tool used to separate strands of rope or wire.

marmalade /ˈmɑːməleɪd/ *noun* preserve of oranges or other citrus fruit.

Marmite /ˈmɑːmaɪt/ *noun proprietary term* thick brown spread made from yeast and vegetable extract.

marmoreal /mɑːˈmɔːrɪəl/ *adjective* of or like marble.

marmoset /ˈmɑːməzet/ *noun* small bushy-tailed monkey.

marmot /ˈmɑːmət/ *noun* burrowing rodent with short bushy tail.

marocain /ˈmærəkeɪn/ *noun* fabric of ribbed crêpe.

maroon[1] /məˈruːn/ *adjective & noun* brownish-crimson.

maroon[2] /məˈruːn/ *verb* put and leave ashore on desolate island or coast; leave stranded.

marquee /mɑːˈkiː/ *noun* large tent.

marquess /ˈmɑːkwəs/ *noun* British nobleman ranking between duke and earl.

marquetry /ˈmɑːkɪtrɪ/ *noun* inlaid work in wood etc.

marquis /'mɑ:kwɪs/ *noun* (*plural* **-quises**) foreign nobleman ranking between duke and count.

marquise /mɑ:'ki:z/ *noun* marquis's wife or widow; woman holding rank of marquis.

marriage /'mærɪdʒ/ *noun* legal union of man and woman for the purpose of living together; act or ceremony establishing this; particular matrimonial union. □ **marriage certificate, lines** certificate stating that marriage has taken place; **marriage guidance** counselling of people with marital problems.

marriageable *adjective* free, ready, or fit for marriage.

marrow /'mærəʊ/ *noun* large fleshy gourd, cooked as vegetable; bone marrow. □ **marrowbone** bone containing edible marrow; **marrowfat** kind of large pea.

marry /'mærɪ/ *verb* (**-ies, -ied**) take, join, or give in marriage; enter into marriage; (+ *into*) become member of (family) by marriage; unite intimately.

Marsala /mɑ:'sɑ:lə/ *noun* dark sweet fortified wine.

Marseillaise /mɑ:seɪ'jeɪz/ *noun* French national anthem.

marsh *noun* low watery ground. □ **marsh gas** methane; **marsh mallow** shrubby herb; **marshmallow** soft sweet made from sugar, albumen, gelatin, etc. □ **marshy** *adjective* (**-ier, -iest**).

marshal /'mɑ:ʃ(ə)l/ ● *noun* (**Marshal**) high-ranking officer of state or in armed forces; officer arranging ceremonies, controlling procedure at races, etc. ● *verb* (**-ll-**) arrange in due order; conduct (person) ceremoniously. □ **marshalling yard** yard in which goods trains etc. are assembled.

marsupial /mɑ:'su:pɪəl/ ● *noun* mammal giving birth to underdeveloped young subsequently carried in pouch. ● *adjective* of or like a marsupial.

mart *noun* trade centre; auction-room; market.

Martello tower /mɑ:'teləʊ/ *noun* small circular coastal fort.

marten /'mɑ:tɪn/ *noun* weasel-like flesh-eating mammal with valuable fur; its fur.

martial /'mɑ:ʃ(ə)l/ *adjective* of warfare; warlike. □ **martial arts** fighting sports such as judo or karate; **martial law** military government with ordinary law suspended.

Martian /'mɑ:ʃ(ə)n/ ● *adjective* of planet Mars. ● *noun* hypothetical inhabitant of Mars.

martin /'mɑ:tɪn/ *noun* bird of swallow family.

martinet /mɑ:tɪ'net/ *noun* strict disciplinarian.

Martini /mɑ:'ti:nɪ/ *noun* (*plural* **-s**) proprietary term type of vermouth; cocktail of gin and vermouth.

martyr /'mɑ:tə/ ● *noun* person who undergoes death or suffering for great cause; (+ *to*) colloquial constant sufferer from. ● *verb* put to death as martyr; torment. □ **martyrdom** noun.

marvel /'mɑ:v(ə)l/ ● *noun* wonderful thing; (+ *of*) wonderful example of. ● *verb* (**-ll-**; US **-l-**) (+ *at, that*) feel surprise or wonder.

marvellous /'mɑ:vələs/ *adjective* (US **marvelous**) astonishing; excellent. □ **marvellously** *adverb*.

Marxism /'mɑ:ksɪz(ə)m/ *noun* doctrines of Marx, predicting common ownership of means of production. □ **Marxist** noun & adjective.

marzipan /'mɑ:zɪpæn/ *noun* paste of ground almonds, sugar, etc.

mascara /mæs'kɑ:rə/ *noun* cosmetic for darkening eyelashes.

mascot /'mæskɒt/ *noun* person, animal, or thing supposed to bring luck.

masculine /'mæskjʊlɪn/ *adjective* of men; manly; Grammar belonging to gender including words for most male people and animals. □ **masculinity** /-'lɪn-/ noun.

maser /'meɪzə/ *noun* device for amplifying or generating microwaves.

mash ● *noun* soft or confused mixture; mixture of boiled bran etc. fed to horses; colloquial mashed potatoes. ● *verb* crush (potatoes etc.) to pulp.

mask /mɑ:sk/ ● *noun* covering for all or part of face, worn as disguise or for protection, or by surgeon etc. to prevent infection of patient; respirator; likeness of person's face, esp. one made by taking mould from face; disguise.

● *verb* cover with mask; conceal; protect.

masochism /'mæsəkız(ə)m/ *noun* pleasure in suffering physical or mental pain, esp. as form of sexual perversion. □ **masochist** *noun*; **masochistic** /-'kıs-/ *adjective*.

mason /'meıs(ə)n/ *noun* person who builds with stone; **(Mason)** Freemason.

Masonic /mə'sɒnık/ *adjective* of Freemasons.

masonry /'meısənrı/ *noun* stonework; mason's work; **(Masonry)** Freemasonry.

masque /mɑːsk/ *noun* musical drama with mime, esp. in 16th & 17th c.

masquerade /mæskə'reıd/ ● *noun* false show, pretence; masked ball. ● *verb* **(-ding)** appear in disguise; assume false appearance.

mass[1] ● *noun* cohesive body of matter; dense aggregation; (in *singular* or *plural*, usually + *of*) large number or amount; (usually + *of*) unbroken expanse (of colour etc.); **(the mass)** the majority; **(the masses)** ordinary people; *Physics* quantity of matter body contains. ● *verb* gather into mass; assemble into one body. ● *adjective* of or relating to large numbers of people or things. □ **mass media** means of communication to large numbers of people; **mass production** mechanical production of large quantities of standardized article.

mass[2] *noun* (often **Mass**) Eucharist, esp. in RC Church; (musical setting of) liturgy used in this.

massacre /'mæsəkə/ ● *noun* general slaughter. ● *verb* **(-ring)** make massacre of.

massage /'mæsɑːʒ/ ● *noun* kneading and rubbing of muscles etc., usually with hands. ● *verb* **(-ging)** treat thus.

masseur /mæ'sɜː/ *noun* (*feminine* **masseuse** /mæ'sɜːz/) person who gives massage.

massif /'mæsiːf/ *noun* mountain heights forming compact group.

massive /'mæsıv/ *adjective* large and heavy or solid; unusually large or severe; substantial. □ **massively** *adverb*.

mast[1] /mɑːst/ *noun* upright to which ship's yards and sails are attached; tall

metal structure supporting radio or television aerial; flag-pole.

mast[2] /mɑːst/ *noun* fruit of beech, oak, etc., esp. as food for pigs.

mastectomy /mæ'stektəmı/ *noun* (*plural* **-ies**) surgical removal of a breast.

master /'mɑːstə/ ● *noun* person having control or ownership; ship's captain; male teacher; prevailing person; skilled workman; skilled practitioner; holder of university degree above bachelor's; revered teacher; great artist; *Chess etc.* player at international level; thing from which series of copies is made; **(Master)** *title prefixed to name of boy.* ● *adjective* commanding; main, principal; controlling others. ● *verb* overcome, conquer; acquire complete knowledge of. □ **master-key** one opening several different locks; **mastermind** *noun* person with outstanding intellect, *verb* plan and direct (enterprise); **Master of Ceremonies** person introducing speakers at banquet or entertainers at variety show; **masterpiece** outstanding piece of artistry, one's best work; **master-switch** switch controlling electricity etc. supply to entire system.

masterful *adjective* imperious, domineering; very skilful. □ **masterfully** *adverb*.

■ **Usage** *Masterful* is normally used of a person, whereas *masterly* is used of achievements, abilities, etc.

masterly *adjective* very skilful.

■ **Usage** See note at MASTERFUL.

mastery *noun* control, dominance; (often + *of*) comprehensive skill or knowledge.

mastic /'mæstık/ *noun* gum or resin from certain trees; such tree; waterproof filler and sealant.

masticate /'mæstıkeıt/ *verb* **(-ting)** chew. □ **mastication** *noun*.

mastiff /'mæstıf/ *noun* large strong kind of dog.

mastodon /'mæstədɒn/ *noun* (*plural* same or **-s**) extinct animal resembling elephant.

mastoid /'mæstɔıd/ ● *adjective* shaped like woman's breast. ● *noun* (in full **mastoid process**) conical prominence on temporal bone; (usually in *plural*) *colloquial* inflammation of mastoid.

masturbate /'mæstəbeɪt/ *verb* (**-ting**) produce sexual arousal (of) by manual stimulation of genitals. □ **masturbation** *noun*.

mat¹ ● *noun* piece of coarse fabric on floor, esp. for wiping shoes on; piece of material laid on table etc. to protect surface. ● *verb* (**-tt-**) (esp. as **matted** *adjective*) bring or come into thickly tangled state. □ **on the mat** *slang* being reprimanded.

mat² = MATT.

matador /'mætədɔː/ *noun* bullfighter whose task is to kill bull.

match¹ ● *noun* contest, game; person or thing equal to, exactly resembling, or corresponding to another; marriage; person viewed as marriage prospect. ● *verb* be equal, correspond; be or find match for; (+ *against, with*) place in conflict or competition with. □ **matchboard** tongued and grooved board fitting into others; **matchmaker** person who arranges marriages or schemes to bring couples together; **match point** state of game when one side needs only one point to win match; **match up** (often + *with*) fit to form whole, tally; **match up to** be equal to.

match² *noun* short thin piece of wood etc., tipped with substance that ignites when rubbed on rough or specially prepared surface. □ **matchbox** box for holding matches; **matchstick** stem of match; **matchwood** wood suitable for matches, minute splinters.

matchless *adjective* incomparable.

mate¹ ● *noun* companion, fellow worker; *colloquial form of address, esp. to another man*; each of a breeding pair, esp. of birds; *colloquial* partner in marriage; subordinate officer on merchant ship; assistant to worker. ● *verb* (**-ting**) come or bring together for breeding.

mate² *noun & verb* (**-ting**) checkmate.

material /mə'tɪərɪəl/ ● *noun* that from which thing is made; cloth, fabric; (in *plural*) things needed for activity; person or thing of specified kind or suitable for purpose; (in *singular* or *plural*) information etc. for book etc.; (in *singular* or *plural*) elements. ● *adjective* of matter; not spiritual; of bodily comfort etc.; important, relevant.

materialism *noun* greater interest in material possessions and comfort than in spiritual values; theory that nothing exists but matter. □ **materialist** *noun*; **materialistic** /-'lɪs-/ *adjective*.

materialize *verb* (also **-ise**) (**-zing** or **-sing**) become fact, happen; *colloquial* appear, be present; represent in or assume bodily form. □ **materialization** *noun*.

maternal /mə'tɜːn(ə)l/ *adjective* of or like a mother; motherly; related on mother's side.

maternity /mə'tɜːnɪtɪ/ ● *noun* motherhood; motherliness. ● *adjective* for women in pregnancy or childbirth.

matey *adjective* (also **maty**) (**-tier, -tiest**) familiar and friendly. □ **matily** *adverb*.

math *noun* US *colloquial* mathematics.

mathematics /mæθə'mætɪks/ *plural noun* (also treated as *singular*) science of space, number, and quantity. □ **mathematical** *adjective*; **mathematician** /-mə'tɪʃ(ə)n/ *noun*.

maths *noun colloquial* mathematics.

matinée /'mætɪneɪ/ *noun* (US **matinee**) theatrical etc. performance in afternoon. □ **matinée coat** baby's short coat.

matins /'mætɪnz/ *noun* (also **mattins**) morning prayer.

matriarch /'meɪtrɪɑːk/ *noun* female head of family or tribe. □ **matriarchal** /-'ɑːk(ə)l/ *adjective*.

matriarchy /'meɪtrɪɑːkɪ/ *noun* (*plural* **-ies**) female-dominated system of society.

matrices *plural* of MATRIX.

matricide /'meɪtrɪsaɪd/ *noun* killing of one's mother; person who does this.

matriculate /mə'trɪkjʊleɪt/ *verb* (**-ting**) admit (student) to university; be thus admitted. □ **matriculation** *noun*.

matrimony /'mætrɪmənɪ/ *noun* marriage. □ **matrimonial** /-'məʊnɪəl/ *adjective*.

matrix /'meɪtrɪks/ *noun* (*plural* **matrices** /-siːz/ or **-es**) mould in which thing is cast or shaped; place etc. in which thing is developed; rock in which gems etc. are embedded; *Mathematics* rectangular array of quantities treated as single quantity.

matron /'meɪtrən/ *noun* woman in charge of nursing in hospital; married, esp. staid, woman; woman nurse and housekeeper at school etc.

matronly *adjective* like a matron, esp. portly or staid.

matt *adjective* (also **mat**) dull, not shiny or glossy.

matter /'mætə/ ●*noun* physical substance; thing(s); material; (**the matter**; often + *with*) thing that is amiss; content as opposed to form, substance; affair, concern; purulent discharge. ●*verb* (often + *to*) be of importance. □ **a matter of** approximately, amounting to; **matter of course** natural or expected thing; **matter-of-fact** prosaic, unimaginative, unemotional; **no matter** (+ *when, how,* etc.) regardless of.

matting *noun* fabric for mats.

mattins = MATINS.

mattock /'mætək/ *noun* tool like pickaxe with adze and chisel edge as ends of head.

mattress /'mætrɪs/ *noun* fabric case filled with soft or firm material or springs, used on or as bed.

mature /mə'tʃʊə/ ●*adjective* (**-r, -st**) fully developed, ripe; adult; careful, considered; (of bill etc.) due for payment. ●*verb* (**-ring**) bring to or reach mature state. □ **maturity** *noun.*

matutinal /mætju:'taɪn(ə)l/ *adjective* of or in morning.

maty = MATEY.

maudlin /'mɔ:dlɪn/ *adjective* weakly sentimental.

maul /mɔ:l/ ●*verb* injure by clawing etc.; handle roughly; damage. ●*noun* Rugby loose scrum; brawl; heavy hammer.

maulstick /'mɔ:lstɪk/ *noun* stick held to support hand in painting.

maunder /'mɔ:ndə/ *verb* talk ramblingly.

Maundy /'mɔ:ndɪ/ *noun* distribution of **Maundy money**, silver coins minted for English sovereign to give to the poor on **Maundy Thursday**, Thursday before Easter.

mausoleum /mɔ:sə'li:əm/ *noun* magnificent tomb.

mauve /məʊv/ *adjective & noun* pale purple.

maverick /'mævərɪk/ *noun* unorthodox or independent-minded person; *US* unbranded calf etc.

maw *noun* stomach of animal.

mawkish /'mɔ:kɪʃ/ *adjective* feebly sentimental.

maxillary /mæk'sɪlərɪ/ *adjective* of the jaw.

maxim /'mæksɪm/ *noun* general truth or rule of conduct briefly expressed.

maxima *plural* of MAXIMUM.

maximal /'mæksɪm(ə)l/ *adjective* greatest possible in size, duration, etc.

maximize /'mæksɪmaɪz/ *verb* (also **-ise**) (**-zing** or **-sing**) make as large or great as possible. □ **maximization** *noun.*

■ **Usage** *Maximize* should not be used in standard English to mean 'to make as good as possible' or 'to make the most of'.

maximum /'mæksɪməm/ ●*noun* (*plural* **maxima**) highest possible amount, size, etc. ●*adjective* greatest in amount, size, etc.

May *noun* fifth month of year; (**may**) hawthorn, esp. in blossom. □ **May Day** 1 May as Spring festival or as international holiday in honour of workers; **mayfly** insect living briefly in spring as adult; **maypole** decorated pole danced round on May Day; **May queen** girl chosen to preside over May Day festivities.

may *auxiliary verb* (*3rd singular present* **may**; *past* **might** /maɪt/) *expressing possibility, permission, request, wish, etc.* □ **be that as it may** although that is possible.

■ **Usage** Both *can* and *may* are used for asking permission, as in *Can I move?* and *May I move?*, but *may* is better in formal English because *Can I move?* also means 'Am I physically able to move?'

maybe /'meɪbi:/ *adverb* perhaps.

mayday /'meɪdeɪ/ *noun* international radio distress signal.

mayhem /'meɪhem/ *noun* destruction, havoc.

mayonnaise /meɪə'neɪz/ *noun* creamy dressing of oil, egg yolk, vinegar, etc.; dish dressed with this.

mayor /meə/ *noun* head of corporation of city or borough; head of district council with status of borough. □ **mayoral** *adjective*.

mayoralty /'meərəltɪ/ *noun* (*plural* **-ies**) office of mayor; period of this.

mayoress /'meərɪs/ *noun* woman mayor; wife or consort of mayor.

maze *noun* network of paths and hedges designed as puzzle; labyrinth; confused network, mass, etc.

mazurka /mə'zɜːkə/ *noun* lively Polish dance in triple time; music for this.

MB *abbreviation* Bachelor of Medicine.

MBE *abbreviation* Member of the Order of the British Empire.

MC *abbreviation* Master of Ceremonies; Military Cross.

MCC *abbreviation* Marylebone Cricket Club.

MD *abbreviation* Doctor of Medicine; Managing Director.

me¹ /miː/ *pronoun used by speaker or writer to refer to himself or herself as object of verb; colloquial* I.

■ **Usage** Some people consider it correct to use only *It is I*, but this is very formal or old-fashioned in most situations, and *It is me* is normally quite acceptable. On the other hand, it is not standard English to say *Me and him went* rather than *He and I went*.

me² /miː/ *noun* (also **mi**) *Music* third note of scale in tonic sol-fa.

mead *noun* alcoholic drink of fermented honey and water.

meadow /'medəʊ/ *noun* piece of grassland, esp. used for hay; low ground, esp. near river. □ **meadowsweet** a fragrant flowering plant.

meagre /'miːgə/ *adjective* (*US* **meager**) scanty in amount or quality.

meal¹ *noun* occasion when food is eaten; the food eaten on one occasion. □ **meal-ticket** *colloquial* source of income.

meal² *noun* grain or pulse ground to powder.

mealy *adjective* (**-ier, -iest**) of, like, or containing meal. □ **mealy-mouthed** afraid to speak plainly.

mean¹ *verb* (*past & past participle* **meant** /ment/) have as one's purpose, design;

intend to convey or indicate; involve, portend; (of word) have as equivalent in same or another language; (+ *to*) be of specified significance to.

mean² *adjective* niggardly; not generous; ignoble; of low degree or poor quality; malicious; *US* vicious, aggressive. □ **meanness** *noun*.

mean³ ● *noun* condition, quality, or course of action equally far from two extremes; term midway between first and last terms of progression; quotient of the sum of several quantities and their number. ● *adjective* (of quantity) equally far from two extremes; calculated as mean.

meander /mɪ'ændə/ ● *verb* wander at random; wind about. ● *noun* (in *plural*) sinuous windings; circuitous journey.

meaning ● *noun* what is meant; significance. ● *adjective* expressive; significant. □ **meaningful** *adjective*; **meaningfully** *adverb*; **meaningless** *adjective*; **meaninglessness** *noun*.

means *plural noun* (often treated as *singular*) action, agent, device, or method producing result; money resources. □ **means test** inquiry into financial resources of applicant for assistance etc.

meantime ● *adverb* meanwhile. ● *noun* intervening period.

meanwhile *adverb* in the intervening time; at the same time.

measles /'miːz(ə)lz/ *plural noun* (also treated as *singular*) infectious viral disease with red rash.

measly /'miːzlɪ/ *adjective* (**-ier, -iest**) *colloquial* meagre, contemptible.

measure /'meʒə/ ● *noun* size or quantity found by measuring; system or unit of measuring; vessel, rod, tape, etc., for measuring; degree, extent; factor determining evaluation etc.; (usually in *plural*) suitable action; legislative enactment; prescribed extent or amount; poetic metre. ● *verb* (**-ring**) find size, quantity, proportions, etc. of by comparison with known standard; be of specified size; estimate by some criterion; (often + *off*) mark (line etc. of given length); (+ *out*) distribute in measured quantities; (+ *with, against*) bring into competition with. □ **measurable** *adjective*; **measurement** *noun*.

measured *adjective* rhythmical; (of language) carefully considered.

measureless *adjective* not measurable; infinite.

meat *noun* animal flesh as food; (often + *of*) chief part.

meaty *adjective* (**-ier, -iest**) full of meat; fleshy; of or like meat; substantial, satisfying.

Mecca /'mekə/ *noun* place one aspires to visit.

mechanic /mɪ'kænɪk/ *noun* person skilled in using or repairing machinery.

mechanical *adjective* of, working, or produced by, machines or mechanism; automatic; lacking originality; of mechanics as a science. □ **mechanically** *adverb*.

mechanics /mɪ'kænɪks/ *plural noun* (usually treated as *singular*) branch of applied mathematics dealing with motion; science of machinery; routine technical aspects of thing.

mechanism /'mekənɪz(ə)m/ *noun* structure or parts of machine; system of parts working together; process, method.

mechanize /'mekənaɪz/ *verb* (also **-ise**) (**-zing** or **-sing**) introduce machines in; make mechanical; equip with tanks, armoured cars, etc. □ **mechanization** *noun*.

medal /'med(ə)l/ *noun* commemorative metal disc etc., esp. awarded for military or sporting prowess.

medallion /mɪ'dæljən/ *noun* large medal; thing so shaped, e.g. portrait.

medallist /'medəlɪst/ *noun* (US **medalist**) winner of (specified) medal.

meddle /'med(ə)l/ *verb* (**-ling**) (often + *with, in*) interfere in others' concerns.

meddlesome *adjective* interfering.

media *plural* of MEDIUM.

■ **Usage** It is a mistake to use *media* with a singular verb, as in *The media is biased.*

mediaeval = MEDIEVAL.

median /'miːdɪən/ ● *adjective* situated in the middle. ● *noun* straight line from angle of triangle to middle of opposite side; middle value of series.

mediate /'miːdɪeɪt/ *verb* (**-ting**) act as go-between or peacemaker. □ **mediation** *noun*; **mediator** *noun*.

medical /'medɪk(ə)l/ ● *adjective* of medicine in general or as distinct from surgery. ● *noun* colloquial medical examination. □ **medical certificate** certificate of fitness or unfitness to work etc.; **medical examination** examination to determine person's physical fitness. □ **medically** *adverb*.

medicament /mɪ'dɪkəmənt/ *noun* substance used in curative treatment.

medicate /'medɪkeɪt/ *verb* (**-ting**) treat medically; impregnate with medicinal substance.

medication /medɪ'keɪʃ(ə)n/ *noun* medicinal drug; treatment using drugs.

medicinal /mə'dɪsɪn(ə)l/ *adjective* (of substance) healing.

medicine /'meds(ə)n/ *noun* science or practice of diagnosis, treatment, and prevention of disease, esp. as distinct from surgery; substance, esp. one taken by mouth, used in this. □ **medicine man** witch-doctor.

medieval /medɪ'iːv(ə)l/ *adjective* (also **mediaeval**) of Middle Ages.

mediocre /miːdɪ'əʊkə/ *adjective* indifferent in quality; second-rate.

mediocrity /miːdɪ'ɒkrɪtɪ/ *noun* (*plural* **-ies**) being mediocre; mediocre person.

meditate /'medɪteɪt/ *verb* (**-ting**) engage in (esp. religious) contemplation; plan mentally. □ **meditation** *noun*; **meditative** /-tətɪv/ *adjective*.

Mediterranean /medɪtə'reɪnɪən/ *adjective* of the sea between Europe and N. Africa, or the countries bordering on it.

medium /'miːdɪəm/ ● *noun* (*plural* **media** or **-s**) middle quality, degree, etc. between extremes; environment; means of communication; physical material or form used by artist, composer, etc.; (*plural* **-s**) person claiming to communicate with the dead. ● *adjective* between two qualities etc.; average, moderate. □ **medium-range** (of aircraft, missile, etc.) able to travel medium distance.

medlar /'medlə/ *noun* tree bearing fruit like apple, eaten when decayed; such fruit.

medley /'medlɪ/ *noun* (*plural* **-s**) varied mixture.

medulla /mɪ'dʌlə/ *noun* inner part of certain bodily organs; soft internal tissue of plants. □ **medulla oblongata** /ɒblɒŋ'gɑːtə/ lowest part of brainstem. □ **medullary** *adjective*.

meek *adjective* humble and submissive or gentle. □ **meekly** *adverb*; **meekness** *noun*.

meerschaum /'mɪəʃəm/ *noun* soft white clay-like substance; tobacco pipe with bowl made from this.

meet[1] ● *verb* (*past & past participle* **met**) encounter or (of two or more people) come together; be present at arrival of (person, train, etc.); come into contact (with); make acquaintance of; deal with (demand etc.); (often + *with*) experience, receive. ● *noun* assembly for a hunt; assembly for athletics.

meet[2] *adjective archaic* fitting, proper.

meeting *noun* coming together; assembly of esp. a society, committee, etc.; race meeting.

mega- *combining form* large; one million; *slang* extremely, very big.

megabyte /'megəbaɪt/ *noun* 2^{20} bytes (approx. 1,000,000) as unit of computer storage.

megalith /'megəlɪθ/ *noun* large stone, esp. prehistoric monument. □ **megalithic** /-'lɪθ-/ *adjective*.

megalomania /megələ'meɪnɪə/ *noun* mental disorder producing delusions of grandeur; passion for grandiose schemes. □ **megalomaniac** *adjective & noun*.

megaphone /'megəfəʊn/ *noun* large funnel-shaped device for amplifying voice.

megaton /'megətʌn/ *noun* unit of explosive power equal to that of 1,000,000 tons of TNT.

meiosis /maɪ'əʊsɪs/ *noun* (*plural* **meioses** /-siːz/) cell division resulting in gametes with half normal chromosome number; ironical understatement.

melamine /'meləmiːn/ *noun* crystalline compound producing resins; plastic made from this.

melancholia /melən'kəʊlɪə/ *noun* depression and anxiety.

melancholy /'melənkəlɪ/ ● *noun* pensive sadness; depression; tendency to this.

● *adjective* sad; depressing. □ **melancholic** /-'kɒl-/ *adjective*.

mêlée /'meleɪ/ *noun* (*US* **melee**) confused fight or scuffle; muddle.

mellifluous /mɪ'lɪfluəs/ *adjective* (of voice etc.) pleasing, musical.

mellow /'meləʊ/ ● *adjective* (of sound, colour, light, or flavour) soft and rich, free from harshness; (of character) gentle; mature; genial. ● *verb* make or become mellow.

melodic /mɪ'lɒdɪk/ *adjective* of melody; melodious.

melodious /mɪ'ləʊdɪəs/ *adjective* of, producing, or having melody; sweet-sounding. □ **melodiously** *adverb*.

melodrama /'melədrɑːmə/ *noun* sensational play etc. appealing blatantly to emotions; this type of drama. □ **melodramatic** /-drə'mæt-/ *adjective*.

melody /'melədɪ/ *noun* (*plural* **-ies**) arrangement of notes to make distinctive pattern; tune; principal part in harmonized music; tunefulness.

melon /'melən/ *noun* sweet fleshy fruit of various climbers of gourd family.

melt *verb* become liquid or change from solid to liquid by action of heat; dissolve; (as **molten** *adjective*) (esp. of metals etc.) liquefied by heat; soften, be softened; (usually + *into*) merge; (often + *away*) leave unobtrusively. □ **melt down** melt (esp. metal) for reuse, become liquid and lose structure; **melting point** temperature at which solid melts; **melting pot** place for mixing races, theories, etc.

member /'membə/ *noun* person etc. belonging to society, team, group, etc.; (**Member**) person elected to certain assemblies; part of larger structure; part or organ of body, esp. limb.

membership *noun* being a member; number or group of members.

membrane /'membreɪn/ *noun* pliable tissue connecting or lining organs in plants and animals; pliable sheet or skin. □ **membranous** /-brən-/ *adjective*.

memento /mɪ'mentəʊ/ *noun* (*plural* **-es** or **-s**) souvenir of person or event.

memo /'meməʊ/ *noun* (*plural* **-s**) *colloquial* memorandum.

memoir /'memwɑː/ noun historical account etc. written from personal knowledge or special sources; (in plural) autobiography.

memorable /'memərəb(ə)l/ adjective worth remembering; easily remembered. □ **memorably** adverb.

memorandum /memə'rændəm/ noun (plural **-da** or **-s**) note or record for future use; informal written message, esp. in business etc.

memorial /mɪ'mɔːrɪəl/ ● noun object etc. established in memory of person or event. ● adjective commemorative.

memoriam see IN MEMORIAM.

memorize /'meməraɪz/ verb (also **-ise**) (**-zing** or **-sing**) commit to memory.

memory /'meməri/ noun (plural **-ies**) faculty by which things are recalled to or kept in mind; store of things remembered; remembrance, esp. of person etc.; storage capacity of computer etc.; posthumous reputation.

memsahib /'memsɑːb/ noun historical European married woman in India.

men plural of MAN.

menace /'menɪs/ ● noun threat; dangerous thing or person; jocular nuisance. ● verb (**-cing**) threaten. □ **menacingly** adverb.

ménage /meɪ'nɑːʒ/ noun household.

menagerie /mɪ'nædʒəri/ noun small zoo.

mend ● verb restore to good condition; repair; regain health; improve. ● noun darn or repair in material etc. □ **on the mend** recovering, esp. in health.

mendacious /men'deɪʃəs/ adjective lying, untruthful. □ **mendacity** /-'dæs-/ noun (plural **-ies**).

mendicant /'mendɪkənt/ ● adjective begging; (of friar) living solely on alms. ● noun beggar; mendicant friar.

menfolk plural noun men, esp. men of family.

menhir /'menhɪə/ noun usually prehistoric monument of tall upright stone.

menial /'miːnɪəl/ ● adjective (of work) degrading, servile. ● noun domestic servant.

meningitis /menɪn'dʒaɪtɪs/ noun (esp. viral) infection and inflammation of membranes enclosing brain and spinal cord.

meniscus /mɪ'nɪskəs/ noun (plural **menisci** /-saɪ/) curved upper surface of liquid in tube; lens convex on one side and concave on the other.

menopause /'menəpɔːz/ noun ceasing of menstruation; period in woman's life when this occurs. □ **menopausal** /-'pɔːz(ə)l/ adjective.

menses /'mensiːz/ plural noun flow of menstrual blood etc.

menstrual /'menstruəl/ adjective of menstruation.

menstruate /'menstrueɪt/ verb (**-ting**) undergo menstruation.

menstruation noun discharge of blood etc. from uterus, usually at monthly intervals.

mensuration /mensjʊə'reɪʃ(ə)n/ noun measuring; measuring of lengths, areas, and volumes.

mental /'ment(ə)l/ adjective of, in, or done by mind; caring for mental patients; colloquial insane. □ **mental age** degree of mental development in terms of average age at which such development is attained; **mental deficiency** abnormally low intelligence; **mental patient** sufferer from mental illness. □ **mentally** adverb.

mentality /men'tælɪtɪ/ noun (plural **-ies**) mental character or disposition.

menthol /'menθɒl/ noun mint-tasting organic alcohol found in oil of peppermint etc., used as flavouring and to relieve local pain.

mention /'menʃ(ə)n/ ● verb refer to briefly or by name; disclose. ● noun reference, esp. by name.

mentor /'mentɔː/ noun experienced and trusted adviser.

menu /'menjuː/ noun (plural **-s**) list of dishes available in restaurant etc., or to be served at meal; Computing list of options displayed on VDU.

MEP abbreviation Member of European Parliament.

mercantile /'mɜːkəntaɪl/ adjective of trade, trading; commercial. □ **mercantile marine** merchant shipping.

mercenary /'mɜːsɪnəri/ ● adjective primarily concerned with or working for money etc. ● noun (plural **-ies**) hired soldier in foreign service.

mercer /'mɜːsə/ *noun* dealer in textile fabrics.

mercerize /'mɜːsəraɪz/ *verb* (also **-ise**) (**-zing** or **-sing**) treat (cotton) with caustic alkali to strengthen and make lustrous.

merchandise /'mɜːtʃəndaɪz/ ● *noun* goods for sale. ● *verb* (**-sing**) trade (in); promote (goods, ideas, etc.).

merchant /'mɜːtʃ(ə)nt/ *noun* wholesale trader, esp. with foreign countries; *esp.* US & Scottish retail trader. □ **merchant bank** bank dealing in commercial loans and finance; **merchantman** merchant ship; **merchant navy** nation's commercial shipping; **merchant ship** ship carrying merchandise.

merchantable *adjective* saleable.

merciful /'mɜːsɪfʊl/ *adjective* showing mercy. □ **mercifulness** *noun*.

mercifully *adverb* in a merciful way; fortunately.

merciless /'mɜːsɪləs/ *adjective* showing no mercy. □ **mercilessly** *adverb*.

mercurial /mɜːˈkjʊərɪəl/ *adjective* (of person) volatile; of or containing mercury.

mercury /'mɜːkjʊrɪ/ *noun* silvery heavy liquid metal used in barometers, thermometers, etc.; (**Mercury**) planet nearest to the sun. □ **mercuric** /-ˈkjʊər-/ *adjective*; **mercurous** *adjective*.

mercy /'mɜːsɪ/ *noun* (*plural* **-ies**) compassion towards defeated enemies or offenders or as quality; act of mercy; thing to be thankful for. □ **at the mercy of** in the power of; **mercy killing** killing done out of pity.

mere[1] /mɪə/ *adjective* (**-st**) being only what is specified. □ **merely** *adverb*.

mere[2] /mɪə/ *noun dialect or poetical* lake.

meretricious /merə'trɪʃəs/ *adjective* showily but falsely attractive.

merganser /mɜːˈɡænsə/ *noun* (*plural* same or **-s**) a diving duck.

merge *verb* (**-ging**) (often + *with*) combine, join or blend gradually; (+ *in*) (cause to) lose character and identity in (something else).

merger *noun* combining, esp. of two commercial companies etc. into one.

meridian /mə'rɪdɪən/ *noun* circle of constant longitude passing through given place and N. & S. Poles; corresponding line on map etc.

meridional /mə'rɪdɪən(ə)l/ *adjective* of or in the south (esp. of Europe); of a meridian.

meringue /mə'ræŋ/ *noun* sugar, whipped egg whites, etc. baked crisp; cake of this.

merino /mə'riːnəʊ/ *noun* (*plural* **-s**) variety of sheep with long fine wool; soft material, originally of merino wool; fine woollen yarn.

merit /'merɪt/ ● *noun* quality of deserving well; excellence, worth; (usually in *plural*) thing that entitles to reward or gratitude. ● *verb* (**-t-**) deserve.

meritocracy /merɪ'tɒkrəsɪ/ *noun* (*plural* **-ies**) government by those selected for merit; group selected in this way.

meritorious /merɪ'tɔːrɪəs/ *adjective* praiseworthy.

merlin /'mɜːlɪn/ *noun* kind of small falcon.

mermaid /'mɜːmeɪd/ *noun* legendary creature with woman's head and trunk and fish's tail.

merry /'merɪ/ *adjective* (**-ier, -iest**) joyous; full of laughter or gaiety; *colloquial* slightly drunk. □ **merry-go-round** fairground ride with revolving model horses, cars, etc.; **merrymaking** festivity. □ **merrily** *adverb*; **merriment** *noun*.

mésalliance /meɪˈzælɪɑ̃s/ *noun* marriage with social inferior. [French]

mescal /'meskæl/ *noun* peyote cactus. □ **mescal buttons** disc-shaped dried tops from mescal, esp. as intoxicant.

mescaline /'meskəlɪn/ *noun* (also **mescalin**) hallucinogenic alkaloid present in mescal buttons.

Mesdames, Mesdemoiselles *plural* of MADAME, MADEMOISELLE.

mesh ● *noun* network structure; each of open spaces in net, sieve, etc.; (in *plural*) network, snare. ● *verb* (often + *with*) (of teeth of wheel) be engaged; be harmonious; catch in net.

mesmerize /'mezməraɪz/ *verb* (also **-ise**) (**-zing** or **-sing**) hypnotize; fascinate. □ **mesmerism** *noun*.

meso- *combining form* middle, intermediate.

mesolithic /mezəʊ'lɪθɪk/ *adjective* of Stone Age between palaeolithic and neolithic periods.

meson /'miːzɒn/ *noun* elementary particle with mass between that of electron and proton.

Mesozoic /mesəʊ'zəʊɪk/ ● *adjective* of geological era marked by development of dinosaurs. ● *noun* this era.

mess ● *noun* dirty or untidy state; state of confusion or trouble; something spilt etc.; disagreeable concoction; soldiers etc. dining together; army dining-hall; meal taken there; domestic animal's excreta; *archaic* portion of liquid or pulpy food. ● *verb* (often + *up*) make mess of, dirty, muddle; *US* (+ *with*) interfere with; take one's meals; *colloquial* defecate. □ **make a mess of** bungle; **mess about, around** potter.

message /'mesɪdʒ/ *noun* communication sent by one person to another; exalted or spiritual communication.

messenger /'mesɪndʒə/ *noun* person who carries message(s).

Messiah /mɪ'saɪə/ *noun* promised deliverer of Jews; Jesus regarded as this. □ **Messianic** /mesɪ'ænɪk/ *adjective*.

Messieurs *plural of* MONSIEUR.

Messrs /'mesəz/ *plural of* MR.

messy *adjective* (**-ier, -iest**) untidy, dirty; causing or accompanied by a mess; difficult to deal with; awkward. □ **messily** *adverb*.

met *past & past participle of* MEET[1].

metabolism /mɪ'tæbəlɪz(ə)m/ *noun* all chemical processes in living organism producing energy and growth. □ **metabolic** /metə'bɒlɪk/ *adjective*.

metacarpus /metə'kɑːpəs/ *noun* (*plural* **-carpi** /-paɪ/) set of bones forming part of hand between wrist and fingers. □ **metacarpal** *adjective*.

metal /'met(ə)l/ ● *noun* any of class of mainly workable elements such as gold, silver, iron, or tin; alloy of any of these; (in *plural*) rails of railway; road-metal. ● *adjective* made of metal. ● *verb* (**-ll-**; *US* **-l-**) make or mend (road) with road-metal; cover or fit with metal.

metallic /mɪ'tælɪk/ *adjective* of or like metal(s); sounding like struck metal.

metallurgy /mɪ'tælədʒɪ/ *noun* science of metals and their application; extraction and purification of metals. □ **metallurgic** /metə'lɜːdʒɪk/ *adjective*; **metallurgical** /metə'lɜːdʒɪk(ə)l/ *adjective*; **metallurgist** *noun*.

metamorphic /metə'mɔːfɪk/ *adjective* of metamorphosis; (of rock) transformed naturally. □ **metamorphism** *noun*.

metamorphose /metə'mɔːfəʊz/ *verb* (**-sing**) (often + *to, into*) change in form or nature.

metamorphosis /metə'mɔːfəsɪs/ *noun* (*plural* **-phoses** /-siːz/) change of form, esp. from pupa to insect; change of character, conditions, etc.

metaphor /'metəfə:/ *noun* application of name or description to something to which it is not literally applicable (see panel). □ **metaphoric** /-'fɒr-/ *adjective*; **metaphorical** /-'fɒr-/ *adjective*; **metaphorically** /-'fɒr-/ *adverb*.

metaphysics /metə'fɪzɪks/ *plural noun* (usually treated as *singular*) philosophy dealing with nature of existence, truth, and knowledge. □ **metaphysical** *adjective*.

metatarsus /metə'tɑːsəs/ *noun* (*plural* **-tarsi** /-saɪ/) set of bones forming part of foot between ankle and toes. □ **metatarsal** *adjective*.

....

Metaphor

A metaphor is a figure of speech that goes further than a simile, either by saying that something is something else that it could not normally be called, e.g.

> *The moon was a ghostly galleon tossed upon cloudy seas.*
> *Stockholm, the Venice of the North*

or by suggesting that something appears, sounds, or behaves like something else, e.g.

> *burning ambition*   *blindingly obvious*
> *the long arm of the law*

....

mete *verb* (**-ting**) (usually + *out*) *literary* apportion, allot.

meteor /ˈmiːtɪə/ *noun* small solid body from outer space becoming incandescent when entering earth's atmosphere.

meteoric /miːtˈɒrɪk/ *adjective* rapid; dazzling; of meteors.

meteorite /ˈmiːtɪəraɪt/ *noun* fallen meteor; fragment of rock or metal from outer space.

meteorology /miːtɪəˈrɒlədʒɪ/ *noun* study of atmospheric phenomena, esp. for forecasting weather. □ **meteorological** /-rəˈlɒdʒ-/ *adjective*; **meteorologist** *noun*.

meter¹ /ˈmiːtə/ • *noun* instrument that measures or records, esp. gas, electricity, etc. used, distance travelled, etc.; parking meter. • *verb* measure or record by meter.

meter² *US* = METRE.

methane /ˈmiːθeɪn/ *noun* colourless odourless inflammable gaseous hydrocarbon, the main constituent of natural gas.

methanol /ˈmeθənɒl/ *noun* colourless inflammable organic liquid, used as solvent.

methinks /mɪˈθɪŋks/ *verb* (*past* **methought** /mɪˈθɔːt/) *archaic* it seems to me.

method /ˈmeθəd/ *noun* way of doing something; procedure; orderliness.

methodical /mɪˈθɒdɪk(ə)l/ *adjective* characterized by method or order. □ **methodically** *adverb*.

Methodist /ˈmeθədɪst/ • *noun* member of Protestant denomination originating in 18th-c. Wesleyan evangelistic movement. • *adjective* of Methodists or Methodism. □ **Methodism** *noun*.

methought *past* of METHINKS.

meths *noun colloquial* methylated spirit.

methyl /ˈmeθɪl/ *noun* hydrocarbon radical CH_3. □ **methyl alcohol** methanol.

methylate /ˈmeθɪleɪt/ *verb* (**-ting**) mix or impregnate with methanol; introduce methyl group into (molecule).

meticulous /məˈtɪkjʊləs/ *adjective* giving great attention to detail; very careful and precise. □ **meticulously** *adverb*.

métier /ˈmetjeɪ/ *noun* one's trade, profession, or field of activity; one's forte. [French]

metonymy /mɪˈtɒnɪmɪ/ *noun* substitution of name of attribute for that of thing meant.

metre /ˈmiːtə/ *noun* (*US* **meter**) SI unit of length (about 39.4 in.); any form of poetic rhythm; basic rhythm of music.

metric /ˈmetrɪk/ *adjective* of or based on the metre. □ **metric system** decimal measuring system with metre, litre, and gram or kilogram as units of length, volume, and mass; **metric ton** 1,000 kg.

metrical *adjective* of or composed in metre; of or involving measurement. □ **metrically** *adverb*.

metronome /ˈmetrənəʊm/ *noun* device ticking at selected rate to mark musical time.

metropolis /mɪˈtrɒpəlɪs/ *noun* chief city, capital.

metropolitan /metrəˈpɒlɪt(ə)n/ • *adjective* of metropolis; of mother country as distinct from colonies. • *noun* bishop with authority over bishops of province.

mettle /ˈmet(ə)l/ *noun* quality or strength of character; spirit, courage. □ **mettlesome** *adjective*.

mew¹ • *noun* cat's cry. • *verb* utter this sound.

mew² *noun* gull, esp. common gull.

mews /mjuːz/ *noun* (treated as *singular*) stabling round yard etc., now used esp. for housing.

mezzanine /ˈmetsəniːn/ *noun* storey between two others (usually ground and first floors).

mezzo /ˈmetsəʊ/ *Music* • *adverb* moderately. • *noun* (in full **mezzo-soprano**) (*plural* **-s**) female singing voice between soprano and contralto, singer with this voice. □ **mezzo forte** fairly loud(ly); **mezzo piano** fairly soft(ly).

mezzotint /ˈmetsəʊtɪnt/ *noun* method of copper or steel engraving; print so produced.

mf *abbreviation* mezzo forte.

mg *abbreviation* milligram(s).

Mgr. *abbreviation* Manager; *Monseigneur*; Monsignor.

MHz *abbreviation* megahertz.

mi = ME².

miaow /mɪˈaʊ/ • *noun* characteristic cry of cat. • *verb* make this cry.

miasma /mɪˈæzmə/ *noun* (*plural* **-mata** or **-s**) *archaic* infectious or noxious vapour.

mica /ˈmaɪkə/ *noun* silicate mineral found as glittering scales in granite etc. or crystals separable into thin plates.

mice *plural of* MOUSE.

Michaelmas /ˈmɪkəlməs/ *noun* feast of St Michael, 29 Sept. □ **Michaelmas daisy** autumn-flowering aster.

mickey /ˈmɪkɪ/ *noun* (also **micky**) □ **take the mickey** (often + *out of*) *slang* tease, mock.

micro /ˈmaɪkrəʊ/ *noun* (*plural* **-s**) *colloquial* microcomputer; microprocessor.

micro- *combining form* small; one-millionth.

microbe /ˈmaɪkrəʊb/ *noun* micro-organism (esp. bacterium) causing disease or fermentation. □ **microbial** /-ˈkrəʊb-/ *adjective*.

microbiology /maɪkrəʊbaɪˈɒlədʒɪ/ *noun* study of micro-organisms. □ **microbiologist** *noun*.

microchip /ˈmaɪkrəʊtʃɪp/ *noun* small piece of semiconductor used to carry integrated circuits.

microcomputer /ˈmaɪkrəʊkəmpjuːtə/ *noun* small computer with microprocessor as central processor.

microcosm /ˈmaɪkrəkɒz(ə)m/ *noun* (often + *of*) miniature representation, e.g. humankind seen as small-scale model of universe; epitome. □ **microcosmic** /-ˈkɒz-/ *adjective*.

microdot /ˈmaɪkrəʊdɒt/ *noun* microphotograph of document etc. reduced to size of dot.

microfiche /ˈmaɪkrəʊfiːʃ/ *noun* small flat piece of film bearing microphotographs of documents etc.

microfilm /ˈmaɪkrəʊfɪlm/ • *noun* length of film bearing microphotographs of documents etc. • *verb* photograph on microfilm.

microlight /ˈmaɪkrəʊlaɪt/ *noun* kind of motorized hang-glider.

micrometer /maɪˈkrɒmɪtə/ *noun* gauge for accurate small-scale measurement.

micron /ˈmaɪkrɒn/ *noun* millionth of a metre.

micro-organism /maɪkrəʊˈɔːgənɪz(ə)m/ *noun* microscopic organism.

microphone /ˈmaɪkrəfəʊn/ *noun* instrument for converting sound waves into electrical energy for reconversion into sound.

microphotograph /maɪkrəʊˈfəʊtəɡrɑːf/ *noun* photograph reduced to very small size.

microprocessor /maɪkrəʊˈprəʊsesə/ *noun* data processor using integrated circuits contained on microchip(s).

microscope /ˈmaɪkrəskəʊp/ *noun* instrument with lenses for magnifying objects or details invisible to naked eye.

microscopic /maɪkrəˈskɒpɪk/ *adjective* visible only with microscope; extremely small; of the microscope. □ **microscopically** *adverb*.

microscopy /maɪˈkrɒskəpɪ/ *noun* use of microscopes.

microsurgery /ˈmaɪkrəʊsɜːdʒərɪ/ *noun* intricate surgery using microscopes.

microwave /ˈmaɪkrəʊweɪv/ • *noun* electromagnetic wave of length between 1 mm and 30 cm; (in full **microwave oven**) oven using microwaves to cook or heat food quickly. • *verb* (**-ving**) cook in microwave oven.

micturition /mɪktjʊəˈrɪʃ(ə)n/ *noun formal* urination.

mid- *combining form* middle of. □ **midday** middle of day, noon; **mid-life** middle age; **mid-off, -on** *Cricket* position of fielder near bowler on off or on side.

midden /ˈmɪd(ə)n/ *noun* dunghill; refuse heap.

middle /ˈmɪd(ə)l/ • *adjective* at equal distance, time, or number from extremities; central; intermediate in rank, quality, etc.; average. • *noun* (often + *of*) middle point, position, or part; waist. □ **in the middle of** in the process of; **middle age** period between youth and old age; **the Middle Ages** period of European history from *c.* 1000 to 1453; **middle class** *noun* social class between upper and lower, including professional and business workers; **middle-class** *adjective*; **the Middle East** countries from Egypt to Iran inclusive;

middleman trader who handles commodity between producer and consumer; **middleweight** amateur boxing weight (71–75 kg).

middling ● adjective moderately good. ● adverb fairly, moderately.

midge noun gnatlike insect.

midget /ˈmɪdʒɪt/ noun extremely small person or thing.

midland /ˈmɪdlənd/ ● noun (**the Midlands**) inland counties of central England; middle part of country. ● adjective of or in midland or Midlands.

midnight noun middle of night; 12 o'clock at night. □ **midnight sun** sun visible at midnight during summer in polar regions.

midriff /ˈmɪdrɪf/ noun front of body just above waist.

midshipman /ˈmɪdʃɪpmən/ noun naval officer ranking next above cadet.

midst noun middle. □ **in the midst of** among.

midsummer noun period of or near summer solstice, about 21 June. □ **Midsummer Day, Midsummer's Day** 24 June.

midwife /ˈmɪdwaɪf/ noun (plural -**wives**) person trained to assist at childbirth. □ **midwifery** /-ˈwɪfrɪ/ noun.

midwinter noun period of or near winter solstice, about 22 Dec.

mien /miːn/ noun literary person's look or bearing.

might[1] past of MAY.

might[2] /maɪt/ noun strength, power.

mightn't /ˈmaɪt(ə)nt/ might not.

mighty ● adjective (-**ier**, -**iest**) powerful, strong; massive. ● adverb colloquial very. □ **mightily** adverb.

mignonette /mɪnjəˈnet/ noun plant with fragrant grey-green flowers.

migraine /ˈmiːɡreɪn/ noun recurrent throbbing headache often with nausea and visual disturbance.

migrant /ˈmaɪɡrənt/ ● adjective migrating. ● noun migrant person or animal, esp. bird.

migrate /maɪˈɡreɪt/ verb (-**ting**) move from one place, esp. one country, to settle in another; (of bird etc.) change habitation seasonally. □ **migration** noun; **migratory** /ˈmaɪɡrətərɪ/ adjective.

mikado /mɪˈkɑːdəʊ/ noun (plural -**s**) historical emperor of Japan.

mike noun colloquial microphone.

milch adjective (of cow etc.) giving milk.

mild /maɪld/ adjective (esp. of person) gentle; not severe or harsh; (of weather) moderately warm; (of flavour) not sharp or strong. □ **mild steel** tough low-carbon steel. □ **mildly** adverb; **mildness** noun.

mildew /ˈmɪldjuː/ ● noun destructive growth of minute fungi on plants, damp paper, leather, etc. ● verb taint or be tainted with mildew.

mile noun unit of linear measure (1,760 yds, approx. 1.6 km); (in plural) colloquial great distance or amount; race extending over one mile. □ **milestone** stone beside road to mark distance in miles, significant point (in life, history, etc.).

mileage noun number of miles travelled; colloquial profit, advantage.

miler noun colloquial person or horse specializing in races of one mile.

milfoil /ˈmɪlfɔɪl/ noun common yarrow.

milieu /ˈmiːljɜː/ noun (plural -**x** or -**s** /-z/) person's environment or social surroundings.

militant /ˈmɪlɪt(ə)nt/ ● adjective combative; aggressively active in support of cause; engaged in warfare. ● noun militant person. □ **militancy** noun; **militantly** adverb.

militarism /ˈmɪlɪtərɪz(ə)m/ noun aggressively military policy etc.; military spirit. □ **militarist** noun; **militaristic** /-ˈrɪst-/ adjective.

military /ˈmɪlɪtərɪ/ ● adjective of or characteristic of soldiers or armed forces. ● noun (treated as singular or plural; **the military**) the army.

militate /ˈmɪlɪteɪt/ verb (-**ting**) (usually + against) have force or effect.

■ **Usage** Militate is often confused with mitigate, which means 'to make less intense or severe'.

militia /mɪˈlɪʃə/ noun military force, esp. one conscripted in emergency. □ **militiaman** noun.

milk ● noun opaque white fluid secreted by female mammals for nourishing young; milk of cows, goats, etc. as food;

milklike liquid of coconut etc. • *verb* draw milk from (cow etc.); exploit (person, situation). □ **milk chocolate** chocolate made with milk; **milk float** small usually electric vehicle used in delivering milk; **milkmaid** woman who milks cows or works in dairy; **milkman** person who sells or delivers milk; **milk run** routine expedition etc.; **milk shake** drink of whisked milk, flavouring, etc.; **milksop** weak or timid man or youth; **milk tooth** temporary tooth in young mammals.

milky *adjective* (**-ier**, **-iest**) of, like, or mixed with milk; (of gem or liquid) cloudy. □ **Milky Way** luminous band of stars, the Earth's galaxy.

mill • *noun* building fitted with mechanical device for grinding corn; such device; device for grinding any solid to powder; building fitted with machinery for manufacturing processes etc.; such machinery. • *verb* grind or treat in mill; (esp. as **milled** *adjective*) produce ribbed edge on (coin); (often + *about*, *round*) move aimlessly. □ **millpond** pond retained by dam for operating mill-wheel; **mill-race** current of water driving mill-wheel; **millstone** each of two circular stones for grinding corn, heavy burden, great responsibility; **mill-wheel** wheel used to drive water-mill.

millennium /mɪˈlenɪəm/ *noun* (*plural* **-s** or **millennia**) thousand-year period; (esp. future) period of happiness on earth. □ **millennial** *adjective*.

miller /ˈmɪlə/ *noun* person who owns or works mill, esp. corn-mill; person operating milling machine.

millesimal /mɪˈlesɪm(ə)l/ • *adjective* thousandth; of, belonging to, or dealing with, thousandth or thousandths. • *noun* thousandth part.

millet /ˈmɪlɪt/ *noun* cereal plant bearing small nutritious seeds; seed of this.

milli- *combining form* one-thousandth.

millibar /ˈmɪlɪbɑː/ *noun* unit of atmospheric pressure equivalent to 100 pascals.

milligram /ˈmɪlɪɡræm/ *noun* (also **-gramme**) one-thousandth of a gram.

millilitre /ˈmɪlɪliːtə/ *noun* (US **-liter**) one-thousandth of a litre (0.002 pint).

millimetre /ˈmɪlɪmiːtə/ *noun* (US **-meter**) one-thousandth of a metre.

milliner /ˈmɪlɪnə/ *noun* maker or seller of women's hats. □ **millinery** *noun*.

million /ˈmɪljən/ *noun* (*plural* same) one thousand thousand; (**millions**) *colloquial* very large number. □ **millionth** *adjective & noun*.

millionaire /mɪljəˈneə/ *noun* (*feminine* **millionairess**) person possessing over a million pounds, dollars, etc.

millipede /ˈmɪlɪpiːd/ *noun* (also **millepede**) small crawling invertebrate with many legs.

millisecond /ˈmɪlɪsekənd/ *noun* one-thousandth of a second.

milometer /maɪˈlɒmɪtə/ *noun* instrument for measuring number of miles travelled by vehicle.

milt *noun* spleen in mammals; reproductive gland or sperm of male fish.

mime • *noun* acting without words, using only gestures; performance using mime. • *verb* (**-ming**) express or represent by mime.

mimeograph /ˈmɪmɪəɡrɑːf/ • *noun* machine which duplicates from stencil; copy so produced. • *verb* reproduce in this way.

mimetic /mɪˈmetɪk/ *adjective* of or practising imitation or mimicry.

mimic /ˈmɪmɪk/ • *verb* (**-ck-**) imitate (person, gesture, etc.), esp. to entertain or ridicule; copy minutely or servilely; resemble closely. • *noun* person who mimics. □ **mimicry** *noun*.

mimosa /mɪˈməʊzə/ *noun* shrub with globular usually yellow flowers; acacia plant.

Min. *abbreviation* Minister; Ministry.

min. *abbreviation* minute(s); minimum; minim (fluid measure).

minaret /mɪnəˈret/ *noun* tall slender turret next to mosque, used by muezzin.

minatory /ˈmɪnətərɪ/ *adjective* *formal* threatening.

mince • *verb* (**-cing**) cut or grind (meat etc.) finely; (usually as **mincing** *adjective*) walk or speak in affected way. • *noun* minced meat. □ **mincemeat** mixture of currants, sugar, spices, suet, etc.; **mince pie** (usually small) pie containing mincemeat. □ **mincer** *noun*.

mind /maɪnd/ ● *noun* seat of consciousness, thought, volition, and feeling; attention, concentration; intellect; memory; opinion; sanity. ● *verb* object to; be upset; (often + *out*) heed, take care; look after; concern oneself with. □ **be in two minds** be undecided.

minded *adjective* (usually + *to do*) disposed, inclined. □ **-minded** inclined to think in specified way, or with specified interest.

minder *noun* person employed to look after person or thing; *slang* bodyguard.

mindful *adjective* (often + *of*) taking heed or care.

mindless *adjective* lacking intelligence; brutish; not requiring thought or skill. □ **mindlessly** *adverb;* **mindlessness** *noun.*

mine[1] *pronoun* the one(s) belonging to me.

mine[2] ● *noun* hole dug to extract metal, coal, salt, etc.; abundant source (of information etc.); *military* explosive device placed in ground or water. ● *verb* (**-ning**) obtain (minerals) from mine; (often + *for*) dig in (earth etc) for ore etc. or to tunnel; lay explosive mines under or in. □ **minefield** area planted with explosive mines; **minesweeper** ship for clearing explosive mines from sea. □ **mining** *noun.*

miner *noun* worker in mine.

mineral /ˈmɪnər(ə)l/ *noun* inorganic substance; substance obtained by mining; (often in *plural*) artificial mineral water or other carbonated drink. □ **mineral water** water naturally or artificially impregnated with dissolved salts.

mineralogy /mɪnəˈrælədʒɪ/ *noun* study of minerals. □ **mineralogical** /-rəˈlɒdʒ-/ *adjective;* **mineralogist** *noun.*

minestrone /mɪnɪˈstrəʊnɪ/ *noun* soup containing vegetables and pasta, beans, or rice.

mingle /ˈmɪŋɡ(ə)l/ *verb* (**-ling**) mix, blend.

mingy /ˈmɪndʒɪ/ *adjective* (**-ier, -iest**) *colloquial* stingy.

mini /ˈmɪnɪ/ *noun* (*plural* **-s**) *colloquial* miniskirt; (**Mini**) *proprietary term* make of small car.

mini- *combining form* miniature; small of its kind.

miniature /ˈmɪnɪtʃə/ ● *adjective* much smaller than normal; represented on small scale. ● *noun* miniature object; detailed small-scale portrait. □ **in miniature** on small scale.

miniaturist *noun* painter of miniatures.

miniaturize *verb* (also **-ise**) (**-zing** or **-sing**) produce in smaller version; make small. □ **miniaturization** *noun.*

minibus /ˈmɪnɪbʌs/ *noun* small bus for about 12 passengers.

minicab /ˈmɪnɪkæb/ *noun* car used as taxi, hireable only by telephone.

minim /ˈmɪnɪm/ *noun Music* note equal to two crotchets or half a semibreve; one-sixtieth of fluid drachm.

minimal /ˈmɪnɪm(ə)l/ *adjective* very minute or slight; being a minimum. □ **minimally** *adverb.*

minimize /ˈmɪnɪmaɪz/ *verb* (also **-ise**) (**-zing** or **-sing**) reduce to or estimate at minimum; estimate or represent at less than true value etc.

minimum /ˈmɪnɪməm/ ● *noun* (*plural* **minima**) least possible or attainable amount. ● *adjective* that is a minimum. □ **minimum wage** lowest wage permitted by law or agreement.

minion /ˈmɪnjən/ *noun derogatory* servile subordinate.

miniskirt /ˈmɪnɪskɜ:t/ *noun* very short skirt.

minister /ˈmɪnɪstə/ ● *noun* head of government department; member of clergy, esp. in Presbyterian and Nonconformist Churches; diplomat, usually ranking below ambassador. ● *verb* (usually + *to*) help, serve, look after. □ **ministerial** /-ˈstɪər-/ *adjective.*

ministration /mɪnɪˈstreɪʃ(ə)n/ *noun* (usually in *plural*) help, service; ministering, esp. in religious matters.

ministry /ˈmɪnɪstrɪ/ *noun* (*plural* **-ies**) government department headed by minister; building for this; (**the ministry**) profession of religious minister, ministers of government or religion.

mink *noun* (*plural* same or **-s**) small semiaquatic stoatlike animal; its fur; coat of this.

minke /ˈmɪŋkɪ/ *noun* small whale.

minnow /ˈmɪnəʊ/ *noun* (*plural* same or **-s**) small freshwater carp.

Minoan /mɪˈnəʊən/ ● *adjective* of Cretan Bronze Age civilization. ● *noun* person of this civilization.

minor /ˈmaɪnə/ ● *adjective* lesser or comparatively small in size or importance; *Music* (of scale) having semitone above second, fifth, and seventh notes; (of key) based on minor scale. ● *noun* person under full legal age; *US* student's subsidiary subject or course. ● *verb US* (+ *in*) study (subject) as subsidiary.

minority /maɪˈnɒrɪtɪ/ *noun* (*plural* -**ies**) (often + *of*) smaller number or part, esp. in politics; smaller group of people differing from larger in race, religion, language, etc.; being under full legal age; period of this.

minster /ˈmɪnstə/ *noun* large or important church; church of monastery.

minstrel /ˈmɪnstr(ə)l/ *noun* medieval singer or musician; musical entertainer with blacked face.

mint¹ *noun* aromatic herb used in cooking; peppermint; peppermint sweet. □ **minty** *adjective* (-**ier**, -**iest**).

mint² ● *noun* (esp. state) establishment where money is coined; *colloquial* vast sum. ● *verb* make (coin); invent (word, phrase, etc.).

minuet /mɪnjʊˈet/ *noun* slow stately dance in triple time; music for this.

minus /ˈmaɪnəs/ ● *preposition* with subtraction of; less than zero; *colloquial* lacking. ● *adjective Mathematics* negative. ● *noun* minus sign; negative quantity; *colloquial* disadvantage. □ **minus sign** symbol (−) indicating subtraction or negative value.

minuscule /ˈmɪnəskjuːl/ *adjective colloquial* extremely small or unimportant.

minute¹ /ˈmɪnɪt/ ● *noun* sixtieth part of hour; distance covered in minute; moment; sixtieth part of angular degree; (in *plural*) summary of proceedings of meeting; official memorandum. ● *verb* (-**ting**) record in minutes; send minutes to. □ **up to the minute** up to date.

minute² /maɪˈnjuːt/ *adjective* (-**est**) very small; accurate, detailed. □ **minutely** *adverb*.

minutiae /maɪˈnjuːʃɪ/ *plural noun* very small, precise, or minor details.

minx /mɪŋks/ *noun* pert, sly, or playful girl.

miracle /ˈmɪrək(ə)l/ *noun* extraordinary, supposedly supernatural, event; remarkable happening. □ **miracle play** medieval play on biblical themes.

miraculous /mɪˈrækjʊləs/ *adjective* being a miracle; supernatural; surprising. □ **miraculously** *adverb*.

mirage /ˈmɪrɑːʒ/ *noun* optical illusion caused by atmospheric conditions, esp. appearance of water in desert; illusory thing.

mire ● *noun* area of swampy ground; mud. ● *verb* (-**ring**) sink in mire; bespatter with mud. □ **miry** *adjective*.

mirror /ˈmɪrə/ ● *noun* polished surface, usually of coated glass, reflecting images; anything reflecting state of affairs etc. ● *verb* reflect in or as in mirror. □ **mirror image** identical image or reflection with left and right reversed.

mirth *noun* merriment, laughter. □ **mirthful** *adjective*.

misadventure /mɪsədˈventʃə/ *noun Law* accident without crime or negligence; bad luck.

misalliance /mɪsəˈlaɪəns/ *noun* unsuitable alliance, esp. marriage.

misanthrope /ˈmɪsənθrəʊp/ *noun* (also **misanthropist** /mɪˈsænθrəpɪst/) person who hates humankind. □ **misanthropic** /-ˈθrɒp-/ *adjective*.

misanthropy /mɪˈsænθrəpɪ/ *noun* condition or habits of misanthrope.

misapply /mɪsəˈplaɪ/ *verb* (-**ies**, -**ied**) apply (esp. funds) wrongly. □ **misapplication** /-æplɪˈkeɪ-/ *noun*.

misapprehend /mɪsæprɪˈhend/ *verb* misunderstand (words, person). □ **misapprehension** *noun*.

misappropriate /mɪsəˈprəʊprɪeɪt/ *verb* (-**ting**) take (another's money etc.) for one's own use; embezzle. □ **misappropriation** *noun*.

misbegotten /mɪsbɪˈgɒt(ə)n/ *adjective* illegitimate, bastard; contemptible.

misbehave /mɪsbɪˈheɪv/ *verb* (-**ving**) behave badly. □ **misbehaviour** *noun*.

miscalculate /mɪsˈkælkjʊleɪt/ *verb* (-**ting**) calculate wrongly. □ **miscalculation** *noun*.

miscarriage /ˈmɪskærɪdʒ/ *noun* spontaneous abortion. □ **miscarriage of justice** failure of judicial system.

miscarry /mɪsˈkærɪ/ *verb* (**-ies**, **-ied**) (of woman) have miscarriage; (of plan etc.) fail.

miscast /mɪsˈkɑːst/ *verb* (*past & past participle* **-cast**) allot unsuitable part to (actor) or unsuitable actors to (play etc.).

miscegenation /mɪsɪdʒɪˈneɪʃ(ə)n/ *noun* interbreeding of races.

miscellaneous /mɪsəˈleɪnɪəs/ *adjective* of mixed composition or character; (+ *plural noun*) of various kinds. □ **miscellaneously** *adverb*.

miscellany /mɪˈselənɪ/ *noun* (*plural* **-ies**) mixture, medley.

mischance /mɪsˈtʃɑːns/ *noun* bad luck; instance of this.

mischief /ˈmɪstʃɪf/ *noun* troublesome, but not malicious, conduct, esp. of children; playfulness; malice; harm, injury. □ **mischievous** /ˈmɪstʃɪvəs/ *adjective*; **mischievously** /ˈmɪstʃɪvəslɪ/ *adverb*.

misconceive /mɪskənˈsiːv/ *verb* (**-ving**) (often + *of*) have wrong idea or conception; (as **misconceived** *adjective*) badly organized etc. □ **misconception** /-ˈsep-/ *noun*.

misconduct /mɪsˈkɒndʌkt/ *noun* improper or unprofessional conduct.

misconstrue /mɪskənˈstruː/ *verb* (**-strues**, **-strued**, **-struing**) interpret wrongly. □ **misconstruction** /-ˈstrʌk-/ *noun*.

miscount /mɪsˈkaʊnt/ ● *verb* count inaccurately. ● *noun* inaccurate count.

miscreant /ˈmɪskrɪənt/ *noun* vile wretch, villain.

misdeed /mɪsˈdiːd/ *noun* evil deed, wrongdoing.

misdemeanour /mɪsdɪˈmiːnə/ *noun* (*US* **misdemeanor**) misdeed; *historical* indictable offence less serious than felony.

misdirect /mɪsdaɪˈrekt/ *verb* direct wrongly. □ **misdirection** *noun*.

miser /ˈmaɪzə/ *noun* person who hoards wealth and lives miserably. □ **miserly** *adjective*.

miserable /ˈmɪzərəb(ə)l/ *adjective* wretchedly unhappy or uncomfortable; contemptible, mean; causing discomfort. □ **miserably** *adverb*.

misericord /mɪˈzerɪkɔːd/ *noun* projection under hinged choir stall seat to support person standing.

misery /ˈmɪzərɪ/ *noun* (*plural* **-ies**) condition or feeling of wretchedness; cause of this; *colloquial* constantly grumbling person.

misfire /mɪsˈfaɪə/ ● *verb* (**-ring**) (of gun, motor engine, etc.) fail to go off, start, or function smoothly; (of plan etc.) fail to be effective. ● *noun* such failure.

misfit /ˈmɪsfɪt/ *noun* person unsuited to surroundings, occupation, etc.; garment etc. that does not fit.

misfortune /mɪsˈfɔːtʃ(ə)n/ *noun* bad luck; instance of this.

misgiving *noun* (usually in *plural*) feeling of mistrust or apprehension.

misgovern /mɪsˈɡʌv(ə)n/ *verb* govern badly. □ **misgovernment** *noun*.

misguided /mɪsˈɡaɪdɪd/ *adjective* mistaken in thought or action. □ **misguidedly** *adverb*.

mishandle /mɪsˈhænd(ə)l/ *verb* (**-ling**) deal with incorrectly or inefficiently; handle roughly.

mishap /ˈmɪshæp/ *noun* unlucky accident.

mishear /mɪsˈhɪə/ *verb* (*past & past participle* **-heard** /-ˈhɜːd/) hear incorrectly or imperfectly.

mishmash /ˈmɪʃmæʃ/ *noun* confused mixture.

misinform /mɪsɪnˈfɔːm/ *verb* give wrong information to, mislead. □ **misinformation** /-fəˈm-/ *noun*.

misinterpret /mɪsɪnˈtɜːprɪt/ *verb* (**-t-**) interpret wrongly. □ **misinterpretation** *noun*.

misjudge /mɪsˈdʒʌdʒ/ *verb* (**-ging**) judge wrongly. □ **misjudgement** *noun*.

mislay /mɪsˈleɪ/ *verb* (*past & past participle* **-laid**) accidentally put (thing) where it cannot readily be found.

mislead /mɪsˈliːd/ *verb* (*past & past participle* **-led**) cause to infer what is not true; deceive. □ **misleading** *adjective*.

mismanage /mɪsˈmænɪdʒ/ *verb* (**-ging**) manage badly or wrongly. □ **mismanagement** *noun*.

misnomer /mɪsˈnəʊmə/ *noun* wrongly used name or term.

misogyny /mɪˈsɒdʒɪnɪ/ *noun* hatred of women. □ **misogynist** *noun*.

misplace /mɪsˈpleɪs/ *verb* (**-cing**) put in wrong place; bestow (affections, confidence, etc.) on inappropriate object. □ **misplacement** *noun*.

misprint ● *noun* /ˈmɪsprɪnt/ printing error. ● *verb* /mɪsˈprɪnt/ print wrongly.

mispronounce /mɪsprəˈnaʊns/ *verb* (**-cing**) pronounce (word etc.) wrongly. □ **mispronunciation** /-nʌnsɪˈeɪ-/ *noun*.

misquote /mɪsˈkwəʊt/ *verb* (**-ting**) quote inaccurately. □ **misquotation** *noun*.

misread /mɪsˈriːd/ *verb* (*past & past participle* **-read** /-ˈred/) read or interpret wrongly.

misrepresent /mɪsreprɪˈzent/ *verb* represent wrongly; give false account of. □ **misrepresentation** *noun*.

misrule /mɪsˈruːl/ ● *noun* bad government. ● *verb* (**-ling**) govern badly.

Miss *noun* title of girl or unmarried woman.

miss ● *verb* fail to hit, reach, meet, find, catch, or perceive; fail to seize (opportunity etc.); regret absence of; avoid; (of engine etc.) misfire. ● *noun* failure. □ **give (thing) a miss** *colloquial* avoid; **miss out** omit.

missal /ˈmɪs(ə)l/ *noun* RC Church book of texts for Mass; book of prayers.

misshapen /mɪsˈʃeɪpən/ *adjective* deformed, distorted.

missile /ˈmɪsaɪl/ *noun* object, esp. weapon, suitable for throwing at target or discharging from machine; weapon directed by remote control or automatically.

missing *adjective* not in its place; lost; (of person) not traced but not known to be dead.

mission /ˈmɪʃ(ə)n/ *noun* task or goal assigned to person or group; journey undertaken as part of this; military or scientific expedition; group of people sent to conduct negotiations or to evangelize; missionary post.

missionary /ˈmɪʃənərɪ/ ● *adjective* of or concerned with religious missions, esp. abroad. ● *noun* (*plural* **-ies**) person doing missionary work.

missis = MISSUS.

missive /ˈmɪsɪv/ *noun* jocular letter; official letter.

misspell /mɪsˈspel/ *verb* (*past & past participle* **-spelt** or **-spelled**) spell wrongly.

misspend /mɪsˈspend/ *verb* (*past & past participle* **-spent**) (esp. as **misspent** *adjective*) spend wrongly or wastefully.

misstate /mɪsˈsteɪt/ *verb* (**-ting**) state wrongly or inaccurately. □ **misstatement** *noun*.

missus /ˈmɪsɪz/ *noun* (also **missis**) *colloquial or jocular form of address to woman*; (**the missis**) *colloquial* my or your wife.

mist ● *noun* water vapour in minute drops limiting visibility; condensed vapour obscuring glass etc.; dimness or blurring of sight caused by tears etc. ● *verb* cover or be covered (as) with mist.

mistake /mɪˈsteɪk/ ● *noun* incorrect idea or opinion; thing incorrectly done, thought, or judged. ● *verb* (**-king**; *past* **mistook** /-ˈstʊk/; *past participle* **mistaken**) misunderstand meaning of; (+ *for*) wrongly take (person, thing) for another.

mistaken /mɪˈsteɪkən/ *adjective* wrong in opinion or judgement; based on or resulting from error. □ **mistakenly** *adverb*.

mister /ˈmɪstə/ *noun colloquial or jocular form of address to man*.

mistime /mɪsˈtaɪm/ *verb* (**-ming**) say or do at wrong time.

mistle thrush /ˈmɪs(ə)l/ *noun* large thrush that eats mistletoe berries.

mistletoe /ˈmɪs(ə)ltəʊ/ *noun* parasitic white-berried plant.

mistook *past of* MISTAKE.

mistral /ˈmɪstr(ə)l/ *noun* cold N or NW wind in S. France.

mistreat /mɪsˈtriːt/ *verb* treat badly. □ **mistreatment** *noun*.

mistress /ˈmɪstrɪs/ *noun* female head of household; woman in authority; female owner of pet; female teacher; woman having illicit sexual relationship with (usually married) man.

mistrial /mɪsˈtraɪəl/ *noun* trial made invalid by error.

mistrust /mɪsˈtrʌst/ ● *verb* be suspicious of; feel no confidence in. ● *noun* suspicion; lack of confidence. □ **mistrustful** *adjective*; **mistrustfully** *adverb*.

misty *adjective* (**-ier**, **-iest**) of or covered with mist; dim in outline; obscure. □ **mistily** *adverb*.

misunderstand /mɪsʌndəˈstænd/ *verb* (*past & past participle* **-stood** /-ˈstʊd/) understand incorrectly; misinterpret

misuse | mock

words or actions of (person). □ **misunderstanding** noun.

misuse ● verb /mɪs'juːz/ (**-sing**) use wrongly; ill-treat. ● noun /mɪs'juːs/ wrong or improper use.

mite[1] noun small arachnid, esp. of kind found in cheese etc.

mite[2] noun small monetary unit; small object or child; modest contribution.

miter US = MITRE.

mitigate /'mɪtɪgeɪt/ verb (**-ting**) make less intense or severe. □ **mitigation** noun.

■ Usage Mitigate is often confused with militate, which means 'to have force or effect'.

mitre /'maɪtə/ (US **miter**) ● noun bishop's or abbot's tall deeply cleft headdress; joint of two pieces of wood at angle of 90°, such that line of junction bisects this angle. ● verb (**-ring**) bestow mitre on; join with mitre.

mitt noun (also **mitten**) glove with only one compartment for the 4 fingers and another for thumb; glove leaving fingers and thumb-tip bare; slang hand; baseball glove.

mix ● verb combine or put together (two or more substances or things) so that constituents of each are diffused among those of the other(s); prepare (compound, cocktail, etc.) by combining ingredients; combine (activities etc.); join, be mixed, combine; be compatible; be sociable; (+ *with*) be harmonious with; combine (two or more sound signals) into one. ● noun mixing, mixture; proportion of materials in mixture; ingredients prepared commercially for making cake, concrete, etc.

mixed /mɪkst/ adjective of diverse qualities or elements; containing people from various backgrounds, of both sexes, etc. □ **mixed marriage** marriage between people of different race or religion; **mixed-up** colloquial mentally or emotionally confused, socially ill-adjusted.

mixer noun machine for mixing foods etc.; person who manages socially in specified way; (usually soft) drink to be mixed with spirit; device combining separate signals from microphones etc.

mixture /'mɪkstʃə/ noun process or result of mixing; combination of ingredients, qualities, etc.

mizen-mast /'mɪz(ə)n/ noun mast next aft of mainmast.

ml abbreviation millilitre(s); mile(s).

Mlle abbreviation (plural **-s**) Mademoiselle.

MM abbreviation Messieurs; Military Medal.

mm abbreviation millimetre(s).

Mme abbreviation (plural **-s**) Madame.

mnemonic /nɪ'mɒnɪk/ ● adjective of or designed to aid memory. ● noun mnemonic word, verse, etc. □ **mnemonically** adverb.

MO abbreviation Medical Officer; money order.

mo /məʊ/ noun (plural **-s**) colloquial moment.

moan ● noun low murmur expressing physical or mental suffering or pleasure; colloquial complaint. ● verb make moan or moans; colloquial complain, grumble. □ **moaner** noun.

moat noun defensive ditch round castle etc., usually filled with water.

mob ● noun disorderly crowd; rabble; (**the mob**) usually derogatory the populace; colloquial gang, group. ● verb (**-bb-**) crowd round to attack or admire.

mob-cap noun historical woman's indoor cap covering all the hair.

mobile /'məʊbaɪl/ ● adjective movable; able to move easily; (of face etc.) readily changing expression; (of shop etc.) accommodated in vehicle to serve various places; (of person) able to change social status. ● noun decoration that may be hung so as to turn freely. □ **mobility** /məˈbɪl-/ noun.

mobilize /'məʊbɪlaɪz/ verb (also **-ise**) (**-zing** or **-sing**) make or become ready for (esp. military) service or action. □ **mobilization** noun.

mobster /'mɒbstə/ noun slang gangster.

moccasin /'mɒkəsɪn/ noun soft flat-soled shoe originally worn by N. American Indians.

mock ● verb (often + *at*) ridicule, scoff (at); treat with scorn or contempt; mimic contemptuously. ● adjective sham; imitation; as a trial run. □ **mock turtle soup** soup made from calf's head etc.; **mock-up** experimental model of proposed structure etc. □ **mockingly** adverb.

mockery noun (plural **-ies**) derision; counterfeit or absurdly inadequate representation; travesty.

mode noun way in which thing is done; prevailing fashion; Music any of several types of scale.

model /'mɒd(ə)l/ ● noun representation in 3 dimensions of existing person or thing or of proposed structure, esp. on smaller scale; simplified description of system etc.; clay, wax, etc. figure for reproduction in another material; particular design or style, esp. of car; exemplary person or thing; person employed to pose for artist or photographer, or to wear clothes etc. for display; (copy of) garment etc. by well-known designer. ● adjective exemplary; ideally perfect. ● verb (**-ll-**; US **-l-**) fashion or shape (figure) in clay, wax, etc.; (+ after, on, etc.) form (thing) in imitation of; act or pose as model; (of person acting as model) display (garment).

modem /'məʊdem/ noun device for sending and receiving computer data by means of telephone line.

moderate /'mɒdərət/ ● adjective avoiding extremes, temperate in conduct or expression; fairly large or good; (of wind) of medium strength; (of prices) fairly low. ● noun person of moderate views. ● verb /-reɪt/ (**-ting**) make or become less violent, intense, rigorous, etc.; act as moderator of or to. □ **moderately** /-rətlɪ/ adverb; **moderation** noun.

moderator noun arbitrator, mediator; presiding officer; Presbyterian minister presiding over ecclesiastical body.

modern /'mɒd(ə)n/ ● adjective of present and recent times; in current fashion, not antiquated. ● noun person living in modern times. □ **modernity** /mə'dɜːn-/ noun.

modernism noun modern ideas or methods, esp. in art. □ **modernist** noun & adjective.

modernize verb (also **-ise**) (**-zing** or **-sing**) make modern; adapt to modern needs or habits. □ **modernization** noun.

modest /'mɒdɪst/ adjective having humble or moderate estimate of one's own merits; bashful; decorous; not excessive; unpretentious, not extravagant. □ **modestly** adverb; **modesty** noun.

modicum /'mɒdɪkəm/ noun (+ of) small quantity.

modify /'mɒdɪfaɪ/ verb (**-ies**, **-ied**) make less severe; make partial changes in. □ **modification** noun.

modish /'məʊdɪʃ/ adjective fashionable. □ **modishly** adverb.

modulate /'mɒdjʊleɪt/ verb (**-ting**) regulate, adjust; moderate; adjust or vary tone or pitch of (speaking voice); alter amplitude or frequency of (wave) by using wave of lower frequency to convey signal; Music pass from one key to another. □ **modulation** noun.

module /'mɒdjuːl/ noun standardized part or independent unit in construction, esp. of furniture, building, spacecraft, or electronic system; unit or period of training or education. □ **modular** adjective.

modus operandi /məʊdəs ɒpə'rændɪ/ noun (plural **modi operandi** /məʊdɪ/) method of working. [Latin]

modus vivendi /məʊdəs vɪ'vendɪ/ noun (plural **modi vivendi** /məʊdɪ/) way of living or coping; compromise between people agreeing to differ. [Latin]

mog noun (also **moggie**) slang cat.

mogul /'məʊg(ə)l/ noun colloquial important or influential person.

mohair /'məʊheə/ noun hair of angora goat; yarn or fabric from this.

Mohammedan = MUHAMMADAN.

moiety /'mɔɪətɪ/ noun (plural **-ies**) half; each of two parts of thing.

moiré /'mwɑːreɪ/ adjective (of silk) watered; (of metal) having clouded appearance.

moist adjective slightly wet; damp. □ **moisten** verb.

moisture /'mɔɪstʃə/ noun water or other liquid diffused as vapour or within solid, or condensed on surface.

moisturize verb (also **-ise**) (**-zing** or **-sing**) make less dry (esp. skin by use of cosmetic). □ **moisturizer** noun.

molar /'məʊlə/ ● adjective (usually of mammal's back teeth) serving to grind. ● noun molar tooth.

molasses /mə'læsɪz/ *plural noun* (treated as *singular*) uncrystallized syrup extracted from raw sugar; *US* treacle.

mold *US* = MOULD[1,2,3].

molder *US* = MOULDER.

molding *US* = MOULDING.

moldy *US* = MOULDY.

mole[1] *noun* small burrowing animal with dark velvety fur and very small eyes; *slang* spy established in position of trust in organization. □ **molehill** small mound thrown up by mole in burrowing.

mole[2] *noun* small permanent dark spot on skin.

mole[3] *noun* massive structure as pier, breakwater, or causeway; artificial harbour.

mole[4] *noun* SI unit of amount of substance.

molecule /'mɒlɪkjuːl/ *noun* group of atoms forming smallest fundamental unit of chemical compound. □ **molecular** /mə'lekjʊlə/ *adjective*.

molest /mə'lest/ *verb* annoy or pester (person); attack or interfere with (person), esp. sexually. □ **molestation** *noun*; **molester** *noun*.

moll *noun slang* gangster's female companion; prostitute.

mollify /'mɒlɪfaɪ/ *verb* (**-ies**, **-ied**) soften, appease. □ **mollification** *noun*.

mollusc /'mɒləsk/ *noun* (*US* **mollusk**) invertebrate with soft body and usually hard shell, e.g. snail or oyster.

mollycoddle /'mɒlɪkɒd(ə)l/ *verb* (**-ling**) coddle, pamper.

molt *US* = MOULT.

molten /'məʊlt(ə)n/ *adjective* melted, esp. made liquid by heat.

molto /'mɒltəʊ/ *adverb Music* very.

molybdenum /mə'lɪbdɪnəm/ *noun* silver-white metallic element added to steel to give strength and resistance to corrosion.

moment /'məʊmənt/ *noun* very brief portion of time; exact point of time; importance; product of force and distance from its line of action to a point.

momentary *adjective* lasting only a moment; transitory. □ **momentarily** *adverb*.

momentous /mə'mentəs/ *adjective* very important.

momentum /mə'mentəm/ *noun* (*plural* **-ta**) quantity of motion of moving body, the product of its mass and velocity; impetus gained by movement or initial effort.

Mon. *abbreviation* Monday.

monarch /'mɒnək/ *noun* sovereign with title of king, queen, emperor, empress, or equivalent. □ **monarchic** /mə'naːk-/ *adjective*; **monarchical** /mə'naːk-/ *adjective*.

monarchist *noun* advocate of monarchy.

monarchy *noun* (*plural* **-ies**) government headed by monarch; state with this.

monastery /'mɒnəstrɪ/ *noun* (*plural* **-ies**) residence of community of monks.

monastic /mə'næstɪk/ *adjective* of or like monasteries or monks, nuns, etc. □ **monastically** *adverb*; **monasticism** /-sɪz(ə)m/ *noun*.

Monday /'mʌndeɪ/ *noun* day of week following Sunday.

monetarism /'mʌnɪtərɪz(ə)m/ *noun* control of supply of money as chief method of stabilizing economy. □ **monetarist** *adjective* & *noun*.

monetary /'mʌnɪtərɪ/ *adjective* of the currency in use; of or consisting of money.

money /'mʌnɪ/ *noun* (*plural* **-s** or **monies**) coins and banknotes as medium of exchange; (in *plural*) sums of money; wealth. □ **moneylender** person lending money at interest; **money market** trade in short-term stocks, loans, etc.; **money order** order for payment of specified sum, issued by bank or Post Office; **money-spinner** thing that brings in a profit.

moneyed /'mʌnɪd/ *adjective* rich.

Mongol /'mɒŋg(ə)l/ ● *adjective* of Asian people now inhabiting Mongolia; resembling this people. ● *noun* Mongolian.

Mongolian /mɒŋ'gəʊlɪən/ ● *noun* native, national, or language of Mongolia. ● *adjective* of or relating to Mongolia or its people or language.

Mongoloid /'mɒŋgəlɔɪd/ ● *adjective* characteristic of Mongolians, esp. in having broad flat yellowish face. ● *noun* Mongoloid person.

mongoose /'mɒŋguːs/ noun (plural **-s**) small flesh-eating civet-like mammal.

mongrel /'mʌŋɡr(ə)l/ ● noun dog of no definable type or breed; any animal or plant resulting from crossing of different breeds or types. ● adjective of mixed origin or character.

monies plural of MONEY.

monitor /'mɒnɪtə/ ● noun person or device for checking; school pupil with disciplinary etc. duties; television set used to select or verify picture being broadcast or to display computer data; person who listens to and reports on foreign broadcasts etc.; detector of radioactive contamination. ● verb act as monitor of; maintain regular surveillance over.

monk /mʌŋk/ noun member of religious community of men living under vows. □ **monkish** adjective.

monkey /'mʌŋkɪ/ ● noun (plural **-eys**) any of various primates, e.g. baboons, marmosets; mischievous person, esp. child. ● verb (**-eys, -eyed**) (often + with) play mischievous tricks. □ **monkey-nut** peanut; **monkey-puzzle** tree with hanging prickly branches; **monkey wrench** wrench with adjustable jaw.

monkshood /'mʌŋkshʊd/ noun poisonous plant with hood-shaped flowers.

mono /'mɒnəʊ/ colloquial ● adjective monophonic. ● noun monophonic reproduction.

mono- combining form (usually **mon-** before vowel) one, alone, single.

monochromatic /mɒnəkrə'mætɪk/ adjective (of light or other radiation) of single colour or wavelength; containing only one colour.

monochrome /'mɒnəkrəʊm/ ● noun photograph or picture in one colour, or in black and white only. ● adjective having or using one colour or black and white only.

monocle /'mɒnək(ə)l/ noun single eyeglass.

monocular /mə'nɒkjʊlə/ adjective with or for one eye.

monody /'mɒnədɪ/ noun (plural **-ies**) ode sung by one actor in Greek tragedy; poem lamenting person's death.

monogamy /mə'nɒɡəmɪ/ noun practice or state of being married to one person at a time. □ **monogamous** adjective.

monogram /'mɒnəɡræm/ noun two or more letters, esp. initials, interwoven.

monograph /'mɒnəɡrɑːf/ noun treatise on single subject.

monolith /'mɒnəlɪθ/ noun single block of stone, esp. shaped into pillar etc.; person or thing like monolith in being massive, immovable, or solidly uniform. □ **monolithic** /-'lɪθ-/ adjective.

monologue /'mɒnəlɒɡ/ noun scene in drama in which person speaks alone; dramatic composition for one performer; long speech by one person in conversation etc.

monomania /mɒnə'meɪnɪə/ noun obsession by single idea or interest. □ **monomaniac** noun & adjective.

monophonic /mɒnə'fɒnɪk/ adjective (of sound-reproduction) using only one channel of transmission.

monoplane /'mɒnəpleɪn/ noun aeroplane with one set of wings.

monopolist /mə'nɒpəlɪst/ noun person who has or advocates monopoly. □ **monopolistic** /-'lɪs-/ adjective.

monopolize /mə'nɒpəlaɪz/ verb (also **-ise**) (**-zing** or **-sing**) obtain exclusive possession or control of (trade etc.); dominate (conversation etc.). □ **monopolization** noun; **monopolizer** noun.

monopoly /mə'nɒpəlɪ/ noun (plural **-ies**) exclusive possession or control of trade in commodity or service; (+ of, US on) sole possession or control.

monorail /'mɒnəreɪl/ noun railway with single-rail track.

monosodium glutamate /mɒnəʊ-'səʊdɪəm 'ɡluːtəmeɪt/ noun sodium salt of glutamic acid used to enhance flavour of food.

monosyllable /'mɒnəsɪləb(ə)l/ noun word of one syllable. □ **monosyllabic** /-'læb-/ adjective.

monotheism /'mɒnəʊθiːɪz(ə)m/ noun doctrine that there is only one God. □ **monotheist** noun; **monotheistic** /-'ɪst-/ adjective.

monotone /'mɒnətəʊn/ noun sound continuing or repeated on one note or without change of pitch.

monotonous /mə'nɒtənəs/ adjective lacking in variety, tedious through sameness. □ **monotonously** adverb; **monotony** noun.

monoxide /mə'nɒksaɪd/ noun oxide containing one oxygen atom.

Monseigneur /mɒnsen'jɜ:/ noun (plural **Messeigneurs** /mesen'jɜ:/) title given to eminent French person, esp. prince, cardinal, etc. [French]

Monsieur /mə'sjɜ:/ noun (plural **Messieurs** /mes'jɜ:/) title used of or to French-speaking man.

Monsignor /mɒn'si:njə/ noun (plural **-nori** /-'njɔ:rɪ/) title of various RC priests and officials.

monsoon /mɒn'su:n/ noun wind in S. Asia, esp. in Indian Ocean; rainy season accompanying summer monsoon.

monster /'mɒnstə/ ● noun imaginary creature, usually large and frightening; inhumanly wicked person; misshapen animal or plant; large, usually ugly, animal or thing. ● adjective huge.

monstrance /'mɒnstrəns/ noun RC Church vessel in which host is exposed for veneration.

monstrosity /mɒn'strɒsɪtɪ/ noun (plural **-ies**) huge or outrageous thing.

monstrous /'mɒnstrəs/ adjective like a monster; abnormally formed; huge; outrageously wrong; atrocious. □ **monstrously** adverb.

montage /mɒn'tɑ:ʒ/ noun selection, cutting, and arrangement as consecutive whole, of separate sections of cinema or television film; composite whole made from juxtaposed photographs etc.

month /mʌnθ/ noun (in full **calendar month**) each of 12 divisions of year; period of time between same dates in successive calendar months; period of 28 days.

monthly ● adjective done, produced, or occurring once every month. ● adverb every month. ● noun (plural **-ies**) monthly periodical.

monument /'mɒnjʊmənt/ noun anything enduring that serves to commemorate, esp. structure, building, or memorial stone.

monumental /mɒnjʊ'ment(ə)l/ adjective extremely great; stupendous; massive and permanent; of or serving as monument.

moo ● noun (plural **-s**) characteristic sound of cattle. ● verb (**moos**, **mooed**) make this sound.

mooch verb colloquial (usually + about, around) wander aimlessly; esp. US cadge.

mood[1] noun state of mind or feeling; fit of bad temper or depression.

mood[2] noun Grammar form(s) of verb indicating whether it expresses fact, command, wish, etc.

moody adjective (**-ier**, **-iest**) given to changes of mood; gloomy, sullen.

moon ● noun natural satellite of the earth, orbiting it monthly, illuminated by and reflecting sun; satellite of any planet. ● verb (often + about, around) wander aimlessly or listlessly. □ **moonbeam** ray of moonlight; **moonlight** noun light of moon, verb colloquial have other paid occupation, esp. one by night as well as one by day; **moonlit** lit by the moon; **moonshine** foolish or visionary talk, illicit alcohol; **moonshot** launching of spacecraft to moon; **moonstone** feldspar of pearly appearance; **moonstruck** slightly mad.

moony adjective (**-ier**, **-iest**) listless; stupidly dreamy.

Moor /mʊə/ noun member of a Muslim people of NW Africa. □ **Moorish** adjective.

moor[1] /mʊə/ noun open uncultivated upland, esp. when covered with heather. □ **moorhen** small waterfowl; **moorland** large area of moor.

moor[2] /mʊə/ verb attach (boat etc.) to fixed object. □ **moorage** noun.

mooring noun (often in plural) place where boat etc. is moored; (in plural) set of permanent anchors and chains.

moose noun (plural same) N. American deer; elk.

moot ● adjective debatable, undecided. ● verb raise (question) for discussion. ● noun historical assembly.

mop ● noun bundle of yarn or cloth or a sponge on end of stick for cleaning floors etc.; thick mass of hair. ● verb (**-pp-**) wipe or clean (as) with mop. □ **mop up** wipe with mop, colloquial absorb, dispose of, complete occupation of (area etc.) by capturing or killing enemy troops left there.

mope ● verb (**-ping**) be depressed or listless. ● noun person who mopes. □ **mopy** adjective (**-ier**, **-iest**).

moped /'məʊped/ *noun* low-powered motorized bicycle.

moquette /mɒˈket/ *noun* thick pile or looped material used for upholstery etc.

moraine /məˈreɪn/ *noun* area of debris carried down and deposited by glacier.

moral /'mɒr(ə)l/ ● *adjective* concerned with goodness or badness of character or behaviour, or with difference between right and wrong; virtuous in conduct. ● *noun* moral lesson of story etc.; (in *plural*) moral principles or behaviour. □ **moral support** psychological rather than physical help. □ **morally** *adverb*.

morale /məˈrɑːl/ *noun* confidence, determination, etc. of person or group.

moralist /'mɒrəlɪst/ *noun* person who practises or teaches morality. □ **moralistic** /-'lɪs-/ *adjective*.

morality /məˈrælɪtɪ/ *noun* (*plural* **-ies**) degree of conformity to moral principles; moral conduct; science of morals.

moralize /'mɒrəlaɪz/ *verb* (also **-ise**) (**-zing** or **-sing**) (often + *on*) indulge in moral reflection or talk. □ **moralization** *noun*.

morass /məˈræs/ *noun* entanglement; *literary* bog.

moratorium /mɒrəˈtɔːrɪəm/ *noun* (*plural* **-s** or **-ria**) (often + *on*) temporary prohibition or suspension (of activity); legal authorization to debtors to postpone payment.

morbid /'mɔːbɪd/ *adjective* (of mind, ideas, etc.) unwholesome; *colloquial* melancholy; of or indicative of disease. □ **morbidity** /-'bɪd-/ *noun*; **morbidly** *adverb*.

mordant /'mɔːd(ə)nt/ ● *adjective* (of sarcasm etc.) caustic, biting; smarting; corrosive, cleansing. ● *noun* mordant substance.

more /mɔː/ ● *adjective* greater in quantity or degree; additional. ● *noun* greater quantity, number, or amount. ● *adverb* to greater degree or extent; *forming comparative of adjectives and adverbs*.

morello /məˈreləʊ/ *noun* (*plural* **-s**) sour kind of dark cherry.

moreover /mɔːˈrəʊvə/ *adverb* besides, in addition.

mores /'mɔːreɪz/ *plural noun* customs or conventions of community.

morganatic /mɔːɡəˈnætɪk/ *adjective* (of marriage) between person of high rank and one of lower rank, the latter and the latter's children having no claim to possessions of former.

morgue /mɔːɡ/ *noun* mortuary; room or file of miscellaneous information kept by newspaper office.

moribund /'mɒrɪbʌnd/ *adjective* at point of death; lacking vitality.

Mormon /'mɔːmən/ *noun* member of Church of Jesus Christ of Latter-Day Saints. □ **Mormonism** *noun*.

morn *noun* poetical morning.

morning /'mɔːnɪŋ/ *noun* early part of day till noon or lunchtime. □ **morning coat** tailcoat with front cut away; **morning dress** man's morning coat and striped trousers; **morning glory** climbing plant with trumpet-shaped flowers; **morning sickness** nausea felt in morning in pregnancy; **morning star** planet, usually Venus, seen in east before sunrise.

morocco /məˈrɒkəʊ/ *noun* (*plural* **-s**) fine flexible leather of goatskin tanned with sumac.

moron /'mɔːrɒn/ *noun* *colloquial* very stupid person; adult with mental age of 8–12. □ **moronic** /məˈr-/ *adjective*.

morose /məˈrəʊs/ *adjective* sullen, gloomy. □ **morosely** *adverb*; **moroseness** *noun*.

morphia /'mɔːfɪə/ *noun* morphine.

morphine /'mɔːfiːn/ *noun* narcotic drug from opium.

morphology /mɔːˈfɒlədʒɪ/ *noun* study of forms of things, esp. of animals and plants and of words and their structure. □ **morphological** /-fəˈlɒdʒ-/ *adjective*.

morris dance /'mɒrɪs/ *noun* traditional English dance in fancy costume. □ **morris dancer** *noun*; **morris dancing** *noun*.

morrow /'mɒrəʊ/ *noun* (usually **the morrow**) *literary* following day.

Morse /mɔːs/ *noun* (in full **Morse code**) code in which letters, numbers, etc. are represented by combinations of long and short light or sound signals.

morsel /'mɔːs(ə)l/ *noun* mouthful; small piece (esp. of food).

mortal /'mɔːt(ə)l/ ● *adjective* subject to or causing death; (of combat) fought to the death; (of enemy) implacable. ● *noun* human being. □ **mortal sin** sin depriving soul of salvation. □ **mortally** *adverb*.

mortality /mɔː'tælɪtɪ/ *noun* (*plural* **-ies**) being subject to death; loss of life on large scale; (in full **mortality rate**) death rate.

mortar /'mɔːtə/ *noun* mixture of lime and cement, sand, and water, for bonding bricks or stones; short cannon for firing shells at high angles; vessel in which ingredients are pounded with pestle. □ **mortarboard** stiff flat square-topped academic cap, flat board for holding mortar.

mortgage /'mɔːgɪdʒ/ ● *noun* conveyance of property to creditor as security for debt (usually one incurred by purchase of property); sum of money lent by this. ● *verb* (**-ging**) convey (property) by mortgage.

mortgagee /mɔːgɪ'dʒiː/ *noun* creditor in mortgage.

mortgager /'mɔːgɪdʒə/ *noun* (also **mortgagor** /-'dʒɔː/) debtor in mortgage.

mortice = MORTISE.

mortician /mɔː'tɪʃ(ə)n/ *noun* US undertaker.

mortify /'mɔːtɪfaɪ/ *verb* (**-ies**, **-ied**) humiliate; wound (person's feelings); bring (body etc.) into subjection by self-denial; (of flesh) affected by gangrene. □ **mortification** *noun*; **mortifying** *adjective*.

mortise /'mɔːtɪs/ (also **mortice**) ● *noun* hole in framework to receive end of another part, esp. tenon. ● *verb* (**-sing**) join, esp. by mortise and tenon; cut mortise in. □ **mortise lock** lock recessed in frame of door etc.

mortuary /'mɔːtjʊərɪ/ ● *noun* (*plural* **-ies**) room or building in which dead bodies are kept until burial or cremation. ● *adjective* of death or burial.

Mosaic /məʊ'zeɪɪk/ *adjective* of Moses.

mosaic /məʊ'zeɪɪk/ *noun* picture or pattern made with small variously coloured pieces of glass, stone, etc.; diversified thing.

moselle /məʊ'zel/ *noun* dry German white wine.

Moslem = MUSLIM.

mosque /mɒsk/ *noun* Muslim place of worship.

mosquito /mɒs'kiːtəʊ/ *noun* (*plural* **-es**) biting insect, esp. with long proboscis to suck blood. □ **mosquito-net** net to keep off mosquitoes.

moss *noun* small flowerless plant growing in dense clusters in bogs and on trees, stones, etc.; *Scottish & Northern English* peatbog. □ **mossy** *adjective* (**-ier**, **-iest**).

most /məʊst/ ● *adjective* greatest in quantity or degree; the majority of. ● *noun* greatest quantity or number; the majority. ● *adverb* in highest degree; *forming superlative of adjectives and adverbs*.

mostly *adverb* mainly; usually.

MOT *abbreviation* (in full **MOT test**) compulsory annual test, instituted by Ministry of Transport, of vehicles over specified age.

mot /məʊ/ *noun* (*plural* **mots** same pronunciation) (usually **bon mot** /bɔ̃/) witty saying. □ **mot juste** /ʒuːst/ most appropriate expression. [French]

mote *noun* speck of dust.

motel /məʊ'tel/ *noun* roadside hotel for motorists.

moth /mɒθ/ *noun* nocturnal insect like butterfly; insect of this type breeding in cloth etc., on which its larva feeds. □ **mothball** ball of naphthalene etc. kept with stored clothes to deter moths; **moth-eaten** damaged by moths, time-worn.

mother /'mʌðə/ ● *noun* female parent; woman or condition etc. giving rise to something else; (in full **Mother Superior**) head of female religious community. ● *verb* treat as mother does. □ **mother country** country in relation to its colonies; **mother-in-law** (*plural* **mothers-in-law**) husband's or wife's mother; **motherland** native country; **mother-of-pearl** iridescent substance forming lining of oyster and other shells; **mother tongue** native language. □ **motherhood** *noun*; **motherly** *adjective*.

motif /məʊ'tiːf/ *noun* theme repeated and developed in artistic work; decorative design; ornament sewn separately on garment.

motion /'məʊʃ(ə)n/ ●noun moving; changing position; gesture; formal proposal put to committee etc.; application to court for order; evacuation of bowels. ●verb (often + to do) direct (person) by gesture. □ **motion picture** esp. US cinema film. □ **motionless** adjective.

motivate /'məʊtɪveɪt/ verb (-ting) supply motive to, be motive of; cause (person) to act in particular way; stimulate interest of (person in activity). □ **motivation** noun.

motive /'məʊtɪv/ ●noun what induces person to act; motif. ●adjective tending to initiate movement.

motley /'mɒtlɪ/ ●adjective (-ier, -iest) diversified in colour; of varied character. ●noun historical jester's particoloured costume.

motor /'məʊtə/ ●noun thing that imparts motion; machine (esp. using electricity or internal combustion) supplying motive power for vehicle or other machine; car. ●adjective giving, imparting, or producing motion; driven by motor; of or for motor vehicles. ●verb go or convey by motor vehicle. □ **motor bike** colloquial, **motorcycle** two-wheeled motor vehicle without pedal propulsion; **motor car** car; **motorway** fast road with separate carriageways limited to motor vehicles.

motorcade /'məʊtəkeɪd/ noun procession of motor vehicles.

motorist noun driver of car.

motorize verb (also **-ise**) (**-zing** or **-sing**) equip with motor transport; provide with motor.

mottle /'mɒt(ə)l/ verb (**-ling**) (esp. as **mottled** adjective) mark with spots or smears of colour.

motto /'mɒtəʊ/ noun (plural **-es**) maxim adopted as rule of conduct; words accompanying coat of arms; appropriate inscription; joke, maxim, etc. in paper cracker.

mould[1] /məʊld/ ●noun (US **mold**) hollow container into which substance is poured or pressed to harden into required shape; pudding etc. shaped in mould; form, shape; character, type. ●verb shape (as) in mould; give shape to; influence development of.

mould[2] /məʊld/ noun (US **mold**) furry growth of fungi, esp. in moist warm conditions.

mould[3] /məʊld/ noun (US **mold**) loose earth; upper soil of cultivated land, esp. when rich in organic matter.

moulder /'məʊldə/ verb (US **molder**) decay to dust; (+ away) rot, crumble.

moulding noun (US **molding**) ornamental strip of plaster etc. applied as architectural feature, esp. in cornice; similar feature in woodwork etc.

mouldy adjective (US **moldy**) (**-ier, -iest**) covered with mould; stale; out of date; colloquial dull, miserable.

moult /məʊlt/ (US **molt**) ●verb shed (feathers, hair, shell, etc.) in renewing plumage, coat, etc. ●noun moulting.

mound /maʊnd/ noun raised mass of earth, stones, etc.; heap, pile; hillock.

mount[1] ●verb ascend; climb on to; get up on (horse etc.); set on horseback; (as **mounted** adjective) serving on horseback; (often + up) accumulate, increase; set in frame etc., esp. for viewing; organize, arrange (exhibition, attack, etc.). ●noun backing etc. on which picture etc. is set for display; horse for riding; setting for gem etc.

mount[2] noun (poetical except before name) mountain, hill.

mountain /'maʊntɪn/ noun large abrupt elevation of ground; large heap or pile; huge quantity; large surplus stock. □ **mountain ash** tree with scarlet berries; **mountain bike** sturdy bicycle with straight handlebars and many gears.

mountaineer /maʊntɪ'nɪə/ ●noun person practising mountain climbing. ●verb climb mountains as sport. □ **mountaineering** noun.

mountainous adjective having many mountains; huge.

mountebank /'maʊntɪbæŋk/ noun swindler, charlatan.

Mountie /'maʊntɪ/ noun colloquial member of Royal Canadian Mounted Police.

mourn /mɔːn/ verb (often + for, over) feel or show sorrow or regret; grieve for loss of (dead person etc.).

mourner noun person who mourns, esp. at funeral.

mournful *adjective* doleful, sad. □ **mournfully** *adverb*.

mourning *noun* expression of sorrow for dead, esp. by wearing black clothes; such clothes.

mouse /maʊs/ ● *noun* (*plural* **mice**) small rodent; timid or feeble person; *Computing* small device controlling cursor on VDU screen. ● *verb* (also /maʊz/) (**-sing**) (of cat etc.) hunt mice. □ **mouser** *noun*; **mousy** *adjective*.

mousse /muːs/ *noun* dish of whipped cream, eggs, etc., flavoured with fruit, chocolate, etc., or with meat or fish purée.

moustache /məˈstɑːʃ/ *noun* (*US* **mustache**) hair left to grow on upper lip.

mouth ● *noun* /maʊθ/ (*plural* **mouths** /maʊðz/) external opening in head, for taking in food and emitting sound; cavity behind it containing teeth and vocal organs; opening of container, cave, trumpet, volcano, etc.; place where river enters sea. ● *verb* /maʊð/ (**-thing**) say or speak by moving lips silently; utter insincerely or without understanding. □ **mouth-organ** harmonica; **mouthpiece** part of musical instrument, telephone, etc., placed next to lips; **mouthwash** liquid antiseptic etc. for rinsing mouth.

mouthful *noun* (*plural* **-s**) quantity of food etc. that fills the mouth; *colloquial* something difficult to say.

move /muːv/ ● *verb* (**-ving**) (cause to) change position, posture, home, or place of work; put or keep in motion; rouse, stir; (often + *about, away, off,* etc.) go, proceed; take action; (+ *in*) be socially active in; affect with emotion; (cause to) change attitude; propose as resolution. ● *noun* act or process of moving; change of house, premises, etc.; step taken to secure object; moving of piece in board game. □ **move in with** start to share accommodation with; **move out** leave one's home. □ **movable** *adjective*.

movement *noun* moving, being moved; moving parts of mechanism; group of people with common object; (in *plural*) person's activities and whereabouts; chief division of longer musical work; bowel motion; rise or fall of stockmarket prices.

movie /ˈmuːvɪ/ *noun esp. US colloquial* cinema film.

moving *adjective* emotionally affecting.

mow /məʊ/ *verb* (*past participle* **mowed** or **mown**) cut (grass, hay, etc.) with scythe or machine. □ **mower** *noun*.

MP *abbreviation* Member of Parliament.

mp *abbreviation* mezzo piano.

m.p.g. *abbreviation* miles per gallon.

m.p.h. *abbreviation* miles per hour.

Mr /ˈmɪstə/ *noun* (*plural* **Messrs**) *title prefixed to name of man or to designation of office etc.*

Mrs /ˈmɪsɪz/ *noun* (*plural* same) *title of married woman.*

MS *abbreviation* (*plural* **MSS** /emˈesɪz/) manuscript; multiple sclerosis.

Ms /mɪz/ *noun title of married or unmarried woman.*

M.Sc. *abbreviation* Master of Science.

Mt. *abbreviation* Mount.

much ● *adjective* existing or occurring in great quantity. ● *noun* great quantity; (usually in negative) noteworthy example. ● *adverb* in great degree; for large part of one's time; often. □ **a bit much** *colloquial* excessive; **much of a muchness** very nearly the same.

mucilage /ˈmjuːsɪlɪdʒ/ *noun* viscous substance obtained from plants; adhesive gum.

muck ● *noun colloquial* dirt; filth; anything disgusting; manure. ● *verb* (usually + *up*) *colloquial* bungle; make dirty; (+ *out*) remove manure from. □ **muck about, around** *colloquial* potter or fool about; **muck in** (often + *with*) *colloquial* share tasks etc.; **muckraking** seeking out and revealing of scandals etc. □ **mucky** *adjective* (**-ier, -iest**).

mucous /ˈmjuːkəs/ *adjective* of or covered with mucus. □ **mucous membrane** mucus-secreting tissue lining body cavities etc.

mucus /ˈmjuːkəs/ *noun* slimy substance secreted by mucous membrane.

mud *noun* soft wet earth. □ **mudguard** curved strip over wheel to protect against mud; **mud-slinging** abuse, slander.

muddle /ˈmʌd(ə)l/ ● *verb* (**-ling**) (often + *up*) bring into disorder; bewilder; confuse. ● *noun* disorder; confusion.

□ **muddle along** progress in haphazard way.

muddy ● adjective (-ier, -iest) like mud; covered in or full of mud; (of liquid, colour, or sound) not clear; confused. ● verb (-ies, -ied) make muddy.

muesli /'mju:zlɪ/ noun breakfast food of crushed cereals, dried fruit, nuts, etc.

muezzin /mu:'ezɪn/ noun Muslim crier who proclaims hours of prayer.

muff[1] noun covering, esp. of fur, for keeping hands or ears warm.

muff[2] verb colloquial bungle; miss (catch etc.).

muffin /'mʌfɪn/ noun light flat round spongy cake, eaten toasted and buttered; US similar cake made from batter or dough.

muffle /'mʌf(ə)l/ verb (-ling) (often + up) wrap for warmth or to deaden sound.

muffler noun wrap or scarf worn for warmth; thing used to deaden sound.

mufti /'mʌftɪ/ noun civilian clothes.

mug[1] ● noun drinking vessel, usually cylindrical with handle and no saucer; its contents; gullible person; slang face, mouth. ● verb (-gg-) attack and rob, esp. in public place. □ **mugger** noun; **mugging** noun.

mug[2] verb (-gg-) (usually + up) slang learn (subject) by concentrated study.

muggins /'mʌgɪnz/ noun (plural same or **mugginses**) colloquial gullible person (often meaning oneself).

muggy /'mʌgɪ/ adjective (-ier, -iest) (of weather etc.) oppressively humid.

Muhammadan /mə'hæməd(ə)n/ noun & adjective (also **Mohammedan**) Muslim.

■ **Usage** The term Muhammadan is not used by Muslims and is often regarded as offensive.

mulatto /mju:'lætəʊ/ noun (plural -s or -es) person of mixed white and black parentage.

mulberry /'mʌlbərɪ/ noun (plural -ies) tree bearing edible purple or white berries; its fruit; dark red, purple.

mulch ● noun layer of wet straw, leaves, plastic, etc., put round plant's roots to enrich or insulate soil. ● verb treat with mulch.

mule[1] /mju:l/ noun offspring of male donkey and female horse or (in general use) vice versa; obstinate person; kind of spinning machine.

mule[2] /mju:l/ noun backless slipper.

muleteer /mju:lə'tɪə/ noun mule driver.

mulish adjective stubborn.

mull[1] verb (often + over) ponder.

mull[2] verb heat and spice (wine, beer).

mullah /'mʌlə/ noun Muslim learned in theology and sacred law.

mullet /'mʌlɪt/ noun (plural same) edible sea fish.

mulligatawny /mʌlɪgə'tɔ:nɪ/ noun highly seasoned soup originally from India.

mullion /'mʌljən/ noun vertical bar between panes in window. □ **mullioned** adjective.

multi- combining form many.

multicoloured /'mʌltɪkʌləd/ adjective of many colours.

multifarious /mʌltɪ'feərɪəs/ adjective many and various; of great variety.

multiform /'mʌltɪfɔ:m/ adjective having many forms; of many kinds.

multilateral /mʌltɪ'lætər(ə)l/ adjective (of agreement etc.) in which 3 or more parties participate; having many sides. □ **multilaterally** adverb.

multilingual /mʌltɪ'lɪŋgw(ə)l/ adjective in, speaking, or using many languages.

multinational /mʌltɪ'næʃən(ə)l/ ● adjective operating in several countries; of several nationalities. ● noun multinational company.

multiple /'mʌltɪp(ə)l/ ● adjective having several parts, elements, or components; many and various. ● noun quantity exactly divisible by another. □ **multiple sclerosis** see SCLEROSIS.

multiplicand /mʌltɪplɪ'kænd/ noun quantity to be multiplied.

multiplication /mʌltɪplɪ'keɪʃ(ə)n/ noun multiplying.

multiplicity /mʌltɪ'plɪsɪtɪ/ noun (plural -ies) manifold variety; (+ of) great number.

multiplier /'mʌltɪplaɪə/ noun quantity by which given number is multiplied.

multiply /'mʌltɪplaɪ/ verb (-ies, -ied) obtain from (number) another a specified number of times its value; increase in number, esp. by procreation.

multi-purpose /mʌltɪˈpɜːpəs/ *adjective* having several purposes.

multiracial /mʌltɪˈreɪʃ(ə)l/ *adjective* of several races.

multitude /ˈmʌltɪtjuːd/ *noun* (often + *of*) great number; large gathering of people; (**the multitude**) the common people. □ **multitudinous** /-ˈtjuːdɪnəs/ *adjective*.

mum[1] *noun colloquial* mother.

mum[2] *adjective colloquial* silent. □ **mum's the word** say nothing.

mumble /ˈmʌmb(ə)l/ ● *verb* (**-ling**) speak or utter indistinctly. ● *noun* indistinct utterance.

mumbo-jumbo /mʌmbəʊˈdʒʌmbəʊ/ *noun* (*plural* **-s**) meaningless ritual; meaningless or unnecessarily complicated language; nonsense.

mummer /ˈmʌmə/ *noun* actor in traditional play or mime.

mummery /ˈmʌmərɪ/ *noun* (*plural* **-ies**) ridiculous (esp. religious) ceremonial; performance by mummers.

mummify /ˈmʌmɪfaɪ/ *verb* (**-ies, -ied**) preserve (body) as mummy. □ **mummification** *noun*.

mummy[1] /ˈmʌmɪ/ *noun* (*plural* **-ies**) *colloquial* mother.

mummy[2] /ˈmʌmɪ/ *noun* (*plural* **-ies**) dead body preserved by embalming, esp. in ancient Egypt.

mumps *plural noun* (treated as *singular*) infectious disease with swelling of neck and face.

munch *verb* chew steadily.

mundane /mʌnˈdeɪn/ *adjective* dull, routine; of this world. □ **mundanely** *adverb*.

municipal /mjuːˈnɪsɪp(ə)l/ *adjective* of municipality or its self-government.

municipality /mjuːnɪsɪˈpælɪtɪ/ *noun* (*plural* **-ies**) town or district with local self-government; its governing body.

munificent /mjuːˈnɪfɪs(ə)nt/ *adjective* (of giver or gift) splendidly generous. □ **munificence** *noun*.

muniment /ˈmjuːnɪmənt/ *noun* (usually in *plural*) document kept as evidence of rights or privileges.

munition /mjuːˈnɪʃ(ə)n/ *noun* (usually in *plural*) military weapons, ammunition, etc.

mural /ˈmjʊər(ə)l/ ● *noun* painting executed directly on wall. ● *adjective* of, on, or like wall.

murder /ˈmɜːdə/ ● *noun* intentional unlawful killing of human being by another; *colloquial* unpleasant or dangerous state of affairs. ● *verb* kill (human being) intentionally and unlawfully; *colloquial* utterly defeat; spoil by bad performance, mispronunciation, etc. □ **murderer, murderess** *noun;* **murderous** *adjective.*

murky /ˈmɜːkɪ/ (**-ier, -iest**) *adjective* dark, gloomy; (of liquid etc.) dirty.

murmur /ˈmɜːmə/ ● *noun* subdued continuous sound; softly spoken utterance; subdued expression of discontent. ● *verb* make murmur; utter in low voice.

murrain /ˈmʌrɪn/ *noun* infectious disease of cattle.

Muscadet /ˈmʌskədeɪ/ *noun* dry white wine of France from Loire region; variety of grape used for this.

muscat /ˈmʌskət/ *noun* sweet usually fortified white wine made from musk-flavoured grapes; this grape.

muscatel /mʌskəˈtel/ *noun* muscat wine or grape; raisin made from muscat grape.

muscle /ˈmʌs(ə)l/ ● *noun* fibrous tissue producing movement in or maintaining position of animal body; part of body composed of muscles; strength, power. ● *verb* (**-ling**) (+ *in, in on*) *colloquial* force oneself on others. □ **muscle-bound** with muscles stiff and inelastic through excessive exercise; **muscle-man** man with highly developed muscles.

Muscovite /ˈmʌskəvaɪt/ ● *noun* native or citizen of Moscow. ● *adjective* of Moscow.

muscular /ˈmʌskjʊlə/ *adjective* of or affecting muscles; having well-developed muscles. □ **muscular dystrophy** hereditary progressive wasting of muscles. □ **muscularity** /-ˈlær-/ *noun.*

muse[1] /mjuːz/ *verb* (**-sing**) (usually + *on, upon*) ponder, reflect.

muse[2] /mjuːz/ *noun Greek & Roman Mythology* any of 9 goddesses inspiring poetry, music, etc.; (usually **the muse**) poet's inspiration.

museum /mju:'zi:əm/ noun building for storing and exhibiting objects of historical, scientific, or cultural interest. □ **museum piece** object fit for museum, derogatory old-fashioned person etc.

mush noun soft pulp; feeble sentimentality; US maize porridge. □ **mushy** adjective (**-ier, -iest**).

mushroom /'mʌʃrʊm/ ● noun edible fungus with stem and domed cap; pinkish-brown colour. ● verb appear or develop rapidly. □ **mushroom cloud** mushroom-shaped cloud from nuclear explosion.

music /'mju:zɪk/ noun art of combining vocal or instrumental sounds in harmonious or expressive way; sounds so produced; musical composition; written or printed score of this; pleasant sound. □ **music centre** equipment combining radio, record player, tape recorder, etc.; **music-hall** variety entertainment, theatre for this.

musical ● adjective of music; (of sounds) melodious, harmonious; fond of or skilled in music; set to or accompanied by music. ● noun musical film or play. □ **musicality** /-'kæl-/ noun; **musically** adverb.

musician /mju:'zɪʃ(ə)n/ noun person skilled in practice of music, esp. professional instrumentalist. □ **musicianship** noun.

musicology /mju:zɪ'kɒlədʒɪ/ noun study of history and forms of music. □ **musicological** /-kə'lɒdʒ-/ adjective; **musicologist** noun.

musk noun substance secreted by male musk deer and used in perfumes; plant which originally had smell of musk. □ **musk deer** small hornless Asian deer; **muskrat** large N. American aquatic rodent with smell like musk, its fur; **musk-rose** rambling rose smelling of musk. □ **musky** adjective (**-ier, -iest**).

musket /'mʌskɪt/ noun historical infantryman's (esp. smooth-bored) light gun.

musketeer /mʌskɪ'tɪə/ noun historical soldier armed with musket.

musketry /'mʌskɪtrɪ/ noun muskets; soldiers armed with muskets; knowledge of handling small arms.

Muslim /'mʊzlɪm/ (also **Moslem** /'mɒzləm/) ● noun follower of Islamic religion. ● adjective of Muslims or their religion.

muslin /'mʌzlɪn/ noun fine delicately woven cotton fabric.

musquash /'mʌskwɒʃ/ noun muskrat; its fur.

mussel /'mʌs(ə)l/ noun edible bivalve mollusc.

must[1] ● auxiliary verb (3rd singular present **must**; past **had to**) be obliged to; be certain to; ought to. ● noun colloquial thing that should not be missed.

■ **Usage** The negative I must not go means 'I am not allowed to go'. To express a lack of obligation, use I am not obliged to go, I need not go, or I haven't got to go.

must[2] noun grape juice before fermentation is complete.

mustache US = MOUSTACHE.

mustang /'mʌstæŋ/ noun small wild horse of Mexico and California.

mustard /'mʌstəd/ noun plant with yellow flowers; seeds of this crushed into paste and used as spicy condiment. □ **mustard gas** colourless oily liquid whose vapour is powerful irritant.

muster /'mʌstə/ ● verb collect (originally soldiers); come together; summon (courage etc.). ● noun assembly of people for inspection. □ **pass muster** be accepted as adequate.

mustn't /'mʌs(ə)nt/ must not.

musty /'mʌstɪ/ adjective (**-ier, -iest**) mouldy, stale; dull, antiquated. □ **mustiness** noun.

mutable /'mju:təb(ə)l/ adjective literary liable to change. □ **mutability** noun.

mutant /'mju:t(ə)nt/ ● adjective resulting from mutation. ● noun mutant organism or gene.

mutate /mju:'teɪt/ (cause to) undergo mutation.

mutation noun change; genetic change which when transmitted to offspring gives rise to heritable variations.

mute /mju:t/ ● adjective silent; refraining from or temporarily bereft of speech; dumb; soundless. ● noun dumb person; device for damping sound of musical instrument. ● verb (**-ting**) muffle or deaden sound of; (as **muted** *adjective*) (of colours etc.) subdued. □ **mute swan** common white swan. □ **mutely** *adverb*.

mutilate /'mjuːtɪleɪt/ *verb* (**-ting**) deprive (person, animal) of limb etc.; destroy usefulness of (limb etc.); excise or damage part of (book etc.). □ **mutilation** *noun*.

mutineer /mjuːtɪ'nɪə/ *noun* person who mutinies.

mutinous /'mjuːtɪnəs/ *adjective* rebellious.

mutiny /'mjuːtɪnɪ/ ● *noun* (*plural* **-ies**) open revolt, esp. by soldiers or sailors against officers. ● *verb* (**-ies**, **-ied**) engage in mutiny.

mutt *noun slang* stupid person.

mutter /'mʌtə/ ● *verb* speak in barely audible manner; (often + *against, at*) grumble. ● *noun* muttered words etc.; muttering.

mutton /'mʌt(ə)n/ *noun* flesh of sheep as food.

mutual /'mjuːtʃʊəl/ *adjective* (of feelings, actions, etc.) experienced or done by each of two or more parties to the other(s); *colloquial* common to two or more people; having same (specified) relationship to each other. □ **mutuality** /-'æl-/ *noun*; **mutually** *adverb*.

■ **Usage** The use of *mutual* to mean 'common to two or more people' is considered incorrect by some people, who use *common* instead.

muzzle /'mʌz(ə)l/ ● *noun* projecting part of animal's face, including nose and mouth; guard put over animal's nose and mouth; open end of firearm. ● *verb* (**-ling**) put muzzle on; impose silence on.

muzzy /'mʌzɪ/ *adjective* (**-ier**, **-iest**) confused, dazed; blurred, indistinct. □ **muzzily** *adverb*.

MW *abbreviation* megawatt(s); medium wave.

my /maɪ/ *adjective* of or belonging to me.

mycology /maɪ'kɒlədʒɪ/ *noun* study of fungi; fungi of particular region.

mynah /'maɪnə/ *noun* (also **myna**) talking bird of starling family.

myopia /maɪ'əʊpɪə/ *noun* short-sightedness; lack of imagination. □ **myopic** /-'ɒp-/ *adjective*.

myriad /'mɪrɪəd/ *literary* ● *noun* indefinitely great number. ● *adjective* innumerable.

myrrh /mɜː/ *noun* gum resin used in perfume, medicine, incense, etc.

myrtle /'mɜːt(ə)l/ *noun* evergreen shrub with shiny leaves and white scented flowers.

myself /maɪ'self/ *pronoun: emphatic form of* I[2] *or* ME[1]; *reflexive form of* ME[1].

mysterious /mɪs'tɪərɪəs/ *adjective* full of or wrapped in mystery. □ **mysteriously** *adverb*.

mystery /'mɪstərɪ/ *noun* (*plural* **-ies**) hidden or inexplicable matter; secrecy, obscurity; fictional work dealing with puzzling event, esp. murder; religious truth divinely revealed; (in *plural*) secret ancient religious rites. □ **mystery play** miracle play; **mystery tour** pleasure trip to unspecified destination.

mystic /'mɪstɪk/ ● *noun* person who seeks unity with deity through contemplation etc., or believes in spiritual apprehension of truths beyond understanding. □ **mysticism** /-sɪz(ə)m/ *noun*.

mystical *adjective* of mystics or mysticism; of hidden meaning; spiritually symbolic.

mystify /'mɪstɪfaɪ/ *verb* (**-ies**, **-ied**) bewilder, confuse. □ **mystification** *noun*.

mystique /mɪs'tiːk/ *noun* atmosphere of mystery and veneration attending some activity, person, profession, etc.

myth /mɪθ/ *noun* traditional story usually involving supernatural or imaginary people and embodying popular ideas on natural or social phenomena; widely held but false idea; fictitious person, thing, or idea. □ **mythical** *adjective*.

mythology /mɪ'θɒlədʒɪ/ *noun* (*plural* **-ies**) body or study of myths. □ **mythological** /-θə'lɒdʒ-/ *adjective*; **mythologize** *verb* (also **-ise**) (**-zing** or **-sing**).

myxomatosis /mɪksəmə'təʊsɪs/ *noun* viral disease of rabbits.

N *abbreviation* (also **N.**) north(ern).

n *noun* indefinite number.

n. *abbreviation* (also **n**) noun; neuter.

NAAFI /'næfɪ/ *abbreviation* Navy, Army, and Air Force Institutes (canteen for servicemen).

nab *verb* (**-bb-**) *slang* arrest; catch in wrongdoing; grab.

nacre /'neɪkə/ *noun* mother-of-pearl from any shelled mollusc. □ **nacreous** /'neɪkrɪəs/ *adjective*.

nadir /'neɪdɪə/ *noun* point on celestial sphere directly below observer; lowest point; time of despair.

naff *adjective slang* unfashionable; rubbishy.

nag [1] *verb* (**-gg-**) persistently criticize or scold; (often + *at*) find fault or urge, esp. continually; (of pain) be persistent.

nag [2] *noun colloquial* horse.

naiad /'naɪæd/ *noun* water nymph.

nail ● *noun* small metal spike hammered in to fasten things; horny covering on upper surface of tip of human finger or toe. ● *verb* fasten with nail(s); fix or hold tight; secure, catch (person, thing).

naïve /naɪˈiːv/ *adjective* (also **naive**) innocent, unaffected; foolishly credulous. □ **naïvely** *adverb*; **naïvety** *noun*.

naked /'neɪkɪd/ *adjective* unclothed, nude; without usual covering; undisguised; (of light, flame, sword, etc.) unprotected. □ **nakedly** *adverb*; **nakedness** *noun*.

namby-pamby /næmbɪˈpæmbɪ/ ● *adjective* insipidly pretty or sentimental; weak. ● *noun* (*plural* **-ies**) namby-pamby person.

name ● *noun* word by which individual person, animal, place, or thing is spoken of etc.; (usually abusive) term used of person; word denoting object or class of objects; reputation, esp. good. ● *verb* (**-ming**) give name to; state name of; mention; specify; cite. □ **name-day** feast-day of saint after whom person is named; **namesake** person or thing having same name as another.

nameless *adjective* having, or showing, no name; left unnamed.

namely *adverb* that is to say; in other words.

nanny /'nænɪ/ *noun* (*plural* **-ies**) child's nurse; *colloquial* grandmother; (in full **nanny goat**) female goat.

nano- /'nænəʊ/ *combining form* one thousand millionth.

nap [1] ● *noun* short sleep, esp. by day. ● *verb* (**-pp-**) have nap.

nap [2] *noun* raised pile on cloth, esp. velvet.

nap [3] ● *noun* card game; racing tip claimed to be almost a certainty. ● *verb* (**-pp-**) name (horse) as probable winner. □ **go nap** try to take all 5 tricks in nap, risk everything.

napalm /'neɪpɑːm/ *noun* thick jellied hydrocarbon mixture used in bombs.

nape *noun* back of neck.

naphtha /'næfθə/ *noun* inflammable hydrocarbon distilled from coal etc.

naphthalene /'næfθəliːn/ *noun* white crystalline substance produced by distilling tar.

napkin /'næpkɪn/ *noun* piece of linen etc. for wiping lips, fingers, etc. at table; baby's nappy.

nappy /'næpɪ/ *noun* (*plural* **-ies**) piece of towelling etc. wrapped round baby to absorb urine and faeces.

narcissism /'nɑːsɪsɪz(ə)m/ *noun* excessive or erotic interest in oneself. □ **narcissistic** /-'sɪstɪk/ *adjective*.

narcissus /nɑːˈsɪsəs/ *noun* (*plural* **-cissi** /-saɪ/) any of several flowering bulbs, including daffodil.

narcosis /nɑːˈkəʊsɪs/ *noun* unconsciousness; induction of this.

narcotic /nɑːˈkɒtɪk/ ● *adjective* (of substance) inducing drowsiness etc.; (of drug) affecting the mind. ● *noun* narcotic substance or drug.

nark *slang* ● *noun* police informer. ● *verb* annoy.

narrate /nəˈreɪt/ *verb* (**-ting**) give continuous story or account of; provide spoken accompaniment for (film etc.). □ **narration** *noun*; **narrator** *noun*.

narrative /ˈnærətɪv/ ● *noun* ordered account of connected events. ● *adjective* of or by narration.

narrow /ˈnærəʊ/ ● *adjective* (**-er, -est**) of small width; restricted; of limited scope; with little margin; precise, exact; narrow-minded. ● *noun* (usually in *plural*) narrow part of strait, river, pass, etc. ● *verb* become or make narrower; contract; lessen. □ **narrow boat** canal boat; **narrow-minded** rigid or restricted in one's views, intolerant. □ **narrowly** *adverb*; **narrowness** *noun*.

narwhal /ˈnɑːw(ə)l/ *noun* Arctic white whale, male of which has long tusk.

nasal /ˈneɪz(ə)l/ ● *adjective* of nose; (of letter or sound) pronounced with breath passing through nose, e.g. *m, n, ng*; (of voice etc.) having many nasal sounds. ● *noun* nasal letter or sound. □ **nasally** *adverb*.

nascent /ˈnæs(ə)nt/ *adjective* in act of being born; just beginning to be. □ **nascency** /-ənsɪ/ *noun*.

nasturtium /nəˈstɜːʃəm/ *noun* trailing garden plant with edible leaves and bright orange, red, or yellow flowers.

nasty /ˈnɑːstɪ/ ● *adjective* (**-ier, -iest**) unpleasant; difficult to negotiate; (of person or animal) ill-natured, spiteful. ● *noun* (*plural* **-ies**) *colloquial* violent horror film, esp. on video. □ **nastily** *adverb*; **nastiness** *noun*.

Nat. *abbreviation* National(ist); Natural.

natal /ˈneɪt(ə)l/ *adjective* of or from birth.

nation /ˈneɪʃ(ə)n/ *noun* community of people having mainly common descent, history, language, etc., forming state or inhabiting territory. □ **nationwide** extending over whole nation.

national /ˈnæʃən(ə)l/ ● *adjective* of nation; characteristic of particular nation. ● *noun* citizen of specified country. □ **national anthem** song adopted by nation, intended to inspire patriotism; **national grid** network of high-voltage electric power lines between major power stations; **National Insurance** system of compulsory payments from employee and employer to provide state assistance in sickness, retirement, etc.; **national service** *historical* conscripted peacetime military service. □ **nationally** *adverb*.

nationalism *noun* patriotic feeling, principles, etc.; policy of national independence. □ **nationalist** *noun*; **nationalistic** /-ˈlɪs-/ *adjective*.

nationality /næʃəˈnælɪtɪ/ *noun* (*plural* **-ies**) membership of nation; being national; ethnic group within one or more political nations.

nationalize /ˈnæʃənəlaɪz/ *verb* (also **-ise**) (**-zing** or **-sing**) take (industry etc.) into state ownership; make national. □ **nationalization** *noun*.

native /ˈneɪtɪv/ ● *noun* (usually + *of*) person born in specified place; local inhabitant; indigenous animal or plant. ● *adjective* inherent; innate; of one's birth; (usually + *to*) belonging to specified place; born in a place.

nativity /nəˈtɪvɪtɪ/ *noun* (*plural* **-ies**) (esp. **the Nativity**) Christ's birth; birth.

NATO /ˈneɪtəʊ/ *abbreviation* (also **Nato**) North Atlantic Treaty Organization.

natter /ˈnætə/ *colloquial* ● *verb* chatter idly. ● *noun* aimless chatter.

natty /ˈnætɪ/ *adjective* (**-ier, -iest**) trim; smart.

natural /ˈnætʃər(ə)l/ ● *adjective* existing in or caused by nature; not surprising; to be expected; unaffected; innate; physically existing; *Music* not flat or sharp. ● *noun colloquial* (usually + *for*) person or thing naturally suitable, adept, etc.; *Music* sign (♮) showing return to natural pitch, natural note. □ **natural gas** gas found in earth's crust; **natural history** study of animals and plants; **natural number** whole number greater than 0; **natural selection** process favouring survival of organisms best adapted to environment.

naturalism *noun* realistic representation in art and literature; philosophy based on nature alone. □ **naturalistic** /-ˈlɪs-/ *adjective*.

naturalist *noun* student of natural history.

naturalize *verb* (also **-ise**) (**-zing** or **-sing**) admit (foreigner) to citizenship;

introduce (plant etc.) into another region; adopt (foreign word, custom, etc.). □ **naturalization** noun.

naturally adverb in a natural way; as might be expected, of course.

nature /ˈneɪtʃə/ noun thing's or person's essential qualities or character; physical power causing material phenomena; these phenomena; kind, class.

naturism noun nudism. □ **naturist** noun.

naught /nɔːt/ archaic ● noun nothing. ● adjective worthless.

naughty /ˈnɔːtɪ/ adjective (**-ier, -iest**) (esp. of children) disobedient; badly behaved; colloquial jocular indecent. □ **naughtily** adverb; **naughtiness** noun.

nausea /ˈnɔːsɪə/ noun inclination to vomit; revulsion.

nauseate /ˈnɔːsɪeɪt/ verb (**-ting**) affect with nausea. □ **nauseating** adjective.

nauseous /ˈnɔːsɪəs/ adjective causing or inclined to vomit; disgusting.

nautical /ˈnɔːtɪk(ə)l/ adjective of sailors or navigation. □ **nautical mile** unit of approx. 2,025 yards (1,852 metres).

nautilus /ˈnɔːtɪləs/ noun (plural **nautiluses** or **nautili** /-laɪ/) kind of mollusc with spiral shell.

naval /ˈneɪv(ə)l/ adjective of navy; of ships.

nave¹ noun central part of church excluding chancel and side aisles.

nave² noun hub of wheel.

navel /ˈneɪv(ə)l/ noun depression in belly marking site of attachment of umbilical cord. □ **navel orange** one with navel-like formation at top.

navigable /ˈnævɪɡəb(ə)l/ adjective of river etc.) suitable for ships; seaworthy; steerable. □ **navigability** noun.

navigate /ˈnævɪɡeɪt/ verb (**-ting**) manage or direct course of (ship, aircraft); sail on (sea, river, etc.); fly through (air); help car-driver etc. by map-reading etc. □ **navigator** noun.

navigation noun act or process of navigating; art or science of navigating.

navvy /ˈnævɪ/ noun (plural **-ies**) labourer employed in building roads, canals, etc.

navy /ˈneɪvɪ/ noun (plural **-ies**) state's warships with their crews, maintenance systems, etc.; (in full **navy blue**) dark blue colour.

nay ● adverb or rather; and even; archaic no. ● noun 'no' vote.

Nazi /ˈnɑːtsɪ/ ● noun (plural **-s**) historical member of German National Socialist party. ● adjective of Nazis or Nazism. □ **Nazism** noun.

NB abbreviation note well (nota bene).

NCB abbreviation historical National Coal Board.

NCO abbreviation non-commissioned officer.

NE abbreviation north-east(ern).

Neanderthal /nɪˈændətɑːl/ adjective of type of human found in palaeolithic Europe.

neap noun (in full **neap tide**) tide with smallest rise and fall.

Neapolitan /nɪəˈpɒlɪt(ə)n/ ● noun native of Naples. ● adjective of Naples.

near /nɪə/ ● adverb (often + to) to or at short distance in space or time; closely. ● preposition to or at a short distance from in space, time, condition, or resemblance. ● adjective close (to); not far in place or time; closely related; (of part of vehicle, animal, or road) on left side; colloquial stingy; with little margin. ● verb approach, draw near to. □ **the Near East** countries of eastern Mediterranean; **near-sighted** short-sighted.

nearby ● adjective near in position. ● adverb close.

nearly adverb almost; closely. □ **not nearly** nothing like, far from.

neat adjective tidy, methodical; elegantly simple; brief and clear; cleverly done; dexterous; (of alcoholic liquor) undiluted. □ **neaten** verb; **neatly** adverb; **neatness** noun.

neath preposition poetical beneath.

nebula /ˈnebjʊlə/ noun (plural **nebulae** /-liː/) cloud of gas and dust seen in night sky, appearing luminous or as dark silhouette. □ **nebular** adjective.

nebulous /ˈnebjʊləs/ adjective cloudlike; indistinct, vague.

necessary /ˈnesəsərɪ/ ● adjective requiring to be done; essential; inevitable. ● noun (plural **-ies**) (usually in plural) any of basic requirements of life. □ **necessarily** adverb.

necessitate /nɪˈsesɪteɪt/ verb (**-ting**) make necessary (esp. as result).

necessitous /nɪˈsesɪtəs/ *adjective* poor, needy.

necessity /nɪˈsesɪtɪ/ *noun* (*plural* **-ies**) indispensable thing; pressure of circumstances; imperative need; poverty; constraint or compulsion seen as natural law governing human action.

neck ● *noun* part of body connecting head to shoulders; part of garment round neck; narrow part of anything. ● *verb colloquial* kiss and caress amorously. □ **neckline** outline of garment-opening at neck; **necktie** strip of material worn round shirt-collar, knotted at front.

necklace /ˈneklas/ *noun* string of beads, precious stones, etc. worn round neck; *South African* petrol-soaked tyre placed round victim's neck and lighted.

necromancy /ˈnekrəʊmænsɪ/ *noun* divination by supposed communication with the dead; magic. □ **necromancer** *noun*.

necrophilia /nekrəˈfɪlɪə/ *noun* morbid esp. sexual attraction to corpses.

necropolis /neˈkrɒpəlɪs/ *noun* ancient cemetery.

necrosis /neˈkrəʊsɪs/ *noun* death of tissue. □ **necrotic** /-ˈkrɒt-/ *adjective*.

nectar /ˈnektə/ *noun* sugary substance produced by plants and made into honey by bees; *Mythology* drink of gods.

nectarine /ˈnektərɪn/ *noun* smooth-skinned variety of peach.

NEDC *abbreviation* National Economic Development Council.

née /neɪ/ *adjective* (*US* **nee**) (before married woman's maiden name) born.

need ● *verb* stand in want of; require; (usually + *to do*) be under necessity or obligation. ● *noun* requirement; circumstances requiring action; destitution; poverty; emergency.

needful *adjective* requisite.

needle ● *noun* very thin pointed rod with slit ('eye') for thread, used in sewing; knitting-needle; pointer on dial; any small thin pointed instrument, esp. end of hypodermic syringe; obelisk; pointed rock or peak; leaf of fir or pine. ● *verb* (**-ling**) *colloquial* annoy, provoke. □ **needlecord** fine-ribbed corduroy fabric; **needlework** sewing or embroidery.

needless *adjective* unnecessary. □ **needlessly** *adverb*.

needy *adjective* (**-ier**, **-iest**) poor, destitute.

ne'er /neə/ *adverb poetical* never. □ **ne'er-do-well** good-for-nothing person.

nefarious /nɪˈfeərɪəs/ *adjective* wicked.

negate /nɪˈgeɪt/ *verb* (**-ting**) nullify; deny existence of.

negation *noun* absence or opposite of something positive; act of denying; negative statement; negative or unreal thing.

negative /ˈnegətɪv/ ● *adjective* expressing or implying denial, prohibition, or refusal; lacking positive attributes; opposite to positive; (of quantity) less than zero, to be subtracted; *Electricity* of, containing, or producing, kind of charge carried by electrons. ● *noun* negative statement or word; *Photography* image with black and white reversed or colours replaced by complementary ones. ● *verb* (**-ving**) refuse to accept; veto; disprove; contradict; neutralize. □ **negatively** *adverb*.

neglect /nɪˈglekt/ ● *verb* fail to care for or do; (+ *to do*) fail; pay no attention to; disregard. ● *noun* negligence; neglecting, being neglected. □ **neglectful** *adjective*; **neglectfully** *adverb*.

negligée /ˈneglɪʒeɪ/ *noun* (also **négligé**) woman's flimsy dressing gown.

negligence /ˈneglɪdʒ(ə)ns/ *noun* lack of proper care or attention; culpable carelessness. □ **negligent** *adjective*; **negligently** *adverb*.

negligible /ˈneglɪdʒɪb(ə)l/ *adjective* not worth considering; insignificant.

negotiate /nɪˈgəʊʃɪeɪt/ *verb* (**-ting**) confer in order to reach agreement; obtain (result) by negotiating; deal successfully with (obstacle etc.); convert (cheque etc.) into money. □ **negotiable** /-ʃəb-/ *adjective*; **negotiation** *noun*; **negotiator** *noun*.

Negress /ˈniːgrɪs/ *noun* female Negro.

■ **Usage** The term *Negress* is often considered offensive; *black* is usually preferred.

Negro /ˈniːgrəʊ/ ● *noun* (*plural* **-es**) member of dark-skinned (originally) African race; black. ● *adjective* of this race; black.

■ **Usage** The term *Negro* is often considered offensive; *black* is usually preferred.

Negroid /'niːgrɔɪd/ ● *adjective* (of physical features etc.) characteristic of black people. ● *noun* black person.

neigh /neɪ/ ● *noun* cry of horse. ● *verb* make a neigh.

neighbour /'neɪbə/ (*US* **neighbor**) *noun* person living next door or nearby; fellow human being. ● *verb* border on, adjoin.

neighbourhood *noun* (*US* **neighborhood**) district; vicinity; people of a district.

neighbourly *adjective* (*US* **neighborly**) like good neighbour, friendly, helpful. □ **neighbourliness** *noun*.

neither /'naɪðə/ *adjective, pronoun & adverb* not either.

nelson /'nels(ə)n/ *noun* wrestling hold in which arm is passed under opponent's arm from behind and hand applied to neck (**half nelson**), or both arms and hands are applied (**full nelson**).

nem. con. *abbreviation* with no one dissenting (*nemine contradicente*). [Latin]

nemesis /'nemɪsɪs/ *noun* justice bringing deserved punishment.

neo- *combining form* new; new form of.

neolithic /niːə'lɪθɪk/ *adjective* of later Stone Age.

neologism /niː'ɒlədʒɪz(ə)m/ *noun* new word; coining of new words.

neon /'niːɒn/ *noun* inert gas giving orange glow when electricity is passed through it.

neophyte /'niːəfaɪt/ *noun* new convert; novice of religious order; beginner.

nephew /'nefjuː/ *noun* son of one's brother or sister or of one's spouse's brother or sister.

nephritic /nɪ'frɪtɪk/ *adjective* of or in kidneys.

nephritis /nɪ'fraɪtɪs/ *noun* inflammation of kidneys.

nepotism /'nepətɪz(ə)m/ *noun* favouritism to relatives in conferring offices.

nereid /'nɪərɪɪd/ *noun* sea nymph.

nerve ● *noun* fibre or bundle of fibres conveying impulses of sensation or motion between brain and other parts of body; coolness in danger; *colloquial* impudence; (in *plural*) nervousness, mental or physical stress. ● *verb* (*-ving*) (usually **nerve oneself**) brace or prepare (oneself). □ **nerve-cell** cell transmitting impulses in nerve tissue.

nerveless *adjective* lacking vigour.

nervous *adjective* easily upset, timid, highly strung; anxious; affecting the nerves; (+ *of*) afraid of. □ **nervous breakdown** period of mental illness, usually after stress; **nervous system** body's network of nerves. □ **nervously** *adverb*; **nervousness** *noun*.

nervy *adjective* (**-ier, -iest**) *colloquial* nervous; easily excited.

nest ● *noun* structure or place where bird lays eggs and shelters young; breeding-place, lair; snug retreat, shelter; brood, swarm; group or set of similar objects. ● *verb* use or build nest; (of objects) fit one inside another. □ **nest egg** money saved up as reserve.

nestle /'nes(ə)l/ *verb* (**-ling**) settle oneself comfortably; press oneself against another in affection etc.; (+ *in, into,* etc.) push (head, shoulders, etc.) affectionately or snugly; lie half hidden or embedded.

nestling /'nestlɪŋ/ *noun* bird too young to leave nest.

net[1] ● *noun* open-meshed fabric of cord, rope, etc.; piece of net used esp. to contain, restrain, or delimit, or to catch fish; structure with net used in various games. ● *verb* (**-tt-**) cover, confine, or catch with net; hit (ball) into net, esp. of goal. □ **netball** game similar to basketball.

net[2] (also **nett**) ● *adjective* remaining after necessary deductions; (of price) not reducible; (of weight) excluding packaging etc. ● *verb* (**-tt-**) gain or yield (sum) as net profit.

nether /'neðə/ *adjective archaic* lower.

nett = NET[2].

netting *noun* meshed fabric of cord or wire.

nettle /'net(ə)l/ ● *noun* plant covered with stinging hairs; plant resembling this. ● *verb* (**-ling**) irritate, provoke. □ **nettle-rash** skin eruption like nettle stings.

network ● *noun* arrangement of intersecting horizontal and vertical lines;

complex system of railways etc.; people connected by exchange of information etc.; group of broadcasting stations connected for simultaneous broadcast of a programme; system of interconnected computers. ● *verb* broadcast on network.

neural /'njʊər(ə)l/ *adjective* of nerve or central nervous system.

neuralgia /njʊə'rældʒə/ *noun* intense pain along a nerve, esp. in face or head. □ **neuralgic** *adjective.*

neuritis /njʊə'raɪtɪs/ *noun* inflammation of nerve(s).

neuro- /'njʊərəʊ/ *combining form* nerve(s).

neurology /njʊə'rɒlədʒɪ/ *noun* study of nerve systems. □ **neurological** /-rə-'lɒdʒ-/ *adjective;* **neurologist** *noun.*

neuron /'njʊərɒn/ *noun* (also **neurone** /-rəʊn/) nerve cell.

neurosis /njʊə'rəʊsɪs/ *noun* (*plural* **-roses** /-siːz/) disturbed behaviour pattern associated with nervous distress.

neurotic /njʊə'rɒtɪk/ ● *adjective* caused by or relating to neurosis; suffering from neurosis; *colloquial* abnormally sensitive or obsessive. ● *noun* neurotic person.

neuter /'njuːtə/ ● *adjective* neither masculine nor feminine. ● *verb* castrate, spay.

neutral /'njuːtr(ə)l/ ● *adjective* supporting neither of two opposing sides, impartial; vague, indeterminate; (of a gear) in which engine is disconnected from driven parts; (of colours) not strong or positive; *Chemistry* neither acid nor alkaline; *Electricity* neither positive nor negative. ● *noun* neutral state or person. □ **neutrality** /-'træl-/ *noun.*

neutralize *verb* (also **-ise**) (**-zing** or **-sing**) make neutral; make ineffective by opposite force. □ **neutralization** *noun.*

neutrino /njuː'triːnəʊ/ *noun* (*plural* **-s**) elementary particle with zero electric charge and probably zero mass.

neutron /'njuːtrɒn/ *noun* elementary particle of about same mass as proton but without electric charge.

never /'nevə/ *adverb* at no time, on no occasion; not ever; not at all; *colloquial* surely not. □ **the never-never** *colloquial* hire purchase.

nevermore *adverb* at no future time.

nevertheless /nevəðə'les/ *adverb* in spite of that; notwithstanding.

new *adjective* of recent origin or arrival; made, discovered, acquired, or experienced for first time; not worn; renewed; reinvigorated; different; unfamiliar. □ **New Age** set of alternative beliefs replacing traditional Western culture; **newborn** recently born; **newcomer** person recently arrived; **newfangled** different from what one is used to; **new moon** moon when first seen as crescent; **New Testament** part of Bible concerned with Christ and his followers; **New World** N. & S. America; **New Year's Day, Eve** 1 Jan., 31 Dec.

newel /'njuːəl/ *noun* supporting central post of winding stairs; top or bottom post of stair-rail.

newly *adverb* recently; afresh.

news /njuːz/ *plural noun* (usually treated as *singular*) information about important or interesting recent events, esp. when published or broadcast; (**the news**) broadcast report of news. □ **newsagent** seller of newspapers etc.; **newscast** radio or television broadcast of news reports; **newsletter** informal printed bulletin of club etc.; **newspaper** /'njuːs-/ printed publication of loose folded sheets with news etc.; **newsprint** low-quality paper for printing newspapers; **newsreader** person who reads out broadcast news bulletins; **newsreel** short cinema film of recent events; **news room** room where news is prepared for publication or broadcasting; **newsworthy** topical, worth reporting as news.

newsy *adjective* (**-ier, -iest**) *colloquial* full of news.

newt /njuːt/ *noun* small tailed amphibian.

newton /'njuːt(ə)n/ *noun* SI unit of force.

next ● *adjective* (often + *to*) being, placed, or living nearest; nearest in time. ● *adverb* (often + *to*) nearest in place or degree, on first or soonest occasion. ● *noun* next person or thing. ● *preposition colloquial* next to. □ **next door** in next house or room; **next of kin** closest living relative(s).

nexus /'neksəs/ *noun* (*plural* same) connected group or series.

NHS *abbreviation* National Health Service.

NI *abbreviation* Northern Ireland; National Insurance.

niacin /ˈnaɪəsɪn/ *noun* nicotinic acid.

nib *noun* pen-point; (in *plural*) crushed coffee or cocoa beans.

nibble /ˈnɪb(ə)l/ • *verb* (**-ling**) (+ *at*) take small bites at; eat in small amounts; bite gently or playfully. • *noun* act of nibbling; very small amount of food.

nice *adjective* pleasant, satisfactory; kind, good-natured; fine, (of distinctions) subtle; fastidious. □ **nicely** *adverb*; **niceness** *noun*.

nicety /ˈnaɪsɪtɪ/ *noun* (*plural* **-ies**) subtle distinction or detail; precision. □ **to a nicety** exactly.

niche /niːʃ/ *noun* shallow recess, esp. in wall; comfortable or apt position in life or employment.

nick • *noun* small cut or notch; *slang* prison, police station; *colloquial* state, condition. • *verb* make nick(s) in; *slang* steal, arrest, catch. □ **in the nick of time** only just in time.

nickel /ˈnɪk(ə)l/ *noun* silver-white metallic element used esp. in magnetic alloys; *colloquial* US 5-cent coin.

nickname /ˈnɪkneɪm/ • *noun* familiar or humorous name added to or substituted for real name of person or thing. • *verb* (**-ming**) give nickname to.

nicotine /ˈnɪkətiːn/ *noun* poisonous alkaloid present in tobacco.

nicotinic acid /nɪkəˈtɪnɪk/ *noun* vitamin of B group.

nictitate /ˈnɪktɪteɪt/ *verb* (**-ting**) blink, wink. □ **nictitation** *noun*.

niece /niːs/ *noun* daughter of one's brother or sister or of one's spouse's brother or sister.

nifty /ˈnɪftɪ/ *adjective* (**-ier, -iest**) *colloquial* clever, adroit; smart, stylish.

niggard /ˈnɪɡəd/ *noun* stingy person.

niggardly *adjective* stingy. □ **niggardliness** *noun*.

niggle /ˈnɪɡ(ə)l/ *verb* (**-ling**) fuss over details, find fault in petty way; *colloquial* nag. □ **niggling** *adjective*.

nigh /naɪ/ *adverb* & *preposition archaic* near.

night /naɪt/ *noun* period of darkness from one day to next; time from sunset to sunrise; nightfall; darkness of night; evening. □ **nightcap** *historical* cap worn in bed, drink before going to bed; **nightclub** club providing entertainment etc. late at night; **nightdress** woman's or child's loose garment worn in bed; **nightfall** end of daylight; **nightjar** nocturnal bird with harsh cry; **night-life** entertainment available at night; **nightmare** terrifying dream or *colloquial* experience; **night safe** safe with access from outer wall of bank for deposit of money when bank is closed; **nightshade** any of various plants with poisonous berries; **nightshirt** long shirt worn in bed.

nightingale /ˈnaɪtɪŋɡeɪl/ *noun* small reddish-brown bird, of which the male sings tunefully, esp. at night.

nightly • *adjective* happening, done, or existing in the night; recurring every night. • *adverb* every night.

nihilism /ˈnaɪɪlɪz(ə)m/ *noun* rejection of all religious and moral principles. □ **nihilist** *noun*; **nihilistic** /-ˈlɪs-/ *adjective*.

nil *noun* nothing.

nimble /ˈnɪmb(ə)l/ *adjective* (**-r, -st**) quick and light in movement or function; agile. □ **nimbly** *adverb*.

nimbus /ˈnɪmbəs/ *noun* (*plural* **nimbi** /-baɪ/ or **nimbuses**) halo; rain-cloud.

nincompoop /ˈnɪŋkəmpuːp/ *noun* foolish person.

nine *adjective* & *noun* one more than eight. □ **ninepins** (usually treated as *singular*) kind of skittles. □ **ninth** /naɪnθ/ *adjective* & *noun*.

nineteen /naɪnˈtiːn/ *adjective* & *noun* one more than eighteen. □ **nineteenth** *adjective* & *noun*.

ninety /ˈnaɪntɪ/ *adjective* & *noun* (*plural* **-ies**) nine times ten. □ **ninetieth** *adjective* & *noun*.

ninny /ˈnɪnɪ/ *noun* (*plural* **-ies**) foolish person.

nip¹ • *verb* (**-pp-**) pinch, squeeze sharply, bite; (often + *off*) remove by pinching etc.; *colloquial* go nimbly. • *noun* pinch, sharp squeeze, bite; biting cold. □ **nip in the bud** suppress or destroy at very beginning.

nip² *noun* small quantity of spirits.

nipper *noun* person or thing that nips; claw of crab etc.; *colloquial* young child; (in *plural*) tool with jaws for gripping or cutting.

nipple /'nɪp(ə)l/ *noun* small projection in mammals from which in females milk for young is secreted; teat of feeding-bottle; device like nipple in function; nipple-like protuberance.

nippy *adjective* (**-ier, -iest**) *colloquial* quick, nimble; chilly.

nirvana /nɪə'vɑːnə/ *noun* (in Buddhism) perfect bliss attained by extinction of individuality.

nit *noun* egg or young of louse or other parasitic insect; *slang* stupid person. □ **nit-picking** *colloquial* fault-finding in a petty way.

niter *US* = NITRE.

nitrate /'naɪtreɪt/ *noun* salt of nitric acid; potassium or sodium nitrate as fertilizer.

nitre /'naɪtə/ *noun* (*US* **niter**) saltpetre.

nitric acid /'naɪtrɪk/ *noun* colourless corrosive poisonous liquid.

nitrogen /'naɪtrədʒ(ə)n/ *noun* gaseous element forming four-fifths of atmosphere. □ **nitrogenous** /-'trɒdʒɪnəs/ *adjective*.

nitroglycerine /naɪtrəʊ'glɪsərɪn/ *noun* (*US* **nitroglycerin**) explosive yellow liquid.

nitrous oxide /'naɪtrəs/ *noun* colourless gas used as anaesthetic.

nitty-gritty /nɪtɪ'grɪtɪ/ *noun slang* realities or practical details of a matter.

nitwit *noun colloquial* stupid person.

NNE *abbreviation* north-north-east.

NNW *abbreviation* north-north-west.

No = NOH.

No. *abbreviation* number.

no /nəʊ/ ● *adjective* not any; not a; hardly any; *used to forbid thing specified.* ● *adverb* by no amount, not at all. ● *interjection expressing negative reply to question, request, etc.* ● *noun* (*plural* **noes**) utterance of word *no*, denial or refusal; 'no' vote. □ **no-ball** unlawfully delivered ball in cricket etc.; **no longer** not now as formerly; **no one** nobody; **no way** *colloquial* it is impossible.

nob[1] *noun slang* person of wealth or high social position.

nob[2] *noun slang* head.

nobble /'nɒb(ə)l/ *verb* (**-ling**) *slang* try to influence (e.g. judge); tamper with (racehorse etc.); steal; seize; catch.

nobility /nəʊ'bɪlɪtɪ/ *noun* (*plural* **-ies**) nobleness of character, birth, or rank; class of nobles.

noble /'nəʊb(ə)l/ ● *adjective* (**-r, -st**) belonging to the aristocracy; of excellent character; magnanimous; of imposing appearance. ● *noun* nobleman; noblewoman. □ **nobleman** peer; **noblewoman** peeress. □ **nobly** *adverb*.

noblesse oblige /nəʊbles ɒ'bliːʒ/ *noun* privilege entails responsibility. [French]

nobody /'nəʊbədɪ/ ● *pronoun* no person. ● *noun* (*plural* **-ies**) person of no importance.

nocturnal /nɒk'tɜːn(ə)l/ *adjective* of or in the night; done or active by night.

nocturne /'nɒktɜːn/ *noun Music* short romantic composition, usually for piano; picture of night scene.

nod ● *verb* (**-dd-**) incline head slightly and briefly; let head droop in drowsiness; be drowsy; show (assent etc.) by nod; (of flowers etc.) bend and sway; make momentary slip or mistake. ● *noun* nodding of head. □ **nod off** *colloquial* fall asleep.

noddle /'nɒd(ə)l/ *noun colloquial* head.

node *noun* part of plant stem from which leaves emerge; knob on root or branch; natural swelling; intersecting point, esp. of planet's orbit with plane of celestial equator; point or line of least disturbance in vibrating system; point at which curve crosses itself; component in computer network. □ **nodal** *adjective*.

nodule /'nɒdjuːl/ *noun* small rounded lump of anything; small tumour, ganglion, swelling on legume root. □ **nodular** *adjective*.

noggin /'nɒgɪn/ *noun* small mug; small measure of spirits.

Noh /nəʊ/ *noun* (also **No**) traditional Japanese drama.

noise /nɔɪz/ ● *noun* sound, esp. loud or unpleasant one; confusion of loud sounds. ● *verb* (**-sing**) (usually in *passive*) make public, spread abroad.

noisome /'nɔɪsəm/ *adjective literary* harmful, noxious; evil-smelling.

noisy *adjective* (**-ier, -iest**) making much noise; full of noise. □ **noisily** *adverb*.

nomad /ˈnəʊmæd/ noun member of tribe roaming from place to place for pasture; wanderer. □ **nomadic** /-ˈmæd-/ adjective.

nom de plume /nɒm də ˈpluːm/ noun (plural **noms de plume** same pronunciation) writer's assumed name. [French]

nomenclature /nəʊˈmenklətʃə/ noun system of names for things; terminology of a science etc.

nominal /ˈnɒmɪn(ə)l/ adjective existing in name only; not real or actual; (of sum of money etc.) very small; of, as, or like noun. □ **nominally** adverb.

nominate /ˈnɒmɪneɪt/ verb (**-ting**) propose (candidate) for election; appoint to office; appoint (date or place). □ **nomination** noun; **nominator** noun.

nominative /ˈnɒmɪnətɪv/ Grammar • noun case expressing subject of verb. • adjective of or in this case.

nominee /nɒmɪˈniː/ noun person who is nominated.

non- prefix not. For words starting with non- that are not found below, the root-words should be consulted.

nonagenarian /nəʊnədʒɪˈneərɪən/ noun person from 90 to 99 years old.

non-belligerent /nɒnbəˈlɪdʒərənt/ • adjective not engaged in hostilities. • noun non-belligerent state etc.

nonce /nɒns/ noun □ **for the nonce** for the time being, for the present; **nonce-word** word coined for one occasion.

nonchalant /ˈnɒnʃələnt/ adjective calm and casual. □ **nonchalance** noun; **nonchalantly** adverb.

non-combatant /nɒnˈkɒmbət(ə)nt/ noun person not fighting in a war, esp. civilian, army chaplain, etc.

non-commissioned /nɒnkəˈmɪʃ(ə)nd/ adjective (of officer) not holding commission.

noncommittal /nɒnkəˈmɪt(ə)l/ adjective avoiding commitment to definite opinion or course of action.

non-conductor /nɒnkənˈdʌktə/ noun substance that does not conduct heat or electricity.

nonconformist /nɒnkənˈfɔːmɪst/ noun person who does not conform to doctrine of established Church, esp. (**Non-conformist**) member of Protestant sect dissenting from Anglican Church; person not conforming to prevailing principle.

nonconformity /nɒnkənˈfɔːmɪtɪ/ noun nonconformists as body; (+ to) failure to conform.

non-contributory /nɒnkənˈtrɪbjʊtərɪ/ adjective not involving contributions.

nondescript /ˈnɒndɪskrɪpt/ • adjective lacking distinctive characteristics, not easily classified. • noun such person or thing.

none /nʌn/ pronoun (often + of) not any; no person(s). □ **none the** (+ comparative), **none too** not in the least.

■ **Usage** The verb following none can be singular or plural when it means 'not any of several', e.g. None of us knows or None of us know.

nonentity /nɒˈnentɪtɪ/ noun (plural **-ies**) person or thing of no importance; non-existence; non-existent thing.

nonet /nəʊˈnet/ noun musical composition for 9 performers; the performers; any group of 9.

nonetheless /nʌnðəˈles/ adverb nevertheless.

non-event /nɒnɪˈvent/ noun insignificant event, esp. contrary to hopes or expectations.

non-existent /nɒnɪgˈzɪst(ə)nt/ adjective not existing. □ **non-existence** noun.

non-fiction /nɒnˈfɪkʃ(ə)n/ noun literary work other than fiction.

non-interference /nɒnɪntəˈfɪərəns/ noun non-intervention.

non-intervention /nɒnɪntəˈvenʃ(ə)n/ noun policy of not interfering in others' affairs.

nonpareil /nɒnpəˈreɪl/ • adjective unrivalled, unique. • noun such person or thing.

non-party /nɒnˈpɑːtɪ/ adjective independent of political parties.

nonplus /nɒnˈplʌs/ verb (**-ss-**) completely perplex.

nonsense /ˈnɒns(ə)ns/ noun (often as interjection) absurd or meaningless words or ideas; foolish conduct. □ **nonsensical** /-ˈsen-/ adjective.

non sequitur /nɒn ˈsekwɪtə/ noun conclusion that does not logically follow from the premisses. [Latin]

non-slip /nɒnˈslɪp/ *adjective* that does not slip; that prevents slipping.

non-smoker /nɒnˈsməʊkə/ *noun* person who does not smoke; train compartment etc. where smoking is forbidden. □ **non-smoking** *adjective*.

non-starter /nɒnˈstɑːtə/ *noun colloquial* person or scheme not worth considering.

non-stick /nɒnˈstɪk/ *adjective* that does not allow things to stick to it.

non-stop /nɒnˈstɒp/ • *adjective* (of train etc.) not stopping at intermediate stations; done without stopping. • *adverb* without stopping.

noodle[1] /ˈnuːd(ə)l/ *noun* strip or ring of pasta.

noodle[2] /ˈnuːd(ə)l/ *noun* simpleton.

nook /nʊk/ *noun* corner or recess; secluded place.

noon *noun* 12 o'clock in day, midday. □ **noonday** midday.

noose • *noun* loop with running knot; snare. • *verb* (**-sing**) catch with or enclose in noose.

nor *conjunction* and not.

Nordic /ˈnɔːdɪk/ *adjective* of tall blond Germanic people of Scandinavia.

norm *noun* standard, type; standard amount of work etc.; customary behaviour.

normal /ˈnɔːm(ə)l/ • *adjective* conforming to standard; regular, usual, typical; *Geometry* (of line) at right angles. • *noun* normal value of a temperature etc.; usual state, level, etc. □ **normalcy** *noun esp. US*; **normality** /-ˈmæl-/ *noun*; **normalize** *verb* (also **-ise**) (**-zing** or **-sing**); **normally** *adverb*.

Norman /ˈnɔːmən/ • *noun* (*plural* **-s**) native of medieval Normandy; descendant of people established there in 10th c. • *adjective* of Normans; of style of medieval architecture found in Britain under Normans.

Norse • *noun* Norwegian language; Scandinavian language group. • *adjective* of ancient Scandinavia, esp. Norway. □ **Norseman** *noun*.

north • *noun* point of horizon 90° anticlockwise from east; corresponding compass point; (usually **the North**) northern part of world, country, town, etc. • *adjective* towards, at, near, or facing north; (of wind) from north. • *adverb* towards, at, or near north; (+ *of*) further north than. □ **northbound** travelling or leading north; **north-east**, **-west** point midway between north and east or west; **north-north-east**, **north-north-west** point midway between north and north-east or north-west; **North Star** pole star. □ **northward** *adjective*, *adverb*, & *noun*; **northwards** *adverb*.

northerly /ˈnɔːðəlɪ/ *adjective* & *adverb* in northern position or direction; (of wind) from north.

northern /ˈnɔːð(ə)n/ *adjective* of or in the north. □ **northern lights** aurora borealis. □ **northernmost** *adjective*.

northerner *noun* native or inhabitant of north.

Norwegian /nɔːˈwiːdʒ(ə)n/ • *noun* native, national, or language of Norway. • *adjective* of or relating to Norway.

nose /nəʊz/ • *noun* organ above mouth, used for smelling and breathing; sense of smell; odour or perfume of wine etc.; projecting part or front end of car, aircraft, etc. • *verb* (**-sing**) (usually + *about* etc.) search; (often + *out*) perceive smell of, discover by smell; thrust nose against or into; make one's way cautiously forward. □ **nosebag** fodder-bag hung on horse's head; **nosebleed** bleeding from nose; **nosedive** (make) steep downward plunge.

nosegay *noun* small bunch of flowers.

nosh *slang* • *verb* eat. • *noun* food or drink. □ **nosh-up** large meal.

nostalgia /nɒsˈtældʒə/ *noun* (often + *for*) yearning for past period; homesickness. □ **nostalgic** *adjective*.

nostril /ˈnɒstr(ə)l/ *noun* either of two openings in nose.

nostrum /ˈnɒstrəm/ *noun* quack remedy, patent medicine; pet scheme.

nosy *adjective* (**-ier**, **-iest**) *colloquial* inquisitive, prying.

not *adverb* expressing negation, refusal, or denial. □ **not half** *slang* very much, very, not nearly, *colloquial* not at all; **not quite** almost.

notable /ˈnəʊtəb(ə)l/ ● *adjective* worthy of note; remarkable; eminent. ● *noun* eminent person. □ **notability** *noun*; **notably** *adverb*.

notary /ˈnəʊtəri/ *noun* (*plural* **-ies**) solicitor etc. who certifies deeds etc. □ **notarial** /-ˈteər-/ *adjective*.

notation /nəʊˈteɪʃ(ə)n/ *noun* representation of numbers, quantities, musical notes, etc. by symbols; set of such symbols.

notch ● *noun* V-shaped indentation on edge or surface. ● *verb* make notches in; (usually + *up*) score, win, achieve (esp. amount or quantity).

note ● *noun* brief written record as memory aid; short letter; formal diplomatic message; additional explanation in book; banknote; notice, attention; eminence; single musical tone of definite pitch; written sign representing its pitch and duration; quality or tone of speaking. ● *verb* (**-ting**) observe, notice; (often + *down*) record as thing to be remembered; (in *passive*; often + *for*) be well known. □ **notebook** book for making notes in; **notecase** wallet for banknotes; **notelet** small folded card for informal letter; **notepaper** paper for writing letters; **noteworthy** worthy of attention, remarkable.

nothing /ˈnʌθɪŋ/ ● *noun* no thing, not anything; person or thing of no importance; non-existence; no amount; nought. ● *adverb* not at all; in no way.

nothingness *noun* non-existence; worthlessness.

notice /ˈnəʊtɪs/ ● *noun* attention; displayed sheet etc. with announcement; intimation; warning; formal declaration of intention to end agreement or employment at specified time; short published review of new play, book, etc. ● *verb* (**-cing**) (often + *that, how,* etc.) perceive, observe. □ **noticeable** *adjective*; **noticeably** *adverb*.

notifiable /ˈnəʊtɪfaɪəb(ə)l/ *adjective* (esp. of disease) that must be notified to authorities.

notify /ˈnəʊtɪfaɪ/ *verb* (**-ies, -ied**) (often + *of, that*) inform, give notice to (person); make known. □ **notification** *noun*.

notion /ˈnəʊʃ(ə)n/ *noun* concept, idea; opinion; vague understanding; intention.

notional *adjective* hypothetical, imaginary. □ **notionally** *adverb*.

notorious /nəʊˈtɔːrɪəs/ *adjective* well known, esp. unfavourably. □ **notoriety** /-təˈraɪətɪ/ *noun*; **notoriously** *adverb*.

notwithstanding /nɒtwɪðˈstændɪŋ/ ● *preposition* in spite of. ● *adverb* nevertheless.

nougat /ˈnuːgɑː/ *noun* sweet made from nuts, egg white, and sugar or honey.

nought /nɔːt/ *noun* digit 0; cipher; *poetical or archaic* nothing.

noun /naʊn/ *noun* word used to name person or thing (see panel).

nourish /ˈnʌrɪʃ/ *verb* sustain with food; foster, cherish (feeling etc.). □ **nourishing** *adjective*.

nourishment *noun* sustenance, food.

nous /naʊs/ *noun* colloquial common sense.

Nov. *abbreviation* November.

nova /ˈnəʊvə/ *noun* (*plural* **novae** /-viː/ or **-s**) star showing sudden burst of brightness and then subsiding.

novel /ˈnɒv(ə)l/ ● *noun* fictitious prose story of book length. ● *adjective* of new kind or nature.

novelette /nɒvəˈlet/ *noun* short (esp. romantic) novel.

novelist /ˈnɒvəlɪst/ *noun* writer of novels.

novella /nəˈvelə/ *noun* (*plural* **-s**) short novel or narrative story.

novelty /ˈnɒvəltɪ/ *noun* (*plural* **-ies**) newness; new thing or occurrence; small toy etc.

November /nəʊˈvembə/ *noun* eleventh month of year.

novena /nəˈviːnə/ *noun* RC Church special prayers or services on 9 successive days.

novice /ˈnɒvɪs/ *noun* probationary member of religious order; beginner.

noviciate /nəˈvɪʃɪət/ *noun* (also **novitiate**) period of being a novice; religious novice; novices' quarters.

now ● *adverb* at present or mentioned time; immediately; by this time; in the immediate past. ● *conjunction* (often + *that*) because. ● *noun* this time; the present. □ **now and again** or **then** occasionally.

nowadays /'naʊədeɪz/ ● *adverb* at present time or age. ● *noun* the present time.

nowhere /'nəʊweə/ ● *adverb* in or to no place. ● *pronoun* no place.

nowt *noun colloquial or dialect* nothing.

noxious /'nɒkʃəs/ *adjective* harmful, unwholesome.

nozzle /'nɒz(ə)l/ *noun* spout on hose etc.

nr. *abbreviation* near.

NSPCC *abbreviation* National Society for Prevention of Cruelty to Children.

NSW *abbreviation* New South Wales.

NT *abbreviation* New Testament; Northern Territory (of Australia); National Trust.

nuance /'nju:ãs/ *noun* subtle shade of meaning, feeling, colour, etc.

nub *noun* point or gist (of matter or story).

nubile /'nju:baɪl/ *adjective* (of woman) marriageable, sexually attractive. □ **nubility** *noun*.

nuclear /'nju:klɪə/ *adjective* of, relating to, or constituting a nucleus; using nuclear energy. □ **nuclear energy**

energy obtained by nuclear fission or fusion; **nuclear family** couple and their child(ren); **nuclear fission** nuclear reaction in which heavy nucleus splits with release of energy; **nuclear fuel** source of nuclear energy; **nuclear fusion** nuclear reaction in which nuclei of low atomic number fuse with release of energy; **nuclear physics** physics of atomic nuclei; **nuclear power** power derived from nuclear energy, country that has nuclear weapons.

nucleic acid /nju:'kli:ɪk/ *noun* either of two complex organic molecules (DNA and RNA) present in all living cells.

nucleon /'nju:klɒn/ *noun* proton or neutron.

nucleus /'nju:klɪəs/ *noun* (*plural* **nuclei** /-lɪaɪ/) central part or thing round which others collect; kernel; initial part; central core of atom; part of cell containing genetic material.

nude /nju:d/ ● *adjective* naked, unclothed. ● *noun* painting etc. of nude human figure; nude person. □ **in the nude** naked. □ **nudity** *noun*.

Noun

A noun is the name of a person or thing. There are four kinds:

1 common nouns (the words for articles and creatures), e.g.

shoe	in	*The red shoe was left on the shelf.*
box	in	*The large box stood in the corner.*
plant	in	*The plant grew to two metres.*
horse	in	*A horse and rider galloped by.*

2 proper nouns (the names of people, places, ships, institutions, and animals, which always begin with a capital letter), e.g.

Jane	*USS Enterprise*	*Bambi*
London	*Grand Hotel*	

3 abstract nouns (the words for qualities, things we cannot see or touch, and things which have no physical reality), e.g.

truth	*absence*
explanation	*warmth*

4 collective nouns (the words for groups of things), e.g.

committee	*squad*	*the Cabinet*
herd	*swarm*	*the clergy*
majority	*team*	*the public*

nudge ● *verb* (**-ging**) prod gently with elbow to draw attention; push gradually. ● *noun* gentle push.

nudist /'njuːdɪst/ *noun* person who advocates or practises going unclothed. □ **nudism** *noun*.

nugatory /'njuːgətərɪ/ *adjective* futile, trifling; inoperative, not valid.

nugget /'nʌgɪt/ *noun* lump of gold etc., as found in earth; lump of anything.

nuisance /'njuːs(ə)ns/ *noun* person, thing, or circumstance causing annoyance.

null *adjective* (esp. **null and void**) invalid; non-existent; expressionless. □ **nullity** *noun*.

nullify /'nʌlɪfaɪ/ *verb* (**-ies, -ied**) neutralize; invalidate. □ **nullification** *noun*.

numb /nʌm/ ● *adjective* deprived of feeling; paralysed. ● *verb* make numb; stupefy, paralyse. □ **numbness** *noun*.

number /'nʌmbə/ ● *noun* arithmetical value representing a quantity; word, symbol, or figure representing this; total count or aggregate; numerical reckoning; quantity; amount; person or thing having place in a series, esp. single issue of magazine, item in programme, etc. ● *verb* include; assign number(s) to; amount to specified number. □ **number one** *colloquial* oneself; **number plate** plate bearing number esp. of motor vehicle.

■ **Usage** The phrase *a number of* is normally used with a plural verb, as in *a number of problems remain.*

numberless *adjective* innumerable.

numeral /'njuːmər(ə)l/ ● *noun* symbol or group of symbols denoting a number. ● *adjective* of or denoting a number.

numerate /'njuːmərət/ *adjective* familiar with basic principles of mathematics. □ **numeracy** *noun*.

numeration /njuːmə'reɪʃ(ə)n/ *noun* process of numbering; calculation.

numerator /'njuːməreɪtə/ *noun* number above line in vulgar fraction.

numerical /njuː'merɪk(ə)l/ *adjective* of or relating to number(s). □ **numerically** *adverb*.

numerology /njuːmə'rɒlədʒɪ/ *noun* study of supposed occult significance of numbers.

numerous /'njuːmərəs/ *adjective* many; consisting of many.

numinous /'njuːmɪnəs/ *adjective* indicating presence of a god; awe-inspiring.

numismatic /njuːmɪz'mætɪk/ *adjective* of or relating to coins or medals.

numismatics *plural noun* (usually treated as *singular*) study of coins and medals. □ **numismatist** /-'mɪzmətɪst/ *noun*.

nun *noun* member of community of women living under religious vows.

nuncio /'nʌnsɪəʊ/ *noun* (*plural* **-s**) papal ambassador.

nunnery *noun* (*plural* **-ies**) religious house of nuns.

nuptial /'nʌpʃ(ə)l/ ● *adjective* of marriage or weddings. ● *noun* (usually in *plural*) wedding.

nurse /nɜːs/ ● *noun* person trained to care for sick and help doctors or dentists; nursemaid. ● *verb* (**-sing**) work as nurse; attend to (sick person); feed or be fed at breast; hold or treat carefully; foster; harbour. □ **nursing home** private hospital or home.

nursemaid *noun* woman in charge of child(ren).

nursery /'nɜːsərɪ/ *noun* (*plural* **-ies**) room or place equipped for young children; place where plants are reared for sale. □ **nurseryman** grower of plants for sale; **nursery rhyme** traditional song or rhyme for young children; **nursery school** school for children between ages of 3 and 5.

nurture /'nɜːtʃə/ ● *noun* bringing up, fostering care; nourishment. ● *verb* (**-ring**) bring up, rear.

nut *noun* fruit consisting of hard shell or pod around edible kernel or seeds; this kernel; small usually hexagonal flat piece of metal with threaded hole through it for screwing on end of bolt to secure it; *slang* head; *slang* crazy person; small lump of (coal etc.). □ **nutcase** *slang* crazy person; **nutcracker** (usually in *plural*) device for cracking nuts; **nuthatch** small bird climbing up and down tree trunks; **nuts** *slang* crazy.

nutmeg /'nʌtmeg/ *noun* hard aromatic seed used as spice etc.; E. Indian tree bearing this.

nutria /'njuːtrɪə/ *noun* coypu fur.

nutrient /'njuːtrɪənt/ ●*noun* substance providing essential nourishment. ●*adjective* serving as or providing nourishment.

nutriment /'njuːtrɪmənt/ *noun* nourishing food.

nutrition /njuː'trɪʃ(ə)n/ *noun* food, nourishment. □ **nutritional** *adjective*; **nutritionist** *noun*.

nutritious /njuː'trɪʃəs/ *adjective* efficient as food.

nutritive /'njuːtrɪtɪv/ *adjective* of nutrition; nutritious.

nutshell *noun* hard covering of nut. □ **in a nutshell** in few words.

nutter *noun slang* crazy person.

nutty *adjective* (**-ier**, **-iest**) full of nuts; tasting like nuts; *slang* crazy.

nux vomica /nʌks 'vɒmɪkə/ *noun* E. Indian tree; its seeds, containing strychnine.

nuzzle /'nʌz(ə)l/ *verb* (**-ling**) prod or rub gently with nose; nestle, lie snug.

NW *abbreviation* north-west(ern).

NY *abbreviation US* New York.

nylon /'naɪlɒn/ *noun* strong light synthetic fibre; nylon fabric; (in *plural*) stockings of nylon.

nymph /nɪmf/ *noun* mythological semidivine female spirit associated with rivers, woods, etc.; immature form of some insects.

nymphomania /nɪmfə'meɪnɪə/ *noun* excessive sexual desire in a woman. □ **nymphomaniac** *noun & adjective*.

NZ *abbreviation* New Zealand.

Oo

O¹ □ **O level** *historical* ordinary level in GCE exam.

O² /əʊ/ *interjection* = OH; *used before name in exclamation.*

oaf *noun* (*plural* **-s**) awkward lout. □ **oafish** *adjective*; **oafishly** *adverb*; **oafishness** *noun*.

oak *noun* acorn-bearing hardwood tree with lobed leaves; its wood. □ **oak-apple**, **-gall** abnormal growth produced on oak trees by insects.

oakum /'əʊkəm/ *noun* loose fibre got by picking old rope to pieces.

OAP *abbreviation* old-age pensioner.

oar /ɔː/ *noun* pole with blade used to propel boat by leverage against water; rower.

oarsman /'ɔːzmən/ *noun* (*feminine* **-woman**) rower. □ **oarsmanship** *noun*.

oasis /əʊ'eɪsɪs/ *noun* (*plural* **oases** /-siːz/) fertile spot in desert.

oast *noun* hop-drying kiln. □ **oast house** building containing this.

oat *noun* cereal plant grown as food; (in *plural*) grain of this; tall grass resembling this. □ **oatcake** thin oatmeal biscuit; **oatmeal** meal ground from oats,

greyish-fawn colour; **sow one's wild oats** indulge in youthful follies before becoming steady. □ **oaten** *adjective*.

oath /əʊθ/ *noun* (*plural* **-s** /əʊðz/) solemn declaration naming God etc. as witness; curse. □ **on**, **under oath** having sworn solemn oath.

ob. *abbreviation* died (*obiit*).

obbligato /ɒblɪ'gɑːtəʊ/ *noun* (*plural* **-s**) *Music* accompaniment forming integral part of a composition.

obdurate /'ɒbdjʊrət/ *adjective* stubborn; hardened. □ **obduracy** *noun*.

OBE *abbreviation* Officer of the Order of the British Empire.

obedient /əʊ'biːdɪənt/ *adjective* obeying or ready to obey; submissive to another's will. □ **obedience** *noun*; **obediently** *adverb*.

obeisance /əʊ'beɪs(ə)ns/ *noun* gesture expressing submission, respect, etc.; homage. □ **obeisant** *adjective*.

obelisk /'ɒbəlɪsk/ *noun* tapering usually 4-sided stone pillar.

obelus /'ɒbələs/ *noun* (*plural* **obeli** /-laɪ/) dagger-shaped mark of reference (†).

obese /əʊ'biːs/ *adjective* very fat. □ **obesity** *noun*.

obey /əʊ'beɪ/ *verb* carry out command of; do what one is told to do.

obfuscate /'ɒbfʌskeɪt/ *verb* (**-ting**) obscure, confuse; bewilder. □ **obfuscation** *noun*.

obituary /ə'bɪtjʊərɪ/ ● *noun* (*plural* **-ies**) notice of death(s); brief biography of deceased person. ● *adjective* of or serving as obituary.

object ● *noun* /'ɒbdʒɪkt/ material thing; person or thing to which action or feeling is directed; thing sought or aimed at; word or phrase representing person or thing affected by action of verb (see panel). ● *verb* /əb'dʒekt/ (often + *to, against*) express opposition, disapproval, or reluctance; protest. □ **no object** not an important factor. □ **objector** *noun*.

objectify /əb'dʒektɪfaɪ/ *verb* (**-ies, -ied**) present as an object, embody.

objection /əb'dʒekʃ(ə)n/ *noun* expression of disapproval or opposition; objecting; adverse reason or statement.

objectionable *adjective* unpleasant, offensive; open to objection. □ **objectionably** *adverb*.

objective /əb'dʒektɪv/ ● *adjective* external to the mind; actually existing; dealing with outward things uncoloured by opinions or feelings; *Grammar* (of case or word) in form appropriate to object. ● *noun* object or purpose; *Grammar* objective case. □ **objectively** *adverb*; **objectivity** /ɒbdʒek'tɪvɪtɪ/ *noun*.

objet d'art /ɒbʒeɪ 'dɑ:/ *noun* (*plural* **objets d'art** same pronunciation) small decorative object. [French]

oblate /'ɒbleɪt/ *adjective* (of spheroid) flattened at poles.

oblation /əʊ'bleɪʃ(ə)n/ *noun* thing offered to a divine being.

obligate /'ɒblɪgeɪt/ *verb* (**-ting**) bind (person) legally or morally.

obligation /ɒblɪ'geɪʃ(ə)n/ *noun* compelling power of law, duty, etc.; duty; binding agreement; indebtedness for service or benefit.

obligatory /ə'blɪgətərɪ/ *adjective* binding, compulsory. □ **obligatorily** *adverb*.

oblige /ə'blaɪdʒ/ *verb* (**-ging**) compel, require; be binding on; do (person) small favour; (as **obliged** *adjective*) grateful.

obliging *adjective* helpful, accommodating. □ **obligingly** *adverb*.

oblique /ə'bli:k/ ● *adjective* slanting; at an angle; not going straight to the point, indirect; *Grammar* (of case) other than nominative or vocative. ● *noun* oblique stroke. □ **obliquely** *adverb*; **obliqueness** *noun*; **obliquity** /ə'blɪkwɪtɪ/ *noun*.

Object

There are two types of object:

1 A direct object is a person or thing directly affected by the verb and can usually be found by asking the question 'whom or what?' after the verb, e.g.

The electors chose Mr Smith.

Charles wrote a letter.

2 An indirect object is usually a person or thing receiving something from the subject of the verb, e.g.

He gave me the pen.

(*me* is the indirect object, and *the pen* is the direct object.)

I sent my bank a letter.

(*my bank* is the indirect object, and *a letter* is the direct object.)

Sentences containing an indirect object usually contain a direct object as well, but not always, e.g.

Pay me.

'Object' on its own usually means a direct object.

obliterate /əˈblɪtəreɪt/ *verb* (**-ting**) blot out, leave no clear trace of. □ **obliteration** *noun*.

oblivion /əˈblɪvɪən/ *noun* state of having or being forgotten.

oblivious /əˈblɪvɪəs/ *adjective* unaware or unconscious. □ **obliviously** *adverb*; **obliviousness** *noun*.

oblong /ˈɒblɒŋ/ ● *adjective* rectangular with adjacent sides unequal. ● *noun* oblong figure or object.

obloquy /ˈɒbləkwɪ/ *noun* abuse, being ill spoken of.

obnoxious /əbˈnɒkʃəs/ *adjective* offensive, objectionable. □ **obnoxiously** *adverb*; **obnoxiousness** *noun*.

oboe /ˈəʊbəʊ/ *noun* double-reeded woodwind instrument. □ **oboist** *noun*.

obscene /əbˈsiːn/ *adjective* offensively indecent; *colloquial* highly offensive; *Law* (of publication) tending to deprave and corrupt. □ **obscenely** *adverb*; **obscenity** /-ˈsen-/ *noun* (*plural* **-ies**).

obscure /əbˈskjʊə/ ● *adjective* not clearly expressed or easily understood; unexplained; dark, indistinct; hidden, undistinguished. ● *verb* (**-ring**) make obscure or invisible. □ **obscurity** *noun*.

obsequies /ˈɒbsɪkwɪz/ *plural noun* funeral.

obsequious /əbˈsiːkwɪəs/ *adjective* fawning, servile. □ **obsequiously** *adverb*; **obsequiousness** *noun*.

observance /əbˈzɜːv(ə)ns/ *noun* keeping or performance of law, duty, etc.; rite, ceremonial act.

observant *adjective* good at observing. □ **observantly** *adverb*.

observation /ɒbzəˈveɪʃ(ə)n/ *noun* observing, being observed; comment, remark; power of perception. □ **observational** *adjective*.

observatory /əbˈzɜːvətərɪ/ *noun* (*plural* **-ies**) building for astronomical or other observation.

observe /əbˈzɜːv/ *verb* (**-ving**) perceive, become aware of; watch; keep (rules etc.); celebrate (rite etc.); remark; take note of scientifically. □ **observable** *adjective*.

observer *noun* person who observes; interested spectator; person attending meeting to note proceedings but without participating.

obsess /əbˈses/ *verb* fill mind of (person) all the time; preoccupy. □ **obsession** *noun*; **obsessional** *adjective*; **obsessive** *adjective*; **obsessively** *adverb*; **obsessiveness** *noun*.

obsidian /əbˈsɪdɪən/ *noun* dark glassy rock formed from lava.

obsolescent /ɒbsəˈles(ə)nt/ *adjective* becoming obsolete. □ **obsolescence** *noun*.

obsolete /ˈɒbsəliːt/ *adjective* no longer used, antiquated.

obstacle /ˈɒbstək(ə)l/ *noun* thing obstructing progress.

obstetrics /əbˈstetrɪks/ *plural noun* (usually treated as *singular*) branch of medicine or surgery dealing with childbirth. □ **obstetric** *adjective*; **obstetrician** /ɒbstəˈtrɪʃ(ə)n/ *noun*.

obstinate /ˈɒbstɪnət/ *adjective* stubborn, intractable. □ **obstinacy** *noun*; **obstinately** *adverb*.

obstreperous /əbˈstrepərəs/ *adjective* noisy, unruly. □ **obstreperously** *adverb*; **obstreperousness** *noun*.

obstruct /əbˈstrʌkt/ *verb* block up; make hard or impossible to pass along or through; retard or prevent progress of.

obstruction /əbˈstrʌkʃ(ə)n/ *noun* obstructing, being obstructed; thing that obstructs; *Sport* unlawfully obstructing another player.

obstructive *adjective* causing or meant to cause obstruction.

obtain /əbˈteɪn/ *verb* acquire; get; have granted to one; be prevalent or established. □ **obtainable** *adjective*.

obtrude /əbˈtruːd/ *verb* (**-ding**) (often + *on*, *upon*) thrust (oneself etc.) importunately forward. □ **obtrusion** *noun*.

obtrusive /əbˈtruːsɪv/ *adjective* unpleasantly noticeable; obtruding oneself. □ **obtrusively** *adverb*; **obtrusiveness** *noun*.

obtuse /əbˈtjuːs/ *adjective* dull-witted; (of angle) between 90° and 180°; blunt, not sharp or pointed. □ **obtuseness** *noun*.

obverse /ˈɒbvɜːs/ *noun* counterpart, opposite; side of coin or medal that bears head or principal design; front or top side.

obviate /ˈɒbvɪeɪt/ *verb* (**-ting**) get round or do away with (need, inconvenience, etc.).

obvious /'ɒbvɪəs/ *adjective* easily seen, recognized, or understood. □ **obviously** *adverb*; **obviousness** *noun*.

OC *abbreviation* Officer Commanding.

ocarina /ɒkə'riːnə/ *noun* egg-shaped musical wind instrument.

occasion /ə'keɪʒ(ə)n/ ● *noun* special event or happening; time of this; reason, need; suitable juncture, opportunity. ● *verb* cause, esp. incidentally.

occasional *adjective* happening irregularly and infrequently; made or meant for, acting on, etc. special occasion(s). □ **occasional table** small table for use as required. □ **occasionally** *adverb*.

Occident /'ɒksɪd(ə)nt/ *noun* (**the Occident**) West, esp. Europe and America as distinct from the Orient. □ **occidental** /-'den-/ *adjective*.

occiput /'ɒksɪpʌt/ *noun* back of head. □ **occipital** /-'sɪpɪt-/ *adjective*.

occlude /ə'kluːd/ *verb* (**-ding**) stop up; obstruct; *Chemistry* absorb (gases); (as **occluded** *adjective*) *Meteorology* (of frontal system) formed when cold front overtakes warm front, raising warm air. □ **occlusion** *noun*.

occult /ɒ'kʌlt, 'ɒkʌlt/ *adjective* involving the supernatural, mystical; esoteric. □ **the occult** occult phenomena generally.

occupant /'ɒkjʊpənt/ *noun* person occupying dwelling, office, or position. □ **occupancy** *noun* (*plural* **-ies**).

occupation /ɒkjʊ'peɪʃ(ə)n/ *noun* profession or employment; pastime; occupying or being occupied, esp. by armed forces of another country.

occupational *adjective* of or connected with one's occupation. □ **occupational disease**, **hazard** one to which a particular occupation renders someone especially liable; **occupational therapy** programme of mental or physical activity to assist recovery from disease or injury.

occupier /'ɒkjʊpaɪə/ *noun* person living in house etc. as owner or tenant.

occupy /'ɒkjʊpaɪ/ *verb* (**-ies**, **-ied**) live in; be tenant of; take up, fill (space, time, or place); take military possession of; place oneself in (building etc.) without authority as protest etc.; hold (office); keep busy.

occur /ə'kɜː/ *verb* (**-rr-**) take place, happen; be met with or found in some place or conditions; (+ *to*) come into one's mind.

occurrence /ə'kʌrəns/ *noun* happening; incident.

ocean /'əʊʃ(ə)n/ *noun* large expanse of sea, esp. one of the 5 named divisions of this, e.g. Atlantic Ocean; (often in *plural*) *colloquial* immense expanse or quantity. □ **oceanic** /əʊʃɪ'ænɪk/ *adjective*.

oceanography /əʊʃə'nɒgrəfɪ/ *noun* study of the oceans. □ **oceanographer** *noun*.

ocelot /'ɒsɪlɒt/ *noun* S. American leopard-like cat.

ochre /'əʊkə/ *noun* (*US* **ocher**) earth used as pigment; pale brownish-yellow colour. □ **ochreous** /'əʊkrɪəs/ *adjective*.

o'clock /ə'klɒk/ *adverb* of the clock (used to specify hour).

Oct. *abbreviation* October.

octa- *combining form* (also **oct-** before vowel) eight.

octagon /'ɒktəgən/ *noun* plane figure with 8 sides and angles. □ **octagonal** /-'tæg-/ *adjective*.

octahedron /ɒktə'hiːdrən/ *noun* (*plural* **-s**) solid figure contained by 8 (esp. triangular) plane faces. □ **octahedral** *adjective*.

octane /'ɒkteɪn/ *noun* colourless inflammable hydrocarbon occurring in petrol. □ **high-octane** (of fuel) used in internal-combustion engines) not detonating rapidly during power stroke; **octane number**, **rating** figure indicating antiknock properties of fuel.

octave /'ɒktɪv/ *noun* *Music* interval of 8 diatonic degrees between two notes, 8 notes occupying this interval, each of two notes at this interval's extremes; 8-line stanza.

octavo /ɒk'teɪvəʊ/ *noun* (*plural* **-s**) size of book or page with sheets folded into 8 leaves.

octet /ɒk'tet/ *noun* musical composition for 8 performers; the performers; any group of 8.

octo- *combining form* (also **oct-** before vowel) eight.

October /ɒk'təʊbə/ *noun* tenth month of year.

octogenarian /ˌɒktəʊdʒɪˈneərɪən/ noun person from 80 to 89 years old.

octopus /ˈɒktəpəs/ noun (plural **-puses**) mollusc with 8 suckered tentacles.

ocular /ˈɒkjʊlə/ adjective of, for, or by the eyes; visual.

oculist /ˈɒkjʊlɪst/ noun specialist in treatment of eyes.

OD /əʊˈdiː/ slang ● noun drug overdose. ● verb (**OD's, OD'd, Od'ing**) take overdose.

odd adjective extraordinary, strange; (of job etc.) occasional, casual; not normally considered, unconnected; (of numbers) not divisible by 2; left over, detached from set etc.; (added to weight, sum, etc.) rather more than. □ **oddball** colloquial eccentric person. □ **oddly** adverb; **oddness** noun.

oddity /ˈɒdɪtɪ/ noun (plural **-ies**) strange person, thing, or occurrence; peculiar trait; strangeness.

oddment noun odd article; something left over.

odds plural noun ratio between amounts staked by parties to a bet; chances in favour of or against result; balance of advantage; difference giving an advantage. □ **at odds** (often + with) in conflict; **odds and ends** remnants, stray articles; **odds-on** state when success is more likely than failure; **over the odds** above general price etc.

ode noun lyric poem of exalted style and tone.

odious /ˈəʊdɪəs/ adjective hateful, repulsive. □ **odiously** adverb; **odiousness** noun.

odium /ˈəʊdɪəm/ noun general dislike or disapproval.

odor US = ODOUR.

odoriferous /ˌəʊdəˈrɪfərəs/ adjective diffusing (usually pleasant) odours.

odour /ˈəʊdə/ noun (US **odor**) smell or fragrance; favour or repute. □ **odorous** adjective; **odourless** adjective.

odyssey /ˈɒdɪsɪ/ noun (plural **-s**) long adventurous journey.

OED abbreviation Oxford English Dictionary.

oedema /ɪˈdiːmə/ noun (US **edema**) excess fluid in body cavities or tissues.

Oedipus complex /ˈiːdɪpəs/ noun attraction of child to parent of opposite

sex (esp. son to mother). □ **Oedipal** adjective.

oesophagus /iːˈsɒfəgəs/ noun (US **esophagus**) (plural **-gi** /-dʒaɪ/ or **-guses**) passage from mouth to stomach, gullet.

oestrogen /ˈiːstrədʒ(ə)n/ noun (US **estrogen**) hormone producing female physical characteristics.

oeuvre /ˈɜːvr/ noun works of creative artist considered collectively. [French]

of /ɒv/ preposition belonging to, from; concerning; out of; among; relating to; US (of time in relation to following hour) to. □ **be of** possess, give rise to; **of late** recently; **of old** formerly.

off ● adverb away, at or to distance; out of position; loose, separate, gone; so as to be rid of; discontinued, stopped; not available on menu. ● preposition from; not on. ● adjective further; far; righthand; colloquial annoying; not acceptable; Cricket of, in, or into half of field which batsman faces. ● noun start of race; Cricket the off side. □ **off and on** now and then; **offbeat** unconventional, Music not coinciding with beat; **off chance** remote possibility; **off colour** unwell, US rather indecent; **offhand** without preparation, casual, curt; **off-licence** shop selling alcoholic drink for consumption away from premises; **offline** Computing adjective not online, adverb with delay between data production and its processing; **off-peak** (of electricity, traffic, etc.) used or for use at times of lesser demand; **offprint** reprint of part of publication; **offshoot** side-shoot or branch, derivative; **offside** (of player in field game) in position where he or she may not play the ball; **off the wall** slang crazy, absurd; **off white** white with grey or yellowish tinge.

offal /ˈɒf(ə)l/ noun edible organs of animal, esp. heart, liver, etc.; refuse, scraps.

offence /əˈfens/ noun (US **offense**) illegal act; transgression; upsetting of person's feelings, insult; aggressive action.

offend /əˈfend/ verb cause offence to, upset; displease, anger; (often + against) do wrong. □ **offender** noun; **offending** adjective.

offense US = OFFENCE.

offensive /ə'fensɪv/ ● *adjective* causing offence; insulting; disgusting; aggressive; (of weapon) for attacking. ● *noun* aggressive attitude, action, or campaign. □ **offensively** *adverb*; **offensiveness** *noun*.

offer /'ɒfə/ ● *verb* present for acceptance, refusal, or consideration; (+ *to do*) express readiness, show intention; attempt; present by way of sacrifice. ● *noun* expression of readiness to do or give if desired, or buy or sell; amount offered; proposal, esp. of marriage; bid. □ **on offer** for sale at certain (esp. reduced) price.

offering *noun* contribution; gift; thing offered.

offertory /'ɒfətərɪ/ *noun* (*plural* **-ies**) offering of bread and wine at Eucharist; collection of money at religious service.

office /'ɒfɪs/ *noun* room or building where administrative or clerical work is done; place for transacting business; department or local branch, esp. for specified purpose; position with duties attached to it; tenure of official position; duty, task, function; (usually in *plural*) piece of kindness, service; authorized form of worship.

officer /'ɒfɪsə/ *noun* person holding position of authority or trust, esp. one with commission in armed forces; policeman or policewoman; president, treasurer, etc. of society etc.

official /ə'fɪʃ(ə)l/ ● *adjective* of office or its tenure; characteristic of people in office; properly authorized. ● *noun* person holding office or engaged in official duties. □ **official secrets** confidential information involving national security. □ **officialdom** *noun*; **officially** *adverb*.

officialese /əfɪʃə'li:z/ *noun* derogatory officials' jargon.

officiate /ə'fɪʃɪeɪt/ *verb* (**-ting**) act in official capacity; conduct religious service.

officious /ə'fɪʃəs/ *adjective* domineering; intrusive in correcting etc. □ **officiously** *adverb*; **officiousness** *noun*.

offing /'ɒfɪŋ/ *noun* □ **in the offing** at hand, ready or likely to happen etc.

offset ● *noun* side-shoot of plant used for propagation; compensation; sloping ledge. ● *verb* (**-setting**; *past & past participle* **-set**) counterbalance, compensate.

offspring *noun* (*plural* same) person's child, children, or descendants; animal's young or descendants.

oft *adverb* archaic often.

often /'ɒf(ə)n/ *adverb* (**oftener**, **oftenest**) frequently; many times; at short intervals; in many instances.

ogee /'əʊdʒiː/ *noun* S-shaped curve or moulding.

ogive /'əʊdʒaɪv/ *noun* pointed arch; diagonal rib of vault.

ogle /'əʊg(ə)l/ ● *verb* (**-ling**) look lecherously or flirtatiously (at). ● *noun* flirtatious glance.

ogre /'əʊgə/ *noun* (*feminine* **ogress** /-grɪs/) man-eating giant. □ **ogreish**, **ogrish** /'əʊgərɪʃ/ *adjective*.

oh /əʊ/ *interjection* (also **O**) *expressing surprise, pain, etc.*

ohm /əʊm/ *noun* SI unit of electrical resistance.

OHMS *abbreviation* On Her or His Majesty's Service.

oho /əʊ'həʊ/ *interjection expressing surprise or exultation.*

OHP *abbreviation* overhead projector.

oil ● *noun* viscous usually inflammable liquid insoluble in water; petroleum. ● *verb* apply oil to, lubricate; treat with oil. □ **oilcake** compressed linseed etc. as cattle food or manure; **oilfield** district yielding mineral oil; **oil paint** paint made by mixing pigment with oil; **oil painting** use of or picture in oil paints; **oil rig** equipment for drilling an oil well; **oilskin** cloth waterproofed with oil, garment or (in *plural*) suit of it; **oil slick** patch of oil, esp. on sea; **oil well** well from which mineral oil is drawn.

oily *adjective* (**-ier**, **-iest**) of, like, covered or soaked with, oil; (of manner) fawning.

ointment /'ɔɪntmənt/ *noun* smooth greasy healing or cosmetic preparation for skin.

OK /əʊ'keɪ/ (also **okay**) colloquial ● *adjective & adverb* all right. ● *noun* (*plural* **OKs**) approval, sanction. ● *verb* (**OK's**, **OK'd**, **OK'ing**) approve, sanction.

okapi /əʊ'kɑːpɪ/ *noun* (*plural* same or **-s**) African partially striped ruminant mammal.

okay = OK.

okra /'ɒkrə/ *noun* tall originally African plant with edible seed pods.

old /əʊld/ *adjective* (**-er, -est**) advanced in age; not young or near its beginning; worn, dilapidated, or shabby from age; practised, inveterate; dating from far back; long established; former; *colloquial* used to indicate affection. □ **old age** later part of normal lifetime; **old-age pension** state retirement pension; **old-age pensioner** person receiving this; **Old Bill** *slang* the police; **old boy** former male pupil of school, *colloquial* elderly man; **old-fashioned** in or according to fashion no longer current, antiquated; **old girl** former female pupil of school, *colloquial* elderly woman; **Old Glory** *US* Stars and Stripes; **old guard** original, past, or conservative members of group; **old hand** experienced or practised person; **old hat** *colloquial* hackneyed; **old maid** *derogatory* elderly unmarried woman, prim and fussy person; **old man** *colloquial* one's father, husband, or employer etc.; **old man's beard** wild clematis; **old master** great painter of former times, painting by such painter; **Old Testament** part of Bible dealing with pre-Christian times; **old wives' tale** unscientific belief; **old woman** *colloquial* one's wife or mother, fussy or timid man; **Old World** Europe, Asia, and Africa. □ **oldish** *adjective*; **oldness** *noun*.

olden *adjective* archaic old, of old.

oldie *noun colloquial* old person or thing.

oleaginous /əʊlɪ'ædʒɪnəs/ *adjective* like or producing oil; oily.

oleander /əʊlɪ'ændə/ *noun* evergreen flowering Mediterranean shrub.

olfactory /ɒl'fæktərɪ/ *adjective* of the sense of smell.

oligarch /'ɒlɪgɑːk/ *noun* member of oligarchy.

oligarchy /'ɒlɪgɑːkɪ/ *noun* (*plural* **-ies**) government by small group of people; members of such government; state so governed. □ **oligarchic(al)** /-'gɑːk-/ *adjective*.

olive /'ɒlɪv/ ● *noun* oval hard-stoned fruit yielding oil; tree bearing this; dull yellowish green. ● *adjective* olive-green; (of complexion) yellowish-brown. □ **olive branch** gesture of peace or reconciliation.

Olympiad /ə'lɪmpɪæd/ *noun* period of 4 years between Olympic Games; celebration of modern Olympic Games.

Olympian /ə'lɪmpɪən/ *adjective* of Olympus; magnificent, condescending; aloof.

Olympic /ə'lɪmpɪk/ ● *adjective* of the Olympic Games. ● *plural noun* (**the Olympics**) Olympic Games. □ **Olympic Games** ancient Greek athletic festival held every 4 years, or modern international revival of this.

OM *abbreviation* Order of Merit.

ombudsman /'ɒmbʊdzmən/ *noun* official appointed to investigate complaints against public authorities.

omega /'əʊmɪgə/ *noun* last letter of Greek alphabet (Ω, ω); last of series.

omelette /'ɒmlɪt/ *noun* beaten eggs fried and often folded over filling.

omen /'əʊmən/ *noun* event supposedly warning of good or evil; prophetic significance.

ominous /'ɒmɪnəs/ *adjective* threatening; inauspicious. □ **ominously** *adverb*.

omit /əʊ'mɪt/ *verb* (**-tt-**) leave out; not include; leave undone; (+ *to do*) neglect. □ **omission** /əʊ'mɪʃ(ə)n/ *noun*.

omni- *combining form* all.

omnibus /'ɒmnɪbəs/ ● *noun formal* bus; volume containing several novels etc. previously published separately. ● *adjective* serving several purposes at once; comprising several items.

omnipotent /ɒm'nɪpət(ə)nt/ *adjective* all-powerful. □ **omnipotence** *noun*.

omnipresent /ɒmnɪ'prez(ə)nt/ *adjective* present everywhere. □ **omnipresence** *noun*.

omniscient /ɒm'nɪsɪənt/ *adjective* knowing everything. □ **omniscience** *noun*.

omnivorous /ɒm'nɪvərəs/ *adjective* feeding on both plant and animal material; *jocular* reading everything that comes one's way. □ **omnivore** /'ɒmnɪvɔː/ *noun*; **omnivorousness** *noun*.

on ● *preposition* (so as to be) supported by, covering, attached to, etc.; (of time) exactly at; during; close to, in direction of; at, near, concerning, about; added to. ● *adverb* (so as to be) on something; in some direction, forward; in advance; with movement; in operation or activity; *colloquial* willing to participate, approve, bet, etc.; *colloquial* practicable, acceptable; being shown or performed. ● *adjective Cricket* of, in, or into half of field behind batsman's back. ● *noun Cricket* the on side. □ **be on about** *colloquial* discuss, esp. tiresomely; **online** directly controlled by or connected to computer; **onscreen** when being filmed; **on to** to a position on.

■ **Usage** See note at ONTO.

ONC *abbreviation* Ordinary National Certificate.

once /wʌns/ ● *adverb* on one occasion only; at some time in past; ever or at all. ● *conjunction* as soon as. ● *noun* one time or occasion. □ **at once** immediately, simultaneously; **once-over** *colloquial* rapid inspection.

oncology /ɒŋˈkɒlədʒɪ/ *noun* study of tumours.

oncoming *adjective* approaching from the front.

OND *abbreviation* Ordinary National Diploma.

one /wʌn/ ● *adjective* single and integral in number; only such; without others; identical; forming a unity. ● *noun* lowest cardinal numeral; thing numbered with it; unit, unity; single thing, person, or example; *colloquial* single drink. ● *pronoun* any person. □ **one-armed bandit** *colloquial* fruit machine with long handle; **one-horse** *colloquial* small, poorly equipped; **one-man** involving or operated by one person only; **one-off** made as the only one, not repeated; **one-sided** unfair, partial; **one-way** allowing movement etc. in one direction only.

oneness *noun* singleness; uniqueness; agreement, sameness.

onerous /ˈəʊnərəs/ *adjective* burdensome. ● **onerousness** *noun*.

oneself *pronoun*: emphatic & reflexive form of ONE. □ **be oneself** act in one's natural manner.

ongoing *adjective* continuing, in progress.

onion /ˈʌnjən/ *noun* vegetable with edible bulb of pungent smell and flavour.

onlooker *noun* spectator. □ **onlooking** *adjective*.

only /ˈəʊnlɪ/ ● *adverb* solely, merely, exclusively. ● *adjective* existing alone of its or their kind. ● *conjunction colloquial* except that; but then. □ **if only** even if for no other reason than, I wish that.

o.n.o. *abbreviation* or near offer.

onomatopoeia /ɒnəmætəˈpiːə/ *noun* formation of word from sound associated with thing named, e.g. *whizz*, *cuckoo*. □ **onomatopoeic** *adjective*.

onset *noun* attack; impetuous beginning.

onslaught /ˈɒnslɔːt/ *noun* fierce attack.

onto *preposition* = ON TO.

■ **Usage** *Onto* is much used but is still not as widely accepted as *into*. It is, however, useful in distinguishing between, e.g., *We drove on to the beach* (i.e. towards it) and *we drove onto the beach* (i.e. into contact with it).

ontology /ɒnˈtɒlədʒɪ/ *noun* branch of metaphysics concerned with the nature of being. □ **ontological** /-təˈlɒdʒ-/ *adjective*; **ontologically** /-təˈlɒdʒ-/ *adverb*; **ontologist** *noun*.

onus /ˈəʊnəs/ *noun* (*plural* **onuses**) burden, duty, responsibility.

onward /ˈɒnwəd/ ● *adverb* (also **onwards**) advancing; into the future. ● *adjective* forward, advancing.

onyx /ˈɒnɪks/ *noun* semiprecious variety of agate with coloured layers.

oodles /ˈuːd(ə)lz/ *plural noun colloquial* very great amount.

ooh /uː/ *interjection* expressing surprised pleasure, pain, excitement, etc.

oolite /ˈəʊəlaɪt/ *noun* granular limestone. □ **oolitic** /-ˈlɪt-/ *adjective*.

oomph /ʊmf/ *noun slang* energy, enthusiasm; attractiveness, esp. sex appeal.

ooze[1] ● *verb* (**-zing**) trickle or leak slowly out; (of substance) exude fluid; (often + *with*) give off (a feeling) freely. ● *noun* sluggish flow. □ **oozy** *adjective*.

ooze[2] *noun* wet mud. □ **oozy** *adjective*.

op *noun colloquial* operation.

op. *abbreviation* opus.

opacity /əʊˈpæsɪtɪ/ *noun* opaqueness.

opal /ˈəʊp(ə)l/ *noun* semiprecious milk-white or bluish stone with iridescent reflections.

opalescent /əʊpəˈles(ə)nt/ *adjective* iridescent. □ **opalescence** *noun*.

opaline /ˈəʊpəlaɪn/ *adjective* opal-like; opalescent.

opaque /əʊˈpeɪk/ *adjective* (**-r, -st**) not transmitting light; impenetrable to sight; unintelligible; stupid. □ **opaquely** *adverb*; **opaqueness** *noun*.

op. cit. *abbreviation* in the work already quoted (*opere citato*).

OPEC /ˈəʊpek/ *abbreviation* Organization of Petroleum Exporting Countries.

open /ˈəʊpən/ ● *adjective* not closed, locked, or blocked up; not covered or confined; exposed; (of goal etc.) undefended; undisguised, public; unfolded, spread out; (of fabric) with gaps; frank; open-minded; accessible to visitors or customers; (of meeting, competition, etc.) not restricted; (+ *to*) willing to receive, vulnerable to. ● *verb* make or become open or more open; (+ *into* etc.) give access; establish, set going; start; ceremonially declare open. ● *noun* (**the open**) open air; open competition etc. □ **open air** *noun* outdoors; **open-air** *adjective* outdoor; **open day** day when public may visit place normally closed to them; **open-ended** with no limit or restriction; **open-handed** generous; **open-heart surgery** surgery with heart exposed and blood made to bypass it; **open house** hospitality for all visitors; **open letter** one addressed to individual and printed in newspaper etc.; **open-minded** accessible to new ideas, unprejudiced; **open-plan** (of house, office, etc.) having large undivided rooms; **open prison** one with few physical restraints on prisoners; **open question** matter on which different views are legitimate; **open sandwich** one without bread on top; **open sea** expanse of sea away from land. □ **openness** *noun*.

opener *noun* device for opening tins or bottles etc.

opening ● *noun* gap, aperture; opportunity; beginning, initial part. ● *adjective* initial, first.

openly *adverb* publicly, frankly.

opera[1] /ˈɒpərə/ *noun* musical drama with sung or spoken dialogue.

□ **opera-glasses** small binoculars for use in theatres etc.; **opera house** theatre for operas.

opera[2] *plural of* OPUS.

operable /ˈɒpərəb(ə)l/ *adjective* that can be operated; suitable for treatment by surgical operation.

operate /ˈɒpəreɪt/ *verb* (**-ting**) work, control (machine etc.); be in action; perform surgical operation(s); direct military etc. action. □ **operating theatre** room for surgical operations.

operatic /ɒpəˈrætɪk/ *adjective* of or like opera.

operation *noun* action, working; performance of surgery on a patient; military manoeuvre; financial transaction. □ **operational** *adjective*; **operationally** *adverb*.

operative /ˈɒpərətɪv/ ● *adjective* in operation; having principal relevance; of or by surgery. ● *noun* worker, artisan.

operator *noun* person operating machine, esp. connecting lines in telephone exchange; person engaging in business.

operetta /ɒpəˈretə/ *noun* light opera.

ophidian /əʊˈfɪdɪən/ ● *noun* member of suborder of reptiles including snakes. ● *adjective* of this order.

ophthalmia /ɒfˈθælmɪə/ *noun* inflammation of eye.

ophthalmic /ɒfˈθælmɪk/ *adjective* of or relating to the eye and its diseases. □ **ophthalmic optician** one qualified to prescribe as well as dispense spectacles.

ophthalmology /ɒfθælˈmɒlədʒɪ/ *noun* study of the eye. □ **ophthalmologist** *noun*.

ophthalmoscope /ɒfˈθælməskəʊp/ *noun* instrument for examining the eye.

opiate /ˈəʊpɪət/ ● *adjective* containing opium; soporific. ● *noun* drug containing opium, usually to ease pain or induce sleep; soothing influence.

opine /əʊˈpaɪn/ *verb* (**-ning**) (often + *that*) express or hold as opinion.

opinion /əˈpɪnjən/ *noun* unproven belief; view held as probable; professional advice; estimation. □ **opinion poll** assessment of public opinion by questioning representative sample.

opinionated /ə'pɪnjəneɪtɪd/ *adjective* unduly confident in one's opinions.

opium /'əʊpɪəm/ *noun* drug made from juice of certain poppy, used as narcotic or sedative.

opossum /ə'pɒsəm/ *noun* tree-living American marsupial; *Australian & NZ* marsupial resembling this.

opponent /ə'pəʊnənt/ *noun* person who opposes.

opportune /'ɒpətjuːn/ *adjective* well-chosen, specially favourable; (of action, event, etc.) well-timed.

opportunism /ɒpə'tjuːnɪz(ə)m/ *noun* adaptation of policy to circumstances, esp. regardless of principle. □ **opportunist** *noun*; **opportunistic** /-'nɪs-/ *adjective*; **opportunistically** /-'nɪs-/ *adverb*.

opportunity /ɒpə'tjuːnɪtɪ/ *noun* (*plural* **-ies**) favourable chance or opening offered by circumstances.

oppose /ə'pəʊz/ *verb* (**-sing**) set oneself against; resist; argue against; (+ *to*) place in opposition or contrast. □ **as opposed to** in contrast with. □ **opposer** *noun*.

opposite /'ɒpəzɪt/ ● *adjective* facing, on other side; (often + *to*, *from*) contrary; diametrically different. ● *noun* opposite thing, person, or term. ● *adverb* in opposite position. ● *preposition* opposite to. □ **opposite number** person in corresponding position in another group etc.; **the opposite sex** either sex in relation to the other.

opposition /ɒpə'zɪʃ(ə)n/ *noun* antagonism, resistance; being in conflict or disagreement; contrast; group or party of opponents; chief parliamentary party, or group of parties, opposed to party in office; act of placing opposite.

oppress /ə'pres/ *verb* govern tyrannically; treat with gross harshness or injustice; weigh down. □ **oppression** *noun*; **oppressor** *noun*.

oppressive *adjective* that oppresses; (of weather) sultry, close. □ **oppressively** *adverb*; **oppressiveness** *noun*.

opprobrious /ə'prəʊbrɪəs/ *adjective* (of language) severely scornful; abusive.

opprobrium /ə'prəʊbrɪəm/ *noun* disgrace; cause of this.

opt *verb* (usually + *for*) make choice; decide. □ **opt out** (**of**) choose not to take part etc. (in).

optic /'ɒptɪk/ *adjective* of eye or sight.

optical *adjective* visual; of or according to optics; aiding sight. □ **optical fibre** thin glass fibre used to carry light signals; **optical illusion** image which deceives the eye, mental misapprehension caused by this.

optician /ɒp'tɪʃ(ə)n/ *noun* maker, seller, or prescriber of spectacles, contact lenses, etc.

optics *plural noun* (treated as *singular*) science of light and vision.

optimal /'ɒptɪm(ə)l/ *adjective* best, most favourable.

optimism /'ɒptɪmɪz(ə)m/ *noun* inclination to hopefulness and confidence. □ **optimist** *noun*; **optimistic** /-'mɪs-/ *adjective*; **optimistically** /-'mɪs-/ *adverb*.

optimize /'ɒptɪmaɪz/ *verb* (also **-ise**) (**-zing** or **-sing**) make best or most effective use of. □ **optimization** *noun*.

optimum /'ɒptɪməm/ ● *noun* (*plural* **-ma**) most favourable conditions; best practical solution. ● *adjective* optimal.

option /'ɒpʃ(ə)n/ *noun* choice, choosing; right to choose; right to buy, sell, etc., on specified conditions at specified time. □ **keep, leave one's options open** not commit oneself.

optional *adjective* not obligatory. □ **optionally** *adverb*.

opulent /'ɒpjʊlənt/ *adjective* wealthy; luxurious; abundant. □ **opulence** *noun*.

opus /'əʊpəs/ *noun* (*plural* **opuses** or **opera** /'ɒpərə/) musical composition numbered as one of composer's works; any artistic work.

or *conjunction introducing alternatives*. □ **or else** otherwise, *colloquial* expressing threat.

oracle /'ɒrək(ə)l/ *noun* place at which ancient Greeks etc. consulted gods for advice or prophecy; response received there; person or thing regarded as source of wisdom etc. □ **oracular** /ɒ'rækjʊlə/ *adjective*.

oral /'ɔːr(ə)l/ ● *adjective* spoken, verbal; by word of mouth; done or taken by mouth. ● *noun colloquial* spoken exam. □ **orally** *adverb*.

orange /'ɒrɪndʒ/ ●*noun* roundish reddish-yellow citrus fruit; its colour; tree bearing it. ●*adjective* orange-coloured.

orangeade /ɒrɪndʒ'eɪd/ *noun* drink made from or flavoured like oranges, usually fizzy.

orang-utan /ɔːˈræŋuːˈtæn/ *noun* (also **orang-outang** /-uːˈtæŋ/) large anthropoid ape.

oration /ɔːˈreɪʃ(ə)n/ *noun* formal or ceremonial speech.

orator /'ɒrətə/ *noun* maker of a formal speech; eloquent public speaker.

oratorio /ɒrəˈtɔːrɪəʊ/ *noun* (*plural* **-s**) semi-dramatic musical composition usually on sacred theme.

oratory /'ɒrətərɪ/ *noun* (*plural* **-ies**) art of or skill in public speaking; small private chapel. □ **oratorical** /-ˈtɒr-/ *adjective*.

orb *noun* globe surmounted by cross as part of coronation regalia; sphere, globe; *poetical* celestial body; *poetical* eye.

orbicular /ɔːˈbɪkjʊlə/ *adjective* formal spherical, circular.

orbit /'ɔːbɪt/ ●*noun* curved course of planet, comet, satellite, etc.; one complete passage round another body; range or sphere of action. ●*verb* (**-t-**) go round in orbit; put into orbit. □ **orbiter** *noun*.

orbital *adjective* of orbits; (of road) passing round outside of city.

Orcadian /ɔːˈkeɪdɪən/ ●*adjective* of Orkney. ●*noun* native of Orkney.

orchard /'ɔːtʃəd/ *noun* enclosed piece of land with fruit trees.

orchestra /'ɔːkɪstrə/ *noun* large group of instrumental performers. □ **orchestra pit** part of theatre where orchestra plays. □ **orchestral** /ɔːˈkestr(ə)l/ *adjective*.

orchestrate /'ɔːkɪstreɪt/ *verb* (**-ting**) compose or arrange for orchestral performance; arrange (elements) for desired effect.

orchid /'ɔːkɪd/ *noun* any of various plants, often with brilliantly coloured or grotesquely shaped flowers.

ordain /ɔːˈdeɪn/ *verb* confer holy orders on; decree, order.

ordeal /ɔːˈdiːl/ *noun* severe trial; painful or horrific experience.

order /'ɔːdə/ ●*noun* condition in which every part, unit, etc. is in its right place; tidiness; specified sequence; authoritative direction or instruction; state of obedience to law, authority, etc.; direction to supply something, thing(s) (to be) supplied; social class or rank; kind, sort; constitution or nature of the world, society, etc.; *Biology* grouping of animals or plants below class and above family; religious fraternity; grade of Christian ministry; any of 5 classical styles of architecture; company of people distinguished by particular honour, etc., insignia worn by its members; stated form of divine service; system of rules etc. (at meetings etc.). ●*verb* command, prescribe; command or direct (person) to specified destination; direct manufacturer, tradesman, etc. to supply; direct waiter to serve; (often as **ordered** *adjective*) put in order; (of God, fate, etc.) ordain. □ **in** or **out of order** in correct or incorrect sequence; **of** or **in the order of** approximately.

orderly ●*adjective* methodically arranged; tidy; not unruly. ●*noun* (*plural* **-ies**) soldier in attendance on officer; hospital attendant. □ **orderly room** room in barracks for company's business.

ordinal /'ɔːdɪn(ə)l/ *noun* (in full **ordinal number**) number defining position in a series; compare CARDINAL NUMBER.

ordinance /'ɔːdɪnəns/ *noun* decree; religious rite.

ordinand /'ɔːdɪnænd/ *noun* candidate for ordination.

ordinary /'ɔːdɪnərɪ/ *adjective* normal; not exceptional; commonplace. □ **ordinary level** *historical* lowest in GCE exam; **ordinary seaman** sailor of lowest rank. □ **ordinarily** *adverb*; **ordinariness** *noun*.

ordination /ɔːdɪˈneɪʃ(ə)n/ *noun* conferring of holy orders; ordaining.

ordnance /'ɔːdnəns/ *noun* artillery and military supplies; government service dealing with these. □ **Ordnance Survey** government survey of UK producing detailed maps.

ordure /'ɔːdjʊə/ *noun* dung.

ore *noun* naturally occurring mineral yielding metal or other valuable minerals.

oregano /ɒrɪˈgɑːnəʊ/ *noun* dried wild marjoram as seasoning.

organ /ˈɔːgən/ *noun* musical instrument consisting of pipes that sound when air is forced through them, operated by keys and pedals; similar instrument producing sound electronically; part of body serving some special function; medium of opinion, esp. newspaper. □ **organ-grinder** player of barrel organ.

organdie /ˈɔːgəndɪ/ *noun* fine translucent muslin, usually stiffened.

organic /ɔːˈgænɪk/ *adjective* of or affecting bodily organ(s); (of animals and plants) having organs or organized physical structure; (of food) produced without artificial fertilizers or pesticides; (of chemical compound etc.) containing carbon; organized; inherent, structural. □ **organic chemistry** that of carbon compounds. □ **organically** *adverb*.

organism /ˈɔːgənɪz(ə)m/ *noun* individual animal or plant; living being with interdependent parts; system made up of interdependent parts.

organist *noun* player of organ.

organization /ɔːgənaɪˈzeɪʃ(ə)n/ *noun* (also **-isation**) organized body, system, or society; organizing, being organized.

organize /ˈɔːgənaɪz/ *verb* (also **-ise**) (**-zing** or **-sing**) give orderly structure to; make arrangements for (person, oneself); initiate, arrange for; (as **organized** *adjective*) make organic or into living tissue. □ **organizer** *noun*.

orgasm /ˈɔːgæz(ə)m/ ● *noun* climax of sexual excitement. ● *verb* have sexual orgasm. □ **orgasmic** /-ˈgæz-/ *adjective*.

orgy /ˈɔːdʒɪ/ *noun* (*plural* **-ies**) wild party with indiscriminate sexual activity; excessive indulgence in an activity. □ **orgiastic** /-ˈæs-/ *adjective*.

oriel /ˈɔːrɪəl/ *noun* window projecting from wall at upper level.

orient /ˈɔːrɪənt/ ● *noun* (**the Orient**) the East, countries east of Mediterranean, esp. E. Asia. ● *verb* place or determine position of with aid of compass; find bearings of; (often + *towards*) direct; place (building etc.) to face east; turn eastward or in specified direction.

oriental /ɔːrɪˈent(ə)l/ (often **Oriental**) ● *adjective* of the East, esp. E. Asia; of the Orient. ● *noun* native of Orient.

orientate /ˈɔːrɪənteɪt/ *verb* (**-ting**) orient.

orientation *noun* orienting, being oriented; relative position; person's adjustment in relation to circumstances; briefing.

orienteering /ɔːrɪənˈtɪərɪŋ/ *noun* competitive sport of running across rough country with map and compass.

orifice /ˈɒrɪfɪs/ *noun* aperture; mouth of cavity.

origami /ɒrɪˈgɑːmɪ/ *noun* Japanese art of folding paper into decorative shapes.

origan /ˈɒrɪgən/ *noun* (also **origanum** /əˈrɪgənəm/) wild marjoram.

origin /ˈɒrɪdʒɪn/ *noun* source; starting point; (often in *plural*) parentage.

original /əˈrɪdʒɪn(ə)l/ ● *adjective* existing from the beginning; earliest; innate; not imitative or derived; creative not copied; by artist etc. himself or herself. ● *noun* original pattern, picture, etc. from which another is copied or translated. □ **original sin** innate sinfulness held to be common to all human beings after the Fall. □ **originality** /-ˈnæl-/ *noun*; **originally** *adverb*.

originate /əˈrɪdʒɪneɪt/ *verb* (**-ting**) begin; initiate or give origin to, be origin of. □ **origination** *noun*; **originator** *noun*.

oriole /ˈɔːrɪəʊl/ *noun* kind of bird, esp. **golden oriole** with black and yellow plumage in male.

ormolu /ˈɔːməluː/ *noun* gilded bronze; gold-coloured alloy; articles made of or decorated with these.

ornament ● *noun* /ˈɔːnəmənt/ thing used to adorn or decorate; decoration; quality or person bringing honour or distinction. ● *verb* /-ment/ adorn, beautify. □ **ornamental** /-ˈmen-/ *adjective*; **ornamentation** /-men-/ *noun*.

ornate /ɔːˈneɪt/ *adjective* elaborately adorned; (of literary style) flowery. □ **ornately** *adverb*.

ornithology /ɔːnɪˈθɒlədʒɪ/ *noun* study of birds. □ **ornithological** /-θəˈlɒdʒ-/ *adjective*; **ornithologist** *noun*.

orotund /ˈɒrətʌnd/ *adjective* (of voice) full, round, imposing; (of writing, style, etc.) pompous; pretentious.

orphan /'ɔːf(ə)n/ ● *noun* child whose parents are dead. ● *verb* bereave of parents.

orphanage *noun* home for orphans.

orrery /'ɒrərɪ/ *noun* (*plural* **-ies**) clockwork model of solar system.

orris root /'ɒrɪs/ *noun* fragrant iris root used in perfumery.

ortho- *combining form* straight, correct.

orthodontics /ɔːθə'dɒntɪks/ *plural noun* (usually treated as *singular*) correction of irregularities in teeth and jaws.

orthodox /'ɔːθədɒks/ *adjective* holding usual or accepted views, esp. on religion, morals, etc.; conventional. □ **Orthodox Church** Eastern Church headed by Patriarch of Constantinople, including Churches of Russia, Romania, Greece, etc. □ **orthodoxy** *noun*.

orthography /ɔː'θɒɡrəfɪ/ *noun* (*plural* **-ies**) spelling, esp. with reference to its correctness. □ **orthographic** /-'ɡræf-/ *adjective*.

orthopaedics /ɔːθə'piːdɪks/ *plural noun* (treated as *singular*) (*US* **-pedics**) branch of medicine dealing with correction of diseased or injured bones or muscles. □ **orthopaedic** *adjective*; **orthopaedist** *noun*.

OS *abbreviation* old style; Ordinary Seaman; Ordnance Survey; outsize.

Oscar /'ɒskə/ *noun* statuette awarded annually in US for excellence in film acting, directing, etc.

oscillate /'ɒsɪleɪt/ *verb* (**-ting**) (cause to) swing to and fro; vacillate; *Electricity* (of current) undergo high-frequency alternations. □ **oscillation** *noun*; **oscillator** *noun*.

oscilloscope /ə'sɪləskəʊp/ *noun* device for viewing oscillations usually on screen of cathode ray tube.

osier /'əʊzɪə/ *noun* willow used in basketwork; shoot of this.

osmosis /ɒz'məʊsɪs/ *noun* passage of solvent through semipermeable partition into another solution; process by which something is acquired by absorption. □ **osmotic** /-'mɒt-/ *adjective*.

osprey /'ɒspreɪ/ *noun* (*plural* **-s**) large bird preying on fish.

osseous /'ɒsɪəs/ *adjective* of bone; bony; having bones.

ossify /'ɒsɪfaɪ/ *verb* (**-ies**, **-ied**) turn into bone; harden; make or become rigid or unprogressive. □ **ossification** *noun*.

ostensible /ɒ'stensɪb(ə)l/ *adjective* professed; used to conceal real purpose or nature. □ **ostensibly** *adverb*.

ostentation /ɒsten'teɪʃ(ə)n/ *noun* pretentious display of wealth; showing off. □ **ostentatious** *adjective*.

osteoarthritis /ɒstɪəʊɑː'θraɪtɪs/ *noun* degenerative disease of the joints. □ **osteoarthritic** /-'θrɪt-/ *adjective*.

osteopath /'ɒstɪəpæθ/ *noun* person who treats disease by manipulation of bones. □ **osteopathy** /-'ɒp-/ *noun*.

osteoporosis /ɒstɪəʊpə'rəʊsɪs/ *noun* brittle bones caused by hormonal change or deficiency of calcium or vitamin D.

ostler /'ɒslə/ *noun historical* stableman at inn.

ostracize /'ɒstrəsaɪz/ *verb* (also **-ise**) (**-zing** or **-sing**) exclude from society, refuse to associate with. □ **ostracism** /-sɪz(ə)m/ *noun*.

ostrich /'ɒstrɪtʃ/ *noun* large flightless swift-running African bird; person refusing to acknowledge awkward truth.

OT *abbreviation* Old Testament.

other /'ʌðə/ ● *adjective* further, additional; different; (**the other**) the only remaining. ● *noun* other person or thing. □ **the other day**, **week**, etc. a few days etc. ago; **other half** *colloquial* one's wife or husband; **other than** apart from.

otherwise /'ʌðəwaɪz/ ● *adverb* or else; in different circumstances; in other respects; in a different way; as an alternative. ● *adjective* different.

otiose /'əʊtɪəʊs/ *adjective* not required, serving no practical purpose.

OTT *abbreviation colloquial* over-the-top.

otter /'ɒtə/ *noun* furred aquatic fish-eating mammal.

Ottoman /'ɒtəmən/ ● *adjective historical* of Turkish Empire. ● *noun* (*plural* **-s**) Turk of Ottoman period; (**ottoman**) cushioned seat without back or arms, storage-box with padded top.

OU *abbreviation* Open University; Oxford University.

oubliette /uːblɪ'et/ *noun* secret dungeon with trapdoor entrance.

ouch /aʊtʃ/ *interjection expressing sharp or sudden pain*.

ought /ɔːt/ *auxiliary verb expressing duty, rightness, probability, etc.*

oughtn't /ˈɔːt(ə)nt/ ought not.

Ouija /ˈwiːdʒə/ *noun* (in full **Ouija board**) *proprietary term* board marked with letters or signs used with movable pointer to try to obtain messages in seances.

ounce /aʊns/ *noun* unit of weight (1/16 lb, 28.35 g); very small quantity.

our /aʊə/ *adjective* of or belonging to us.

ours /aʊəz/ *pronoun* the one(s) belonging to us.

ourselves /aʊəˈselvz/ *pronoun: emphatic form of* WE *or* US; *reflexive form of* US.

ousel = OUZEL.

oust /aʊst/ *verb* drive out of office or power, esp. by seizing place of.

out /aʊt/ ● *adverb* away from or not in place, not at home, office, etc.; into open, sight, notice, etc.; to or at an end; not burning; in error; *colloquial* unconscious; (+ *to do*) determined; (of limb etc.) dislocated. ● *preposition* out of. ● *noun* way of escape. ● *verb* emerge. □ **out for** intent on, determined to get; **out of** from inside, not inside, from among, lacking, having no more of, because of.

■ **Usage** The use of *out* as a preposition, as in *He walked out the room*, is not standard English. *Out of* should be used instead.

---

out- *prefix* so as to surpass; external; out of.

outback *noun Australian* remote inland areas.

outbalance /aʊtˈbæləns/ *verb* (**-cing**) outweigh.

outbid /aʊtˈbɪd/ *verb* (**-dd-**; *past & past participle* **-bid**) bid higher than.

outboard motor *noun* portable engine attached to outside of boat.

outbreak /ˈaʊtbreɪk/ *noun* sudden eruption of emotion, war, disease, fire, etc.

outbuilding *noun* shed, barn, etc. detached from main building.

outburst *noun* bursting out, esp. of emotion in vehement words.

outcast ● *noun* person cast out from home and friends. ● *adjective* homeless; rejected.

outclass /aʊtˈklɑːs/ *verb* surpass in quality.

outcome *noun* result.

outcrop *noun* rock etc. emerging at surface; noticeable manifestation.

outcry *noun* (*plural* **-ies**) loud public protest.

outdated /aʊtˈdeɪtɪd/ *adjective* out of date, obsolete.

outdistance /aʊtˈdɪst(ə)ns/ *verb* (**-cing**) leave (competitor) behind completely.

outdo /aʊtˈduː/ *verb* (**-doing**; *3rd singular present* **-does**; *past* **-did**; *past participle* **-done**) surpass, excel.

outdoor *adjective* done, existing, or used out of doors; fond of the open air.

outdoors /aʊtˈdɔːz/ ● *adverb* in(to) the open air. ● *noun* the open air.

outer *adjective* outside, external; farther from centre or inside. □ **outer space** universe beyond earth's atmosphere. □ **outermost** *adjective*.

outface /aʊtˈfeɪs/ *verb* (**-cing**) disconcert by staring or by confident manner.

outfall *noun* outlet of river, drain, etc.

outfield *noun* outer part of cricket or baseball pitch. □ **outfielder** *noun*.

outfit *noun* set of equipment or clothes; *colloquial* (organized) group or company.

outfitter *noun* supplier of clothing.

outflank /aʊtˈflæŋk/ *verb* get round the flank of (enemy); outmanoeuvre.

outflow *noun* outward flow; what flows out.

outgoing ● *adjective* friendly; retiring from office; going out. ● *noun* (in *plural*) expenditure.

outgrow /aʊtˈɡrəʊ/ *verb* (*past* **-grew**; *past participle* **-grown**) get too big for (clothes etc.); leave behind (childish habit etc.), grow faster or taller than.

outgrowth *noun* offshoot.

outhouse *noun* shed etc., esp. adjoining main house.

outing *noun* pleasure trip.

outlandish /aʊtˈlændɪʃ/ *adjective* bizarre, strange. □ **outlandishly** *adverb*; **outlandishness** *noun*.

outlast /aʊtˈlɑːst/ *verb* last longer than.

outlaw ● *noun* fugitive from law; *historical* person deprived of protection of law. ● *verb* declare (person) an outlaw; make illegal; proscribe.

outlay *noun* expenditure.

outlet *noun* means of exit; means of expressing feelings; market for goods.

outline ● *noun* rough draft; summary; line(s) enclosing visible object; contour; external boundary; (in *plural*) main features. ● *verb* (**-ning**) draw or describe in outline; mark outline of.

outlive /aʊtˈlɪv/ *verb* (**-ving**) live longer than, beyond, or through.

outlook *noun* view, prospect; mental attitude.

outlying *adjective* far from centre; remote.

outmanoeuvre /aʊtməˈnuːvə/ *verb* (**-ring**) (*US* **-maneuver**) outdo by skilful manoeuvring.

outmatch /aʊtˈmætʃ/ *verb* be more than a match for.

outmoded /aʊtˈməʊdɪd/ *adjective* outdated; out of fashion.

outnumber /aʊtˈnʌmbə/ *verb* exceed in number.

outpace /aʊtˈpeɪs/ *verb* (**-cing**) go faster than; outdo in contest.

outpatient *noun* non-resident hospital patient.

outplacement *noun* help in finding new job after redundancy.

outpost *noun* detachment on guard at some distance from army; outlying settlement etc.

outpouring *noun* (usually in *plural*) copious expression of emotion.

output ● *noun* amount produced (by machine, worker, etc.); electrical power etc. supplied by apparatus; printout, results, etc. from computer; place where energy, information, etc., leaves a system. ● *verb* (**-tt-**; *past & past participle* **-put** or **-putted**) (of computer) supply (results etc.).

outrage ● *noun* forcible violation of others' rights, sentiments, etc.; gross offence or indignity; fierce resentment. ● *verb* (**-ging**) subject to outrage; insult; shock and anger.

outrageous /aʊtˈreɪdʒəs/ *adjective* immoderate; shocking; immoral, offensive. □ **outrageously** *adverb*.

outrank /aʊtˈræŋk/ *verb* be superior in rank to.

outré /ˈuːtreɪ/ *adjective* eccentric, violating decorum. [French]

outrider *noun* motorcyclist or mounted guard riding ahead of car(s) etc.

outrigger *noun* spar or framework projecting from or over side of ship, canoe, etc. to give stability; boat with this.

outright ● *adverb* altogether, entirely; not gradually; without reservation. ● *adjective* downright, complete; undisputed.

outrun /aʊtˈrʌn/ *verb* (**-nn-**; *past* **-ran**; *past participle* **-run**) run faster or farther than; go beyond.

outsell /aʊtˈsel/ *verb* (*past & past participle* **-sold**) sell more than; be sold in greater quantities than.

outset *noun* □ **at, from the outset** at or from the beginning.

outshine /aʊtˈʃaɪn/ *verb* (**-ning**; *past & past participle* **-shone**) be more brilliant than.

outside ● *noun* /aʊtˈsaɪd, ˈaʊtsaɪd/ external surface, outer part(s); external appearance; position on outer side. ● *adjective* /ˈaʊtsaɪd/ of, on, or nearer outside; not belonging to particular circle or institution; (of chance etc.) remote; greatest existent or possible. ● *adverb* /aʊtˈsaɪd/ on or to outside; out of doors; not within or enclosed. ● *preposition* /aʊtˈsaɪd/ not in; to or at the outside of; external to; beyond limits of. □ **at the outside** (of estimate etc.) at the most; **outside interest** hobby etc. unconnected with one's work.

outsider /aʊtˈsaɪdə/ *noun* non-member of circle, party, profession, etc.; competitor thought to have little chance.

outsize *adjective* unusually large.

outskirts *plural noun* outer area of town etc.

outsmart /aʊtˈsmɑːt/ *verb* outwit; be too clever for.

outspoken /aʊtˈspəʊkən/ *adjective* saying openly what one thinks; frank. □ **outspokenly** *adverb*; **outspokenness** *noun*.

outspread /aʊtˈspred/ *adjective* spread out.

outstanding /aʊtˈstændɪŋ/ *adjective* conspicuous, esp. from excellence; still to be dealt with; (of debt) not yet settled. □ **outstandingly** *adverb*.

outstation *noun* remote branch or outpost.

outstay /aʊt'steɪ/ *verb* stay longer than (one's welcome etc.).

outstretched /aʊt'stretʃt/ *adjective* stretched out.

outstrip /aʊt'strɪp/ *verb* (**-pp-**) go faster than; surpass in progress, competition, etc.

out-take *noun* film or tape sequence cut out in editing.

out-tray *noun* tray for outgoing documents.

outvote /aʊt'vəʊt/ *verb* (**-ting**) defeat by majority of votes.

outward /'aʊtwəd/ ● *adjective* directed towards outside; going out; physical; external, apparent. ● *adverb* (also **outwards**) in outward direction, towards outside. □ **outwardly** *adverb*.

outweigh /aʊt'weɪ/ *verb* exceed in weight, value, influence, etc.

outwit /aʊt'wɪt/ *verb* (**-tt-**) be too clever for; overcome by greater ingenuity.

outwith /aʊt'wɪθ/ *preposition Scottish* outside.

outwork *noun* advanced or detached part of fortress etc.; work done off premises of shop, factory, etc. supplying it.

outworn /aʊt'wɔːn/ *adjective* worn out; obsolete.

ouzel /'uːz(ə)l/ *noun* (also **ousel**) small bird of thrush family.

ouzo /'uːzəʊ/ *noun* (*plural* **-s**) Greek aniseed-flavoured alcoholic spirit.

ova *plural* of OVUM.

oval /'əʊv(ə)l/ ● *adjective* shaped like egg, elliptical. ● *noun* elliptical closed curve; thing with oval outline.

ovary /'əʊvərɪ/ *noun* (*plural* **-ies**) either of two ovum-producing organs in female; seed vessel in plant. □ **ovarian** /əʊ'veər-/ *adjective*.

ovation /əʊ'veɪʃ(ə)n/ *noun* enthusiastic applause or reception.

oven /'ʌv(ə)n/ *noun* enclosed chamber for cooking food in. □ **ovenproof** heat-resistant; **oven-ready** (of food) prepared before sale for immediate cooking; **ovenware** dishes for cooking food in oven.

over /'əʊvə/ ● *adverb* outward and downward from brink or from erect position; so as to cover whole surface; so as to

produce fold or reverse position; above in place or position; from one side, end, etc. to other; from beginning to end with repetition; in excess; settled, finished. ● *preposition* above; out and down from; so as to cover; across; on or to other side, end, etc. of; concerning. ● *noun Cricket* sequence of 6 balls bowled from one end before change is made to other; play during this time. □ **over the way** (in street etc.) facing or across from.

over- *prefix* excessively; upper, outer; over; completely.

overact /əʊvə'rækt/ *verb* act (a role) with exaggeration.

over-active /əʊvə'ræktɪv/ *adjective* too active.

overall ● *adjective* /'əʊvərɔːl/ taking everything into account, inclusive, total. ● *adverb* /əʊvər'ɔːl/ including everything; on the whole. ● *noun* /'əʊvərɔːl/ protective outer garment; (in *plural*) protective trousers or suit.

overarm *adjective & adverb* with arm raised above shoulder.

overawe /əʊvə'rɔː/ *verb* (**-wing**) awe into submission.

overbalance /əʊvə'bæləns/ *verb* (**-cing**) lose balance and fall; cause to do this.

overbearing /əʊvə'beərɪŋ/ *adjective* domineering; oppressive.

overblown /əʊvə'bləʊn/ *adjective* inflated, pretentious; (of flower etc.) past its prime.

overboard *adverb* from ship into water. □ **go overboard** *colloquial* show extreme enthusiasm, behave immoderately.

overbook /əʊvə'bʊk/ *verb* make too many bookings for (aircraft, hotel, etc.).

overcame *past* of OVERCOME.

overcast *adjective* (of sky) covered with cloud; (in sewing) edged with stitching.

overcharge /əʊvə'tʃɑːdʒ/ *verb* (**-ging**) charge too high a price to; put too much charge into (battery, gun, etc.).

overcoat *noun* warm outdoor coat.

overcome /əʊvə'kʌm/ *verb* (**-coming**; *past* **-came**; *past participle* **-come**) prevail over, master; be victorious; (usually as **overcome** *adjective*) make faint; (often + *with*) make weak or helpless.

overcrowd /əʊvəˈkraʊd/ verb (usually as **overcrowded** adjective) cause too many people or things to be in (a place). □ **overcrowding** noun.

overdevelop /əʊvədɪˈveləp/ verb (**-p-**) develop too much.

overdo /əʊvəˈduː/ verb (**-doing**; 3rd singular present **-does**; past **-did**; past participle **-done**) carry to excess; (as **overdone** adjective) overcooked. □ **overdo it, things** colloquial exhaust oneself.

overdose ● noun excessive dose of drug etc. ● verb (**-sing**) take overdose.

overdraft noun overdrawing of bank account; amount by which account is overdrawn.

overdraw /əʊvəˈdrɔː/ verb (past **-drew**; past participle **-drawn**) draw more from (bank account) than amount in credit; (as **overdrawn** adjective) having overdrawn one's account.

overdress /əʊvəˈdres/ verb dress ostentatiously or with too much formality.

overdrive noun mechanism in vehicle providing gear above top gear for economy at high speeds; state of high activity.

overdue /əʊvəˈdjuː/ adjective past the time when due or ready; late, in arrears.

overestimate ● verb /əʊvərˈestɪmeɪt/ (**-ting**) form too high an estimate of. ● noun /əʊvərˈestɪmət/ too high an estimate. □ **overestimation** noun.

overexpose /əʊvərɪkˈspəʊz/ verb (**-sing**) expose too much to public; expose (film) for too long.

overfish /əʊvəˈfɪʃ/ verb deplete (stream etc.) by too much fishing.

overflow ● verb /əʊvəˈfləʊ/ flow over; be so full that contents overflow; (of crowd etc.) extend beyond limits or capacity of; flood; (of kindness, harvest, etc.) be very abundant. ● noun /ˈəʊvəfləʊ/ what overflows or is superfluous; outlet for excess liquid.

overgrown /əʊvəˈgrəʊn/ adjective grown too big; covered with weeds etc. □ **overgrowth** noun.

overhang ● verb /əʊvəˈhæŋ/ (past & past participle **-hung**) project or hang over. ● noun /ˈəʊvəhæŋ/ fact or amount of overhanging.

overhaul verb /əʊvəˈhɔːl/ check over thoroughly and make repairs to if necessary; overtake. ● noun /ˈəʊvəhɔːl/ thorough examination, with repairs if necessary.

overhead ● adverb /əʊvəˈhed/ above one's head; in sky. ● adjective /ˈəʊvəhed/ placed overhead. ● noun /ˈəʊvəhed/ (in plural) routine administrative and maintenance expenses of a business. □ **overhead projector** projector for producing enlarged image of transparency above and behind user.

overhear /əʊvəˈhɪə/ verb (past & past participle **-heard**) hear as hidden or unintentional listener.

overindulge /əʊvərɪnˈdʌldʒ/ noun (**-ging**) indulge to excess.

overjoyed /əʊvəˈdʒɔɪd/ adjective filled with great joy.

overkill noun excess of capacity to kill or destroy; excess.

overland adjective & adverb by land and not sea.

overlap ● verb /əʊvəˈlæp/ (**-pp-**) partly cover; cover and extend beyond; partly coincide. ● noun /ˈəʊvəlæp/ overlapping; overlapping part or amount.

overlay ● verb /əʊvəˈleɪ/ (past & past participle **-laid**) lay over; (+ with) cover (thing) with (coating etc.). ● noun /ˈəʊvəleɪ/ thing laid over another.

overleaf /əʊvəˈliːf/ adverb on other side of page of book.

overlie /əʊvəˈlaɪ/ verb (**-lying**; past **-lay**; past participle **-lain**) lie on top of.

overload ● verb /əʊvəˈləʊd/ load too heavily (with baggage, work, etc.); put too great a demand on (electrical circuit etc.). ● noun /ˈəʊvələʊd/ excessive quantity or demand.

overlook /əʊvəˈlʊk/ verb fail to observe; tolerate; have view of from above.

overlord noun supreme lord.

overly adverb excessively.

overman /əʊvəˈmæn/ verb (**-nn-**) provide with too large a crew, staff, etc.

overmuch /əʊvəˈmʌtʃ/ adverb & adjective too much.

overnight ● adverb /əʊvəˈnaɪt/ for a night; during the night; suddenly. ● adjective for use or done etc. overnight; instant.

over-particular /əʊvəpəˈtɪkjʊlə/ adjective fussy or excessively particular.

overpass noun esp. US bridge by which road or railway line crosses another.

overplay /əʊvəˈpleɪ/ verb give undue importance or emphasis to. □ **overplay one's hand** act on unduly optimistic estimate of one's chances.

overpower /əʊvəˈpaʊə/ verb subdue, reduce to submission; (esp. as **overpowering** adjective) be too intense or overwhelming for.

overproduce /əʊvəprəˈdjuːs/ verb (-cing) produce in excess of demand or of defined amount. □ **overproduction** noun.

overrate /əʊvəˈreɪt/ verb (-ting) assess or value too highly; (as **overrated** adjective) not as good as it is said to be.

overreach /əʊvəˈriːtʃ/ verb (**overreach oneself**) fail by attempting too much.

overreact /əʊvərɪˈækt/ verb respond more violently etc. than is justified. □ **overreaction** noun.

override ● verb /əʊvəˈraɪd/ (-ding; past -rode; past participle -ridden) have priority over; intervene and make ineffective; interrupt action of (automatic device). ● noun /ˈəʊvəraɪd/ suspension of automatic function.

overrider noun each of pair of projecting pieces on bumper of car.

overrule /əʊvəˈruːl/ verb (-ling) set aside (decision etc.) by superior authority; reject proposal of (person) in this way.

overrun /əʊvəˈrʌn/ verb (-nn-; past -ran; past participle -run) spread over; conquer (territory) by force; exceed time etc. allowed.

overseas ● adverb /əʊvəˈsiːz/ across or beyond sea. ● adjective /ˈəʊvəsiːz/ of places across sea; foreign.

oversee /əʊvəˈsiː/ verb (-sees; past -saw; past participle -seen) superintend (workers etc.). □ **overseer** noun.

over-sensitive /əʊvəˈsensɪtɪv/ adjective excessively sensitive; easily hurt; quick to react. □ **over-sensitiveness** noun, **over-sensitivity** /-ˈtɪv-/ noun.

oversew verb (past participle -sewn or -sewed) sew (two edges) with stitches lying over them.

oversexed /əʊvəˈsekst/ adjective having unusually strong sexual desires.

overshadow /əʊvəˈʃædəʊ/ verb appear much more prominent or important than; cast into shade.

overshoe noun shoe worn over another for protection in wet weather etc.

overshoot /əʊvəˈʃuːt/ verb (past & past participle -shot) pass or send beyond (target or limit); go beyond runway when landing or taking off. □ **overshoot the mark** go beyond what is intended or proper.

oversight noun failure to notice; inadvertent omission or mistake; supervision.

oversimplify /əʊvəˈsɪmplɪfaɪ/ verb (-ies, -ied) distort (problem etc.) by putting it in too simple terms. □ **oversimplification** noun.

oversleep /əʊvəˈsliːp/ verb (past & past participle -slept) sleep beyond intended time of waking.

overspend /əʊvəˈspend/ verb (past & past participle -spent) spend beyond one's means.

overspill noun what is spilt over or overflows; surplus population leaving one area for another.

overspread /əʊvəˈspred/ verb (past & past participle -spread) cover surface of; (as **overspread** adjective) (usually + with) covered.

overstate /əʊvəˈsteɪt/ verb (-ting) state too strongly; exaggerate. □ **overstatement** noun.

overstep /əʊvəˈstep/ verb (-pp-) pass beyond. □ **overstep the mark** go beyond conventional behaviour.

overstrain /əʊvəˈstreɪn/ verb damage by exertion; stretch too far.

overstrung adjective /əʊvəˈstrʌŋ/ (of person, nerves, etc.) too highly strung; /ˈəʊvəstrʌŋ/ (of piano) with strings crossing each other obliquely.

oversubscribe /əʊvəsəbˈskraɪb/ verb (-bing) (usually as **oversubscribed** adjective) subscribe for more than available amount or number of (offer, shares, places, etc.).

overt /əʊˈvɜːt/ adjective openly done, unconcealed. □ **overtly** adverb.

overtake /əʊvəˈteɪk/ verb (-king; past -took; past participle -taken) catch up and pass; (of bad luck etc.) come suddenly upon.

overtax /əʊvə'tæks/ *verb* make excessive demands on; tax too highly.

over-the-top *adjective colloquial* excessive.

overthrow • *verb* /əʊvə'θrəʊ/ (*past* **-threw**; *past participle* **-thrown**) remove forcibly from power; conquer. • *noun* /'əʊvəθrəʊ/ defeat; downfall.

overtime • *noun* time worked in addition to regular hours; payment for this. • *adverb* in addition to regular hours.

overtone *noun Music* any of tones above lowest in harmonic series; subtle extra quality or implication.

overture /'əʊvətjʊə/ *noun* orchestral prelude; (usually in *plural*) opening of negotiations; formal proposal or offer.

overturn /əʊvə'tɜːn/ *verb* (cause to) fall down or over; upset, overthrow.

overview *noun* general survey.

overweening /əʊvə'wiːnɪŋ/ *adjective* arrogant.

overweight • *adjective* /əʊvə'weɪt/ above the weight allowed or desirable. • *noun* /'əʊvəweɪt/ excess weight.

overwhelm /əʊvə'welm/ *verb* overpower with emotion; overcome by force of numbers; bury, submerge utterly.

overwhelming *adjective* too great to resist or overcome; by a great number. □ **overwhelmingly** *adverb*.

overwork /əʊvə'wɜːk/ • *verb* (cause to) work too hard; weary or exhaust with work; (esp. as **overworked** *adjective*) make excessive use of. • *noun* excessive work.

overwrought /əʊvə'rɔːt/ *adjective* overexcited, nervous, distraught; too elaborate.

oviduct /'əʊvɪdʌkt/ *noun* tube through which ova pass from ovary.

oviform /'əʊvɪfɔːm/ *adjective* egg-shaped.

ovine /'əʊvaɪn/ *adjective* of or like sheep.

oviparous /əʊ'vɪpərəs/ *adjective* egglaying.

ovoid /'əʊvɔɪd/ *adjective* (of solid) eggshaped.

ovulate /'ɒvjʊleɪt/ *verb* (**-ting**) produce ova or ovules, or discharge them from ovary. □ **ovulation** *noun*.

ovule /'ɒvjuːl/ *noun* structure containing germ cell in female plant.

ovum /'əʊvəm/ *noun* (*plural* **ova** /'əʊvə/) female egg cell from which young develop after fertilization with male sperm.

ow /aʊ/ *interjection* expressing sudden pain.

owe /əʊ/ *verb* (**owing**) be under obligation to (re)pay or render; (usually + *for*) be in debt; (usually + *to*) be indebted to person, thing, etc. for.

owing /'əʊɪŋ/ *adjective* owed, yet to be paid; (+ *to*) caused by, because of.

owl /aʊl/ *noun* night bird of prey; solemn or wise-looking person. □ **owlish** *adjective*.

owlet /'aʊlɪt/ *noun* small or young owl.

own /əʊn/ • *adjective* (after *my*, *your*, etc.) belonging to myself, yourself, etc.; not another's. • *verb* have as property, possess; acknowledge as true or belonging to one. □ **come into one's own** achieve recognition, receive one's due; **hold one's own** maintain one's position, not be defeated; **on one's own** alone, independently, unaided; **own goal** goal scored by mistake against scorer's own side, action etc. having unintended effect of harming person's own interests; **own up** confess.

owner *noun* possessor. □ **owner-occupier** person who owns and occupies house. □ **ownership** *noun*.

ox *noun* (*plural* **oxen**) large usually horned ruminant; castrated male of domestic species of cattle. □ **ox-eye daisy** daisy with large white petals and yellow centre; **oxtail** tail of ox, often used in making soup.

oxalic acid /ɒk'sælɪk/ *noun* intensely sour poisonous acid found in wood sorrel and rhubarb leaves.

oxidation /ɒksɪ'deɪʃ(ə)n/ *noun* oxidizing, being oxidized.

oxide /'ɒksaɪd/ *noun* compound of oxygen with another element.

oxidize /'ɒksɪdaɪz/ *verb* (also **-ise**) (**-zing** or **-sing**) combine with oxygen; rust; cover with coating of oxide. □ **oxidization** *noun*.

oxyacetylene /ɒksɪə'setɪliːn/ *adjective* of or using mixture of oxygen and acetylene, esp. in cutting or welding metals.

oxygen /'ɒksɪdʒ(ə)n/ *noun* colourless odourless tasteless gaseous element essential to life and to combustion.

□ **oxygen tent** enclosure to allow patient to breathe air with increased oxygen content.

oxygenate /'ɒksɪdʒəneɪt/ *verb* (**-ting**) supply, treat, or mix with oxygen; oxidize.

oyez /əʊˈjes/ *interjection* (also **oyes**) *uttered by public crier or court officer to call for attention.*

oyster /'ɔɪstə/ ● *noun* bivalve mollusc living on seabed, esp. edible kind. ● *adjective* (in full **oyster-white**) greyish white.

oz *abbreviation* ounce(s).

ozone /'əʊzəʊn/ *noun* form of oxygen with pungent odour; *colloquial* invigorating seaside air. □ **ozone-friendly** not containing chemicals destructive to ozone layer; **ozone layer** layer of ozone in stratosphere that absorbs most of sun's ultraviolet radiation.

Pp

p *abbreviation* (also **p.**) penny, pence; page; piano (softly). □ **p. & p.** postage and packing.

PA *abbreviation* personal assistant; public address.

pa /pɑː/ *noun colloquial* father.

p.a. *abbreviation* per annum.

pace[1] ● *noun* single step in walking or running; distance covered in this; speed, rate of progression; gait. ● *verb* (**-cing**) walk (over, about), esp. with slow or regular step; set pace for; (+ *out*) measure (distance) by pacing. □ **pacemaker** person who sets pace, natural or electrical device for stimulating heart muscle.

pace[2] /'pɑːtʃeɪ/ *preposition* with all due deference to. [Latin]

pachyderm /'pækɪdɜːm/ *noun* large thick-skinned mammal, esp. elephant or rhinoceros. □ **pachydermatous** /-'dɜːmətəs/ *adjective.*

pacific /pə'sɪfɪk/ ● *adjective* tending to peace, peaceful; (**Pacific**) of or adjoining the Pacific. ● *noun* (**the Pacific**) ocean between America to the east and Asia to the west.

pacifist /'pæsɪfɪst/ *noun* person opposed to war. □ **pacifism** *noun.*

pacify /'pæsɪfaɪ/ *verb* (**-ies, -ied**) appease (person, anger, etc.); bring (country etc.) to state of peace. □ **pacification** *noun.*

pack ● *noun* collection of things tied or wrapped together for carrying; back-

pack; set of packaged items; set of playing cards; *usually derogatory* lot, set; group of wild animals or hounds; organized group of Cub Scouts or Brownies; forwards of Rugby team; area of large crowded pieces of floating ice in sea. ● *verb* put together into bundle, box, etc., fill with clothes etc. for transport or storing; cram, crowd together, form into pack; (esp. in *passive*; often + *with*) fill; wrap tightly. □ **packed out** full, crowded; **packhorse** horse for carrying loads; **pack in** *colloquial* stop, give up; **pack it in, up** *colloquial* end or stop it; **pack up** *colloquial* stop working, break down, retire from contest, activity, etc.; **send packing** *colloquial* dismiss summarily.

package ● *noun* parcel; box etc. in which goods are packed; (in full **package deal**) set of proposals or items offered or agreed to as a whole. ● *verb* (**-ging**) make up into or enclose in package. □ **package holiday, tour**, etc., one with fixed inclusive price. □ **packaging** *noun.*

packet /'pækɪt/ *noun* small package; *colloquial* large sum of money; *historical* mail-boat.

pact *noun* agreement, treaty.

pad[1] ● *noun* piece of soft stuff used to diminish jarring, raise surface, absorb fluid, etc.; sheets of blank paper fastened together at one edge; fleshy cushion forming sole of foot of some animals; leg-guard in games; flat surface for helicopter take-off or rocket-launching; *slang* lodging. ● *verb* (**-dd-**) provide with pad or padding, stuff; (+ *out*) fill out (book etc.) with superfluous matter.

pad² ● *verb* (**-dd-**) walk softly; tramp (along) on foot; travel on foot. ● *noun* sound of soft steady steps.

padding *noun* material used to pad.

paddle¹ /'pæd(ə)l/ ● *noun* short oar with broad blade at one or each end; paddle-shaped instrument; fin, flipper; board on paddle-wheel or mill-wheel; action or spell of paddling. ● *verb* (**-ling**) move on water or propel (boat etc.) with paddle(s); row gently. □ **paddle-wheel** wheel for propelling ship, with boards round circumference.

paddle² /'pæd(ə)l/ ● *verb* (**-ling**) wade about in shallow water. ● *noun* action or spell of paddling.

paddock /'pædək/ *noun* small field, esp. for keeping horses in; enclosure where horses or cars are assembled before race.

paddy¹ /'pædɪ/ *noun* (*plural* **-ies**) (in full **paddy field**) field where rice is grown; rice before threshing or in the husk.

paddy² /'pædɪ/ *noun* (*plural* **-ies**) *colloquial* rage, temper.

padlock /'pædlɒk/ ● *noun* detachable lock hanging by pivoted hook. ● *verb* secure with padlock.

padre /'pɑːdrɪ/ *noun* chaplain in army etc.

paean /'piːən/ *noun* (*US* **pean**) song of praise or triumph.

paediatrics /piːdɪˈætrɪks/ *plural noun* (treated as *singular*) (*US* **pediatrics**) branch of medicine dealing with children's diseases. □ **paediatric** *adjective*; **paediatrician** /-əˈtrɪʃ(ə)n/ *noun*.

paedophile /'piːdəfaɪl/ *noun* (*US* **pedophile**) person feeling sexual attraction towards children.

paella /paɪˈelə/ *noun* Spanish dish of rice, saffron, chicken, seafood, etc.

paeony = PEONY.

pagan /'peɪgən/ ● *noun* heathen, pantheist, etc. ● *adjective* of pagans; heathen; pantheistic. □ **paganism** *noun*.

page¹ ● *noun* leaf of book etc.; each side of this. ● *verb* (**-ging**) number pages of.

page² ● *noun* boy or man employed as liveried servant or personal attendant. ● *verb* (**-ging**) call name of (person sought) in public rooms of hotel etc. □ **page-boy** boy attending bride etc., woman's short hairstyle.

pageant /'pædʒ(ə)nt/ *noun* spectacular performance, usually illustrative of historical events; any brilliant show.

pageantry *noun* spectacular show or display.

pager *noun* bleeping device calling bearer to telephone etc.

paginate /'pædʒɪneɪt/ *verb* (**-ting**) number pages of (book etc.). □ **pagination** *noun*.

pagoda /pəˈgəʊdə/ *noun* temple or sacred tower in China etc.; ornamental imitation of this.

pah *interjection expressing disgust.*

paid past & past participle of PAY.

pail *noun* bucket.

pain ● *noun* bodily suffering caused by injury, pressure, illness, etc.; mental suffering; *colloquial* troublesome person or thing. ● *verb* cause pain to. □ **be at** or **take pains** take great care; **in pain** suffering pain; **painkiller** pain-relieving drug.

painful *adjective* causing or (esp. of part of the body) suffering pain; causing trouble or difficulty. □ **painfully** *adverb*.

painless *adjective* not causing pain. □ **painlessly** *adverb*.

painstaking /'peɪnzteɪkɪŋ/ *adjective* careful, industrious, thorough. □ **painstakingly** *adverb*.

paint ● *noun* colouring matter, esp. in liquid form, for applying to surface. ● *verb* cover surface of with paint; portray or make pictures in colours; describe vividly; apply liquid or cosmetic to. □ **paintbox** box holding dry paints for painting pictures; **painted lady** butterfly with spotted orange-red wings; **paintwork** painted, esp. wooden, surface or area in building etc.

painter¹ *noun* person who paints, esp. as artist or decorator.

painter² *noun* rope at bow of boat for tying it up.

painting *noun* process or art of using paint; painted picture.

pair •*noun* set of two people or things; thing with two joined or corresponding parts; engaged or married or mated couple; two playing cards of same denomination; (either of) two MPs etc. on opposite sides agreeing not to vote on certain occasions. •*verb* (often + *off*) arrange or unite as pair, in pairs, or in marriage; mate.

Paisley /'peɪzlɪ/ *noun* (*plural* -s) pattern of curved feather-shaped figures.

pajamas *US* = PYJAMAS.

Pakistani /pɑːkɪs'tɑːnɪ/ •*noun* (*plural* -s) native or national of Pakistan; person of Pakistani descent. •*adjective* of Pakistan.

pal *colloquial* •*noun* friend. •*verb* (-ll-) (+ *up*) make friends.

palace /'pælɪs/ *noun* official residence of sovereign, president, archbishop, or bishop; stately or spacious building.

palaeo- *combining form* (*US* **paleo-**) ancient; prehistoric.

palaeography /pælɪ'ɒɡrəfɪ/ *noun* (*US* **paleography**) study of ancient writing and documents.

palaeolithic /pælɪəʊ'lɪθɪk/ *adjective* (*US* **paleolithic**) of earlier Stone Age.

palaeontology /pælɪɒn'tɒlədʒɪ/ *noun* (*US* **paleontology**) study of life in geological past. □ **palaeontologist** *noun*.

Palaeozoic /pælɪəʊ'zəʊɪk/ (*US* **Paleozoic**) •*adjective* of geological era marked by appearance of plants and animals, esp. invertebrates. •*noun* this era.

palais /'pæleɪ/ *noun colloquial* public dance hall.

palanquin /pælən'kiːn/ *noun* (also **palankeen**) Eastern covered litter for one.

palatable /'pælətəb(ə)l/ *adjective* pleasant to taste; (of idea etc.) acceptable, satisfactory.

palatal /'pælət(ə)l/ •*adjective* of the palate; (of sound) made with tongue against palate. •*noun* palatal sound.

palate /'pælət/ *noun* roof of mouth in vertebrates; sense of taste; liking.

palatial /pə'leɪʃ(ə)l/ *adjective* like palace, splendid.

palaver /pə'lɑːvə/ *noun colloquial* tedious fuss and bother.

pale¹ •*adjective* (of complexion etc.) whitish; faintly coloured; (of colour) faint, (of light) dim. •*verb* (**-ling**) grow or make pale; (often + *before, beside*) seem feeble in comparison (with). □ **palely** *adverb*.

pale² *noun* pointed piece of wood for fencing etc.; stake; boundary. □ **beyond the pale** outside bounds of acceptable behaviour.

paleo- *US* = PALAEO-.

Palestinian /pælɪ'stɪnɪən/ •*adjective* of Palestine. •*noun* native or inhabitant of Palestine.

palette /'pælɪt/ *noun* artist's flat tablet for mixing colours on; range of colours used by artist. □ **palette-knife** knife with long round-ended flexible blade, esp. for mixing colours or applying or removing paint.

palimony /'pælɪmənɪ/ *noun esp. US colloquial* allowance paid by either of a separated unmarried couple to the other.

palimpsest /'pælɪmpsest/ *noun* writing material used for second time after original writing has been erased.

palindrome /'pælɪndrəʊm/ *noun* word or phrase that reads same backwards as forwards. □ **palindromic** /-'drɒm-/ *adjective*.

paling *noun* (in *singular* or *plural*) fence of pales; pale.

palisade /pælɪ'seɪd/ •*noun* fence of pointed stakes. •*verb* (**-ding**) enclose or provide with palisade.

pall¹ /pɔːl/ *noun* cloth spread over coffin etc.; ecclesiastical vestment; dark covering. □ **pallbearer** person helping to carry or escort coffin at funeral.

pall² /pɔːl/ *verb* become uninteresting.

pallet¹ /'pælɪt/ *noun* straw mattress; makeshift bed.

pallet² /'pælɪt/ *noun* portable platform for transporting and storing loads.

palliasse /'pælɪæs/ *noun* straw mattress.

palliate /'pælɪeɪt/ *verb* (**-ting**) alleviate without curing; excuse, extenuate. □ **palliative** /-ətɪv/ *adjective & noun*.

pallid /'pælɪd/ *adjective* pale, sickly-looking.

pallor /'pælə/ *noun* paleness.

pally *adjective* (**-ier**, **-iest**) *colloquial* friendly.

palm[1] /pɑːm/ *noun* (also **palm tree**) (usually tropical) treelike plant with unbranched stem and crown of large esp. sickle- or fan-shaped leaves; leaf of this as symbol of victory. □ **Palm Sunday** Sunday before Easter.

palm[2] /pɑːm/ ● *noun* inner surface of hand between wrist and fingers. ● *verb* conceal in hand. □ **palm off** (often + *on*) impose fraudulently (on person).

palmate /ˈpælmeɪt/ *adjective* shaped like open hand.

palmetto /pælˈmetəʊ/ *noun* (*plural* **-s**) small palm tree.

palmist /ˈpɑːmɪst/ *noun* teller of character or fortune from lines etc. in palm of hand. □ **palmistry** *noun*.

palmy /ˈpɑːmɪ/ *adjective* (**-ier**, **-iest**) of, like, or abounding in palms; flourishing.

palomino /pæləˈmiːnəʊ/ *noun* (*plural* **-s**) golden or cream-coloured horse with light-coloured mane and tail.

palpable /ˈpælpəb(ə)l/ *adjective* that can be touched or felt; readily perceived. □ **palpably** *adverb*.

palpate /ˈpælpeɪt/ *verb* (**-ting**) examine (esp. medically) by touch. □ **palpation** *noun*.

palpitate /ˈpælpɪteɪt/ *verb* (**-ting**) pulsate, throb; tremble. □ **palpitation** *noun*.

palsy /ˈpɔːlzɪ/ ● *noun* (*plural* **-ies**) paralysis, esp. with involuntary tremors. ● *verb* (**-ies**, **-ied**) affect with palsy.

paltry /ˈpɔːltrɪ/ *adjective* (**-ier**, **-iest**) worthless, contemptible, trifling.

pampas /ˈpæmpəs/ *plural noun* large treeless S. American plains. □ **pampas grass** large ornamental grass.

pamper /ˈpæmpə/ *verb* overindulge.

pamphlet /ˈpæmflɪt/ *noun* small unbound booklet, esp. controversial treatise.

pamphleteer /pæmflɪˈtɪə/ *noun* writer of (esp. political) pamphlets.

pan[1] ● *noun* flat-bottomed usually metal vessel used in cooking etc.; shallow receptacle or tray; bowl of scales or of lavatory. ● *verb* (**-nn-**) *colloquial* criticize harshly; (+ *off*, *out*) wash (gold-bearing gravel) in pan; search for gold in this way. □ **pan out** turn out, work out well or in specified way.

pan[2] ● *verb* (**-nn-**) swing (film-camera) horizontally to give panoramic effect or follow moving object; (of camera) be moved thus. ● *noun* panning movement.

pan- *combining form* all; the whole of (esp. referring to a continent, racial group, religion, etc.).

panacea /pænəˈsiːə/ *noun* universal remedy.

panache /pəˈnæʃ/ *noun* assertively flamboyant or confident style.

panama /ˈpænəmɑː/ *noun* hat of straw-like material with brim and indented crown.

panatella /pænəˈtelə/ *noun* long thin cigar.

pancake *noun* thin flat cake of fried batter, usually folded or rolled up with filling. □ **Pancake Day** Shrove Tuesday (when pancakes are traditionally eaten); **pancake landing** *colloquial* emergency aircraft landing with undercarriage still retracted.

panchromatic /pænkrəʊˈmætɪk/ *adjective* (of film etc.) sensitive to all visible colours of spectrum.

pancreas /ˈpæŋkrɪəs/ *noun* gland near stomach supplying digestive fluid and insulin. □ **pancreatic** /-ˈæt-/ *adjective*.

panda /ˈpændə/ *noun* (also **giant panda**) large rare bearlike black and white mammal native to China and Tibet; (also **red panda**) racoon-like Himalayan mammal. □ **panda car** police patrol car.

pandemic /pænˈdemɪk/ *adjective* (of disease) widespread; universal.

pandemonium /pændɪˈməʊnɪəm/ *noun* uproar; utter confusion; scene of this.

pander /ˈpændə/ ● *verb* (+ *to*) indulge (person or weakness). ● *noun* procurer, pimp.

pandit = PUNDIT.

pane *noun* single sheet of glass in window or door.

panegyric /pænɪˈdʒɪrɪk/ *noun* eulogy; speech or essay of praise.

panel /ˈpæn(ə)l/ ● *noun* distinct, usually rectangular, section of surface, esp. of wall, door, or vehicle; group or team of people assembled for consultation, etc.; strip of material in garment; list of available jurors; jury.

● verb (**-ll-**; *US* **-l-**) fit with panels.
□ **panel game** broadcast quiz etc.
played by panel. □ **panelling** noun.

panellist noun (*US* **panelist**) member of
panel.

pang noun sudden sharp pain or distressing emotion.

pangolin /pæŋ'gəʊlɪn/ noun scaly
anteater.

panic /'pænɪk/ ● noun sudden alarm; infectious fright. ● verb (**-ck-**) (often +
into) affect or be affected with panic.
□ **panic-stricken**, **-struck** affected
with panic. □ **panicky** adjective.

panicle /'pænɪk(ə)l/ noun loose branching cluster of flowers.

panjandrum /pæn'dʒændrəm/ noun:
mock title of great personage.

pannier /'pænɪə/ noun one of pair of
baskets or bags etc. carried by beast of
burden or on bicycle or motorcycle.

panoply /'pænəplɪ/ noun (*plural* **-ies**) complete or splendid array; full armour.

panorama /pænə'rɑːmə/ noun unbroken
view of surrounding region; picture or
photograph containing wide view.
□ **panoramic** /-'ræm-/ adjective.

pansy /'pænzɪ/ noun (*plural* **-ies**) garden
plant of violet family with richly coloured flowers.

pant ● verb breathe with quick breaths;
yearn. ● noun panting breath.

pantaloons /pæntə'luːnz/ plural noun
baggy trousers gathered at ankles.

pantechnicon /pæn'teknɪkən/ noun
large furniture van.

pantheism /'pænθiːɪz(ə)m/ noun doctrine
that God is everything and everything
is God. □ **pantheist** noun; **pantheistic**
/-'ɪs-/ adjective.

pantheon /'pænθɪən/ noun building with
memorials of illustrious dead; deities
of a people collectively; temple of all
gods.

panther /'pænθə/ noun leopard, esp.
black; *US* puma.

panties /'pæntɪz/ plural noun colloquial
short-legged or legless knickers.

pantile /'pæntaɪl/ noun curved roof-tile.

pantograph /'pæntəɡrɑːf/ noun instrument for copying plan etc. on any scale.

pantomime /'pæntəmaɪm/ noun dramatic usually Christmas entertainment based on fairy tale; colloquial absurd or outrageous behaviour; gestures and facial expressions conveying
meaning.

pantry /'pæntrɪ/ noun (*plural* **-ies**) room in
which provisions, crockery, cutlery,
etc. are kept.

pants plural noun underpants; knickers;
US trousers.

pap[1] noun soft or semi-liquid food; trivial reading matter.

pap[2] noun archaic nipple.

papa /pə'pɑː/ noun archaic; child's name
for father.

papacy /'peɪpəsɪ/ noun (*plural* **-ies**) Pope's
office or tenure; papal system.

papal /'peɪp(ə)l/ adjective of the Pope or
his office.

paparazzo /pæpə'rætsəʊ/ noun (*plural*
-zzi /-tsɪ/) freelance photographer who
pursues celebrities to photograph
them.

papaya = PAWPAW.

paper /'peɪpə/ ● noun substance made in
very thin sheets from pulp of wood etc.,
used for writing, printing, wrapping,
etc.; newspaper; (in *plural*) documents;
set of exam questions or answers; wallpaper; essay. ● adjective not actual,
theoretical. ● verb decorate (wall etc.)
with paper. □ **paper-boy**, **-girl** one
who delivers or sells newspapers;
paper-clip clip of bent wire or plastic
for holding sheets of paper together;
paper-knife blunt knife for opening
envelopes etc.; **paper money** banknotes etc.; **paper round** job of regularly
delivering newspapers, route for
doing this; **paperweight** small heavy object to hold papers down; **paperwork**
office record-keeping and administration.

paperback ● adjective bound in stiff
paper, not boards. ● noun paperback
book.

papier mâché /pæpɪeɪ 'mæʃeɪ/ noun
moulded paper pulp used for making
models etc.

papilla /pə'pɪlə/ noun (*plural* **papillae**
/-liː/) small nipple-like protuberance.
□ **papillary** adjective.

papoose /pə'puːs/ noun young N. American Indian child.

paprika /ˈpæprɪkə/ *noun* ripe red pepper; condiment made from this.

papyrus /pəˈpaɪərəs/ *noun* (*plural* **papyri** /-raɪ/) aquatic plant of N. Africa; ancient writing material needed made from stem of this; manuscript written on this.

par *noun* average or normal value, degree, condition, etc.; equality, equal footing; *Golf* number of strokes needed by first-class player for hole or course; face value. □ **par for the course** *colloquial* what is normal or to be expected.

para /ˈpærə/ *noun colloquial* paratrooper.

para- *prefix* beside, beyond.

parable /ˈpærəb(ə)l/ *noun* story used to illustrate moral or spiritual truth.

parabola /pəˈræbələ/ *noun* plane curve formed by intersection of cone with plane parallel to its side. □ **parabolic** /pærəˈbɒlɪk/ *adjective*.

paracetamol /pærəˈsiːtəmɒl/ *noun* compound used to relieve pain and reduce fever; tablet of this.

parachute /ˈpærəʃuːt/ ● *noun* usually umbrella-shaped apparatus allowing person or heavy object to descend safely from a height, esp. from aircraft. ● *verb* (**-ting**) convey or descend by parachute. □ **parachutist** *noun*.

parade /pəˈreɪd/ ● *noun* public procession; muster of troops etc. for inspection; parade ground; display, ostentation; public square, row of shops. ● *verb* (**-ding**) march ceremonially; assemble for parade; display ostentatiously. □ **parade ground** place for muster of troops.

paradigm /ˈpærədaɪm/ *noun* example or pattern, esp. of inflection of word.

paradise /ˈpærədaɪs/ *noun* heaven; place or state of complete bliss; garden of Eden.

paradox /ˈpærədɒks/ *noun* seemingly absurd or self-contradictory though often true statement etc. □ **paradoxical** /-ˈdɒks-/ *adjective*; **paradoxically** /-ˈdɒks-/ *adverb*.

paraffin /ˈpærəfɪn/ *noun* inflammable waxy or oily substance got by distillation from petroleum etc., used in liquid form esp. as fuel. □ **paraffin wax** solid paraffin.

paragon /ˈpærəgən/ *noun* (often + *of*) model of excellence.

paragraph /ˈpærəgrɑːf/ *noun* distinct passage in book etc. usually marked by indentation of first line; mark of reference (¶); short separate item in newspaper etc.

parakeet /ˈpærəkiːt/ *noun* small usually long-tailed parrot.

parallax /ˈpærəlæks/ *noun* apparent difference in position or direction of object caused by change of observer's position; angular amount of this.

parallel /ˈpærəlel/ ● *adjective* (of lines) continuously equidistant; precisely similar, analogous, or corresponding; (of processes etc.) occurring or performed simultaneously. ● *noun* person or thing analogous to another; comparison; imaginary line on earth's surface or line on map marking degree of latitude. ● *verb* (**-l-**) be parallel or correspond to; represent as similar; compare. □ **parallelism** *noun*.

parallelepiped /pærəleləˈpaɪped/ *noun* solid bounded by parallelograms.

parallelogram /pærəˈleləgræm/ *noun* 4-sided rectilinear figure whose opposite sides are parallel.

paralyse /ˈpærəlaɪz/ *verb* (**-sing**) (*US* **-lyze**; **-zing**) affect with paralysis; render powerless, cripple.

paralysis /pəˈrælɪsɪs/ *noun* impairment or loss of esp. motor function of nerves, causing immobility; powerlessness.

paralytic /pærəˈlɪtɪk/ ● *adjective* affected with paralysis; *slang* very drunk. ● *noun* person affected with paralysis.

paramedic /pærəˈmedɪk/ *noun* paramedical worker.

paramedical /pærəˈmedɪk(ə)l/ *adjective* supplementing and supporting medical work.

parameter /pəˈræmɪtə/ *noun Mathematics* quantity constant in case considered, but varying in different cases; (esp. measurable or quantifiable) characteristic or feature; (loosely) boundary, esp. of subject for discussion.

paramilitary /pærəˈmɪlɪtərɪ/ ● *adjective* similarly organized to military forces. ● *noun* (*plural* **-ies**) member of unofficial paramilitary organization.

paramount /ˈpærəmaʊnt/ *adjective* supreme; most important or powerful.

paramour /ˈpærəmʊə/ *noun archaic* illicit lover of married person.

paranoia /pærəˈnɔɪə/ noun mental derangement with delusions of grandeur, persecution, etc.; abnormal tendency to suspect and mistrust others. □ **paranoiac** adjective & noun; **paranoid** /ˈpærənɔɪd/ adjective & noun.

paranormal /pærəˈnɔːm(ə)l/ adjective beyond the scope of normal scientific investigations etc.

parapet /ˈpærəpɪt/ noun low wall at edge of roof, balcony, bridge, etc.; mound along front of trench etc.

paraphernalia /pærəfəˈneɪlɪə/ plural noun (also treated as singular) personal belongings, miscellaneous accessories, etc.

paraphrase /ˈpærəfreɪz/ noun restatement of sense of passage etc. in other words. verb (**-sing**) express meaning of in other words.

paraplegia /pærəˈpliːdʒə/ noun paralysis below waist. □ **paraplegic** adjective & noun.

parapsychology /pærəsaɪˈkɒlədʒɪ/ noun study of mental phenomena outside sphere of ordinary psychology.

paraquat /ˈpærəkwɒt/ noun quick-acting highly toxic herbicide.

parasite /ˈpærəsaɪt/ noun animal or plant living in or on another and feeding on it; person exploiting another or others. □ **parasitic** /-ˈsɪt-/ adjective; **parasitism** noun.

parasol /ˈpærəsɒl/ noun light umbrella giving shade from the sun.

paratroops /ˈpærətruːps/ plural noun airborne troops landing by parachute. □ **paratrooper** noun.

paratyphoid /pærəˈtaɪfɔɪd/ noun fever resembling typhoid.

parboil /ˈpɑːbɔɪl/ verb partly cook by boiling.

parcel /ˈpɑːs(ə)l/ • noun goods etc. packed up in single wrapping; piece of land. • verb (**-ll-**; US **-l-**) (+ up) wrap into parcel; (+ out) divide into portions.

parch verb make or become hot and dry; slightly roast.

parchment /ˈpɑːtʃmənt/ noun skin, esp. of sheep or goat, prepared for writing etc.; manuscript written on this.

pardon /ˈpɑːd(ə)n/ • noun forgiveness; remission of punishment. • verb forgive; excuse; release from legal consequences of offence etc. • interjection (also **pardon me** or **I beg your pardon**) formula of apology or disagreement; request to repeat something said. □ **pardonable** adjective.

pare /peə/ verb (**-ring**) trim or reduce by cutting away edge or surface of; (often + away, down) whittle away.

parent /ˈpeərənt/ noun person who has had or adopted a child; father, mother; source, origin. □ **parent company** company of which others are subsidiaries; **parent-teacher association** social and fund-raising organization of school's teachers and parents. □ **parental** /pəˈrent(ə)l/ adjective; **parenthood** noun.

parentage noun lineage, descent from or through parents.

parenthesis /pəˈrenθəsɪs/ noun (plural **-theses** /-siːz/) word, clause, or sentence inserted as explanation etc. into passage independently of grammatical sequence; (in plural) round brackets used to mark this; interlude. □ **parenthetic** /pærənˈθetɪk/ adjective.

par excellence /pɑːr eksəˈlɑ̃s/ adverb superior to all others so called. [French]

parfait /ˈpɑːfeɪ/ noun rich iced pudding of whipped cream, eggs, etc.; layers of ice cream, meringue, etc., served in tall glass.

pariah /pəˈraɪə/ noun social outcast; historical member of low or no caste.

parietal /pəˈraɪət(ə)l/ adjective of wall of body or any of its cavities. □ **parietal bone** either of pair forming part of skull.

paring noun strip pared off.

parish /ˈpærɪʃ/ noun division of diocese having its own church and clergyman; local government district; inhabitants of parish.

parishioner /pəˈrɪʃənə/ noun inhabitant of parish.

parity /ˈpærɪtɪ/ noun (plural **-ies**) equality; equal status etc.; equivalence; being at par.

park • noun large public garden in town; large enclosed piece of ground attached to country house or laid out or preserved for public use; place where vehicles may be parked; area for specified purpose. • verb place and leave (esp.

vehicle) temporarily. □ **parking-lot** *US* outdoor car park; **parking meter** coin-operated meter allocating period of time for which a vehicle may be parked in street; **parking ticket** notice of fine etc. imposed for parking vehicle illegally.

parka /ˈpɑːkə/ *noun* jacket with hood, as worn by Eskimos, mountaineers, etc.

parkin /ˈpɑːkɪn/ *noun* oatmeal gingerbread.

parky /ˈpɑːkɪ/ *adjective* (**-ier, -iest**) *colloquial or dialect* chilly.

parlance /ˈpɑːləns/ *noun* way of speaking.

parley /ˈpɑːlɪ/ ● *noun* (*plural* **-s**) meeting between representatives of opposed forces to discuss terms. ● *verb* (**-leys, -leyed**) (often + *with*) hold parley.

parliament /ˈpɑːləmənt/ *noun* body consisting of House of Commons and House of Lords and forming (with Sovereign) legislature of UK; similar legislature in other states.

parliamentarian /pɑːləmənˈteərɪən/ *noun* member of parliament.

parliamentary /pɑːləˈmentərɪ/ *adjective* of, in, concerned with, or enacted by parliament.

parlour /ˈpɑːlə/ *noun* (*US* **parlor**) *archaic* sitting-room in private house; *esp. US* shop providing specified goods or services. □ **parlour game** indoor game, esp. word game.

parlous /ˈpɑːləs/ *adjective archaic* perilous; hard to deal with.

Parmesan /pɑːmɪˈzæn/ *noun* hard Italian cheese usually used grated as flavouring.

parochial /pəˈrəʊkɪəl/ *adjective* of a parish; of narrow range, merely local. □ **parochialism** *noun*.

parody /ˈpærədɪ/ ● *noun* (*plural* **-ies**) humorous exaggerated imitation of author, style, etc.; travesty. ● *verb* (**-ies, -ied**) write parody of; mimic humorously. □ **parodist** *noun*.

parole /pəˈrəʊl/ ● *noun* temporary or permanent release of prisoner before end of sentence, on promise of good behaviour; such promise. ● *verb* (**-ling**) put (prisoner) on parole.

parotid /pəˈrɒtɪd/ ● *adjective* situated near ear. ● *noun* (in full **parotid gland**) salivary gland in front of ear.

paroxysm /ˈpærəksɪz(ə)m/ *noun* (often + *of*) fit (of pain, rage, coughing, etc.).

parquet /ˈpɑːkeɪ/ ● *noun* flooring of wooden blocks arranged in a pattern. ● *verb* (**-eted** /-eɪd/, **-eting** /-eɪɪŋ/) floor (room) thus.

parricide /ˈpærɪsaɪd/ *noun* person who kills his or her parent; such a killing. □ **parricidal** /-ˈsaɪd(ə)l/ *adjective*.

parrot /ˈpærət/ ● *noun* mainly tropical bird with short hooked bill, of which some species can be taught to repeat words; unintelligent imitator or chatterer. ● *verb* (**-t-**) repeat mechanically. □ **parrot-fashion** (learning or repeating) mechanically, by rote.

parry /ˈpærɪ/ ● *verb* (**-ies, -ied**) ward off, avert. ● *noun* (*plural* **-ies**) act of parrying.

parse /pɑːz/ *verb* (**-sing**) describe (word) or analyse (sentence) in terms of grammar.

parsec /ˈpɑːsek/ *noun* unit of stellar distance, about 3.25 light years.

parsimony /ˈpɑːsɪmənɪ/ *noun* carefulness in use of money etc.; meanness. □ **parsimonious** /-ˈməʊn-/ *adjective*.

parsley /ˈpɑːslɪ/ *noun* herb used for seasoning and garnishing.

parsnip /ˈpɑːsnɪp/ *noun* plant with pale yellow tapering root used as vegetable; this root.

parson /ˈpɑːs(ə)n/ *noun* parish clergyman; *colloquial* any clergyman. □ **parson's nose** fatty flesh at rump of cooked fowl.

parsonage *noun* parson's house.

part ● *noun* some but not all; component, division, portion; share, allotted portion; person's share in an action etc.; assigned character or role; *Music* one of melodies making up harmony of concerted music; side in agreement or dispute; (usually in *plural*) region, direction, way; (in *plural*) abilities. ● *verb* divide into parts; separate; (+ *with*) give up, hand over; make parting in (hair). ● *adverb* partly, in part. □ **on the part of** made or done by; **part and parcel** (usually + *of*) essential part; **part-exchange** *noun* transaction in which article is given as part of payment for more expensive one, *verb* give (article) thus; **part of speech** grammatical class of words (noun, pronoun, adjective, adverb, verb, etc.); **part-song** song for 3 or more voice parts; **part-time** employed for or occupying less than normal working week etc.; **part-timer** part-time worker.

partake /pɑːˈteɪk/ verb (**-king**; past **partook**; past participle **partaken**) (+ *of*, *in*) take share of; (+ *of*) eat or drink some of.

parterre /pɑːˈteə/ noun level garden space filled with flower-beds etc.; *US* pit of theatre.

partial /ˈpɑːʃ(ə)l/ adjective not total or complete; biased, unfair; (+ *to*) having a liking for. □ **partiality** /-ʃɪˈæl-/ noun; **partially** adverb.

participate /pɑːˈtɪsɪpeɪt/ verb (**-ting**) (often + *in*) have share or take part. □ **participant** noun; **participation** noun.

participle /ˈpɑːtɪsɪp(ə)l/ noun word (either **present participle**, e.g. *writing*, or **past participle**, e.g. *written*) formed from verb and used in complex verb-forms or as adjective. □ **participial** /-ˈsɪp-/ adjective.

particle /ˈpɑːtɪk(ə)l/ noun minute portion of matter; smallest possible amount; minor esp. indeclinable part of speech.

particoloured /ˈpɑːtɪkʌləd/ adjective (*US* **-colored**) of more than one colour.

particular /pəˈtɪkjʊlə/ adjective relating to or considered as one as distinct from others; special; scrupulously exact; fastidious. ● noun detail, item; (in *plural*) detailed account. □ **in particular** specifically. □ **particularity** /-ˈlær-/ noun.

particularize /pəˈtɪkjʊləraɪz/ verb (also **-ise**) (**-zing** or **-sing**) name specially or one by one; specify (items). □ **particularization** noun.

particularly adverb very; specifically; in a fastidious way.

parting noun leave-taking; dividing line of combed hair.

partisan /pɑːtɪˈzæn/ ● noun strong supporter of party, side, or cause; guerrilla. ● adjective of partisans; biased. □ **partisanship** noun.

partition /pɑːˈtɪʃ(ə)n/ ● noun structure dividing a space, esp. light interior wall; division into parts. ● verb divide into parts; (+ *off*) separate with partition.

partitive /ˈpɑːtɪtɪv/ ● adjective (of word) denoting part of collective whole. ● noun partitive word.

partly adverb with respect to a part; to some extent.

partner /ˈpɑːtnə/ ● noun sharer; person associated with others in business; either of pair in marriage etc. or dancing or game. ● verb be partner of. □ **partnership** noun.

partridge /ˈpɑːtrɪdʒ/ noun (*plural* same or **-s**) kind of game bird.

parturition /pɑːtjʊˈrɪʃ(ə)n/ noun formal childbirth.

party /ˈpɑːtɪ/ noun (*plural* **-ies**) social gathering; group of people travelling or working together; political group putting forward candidates in elections and usually organized on national basis; each side in agreement or dispute. □ **party line** set policy of political party etc., shared telephone line; **party wall** wall common to adjoining rooms, buildings, etc.

parvenu /ˈpɑːvənjuː/ noun (*plural* **-s**; *feminine* **parvenue**, *plural* **-s**) newly rich social climber; upstart.

pascal /ˈpæsk(ə)l/ noun SI unit of pressure; (**Pascal** /ˈpæskɑːl/) computer language designed for training.

paschal /ˈpæsk(ə)l/ adjective of Passover; of Easter.

pasha /ˈpɑːʃə/ noun historical Turkish officer of high rank.

pasque-flower /ˈpæskflaʊə/ noun kind of anemone.

pass[1] /pɑːs/ ● verb move onward, proceed; go past; leave on one side or behind; (cause to) be transferred from one person or place to another; surpass; go unremarked or uncensured; move; cause to go; be successful in (exam); allow (bill in Parliament) to proceed; be approved; elapse; happen; spend (time etc.); *Football etc.* kick, hand, or hit (ball etc.) to player of one's own side; (+ *into*, *from*) change; come to an end; be accepted as adequate; discharge from body as or with excreta; utter (judgement etc.). ● noun passing, esp. of exam; status of degree without honours; written permission, ticket, or order; *Football etc.* passing of ball; critical position. □ **make a pass at** *colloquial* make sexual advances to; **pass away** die; **passbook** book recording customer's transactions with bank etc.; **passer-by** (*plural* **passers-by**) person who goes past, esp. by chance; **pass for** be accepted as; **passkey** private key to gate etc., master-key; **pass off** fade away, be carried through (in specified way), lightly dismiss, (+ *as*) misrepresent as something false; **pass on** proceed, die, transmit to next person in a series; **pass out** become unconscious, complete military training; **pass over** omit, overlook, make no remark on, die; **pass round** distribute, give to one person after another; **pass up** *colloquial* refuse or neglect (opportunity etc.); **password** prearranged word or phrase to secure recognition, admission, etc.

pass² /pɑːs/ *noun* narrow way through mountains.

passable *adjective* adequate, fairly good.

passage /ˈpæsɪdʒ/ *noun* process or means of passing, transit; passageway; right to pass through; journey by sea or air; transition from one state to another; short part of book or piece of music etc.; duct etc. in body.

passageway *noun* narrow way for passing along; corridor.

passé /ˈpæseɪ/ *adjective* (*feminine* **passée**) outmoded; past its prime.

passenger /ˈpæsɪndʒə/ *noun* traveller in or on vehicle (other than driver, pilot, crew, etc.); *colloquial* idle member of team etc.

passerine /ˈpæsəriːn/ • *noun* bird able to grip branch etc. with claws. • *adjective* of passerines.

passim /ˈpæsɪm/ *adverb* throughout. [Latin]

passion /ˈpæʃ(ə)n/ *noun* strong emotion; outburst of anger; intense sexual love; strong enthusiasm; object arousing this; **(the Passion)** sufferings of Christ during his last days, Gospel narrative of this or musical setting of it. □ **passion-flower** plant with flower supposed to suggest instruments of Crucifixion; **passion-fruit** edible fruit of some species of passion-flower. □ **passionless** *adjective*.

passionate /ˈpæʃənət/ *adjective* dominated by, easily moved to, or showing passion. □ **passionately** *adverb*.

passive /ˈpæsɪv/ *adjective* acted upon, not acting; submissive; inert; *Grammar* (of verb) of which subject undergoes action (e.g. *was written* in it *was written by me*). □ **passive smoking** involuntary inhalation of others' cigarette smoke. □ **passively** *adverb*; **passivity** /-ˈsɪv-/ *noun*.

Passover /ˈpɑːsəʊvə/ *noun* Jewish spring festival commemorating Exodus from Egypt.

passport /ˈpɑːspɔːt/ *noun* official document showing holder's identity and nationality etc. and authorizing travel abroad.

past /pɑːst/ • *adjective* gone by; just over; of former time; *Grammar* expressing past action or state. • *noun* past time or events; person's past life or career; past tense. • *preposition* beyond. • *adverb* so as to pass by. □ **past it** *colloquial* old and useless; **past master** expert.

pasta /ˈpæstə/ *noun* dried flour paste in various shapes.

paste /peɪst/ • *noun* any moist fairly stiff mixture; dough of flour with fat, water, etc.; flour and water or other mixture as adhesive; meat or fish spread; hard glasslike material used for imitation gems. • *verb* (**-ting**) fasten or coat with paste; *slang* beat, thrash. □ **pasteboard** stiff substance made by pasting together sheets of paper. □ **pasting** *noun*.

pastel /ˈpæst(ə)l/ • *noun* pale shade of colour; crayon made of dry pigment-paste; drawing in pastel. • *adjective* of pale shade of colour.

pastern /ˈpæst(ə)n/ *noun* part of horse's foot between fetlock and hoof.

pasteurize /ˈpɑːstʃəraɪz/ *verb* (also **-ise**) (**-zing** or **-sing**) partially sterilize (milk etc.) by heating. □ **pasteurization** *noun*.

pastiche /pæsˈtiːʃ/ *noun* picture or musical composition made up from various sources; literary or other work imitating style of author or period etc.

pastille /ˈpæstɪl/ *noun* small sweet or lozenge.

pastime /ˈpɑːstaɪm/ *noun* recreation; hobby.

pastor /ˈpɑːstə/ *noun* minister, esp. of Nonconformist church.

pastoral /ˈpɑːstər(ə)l/ • *adjective* of shepherds; of (esp. romanticized) rural life; of pastor. ● *noun* pastoral poem, play, picture, etc; letter from bishop or other pastor to clergy or people.

pastrami /pæ'strɑːmɪ/ *noun* seasoned smoked beef.

pastry /'peɪstrɪ/ *noun* (*plural* **-ies**) dough of flour, fat, and water; (item of) food made wholly or partly of this.

pasturage *noun* pasture land; pasturing.

pasture /'pɑːstʃə/ ● *noun* land covered with grass etc. for grazing animals; herbage for animals. ● *verb* (**-ring**) put (animals) to pasture; graze.

pasty¹ /'pæstɪ/ *noun* (*plural* **-ies**) pie of meat etc. wrapped in pastry and baked without dish.

pasty² /'peɪstɪ/ *adjective* (**-ier**, **-iest**) pallid.

pat¹ ● *verb* (**-tt-**) strike gently with flat palm or other flat surface, esp. in affection etc. ● *noun* light stroke or tap, esp. with hand in affection etc.; patting sound; small mass, esp. of butter, made (as) by patting.

pat² ● *adjective* known thoroughly; apposite, opportune, esp. glibly so. ● *adverb* in a pat way. □ **have off pat** have memorized perfectly.

patch ● *noun* piece put on in mending or as reinforcement; cover protecting injured eye; large or irregular spot on surface; distinct area or period; small plot of ground. ● *verb* mend with patch(es); (often + *up*) piece together; (+ *up*) settle (quarrel etc.), esp. hastily. □ **not a patch on** *colloquial* very much inferior to; **patchwork** stitching together of small pieces of differently coloured cloth to form pattern.

patchy *adjective* (**-ier**, **-iest**) uneven in quality; having patches. □ **patchily** *adverb*.

pate *noun colloquial* head.

pâté /'pæteɪ/ *noun* smooth paste of meat etc. □ **pâté de foie gras** /də fwɑː 'grɑː/ pâté made from livers of fatted geese.

patella /pə'telə/ *noun* (*plural* **patellae** /-liː/) kneecap.

paten /'pæt(ə)n/ *noun* plate for bread at Eucharist.

patent /'peɪt(ə)nt, 'pæt-/ ● *noun* official document conferring right, title, etc., esp. sole right to make, use, or sell some invention; invention or process so protected. ● *adjective* /'peɪt(ə)nt/ plain, obvious; conferred or protected by patent; (of food, medicine, etc.) proprietary. ● *verb* obtain patent for (invention). □ **patent leather** glossy varnished leather. □ **patently** *adverb*.

patentee /peɪtən'tiː/ *noun* holder of patent.

paterfamilias /peɪtəfə'mɪlɪæs/ *noun* male head of family etc.

paternal /pə'tɜːn(ə)l/ *adjective* of father, fatherly; related through father.

paternalism *noun* policy of restricting freedom and responsibility by well-meant regulations. □ **paternalistic** /-'lɪs-/ *adjective*.

paternity /pə'tɜːnɪtɪ/ *noun* fatherhood; one's paternal origin.

paternoster /pætə'nɒstə/ *noun* Lord's Prayer, esp. in Latin.

path /pɑːθ/ *noun* (*plural* **paths** /pɑːðz/ footway, track; line along which person or thing moves. □ **pathway** path, its course.

pathetic /pə'θetɪk/ *adjective* exciting pity, sadness, or contempt. □ **pathetically** *adverb*.

pathogen /'pæθədʒ(ə)n/ *noun* agent causing disease. □ **pathogenic** /-'dʒen-/ *adjective*.

pathological /pæθə'lɒdʒɪk(ə)l/ *adjective* of pathology; or of caused by mental or physical disorder. □ **pathologically** *adverb*.

pathology /pə'θɒlədʒɪ/ *noun* study of disease. □ **pathologist** *noun*.

pathos /'peɪθɒs/ *noun* quality that excites pity or sadness.

patience /'peɪʃ(ə)ns/ *noun* ability to endure delay, hardship, provocation, pain, etc.; perseverance; solo card game.

patient ● *adjective* having or showing patience. ● *noun* person under medical etc. treatment. □ **patiently** *adverb*.

patina /'pætɪnə/ *noun* (*plural* **-s**) film, usually green, on surface of old bronze etc.; gloss produced by age on woodwork etc.

patio /'pætɪəʊ/ *noun* (*plural* **-s**) paved usually roofless area adjoining house; roofless inner courtyard.

patisserie /pəˈtiːsərɪ/ noun shop where pastries are made and sold; pastries collectively.

patois /ˈpætwɑː/ noun (plural same /-wɑːz/) regional dialect differing from literary language.

patriarch /ˈpeɪtrɪɑːk/ noun male head of family or tribe; chief bishop in Orthodox and RC Churches; venerable old man. □ **patriarchal** /-ˈɑːk-/ adjective.

patriarchate /ˈpeɪtrɪɑːkət/ noun office, see, or residence of patriarch; rank of tribal patriarch.

patriarchy /ˈpeɪtrɪɑːkɪ/ noun (plural **-ies**) male-dominated social system, with descent reckoned through male line.

patrician /pəˈtrɪʃ(ə)n/ ● noun person of noble birth, esp. in ancient Rome. ● adjective of nobility; aristocratic.

patricide /ˈpætrɪsaɪd/ noun parricide. □ **patricidal** /-ˈsaɪd(ə)l/ adjective.

patrimony /ˈpætrɪmənɪ/ noun (plural **-ies**) property inherited from father or ancestors; heritage.

patriot /ˈpeɪtrɪət/ noun person devoted to and ready to defend his or her country. □ **patriotic** /-ˈɒt-/ adjective; **patriotism** noun.

patrol /pəˈtrəʊl/ ● noun act of walking or travelling round area etc. to protect or supervise it; person(s) or vehicle(s) sent out on patrol; unit of usually 6 in Scout troop or Guide company. ● verb (**-ll-**) carry out patrol of; act as patrol. □ **patrol car** car used by police etc. for patrol.

patron /ˈpeɪtr(ə)n/ noun (feminine **patroness**) person who gives financial or other support; customer of shop etc. □ **patron saint** saint regarded as protecting person, place, activity, etc.

patronage /ˈpætrənɪdʒ/ noun patron's or customer's support; right of bestowing or recommending for appointments; condescending manner.

patronize /ˈpætrənaɪz/ verb (also **-ise**) (**-zing** or **-sing**) treat condescendingly; act as patron to; be customer of. □ **patronizing** adjective.

patronymic /pætrəˈnɪmɪk/ noun name derived from that of father or ancestor.

patten /ˈpæt(ə)n/ noun historical wooden sole mounted on iron ring for raising wearer's shoe above mud etc.

patter[1] /ˈpætə/ ● noun sound of quick light taps or steps. ● verb (of rain etc.) make this sound.

patter[2] /ˈpætə/ ● noun rapid often glib or deceptive talk. ● verb say or talk glibly.

pattern /ˈpæt(ə)n/ ● noun decorative design on surface; regular or logical form, order, etc.; model, design, or instructions from which thing is to be made; excellent example. ● verb decorate with pattern; model (thing) on design etc.

patty /ˈpætɪ/ noun (plural **-ies**) small pie or pasty.

paucity /ˈpɔːsɪtɪ/ noun smallness of number or quantity.

paunch /pɔːntʃ/ noun belly, stomach. □ **paunchy** adjective.

pauper /ˈpɔːpə/ noun very poor person. □ **pauperism** noun.

pause /pɔːz/ ● noun temporary stop or silence; Music mark denoting lengthening of note or rest. ● verb (**-sing**) make a pause; wait.

pavane /pəˈvɑːn/ noun (also **pavan** /ˈpæv(ə)n/) historical stately dance; music for this.

pave verb (**-ving**) cover (street, floor, etc.) with durable surface. □ **pave the way** (usually + for) make preparations. □ **paving** noun.

pavement noun paved footway at side of road. □ **pavement artist** artist who draws in chalk on pavement for tips.

pavilion /pəˈvɪljən/ noun building on sports ground for spectators or players; summerhouse etc. in park; large tent; building or stand at exhibition.

pavlova /pævˈləʊvə/ noun meringue dessert with cream and fruit filling.

paw ● noun foot of animal with claws; colloquial person's hand. ● verb touch with paw; colloquial fondle awkwardly or indecently.

pawn[1] noun chessman of smallest size and value; person subservient to others' plans.

pawn[2] verb deposit (thing) as security for money borrowed; pledge. □ **in pawn** held as security; **pawnbroker** person who lends money at interest on security of personal property;

pawnshop pawnbroker's place of business.

pawpaw /'pɔ:pɔ:/ noun (also **papaya** /pə'paɪə/) pear-shaped mango-like fruit with pulpy orange flesh; tropical tree bearing this.

pay • verb (past & past participle **paid**) discharge debt to; give as due; render, bestow (attention etc.); yield adequate return; let out (rope) by slackening it; reward or punish. • noun wages. □ **in the pay of** employed by; **pay-as-you-earn** collection of income tax by deduction at source from wages etc.; **pay-claim** demand for increase in pay; **payday** day on which wages are paid; **pay for** hand over money for, bear cost of, suffer or be punished for; **paying guest** lodger; **payload** part of (esp. aircraft's) load from which revenue is derived; **paymaster** official who pays troops, workmen, etc.; **Paymaster General** Treasury minister responsible for payments; **pay off** pay in full and discharge, colloquial yield good results; **pay-off** slang payment, climax, end result; **pay phone** coin box telephone; **payroll** list of employees receiving regular pay. □ **payee** /peɪ'iː/ noun.

payable adjective that must or may be paid.

PAYE abbreviation pay-as-you-earn.

payment noun paying, amount paid; recompense.

payola /peɪ'əʊlə/ noun esp. US slang bribe offered for unofficial media promotion of product etc.

PC abbreviation Police Constable; personal computer; politically correct; political correctness; Privy Councillor.

p.c. abbreviation per cent; postcard.

pd. abbreviation paid.

PE abbreviation physical education.

pea noun climbing plant bearing round edible seeds in pods; one of its seeds; similar plant. □ **pea-souper** colloquial thick yellowish fog.

peace noun quiet, calm; freedom from or cessation of war; civil order. □ **peacemaker** person who brings about peace; **peacetime** time when country is not at war.

peaceable adjective disposed or tending to peace, peaceful.

peaceful adjective characterized by or not infringing peace. □ **peacefully** adverb; **peacefulness** noun.

peach¹ noun roundish juicy fruit with downy yellow or rosy skin; tree bearing it; yellowish-pink colour; colloquial person or thing of superlative merit. □ **peach Melba** dish of ice cream and peaches. □ **peachy** adjective (**-ier, -iest**).

peach² verb colloquial turn informer; inform.

peacock /'piːkɒk/ noun (plural same or **-s**) male peafowl, bird with brilliant plumage and erectile fanlike tail. □ **peacock blue** bright lustrous greenish blue of peacock's neck; **peacock butterfly** butterfly with eyelike markings resembling those on peacock's tail.

peafowl /'piːfaʊl/ noun kind of pheasant, peacock or peahen.

peahen /'piːhen/ noun female peafowl.

peak¹ • noun pointed top, esp. of mountain; stiff projecting brim at front of cap; highest point of achievement, intensity, etc. • verb reach highest value, quality, etc.

peak² verb waste away; (as **peaked** adjective) pinched-looking.

peaky adjective (**-ier, -iest**) sickly, puny.

peal • noun loud ringing of bell(s); set of bells; loud repeated sound. • verb (cause to) sound in peal; utter sonorously.

peanut noun plant bearing underground pods containing seeds used as food and yielding oil; its seed; (in plural) colloquial trivial amount, esp. of money. □ **peanut butter** paste of ground roasted peanuts.

pear /peə/ noun fleshy fruit tapering towards stalk; tree bearing it.

pearl /pɜːl/ • noun rounded lustrous usually white solid formed in shell of certain oysters and prized as gem; imitation of this; precious thing, finest example. • verb poetical (of moisture) form drops, form drops on; fish for pearls. □ **pearl barley** barley rubbed into small rounded grains; **pearl button** button of (real or imitation) mother-of-pearl.

pearly • adjective (**-ier, -iest**) resembling a pearl; adorned with pearls. • noun (plural **-ies**) pearly king or queen; (in *plural*) pearly king's or queen's clothes. □ **Pearly Gates** *colloquial* gates of Heaven; **pearly king, queen** London costermonger, or his wife, wearing clothes covered with pearl buttons.

peasant /'pez(ə)nt/ *noun* (in some countries) worker on land, farm labourer; small farmer; *derogatory* lout, boor. □ **peasantry** *noun* (*plural* **-ies**).

pease-pudding /pi:z/ *noun* dried peas boiled in cloth.

peat *noun* vegetable matter decomposed by water and partly carbonized; piece of this as fuel. □ **peatbog** bog composed of peat. □ **peaty** *adjective*.

pebble /'peb(ə)l/ *noun* small stone made smooth by action of water. □ **pebble-dash** mortar with pebbles in it as wall-coating. □ **pebbly** *adjective*.

pecan /'pi:kən/ *noun* pinkish-brown smooth nut; kind of hickory producing it.

peccadillo /pekə'dɪləʊ/ *noun* (*plural* **-es** or **-s**) trivial offence.

peck[1] • *verb* strike, pick up, pluck out, or make (hole) with beak; kiss hastily or perfunctorily; *colloquial* (+ *at*) eat (meal) listlessly or fastidiously. • *noun* stroke with beak; hasty or perfunctory kiss. □ **pecking order** social hierarchy.

peck[2] *noun* measure of capacity for dry goods (2 gallons, 9.092 litres).

pecker *noun* □ **keep your pecker up** *colloquial* stay cheerful.

peckish *adjective colloquial* hungry.

pectin /'pektɪn/ *noun* soluble gelatinous substance in ripe fruits, causing jam etc. to set.

pectoral /'pektər(ə)l/ • *adjective* of or for breast or chest. • *noun* pectoral fin or muscle.

peculiar /pɪ'kju:lɪə/ *adjective* odd; (usually + *to*) belonging exclusively; belonging to the individual; particular, special.

peculiarity /pɪkju:lɪ'ærɪtɪ/ *noun* (*plural* **-ies**) oddity; characteristic; being peculiar.

peculiarly *adverb* more than usually, especially; oddly.

pecuniary /pɪ'kju:nɪərɪ/ *adjective* of or in money.

pedagogue /'pedəɡɒɡ/ *noun archaic or derogatory* schoolmaster.

pedagogy /'pedəɡɒdʒɪ/ *noun* science of teaching. □ **pedagogic(al)** /-'ɡɒg-/ *adjective*.

pedal /'ped(ə)l/ • *noun* lever or key operated by foot, eg in bicycle, motor vehicle, or some musical instruments. • *verb* (**-ll-**; *US* **-l-**) work pedals (of); ride bicycle. • *adjective* /'pi:d(ə)l/ of foot or feet.

pedant /'ped(ə)nt/ *noun derogatory* person who insists on strict adherence to literal meaning or formal rules. □ **pedantic** /pɪ'dæntɪk/ *adjective*; **pedantry** *noun*.

peddle /'ped(ə)l/ *verb* (**-ling**) sell as pedlar; advocate; sell (drugs) illegally; engage in selling, esp. as pedlar.

peddler *noun* person who sells drugs illegally; *US* = PEDLAR.

pedestal /'pedɪst(ə)l/ *noun* base of column; block on which something stands.

pedestrian /pɪ'destrɪən/ • *noun* walker, esp. in town. • *adjective* prosaic, dull. □ **pedestrian crossing** part of road where crossing pedestrians have right of way.

pedicure /'pedɪkjʊə/ *noun* care or treatment of feet, esp. of toenails.

pedigree /'pedɪgri:/ *noun* recorded (esp. distinguished) line of descent of person or animal; genealogical table; *colloquial* thing's history.

pediment /'pedɪmənt/ *noun* triangular part crowning front of building, esp. over portico.

pedlar /'pedlə/ *noun* (*US* **peddler**) travelling seller of small wares.

pedometer /pɪ'dɒmɪtə/ *noun* instrument for estimating distance travelled on foot.

pedophile *US* = PAEDOPHILE.

peduncle /pɪ'dʌŋk(ə)l/ *noun* stalk of flower, fruit, or cluster, esp. main stalk bearing solitary flower.

pee *colloquial* • *verb* (**pees, peed**) urinate. • *noun* urination; urine.

peek *noun & verb* peep, glance.

peel • *verb* strip rind etc. from; (usually + *off*) take off (skin etc.); become bare of bark, skin, etc.; (often + *off*) flake off. ● *noun* rind or outer coating of fruit, potato, etc.

peeling *noun* (usually in *plural*) piece peeled off.

peep[1] ● *verb* look furtively or through narrow aperture; come cautiously or partly into view; emerge. ● *noun* furtive or peering glance; (usually + *of*) first light of dawn. □ **peep-hole** small hole to peep through; **Peeping Tom** furtive voyeur; **peep-show** exhibition of pictures etc. viewed through lens or peep-hole.

peep[2] ● *verb* cheep, squeak. ● *noun* cheep, squeak; slight sound, utterance, or complaint.

peer[1] *verb* look closely or with difficulty.

peer[2] *noun* (*feminine* **peeress**) duke, marquis, earl, viscount, or baron; equal (esp. in civil standing or rank). □ **peer group** person's associates of same status.

peerage *noun* peers as a class; rank of peer or peeress.

peerless *adjective* unequalled.

peeve *colloquial* ● *verb* (**-ving**) (usually as **peeved** *adjective*) irritate. ● *noun* cause or state of annoyance.

peevish *adjective* querulous, irritable. □ **peevishly** *adverb*.

peewit /'piːwɪt/ *noun* lapwing.

peg ● *noun* wooden, metal, etc. bolt or pin for holding things together, hanging things on, etc.; each of pins used to tighten or loosen strings of violin etc.; forked wooden peg etc. for hanging washing on line; drink, esp. of spirits. ● *verb* (**-gg-**) (usually + *down*, *in*, etc.) fix, mark, or hang out (as with peg(s); keep (prices etc.) stable. □ **off the peg** (of clothes) ready-made; **peg away** (often + *at*) work persistently; **pegboard** board with holes for pegs; **peg out** *slang* die, mark out boundaries of.

pejorative /prɪˈdʒɒrətɪv/ ● *adjective* derogatory. ● *noun* derogatory word.

peke *noun colloquial* Pekingese.

Pekingese /piːkɪˈniːz/ *noun* (also **Pekinese**) (*plural* same) dog of small short-legged snub-nosed breed with long silky hair.

pelargonium /pelɑːˈɡəʊnɪəm/ *noun* plant with showy flowers; geranium.

pelf *noun* money, wealth.

pelican /'pelɪkən/ *noun* large waterfowl with pouch below bill for storing fish. □ **pelican crossing** road crossing-place with traffic lights operated by pedestrians.

pellagra /pəˈlæɡrə/ *noun* deficiency disease with cracking of skin.

pellet /'pelɪt/ *noun* small compressed ball of a substance; pill; small shot.

pellicle /'pelɪk(ə)l/ *noun* thin skin; membrane; film.

pell-mell /pel'mel/ *adverb* headlong; in disorder.

pellucid /prɪˈluːsɪd/ *adjective* transparent, clear.

pelmet /'pelmɪt/ *noun* hanging border concealing curtain-rods etc.

pelt[1] ● *verb* assail with missiles, abuse, etc.; (of rain) come down hard; run at full speed. ● *noun* pelting.

pelt[2] *noun* skin of animal, esp. with hair or fur still on it.

pelvis /'pelvɪs/ *noun* lower abdominal cavity in most vertebrates, formed by haunch bones etc. □ **pelvic** *adjective*.

pen[1] ● *noun* implement for writing with ink. ● *verb* (**-nn-**) write. □ **penfriend** friend with whom one communicates by letter only; **penknife** small folding knife; **pen-name** literary pseudonym; **pen-pal** *colloquial* penfriend.

pen[2] ● *noun* small enclosure for cows, sheep, poultry, etc. ● *verb* (**-nn-**) enclose; put or keep in confined space.

pen[3] *noun* female swan.

penal /'piːn(ə)l/ *adjective* of or involving punishment; punishable.

penalize /'piːnəlaɪz/ *verb* (also **-ise**) (**-zing** or **-sing**) subject to penalty or disadvantage; make punishable.

penalty /'penltɪ/ *noun* (*plural* **-ies**) fine or other punishment; disadvantage, loss, etc., esp. as result of one's own actions; disadvantage imposed in sports for breach of rules etc. □ **penalty area** *Football* area in front of goal within which breach of rules involves award of penalty kick for opposing team; **penalty kick** free kick at goal from close range.

penance /'penəns/ *noun* act of self-punishment, esp. imposed by priest, performed as expression of penitence.

pence *plural* of PENNY.

penchant /ˈpɑ̃ʃɑ̃/ noun (+ for) inclination or liking for.

pencil /ˈpens(ə)l/ •noun instrument for drawing or writing, esp. of graphite enclosed in wooden cylinder or metal case with tapering end; something used or shaped like this. •verb (-ll-; US -l-) write, draw, or mark with pencil.

pendant /ˈpend(ə)nt/ noun ornament hung from necklace etc.

pendent /ˈpend(ə)nt/ adjective formal hanging; overhanging; pending.

pending /ˈpendɪŋ/ •adjective awaiting decision or settlement. •preposition until; during.

pendulous /ˈpendjʊləs/ adjective hanging down; swinging.

pendulum /ˈpendjʊləm/ noun (plural -s) body suspended so as to be free to swing, esp. regulating movement of clock's works.

penetrate /ˈpenɪtreɪt/ verb (-ting) make way into or through; pierce; permeate; see into or through; be absorbed by the mind; (as **penetrating** adjective) having or suggesting insight, (of voice) easily heard above other sounds, piercing. □ **penetrable** /-trəb(ə)l/ adjective; **penetration** noun.

penguin /ˈpeŋgwɪn/ noun flightless seabird of southern hemisphere.

penicillin /penɪˈsɪlɪn/ noun antibiotic obtained from mould.

peninsula /pɪˈnɪnsjʊlə/ noun piece of land almost surrounded by water or projecting far into sea etc. □ **peninsular** adjective.

penis /ˈpiːnɪs/ noun sexual and (in mammals) urinary organ of male animal.

penitent /ˈpenɪt(ə)nt/ •adjective repentant. •noun penitent person; person doing penance. □ **penitence** noun, **penitently** adverb.

penitential /penɪˈtenʃ(ə)l/ adjective of penitence or penance.

penitentiary /penɪˈtenʃərɪ/ •noun (plural -ies) US prison. •adjective of penance or reformatory treatment.

pennant /ˈpenənt/ noun tapering flag, esp. that at masthead of ship in commission.

penniless /ˈpenɪlɪs/ adjective destitute.

pennon /ˈpenən/ noun long narrow triangular or swallow-tailed flag; long pointed streamer on ship.

penny /ˈpenɪ/ noun (plural **pence** or, for separate coins only, **pennies**) British coin worth 1/100 of pound, or formerly 1/240 of pound. □ **penny-farthing** early kind of bicycle with large front wheel and small rear one; **penny-pinching** noun meanness, adjective mean; **a pretty penny** a large sum of money.

pennyroyal /penɪˈrɔɪəl/ noun creeping kind of mint.

penology /piːˈnɒlədʒɪ/ noun study of punishment and prison management.

pension[1] /ˈpenʃ(ə)n/ •noun periodic payment made by government, exemployer, private fund, etc. to person above specified age or to retired, widowed, disabled, etc. person. •verb grant pension to. □ **pension off** dismiss with pension.

pension[2] /pɑ̃ˈsjɔ̃/ noun European, esp. French, boarding house. [French]

pensionable adjective entitled or entitling person to pension.

pensioner noun recipient of (esp. retirement) pension.

pensive /ˈpensɪv/ adjective deep in thought. □ **pensively** adverb.

pent adjective (often + in, up) closely confined; shut in.

penta- combining form five.

pentacle /ˈpentək(ə)l/ noun figure used as symbol, esp. in magic, e.g. pentagram.

pentagon /ˈpentəgən/ noun plane figure with 5 sides and angles; (**the Pentagon**) (pentagonal headquarters of) leaders of US defence forces. □ **pentagonal** /-ˈtæg-/ adjective.

pentagram /ˈpentəgræm/ noun 5-pointed star.

pentameter /penˈtæmɪtə/ noun line of verse with 5 metrical feet.

Pentateuch /ˈpentətjuːk/ noun first 5 books of Old Testament.

pentathlon /penˈtæθlən/ noun athletic contest of 5 events. □ **pentathlete** noun.

Pentecost /ˈpentɪkɒst/ noun Whit Sunday; Jewish harvest festival 50 days after second day of Passover.

pentecostal /pentɪˈkɒst(ə)l/ adjective (of religious group) emphasizing divine gifts, esp. healing, and often fundamentalist.

penthouse /'penthaʊs/ *noun* flat on roof or top floor of tall building.

penultimate /pɪ'nʌltɪmət/ *adjective & noun* last but one.

penumbra /pɪ'nʌmbrə/ *noun* (*plural* **-s** or **-brae** /-briː/) partly shaded region round shadow of opaque body; partial shadow. □ **penumbral** *adjective*.

penurious /pɪ'njʊərɪəs/ *adjective* poor; stingy.

penury /'penjʊrɪ/ *noun* (*plural* **-ies**) destitution, poverty.

peon /'piːən/ *noun* Spanish-American day-labourer.

peony /'piːənɪ/ *noun* (also **paeony**) (*plural* **-ies**) plant with large globular red, pink, or white flowers.

people /'piːp(ə)l/ ● *plural noun* persons in general; (*singular*) race or nation; (**the people**) ordinary people, esp. as electorate; parents or other relatives; subjects. ● *verb* (**-ling**) (usually + *with*) fill with people; populate; (esp. as **peopled** *adjective*) inhabit.

PEP /pep/ *abbreviation* Personal Equity Plan.

pep *colloquial* ● *noun* vigour, spirit. ● *verb* (**-pp-**) (usually + *up*) fill with vigour. □ **pep pill** one containing stimulant drug; **pep talk** exhortation to greater effort or courage.

pepper /'pepə/ ● *noun* hot aromatic condiment from dried berries of some plants; capsicum plant, its fruit. ● *verb* sprinkle or flavour with pepper; pelt with missiles. □ **pepper-and-salt** of closely mingled dark and light colour; **peppercorn** dried pepper berry, (in full **peppercorn rent**) nominal rent; **pepper-mill** mill for grinding peppercorns by hand.

peppermint *noun* species of mint grown for its strong-flavoured oil; sweet flavoured with this oil; the oil.

pepperoni /pepə'rəʊnɪ/ *noun* sausage seasoned with pepper.

peppery *adjective* of, like, or abounding in pepper; hot-tempered.

pepsin /'pepsɪn/ *noun* enzyme contained in gastric juice.

peptic /'peptɪk/ *adjective* digestive. □ **peptic ulcer** one in stomach or duodenum.

per *preposition* for each; by, by means of, through.

peradventure /pərəd'ventʃə/ *adverb* archaic perhaps.

perambulate /pə'ræmbjʊleɪt/ *verb* (**-ting**) walk through, over, or about. □ **perambulation** *noun*.

perambulator *noun* formal pram.

per annum /pər 'ænəm/ *adverb* for each year.

per capita /pə 'kæpɪtə/ *adverb & adjective* for each person.

perceive /pə'siːv/ *verb* (**-ving**) become aware of by one of senses; apprehend; understand. □ **perceivable** *adjective*.

per cent /pə 'sent/ (*US* **percent**) ● *adverb* in every hundred. ● *noun* percentage; one part in every hundred.

percentage *noun* rate or proportion per cent; proportion.

percentile /pə'sentaɪl/ *noun* each of 99 points at which a range of data is divided to make 100 groups of equal size; each of these groups.

perceptible /pə'septɪb(ə)l/ *adjective* that can be perceived. □ **perceptibility** *noun*; **perceptibly** *adverb*.

perception /pə'sepʃ(ə)n/ *noun* act or faculty of perceiving. □ **perceptual** /-'septʃʊəl/ *adjective*.

perceptive /pə'septɪv/ *adjective* sensitive; discerning; capable of perceiving. □ **perceptively** *adverb*; **perceptiveness** *noun*.

perch[1] ● *noun* bird's resting-place above ground; high place for person or thing to rest on; *historical* measure of length (5½ yds). ● *verb* rest or place on perch.

perch[2] *noun* (*plural* same or **-es**) edible spiny-finned freshwater fish.

perchance /pə'tʃɑːns/ *adverb* archaic maybe.

percipient /pə'sɪpɪənt/ *adjective* perceiving; conscious.

percolate /'pɜːkəleɪt/ *verb* (**-ting**) (often + *through*) filter gradually; (of idea etc.) permeate gradually; prepare (coffee) in percolator. □ **percolation** *noun*.

percolator *noun* apparatus for making coffee by circulating boiling water through ground beans.

percussion /pə'kʌʃ(ə)n/ *noun* playing of music by striking instruments with sticks etc.; such instruments collectively; gentle tapping of body in medical diagnosis; forcible striking of body against another. □ **percussionist** noun; **percussive** adjective.

perdition /pə'dɪʃ(ə)n/ noun damnation.

peregrine /'perɪgrɪn/ noun (in full **peregrine falcon**) kind of falcon.

peremptory /pə'remptərɪ/ adjective admitting no denial or refusal; imperious. □ **peremptorily** adverb.

perennial /pə'renɪəl/ ● adjective lasting through the year; (of plant) living several years; lasting long or for ever. ● noun perennial plant. □ **perennially** adverb.

perestroika /perɪ'strɔɪkə/ noun (in former USSR) reform of economic and political system.

perfect ● adjective /'pɜːfɪkt/ complete; faultless; not deficient; very enjoyable; exact, precise; entire, unqualified; Grammar (of tense) expressing completed action. ● verb /pə'fekt/ make perfect; complete. ● noun /'pɜːfɪkt/ perfect tense. □ **perfect pitch** Music ability to recognize pitch of note.

perfection /pə'fekʃ(ə)n/ noun being or making perfect; perfect state; perfect person, specimen, etc.

perfectionism noun uncompromising pursuit of perfection. □ **perfectionist** noun.

perfectly adverb quite, completely; in a perfect way.

perfidy /'pɜːfɪdɪ/ noun breach of faith, treachery. □ **perfidious** /-'fɪd-/ adjective.

perforate /'pɜːfəreɪt/ verb (-ting) pierce, make hole(s) through; make row of small holes in (paper etc.). □ **perforation** noun.

perforce /pə'fɔːs/ adverb archaic unavoidably, necessarily.

perform /pə'fɔːm/ verb carry into effect; go through, execute; act, sing, etc., esp. in public; (of animals) do tricks etc. □ **performing arts** drama, music, dance, etc. □ **performer** noun.

performance noun act, process, or manner of doing or functioning; execution (of duty etc.); performing of or in play etc.; colloquial fuss, emotional scene.

perfume /'pɜːfjuːm/ ● noun sweet smell; fragrant liquid, esp. for application to the body, scent. ● verb (-ming) impart perfume to.

perfumer /pə'fjuːmə/ noun maker or seller of perfumes. □ **perfumery** noun (plural -ies).

perfunctory /pə'fʌŋktərɪ/ adjective done merely out of duty; superficial. □ **perfunctorily** adverb; **perfunctoriness** noun.

pergola /'pɜːgələ/ noun arbour or covered walk arched with climbing plants.

perhaps /pə'hæps/ adverb it may be, possibly.

perianth /'perɪænθ/ noun outer part of flower.

perigee /'perɪdʒiː/ noun point nearest to earth in orbit of moon etc.

perihelion /perɪ'hiːlɪən/ noun (plural -lia) point nearest to sun in orbit of planet, comet, etc. round it.

peril /'perɪl/ noun serious and immediate danger. □ **perilous** adjective; **perilously** adverb.

perimeter /pə'rɪmɪtə/ noun circumference or outline of closed figure; length of this; outer boundary.

period /'pɪərɪəd/ ● noun amount of time during which something runs its course; distinct portion of history, life, etc.; occurrence of menstruation, time of this; complete sentence; esp. US full stop. ● adjective characteristic of past period.

periodic /pɪərɪ'ɒdɪk/ adjective appearing or recurring at intervals. □ **periodic table** arrangement of chemical elements by atomic number and chemical properties. □ **periodicity** /-rɪə'dɪsɪtɪ/ noun.

periodical ● noun magazine etc. published at regular intervals. ● adjective periodic. □ **periodically** adverb.

peripatetic /perɪpə'tetɪk/ adjective (of teacher) working in more than one establishment; going from place to place; itinerant.

peripheral /pə'rɪfər(ə)l/ ● adjective of minor importance; of periphery. ● noun input, output, or storage device connected to computer.

periphery /pə'rɪfərɪ/ noun (plural -ies) bounding line, esp. of round surface; outer or surrounding area.

periphrasis /pə'rɪfrəsɪs/ noun (plural -phrases /-siːz/) circumlocution, roundabout speech or phrase. □ **periphrastic** /perɪ'fræstɪk/ adjective.

periscope /'perɪskəʊp/ *noun* apparatus with tube and mirrors or prisms for viewing objects otherwise out of sight.

perish /'perɪʃ/ *verb* suffer destruction, die; lose natural qualities; (cause to) rot or deteriorate; (in *passive*) suffer from cold.

perishable ● *adjective* subject to speedy decay; liable to perish. ● *noun* perishable thing (esp. food).

perisher *noun slang* annoying person.

perishing *colloquial* ● *adjective* confounded; intensely cold. ● *adverb* confoundedly.

peritoneum /perɪtə'ni:əm/ *noun* (*plural* -**s** or -**nea**) membrane lining abdominal cavity. □ **peritoneal** *adjective*.

peritonitis /perɪtə'naɪtɪs/ *noun* inflammation of peritoneum.

periwig /'perɪwɪg/ *noun historical* wig.

periwinkle¹ /'perɪwɪŋk(ə)l/ *noun* evergreen trailing plant with blue or white flower.

periwinkle² /'perɪwɪŋk(ə)l/ *noun* winkle.

perjure /'pɜːdʒə/ *verb* (-**ring**) (**perjure oneself**) commit perjury; (as **perjured** *adjective*) guilty of perjury. □ **perjurer** *noun*.

perjury /'pɜːdʒərɪ/ *noun* (*plural* -**ies**) wilful lying while on oath.

perk¹ *verb* □ **perk up** (cause to) recover courage, smarten up, raise (head etc.) briskly.

perk² *noun colloquial* perquisite.

perky *adjective* (-**ier**, -**iest**) lively and cheerful.

perm¹ ● *noun* permanent wave. ● *verb* give permanent wave to.

perm² *colloquial* ● *noun* permutation. ● *verb* make permutation of.

permafrost /'pɜːməfrɒst/ *noun* permanently frozen subsoil, as in polar regions.

permanent /'pɜːmənənt/ *adjective* lasting or intended to last permanently. □ **permanent wave** long-lasting artificial wave in hair. □ **permanence** *noun*, **permanently** *adverb*.

permeable /'pɜːmɪəb(ə)l/ *adjective* capable of being permeated. □ **permeability** *noun*.

permeate /'pɜːmɪeɪt/ *verb* (-**ting**) penetrate, saturate, pervade; be diffused. □ **permeation** *noun*.

permissible /pə'mɪsɪb(ə)l/ *adjective* allowable. □ **permissibility** *noun*.

permission /pə'mɪʃ(ə)n/ *noun* consent, authorization.

permissive /pə'mɪsɪv/ *adjective* tolerant, liberal; giving permission. □ **permissiveness** *noun*.

permit ● *verb* /pə'mɪt/ (-**tt**-) give consent to; authorize; allow; give opportunity; (+ *of*) allow as possible. ● *noun* /'pɜːmɪt/ written order giving permission or allowing entry.

permutation /pɜːmjʊ'teɪʃ(ə)n/ *noun* one of possible ordered arrangements of set of things; combination or selection of specified number of items from larger group.

pernicious /pə'nɪʃəs/ *adjective* destructive, injurious. □ **pernicious anaemia** defective formation of red blood cells through lack of vitamin B.

pernickety /pə'nɪkɪtɪ/ *adjective colloquial* fastidious, over-precise.

peroration /perə'reɪʃ(ə)n/ *noun* concluding part of speech.

peroxide /pə'rɒksaɪd/ ● *noun* (in full **hydrogen peroxide**) colourless liquid used in water solution, esp. to bleach hair; oxide containing maximum proportion of oxygen. ● *verb* (-**ding**) bleach (hair) with peroxide.

perpendicular /pɜːpən'dɪkjʊlə/ ● *adjective* (usually + *to*) at right angles; upright; very steep; (**Perpendicular**) of or in style of English Gothic architecture of 15th & 16th c. ● *noun* perpendicular line etc. □ **perpendicularity** /-'lærɪtɪ/ *noun*.

perpetrate /'pɜːpɪtreɪt/ *verb* (-**ting**) commit. □ **perpetration** *noun*, **perpetrator** *noun*.

perpetual /pə'petʃʊəl/ *adjective* lasting for ever or indefinitely; continuous; *colloquial* frequent. □ **perpetually** *adverb*.

perpetuate /pə'petʃʊeɪt/ *verb* (-**ting**) make perpetual; cause to be always remembered. □ **perpetuation** *noun*.

perpetuity /pɜːpɪ'tjuːɪtɪ/ *noun* (*plural* -**ies**) perpetual continuance or possession. □ **in perpetuity** for ever.

perplex /pə'pleks/ *verb* bewilder, puzzle; complicate, tangle. □ **perplexing** *adjective*, **perplexity** *noun*.

per pro. /pɜː 'prəʊ/ *abbreviation* through the agency of (used in signatures) (*per procurantionem*). [Latin].

■ **Usage** The abbreviation *per pro.* (or *p.p.*) is frequently written before the wrong name: "T. Jones, *p.p.* P. Smith" means that P. Smith is signing on behalf of T. Jones.

perquisite /'pɜːkwɪzɪt/ *noun* extra profit additional to main income etc.; customary extra right or privilege.

■ **Usage** *Perquisite* is sometimes confused with *prerequisite*, which means 'a thing required as a precondition'.

perry /'peri/ *noun* (*plural* **-ies**) drink made from fermented pear juice.

per se /pɜː 'seɪ/ *adverb* by or in itself, intrinsically. [Latin]

persecute /'pɜːsɪkjuːt/ *verb* (**-ting**) subject to constant hostility and ill-treatment; harass, worry. □ **persecution** /-'kjuːʃ(ə)n/ *noun*; **persecutor** *noun*.

persevere /pɜːsɪ'vɪə/ *verb* (**-ring**) continue steadfastly, persist. □ **perseverance** *noun*.

Persian /'pɜːʃ(ə)n/ ●*noun* native, national, or language of Persia (now Iran); (in full **Persian cat**) cat with long silky hair. ●*adjective* of Persia (Iran). □ **Persian lamb** silky curled fur of young karakul.

persiflage /'pɜːsɪflɑːʒ/ *noun* banter; light raillery.

persimmon /pɜː'sɪmən/ *noun* tropical tree; its edible orange tomato-like fruit.

persist /pə'sɪst/ *verb* (often + *in*) continue to exist or do something in spite of obstacles. □ **persistence** *noun*, **persistent** *adjective*; **persistently** *adverb*.

person /'pɜːs(ə)n/ *noun* individual human being; living body of human being; *Grammar* one of 3 classes of pronouns, verb-forms, etc., denoting person etc. speaking, spoken to, or spoken of. □ **in person** physically present.

persona /pə'səʊnə/ *noun* (*plural* **-nae** /-niː/) aspect of personality as perceived by others. □ **persona grata** /'grɑːtə/ (*plural* **personae gratae** /-niː, -tiː/) person acceptable to certain others; **persona non grata** /nɒn/ (*plural* **personae non gratae**) person not acceptable.

personable *adjective* pleasing in appearance or demeanour.

personage *noun* person, esp. important one.

personal /'pɜːsən(ə)l/ *adjective* one's own; individual, private; done etc. in person; directed to or concerning individual; referring (esp. in hostile way) to individual's private life; *Grammar* of or denoting one of the 3 persons. □ **personal column** part of newspaper devoted to private advertisements and messages; **personal computer** computer designed for use by single individual; **personal equity plan** scheme for tax-free personal investments; **personal organizer** means of keeping track of personal affairs, esp. loose-leaf notebook divided into sections; **personal pronoun** pronoun replacing subject, object, etc., of clause etc.; **personal property** all property except land.

personality /pɜːsə'nælɪtɪ/ *noun* (*plural* **-ies**) distinctive personal character; well-known person; (in *plural*) personal remarks.

personalize *verb* (also **-ise**) (**-zing** or **-sing**) identify as belonging to particular person.

personally *adverb* in person; for one's own part; in a personal way.

personification /pəsɒnɪfɪ'keɪʃ(ə)n/ *noun* type of metaphor in which human qualities are attributed to object, plant, animal, nature, etc., e.g. *Life can play some nasty tricks.*

personify /pə'sɒnɪfaɪ/ *verb* (**-ies**, **-ied**) attribute human characteristics to; symbolize by human figure; (usually as **personified** *adjective*) embody, exemplify typically. □ **personification** *noun*.

personnel /pɜːsə'nel/ *noun* staff of an organization; people engaged in particular service, profession, etc. □ **personnel department** department of firm etc. dealing with appointment, training, and welfare of employees.

perspective /pə'spektɪv/ ●*noun* art of drawing so as to give effect of solidity and relative position and size; relation as to position and distance, or proportion between visible objects, parts of subject, etc.; mental view of relative importance of things; view, prospect. ●*adjective* of or in perspective. □ **in** or **out of perspective** according or not according to rules of perspective, in or not in proportion.

Perspex /'pɜːspeks/ *noun* proprietary term tough light transparent plastic.

perspicacious /pɜːspɪˈkeɪʃəs/ adjective having mental penetration or discernment. □ **perspicacity** /-ˈkæs-/ noun.

perspicuous /pəˈspɪkjuəs/ adjective lucid; clearly expressed. □ **perspicuity** /-ˈkjuː-/ noun.

perspire /pəˈspaɪə/ verb (**-ring**) sweat. □ **perspiration** /pɜːspɪˈreɪʃ(ə)n/ noun.

persuade /pəˈsweɪd/ verb (**-ding**) cause (person) by argument etc. to believe or do something; convince.

persuasion /pəˈsweɪʒ(ə)n/ noun persuading; conviction; religious belief or sect.

persuasive /pəˈsweɪsɪv/ adjective able or tending to persuade. □ **persuasively** adverb; **persuasiveness** noun.

pert adjective saucy, impudent; jaunty. □ **pertly** adverb; **pertness** noun.

pertain /pəˈteɪn/ verb belong, relate.

pertinacious /pɜːtɪˈneɪʃəs/ adjective persistent, obstinate. □ **pertinacity** /-ˈnæs-/ noun.

pertinent /ˈpɜːtɪnənt/ adjective relevant. □ **pertinence** noun, **pertinency** noun.

perturb /pəˈtɜːb/ verb throw into agitation; disquiet. □ **perturbation** noun.

peruke /pəˈruːk/ noun historical wig.

peruse /pəˈruːz/ verb (**-sing**) read; scan. □ **perusal** noun.

pervade /pəˈveɪd/ verb (**-ding**) spread through, permeate; be rife among. □ **pervasion** noun, **pervasive** adjective.

perverse /pəˈvɜːs/ adjective obstinately or wilfully in the wrong; wayward. □ **perversely** adverb; **perversity** noun.

perversion /pəˈvɜːʃ(ə)n/ noun perverting, being perverted; preference for abnormal form of sexual activity.

pervert ● verb /pəˈvɜːt/ turn (thing) aside from proper or normal use; lead astray from right behaviour or belief etc.; (as **perverted** adjective) showing perversion. ● noun /ˈpɜːvɜːt/ person who is perverted, esp. sexually.

pervious /ˈpɜːvɪəs/ adjective permeable; allowing passage or access.

peseta /pəˈseɪtə/ noun Spanish monetary unit.

peso /ˈpeɪsəʊ/ noun (plural **-s**) monetary unit in several Latin American countries.

pessary /ˈpesərɪ/ noun (plural **-ies**) device worn in vagina; vaginal suppository.

pessimism /ˈpesɪmɪz(ə)m/ noun tendency to take worst view or expect worst outcome. □ **pessimist** noun; **pessimistic** /-ˈmɪst-/ adjective.

pest noun troublesome or destructive person, animal, or thing.

pester /ˈpestə/ verb trouble or annoy, esp. with persistent requests.

pesticide /ˈpestɪsaɪd/ noun substance for destroying harmful insects etc.

pestilence /ˈpestɪləns/ noun fatal epidemic disease, esp. bubonic plague.

pestilent /ˈpestɪlənt/ adjective deadly; harmful or morally destructive.

pestilential /pestɪˈlenʃ(ə)l/ adjective of pestilence; pestilent.

pestle /ˈpes(ə)l/ noun instrument for pounding substances in a mortar.

pet[1] ● noun domestic animal kept for pleasure or companionship; favourite. ● adjective as, of, or for a pet; favourite; expressing fondness. ● verb (**-tt-**) fondle, esp. erotically; treat as pet.

pet[2] noun fit of ill humour.

petal /ˈpet(ə)l/ noun each division of flower corolla.

peter /ˈpiːtə/ verb □ **peter out** diminish, come to an end.

petersham /ˈpiːtəʃəm/ noun thick ribbed silk ribbon.

petiole /ˈpetɪəʊl/ noun leaf-stalk.

petite /pəˈtiːt/ adjective (of woman) of small dainty build. [French]

petit four /petɪ ˈfɔː/ noun (plural **petits fours** /ˈfɔːz/) very small fancy cake.

petition /pəˈtɪʃ(ə)n/ ● noun request, supplication; formal written request, esp. one signed by many people, to authorities etc. ● verb make petition to; ask humbly.

petit point /petɪ ˈpwæ̃/ noun embroidery on canvas using small stitches.

petrel /ˈpetr(ə)l/ noun seabird, usually flying far from land.

petrify /ˈpetrɪfaɪ/ verb (**-ies**, **-ied**) paralyse with terror or astonishment etc.; turn or be turned into stone. □ **petrifaction** /-ˈfækʃ(ə)n/ noun.

petrochemical /petrəʊˈkemɪk(ə)l/ noun substance obtained from petroleum or natural gas.

petrodollar /ˈpetrəʊdɒlə/ noun notional unit of currency earned by petroleum-exporting country.

petrol /'petr(ə)l/ *noun* refined petroleum used as fuel in motor vehicles, aircraft, etc.

petroleum /pɪ'trəʊlɪəm/ *noun* hydrocarbon oil found in upper strata of earth, refined for use as fuel etc. □ **petroleum jelly** translucent solid mixture of hydrocarbons got from petroleum and used as lubricant etc.

petticoat /'petɪkəʊt/ *noun* woman's or girl's undergarment hanging from waist or shoulders.

pettifogging /'petɪfɒgɪŋ/ *adjective* quibbling; petty; dishonest.

pettish *adjective* fretful, peevish.

petty /'petɪ/ *adjective* (**-ier, -iest**) unimportant, trivial; small-minded; minor, inferior. □ **petty cash** money kept for small items of expenditure; **petty officer** naval NCO. □ **pettiness** *noun.*

petulant /'petjʊlənt/ *adjective* peevishly impatient or irritable. □ **petulance** *noun*; **petulantly** *adverb.*

petunia /pɪ'tju:nɪə/ *noun* cultivated plant with vivid funnel-shaped flowers.

pew *noun* (in church) enclosed compartment or fixed bench with back; *colloquial* seat.

pewter /'pju:tə/ *noun* grey alloy of tin, antimony, and copper; articles made of this.

peyote /peɪ'əʊtɪ/ *noun* a Mexican cactus; hallucinogenic drug prepared from it.

pfennig /'fenɪg/ *noun* one-hundredth of Deutschmark.

PG *abbreviation* (of film) classified as suitable for children subject to parental guidance.

pH /piː'eɪtʃ/ *noun* measure of acidity or alkalinity of a solution.

phagocyte /'fægəsaɪt/ *noun* blood corpuscle etc. capable of absorbing foreign matter.

phalanx /'fælæŋks/ *noun* (*plural* **phalanxes** or **phalanges** /fə'lændʒiːz/) group of infantry in close formation; united or organized party or company.

phallus /'fæləs/ *noun* (*plural* **phalli** /-laɪ/ or **phalluses**) (esp. erect) penis; image of this. □ **phallic** *adjective.*

phantasm /'fæntæz(ə)m/ *noun* illusion; phantom. □ **phantasmal** /-'tæzm(ə)l/ *adjective.*

phantasmagoria /fæntæzmə'gɔːrɪə/ *noun* shifting scene of real or imaginary figures. □ **phantasmagoric** /-'gɒrɪk/ *adjective.*

phantom /'fæntəm/ ● *noun* spectre, apparition; mental illusion. ● *adjective* illusory.

Pharaoh /'feərəʊ/ *noun* ruler of ancient Egypt.

Pharisee /'færɪsiː/ *noun* member of ancient Jewish sect distinguished by strict observance of traditional and written law; self-righteous person; hypocrite. □ **Pharisaic** /-'seɪk/ *adjective.*

pharmaceutical /fɑːmə'sjuːtɪk(ə)l/ *adjective* of pharmacy; of use or sale of medicinal drugs. □ **pharmaceutics** *noun.*

pharmacist /'fɑːməsɪst/ *noun* person qualified to practise pharmacy.

pharmacology /fɑːmə'kɒlədʒɪ/ *noun* study of action of drugs on the body. □ **pharmacological** /-kə'lɒdʒ-/ *adjective*; **pharmacologist** *noun.*

pharmacopoeia /fɑːməkə'piːə/ *noun* book with list of drugs and directions for use; stock of drugs.

pharmacy /'fɑːməsɪ/ *noun* (*plural* **-ies**) preparation and dispensing of drugs; pharmacist's shop; dispensary.

pharynx /'færɪŋks/ *noun* (*plural* **pharynges** /-rɪndʒiːz/ or **-xes**) cavity behind mouth and nose. □ **pharyngeal** /færɪn'dʒiːəl/ *adjective.*

phase /feɪz/ ● *noun* stage of development, process, or recurring sequence; aspect of moon or planet. ● *verb* (**-sing**) carry out by phases. □ **phase in, out** bring gradually into or out of use.

Ph.D. *abbreviation* Doctor of Philosophy.

pheasant /'fez(ə)nt/ *noun* long-tailed game bird.

phenomenal /fɪ'nɒmɪn(ə)l/ *adjective* extraordinary, remarkable; of or concerned with phenomena. □ **phenomenally** *adverb.*

phenomenon /fɪ'nɒmɪnən/ *noun* (*plural* **-mena**) observed or apparent object, fact, or occurrence; remarkable person or thing.

■ **Usage** It is a mistake to use the plural form *phenomena* when only one phenomenon is meant.

phew /fju:/ *interjection expressing disgust, relief, etc.*

phial /'faɪəl/ *noun* small glass bottle.

philander /fɪ'lændə/ *verb* flirt or have casual affairs with women. □ **philanderer** *noun.*

philanthropy /fɪ'lænθrəpɪ/ *noun* love of all humankind; practical benevolence. □ **philanthropic** /-'θrɒp-/ *adjective;* **philanthropist** *noun.*

philately /fɪ'lætəlɪ/ *noun* stamp-collecting. □ **philatelist** *noun.*

philharmonic /fɪlhɑ:'mɒnɪk/ *adjective* devoted to music.

philippic /fɪ'lɪpɪk/ *noun* bitter verbal attack.

philistine /'fɪlɪstaɪn/ ● *noun* person who is hostile or indifferent to culture. ● *adjective* hostile or indifferent to culture. □ **philistinism** /-stɪn-/ *noun.*

Phillips /'fɪlɪps/ *noun proprietary term* □ **Phillips screw, screwdriver** screw with cross-shaped slot, corresponding screwdriver.

philology /fɪ'lɒlədʒɪ/ *noun* study of language. □ **philological** /-lə'lɒdʒ-/ *adjective;* **philologist** *noun.*

philosopher /fɪ'lɒsəfə/ *noun* expert in or student of philosophy; person who acts philosophically.

philosophical /fɪlə'sɒfɪk(ə)l/ *adjective* (also **philosophic**) of or according to philosophy; calm under adverse circumstances. □ **philosophically** *adverb.*

philosophize /fɪ'lɒsəfaɪz/ *verb* (also **-ise**) (**-zing** or **-sing**) reason like philosopher; theorize.

philosophy /fɪ'lɒsəfɪ/ *noun* (*plural* **-ies**) use of reason and argument in seeking truth and knowledge, esp. of ultimate reality or of general causes and principles; philosophical system; system for conduct of life.

philtre /'fɪltə/ *noun* (*US* **philter**) love potion.

phlebitis /flɪ'baɪtɪs/ *noun* inflammation of vein. □ **phlebitic** /-'bɪt-/ *adjective.*

phlegm /flem/ *noun* bronchial mucus ejected by coughing; calmness; sluggishness.

phlegmatic /fleg'mætɪk/ *adjective* calm; sluggish.

phlox /flɒks/ *noun* (*plural* same or **-es**) plant with clusters of white or coloured flowers.

phobia /'fəʊbɪə/ *noun* abnormal fear or aversion. □ **phobic** *adjective & noun.*

phoenix /'fi:nɪks/ *noun* bird, the only one of its kind, fabled to burn itself and rise from its ashes.

phone *noun & verb* (**-ning**) *colloquial* telephone. □ **phone book** telephone directory; **phonecard** card holding prepaid units for use with cardphone; **phone-in** broadcast programme in which listeners or viewers participate by telephone.

phonetic /fə'netɪk/ *adjective* of or representing vocal sounds; (of spelling) corresponding to pronunciation. □ **phonetically** *adverb.*

phonetics /fə'netɪks/ *plural noun* (usually treated as *singular*) study or representation of vocal sounds. □ **phonetician** /fəʊnɪ'tɪʃ(ə)n/ *noun.*

phoney /'fəʊnɪ/ (also **phony**) *colloquial* ● *adjective* (**-ier, -iest**) false, sham, counterfeit. ● *noun* (*plural* **-eys** or **-ies**) phoney person or thing. □ **phoniness** *noun.*

phonic /'fɒnɪk/ *adjective* of (vocal) sound.

phonograph /'fəʊnəgrɑ:f/ *noun* early form of gramophone.

phonology /fə'nɒlədʒɪ/ *noun* study of sounds in language. □ **phonological** /fəʊnə'lɒdʒɪk(ə)l/ *adjective.*

phony = PHONEY.

phosphate /'fɒsfeɪt/ *noun* salt of phosphoric acid, esp. used as fertilizer.

phosphorescence /fɒsfə'res(ə)ns/ *noun* emission of light without combustion or perceptible heat. □ **phosphoresce** *verb* (**-cing**); **phosphorescent** *adjective.*

phosphorus /'fɒsfərəs/ *noun* nonmetallic element occurring esp. as waxlike substance appearing luminous in dark. □ **phosphoric** /-'fɒrɪk/ *adjective;* **phosphorous** *adjective.*

photo /'fəʊtəʊ/ *noun* (*plural* **-s**) photograph. □ **photo finish** close finish of race in which winner is distinguishable only on photograph; **photofit** picture of suspect constructed from composite photographs.

photo- *combining form* light; photography.

photocopier /'fəʊtəʊkɒpɪə/ *noun* machine for photocopying documents.

photocopy /ˈfəʊtəʊkɒpɪ/ ● *noun* (*plural* **-ies**) photographic copy of document. ● *verb* (**-ies, -ied**) make photocopy of.

photoelectric /fəʊtəʊɪˈlektrɪk/ *adjective* with or using emission of electrons from substances exposed to light. □ **photoelectric cell** device using this effect to generate current. □ **photoelectricity** /-ˈtrɪsɪtɪ/ *noun*.

photogenic /fəʊtəʊˈdʒenɪk/ *adjective* looking attractive in photographs; producing or emitting light.

photograph /ˈfəʊtəgrɑːf/ ● *noun* picture formed by chemical action of light on sensitive film. ● *verb* take photograph (of). □ **photographer** /fəˈtɒgrəfə/ *noun*; **photographic** /-ˈgræf-/ *adjective*; **photography** /fəˈtɒgrəfɪ/ *noun*.

photogravure /fəʊtəʊgrəˈvjʊə/ *noun* picture produced from photographic negative transferred to metal plate and etched in; this process.

photojournalism /fəʊtəʊˈdʒɜːnəlɪz(ə)m/ *noun* reporting of news by photographs in magazines etc.

photolithography /fəʊtəʊlɪˈθɒgrəfɪ/ *noun* lithography using plates made photographically.

photometer /fəʊˈtɒmɪtə/ *noun* instrument for measuring light. □ **photometric** /fəʊtəʊˈmetrɪk/ *adjective*; **photometry** /-ˈtɒmɪtrɪ/ *noun*.

photon /ˈfəʊtɒn/ *noun* quantum of electromagnetic radiation energy.

Photostat /ˈfəʊtəʊstæt/ ● *noun proprietary term* type of photocopier; copy made by it. ● *verb* (**photostat**) (**-tt-**) make Photostat of.

photosynthesis /fəʊtəʊˈsɪnθəsɪs/ *noun* process in which energy of sunlight is used by green plants to form carbohydrates from carbon dioxide and water. □ **photosynthesize** *verb* (also **-ise**) (**-zing** or **-sing**).

phrase /freɪz/ ● *noun* group of words forming conceptual unit but not sentence (see panel); short pithy expression; *Music* short sequence of notes. ● *verb* (**-sing**) express in words; divide (music) into phrases. □ **phrase book** book listing phrases and their foreign equivalents, for use by tourists etc. □ **phrasal** *adjective*.

phraseology /freɪzɪˈɒlədʒɪ/ *noun* (*plural* **-ies**) choice or arrangement of words. □ **phraseological** /-zɪəˈlɒdʒ-/ *adjective*.

phrenology /frɪˈnɒlədʒɪ/ *noun historical* study of external form of cranium as supposed indication of mental faculties etc. □ **phrenologist** *noun*.

phut /fʌt/ *adverb colloquial* □ **go phut** collapse, break down.

phylactery /fɪˈlæktərɪ/ *noun* (*plural* **-ies**) small box containing Hebrew texts, worn by Jewish man at prayer.

phylum /ˈfaɪləm/ *noun* (*plural* **phyla**) major division of plant or animal kingdom.

physic /ˈfɪzɪk/ *noun esp. archaic* medicine; medical art or profession.

physical /ˈfɪzɪk(ə)l/ ● *adjective* of the body; of matter; of nature or according

....

Phrase

A phrase is a group of words that has meaning but does not have a subject, verb, or object (unlike a clause or sentence). It can be:

1 a noun phrase, functioning as a noun, e.g.

I went to see my friend Tom.
The only ones they have *are too small*.

2 an adjective phrase, functioning as an adjective, e.g.

I was very pleased indeed.
This one is better than mine.

3 an adverb phrase, functioning as an adverb, e.g.

They drove off in their car.
I was there ten days ago.

....

to its laws; of physics. ● noun US medical examination. □ **physically** adverb.

physician /fɪˈzɪʃ(ə)n/ noun doctor, esp. specialist in medical diagnosis and treatment.

physics /ˈfɪzɪks/ plural noun (usually treated as singular) science of properties and interaction of matter and energy. □ **physicist** noun.

physiognomy /fɪzɪˈɒnəmɪ/ noun (plural -ies) features or type of face; art of judging character from face etc.

physiology /fɪzɪˈɒlədʒɪ/ noun science of functioning of living organisms. □ **physiological** /-əˈlɒdʒ-/ adjective; **physiologist** noun.

physiotherapy /fɪzɪəˈθerəpɪ/ noun treatment of injury or disease by exercise, heat, or oᴛher physical agencies. □ **physiotherapist** noun.

physique /fɪˈziːk/ noun bodily structure and development.

pi /paɪ/ noun sixteenth letter of Greek alphabet (Π, π); (as π) symbol of ratio of circumference of circle to diameter (approx. 3.14).

pia mater /paɪə ˈmeɪtə/ noun inner membrane enveloping brain and spinal cord.

pianissimo /pɪəˈnɪsɪməʊ/ Music ● adjective very soft. ● adverb very softly. ● noun (plural -s or -mi /-mɪ/) very soft playing, singing, or passage.

pianist /ˈpɪənɪst/ noun player of piano.

piano[1] /ˈpjænəʊ/ noun (plural -s) keyboard instrument with metal strings struck by hammers. □ **piano-accordion** accordion with small keyboard like that of piano.

piano[2] /ˈpjɑːnəʊ/ Music ● adjective soft. ● adverb softly. ● noun (plural -s or -ni /-nɪ/) soft playing, singing, or passage.

pianoforte /pjænəʊˈfɔːtɪ/ noun formal or archaic = PIANO[1].

piazza /pɪˈætsə/ noun public square or market-place.

pibroch /ˈpiːbrɒk/ noun martial or funeral bagpipe music.

picador /ˈpɪkədɔː/ noun mounted man with lance in bullfight.

picaresque /pɪkəˈresk/ adjective (of style of fiction) dealing with episodic adventures of rogues.

piccalilli /pɪkəˈlɪlɪ/ noun (plural -s) pickle of chopped vegetables, mustard, and spices.

piccolo /ˈpɪkələʊ/ noun (plural -s) small high-pitched flute.

pick ● verb select carefully; pluck, gather (flower, fruit, etc.); probe with fingers or instrument to remove unwanted matter; clear (bone etc.) of scraps of meat etc.; eat (food, meal, etc.) in small bits. ● noun picking, selection; (usually + of) best; pickaxe; colloquial plectrum; instrument for picking. □ **pick a lock** open lock with instrument other than proper key, esp. with criminal intent; **pick on** nag at, find fault with, select; **pickpocket** person who steals from pockets; **pick up** take hold of and lift, acquire casually, learn routinely, stop for and take with one, make acquaintance of casually, recover, improve, arrest, detect, manage to receive (broadcast signal etc.), accept responsibility of paying (bill etc.), resume; **pick-up** person met casually, small open truck, part of record player carrying stylus, device on electric guitar etc. that converts string vibrations into electrical signals, act of picking up; **pick-your-own** (of fruit and vegetables) dug or picked by customer at farm etc.

pickaxe /ˈpɪkæks/ noun (US **pickax**) tool with sharp-pointed iron cross-bar for breaking up ground etc.

picket /ˈpɪkɪt/ ● noun one or more people stationed to dissuade workers from entering workplace during strike etc.; pointed stake driven into ground; small group of troops sent to watch for enemy. ● verb (-t-) place or act as picket outside; post as military picket; secure with stakes. □ **picket line** boundary established by workers on strike, esp. at workplace entrance, which others are asked not to cross.

pickings plural noun perquisites, gleanings.

pickle /ˈpɪk(ə)l/ ● noun (often in plural) vegetables etc. preserved in vinegar etc.; liquid used for this; colloquial plight. ● verb (-ling) preserve in or treat with pickle; (as **pickled** adjective) slang drunk.

picky adjective (-ier, -iest) colloquial highly fastidious.

picnic /'pɪknɪk/ ● *noun* outing including outdoor meal; such meal; something pleasantly or easily accomplished. ● *verb* (**-ck-**) eat meal outdoors.

pictograph /'pɪktəgrɑːf/ *noun* (also **pictogram** /-græm/) pictorial symbol used as form of writing.

pictorial /pɪk'tɔːrɪəl/ *adjective* of, expressed in, or illustrated with a picture or pictures. □ **pictorially** *adverb*.

picture /'pɪktʃə/ ● *noun* painting, drawing, photograph, etc., esp. as work of art; portrait; beautiful object; scene; mental image; cinema film; (**the pictures**) cinema (performance). ● *verb* (**-ring**) imagine; represent in picture; describe graphically. □ **picture postcard** postcard with picture on one side; **picture window** large window of one pane of glass.

picturesque /pɪktʃə'resk/ *adjective* striking and pleasant to look at; (of language etc.) strikingly graphic.

piddle /'pɪd(ə)l/ *verb* (**-ling**) *colloquial* urinate; (as **piddling** *adjective*) *colloquial* trivial; work or act in trifling way.

pidgin /'pɪdʒɪn/ *noun* simplified language, esp. used between speakers of different languages.

pie *noun* dish of meat, fruit, etc., encased in or covered with pastry etc. and baked. □ **pie chart** diagram representing relative quantities as sectors of circle; **pie-eyed** *slang* drunk.

piebald /'paɪbɔːld/ ● *adjective* having irregular patches of two colours, esp. black and white. ● *noun* piebald animal.

piece /piːs/ ● *noun* distinct portion forming part of or broken off from larger object; coin; picture, literary or musical composition; example, item; chessman, man at draughts, etc. ● *verb* (**-cing**) (usually + *together*) form into a whole; join. □ **of a piece** uniform or consistent; **piece-work** work paid for according to amount done.

pièce de résistance /pjes də reɪ'ziːstɑ̃s/ *noun* (*plural* **pièces de résistance** same pronunciation) most important or remarkable item.

piecemeal ● *adverb* piece by piece, part at a time. ● *adjective* gradual; unsystematic.

pied /paɪd/ *adjective* of mixed colours.

pied-à-terre /pjeɪdɑː'teə/ *noun* (*plural* **pieds-** same pronunciation) (usually small) flat, house, etc. kept for occasional use. [French]

pier /pɪə/ *noun* structure built out into sea etc. used as promenade and landing-stage or breakwater; support of arch or of span of bridge; pillar; solid part of wall between windows etc. □ **pier-glass** large tall mirror.

pierce /pɪəs/ *verb* (**-cing**) go through or into like spear or needle; make hole in; make (hole etc.).

pierrot /'pɪərəʊ/ *noun* (*feminine* **pierrette** /pɪə'ret/) French white-faced pantomime character with clown's costume; itinerant entertainer so dressed.

pietà /pɪe'tɑː/ *noun* representation of Virgin Mary holding dead body of Christ. [Italian]

pietism /'paɪətɪz(ə)m/ *noun* extreme or affected piety.

piety /'paɪətɪ/ *noun* piousness.

piffle /'pɪf(ə)l/ *colloquial* ● *noun* nonsense. ● *verb* (**-ling**) talk or act feebly.

pig ● *noun* wild or domesticated animal with broad snout and stout bristly body; *colloquial* greedy, dirty, obstinate, or annoying person; oblong mass of smelted iron or other metal. ● *verb* (**-gg-**) *colloquial* eat (food) greedily. □ **pigheaded** obstinate; **pig-iron** crude iron from smelting-furnace; **pig it** *colloquial* live in disorderly fashion; **pig out** *esp. US slang* eat greedily; **pigsty** sty for pigs; **pigtail** plait of hair hanging from back or each side of head.

pigeon /'pɪdʒ(ə)n/ *noun* bird of dove family. □ **pigeon-hole** *noun* each of set of compartments in cabinet etc. for papers etc., *verb* classify mentally, put in pigeon-hole, put aside for future consideration; **pigeon-toed** having toes turned inwards.

piggery *noun* (*plural* **-ies**) pig farm; pigsty.

piggish *adjective* greedy; dirty; mean.

piggy ● *noun* (*plural* **-ies**) *colloquial* little pig. ● *adjective* (**-ier**, **-iest**) like a pig; (of features etc.) like those of a pig. □ **piggyback** (a ride) on shoulders and back of another person; **piggy bank** pig-shaped money box.

piglet /'pɪglɪt/ *noun* young pig.

pigment /ˈpɪgmənt/ ● *noun* coloured substance used as paint etc., or occurring naturally in plant or animal tissue. ● *verb* colour (as) with natural pigment. □ **pigmentation** *noun*.

pigmy = PYGMY.

pike *noun* (*plural* same or **-s**) large voracious freshwater fish; spear formerly used by infantry. □ **pikestaff** wooden shaft of pike (**plain as a pikestaff** quite obvious).

pilaff = PILAU.

pilaster /pɪˈlæstə/ *noun* rectangular column, esp. one fastened into wall.

pilau /pɪˈlaʊ/ *noun* (also **pilaff** /pɪˈlɑːf/) Middle Eastern or Indian dish of rice with meat, spices, etc.

pilchard /ˈpɪltʃəd/ *noun* small sea fish related to herring.

pile¹ ● *noun* heap of things laid on one another; large imposing building; *colloquial* large amount, esp. of money; series of plates of dissimilar metals laid alternately for producing electric current; nuclear reactor; pyre. ● *verb* (**-ling**) heap; (+ *with*) load with thing; (+ *in, into, on, out of*, etc.) crowd. □ **pile up** accumulate, heap up; **pile-up** *colloquial* collision of several motor vehicles.

pile² *noun* heavy beam driven vertically into ground as support for building etc.

pile³ *noun* soft projecting surface of velvet, carpet, etc.

piles *plural noun colloquial* haemorrhoids.

pilfer /ˈpɪlfə/ *verb* steal or thieve in petty way.

pilgrim /ˈpɪlgrɪm/ *noun* person who journeys to sacred place; traveller. □ **Pilgrim Fathers** English Puritans who founded colony in Massachusetts in 1620.

pilgrimage *noun* pilgrim's journey.

pill *noun* ball or flat piece of medicinal substance to be swallowed whole; (usually **the pill**) *colloquial* contraceptive pill. □ **pillbox** small round shallow box for pills, hat shaped like this, *Military* round concrete shelter, mainly underground.

pillage /ˈpɪlɪdʒ/ *verb* (**-ging**) & *noun* plunder.

pillar /ˈpɪlə/ *noun* slender upright structure used as support or ornament; person regarded as mainstay; upright mass. □ **pillar-box** public postbox shaped like pillar.

pillion /ˈpɪljən/ *noun* seat for passenger behind motorcyclist etc.

pillory /ˈpɪlərɪ/ ● *noun* (*plural* **-ies**) *historical* frame with holes for head and hands, allowing an offender to be exposed to public ridicule. ● *verb* (**-ies, -ied**) expose to ridicule; *historical* set in pillory.

pillow /ˈpɪləʊ/ ● *noun* cushion as support for head, esp. in bed; pillow-shaped support. ● *verb* rest (as) on pillow. □ **pillowcase**, **pillowslip** washable cover for pillow.

pilot /ˈpaɪlət/ ● *noun* person operating controls of aircraft; person in charge of ships entering or leaving harbour etc.; experimental or preliminary study or undertaking; guide, leader. ● *adjective* experimental, preliminary. ● *verb* (**-t-**) act as pilot to; guide course of. □ **pilot-light** small gas burner kept alight to light another; **pilot officer** lowest commissioned rank in RAF.

pimento /pɪˈmentəʊ/ *noun* (*plural* **-s**) allspice; sweet pepper.

pimiento /pɪmɪˈentəʊ/ *noun* (*plural* **-s**) sweet pepper.

pimp ● *noun* person who lives off earnings of prostitute or brothel. ● *verb* act as pimp, esp. procure clients for prostitute.

pimpernel /ˈpɪmpənel/ *noun* scarlet pimpernel.

pimple /ˈpɪmp(ə)l/ *noun* small hard inflamed spot on skin. □ **pimply** *adjective*.

pin ● *noun* small thin pointed piece of metal with head, used as fastening; wooden or metal peg, rivet, etc.; (in *plural*) *colloquial* legs. ● *verb* (**-nn-**) fasten with pin(s); transfix with pin, lance, etc.; (usually + *on*) fix (responsibility, blame, etc.); seize and hold fast. □ **pinball** game in which small metal balls are shot across board and strike obstacles; **pincushion** small pad for holding pins; **pin down** (often + *to*) bind (person etc.) to promise, arrangement, etc., make (person) declare position or intentions; **pin-money** small sum of money, esp. earned by woman; **pinpoint** *noun* very small or sharp thing, *adjective* precise, *verb* locate with precision; **pinprick** petty irritation; **pins and needles** tingling sensation in limb recovering from numbness; **pinstripe** very narrow stripe in cloth; **pin-table** table used in pinball; **pintail** duck or grouse with pointed tail; **pin-tuck** narrow ornamental tuck; **pin-up** picture of attractive or famous person, pinned up on wall etc.; **pinwheel** small Catherine wheel.

pina colada /piːnə kəˈlɑːdə/ noun cocktail of pineapple juice, rum, and coconut.

pinafore /ˈpɪnəfɔː/ noun apron, esp. with bib; (in full **pinafore dress**) dress without collar or sleeves, worn over blouse or jumper.

pince-nez /ˈpænsneɪ/ noun (plural same) pair of eyeglasses with spring that clips on nose.

pincers /ˈpɪnsəz/ plural noun gripping-tool forming pair of jaws; pincer-shaped claw in crustaceans etc. □ **pincer movement** converging movement by two wings of army against enemy position.

pinch ● verb grip tightly, esp. between finger and thumb; constrict painfully; (of cold etc.) affect painfully; slang steal, arrest; stint, be niggardly. ● noun pinching; (as **pinched** adjective) (of features) drawn; amount that can be taken up with fingers and thumb; stress of poverty etc. □ **at a pinch** in an emergency.

pinchbeck /ˈpɪntʃbek/ ● noun goldlike copper and zinc alloy used in cheap jewellery etc. ● adjective spurious, sham.

pine[1] noun evergreen needle-leaved coniferous tree; its wood. □ **pine cone** fruit of pine; **pine nut**, **kernel** edible seed of some pines.

pine[2] verb (**-ning**) (often + away) waste away with grief, disease, etc.; (usually + for) long.

pineal /ˈpɪnɪəl/ adjective shaped like pine cone. □ **pineal gland**, **body** conical gland in brain, secreting hormone-like substance.

pineapple /ˈpaɪnæp(ə)l/ noun large juicy tropical fruit with yellow flesh and tough skin.

ping ● noun abrupt single ringing sound. ● verb (cause to) emit ping.

ping-pong noun colloquial table tennis.

pinion[1] /ˈpɪnjən/ ● noun outer part of bird's wing; poetical wing; flight feather. ● verb cut off pinion (of wing or bird) to prevent flight; restrain by binding arms to sides.

pinion[2] /ˈpɪnjən/ noun small cogwheel engaging with larger.

pink[1] ● noun pale red colour; garden plant with clove-scented flowers; (**the pink**) the most perfect condition. ● adjective pink-coloured; colloquial mildly socialist. □ **in the pink** colloquial in very good health. □ **pinkish** adjective; **pinkness** noun.

pink[2] verb pierce slightly; cut scalloped or zigzag edge on. □ **pinking shears** dressmaker's serrated shears for cutting zigzag edge.

pink[3] verb (of vehicle engine) emit high-pitched explosive sounds caused by faulty combustion.

pinnace /ˈpɪnɪs/ noun ship's small boat.

pinnacle /ˈpɪnək(ə)l/ noun culmination, climax; natural peak; small ornamental turret crowning buttress, roof, etc.

pinnate /ˈpɪneɪt/ adjective (of compound leaf) with leaflets on each side of leaf-stalk.

pinny /ˈpɪnɪ/ noun (plural **-ies**) colloquial pinafore.

pint /paɪnt/ noun measure of capacity (1/8 gal., 0.568 litre); colloquial pint of beer. □ **pint-sized** colloquial very small.

pinta /ˈpaɪntə/ noun colloquial pint of milk.

pintle /ˈpɪnt(ə)l/ noun bolt or pin, esp. one on which some other part turns.

Pinyin /pɪnˈjɪn/ noun system of romanized spelling for transliterating Chinese.

pioneer /paɪəˈnɪə/ ● noun beginner of enterprise etc.; explorer or settler. ● verb initiate (enterprise etc.) for others to follow; act as pioneer.

pious /ˈpaɪəs/ adjective devout, religious; sanctimonious; dutiful. □ **piously** adverb.

pip[1] noun seed of apple, pear, orange, etc.

pip[2] noun short high-pitched sound.

pip[3] verb (**-pp-**) colloquial hit with a shot; (also **pip at** or **to the post**) defeat narrowly.

pip[4] *noun* each spot on dominoes, dice, or playing cards; star on army officer's shoulder.

pip[5] *noun* disease of poultry etc.; (esp. **the pip**) *colloquial* (fit of) depression, boredom, or bad temper.

pipe ● *noun* tube of earthenware, metal, etc., esp. for carrying gas, water, etc.; narrow tube with bowl at one end containing tobacco for smoking; quantity of tobacco held by this; wind instrument of single tube; each tube by which sound is produced in organ; (in *plural*) bagpipes; tubular organ etc. in body; high note or song, esp. of bird; boatswain's whistle; measure of capacity for wine (105 gals., 477 litres). ● *verb* (**-ping**) convey (as) through pipes; play on pipe; (esp. as **piped** *adjective*) transmit (recorded music etc.) by wire or cable; utter shrilly; summon, lead, etc. by sound of pipe or whistle; trim with piping; furnish with pipe(s). □ **pipeclay** fine white clay for tobacco pipes or for whitening leather etc.; **pipe-cleaner** piece of flexible tuft-covered wire to clean inside tobacco pipe; **pipe down** *colloquial* be quiet; **pipedream** extravagant fancy, impossible wish, etc.; **pipeline** pipe conveying oil etc. across country, channel of supply or communication; **pipe up** begin to play, sing, etc.

piper *noun* person who plays on pipe, esp. bagpipes.

pipette /pɪˈpet/ *noun* slender tube for transferring or measuring small quantities of liquid.

piping *noun* ornamentation of dress, upholstery, etc. by means of cord enclosed in pipelike fold; ornamental cordlike lines of sugar etc. on cake etc.; length or system of pipes. □ **piping hot** (of food, water, etc.) very or suitably hot.

pipit /ˈpɪpɪt/ *noun* small bird resembling lark.

pippin /ˈpɪpɪn/ *noun* apple grown from seed; dessert apple.

piquant /ˈpiːkənt/ *adjective* agreeably pungent, sharp, appetizing, stimulating. □ **piquancy** *noun*.

pique /piːk/ ● *verb* (**piques, piqued, piquing**) wound pride of; stir (curiosity). ● *noun* resentment; hurt pride.

piquet /pɪˈket/ *noun* card game for two players.

piracy /ˈpaɪrəsɪ/ *noun* (*plural* **-ies**) activity of pirate.

piranha /pɪˈrɑːnə/ *noun* voracious S. American freshwater fish.

pirate /ˈpaɪərət/ ● *noun* seafaring robber attacking ships; ship used by pirate; person who infringes copyright or regulations or encroaches on rights of others etc. ● *verb* (**-ting**) reproduce (book etc.) or trade (goods) without permission. □ **piratical** /-ˈræt-/ *adjective*.

pirouette /pɪruˈet/ ● *noun* dancer's spin on one foot or point of toe. ● *verb* (**-tting**) perform pirouette.

piscatorial /pɪskəˈtɔːrɪəl/ *adjective* of fishing.

Pisces /ˈpaɪsiːz/ *noun* twelfth sign of zodiac.

piscina /pɪˈsiːnə/ *noun* (*plural* **-nae** /-niː/ or **-s**) stone basin near altar in church, for draining water after use.

pistachio /pɪsˈtɑːʃɪəʊ/ *noun* (*plural* **-s**) kind of nut with green kernel.

piste /piːst/ *noun* ski run of compacted snow.

pistil /ˈpɪstɪl/ *noun* female organ in flowers. □ **pistillate** *adjective*.

pistol /ˈpɪst(ə)l/ *noun* small firearm.

piston /ˈpɪst(ə)n/ *noun* sliding cylinder fitting closely in tube and moving up and down in it, used in steam or petrol engine to impart motion; sliding valve in trumpet etc. □ **piston rod** rod connecting piston to other parts of machine.

pit[1] ● *noun* large hole in ground; coal mine; covered hole as trap; depression in skin or any surface; orchestra pit; (**the pits**) *slang* worst imaginable place, situation, person, etc.; area to side of track where racing cars are refuelled etc. during race; sunken area in floor of workshop etc. for inspection or repair of underside of vehicle etc. ● *verb* (**-tt-**) (usually + *against*) set (one's wits, strength, etc.) in competition; (usually as **pitted** *adjective*) make pit(s) in; store in pit. □ **pit bull terrier** small American dog noted for ferocity; **pitfall** unsuspected danger or drawback, covered pit as trap; **pit-head** top of shaft of coal mine, area surrounding this; **pit**

of the stomach hollow below base of breastbone.

pit² verb (-tt-) (usually as **pitted** adjective) remove stones from (fruit).

pita = PITTA.

pit-a-pat /ˈpɪtəpæt/ (also **pitter-patter** /ˈpɪtəpætə/) • adverb with sound as of light quick steps; falteringly. • noun such sound.

pitch¹ • verb set up (esp. tent, camp, etc.) in chosen position; throw; express in particular style or at particular level; fall heavily; (of ship etc.) plunge in lengthwise direction; set at particular musical pitch. • noun area of play in esp. outdoor game; height, degree, intensity, etc.; gradient, esp. of roof; Music degree of highness or lowness of tone; act or process of pitching; colloquial salesman's persuasive talk; place, esp. in street or market, where one is stationed; distance between successive points, lines, etc. □ **pitched battle** vigorous argument etc., planned battle between sides in prepared positions; **pitched roof** sloping roof; **pitchfork** noun fork with long handle and two prongs for tossing hay etc., verb (+ into) thrust forcibly or hastily into office, position, etc.; **pitch in** colloquial set to work vigorously; **pitch into** colloquial attack vigorously.

pitch² • noun dark resinous tarry substance. • verb coat with pitch. □ **pitch-black, -dark** intensely dark; **pitch pine** resinous kinds of pine. □ **pitchy** adjective (-ier, -iest).

pitchblende /ˈpɪtʃblend/ noun uranium oxide yielding radium.

pitcher¹ /ˈpɪtʃə/ noun large jug, ewer.

pitcher² noun player who delivers ball in baseball.

piteous /ˈpɪtɪəs/ adjective deserving or arousing pity. □ **piteously** adverb; **piteousness** noun.

pith noun spongy tissue in stems of plants or lining rind of orange etc.; chief part; vigour, energy. □ **pith helmet** sun-helmet made from dried pith of plants.

pithy /ˈpɪθɪ/ adjective (-ier, -iest) condensed and forcible, terse. □ **pithily** adverb; **pithiness** noun.

pitiable /ˈpɪtɪəb(ə)l/ adjective deserving or arousing pity or contempt. □ **pitiably** adverb.

pitiful /ˈpɪtɪfʊl/ adjective arousing pity; contemptible. □ **pitifully** adverb.

pitiless /ˈpɪtɪlɪs/ adjective showing no pity. □ **pitilessly** adverb.

piton /ˈpiːtɒn/ noun peg driven in to support climber or rope.

pitta /ˈpɪtə/ noun (also **pita**) originally Turkish unleavened bread which can be split and filled.

pittance /ˈpɪt(ə)ns/ noun scanty allowance, small amount.

pitter-patter = PIT-A-PAT.

pituitary /pɪˈtjuːɪtərɪ/ noun (plural -ies) (in full **pituitary gland**) small ductless gland at base of brain.

pity /ˈpɪtɪ/ • noun sorrow for another's suffering; cause for regret. • verb (-ies, -ied) feel pity for. □ **pitying** adjective.

pivot /ˈpɪvət/ • noun shaft or pin on which something turns; crucial person or point. • verb (-t-) turn (as) on pivot; provide with pivot. □ **pivotal** adjective.

pixie /ˈpɪksɪ/ noun (also **pixy**) (plural -ies) fairy-like being.

pizza /ˈpiːtsə/ noun flat piece of dough baked with topping of cheese, tomatoes, etc.

pizzeria /piːtsəˈriːə/ noun pizza restaurant.

pizzicato /pɪtsɪˈkɑːtəʊ/ Music • adverb plucking. • adjective performed thus. • noun (plural -s or -ti /-tɪ/) pizzicato note or passage.

pl. abbreviation plural; place; plate.

placable /ˈplækəb(ə)l/ adjective easily appeased; mild-tempered. □ **placability** noun.

placard /ˈplækɑːd/ • noun large notice for public display. • verb post placards on.

placate /pləˈkeɪt/ verb (-ting) conciliate, pacify. □ **placatory** adjective.

place • noun particular part of space; space or room of or for person etc.; city, town, village, residence, building; rank, station, position; building or spot devoted to specified purpose; office, employment; duties of this. • verb (-cing) put or dispose in place; assign rank, order, or class to; give (order for goods etc.) to firm etc.; (in *passive*) be among first 3 (or 4) in race. □ **in place** suitable, in the right position; **in place of** instead of; **out of place** unsuitable, in the wrong position; **place-kick** *Football* kick made with ball placed on ground; **place-mat** small mat on table at person's place; **place setting** set of cutlery etc. for one person to eat with; **take place** happen; **take the place of** be substituted for. □ **placement** noun.

placebo /pləˈsiːbəʊ/ noun (*plural* **-s**) medicine with no physiological effect prescribed for psychological reasons; dummy pill etc. used in controlled trial.

placenta /pləˈsentə/ noun (*plural* **-tae** /-tiː/ or **-s**) organ in uterus of pregnant mammal that nourishes foetus. □ **placental** adjective.

placid /ˈplæsɪd/ adjective calm, unruffled; not easily disturbed. □ **placidity** /pləˈsɪdɪtɪ/ noun; **placidly** adverb.

placket /ˈplækɪt/ noun opening or slit in garment, for fastenings or access to pocket.

plagiarize /ˈpleɪdʒəraɪz/ verb (also **-ise**) (**-zing** or **-sing**) take and use (another's writings etc.) as one's own. □ **plagiarism** noun; **plagiarist** noun; **plagiarizer** noun.

plague /pleɪg/ ● noun deadly contagious disease; (+ *of*) colloquial infestation; great trouble or affliction. ● verb (**plaguing**) colloquial annoy, bother; afflict, hinder; affect with plague.

plaice /pleɪs/ noun (*plural* same) marine flatfish.

plaid /plæd/ noun chequered or tartan, esp. woollen, cloth; long piece of this as part of Highland costume.

plain ● adjective clear, evident; readily understood; simple; not beautiful or distinguished-looking; straightforward in speech; not luxurious. ● adverb clearly; simply. ● noun level tract of country; ordinary stitch in knitting. □ **plain chocolate** chocolate made without milk; **plain clothes** ordinary clothes as distinct from esp. police uniform; **plain flour** flour with no raising agent; **plain sailing** simple situation or course of action; **plainsong** traditional church music sung in unison in medieval modes and free rhythm; **plain-spoken** frank. □ **plainly** adverb.

plaint noun Law accusation, charge; *literary* lamentation.

plaintiff /ˈpleɪntɪf/ noun person who brings case against another in law court.

plaintive /ˈpleɪntɪv/ adjective mournful-sounding. □ **plaintively** adverb.

plait /plæt/ ● noun length of hair, straw, etc. in 3 or more interlaced strands. ● verb form into plait.

plan ● noun method or procedure for doing something; drawing exhibiting relative position and size of parts of building etc.; diagram; map. ● verb (**-nn-**) arrange beforehand, scheme; make plan of; design; (as **planned** adjective) in accordance with plan; make plans. □ **plan on** (often + present participle) colloquial aim at, intend. □ **planning** noun.

planchette /plɑːnˈʃet/ noun small board on castors, with pencil, said to write messages from spirits when person's fingers rest on it.

plane[1] ● noun flat surface (not necessarily horizontal); colloquial aeroplane; level of attainment etc. ● adjective level as or lying in a plane.

plane[2] ● noun tool for smoothing surface of wood by paring shavings from it. ● verb (**-ning**) smooth or pare with plane.

plane[3] noun tall spreading broad-leaved tree.

planet /ˈplænɪt/ noun heavenly body orbiting star. □ **planetary** adjective.

planetarium /plænɪˈteərɪəm/ noun (*plural* **-s** or **-ria**) building in which image of night sky as seen at various times and places is projected; device for such projection.

plangent /ˈplændʒ(ə)nt/ adjective literary loudly lamenting; plaintive; reverberating.

plank ● noun long flat piece of timber; item of political or other programme. ● verb provide or cover with planks; (usually + *down*) colloquial put down roughly, deposit (esp. money).

plankton /ˈplæŋkt(ə)n/ noun chiefly microscopic organisms drifting in sea or fresh water.

planner *noun* person who plans new town etc.; person who makes plans; list, table, chart, etc. with information helpful in planning.

plant /plɑːnt/ ● *noun* organism capable of living wholly on inorganic substances and lacking power of locomotion; small plant (other than trees and shrubs); equipment for industrial process; *colloquial* thing deliberately placed for discovery, esp. to incriminate another. ● *verb* place (seed etc.) in ground to grow; fix firmly, establish; cause (idea etc.) to be established, esp. in another person's mind; deliver (blow etc.); *colloquial* place (something incriminating) for later discovery.

plantain[1] /'plæntɪn/ *noun* herb yielding seed used as food for birds.

plantain[2] /'plæntɪn/ *noun* plant related to banana; banana-like fruit of this.

plantation /plɑː'teɪʃ(ə)n/ *noun* estate for cultivation of cotton, tobacco, etc.; number of growing plants, esp. trees, planted together; *historical* colony.

planter *noun* owner or manager of plantation; container for house-plants.

plaque /plæk/ *noun* ornamental tablet of metal, porcelain, etc.; deposit on teeth, where bacteria proliferate.

plasma /'plæzmə/ *noun* (also **plasm** /'plæz(ə)m/) colourless fluid part of blood etc. in which corpuscles etc. float; protoplasm; gas of positive ions and free electrons in about equal numbers. □ **plasmic** *adjective*.

plaster /'plɑːstə/ ● *noun* mixture esp. of lime, sand, and water spread on walls etc.; sticking plaster; plaster of Paris. ● *verb* cover with or like plaster; apply, stick, etc. like plaster to; (as **plastered** *adjective*) *slang* drunk. □ **plasterboard** two boards with core of plaster used for walls etc.; **plaster cast** bandage stiffened with plaster of Paris and wrapped round broken limb etc.; **plaster of Paris** fine white gypsum powder for plaster casts etc. □ **plasterer** *noun*.

plastic /'plæstɪk/ ● *noun* synthetic resinous substance that can be given any shape; (in full **plastic money**) *colloquial* credit card(s). ● *adjective* made of plastic; capable of being moulded; giving form to clay, wax, etc. □ **plastic arts** those

involving modelling; **plastic explosive** putty-like explosive; **plastic surgery** repair or restoration of lost or damaged etc. tissue. □ **plasticity** /-'tɪs-/ *noun*; **plasticize** /-saɪz/ *verb* (also **-ise**) (**-zing** or **-sing**); **plasticky** *adjective*.

Plasticine /'plæstəsiːn/ *noun proprietary term* pliant substance used for modelling.

plate ● *noun* shallow usually circular vessel from which food is eaten or served; similar vessel used for collection in church etc.; table utensils of gold, silver, or other metal; objects of plated metal; piece of metal with inscription, for fixing to door etc.; illustration on special paper in book; thin sheet of metal, glass, etc. coated with sensitive film for photography; flat thin sheet of metal etc.; part of denture fitting to mouth and holding teeth; each of several sheets of rock thought to form earth's crust. ● *verb* (**-ting**) cover (other metal) with thin coating of silver, gold, etc.; cover with plates of metal. □ **plate glass** thick fine-quality glass for mirrors, windows, etc.; **platelayer** workman laying and repairing railway lines. □ **plateful** *noun* (*plural* **-s**).

plateau /'plætəʊ/ ● *noun* (*plural* **-x** or **-s** /-z/) area of level high ground; state of little variation following an increase. ● *verb* (**plateaus, plateaued, plateauing**) (often + *out*) reach level or static state after period of increase.

platelet /'pleɪtlɪt/ *noun* small disc in blood, involved in clotting.

platen /'plæt(ə)n/ *noun* plate in printing press by which paper is pressed against type; corresponding part in typewriter etc.

platform /'plætfɔːm/ *noun* raised level surface, esp. one from which speaker addresses audience, or one along side of line at railway station; floor area at entrance to bus etc.; thick sole of shoe; declared policy of political party.

platinum /'plætɪnəm/ *noun* white heavy precious metallic element that does not tarnish. □ **platinum blonde** *adjective* silvery-blond, *noun* person with such hair.

platitude /'plætɪtjuːd/ *noun* commonplace remark. □ **platitudinous** /-'tjuːd-/ *adjective*.

Platonic /pləˈtɒnɪk/ *adjective* of Plato or his philosophy; (**platonic**) (of love or friendship) not sexual.

platoon /pləˈtuːn/ *noun* subdivision of infantry company.

platter /ˈplætə/ *noun* flat plate or dish.

platypus /ˈplætɪpəs/ *noun* (*plural* **-puses**) Australian aquatic egg-laying mammal with ducklike beak.

plaudit /ˈplɔːdɪt/ *noun* (usually in *plural*) round of applause; commendation.

plausible /ˈplɔːzɪb(ə)l/ *adjective* reasonable, probable; (of person) persuasive but deceptive. □ **plausibility** *noun*; **plausibly** *adverb*.

play ● *verb* occupy or amuse oneself pleasantly; (+ *with*) act light-heartedly or flippantly with (feelings etc.); perform on (musical instrument), perform (piece of music etc.); cause (record etc.) to produce sounds; perform (drama, role); (+ *on*) perform (trick or joke etc.) on; *colloquial* cooperate, do what is wanted; take part in (game); have as opponent in game; move (piece) in game, put (card) on table, strike (ball), etc.; move about in lively or unrestrained way; (often + *on*) touch gently; pretend to (an emotion); allow (fish) to exhaust itself pulling against line. ● *noun* recreation; amusement; playing of game; dramatic piece for stage etc.; freedom of movement; fitful or light movement; gambling. □ **play along** pretend to cooperate; **play back** play (what has been recorded); **play-back** *noun*; **play ball** *colloquial* cooperate; **playbill** poster announcing play etc.; **playboy** pleasure-seeking usually wealthy man; **play by ear** perform (music) without having seen it written down, (also **play it by ear**) *colloquial* proceed gradually according to results; **play one's cards right** *colloquial* make best use of opportunities and advantages; **play down** minimize; **playfellow** playmate; **play the game** behave honourably; **playground** outdoor area for children to play in; **playgroup** group of preschool children who play together under supervision; **playhouse** theatre; **playing card** small usually oblong card used in games, one of set of usually 52 divided into 4 suits; **play it cool** *colloquial* appear relaxed or indifferent; **playmate**

child's companion in play; **play-off** extra match played to decide draw or tie; **plaything** toy; **play up** behave mischievously, annoy in this way, cause trouble; **play with fire** take foolish risks; **playwright** dramatist. □ **player** *noun*.

playful *adjective* fond of or inclined to play; done in fun. □ **playfully** *adverb*; **playfulness** *noun*.

plc *abbreviation* (also **PLC**) Public Limited Company.

plea *noun* appeal, entreaty; *Law* formal statement by or on behalf of defendant; excuse.

pleach *verb* entwine or interlace (esp. branches to form a hedge).

plead *verb* (+ *with*) make earnest appeal to; address court as advocate or party; allege as excuse; (+ *guilty, not guilty*) declare oneself to be guilty or not guilty of a charge; make appeal or entreaty.

pleading *noun* (usually in *plural*) formal statement of cause of action or defence.

pleasant /ˈplez(ə)nt/ *adjective* (**-er**, **-est**) agreeable; giving pleasure. □ **pleasantly** *adverb*.

pleasantry *noun* (*plural* **-ies**) joking remark; polite remark.

please /pliːz/ *verb* (**-sing**) be agreeable to; give joy or gratification to; think fit; (in *passive*) be willing, like; *used in polite requests*. □ **pleased** *adjective*; **pleasing** *adjective*.

pleasurable /ˈpleʒərəb(ə)l/ *adjective* causing pleasure. □ **pleasurably** *adverb*.

pleasure /ˈpleʒə/ ● *noun* satisfaction, delight; sensuous enjoyment; source of gratification; will, choice. ● *adjective* done or used for pleasure.

pleat ● *noun* flattened fold in cloth etc. ● *verb* make pleat(s) in.

pleb *noun* *colloquial* plebeian.

plebeian /plɪˈbiːən/ ● *noun* commoner, esp. in ancient Rome; working-class person (esp. uncultured). ● *adjective* of the common people; uncultured, coarse.

plebiscite /ˈplebɪsaɪt/ *noun* referendum.

plectrum /ˈplektrəm/ *noun* (*plural* **-s** or **-tra**) thin flat piece of plastic etc. for

plucking strings of musical instrument.

pledge ● *noun* solemn promise; thing given as security for payment of debt etc.; thing put in pawn; token; drinking of health. ● *verb* (**-ging**) deposit as security, pawn; promise solemnly by pledge; bind by solemn promise; drink to the health of.

Pleiades /ˈplaɪədiːz/ *plural noun* cluster of stars in constellation Taurus.

plenary /ˈpliːnərɪ/ *adjective* (of assembly) to be attended by all members; entire, unqualified.

plenipotentiary /plenɪpəˈtenʃərɪ/ ● *noun* (*plural* **-ies**) person (esp. diplomat) having full authority to act. ● *adjective* having such power.

plenitude /ˈplenɪtjuːd/ *noun literary* fullness; completeness; abundance.

plenteous /ˈplentɪəs/ *adjective literary* plentiful.

plentiful /ˈplentɪfʊl/ *adjective* existing in ample quantity. □ **plentifully** *adverb.*

plenty /ˈplentɪ/ ● *noun* abundance; quite enough. ● *adjective colloquial* plentiful. ● *adverb colloquial* fully.

plenum /ˈpliːnəm/ *noun* full assembly of people or a committee etc.

pleonasm /ˈpliːənæz(ə)m/ *noun* use of more words than are needed. □ **pleonastic** /-ˈnæstɪk/ *adjective.*

plesiosaur /ˈpliːsɪəsɔː/ *noun* large extinct reptile with flippers and long neck.

plethora /ˈpleθərə/ *noun* overabundance.

pleurisy /ˈplʊərəsɪ/ *noun* inflammation of membrane enclosing lungs. □ **pleuritic** /-ˈrɪt-/ *adjective.*

plexus /ˈpleksəs/ *noun* (*plural* same or **plexuses**) network of nerves or blood vessels.

pliable /ˈplaɪəb(ə)l/ *adjective* easily bent or influenced; supple; compliant. □ **pliability** *noun.*

pliant /ˈplaɪənt/ *adjective* pliable. □ **pliancy** *noun.*

pliers /ˈplaɪəz/ *plural noun* pincers with parallel flat surfaces for bending wire etc.

plight¹ /plaɪt/ *noun* unfortunate condition or state.

plight² /plaɪt/ *verb archaic* pledge. □ **plight one's troth** promise to marry.

plimsoll /ˈplɪms(ə)l/ *noun* rubber-soled canvas shoe. □ **Plimsoll line**, **mark** marking on ship's side showing limit of legal submersion under various conditions.

plinth *noun* base supporting column, vase, statue, etc.

plod *verb* (**-dd-**) walk or work laboriously. □ **plodder** *noun.*

plonk¹ ● *verb* set down hurriedly or clumsily; (usually + *down*) set down firmly. ● *noun* heavy thud.

plonk² *noun colloquial* cheap or inferior wine.

plop ● *noun* sound as of smooth object dropping into water. ● *verb* (**-pp-**) (cause to) fall with plop. ● *adverb* with a plop.

plot ● *noun* small piece of land; plan or interrelationship of main events of tale, play, etc.; secret plan, conspiracy. ● *verb* (**-tt-**) make chart, diagram, graph, etc. of; hatch secret plans; devise secretly; mark on chart or diagram. □ **plotter** *noun.*

plough /plaʊ/ (*US* **plow**) ● *noun* implement for furrowing and turning over soil; similar instrument for clearing away snow etc. ● *verb* (often + *up, out,* etc.) turn up or extract with plough; furrow, make (furrow); (+ *through*) advance laboriously or cut or force way through; *colloquial* fail in exam. □ **plough back** reinvest (profits) in business; **ploughman** user of plough; **ploughman's lunch** meal of bread, cheese, pickles, etc.; **ploughshare** blade of plough.

plover /ˈplʌvə/ *noun* plump-breasted wading bird.

plow *US* = PLOUGH.

ploy *noun* manoeuvre to gain advantage.

pluck ● *verb* pick or pull out or away; strip (bird) of feathers; pull at, twitch; (+ *at*) tug or snatch at; sound (string of musical instrument) with finger or plectrum. ● *noun* courage; twitch; animal's heart, liver, and lungs. □ **pluck up** summon up (one's courage etc.).

plucky *adjective* (**-ier**, **-iest**) brave, spirited.

plug ● *noun* something fitting into hole or filling cavity; device of metal pins etc. for making electrical connection; spark plug; *colloquial* piece of free publicity; cake or stick of tobacco. ● *verb* (**-gg-**) (often + *up*) stop with plug; *slang* shoot; *colloquial* seek to popularize by frequent recommendation. □ **plug away** (often + *at*) *colloquial* work steadily; **plug-hole** hole for plug, esp. in sink or bath; **plug in** *verb* connect electrically by inserting plug into socket; **plug-in** *adjective* designed to be plugged into socket; **pull the plug** *colloquial* flush toilet; (+ *on*) put an end to by withdrawing resources etc.

plum *noun* roundish fleshy stone fruit; tree bearing this; reddish-purple colour; raisin; *colloquial* prized thing. □ **plum pudding** Christmas pudding.

plumage /ˈpluːmɪdʒ/ *noun* bird's feathers.

plumb /plʌm/ ● *noun* lead ball attached to line for testing water's depth or whether wall etc. is vertical. ● *adverb* exactly; vertically; *US slang* quite, utterly. ● *adjective* vertical. ● *verb* provide with plumbing; fit as part of plumbing system; work as plumber; test with plumb; experience (extreme feeling); learn detailed facts about. □ **plumb line** string with plumb attached.

plumber *noun* person who fits and repairs apparatus of water supply, heating, etc.

plumbing *noun* system or apparatus of water supply etc.; plumber's work.

plume /pluːm/ ● *noun* feather, esp. large and showy one; feathery ornament in hat, hair, etc.; feather-like formation, esp. of smoke. ● *verb* (**-ming**) furnish with plume(s); (**plume oneself on**, **upon**) pride oneself on.

plummet /ˈplʌmɪt/ ● *noun* plumb, plumb line; sounding line. ● *verb* (**-t-**) fall rapidly.

plummy *adjective* (**-ier**, **-iest**) *colloquial* (of voice) affectedly rich in tone; *colloquial* good, desirable.

plump[1] ● *adjective* having full rounded shape; fleshy. ● *verb* (often + *up*, *out*) make or become plump. □ **plumpness** *noun*.

plump[2] ● *verb* (+ *for*) decide on, choose. ● *noun* abrupt or heavy fall. ● *adverb* *colloquial* with plump.

plunder /ˈplʌndə/ ● *verb* rob or steal, esp. in war; embezzle. ● *noun* plundering; property plundered.

plunge ● *verb* (**-ging**) (usually + *in*, *into*) throw forcefully, dive, (cause to) enter into impetuously, immerse completely; move suddenly downward; move with a rush; *colloquial* run up gambling debts. ● *noun* plunging; dive; decisive step.

plunger *noun* part of mechanism that works with plunging or thrusting motion; rubber cup on handle for removing blockages by plunging action.

pluperfect /pluːˈpɜːfɪkt/ *Grammar* ● *adjective* expressing action completed prior to some past point of time. ● *noun* pluperfect tense.

plural /ˈplʊər(ə)l/ ● *adjective* more than one in number; denoting more than one. ● *noun* plural word, form, or number.

pluralism *noun* form of society in which minority groups retain independent traditions; holding of more than one office at a time. □ **pluralist** *noun*; **pluralistic** /-ˈlɪst-/ *adjective*.

plurality /plʊəˈrælɪtɪ/ *noun* (*plural* **-ies**) state of being plural; pluralism; large number; non-absolute majority (of votes etc.).

pluralize *verb* (also **-ise**) (**-zing** or **-sing**) make plural; express as plural.

plus ● *preposition* with addition of; (of temperature) above zero; *colloquial* having gained. ● *adjective* (after number) at least, (after grade) better than; *Mathematics* positive; additional, extra. ● *noun* plus sign; advantage. □ **plus sign** symbol (+) indicating addition or positive value.

■ **Usage** The use of *plus* as a conjunction, as in *they arrived late, plus they wanted a meal*, is considered incorrect except in very informal use.

plush ● *noun* cloth of silk, cotton, etc., with long soft pile. ● *adjective* made of plush; *colloquial* plushy.

plushy *adjective* (**-ier**, **-iest**) *colloquial* stylish, luxurious.

plutocracy /pluːˈtɒkrəsɪ/ *noun* (*plural* **-ies**) state in which power belongs to rich; wealthy élite. □ **plutocrat** /'plu:tə-kræt/ *noun*; **plutocratic** /-tə'kræt-/ *adjective*.

plutonium /plu:'təʊnɪəm/ *noun* radioactive metallic element.

pluvial /'plu:vɪəl/ *adjective* of or caused by rain.

ply[1] /plaɪ/ *noun* (*plural* **-ies**) thickness; layer; strand.

ply[2] /plaɪ/ *verb* (**-ies**, **-ied**) wield; work at; (+ *with*) supply continuously or approach repeatedly with; (often + *between*) (of vehicle etc.) go to and fro.

plywood *noun* strong thin board made by gluing layers of wood with the direction of the grain alternating.

PM *abbreviation* prime minister.

p.m. *abbreviation* after noon (*post meridiem*).

PMS *abbreviation* premenstrual syndrome.

PMT *abbreviation* premenstrual tension.

pneumatic /nju:'mætɪk/ *adjective* filled with air or wind; operated by compressed air.

pneumonia /nju:'məʊnɪə/ *noun* inflammation of lung(s).

PO *abbreviation* Post Office; postal order; Petty Officer; Pilot Officer.

po *noun* (*plural* **-s**) *colloquial* chamber pot. □ **po-faced** solemn-faced, humourless, smug.

poach[1] *verb* cook (egg) without shell in boiling water; cook (fish etc.) by simmering in small amount of liquid. □ **poacher** *noun*.

poach[2] *verb* catch (game or fish) illicitly; (often + *on*) trespass, encroach; appropriate (another's ideas, staff, etc.). □ **poacher** *noun*.

pock *noun* (also **pock-mark**) small pus-filled spot, esp. in smallpox. □ **pock-marked** *adjective*.

pocket /'pɒkɪt/ ● *noun* small bag sewn into or on garment for carrying small articles; pouchlike compartment in suitcase, car door, etc.; financial resources; isolated group or area; cavity in earth etc. containing ore; pouch at corner or on side of billiard or snooker table into which balls are driven. ● *adjective* small, esp. small enough for carrying in pocket. ● *verb* (**-t-**) put into pocket; appropriate; submit to (affront

etc.); conceal (feelings). □ **in** or **out of pocket** having gained or lost in transaction; **pocketbook** notebook, folding case for papers, paper money, etc.; **pocket knife** small folding knife; **pocket money** money for minor expenses, esp. given to child.

pod ● *noun* long seed vessel, esp. of pea or bean. ● *verb* (**-dd-**) form pods; remove (peas etc.) from pods.

podgy /'pɒdʒɪ/ *adjective* (**-ier**, **-iest**) short and fat.

podium /'pəʊdɪəm/ *noun* (*plural* **-s** or **podia**) rostrum.

poem /'pəʊɪm/ *noun* metrical composition; elevated composition in verse or prose; something with poetic qualities.

poesy /'pəʊəzɪ/ *noun archaic* poetry.

poet /'pəʊɪt/ *noun* (*feminine* **poetess**) writer of poems. □ **Poet Laureate** poet appointed to write poems for state occasions.

poetaster /pəʊɪ'tæstə/ *noun* inferior poet.

poetic /pəʊ'etɪk/ *adjective* (also **poetical**) of or like poetry or poets. □ **poetic justice** well-deserved punishment or reward; **poetic licence** departure from truth etc. for effect. □ **poetically** *adverb*.

poetry /'pəʊɪtrɪ/ *noun* poet's art or work; poems; poetic or tenderly pleasing quality.

pogo /'pəʊgəʊ/ *noun* (*plural* **-s**) (also **pogo stick**) stiltlike toy with spring, used to jump about on.

pogrom /'pɒgrəm/ *noun* organized massacre (originally of Jews in Russia).

poignant /'pɔɪnjənt/ *adjective* painfully sharp, deeply moving; arousing sympathy; pleasantly piquant. □ **poignance** *noun*; **poignancy** *noun*; **poignantly** *adverb*.

poinsettia /pɔɪn'setɪə/ *noun* plant with large scarlet bracts surrounding small yellowish flowers.

point ● *noun* sharp end, tip; geometric entity with position but no magnitude; particular place; precise moment; very small mark on surface; decimal point; stage or degree in progress or increase; single item or particular; unit of scoring in games etc., or in evaluation etc.;

significant thing, thing actually intended or under discussion; sense, purpose, advantage; characteristic; each of 32 directions marked on compass; (usually in plural) pair of tapering movable rails to direct train from one line to another; power point; Cricket (position of) fielder near batsman on off side; promontory. ● verb (usually + to, at) direct (finger, weapon, etc.); direct attention; (+ at, towards) aim or be directed to; (+ to) indicate; give force to (words, action); fill joints of (brickwork) with smoothed mortar or cement; (of dog) indicate presence of game by acting as pointer. □ at or on the point of on the verge of; point-blank at close range, directly, flatly; point-duty traffic control by police officer; point of view position from which thing is viewed, way of considering a matter; point out indicate, draw attention to; point-to-point steeplechase for hunting horses; point up emphasize.

pointed adjective having point; (of remark etc.) cutting, emphasized. □ **pointedly** adverb.

pointer noun indicator on gauge etc.; rod for pointing at features on screen etc.; colloquial hint; dog of breed trained to stand rigid looking at game.

pointless adjective purposeless, meaningless; ineffective. ● **pointlessly** adverb; **pointlessness** noun.

poise /pɔɪz/ ● noun composure; equilibrium; carriage (of head etc.). ● verb (-sing) balance, hold suspended or supported; be balanced or suspended.

poised adjective self-assured; carrying oneself with dignity; (often + for) ready.

poison /ˈpɔɪz(ə)n/ ● noun substance that when absorbed by living organism kills or injures it; colloquial harmful influence. ● verb administer poison to; kill or injure with poison; treat (weapon) with poison; corrupt, pervert; spoil. □ **poison ivy** N. American climbing plant secreting irritant oil from leaves; **poison-pen letter** malicious anonymous letter. □ **poisoner** noun; **poisonous** adjective.

poke ● verb (-king) push with (end of) finger, stick, etc.; (+ out, up, etc.) (be)

thrust forward; (+ at etc.) make thrusts; (+ in) produce (hole etc.) in by poking; stir (fire). ● noun poking; thrust, nudge. □ **poke fun at** ridicule.

poker[1] noun metal rod for stirring fire.

poker[2] /ˈpəʊkə/ noun card game in which players bet on value of their hands. □ **poker-face** impassive countenance assumed by poker player.

poky /ˈpəʊkɪ/ adjective (-ier, -iest) (of room etc.) small and cramped.

polar /ˈpəʊlə/ adjective of or near either pole of earth etc.; having magnetic or electric polarity; directly opposite in character. □ **polar bear** large white bear living in Arctic.

polarity /pəˈlærɪtɪ/ noun (plural -ies) tendency of magnet etc. to point to earth's magnetic poles or of body to lie with axis in particular direction; possession of two poles having contrary qualities; possession of two opposite tendencies, opinions, etc.; electrical condition of body (positive or negative).

polarize /ˈpəʊləraɪz/ verb (also -ise) (-zing or -sing) restrict vibrations of (light-waves etc.) to one direction; give polarity to; divide into two opposing groups. □ **polarization** noun.

Polaroid /ˈpəʊlərɔɪd/ noun proprietary term material in thin sheets polarizing light passing through it; camera that produces print immediately after each exposure; (in plural) sunglasses with Polaroid lenses.

Pole noun native or national of Poland.

pole[1] noun long slender rounded piece of wood, metal, etc., esp. as support etc.; historical measure of length ($5\frac{1}{2}$ yds). □ **pole-vault** jump over high bar with aid of pole held in hands.

pole[2] noun each of two points in celestial sphere (in full **north**, **south pole**) about which stars appear to revolve; each end of axis of earth (in full **North**, **South Pole**) or of other body; each of two opposite points on surface of magnet at which magnetic forces are strongest; positive or negative terminal of electric cell, battery, etc.; each of two opposed principles. □ **pole star** star near N. pole of heavens, thing serving as guide.

poleaxe /ˈpəʊlæks/ (US **-ax**) ● noun historical battleaxe; butcher's axe. ● verb

(-xing) hit or kill with poleaxe; (esp. as **poleaxed** *adjective*) *colloquial* dumbfound, overwhelm.

polecat /'pəʊlkæt/ *noun* small dark brown mammal of weasel family.

polemic /pə'lemɪk/ ● *noun* verbal attack; controversy; (in *plural*) art of controversial discussion. ● *adjective* (also **polemical**) involving dispute, controversial. □ **polemicist** /-sɪst/ *noun*.

police /pə'liːs/ ● *noun* (treated as *plural*) civil force responsible for maintaining public order; its members; force with similar functions. ● *verb* (**-cing**) control or provide with police; keep in order, control, administer. □ **police dog** dog used in police work; **police force** body of police of country, district, or town; **policeman**, **policewoman**, **police officer** member of police force; **police state** totalitarian state controlled by political police; **police station** office of local police force.

policy[1] /'pɒlɪsɪ/ *noun* (*plural* **-ies**) course of action adopted by government, business, etc.; prudent conduct.

policy[2] /'pɒlɪsɪ/ *noun* (*plural* **-ies**) (document containing) contract of insurance. □ **policyholder** person or body holding insurance policy.

polio /'pəʊlɪəʊ/ *noun* poliomyelitis.

poliomyelitis /ˌpəʊlɪəʊmaɪə'laɪtɪs/ *noun* infectious viral disease of grey matter of central nervous system, with temporary or permanent paralysis.

Polish /'pəʊlɪʃ/ ● *adjective* of Poland. ● *noun* language of Poland.

polish /'pɒlɪʃ/ ● *verb* (often + *up*) make or become smooth or glossy by rubbing; (esp. as **polished** *adjective*) refine, improve. ● *noun* substance used for polishing; smoothness, glossiness; refinement. □ **polish off** finish quickly.

polite /pə'laɪt/ *adjective* (**-r**, **-st**) having good manners, courteous, cultivated, refined. □ **politely** *adverb*; **politeness** *noun*.

politic /'pɒlɪtɪk/ ● *adjective* judicious, expedient; prudent, sagacious. ● *verb* (**-ck-**) engage in politics.

political /pə'lɪtɪk(ə)l/ *adjective* of state or its government; of public affairs; of, engaged in, or taking a side in politics; relating to pursuit of power, status, etc.;

□ **political asylum** state protection for foreign refugee; **political correctness** avoidance of language or action which excludes ethnic or cultural minorities; **political economy** study of economic aspects of government; **political geography** geography dealing with boundaries etc. of states; **political prisoner** person imprisoned for political reasons.

politically *adverb* in a political way. □ **politically correct** exhibiting political correctness.

politician /ˌpɒlɪ'tɪʃ(ə)n/ *noun* person engaged in politics.

politicize /pə'lɪtɪsaɪz/ *verb* (also **-ise**) (**-zing** or **-sing**) give political character or awareness to.

politics /'pɒlɪtɪks/ *plural noun* (treated as *singular* or *plural*) art and science of government; political life, affairs, principles, etc.; activities relating to pursuit of power, status, etc.

polity /'pɒlɪtɪ/ *noun* (*plural* **-ies**) form of civil administration; organized society, state.

polka /'pɒlkə/ ● *noun* lively dance; music for this. ● *verb* (**-kas**, **-kaed** /-kəd/ or **-ka'd**, **-kaing** /-kəɪŋ/) dance polka. □ **polka dot** round dot as one of many forming regular pattern on textile fabric etc.

poll /pəʊl/ ● *noun* (often in *plural*) voting; counting of votes; result of voting, number of votes recorded; questioning of sample of population to estimate trend of public opinion; head. ● *verb* take or receive vote(s) of, vote; record opinion of (person, group); cut off top of (tree etc.) or (esp. as **polled** *adjective*) horns of (cattle). □ **polling booth** cubicle where voter stands to mark ballot paper; **polling station** building used for voting; **poll tax** *historical* tax levied on every adult.

pollack /'pɒlək/ *noun* (also **pollock**) (*plural* same or **-s**) edible marine fish related to cod.

pollard /'pɒləd/ ● *noun* hornless animal; tree polled to produce close head of young branches. ● *verb* make pollard of (tree).

pollen /'pɒlən/ *noun* fertilizing powder discharged from flower's anther.

□ **pollen count** index of amount of pollen in air.

pollinate /ˈpɒlɪneɪt/ *verb* (**-ting**) sprinkle (stigma of flower) with pollen. □ **pollination** *noun*.

pollock = POLLACK.

pollster *noun* person who organizes opinion poll.

pollute /pəˈluːt/ *verb* (**-ting**) contaminate; make impure. □ **pollutant** *noun*; **polluter** *noun*; **pollution** *noun*.

polo /ˈpəʊləʊ/ *noun* game like hockey played on horseback. □ **polo-neck** (sweater with) high round turned-over collar.

polonaise /pɒləˈneɪz/ *noun* slow processional dance; music for this.

poltergeist /ˈpɒltəɡaɪst/ *noun* noisy mischievous ghost.

poltroon /pɒlˈtruːn/ *noun* coward. □ **poltroonery** *noun*.

poly- *combining form* many; polymerized.

polyandry /ˈpɒliændrɪ/ *noun* polygamy in which one woman has more than one husband.

polyanthus /pɒliˈænθəs/ *noun* (*plural* **-thuses**) cultivated primula.

polychromatic /pɒlikrəʊˈmætɪk/ *adjective* many-coloured.

polychrome /ˈpɒlikrəʊm/ ● *adjective* in many colours. ● *noun* polychrome work of art.

polyester /pɒliˈestə/ *noun* synthetic fibre or resin.

polyethylene /pɒliˈeθɪliːn/ *noun* polythene.

polygamy /pəˈlɪɡəmɪ/ *noun* practice of having more than one wife or husband at once. □ **polygamist** *noun*, **polygamous** *adjective*.

polyglot /ˈpɒliɡlɒt/ ● *adjective* knowing, using, or written in several languages. ● *noun* polyglot person.

polygon /ˈpɒliɡən/ *noun* figure with many sides and angles. □ **polygonal** /pəˈlɪɡ-/ *adjective*.

polyhedron /pɒliˈhiːdrən/ *noun* (*plural* **-dra**) solid figure with many faces. □ **polyhedral** *adjective*.

polymath /ˈpɒlimæθ/ *noun* person of great or varied learning.

polymer /ˈpɒlimə/ *noun* compound of molecule(s) formed from repeated units of smaller molecules. □ **polymeric** /-ˈmer-/ *adjective*; **polymerization** *noun*; **polymerize** *verb* (also **-ise**) (**-zing** or **-sing**).

polyp /ˈpɒlɪp/ *noun* simple organism with tube-shaped body; small growth on mucous membrane.

polyphony /pəˈlɪfənɪ/ *noun* (*plural* **-ies**) contrapuntal music. □ **polyphonic** /pɒliˈfɒnɪk/ *adjective*.

polypropylene /pɒliˈprəʊpɪliːn/ *noun* any of various thermoplastic materials used for films, fibres, or moulding.

polystyrene /pɒliˈstaɪəriːn/ *noun* kind of hard plastic.

polysyllabic /pɒlɪsɪˈlæbɪk/ *adjective* having many syllables; using polysyllables.

polysyllable /ˈpɒlɪsɪləb(ə)l/ *noun* polysyllabic word.

polytechnic /pɒliˈteknɪk/ *noun* college providing courses in esp. vocational subjects up to degree level.

polytheism /ˈpɒliθiːɪz(ə)m/ *noun* belief in or worship of more than one god. □ **polytheistic** /-ˈɪst-/ *adjective*.

polythene /ˈpɒliθiːn/ *noun* a tough light plastic.

polyunsaturated /pɒliʌnˈsætʃəreɪtɪd/ *adjective* (of fat) containing several double or triple bonds in each molecule and therefore capable of combining with hydrogen and not associated with accumulation of cholesterol.

polyurethane /pɒliˈjʊərəθeɪn/ *noun* synthetic resin or plastic used esp. in paints or foam.

polyvinyl chloride /pɒliˈvaɪnɪl/ *noun* see PVC.

pomade /pəˈmɑːd/ *noun* scented ointment for hair.

pomander /pəˈmændə/ *noun* ball of mixed aromatic substances; container for this.

pomegranate /ˈpɒmɪɡrænɪt/ *noun* tropical tough-rinded many-seeded fruit; tree bearing this.

pommel /ˈpʌm(ə)l/ *noun* knob of sword hilt; projecting front of saddle.

pomp *noun* splendid display, splendour; specious glory.

pom-pom /ˈpɒmpɒm/ *noun* automatic quick-firing gun.

pompon /ˈpɒmpɒn/ *noun* (also **pompom**) decorative tuft or ball on hat, shoe, etc.

pompous /ˈpɒmpəs/ *adjective* self-important, affectedly grand or solemn. □ **pomposity** /-ˈpɒs-/ *noun* (*plural* **-ies**); **pompously** *adverb*; **pompousness** *noun*.

ponce *slang* ● *noun* man who lives off prostitute's earnings. ● *verb* (**-cing**) act as ponce. □ **ponce about** move about effeminately.

poncho /ˈpɒntʃəʊ/ *noun* (*plural* **-s**) cloak of rectangular piece of material with slit in middle for head.

pond *noun* small body of still water.

ponder /ˈpɒndə/ *verb* think over; muse.

ponderable /ˈpɒndərəb(ə)l/ *adjective literary* having appreciable weight.

ponderous /ˈpɒndərəs/ *adjective* heavy and unwieldy; laborious, dull. □ **ponderously** *adverb*; **ponderousness** *noun*.

pong *noun & verb colloquial* stink. □ **pongy** *adjective* (**-ier**, **-iest**).

poniard /ˈpɒnjəd/ *noun* dagger.

pontiff /ˈpɒntɪf/ *noun* Pope.

pontifical /pɒnˈtɪfɪk(ə)l/ *adjective* papal; pompously dogmatic.

pontificate ● *verb* /pɒnˈtɪfɪkeɪt/ (**-ting**) be pompously dogmatic. ● *noun* /pɒnˈtɪfɪkət/ office of bishop or Pope; period of this.

pontoon[1] /pɒnˈtuːn/ *noun* card game in which players try to acquire cards with face value totalling 21.

pontoon[2] /pɒnˈtuːn/ *noun* flat-bottomed boat; boat etc. as one of supports for temporary bridge.

pony /ˈpəʊnɪ/ *noun* (*plural* **-ies**) horse of any small breed. □ **pony-tail** hair drawn back, tied, and hanging down behind head; **pony-trekking** travelling across country on ponies for pleasure.

poodle /ˈpuːd(ə)l/ *noun* dog of breed with thick curling hair.

pooh /puː/ *interjection expressing contempt or disgust.* □ **pooh-pooh** express contempt for, ridicule.

pool[1] *noun* small body of still water; small shallow body of any liquid; swimming pool; deep place in river.

pool[2] ● *noun* common supply of people, vehicles, etc., for sharing by group; group of people sharing duties etc.; common fund, e.g. of profits or of gamblers' stakes; arrangement between competing parties to fix prices and share business; game like billiards with usually 16 balls; (**the pools**) football pool. ● *verb* put into common fund; share in common.

poop *noun* stern of ship; furthest aft and highest deck.

poor /pʊə/ *adjective* having little money or means; (+ *in*) deficient in; inadequate; inferior; deserving pity; despicable. □ **poor man's** inferior substitute for.

poorly ● *adverb* in poor manner; badly. ● *adjective* unwell.

pop[1] ● *noun* abrupt explosive sound; *colloquial* effervescent drink. ● *verb* (**-pp-**) (cause to) make pop; (+ *in*, *out*, *up*, etc.) move, come, or put unexpectedly or suddenly; *slang* pawn. ● *adverb* with the sound pop. □ **popcorn** maize kernels which burst open when heated; **pop-eyed** *colloquial* with eyes bulging or wide open; **popgun** toy gun shooting pellet etc. by compressed air or spring; **popping crease** *Cricket* line in front of and parallel to wicket; **pop-up** involving parts that pop up automatically.

pop[2] *noun colloquial* (in full **pop music**) highly successful commercial music; pop record or song. □ **pop art** art based on modern popular culture and the mass media; **pop culture** commercial culture based on popular taste; **pop group** ensemble playing pop music.

pop[3] *noun esp. US colloquial* father.

popadam = POPPADAM.

pope *noun* (also **Pope**) head of RC Church.

popinjay /ˈpɒpɪndʒeɪ/ *noun* fop, conceited person.

poplar /ˈpɒplə/ *noun* slender tree with straight trunk and often tremulous leaves.

poplin /ˈpɒplɪn/ *noun* closely woven corded fabric.

poppadam /ˈpɒpədəm/ *noun* (also **poppadom**, **popadam**) thin crisp spiced Indian bread.

popper *noun colloquial* press-stud; thing that pops.

poppet /ˈpɒpɪt/ *noun colloquial* (esp. as term of endearment) small or dainty person.

poppy /'pɒpɪ/ *noun* (*plural* **-ies**) plant with bright flowers and milky narcotic juice; artificial poppy worn on Remembrance Sunday. □ **Poppy Day** Remembrance Sunday.

poppycock /'pɒpɪkɒk/ *noun slang* nonsense.

populace /'pɒpjʊləs/ *noun* the common people.

popular /'pɒpjʊlə/ *adjective* generally liked or admired; of, for, or prevalent among the general public. □ **popularity** /-'lærɪtɪ/ *noun*; **popularize** *verb* (also **-ise**) (**-zing** or **-sing**); **popularly** *adverb*.

populate /'pɒpjʊleɪt/ *verb* (**-ting**) form population of; supply with inhabitants.

population /pɒpjʊ'leɪʃ(ə)n/ *noun* inhabitants of town, country, etc.; total number of these.

populous /'pɒpjʊləs/ *adjective* thickly inhabited.

porcelain /'pɔːsəlɪn/ *noun* fine translucent ceramic; things made of this.

porch *noun* covered entrance to building.

porcine /'pɔːsaɪn/ *adjective* of or like pigs.

porcupine /'pɔːkjʊpaɪn/ *noun* large rodent with body and tail covered with erectile spines.

pore[1] *noun* minute opening in surface through which fluids may pass.

pore[2] *verb* (**-ring**) (+ *over*) be absorbed in studying (book etc.).

pork *noun* flesh of pig used as food.

porker *noun* pig raised for food.

porn (also **porno**) *colloquial* ● *noun* pornography. ● *adjective* pornographic.

pornography /pɔː'nɒɡrəfɪ/ *noun* explicit presentation of sexual activity in literature, films, etc., to stimulate erotic rather than aesthetic feelings. □ **pornographic** /-nə'ɡræf-/ *adjective*.

porous /'pɔːrəs/ *adjective* having pores; permeable. □ **porosity** /-'rɒs-/ *noun*.

porphyry /'pɔːfɪrɪ/ *noun* (*plural* **-ies**) hard rock with feldspar crystals in fine-grained red mass.

porpoise /'pɔːpəs/ *noun* sea mammal of whale family.

porridge /'pɒrɪdʒ/ *noun* oatmeal or other cereal boiled in water or milk.

porringer /'pɒrɪndʒə/ *noun* small soup-bowl.

port[1] *noun* harbour; town possessing harbour.

port[2] *noun* strong sweet fortified wine.

port[3] ● *noun* left-hand side of ship or aircraft looking forward. ● *verb* turn (helm) to port.

port[4] *noun* opening in ship's side for entrance, loading, etc.; porthole. □ **porthole** (esp. glazed) aperture in ship's side to admit light.

portable /'pɔːtəb(ə)l/ *adjective* easily movable, convenient for carrying; adaptable in altered circumstances. □ **portability** *noun*.

portage /'pɔːtɪdʒ/ *noun* carrying of boats or goods between two navigable waters.

Portakabin /'pɔːtəkæbɪn/ *noun proprietary term* prefabricated small building.

portal /'pɔːt(ə)l/ *noun* doorway, gate.

portcullis /pɔːt'kʌlɪs/ *noun* strong heavy grating lowered in defence of fortress gateway.

portend /pɔː'tend/ *verb* foreshadow as an omen; give warning of.

portent /'pɔːtent/ *noun* omen, significant sign; marvellous thing.

portentous /pɔː'tentəs/ *adjective* like or being portent; pompously solemn.

porter[1] /'pɔːtə/ *noun* person employed to carry luggage etc.; dark beer brewed from charred or browned malt. □ **porterhouse steak** choice cut of beef.

porter[2] /'pɔːtə/ *noun* gatekeeper or doorkeeper, esp. of large building.

porterage *noun* (charge for) hire of porters.

portfolio /pɔːt'fəʊlɪəʊ/ *noun* (*plural* **-s**) folder for loose sheets of paper, drawings, etc.; samples of artist's work; list of investments held by investor etc.; office of government minister. □ **Minister without Portfolio** government minister not in charge of department.

portico /'pɔːtɪkəʊ/ *noun* (*plural* **-es** or **-s**) colonnade; roof supported by columns, usually serving as porch to building.

portion /'pɔːʃ(ə)n/ ● *noun* part, share; helping; destiny or lot. ● *verb* divide into portions; (+ *out*) distribute.

Portland /'pɔːtlənd/ *noun* □ **Portland cement** cement manufactured from chalk and clay; **Portland stone** a valuable building limestone.

portly /'pɔːtlɪ/ *adjective* (**-ier**, **-iest**) corpulent.

portmanteau /pɔːt'mæntəʊ/ *noun* (*plural* **-s** or **-x** /-z/) case for clothes etc., opening into two equal parts. □ **portmanteau word** word combining sounds and meanings of two others.

portrait /'pɔːtrɪt/ *noun* drawing, painting, photograph, etc. of person or animal; description.

portraiture /'pɔːtrɪtʃə/ *noun* portraying; description; portrait.

portray /pɔː'treɪ/ *verb* make likeness of; describe. □ **portrayal** *noun*.

Portuguese /pɔːtʃʊ'giːz/ *noun* (*plural* same) native, national, or language of Portugal. ● *adjective* of Portugal.

pose /pəʊz/ ● *verb* (**-sing**) assume attitude, esp. for artistic purpose; (+ *as*) pretend to be; behave affectedly for effect; propound (question, problem); arrange in required attitude. ● *noun* attitude of body or mind; affectation, pretence.

poser *noun* poseur; *colloquial* puzzling question or problem.

poseur /pəʊ'zɜː/ *noun* person who behaves affectedly.

posh *colloquial* ● *adjective* smart; upperclass. ● *adverb* in an upper-class way. □ **poshly** *adverb*; **poshness** *noun*.

posit /'pɒzɪt/ *verb* (**-t-**) assume as fact, postulate.

position /pə'zɪʃ(ə)n/ ● *noun* place occupied by person or thing; way thing is placed; proper place; advantage; mental attitude; situation; rank, status; paid employment; strategic location. ● *verb* place in position. □ **in a position to** able to. □ **positional** *adjective*.

positive /'pɒzɪtɪv/ ● *adjective* explicit, definite, unquestionable; convinced, confident, cocksure; absolute, not relative; *Grammar* (of adjective or adverb) expressing simple quality without comparison; constructive; marked by presence and not absence of qualities; favourable; dealing only with matters of fact, practical; *Mathematics* (of quantity) greater than zero; *Electricity* of, containing, or producing kind of charge produced by rubbing glass with silk;

Photography showing lights and shades or colours as seen in original image. ● *noun* positive adjective, photograph, quantity, etc. □ **positive discrimination** making distinctions in favour of groups believed to be underprivileged; **positive vetting** inquiry into background etc. of candidate for post involving national security. □ **positively** *adverb*; **positiveness** *noun*.

positivism *noun* philosophical system recognizing only facts and observable phenomena. □ **positivist** *noun & adjective*.

positron /'pɒzɪtrɒn/ *noun* elementary particle with same mass as but opposite charge to electron.

posse /'pɒsɪ/ *noun* strong force or company; group of law-enforcers.

possess /pə'zes/ *verb* hold as property, own; have; occupy, dominate mind of. □ **possessor** *noun*.

possession /pə'zeʃ(ə)n/ *noun* possessing, being possessed; thing possessed; occupancy; (in *plural*) property; control of ball by player.

possessive /pə'zesɪv/ ● *adjective* wanting to retain what one possesses; jealous and domineering; *Grammar* indicating possession. ● *noun Grammar* possessive case or word. □ **possessiveness** *noun*.

possibility /pɒsɪ'bɪlɪtɪ/ *noun* (*plural* **-ies**) state or fact of being possible; thing that may exist or happen; (usually in *plural*) capability of being used.

possible /'pɒsɪb(ə)l/ ● *adjective* capable of existing, happening, being done, etc.; potential. ● *noun* possible candidate, member of team, etc.; highest possible score.

possibly *adverb* perhaps; in accordance with possibility.

possum /'pɒsəm/ *noun colloquial* opossum. □ **play possum** *colloquial* pretend to be unconscious or unaware.

post[1] /pəʊst/ ● *noun* upright of timber or metal as support in building, to mark boundary, carry notices, etc.; pole etc. marking start or finish of race. ● *verb* (often + *up*) display (notice etc.) in prominent place; advertise by poster or list.

post[2] /pəʊst/ ● *noun* official conveying of parcels, letters, etc.; single collection or delivery of these; letters etc. dispatched; place where letters etc. are collected. ● *verb* put (letter etc.) into post; (esp. as **posted** *adjective*) (often + *up*) supply with information; enter in ledger. □ **postbox** public box for posting mail; **postcard** card for posting without envelope; **postcode** group of letters and figures in postal address to assist sorting; **post-haste** with great speed; **postman**, **postwoman** person who collects or delivers post; **postmark** official mark on letters to cancel stamp; **postmaster**, **postmistress** official in charge of post office; **post office** room or building for postal business; **Post Office** public department or corporation providing postal services.

post³ /pəʊst/ ● *noun* appointed place of soldier etc. on duty; occupying force; fort; paid employment; trading post. ● *verb* place (soldier etc.) at post; appoint to post or command.

post- *prefix* after, behind.

postage *noun* charge for sending letter etc. by post. □ **postage stamp** small adhesive label indicating amount of postage paid.

postal *adjective* of or by post. □ **postal order** money order issued by Post Office.

postdate /pəʊst'deɪt/ *verb* (**-ting**) give later than actual date to; follow in time.

poster *noun* placard in public place; large printed picture. □ **poster paint** gummy opaque paint.

poste restante /pəʊst re'stɑ̃t/ *noun* department in post office where letters are kept till called for.

posterior /pɒ'stɪərɪə/ ● *adjective* later in time or order; at the back. ● *noun* (in *singular* or *plural*) buttocks.

posterity /pɒ'sterɪtɪ/ *noun* later generations; descendants.

postern /'pɒst(ə)n/ *noun archaic* back or side entrance.

postgraduate /pəʊst'grædjʊət/ ● *noun* person on course of study after taking first degree. ● *adjective* relating to postgraduates.

posthumous /'pɒstjʊməs/ *adjective* occurring after death; published after author's death; born after father's death. □ **posthumously** *adverb*.

postilion /pɒ'stɪljən/ *noun* (also **postillion**) rider on near horse of team drawing coach etc. without coachman.

post-impressionism /pəʊstɪm'preʃənɪz(ə)m/ *noun* art intending to express individual artist's conception of objects represented. □ **post-impressionist** *noun & adjective*.

post-industrial /pəʊstɪn'dʌstrɪəl/ *adjective* of society or economy no longer reliant on heavy industry.

post-mortem /pəʊst'mɔːtəm/ ● *noun* examination of body made after death; *colloquial* discussion after conclusion (of game etc.). ● *adverb & adjective* after death.

postnatal /pəʊst'neɪt(ə)l/ *adjective* existing or occurring after birth.

postpone /pəʊst'pəʊn/ *verb* (**-ning**) cause to take place at later time. □ **postponement** *noun*.

postscript /'pəʊstskrɪpt/ *noun* addition at end of letter etc. after signature.

postulant /'pɒstjʊlənt/ *noun* candidate, esp. for admission to religious order.

postulate ● *verb* /'pɒstjʊleɪt/ (**-ting**) (often + *that*) assume or require to be true, take for granted; claim. ● *noun* /'pɒstjʊlət/ thing postulated; prerequisite.

posture /'pɒstʃə/ ● *noun* relative position of parts, esp. of body; bearing; mental attitude; condition or state (of affairs etc.). ● *verb* (**-ring**) assume posture, esp. for effect; pose (person).

postwar /pəʊst'wɔː/ *adjective* occurring or existing after a war.

posy /'pəʊzɪ/ *noun* (*plural* **-ies**) small bunch of flowers.

pot¹ ● *noun* rounded ceramic, metal, or glass vessel; flowerpot, teapot, etc.; contents of pot; chamber pot; total amount bet in game etc.; (usually in *plural*) *colloquial* large sum; *slang* cup etc. as prize. ● *verb* (**-tt-**) plant in pot; (usually as **potted** *adjective*) preserve (food) in sealed pot; pocket (ball) in billiards etc.; abridge, epitomize; shoot at, hit, or kill (animal). □ **go to pot** *colloquial* be ruined; **pot-belly** protuberant belly; **pot-boiler** work of literature etc. done merely to earn money; **pot-herb** herb grown in kitchen garden; **pothole** deep hole in rock, hole in road surface; **potluck** whatever is available; **pot**

plant plant grown in flowerpot; **pot roast** piece of braised meat; **pot-roast** braise; **potsherd** broken piece of ceramic material; **pot-shot** random shot. □ **potful** noun (plural **-s**).

pot² noun slang marijuana.

potable /'pəʊtəb(ə)l/ adjective drinkable.

potash /'pɒtæʃ/ noun any of various compounds of potassium.

potassium /pə'tæsɪəm/ noun soft silver-white metallic element.

potation /pə'teɪʃ(ə)n/ noun a drink; drinking.

potato /pə'teɪtəʊ/ noun (plural **-es**) edible plant tuber; plant bearing this. □ **potato crisp** crisp.

poteen /pɒ'tʃiːn/ noun Irish illicit distilled spirit.

potent /'pəʊt(ə)nt/ adjective powerful, strong; cogent; (of male) able to achieve erection of penis or have sexual intercourse. □ **potency** noun.

potentate /'pəʊtənteɪt/ noun monarch, ruler.

potential /pə'tenʃ(ə)l/ ● adjective capable of coming into being; latent. ● noun capability for use or development; usable resources; quantity determining energy of mass in gravitational field or of charge in electric field. □ **potentiality** /-ʃɪ'æl-/ noun; **potentially** adverb.

pother /'pɒðə/ noun literary din, fuss.

potion /'pəʊʃ(ə)n/ noun liquid dose of medicine, poison, etc.

pot-pourri /pəʊ'pʊərɪ/ noun (plural **-s**) scented mixture of dried petals and spices; musical or literary medley.

pottage /'pɒtɪdʒ/ noun archaic soup, stew.

potter¹ /'pɒtə/ verb (often + about, around) work etc. in aimless or desultory manner; go slowly.

potter² /'pɒtə/ noun maker of ceramic vessels.

pottery /'pɒtərɪ/ noun (plural **-ies**) vessels etc. made of baked clay; potter's work or workshop.

potty¹ /'pɒtɪ/ adjective (**-ier**, **-iest**) slang crazy; insignificant. □ **pottiness** noun.

potty² noun (plural **-ies**) colloquial chamber pot, esp. for child.

pouch ● noun small bag, detachable pocket; baggy area of skin under eyes

etc.; baglike receptacle in which marsupials carry undeveloped young, other baglike natural structure. ● verb put or make into pouch; take possession of.

pouffe /puːf/ noun firm cushion as low seat or footstool.

poulterer /'pəʊltərə/ noun dealer in poultry and usually game.

poultice /'pəʊltɪs/ ● noun soft usually hot dressing applied to sore or inflamed part of body. ● verb (**-cing**) apply poultice to.

poultry /'pəʊltrɪ/ noun domestic fowls.

pounce ● verb (**-cing**) spring, swoop; (often + on, upon) make sudden attack, seize eagerly. ● noun act of pouncing.

pound¹ noun unit of weight equal to 16 oz (454 g); (in full **pound sterling**) monetary unit of UK etc.

pound² verb crush or beat with repeated strokes; (+ at, on) deliver heavy blows or gunfire to; (+ along etc.) walk, run, etc. heavily.

pound³ noun enclosure where stray animals or officially removed vehicles are kept until claimed.

poundage noun commission or fee of so much per pound sterling or weight.

-pounder combining form thing or person weighing specified number of pounds; gun firing shell weighing specified number of pounds.

pour /pɔː/ verb (usually + down, out, over, etc.) (cause to) flow in stream or shower; dispense (drink); rain heavily; (usually + in, out, etc.) come or go in profusion or in a rush; discharge copiously.

pout ● verb push lips forward, esp. as sign of displeasure; (of lips) be pushed forward. ● noun pouting expression.

pouter noun kind of pigeon able to inflate crop.

poverty /'pɒvətɪ/ noun being poor, want; (often + of, in) scarcity, lack; inferiority, poorness. □ **poverty-stricken** very poor; **poverty trap** situation in which increase of income incurs greater loss of state benefits.

POW abbreviation prisoner of war.

powder /'paʊdə/ ● noun mass of fine dry particles; medicine or cosmetic in this form; gunpowder. ● *verb* apply powder to; (esp. as **powdered** *adjective*) reduce to powder. □ **powder blue** pale blue; **powder-puff** soft pad for applying cosmetic powder to skin; **powder-room** *euphemistic* women's lavatory. □ **powdery** *adjective*.

power /'paʊə/ ● *noun* ability to do or act; mental or bodily faculty; influence, authority; ascendancy; authorization; influential person etc.; state with international influence; vigour, energy; *colloquial* large number or amount; capacity for exerting mechanical force; mechanical or electrical energy; electricity supply; particular source or form of energy; product obtained by multiplying a number by itself a specified number of times; magnifying capacity of lens. ● *verb* supply with mechanical or electrical energy; (+ *up, down*) increase or decrease power supplied to (device), switch on or off. □ **power cut** temporary withdrawal or failure of electric power supply; **powerhouse** power station, person or thing of great energy; **power of attorney** authority to act for another in legal and financial matters; **power point** socket for connection of electrical appliance etc. to mains; **power-sharing** coalition government; **power station** building where electric power is generated for distribution.

powerful *adjective* having great power or influence. □ **powerfully** *adverb*; **powerfulness** *noun*.

powerless *adjective* without power; wholly unable. □ **powerlessness** *noun*.

powwow /'paʊwaʊ/ ● *noun* meeting for discussion (originally among N. American Indians). ● *verb* hold powwow.

pox *noun* virus disease leaving pocks; *colloquial* syphilis.

pp *abbreviation* pianissimo.

pp. *abbreviation* pages.

p.p. *abbreviation* (also **pp**) *per pro*.

PPS *abbreviation* Parliamentary Private Secretary; further postscript (*post-postscriptum*).

PR *abbreviation* public relations; proportional representation.

practicable /'præktɪkəb(ə)l/ *adjective* that can be done or used. □ **practicability** *noun*.

practical /'præktɪk(ə)l/ ● *adjective* of or concerned with practice rather than theory; functional; good at making, organizing, or mending things; realistic; that is such in effect, virtual. ● *noun* practical exam. □ **practical joke** trick played on person. □ **practicality** /-'kæl-/ *noun* (*plural* **-ies**).

practically *adverb* virtually, almost; in a practical way.

practice /'præktɪs/ *noun* habitual action; repeated exercise to improve skill; action as opposed to theory; doctor's or lawyer's professional business etc.; procedure, esp. of specified kind. □ **in practice** when applied, in reality, skilled from recent practice; **out of practice** lacking former skill.

practise /'præktɪs/ *verb* (**-sing**; *US* **-tice**; **-cing**) carry out in action; do repeatedly to improve skill; exercise oneself in or on; (as **practised** *adjective*) expert; engage in (profession, religion, etc.).

practitioner /præk'tɪʃənə/ *noun* professional worker, esp. in medicine.

praesidium = PRESIDIUM.

praetorian guard /priː'tɔːrɪən/ *noun* bodyguard of ancient Roman emperor etc.

pragmatic /præg'mætɪk/ *adjective* dealing with matters from a practical point of view. □ **pragmatically** *adverb*.

pragmatism /'prægmətɪz(ə)m/ *noun* pragmatic attitude or procedure; *Philosophy* doctrine that evaluates assertions according to their practical consequences. □ **pragmatist** *noun*.

prairie /'preərɪ/ *noun* large treeless tract of grassland, esp. in N. America.

praise /preɪz/ ● *verb* (**-sing**) express warm approval or admiration of; glorify. ● *noun* praising; commendation. □ **praiseworthy** worthy of praise.

praline /'prɑːliːn/ *noun* sweet made of nuts browned in boiling sugar.

pram *noun* carriage for baby, pushed by person on foot.

prance /prɑːns/ ● *verb* (**-cing**) (of horse) spring from hind legs; walk or behave in an elated or arrogant way. ● *noun* prancing; prancing movement.

prank *noun* practical joke.

prat *noun* *slang* fool.

prate ● verb (**-ting**) talk too much; chatter foolishly. ● noun idle talk.

prattle /'præt(ə)l/ ● verb (**-ling**) talk in childish or inconsequential way. ● noun prattling talk.

prawn noun edible shellfish like large shrimp.

pray verb (often + for, to do, that) say prayers; make devout supplication; entreat.

prayer /preə/ noun request or thanksgiving to God or object of worship; formula used in praying; entreaty. □ **prayer book** book of set prayers; **prayer-mat** small carpet on which Muslims kneel when praying; **prayer-shawl** one worn by male Jews when praying.

pre- prefix before (in time, place, order, degree, or importance).

preach verb deliver (sermon); proclaim (the gospel etc.); give moral advice obtrusively; advocate, inculcate. □ **preacher** noun.

preamble /pri:'æmb(ə)l/ noun preliminary statement; introductory part of statute, deed, etc.

prearrange /pri:ə'reɪndʒ/ verb (**-ging**) arrange beforehand. □ **prearrangement** noun.

prebend /'prebənd/ noun stipend of canon or member of chapter; portion of land etc. from which this is drawn. □ **prebendal** /prɪ'bend(ə)l/ adjective.

prebendary /'prebəndərɪ/ noun (plural **-ies**) holder of prebend; honorary canon.

Precambrian /pri:'kæmbrɪən/ ● adjective of earliest geological era. ● noun this era.

precarious /prɪ'keərɪəs/ adjective uncertain, dependent on chance; perilous. □ **precariously** adverb; **precariousness** noun.

precast /pri:'kɑːst/ adjective (of concrete) cast in required shape before positioning.

precaution /prɪ'kɔːʃ(ə)n/ noun action taken beforehand to avoid risk or ensure good result. □ **precautionary** adjective.

precede /prɪ'siːd/ verb (**-ding**) come or go before in time, order, importance, etc.; (+ by) cause to be preceded by.

precedence /'presɪd(ə)ns/ noun priority; right of preceding others. □ **take precedence** (often + over, of) have priority.

precedent ● noun /'presɪd(ə)nt/ previous case taken as guide or justification etc. ● adjective /prɪ'siːd(ə)nt/ preceding.

precentor /prɪ'sentə/ noun leader of singing or (in synagogue) prayers of congregation.

precept /'priːsept/ noun rule for action or conduct.

preceptor /prɪ'septə/ noun teacher, instructor. □ **preceptorial** /priːsep'tɔːrɪəl/ adjective.

precession /prɪ'seʃ(ə)n/ noun slow movement of axis of spinning body around another axis; such change causing equinoxes to occur earlier in each successive sidereal year.

precinct /'priːsɪŋkt/ noun enclosed area, esp. around building; district in town, esp. where traffic is excluded; (in plural) environs.

preciosity /preʃɪ'ɒsɪtɪ/ noun affected refinement in art.

precious /'preʃəs/ ● adjective of great value; much prized; affectedly refined. ● adverb colloquial extremely, very.

precipice /'presɪpɪs/ noun vertical or steep face of rock, cliff, mountain, etc.

precipitate ● verb /prɪ'sɪpɪteɪt/ (**-ting**) hasten occurrence of; (+ into) cause to go into (war etc.) hurriedly or violently; throw down headlong; Chemistry cause (substance) to be deposited in solid form from solution; Physics condense (vapour) into drops. ● adjective /prɪ'sɪpɪtət/ headlong; hasty, rash. ● noun /prɪ'sɪpɪtət/ solid matter precipitated; moisture condensed from vapour.

precipitation /prɪsɪpɪ'teɪʃ(ə)n/ noun precipitating, being precipitated; rash haste; rain, snow, etc., falling to ground.

precipitous /prɪ'sɪpɪtəs/ adjective of or like precipice; steep.

précis /'preɪsiː/ ● noun (plural same /-siːz/) summary, abstract. ● verb (**-cises** /-siːz/, **-cised** /-siːd/, **-cising** /-siːɪŋ/) make précis of.

precise /prɪ'saɪs/ adjective accurately worded; definite, exact; punctilious.

precisely *adverb* in a precise way, exactly; quite so.

precision /prɪ'sɪʒ(ə)n/ ● *noun* accuracy. ● *adjective* designed for or produced by precise work.

preclude /prɪ'kluːd/ *verb* (**-ding**) (+ *from*) prevent; make impossible.

precocious /prɪ'kəʊʃəs/ *adjective* prematurely developed in some respect. □ **precociously** *adverb*; **precociousness** *noun*; **precocity** /-'kɒs-/ *noun*.

precognition /priːkɒg'nɪʃ(ə)n/ *noun* (esp. supernatural) foreknowledge.

preconceive /priːkən'siːv/ *verb* (**-ving**) form (opinion etc.) beforehand.

preconception /priːkən'sepʃ(ə)n/ *noun* preconceived idea; prejudice.

precondition /priːkən'dɪʃ(ə)n/ *noun* condition that must be fulfilled beforehand.

precursor /priː'kɜːsə/ *noun* forerunner; person who precedes in office etc.; harbinger.

predate /priː'deɪt/ *verb* (**-ting**) precede in time.

predator /'predətə/ *noun* predatory animal; exploiter of others.

predatory /'predətərɪ/ *adjective* (of animal) preying naturally on others; plundering or exploiting others.

predecease /priːdɪ'siːs/ *verb* (**-sing**) die before (another).

predecessor /'priːdɪsesə/ *noun* previous holder of office or position; ancestor; thing to which another has succeeded.

predestine /priː'destɪn/ *verb* (**-ning**) determine beforehand; ordain by divine will or as if by fate. □ **predestination** *noun*.

predetermine /priːdɪ'tɜːmɪn/ *verb* (**-ning**) decree beforehand; predestine.

predicament /prɪ'dɪkəmənt/ *noun* difficult or unpleasant situation.

predicate ● *verb* /'predɪkeɪt/ (**-ting**) assert (something) about subject of proposition; (+ *on*) base (statement etc.) on. ● *noun* /'predɪkət/ *Grammar & Logic* what is said about subject of sentence or proposition. □ **predicable** *adjective*; **predication** *noun*.

predicative /prɪ'dɪkətɪv/ *adjective Grammar* (of adjective or noun) forming part or all of predicate; that predicates.

predict /prɪ'dɪkt/ *verb* forecast; prophesy. □ **predictable** *adjective*; **predictably** *adverb*; **prediction** *noun*.

predilection /priːdɪ'lekʃ(ə)n/ *noun* (often + *for*) preference, special liking.

predispose /priːdɪs'pəʊz/ *verb* (**-sing**) influence favourably in advance; (+ *to, to do*) render liable or inclined beforehand to. □ **predisposition** /-pə'zɪʃ(ə)n/ *noun*.

predominate /prɪ'dɒmɪneɪt/ *verb* (**-ting**) (+ *over*) have control over; prevail; preponderate. □ **predominance** *noun*; **predominant** *adjective*; **predominantly** *adverb*.

pre-eminent /priː'emɪnənt/ *adjective* excelling others; outstanding. □ **pre-eminence** *noun*; **pre-eminently** *adverb*.

pre-empt /priː'empt/ *verb* forestall; obtain by pre-emption.

■ **Usage** *Pre-empt* is sometimes used to mean *prevent*, but this is considered incorrect in standard English.

pre-emption /priː'empʃ(ə)n/ *noun* purchase or taking of thing before it is offered to others.

pre-emptive /priː'emptɪv/ *adjective* pre-empting; *Military* intended to prevent attack by disabling enemy.

preen *verb* (of bird) tidy (feathers, itself) with beak; (of person) smarten or admire (oneself, one's hair, clothes, etc.); (often + *on*) pride (oneself).

prefab /'priːfæb/ *noun colloquial* prefabricated building.

prefabricate /priː'fæbrɪkeɪt/ *verb* (**-ting**) manufacture sections of (building etc.) prior to assembly on site.

preface /'prefəs/ ● *noun* introduction to book stating subject, scope, etc.; preliminary part of speech. ● *verb* (**-cing**) (often + *with*) introduce or begin (as) with preface; (of event etc.) lead up to (another). □ **prefatory** *adjective*.

prefect /'priːfekt/ *noun* chief administrative officer of district in France etc.; senior pupil in school, authorized to maintain discipline.

prefecture /'priːfektʃə/ *noun* district under government of prefect; prefect's office or tenure.

prefer /prɪ'fɜː/ *verb* (**-rr-**) (often + *to, to do*) like better; submit (information, accusation, etc.); promote (person).

preferable /'prefərəb(ə)l/ *adjective* to be preferred, more desirable. □ **preferably** *adverb*.

preference /'prefərəns/ *noun* preferring, being preferred; thing preferred; favouring of one person etc. before others; prior right.

preferential /prefə'renʃ(ə)l/ *adjective* of, giving, or receiving preference. □ **preferentially** *adverb*.

preferment /pri'fɜ:mənt/ *noun formal* promotion to higher office.

prefigure /pri:'fɪgə/ *verb* (**-ring**) represent or imagine beforehand.

prefix /'pri:fɪks/ •*noun* part-word added to beginning of word to alter meaning, e.g. *re-* in *retake*, *ex-* in *ex-president*; title before name. •*verb* (often + *to*) add as introduction; join (word, element) as prefix.

pregnant /'pregnənt/ *adjective* having child or young developing in womb; significant, suggestive. □ **pregnancy** *noun* (*plural* **-ies**).

preheat /pri:'hi:t/ *verb* heat beforehand.

prehensile /pri:'hensaɪl/ *adjective* (of tail, limb, etc.) capable of grasping.

prehistoric /pri:hɪs'tɒrɪk/ *adjective* of period before written records. □ **prehistory** /-'hɪstərɪ/ *noun*.

prejudge /pri:'dʒʌdʒ/ *verb* (**-ging**) form premature judgement on (person etc.).

prejudice /'predʒʊdɪs/ •*noun* preconceived opinion; (+ *against, in favour of*) bias; harm (possibly) resulting from action or judgement. •*verb* (**-cing**) impair validity of; (esp. as **prejudiced** *adjective*) cause (person) to have prejudice. □ **prejudicial** /-'dɪʃ-/ *adjective*.

prelacy /'preləsɪ/ *noun* (*plural* **-ies**) church government by prelates; (**the prelacy**) prelates collectively; office or rank of prelate.

prelate /'prelət/ *noun* high ecclesiastical dignitary, e.g. bishop.

preliminary /prɪ'lɪmɪnərɪ/ •*adjective* introductory, preparatory. •*noun* (*plural* **-ies**) (usually in *plural*) preliminary action or arrangement; preliminary trial or contest.

prelude /'prelju:d/ •*noun* (often + *to*) action, event, etc. serving as introduction; introductory part of poem etc.; *Music* introductory piece of suite, short piece of similar type. •*verb* (**-ding**) serve as prelude to; introduce with prelude.

premarital /pri:'mærɪt(ə)l/ *adjective* occurring etc. before marriage.

premature /'premətʃə/ *adjective* occurring or done before usual or right time; too hasty; (of baby) born 3 or more weeks before expected time. □ **prematurely** *adverb*.

premed /pri:'med/ *noun colloquial* premedication.

premedication /pri:medɪ'keɪʃ(ə)n/ *noun* medication in preparation for operation.

premeditate /pri:'medɪteɪt/ *verb* (**-ting**) think out or plan beforehand. □ **premeditation** *noun*.

premenstrual /pri:'menstrʊəl/ *adjective* of the time immediately before menstruation.

premier /'premɪə/ •*noun* prime minister. •*adjective* first in importance, order, or time. □ **premiership** *noun*.

première /'premɪeə/ •*noun* first performance or showing of play or film. •*verb* (**-ring**) give première of.

premise /'premɪs/ *noun* premiss; (in *plural*) house or other building with its grounds etc.; (in *plural*) *Law* previously specified houses, lands, or tenements. □ **on the premises** in the house etc. concerned.

premiss /'premɪs/ *noun* previous statement from which another is inferred.

premium /'pri:mɪəm/ •*noun* amount to be paid for contract of insurance; sum added to interest, wages, etc.; reward, prize. •*adjective* of best quality and highest price. □ **at a premium** highly valued, above usual or nominal price; **Premium (Savings) Bond** government security not bearing interest but with periodic prize draw.

premonition /premə'nɪʃ(ə)n/ *noun* forewarning; presentiment. □ **premonitory** /prɪ'mɒnɪtərɪ/ *adjective*.

prenatal /pri:'neɪt(ə)l/ *adjective* existing or occurring before birth.

preoccupy /pri:'ɒkjʊpaɪ/ *verb* (**-ies**, **-ied**) dominate mind of; (as **preoccupied** *adjective*) otherwise engrossed. □ **preoccupation** *noun*.

preordain /pri:ɔ:'deɪn/ *verb* ordain or determine beforehand.

prep *noun colloquial* homework; time when this is done.

prepack /priː'pæk/ *verb* (also **prepackage** /-'pækɪdʒ/) pack (goods) before retail.

preparation /prepə'reɪʃ(ə)n/ *noun* preparing, being prepared; (often in *plural*) thing done to make ready; substance specially prepared.

preparatory /prɪ'pærətərɪ/ ● *adjective* (often + *to*) serving to prepare; introductory. ● *adverb* (often + *to*) as a preparation. □ **preparatory school** private primary or (*US*) secondary school.

prepare /prɪ'peə/ *verb* (**-ring**) make or get ready; get oneself ready.

prepay /priː'peɪ/ *verb* (*past & past participle* **prepaid**) pay (charge) beforehand; pay postage on beforehand. □ **prepayment** *noun*.

preponderate /prɪ'pɒndəreɪt/ *verb* (**-ting**) (often + *over*) be superior in influence, quantity, or number; predominate. □ **preponderance** *noun*; **preponderant** *adjective*.

preposition /prepə'zɪʃ(ə)n/ *noun* word used before noun or pronoun to indicate its relationship to another word (see panel). □ **prepositional** *adjective*.

prepossess /priːpə'zes/ *verb* (usually in *passive*) take possession of; prejudice, usually favourably; (as **prepossessing** *adjective*) attractive. □ **prepossession** *noun*.

preposterous /prɪ'pɒstərəs/ *adjective* utterly absurd; contrary to nature or reason. □ **preposterously** *adverb*.

prepuce /'priːpjuːs/ *noun* foreskin.

Pre-Raphaelite /priː'ræfəlaɪt/ ● *noun* member of group of 19th-c. English artists. ● *adjective* of Pre-Raphaelites; (**pre-Raphaelite**) (esp. of woman) of type painted by Pre-Raphaelites.

pre-record /priːrɪ'kɔːd/ *verb* record in advance.

prerequisite /priː'rekwɪzɪt/ ● *adjective* required as precondition. ● *noun* prerequisite thing.

■ **Usage** *Prerequisite* is sometimes confused with *perquisite* which means 'an extra profit, right, or privilege'.

prerogative /prɪ'rɒgətɪv/ *noun* right or privilege exclusive to individual or class.

Pres. *abbreviation* President.

presage /'presɪdʒ/ ● *noun* omen; presentiment. ● *verb* (**-ging**) portend; indicate (future event etc.); foretell, foresee.

presbyopia /prezbɪ'əʊpɪə/ *noun* long-sightedness. □ **presbyopic** *adjective*.

presbyter /'prezbɪtə/ *noun* priest of Episcopal Church; elder of Presbyterian Church.

Presbyterian /prezbɪ'tɪərɪən/ ● *adjective* (of Church, esp. Church of Scotland) governed by elders all of equal rank.

Preposition

A preposition is used in front of a noun or pronoun to form a phrase. It often describes the position of something, e.g. *under the chair*, or the time at which something happens, e.g. *in the evening*.

Prepositions in common use are:

about	*behind*	*into*	*through*
above	*beside*	*like*	*till*
across	*between*	*near*	*to*
after	*by*	*of*	*towards*
against	*down*	*off*	*under*
along	*during*	*on*	*underneath*
among	*except*	*outside*	*until*
around	*for*	*over*	*up*
as	*from*	*past*	*upon*
at	*in*	*round*	*with*
before	*inside*	*since*	*without*

• *noun* member of Presbyterian Church. □ **Presbyterianism** *noun*.

presbytery /'prezbɪtərɪ/ *noun* (*plural* -**ies**) eastern part of chancel; body of presbyters; RC priest's house.

prescient /'presɪənt/ *adjective* having foreknowledge or foresight. □ **prescience** *noun*.

prescribe /prɪ'skraɪb/ *verb* (-**bing**) advise use of (medicine etc.); lay down authoritatively.

■ **Usage** *Prescribe* is sometimes confused with *proscribe*, which means 'forbid'.

prescript /'priːskrɪpt/ *noun* ordinance, command.

prescription /prɪ'skrɪpʃ(ə)n/ *noun* prescribing; doctor's (usually written) instruction for composition and use of medicine; medicine thus prescribed.

prescriptive /prɪ'skrɪptɪv/ *adjective* prescribing, laying down rules; arising from custom.

presence /'prez(ə)ns/ *noun* being present; place where person is; personal appearance; person or spirit that is present. □ **presence of mind** calmness and quick-wittedness in sudden difficulty etc.

present[1] /'prez(ə)nt/ • *adjective* being in place in question; now existing, occurring, or being dealt with etc.; *Grammar* expressing present action or state. • *noun* (**the present**) now; present tense. □ **at present** now; **for the present** just now; **present-day** of this time, now.

present[2] /prɪ'zent/ *verb* introduce; exhibit; offer or give (thing) to; (+ *with*) provide (person) with; put (play, film, etc.) before public; reveal; deliver (cheque etc.) for payment etc. □ **present arms** hold rifle etc. in saluting position.

present[3] /'prez(ə)nt/ *noun* gift.

presentable /prɪ'zentəb(ə)l/ *adjective* of good appearance; fit to be shown. □ **presentability** *noun*; **presentably** *adverb*.

presentation /prezən'teɪʃ(ə)n/ *noun* presenting, being presented; thing presented; manner or quality of presenting; demonstration of materials etc., lecture.

presenter *noun* person introducing broadcast programme.

presentiment /prɪ'zentɪmənt/ *noun* vague expectation, foreboding.

presently *adverb* before long; *US & Scottish* at present.

preservative /prɪ'zɜːvətɪv/ • *noun* substance for preserving food etc. • *adjective* tending to preserve.

preserve /prɪ'zɜːv/ • *verb* (-**ving**) keep safe or free from decay; maintain, retain; treat (food) to prevent decomposition or fermentation; keep (game etc.) undisturbed for private use. • *noun* (in *singular* or *plural*) preserved fruit, jam; place where game etc. is preserved; sphere of activity regarded by person as his or hers alone. □ **preservation** /prezə'veɪʃ(ə)n/ *noun*.

preshrunk /priː'ʃrʌŋk/ *adjective* (of fabric etc.) treated so as to shrink during manufacture and not in use.

preside /prɪ'zaɪd/ *verb* (-**ding**) (often + *at*, *over*) be chairperson or president; exercise control or authority.

presidency /'prezɪdənsɪ/ *noun* (*plural* -**ies**) office of president; period of this.

president /'prezɪd(ə)nt/ *noun* head of republic; head of society or council etc., of certain colleges, or (*US*) of university, company, etc.; person in charge of meeting. □ **presidential** /-'den-/ *adjective*.

presidium /prɪ'sɪdɪəm/ *noun* (also **praesidium**) standing committee, esp. in Communist country.

press[1] • *verb* apply steady force to; flatten, shape, smooth (esp. clothes); (+ *out of*, *from*, etc.) squeeze (juice etc.); embrace, caress firmly; (+ *on*, *against*, etc.) exert pressure on; be urgent, urge; (+ *for*) demand insistently; (+ *up*, *round*, etc.) crowd; (+ *on*, *forward*, etc.) hasten; (+ *on*, *upon*) force (offer etc.) on; manufacture (gramophone record, car part, etc.) using pressure. • *noun* pressing; device for compressing, flattening, extracting juice, etc.; machine for printing; (**the press**) newspapers; publicity in newspapers; printing house; publishing company; crowding, crowd; pressure of affairs; large usually shelved cupboard. □ **press agent** person employed to manage advertising and press publicity; **press**

conference meeting with journalists; **press gallery** gallery for reporters, esp. in legislative assembly; **press release** statement issued to newspapers etc.; **press-stud** small device fastened by pressing to engage two parts; **press-up** exercise in which prone body is raised by pressing down on hands to straighten arms.

press² verb historical force to serve in army or navy; bring into use as makeshift. □ **press-gang** noun historical group of men employed to press men for navy, verb force into service.

pressing ● adjective urgent; insistent. ● noun thing made by pressing, e.g. gramophone record; series of these made at one time; act of pressing. □ **pressingly** adverb.

pressure /'preʃə/ ● noun exertion of continuous force, force so exerted, amount of this; urgency; affliction, difficulty; constraining or compelling influence. ● verb (-ring) (often + into) apply pressure to, coerce, persuade. □ **pressure-cooker** pan for cooking quickly under high pressure; **pressure group** group formed to influence public policy.

pressurize verb (also -ise) (-zing or -sing) (esp. as **pressurized** adjective) maintain normal atmospheric pressure in (aircraft cabin etc.) at high altitude; raise to high pressure; pressure (person).

prestidigitator /prestɪ'dɪdʒɪteɪtə/ noun formal conjuror. □ **prestidigitation** noun.

prestige /pres'tiːʒ/ ● noun respect or reputation. ● adjective having or conferring prestige. □ **prestigious** /-'stɪdʒəs/ adjective.

presto /'prestəʊ/ Music ● adverb & adjective in quick tempo. ● noun (plural -s) presto movement or passage.

prestressed /priː'strest/ adjective (of concrete) strengthened by stretched wires in it.

presumably /prɪ'zjuːməblɪ/ adverb as may reasonably be presumed.

presume /prɪ'zjuːm/ verb (-ming) (often + that) suppose to be true, take for granted; (often + to do) venture; be presumptuous; (+ on, upon) make unscrupulous use of.

presumption /prɪ'zʌmpʃ(ə)n/ noun arrogance, presumptuous behaviour; taking for granted; thing presumed to be true; ground for presuming.

presumptive /prɪ'zʌmptɪv/ adjective giving grounds for presumption.

presumptuous /prɪ'zʌmptʃʊəs/ adjective unduly confident, arrogant. □ **presumptuously** adverb; **presumptuousness** noun.

presuppose /priːsə'pəʊz/ verb (-sing) assume beforehand; imply. □ **presupposition** /-sʌpə'zɪʃ(ə)n/ noun.

pre-tax /priː'tæks/ adjective (of income) before deduction of taxes.

pretence /prɪ'tens/ noun (US **pretense**) pretending, make-believe; pretext; (+ to) (esp. false) claim; ostentation.

pretend /prɪ'tend/ ● verb claim or assert falsely; imagine in play; (as **pretended** adjective) falsely claimed to be; (+ to) profess to have. ● adjective colloquial pretended.

pretender noun person who claims throne, title, etc.

pretense US = PRETENCE.

pretension /prɪ'tenʃ(ə)n/ noun (often + to) assertion of claim; pretentiousness.

pretentious /prɪ'tenʃəs/ adjective making excessive claim to merit or importance; ostentatious. □ **pretentiously** adverb; **pretentiousness** noun.

preternatural /priːtə'nætʃər(ə)l/ adjective extraordinary; supernatural.

pretext /'priːtekst/ noun ostensible reason; excuse.

pretty /'prɪtɪ/ ● adjective (-ier, -iest) attractive in delicate way; fine, good; considerable. ● adverb colloquial fairly, moderately. ● verb (-ies, -ied) (often + up) make pretty. □ **pretty-pretty** colloquial too pretty. □ **prettify** verb (-ies, -ied); **prettily** adverb; **prettiness** noun.

pretzel /'prets(ə)l/ noun crisp knot-shaped salted biscuit.

prevail /prɪ'veɪl/ verb (often + against, over) be victorious; be the more usual or predominant; exist or occur in general use; (+ on, upon) persuade.

prevalent /'prevələnt/ adjective generally existing or occurring. □ **prevalence** noun.

prevaricate /prɪ'værɪkeɪt/ verb (-ting) speak or act evasively or misleadingly.

□ **prevarication** *noun*; **prevaricator** *noun*.

■ *Usage* *Prevaricate* is often confused with *procrastinate*, which means 'to defer action'.

prevent /prɪ'vent/ *verb* (often + *from doing*) stop, hinder. □ **preventable** *adjective* (also **preventible**); **prevention** *noun*.

■ *Usage* The use of *prevent* without 'from' as in *She prevented me going* is informal. An acceptable further alternative is *She prevented my going*.

preventative /prɪ'ventətɪv/ *adjective & noun* preventive.

preventive /prɪ'ventɪv/ ● *adjective* serving to prevent, esp. disease. ● *noun* preventive agent, measure, drug, etc.

preview /'priːvjuː/ ● *noun* showing of film, play, etc. before it is seen by general public. ● *verb* view or show in advance.

previous /'priːvɪəs/ ● *adjective* (often + *to*) coming before in time or order; *colloquial* hasty, premature. ● *adverb* (+ *to*) before. □ **previously** *adverb*.

pre-war /priː'wɔː/ *adjective* existing or occurring before a war.

prey /preɪ/ ● *noun* animal hunted or killed by another for food; (often + *to*) victim. ● *verb* (+ *on, upon*) seek or take as prey; exert harmful influence.

price ● *noun* amount of money for which thing is bought or sold; what must be given, done, etc. to obtain thing; odds. ● *verb* (-**cing**) fix or find price of; estimate value of. □ **at a price** at high cost; **price tag** label on item showing its price.

priceless *adjective* invaluable; *colloquial* very amusing or absurd.

pricey *adjective* (**pricier, priciest**) *colloquial* expensive.

prick ● *verb* pierce slightly, make small hole in; (+ *off, out*) mark with pricks or dots; trouble mentally; tingle. ● *noun* pricking, mark of it; pain caused as by pricking, mental pain. □ **prick out** plant (seedlings etc.) in small holes pricked in earth; **prick up one's ears** (of dog) erect the ears when alert, (of person) become suddenly attentive.

prickle /'prɪk(ə)l/ ● *noun* small thorn; hard-pointed spine; prickling sensation. ● *verb* (-**ling**) cause or feel sensation as of prick(s).

prickly *adjective* (-**ier**, -**iest**) having prickles; irritable; tingling. □ **prickly heat** itchy inflammation of skin near sweat glands; **prickly pear** cactus with pear-shaped edible fruit, its fruit. □ **prickliness** *noun*.

pride ● *noun* elation or satisfaction at one's achievements, possessions, etc.; object of this; unduly high opinion of oneself; proper sense of one's own worth, position, etc.; group (of lions etc.). ● *verb* (-**ding**) (**pride oneself on**, **upon**) be proud of. □ **pride of place** most important position; **take (a) pride in** be proud of.

prie-dieu /priː'djɜː/ *noun* (*plural* -**x** same pronunciation) kneeling-desk for prayer.

priest /priːst/ *noun* ordained minister of some Christian churches (above deacon and below bishop); (*feminine* **priestess**) official minister of non-Christian religion. □ **priesthood** *noun*; **priestly** *adjective*.

prig *noun* self-righteous or moralistic person. □ **priggish** *adjective*; **priggishness** *noun*.

prim *adjective* (-**mm**-) stiffly formal and precise; prudish. □ **primly** *adverb*; **primness** *noun*.

prima /'priːmə/ *adjective* □ **prima ballerina** chief female dancer in ballet; **prima donna** chief female singer in opera, temperamental person.

primacy /'praɪməsɪ/ *noun* (*plural* -**ies**) pre-eminence; office of primate.

prima facie /praɪmə 'feɪʃɪ/ ● *adverb* at first sight. ● *adjective* (of evidence) based on first impression.

primal /'praɪm(ə)l/ *adjective* primitive, primeval; fundamental.

primary /'praɪmərɪ/ ● *adjective* of first importance; fundamental; original. ● *noun* (*plural* -**ies**) primary colour, feather, school, etc.; *US* primary election. □ **primary colour** one not obtained by mixing others; **primary education** education for children under 11; **primary election** *US* election to select candidate(s) for principal election;

primary feather large flight feather of bird's wing; **primary school** school for primary education. □ **primarily** /ˈpraɪmərɪlɪ, praɪˈmeərɪlɪ/ *adverb*.

primate /ˈpraɪmeɪt/ *noun* member of highest order of mammals, including apes, man, etc.; archbishop.

prime[1] ● *adjective* chief, most important; of highest quality; primary, fundamental; (of number etc.) divisible only by itself and unity. ● *noun* best or most vigorous stage. □ **prime minister** chief minister of government; **prime time** time when television etc. audience is largest.

prime[2] *verb* (**-ming**) prepare (thing) for use; prepare (gun) for firing or (explosive) for detonation; pour liquid into (pump) to start it working; cover (wood, metal, etc.) with primer; equip (person) with information etc.

primer[1] *noun* substance applied to bare wood, metal, etc. before painting.

primer[2] *noun* elementary school-book; introductory book.

primeval /praɪˈmiːv(ə)l/ *adjective* of first age of world; ancient, primitive.

primitive /ˈprɪmɪtɪv/ ● *adjective* at early stage of civilization; crude, simple. ● *noun* untutored painter with naïve style; picture by such painter. □ **primitively** *adverb*; **primitiveness** *noun*.

primogeniture /praɪməʊˈdʒenɪtʃə/ *noun* being first-born; first-born's right to inheritance.

primordial /praɪˈmɔːdɪəl/ *adjective* existing at or from beginning, primeval.

primrose /ˈprɪmrəʊz/ *noun* plant bearing pale yellow spring flower; this flower; pale yellow. □ **primrose path** pursuit of pleasure.

primula /ˈprɪmjʊlə/ *noun* cultivated plant with flowers of various colours.

Primus /ˈpraɪməs/ *noun proprietary term* portable cooking stove burning vaporized oil.

prince *noun* (as title usually **Prince**) male member of royal family other than king; ruler of small state; nobleman of some countries; (often + *of*) the greatest. □ **Prince Consort** husband of reigning queen who is himself a prince.

princely *adjective* (**-ier**, **-iest**) of or worthy of a prince; sumptuous, splendid.

princess /prɪnˈses/ *noun* (as title usually **Princess** /ˈprɪnses/) prince's wife; female member of royal family other than queen.

principal /ˈprɪnsɪp(ə)l/ ● *adjective* first in importance, chief; leading. ● *noun* chief person; head of some institutions; principal actor, singer, etc.; capital sum lent or invested; person for whom another is agent etc. □ **principal boy** (usually actress playing) leading male role in pantomime. □ **principally** *adverb*.

principality /prɪnsɪˈpælɪtɪ/ *noun* (*plural* **-ies**) state ruled by prince; (**the Principality**) Wales.

principle /ˈprɪnsɪp(ə)l/ *noun* fundamental truth or law as basis of reasoning or action; personal code of conduct; fundamental source or element. □ **in principle** in theory; **on principle** from moral motive.

principled *adjective* based on or having (esp. praiseworthy) principles of behaviour.

prink *verb* (usually **prink oneself**; often + *up*) smarten, dress up.

print ● *verb* produce by applying inked type, plates, etc. to paper etc.; express or publish in print; (often + *on, with*) impress, stamp; write in letters that are not joined; produce (photograph) from negative; (usually + *out*) produce computer output in printed form; mark (fabric) with design. ● *noun* mark left on surface by pressure; printed lettering, words, or publication (esp. newspaper); engraving; photograph; printed fabric. □ **in print** (of book etc.) available from publisher, in printed form; **out of print** (of book etc.) no longer available from publisher; **printed circuit** electric circuit with thin conducting strips printed on flat sheet; **printing press** machine for printing from type, plates, etc.; **printout** computer output in printed form.

printer *noun* person who prints books etc.; owner of printing business; device that prints esp. computer output.

prior /ˈpraɪə/ ● *adjective* earlier; (often + *to*) coming before in time, order, or importance. • *adverb* (+ *to*) before. • *noun* (*feminine* **prioress**) superior of religious house; (in abbey) deputy of abbot.

priority /praɪˈɒrɪtɪ/ *noun* (*plural* **-ies**) thing considered more important than others; precedence in time, rank, etc.; right to do something before other people. □ **prioritize** *verb* (also **-ise**) (**-zing** or **-sing**).

priory /ˈpraɪərɪ/ *noun* (*plural* **-ies**) religious house governed by prior or prioress.

prise /praɪz/ *verb* (also **prize**) (**-sing** or **-zing**) force open or out by leverage.

prism /ˈprɪz(ə)m/ *noun* solid figure whose two ends are equal parallel rectilinear figures, and whose sides are parallelograms; transparent body of this form with refracting surfaces.

prismatic /prɪzˈmætɪk/ *adjective* of, like, or using prism; (of colours) distributed (as if) by transparent prism.

prison /ˈprɪz(ə)n/ *noun* place of captivity, esp. building to which people are consigned while awaiting trial or for punishment.

prisoner /ˈprɪznə/ *noun* person kept in prison; person or thing confined by illness, another's grasp, etc.; (in full **prisoner of war**) person captured in war.

prissy /ˈprɪsɪ/ *adjective* (**-ier**, **-iest**) prim, prudish. □ **prissily** *adverb*; **prissiness** *noun*.

pristine /ˈprɪstiːn/ *adjective* in original condition, unspoilt; ancient.

privacy /ˈprɪvəsɪ/ *noun* (right to) being private; freedom from intrusion or publicity.

private /ˈpraɪvət/ • *adjective* belonging to an individual, personal; confidential, secret; not public; secluded; not holding public office or official position; not supported, managed, or provided by state. • *noun* private soldier; (in *plural*) *colloquial* genitals. □ **in private** privately; **private detective** detective outside police force; **private enterprise** business(es) not under state control; **private eye** *colloquial* private detective; **private means** unearned income from investments etc.; **private member** MP not holding government office; **private parts** *euphemistic* genitals; **private sol-**

-dier ordinary soldier, not officer. □ **privately** *adverb*.

privateer /praɪvəˈtɪə/ *noun* (commander of) privately owned and government-commissioned warship.

privation /praɪˈveɪʃ(ə)n/ *noun* lack of comforts or necessities.

privatize /ˈpraɪvətaɪz/ *verb* (also **-ise**) (**-zing** or **-sing**) transfer from state to private ownership. □ **privatization** *noun*.

privet /ˈprɪvɪt/ *noun* bushy evergreen shrub used for hedges.

privilege /ˈprɪvɪlɪdʒ/ • *noun* right, advantage, or immunity belonging to person, class, or office; special benefit or honour. • *verb* (**-ging**) invest with privilege.

privy /ˈprɪvɪ/ • *adjective* (+ *to*) sharing secret of; *archaic* hidden, secret. • *noun* (*plural* **-ies**) lavatory. □ **Privy Council** group of advisers appointed by sovereign; **Privy Councillor**, **Counsellor** member of this; **privy purse** allowance from public revenue for monarch's private expenses; **privy seal** state seal formerly affixed to minor documents.

prize¹ • *noun* reward in competition, lottery, etc.; reward given as symbol of victory or superiority; thing (to be) striven for. • *adjective* to which prize is awarded; excellent of its kind. • *verb* (**-zing**) value highly. □ **prizefight** boxing match for money.

prize² *noun* ship or property captured in naval warfare.

prize³ = PRISE.

PRO *abbreviation* Public Record Office; public relations officer.

pro¹ *noun* (*plural* **-s**) *colloquial* professional.

pro² • *adjective* in favour. • *noun* (*plural* **-s**) reason in favour. • *preposition* in favour of. □ **pros and cons** reasons for and against.

proactive /prəʊˈæktɪv/ *adjective* (of person, policy, etc.) taking the initiative.

probability *noun* (*plural* **-ies**) being probable; likelihood; (most) probable event; extent to which thing is likely to occur, measured by ratio of favourable cases to all cases possible. □ **in all probability** most probably.

probable /ˈprɒbəb(ə)l/ • *adjective* (often + *that*) that may be expected to happen or prove true; likely. ● *noun* probable candidate, member of team, etc. □ **probably** *adverb*.

probate /ˈprəʊbeɪt/ *noun* official proving of will; verified copy of will.

probation /prəˈbeɪʃ(ə)n/ *noun* system of supervising behaviour of offenders as alternative to prison; testing of character and abilities of eg. new employee. □ **probation officer** official supervising offenders on probation. □ **probationary** *adjective*.

probationer *noun* person on probation.

probe ● *noun* investigation; device for measuring, testing, etc.; blunt-ended surgical instrument for exploring wound etc.; unmanned exploratory spacecraft. ● *verb* (**-bing**) examine closely; explore with probe.

probity /ˈprəʊbɪtɪ/ *noun* uprightness, honesty.

problem /ˈprɒbləm/ ● *noun* doubtful or difficult question; thing hard to understand or deal with. ● *adjective* causing problems.

problematic /prɒbləˈmætɪk/ *adjective* (also **problematical**) attended by difficulty; doubtful, questionable.

proboscis /prəˈbɒsɪs/ *noun* (*plural* **-sces**) long flexible trunk or snout, e.g. of elephant; elongated mouth-parts of some insects.

procedure /prəˈsiːdʒə/ *noun* way of conducting business etc. or performing task; set series of actions. □ **procedural** *adjective*.

proceed /prəˈsiːd/ *verb* (often + *to*) go forward or on further, make one's way; (often + *with, to do*) continue or resume; adopt course of action; go on to say; (+ *against*) start lawsuit against; (often + *from*) originate.

proceeding *noun* action, piece of conduct; (in *plural*) legal action, published report of discussions or conference.

proceeds /ˈprəʊsiːdz/ *plural noun* profits from sale etc.

process[1] /ˈprəʊses/ ● *noun* course of action or proceeding, esp. series of stages in manufacture etc.; progress or course; natural or involuntary course of change; action at law; summons, writ; *Biology* natural appendage or outgrowth of organism. ● *verb* subject to

particular process; (as **processed** *adjective*) (of food) treated, esp. to prevent decay.

process[2] /prəˈses/ *verb* walk in procession.

procession /prəˈseʃ(ə)n/ *noun* people etc. advancing in orderly succession, esp. at ceremony, demonstration, or festivity.

processional ● *adjective* of processions; used, carried, or sung in processions. ● *noun* processional hymn (book).

processor /ˈprəʊsesə/ *noun* machine that processes things; central processor; food processor.

proclaim /prəˈkleɪm/ *verb* (often + *that*) announce publicly or officially; declare to be. □ **proclamation** /prɒklə-/ *noun*.

proclivity /prəˈklɪvɪtɪ/ *noun* (*plural* **-ies**) natural tendency.

procrastinate /prəʊˈkræstɪneɪt/ *verb* (**-ting**) defer action. □ **procrastination** *noun*.

■ Usage *Procrastinate* is often confused with *prevaricate*, which means 'to speak or act evasively or misleadingly'.

procreate /ˈprəʊkrɪeɪt/ *verb* (**-ting**) produce (offspring) naturally. □ **procreation** *noun*; **procreative** /-krɪˈeɪ-/ *adjective*.

proctor /ˈprɒktə/ *noun* university disciplinary official. □ **proctorial** /-ˈtɔːrɪəl/ *adjective*.

procuration /prɒkjʊˈreɪʃ(ə)n/ *noun formal* procuring; action of attorney.

procurator /ˈprɒkjʊreɪtə/ *noun* agent or proxy, esp. with power of attorney. □ **procurator fiscal** (in Scotland) local coroner and public prosecutor.

procure /prəˈkjʊə/ *verb* (**-ring**) succeed in getting; bring about; act as procurer. □ **procurement** *noun*.

procurer *noun* (*feminine* **procuress**) person who obtains women for prostitution.

prod ● *verb* (**-dd-**) poke with finger, stick, etc.; stimulate to action. ● *noun* poke, thrust; stimulus to action.

prodigal /ˈprɒdɪg(ə)l/ ● *adjective* wasteful; (+ *of*) lavish of. ● *noun* spendthrift. □ **prodigal son** repentant wastrel. □ **prodigality** /-ˈgæl-/ *noun*.

prodigious /prəˈdɪdʒəs/ *adjective* marvellous; enormous; abnormal.

prodigy /ˈprɒdɪdʒɪ/ *noun* (*plural* **-ies**) exceptionally gifted person, esp. precocious child; marvellous thing; (+ *of*) wonderful example of.

produce ● *verb* /prəˈdjuːs/ (**-cing**) manufacture or prepare; bring forward for inspection etc.; bear, yield, or bring into existence; cause or bring about; *Geometry* extend or continue (line); bring (play etc.) before public. ● *noun* /ˈprɒdjuːs/ what is produced, esp. agricultural products; amount produced; (often + *of*) result.

producer *noun* person who produces goods etc.; person who supervises production of play, film, broadcast, etc.

product /ˈprɒdʌkt/ *noun* thing or substance produced, esp. by manufacture; result; *Mathematics* quantity obtained by multiplying.

production /prəˈdʌkʃ(ə)n/ *noun* producing, being produced; total yield; thing produced, esp. play etc. □ **production line** systematized sequence of operations to produce commodity.

productive /prəˈdʌktɪv/ *adjective* producing, esp. abundantly. □ **productively** *adverb*; **productiveness** *noun*.

productivity /prɒdʌkˈtɪvɪtɪ/ *noun* capacity to produce; effectiveness of industry, workforce, etc.

Prof. *abbreviation* Professor.

profane /prəˈfeɪn/ ● *adjective* irreverent, blasphemous; obscene; not sacred. ● *verb* (**-ning**) treat irreverently; violate, pollute. □ **profanation** /prɒfə-/ *noun*.

profanity /prəˈfænɪtɪ/ *noun* (*plural* **-ies**) blasphemy; swear-word.

profess /prəˈfes/ *verb* claim openly to have; (often + *to do*) pretend, declare; affirm one's faith in or allegiance to.

professed *adjective* self-acknowledged; alleged, ostensible. □ **professedly** /-sɪdlɪ/ *adverb*.

profession /prəˈfeʃ(ə)n/ *noun* occupation or calling, esp. learned or scientific; people in a profession; declaration, avowal.

professional ● *adjective* of, belonging to, or connected with a profession; competent, worthy of professional; engaged in specified activity as paid occupation,

or (*derogatory*) fanatically. ● *noun* professional person. □ **professionally** *adverb*.

professionalism *noun* qualities of professionals, esp. competence, skill, etc.

professor /prəˈfesə/ *noun* highest-ranking academic in university department, *US* university teacher; person who professes a religion etc. □ **professorial** /prɒfɪˈsɔːrɪəl/ *adjective*; **professorship** *noun*.

proffer /ˈprɒfə/ *verb* offer.

proficient /prəˈfɪʃ(ə)nt/ *adjective* (often + *in*, *at*) adept, expert. □ **proficiency** *noun*; **proficiently** *adverb*.

profile /ˈprəʊfaɪl/ ● *noun* side view or outline, esp. of human face; short biographical sketch. ● *verb* (**-ling**) represent by profile. □ **keep a low profile** remain inconspicuous.

profit /ˈprɒfɪt/ ● *noun* advantage, benefit; financial gain, excess of returns over outlay. ● *verb* (**-t-**) be beneficial to; obtain advantage. □ **at a profit** with financial gain; **profit margin** profit after deduction of costs.

profitable *adjective* yielding profit; beneficial. □ **profitability** *noun*; **profitably** *adverb*.

profiteer /prɒfɪˈtɪə/ ● *verb* make or seek excessive profits, esp. illegally. ● *noun* person who profiteers.

profiterole /prəˈfɪtərəʊl/ *noun* small hollow cake of choux pastry with filling.

profligate /ˈprɒflɪgət/ ● *adjective* recklessly extravagant; licentious, dissolute. ● *noun* profligate person. □ **profligacy** *noun*; **profligately** *adverb*.

pro forma /prəʊ ˈfɔːmə/ ● *adverb & adjective* for form's sake. ● *noun* (in full **pro forma invoice**) invoice sent in advance of goods supplied.

profound /prəˈfaʊnd/ *adjective* (**-er**, **-est**) having or demanding great knowledge, study, or insight; intense, thorough; deep. □ **profoundly** *adverb*; **profoundness** *noun*; **profundity** /-ˈfʌndɪtɪ/ *noun* (*plural* **-ies**).

profuse /prəˈfjuːs/ *adjective* (often + *in*, *of*) lavish, extravagant, copious. □ **profusely** *adverb*; **profusion** *noun*.

progenitor /prəʊˈdʒenɪtə/ *noun* ancestor; predecessor; original.

progeny /ˈprɒdʒɪnɪ/ *noun* offspring, descendants; outcome, issue.

progesterone /prəʊˈdʒestərəʊn/ noun a sex hormone that helps to initiate and maintains pregnancy.

prognosis /prɒgˈnəʊsɪs/ noun (plural **-noses** /-siːz/) forecast, esp. of course of disease.

prognostic /prɒgˈnɒstɪk/ • noun (often + of) advance indication; prediction. • adjective (often + of) foretelling, predictive.

prognosticate /prɒgˈnɒstɪkeɪt/ verb (**-ting**) (often + that) foretell; betoken. □ **prognostication** noun.

programme /ˈprəʊɡræm/ (US **program**) • noun list of events, performers, etc.; radio or television broadcast; plan of events; course or series of studies, lectures, etc.; (usually **program**) series of instructions for computer. • verb (**-mm-**; US **-m-**) make programme of; (usually **program**) express (problem) or instruct (computer) by means of program. □ **programmable** adjective; **programmer** noun.

progress • noun /ˈprəʊɡres/ forward movement; advance, development, improvement; historical state journey, esp. by royalty. • verb /prəˈɡres/ move forward or onward; advance, develop, improve. □ **in progress** developing, going on.

progression /prəˈɡreʃ(ə)n/ noun progressing; succession, series.

progressive /prəˈɡresɪv/ • adjective moving forward; proceeding step by step; cumulative; favouring rapid reform; modern, efficient; (of disease etc.) increasing in severity or extent; (of taxation) increasing with the sum taxed. • noun (also **Progressive**) advocate of progressive policy. □ **progressively** adverb.

prohibit /prəˈhɪbɪt/ verb (**-t-**) (often + from) forbid; prevent.

prohibition /prəʊhɪˈbɪʃ(ə)n/ noun forbidding, being forbidden; edict or order that forbids; (usually **Prohibition**) legal ban on manufacture and sale of alcohol. □ **prohibitionist** noun.

prohibitive /prəˈhɪbɪtɪv/ adjective prohibiting; (of prices, taxes, etc.) extremely high. □ **prohibitively** adverb.

project • noun /ˈprɒdʒekt/ plan, scheme; extensive essay, piece of research, etc.

by student(s). • verb /prəˈdʒekt/ protrude, jut out; throw, impel; forecast; plan; cause (light, image, etc.) to fall on surface; cause (voice etc.) to be heard at distance.

projectile /prəˈdʒektaɪl/ • noun object to be fired (esp. by rocket) or hurled. • adjective of or serving as projectile; projecting, impelling.

projection /prəˈdʒekʃ(ə)n/ noun projecting, being projected; thing that protrudes; presentation of image(s) etc. on surface; forecast, estimate; mental image viewed as objective reality; transfer of feelings to other people etc.; representation of earth etc. on plane surface.

projectionist noun person who operates projector.

projector /prəˈdʒektə/ noun apparatus for projecting image or film on screen.

prolactin /prəʊˈlæktɪn/ noun hormone that stimulates milk production after childbirth.

prolapse • noun /ˈprəʊlæps/ (also **prolapsus** /-ˈlæpsəs/) slipping forward or downward of part or organ; prolapsed womb, rectum, etc. • verb /prəˈlæps/ (**-sing**) undergo prolapse.

prolate /ˈprəʊleɪt/ adjective (of spheroid) lengthened along polar diameter.

prolegomenon /prəʊlɪˈɡɒmɪnən/ noun (plural **-mena**) (usually in plural) preface to book etc., esp. discursive or critical.

proletarian /prəʊlɪˈteərɪən/ • adjective of proletariat. • noun member of proletariat.

proletariat /prəʊlɪˈteərɪət/ noun working class; esp. derogatory lowest class.

proliferate /prəˈlɪfəreɪt/ verb (**-ting**) reproduce; produce (cells etc.) rapidly; increase rapidly, multiply. □ **proliferation** noun.

prolific /prəˈlɪfɪk/ adjective producing many offspring or much output; (often + of) abundantly productive; copious.

prolix /ˈprəʊlɪks/ adjective lengthy; tedious. □ **prolixity** /-ˈlɪks-/ noun.

prologue /ˈprəʊlɒɡ/ noun introduction to poem, play, etc.; (usually + to) introductory event.

prolong /prəˈlɒŋ/ verb extend; (as **prolonged** adjective) (tediously) lengthy. □ **prolongation** /prəʊlɒŋˈɡeɪʃ(ə)n/ noun.

prom *noun colloquial* promenade; promenade concert.

promenade /prɒməˈnɑːd/ • *noun* paved public walk, esp. at seaside; leisure walk. • *verb* (**-ding**) make promenade (through); lead about, esp. for display. □ **promenade concert** one at which (part of) audience is not seated; **promenade deck** upper deck on liner.

promenader *noun* person who promenades; regular attender at promenade concerts.

prominent /ˈprɒmɪnənt/ *adjective* jutting out; conspicuous; distinguished. □ **prominence** *noun*.

promiscuous /prəˈmɪskjʊəs/ *adjective* having frequent casual sexual relationships; mixed and indiscriminate; *colloquial* casual. □ **promiscuously** *adverb*; **promiscuity** /prɒmɪsˈkjuːɪtɪ/ *noun*.

promise /ˈprɒmɪs/ • *noun* explicit undertaking to do or not to do something; favourable indications. • *verb* (**-sing**) (usually + *to do, that*) make promise; (often + *to do*) seem likely; *colloquial* assure.

promising *adjective* likely to turn out well; hopeful, full of promise. □ **promisingly** *adverb*.

promissory /ˈprɒmɪsərɪ/ *adjective* expressing or implying promise. □ **promissory note** signed document containing promise to pay stated sum.

promontory /ˈprɒməntərɪ/ *noun* (*plural* **-ies**) point of high land jutting out into sea etc.; headland.

promote /prəˈməʊt/ *verb* (**-ting**) (often + *to*) advance (person) to higher office or position; help forward, encourage; publicize and sell. □ **promotion** *noun*; **promotional** *adjective*.

promoter *noun* person who promotes, esp. sporting event, theatrical production, etc., or formation of joint-stock company.

prompt • *adjective* acting, made, or done immediately; ready. • *adverb* punctually. • *verb* (usually + *to, to do*) incite; supply (actor, speaker) with next words or with suggestion; inspire. • *noun* prompting; thing said to prompt actor etc.; sign on computer screen inviting input. □ **promptitude** *noun*; **promptly** *adverb*; **promptness** *noun*.

prompter *noun* person who prompts actors.

promulgate /ˈprɒmʌlgeɪt/ *verb* (**-ting**) make known to the public; proclaim. □ **promulgation** *noun*.

prone *adjective* lying face downwards; prostrate; (usually + *to, to do*) disposed, liable. □ **-prone** likely to suffer. □ **proneness** *noun*.

prong *noun* spike of fork.

pronominal /prəʊˈnɒmɪn(ə)l/ *adjective* of, concerning, or being a pronoun.

pronoun /ˈprəʊnaʊn/ *noun* word used as substitute for noun or noun phrase usually already mentioned or known (see panel).

pronounce /prəˈnaʊns/ *verb* (**-cing**) utter or speak, esp. in approved manner; utter formally; state (as) one's opinion; (usually + *on, for, against,* etc.) pass judgement. □ **pronounceable** *adjective*; **pronouncement** *noun*.

pronounced *adjective* strongly marked.

Pronoun

A pronoun is used as a substitute for a noun or a noun phrase, e.g.

> He *was* upstairs.   *Did you see* that?
> Anything *can happen* now.   It's *lovely weather*.

Using a pronoun often avoids repetition, e.g.

> *I found Jim—he was upstairs.*
> (instead of *I found Jim—Jim was upstairs.*)
>
> *Where are your keys?—I've got them.*
> (instead of *Where are your keys?—I've got my keys.*)

---

pronto /ˈprɒntəʊ/ adverb colloquial promptly, quickly.

pronunciation /prənʌnsɪˈeɪʃ(ə)n/ noun pronouncing of word, esp. with reference to standard; act of pronouncing; way of pronouncing words.

proof /pruːf/ ● noun fact, evidence, reasoning, or demonstration that proves something; test, trial; standard of strength of distilled alcohol; trial impression of printed matter for correction. ● adjective (often + against) impervious to penetration, damage, etc. by a specified thing. ● verb make proof, esp. against water or bullets. □ **proofread** read and correct (printed proof); **proofreader** person who does this.

prop[1] ● noun rigid support; person or thing that supports, comforts, etc. ● verb (-pp-) (often + against, up, etc.) support (as) with prop.

prop[2] noun colloquial stage property.

prop[3] noun colloquial propeller.

propaganda /prɒpəˈɡændə/ noun organized propagation of a doctrine etc.; usually derogatory ideas etc. so propagated. □ **propagandist** noun.

propagate /ˈprɒpəɡeɪt/ verb (-ting) breed from parent stock; (often **propagate itself**) (of plant etc.) reproduce itself; disseminate; transmit. □ **propagation** noun; **propagator** noun.

propane /ˈprəʊpeɪn/ noun gaseous hydrocarbon used as fuel.

propel /prəˈpel/ verb (-ll-) drive or push forward; urge on. □ **propellant** noun & adjective.

propeller noun revolving shaft with blades, esp. for propelling ship or aircraft.

propensity /prəˈpensɪtɪ/ noun (plural -ies) inclination, tendency.

proper /ˈprɒpə/ adjective accurate, correct; suitable, appropriate; decent, respectable; (usually + to) belonging, relating; strictly so called, genuine; colloquial thorough. □ **proper name**, noun name of person, place, etc. □ **properly** adverb.

property /ˈprɒpətɪ/ noun (plural -ies) thing(s) owned; landed estate; quality, characteristic; movable article used on theatre stage or in film.

prophecy /ˈprɒfɪsɪ/ noun (plural -ies) prophetic utterance; prediction; prophesying.

prophesy /ˈprɒfɪsaɪ/ verb (-ies, -ied) (usually + that, who, etc.) foretell; speak as prophet.

prophet /ˈprɒfɪt/ noun (feminine **prophetess**) teacher or interpreter of divine will; person who predicts; (**the Prophet**) Muhammad.

prophetic /prəˈfetɪk/ adjective (often + of) containing a prediction, predicting; of prophet.

prophylactic /prɒfɪˈlæktɪk/ ● adjective tending to prevent disease etc. ● noun preventive medicine or action; esp. US condom.

prophylaxis /prɒfɪˈlæksɪs/ noun preventive treatment against disease.

propinquity /prəˈpɪŋkwɪtɪ/ noun nearness; close kinship; similarity.

propitiate /prəˈpɪʃɪeɪt/ verb (-ting) appease. □ **propitiation** noun; **propitiatory** /-ʃətərɪ/ adjective.

propitious /prəˈpɪʃəs/ adjective favourable, auspicious; (often + for, to) suitable.

proponent /prəˈpəʊnənt/ noun person advocating proposal etc.

proportion /prəˈpɔːʃ(ə)n/ ● noun comparative part, share; comparative ratio; correct relation between things or parts of thing; (in plural) dimensions. ● verb (usually + to) make proportionate.

proportional adjective in correct proportion; comparable. □ **proportional representation** representation of parties in parliament in proportion to votes they receive. □ **proportionally** adverb.

proportionate /prəˈpɔːʃənət/ adjective proportional. □ **proportionately** adverb.

proposal /prəˈpəʊz(ə)l/ noun proposing; scheme etc. proposed; offer of marriage.

propose /prəˈpəʊz/ verb (-sing) put forward for consideration; (usually + do) purpose; (usually + to) offer marriage; nominate as member of society etc. □ **propose a toast** ask people to drink to health or in honour of person or thing. □ **proposer** noun.

proposition /prɒpə'zɪʃ(ə)n/ ● *noun* statement, assertion; scheme proposed, proposal; statement subject to proof or disproof; *colloquial* problem, opponent, prospect, etc.; *Mathematics* formal statement of theorem or problem; likely commercial enterprise, person, etc.; sexual proposal. ● *verb colloquial* put (esp. sexual) proposal to.

propound /prə'paʊnd/ *verb* offer for consideration.

proprietary /prə'praɪətərɪ/ *adjective* of or holding property; of property; held in private ownership; manufactured by one particular firm. □ **proprietary name**, **term** name of product etc. registered as trade mark.

proprietor /prə'praɪətə/ *noun* (*feminine* **proprietress**) owner. □ **proprietorial** /-'tɔːr-/ *adjective*.

propriety /prə'praɪɪtɪ/ *noun* (*plural* **-ies**) fitness, rightness; correctness of behaviour or morals; (in *plural*) rules of polite behaviour.

propulsion /prə'pʌlʃ(ə)n/ *noun* driving or pushing forward; force causing this. □ **propulsive** /-'pʌlsɪv/ *adjective*.

pro rata /prəʊ 'rɑːtə/ ● *adjective* proportional. ● *adverb* proportionally. [Latin]

prorogue /prə'rəʊg/ *verb* (**-gues**, **-gued**, **-guing**) discontinue meetings of (parliament etc.) without dissolving it; be prorogued. □ **prorogation** /prəʊrə-/ *noun*.

prosaic /prə'zeɪɪk/ *adjective* like prose; unromantic; commonplace. □ **prosaically** *adverb*.

proscenium /prə'siːnɪəm/ *noun* (*plural* **-s** or **-nia**) part of theatre stage in front of curtain and enclosing arch.

proscribe /prə'skraɪb/ *verb* (**-bing**) forbid; denounce; outlaw. □ **proscription** /-'skrɪp-/ *noun*; **proscriptive** /-'skrɪp-/ *adjective*.

■ **Usage** *Proscribe* is sometimes confused with *prescribe* which means 'to impose'.

prose /prəʊz/ ● *noun* ordinary language not in verse; passage of this, esp. for translation; dullness. ● *verb* (**-sing**) talk tediously.

prosecute /'prɒsɪkjuːt/ *verb* (**-ting**) institute legal proceedings against; *formal* carry on (trade etc.). □ **prosecutor** *noun*.

prosecution /prɒsɪ'kjuːʃ(ə)n/ *noun* prosecuting, being prosecuted; prosecuting party.

proselyte /'prɒsəlaɪt/ *noun* convert, esp. recent; convert to Jewish faith. □ **proselytism** /-lɪtɪz(ə)m/ *noun*.

proselytize /'prɒsəlɪtaɪz/ *verb* (also **-ise**) (**-zing** or **-sing**) (seek to) convert.

prosody /'prɒsədɪ/ *noun* science of versification. □ **prosodist** *noun*.

prospect ● *noun* /'prɒspekt/ (often in *plural*) expectation; extensive view; mental picture; possible or likely customer etc. ● *verb* /prə'spekt/ (usually + *for*) explore (for gold etc.). □ **prospector** *noun*.

prospective /prə'spektɪv/ *adjective* some day to be, expected; future.

prospectus /prə'spektəs/ *noun* (*plural* **-tuses**) pamphlet etc. advertising or describing school, business, etc.

prosper /'prɒspə/ *verb* succeed, thrive.

prosperity /prɒ'sperɪtɪ/ *noun* prosperous state.

prosperous /'prɒspərəs/ *adjective* successful, rich, thriving; auspicious. □ **prosperously** *adverb*.

prostate /'prɒsteɪt/ *noun* (in full **prostate gland**) gland secreting component of semen. □ **prostatic** /-'stæt-/ *adjective*.

prostitute /'prɒstɪtjuːt/ ● *noun* person who offers sexual intercourse for payment. ● *verb* (**-ting**) make prostitute of; misuse, offer for sale unworthily. □ **prostitution** *noun*.

prostrate ● *adjective* /'prɒstreɪt/ lying face downwards, esp. in submission; lying horizontally; overcome, esp. exhausted. ● *verb* /prɒs'treɪt/ (**-ting**) lay or throw flat; overcome, make weak. □ **prostration** *noun*.

prosy /'prəʊzɪ/ *adjective* (**-ier**, **-iest**) tedious, commonplace, dull.

protagonist /prə'tægənɪst/ *noun* chief person in drama, story, etc.; supporter of cause.

■ **Usage** The use of *protagonist* to mean 'a supporter of a cause' is considered incorrect by some people.

protean /ˈprəʊtiən/ *adjective* variable, versatile.

protect /prəˈtekt/ *verb* (often + *from*, *against*) keep (person etc.) safe; shield.

protection /prəˈtekʃ(ə)n/ *noun* protecting, being protected; defence; person etc. that protects; protectionism; *colloquial* immunity from violence etc. by paying gangsters etc.

protectionism *noun* theory or practice of protecting home industries. □ **protectionist** *noun & adjective*.

protective /prəˈtektɪv/ *adjective* protecting; intended for or giving protection. □ **protective custody** detention of person for his or her own protection. □ **protectively** *adverb*; **protectiveness** *noun*.

protector *noun* (*feminine* **protectress**) person or thing that protects; *historical* regent ruling during minority or absence of sovereign. □ **protectorship** *noun*.

protectorate /prəˈtektərət/ *noun* state controlled and protected by another; such protectorship; *historical* office of protector of kingdom or state; period of this.

protégé /ˈprɒtɪʒeɪ/ *noun* (*feminine* **protégée** same pronunciation) person under protection, patronage, etc. of another.

protein /ˈprəʊtiːn/ *noun* any of a class of nitrogenous compounds essential in all living organisms.

pro tem /prəʊ ˈtem/ *adjective & adverb* *colloquial* for the time being (*pro tempore*).

protest ● *noun* /ˈprəʊtest/ expression of dissent or disapproval; legal written refusal to pay or accept bill. ● *verb* /prəˈtest/ (usually + *against, at, about*, etc.) make protest; affirm (innocence etc.); write or get protest relating to (bill); *US* object to. □ **protester, protestor** *noun*.

Protestant /ˈprɒtɪst(ə)nt/ ● *noun* member or adherent of any of Churches separated from RC Church in Reformation. ● *adjective* of Protestant Churches or Protestants. □ **Protestantism** *noun*.

protestation /prɒtɪsˈteɪʃ(ə)n/ *noun* strong affirmation; protest.

proto- *combining form* first.

protocol /ˈprəʊtəkɒl/ ● *noun* official formality and etiquette; draft. esp. of terms of treaty. ● *verb* (-**ll**-) draft or record in protocol.

proton /ˈprəʊtɒn/ *noun* elementary particle with positive electric charge equal to electron's, and occurring in all atomic nuclei.

protoplasm /ˈprəʊtəplæz(ə)m/ *noun* viscous translucent substance comprising living part of cell in organism. □ **protoplasmic** /-ˈplæzmɪk/ *adjective*.

prototype /ˈprəʊtətaɪp/ *noun* original as pattern for copy, improved form, etc.; trial model of vehicle, machine, etc. □ **prototypic** /-ˈtɪp-/ *adjective*; **prototypical** /-ˈtɪp-/ *adjective*.

protozoan /prəʊtəˈzəʊən/ ● *noun* (*plural* **-s**) (also **protozoon** /-ˈzəʊɒn/, *plural* **-zoa** /-ˈzəʊə/) one-celled microscopic organism. ● *adjective* (also **protozoic** /-ˈzəʊɪk/) of protozoa.

protract /prəˈtrækt/ *verb* (often as **protracted** *adjective*) prolong, lengthen. □ **protraction** *noun*.

protractor *noun* instrument for measuring angles, usually in form of graduated semicircle.

protrude /prəˈtruːd/ *verb* (**-ding**) thrust forward; stick out. □ **protrusion** *noun*; **protrusive** *adjective*.

protuberant /prəˈtjuːbərənt/ *adjective* bulging out; prominent. □ **protuberance** *noun*.

proud /praʊd/ *adjective* feeling greatly honoured; haughty, arrogant; (often + *of*) feeling or showing (proper) pride; imposing, splendid; (often + *of*) slightly projecting. □ **do** (**person**) **proud** *colloquial* treat with great generosity or honour. □ **proudly** *adverb*.

prove /pruːv/ *verb* (**-ving**; *past participle* **proved** or *esp. US & Scottish* **proven** /ˈpruːv(ə)n/) (often + *that*) demonstrate to be true by evidence or argument; (**prove oneself**) show one's abilities etc.; (usually + *to be*) be found; test accuracy of; establish validity of (will); (of dough) rise. □ **provable** *adjective*.

■ **Usage** The use of *proven* as the past participle is uncommon except in certain expressions, such as *of proven ability*. It is, however, standard in Scots and American English.

provenance /ˈprɒvɪnəns/ *noun* (place of) origin; history.

provender /ˈprɒvɪndə/ *noun* fodder; *jocular* food.

proverb /ˈprɒvɜːb/ *noun* short pithy saying in general use.

proverbial /prəˈvɜːbɪəl/ *adjective* notorious; of or referred to in proverbs. □ **proverbially** *adverb*.

provide /prəˈvaɪd/ *verb* (-ding) supply; (usually + *for, against*) make due preparation; (usually + *for*) take care of person etc. with money, food, etc.; (often + *that*) stipulate. □ **provided, providing** (often + *that*) on condition or understanding that.

providence /ˈprɒvɪd(ə)ns/ *noun* protective care of God or nature; (**Providence**) God; foresight, thrift.

provident /ˈprɒvɪd(ə)nt/ *adjective* having or showing foresight, thrifty.

providential /prɒvɪˈden(ʃ)(ə)l/ *adjective* of or by divine foresight or intervention; opportune, lucky. □ **providentially** *adverb*.

province /ˈprɒvɪns/ *noun* principal administrative division of country etc.; (**the provinces**) whole of country outside capital; sphere of action; branch of learning.

provincial /prəˈvɪnʃ(ə)l/ ● *adjective* of province(s); unsophisticated, uncultured. ● *noun* inhabitant of province(s); unsophisticated or uncultured person. □ **provincialism** *noun*.

provision /prəˈvɪʒ(ə)n/ ● *noun* providing; (in *plural*) food and drink, esp. for expedition; legal or formal stipulation. ● *verb* supply with provisions.

provisional ● *adjective* providing for immediate needs only, temporary; (**Provisional**) of the unofficial wing of the IRA. ● *noun* (**Provisional**) member of unofficial wing of IRA. □ **provisionally** *adverb*.

proviso /prəˈvaɪzəʊ/ *noun* (*plural* -**s**) stipulation; limiting clause. □ **provisory** *adjective*.

provocation /prɒvəˈkeɪʃ(ə)n/ *noun* provoking, being provoked; cause of annoyance.

provocative /prəˈvɒkətɪv/ *adjective* (usually + *of*) tending or intended to provoke anger, lust, etc. □ **provocatively** *adverb*.

provoke /prəˈvəʊk/ *verb* (-king) (often + *to, to do*) rouse, incite; call forth, cause; (usually + *into*) irritate, stimulate; tempt.

provost /ˈprɒvəst/ *noun* head of some colleges; head of cathedral chapter; /prəˈvəʊ/ (in full **provost marshal**) head of military police in camp or on active service.

prow /praʊ/ *noun* bow of ship; pointed or projecting front part.

prowess /ˈpraʊɪs/ *noun* skill, expertise; valour, gallantry.

prowl /praʊl/ ● *verb* (often + *about, around*) roam, esp. stealthily in search of prey, plunder, etc. ● *noun* prowling. □ **prowler** *noun*.

prox. *abbreviation* proximo.

proximate /ˈprɒksɪmət/ *adjective* nearest, next before or after.

proximity /prɒkˈsɪmɪtɪ/ *noun* nearness.

proximo /ˈprɒksɪməʊ/ *adjective* of next month.

proxy /ˈprɒksɪ/ *noun* (*plural* -**ies**) authorization given to deputy; person authorized to deputize; document authorizing person to vote on another's behalf; vote so given.

prude *noun* excessively squeamish or sexually modest person. □ **prudery** *noun*; **prudish** *adjective*; **prudishly** *adverb*; **prudishness** *noun*.

prudent /ˈpruːd(ə)nt/ *adjective* cautious; politic. □ **prudence** *noun*; **prudently** *adverb*.

prudential /pruːˈden(ʃ)(ə)l/ *adjective* of or showing prudence.

prune[1] *noun* dried plum.

prune[2] *verb* (-ning) (often + *down*) trim (tree etc.) by cutting away dead or overgrown parts; (usually + *off, away*) remove (branches etc.) thus; reduce (costs etc.); (often + *of*) clear superfluities from; remove (superfluities).

prurient /ˈprʊərɪənt/ *adjective* having or encouraging unhealthy sexual curiosity. □ **prurience** *noun*.

Prussian /ˈprʌʃ(ə)n/ ● *adjective* of Prussia. ● *noun* native of Prussia. □ **Prussian blue** deep blue (pigment).

prussic acid /ˈprʌsɪk/ *noun* highly poisonous liquid.

pry /praɪ/ *verb* (**pries**, **pried**) (usually + *into* etc.) inquire impertinently, look inquisitively.

PS *abbreviation* postscript.

psalm /sɑːm/ *noun* (also **Psalm**) sacred song; (**the (Book of) Psalms**) book of these in Old Testament.

psalmist /'sɑːmɪst/ *noun* author or composer of psalm(s).

psalmody /'sɑːmədɪ/ *noun* practice or art of singing psalms.

Psalter /'sɔːltə/ *noun* Book of Psalms; (**psalter**) version or copy of this.

psaltery /'sɔːltərɪ/ *noun* (*plural* **-ies**) ancient and medieval plucked stringed instrument.

psephology /sɪ'fɒlədʒɪ/ *noun* statistical study of voting etc. □ **psephologist** *noun*.

pseudo- *combining form* (also **pseud-** before vowel) false, not genuine; resembling, imitating.

pseudonym /'sjuːdənɪm/ *noun* fictitious name, esp. of author.

psoriasis /sə'raɪəsɪs/ *noun* skin disease with red scaly patches.

PSV *abbreviation* public service vehicle.

psych /saɪk/ *verb colloquial* (usually + *up*) prepare mentally; (often + *out*) intimidate; (usually + *out*) analyse (person's motivation etc.).

psyche /'saɪkɪ/ *noun* soul, spirit, mind.

psychedelic /saɪkə'delɪk/ *adjective* expanding the mind's awareness, hallucinatory; vivid in colour, design, etc.

psychiatry /saɪ'kaɪətrɪ/ *noun* study and treatment of mental disease. □ **psychiatric** /-kɪ'ætrɪk/ *adjective*; **psychiatrist** *noun*.

psychic /'saɪkɪk/ ● *adjective* (of person) regarded as having paranormal powers, clairvoyant; of the soul or mind. ● *noun* psychic person, medium.

psychical *adjective* concerning psychic phenomena or faculties; of the soul or mind.

psycho- *combining form* of mind or psychology.

psychoanalysis /saɪkəʊə'nælɪsɪs/ *noun* treatment of mental disorders by bringing repressed fears etc. into conscious mind. □ **psychoanalyse** /-'ænəl-/ *verb* (**-sing**); **psychoanalyst** /-'ænəl-/ *noun*; **psychoanalytical** /-ænə'lɪt-/ *adjective*.

psychokinesis /saɪkəʊkɪ'niːsɪs/ *noun* movement of objects by telepathy.

psychological /saɪkə'lɒdʒɪk(ə)l/ *adjective* of the mind; of psychology; *colloquial* imaginary. □ **psychological block** inhibition caused by emotion; **psychological moment** best time to achieve purpose; **psychological warfare** campaign to reduce enemy's morale. □ **psychologically** *adverb*.

psychology /saɪ'kɒlədʒɪ/ *noun* (*plural* **-ies**) study of human mind; treatise on or theory of this; mental characteristics. □ **psychologist** *noun*.

psychopath /'saɪkəpæθ/ *noun* mentally deranged person, esp. with abnormal social behaviour; mentally or emotionally unstable person. □ **psychopathic** /-'pæθ-/ *adjective*.

psychosis /saɪ'kəʊsɪs/ *noun* (*plural* **-choses** /-siːz/) severe mental derangement involving loss of contact with reality.

psychosomatic /saɪkəʊsə'mætɪk/ *adjective* (of disease) mental, not physical, in origin; of both mind and body.

psychotherapy /saɪkəʊ'θerəpɪ/ *noun* treatment of mental disorder by psychological means. □ **psychotherapist** *noun*.

psychotic /saɪ'kɒtɪk/ ● *adjective* of or suffering from psychosis. ● *noun* psychotic person.

PT *abbreviation* physical training.

pt *abbreviation* part; pint; point; port.

PTA *abbreviation* parent–teacher association.

ptarmigan /'tɑːmɪgən/ *noun* bird of grouse family.

Pte. *abbreviation* Private (soldier).

pteridophyte /'terɪdəfaɪt/ *noun* flowerless plant.

pterodactyl /terə'dæktɪl/ *noun* large extinct flying reptile.

PTO *abbreviation* please turn over.

ptomaine /'təʊmeɪn/ *noun* any of a group of compounds (some toxic) in putrefying matter.

pub *noun colloquial* public house.

puberty /'pjuːbətɪ/ *noun* period of sexual maturing.

pubes[1] /'pju:bi:z/ noun (plural same) lower part of abdomen.

pubes[2] plural of PUBIS.

pubescence /pju:'bes(ə)ns/ noun beginning of puberty; soft down on plant or animal. □ **pubescent** adjective.

pubic /'pju:bɪk/ adjective of pubes or pubis.

pubis /'pju:bɪs/ noun (plural **pubes** /-bi:z/) front portion of hip bone.

public /'pʌblɪk/ ● adjective of the people as a whole; open to or shared by all; done or existing openly; of or from government; involved in community affairs. ● noun (treated as singular or plural) (members of) community as a whole; section of community. □ **go public** (of company) start selling shares on open market, reveal one's plans; **in public** publicly, openly; **public address system** equipment of loudspeakers etc.; **public convenience** public lavatory; **public figure** famous person; **public house** place selling alcoholic drink for consumption on premises; **public lending right** right of authors to payment when their books are lent by public libraries; **public relations** professional promotion of company, product, etc.; **public school** independent fee-paying school; US, Australian, Scottish, etc. non-fee-paying school; **public-spirited** ready to do things for the community; **public transport** buses, trains, etc. available for public use on fixed routes; **public utility** organization supplying water, gas, etc. to community. □ **publicly** adverb.

publican /'pʌblɪkən/ noun keeper of public house.

publication /pʌblɪ'keɪʃ(ə)n/ noun publishing; published book, periodical, etc.

publicist /'pʌblɪsɪst/ noun publicity agent, public relations officer.

publicity /pʌb'lɪsɪtɪ/ noun (means of attracting) public attention; (material used for) advertising.

publicize /'pʌblɪsaɪz/ verb (also **-ise**) (**-zing** or **-sing**) advertise, make publicly known.

publish /'pʌblɪʃ/ verb prepare and issue (book, magazine, etc.) for public sale; make generally known; formally announce.

publisher noun person or firm that publishes books etc.

puce /pju:s/ adjective & noun purplebrown.

puck[1] noun rubber disc used in ice hockey.

puck[2] noun mischievous sprite. □ **puckish** adjective, **puckishly** adverb; **puckishness** noun.

pucker /'pʌkə/ ● verb (often + up) gather into wrinkles, folds, or bulges. ● noun such wrinkle etc.

pudding /'pʊdɪŋ/ noun sweet cooked dish; savoury dish containing flour, suet, etc.; sweet course of meal; kind of sausage.

puddle /'pʌd(ə)l/ noun small (dirty) pool; clay made into watertight coating.

pudenda /pju:'dendə/ plural noun genitals, esp. of woman.

pudgy /'pʌdʒɪ/ adjective (**-ier**, **-iest**) colloquial plump, podgy.

puerile /'pjʊəraɪl/ adjective childish, immature. □ **puerility** /-'rɪl-/ noun (plural **-ies**).

puerperal /pju:'ɜ:pər(ə)l/ adjective of or due to childbirth.

puff ● noun short quick blast of breath or wind; sound (as) of this; vapour or smoke sent out in one blast; light pastry cake; gathered material in dress etc.; unduly enthusiastic review, advertisement, etc. ● verb emit puff(s); smoke or move with puffs; (usually in passive; often + out) colloquial put out of breath; pant; (usually + up, out) inflate; (usually as **puffed up** adjective) elate, make boastful; advertise in exaggerated terms. □ **puff-adder** large venomous African viper; **puffball** ballshaped fungus; **puff pastry** pastry consisting of thin layers.

puffin /'pʌfɪn/ noun N. Atlantic and N. Pacific auk with short striped bill.

puffy adjective (**-ier**, **-iest**) swollen, puffed out; colloquial short-winded.

pug noun (in full **pug-dog**) dog of small breed with flat nose. □ **pug-nose** short flat or snub nose.

pugilist /'pju:dʒɪlɪst/ noun boxer. □ **pugilism** noun; **pugilistic** /-'lɪs-/ adjective.

pugnacious /pʌg'neɪʃəs/ adjective disposed to fight. □ **pugnaciously** adverb; **pugnacity** /-'næs-/ noun.

puissance /ˈpwiːsãs/ noun jumping of large obstacles in showjumping.

puissant /ˈpwiːsɒnt/ adjective literary powerful; mighty.

puke /pjuːk/ verb & noun (-king) slang vomit. □ **pukey** adjective.

pukka /ˈpʌkə/ adjective colloquial genuine; reliable.

pulchritude /ˈpʌlkrɪtjuːd/ noun literary beauty. □ **pulchritudinous** /-ˈtjuːdɪnəs/ adjective.

pull /pʊl/ ● verb exert force on (thing etc.) to move it to oneself or origin of force; exert pulling force; extract by pulling; damage (muscle etc.) by abnormal strain; proceed with effort; (+ on) draw (weapon) against (person); attract; draw (liquor) from barrel etc.; (+ at) pluck at; (often + on, at) inhale or drink deeply, suck. ● noun act of pulling; force thus exerted; influence; advantage; attraction; deep draught of liquor; prolonged effort; handle etc. for applying ball; printer's rough proof; suck at cigarette. □ **pull back** retreat; **pull down** demolish; **pull in** arrive to take passengers, move to side of or off road, colloquial earn, colloquial arrest; **pull-in** roadside café etc.; **pull off** remove, win, manage successfully; **pull oneself together** recover control of oneself; **pull out** take out, depart, withdraw, leave station or stop, move towards off side; **pull-out** removable section of magazine; **pull round, through** (cause to) recover from illness; **pull strings** exert (esp. clandestine) influence; **pull together** work in harmony; **pull up** (cause to) stop moving, pull out of ground, reprimand, check oneself.

pullet /ˈpʊlɪt/ noun young hen, esp. less than one year old.

pulley /ˈpʊlɪ/ noun (plural **-s**) grooved wheel(s) for cord etc. to run over, mounted in block and used to lift weight etc.; wheel or drum mounted on shaft and turned by belt, used to increase speed or power.

Pullman /ˈpʊlmən/ noun (plural **-s**) luxurious railway carriage or motor coach; sleeping car.

pullover noun knitted garment put on over the head.

pullulate /ˈpʌljʊleɪt/ verb (**-ting**) sprout; swarm; develop; (+ with) abound with. □ **pullulation** noun.

pulmonary /ˈpʌlmənərɪ/ adjective of lungs; having (organs like) lungs; affected with or subject to lung disease.

pulp ● noun fleshy part of fruit etc.; soft shapeless mass, esp. of materials for papermaking; cheap fiction. ● verb reduce to or become pulp. □ **pulpy** adjective, **pulpiness** noun.

pulpit /ˈpʊlpɪt/ noun raised enclosed platform for preaching from; (**the pulpit**) preachers collectively, preaching.

pulsar /ˈpʌlsɑː/ noun cosmic source of regular rapid pulses of radiation.

pulsate /pʌlˈseɪt/ verb (**-ting**) expand and contract rhythmically; throb, vibrate, quiver. □ **pulsation** noun.

pulse[1] ● noun rhythmical throbbing of arteries; each beat of arteries or heart; throb or thrill of life or emotion; general feeling; single vibration of sound, electromagnetic radiation, etc.; rhythmical (esp. musical) beat. ● verb (**-sing**) pulsate.

pulse[2] noun (treated as singular or plural) (plant producing) edible seeds of peas, beans, lentils, etc.

pulverize /ˈpʌlvəraɪz/ verb (also **-ise**) (**-zing** or **-sing**) reduce or crumble to powder or dust; colloquial demolish, crush. □ **pulverization** noun.

puma /ˈpjuːmə/ noun large tawny American feline.

pumice /ˈpʌmɪs/ noun (in full **pumice stone**) light porous lava used as abrasive; piece of this.

pummel /ˈpʌm(ə)l/ verb (**-ll-**; US **-l-**) strike repeatedly, esp. with fists.

pump[1] ● noun machine or device for raising or moving liquids or gases; act of pumping. ● verb (often + in, out, up, etc.) raise, remove, inflate, empty, etc. (as) with pump; work pump; persistently question (person) to elicit information; move vigorously up and down. □ **pump iron** colloquial exercise with weights.

pump[2] noun plimsoll; light shoe for dancing etc.

pumpernickel /ˈpʌmpənɪk(ə)l/ noun wholemeal rye bread.

pumpkin /ˈpʌmpkɪn/ noun large yellow or orange fruit used as vegetable; plant bearing it.

pun ● *noun* humorous use of word(s) with two or more meanings, play on words. ● *verb* (**-nn-**) (usually + *on*) make pun(s).

Punch *noun* grotesque humpbacked puppet in *Punch and Judy* shows.

punch[1] ● *verb* strike with fist; make hole in (as) with punch; pierce (hole) thus. ● *noun* blow with fist; *colloquial* vigour, effective force; instrument or machine for piercing holes or impressing design in leather, metal, etc. □ **pull one's punches** avoid using full force; **punchball** stuffed or inflated ball used for practice in punching; **punch-drunk** stupefied (as) with repeated punches; **punchline** words giving point of joke etc.; **punch-up** *colloquial* fist-fight, brawl. □ **puncher** *noun*.

punch[2] *noun* hot or cold mixture of wine or spirit with water, fruit, spices, etc. □ **punch-bowl** bowl for punch; deep round hollow in hill.

punchy *adjective* (**-ier, -iest**) vigorous, forceful.

punctilio /pʌŋkˈtɪliəʊ/ *noun* (*plural* **-s**) delicate point of ceremony or honour; petty formality.

punctilious /pʌŋkˈtɪliəs/ *adjective* attentive to formality or etiquette; precise in behaviour. □ **punctiliously** *adverb*; **punctiliousness** *noun*.

punctual /ˈpʌŋktʃʊəl/ *adjective* observing appointed time; prompt. □ **punctuality** /-ˈæl-/ *noun*; **punctually** *adverb*.

punctuate /ˈpʌŋktʃʊeɪt/ *verb* (**-ting**) insert punctuation marks in; interrupt at intervals.

punctuation *noun* (system of) punctuating. □ **punctuation mark** any of the marks used in writing to separate sentences, phrases, etc.

puncture /ˈpʌŋktʃə/ ● *noun* prick, pricking; hole made by this. ● *verb* (**-ring**) make or suffer puncture (in); deflate.

pundit /ˈpʌndɪt/ *noun* (also **pandit**) learned Hindu; expert.

pungent /ˈpʌndʒ(ə)nt/ *adjective* having sharp or strong taste or smell; biting, caustic. □ **pungency** *noun*.

punish /ˈpʌnɪʃ/ *verb* inflict penalty on (offender) or for (offence); tax, abuse, or treat severely. □ **punishable** *adjective*; **punishment** *noun*.

punitive /ˈpjuːnɪtɪv/ *adjective* inflicting or intended to inflict punishment; extremely severe.

punk *noun* (in full **punk rock**) deliberately outrageous style of rock music; (in full **punk rocker**) fan of this; *esp. US* hooligan, lout.

punkah /ˈpʌŋkə/ *noun* large swinging fan on frame worked by cord or electrically.

punnet /ˈpʌnɪt/ *noun* small basket for fruit etc.

punster /ˈpʌnstə/ *noun* maker of puns.

punt[1] ● *noun* square-ended flat-bottomed boat propelled by long pole. ● *verb* travel or carry in punt.

punt[2] ● *verb* kick (football) dropped from hands before it reaches ground. ● *noun* such kick.

punt[3] *verb* *colloquial* bet, speculate in shares etc.; (in some card games) lay stake against bank.

punt[4] /pʊnt/ *noun* chief monetary unit of Republic of Ireland.

punter *noun* *colloquial* person who gambles or bets; customer, client.

puny /ˈpjuːnɪ/ *adjective* (**-ier, -iest**) undersized; feeble.

pup ● *noun* young dog, wolf, rat, seal, etc. ● *verb* (**-pp-**) give birth to (pups).

pupa /ˈpjuːpə/ *noun* (*plural* **pupae** /-piː/) insect in stage between larva and imago.

pupil[1] /ˈpjuːpɪl/ *noun* person being taught.

pupil[2] /ˈpjuːpɪl/ *noun* opening in centre of iris of eye.

puppet /ˈpʌpɪt/ *noun* small figure moved esp. by strings as entertainment; person controlled by another. □ **puppet state** country apparently independent but actually under control of another power. □ **puppetry** *noun*.

puppy /ˈpʌpɪ/ *noun* (*plural* **-ies**) young dog; conceited young man. □ **puppy fat** temporary fatness of child or adolescent; **puppy love** calf love.

purblind /ˈpɜːblaɪnd/ *adjective* partly blind, dim-sighted; obtuse, dull. □ **purblindness** *noun*.

purchase /ˈpɜːtʃəs/ ● *verb* (**-sing**) buy. ● *noun* buying; thing bought; firm hold on thing, leverage; equipment for moving heavy objects. □ **purchaser** noun.

purdah /ˈpɜːdə/ noun screening of Muslim or Hindu women from strangers.

pure /pjʊə/ adjective unmixed, unadulterated; chaste; not morally corrupt; guiltless; sincere; not discordant; (of science) abstract, not applied. □ **pureness** noun; **purity** noun.

purée /ˈpjʊəreɪ/ ● noun smooth pulp of vegetables or fruit etc. ● verb (**-ées**, **-éed**) make purée of.

purely adverb in a pure way; merely, solely, exclusively.

purgative /ˈpɜːgətɪv/ ● adjective serving to purify; strongly laxative. ● noun purgative thing.

purgatory /ˈpɜːgətərɪ/ noun (plural **-ies**) place or state of spiritual cleansing, esp. after death and before entering heaven; place or state of temporary suffering or expiation. ● adjective purifying. □ **purgatorial** /-ˈtɔːrɪəl/ adjective.

purge /pɜːdʒ/ ● verb (**-ging**) (often + of, from) make physically or spiritually clean; remove by cleansing; rid of unacceptable members; empty (bowels); Law atone for (offence). ● noun purging; purgative.

purify /ˈpjʊərɪfaɪ/ verb (**-ies**, **-ied**) clear of extraneous elements, make pure; (often + of, from) cleanse. □ **purification** noun; **purificatory** /-fɪkeɪtərɪ/ adjective.

purist /ˈpjʊərɪst/ noun stickler for correctness, esp. in language. □ **purism** noun.

puritan /ˈpjʊərɪt(ə)n/ ● noun (**Puritan**) historical member of English Protestant group regarding Reformation as incomplete; purist member of any party; strict observer of religion or morals. ● adjective (**Puritan**) historical of Puritans; scrupulous in religion or morals. □ **puritanical** /-ˈtæn-/ adjective; **puritanically** /-ˈtæn-/ adverb; **puritanism** noun.

purl[1] ● noun knitting stitch with needle moved in opposite to normal direction; chain of minute loops. ● verb knit with purl stitch.

purl[2] verb flow with babbling sound.

purler /ˈpɜːlə/ noun colloquial heavy fall.

purlieu /ˈpɜːljuː/ noun (plural **-s**) person's limits or usual haunts; historical tract on border of forest; (in plural) outskirts, outlying region.

purlin /ˈpɜːlɪn/ noun horizontal beam along length of roof.

purloin /pəˈlɔɪn/ verb formal or jocular steal, pilfer.

purple /ˈpɜːp(ə)l/ ● noun colour between red and blue; purple robe, esp. of emperor etc.; cardinal's scarlet official dress. ● adjective of purple. ● verb (**-ling**) make or become purple. □ **purplish** adjective.

purport ● verb /pəˈpɔːt/ profess, be intended to seem; (often + that) have as its meaning. ● noun /ˈpɜːpɔːt/ ostensible meaning; tenor of document or statement. □ **purportedly** adverb.

purpose /ˈpɜːpəs/ ● noun object to be attained, thing intended; intention to act; resolution, determination. ● verb (**-sing**) have as one's purpose, intend. □ **on purpose** intentionally; **to good, little, no,** etc. **purpose** with good, little, no, etc., effect or result; **to the purpose** relevant, useful.

purposeful adjective having or indicating purpose; intentional. □ **purposefully** adverb; **purposefulness** noun.

purposeless adjective having no aim or plan.

purposely adverb on purpose.

purposive /ˈpɜːpəsɪv/ adjective having, serving, or done with a purpose; purposeful.

purr /pɜː/ ● verb make low vibratory sound of cat expressing pleasure; (of machinery etc.) run smoothly and quietly. ● noun purring sound.

purse /pɜːs/ ● noun small pouch for carrying money in; US handbag; funds; sum given as present or prize. ● verb (**-sing**) (often + up) contract (esp. lips); become wrinkled. □ **hold the purse-strings** have control of expenditure.

purser /ˈpɜːsə/ noun ship's officer who keeps accounts, esp. head steward in passenger vessel.

pursuance /pəˈsjuːəns/ noun (+ of) carrying out or observance (of plan, rules, etc.).

pursuant /pəˈsjuːənt/ adverb (+ to) in accordance with.

pursue /pə'sjuː/ *verb* (**-sues, -sued, -suing**) follow with intent to overtake, capture, or harm; proceed along; engage in (study etc.); carry out (plan etc.); seek after; continue to investigate etc.; persistently importune or assail. □ **pursuer** *noun*.

pursuit /pə'sjuːt/ *noun* pursuing; occupation or activity pursued. □ **in pursuit of** pursuing.

purulent /'pjʊərʊlənt/ *adjective* of, containing, or discharging pus. □ **purulence** *noun*.

purvey /pə'veɪ/ *verb* provide or supply food etc. as one's business. □ **purveyor** *noun*.

purview /'pɜːvjuː/ *noun* scope of document etc.; range of physical or mental vision.

pus /pʌs/ *noun* thick yellowish liquid produced from infected tissue.

push /pʊʃ/ ● *verb* exert force on (thing) to move it away, cause to move thus; exert such force; thrust forward or upward; (cause to) project; make (one's way) forcibly or persistently; exert oneself; (often + *on, into, to do*) urge, impel; (often + *for*) pursue (claim etc.) persistently; promote, advertise; *colloquial* sell (drug) illegally. ● *noun* act of pushing; force thus exerted; vigorous effort; determination; use of influence to advance person. □ **give** or **get the push** *colloquial* dismiss, be dismissed; **push-bike** *colloquial* bicycle; **pushchair** child's folding chair on wheels; **push off** *colloquial* go away; **pushover** *colloquial* opponent or difficulty easily overcome.

pusher *noun colloquial* seller of illegal drugs.

pushing *adjective* pushy; *colloquial* having nearly reached (specified age).

pushy *adjective* (**-ier, -iest**) *colloquial* excessively self-assertive. □ **pushily** *adverb*; **pushiness** *noun*.

pusillanimous /pjuːsɪ'lænɪməs/ *adjective formal* cowardly, timid. □ **pusillanimity** /-lə'nɪm-/ *noun*.

puss /pʊs/ *noun colloquial* cat; sly or coquettish girl.

pussy /'pʊsɪ/ *noun* (*plural* **-ies**) (also **pussy-cat**) *colloquial* cat. □ **pussyfoot** *colloquial* move stealthily, equivocate; **pussy willow** willow with furry catkins.

pustulate /'pʌstjʊleɪt/ *verb* (**-ting**) form into pustules.

pustule /'pʌstjuːl/ *noun* pimple containing pus. □ **pustular** *adjective*.

put /pʊt/ ● *verb* (**-tt-**; *past & past participle* **put**) move to or cause to be in specified place, position, or state; (often + *on, to*) impose; (+ *for*) substitute (thing) for (another); express in specified way; (+ *at*) estimate; (+ *into*) express or translate in (words etc.); (+ *into*) invest (money) in; (+ *on*) stake (money) on; (+ *to*) submit for attention; hurl (shot etc.) as sport. ● *noun* throw of shot. □ **put about** spread (rumour etc.); **put across** make understood, achieve by deceit; **put away** restore to usual place, lay aside for future, imprison, consume (food or drink); **put back** restore to usual place, change (meeting etc.) to later time, move back hands of (clock or watch); **put by** lay aside for future; **put down** suppress, *colloquial* snub, record in writing, enter on list, (+ *as, for*) account or reckon, (+ *to*) attribute to, kill (old etc. animal), pay as deposit; **put in** submit (claim), (+ *for*) be candidate for (election etc.), spend (time); **put off** postpone, evade (person) with excuse, dissuade, disconcert; **put on** clothe oneself with, cause (light etc.) to operate, make (transport) available, stage (play etc.), advance hands of (clock or watch), feign, increase one's weight by (specified amount); **put out** disconcert, annoy, inconvenience, extinguish; **put over** put across; **put through** complete, connect by telephone; **put together** make from parts, combine (parts) into whole; **put up** *verb* build, raise, lodge (person), engage in (fight etc.), propose, provide (money) as backer, display (notice), offer for sale etc.; **put-up** *adjective* fraudulent; **put upon** (usually in *passive*) *colloquial* unfairly burden or deceive; **put (person) up to** instigate him or her to; **put up with** endure, tolerate.

putative /'pjuːtətɪv/ *adjective formal* reputed, supposed.

putrefy /'pjuːtrɪfaɪ/ *verb* (**-ies, -ied**) become or make putrid, go bad; fester; become morally corrupt. □ **putrefaction** /-'fæk-/ *noun*; **putrefactive** /-'fæk-/ *adjective*.

putrescent /pju:'tres(ə)nt/ *adjective* rotting. □ **putrescence** *noun*.

putrid /'pju:trɪd/ *adjective* decomposed, rotten; noxious; corrupt; *slang* contemptible, very unpleasant. □ **putridity** /-'trɪd-/ *noun*.

putsch /pʊtʃ/ *noun* attempt at revolution.

putt /pʌt/ • *verb* (-**tt**-) strike (golf ball) on putting green. • *noun* putting stroke. □ **putting green** smooth turf round hole on golf course.

puttee /'pʌtɪ/ *noun historical* long strip of cloth wound round leg for protection and support.

putter[1] *noun* golf club used in putting.

putter[2] *US* = POTTER[1].

putty /'pʌtɪ/ • *noun* paste of chalk, linseed oil, etc. for fixing panes of glass etc. • *verb* (-**ies**, -**ied**) fix, fill, etc. with putty.

puzzle /'pʌz(ə)l/ • *noun* difficult or confusing problem; problem or toy designed to test ingenuity etc. • *verb* (-**ling**) perplex, (usually + *over* etc.) be perplexed; (usually as **puzzling** *adjective*) require much mental effort; (+ *out*) solve using ingenuity etc. □ **puzzlement** *noun*.

PVC *abbreviation* polyvinyl chloride, a plastic used for pipes, electrical insulation, etc.

pyaemia /paɪ'i:mɪə/ *noun* (*US* **pyemia**) severe bacterial infection of blood.

pygmy /'pɪgmɪ/ (also **pigmy**) • *noun* (*plural* -**ies**) member of dwarf people of esp. equatorial Africa; very small person, animal, or thing. • *adjective* very small.

pyjamas /pə'dʒɑ:məz/ *plural noun* (*US* **pajamas**) suit of trousers and top for sleeping in etc.; loose trousers worn in some Asian countries.

pylon /'paɪlən/ *noun* tall structure esp. as support for electric cables.

pyorrhoea /paɪə'rɪə/ *noun* (*US* **pyorrhea**) gum disease; discharge of pus.

pyramid /'pɪrəmɪd/ *noun* monumental (esp. ancient Egyptian) stone structure with square base and sloping sides meeting at apex; solid of this shape with base of 3 or more sides; pyramid-shaped thing. □ **pyramidal** /-'ræm-/ *adjective*.

pyre /'paɪə/ *noun* pile of combustible material, esp. for burning corpse.

pyrethrum /paɪ'ri:θrəm/ *noun* aromatic chrysanthemum; insecticide from its dried flowers.

Pyrex /'paɪəreks/ *noun proprietary term* a hard heat-resistant glass.

pyrites /paɪ'raɪti:z/ *noun* (in full **iron pyrites**) yellow sulphide of iron.

pyromania /paɪərəʊ'meɪnɪə/ *noun* obsessive desire to start fires. □ **pyromaniac** *noun & adjective*.

pyrotechnics /paɪərəʊ'tekniks/ *plural noun* art of making fireworks; display of fireworks. □ **pyrotechnic** *adjective*.

pyrrhic /'pɪrɪk/ *adjective* (of victory) achieved at too great cost.

python /'paɪθ(ə)n/ *noun* large snake that crushes its prey.

pyx /pɪks/ *noun* vessel for consecrated bread of Eucharist.

Qq

Q *abbreviation* (also **Q.**) question.

QC *abbreviation* Queen's Counsel.

QED *abbreviation* which was to be proved (*quod erat demonstrandum*).

QM *abbreviation* Quartermaster.

qr. *abbreviation* quarter(s).

qt *abbreviation* quart(s).

qua /kwɑː, kweɪ/ *conjunction* in the capacity of.

quack[1] ● *noun* harsh sound made by ducks. ● *verb* utter this sound.

quack[2] *noun* unqualified practitioner, esp. of medicine; *slang* any doctor. □ **quackery** *noun*.

quad /kwɒd/ *colloquial* ● *noun* quadrangle; quadruplet; quadraphonics. ● *adjective* quadraphonic.

quadrangle /'kwɒdræŋg(ə)l/ *noun* 4-sided plane figure, esp. square or rectangle; 4-sided court, esp. in college etc. □ **quadrangular** /-'ræŋgjʊlə/ *adjective*.

quadrant /'kwɒdrənt/ *noun* quarter of circle or sphere or of circle's circumference; optical instrument for measuring angle between distant objects.

quadraphonic /kwɒdrə'fɒnɪk/ *adjective* (of sound reproduction) using 4 transmission channels. □ **quadraphonically** *adverb*; **quadraphonics** *plural noun*.

quadrate ● *adjective* /'kwɒdrət/ square, rectangular. ● *noun* /'kwɒdrət, -dreɪt/ rectangular object. ● *verb* /kwɒ'dreɪt/ (**-ting**) make square.

quadratic /kwɒ'drætɪk/ *Mathematics* ● *adjective* involving the square (and no higher power) of unknown quantity or variable. ● *noun* quadratic equation.

quadriceps /'kwɒdrɪseps/ *noun* 4-headed muscle at front of thigh.

quadrilateral /kwɒdrɪ'lætər(ə)l/ ● *adjective* having 4 sides. ● *noun* 4-sided figure.

quadrille /kwɒ'drɪl/ *noun* square dance, music for this.

quadruped /'kwɒdruped/ *noun* 4-footed animal, esp. mammal.

quadruple /'kwɒdrʊp(ə)l/ ● *adjective* fourfold; having 4 parts; (of time in music) having 4 beats in bar. ● *noun* fourfold number or amount. ● *verb* /kwɒ'druːp(ə)l/ multiply by 4.

quadruplet /'kwɒdrʊplɪt/ *noun* each of 4 children born at one birth.

quadruplicate ● *adjective* /kwɒ'druːplɪkət/ fourfold; of which 4 copies are made. ● *verb* /-keɪt/ (**-ting**) multiply by 4.

quaff /kwɒf/ *verb literary* drink deeply; drain (cup etc.) in long draughts.

quagmire /'kwɒgmaɪə, 'kwæg-/ *noun* muddy or boggy area; hazardous situation.

quail[1] *noun* (*plural* same or **-s**) small game bird related to partridge.

quail[2] *verb* flinch, show fear.

quaint *adjective* attractively odd or old-fashioned. □ **quaintly** *adverb*; **quaintness** *noun*.

quake ● *verb* (**-king**) shake, tremble. ● *noun colloquial* earthquake.

Quaker *noun* member of Society of Friends. □ **Quakerism** *noun*.

qualification /kwɒlɪfɪ'keɪʃ(ə)n/ *noun* accomplishment fitting person for position or purpose; thing that modifies or limits; qualifying, being qualified. □ **qualificatory** /'kwɒl-/ *adjective*.

qualify /'kwɒlɪfaɪ/ *verb* (**-ies, -ied**) (often as **qualified** *adjective*) make competent or fit for purpose or position; make legally entitled; (usually + *for*) satisfy conditions; modify, limit; *Grammar* (of word) attribute quality to (esp. noun); moderate, mitigate; (+ *as*) be describable as. □ **qualifier** *noun*.

qualitative /'kwɒlɪtətɪv/ *adjective* concerned with quality as opposed to quantity. □ **qualitatively** *adverb*.

quality /'kwɒlɪtɪ/ ● *noun* (*plural* **-ies**) excellence; degree of excellence; attribute, faculty; relative nature or character; timbre. ● *adjective* of high quality.

qualm /kwɑːm/ *noun* misgiving; scruple of conscience; momentary faint or sick feeling.

quandary /ˈkwɒndərɪ/ *noun* (*plural* **-ies**) perplexed state; practical dilemma.

quango /ˈkwæŋɡəʊ/ *noun* (*plural* **-s**) semi-public administrative body appointed by government.

quanta *plural of* QUANTUM.

quantify /ˈkwɒntɪfaɪ/ *verb* (**-ies, -ied**) determine quantity of; express as quantity. □ **quantifiable** *adjective*.

quantitative /ˈkwɒntɪtətɪv/ *adjective* concerned with quantity as opposed to quality; measured or measurable by quantity.

quantity /ˈkwɒntɪtɪ/ *noun* (*plural* **-ies**) property of things that is measurable; size, extent, weight, amount, or number; (in *plural*) large amounts or numbers; length or shortness of vowel sound or syllable; *Mathematics* value, component, etc. that may be expressed in numbers. □ **quantity surveyor** person who measures and prices building work.

quantum /ˈkwɒntəm/ *noun* (*plural* **-ta**) discrete amount of energy proportional to frequency of radiation it represents; required or allowed amount. □ **quantum mechanics, theory** theory assuming that energy exists in discrete units.

quarantine /ˈkwɒrəntiːn/ *noun* isolation imposed on person or animal to prevent infection or contagion; period of this. *verb* (**-ning**) put in quarantine.

quark[1] /kwɑːk/ *noun Physics* component of elementary particles.

quark[2] /kwɑːk/ *noun* kind of low-fat curd cheese.

quarrel /ˈkwɒr(ə)l/ *noun* severe or angry dispute; break in friendly relations; cause of complaint. *verb* (**-ll-**; *US* **-l-**) (often + *with*) find fault; dispute; break off friendly relations. □ **quarrelsome** *adjective*.

quarry[1] /ˈkwɒrɪ/ *noun* (*plural* **-ies**) place from which stone etc. is extracted. *verb* (**-ies, -ied**) extract (stone etc.) from quarry. □ **quarry tile** unglazed floor-tile.

quarry[2] /ˈkwɒrɪ/ *noun* (*plural* **-ies**) intended victim or prey; object of pursuit.

quart /kwɔːt/ *noun* liquid measure equal to quarter of gallon; two pints (1.136 litre).

quarter /ˈkwɔːtə/ *noun* each of 4 equal parts; period of 3 months; point of time 15 minutes before or after any hour; 25 US or Canadian cents, coin worth this; part of town, esp. as occupied by particular class; point of compass, region at this; direction; district; source of supply; (in *plural*) lodgings, accommodation of troops etc.; one-fourth of a lunar month; mercy towards enemy etc. on condition of surrender; grain measure equivalent to 8 bushels, *colloquial* one-fourth of a pound weight. *verb* divide into quarters; put (troops etc.) into quarters; provide with lodgings; *Heraldry* place (coats of arms) on 4 quarters of shield. □ **quarterback** player in American football who directs attacking play; **quarter day** day on which quarterly payments are due; **quarterdeck** part of ship's upper deck near stern; **quarter-final** *Sport* match or round preceding semifinal; **quarter-hour** period of 15 minutes; **quartermaster** regimental officer in charge of quartering, rations, etc., naval petty officer in charge of steering, signals, etc.

quarterly *adjective* produced or occurring once every quarter of year. *adverb* once every quarter of year. *noun* (*plural* **-ies**) quarterly journal.

quartet /kwɔːˈtet/ *noun* musical composition for 4 performers; the performers; any group of 4.

quarto /ˈkwɔːtəʊ/ *noun* (*plural* **-s**) size of book or page made by folding sheet of standard size twice to form 4 leaves.

quartz /kwɔːts/ *noun* silica in various mineral forms. *adjective* (of clock or watch) operated by vibrations of electrically driven quartz crystal.

quasar /ˈkweɪzɑː/ *noun* starlike object with large red shift.

quash /kwɒʃ/ *verb* annul; reject as not valid; suppress, crush.

quasi- /ˈkweɪzaɪ/ *combining form* seemingly, not really; almost.

quaternary /kwəˈtɜːnərɪ/ *adjective* having 4 parts.

quatrain /ˈkwɒtreɪn/ *noun* 4-line stanza.

quatrefoil /ˈkætrəfɔɪl/ *noun* leaf consisting of 4 leaflets; design or ornament in this shape.

quaver /ˈkweɪvə/ *verb* (esp. of voice or sound) vibrate, shake, tremble; sing or say with quavering voice. ● *noun Music* note half as long as crotchet; trill in singing; tremble in speech. □ **quavery** *adjective.*

quay /kiː/ *noun* artificial landing-place for loading and unloading ships. □ **quayside** land forming or near quay.

queasy /ˈkwiːzɪ/ *adjective* (**-ier, -iest**) (of person) nauseous; (of stomach) easily upset; (of the conscience etc.) overscrupulous. □ **queasily** *adverb*; **queasiness** *noun.*

queen ● *noun* (as title usually **Queen**) female sovereign; (in full **queen consort**) king's wife; woman, country, or thing pre-eminent of its kind; fertile female among bees, ants, etc.; most powerful piece in chess; court card depicting queen; (**the Queen**) national anthem when sovereign is female; *offensive slang* male homosexual. ● *verb* convert (pawn in chess) to queen when it reaches opponent's side of board. □ **queen mother** king's widow who is mother of sovereign; **Queen's Bench** division of High Court of Justice; **Queen's Counsel** counsel to the Crown, taking precedence over other barristers; **the Queen's English** English language correctly written or spoken. □ **queenly** *adjective* (**-ier, -iest**).

Queensberry Rules /ˈkwiːnzbərɪ/ *plural noun* standard rules, esp. of boxing.

queer ● *adjective* strange, odd, eccentric; suspect, of questionable character; slightly ill, faint; *offensive slang* (esp. of a man) homosexual. ● *noun offensive slang* homosexual. ● *verb slang* spoil, put out of order. □ **in Queer Street** *slang* in difficulty, esp. in debt.

quell *verb* suppress, crush.

quench *verb* satisfy (thirst) by drinking; extinguish (fire or light); cool, esp. with water; stifle, suppress.

quern *noun* hand mill for grinding corn.

querulous /ˈkwerʊləs/ *adjective* complaining; peevish. □ **querulously** *adverb.*

query /ˈkwɪərɪ/ ● *noun* (*plural* **-ies**) question; question mark. ● *verb* (**-ies, -ied**) ask, inquire; call in question; dispute accuracy of.

quest ● *noun* search, seeking; thing sought, esp. by medieval knight. ● *verb* (often + *about*) go about in search of something.

question /ˈkwestʃ(ə)n/ ● *noun* sentence worded or expressed so as to seek information or answer; doubt or dispute about matter, raising of such doubt etc.; matter to be discussed or decided; problem requiring solution. ● *verb* ask questions of; subject (person) to examination; throw doubt on. □ **be just a question of time** be certain to happen sooner or later; **be a question of** be at issue, be a problem; **call in** or **into question** express doubts about; **in question** being discussed or referred to; **out of the question** not worth questioning, impossible; **question mark** punctuation mark (?) indicating question (see panel); **question-master** person presiding over quiz game etc.; **question time** period in Parliament when MPs may question ministers. □ **questioner** *noun*; **questioning** *adjective & noun*; **questioningly** *adverb.*

questionable *adjective* doubtful as regards truth, quality, honesty, wisdom, etc.

....

Question mark ?

This is used instead of a full stop at the end of a sentence to show that it is a question, e.g.

Have you seen the film yet?
You didn't lose my purse, did you?

It is **not** used at the end of a reported question, e.g.

I asked you whether you'd seen the film yet.

....

questionnaire /kwestʃəˈneə/ noun list of questions for obtaining information esp. for statistical analysis.

queue /kjuː/ ● noun line or sequence of people, vehicles, etc. waiting their turn. ● verb (**-s, -d, queuing** or **queue-ing**) (often + **up**) form or join queue. □ **queue-jump** push forward out of turn in queue.

quibble /ˈkwɪb(ə)l/ ● noun petty objection, trivial point of criticism; evasion. ● verb (**-ling**) use quibbles.

quiche /kiːʃ/ noun savoury flan.

quick ● adjective taking only a short time; arriving after only a short time, prompt; with only a short interval; lively, alert, intelligent; (of temper) easily roused. ● adverb quickly. ● noun soft sensitive flesh, esp. below nails or skin; seat of emotion. □ **quicklime** unslaked lime; **quicksand** (often in plural) area of loose wet sand that sucks in anything placed on it, treacherous situation etc.; **quickset** (of hedge etc.) formed of cuttings, esp. hawthorn; **quicksilver** mercury; **quickstep** fast foxtrot; **quick-tempered** easily angered; **quick-witted** quick to grasp situation, make repartee, etc.; **quick-wittedness** noun. □ **quickly** adverb.

quicken verb make or become quicker, accelerate; give life or vigour to, rouse; (of woman) reach stage in pregnancy when movements of foetus can be felt; (of foetus) begin to show signs of life.

quid[1] noun slang (plural same) one pound sterling.

quid[2] noun lump of tobacco for chewing.

quid pro quo /ˌkwɪd prəʊ ˈkwəʊ/ noun (plural **quid pro quos**) gift, favour, etc. exchanged for another.

quiescent /kwɪˈes(ə)nt/ adjective inert, dormant. □ **quiescence** noun.

quiet /ˈkwaɪət/ ● adjective with little or no sound or motion; of gentle or peaceful disposition; unobtrusive, not showy; not overt, disguised; undisturbed, uninterrupted; not busy. ● noun silence, stillness; undisturbed state, tranquillity. ● verb (often + **down**) make or become quiet, calm. □ **be quiet** (esp. in imperative) cease talking etc.; **keep quiet** (often + **about**) say nothing; **on the quiet** secretly. □ **quietly** adverb; **quietness** noun.

quieten verb (often + **down**) make or become quiet or calm.

quietism noun passive contemplative attitude towards life. □ **quietist** noun & adjective.

quietude /ˈkwaɪɪtjuːd/ noun state of quiet.

quietus /kwaɪˈiːtəs/ noun release from life; death, final riddance.

quiff noun man's tuft of hair brushed upwards in front.

quill noun (in full **quill-feather**) large feather in wing or tail; hollow stem of this; (in full **quill pen**) pen made of quill; (usually in plural) porcupine's spine.

quilt ● noun bedspread, esp. of quilted material. ● verb line bedspread or garment with padding enclosed between layers of fabric by lines of stitching. □ **quilter** noun; **quilting** noun.

quin noun colloquial quintuplet.

quince noun (tree bearing) acid pear-shaped fruit used in jams etc.

quincentenary /kwɪnsenˈtiːnərɪ/ ● noun (plural **-ies**) 500th anniversary; celebration of this. ● adjective of this anniversary.

quinine /ˈkwɪniːn/ noun bitter drug used as a tonic and to reduce fever.

Quinquagesima /ˌkwɪŋkwəˈdʒesɪmə/ noun Sunday before Lent.

quinquennial /kwɪŋˈkwenɪəl/ adjective lasting 5 years; recurring every 5 years. □ **quinquennially** adverb.

quintessence /kwɪnˈtes(ə)ns/ noun (usually + of) purest and most perfect form, manifestation, or embodiment of quality etc.; highly refined extract. □ **quintessential** /-tɪˈsen-/ adjective; **quintessentially** /-tɪˈsen-/ adverb.

quintet /kwɪnˈtet/ noun musical composition for 5 performers; the performers; any group of 5.

quintuple /ˈkwɪntjʊp(ə)l/ ● adjective fivefold, having 5 parts. ● noun fivefold number or amount. ● verb (**-ling**) multiply by 5.

quintuplet /ˈkwɪntjʊplɪt/ noun each of 5 children born at one birth.

quip ● noun clever saying, epigram. ● verb (**-pp-**) make quips.

quire noun 25 sheets of paper.

quirk *noun* peculiar feature; trick of fate. □ **quirky** *adjective* (**-ier, -iest**).

quisling /'kwɪzlɪŋ/ *noun* collaborator with invading enemy.

quit ● *verb* (**-tting**; *past & past participle* **quitted** or **quit**) give up, let go, abandon; *US* cease, stop; leave or depart from. ● *adjective* (+ *of*) rid of.

quitch *noun* couch grass.

quite *adverb* completely, altogether, absolutely; rather, to some extent; (often + *so*) *said to indicate agreement.* □ **quite a, quite some** a remarkable; **quite a few** *colloquial* a fairly large number (of); **quite something** *colloquial* a remarkable thing or person.

quits *adjective* on even terms by retaliation or repayment. □ **call it quits** acknowledge that things are now even, agree to stop quarrelling.

quiver[1] /'kwɪvə/ ● *verb* tremble or vibrate with slight rapid motion. ● *noun* quivering motion or sound.

quiver[2] /'kwɪvə/ *noun* case for arrows.

quixotic /kwɪk'sɒtɪk/ *adjective* extravagantly and romantically chivalrous. □ **quixotically** *adverb*.

quiz ● *noun* (*plural* **quizzes**) test of knowledge, esp. as entertainment; interrogation, examination. ● *verb* examine by questioning.

quizzical /'kwɪzɪk(ə)l/ *adjective* mocking, gently amused. □ **quizzically** *adverb*.

quod *noun slang* prison.

quoin /kɔɪn/ *noun* external angle of building; cornerstone; wedge used in printing or gunnery.

quoit /kɔɪt/ *noun* ring thrown to encircle peg; (in *plural*) game using these.

quondam /'kwɒndæm/ *adjective* that once was, former.

quorate /'kwɔːreɪt/ *adjective* constituting or having quorum.

Quorn /kwɔːn/ *noun proprietary term* vegetable protein food made from fungus.

quorum /'kwɔːrəm/ *noun* minimum number of members that must be present to constitute valid meeting.

Quotation marks ' ' " "

Also called inverted commas, these are used:

1 round a direct quotation (closing quotation marks come after any punctuation which is part of the quotation), e.g.

> *He said, 'That is nonsense.'*
> *'That', he said, 'is nonsense.'*
> *'That, however,' he said, 'is nonsense.'*
> *Did he say, 'That is nonsense'?*
> *He asked, 'Is that nonsense?'*

2 round a quoted word or phrase, e.g.

> *What does 'integrated circuit' mean?*

3 round a word or phrase that is not being used in its central sense, e.g.

> *the 'king' of jazz*
> *He said he had enough 'bread' to buy a car.*

4 round the title of a book, song, poem, magazine article, television programme, etc. (but not a book of the Bible), e.g.

> *'Hard Times' by Charles Dickens*

5 as double quotation marks round a quotation within a quotation, e.g.

> *He asked, 'Do you know what "integrated circuit" means?'*

In handwriting, double quotation marks are usual.

---

quota /ˈkwəʊtə/ *noun* share to be contributed to or received from total; number of goods, people, etc. stipulated or permitted.

quotable *adjective* worth quoting.

quotation /kwəʊˈteɪʃ(ə)n/ *noun* passage or remark quoted; quoting, being quoted; contractor's estimate. □ **quotation marks** inverted commas (' ' or " ") used at beginning and end of quotation etc. (see panel).

quote ● *verb* (**-ting**) cite or appeal to as example, authority, etc.; repeat or copy out passage from; (+ *from*) cite (author, book, etc.); (+ *as*) cite (author

etc.) as proof, evidence, etc.; (as *interjection*) used in dictation etc. to indicate opening quotation marks; (often + *at*) state price of; state (price) for job. ● *noun colloquial* passage quoted; (usually in *plural*) quotation marks.

quoth /kwəʊθ/ *verb* (only in 1st & 3rd persons) *archaic* said.

quotidian /kwɒˈtɪdɪən/ *adjective* occurring or recurring daily; commonplace, trivial.

quotient /ˈkwəʊʃ(ə)nt/ *noun* result of division sum.

q.v. *abbreviation* which see (*quod vide*).

···············

Rr

···············

R *abbreviation* (also **R.**) *Regina*; *Rex*; River; (also ®) registered as trademark. □ **R & D** research and development.

r. *abbreviation* (also **r**) right; radius.

RA *abbreviation* Royal Academy or Academician; Royal Artillery.

rabbet /ˈræbɪt/ ● *noun* step-shaped channel cut along edge or face of wood etc. to receive edge or tongue of another piece. ● *verb* (**-t-**) join with rabbet; make rabbet in.

rabbi /ˈræbaɪ/ *noun* (*plural* **-s**) Jewish religious leader; Jewish scholar or teacher, esp. of the law. □ **rabbinical** /rəˈbɪn-/ *adjective*.

rabbit /ˈræbɪt/ ● *noun* burrowing mammal of hare family; its fur. ● *verb* (**-t-**) hunt rabbits; (often + *on*, *away*) *colloquial* talk pointlessly; chatter. □ **rabbit punch** blow with edge of hand on back of neck.

rabble /ˈræb(ə)l/ *noun* disorderly crowd, mob; contemptible or inferior set of people. □ **rabble-rouser** person who stirs up rabble, esp. to agitate for social change.

Rabelaisian /ræbəˈleɪzɪən/ *adjective* exuberantly and coarsely humorous.

rabid /ˈræbɪd/ *adjective* affected with rabies, mad; violent, fanatical. □ **rabidity** /rəˈbɪd-/ *noun*.

rabies /ˈreɪbiːz/ *noun* contagious viral disease of esp. dogs; hydrophobia.

RAC *abbreviation* Royal Automobile Club.

raccoon /rəˈkuːn/ *noun* (also **racoon**) (*plural* same or **-s**) N. American mammal with bushy tail; its fur.

race¹ ● *noun* contest of speed or to be first to achieve something; (in *plural*) series of races for horses etc.; strong current in sea or river; channel. ● *verb* (**-cing**) take part in race; have race with; (+ *with*) compete in speed; cause to race; go at full speed; (usually as **racing** *adjective*) follow or take part in horse racing. □ **racecourse** ground for horse racing; **racehorse** one bred or kept for racing; **race meeting** sequence of horse races at one place; **racetrack** racecourse, track for motor racing; **racing car** one built for racing; **racing driver** driver of racing car.

race² *noun* each of the major divisions of humankind, each having distinct physical characteristics; group of people, animals, or plants connected by common descent; any great division of living creatures. □ **race relations** relations between members of different races in same country.

raceme /rəˈsiːm/ *noun* flower cluster with flowers attached by short stalks at equal distances along stem.

racial /'reɪʃ(ə)l/ *adjective* of or concerning race; on grounds of or connected with difference in race. □ **racially** *adverb*.

racialism *noun* = RACISM. □ **racialist** *noun & adjective*.

racism *noun* (prejudice based on) belief in superiority of particular race; antagonism towards other races. □ **racist** *noun & adjective*.

rack[1] ● *noun* framework, usually with rails, bars, etc., for holding things; cogged or toothed rail or bar engaging with wheel, pinion, etc.; *historical* instrument of torture stretching victim's joints. ● *verb* inflict suffering on; *historical* torture on rack. □ **rack one's brains** make great mental effort; **rack-rent** extortionate rent.

rack[2] *noun* destruction (esp. in **rack and ruin**).

rack[3] *verb* (often + *off*) draw off (wine etc.) from lees.

racket[1] /'rækɪt/ *noun* (also **racquet**) bat with round or oval frame strung with catgut, nylon, etc., used in tennis etc.; (in *plural*) game like squash but in larger court.

racket[2] ● *noun* uproar, din; *slang* scheme for obtaining money etc. by dishonest means; dodge; sly game; *colloquial* line of business.

racketeer /rækɪ'tɪə/ *noun* person who operates dishonest business. □ **racketeering** *noun*.

raconteur /rækɒn'tɜː/ *noun* teller of anecdotes.

racoon = RACCOON.

racy *adjective* (**-ier**, **-iest**) lively and vigorous in style; risqué; of distinctive quality. □ **raciness** *noun*.

rad *noun* unit of absorbed dose of ionizing radiation.

RADA /'rɑːdə/ *abbreviation* Royal Academy of Dramatic Art.

radar /'reɪdɑː/ *noun* radio system for detecting the direction, range, or presence of objects; apparatus for this. □ **radar trap** device using radar to detect speeding vehicles.

raddled /'ræd(ə)ld/ *adjective* worn out.

radial /'reɪdɪəl/ ● *adjective* of or arranged like rays or radii; having spokes or radiating lines; acting or moving along

such lines; (in full **radial-ply**) (of tyre) having fabric layers arranged radially. ● *noun* radial-ply tyre. □ **radially** *adverb*.

radian /'reɪdɪən/ *noun* SI unit of plane angle (about 57°).

radiant /'reɪdɪənt/ ● *adjective* emitting or issuing in rays; beaming with joy etc.; splendid; dazzling. ● *noun* point or object from which heat or light radiates. □ **radiance** *noun*; **radiantly** *adverb*.

radiate /'reɪdɪeɪt/ *verb* (**-ting**) emit rays of light, heat, etc.; be emitted in rays; emit or spread from a centre; transmit or demonstrate.

radiation *noun* radiating; emission of energy as electromagnetic waves; energy thus transmitted, esp. invisibly; (in full **radiation therapy**) treatment of cancer etc. using e.g. X-rays or ultraviolet light. □ **radiation sickness** sickness caused by exposure to radiation such as gamma rays.

radiator *noun* device for heating room etc. by circulation of hot water etc.; engine-cooling device in motor vehicle or aircraft.

radical /'rædɪk(ə)l/ ● *adjective* fundamental; far-reaching, thorough; advocating fundamental reform; forming the basis; primary; of the root of a number or plant. ● *noun* person holding radical views; atom or group of atoms forming base of compound and remaining unchanged during reactions; quantity forming or expressed as root of another. □ **radicalism** *noun*; **radically** *adverb*.

radicchio /rə'diːkɪəʊ/ *noun* (*plural* **-s**) chicory with purplish leaves.

radicle /'rædɪk(ə)l/ *noun* part of seed that develops into root.

radii *plural* of RADIUS.

radio /'reɪdɪəʊ/ ● *noun* (*plural* **-s**) transmission and reception of messages etc. by electromagnetic waves of radio frequency; apparatus for receiving, broadcasting, or transmitting radio signals; sound broadcasting (station or channel). ● *verb* (**-es**, **-ed**) send (message) by radio; send message to (person) by radio; communicate or broadcast by radio. □ **radio-controlled** controlled from a distance by radio; **radio telephone** one operating by radio; **radio**

telescope aerial system for analysing radiation in the radio-frequency range from stars etc.

radioactive *adjective* of or exhibiting radioactivity.

radioactivity *noun* spontaneous disintegration of atomic nuclei, with emission of usually penetrating radiation or particles.

radiocarbon *noun* radioactive isotope of carbon.

radiogram /ˈreɪdɪəʊgræm/ *noun* combined radio and record player; picture obtained by X-rays etc.; telegram sent by radio.

radiograph /ˈreɪdɪəʊgrɑːf/ ● *noun* instrument recording intensity of radiation; picture obtained by X-rays etc. ● *verb* obtain picture of by X-rays, gamma rays, etc. □ **radiographer** /-ˈɒgrəfə/ *noun*, **radiography** /-ˈɒgrəfɪ/ *noun*.

radiology /reɪdɪˈɒlədʒɪ/ *noun esp. Medicine* study of X-rays and other high-energy radiation. □ **radiologist** *noun*.

radiophonic *adjective* of electronically produced sound, esp. music.

radioscopy /reɪdɪˈɒskəpɪ/ *noun* examination by X-rays etc. of objects opaque to light.

radiotherapy *noun* treatment of disease by X-rays or other forms of radiation.

radish /ˈrædɪʃ/ *noun* plant with crisp pungent root; this root, esp. eaten raw.

radium /ˈreɪdɪəm/ *noun* radioactive metallic element.

radius /ˈreɪdɪəs/ *noun* (*plural* **radii** /-dɪaɪ/ or **-es**) straight line from centre to circumference of circle or sphere; distance from a centre; bone of forearm on same side as thumb.

radon /ˈreɪdɒn/ *noun* gaseous radioactive inert element arising from disintegration of radium.

RAF *abbreviation* Royal Air Force.

raffia /ˈræfɪə/ *noun* palm tree native to Madagascar; fibre from its leaves.

raffish /ˈræfɪʃ/ *adjective* disreputable, rakish; tawdry.

raffle /ˈræf(ə)l/ ● *noun* fund-raising lottery with prizes. ● *verb* (**-ling**) (often + *off*) sell by raffle.

raft /rɑːft/ *noun* flat floating structure of wood etc., used for transport.

rafter /ˈrɑːftə/ *noun* any of sloping beams forming framework of roof.

rag [1] *noun* torn, frayed, or worn piece of woven material; remnant; (in *plural*) old or worn clothes; *derogatory* newspaper. □ **rag-bag** miscellaneous collection; **rag doll** stuffed cloth doll; **ragtime** form of highly syncopated early jazz; **the rag trade** *colloquial* the clothing business; **ragwort** yellow-flowered ragged-leaved plant.

rag [2] ● *noun* fund-raising programme of stunts etc. staged by students; prank; rowdy celebration, disorderly scene. ● *verb* (**-gg-**) tease; play rough jokes on; engage in rough play.

ragamuffin /ˈrægəmʌfɪn/ *noun* child in ragged dirty clothes.

rage ● *noun* violent anger; fit of this. ● *verb* (**-ging**) be full of anger; (often + *at, against*) speak furiously; be violent, be at its height; (as **raging** *adjective*) extreme, very painful. □ **all the rage** very popular, fashionable.

ragged /ˈrægɪd/ *adjective* torn; frayed; in ragged clothes; with a broken or jagged outline or surface; lacking finish, smoothness, or uniformity.

raglan /ˈræglən/ *adjective* (of sleeve) running up to neck of garment.

ragout /ræˈguː/ *noun* highly seasoned stew of meat and vegetables.

raid ● *noun* rapid surprise attack by armed forces or thieves; surprise visit by police etc. to arrest suspects or seize illicit goods. ● *verb* make raid on. □ **raider** *noun*.

rail [1] ● *noun* bar used to hang things on or as protection, part of fence, top of banisters, etc.; steel bar(s) making railway track; railway. ● *verb* provide or enclose with rail(s). □ **railcard** pass entitling holder to reduced rail fares.

rail [2] *verb* (often + *at, against*) complain or protest strongly; rant.

rail [3] *noun* marsh wading bird.

railing *noun* (often in *plural*) fence or barrier made of rails.

raillery /ˈreɪlərɪ/ *noun* good-humoured ridicule.

railroad ● *noun esp. US* railway. ● *verb* (often + *into, through*) coerce, rush.

railway /ˈreɪlweɪ/ *noun* track or set of tracks of steel rails on which trains run; organization and people required to work such a system. □ **railwayman** male railway employee.

raiment /'reɪmənt/ *noun archaic* clothing.

rain ●*noun* condensed atmospheric moisture falling in drops; fall of these; falling liquid or objects; **(the rains)** rainy season. ●*verb* (after *it*) rain falls, send in large quantities; fall or send down like rain; lavishly bestow. □ **raincoat** waterproof or water-resistant coat; **rainfall** total amount of rain falling within given area in given time; **rainforest** tropical forest with heavy rainfall; **take a rain check on** reserve right to postpone taking up (offer) until convenient.

rainbow /'reɪnbəʊ/ ●*noun* arch of colours formed in sky by reflection, refraction, and dispersion of sun's rays in falling rain etc. ●*adjective* many-coloured. □ **rainbow trout** large trout originally of N. America.

rainy *adjective* (**-ier, -iest**) (of weather, day, climate, etc.) in or on which rain is falling or much rain usually falls. □ **rainy day** time of need in the future.

raise /reɪz/ ●*verb* (**-sing**) put or take into higher position; (often + *up*) cause to rise or stand up or be vertical; increase amount, value, or strength of; (often + *up*) build up; levy, collect; cause to be heard or considered; bring up, educate; breed; remove (barrier); rouse. ●*noun Cards* increase in stake or bid; *US* rise in salary. □ **raise Cain, hell, the roof** be very angry, cause an uproar; **raise a laugh** cause others to laugh.

raisin /'reɪz(ə)n/ *noun* dried grape.

raison d'être /reɪzɔ̃ 'detr/ *noun* (*plural* **raisons d'être** *same pronunciation*) purpose that accounts for, justifies, or originally caused thing's existence. [French]

raj /rɑːdʒ/ *noun* (**the raj**) *historical* British rule in India.

raja /'rɑːdʒə/ *noun* (also **rajah**) *historical* Indian king or prince.

rake¹ ●*noun* implement with long handle and toothed crossbar for drawing hay etc. together, smoothing loose soil, etc.; similar implement. ●*verb* (**-king**) collect or gather (as) with rake; ransack, search thoroughly; direct

gunfire along (line) from end to end. □ **rake in** *colloquial* amass (profits etc.); **rake-off** *colloquial* commission or share; **rake up** revive (unwelcome) memory of.

rake² *noun* dissolute man of fashion.

rake³ ●*verb* (**-king**) set or be set at sloping angle. ●*noun* raking position or build; amount by which thing rakes.

rakish *adjective* dashing, jaunty; dissolute. □ **rakishly** *adverb*.

rallentando /rælən'tændəʊ/ *Music* ●*adverb & adjective* with gradual decrease of speed. ●*noun* (*plural* **-s** or **-di** /-diː/) rallentando passage.

rally /'rælɪ/ ●*verb* (**-ies, -ied**) (often + *round*) bring or come together as support or for action; recover after illness etc., revive; (of prices etc.) increase after fall. ●*noun* (*plural* **-ies**) rallying, being rallied; mass meeting; competition for motor vehicles over public roads; extended exchange of strokes in tennis etc. □ **rallycross** motor racing across country.

RAM *abbreviation* Royal Academy of Music; random-access memory.

ram ●*noun* uncastrated male sheep; **(the Ram)** zodiacal sign or constellation Aries; falling weight of pile-driving machine; hydraulic water pump. ●*verb* (**-mm-**) force into place; (usually + *down, in,* etc.) beat down or drive in by blows; (of ship, vehicle, etc.) strike, crash against. □ **ram-raid** crashing vehicle into shop front in order to steal contents; **ram-raider** *noun*; **ram-raiding** *noun*.

Ramadan /'ræmədæn/ *noun* ninth month of Muslim year, with strict fasting from sunrise to sunset.

ramble /'ræmb(ə)l/ ●*verb* (**-ling**) walk for pleasure; talk or write incoherently. ●*noun* walk taken for pleasure.

rambler *noun* person who rambles; straggling or spreading rose.

rambling *adjective* wandering; disconnected, incoherent; irregularly arranged; (of plant) straggling, climbing.

RAMC *abbreviation* Royal Army Medical Corps.

ramekin /'ræmɪkɪn/ *noun* small dish for baking and serving individual portion of food.

ramification /ˌræmɪfɪˈkeɪʃ(ə)n/ *noun* (usually in *plural*) consequence; subdivision.

ramify /ˈræmɪfaɪ/ *verb* (**-ies, -ied**) (cause to) form branches or subdivisions; branch out.

ramp *noun* slope joining two levels of ground, floor, etc.; stairs for entering or leaving aircraft; transverse ridge in road making vehicles slow down.

rampage ● *verb* /ræmˈpeɪdʒ/ (**-ging**) (often + *about*) rush wildly; rage, storm. ● *noun* /ˈræmpeɪdʒ/ wild or violent behaviour. □ **on the rampage** rampaging.

rampant /ˈræmpənt/ *adjective* unchecked, flourishing excessively; rank, luxuriant; *Heraldry* (of lion etc.) standing on left hind foot with forepaws in air; fanatical. □ **rampancy** *noun*.

rampart /ˈræmpɑːt/ *noun* defensive broad-topped wall; defence, protection.

ramrod *noun* rod for ramming down charge of muzzle-loading firearm; thing that is very straight or rigid.

ramshackle /ˈræmʃæk(ə)l/ *adjective* rickety, tumbledown.

ran *past of* RUN.

ranch /rɑːntʃ/ ● *noun* cattle-breeding establishment, esp. in US & Canada; farm where other animals are bred. ● *verb* farm on ranch. □ **rancher** *noun*.

rancid /ˈrænsɪd/ *adjective* (of fat or fatty foods) smelling or tasting rank and stale. □ **rancidity** /-ˈsɪd-/ *noun*.

rancour /ˈræŋkə/ *noun* (*US* **rancor**) inveterate bitterness; malignant hate. □ **rancorous** *adjective*.

rand *noun* monetary unit of South Africa.

random /ˈrændəm/ *adjective* made, done, etc. without method or conscious choice. □ **at random** without particular aim; **random-access** (of computer memory) having all parts directly accessible. □ **randomly** *adverb*.

randy /ˈrændɪ/ *adjective* (**-ier, -iest**) eager for sexual satisfaction.

ranee /ˈrɑːniː/ *noun* (also **rani**) (*plural* **-s**) *historical* raja's wife or widow.

rang *past of* RING².

range /reɪndʒ/ ● *noun* region between limits of variation, esp. scope of operation; such limits; area relevant to something; distance attainable by gun or projectile, distance between gun etc. and target; row, series, etc., esp. of mountains; area with targets for shooting; fireplace for cooking; area over which a thing is distributed; distance that can be covered by vehicle without refuelling; stretch of open land for grazing or hunting. ● *verb* (**-ging**) reach; extend; vary between limits; (usually in *passive*) line up, arrange; rove, wander; traverse in all directions. □ **range-finder** instrument for determining distance of object.

ranger *noun* keeper of royal or national park, or of forest; (**Ranger**) senior Guide.

rangy /ˈreɪndʒɪ/ *adjective* (**-ier, -iest**) tall and slim.

rani = RANEE.

rank¹ ● *noun* position in hierarchy; grade of advancement; distinct social class, grade of dignity or achievement; high social position; place in scale; row or line; single line of soldiers drawn up abreast; place where taxis wait for customers. ● *verb* have rank or place; classify, give a certain grade to; arrange in rank. □ **rank and file** (usually treated as *plural*) ordinary members of organization; **the ranks** common soldiers.

rank² *adjective* luxuriant; coarse; choked with weeds etc.; foul-smelling; loathsome; flagrant; gross, complete.

rankle /ˈræŋk(ə)l/ *verb* (**-ling**) cause persistent annoyance or resentment.

ransack /ˈrænsæk/ *verb* pillage, plunder; thoroughly search.

ransom /ˈrænsəm/ ● *noun* sum demanded or paid for release of prisoner. ● *verb* buy freedom or restoration of; hold (prisoner) to ransom; release for a ransom. □ **hold to ransom** keep (prisoner) and demand ransom, demand concessions from by threats.

rant ● *verb* speak loudly, bombastically, or violently. ● *noun* piece of ranting. □ **rant and rave** express anger noisily and forcefully.

ranunculus /rəˈnʌŋkjʊləs/ *noun* (*plural* **-luses** or **-li** /-laɪ/) plant of genus including buttercup.

RAOC *abbreviation* Royal Army Ordnance Corps.

rap[1] ● *noun* smart slight blow; sound of this, tap; *slang* blame, punishment; rhythmic monologue recited to music; (in full **rap music**) style of rock music with words recited. ● *verb* (**-pp-**) strike smartly; make sharp tapping sound; criticize adversely; *Music* perform rap. □ **take the rap** suffer the consequences. □ **rapper** *noun Music*.

rap[2] *noun* the least bit.

rapacious /rə'peɪʃəs/ *adjective* grasping, extortionate, predatory. □ **rapacity** /-'pæs-/ *noun*.

rape[1] ● *noun* act of forcing esp. woman or girl to have sexual intercourse unwillingly; (often + *of*) violation. ● *verb* (**-ping**) commit rape on.

rape[2] *noun* plant grown as fodder and for oil from its seed.

rapid /'ræpɪd/ ● *adjective* (**-er, -est**) quick, swift. ● *noun* (usually in *plural*) steep descent in river bed, with swift current. □ **rapid eye movement** jerky movement of eyes during dreaming. □ **rapidity** /rə'pɪd-/ *noun*; **rapidly** *adverb*.

rapier /'reɪpɪə/ *noun* light slender sword for thrusting.

rapine /'ræpaɪn/ *noun rhetorical* plundering.

rapist *noun* person who commits rape.

rapport /ræ'pɔː/ *noun* communication or relationship, esp. when useful and harmonious.

rapprochement /ræ'prɒʃmɑ̃/ *noun* resumption of harmonious relations, esp. between states. [French]

rapscallion /ræp'skælɪən/ *noun archaic* rascal.

rapt *adjective* absorbed; intent; carried away with feeling or thought.

rapture /'ræptʃə/ *noun* ecstatic delight; (in *plural*) great pleasure or enthusiasm or expression of it. □ **rapturous** *adjective*.

rare[1] *adjective* (**-r, -st**) seldom done, found, or occurring; uncommon; exceptionally good; of less than usual density. □ **rareness** *noun*.

rare[2] *adjective* (**-r, -st**) (of meat) underdone.

rarebit *noun* see WELSH RAREBIT.

rarefy /'reərɪfaɪ/ *verb* (**-ies, -ied**) (often as **rarefied** *adjective*) make or become less dense or solid; refine, make (idea etc.) subtle. □ **rarefaction** /-'fækʃ(ə)n/ *noun*.

rarely *adverb* seldom, not often.

raring /'reərɪŋ/ *adjective colloquial* eager (esp. in **raring to go**).

rarity /'reərətɪ/ *noun* (*plural* **-ies**) rareness; uncommon thing.

rascal /'rɑːsk(ə)l/ *noun* dishonest or mischievous person. □ **rascally** *adjective*.

rase = RAZE.

rash[1] *adjective* reckless; hasty, impetuous. □ **rashly** *adverb*; **rashness** *noun*.

rash[2] *noun* skin eruption in spots or patches; (usually + *of*) sudden widespread phenomenon.

rasher /'ræʃə/ *noun* thin slice of bacon or ham.

rasp /rɑːsp/ ● *noun* coarse file; grating noise or utterance. ● *verb* scrape roughly or with rasp; make grating sound; say gratingly; grate on.

raspberry /'rɑːzbərɪ/ *noun* (*plural* **-ies**) red fruit like blackberry; shrub bearing this; *colloquial* sound made by blowing through lips, expressing derision or disapproval.

Rastafarian /ræstə'feərɪən/ (also **Rasta** /'ræstə/) ● *noun* member of Jamaican sect regarding Haile Selassie of Ethiopia (d. 1975) as God. ● *adjective* of this sect.

rat ● *noun* large mouselike rodent; *colloquial* unpleasant or treacherous person. ● *verb* (**-tt-**) hunt or kill rats; (also + *on*) inform (on), desert, betray. □ **ratbag** *slang* obnoxious person; **rat race** *colloquial* fiercely competitive struggle.

ratable = RATEABLE.

ratatouille /rætə'tuː/ *noun* dish of stewed onions, courgettes, tomatoes, aubergines, and peppers.

ratchet /'rætʃɪt/ *noun* set of teeth on edge of bar or wheel with catch ensuring motion in one direction only; (in full **ratchet-wheel**) wheel with rim so toothed.

rate ● *noun* numerical proportion between two sets of things or as basis of calculating amount or value; charge, cost, or value; measure of this; pace of movement or change; (in *plural*) tax levied by local authorities according to

value of buildings and land occupied.
● verb (-ting) estimate worth or value of; assign value to; consider, regard as; (+ as) rank or be considered as; subject to payment of local rate; deserve. □ **at any rate** in any case, whatever happens; **at this rate** if this example is typical; **rate-capping** historical imposition of upper limit on local authority rates; **ratepayer** person liable to pay rates.

rateable /ˈreɪtəb(ə)l/ adjective (also **ratable** /ˈreɪtəb(ə)l/) liable to rates. □ **rateable value** value at which business etc. is assessed for rates.

rather /ˈrɑːðə/ adverb by preference; (usually + than) more truly; as a more likely alternative; more precisely; to some extent; /rɑːˈðɜː/ most emphatically.

ratify /ˈrætɪfaɪ/ verb (-ies, -ied) confirm or accept by formal consent, signature, etc. □ **ratification** noun.

rating /ˈreɪtɪŋ/ noun placing in rank or class; estimated standing of person as regards credit etc.; non-commissioned sailor; (usually in plural) popularity of a broadcast as determined by estimated size of audience.

ratio /ˈreɪʃɪəʊ/ noun (plural **-s**) quantitative relation between similar magnitudes.

ratiocinate /rætɪˈɒsɪneɪt/ verb (-ting) literary reason, esp. using syllogisms. □ **ratiocination** noun.

ration /ˈræʃ(ə)n/ ● noun official allowance of food, clothing, etc., in time of shortage; (usually in plural) fixed daily allowance of food. ● verb limit (food etc. or people) to fixed ration; (usually + out) share (out) in fixed quantities.

rational /ˈræʃən(ə)l/ adjective of or based on reason; sensible; endowed with reason; rejecting what is unreasonable; Mathematics expressible as ratio of whole numbers. □ **rationality** /-ˈnæl-/ noun; **rationally** adverb.

rationale /ræʃəˈnɑːl/ noun fundamental reason, logical basis.

rationalism noun practice of treating reason as basis of belief and knowledge. □ **rationalist** noun & adjective; **rationalistic** /-ˈlɪs-/ adjective.

rationalize verb (also **-ise**) (**-zing** or **-sing**) (often + away) offer rational but specious explanation of (behaviour or attitude); make logical and consistent; make (industry etc.) more efficient by reducing waste. □ **rationalization** noun.

ratline /ˈrætlɪn/ noun (also **ratlin**) (usually in plural) any of the small lines fastened across ship's shrouds like ladder rungs.

rattan /rəˈtæn/ noun palm with long thin many-jointed stems; cane of this.

rattle /ˈræt(ə)l/ ● verb (-ling) (cause to) give out rapid succession of short sharp sounds; cause such sounds by shaking something; move or travel with rattling noise; (usually + off) say or recite rapidly; (usually + on) talk in lively thoughtless way; colloquial disconcert, alarm. ● noun rattling sound; device or plaything made to rattle. □ **rattlesnake** poisonous American snake with rattling rings on tail. □ **rattly** adjective.

rattling ● adjective that rattles; brisk, vigorous. ● adverb colloquial remarkably (good etc.).

raucous /ˈrɔːkəs/ adjective harsh-sounding; hoarse. □ **raucously** adverb; **raucousness** noun.

raunchy /ˈrɔːntʃɪ/ adjective (**-ier**, **-iest**) colloquial sexually boisterous.

ravage /ˈrævɪdʒ/ ● verb (-ging) devastate, plunder. ● noun (usually in plural, + of) destructive effect.

rave ● verb (-ving) talk wildly or deliriously; (usually + about, over) speak with rapturous admiration; colloquial enjoy oneself freely. ● noun colloquial highly enthusiastic review; (also **rave-up**) lively party.

ravel /ˈræv(ə)l/ verb (**-ll-**; US **-l-**) entangle, become entangled; fray out.

raven /ˈreɪv(ə)n/ ● noun large glossy black crow with hoarse cry. ● adjective glossy black.

ravening /ˈrævənɪŋ/ adjective hungrily seeking prey; voracious.

ravenous /ˈrævənəs/ adjective very hungry; voracious; rapacious. □ **ravenously** adverb.

raver noun colloquial uninhibited pleasure-loving person.

ravine /rəˈviːn/ noun deep narrow gorge.

raving • *noun* (usually in *plural*) wild or delirious talk. • *adjective colloquial* utter, absolute. • *adverb colloquial* utterly, absolutely.

ravioli /ˌrævɪˈəʊlɪ/ *noun* small square pasta envelopes containing meat, spinach, etc.

ravish /ˈrævɪʃ/ *verb archaic* rape (woman); enrapture.

ravishing *adjective* lovely, beautiful. □ **ravishingly** *adverb*.

raw *adjective* uncooked; in natural state, not processed or manufactured; inexperienced, untrained; stripped of skin; unhealed; sensitive to touch; (of weather) cold and damp; crude. □ **in the raw** in its natural state, naked; **raw-boned** gaunt; **raw deal** unfair treatment; **rawhide** untanned hide, rope or whip of this; **raw material** material from which manufactured goods are made.

Rawlplug /ˈrɔːlplʌg/ *noun proprietary term* cylindrical plug for holding screw in masonry.

ray[1] *noun* single line or narrow beam of light; straight line in which radiation travels; (in *plural*) radiation; trace or beginning of enlightening influence; any of set of radiating lines, parts, or things; marginal part of daisy etc.

ray[2] *noun* large edible marine fish with flat body.

ray[3] *noun* (also **re**) *Music* second note of scale in tonic sol-fa.

rayon /ˈreɪɒn/ *noun* textile fibre or fabric made from cellulose.

raze *verb* (also **rase**) (**-zing** or **-sing**) completely destroy, tear down.

razor /ˈreɪzə/ *noun* instrument for shaving. □ **razorbill** auk with sharp-edged bill; **razor-blade** flat piece of metal with sharp edge, used in safety razor; **razor-edge**, **razor's edge** keen edge, sharp mountain ridge, critical situation, sharp line of division.

razzle /ˈræz(ə)l/ *noun colloquial* spree. □ **razzle-dazzle** excitement, bustle, extravagant publicity.

razzmatazz /ˌræzməˈtæz/ *noun* (also **razzamatazz** /ˌræzə-/) *colloquial* glamorous excitement; insincere activity.

RC *abbreviation* Roman Catholic.

Rd. *abbreviation* Road.

RE *abbreviation* Religious Education; Royal Engineers.

re[1] /riː/ *preposition* in the matter of; about, concerning.

re[2] = RAY[3].

re- *prefix attachable to almost any verb or its derivative, meaning:* once more, anew, afresh; back. For words starting with *re-* that are not found below, the root-words should be consulted.

reach • *verb* (often + *out*) stretch out, extend; (often + *for*) stretch hand etc.; get as far as, get to or attain; make contact with; pass, hand; take with outstretched hand; *Nautical* sail with wind abeam. • *noun* extent to which hand etc. can be reached out, influence exerted, etc.; act of reaching out; continuous extent, esp. of river or canal. □ **reach-me-down** *colloquial* ready-made garment. □ **reachable** *adjective*.

react /rɪˈækt/ *verb* (often + *to*) respond to stimulus; change or behave differently due to some influence; (often + *with*) undergo chemical reaction (with other substance); (often + *against*) respond with repulsion to; tend in reverse or contrary direction.

reaction /rɪˈæk∫(ə)n/ *noun* reacting; response; bad physical response to drug etc.; occurrence of condition after its opposite; tendency to oppose change or reform; interaction of substances undergoing chemical change.

reactionary • *adjective* tending to oppose (esp. political) change or reform. • *noun* (*plural* **-ies**) reactionary person.

reactivate /rɪˈæktɪveɪt/ *verb* (**-ting**) restore to state of activity. □ **reactivation** *noun*.

reactive /rɪˈæktɪv/ *adjective* showing reaction; reacting rather than taking initiative; susceptible to chemical reaction.

reactor *noun* (in full **nuclear reactor**) device in which nuclear chain reaction is used to produce energy.

read • *verb* (*past & past participle* **read** /red/) reproduce (written or printed words) mentally or (often + *aloud*, *out*, *off*, etc.) vocally; (be able to) convert (written or printed words or other symbols) into intended words or meaning; interpret; (of meter) show (figure); interpret state of (meter); study (subject) at university; (as **read** /red/ *adjective*) versed in subject (esp. literature) by reading; (of computer) copy or transfer (data); hear and understand (over radio); substitute (word etc.) for incorrect one. ● *noun* spell of reading; *colloquial* book etc. as regards readability. □ **take as read** treat (thing) as if it has been agreed.

readable *adjective* able to be read; interesting to read. □ **readability** *noun*.

reader *noun* person who reads; book intended for reading pratice; device for producing image that can be read from microfilm etc.; (also **Reader**) university lecturer of highest grade below professor; publisher's employee who reports on submitted manuscripts; printer's proof-corrector.

readership *noun* readers of a newspaper etc.; (also **Readership**) position of Reader.

readily *adverb* without reluctance; willingly; easily.

readiness *noun* prepared state; willingness; facility; promptness in argument or action.

reading *noun* act of reading; matter to be read; literary knowledge; entertainment at which something is read; figure etc. shown by recording instrument; interpretation or view taken; interpretation made (of music etc.); presentation of bill to legislature.

ready /'redɪ/ ● *adjective* (**-ier**, **-iest**) with preparations complete; in fit state; willing; (of income etc.) easily secured; fit for immediate use; prompt, enthusiastic; (+ *to do*) about to; provided beforehand. ● *adverb* usually in combination beforehand; in readiness. ● *noun slang* (**the ready**) ready money; (**readies**) bank notes. ● *verb* (**-ies**, **-ied**) prepare. □ **at the ready** ready for action; **ready-made**, **ready-to-wear** (esp. of clothes) made in standard size, not to measure; **ready money** cash, actual coin; **ready reckoner** book or table listing standard numerical calculations.

reagent /riː'eɪdʒ(ə)nt/ *noun* substance used to produce chemical reaction.

real ● *adjective* actually existing or occurring; genuine; appraised by purchasing power. ● *adverb* *Scottish & US colloquial*

really, very. □ **real ale** beer regarded as brewed in traditional way; **real estate** property such as land and houses; **real tennis** original form of tennis played on indoor court.

realism *noun* practice of regarding things in their true nature and dealing with them as they are; fidelity to nature in representation. □ **realist** *noun*.

realistic /rɪə'lɪstɪk/ *adjective* regarding things as they are; based on facts rather than ideals. □ **realistically** *adverb*.

reality /rɪ'ælɪtɪ/ *noun* (*plural* **-ies**) what is real or existent or underlies appearances; (+ *of*) real nature of; real existence; being real; likeness to original. □ **in reality** in fact.

realize *verb* (also **-ise**) (**-zing** or **-sing**) (often + *that*) be or become fully aware of; understand clearly; convert into actuality; convert into money; acquire (profit); be sold for. □ **realizable** *adjective*; **realization** *noun*.

really /'rɪəlɪ/ *adverb* in fact; very; I assure you; *expression of mild protest or surprise*.

realm /relm/ *noun formal* kingdom; domain.

realty /'riːəltɪ/ *noun* real estate.

ream *noun* 500 sheets of paper; (in *plural*) large quantity of writing.

reap *verb* cut (grain etc.) as harvest; receive as consequences of actions. □ **reaper** *noun*.

rear[1] ● *noun* back part of anything; space or position at back. ● *adjective* at the back. □ **bring up the rear** come last; **rear admiral** naval officer below vice admiral. □ **rearmost** *adjective*.

rear[2] *verb* bring up and educate; breed and care for; (of horse etc.) raise itself on hind legs; raise, build.

rearguard *noun* troops detached to protect rear, esp. in retreat. □ **rearguard action** engagement undertaken by rearguard, defensive stand or struggle, esp. when losing.

rearm /riː'ɑːm/ *verb* arm again, esp. with improved weapons. □ **rearmament** *noun*.

rearward /'rɪəwəd/ ● *noun* rear. ● *adjective* to the rear. ● *adverb* (also **rearwards**) towards the rear.

reason /'ri:z(ə)n/ ● *noun* motive, cause, or justification; fact adduced or serving as this; intellectual faculty by which conclusions are drawn; sanity; sense, sensible conduct; moderation. ● *verb* form or try to reach conclusions by connected thought; (+ *with*) use argument with person by way of persuasion; (+ *that*) conclude or assert in argument; (+ *out*) think out.

reasonable *adjective* having sound judgement; moderate; ready to listen to reason; sensible; inexpensive; tolerable. □ **reasonableness** *noun*; **reasonably** *adverb*.

reassure /ri:ə'ʃʊə/ *verb* (**-ring**) restore confidence to; confirm in opinion etc. □ **reassurance** *noun*; **reassuring** *adjective*.

rebate[1] /'ri:beɪt/ *noun* partial refund; deduction from sum to be paid, discount.

rebate[2] /'ri:beɪt/ *noun* & *verb* (**-ting**) rabbet.

rebel ● *noun* /'reb(ə)l/ person who fights against, resists, or refuses allegiance to, established government; person etc. who resists authority or control. ● *verb* /rɪ'bel/ (**-ll-**) (usually + *against*) act as rebel; feel or show repugnance.

rebellion /rɪ'beljən/ *noun* open resistance to authority, esp. organized armed resistance to established government.

rebellious /rɪ'beljəs/ *adjective* disposed to rebel; in rebellion; unmanageable. □ **rebelliously** *adverb*; **rebelliousness** *noun*.

rebound ● *verb* /rɪ'baʊnd/ spring back after impact; (+ *upon*) have adverse effect on (doer). ● *noun* /'ri:baʊnd/ rebounding, recoil; reaction. □ **on the rebound** while still recovering from emotional shock, esp. rejection by lover.

rebuff /rɪ'bʌf/ ● *noun* rejection of person who makes advances, offers help, etc.; snub. ● *verb* give rebuff to.

rebuke /rɪ'bju:k/ ● *verb* (**-king**) express sharp disapproval to (person) for fault; censure. ● *noun* rebuking, being rebuked.

rebus /'ri:bəs/ *noun* (*plural* **rebuses**) representation of word (esp. name) by pictures etc. suggesting its parts.

rebut /rɪ'bʌt/ *verb* (**-tt-**) refute, disprove; force back. □ **rebuttal** *noun*.

recalcitrant /rɪ'kælsɪtrənt/ *adjective* obstinately disobedient; objecting to restraint. □ **recalcitrance** *noun*.

recall /rɪ'kɔ:l/ ● *verb* summon to return; recollect, remember; bring back to memory; revoke, annul; revive, resuscitate. ● *noun* (also /'ri:kɔ:l/) summons to come back; act of remembering; ability to remember; possibility of recalling.

recant /rɪ'kænt/ *verb* withdraw and renounce (belief or statement) as erroneous or heretical. □ **recantation** /ri:kæn'teɪʃ(ə)n/ *noun*.

recap /'ri:kæp/ *colloquial* ● *verb* (**-pp-**) recapitulate. ● *noun* recapitulation.

recapitulate /ri:kə'pɪtjʊleɪt/ *verb* (**-ting**) summarize, restate briefly. □ **recapitulation** *noun*.

recast /ri:'kɑ:st/ ● *verb* (*past & past participle* **recast**) cast again; put into new form; improve arrangement of. ● *noun* recasting; recast form.

recce /'rekɪ/ *colloquial* ● *noun* reconnaissance. ● *verb* (**recced**, **recceing**) reconnoitre.

recede /rɪ'si:d/ *verb* (**-ding**) go or shrink back; be left at an increasing distance; slope backwards; decline in force or value.

receipt /rɪ'si:t/ ● *noun* receiving, being received; written or printed acknowledgement of payment received; (usually in *plural*) amount of money received. ● *verb* place written or printed receipt on (bill). □ **in receipt of** having received.

receive /rɪ'si:v/ *verb* (**-ving**) take or accept (thing offered, sent, or given); acquire; have conferred etc. on one; react to (news etc.) in particular way; stand force or weight of; consent to hear or consider; admit, entertain as guest, greet, welcome; be able to hold; convert (broadcast signals) into sound or pictures; (as **received** *adjective*) accepted as authoritative or true. □ **Received Pronunciation** standard pronunciation of English in Britain (see panel at ACCENT).

receiver noun part of telephone containing earpiece; (in full **official receiver**) person appointed to administer property of bankrupt person etc. or property under litigation; radio or television receiving apparatus; person who receives stolen goods.

receivership noun □ **in receivership** being dealt with by receiver.

recent /ˈriːs(ə)nt/ adjective not long past, that happened or existed lately; not long established, modern. □ **recently** adverb.

receptacle /rɪˈsɛptək(ə)l/ noun object or space used to contain something.

reception /rɪˈsɛpʃ(ə)n/ noun receiving, being received; way in which person or thing is received; social occasion for receiving guests, esp. after wedding; place where visitors register on arriving at hotel, office, etc.; (quality of) receiving of broadcast signals. □ **reception room** room for receiving guests, clients, etc.

receptionist noun person employed to receive guests, clients, etc.

receptive /rɪˈsɛptɪv/ adjective able or quick to receive ideas etc. □ **receptively** adverb; **receptiveness** noun; **receptivity** /riːsɛpˈtɪv-/ noun.

recess /rɪˈsɛs/ ● noun space set back in wall; (often in plural) remote or secret place; temporary cessation from work, esp. of Parliament. ● verb make recess in; place in recess; US take recess, adjourn.

recession /rɪˈsɛʃ(ə)n/ noun temporary decline in economic activity or prosperity; receding, withdrawal.

recessive /rɪˈsɛsɪv/ adjective tending to recede; (of inherited characteristic) appearing in offspring only when not masked by inherited dominant characteristic.

recherché /rəˈʃɛəʃeɪ/ adjective carefully sought out; far-fetched.

recidivist /rɪˈsɪdɪvɪst/ noun person who relapses into crime. □ **recidivism** noun.

recipe /ˈrɛsɪpɪ/ noun statement of ingredients and procedure for preparing dish etc.; (+ for) certain means to.

recipient /rɪˈsɪpɪənt/ noun person who receives something.

reciprocal /rɪˈsɪprək(ə)l/ ● adjective in return; mutual; Grammar expressing mutual relation. ● noun Mathematics function or expression so related to another that their product is unity. □ **reciprocally** adverb.

reciprocate /rɪˈsɪprəkeɪt/ verb (-ting) requite, return; (+ with) give in return; interchange; (of machine part) move backwards and forwards. □ **reciprocation** noun.

reciprocity /rɛsɪˈprɒsɪtɪ/ noun condition of being reciprocal; mutual action; give and take.

recital /rɪˈsaɪt(ə)l/ noun reciting, being recited; concert of classical music by soloist or small group; (+ of) detailed account of (facts etc.); narrative.

recitation /rɛsɪˈteɪʃ(ə)n/ noun reciting; piece recited.

recitative /rɛsɪtəˈtiːv/ noun passage of singing in speech rhythm, esp. in narrative or dialogue section of opera or oratorio.

recite /rɪˈsaɪt/ verb (-ting) repeat aloud or declaim from memory; enumerate.

reckless /ˈrɛklɪs/ adjective disregarding consequences or danger etc. □ **recklessly** adverb; **recklessness** noun.

reckon /ˈrɛkən/ verb (often + that) think, consider; count or compute by calculation; (+ on) rely or base plans on; (+ with, without) take (or fail to take) into account.

reckoning noun calculating; opinion; settlement of account.

reclaim /rɪˈkleɪm/ verb seek return of (one's property etc.); bring (land) under cultivation from sea etc.; win back from vice, error, or waste condition. □ **reclaimable** adjective; **reclamation** /rɛklə-/ noun.

recline /rɪˈklaɪn/ verb (-ning) assume or be in horizontal or leaning position.

recluse /rɪˈkluːs/ noun person given to or living in seclusion. □ **reclusive** adjective.

recognition /rɛkəgˈnɪʃ(ə)n/ noun recognizing, being recognized.

recognizance /rɪˈkɒgnɪz(ə)ns/ noun Law bond by which person undertakes to observe some condition; sum pledged as surety for this.

recognize /'rekəgnaɪz/ *verb* (also **-ise**) (**-zing** or **-sing**) identify as already known; realize or discover nature of; (+ *that*) realize or admit; acknowledge existence, validity, character, or claims of; show appreciation of; reward. □ **recognizable** *adjective*.

recoil ● *verb* /rɪˈkɔɪl/ jerk or spring back in horror, disgust, or fear; shrink mentally in this way; rebound; (of gun) be driven backwards by discharge. ● *noun* /'riːkɔɪl/ act or sensation of recoiling.

recollect /rekəˈlekt/ *verb* remember; call to mind.

recollection /rekəˈlekʃən/ *noun* act or power of recollecting; thing recollected; person's memory, time over which it extends.

recommend /rekəˈmend/ *verb* suggest as fit for purpose or use; advise (course of action etc.); (of qualities etc.) make acceptable or desirable; (+ *to*) commend or entrust. □ **recommendation** *noun*.

recompense /'rekəmpens/ ● *verb* (**-sing**) make amends to; compensate; reward or punish. ● *noun* reward; compensation; retribution.

reconcile /'rekənsaɪl/ *verb* (**-ling**) make friendly again after estrangement; (usually **reconcile oneself** or in *passive*; + *to*) make resigned to; settle (quarrel etc.); harmonize; make compatible; show compatibility of. □ **reconcilable** /-ˈsaɪl-/ *adjective*; **reconciliation** /-sɪlɪ-/ *noun*.

recondite /'rekəndaɪt/ *adjective* abstruse; obscure.

recondition /riːkənˈdɪʃ(ə)n/ *verb* overhaul, renovate, make usable again.

reconnaissance /rɪˈkɒnɪs(ə)ns/ *noun* survey of region to locate enemy or ascertain strategic features; preliminary survey.

reconnoitre /rekəˈnɔɪtə/ *verb* (US **reconnoiter**) (**-ring**) make reconnaissance (of).

reconsider /riːkənˈsɪdə/ *verb* consider again, esp. for possible change of decision.

reconstitute /riːˈkɒnstɪtjuːt/ *verb* (**-ting**) reconstruct; reorganize; rehydrate (dried food etc.). □ **reconstitution** /-ˈtjuː-ʃ(ə)n/ *noun*.

reconstruct /riːkənˈstrʌkt/ *verb* build again; form impression of (past events) by assembling evidence; re-enact (crime); reorganize. □ **reconstruction** *noun*.

record ● *noun* /'rekɔːd/ evidence etc. constituting account of occurrence, statement, etc.; document etc. preserving this; (in full **gramophone record**) disc carrying recorded sound in grooves, for reproduction by record player; facts known about person's past, esp. criminal convictions; best performance or most remarkable event of its kind. ● *verb* /rɪˈkɔːd/ put in writing or other permanent form for later reference; convert (sound etc.) into permanent form for later reproduction. □ **have a record** have criminal conviction; **off the record** unofficially, confidentially; **on record** officially recorded, publicly known; **recorded delivery** Post Office service in which dispatch and receipt are recorded; **record player** apparatus for reproducing sounds from gramophone records.

recorder /rɪˈkɔːdə/ *noun* apparatus for recording; woodwind instrument; (also **Recorder**) barrister or solicitor serving as part-time judge.

recording /rɪˈkɔːdɪŋ/ *noun* process of recording sound etc. for later reproduction; material or programme recorded.

recordist /rɪˈkɔːdɪst/ *noun* person who records sound.

recount /rɪˈkaʊnt/ *verb* narrate; tell in detail.

re-count ● *verb* /riːˈkaʊnt/ count again. ● *noun* /'riːkaʊnt/ re-counting, esp. of votes.

recoup /rɪˈkuːp/ *verb* recover or regain (loss); compensate or reimburse for loss.

recourse /rɪˈkɔːs/ *noun* resort to possible source of help; person or thing resorted to.

recover /rɪˈkʌvə/ *verb* regain possession, use, or control of; return to health, consciousness, or normal state or position; secure by legal process; make up for; retrieve. □ **recoverable** *adjective*.

re-cover /riːˈkʌvə/ *verb* cover again; provide (chairs etc.) with new cover.

recovery noun (plural **-ies**) recovering, being recovered.

recreant /'rekrıənt/ literary ● adjective cowardly. ● noun coward.

re-create /riːkrɪ'eɪt/ verb (**-ting**) create anew; reproduce. □ **re-creation** noun.

recreation /rekrɪ'eɪʃ(ə)n/ noun (means of) entertaining oneself; pleasurable activity. □ **recreation ground** public land for sports etc. □ **recreational** adjective.

recriminate /rɪ'krɪmɪneɪt/ verb (**-ting**) make mutual or counter accusations. □ **recrimination** noun; **recriminatory** adjective.

recrudesce /riːkruː'des/ verb (**-cing**) formal (of disease, problem, etc.) break out again. □ **recrudescence** noun; **recrudescent** adjective.

recruit /rɪ'kruːt/ ● noun newly enlisted serviceman or servicewoman; new member of a society etc. ● verb enlist (person) as recruit; form (army etc.) by enlisting recruits; replenish, reinvigorate. □ **recruitment** noun.

rectal /'rekt(ə)l/ adjective of or by means of rectum.

rectangle /'rektæŋg(ə)l/ noun plane figure with 4 straight sides and 4 right angles. □ **rectangular** /-'tæŋgjʊlə/ adjective.

rectify /'rektɪfaɪ/ verb (**-ies, -ied**) adjust or make right; purify, esp. by repeated distillation; convert (alternating current) to direct current. □ **rectifiable** adjective; **rectification** noun.

rectilinear /rektɪ'lɪnɪə/ adjective bounded or characterized by straight lines; in or forming straight line.

rectitude /'rektɪtjuːd/ noun moral uprightness.

recto /'rektəʊ/ noun (plural **-s**) right-hand page of open book; front of printed leaf.

rector /'rektə/ noun incumbent of C. of E. parish where in former times all tithes passed to incumbent; head priest of church or religious institution; head of university or college. □ **rectorship** noun.

rectory noun (plural **-ies**) rector's house.

rectum /'rektəm/ noun (plural **-s**) final section of large intestine.

recumbent /rɪ'kʌmbənt/ adjective lying down, reclining.

recuperate /rɪ'kuːpəreɪt/ verb (**-ting**) recover from illness, exhaustion, loss, etc.; regain (health, loss, etc.). □ **recuperation** noun; **recuperative** /-rətɪv/ adjective.

recur /rɪ'kɜː/ verb (**-rr-**) occur again or repeatedly; (+ to) go back to in thought or speech; (as **recurring** adjective) (of decimal fraction) with same figure(s) repeated indefinitely.

recurrent /rɪ'kʌrənt/ adjective recurring. □ **recurrence** noun.

recusant /'rekjʊz(ə)nt/ noun person refusing submission or compliance, esp. (historical) one who refused to attend services of the Church of England. □ **recusancy** noun.

recycle /riː'saɪk(ə)l/ verb (**-ling**) convert (waste) to reusable material. □ **recyclable** adjective.

red ● adjective (**-dd-**) of colour from that of blood to deep pink or orange; flushed; bloodshot; (of hair) reddish-brown; having to do with bloodshed, burning, violence, or revolution; colloquial Communist. ● noun red colour, paint, clothes, etc.; colloquial Communist. □ **in the red** in debt or deficit; **red admiral** butterfly with red bands; **red-blooded** virile, vigorous; **redbrick** (of university) founded in the 19th or early 20th c.; **red card** Football card shown by referee to player being sent off; **red carpet** privileged treatment of eminent visitor; **redcoat** historical British soldier; **Red Crescent** equivalent of Red Cross in Muslim countries; **Red Cross** international relief organization; **redcurrant** small red edible berry, shrub bearing it; **red flag** symbol of revolution, danger signal; **red-handed** in act of crime; **redhead** person with red hair; **red herring** irrelevant diversion; **red-hot** heated until red, colloquial highly exciting or excited, colloquial (of news) completely new; **red lead** red oxide of lead as pigment; **red-letter day** joyfully noteworthy or memorable day; **red light** stop signal, warning; **red meat** meat that is red when raw (e.g. beef); **red neck** conservative working-class white in southern US; **red pepper** cayenne pepper, red fruit of capsicum; **red rag** thing that excites rage; **redshank** sandpiper with bright red legs; **red shift** displacement of spectrum to longer wavelengths in light from receding galaxies; **redstart** red-tailed songbird; **red tape** excessive bureaucracy or formality; **redwing** thrush with red underwings; **redwood** tree with red wood. □ **reddish** *adjective*; **redness** *noun*.

redden *verb* make or become red; blush.

redeem /rɪˈdiːm/ *verb* recover by expenditure of effort; make single payment to cancel (regular charge etc.); convert (tokens or bonds) into goods or cash; deliver from sin and damnation; (often as **redeeming** *adjective*) make amends or compensate for; save, rescue, reclaim; fulfil (promise). □ **redeemable** *adjective*.

redeemer *noun* one who redeems, esp. Christ.

redemption /rɪˈdempʃ(ə)n/ *noun* redeeming, being redeemed.

redeploy /riːdɪˈplɔɪ/ *verb* send (troops, workers, etc.) to new place or task. □ **redeployment** *noun*.

rediffusion /riːdɪˈfjuːʒ(ə)n/ *noun* relaying of broadcast programmes, esp. by cable from central receiver.

redolent /ˈredələnt/ *adjective* (+ *of*, *with*) strongly smelling or suggestive of. □ **redolence** *noun*.

redouble /riːˈdʌb(ə)l/ *verb* (**-ling**) make or grow greater or more intense or numerous; double again.

redoubt /rɪˈdaʊt/ *noun* *Military* outwork or fieldwork without flanking defences.

redoubtable /rɪˈdaʊtəb(ə)l/ *adjective* formidable.

redound /rɪˈdaʊnd/ *verb* (+ *to*) make great contribution to (one's advantage etc.); (+ *upon*, *on*) come back or recoil upon.

redress /rɪˈdres/ ● *verb* remedy; put right again. ● *noun* reparation; (+ *of*) redressing.

reduce /rɪˈdjuːs/ *verb* (**-cing**) make or become smaller or less; (+ *to*) bring by force or necessity; convert to another (esp. simpler) form; bring lower in status, rank, or price; lessen one's weight or size; make (sauce etc.) more concentrated by boiling; weaken; impoverish; subdue. □ **reduced circumstances** poverty after relative prosperity. □ **reducible** *adjective*.

reduction /rɪˈdʌkʃ(ə)n/ *noun* reducing, being reduced; amount by which prices etc. are reduced; smaller copy of picture etc. □ **reductive** *adjective*.

redundant /rɪˈdʌnd(ə)nt/ *adjective* superfluous; that can be omitted without loss of significance; no longer needed at work and therefore unemployed. □ **redundancy** *noun* (*plural* **-ies**).

reduplicate /rɪˈdjuːplɪkeɪt/ *verb* (**-ting**) make double; repeat. □ **reduplication** *noun*.

re-echo /riːˈekəʊ/ *verb* (**-es**, **-ed**) echo repeatedly; resound.

reed *noun* firm-stemmed water or marsh plant; tall straight stalk of this; vibrating part of some wind instruments. □ **reedy** *adjective* (**-ier**, **-iest**).

reef[1] *noun* ridge of rock or coral etc. at or near surface of sea; lode of ore, bedrock surrounding this.

reef[2] ● *noun* each of several strips across sail, for taking it in etc. ● *verb* take in reef(s) of (sail). □ **reef-knot** symmetrical double knot.

reefer *noun* *slang* marijuana cigarette; thick double-breasted jacket.

reek ● *verb* (often + *of*) smell unpleasantly; have suspicious associations. ● *noun* foul or stale smell; *esp. Scottish* smoke; vapour, exhalation.

reel ● *noun* cylindrical device on which thread, paper, film, wire, etc. are wound; device for winding and unwinding line as required, esp. in fishing; lively folk or Scottish dance, music for this. ● *verb* wind on reel; (+ *in*, *up*) draw in or up with reel; stand, walk, etc. unsteadily; be shaken physically or mentally; dance reel. □ **reel off** recite rapidly and without apparent effort.

re-entrant /riːˈentrənt/ *adjective* (of angle) pointing inwards.

re-entry /riːˈentrɪ/ *noun* (*plural* **-ies**) act of entering again, esp. (of spacecraft etc.) of re-entering earth's atmosphere.

reeve *noun* *historical* chief magistrate of town or district; official supervising landowner's estate.

ref[1] *noun* *colloquial* referee.

ref[2] *noun* *colloquial* reference.

refectory /rɪˈfɛktərɪ/ *noun* (*plural* **-ies**) dining-room, esp. in monastery or college. □ **refectory table** long narrow table.

refer /rɪˈfɜː/ *verb* (**-rr-**) (usually + *to*) have recourse to (some authority or source of information); send on or direct; make allusion or be relevant. □ **referred pain** pain felt in part of body other than actual source. □ **referable** *adjective*.

referee /rɛfəˈriː/ ● *noun* umpire, esp. in football or boxing; person referred to for decision in dispute etc.; person willing to testify to character of applicant for employment etc. ● *verb* (**-rees**, **-reed**) act as referee (for).

reference /ˈrɛfərəns/ *noun* referring to some authority; scope given to such authority; (+ *to*) relation, respect, or allusion to; direction to page, book, etc. for information; written testimonial, person giving it. □ **reference book** book for occasional consultation. □ **referential** /-ˈrɛn-/ *adjective*.

referendum /rɛfəˈrɛndəm/ *noun* (*plural* **-s** or **-da**) vote on political question open to entire electorate.

referral /rɪˈfɜːr(ə)l/ *noun* referring of person to medical specialist etc.

refill ● *verb* /riːˈfɪl/ fill again. ● *noun* /ˈriːfɪl/ thing that refills; act of refilling. □ **refillable** *adjective*.

refine /rɪˈfaɪn/ *verb* (**-ning**) free from impurities or defects; (esp. as **refined** *adjective*) make or become more elegant or cultured.

refinement *noun* refining, being refined; fineness of feeling or taste; elegance; added development or improvement; subtle reasoning; fine distinction.

refiner *noun* person or firm refining crude oil, metal, sugar, etc.

refinery *noun* (*plural* **-ies**) place where oil etc. is refined.

refit ● *verb* /riːˈfɪt/ (**-tt-**) *esp. Nautical* make or become serviceable again by repairs etc. ● *noun* /ˈriːfɪt/ refitting.

reflate /riːˈfleɪt/ *verb* (**-ting**) cause reflation of (currency, economy, etc.).

reflation *noun* inflation of financial system to restore previous condition after deflation. □ **reflationary** *adjective*.

reflect /rɪˈflɛkt/ *verb* throw back (light, heat, sound, etc.); (of mirror etc.) show image of, reproduce to eye or mind; correspond in appearance or effect to; bring (credit, discredit, etc.); (usually + *on*, *upon*) bring discredit; (often + *on*, *upon*) meditate; (+ *that*, *how*, etc.) consider.

reflection /rɪˈflɛkʃ(ə)n/ *noun* reflecting, being reflected; reflected light, heat, colour, or image; reconsideration; (often + *on*) thing bringing discredit; (often + *on*, *upon*) comment.

reflective *adjective* (of surface) reflecting; (of mental faculties) concerned in reflection or thought; thoughtful. □ **reflectively** *adverb*.

reflector *noun* piece of glass or metal for reflecting light in required direction; telescope etc. using mirror to produce images.

reflex /ˈriːflɛks/ ● *adjective* (of action) independent of will; (of angle) larger than 180°. ● *noun* reflex action; sign, secondary manifestation; reflected light or image. □ **reflex camera** camera in which image is reflected by mirror to enable correct focusing.

reflexive /rɪˈflɛksɪv/ *Grammar* ● *adjective* (of word or form) referring back to subject (e.g. *myself* in *I hurt myself*); (of verb) having reflexive pronoun as object. ● *noun* reflexive word or form.

reflexology /riːflɛkˈsɒlədʒɪ/ *noun* massage to areas of soles of feet. □ **reflexologist** *noun*.

reform /rɪˈfɔːm/ ● *verb* make or become better; abolish or cure (abuse etc.). ● *noun* removal of abuses, esp. political; improvement. □ **reformative** *adjective*.

reformation /rɛfəˈmeɪʃ(ə)n/ *noun* reforming or being reformed, esp. radical improvement in political, religious, or social affairs; (**the Reformation**) 16th-c. movement for reform of abuses in Roman Church ending in establishment of Reformed or Protestant Churches.

reformatory /rɪˈfɔːmətərɪ/ ● *noun* (*plural* **-ies**) *US historical* institution for reform of young offenders. ● *adjective* producing reform.

reformer *noun* advocate of reform.

reformism *noun* policy of reform rather than abolition or revolution. □ **reformist** *noun & adjective.*

refract /rɪ'frækt/ *verb* deflect (light) at certain angle when it enters obliquely from another medium. □ **refraction** *noun;* **refractive** *adjective.*

refractor *noun* refracting medium or lens; telescope using lens to produce image.

refractory /rɪ'fræktərɪ/ *adjective* stubborn, unmanageable, rebellious; resistant to treatment; hard to fuse or work.

refrain[1] /rɪ'freɪn/ *verb* (+ *from*) avoid doing (action).

refrain[2] /rɪ'freɪn/ *noun* recurring phrase or lines, esp. at ends of stanzas.

refresh /rɪ'freʃ/ *verb* give fresh spirit or vigour to; revive (memory). □ **refreshing** *adjective,* **refreshingly** *adverb.*

refresher *noun* something that refreshes, esp. drink; extra fee to counsel in prolonged lawsuit. □ **refresher course** course reviewing or updating previous studies.

refreshment *noun* refreshing, being refreshed; (usually in *plural*) food or drink.

refrigerant /rɪ'frɪdʒərənt/ ● *noun* substance used for refrigeration. ● *adjective* cooling.

refrigerate /rɪ'frɪdʒəreɪt/ *verb* (**-ting**) cool or freeze (esp. food). □ **refrigeration** *noun.*

refrigerator *noun* cabinet or room in which food etc. is refrigerated.

refuge /'refjuːdʒ/ *noun* shelter from pursuit, danger, or trouble; person or place offering this.

refugee /refjʊ'dʒiː/ *noun* person taking refuge, esp. in foreign country, from war, persecution, etc.

refulgent /rɪ'fʌldʒ(ə)nt/ *adjective literary* shining, gloriously bright. □ **refulgence** *noun.*

refund ● *verb* /rɪ'fʌnd/ pay back (money etc.); reimburse. ● *noun* /'riːfʌnd/ act of refunding; sum refunded. □ **refundable** /rɪ'fʌn-/ *adjective.*

refurbish /riː'fɜːbɪʃ/ *verb* brighten up, redecorate. □ **refurbishment** *noun.*

refusal /rɪ'fjuːz(ə)l/ *noun* refusing, being refused; (in full **first refusal**) chance of taking thing before it is offered to others.

refuse[1] /rɪ'fjuːz/ *verb* (**-sing**) withhold acceptance of or consent to; (often + *to do*) indicate unwillingness; not grant (request) made by (person); (of horse) be unwilling to jump (fence etc.).

refuse[2] /'refjuːs/ *noun* items rejected as worthless; waste.

refusenik /rɪ'fjuːznɪk/ *noun historical* Soviet Jew refused permission to emigrate to Israel.

refute /rɪ'fjuːt/ *verb* (**-ting**) prove falsity or error of; rebut by argument; deny or contradict (without argument). □ **refutation** /refjʊ'teɪʃ(ə)n/ *noun.*

■ **Usage** The use of *refute* to mean 'deny, contradict' is considered incorrect by some people. *Repudiate* can be used instead.

reg /redʒ/ *noun colloquial* registration mark.

regain /rɪ'geɪn/ *verb* obtain possession or use of after loss.

regal /'riːg(ə)l/ *adjective* of or by monarch(s); magnificent. □ **regality** /rɪ'gæl-/ *noun;* **regally** *adverb.*

regale /rɪ'geɪl/ *verb* (**-ling**) entertain lavishly with feasting; (+ *with*) entertain with (talk etc.).

regalia /rɪ'geɪlɪə/ *plural noun* insignia of royalty or an order, mayor, etc.

regard /rɪ'gɑːd/ ● *verb* gaze on; heed, take into account; look upon or think of in specified way. ● *noun* gaze; steady look; attention, care; esteem; (in *plural*) expression of friendliness in letter etc. □ **as regards** about, in respect of; **in this regard** on this point; **in, with regard to** in respect of.

regardful *adjective* (+ *of*) mindful of.

regarding *preposition* concerning; in respect of.

regardless ● *adjective* (+ *of*) without regard or consideration for. ● *adverb* without paying attention.

regatta /rɪ'gætə/ *noun* event consisting of rowing or yacht races.

regency /'riːdʒənsɪ/ *noun* (*plural* **-ies**) office of regent; commission acting as regent; regent's or regency commission's period of office; (**Regency**) (in UK) 1811–1820.

regenerate ● *verb* /rɪ'dʒenəreɪt/ (**-ting**) bring or come into renewed existence;

improve moral condition of; impart new, more vigorous, or spiritually higher life or nature to; regrow or cause (new tissue) to regrow. • *adjective* /-rət/ spiritually born again, reformed. □ **regeneration** *noun*; **regenerative** /-rətɪv/ *adjective*.

regent /ˈriːdʒ(ə)nt/ • *noun* person acting as head of state because monarch is absent, ill, or a child. • *adjective* (after *noun*) acting as regent.

reggae /ˈregeɪ/ *noun* W. Indian style of music with strongly accented subsidiary beat.

regicide /ˈredʒɪsaɪd/ *noun* person who kills or helps to kill a king; killing of a king.

regime /reɪˈʒiːm/ *noun* (also **régime**) method of government; prevailing system; regimen.

regimen /ˈredʒɪmən/ *noun* prescribed course of exercise, way of life, and diet.

regiment • *noun* /ˈredʒɪmənt/ permanent unit of army consisting of several companies, troops, or batteries; (usually + *of*) large or formidable array or number. • *verb* /-ment/ organize in groups or according to system; form into regiment(s). □ **regimentation** /-men-/ *noun*.

regimental /redʒɪˈment(ə)l/ • *adjective* of a regiment. • *noun* (in *plural*) military uniform, esp. of particular regiment.

Regina /rɪˈdʒaɪnə/ *noun* (after *name*) reigning queen; *Law* the Crown. [Latin]

region /ˈriːdʒ(ə)n/ *noun* geographical area or division, having definable boundaries or characteristics; administrative area, esp. in Scotland; part of body; sphere, realm. □ **in the region of** approximately. □ **regional** *adjective*; **regionally** *adverb*.

register /ˈredʒɪstə/ • *noun* official list; book in which items are recorded for reference; device recording speed, force, etc.; compass of voice or instrument; form of language used in particular circumstances; adjustable plate for regulating draught etc. • *verb* set down formally, record in writing; enter or cause to be entered in register; send (letter) by registered post; record automatically, indicate; make mental note of; show (emotion etc.) in face etc.;

make impression. □ **registered post** postal procedure with special precautions and compensation in case of loss; **register office** state office where civil marriages are conducted and births, marriages, and deaths are recorded.

registrar /redʒɪˈstrɑː/ *noun* official keeping register; chief administrator in university etc.; hospital doctor training as specialist.

registration /redʒɪˈstreɪʃ(ə)n/ *noun* registering, being registered. □ **registration mark, number** combination of letters and numbers identifying vehicle.

registry /ˈredʒɪstrɪ/ *noun* (*plural* **-ies**) place where registers or records are kept. □ **registry office** register office (the official name).

Regius professor /ˈriːdʒɪəs/ *noun* holder of university chair founded by sovereign or filled by Crown appointment.

regress • *verb* /rɪˈgres/ move backwards; return to former stage or state. • *noun* /ˈriːgres/ act of regressing. □ **regression** /rɪˈgreʃ(ə)n/ *noun*; **regressive** /rɪˈgresɪv/ *adjective*.

regret /rɪˈgret/ • *verb* (**-tt-**) feel or express sorrow, repentance, or distress over (action or loss); say with sorrow or remorse. • *noun* sorrow, repentance, or distress over action or loss. □ **regretful** *adjective*; **regretfully** *adverb*.

regrettable *adjective* undesirable, unwelcome; deserving censure. □ **regrettably** *adverb*.

regular /ˈregjʊlə/ • *adjective* acting, done, or recurring uniformly; habitual, orderly; conforming to rule or principle; symmetrical; conforming to correct procedure etc.; *Grammar* (of verb etc.) following normal type of inflection; *colloquial* absolute, thorough; (of soldier etc.) permanent, professional. • *noun* regular soldier; *colloquial* regular customer, visitor, etc.; one of regular clergy. □ **regularity** /-ˈlærɪtɪ/ *noun*; **regularize** *verb* (also **-ise**) (**-zing** or **-sing**); **regularly** *adverb*.

regulate /ˈregjʊlet/ *verb* (**-ting**) control by rule, subject to restrictions; adapt to requirements; adjust (clock, watch, etc.) to work accurately. □ **regulator** *noun*.

regulation • *noun* regulating, being regulated; prescribed rule. • *adjective* in accordance with regulations, of correct pattern etc.

regulo /'regjʊləʊ/ *noun* (usually + numeral) number on scale denoting temperature in gas oven.

regurgitate /rɪ'gɜːdʒɪteɪt/ *verb* (-ting) bring (swallowed food) up again to mouth; reproduce (information etc.). □ **regurgitation** *noun*.

rehabilitate /ri:hə'bɪlɪteɪt/ *verb* (-ting) restore to normal life by training, etc. esp. after imprisonment or illness; restore to former privileges or reputation or to proper condition. □ **rehabilitation** *noun*.

rehash • *verb* /ri:'hæʃ/ put into new form without significant change or improvement. • *noun* /'ri:hæʃ/ material rehashed; rehashing.

rehearsal /rɪ'hɜːs(ə)l/ *noun* trial performance or practice; rehearsing.

rehearse /rɪ'hɜːs/ *verb* (-sing) practise before performing in public; recite or say over; give list of, enumerate.

Reich /raɪx/ *noun* former German state, esp. Third Reich (1933–45).

reign /reɪn/ • *verb* be king or queen; prevail; (as **reigning** *adjective*) currently holding title. • *noun* sovereignty, rule; sovereign's period of rule.

reimburse /ri:ɪm'bɜːs/ *verb* (-sing) repay (person); refund. □ **reimbursement** *noun*.

rein /reɪn/ • *noun* (in *singular* or *plural*) long narrow strap used to guide horse; means of control. • *verb* (+ *back*, *up*, *in*) pull back or up or hold in (as) with reins; govern, control.

reincarnate • *verb* /ri:ɪn'kɑːneɪt/ (-ting) give esp. human form to again. • *adjective* /-nət/ reincarnated.

reincarnation /ri:ɪnkɑː'neɪʃ(ə)n/ *noun* rebirth of soul in new body.

reindeer /'reɪndɪə/ *noun* (*plural* same or -s) subarctic deer with large antlers.

reinforce /ri:ɪn'fɔːs/ *verb* (-cing) support or strengthen, esp. with additional personnel or material. □ **reinforced concrete** concrete with metal bars etc. embedded in it.

reinforcement *noun* reinforcing, being reinforced; (in *plural*) additional personnel, equipment, etc.

reinstate /ri:ɪn'steɪt/ *verb* (-ting) replace in former position; restore to former privileges. □ **reinstatement** *noun*.

reinsure /ri:ɪn'ʃʊə/ *verb* (-ring) insure again (esp. of insurer transferring risk to another insurer). □ **reinsurance** *noun*.

reiterate /ri:'ɪtəreɪt/ *verb* (-ting) say or do again or repeatedly. □ **reiteration** *noun*.

reject • *verb* /rɪ'dʒekt/ put aside or send back as not to be used, done, or complied with; refuse to accept or believe in; rebuff. • *noun* /'ri:dʒekt/ rejected thing or person. □ **rejection** /rɪ'dʒek-/ *noun*.

rejoice /rɪ'dʒɔɪs/ *verb* (-cing) feel joy, be glad; (+ *in*, *at*) take delight in.

rejoin[1] /ri:'dʒɔɪn/ *verb* join again; reunite.

rejoin[2] /rɪ'dʒɔɪn/ *verb* say in answer; retort.

rejoinder /rɪ'dʒɔɪndə/ *noun* reply, retort.

rejuvenate /rɪ'dʒuːvəneɪt/ *verb* (-ting) make (as if) young again. □ **rejuvenation** *noun*.

relapse /rɪ'læps/ • *verb* (-sing) (usually + *into*) fall back (into worse state after improvement). • *noun* relapsing, esp. deterioration in patient's condition after partial recovery.

relate /rɪ'leɪt/ *verb* (-ting) narrate, recount; (usually + *to*, *with*) connect in thought or meaning; have reference to; (+ *to*) feel connected or sympathetic to.

related *adjective* connected, esp. by blood or marriage.

relation /rɪ'leɪʃ(ə)n/ *noun* connection between people or things; relative; (in *plural*) dealings (with others); narration.

relationship *noun* state of being related; connection, association; *colloquial* emotional association between two people.

relative /'relətɪv/ • *adjective* in relation or proportion to something else; implying comparison or relation; (+ *to*) having application or reference to; *Grammar* (of word, clause, etc.) referring to expressed or implied antecedent, attached to antecedent by such word. • *noun* person connected by blood or marriage; species related to another by common origin; relative word, esp. pronoun. ☐ **relative density** ratio between density of substance and that of a standard (usually water or air). ☐ **relatively** adverb.

relativity /reləˈtɪvɪtɪ/ noun relativeness; Physics theory based on principle that all motion is relative and that light has constant velocity in a vacuum.

relax /rɪˈlæks/ verb make or become less stiff, rigid, tense, formal, or strict; reduce (attention, efforts); cease work or effort; (as **relaxed** adjective) at ease, unperturbed.

relaxation /riːlækˈseɪʃ(ə)n/ noun relaxing; recreation.

relay /ˈriːleɪ/ ● noun fresh set of people etc. to replace tired ones; supply of material similarly used; relay race; device activating electric circuit; device transmitting broadcast; relayed transmission. ● verb /also rɪˈleɪ/ receive (esp. broadcast message) and transmit to others. ☐ **relay race** one between teams of which each member in turn covers part of distance.

release /rɪˈliːs/ ● verb (**-sing**) (often + *from*) set free, liberate, unfasten; allow to move from fixed position; make (information) public; issue (film etc.) generally. ● noun liberation from restriction, duty, or difficulty; handle, catch, etc. that releases part of mechanism; item made available for publication; film, record, etc. that is released; releasing of film etc.

relegate /ˈrelɪɡeɪt/ verb (**-ting**) consign or dismiss to inferior position; transfer (team) to lower division of league. ☐ **relegation** noun.

relent /rɪˈlent/ verb relax severity; yield to compassion.

relentless adjective unrelenting. ☐ **relentlessly** adverb.

relevant /ˈrelɪv(ə)nt/ adjective (often + *to*) bearing on or pertinent to matter in hand. ☐ **relevance** noun.

reliable /rɪˈlaɪəb(ə)l/ adjective that may be relied on. ☐ **reliability** noun; **reliably** adverb.

reliance /rɪˈlaɪəns/ noun (+ *in*, *on*) trust or confidence in. ☐ **reliant** adjective.

relic /ˈrelɪk/ noun object interesting because of its age or associations; part of

holy person's body or belongings kept as object of reverence; surviving custom, belief, etc. from past age; (in *plural*) dead body or remains of person, what has survived.

relict /ˈrelɪkt/ noun object surviving in primitive form.

relief /rɪˈliːf/ noun (feeling accompanying) alleviation of or deliverance from pain, distress, etc.; feature etc. that diversifies monotony or relaxes tension; assistance given to people in special need; replacing of person(s) on duty by another or others; person(s) thus bringing relief; thing supplementing another in some service; method of carving, moulding, etc., in which design projects from surface; piece of sculpture etc. in relief; effect of being done in relief given by colour or shading etc.; vividness, distinctness. ☐ **relief map** one showing hills and valleys by shading or colouring etc.

relieve /rɪˈliːv/ verb (**-ving**) bring or give relief to; mitigate tedium of; release (person) from duty by acting as or providing substitute; (+ *of*) take (burden or duty) away from; (**relieve oneself**) urinate, defecate. ☐ **relieved** adjective.

religion /rɪˈlɪdʒ(ə)n/ noun belief in superhuman controlling power, esp. in personal God or gods entitled to obedience; system of faith and worship.

religiosity /rɪlɪdʒɪˈrɒsɪtɪ/ noun state of being religious or too religious.

religious /rɪˈlɪdʒəs/ ● adjective devoted to religion, devout; of or concerned with religion; of or belonging to monastic order; scrupulous. ● noun (*plural* same) person bound by monastic vows. ☐ **religiously** adverb.

relinquish /rɪˈlɪŋkwɪʃ/ verb give up, let go, resign, surrender. ☐ **relinquishment** noun.

reliquary /ˈrelɪkwərɪ/ noun (*plural* **-ies**) receptacle for relic(s).

relish /ˈrelɪʃ/ ● noun (often + *for*) liking or enjoyment; appetizing flavour, attractive quality; thing eaten with plainer food to add flavour; (+ *of*) distinctive flavour or taste. ● verb get pleasure out of, enjoy greatly; anticipate with pleasure.

reluctant /rɪˈlʌkt(ə)nt/ adjective (often + to do) unwilling, disinclined. □ **reluctance** noun; **reluctantly** adverb.

rely /rɪˈlaɪ/ verb (-ies, -ied) (+ on, upon) depend with confidence on; be dependent on.

REM abbreviation rapid eye movement.

remade past & past participle of REMAKE.

remain /rɪˈmeɪn/ verb be left over; stay in same place or condition; be left behind; continue to be.

remainder /rɪˈmeɪndə/ • noun residue; remaining people or things; number left after subtraction or division; (any of) copies of book left unsold. • verb dispose of remainder of (book) at reduced prices.

remains /rɪˈmeɪnz/ plural noun what remains after other parts have been removed or used; relics of antiquity etc.; dead body.

remake • verb /riːˈmeɪk/ (-king; past & past participle **remade**) make again or differently. • noun /ˈriːmeɪk/ remade thing, esp. cinema film.

remand /rɪˈmɑːnd/ • verb return (prisoner) to custody, esp. to allow further inquiry. • noun recommittal to custody. □ **on remand** in custody pending trial; **remand centre** institution for remand of accused people.

remark /rɪˈmɑːk/ • verb (often + that) say by way of comment; (usually + on, upon) make comment; archaic take notice of. • noun comment, thing said; noticing.

remarkable adjective worth notice; exceptional, striking. □ **remarkably** adverb.

REME /ˈriːmiː/ abbreviation Royal Electrical and Mechanical Engineers.

remedial /rɪˈmiːdɪəl/ adjective affording or intended as a remedy; (of teaching) for slow or disadvantaged pupils.

remedy /ˈremɪdɪ/ • noun (plural -ies) (often + for, against) medicine or treatment; means of removing anything undesirable; redress. • verb (-ies, -ied) rectify, make good. □ **remediable** /rɪˈmiːdɪəb(ə)l/ adjective.

remember /rɪˈmembə/ verb (often + to do, that) keep in the memory; not forget; bring back into one's thoughts; acknowledge in making gift etc.; convey greetings from.

remembrance /rɪˈmembrəns/ noun remembering, being remembered; recollection; keepsake, souvenir; (in plural) greetings conveyed through third person.

remind /rɪˈmaɪnd/ verb (usually + of, to do, that) cause (person) to remember or think of.

reminder noun thing that reminds; (often + of) memento.

reminisce /remɪˈnɪs/ verb (-cing) indulge in reminiscence.

reminiscence /remɪˈnɪs(ə)ns/ noun remembering things past; (in plural) literary account of things remembered.

reminiscent adjective (+ of) reminding or suggestive of; concerned with reminiscence.

remiss /rɪˈmɪs/ adjective careless of duty; negligent.

remission /rɪˈmɪʃ(ə)n/ noun reduction of prison sentence for good behaviour; remittance of debt etc.; diminution of force etc.; (often + of) forgiveness (of sins etc.).

remit • verb /rɪˈmɪt/ (-tt-) refrain from exacting or inflicting (debt, punishment, etc.); abate, slacken; send (esp. money); (+ to) refer to some authority, send back to lower court; postpone, defer; pardon (sins etc.). • noun /ˈriːmɪt/ terms of reference of committee etc.; item remitted.

remittance noun money sent; sending of money.

remittent adjective (of disease etc.) abating at intervals.

remix • verb /riːˈmɪks/ mix again. • noun /ˈriːmɪks/ remixed recording.

remnant /ˈremnənt/ noun small remaining quantity; piece of cloth etc. left when greater part has been used or sold.

remold US = REMOULD.

remonstrate /ˈremənstreɪt/ verb (-ting) (+ with) make protest; argue forcibly. □ **remonstrance** /rɪˈmɒnstrəns/ noun; **remonstration** noun.

remorse /rɪˈmɔːs/ noun bitter repentance; compunction; mercy.

remorseful adjective filled with repentance. □ **remorsefully** adverb.

remorseless *adjective* without compassion. □ **remorselessly** *adverb*.

remote /rɪˈməʊt/ *adjective* (**-r, -st**) distant in place or time; secluded; distantly related; slight, faint; aloof, not friendly. □ **remote control** (device for) control of apparatus etc. from a distance. □ **remotely** *adverb*; **remoteness** *noun*.

remould *verb* /riːˈməʊld/ (*US* **remold**) mould again, refashion; reconstruct tread of (tyre). ● *noun* /ˈriːməʊld/ remoulded tyre.

removal /rɪˈmuːv(ə)l/ *noun* removing, being removed; transfer of furniture etc. on moving house.

remove /rɪˈmuːv/ ● *verb* (**-ving**) take off or away from place occupied; convey to another place; dismiss; cause to be no longer available; (in *passive*; + *from*) be distant in condition; (as **removed** *adjective*) (esp. of cousins) separated by a specified number of generations. ● *noun* distance, degree of remoteness; stage in gradation; form or division in some schools. □ **removable** *adjective*.

remunerate /rɪˈmjuːnəreɪt/ *verb* (**-ting**) pay for service rendered. □ **remuneration** *noun*; **remunerative** /-rətɪv/ *adjective*.

Renaissance /rɪˈneɪs(ə)ns/ *noun* revival of classical art and literature in 14th–16th c.; period of this; style of art and architecture developed by it; (**renaissance**) any similar revival. □ **Renaissance man** person with many talents.

renal /ˈriːn(ə)l/ *adjective* of kidneys.

renascent /rɪˈnæs(ə)nt/ *adjective* springing up anew; being reborn. □ **renascence** *noun*.

rend *verb* (*past & past participle* **rent**) *archaic* tear or wrench forcibly.

render /ˈrendə/ *verb* cause to be or become; give in return; pay as due; (often + *to*) give (assistance), show (obedience etc.); present, submit; represent, portray; perform; translate; (often + *down*) melt (fat) down; cover (stone or brick) with plaster. □ **rendering** *noun*.

rendezvous /ˈrɒndɪvuː/ ● *noun* (*plural* same /-vuːz/) agreed or regular meeting-place; meeting by arrangement. ● *verb* (**rendezvouses** /-vuːz/; **rendezvoused** /-vuːd/; **rendezvousing** /-vuːɪŋ/) meet at rendezvous.

rendition /renˈdɪʃ(ə)n/ *noun* interpretation or rendering of dramatic or musical piece.

renegade /ˈrenɪɡeɪd/ *noun* deserter of party or principles.

renege /rɪˈniːɡ, rɪˈneɪɡ/ *verb* (**-ging**) (often + *on*) go back on promise etc.

renew /rɪˈnjuː/ *verb* make new again; restore to original state; replace; repeat; resume after interruption; grant or be granted continuation of (licence etc.). □ **renewable** *adjective*; **renewal** *noun*.

rennet /ˈrenɪt/ *noun* curdled milk from calf's stomach, or artificial preparation, used in making cheese etc.

renounce /rɪˈnaʊns/ *verb* (**-cing**) consent formally to abandon; repudiate; decline further association with.

renovate /ˈrenəveɪt/ *verb* (**-ting**) restore to good condition; repair. □ **renovation** *noun*; **renovator** *noun*.

renown /rɪˈnaʊn/ *noun* fame, high distinction. □ **renowned** *adjective*.

rent[1] ● *noun* periodical payment for use of land or premises; payment for hire of machinery etc. ● *verb* (often + *from*) take, occupy, or use for rent; (often + *out*) let or hire for rent; (often + *at*) be let at specified rate.

rent[2] *noun* tear in garment etc.; gap, cleft, fissure.

rent[3] *past & past participle* of REND.

rental /ˈrent(ə)l/ *noun* amount paid or received as rent; act of renting.

rentier /ˈrɒ̃tɪeɪ/ *noun* person living on income from property or investments. [French]

renunciation /rɪnʌnsɪˈeɪʃ(ə)n/ *noun* renouncing, self-denial, giving up of things.

rep[1] *noun* *colloquial* representative, esp. commercial traveller.

rep[2] *noun* *colloquial* repertory; repertory theatre or company.

repair[1] /rɪˈpeə/ ● *verb* restore to good condition after damage or wear; set right or make amends for. ● *noun* (result of) restoring to sound condition; good or relative condition for working or using. □ **repairable** *adjective*; **repairer** *noun*.

repair[2] /rɪˈpeə/ *verb* (usually + *to*) resort; go.

reparable /ˈrepərəb(ə)l/ *adjective* that can be made good.

reparation /repəˈreɪʃ(ə)n/ *noun* making amends; (esp. in *plural*) compensation.

repartee /repɑːˈtiː/ *noun* (making of) witty retorts.

repast /rɪˈpɑːst/ *noun formal* meal.

repatriate /riːˈpætrɪeɪt/ *verb* (**-ting**) return (person) to native land. □ **repatriation** *noun*.

repay /riːˈpeɪ/ *verb* (*past & past participle* **repaid**) pay back (money); make repayment to (person); reward (action etc.). □ **repayable** *adjective*; **repayment** *noun*.

repeal /rɪˈpiːl/ ● *verb* annul, revoke. ● *noun* repealing.

repeat /rɪˈpiːt/ ● *verb* say or do over again; recite, report; recur. ● *noun* repeating; thing repeated, esp. broadcast; *Music* passage intended to be repeated. □ **repeatable** *adjective*; **repeatedly** *adverb*.

repeater *noun* person or thing that repeats; firearm that fires several shots without reloading; watch that strikes last quarter etc. again when required; device for retransmitting electrical message.

repel /rɪˈpel/ *verb* drive back; ward off; be repulsive or distasteful to; resist mixing with; push away from itself. □ **repellent** *adjective & noun*.

repent /rɪˈpent/ *verb* (often + *of*) feel sorrow about one's actions etc.; wish one had not done, resolve not to continue (wrongdoing etc.). □ **repentance** *noun*; **repentant** *adjective*.

repercussion /riːpəˈkʌʃ(ə)n/ *noun* indirect effect or reaction following event etc.; recoil after impact.

repertoire /ˈrepətwɑː/ *noun* stock of works that performer etc. knows or is prepared to perform.

repertory /ˈrepətəri/ *noun* (*plural* **-ies**) performance of various plays for short periods by one company; repertory theatres collectively; store of information etc.; repertoire. □ **repertory company** one performing plays from repertoire; **repertory theatre** one with repertoire of plays.

repetition /repəˈtɪʃ(ə)n/ *noun* repeating, being repeated; thing repeated, copy.

□ **repetitious** *adjective*; **repetitive** /rɪˈpetətɪv/ *adjective*.

repine /rɪˈpaɪn/ *verb* (**-ning**) (often + *at*, *against*) fret, be discontented.

replace /rɪˈpleɪs/ *verb* (**-cing**) put back in place; take place of; be or provide substitute for; (often + *with*, *by*) fill up place of.

replacement *noun* replacing, being replaced; person or thing that replaces another.

replay ● *verb* /riːˈpleɪ/ play (match, recording, etc.) again. ● *noun* /ˈriːpleɪ/ replaying of match, recorded incident in game, etc.

replenish /rɪˈplenɪʃ/ *verb* (often + *with*) fill up again. □ **replenishment** *noun*.

replete /rɪˈpliːt/ *adjective* (often + *with*) well-fed; filled or well-supplied. □ **repletion** *noun*.

replica /ˈreplɪkə/ *noun* exact copy, esp. duplicate made by original artist; model, esp. small-scale.

replicate /ˈreplɪkeɪt/ *verb* make replica of. □ **replication** *noun*.

reply /rɪˈplaɪ/ ● *verb* (**-ies**, **-ied**) (often + *to*) make an answer, respond; say in answer. ● *noun* (*plural* **-ies**) replying; what is replied.

report /rɪˈpɔːt/ ● *verb* bring back or give account of; tell as news; describe, give as eyewitness; make official or formal statement; (often + *to*) bring to attention of authorities, present oneself as arrived; take down, write description of, etc. for publication; (+ *to*) be responsible to. ● *noun* account given or opinion formally expressed after investigation; description, reproduction, or summary of speech, law case, scene, etc., esp. for newspaper publication or broadcast; common talk, rumour; repute; periodical statement on (esp. pupil's) work etc.; sound of gunshot. □ **reportedly** *adverb*.

reporter *noun* person employed to report news etc. for media.

repose[1] /rɪˈpəʊz/ ● *noun* rest; sleep; tranquillity. ● *verb* (**-sing**) rest; lie, esp. when dead.

repose[2] /rɪˈpəʊz/ *verb* (**-sing**) (+ *in*) place (trust etc.) in.

repository /rɪˈpɒzɪtəri/ *noun* (*plural* **-ies**) place where things are stored or may be found; receptacle; (often + *of*) book, person, etc. regarded as store of information, recipient of secrets etc.

reprehend /reprɪ'hend/ *verb formal* rebuke, blame.

reprehensible /reprɪ'hensɪb(ə)l/ *adjective* blameworthy.

represent /reprɪ'zent/ *verb* stand for, correspond to; be specimen of; symbolize; present likeness of to mind or senses; (often + *as, to be*) describe or depict, declare; (+ *that*) allege; show or play part of; be substitute or deputy for; be elected by as member of legislature etc.

representation /reprɪzen'teɪʃ(ə)n/ *noun* representing, being represented; thing that represents another.

representational *adjective* (of art) seeking to portray objects etc. realistically.

representative /reprɪ'zentətɪv/ ● *adjective* typical of class; containing typical specimens of all or many classes; (of government etc.) of elected deputies or based on representation. ● *noun* (+ *of*) sample, specimen, or typical embodiment of; agent; commercial traveller; delegate or deputy, esp. in representative assembly.

repress /rɪ'pres/ *verb* keep under; put down; suppress (esp. unwelcome thought). □ **repression** *noun*; **repressive** *adjective*.

reprieve /rɪ'priːv/ ● *verb* (**-ving**) remit or postpone execution of; give respite to. ● *noun* reprieving, being reprieved.

reprimand /'reprɪmɑːnd/ ● *noun* official rebuke. ● *verb* rebuke officially.

reprint ● *verb* /riː'prɪnt/ print again. ● *noun* /'riːprɪnt/ reprinting of book etc.; quantity reprinted.

reprisal /rɪ'praɪz(ə)l/ *noun* act of retaliation.

reprise /rɪ'priːz/ *noun Music* repeated passage or song etc.

repro /'riːprəʊ/ *noun* (*plural* **-s**) *colloquial* reproduction, copy.

reproach /rɪ'prəʊtʃ/ ● *verb* express disapproval to (person) for fault etc. ● *noun* rebuke, censure; (often + *to*) thing that brings discredit.

reproachful *adjective* full of or expressing reproach. □ **reproachfully** *adverb*.

reprobate /'reprəbeɪt/ *noun* unprincipled or immoral person.

reproduce /riːprə'djuːs/ *verb* (**-cing**) produce copy or representation of; produce further members of same species by natural means; (**reproduce itself**) produce offspring. □ **reproducible** *adjective*.

reproduction /riːprə'dʌkʃ(ə)n/ ● *noun* reproducing, esp. of further members of same species; copy of work of art. ● *adjective* (of furniture etc.) imitating earlier style. □ **reproductive** *adjective*.

reproof /rɪ'pruːf/ *noun formal* blame; rebuke.

reprove /rɪ'pruːv/ *verb* (**-ving**) *formal* rebuke.

reptile /'reptaɪl/ *noun* cold-blooded scaly animal of class including snakes, lizards, etc.; grovelling or repulsive person. □ **reptilian** /-'tɪl-/ *adjective*.

republic /rɪ'pʌblɪk/ *noun* state in which supreme power is held by the people or their elected representatives.

republican ● *adjective* of or characterizing republic(s); advocating or supporting republican government. ● *noun* supporter or advocate of republican government; (**Republican**) member of political party styled 'Republican'. □ **republicanism** *noun*.

repudiate /rɪ'pjuːdɪeɪt/ *verb* (**-ting**) disown, disavow, deny; refuse to recognize or obey (authority) or discharge (obligation or debt). □ **repudiation** *noun*.

repugnance /rɪ'pʌgnəns/ *noun* aversion, antipathy; inconsistency or incompatibility of ideas etc.

repugnant /rɪ'pʌgn(ə)nt/ *adjective* distasteful; contradictory.

repulse /rɪ'pʌls/ ● *verb* (**-sing**) drive back; rebuff, reject. ● *noun* defeat, rebuff.

repulsion /rɪ'pʌlʃ(ə)n/ *noun* aversion, disgust; *Physics* tendency of bodies to repel each other.

repulsive /rɪ'pʌlsɪv/ *adjective* causing aversion or loathing. □ **repulsively** *adverb*.

reputable /'repjʊtəb(ə)l/ *adjective* of good reputation, respectable.

reputation /repjʊ'teɪʃ(ə)n/ *noun* what is generally said or believed about character of person or thing; credit, respectability.

repute /rɪ'pjuːt/ ● *noun* reputation. ● *verb* (as **reputed** *adjective*) be generally considered. □ **reputedly** *adverb*.

request /rɪ'kwest/ ● *noun* asking for something, thing asked for. ● *verb* ask to be given, allowed, etc.; (+ *to do*) ask (person) to do something; (+ *that*) ask that.

Requiem /'rekwɪəm/ *noun* (also **requiem**) *esp. RC Church* mass for the dead.

require /rɪ'kwaɪə/ *verb* (**-ring**) need; depend on for success etc.; lay down as imperative; command, instruct; demand, insist on. □ **requirement** *noun*.

requisite /'rekwɪzɪt/ ● *adjective* required, necessary. ● *noun* (often + *for*) thing needed.

requisition /rekwɪ'zɪʃ(ə)n/ ● *noun* official order laying claim to use of property or materials; formal written demand. ● *verb* demand use or supply of.

requite /rɪ'kwaɪt/ *verb* (**-ting**) make return for; reward, avenge; (often + *for*) give in return. □ **requital** *noun*.

reredos /'rɪədɒs/ *noun* ornamental screen covering wall above back of altar.

rescind /rɪ'sɪnd/ *verb* abrogate, revoke, cancel. □ **rescission** /-'sɪʒ-/ *noun*.

rescue /'reskjuː/ ● *verb* (**-ues**, **-ued**, **-uing**) (often + *from*) save or set free from danger or harm. ● *noun* rescuing, being rescued. □ **rescuer** *noun*.

research /rɪ'sɜːtʃ, 'riːsɜːtʃ/ ● *noun* systematic investigation of materials, sources, etc. to establish facts. ● *verb* do research into or for. □ **researcher** *noun*.

resemble /rɪ'zemb(ə)l/ *verb* (**-ling**) be like; have similarity to. □ **resemblance** *noun*.

resent /rɪ'zent/ *verb* feel indignation at; be aggrieved by. □ **resentful** *adjective*; **resentfully** *adverb*; **resentment** *noun*.

reservation /rezə'veɪʃ(ə)n/ *noun* reserving, being reserved; thing reserved (e.g. room in hotel); spoken or unspoken limitation or exception; (in full **central reservation**) strip of land between carriageways of road; area reserved for occupation of aboriginal peoples.

reserve /rɪ'zɜːv/ ● *verb* (**-ving**) put aside or keep back for later occasion or special use; order to be retained or allocated for person at particular time; retain, secure. ● *noun* thing reserved for future use; limitation or exception attached to something; self-restraint, reticence; company's profit added to capital; (in *singular* or *plural*) assets kept readily available, troops withheld from action to reinforce or protect others, forces outside regular ones but available in emergency; extra player chosen as possible substitute in team; land reserved for special use, esp. as habitat.

reserved *adjective* reticent, uncommunicative; set apart for particular use.

reservist *noun* member of reserve forces.

reservoir /'rezəvwɑː/ *noun* large natural or artificial lake as source of water supply; receptacle for fluid; supply of facts etc.

reshuffle /riː'ʃʌf(ə)l/ ● *verb* (**-ling**) shuffle again; change posts of (government ministers etc.). ● *noun* reshuffling.

reside /rɪ'zaɪd/ *verb* (**-ding**) have one's home; (+ *in*) (of right etc.) be vested in, (of quality) be present in.

residence /'rezɪd(ə)ns/ *noun* residing; place where one resides; house, esp. large one. □ **in residence** living or working at specified place.

resident /'rezɪd(ə)nt/ ● *noun* (often + *of*) permanent inhabitant; guest staying at hotel. ● *adjective* residing, in residence; living at one's workplace etc.; (+ *in*) located in.

residential /rezɪ'denʃ(ə)l/ *adjective* suitable for or occupied by dwellings; used as residence; connected with residence.

residual /rɪ'zɪdjʊəl/ *adjective* left as residue or residuum.

residuary /rɪ'zɪdjʊərɪ/ *adjective* of the residue of an estate; residual.

residue /'rezɪdjuː/ *noun* remainder, what is left over; what remains of estate when liabilities have been discharged.

residuum /rɪ'zɪdjʊəm/ *noun* (*plural* **-dua**) substance left after combustion or evaporation; residue.

resign /rɪˈzaɪn/ *verb* (often + *from*) give up job, position, etc.; relinquish, surrender; (**resign oneself to**) accept (situation etc.) reluctantly.

resignation /rezɪgˈneɪʃ(ə)n/ *noun* resigning, esp. from job or office; reluctant acceptance of the inevitable.

resigned *adjective* (often + *to*) having resigned oneself; resolved to endure; indicative of this. □ **resignedly** /-nɪdlɪ/ *adverb*.

resilient /rɪˈzɪlɪənt/ *adjective* resuming original form after compression etc.; readily recovering from setback. □ **resilience** *noun*.

resin /ˈrezɪn/ ● *noun* sticky secretion of trees and plants; (in full **synthetic resin**) organic compound made by polymerization etc. and used in plastics. ● *verb* (**-n-**) rub or treat with resin. □ **resinous** *adjective*.

resist /rɪˈzɪst/ *verb* withstand action or effect of; abstain from (pleasure etc.); strive against, oppose; offer opposition. □ **resistible** *adjective*.

resistance /rɪˈzɪst(ə)ns/ *noun* resisting; power to resist; ability to withstand disease; impeding effect exerted by one thing on another; *Physics* property of hindering passage of electric current, heat, etc.; resistor; secret organization resisting regime, esp. in occupied country. □ **resistant** *adjective*.

resistor *noun* device having resistance to passage of electric current.

resit ● *verb* /riːˈsɪt/ (**-tt-**; *past & past participle* **resat**) sit (exam) again after failing. ● *noun* /ˈriːsɪt/ resitting of exam; exam for this.

resoluble /rɪˈzɒljʊb(ə)l/ *adjective* resolvable; (+ *into*) analysable into.

resolute /ˈrezəluːt/ *adjective* determined, decided; purposeful. □ **resolutely** *adverb*.

resolution /rezəˈluːʃ(ə)n/ *noun* resolute temper or character; thing resolved on; formal expression of opinion of meeting; (+ *of*) solving of question etc.; resolving, being resolved.

resolve /rɪˈzɒlv/ ● *verb* (**-ving**) make up one's mind, decide firmly; cause to do this; solve, settle; (+ *that*) pass resolution by vote; (often + *into*) (cause to) separate into constituent parts, analyse; *Music* convert or be converted into

concord. ● *noun* firm mental decision; determination. □ **resolved** *adjective*.

resonant /ˈrezənənt/ *adjective* echoing, resounding; continuing to sound; causing reinforcement or prolongation of sound, esp. by vibration. □ **resonance** *noun*.

resonate /ˈrezəneɪt/ *verb* (**-ting**) produce or show resonance; resound. □ **resonator** *noun*.

resort /rɪˈzɔːt/ ● *noun* place frequented, esp. for holidays etc.; thing to which recourse is had, expedient; (+ *to*) recourse to, use of. ● *verb* (+ *to*) turn to as expedient; (+ *to*) go often or in numbers to. □ **in the** or **as a last resort** when all else has failed.

resound /rɪˈzaʊnd/ *verb* (often + *with*) ring, echo; produce echoes, go on sounding, fill place with sound; be much talked of, produce sensation.

resounding *adjective* ringing, echoing; unmistakable, emphatic.

resource /rɪˈzɔːs/ ● *noun* expedient, device; (often in *plural*) means available; stock that can be drawn on; (in *plural*) country's collective wealth; person's inner strength; skill in devising expedients. ● *verb* (**-cing**) provide with resources.

resourceful *adjective* good at devising expedients. □ **resourcefully** *adverb*; **resourcefulness** *noun*.

respect /rɪˈspekt/ ● *noun* deferential esteem; (+ *of, for*) heed, regard; detail, aspect; reference, relation; (in *plural*) polite greetings. ● *verb* regard with deference or esteem; treat with consideration, spare. □ **respectful** *adjective*; **respectfully** *adverb*.

respectable *adjective* of acceptable social standing, decent in appearance or behaviour; reasonably good in condition, appearance, size, etc. □ **respectability** *noun*; **respectably** *adverb*.

respecting *preposition* with regard to.

respective /rɪˈspektɪv/ *adjective* of or relating to each of several individually.

respectively *adverb* for each separately or in turn, and in the order mentioned.

respiration /respəˈreɪʃ(ə)n/ *noun* breathing; single breath in or out; plant's absorption of oxygen and emission of carbon dioxide.

respirator /'respəreɪtə/ *noun* apparatus worn over mouth and nose to filter inhaled air; apparatus for maintaining artificial respiration.

respire /rɪ'spaɪə/ *verb* (**-ring**) breathe; inhale and exhale; (of plant) carry out respiration. □ **respiratory** /-'spɪr-/ *adjective*.

respite /'respaɪt/ *noun* interval of rest or relief; delay permitted before discharge of obligation or suffering of penalty.

resplendent /rɪ'splend(ə)nt/ *adjective* brilliant, dazzlingly or gloriously bright. □ **resplendence** *noun*.

respond /rɪ'spɒnd/ *verb* answer, reply; (often + *to*) act etc. in response.

respondent ● *noun* defendant, esp. in appeal or divorce case. ● *adjective* in position of defendant.

response /rɪ'spɒns/ *noun* answer, reply; action, feeling, etc. caused by stimulus etc.; (often in *plural*) part of liturgy said or sung in answer to priest.

responsibility /rɪspɒnsə'bɪlɪtɪ/ *noun* (*plural* **-ies**) (often + *for, of*) being responsible; authority; person or thing for which one is responsible.

responsible /rɪ'spɒnsəb(ə)l/ *adjective* (often + *to, for*) liable to be called to account; morally accountable for actions; of good credit and repute; trustworthy; (often + *for*) being the cause; involving responsibility. □ **responsibly** *adverb*.

responsive /rɪ'spɒnsɪv/ *adjective* (often + *to*) responding readily (to some influence); sympathetic; answering; by way of answer. □ **responsiveness** *noun*.

rest¹ ● *verb* cease from exertion or action; be still, esp. to recover strength; lie in sleep or death; give relief or repose to; be left without further investigation or discussion; (+ *on, upon, against*) place, lie, lean, or depend on; (as **rested** *adjective*) refreshed by resting. ● *noun* repose or sleep; resting; prop or support for steadying something; *Music* (sign denoting) interval of silence. □ **at rest** not moving, not agitated or troubled; **rest-cure** prolonged rest as medical treatment; **rest home** place where elderly or convalescent people are cared for; **rest room** *esp. US* public lavatory; **set at rest** settle, reassure.

rest² ● *noun* (**the rest**) remainder or remaining parts or individuals. ● *verb* remain in specified state; (+ *with*) be left in the charge of. □ **for the rest** as regards anything else.

restaurant /'restərɒnt/ *noun* public premises where meals may be bought and eaten.

restaurateur /restərə'tɜː/ *noun* keeper of restaurant.

restful *adjective* quiet, soothing.

restitution /restɪ'tjuːʃ(ə)n/ *noun* restoring of property etc. to its owner; reparation.

restive /'restɪv/ *adjective* fidgety; intractable, resisting control.

restless *adjective* without rest; uneasy, agitated, fidgeting. □ **restlessly** *adverb*; **restlessness** *noun*.

restoration /restə'reɪʃ(ə)n/ *noun* restoring, being restored; model or drawing representing supposed original form of thing; (**Restoration**) re-establishment of British monarchy in 1660.

restorative /rɪ'stɒrətɪv/ ● *adjective* tending to restore health or strength.. ● *noun* restorative food, medicine, etc.

restore /rɪ'stɔː/ *verb* (**-ring**) bring back to original state by rebuilding, repairing, etc.; give back; reinstate; bring back to former place, condition, or use; make restoration of (extinct animal, ruined building, etc.). □ **restorer** *noun*.

restrain /rɪ'streɪn/ *verb* (usually + *from*) check or hold in; keep under control; repress; confine.

restraint /rɪ'streɪnt/ *noun* restraining, being restrained; restraining agency or influence; self-control, moderation; reserve of manner.

restrict /rɪ'strɪkt/ *verb* confine, limit; withhold from general disclosure. □ **restriction** *noun*.

restrictive /rɪ'strɪktɪv/ *adjective* restricting. □ **restrictive practice** agreement or practice that limits competition or output in industry.

result /rɪ'zʌlt/ ● *noun* consequence; issue; satisfactory outcome; answer etc. got by calculation; (in *plural*) list of scores, winners, etc. in sporting events or exams. ● *verb* (often + *from*) arise as consequence; (+ *in*) end in.

resultant ● *adjective* resulting. ● *noun* force etc. equivalent to two or more acting in different directions at same point.

resume /rɪˈzjuːm/ *verb* (**-ming**) begin again; recommence; take again or back. □ **resumption** /-ˈzʌmp-/ *noun*; **resumptive** /-ˈzʌmp-/ *adjective*.

résumé /ˈrezjʊmeɪ/ *noun* summary.

resurgent /rɪˈsɜːdʒ(ə)nt/ *adjective* rising or arising again. □ **resurgence** *noun*.

resurrect /rezəˈrekt/ *verb colloquial* revive practice or memory of; raise or rise from dead.

resurrection /rezəˈrekʃ(ə)n/ *noun* rising from the dead; revival from disuse or decay etc.

resuscitate /rɪˈsʌsɪteɪt/ *verb* (**-ting**) revive from unconsciousness or apparent death; revive, restore. □ **resuscitation** *noun*.

retail /ˈriːteɪl/ ● *noun* sale of goods to the public in small quantities. ● *adjective & adverb* by retail; at retail price. ● *verb* sell by retail; (often + *at, of*) (of goods) be sold by retail; (also /rɪˈteɪl/) recount. □ **retailer** *noun*.

retain /rɪˈteɪn/ *verb* keep possession of, continue to have, use, etc.; keep in mind; keep in place, hold fixed; secure services of (esp. barrister) by preliminary fee.

retainer *noun* fee for securing person's services; faithful servant; reduced rent paid to retain unoccupied accommodation; person or thing that retains.

retake ● *verb* /riːˈteɪk/ (**-king**; *past* **retook**; *past participle* **retaken**) take (photograph, exam, etc.) again; recapture. ● *noun* /ˈriːteɪk/ filming, recording, etc. again; taking of exam etc. again.

retaliate /rɪˈtælɪeɪt/ *verb* (**-ting**) repay in kind; attack in return. □ **retaliation** *noun*; **retaliatory** /-ˈtæljət-/ *adjective*.

retard /rɪˈtɑːd/ *verb* make slow or late; delay progress or accomplishment of. □ **retardant** *adjective & noun*; **retardation** /riː-/ *noun*.

retarded *adjective* backward in mental or physical development.

retch *verb* make motion of vomiting.

retention /rɪˈtenʃ(ə)n/ *noun* retaining, being retained.

retentive /rɪˈtentɪv/ *adjective* tending to retain; (of memory) not forgetful.

rethink ● *verb* /riːˈθɪŋk/ (*past & past participle* **rethought** /-ˈθɔːt/) consider again, esp. with view to making changes. ● *noun* /ˈriːθɪŋk/ rethinking, reassessment.

reticence /ˈretɪs(ə)ns/ *noun* avoidance of saying all one knows or feels; taciturnity. □ **reticent** *adjective*.

reticulate ● *verb* /rɪˈtɪkjʊleɪt/ (**-ting**) divide or be divided in fact or appearance into network. ● *adjective* /rɪˈtɪkjʊlət/ reticulated. □ **reticulation** *noun*.

retina /ˈretɪnə/ *noun* (*plural* **-s** or **-nae** /-niː/) light-sensitive layer at back of eyeball. □ **retinal** *adjective*.

retinue /ˈretɪnjuː/ *noun* group of people attending important person.

retire /rɪˈtaɪə/ *verb* (**-ring**) leave office or employment, esp. because of age; cause (employee) to retire; withdraw, retreat, seek seclusion or shelter; go to bed; *Cricket* (of batsman) suspend one's innings. □ **retired** *adjective*.

retirement *noun* retiring; period spent as retired person; seclusion. □ **retirement pension** pension paid by state to retired people above certain age.

retiring *adjective* shy, fond of seclusion.

retort[1] /rɪˈtɔːt/ ● *noun* incisive, witty, or angry reply. ● *verb* say by way of retort; repay in kind.

retort[2] /rɪˈtɔːt/ *noun* vessel with long downward-bent neck for distilling liquids; vessel for heating coal to generate gas.

retouch /riːˈtʌtʃ/ *verb* improve (esp. photograph) by minor alterations.

retrace /rɪˈtreɪs/ *verb* (**-cing**) go back over (one's steps etc.); trace back to source or beginning.

retract /rɪˈtrækt/ *verb* withdraw (statement etc.); draw or be drawn back or in. □ **retractable** *adjective*; **retraction** *noun*.

retractile /rɪˈtræktaɪl/ *adjective* retractable.

retread ● *verb* /riːˈtred/ (*past* **retrod**; *past participle* **retrodden**) tread (path etc.) again; (*past & past participle* **retreaded**) put new tread on (tyre). ● *noun* /ˈriːtred/ retreaded tyre.

retreat /rɪˈtriːt/ • verb go back, retire; recede. • noun (signal for) act of retreating; withdrawing into privacy; place of seclusion or shelter; period of seclusion for prayer and meditation.

retrench /rɪˈtrentʃ/ verb cut down expenses; reduce amount of (costs); economize. □ **retrenchment** noun.

retrial /riːˈtraɪəl/ noun retrying of case.

retribution /retrɪˈbjuːʃ(ə)n/ noun recompense, usually for evil; vengeance. □ **retributive** /rɪˈtrɪb-/ adjective.

retrieve /rɪˈtriːv/ verb (**-ving**) regain possession of; find again; obtain (information in computer); (of dog) find and bring in (game); (+ from) rescue from (bad state etc.); restore to good state; repair, set right. □ **retrievable** adjective; **retrieval** noun.

retriever noun dog of breed used for retrieving game.

retro /ˈretrəʊ/ slang • adjective reviving or harking back to past. • noun (plural **retros**) retro fashion or style.

retro- combining form backwards, back.

retroactive /retrəʊˈæktɪv/ adjective having retrospective effect.

retrod past of RETREAD.

retrodden past participle of RETREAD.

retrograde /ˈretrəɡreɪd/ • adjective directed backwards; reverting, esp. to inferior state. • verb move backwards; decline, revert.

retrogress /retrəˈɡres/ verb move backwards; deteriorate. □ **retrogression** noun; **retrogressive** adjective.

retrorocket /ˈretrəʊrɒkɪt/ noun auxiliary rocket for slowing down spacecraft etc.

retrospect /ˈretrəspekt/ noun □ **in retrospect** when looking back.

retrospection /retrəˈspekʃ(ə)n/ noun looking back into the past.

retrospective /retrəˈspektɪv/ • adjective looking back on or dealing with the past; (of statute etc.) applying to the past as well as the future. • noun exhibition etc. showing artist's lifetime development. □ **retrospectively** adverb.

retroussé /rəˈtruːseɪ/ adjective (of nose) turned up at tip.

retroverted /ˈretrəʊvɜːtɪd/ adjective (of womb) inclining backwards.

retry /riːˈtraɪ/ verb (**-ies**, **-ied**) try (defendant, law case) again.

retsina /retˈsiːnə/ noun resin-flavoured Greek white wine.

return /rɪˈtɜːn/ • verb come or go back; bring, put, or send back; give in response; yield (profit); say in reply; send (ball) back in tennis etc.; state in answer to formal demand; elect as MP etc. • noun coming, going, putting, giving, sending, or paying back; what is returned; (in full **return ticket**) ticket for journey to place and back again; (in singular or plural) proceeds, profit; coming in of these; formal statement or report; (in full **return match**, **game**) second game between same opponents; (announcement of) person's election as MP etc. □ **by return** (**of post**) by the next available post in the return direction; **returning officer** official conducting election in constituency etc. and announcing result.

returnee /rɪtɜːˈniː/ noun person who returns home, esp. after war service.

reunify /riːˈjuːnɪfaɪ/ verb (**-ies**, **-ied**) restore to political unity. □ **reunification** noun.

reunion /riːˈjuːnjən/ noun reuniting, being reunited; social gathering, esp. of former associates.

reunite /riːjuːˈnaɪt/ verb (**-ting**) (cause to) come together again.

reuse • verb /riːˈjuːz/ (**-sing**) use again. • noun /riːˈjuːs/ second or further use. □ **reusable** adjective.

Rev. abbreviation Reverend.

rev colloquial • noun (in plural) revolutions of engine per minute. • verb (**-vv-**) (of engine) revolve; (often + up) cause (engine) to run quickly.

revalue /riːˈvæljuː/ verb (**-ues**, **-ued**, **-uing**) give different, esp. higher, value to (currency etc.). □ **revaluation** noun.

revamp /riːˈvæmp/ verb renovate, revise; patch up.

Revd abbreviation Reverend.

reveal /rɪˈviːl/ verb display, show, allow to appear; (often as **revealing** adjective) disclose, divulge.

reveille /rɪˈvæli/ noun military waking-signal.

revel /ˈrev(ə)l/ • verb (**-ll-**; US **-l-**) make merry, be riotously festive; (+ in) take keen delight in. ●*noun* (in *singular* or *plural*) revelling. □ **reveller** *noun*; **revelry** *noun* (*plural* **-ies**).

revelation /revəˈleɪʃ(ə)n/ *noun* revealing; knowledge supposedly disclosed by divine or supernatural agency; striking disclosure or realization; (**Revelation** or *colloquial* **Revelations**) last book of New Testament.

revenge /rɪˈvendʒ/ ●*noun* (act of) retaliation; desire for this. ●*verb* (**-ging**) avenge; (**revenge oneself** or in *passive*; often + *on*, *upon*) inflict retaliation.

revengeful *adjective* eager for revenge.

revenue /ˈrevənjuː/ *noun* income, esp. annual income of state; department collecting state revenue.

reverberate /rɪˈvɜːbəreɪt/ *verb* (**-ting**) (of sound, light, or heat) be returned or reflected repeatedly; return (sound etc.) thus; (of event) produce continuing effect. □ **reverberant** *adjective*; **reverberation** *noun*; **reverberative** /-rətɪv/ *adjective*.

revere /rɪˈvɪə/ *verb* (**-ring**) regard with deep and affectionate or religious respect.

reverence /ˈrevərəns/ ●*noun* revering, being revered; deep respect. ●*verb* (**-cing**) treat with reverence.

reverend /ˈrevərənd/ *adjective* (esp. as title of member of clergy) deserving reverence. □ **Reverend Mother** Mother Superior of convent.

reverent /ˈrevərənt/ *adjective* feeling or showing reverence. □ **reverently** *adverb*.

reverential /revəˈrenʃ(ə)l/ *adjective* of the nature of, due to, or characterized by reverence. □ **reverentially** *adverb*.

reverie /ˈrevərɪ/ *noun* fit of musing; daydream.

revers /rɪˈvɪə/ *noun* (*plural* same /-ˈvɪəz/) (material of) turned-back front edge of garment.

reverse /rɪˈvɜːs/ ●*verb* (**-sing**) turn the other way round or up, turn inside out; convert to opposite character or effect; (cause to) travel backwards; make (engine) work in contrary direction; revoke, annul. ●*adjective* backward, upside down; opposite or contrary in character or order, inverted. ●*noun* opposite or contrary; contrary of usual

manner; piece of misfortune, disaster; reverse gear or motion; reverse side; side of coin etc. bearing secondary design; verso of printed leaf. □ **reverse the charges** have recipient of telephone call pay for it; **reverse gear** gear used to make vehicle etc. go backwards; **reversing light** light at rear of vehicle showing it is in reverse gear. □ **reversal** *noun*; **reversible** *adjective*.

reversion /rɪˈvɜːʃ(ə)n/ *noun* return to previous state or earlier type; legal right (esp. of original owner) to possess or succeed to property on death of present possessor.

revert /rɪˈvɜːt/ *verb* (+ *to*) return to (former condition, practice, subject, opinion, etc.); return by reversion. □ **revertible** *adjective*.

review /rɪˈvjuː/ ●*noun* general survey or assessment; survey of past; revision, reconsideration; published criticism of book, play, etc.; periodical in which events, books, etc. are reviewed; inspection of troops etc. ●*verb* survey, look back on; reconsider, revise; hold review of (troops etc.); write review of (book etc.). □ **reviewer** *noun*.

revile /rɪˈvaɪl/ *verb* (**-ling**) abuse verbally.

revise /rɪˈvaɪz/ *verb* (**-sing**) examine and improve or amend; reconsider and alter (opinion etc.); go over (work etc.) again, esp. for examination. □ **revisory** *adjective*.

revision /rɪˈvɪʒ(ə)n/ *noun* revising, being revised; revised edition or form.

revisionism *noun* often derogatory revision or modification of orthodoxy, esp. of Marxism. □ **revisionist** *noun* & *adjective*.

revitalize /riːˈvaɪtəlaɪz/ *verb* (also **-ise**) (**-zing** or **-sing**) imbue with new vitality.

revival /rɪˈvaɪv(ə)l/ *noun* reviving, being revived; new production of old play etc.; (campaign to promote) reawakening of religious fervour.

revivalism *noun* promotion of esp. religious revival. □ **revivalist** *noun* & *adjective*.

revive /rɪˈvaɪv/ *verb* (**-ving**) come or bring back to consciousness, life, vigour, use, or notice.

revivify /rɪˈvɪvɪfaɪ/ *verb* (**-ies, -ied**) restore to life, strength, or activity. □ **revivification** *noun*.

revoke /rɪˈvəʊk/ ● *verb* (**-king**) rescind, withdraw, cancel; *Cards* fail to follow suit though able to. ● *noun Cards* revoking. □ **revocable** /ˈrevəkəb(ə)l/ *adjective*; **revocation** /revəˈkeɪʃ(ə)n/ *noun*.

revolt /rɪˈvəʊlt/ ● *verb* rise in rebellion; affect with disgust; (often + *at, against*) feel revulsion. ● *noun* insurrection; sense of disgust; rebellious mood.

revolting *adjective* disgusting, horrible. □ **revoltingly** *adverb*.

revolution /revəˈluːʃ(ə)n/ *noun* forcible overthrow of government or social order; fundamental change; revolving; single completion of orbit or rotation.

revolutionary ● *adjective* involving great change; of political revolution. ● *noun* (*plural* **-ies**) instigator or supporter of political revolution.

revolutionize *verb* (also **-ise**) (**-zing** or **-sing**) change fundamentally.

revolve /rɪˈvɒlv/ *verb* (**-ving**) turn round; rotate; move in orbit; ponder in the mind; (+ *around*) be centred on.

revolver *noun* pistol with revolving chambers enabling user to fire several shots without reloading.

revue /rɪˈvjuː/ *noun* theatrical entertainment of usually comic sketches and songs.

revulsion /rɪˈvʌlʃ(ə)n/ *noun* abhorrence; sudden violent change of feeling.

reward /rɪˈwɔːd/ ● *noun* return or recompense for service or merit; requital for good or evil; sum offered for detection of criminal, recovery of lost property, etc. ● *verb* give or serve as reward to. □ **rewarding** *adjective*.

rewind /riːˈwaɪnd/ *verb* (*past & past participle* **rewound** /-ˈwaʊnd/) wind (film, tape, etc.) back.

rewire /riːˈwaɪə/ *verb* (**-ring**) provide with new electrical wiring.

rework /riːˈwɜːk/ *verb* revise, refashion, remake. □ **reworking** *noun*.

Rex *noun* (after name) reigning king; *Law* the Crown. [Latin].

rhapsody /ˈræpsədɪ/ *verb* (also **-ise**) (**-zing** or **-sing**) speak or write rhapsodies.

rhapsody /ˈræpsədɪ/ *noun* (*plural* **-ies**) enthusiastic or extravagant speech or composition; melodic musical piece often based on folk culture. □ **rhapsodic** /-ˈsɒd-/ *adjective*.

rhea /ˈrɪə/ *noun* large flightless S. American bird.

rheostat /ˈriːəstæt/ *noun* instrument used to control electric current by varying resistance.

rhesus /ˈriːsəs/ *noun* (in full **rhesus monkey**) small Indian monkey. □ **rhesus factor** antigen occurring on red blood cells of most humans and some other primates; **rhesus-positive**, **-negative** having or not having rhesus factor.

rhetoric /ˈretərɪk/ *noun* art of persuasive speaking or writing; language intended to impress, esp. seen as inflated, exaggerated, or meaningless.

rhetorical /rɪˈtɒrɪk(ə)l/ *adjective* expressed artificially or extravagantly; of the nature of rhetoric. □ **rhetorical question** question asked not for information but to produce effect. □ **rhetorically** *adverb*.

rheumatic /ruːˈmætɪk/ ● *adjective* of, caused by, or suffering from rheumatism. ● *noun* person suffering from rheumatism; (in *plural*, often treated as *singular*) *colloquial* rheumatism. □ **rheumatic fever** fever with pain in the joints. □ **rheumatically** *adverb*; **rheumaticky** *adjective colloquial*.

rheumatism /ˈruːmətɪz(ə)m/ *noun* disease marked by inflammation and pain in joints etc.

rheumatoid /ˈruːmətɔɪd/ *adjective* having the character of rheumatism. □ **rheumatoid arthritis** chronic progressive disease causing inflammation and stiffening of joints.

rhinestone /ˈraɪnstəʊn/ *noun* imitation diamond.

rhino /ˈraɪnəʊ/ *noun* (*plural* same or **-s**) *colloquial* rhinoceros.

rhinoceros /raɪˈnɒsərəs/ *noun* (*plural* same or **-roses**) large thick-skinned animal with usually one horn on nose.

rhizome /ˈraɪzəʊm/ *noun* underground rootlike stem bearing both roots and shoots.

rhododendron /ˌrəʊdə'dendrən/ noun (plural **-s** or **-dra**) evergreen shrub with large flowers.

rhomboid /'rɒmbɔɪd/ ● adjective (also **rhomboidal** /-'bɔɪd-/) like a rhombus. ● noun quadrilateral of which only opposite sides and angles are equal.

rhombus /'rɒmbəs/ noun (plural **-buses** or **-bi** /-baɪ/) oblique equilateral parallelogram, e.g. diamond on playing card.

rhubarb /'ruːbɑːb/ noun (stalks of) plant with fleshy leaf-stalks cooked and eaten as dessert; colloquial indistinct conversation or noise, from repeated use of word 'rhubarb' by stage crowd.

rhyme /raɪm/ ● noun identity of sound at ends of words or verse-lines; (in singular or plural) rhymed verse; use of rhyme; word providing rhyme. ● verb (**-ming**) (of words or lines) produce rhyme; (+ with) be or use as rhyme; write rhymes; put into rhyme.

rhythm /'rɪð(ə)m/ noun periodical accent and duration of notes in music; type of structure formed by this; measured flow of words in verse or prose; Physiology pattern of successive strong and weak movements; regularly occurring sequence of events. □ **rhythm method** contraception by avoiding sexual intercourse near times of ovulation. □ **rhythmic** adjective; **rhythmical** adjective; **rhythmically** adverb.

rib ● noun each of the curved bones joined to spine and protecting organs of chest; joint of meat from this part of animal; supporting ridge, timber, rod, etc. across surface or through structure; combination of plain and purl stitches producing ribbed design. ● verb (**-bb-**) provide or mark (as) with ribs; colloquial tease. □ **ribcage** wall of bones formed by ribs round chest; **rib-tickler** something amusing. □ **ribbed** adjective; **ribbing** noun.

ribald /'rɪb(ə)ld/ adjective irreverent, coarsely humorous. □ **ribaldry** noun.

riband /'rɪbənd/ noun ribbon.

ribbon /'rɪbən/ noun narrow strip or band of fabric; material in this form; ribbon worn to indicate some honour, membership of sports team, etc.; long narrow strip; (in plural) ragged strips. □ **ribbon development** building of

houses along main road outwards from town.

riboflavin /ˌraɪbəʊ'fleɪvɪn/ noun (also **riboflavine** /-viːn/) vitamin of B complex, found in liver, milk, and eggs.

ribonucleic acid /ˌraɪbəʊnjuːˈkliːɪk/ noun substance controlling protein synthesis in cells.

rice noun (grains from) swamp grass grown esp. in Asia. □ **rice-paper** edible paper made from pith of an oriental tree and used for painting and in cookery.

rich adjective having much wealth; splendid, costly; valuable; abundant, ample; (often + in, with) abounding; fertile; (of food) containing much fat, spice, etc.; mellow, strong and full; highly amusing or ludicrous. □ **richness** noun.

riches plural noun abundant means; valuable possessions.

richly adverb in a rich way; fully, thoroughly.

Richter scale /'rɪktə/ noun scale of 0–10 for representing strength of earthquake.

rick[1] noun stack of hay etc.

rick[2] (also **wrick**) ● noun slight sprain or strain. ● verb slightly strain or sprain.

rickets /'rɪkɪts/ noun (treated as singular or plural) children's deficiency disease with softening of the bones.

rickety /'rɪkɪtɪ/ adjective shaky, insecure; suffering from rickets.

rickshaw /'rɪkʃɔː/ noun (also **ricksha** /-ʃə/) light two-wheeled hooded vehicle drawn by one or more people.

ricochet /'rɪkəʃeɪ/ ● noun rebounding of esp. shell or bullet off surface; hit made after this. ● verb (**-cheted** /-ʃeɪd/ or **-chetted** /-ʃetɪd/; **-cheting** /-ʃeɪɪŋ/ or **-chetting** /-ʃetɪŋ/) (of projectile) make ricochet.

ricotta /rɪ'kɒtə/ noun soft Italian cheese.

rid verb (**-dd-**; past & past participle **rid**) (+ of) make (person, place) free of.

riddance /'rɪd(ə)ns/ noun □ **good riddance** expression of relief at getting rid of something or someone.

ridden past participle of RIDE.

riddle[1] /'rɪd(ə)l/ ● noun verbal puzzle or test, often with trick answer; puzzling fact, thing, or person. ● *verb* **(-ling)** speak in riddles.

riddle[2] /'rɪd(ə)l/ ● *verb* **(-ling)** (usually + *with*) make many holes in, esp. with gunshot; (in *passive*) fill, permeate; pass through riddle. ● *noun* coarse sieve.

ride ● *verb* **(-ding**; *past* **rode**; *past participle* **ridden** /'rɪd(ə)n/) (often + *on, in*) travel or be carried on or in (bicycle, vehicle, horse, etc.); be carried or supported by; cross, be conveyed over; float buoyantly; (as **ridden** *adjective*) (+ *by, with*) dominated by or infested with. ● *noun* journey or spell of riding in vehicle, on horse, etc.; path (esp. through woods) for riding on; amusement for riding on at fairground. □ **ride up** (of garment) work upwards when worn; **take for a ride** *colloquial* hoax, deceive.

rider *noun* person riding; additional remark following statement, verdict, etc.

ridge *noun* line of junction of two surfaces sloping upwards towards each other; long narrow hilltop; mountain range; any narrow elevation across surface. □ **ridge-pole** horizontal pole of long tent; **ridgeway** road along ridge.

ridicule /'rɪdɪkjuːl/ ● *noun* derision, mockery. ● *verb* **(-ling)** make fun of; mock; laugh at.

ridiculous /rɪ'dɪkjʊləs/ *adjective* deserving to be laughed at; unreasonable. □ **ridiculously** *adverb*; **ridiculousness** *noun*.

riding[1] /'raɪdɪŋ/ *noun* sport or pastime of travelling on horseback.

riding[2] /'raɪdɪŋ/ *noun historical* former division of Yorkshire.

Riesling /'riːzlɪŋ/ *noun* (white wine made from) type of grape.

rife *adjective* widespread; (+ *with*) abounding in.

riff *noun* short repeated phrase in jazz etc.

riffle /'rɪf(ə)l/ ● *verb* **(-ling)** (often + *through*) leaf quickly through (pages); shuffle (cards). ● *noun* riffling; *US* patch of ripples in stream etc.

riff-raff /'rɪfræf/ *noun* rabble, disreputable people.

rifle[1] /'raɪf(ə)l/ ● *noun* gun with long rifled barrel; (in *plural*) troops armed

with these. ● *verb* **(-ling)** make spiral grooves in (gun etc.) to make projectile spin. □ **rifle range** place for rifle practice.

rifle[2] /'raɪf(ə)l/ *verb* **(-ling)** (often + *through*) search and rob; carry off as booty.

rift *noun* crack, split; cleft; disagreement, dispute. □ **rift-valley** one formed by subsidence of section of earth's crust.

rig[1] ● *verb* **(-gg-)** provide (ship) with rigging; (often + *out, up*) fit with clothes or equipment; (+ *up*) set up hastily or as makeshift. ● *noun* arrangement of ship's masts, sails, etc.; equipment for special purpose; oil rig; *colloquial* style of dress, uniform. □ **rig-out** *colloquial* outfit of clothes. □ **rigger** *noun*.

rig[2] ● *verb* **(-gg-)** manage or fix fraudulently. ● *noun* trick, swindle.

rigging *noun* ship's spars, ropes, etc.

right /raɪt/ ● *adjective* just, morally or socially correct; correct, true; preferable, suitable; in good or normal condition; on or towards east side of person or thing facing north; (also **Right**) *Politics* of the Right; (of side of fabric etc.) meant to show; *colloquial* real, complete. ● *noun* what is just; fair treatment; fair claim; legal or moral entitlement; right-hand part, region, or direction; *Boxing* right hand, blow with this; (often **Right**) *Politics* conservatives collectively. ● *verb* (often *reflexive*) restore to proper, straight, or vertical position; correct, avenge; set in order; make reparation for. ● *adverb* straight; *colloquial* immediately; (+ *to, round, through,* etc.) all the way; (+ *off, out,* etc.) completely; quite, very; justly, properly, correctly, truly; on or to right side. ● *interjection colloquial: expressing agreement or consent.* □ **by right(s)** if right were done; **in the right** having justice or truth on one's side; **right angle** angle of 90°; **right-hand** on right side; **right-handed** naturally using right hand for writing etc., made by or for right hand, turning to right, (of screw) turning clockwise to tighten; **right-hander** right-handed person or blow; **right-hand man** essential or chief assistant; **Right Honourable** *title of certain high officials, e.g. Privy Counsellors*; **right-minded, -thinking** having sound views and principles; **right**

of way right to pass over another's ground, path subject to such right, precedence granted to one vehicle over another; **Right Reverend** *title of bishop*; **right wing** more conservative section of political party etc., right side of football etc. team; **right-wing** conservative, reactionary; **right-winger** member of right wing. □ **rightward** *adjective & adverb*; **rightwards** *adverb*.

righteous /ˈraɪtʃəs/ *adjective* morally right; virtuous, law-abiding. □ **righteously** *adverb*; **righteousness** *noun*.

rightful *adjective* legitimately entitled to (position etc.); that one is entitled to. □ **rightfully** *adverb*.

rightly *adverb* justly, correctly, properly, justifiably.

rigid /ˈrɪdʒɪd/ *adjective* not flexible, unbendable; inflexible, harsh. □ **rigidity** /-ˈdʒɪd-/ *noun*, **rigidly** *adverb*.

rigmarole /ˈrɪgmərəʊl/ *noun* complicated procedure; rambling tale etc.

rigor *US* = RIGOUR.

rigor mortis /ˌrɪgə ˈmɔːtɪs/ *noun* stiffening of body after death.

rigorous /ˈrɪgərəs/ *adjective* strict, severe; exact, accurate. □ **rigorously** *adverb*, **rigorousness** *noun*.

rigour /ˈrɪgə/ *noun* (*US* **rigor**) severity, strictness, harshness; (in *plural*) harsh conditions; strict application or observance etc.

rile *verb* (**-ling**) *colloquial* anger, irritate.

rill *noun* small stream.

rim *noun* edge or border, esp. of something circular; outer ring of wheel, holding tyre; part of spectacle frames around lens. □ **rimless** *adjective*; **rimmed** *adjective*.

rime ● *noun* frost; hoar-frost. ● *verb* (**-ming**) cover with rime.

rind /raɪnd/ *noun* tough outer layer or covering of fruit and vegetables, cheese, bacon, etc.

ring[1] ● *noun* circular band, usually of metal, worn on finger; circular band of any material; line or band round cylindrical or circular object; mark or part etc. resembling ring; ring in cross-section of tree representing one year's growth; enclosure for circus, boxing, betting at races, etc.; people or things arranged in circle, such arrangement;

combination of traders, politicians, spies, etc. acting together; gas ring; disc or halo round planet, moon, etc. ● *verb* (often + *round*, *about*, *in*) encircle; put ring on (bird etc.). □ **ring-binder** loose-leaf binder with ring-shaped clasps; **ring-dove** woodpigeon; **ring finger** finger next to little finger, esp. on left hand; **ringleader** instigator in crime or mischief etc.; **ringmaster** director of circus performance; **ring-pull** (of tin) having ring for pulling to break seal; **ring road** bypass encircling town; **ringside** area immediately beside boxing or circus ring etc.; **ringworm** skin infection forming circular inflamed patches.

ring[2] ● *verb* (*past* **rang**; *past participle* **rung**) (often + *out* etc.) give clear resonant sound; make (bell) ring; call by telephone; (usually + *with*, *to*) (of place) resound, re-echo; (of ears) be filled with sensation of ringing; (+ *in*, *out*) usher in or out with bell-ringing; give specified impression. ● *noun* ringing sound or tone; act of ringing bell, sound caused by this; *colloquial* telephone call; set of esp. church bells; specified feeling conveyed by words etc.. □ **ring back** make return telephone call to; **ring off** end telephone call; **ring up** make telephone call (to), record (amount) on cash register.

ringlet /ˈrɪŋlɪt/ *noun* curly lock of esp. long hair.

rink *noun* area of ice for skating, curling, etc.; enclosed area for roller-skating; building containing either of these; strip of bowling green; team in bowls or curling.

rinse ● *verb* (**-sing**) (often + *through*, *out*) wash or treat with clean water etc.; wash lightly; put through clean water after washing; (+ *out*, *away*) remove by rinsing. ● *noun* rinsing; temporary hair tint.

riot /ˈraɪət/ ● *noun* disturbance of peace by crowd; loud revelry; (+ *of*) lavish display of; *colloquial* very amusing thing or person. ● *verb* make or engage in riot. □ **run riot** throw off all restraint, spread uncontrolled. □ **rioter** *noun*, **riotous** *adjective*.

RIP *abbreviation* may he, she, or they rest in peace (*requiesca(n)t in pace*).

rip ● verb (**-pp-**) tear or cut quickly or forcibly away or apart; make (hole etc.) thus; make long tear or cut in; come violently apart, split. ● noun long tear or cut; act of ripping. □ **let rip** colloquial (allow) to proceed or act without restraint or interference; **rip-cord** cord for releasing parachute from its pack; **rip off** colloquial swindle, exploit, steal; **rip-off** noun □ **ripper** noun.

riparian /raɪˈpeərɪən/ adjective of or on riverbank.

ripe adjective ready to be reaped, picked, or eaten; mature; (often + for) fit, ready. □ **ripen** verb; **ripeness** noun.

riposte /rɪˈpɒst/ ● noun quick retort; quick return thrust in fencing. ● verb (**-ting**) deliver riposte.

ripple /ˈrɪp(ə)l/ ● noun ruffling of water's surface; small wave(s); gentle lively sound, e.g. of laughter or applause; slight variation in strength of current etc.; ice cream with veins of syrup. ● verb (**-ling**) (cause to) form or flow in ripples; show or sound like ripples.

rise /raɪz/ ● verb (**-sing**; past **rose** /rəʊz/; past participle **risen** /ˈrɪz(ə)n/) come or go up; project or swell upwards; appear above horizon; get up from lying, sitting, or kneeling; get out of bed; (of meeting etc.) adjourn; reach higher level; make social progress; (often + up) rebel; come to surface; react to provocation; ascend, soar; have origin, begin to flow. ● noun rising; upward slope; increase in amount, extent, pitch, etc.; increase in salary; increase in status or power; height of step, incline, etc.; origin. □ **give rise to** cause, induce; **get**, **take a rise out of** colloquial provoke reaction from; **on the rise** on the increase.

riser noun person who rises from bed; vertical piece between treads of staircase.

risible /ˈrɪzɪb(ə)l/ adjective laughable, ludicrous.

rising ● adjective advancing; approaching specified age; going up. ● noun insurrection. □ **rising damp** moisture absorbed from ground into wall.

risk ● noun chance of danger, injury, loss, etc.; person or thing causing risk. ● verb expose to risk; venture on, take chances of. □ **at risk** exposed to danger; **at one's** (**own**) **risk** accepting responsibility for oneself; **at the risk of** with the possibility of (adverse consequences).

risky adjective (**-ier, -iest**) involving risk; risqué. □ **riskily** adverb; **riskiness** noun.

risotto /rɪˈzɒtəʊ/ noun (plural **-s**) Italian savoury rice dish cooked in stock.

risqué /ˈrɪskeɪ/ adjective (of story etc.) slightly indecent.

rissole /ˈrɪsəʊl/ noun fried cake of minced meat coated in breadcrumbs.

ritardando /rɪtɑːˈdændəʊ/ adverb, adjective, & noun (plural **-s** or **-di** /-dɪ/) Music = RALLENTANDO.

rite noun religious or solemn ceremony or observance. □ **rite of passage** (often in plural) event marking change or stage in life.

ritual /ˈrɪtʃʊəl/ ● noun prescribed order esp. of religious ceremony; solemn or colourful pageantry etc.; procedure regularly followed. ● adjective of or done as ritual or rite. □ **ritually** adverb.

ritualism noun regular or excessive practice of ritual. □ **ritualist** noun; **ritualistic** /-ˈlɪs-/ adjective; **ritualistically** /-ˈlɪs-/ adverb.

rival /ˈraɪv(ə)l/ ● noun person or thing that competes with another or equals another in quality. ● verb (**-ll-**; US **-l-**) be rival of or comparable to.

rivalry noun (plural **-ies**) being rivals; competition.

riven /ˈrɪv(ə)n/ adjective literary split, torn.

river /ˈrɪvə/ noun large natural stream of water flowing to sea, lake, etc.; copious flow. □ **riverside** ground along riverbank.

rivet /ˈrɪvɪt/ ● noun nail or bolt for joining metal plates etc. ● verb (**-t-**) join or fasten with rivets; fix, make immovable; (+ on, upon) direct intently; (esp. as **riveting** adjective) engross.

riviera /rɪvɪˈeərə/ noun coastal subtropical region, esp. that of SE France and NW Italy.

rivulet /ˈrɪvjʊlɪt/ noun small stream.

RLC abbreviation Royal Logistics Corps.

RM abbreviation Royal Marines.

rm. abbreviation room.

RN abbreviation Royal Navy.

RNA abbreviation ribonucleic acid.

RNLI *abbreviation* Royal National Lifeboat Institution.

roach *noun* (*plural* same or **-es**) small freshwater fish.

road *noun* way with prepared surface for vehicles, etc.; route; (usually in *plural*) piece of water near shore in which ships can ride at anchor. □ **any road** *dialect* anyway; **in the** or **one's road** *dialect* forming obstruction; **on the road** travelling; **roadbed** foundation of road or railway, *US* part of road for vehicles; **roadblock** barrier on road to detain traffic; **road fund licence** = TAX DISC; **road-hog** *colloquial* reckless or inconsiderate motorist etc.; **roadhouse** inn etc. on main road; **road-metal** broken stone for road-making; **roadshow** touring entertainment etc., esp. radio or television series broadcast from changing venue; **roadstead** sea road for ships; **road tax** tax payable on vehicles; **road test** test of vehicle's roadworthiness; **roadway** part of road used by vehicles; **roadworks** construction or repair of roads; **roadworthy** (of vehicle) fit to be used on road; **roadworthiness** *noun*.

roadie *noun colloquial* assistant of touring band etc., responsible for equipment.

roadster *noun* open car without rear seats.

roam *verb* ramble, wander; travel unsystematically over, through, or around.

roan ● *adjective* (esp. of horse) with coat thickly interspersed with hairs of another colour. ● *noun* roan animal.

roar /rɔː/ ● *noun* loud deep hoarse sound as of lion; loud laugh. ● *verb* (often + *out*) utter loudly, or make roar, roaring laugh, etc.; travel in vehicle at high speed. □ **roaring drunk** very drunk and noisy; **roaring forties** stormy ocean tracts between latitudes 40° and 50°S; **roaring success** great success; **roaring twenties** decade of 1920s.

roast ● *verb* cook or be cooked by exposure to open heat or in oven; criticize severely. ● *adjective* roasted. ● *noun* (dish of) roast meat; meat for roasting; process of roasting.

rob *verb* (**-bb-**) (often + *of*) take unlawfully from, esp. by force; deprive of. □ **robber** *noun*, **robbery** *noun* (*plural* **-ies**).

robe ● *noun* long loose garment, esp. (often in *plural*) as indication of rank,

office, etc.; *esp. US* dressing gown. ● *verb* (**-bing**) clothe in robe; dress.

robin /'rɒbɪn/ *noun* (also **robin redbreast**) small brown red-breasted bird.

Robin Hood *noun* person who steals from rich to give to poor.

robot /'rəʊbɒt/ *noun* automaton resembling or functioning like human; automatic mechanical device; machine-like person. □ **robotic** /-'bɒt-/ *adjective*; **robotize** *verb* (also **-ise**) (**-zing** or **-sing**).

robotics /rəʊ'bɒtɪks/ *plural noun* (usually treated as *singular*) science or study of robot design and operation.

robust /rəʊ'bʌst/ *adjective* (**-er**, **-est**) strong, esp. in health and physique; (of exercise etc.) vigorous; straightforward; (of statement etc.) bold. □ **robustly** *adverb*; **robustness** *noun*.

roc *noun* gigantic bird of Eastern legend.

rock¹ *noun* solid part of earth's crust; material or projecting mass of this; **(the Rock)** Gibraltar; large detached stone; *US* stone of any size; firm support or protection; hard sweet usually as peppermint-flavoured stick; *slang* precious stone, esp. diamond. □ **on the rocks** *colloquial* short of money, (of marriage) broken down, (of drink) served with ice cubes; **rock-bottom** very lowest (level); **rock-cake** bun with rough surface; **rock crystal** crystallized quartz; **rock face** vertical surface of natural rock; **rock-garden** rockery; **rock plant** plant that grows on or among rocks; **rock-salmon** catfish, dogfish, etc.; **rock salt** common salt as solid mineral.

rock² ● *verb* move gently to and fro; set, keep, or be in such motion; (cause to) sway; oscillate; shake, reel. ● *noun* rocking motion; rock and roll, popular music influenced by this. □ **rock and roll**, **rock 'n' roll** popular dance music with heavy beat and blues influence; **rocking-chair** chair on rockers or springs; **rocking-horse** toy horse on rockers or springs.

rocker *noun* device for rocking, esp. curved bar etc. on which something rocks; rocking-chair; rock music devotee, esp. leather-clad motorcyclist.

rockery *noun* (*plural* **-ies**) pile of rough stones with soil between them for growing rock plants on.

rocket /ˈrɒkɪt/ ● *noun* firework or signal propelled to great height after ignition; engine operating on same principle; rocket-propelled missile, spacecraft, etc. ● *verb* (**-t-**) move rapidly upwards or away; bombard with rockets.

rocketry *noun* science or practice of rocket propulsion.

rocky[1] *adjective* (**-ier, -iest**) of, like, or full of rocks.

rocky[2] *adjective* (**-ier, -iest**) *colloquial* unsteady, tottering.

rococo /rəˈkəʊkəʊ/ ● *adjective* of ornate style of art, music, and literature in 18th-c. Europe. ● *noun* this style.

rod *noun* slender straight round stick or bar; cane for flogging; fishing-rod; *historical* measure of length (5½ yds.).

rode *past of* RIDE.

rodent /ˈrəʊd(ə)nt/ *noun* mammal with strong incisors and no canine teeth (e.g. rat, squirrel, beaver).

rodeo /ˈrəʊdɪəʊ/ *noun* (*plural* **-s**) exhibition of cowboys' skills; round-up of cattle for branding etc.

roe[1] *noun* (also **hard roe**) mass of eggs in female fish; (also **soft roe**) male fish's milk.

roe[2] *noun* (*plural* same or **-s**) (also **roe-deer**) small kind of deer. □ **roebuck** male roe.

roentgen /ˈrʌntjən/ *noun* (also **röntgen**) unit of exposure to ionizing radiation.

rogation /rəʊˈɡeɪʃ(ə)n/ *noun* (usually in *plural*) litany of the saints chanted on the 3 days (**Rogation Days**) before Ascension Day.

roger /ˈrɒdʒə/ *interjection* your message has been received and understood; *slang* I agree.

rogue /rəʊɡ/ *noun* dishonest or unprincipled person; *jocular* mischievous person; wild fierce animal driven or living apart from herd; inferior or defective specimen. □ **roguery** *noun* (*plural* **-ies**); **roguish** *adjective*.

roister /ˈrɔɪstə/ *verb* (esp. as **roistering** *adjective*) revel noisily, be uproarious. □ **roisterer** *noun*.

role *noun* (also **rôle**) actor's part; person's or thing's function. □ **role model** person on whom others model themselves; **role-playing, -play** acting of characters or situations as aid in psychotherapy, teaching, etc.; **role-play** *verb*.

roll /rəʊl/ ● *verb* (cause to) move or go in some direction by turning over and over on axis; make cylindrical or spherical by revolving between two surfaces or over on itself; gather into mass; (often + *along*, *by*, etc.) move or be carried on or as if on wheels; flatten with roller; rotate; sway or rock; proceed unsteadily; undulate, show undulating motion or surface; sound with vibration. ● *noun* rolling motion or gait; undulation; act of rolling; rhythmic rumbling sound; anything forming cylinder by being turned over on itself without folding; small loaf of bread for one person; official list or register. □ **roll-call** calling of list of names to establish presence; **rolled gold** thin coating of gold applied by roller to base metal; **rolled oats** husked and crushed oats; **rolling-mill** machine or factory for rolling metal into shape; **rolling-pin** roller for pastry; **rolling-stock** company's railway or (*US*) road vehicles; **rollmop** rolled pickled herring fillet; **roll-neck** having high loosely turned-over collar; **roll-on** applied by means of rotating ball; **roll-on roll-off** (of ship etc.) in which vehicles are driven directly on and off; **roll-top desk** desk with flexible cover sliding in curved grooves; **roll-up** hand-rolled cigarette; **strike off the rolls** debar from practising as solicitor.

roller *noun* revolving cylinder for smoothing, flattening, crushing, spreading, etc.; small cylinder on which hair is rolled for setting; long swelling wave. □ **roller bearing** bearing with cylinders instead of balls; **roller coaster** switchback at fair etc.; **roller-skate** *noun* frame with small wheels, strapped to shoes; boot with small wheels underneath; *verb* move on roller-skates; **roller towel** towel with ends joined.

rollicking /ˈrɒlɪkɪŋ/ *adjective* jovial, exuberant.

roly-poly /ˈrəʊlɪˈpəʊlɪ/ ● *noun* (*plural* **-ies**) (also **roly-poly pudding**) pudding of rolled-up suet pastry covered with jam and boiled or baked. ● *adjective* podgy, plump.

ROM *noun Computing* read-only memory.

Roman /'rəʊmən/ ● *adjective* of ancient Rome or its territory or people; of medieval or modern Rome; Roman Catholic; (**roman**) (of type) plain and upright, used in ordinary print; (of the alphabet etc.) based on the ancient Roman system with letters A–Z. ● *noun* (*plural* **-s**) citizen of ancient Roman Republic or Empire, or of modern Rome; Roman Catholic; (**roman**) roman type. □ **Roman candle** firework discharging coloured sparks; **Roman Catholic** *adjective* of part of Christian Church acknowledging Pope as its head, *noun* member of this; **Roman Catholicism** *noun*; **Roman Empire** *historical* that established in 27 BC and divided in AD 395; **Roman law** law code of ancient Rome, forming basis of many modern codes; **Roman nose** one with high bridge; **roman numerals** numerals expressed in letters of Roman alphabet. □ **romanize** *verb* (also **-ise**) (**-zing** or **-sing**); **romanization** *noun*.

romance /rəʊ'mæns/ ● *noun* (also /'rəʊ-/) idealized, poetic, or unworldly atmosphere or tendency; love affair; (work of) literature concerning romantic love, stirring action, etc.; medieval tale of chivalry; exaggeration, picturesque falsehood. ● *adjective* (**Romance**) (of a language) descended from Latin. ● *verb* (**-cing**) exaggerate, fantasize; woo.

Romanesque /rəʊmə'nesk/ ● *noun* style of European architecture *c.* 900–1200, with massive vaulting and round arches. ● *adjective* of this style.

Romanian /rəʊ'meɪnɪən/ (also **Rumanian** /ruː-/) ● *noun* native, national, or language of Romania. ● *adjective* of Romania or its people or language.

romantic /rəʊ'mæntɪk/ ● *adjective* of, characterized by, or suggestive of romance; imaginative, visionary; (of literature or music etc.) concerned more with emotion than with form; (also **Romantic**) of the 18th–19th-c. romantic movement or style in European arts. ● *noun* romantic person; romanticist. □ **romantically** *adverb*.

romanticism /rəʊ'mæntɪsɪz(ə)m/ *noun* (also **Romanticism**) adherence to romantic style in literature, art, etc. □ **romanticist**, **Romanticist** *noun*.

romanticize /rəʊ'mæntɪsaɪz/ *verb* (also **-ise**) (**-zing** or **-sing**) make romantic; exaggerate; indulge in romance.

Romany /'rɒmənɪ/ ● *noun* (*plural* **-ies**) Gypsy; language of Gypsies. ● *adjective* of Gypsies or Romany language.

Romeo /'rəʊmɪəʊ/ *noun* (*plural* **-s**) passionate male lover or seducer.

romp ● *verb* play roughly and energetically; (+ *along*, *past*, etc.) *colloquial* proceed without effort. ● *noun* spell of romping. □ **romp in**, **home** *colloquial* win easily.

rompers *plural noun* (also **romper suit**) young child's one-piece garment.

rondeau /'rɒndəʊ/ *noun* (*plural* **-x** same pronunciation or /-z/) short poem with two rhymes only, and opening words used as refrains.

rondel /'rɒnd(ə)l/ *noun* rondeau.

rondo /'rɒndəʊ/ *noun* (*plural* **-s**) musical form with recurring leading theme.

röntgen = ROENTGEN.

rood /ruːd/ *noun* crucifix, esp. on roodscreen; quarter-acre. □ **rood-screen** carved screen separating nave and chancel.

roof /ruːf/ ● *noun* (*plural* **roofs** /ruːvz/) upper covering of building; top of covered vehicle etc.; top interior surface of oven, cave, mine, etc. ● *verb* (often + *in*, *over*) cover with roof; be roof of. □ **roof of the mouth** palate; **roof-rack** framework for luggage on top of vehicle; **rooftop** outer surface of roof, (in *plural*) tops of houses etc.

rook[1] /rʊk/ ● *noun* black bird of crow family nesting in colonies. ● *verb* *colloquial* charge (customer) extortionately; win money at cards etc., esp. by swindling.

rook[2] /rʊk/ *noun* chess piece with battlement-shaped top.

rookery *noun* (*plural* **-ies**) colony of rooks, penguins, or seals.

rookie /'rʊkɪ/ *noun slang* recruit.

room /ruːm/ ● *noun* space for, or occupied by, something; capacity; part of building enclosed by walls; (in *plural*) apartments or lodgings. ● *verb US* have room(s), lodge. □ **room service** provision of food etc. in hotel bedroom.

roomy *adjective* (**-ier, -iest**) having much room, spacious. □ **roominess** *noun*.

roost /ruːst/ ● *noun* bird's perch. ● *verb* (of bird) settle for rest or sleep.

rooster *noun* domestic cock.

root[1] /ruːt/ ● *noun* part of plant below ground conveying nourishment from soil; (in *plural*) fibres or branches of this; plant with edible root, such root; (in *plural*) emotional attachment or family ties in a place; embedded part of hair or tooth etc.; basic cause, source; *Mathematics* number which multiplied by itself a given number of times yields a given number, esp. square root; core of a word. ● *verb* (cause to) take root; (esp. as **rooted** *adjective*) fix or establish firmly; pull up by roots. □ **root out** find and get rid of; **rootstock** rhizome, plant into which graft is inserted, source from which offshoots have arisen; **take root** begin to draw nourishment from the soil, become established. □ **rootless** *adjective*.

root[2] /ruːt/ *verb* (often + *up*) turn up (ground) with snout etc. in search of food; (+ *around, in,* etc.) rummage; (+ *out, up*) extract by rummaging; (+ *for*) *US slang* encourage by applause or support.

rope ● *noun* stout cord made by twisting together strands of hemp or wire etc.; (+ *of*) string of onions, pearls etc.; (**the rope**) (halter for) execution by hanging. ● *verb* (**-ping**) fasten or catch with rope; (+ *off, in*) enclose with rope. □ **know, learn,** or **show the ropes** know, learn, show how to do a thing properly; **rope into** persuade to take part (in).

ropy *adjective* (also **ropey**) (**-ier, -iest**) *colloquial* poor in quality. □ **ropiness** *noun*.

Roquefort /ˈrɒkfɔː/ *noun proprietary term* soft blue ewe's-milk cheese.

rorqual /ˈrɔːkw(ə)l/ *noun* whale with dorsal fin.

rosaceous /rəʊˈzeɪʃəs/ *adjective* of plant family including the rose.

rosary /ˈrəʊzərɪ/ *noun* (*plural* **-ies**) *RC Church* repeated sequence of prayers;

string of beads for keeping count in this.

rose[1] /rəʊz/ ● *noun* prickly shrub bearing fragrant red, pink, yellow, or white flowers; this flower; pinkish-red colour or (usually in *plural*) complexion; rose-shaped design; circular fitting on ceiling from which electric light hangs by cable; spray nozzle of watering-can etc.; (in *plural*) *used to express ease, luck, etc.* ● *adjective* rose-coloured. □ **rosebowl** bowl for cut roses, esp. given as prize; **rosebud** bud of rose, pretty girl; **rose-coloured** pinkish-red, cheerful, optimistic; **rose-hip** fruit of rose; **rose-water** perfume made from roses; **rose-window** circular window with roselike tracery; **rosewood** close-grained wood used in making furniture.

rose[2] *past of* RISE.

rosé /ˈrəʊzeɪ/ *noun* light pink wine. [French]

rosemary /ˈrəʊzmərɪ/ *noun* evergreen fragrant shrub used as herb.

rosette /rəʊˈzet/ *noun* rose-shaped ornament made of ribbons etc. or carved in stone etc.

rosin /ˈrɒzɪn/ ● *noun* resin, esp. in solid form. ● *verb* (**-n-**) rub with rosin.

RoSPA /ˈrɒspə/ *abbreviation* Royal Society for the Prevention of Accidents.

roster /ˈrɒstə/ ● *noun* list or plan of turns of duty etc. ● *verb* place on roster.

rostrum /ˈrɒstrəm/ *noun* (*plural* **rostra** or **-s**) platform for public speaking etc.

rosy /ˈrəʊzɪ/ *adjective* (**-ier, -iest**) pink, red; optimistic, hopeful.

rot ● *verb* (**-tt-**) undergo decay by putrefaction; perish, waste away; cause to rot, make rotten. ● *noun* decay, rottenness; *slang* nonsense; decline in standards etc. ● *interjection expressing incredulity or ridicule.* □ **rot-gut** *slang* cheap harmful alcohol.

rota /ˈrəʊtə/ *noun* list of duties to be done or people to do them in turn.

rotary /ˈrəʊtərɪ/ ● *adjective* acting by rotation. ● *noun* (*plural* **-ies**) rotary machine; (**Rotary**; in full **Rotary International**) worldwide charitable society of businessmen.

rotate /rəʊˈteɪt/ *verb* (**-ting**) move round axis or centre, revolve; arrange or take in rotation. □ **rotatory** /ˈrəʊtətərɪ/ adjective.

rotation noun rotating, being rotated; recurrent series or period; regular succession; growing of different crops in regular order. □ **rotational** adjective.

rote noun (usually in **by rote**) mechanical repetition (in order to memorize).

rotisserie /rəʊˈtɪsərɪ/ noun restaurant etc. where meat is roasted; revolving spit for roasting food.

rotor /ˈrəʊtə/ noun rotary part of machine; rotating aerofoil on helicopter.

rotten /ˈrɒt(ə)n/ adjective (**-er, -est**) rotting or rotted; fragile from age etc.; morally or politically corrupt; slang disagreeable, worthless. □ **rotten borough** historical (before 1832) English borough electing MP though having very few voters. □ **rottenness** noun.

rotter noun slang objectionable person.

Rottweiler /ˈrɒtvaɪlə/ noun black-and-tan dog noted for ferocity.

rotund /rəʊˈtʌnd/ adjective plump, podgy. □ **rotundity** noun.

rotunda /rəʊˈtʌndə/ noun circular building, esp. domed.

rouble /ˈruːb(ə)l/ noun (also **ruble**) monetary unit of Russia etc.

roué /ˈruːeɪ/ noun (esp. elderly) debauchee.

rouge /ruːʒ/ ● noun red cosmetic used to colour cheeks. ● verb (**-ging**) colour with or apply rouge; blush.

rough /rʌf/ ● adjective having uneven surface, not smooth or level; shaggy; coarse, violent; not mild, quiet, or gentle; (of wine) harsh; insensitive; unpleasant, severe; lacking finish etc.; approximate, rudimentary. ● adverb in a rough way. ● noun (usually **the rough**) hardship; rough ground; hooligan; unfinished or natural state. ● verb make rough; (+ **out, in**) sketch or plan roughly. □ **rough-and-ready** rough or crude but effective, not over-particular; **rough-and-tumble** adjective irregular, disorderly, noun scuffle; **roughcast** noun plaster of lime and gravel, verb coat with this; **rough diamond** uncut diamond, rough but honest person; **rough house** slang disturbance, rough fight; **rough it** colloquial do without basic comforts; **rough justice** treatment that is

approximately fair, unfair treatment; **roughneck** colloquial worker on oil rig, rough person; **rough up** slang attack violently. □ **roughen** verb; **roughly** adverb; **roughness** noun.

roughage noun fibrous material in food, stimulating intestinal action.

roughshod /ˈrʌfʃɒd/ □ **ride roughshod over** treat arrogantly.

roulade /ruːˈlɑːd/ noun filled rolled piece of meat, sponge, etc.; quick succession of notes.

roulette /ruːˈlet/ noun gambling game with ball dropped on revolving numbered wheel.

round /raʊnd/ ● adjective shaped like circle, sphere, or cylinder; done with circular motion; (of number etc.) without odd units; entire, continuous, complete; candid; (of voice etc.) sonorous. ● noun round object; revolving motion, circular or recurring course, series; route for deliveries, inspection, etc.; drink etc. for each member of group; one bullet, shell, etc.; slice of bread, sandwich made from two slices, joint of beef from haunch; one period of play etc., one stage in competition, playing of all holes in golf course once; song for unaccompanied voices overlapping at intervals; rung of ladder; (+ of) circumference or extent of. ● adverb with circular motion, with return to starting point or change to opposite position; to, at, or affecting circumference, area, group, etc.; in every direction from a centre; measuring (specified distance) in girth. ● preposition so as to encircle or enclose; at or to points on circumference of; with successive visits to; within a radius of; having as central point; so as to pass in curved course, having thus passed. ● verb give or take round shape; pass round (corner etc.); (usually + up, down) express (number) approximately. □ **in the round** with all angles or features shown or considered, with audience all round theatre stage; **Roundhead** historical member of Parliamentary party in English Civil War; **round off** make complete or less angular; **round on** attack unexpectedly; **round out** provide with more details, finish; **round robin** petition with signatures in circle to conceal order of writing, tournament in which each competitor plays every other; **Round Table** international charitable association; **round table** assembly for discussion, esp. at conference; **round trip** trip to one or more places and back; **round up** gather or bring together; **round-up** rounding-up, summary.

roundabout • noun road junction with traffic passing in one direction round central island; revolving device in children's playground; merry-go-round. • adjective circuitous.

roundel /'raʊnd(ə)l/ noun circular mark; small disc, medallion.

roundelay /'raʊndɪleɪ/ noun short simple song with refrain.

rounders /'raʊndəz/ noun team game in which players hit ball and run through round of bases.

roundly adverb bluntly, severely.

rouse /raʊz/ verb (**-sing**) (cause to) wake; (often + up) make or become active or excited; anger; evoke (feelings). □ **rousing** adjective.

roustabout /'raʊstəbaʊt/ noun labourer on oil rig; unskilled or casual labourer.

rout /raʊt/ • noun disorderly retreat of defeated troops; overthrow, defeat. • verb put to flight, defeat.

route /ruːt/ • noun way taken (esp. regularly) from one place to another. • verb (**-teing**) send etc. by particular route. □ **route march** training-march for troops.

routine /ruːˈtiːn/ • noun regular course or procedure, unvarying performance of certain acts; set sequence in dance, comedy act, etc.; sequence of instructions to computer. • adjective performed as routine; of customary or standard kind. □ **routinely** adverb.

roux /ruː/ noun (plural same) mixture of fat and flour used in sauces etc.

rove /raʊv/ verb (**-ving**) wander without settling, roam; (of eyes) look about.

rover noun wanderer.

row¹ /rəʊ/ noun line of people or things; line of seats in theatre etc. □ **in a row** forming a row, colloquial in succession.

row² /rəʊ/ • verb propel (boat) with oars; convey thus. • noun spell of rowing; trip in rowing boat. □ **rowing boat** (US

row-boat) small boat propelled by oars. □ **rower** noun.

row³ /raʊ/ colloquial • noun loud noise, commotion; quarrel, dispute; severe reprimand. • verb make or engage in row; reprimand.

rowan /'rəʊən/ noun (in full **rowan tree**) mountain ash; (in full **rowan-berry**) its scarlet berry.

rowdy /'raʊdɪ/ • adjective (**-ier**, **-iest**) noisy and disorderly. • noun (plural **-ies**) rowdy person. □ **rowdily** adverb; **rowdiness** noun; **rowdyism** noun.

rowel /'raʊəl/ noun spiked revolving disc at end of spur.

rowlock /'rɒlək/ noun device for holding oar in place.

royal /'rɔɪəl/ • adjective of, suited to, or worthy of king or queen; in service or under patronage of king or queen; of family of king or queen; splendid, on great scale. • noun colloquial member of royal family. □ **royal blue** deep vivid blue; **Royal Commission** commission of inquiry appointed by Crown at request of government; **royal flush** straight poker flush headed by ace; **royal jelly** substance secreted by worker bees and fed to future queen bees; **Royal Navy** British navy; **royal 'we'** use of 'we' instead of 'I' by single person. □ **royally** adverb.

royalist noun supporter of monarchy, esp. historical of King's side in English Civil War.

royalty noun (plural **-ies**) being royal; royal people; member of royal family; percentage of profit from book, public performance, patent, etc. paid to author etc.; royal right (now esp. over minerals) granted by sovereign; payment made by producer of minerals etc. to owner of site etc.

RP abbreviation Received Pronunciation.

RPI abbreviation retail price index.

rpm abbreviation revolutions per minute.

RSA abbreviation Royal Society of Arts; Royal Scottish Academy; Royal Scottish Academician.

RSC abbreviation Royal Shakespeare Company.

RSM abbreviation Regimental Sergeant-Major.

RSPB *abbreviation* Royal Society for the Protection of Birds.

RSPCA *abbreviation* Royal Society for the Prevention of Cruelty to Animals.

RSV *abbreviation* Revised Standard Version (of Bible).

RSVP *abbreviation* please answer (*répondez s'il vous plaît*).

Rt. Hon. *abbreviation* Right Honourable.

Rt Revd *abbreviation* (also **Rt. Rev.**) Right Reverend.

rub ● *verb* (**-bb-**) move hand etc. firmly over surface of; (usually + *against, in, on, over*) apply (hand etc.) thus; polish, clean, abrade, chafe, or make dry, sore, or bare by rubbing; (+ *in, into, through, over*) apply by rubbing; (often + *together, against, on*) move with friction or slide (objects) against each other; get frayed or worn by friction. ● *noun* action or spell of rubbing; impediment or difficulty. □ **rub off** (usually + *on*) be transferred by contact, be transmitted; **rub out** erase with rubber; **rub up the wrong way** irritate.

rubato /ruːˈbɑːtəʊ/ *noun Music* (*plural* **-s** or **-ti** /-tɪ/) temporary disregarding of strict tempo.

rubber[1] /ˈrʌbə/ *noun* elastic substance made from latex of plants or synthetically; piece of this or other substance for erasing pencil marks; (in *plural*) *US* galoshes. □ **rubber band** loop of rubber to hold papers etc.; **rubberneck** *colloquial* (be) inquisitive sightseer; **rubber plant** tropical plant often grown as house-plant, (also **rubber tree**) yielding latex; **rubber stamp** device for inking and imprinting on surface, (person giving) mechanical endorsement of actions etc.; **rubber-stamp** approve automatically. □ **rubberize** *verb* (also **-ise**) (**-zing** or **-sing**); **rubbery** *adjective*.

rubber[2] /ˈrʌbə/ *noun* series of games between same sides or people at whist, bridge, cricket, etc.

rubbish /ˈrʌbɪʃ/ ● *noun* waste or worthless matter; litter; trash; (often as *interjection*) nonsense. ● *verb colloquial* criticize contemptuously. □ **rubbishy** *adjective*.

rubble /ˈrʌb(ə)l/ *noun* rough fragments of stone, brick, etc.

rubella /ruːˈbelə/ *noun formal* German measles.

Rubicon /ˈruːbɪkɒn/ *noun* point from which there is no going back.

rubicund /ˈruːbɪkʌnd/ *adjective* ruddy, red-faced.

ruble = ROUBLE.

rubric /ˈruːbrɪk/ *noun* heading or passage in red or special lettering; explanatory words; established custom or rule; direction for conduct of divine service in liturgical book.

ruby /ˈruːbɪ/ ● *noun* (*plural* **-ies**) crimson or rose-coloured precious stone; deep red colour. ● *adjective* ruby-coloured. □ **ruby wedding** 40th wedding anniversary.

RUC *abbreviation* Royal Ulster Constabulary.

ruche /ruːʃ/ *noun* frill or gathering of lace etc. □ **ruched** *adjective*.

ruck[1] *noun* (**the ruck**) main group of competitors not likely to overtake leaders; undistinguished crowd of people or things; *Rugby* loose scrum.

ruck[2] ● *verb* (often + *up*) crease, wrinkle. ● *noun* crease, wrinkle.

rucksack /ˈrʌksæk/ *noun* bag carried on back, esp. by hikers.

ruckus /ˈrʌkəs/ *noun esp. US* row, commotion.

ruction /ˈrʌkʃ(ə)n/ *noun colloquial* disturbance, tumult; (in *plural*) row.

rudder /ˈrʌdə/ *noun* flat piece hinged to vessel's stern or rear of aeroplane for steering. □ **rudderless** *adjective*.

ruddy /ˈrʌdɪ/ *adjective* (**-ier**, **-iest**) freshly or healthily red; reddish; *colloquial* bloody, damnable.

rude *adjective* impolite, offensive; roughly made; primitive, uneducated; abrupt, sudden; *colloquial* indecent, lewd; vigorous, hearty. □ **rudely** *adverb*; **rudeness** *noun*.

rudiment /ˈruːdɪmənt/ *noun* (in *plural*) elements or first principles of subject, imperfect beginning of something undeveloped; vestigial or undeveloped part or organ. □ **rudimentary** /-ˈmentə-/ *adjective*.

rue[1] *verb* (**rues**, **rued**, **rueing** or **ruing**) repent of; wish undone or non-existent.

rue[2] *noun* evergreen shrub with bitter strong-scented leaves.

rueful *adjective* genuinely or humorously sorrowful. □ **ruefully** *adverb*.

ruff[1] *noun* projecting starched frill worn round neck; projecting or coloured ring of feathers or hair round bird's or animal's neck; domestic pigeon.

ruff[2] ● *verb* trump at cards. ● *noun* trumping.

ruffian /'rʌfɪən/ *noun* violent lawless person.

ruffle /'rʌf(ə)l/ ● *verb* (**-ling**) disturb smoothness or tranquillity of; gather into ruffle; (often + *up*) (of bird) erect (feathers) in anger, display, etc. ● *noun* frill of lace etc.

rufous /'ru:fəs/ *adjective* reddish-brown.

rug *noun* floor-mat; thick woollen wrap or coverlet.

Rugby /'rʌgbɪ/ *noun* (in full **Rugby football**) team game played with oval ball that may be kicked or carried. □ **Rugby League** partly professional Rugby with teams of 13; **Rugby Union** amateur Rugby with teams of 15.

rugged /'rʌgɪd/ *adjective* (esp. of ground) rough, uneven; (of features) furrowed, irregular; harsh; robust. □ **ruggedly** *adverb*; **ruggedness** *noun*.

rugger /'rʌgə/ *noun colloquial* Rugby.

ruin /'ru:ɪn/ ● *noun* wrecked or spoiled state; downfall; loss of property or position; (in *singular* or *plural*) remains of building etc. that has suffered ruin; cause of ruin. ● *verb* bring to ruin; spoil, damage; (esp. as **ruined** *adjective*) reduce to ruins. □ **ruination** *noun*.

ruinous *adjective* bringing ruin; disastrous; dilapidated.

rule ● *noun* compulsory principle governing action; prevailing custom, standard, normal state of things; government, dominion; straight measuring device, ruler; code of discipline of religious order; *Printing* thin line or dash. ● *verb* (**-ling**) dominate; keep under control; (often + *over*) have sovereign control of; (often + *that*) pronounce authoritatively; make parallel lines across (paper), make (straight line) with ruler etc. □ **as a rule** usually; **rule of thumb** rule based on experience or practice, not theory; **rule out** exclude.

ruler *noun* person exercising government or dominion; straight strip of plastic etc. used to draw or measure.

ruling *noun* authoritative pronouncement.

rum[1] *noun* spirit distilled from sugar cane or molasses. □ **rum baba** sponge cake soaked in rum syrup.

rum[2] *adjective* (**-mm-**) *colloquial* queer, strange.

Rumanian = ROMANIAN.

rumba /'rʌmbə/ *noun* ballroom dance of Cuban origin; music for this.

rumble /'rʌmb(ə)l/ ● *verb* (**-ling**) make continuous deep sound as of thunder; (+ *along, by, past,* etc.) (esp. of vehicle) move with such sound; *slang* see through, detect. ● *noun* rumbling sound.

rumbustious /rʌm'bʌstʃəs/ *adjective colloquial* boisterous, uproarious.

ruminant /'ru:mɪnənt/ ● *noun* animal that chews the cud. ● *adjective* of ruminants; meditative.

ruminate /'ru:mɪneɪt/ *verb* (**-ting**) meditate, ponder; chew the cud. □ **rumination** *noun*; **ruminative** /-nətɪv/ *adjective*.

rummage /'rʌmɪdʒ/ ● *verb* (**-ging**) search, esp. unsystematically; (+ *up, out*) find among other things. ● *noun* rummaging. □ **rummage sale** *esp. US* jumble sale.

rummy /'rʌmɪ/ *noun* card game played usually with two packs.

rumour /'ru:mə/ (*US* **rumor**) ● *noun* (often + *of, that*) general talk, assertion, or hearsay of doubtful accuracy. ● *verb* (usually in *passive*) report by way of rumour.

rump *noun* hind part of mammal or bird, esp. buttocks; remnant of parliament etc. □ **rump steak** cut of beef from rump.

rumple /'rʌmp(ə)l/ *verb* (**-ling**) crease, ruffle.

rumpus /'rʌmpəs/ *noun colloquial* row, uproar.

run ● *verb* (**-nn-**; *past* **ran**; *past participle* **run**) go at pace faster than walk; flee; go or travel hurriedly, briefly, etc.; advance smoothly or (as) by rolling or on wheels; (cause to) be in action or operation; be current or operative; (of bus, train, etc.) travel on its route; (of play etc.) be presented; extend, have course or tendency; compete in or enter (horse etc.) in race etc.; (often + *for*) seek election; (cause to) flow or emit liquid; spread rapidly; perform (errand); publish (article etc.); direct (business etc.); own and use (vehicle); smuggle; (of thought, the eye, etc.) pass quickly; (of tights etc.) ladder. • *noun* running; short excursion; distance travelled; general tendency; regular route; continuous stretch, spell, or course; (often + *on*) high general demand; quantity produced at one time; general or average type or class; point scored in cricket or baseball; (+ *of*) free use of; animal's regular track; enclosure for fowls etc.; range of pasture; ladder in tights etc.; *Music* rapid scale passage. □ **give (person) the run-around** deceive, evade; **on the run** fleeing; **runabout** light car or aircraft; **run across** happen to meet; **run after** pursue; **run away** (often + *from*) flee, abscond; **runaway** *noun* person, animal, vehicle, etc. running away or out of control; **run down** *verb* knock down, reduce numbers of, (of clock etc.) stop, discover after search, *colloquial* disparage; **run-down** *noun* reduction in numbers, detailed analysis, *adjective* dilapidated, decayed, exhausted; **run dry** cease to flow; **run in** *verb* run (vehicle, engine) carefully when new, *colloquial* arrest; **run-in** *noun colloquial* quarrel; **run into** collide with, encounter, reach as many as; **run low**, **short** become depleted, have too little; **run off** flee, produce (copies) on machine, decide (race) after tie or heats, write or recite fluently; **run-of-the-mill** ordinary, not special; **run on** continue in operation, speak volubly, continue on same line as preceding matter; **run out** come to an end, (+ *of*) exhaust one's stock of, put down wicket of (running batsman); **run out on** *colloquial* desert; **run over** (of vehicle) knock down or crush, overflow, review quickly; **run through** *verb* examine or rehearse briefly, deal successively with, spend money rapidly, pervade, pierce with blade; **run-through** *noun* rehearsal; **run to** have money or ability for, reach (amount etc.), show tendency to; **run up** *verb* accumulate (debt etc.), build or make hurriedly, raise (flag); **run-up** *noun* (often + *to*) preparatory period; **run up against** meet with

(difficulty etc.); **runway** specially prepared airfield surface for taking off and landing.

rune *noun* letter of earliest Germanic alphabet; similar character of mysterious or magic significance. □ **runic** *adjective.*

rung[1] *noun* step of ladder; strengthening crosspiece of chair etc.

rung[2] *past participle of* RING[2].

runnel /ˈrʌn(ə)l/ *noun* brook; gutter.

runner *noun* racer; creeping rooting plant-stem; groove, rod, etc. for thing to slide along or on; sliding ring on rod etc.; messenger; long narrow ornamental cloth or rug; (in full **runner bean**) kind of climbing bean. □ **runner-up** (*plural* **runners-up** or **runner-ups**) competitor taking second place.

running • *noun* act or manner of running race etc. • *adjective* continuous; consecutive; done with a run. □ **in** or **out of the running** with good or poor chance of success; **running commentary** verbal description of events in progress; **running knot** one that slips along rope etc. to allow tightening; **running mate** *US* vice-presidential candidate, horse setting pace for another; **running repairs** minor or temporary repairs; **running water** flowing water, esp. on tap.

runny *adjective* (**-ier**, **-iest**) tending to run or flow; excessively fluid.

runt *noun* smallest pig etc. of litter; undersized person.

rupee /ruːˈpiː/ *noun* monetary unit of India, Pakistan, etc.

rupiah /ruːˈpiːə/ *noun* monetary unit of Indonesia.

rupture /ˈrʌptʃə/ • *noun* breaking, breach; breach in relationship; abdominal hernia. • *verb* (**-ring**) burst (cell, membrane, etc.); sever (connection); affect with or suffer hernia.

rural /ˈrʊər(ə)l/ *adjective* in, of, or suggesting country.

ruse /ruːz/ *noun* stratagem, trick.

rush[1] • *verb* go, move, flow, or act precipitately or with great speed; move or transport with great haste; perform or deal with hurriedly; force (person) to act hastily; attack or capture by sudden assault. • *noun* rushing; violent advance or attack; sudden flow; period of great activity; sudden migration of large numbers; (+ *on, for*) strong demand for a commodity; (in *plural*) *colloquial* first uncut prints of film. ● *adjective* done hastily. □ **rush hour** time each day when traffic is heaviest.

rush² *noun* marsh plant with slender pith-filled stem; its stem esp. used for making basketware etc.

rusk *noun* slice of bread rebaked as light biscuit, esp. for infants.

russet /ˈrʌsɪt/ ● *adjective* reddish-brown. ● *noun* russet colour; rough-skinned russet-coloured apple.

Russian /ˈrʌʃ(ə)n/ ● *noun* native or national of Russia or (loosely) former USSR; person of Russian descent; language of Russia. ● *adjective* of Russia or (loosely) former USSR or its people; of or in Russian. □ **Russian roulette** firing of revolver held to one's head after spinning cylinder with one chamber loaded; **Russian salad** mixed diced cooked vegetables with mayonnaise.

rust ● *noun* reddish corrosive coating formed on iron etc. by oxidation; plant disease with rust-coloured spots; reddish-brown. ● *verb* affect or be affected with rust; become impaired through disuse. □ **rustproof** not susceptible to corrosion by rust.

rustic /ˈrʌstɪk/ ● *adjective* of or like country people or country life; unsoph-

isticated; of rough workmanship; made of untrimmed branches or rough timber; *Architecture* with roughened surface. ● *noun* country person, peasant. □ **rusticity** /-ˈtɪs-/ *noun*.

rusticate /ˈrʌstɪkeɪt/ *verb* (**-ting**) expel temporarily from university; retire to or live in the country; make rustic. □ **rustication** *noun*.

rustle /ˈrʌs(ə)l/ ● *verb* (**-ling**) (cause to) make sound as of dry blown leaves; steal (cattle or horses). ● *noun* rustling sound. □ **rustle up** *colloquial* produce at short notice. □ **rustler** *noun*.

rusty *adjective* (**-ier, -iest**) rusted, affected by rust; stiff with age or disuse; (of knowledge etc.) impaired by neglect; rust-coloured; discoloured by age.

rut¹ ● *noun* deep track made by passage of wheels; fixed (esp. tedious) practice or routine. ● *verb* (**-tt-**) (esp. as **rutted** *adjective*) mark with ruts.

rut² ● *noun* periodic sexual excitement of male deer etc. ● *verb* (**-tt-**) be affected with rut.

ruthless /ˈruːθlɪs/ *adjective* having no pity or compassion. □ **ruthlessly** *adverb*; **ruthlessness** *noun*.

RV *abbreviation* Revised Version (of Bible).

rye /raɪ/ *noun* cereal plant; grain of this, used for bread, fodder, etc.; (in full **rye whisky**) whisky distilled from rye.

Ss

S *abbreviation* (also **S.**) Saint; south(ern).

s. *abbreviation* second(s); *historical* shilling(s); son.

SA *abbreviation* Salvation Army; South Africa; South Australia.

sabbath /'sæbəθ/ *noun* religious rest-day kept by Christians on Sunday and Jews on Saturday.

sabbatical /sə'bætɪk(ə)l/ ● *adjective* (of leave) granted at intervals to university teacher for study or travel. ● *noun* period of sabbatical leave.

saber *US* = SABRE.

sable /'seɪb(ə)l/ ● *noun* (*plural* same or **-s**) small dark-furred mammal; its skin or fur. ● *adjective* Heraldry black; *esp. poetical* gloomy.

sabot /'sæbəʊ/ *noun* wooden or wooden-soled shoe.

sabotage /'sæbətɑːʒ/ ● *noun* deliberate destruction or damage, esp. for political purpose. ● *verb* (**-ging**) commit sabotage on; destroy, spoil.

saboteur /sæbə'tɜː/ *noun* person who commits sabotage.

sabre /'seɪbə/ *noun* (*US* **saber**) curved cavalry sword; light fencing-sword. □ **sabre-rattling** display or threat of military force.

sac *noun* membranous bag in animal or plant.

saccharin /'sækərɪn/ *noun* a sugar substitute.

saccharine /'sækəriːn/ *adjective* excessively sentimental or sweet.

sacerdotal /sækə'dəʊt(ə)l/ *adjective* of priests or priestly office.

sachet /'sæʃeɪ/ *noun* small bag or packet containing shampoo, perfumed substances, etc.

sack¹ ● *noun* large strong bag for coal, food, mail, etc.; amount held by sack; (**the sack**) *colloquial* dismissal, *US slang* bed. ● *verb* put in sack(s); *colloquial* dismiss from employment. □ **sackcloth** coarse fabric of flax or hemp.

sack² ● *verb* plunder and destroy (town etc.). ● *noun* such sacking.

sack³ *noun* *historical* white wine from Spain etc.

sackbut /'sækbʌt/ *noun* early form of trombone.

sacking *noun* sackcloth.

sacral /'seɪkr(ə)l/ *adjective* of sacrum.

sacrament /'sækrɪmənt/ *noun* symbolic Christian ceremony, esp. Eucharist; sacred thing. □ **sacramental** /-'men-/ *adjective*.

sacred /'seɪkrɪd/ *adjective* (often + *to*) dedicated to a god, connected with religion; safeguarded or required, esp. by tradition; inviolable. □ **sacred cow** *colloquial* idea or institution unreasonably held to be above criticism.

sacrifice /'sækrɪfaɪs/ ● *noun* voluntary relinquishing of something valued; thing thus relinquished; loss entailed; slaughter of animal or person, or surrender of possession, as offering to deity; animal, person, or thing thus offered. ● *verb* (**-cing**) give up; (+ *to*) devote to; offer or kill (as) sacrifice. □ **sacrificial** /-'fɪʃ-/ *adjective*.

sacrilege /'sækrɪlɪdʒ/ *noun* violation of what is sacred. □ **sacrilegious** /-'lɪdʒəs/ *adjective*.

sacristan /'sækrɪst(ə)n/ *noun* person in charge of sacristy and church contents.

sacristy /'sækrɪstɪ/ *noun* (*plural* **-ies**) room in church for vestments, vessels, etc.

sacrosanct /'sækrəʊsæŋkt/ *adjective* most sacred; inviolable. □ **sacrosanctity** /-'sæŋkt-/ *noun*.

sacrum /'seɪkrəm/ *noun* (*plural* **sacra** or **-s**) triangular bone between hip-bones.

sad *adjective* (**-dd-**) sorrowful; causing sorrow; regrettable; deplorable. □ **sadden** *verb*; **sadly** *adverb*; **sadness** *noun*.

saddle /'sæd(ə)l/ ● *noun* seat of leather etc. fastened on horse etc.; bicycle etc. seat; joint of meat consisting of the two loins; ridge rising to a summit at each end. ● *verb* (**-ling**) put saddle on (horse etc.); (+ *with*) burden with task etc. □ **saddle-bag** each of pair of bags laid across back of horse etc., bag attached behind bicycle etc. saddle.

saddler *noun* maker of or dealer in saddles etc. □ **saddlery** *noun* (*plural* **-ies**).

sadism /'seɪdɪz(ə)m/ *noun colloquial* enjoyment of cruelty to others; sexual perversion characterized by this. □ **sadist** *noun*, **sadistic** /sə'dɪs-/ *adjective*; **sadistically** /sə'dɪs-/ *adverb*.

sadomasochism /seɪdəʊ'mæsəkɪz(ə)m/ *noun* sadism and masochism in one person. □ **sadomasochist** *noun*; **sadomasochistic** /-'kɪs-/ *adjective*.

s.a.e. *abbreviation* stamped addressed envelope.

safari /sə'fɑːrɪ/ *noun* (*plural* **-s**) expedition, esp. in Africa, to observe or hunt animals. □ **safari park** area where wild animals are kept in open for viewing.

safe ● *adjective* free of danger or injury; secure, not risky; reliable, sure; prevented from escaping or doing harm; cautious. ● *noun* strong lockable cupboard for valuables; ventilated cupboard for provisions. □ **safe conduct** immunity from arrest or harm; **safe deposit** building containing strongrooms and safes for hire. □ **safely** *adverb*.

safeguard ● *noun* protecting proviso, circumstance, etc. ● *verb* guard or protect (rights etc.).

safety /'seɪftɪ/ *noun* being safe; freedom from danger. □ **safety-belt** belt or strap preventing injury, esp. seat-belt; **safety-catch** device preventing accidental operation of gun trigger or machinery; **safety curtain** fireproof curtain to divide theatre auditorium from stage; **safety match** match that ignites only on specially prepared surface; **safety net** net placed to catch acrobat etc. in case of fall; **safety pin** pin with guarded point; **safety razor** razor with guard to prevent user cutting skin; **safety-valve** valve relieving excessive pressure of steam, means of harmlessly venting excitement etc.

saffron /'sæfrən/ ● *noun* deep yellow colouring and flavouring from dried crocus stigmas; colour of this. ● *adjective* deep yellow.

sag ● *verb* (**-gg-**) sink or subside; have downward bulge or curve in middle. ● *noun* state or amount of sagging. □ **saggy** *adjective*.

saga /'sɑːgə/ *noun* long heroic story, esp. medieval Icelandic or Norwegian; long family chronicle; long involved story.

sagacious /sə'geɪʃəs/ *adjective* showing insight or good judgement. □ **sagacity** /-'gæs-/ *noun*.

sage[1] *noun* aromatic herb with dull greyish-green leaves.

sage[2] ● *noun* wise man. ● *adjective* wise, judicious, experienced. □ **sagely** *adverb*.

Sagittarius /sædʒɪ'teərɪəs/ *noun* ninth sign of zodiac.

sago /'seɪgəʊ/ *noun* (*plural* **-s**) starch used in puddings etc.; (in full **sago palm**) any of several tropical trees yielding this.

sahib /sɑːb/ *noun historical form of address to European men in India.*

said *past & past participle* of SAY.

sail ● *noun* piece of material extended on rigging to catch wind and propel vessel; ship's sails collectively; voyage or excursion in sailing vessel; wind-catching apparatus of windmill. ● *verb* travel on water by use of sails or enginepower; begin voyage; navigate (ship etc.); travel on (sea); glide or move smoothly or with dignity; (often + *through*) *colloquial* succeed easily. □ **sailboard** board with mast and sail, used in windsurfing; **sailcloth** material for sails, kind of coarse linen; **sailing boat**, **ship**, etc., vessel moved by sails; **sailplane** kind of glider.

sailor *noun* seaman or mariner, esp. below officer's rank. □ **bad**, **good sailor** person very liable or not liable to seasickness.

sainfoin /'sænfɔɪn/ *noun* pink-flowered plant used as fodder.

saint /seɪnt, before a name usually sənt/ ● *noun* holy or canonized person, regarded as deserving special veneration; very virtuous person. ● *verb* (as **sainted** *adjective*) holy, virtuous.

□ **sainthood** *noun*; **saintlike** *adjective*; **saintliness** *noun*; **saintly** (**-ier**, **-iest**) *adjective*.

sake[1] *noun* □ **for the sake of** out of consideration for, in the interest of, in order to please, get, etc.

sake[2] /'sɑːkɪ/ *noun* Japanese rice wine.

salaam /sə'lɑːm/ ● *noun* (*chiefly as Muslim greeting*) Peace!; low bow. ● *verb* make salaam.

salacious /sə'leɪʃəs/ *adjective* erotic; lecherous. □ **salaciousness** *noun*; **salacity** /-'læs-/ *noun*.

salad /'sæləd/ *noun* cold mixture of usually raw vegetables etc. often with dressing. □ **salad cream** creamy salad dressing; **salad days** period of youthful inexperience; **salad dressing** sauce of oil, vinegar, etc. for salads.

salamander /'sæləmændə/ *noun* newt-like amphibian formerly supposed to live in fire; similar mythical creature.

salami /sə'lɑːmɪ/ *noun* (*plural* **-s**) highly-seasoned sausage, originally Italian.

sal ammoniac /sæl ə'məʊnɪæk/ *noun* ammonium chloride.

salary /'sælərɪ/ ● *noun* (*plural* **-ies**) fixed regular payment by employer to employee. ● *verb* (**-ies**, **-ied**) (usually as **salaried**) pay salary to.

sale *noun* exchange of commodity for money etc.; act or instance of selling; amount sold; temporary offering of goods at reduced prices; event at which goods are sold. □ **on, for sale** offered for purchase; **saleroom** room where auctions are held; **salesman**, **salesperson**, **saleswoman** person employed to sell goods etc.

saleable *adjective* fit or likely to be sold. □ **saleability** *noun*.

salesmanship *noun* skill in selling.

salient /'seɪlɪənt/ ● *adjective* prominent, conspicuous; (of angle) pointing outwards. ● *noun* salient angle; outward bulge in military line.

saline /'seɪlaɪn/ ● *adjective* containing or tasting of salt(s); of salt(s). ● *noun* salt lake, spring, etc.; saline solution. □ **salinity** /-'lɪn-/ *noun*.

saliva /sə'laɪvə/ *noun* colourless liquid produced by glands in mouth. □ **salivary** *adjective*.

salivate /'sælɪveɪt/ *verb* (**-ting**) secrete saliva, esp. in excess.

sallow[1] /'sæləʊ/ *adjective* (**-er**, **-est**) (esp. of complexion) yellowish.

sallow[2] /'sæləʊ/ *noun* low-growing willow; shoot or wood of this.

sally /'sælɪ/ ● *noun* (*plural* **-ies**) witticism; military rush; excursion. ● *verb* (**-ies**, **-ied**) (usually + *out*, *forth*) set out for walk etc., make sally.

salmon /'sæmən/ ● *noun* (*plural* same) large silver-scaled fish with orange-pink flesh. ● *adjective* orange-pink. □ **salmon-pink** orange-pink; **salmon trout** large silver-coloured trout.

salmonella /sælmə'nelə/ *noun* (*plural* **-llae** /-liː/) bacterium causing food poisoning; such food poisoning.

salon /'sælɒn/ *noun* room or establishment of hairdresser, fashion designer, etc.; *historical* meeting of eminent people at fashionable home; reception room of large house.

saloon /sə'luːn/ *noun* large room or hall on ship, in hotel, etc., or for specified purpose; saloon car; *US* drinking bar; saloon bar. □ **saloon bar** more comfortable bar in public house; **saloon car** car with body closed off from luggage area.

salsa /'sælsə/ *noun* dance music of Cuban origin; kind of spicy tomato sauce.

salsify /'sælsɪfɪ/ *noun* (*plural* **-ies**) plant with long fleshy edible root.

salt /sɔːlt/ ● *noun* (also **common salt**) sodium chloride, esp. mined or evaporated from sea water, and used esp. for seasoning or preserving food; *Chemistry* substance formed in reaction of an acid with a base; piquancy, wit; (in *singular* or *plural*) substance resembling salt in taste, form, etc.; (esp. in *plural*) substance used as laxative; (also **old salt**) experienced sailor. ● *adjective* containing, tasting of, or preserved with salt. ● *verb* cure, preserve, or season with salt; sprinkle salt on (road etc.). □ **salt away**, **down** *slang* put (money etc.) by; **salt-cellar** container for salt at table; **salt-mine** mine yielding rock salt; **salt of the earth** finest or most honest people; **salt-pan** vessel, or hollow near sea, used for getting salt by evaporation; **salt-water** of or living in sea;

take with a pinch or **grain of salt** be sceptical about; **worth one's salt** efficient, capable.

salting /noun/ (esp. in *plural*) marsh overflowed by sea.

saltire /'sɔːltaɪə/ *noun* X-shaped cross.

saltpetre /sɔːlt'piːtə/ *noun* (*US* **saltpeter**) white crystalline salty substance used in preserving meat and in gunpowder.

salty *adjective* (**-ier**, **-iest**) tasting of or containing salt; witty, piquant. □ **saltiness** *noun*.

salubrious /sə'luːbrɪəs/ *adjective* healthgiving. □ **salubrity** *noun*.

saluki /sə'luːkɪ/ *noun* (*plural* **-s**) dog of tall slender silky-coated breed.

salutary /'sæljʊtərɪ/ *adjective* producing good effect.

salutation /sælju:'teɪʃ(ə)n/ *noun formal* sign or expression of greeting.

salute /sə'luːt/ ● *noun* gesture of respect, homage, greeting, etc.; *Military etc.* prescribed gesture or use of weapons or flags as sign of respect etc. ● *verb* (**-ting**) make salute (to); greet; commend.

salvage /'sælvɪdʒ/ ● *noun* rescue of property from sea, fire, etc.; saving and utilization of waste materials; property or materials salvaged. ● *verb* (**-ging**) save from wreck etc. □ **salvageable** *adjective*.

salvation /sæl'veɪʃ(ə)n/ *noun* saving, being saved; deliverance from sin and damnation; religious conversion; person or thing that saves. □ **Salvation Army** worldwide quasi-military Christian charitable organization.

Salvationist *noun* member of Salvation Army.

salve[1] ● *noun* healing ointment; (often + *for*) thing that soothes. ● *verb* (**-ving**) soothe.

salve[2] *verb* (**-ving**) save from wreck, fire, etc. □ **salvable** *adjective*.

salver /'sælvə/ *noun* tray for drinks, letters, etc.

salvo /'sælvəʊ/ *noun* (*plural* **-es** or **-s**) simultaneous firing of guns etc.; round of applause.

sal volatile /sæl və'lætɪlɪ/ *noun* solution of ammonium carbonate, used as smelling salts.

SAM *abbreviation* surface-to-air missile.

Samaritan /sə'mærɪt(ə)n/ *noun* (in full **good Samaritan**) charitable or helpful person; member of counselling organization.

samba /'sæmbə/ ● *noun* ballroom dance of Brazilian origin; music for this. ● *verb* (**-bas**, **-baed** or **-ba'd** /-bəd/, **-baing** /-beɪŋ/) dance samba.

same ● *adjective* identical; unvarying; just mentioned. ● *pronoun* (**the same**) the same person or thing. ● *adverb* (**the same**) in the same manner. □ **all** or **just the same** nevertheless; **at the same time** simultaneously, notwithstanding. □ **sameness** *noun*.

samosa /sə'məʊsə/ *noun* Indian fried triangular pastry containing spiced vegetables or meat.

samovar /'sæməvɑː/ *noun* Russian tea-urn.

Samoyed /'sæməjed/ *noun* member of a northern Siberian people; (also **samoyed**) dog of white Arctic breed.

sampan /'sæmpæn/ *noun* small boat used in Far East.

samphire /'sæmfaɪə/ *noun* cliff plant used in pickles.

sample /'sɑːmp(ə)l/ ● *noun* small representative part or quantity; specimen; typical example. ● *verb* (**-ling**) take samples of; try qualities of; experience briefly.

sampler /'sɑːmplə/ *noun* piece of embroidery worked to show proficiency.

samurai /'sæmʊraɪ/ *noun* (*plural* same) Japanese army officer; *historical* member of Japanese military caste.

sanatorium /sænə'tɔːrɪəm/ *noun* (*plural* **-riums** or **-ria**) residential clinic, esp. for convalescents and the chronically sick; accommodation for sick people in school etc.

sanctify /'sæŋktɪfaɪ/ *verb* (**-ies**, **-ied**) consecrate, treat as holy; purify from sin; sanction. □ **sanctification** *noun*.

sanctimonious /sæŋktɪ'məʊnɪəs/ *adjective* ostentatiously pious. □ **sanctimoniously** *adverb*; **sanctimony** /'sæŋktɪmənɪ/ *noun*.

sanction /'sæŋkʃ(ə)n/ ● *noun* approval by custom or tradition; express permission; confirmation of law etc.; penalty or reward attached to law; moral impetus for obedience to rule; (esp. in *plural*) (esp. economic) action to coerce state to conform to agreement etc. ● *verb* authorize, countenance; make (law etc.) binding.

sanctity /'sæŋktɪtɪ/ *noun* holiness, sacredness; inviolability.

sanctuary /'sæŋktʃʊərɪ/ *noun* (*plural* **-ies**) holy place; place where birds, wild animals, etc. are protected; place of refuge.

sanctum /'sæŋktəm/ *noun* (*plural* **-s**) holy place, esp. in temple or church; *colloquial* person's den.

sand ● *noun* fine grains resulting from erosion of esp. siliceous rocks; (in *plural*) grains of sand, expanse of sand, sandbank. ● *verb* smooth or treat with sandpaper or sand. □ **sandbag** *noun* bag filled with sand, esp. for making temporary defences; *verb* defend or hit with sandbag(s); **sandbank** sand forming shallow place in sea or river; **sandblast** *verb* treat with jet of sand driven by compressed air or steam, *noun* this jet; **sandcastle** model castle of sand on beach; **sand-dune**, **-hill** dune; **sand-martin** bird nesting in sandy banks; **sandpaper** paper with abrasive coating for smoothing or polishing wood etc., *verb* treat with this; **sandpiper** bird inhabiting wet sandy places; **sandpit** hollow or box containing sand for children to play in; **sandstone** sedimentary rock of compressed sand; **sandstorm** storm with clouds of sand raised by wind.

sandal /'sænd(ə)l/ *noun* shoe with openwork upper or no upper, fastened with straps.

sandal-tree /'sændəltriː/ *noun* tree yielding sandalwood.

sandalwood /'sændəlwʊd/ *noun* scented wood of sandal-tree.

sandwich /'sænwɪdʒ/ ● *noun* two or more slices of bread with filling; layered cake with jam, cream, etc. ● *verb* put (thing, statement, etc.) between two of different kind; squeeze in between others. □ **sandwich-board** each of two advertising boards worn front and back; **sandwich course** course with alternate periods of study and work experience.

sandy *adjective* (**-ier**, **-iest**) containing or covered with sand; (of hair) reddish; sand-coloured.

sane *adjective* of sound mind, not mad; (of opinion etc.) moderate, sensible.

sang *past of* SING.

sang-froid /sɑ̃'frwɑː/ *noun* calmness in danger or difficulty.

sangria /sæŋ'griːə/ *noun* Spanish drink of red wine with fruit etc.

sanguinary /'sæŋgwɪnərɪ/ *adjective* bloody; bloodthirsty.

sanguine /'sæŋgwɪn/ *adjective* optimistic; (of complexion) florid, ruddy.

Sanhedrin /'sænɪdrɪn/ *noun* court of justice and supreme council in ancient Jerusalem.

sanitarium /sænɪ'teərɪəm/ *noun* (*plural* **-s** or **-ria**) *US* sanatorium.

sanitary /'sænɪtərɪ/ *adjective* (of conditions etc.) affecting health; hygienic. □ **sanitary towel** (*US* **sanitary napkin**) absorbent pad used during menstruation. **sanitariness** *noun*.

sanitation /sænɪ'teɪʃ(ə)n/ *noun* sanitary conditions; maintenance etc. of these; disposal of sewage, refuse, etc.

sanitize /'sænɪtaɪz/ *verb* (also **-ise**) (**-zing** or **-sing**) make sanitary, disinfect; *colloquial* censor.

sanity /'sænɪtɪ/ *noun* being sane; moderation.

sank *past of* SINK.

Sanskrit /'sænskrɪt/ ● *noun* ancient and sacred language of Hindus in India. ● *adjective* of or in Sanskrit.

Santa Claus /'sæntə klɔːz/ *noun* person said to bring children presents at Christmas.

sap[1] ● *noun* vital juice of plants; vitality; *slang* foolish person. ● *verb* (**-pp-**) drain of sap; weaken. □ **sappy** *adjective* (**-ier**, **-iest**).

sap[2] ● *noun* tunnel or trench for concealed approach to enemy. ● *verb* (**-pp-**) dig saps; undermine.

sapient /'seɪpɪənt/ *adjective* *literary* wise; aping wisdom. □ **sapience** *noun*.

sapling /'sæplɪŋ/ *noun* young tree.

sapper *noun* digger of saps; private of Royal Engineers.

sapphire /'sæfaɪə/ ● *noun* transparent blue precious stone; its colour. ● *adjective* (also **sapphire blue**) bright blue.

saprophyte /'sæprəfaɪt/ *noun* plant or micro-organism living on dead organic matter.

saraband/ /ˈsærəbænd/ *noun* slow Spanish dance; music for this.

Saracen /ˈsærəs(ə)n/ *noun* Arab or Muslim of time of Crusades.

sarcasm /ˈsɑːkæz(ə)m/ *noun* ironically scornful remark(s). □ **sarcastic** /sɑːˈkæstɪk/ *adjective*; **sarcastically** /sɑːˈkæstɪkəlɪ/ *adverb*.

sarcophagus /sɑːˈkɒfəgəs/ *noun* (*plural* **-gi** /-gaɪ/) stone coffin.

sardine /sɑːˈdiːn/ *noun* (*plural* same or **-s**) young pilchard etc. tinned tightly packed.

sardonic /sɑːˈdɒnɪk/ *adjective* bitterly mocking; cynical. □ **sardonically** *adverb*.

sardonyx /ˈsɑːdənɪks/ *noun* onyx in which layers alternate with yellow or orange ones.

sargasso /sɑːˈgæsəʊ/ *noun* (*plural* **-s** or **-es**) seaweed with berry-like airvessels.

sarge *noun slang* sergeant.

sari /ˈsɑːrɪ/ *noun* (*plural* **-s**) length of material draped round body, worn traditionally by Hindu etc. women.

sarky /ˈsɑːkɪ/ *adjective* (**-ier**, **-iest**) *slang* sarcastic.

sarong /səˈrɒŋ/ *noun* garment of long strip of cloth tucked round waist or under armpits.

sarsaparilla /sɑːsəpəˈrɪlə/ *noun* dried roots of esp. smilax used to flavour drinks and medicines and formerly as tonic; plant yielding these.

sarsen /ˈsɑːs(ə)n/ *noun* sandstone boulder carried by ice in glacial period.

sarsenet /ˈsɑːsnɪt/ *noun* soft silk fabric used esp. for linings.

sartorial /sɑːˈtɔːrɪəl/ *adjective* of men's clothes or tailoring. □ **sartorially** *adverb*.

SAS *abbreviation* Special Air Service.

sash[1] *noun* strip or loop of cloth worn over one shoulder or round waist.

sash[2] *noun* frame holding glass in window sliding up and down in grooves.

sass *US colloquial* ● *noun* impudence. ● *verb* be impudent to. □ **sassy** *adjective* (**-ier**, **-iest**).

sassafras /ˈsæsəfræs/ *noun* small N. American tree; medicinal preparation from its leaves or bark.

Sassenach /ˈsæsənæk/ *noun Scottish usually derogatory* English person.

Sat. *abbreviation* Saturday.

sat *past & past participle* of SIT.

Satan /ˈseɪt(ə)n/ *noun* the Devil.

satanic /səˈtænɪk/ *adjective* of or like Satan; hellish, evil.

Satanism *noun* worship of Satan. □ **Satanist** *noun*.

satchel /ˈsætʃ(ə)l/ *noun* small bag, esp. for carrying school-books.

sate *verb* (**-ting**) *formal* gratify fully, surfeit.

sateen /sæˈtiːn/ *noun* glossy cotton fabric like satin.

satellite /ˈsætəlaɪt/ ● *noun* heavenly or artificial body orbiting earth or other planet; (in full **satellite state**) small country controlled by another. ● *adjective* transmitted by satellite; receiving signal from satellite.

satiate /ˈseɪʃɪeɪt/ *verb* (**-ting**) sate. □ **satiation** *noun*.

satiety /səˈtaɪɪtɪ/ *noun formal* being sated.

satin /ˈsætɪn/ ● *noun* silk etc. fabric glossy on one side. ● *adjective* smooth as satin. □ **satinwood** kind of yellow glossy timber. ■ **satiny** *adjective*.

satire /ˈsætaɪə/ *noun* ridicule, irony, etc. used to expose folly, vice, etc.; literary work using satire. □ **satirical** /səˈtɪrɪk(ə)l/ *adjective*; **satirically** /səˈtɪrɪkəlɪ/ *adverb*.

satirist /ˈsætərɪst/ *noun* writer of satires; satirical person.

satirize /ˈsætəraɪz/ *verb* (also **-ise**) (**-zing** or **-sing**) attack or describe with satire.

satisfaction /sætɪsˈfæk(ʃ)ən/ *noun* satisfying, being satisfied; thing that satisfies; atonement; compensation.

satisfactory /sætɪsˈfæktərɪ/ *adjective* adequate; causing satisfaction. □ **satisfactorily** *adverb*.

satisfy /ˈsætɪsfaɪ/ *verb* (**-ies**, **-ied**) meet expectations or wishes of; be adequate; meet (an appetite or want); rid (person) of an appetite or want; pay; fulfil, comply with; convince.

satsuma /sætˈsuːmə/ *noun* kind of tangerine.

saturate /ˈsætʃəreɪt/ *verb* (**-ting**) fill with moisture; fill to capacity; cause (substance) to absorb, hold, etc. as much as possible of another substance; supply (market) beyond demand; (as **saturated** *adjective*) (of fat) containing the most possible hydrogen atoms.

saturation *noun* saturating, being saturated. □ **saturation point** stage beyond which no more can be absorbed or accepted.

Saturday /'sætədeɪ/ *noun* day of week following Friday.

Saturnalia /sætə'neɪlɪə/ *noun* (*plural* same or **-s**) ancient Roman festival of Saturn; (**saturnalia**) (treated as *singular* or *plural*) scene of wild revelry.

saturnine /'sætənaɪn/ *adjective* of gloomy temperament or appearance.

satyr /'sætə/ *noun* Greek & Roman Mythology part-human part-animal woodland deity; lecherous man.

sauce /sɔːs/ ● *noun* liquid or viscous accompaniment to food; something that adds piquancy; *colloquial* impudence. ● *verb* (**-cing**) *colloquial* be impudent to. □ **sauce-boat** jug or dish for serving sauce; **saucepan** cooking vessel usually with handle, used on hob.

saucer /'sɔːsə/ *noun* shallow circular dish, esp. for standing cup on.

saucy *adjective* (**-ier, -iest**) impudent, cheeky. □ **saucily** *adverb*; **sauciness** *noun*.

sauerkraut /'saʊəkraʊt/ *noun* German dish of pickled cabbage.

sauna /'sɔːnə/ *noun* period spent in room with steam bath; this room.

saunter /'sɔːntə/ ● *verb* stroll. ● *noun* leisurely walk.

saurian /'sɔːrɪən/ *adjective* of or like a lizard.

sausage /'sɒsɪdʒ/ *noun* seasoned minced meat etc. in edible cylindrical case; sausage-shaped object. □ **sausage meat** minced meat for sausages etc.; **sausage roll** sausage meat in pastry cylinder.

sauté /'səʊteɪ/ ● *adjective* fried quickly in a little fat. ● *noun* food cooked thus. ● *verb* (*past & past participle* **sautéd** or **sautéed**) cook thus.

savage /'sævɪdʒ/ ● *adjective* fierce, cruel; wild, primitive. ● *noun derogatory* member of primitive tribe; brutal or barbarous person. ● *verb* (**-ging**) attack and

maul; attack verbally. □ **savagely** *adverb*; **savagery** *noun* (*plural* **-ies**).

savannah /sə'vænə/ *noun* (also **savanna**) grassy plain in tropical or subtropical region.

savant /'sæv(ə)nt/ *noun* (*feminine* **savante** same pronunciation) learned person.

save[1] ● *verb* (**-ving**) (often + *from*) rescue or preserve from danger or harm; (often + *up*) keep for future use; relieve (person) from spending (money, time, etc.); prevent exposure to (annoyance etc.); prevent need for; rescue spiritually; *Football etc.* avoid losing (match), prevent (goal) from being scored. ● *noun Football etc.* act of saving goal. □ **savable, saveable** *adjective*; **saver** *noun*.

save[2] *preposition & conjunction archaic or poetical* except; but.

saveloy /'sævəlɔɪ/ *noun* highly seasoned sausage.

saving ● *noun* anything saved; an economy; (usually in *plural*) money saved; act of preserving or rescuing. ● *preposition* except; without offence to. □ **-saving** making economical use of specified thing; **saving grace** redeeming feature.

saviour /'seɪvjə/ *noun* (US **savior**) person who saves from danger etc.; (**the, our Saviour**) Christ.

savoir faire /sævwɑː 'feə/ *noun* ability to behave appropriately; tact. [French]

savour /'seɪvə/ (US **savor**) ● *noun* characteristic taste, flavour, etc.; tinge or hint. ● *verb* appreciate, enjoy; (+ *of*) imply, suggest.

savoury /'seɪvərɪ/ (US **savory**) ● *adjective* with appetizing taste or smell; (of food) salty or piquant, not sweet; pleasant. ● *noun* (*plural* **-ies**) savoury dish.

savoy /sə'vɔɪ/ *noun* rough-leaved winter cabbage.

savvy /'sævɪ/ *slang* ● *verb* (**-ies, -ied**) know. ● *noun* knowingness, understanding. ● *adjective* (**-ier, -iest**) US knowing, wise.

saw[1] ● *noun* implement with toothed blade etc. for cutting wood etc. ● *verb* (*past participle* **sawn** or **sawed**) cut or make with saw; use saw; make to-and-fro sawing motion. □ **sawdust** fine wood fragments produced in sawing; **sawfish** (*plural* same or **-es**) large sea fish with toothed flat snout; **sawmill** factory for sawing wood into planks; **sawtooth(ed)** serrated.

saw² *past of* SEE¹.

saw³ *noun* proverb, maxim.

sawyer /'sɔːjə/ *noun* person who saws timber.

sax *noun colloquial* saxophone.

saxe /sæks/ *noun & adjective* (in full **saxe blue**) ● *as adjective* often hyphenated) light greyish-blue.

saxifrage /'sæksɪfreɪdʒ/ *noun* small-flowered rock-plant.

Saxon /'sæks(ə)n/ ● *noun historical* member or language of Germanic people that occupied parts of England in 5th–6th c.; Anglo-Saxon. ● *adjective historical* of the Saxons; Anglo-Saxon.

saxophone /'sæksəfəʊn/ *noun* keyed brass reed instrument used esp. in jazz. □ **saxophonist** /'sɒfən-/ *noun*.

say ● *verb* (*3rd singular present* **says** /sez/; *past & past participle* **said** /sed/) utter, remark; express; state; indicate; (in *passive*; usually + *to do*) be asserted; (+ *to do*) *colloquial* direct, order; convey (information); adduce, plead; decide; take as example or as near enough; **(the said)** *Law or jocular* the previously mentioned. ● *noun* opportunity to express view; share in decision. □ **say-so** *colloquial* power of decision, mere assertion.

saying *noun* maxim, proverb, etc.

sc. *abbreviation* scilicet.

scab ● *noun* crust over healing cut, sore, etc.; skin disease; plant disease; *colloquial derogatory* blackleg. ● *verb* (**-bb-**) form scab; *colloquial derogatory* act as blackleg. □ **scabby** *adjective* (**-ier, -iest**).

scabbard /'skæbəd/ *noun historical* sheath of sword etc.

scabies /'skeɪbiːz/ *noun* contagious skin disease causing itching.

scabious /'skeɪbɪəs/ *noun* plant with pincushion-shaped flowers.

scabrous /'skeɪbrəs/ *adjective* rough, scaly; indecent.

scaffold /'skæfəʊld/ *noun* scaffolding; *historical* platform for execution of criminal.

scaffolding *noun* temporary structure of poles, planks, etc. for building work; materials for this.

scald /skɔːld/ ● *verb* burn (skin etc.) with hot liquid or vapour; heat (esp. milk) to near boiling point; (usually + *out*) clean with boiling water. ● *noun* burn etc. caused by scalding.

scale¹ ● *noun* each of thin horny plates protecting skin of fish and reptiles; thing resembling this; incrustation inside kettle etc.; tartar on teeth. ● *verb* (**-ling**) remove scale(s) from; form or come off in scales. □ **scaly** *adjective* (**-ier, -iest**).

scale² *noun* (often in *plural*) weighing machine; (also **scale-pan**) pan of weighing-balance. □ **tip, turn the scales** be decisive factor, (+ *at*) weigh (specified amount).

scale³ ● *noun* graded classification system; ratio of reduction or enlargement in map, picture, etc.; relative dimensions; *Music* set of notes at fixed intervals, arranged in order of pitch; set of marks on line used in measuring etc., rule determining distances between these, rod on which these are marked. ● *verb* (**-ling**) climb; represent in proportion; reduce to common scale. □ **scale down, up** make or become smaller or larger in proportion; **to scale** uniformly in proportion.

scalene /'skeɪliːn/ *adjective* (of triangle) having unequal sides.

scallion /'skæljən/ *noun esp. US* shallot; spring onion.

scallop /'skæləp/ ● *noun* edible bivalve with fan-shaped ridged shells; (in full **scallop shell**) one shell of this, esp. used for cooking or serving food on; (in *plural*) ornamental edging of semicircular curves. ● *verb* (**-p-**) ornament with scallops.

scallywag /'skælɪwæg/ *noun* scamp, rascal.

scalp ● *noun* skin and hair on head; *historical* this cut off as trophy by N. American Indian. ● *verb historical* take scalp of.

scalpel /'skælp(ə)l/ *noun* small surgical knife.

scam *noun US slang* trick, fraud.

scamp *noun colloquial* rascal, rogue.

scamper /'skæmpə/ • *verb* run and skip. • *noun* act of scampering.

scampi /'skæmpɪ/ *plural noun* large prawns.

scan • *verb* (**-nn-**) look at intently or quickly; (of verse etc.) be metrically correct; examine (surface etc.) for radioactivity etc.; traverse (region) with radar etc. beam; resolve (picture) into elements of light and shade for esp. television transmission; analyse metre of (line etc.); obtain image of (part of body) using scanner. • *noun* scanning; image obtained by scanning.

scandal /'skænd(ə)l/ *noun* disgraceful event; public outrage; malicious gossip. □ **scandalmonger** /-mʌŋgə/ person who spreads scandal. □ **scandalous** *adjective*; **scandalously** *adverb*.

scandalize *verb* (also **-ise**) (**-zing** or **-sing**) offend morally, shock.

Scandinavian /skændɪ'neɪvɪən/ • *noun* native or inhabitant, or family of languages, of Scandinavia. • *adjective* of Scandinavia.

scanner *noun* device for scanning; diagnostic apparatus measuring radiation, ultrasound reflections, etc. from body.

scansion /'skænʃ(ə)n/ *noun* metrical scanning of verse.

scant *adjective* barely sufficient; deficient.

scanty *adjective* (**-ier**, **-iest**) of small extent or amount; barely sufficient. □ **scantily** *adverb*; **scantiness** *noun*.

scapegoat /'skeɪpgəʊt/ *noun* person blamed for others' faults.

scapula /'skæpjʊlə/ *noun* (*plural* **-lae** /-liː/ or **-s**) shoulder blade.

scapular /'skæpjʊlə/ • *adjective* of scapula. • *noun* monastic short cloak.

scar¹ • *noun* mark left on skin etc. by wound etc.; emotional damage. • *verb* (**-rr-**) (esp. as **scarred** *adjective*) mark with or form scar(s).

scar² *noun* (also **scaur**) steep craggy part of mountainside.

scarab /'skærəb/ *noun* kind of beetle; gem cut in form of beetle.

scarce /skeəs/ • *adjective* in short supply; rare. • *adverb* archaic or *literary* scarcely. □ **make oneself scarce** *colloquial* keep out of the way, disappear.

scarcely /'skeəslɪ/ *adverb* hardly, only just.

scarcity *noun* (*plural* **-ies**) lack or shortage.

scare /skeə/ • *verb* (**-ring**) frighten; (as **scared** *adjective*) (usually + *of*) frightened; (usually + *away*, *off*, etc.) drive away by frightening. • *noun* sudden fright or alarm, esp. caused by rumours. □ **scarecrow** human figure used for frightening birds away from crops, *colloquial* badly-dressed or grotesque person; **scaremonger** /-mʌŋgə/ person who spreads scare(s).

scarf¹ *noun* (*plural* **scarves** /skɑːvz/ or **-s**) piece of material worn round neck or over head for warmth or ornament.

scarf² *verb* join ends of (timber etc.) by thinning or notching them and bolting them together. • *noun* (*plural* **-s**) joint made thus.

scarify /'skærɪfaɪ/ *verb* (**-ies**, **-ied**) make slight incisions in; scratch; criticize etc. mercilessly; loosen (soil). □ **scarification** *noun*.

scarlatina /skɑːlə'tiːnə/ *noun* scarlet fever.

scarlet /'skɑːlət/ • *adjective* of brilliant red tinged with orange. • *noun* scarlet colour, pigment, clothes, etc. □ **scarlet fever** infectious fever with scarlet rash; **scarlet pimpernel** wild plant with small esp. scarlet flowers.

scarp • *noun* steep slope, esp. inner side of ditch in fortification. • *verb* make perpendicular or steep.

scarper /'skɑːpə/ *verb* *slang* run away, escape.

scarves *plural* of SCARF¹.

scary *adjective* (**-ier**, **-iest**) *colloquial* frightening.

scat¹ • *noun* wordless jazz singing. • *verb* (**-tt-**) sing scat.

scathing /'skeɪðɪŋ/ *adjective* witheringly scornful. □ **scathingly** *adverb*.

scatology /skæ'tɒlədʒɪ/ *noun* preoccupation with excrement or obscenity. □ **scatological** /-tə'lɒdʒ-/ *adjective*.

scatter /'skætə/ • *verb* throw about, strew; cover by scattering; (cause to) flee; (cause to) disperse; (as **scattered** *adjective*) wide apart, sporadic; *Physics* deflect or diffuse (light, particles, etc.). • *noun* act of scattering; small amount scattered; extent of distribution. □ **scatterbrain** person lacking concentration; **scatterbrained** adjective.

scatty /'skætɪ/ adjective (**-ier, -iest**) colloquial lacking concentration. □ **scattily** adverb; **scattiness** noun.

scavenge /'skævɪndʒ/ verb (**-ging**) (usually + for) search for and collect (discarded items).

scavenger /'skævɪndʒə/ noun person who scavenges; animal etc. feeding on carrion.

SCE abbreviation Scottish Certificate of Education.

scenario /sɪ'nɑːrɪəʊ/ noun (plural **-s**) synopsis of film, play, etc.; imagined sequence of future events.

■ Usage Scenario should not be used in standard English to mean 'situation', as in It was an unpleasant scenario.

scene /siːn/ noun place of actual or fictitious occurrence; incident; public display of emotion, temper, etc.; piece of continuous action in a play, film, book, etc.; piece(s) of scenery for a play; landscape, view; colloquial area of interest or activity. □ **behind the scenes** out of view of audience, secret, secretly; **scene-shifter** person who moves scenery in theatre.

scenery /'siːnərɪ/ noun features (esp. picturesque) of landscape; backcloths, properties, etc. representing scene in a play etc.

scenic /'siːnɪk/ adjective picturesque; of scenery. □ **scenically** adverb.

scent /sent/ ● noun characteristic, esp. pleasant, smell; liquid perfume; smell left by animal; clues etc. leading to discovery; power of scenting. ● verb discern by smell; sense; (esp. as **scented** adjective) make fragrant.

scepter US = SCEPTRE.

sceptic /'skeptɪk/ noun (US **skeptic**) sceptical person; person who questions truth of religions, or the possibility of knowledge. □ **scepticism** /-sɪz(ə)m/ noun.

sceptical /'skeptɪk(ə)l/ adjective (US **skeptical**) inclined to doubt accepted opinions; critical; incredulous. □ **sceptically** adverb.

sceptre /'septə/ noun (US **scepter**) staff borne as symbol of sovereignty.

schedule /'ʃedjuːl/ ● noun timetable; list, esp. of rates or prices. ● verb (**-ling**) include in schedule; make schedule of; list (building) for preservation. □ **on schedule** at time appointed; **scheduled flight**, **service**, etc., regular public one.

schema /'skiːmə/ noun (plural **schemata** or **-s**) synopsis, outline, diagram.

schematic /skɪ'mætɪk/ ● adjective of or as scheme or diagram. ● noun diagram, esp. of electronic circuit.

schematize /'skiːmətaɪz/ verb (also **-ise**) (**-zing** or **-sing**) put in schematic form.

scheme /skiːm/ ● noun systematic arrangement; artful plot; outline, syllabus, etc. ● verb (**-ming**) plan, esp. secretly or deceitfully. □ **scheming** adjective.

scherzo /'skeətsəʊ/ noun (plural **-s**) Music vigorous and lively movement or composition.

schism /'skɪz(ə)m/ noun division of esp. religious group into sects etc. □ **schismatic** /-'mæt-/ adjective & noun.

schist /ʃɪst/ noun layered crystalline rock.

schizo /'skɪtsəʊ/ colloquial ● adjective schizophrenic. ● noun (plural **-s**) schizophrenic person.

schizoid /'skɪtsɔɪd/ ● adjective tending to schizophrenia. ● noun schizoid person.

schizophrenia /skɪtsə'friːnɪə/ noun mental disorder marked by disconnection between thoughts, feelings, and actions. □ **schizophrenic** /-'fren-/ adjective & noun.

schmaltz /ʃmɔːlts/ noun colloquial sickly sentimentality. □ **schmaltzy** adjective (**-ier, -iest**).

schnapps /ʃnæps/ noun any of various spirits drunk in N. Europe.

schnitzel /'ʃnɪts(ə)l/ noun veal escalope.

scholar /'skɒlə/ noun learned person; holder of scholarship; person of specified academic ability. □ **scholarly** adjective.

scholarship noun learning, erudition; award of money etc. towards education.

scholastic /skə'læstɪk/ adjective of schools, education, etc.; academic.

school[1] /skuːl/ ● *noun* educational institution for pupils up to 19 years old or (*US*) at any level; school buildings, pupils, staff, etc; (time given to) teaching; university department or faculty; group of artists, disciples, etc. following or holding similar principles, opinions, etc.; instructive circumstances. ● *verb* send to school; discipline, train, control; (as **schooled** *adjective*) (+ *in*) educated, trained. □ **schoolboy**, **schoolchild**, **schoolgirl** one who attends school; **school-leaver** person who has just left school; **schoolmaster**, **schoolmistress**, **schoolteacher** teacher in school; **schoolroom** room used for lessons, esp. in private house.

school[2] /skuːl/ *noun* shoal of fish, whales, etc.

schooling *noun* education.

schooner /'skuːnə/ *noun* two-masted fore-and-aft rigged ship; large glass, esp. for sherry; *US & Australian* tall beer glass.

schottische /ʃʊ'tiːʃ/ *noun* kind of slow polka.

sciatic /saɪ'ætɪk/ *adjective* of hip or sciatic nerve; of or having sciatica. □ **sciatic nerve** large nerve from pelvis to thigh.

sciatica /saɪ'ætɪkə/ *noun* neuralgia of hip and leg.

science /'saɪəns/ *noun* branch of knowledge involving systematized observation, experiment, and induction; knowledge so gained; pursuit or principles of this; skilful technique. □ **science fiction** fiction with scientific theme; **science park** area containing science-based businesses.

scientific /saɪən'tɪfɪk/ *adjective* following systematic methods of science; systematic, accurate; of or concerned with science.

scientist /'saɪəntɪst/ *noun* student or expert in science.

sci-fi /'saɪfaɪ/ *noun colloquial* science fiction.

scilicet /'saɪlɪset/ *adverb* that is to say.

scimitar /'sɪmɪtə/ *noun* curved oriental sword.

scintillate /'sɪntɪleɪt/ (**-ting**) (esp. as **scintillating** *adjective*) talk or act cleverly; sparkle, twinkle. □ **scintillation** *noun*.

scion /'saɪən/ *noun* shoot cut for grafting; young member of family.

scissors /'sɪzəz/ *plural noun* (also **pair of scissors** *singular*) cutting instrument with pair of pivoted blades.

sclerosis /sklə'rəʊsɪs/ *noun* abnormal hardening of tissue; (in full **multiple sclerosis**) serious progressive disease of nervous system. □ **sclerotic** /-'rɒt-/ *adjective*.

scoff[1] ● *verb* (usually + *at*) speak derisively, mock. ● *noun* mocking words, taunt.

scoff[2] *colloquial* ● *verb* eat (food) greedily. ● *noun* food.

scold /skəʊld/ ● *verb* rebuke; find fault noisily. ● *noun archaic* nagging woman.

sconce *noun* wall-bracket holding candlestick or light-fitting.

scone /skɒn, skəʊn/ *noun* small cake of flour etc. baked quickly.

scoop /skuːp/ ● *noun* short-handled deep shovel; long-handled ladle; excavating part of digging machine etc.; device for serving ice cream etc.; quantity taken up by scoop; scooping movement; exclusive news item; large profit made quickly. ● *verb* (usually + *out*) hollow out or (usually + *up*) lift (as) with scoop; forestall (rival newspaper etc.) with scoop; secure (large profit etc.), esp. suddenly.

scoot /skuːt/ *verb* (esp. in *imperative*) *colloquial* shoot along; depart, flee.

scooter *noun* child's toy with footboard on two wheels and long steering-handle; low-powered motorcycle.

scope *noun* range, opportunity; extent of ability, outlook, etc.

scorch ● *verb* burn or discolour surface of with dry heat; become so discoloured etc.; (as **scorching** *adjective*) *colloquial* (of weather) very hot, (of criticism etc.) stringent. ● *noun* mark of scorching. □ **scorched earth policy** policy of destroying everything that might be of use to invading enemy.

scorcher *noun colloquial* extremely hot day.

score ● *noun* number of points, goals, etc. made by player or side in game etc.; respective scores of competitors; act of gaining esp. goal; (*plural* same or **-s**) (set of) 20; (in *plural*) a great many; reason, motive; *Music* copy of composition with parts arranged one below another; music for film or play; notch, line, etc. made on surface; record of money owing. ● *verb* (**-ring**) win, gain; make (points etc.) in game; keep score; mark with notches etc.; have an advantage; *Music* (often + *for*) orchestrate or arrange (piece of music); *slang* obtain drugs illegally, make sexual conquest. □ **keep (the) score** register points etc. as they are made; **score (points) off** *colloquial* humiliate, esp. verbally; **scoreboard** large board for displaying score in match etc.

scoria /'skɔːrɪə/ *noun* (*plural* **scoriae** /-riːiː/) (fragments of) cellular lava; slag.

scorn ● *noun* disdain, contempt, derision. ● *verb* hold in contempt; reject or refuse to do as unworthy.

scornful *adjective* (often + *of*) contemptuous. □ **scornfully** *adverb*.

Scorpio /'skɔːpɪəʊ/ *noun* eighth sign of zodiac.

scorpion /'skɔːpɪən/ *noun* lobster-like arachnid with jointed stinging tail.

Scot *noun* native of Scotland.

Scotch ● *adjective* Scottish, Scots. ● *noun* Scottish, Scots; Scotch whisky. □ **Scotch broth** meat soup with pearl barley etc.; **Scotch egg** hard-boiled egg in sausage meat; **Scotch fir** Scots pine; **Scotch mist** thick mist and drizzle; **Scotch terrier** small rough-coated terrier; **Scotch whisky** whisky distilled in Scotland.

■ **Usage** Scots or Scottish is preferred to *Scotch* in Scotland, except in the compound nouns given above.

scotch *verb* decisively put an end to; *archaic* wound without killing.

scot-free *adverb* unharmed, unpunished.

Scots ● *adjective* Scottish. ● *noun* Scottish; form of English spoken in (esp. Lowlands of) Scotland. □ **Scotsman, Scotswoman** Scot; **Scots pine** kind of pine tree.

Scottish ● *adjective* of Scotland or its inhabitants. ● *noun* (**the Scottish**) (treated as *plural*) people of Scotland.

scoundrel /'skaʊndr(ə)l/ *noun* unscrupulous villain; rogue.

scour¹ /skaʊə/ ● *verb* rub clean; (usually + *away*, *off*, etc.) clear by rubbing; clear out (pipe etc.) by flushing through. ● *noun* scouring, being scoured. □ **scourer** *noun*.

scour² /skaʊə/ *verb* search thoroughly.

scourge /skɜːdʒ/ ● *noun* person or thing regarded as causing suffering; whip. ● *verb* (**-ging**) whip; punish, oppress.

Scouse /skaʊs/ *colloquial* ● *noun* Liverpool dialect; (also **Scouser**) native of Liverpool. ● *adjective* of Liverpool.

scout /skaʊt/ ● *noun* person sent out to get information or reconnoitre; search for this; talent-scout; (also **Scout**) member of (originally boys') association intended to develop character. ● *verb* (often + *for*) seek information etc.; (often + *about*, *around*) make search; (often + *out*) *colloquial* explore. □ **Scoutmaster** person in charge of group of Scouts. □ **scouting** *noun*.

Scouter *noun* adult leader of Scouts.

scowl /skaʊl/ ● *noun* sullen or bad-tempered look. ● *verb* wear scowl.

scrabble /'skræb(ə)l/ ● *verb* (**-ling**) scratch or grope busily about. ● *noun* scrabbling; (**Scrabble**) *proprietary term* game in which players build up words from letter-blocks on board.

scrag ● *noun* (also **scrag-end**) inferior end of neck of mutton; skinny person or animal. ● *verb* (**-gg-**) *slang* strangle, hang; handle roughly, beat up.

scraggy *adjective* (**-ier, -iest**) thin and bony. □ **scragginess** *noun*.

scram *verb* (**-mm-**) (esp. in *imperative*) *colloquial* go away.

scramble /'skræmb(ə)l/ ● *verb* (**-ling**) clamber, crawl, climb, etc.; (+ *for*, *at*) struggle with competitors (for thing or share); mix indiscriminately; cook (eggs) by stirring in heated pan; alter sound frequencies of (broadcast or telephone conversation) so as to make it unintelligible without special receiver; (of fighter aircraft or pilot) take off rapidly. ● *noun* scrambling; difficult climb or walk; (+ *for*) eager struggle or competition; motorcycle race over rough ground; emergency take-off by fighter aircraft.

scrambler *noun* device for scrambling telephone conversations; motorcycle used for scrambles.

scrap¹ ●*noun* small detached piece, fragment; waste material; discarded metal for reprocessing; (with negative) smallest piece or amount; (in *plural*) odds and ends, bits of uneaten food. ●*verb* (**-pp-**) discard as useless. □ **scrapbook** book in which cuttings etc. are kept; **scrap heap** collection of waste material, state of being discarded as useless; **scrapyard** place where (esp. metal) scrap is collected.

scrap² *colloquial* ●*noun* fight or rough quarrel. ●*verb* (**-pp-**) have scrap.

scrape ●*verb* (**-ping**) move hard edge across (surface), esp. to smooth or clean; (+ *away, off,* etc.) remove by scraping; rub (surface) harshly against another; scratch, damage, or make by scraping; draw or move with sound (as) of scraping; produce such sound from; (often + *along, by, through,* etc.) move while (almost) touching; narrowly achieve; (often + *by, through*) barely manage, pass exam etc. with difficulty; (+ *together, up*) provide or amass with difficulty; be economical; make clumsy bow; (+ *back*) draw (hair) tightly back. ●*noun* act or sound of scraping; scraped place, graze; *colloquial* predicament caused by rashness. □ **scraper** *noun*.

scrapie /'skreɪpɪ/ *noun* viral disease of sheep.

scrappy *adjective* (**-ier, -iest**) consisting of scraps; incomplete.

scratch ●*verb* score or wound superficially, esp. with sharp object; scrape with the nails to relieve itching; make or form by scratching; (+ *out, off, through*) erase; withdraw from race or competition; (often + *about, around,* etc.) scratch ground etc. in search, search haphazardly. ●*noun* mark, wound, or sound made by scratching; act of scratching oneself; *colloquial* trifling wound; starting line for race etc.; position of those receiving no handicap. ●*adjective* collected by chance; collected or made from whatever is available; with no handicap given. □ **from scratch** from the beginning, without help; **up to scratch** up to required standard.

scratchy *adjective* (**-ier, -iest**) tending to make scratches or scratching noise;

causing itchiness; (of drawing etc.) careless. □ **scratchily** *adverb*; **scratchiness** *noun*.

scrawl ●*verb* write in hurried untidy way. ●*noun* hurried writing; scrawled note. ●**scrawly** *adjective* (**-ier, -iest**).

scrawny /'skrɔːnɪ/ *adjective* (**-ier, -iest**) lean, scraggy.

scream ●*noun* piercing cry (as) of terror or pain; *colloquial* hilarious occurrence or person. ●*verb* emit scream; utter in or with scream; move with scream; laugh uncontrollably; be blatantly obvious.

scree *noun* (in *singular* or *plural*) small loose stones; mountain slope covered with these.

screech *noun* harsh scream or squeal. ●*verb* utter with or make screech. □ **screech-owl** barn owl.

screed *noun* long usually tiresome letter or harangue; layer of cement etc. applied to level a surface.

screen ●*noun* fixed or movable upright partition for separating, concealing, or protecting from heat etc.; thing used to conceal or shelter; concealing stratagem; protection thus given; blank surface on which images are projected; (**the screen**) cinema industry, films collectively; windscreen; large sieve; system for detecting disease, ability, attribute, etc. ●*verb* shelter, hide; protect from detection, censure, etc.; (+ *off*) conceal behind screen; show (film etc.); prevent from causing, or protect from, electrical interference; test (person or group) for disease, reliability, loyalty, etc.; sieve. □ **screenplay** film script; **screen printing** printing process with ink forced through areas of sheet of fine mesh; **screen test** audition for film part; **screenwriter** person who writes for cinema.

screw /skruː/ ●*noun* cylinder or cone with spiral ridge running round it outside (**male screw**) or inside (**female screw**); (in full **woodscrew**) metal male screw with slotted head and sharp point; (in full **screw-bolt**) blunt metal male screw on which nut is threaded; straight screw used to exert pressure; (in *singular* or *plural*) instrument of torture acting thus; (in full **screw propeller**) propeller with twisted blades; one turn of screw; (+ *of*) small twisted-up paper (of tobacco etc.); oblique curling motion; *slang* prison warder. ● *verb* fasten or tighten (as) with screw(s); (of ball etc.) swerve; (+ *out*, *of*) extort from; swindle. □ **screwball** *US slang* crazy or eccentric person; **screwdriver** tool for turning screws by putting tool's tip into screw's slot; **screw up** contract, crumple, or contort, summon up (courage etc.), *slang* bungle, spoil, or upset; **screw-up** *slang* bungle.

screwy *adjective* (**-ier**, **-iest**) *slang* mad, eccentric; absurd. □ **screwiness** *noun*.

scribble /'skrɪb(ə)l/ ● *verb* (**-ling**) write or draw carelessly or hurriedly; *jocular* be author or writer. ● *noun* scrawl; hasty note etc.

scribe ● *noun* ancient or medieval copyist of manuscripts; pointed instrument for marking wood etc.; *colloquial* writer. ● *verb* (**-bing**) mark with scribe. □ **scribal** *adjective*.

scrim *noun* open-weave fabric for lining, upholstery, etc.

scrimmage /'skrɪmɪdʒ/ ● *noun* tussle, brawl. ● *verb* (**-ging**) engage in scrimmage.

scrimp *verb* skimp.

scrip *noun* provisional certificate of money subscribed to company etc.; extra share(s) instead of dividend.

script ● *noun* text of play, film, or broadcast (see panel at DIRECT SPEECH); handwriting; typeface imitating handwriting; alphabet or other system of writing; examinee's written answer(s). ● *verb* write script for (film etc.). □ **scriptwriter** person who writes scripts for films, etc.

scripture /'skrɪptʃə/ *noun* sacred writings; (**Scripture, the Scriptures**) the Bible. □ **scriptural** *adjective*.

scrivener /'skrɪvənə/ *noun historical* copyist, drafter of documents; notary.

scrofula /'skrɒfjʊlə/ *noun* disease with glandular swellings. □ **scrofulous** *adjective*.

scroll /skrəʊl/ ● *noun* roll of parchment or paper; book in ancient roll form; ornamental design imitating roll of parchment. ● *verb* (often + *down*, *up*) move (display on VDU screen) to view later or earlier material.

scrotum /'skrəʊtəm/ *noun* (*plural* **scrota** or **-s**) pouch of skin enclosing testicles. □ **scrotal** *adjective*.

scrounge /skraʊndʒ/ *verb* (**-ging**) obtain (things) by cadging. □ **on the scrounge** scrounging. □ **scrounger** *noun*.

scrub[1] ● *verb* (**-bb-**) clean by hard rubbing, esp. with hard brush; (often + *up*) (of surgeon etc.) clean and disinfect hands etc. before operating; *colloquial* cancel; pass (gas etc.) through scrubber. ● *noun* scrubbing, being scrubbed.

scrub[2] *noun* brushwood or stunted trees etc.; land covered with this. □ **scrubby** *adjective* (**-ier**, **-iest**).

scrubber *noun slang* promiscuous woman; apparatus for purifying gases etc.

scruff[1] *noun* back of neck.

scruff[2] *noun colloquial* scruffy person.

scruffy /'skrʌfɪ/ *adjective* (**-ier**, **-iest**) *colloquial* shabby, slovenly, untidy. □ **scruffily** *adverb*; **scruffiness** *noun*.

scrum *noun* scrummage; *colloquial* scrimmage. □ **scrum-half** *Rugby* half-back who puts ball into scrum.

scrummage /'skrʌmɪdʒ/ *noun Rugby* massed forwards on each side pushing to gain possession of ball thrown on ground between them.

scrumptious /'skrʌmpʃəs/ *adjective colloquial* delicious.

scrumpy /'skrʌmpɪ/ *noun colloquial* rough cider.

scrunch ● *verb* (usually + *up*) crumple; crunch. ● *noun* crunch.

scruple /'skru:p(ə)l/ ● *noun* (often in *plural*) moral concern; doubt caused by this. ● *verb* (**-ling**) (+ *to do*; usually in negative) hesitate owing to scruples.

scrupulous /'skru:pjʊləs/ *adjective* conscientious, thorough; careful to avoid doing wrong; over-attentive to details. □ **scrupulously** *adverb*.

scrutineer /skru:tɪ'nɪə/ *noun* person who scrutinizes ballot papers.

scrutinize /'skru:tɪnaɪz/ *verb* (also **-ise**) (**-zing** or **-sing**) subject to scrutiny.

scrutiny /'skru:tɪnɪ/ *noun* (*plural* **-ies**) critical gaze; close examination; official examination of ballot papers.

scuba /'sku:bə/ *noun* (*plural* **-s**) aqualung. □ **scuba-diving** swimming underwater using scuba.

scud • verb (**-dd-**) move straight and fast; skim along; *Nautical* run before wind. • noun scudding; vapoury driving clouds or shower.

scuff • verb graze or brush against; mark or wear out (shoes etc.) thus; shuffle or drag feet. • noun mark of scuffing.

scuffle /'skʌf(ə)l/ • noun confused struggle or fight at close quarters. • verb (**-ling**) engage in scuffle.

scull • noun each of pair of small oars; oar used to propel boat from stern; (in *plural*) sculling race. • verb propel with scull(s).

scullery /'skʌlərɪ/ noun (*plural* **-ies**) back kitchen; room where dishes are washed etc.

sculpt verb sculpture.

sculptor /'skʌlptə/ noun (*feminine* **sculptress**) person who sculptures.

sculpture /'skʌlptʃə/ • noun art of making 3-dimensional forms by chiselling, carving, modelling, casting, etc.; work of sculpture. • verb (**-ring**) represent in or adorn with sculpture; practise sculpture. □ **sculptural** adjective.

scum • noun layer of dirt etc. at surface of liquid; *derogatory* worst person, part, or group. • verb (**-mm-**) remove scum from; form scum (on). □ **scumbag** slang contemptible person. □ **scummy** adjective (**-ier**, **-iest**).

scupper[1] /'skʌpə/ noun hole in ship's side draining water from deck.

scupper[2] /'skʌpə/ verb slang sink (ship, crew); defeat or ruin (plan etc.); kill.

scurf noun dandruff. □ **scurfy** adjective (**-ier**, **-iest**).

scurrilous /'skʌrɪləs/ adjective grossly or obscenely abusive. □ **scurrility** /skə'rɪl-/ noun (*plural* **-ies**); **scurrilously** adverb; **scurrilousness** noun.

scurry /'skʌrɪ/ • verb (**-ies**, **-ied**) run hurriedly, scamper. • noun (*plural* **-ies**) scurrying sound or movement; flurry of rain or snow.

scurvy /'skɜːvɪ/ • noun disease resulting from deficiency of vitamin C. • adjective (**-ier**, **-iest**) paltry, contemptible. □ **scurvily** adverb.

scut noun short tail, esp. of hare, rabbit, or deer.

scutter /'skʌtə/ verb & noun colloquial scurry.

scuttle[1] /'skʌt(ə)l/ noun coal scuttle; part of car body between windscreen and bonnet.

scuttle[2] /'skʌt(ə)l/ • verb (**-ling**) scurry; flee in undignified way. • noun hurried gait; precipitate flight.

scuttle[3] /'skʌt(ə)l/ • noun hole with lid in ship's deck or side. • verb (**-ling**) let water into (ship) to sink it.

scythe /saɪð/ • noun mowing and reaping implement with long handle and curved blade. • verb (**-thing**) cut with scythe.

SDLP abbreviation (in N. Ireland) Social Democratic and Labour Party.

SDP abbreviation (in UK) Social Democratic Party.

SE abbreviation souтн-east(ern).

sea noun expanse of salt water covering most of earth; area of this; large inland lake; (motion or state of) waves of sea; (+ *of*) vast quantity or expanse. □ **at sea** in ship on the sea, confused; **sea anchor** bag to reduce drifting of ship; **sea anemone** polyp with petal-like tentacles; **seabed** ocean floor; **seaboard** coastline, coastal area; **sea dog** old sailor; **seafarer** traveller by sea; **seafood** edible marine fish or shellfish; **sea front** part of seaside town facing sea; **seagoing** designed for open sea; **seagull** = GULL[1]; **sea horse** small fish with head like horse's; **seakale** plant with young shoots used as vegetable; **sea legs** ability to keep one's balance at sea; **sea level** mean level of sea's surface, used in reckoning heights of hills etc. and as barometric standard; **sea lion** large, eared seal; **seaman** person whose work is at sea, sailor, sailor below rank of officer; **seaplane** aircraft designed to take off from and land on water; **seaport** town with harbour; **sea salt** salt got by evaporating sea water; **seascape** picture or view of sea; **seashell** shell of salt-water mollusc; **seashore** land next to sea; **seasick** nauseous from motion of ship at sea; **seasickness** noun; **seaside** sea-coast, esp. as holiday resort; **sea urchin** small marine animal with spiny shell; **seaweed** plant growing in sea; **seaworthy** fit to put to sea.

seal[1] • *noun* piece of stamped wax etc. attached to document or to receptacle, envelope, etc. to guarantee authenticity or security; metal stamp etc. used in making seal; substance or device used to close gap etc.; anything regarded as confirmation or guarantee; decorative adhesive stamp. • *verb* close securely or hermetically; stamp, fasten, or fix with seal; certify as correct with seal; (+ *off*) prevent access to or from; (often + *up*) confine securely; settle, decide. □ **sealing wax** mixture softened by heating and used for seals.

seal[2] • *noun* fish-eating amphibious marine mammal with flippers. • *verb* hunt seals.

sealant *noun* material for sealing, esp. to make watertight.

seam • *noun* line where two edges join, esp. of cloth or boards; fissure between parallel edges; wrinkle; stratum of coal etc. • *verb* join with seam; (esp. as **seamed** *adjective*) mark or score with seam. □ **seamless** *adjective*.

seamstress /ˈsiːmstrɪs/ *noun* woman who sews.

seamy *adjective* (**-ier**, **-iest**) disreputable, sordid; showing seams. □ **seaminess** *noun*.

seance /ˈseɪɑ̃s/ *noun* meeting at which spiritualists attempts to contact the dead.

sear /sɪə/ *verb* scorch, cauterize; cause anguish to; brown (meat) quickly.

search /sɜːtʃ/ • *verb* examine thoroughly to find something; make investigation; (+ *for*, *out*) look for, seek out; (as **searching** *adjective*) keenly questioning. • *noun* act of searching; investigation. □ **searchlight** outdoor lamp designed to throw strong beam of light in any direction, light or beam from this; **search party** group of people conducting organized search; **search warrant** official authorization to enter and search building. □ **searcher** *noun*; **searchingly** *adverb*.

season /ˈsiːz(ə)n/ • *noun* each of climatic divisions of year; proper or suitable time; time when something is plentiful, active, etc.; (**the season**) (also **high season**) busiest period at resort etc.; *colloquial* season ticket. • *verb* flavour with salt, herbs, etc.; enhance with wit

etc.; moderate; (esp. as **seasoned** *adjective*) make or become suitable by exposure to weather or experience. □ **in season** (of food) available plentifully, (of animal) on heat; **season ticket** one entitling holder to unlimited travel, access, etc. in given period.

seasonable *adjective* suitable to season; opportune.

■ **Usage** *Seasonable* is sometimes confused with *seasonal*.

seasonal *adjective* of, depending on, or varying with seasons.

■ **Usage** *Seasonal* is sometimes confused with *seasonable*.

seasoning *noun* salt, herbs, etc. as flavouring for food.

seat • *noun* thing made or used for sitting on; buttocks, part of garment covering them; part of chair etc. on which buttocks rest; place for one person in theatre etc.; position as MP, committee member, etc., or right to occupy it; machine's supporting or guiding part; location; country mansion; posture on horse. • *verb* cause to sit; provide sitting accommodation for; (as **seated** *adjective*) sitting; establish in position. □ **seat belt** belt securing seated person in vehicle or aircraft.

seating *noun* seats collectively; sitting accommodation.

sebaceous /sɪˈbeɪʃəs/ *adjective* fatty; secreting oily matter.

Sec. *abbreviation* (also **sec.**) secretary.

sec. *abbreviation* second(s).

sec[1] *noun colloquial* (in phrases) second, moment.

sec[2] *adjective* (of wine) dry.

secateurs /sekəˈtɜːz/ *plural noun* pruning clippers.

secede /sɪˈsiːd/ *verb* (**-ding**) withdraw formally from political or religious body.

secession /sɪˈseʃ(ə)n/ *noun* seceding. □ **secessionist** *noun & adjective*.

seclude /sɪˈkluːd/ *verb* (**-ding**) keep (person, place) apart from others; (esp. as **secluded** *adjective*) screen from view.

seclusion /sɪˈkluːʒ(ə)n/ *noun* secluded state or place.

second[1] /ˈsekənd/ ● *adjective* next after first; additional; subordinate; inferior; comparable to. ● *noun* runner-up; person or thing coming second; second gear; (in *plural*) inferior goods; *colloquial* second helping or course; assistant to boxer, duellist, etc. ● *verb* formally support (nomination, proposal, etc.). □ **second-best** next after best; **second class** second-best group, category, postal service, or accommodation; **second cousin** child of parent's first cousin; **second fiddle** subordinate position; **second-guess** *colloquial* anticipate by guesswork, criticize with hindsight; **second-hand** (of goods) having had previous owner, (of information etc.) obtained indirectly; **second nature** acquired tendency that has become instinctive; **second-rate** inferior; **second sight** clairvoyance; **second string** alternative course of action etc.; **second thoughts** revised opinion; **second wind** renewed capacity for effort after breathlessness or tiredness. □ **seconder** *noun*.

second[2] /ˈsekənd/ *noun* SI unit of time (1/60 of minute); 1/60 of minute of angle; *colloquial* very short time.

second[3] /sɪˈkɒnd/ *verb* transfer (person) temporarily to another department etc. □ **secondment** *noun*.

secondary /ˈsekəndərɪ/ ● *adjective* coming after or next below what is primary; derived from or supplementing what is primary; (of education etc.) following primary. ● *noun* (*plural* -ies) secondary thing. □ **secondary colour** result of mixing two primary colours.

secondly *adverb* furthermore; as a second item.

secrecy /ˈsiːkrəsɪ/ *noun* being secret; keeping of secrets.

secret /ˈsiːkrɪt/ ● *adjective* not (to be) made known or seen; working etc. secretly; liking secrecy. ● *noun* thing (to be) kept secret; mystery; effective but not widely known method. □ **in secret** secretly; **secret agent** spy; **secret police** police operating secretly for political ends; **secret service** government department concerned with espionage. □ **secretly** *adverb*.

secretariat /ˌsekrɪˈteərɪət/ *noun* administrative office or department; its members or premises.

secretary /ˈsekrɪtərɪ/ *noun* (*plural* -ies) employee who deals with correspondence, records, making appointments, etc.; official of society etc. who writes letters, organizes business, etc.; principal assistant of government minister, ambassador, etc. □ **secretary bird** long-legged crested African bird; **Secretary-General** principal administrative officer of organization; **Secretary of State** head of major government department, (in US) foreign minister. □ **secretarial** /-ˈteərɪəl/ *adjective*.

secrete /sɪˈkriːt/ *verb* (-ting) (of cell, organ, etc.) produce and discharge (substance); conceal. □ **secretory** *adjective*.

secretion /sɪˈkriːʃ(ə)n/ *noun* process or act of secreting; secreted substance.

secretive /ˈsiːkrətɪv/ *adjective* inclined to make or keep secrets, uncommunicative. □ **secretively** *adverb*; **secretiveness** *noun*.

sect *noun* group sharing (usually unorthodox) religious etc. doctrines; religious denomination.

sectarian /sekˈteərɪən/ ● *adjective* of sect(s); bigoted in following one's sect. ● *noun* member of a sect. □ **sectarianism** *noun*.

section /ˈsekʃ(ə)n/ ● *noun* each of parts into which something is divisible or divided; part cut off; subdivision; *US* area of land, district of town; surgical separation or cutting; cutting of solid by plane, resulting figure or area of this; thin slice cut off for microscopic examination. ● *verb* arrange in or divide into sections; compulsorily commit to psychiatric hospital.

sectional *adjective* of a social group; partisan; made in sections; local rather than general. □ **sectionally** *adverb*.

sector /ˈsektə/ *noun* branch of an enterprise, the economy, etc.; *Military* portion of battle area; plane figure enclosed between two radii of circle etc.

secular /ˈsekjʊlə/ *adjective* not concerned with religion, not sacred; (of clerics) not monastic. □ **secularism** *noun*; **secularization** *noun*; **secularize** *verb* (also **-ise**) (**-zing** or **-sing**).

secure /sɪˈkjʊə/ ● *adjective* untroubled by danger or fear; safe; reliable, stable, fixed. ● verb (-ring) make secure or safe; fasten or secure securely; obtain. □ **securely** adverb.

security noun (plural **-ies**) secure condition or feeling; thing that guards or guarantees; safety against espionage, theft, etc.; organization for ensuring this; thing deposited as guarantee for undertaking or loan; (often in plural) document as evidence of loan, certificate of stock, bonds, etc. □ **security risk** person or thing threatening security.

sedan /sɪˈdæn/ noun (in full **sedan chair**) historical enclosed chair for one person, usually carried on poles by two; US saloon car.

sedate /sɪˈdeɪt/ ● adjective tranquil, serious. ● verb (-ting) put under sedation. □ **sedately** adverb; **sedateness** noun.

sedation noun treatment with sedatives.

sedative /ˈsedətɪv/ ● noun calming drug or influence. ● adjective calming, soothing.

sedentary /ˈsedəntəri/ adjective sitting; (of work etc.) done while sitting; (of person) disinclined to exercise.

sedge noun grasslike waterside or marsh plant. □ **sedgy** adjective.

sediment /ˈsedɪmənt/ noun dregs; matter deposited on land by water or wind. □ **sedimentary** /-ˈmen-/ adjective; **sedimentation** noun.

sedition /sɪˈdɪʃ(ə)n/ noun conduct or speech inciting to rebellion. □ **seditious** adjective.

seduce /sɪˈdjuːs/ verb (-cing) entice into sexual activity or wrongdoing; coax or lead astray. □ **seducer** noun.

seduction /sɪˈdʌkʃ(ə)n/ noun seducing, being seduced; tempting or attractive thing.

seductive /sɪˈdʌktɪv/ adjective alluring, enticing. □ **seductively** adverb; **seductiveness** noun.

sedulous /ˈsedjʊləs/ adjective persevering, diligent, painstaking. □ **sedulity** /sɪˈdjuː-/ noun; **sedulously** adverb.

see[1] verb (**sees**; past **saw**; past participle **seen**) perceive with the eyes; have or use this power; discern mentally, understand; watch; experience; ascertain; imagine, foresee; look at; meet; visit, be visited by; meet regularly;

reflect, get clarification; (+ in) find attractive in; escort, conduct; witness (event etc.); ensure; **see about** attend to, consider; **see off** be present at departure of, colloquial get the better of; **see over** inspect, tour; **see red** colloquial become enraged; **see through** not be deceived by, support (person) during difficult time, complete (project); **see-through** translucent; **see to** attend to, repair; **see to it** (+ that) ensure.

see[2] noun area under (arch)bishop's authority; (arch)bishop's office or jurisdiction.

seed ● noun part of plant capable of developing into another such plant; seeds collectively, esp. for sowing; semen; prime cause, beginning; offspring; Tennis etc. seeded player. ● verb place seed(s) in; sprinkle (as) with seed; sow seeds; produce or drop seed; remove seeds from (fruit etc.); place crystal etc. in (cloud) to produce rain; Tennis etc. designate (competitor in knockout tournament) so that strong competitors do not meet each other until later rounds, arrange (order of play) thus. □ **go**, **run to seed** cease flowering as seed develops, become degenerate, unkempt, etc.; **seed-bed** bed prepared for sowing, place of development; **seed-pearl** very small pearl; **seed-potato** potato kept for planting; **seedsman** dealer in seeds.

seedling noun young plant raised from seed.

seedy adjective (**-ier**, **-iest**) shabby; colloquial unwell; full of seed.

seeing conjunction (usually + that) considering that, inasmuch as, because.

seek verb (past & past participle **sought** /sɔːt/) (often + for, after) search, inquire; try or want to obtain or reach; request; endeavour. □ **seek out** search for and find. □ **seeker** noun.

seem verb (often + to do) appear, give the impression.

seeming adjective apparent but doubtful. □ **seemingly** adverb.

seemly /ˈsiːmlɪ/ adjective (**-ier**, **-iest**) in good taste, decorous. □ **seemliness** noun.

seen past participle of SEE[1].

seep verb ooze, percolate.

seepage noun act of seeping; quantity that seeps.

seer /sɪə/ noun person who sees; prophet, visionary.

seersucker /ˈsɪəsʌkə/ noun thin cotton etc. fabric with puckered surface.

see-saw /ˈsiːsɔː/ • noun long board supported in middle so that children etc. sitting on ends move alternately up and down; this game; up-and-down or to-and-fro motion, contest, etc. • verb play or move (as) on see-saw; vacillate. • adjective & adverb with up-and-down or to-and-fro motion.

seethe /siːð/ verb (-thing) boil, bubble; be very angry, resentful, etc.

segment • noun /ˈsegmənt/ part cut off or separable from other parts; part of circle or sphere cut off by intersecting line or plane. • verb /segˈment/ divide into segments. □ **segmental** /-ˈment-/ adjective; **segmentation** noun.

segregate /ˈsegrɪgeɪt/ verb (-ting) put apart, isolate; separate (esp. ethnic group) from the rest of the community. □ **segregation** noun; **segregationist** noun & adjective.

seigneur /seɪnˈjɜː/ noun feudal lord. □ **seigneurial** adjective.

seine /seɪn/ • noun large vertical fishing net. • verb (-ning) fish with seine.

seismic /ˈsaɪzmɪk/ adjective of earthquake(s).

seismograph /ˈsaɪzməgrɑːf/ noun instrument for recording earthquake details. □ **seismographic** /-ˈgræf-/ adjective.

seismology /saɪzˈmɒlədʒɪ/ noun the study of earthquakes. □ **seismological** /-məˈlɒdʒ-/ adjective; **seismologist** noun.

seize /siːz/ verb (-zing) (often + on, upon) take hold or possession of, esp. forcibly, suddenly, or by legal power; take advantage of; comprehend quickly or clearly; affect suddenly; (also **seise**) (usually + of) Law put in possession of. □ **seize up** (of mechanism) become jammed, (of part of body etc.) become stiff.

seizure /ˈsiːʒə/ noun seizing, being seized; sudden attack of epilepsy, apoplexy, etc.

seldom /ˈseldəm/ adverb rarely, not often.

select /sɪˈlekt/ • verb choose, esp. with care. • adjective chosen for excellence or suitability; exclusive. □ **select committee** parliamentary committee conducting special inquiry. □ **selector** noun.

selection /sɪˈlekʃ(ə)n/ noun selecting, being selected; person or thing selected; things from which choice may be made; = NATURAL SELECTION.

selective adjective of or using selection; able to select; selecting what is convenient. □ **selectively** adverb; **selectivity** /-ˈtɪv-/ noun.

selenium /sɪˈliːnɪəm/ noun non-metallic element in some sulphide ores.

self • noun (plural **selves** /selvz/) individuality, essence; object of introspection or reflexive action; one's own interests or pleasure, concentration on these.

self- combining form expressing reflexive action, automatic or independent action, or sameness. □ **self-addressed** addressed to oneself; **self-adhesive** (of envelope etc.) adhesive, esp. without wetting; **self-aggrandizement** enriching oneself, making oneself powerful; **self-assertive** confident or assertive in promoting oneself, one's claims, etc.; **self-assertion** self-confident; **self-assured** self-confident; **self-catering** providing cooking facilities but no food; **self-centred** preoccupied with oneself; **self-confessed** openly admitting oneself to be; **self-confident** having confidence in oneself; **self-confidence** noun; **self-conscious** nervous, shy, embarrassed; **self-consciously** adverb; **self-contained** uncommunicative, complete in itself; **self-control** control of oneself, one's behaviour, etc.; **self-critical** critical of oneself, one's abilities, etc.; **self-defence** defence of oneself, one's reputation, etc.; **self-denial** abstinence, esp. as discipline; **self-deprecating** belittling oneself; **self-destruct** (of device etc.) explode or disintegrate automatically, esp. when pre-set to do so; **self-determination** nation's right to determine own government etc., free will; **self-effacing** retiring, modest; **self-employed** working as freelance or for one's own business etc.; **self-employment** noun; **self-esteem** good opinion of oneself; **self-**

evident needing no proof or explanation; **self-explanatory** not needing explanation; **self-financing** not needing subsidy; **self-fulfilling** (of prophecy etc.) assured fulfilment by its utterance; **self-governing** governing itself or oneself; **self-government** *noun;* **self-help** use of one's own abilities etc. to achieve success etc.; **self-image** one's conception of oneself; **self-important** conceited, pompous; **self-importance** *noun;* **self-indulgent** indulging one's own pleasures, feelings, etc., (of work of art etc.) lacking control; **self-indulgence** *noun;* **self-interest** one's own interest or advantage; **self-interested** *adjective;* **self-made** successful or rich by one's own efforts; **self-opinionated** obstinate in one's opinion; **self-pity** pity for oneself; **self-portrait** portrait of oneself by oneself; **self-possessed** unperturbed, cool; **self-possession** *noun;* **self-preservation** keeping oneself safe, instinct for this; **self-raising** (of flour) containing a raising agent; **self-reliance** reliance on one's own abilities etc.; **self-reliant** *adjective,* **self-respect** respect for oneself; **self-restraint** self-control; **self-righteous** smugly sure of one's righteousness; **self-righteously** *adverb;* **self-righteousness** *noun;* **self-rule** self-government; **self-sacrifice** selflessness, self-denial; **self-satisfied** complacent; **self-satisfaction** *noun;* **self-seeking** selfish; **self-service** with customers helping themselves and paying cashier afterwards; **self-starter** electric device for starting engine, ambitious person with initiative; **self-styled** called so by oneself; **self-sufficient** capable of supplying one's own needs; **self-sufficiency** *noun;* **self-willed** obstinately pursuing one's own wishes; **self-worth** self-esteem.

selfish *adjective* concerned chiefly with one's own interests or pleasure; actuated by or appealing to self-interest. □ **selfishness** *noun.*

selfless *adjective* unselfish.

selfsame /'selfseɪm/ *adjective* (**the selfsame**) the very same, the identical.

sell ● *verb* (*past & past participle* **sold** /səʊld/) exchange or be exchanged for money; stock for sale; (+ *at, for*) have specified price; betray or prostitute for money etc.; advertise, publicize; cause to be sold; *colloquial* make (person) enthusiastic about (idea etc.). ● *noun colloquial* manner of selling; deception, disappointment. □ **sell-by date** latest recommended date of sale; **sell off** sell at reduced prices; **sell out** sell (all one's stock or shares etc.), betray, be treacherous; **sell-out** commercial success, betrayal; **sell short** disparage, underestimate; **sell up** sell one's business, house, etc.

seller *noun* person who sells; thing that sells well or badly as specified. □ **seller's market** time when goods are scarce and expensive.

Sellotape /'seləteɪp/ ● *noun proprietary term* adhesive usually transparent cellulose tape. ● *verb* (**sellotape**) (**-ping**) fix with Sellotape.

selvage /'selvɪdʒ/ *noun* (also **selvedge**) edge of cloth woven to prevent fraying.

selves *plural* of SELF.

semantic /sɪ'mæntɪk/ *adjective* of meaning in language.

semantics *plural noun* (usually treated as *singular*) branch of linguistics concerned with meaning.

semaphore /'seməfɔː/ ● *noun* system of signalling with arms or two flags; railway signalling apparatus with arm(s). ● *verb* (**-ring**) signal or send by semaphore.

semblance /'sembləns/ *noun* (+ *of*) appearance, show.

semen /'siːmən/ *noun* reproductive fluid of males.

semester /sɪ'mestə/ *noun* half-year term in universities.

semi /'semɪ/ *noun colloquial* (*plural* **-s**) semi-detached house.

semi- *prefix* half; partly.

semibreve /'semɪbriːv/ *noun Music* note equal to 4 crotchets.

semicircle /'semɪsɜːk(ə)l/ *noun* half of circle or its circumference. □ **semicircular** /-'sɜːkjʊlə/ *adjective.*

semicolon /semɪ'kəʊlən/ *noun* punctuation mark (;) of intermediate value between comma and full stop (see panel).

semiconductor /semɪkən'dʌktə/ *noun* substance that is a poor electrical conductor when either pure or cold and a good conductor when either impure or hot.

semi-detached /semɪdɪ'tætʃt/ ● *adjective* (of house) joined to another on one side only. ● *noun* such house.

semifinal /semɪ'faɪn(ə)l/ *noun Sport* match or round preceding final. □ **semifinalist** *noun*.

seminal /'semɪn(ə)l/ *adjective* of seed, semen, or reproduction; germinal; (of idea etc.) providing basis for future development.

seminar /'semɪnɑː/ *noun* small class for discussion etc.; short intensive course of study; specialists' conference.

seminary /'semɪnərɪ/ *noun* (*plural* **-ies**) training college for priests etc. □ **seminarist** *noun*.

semipermeable /semɪ'pɜːmɪəb(ə)l/ *adjective* (of membrane etc.) allowing small molecules to pass through.

semiprecious /semɪ'preʃəs/ *adjective* (of gem) less valuable than a precious stone.

semi-professional /semɪprə'feʃ(ə)l/ ● *adjective* (of footballer, musician, etc.) paid for activity but not relying on it for living; of semi-professionals. ● *noun* semi-professional person.

semiquaver /'semɪkweɪvə/ *noun Music* note equal to half a quaver.

semi-skimmed /semɪ'skɪmd/ *adjective* (of milk) with some of cream skimmed off.

Semite /'siːmaɪt/ *noun* member of peoples supposedly descended from Shem, including Jews and Arabs.

Semitic /sɪ'mɪtɪk/ *adjective* of Semites, esp. Jews; of languages of family including Hebrew and Arabic.

semitone /'semɪtəʊn/ *noun* half a tone in musical scale.

semivowel /'semɪvaʊəl/ *noun* sound intermediate between vowel and consonant; letter representing this.

semolina /semə'liːnə/ *noun* hard round grains of wheat used for puddings etc.; pudding of this.

Semtex /'semteks/ *noun* proprietary term odourless plastic explosive.

SEN *abbreviation* State Enrolled Nurse.

Sen. *abbreviation* Senior; Senator.

senate /'senɪt/ *noun* upper house of legislature in some countries; governing body of some universities or (*US*) colleges; ancient Roman state council.

senator /'senətə/ *noun* member of senate. □ **senatorial** /-'tɔː-/ *adjective*.

send *verb* (*past & past participle* **sent**) order or cause to go or be conveyed; cause to become; send message etc.; grant, bestow, inflict, cause to be. □ **send away for** order (goods) by post; **send down** rusticate or expel from university, send to prison; **send for** summon, order by post; **send off** dispatch, attend departure of; **send-off** party etc. at departure of person; **send off for** send away for; **send on** transmit further or in advance of oneself; **send up** *colloquial* ridicule (by mimicking); **send-up** *noun* □ **sender** *noun*.

senescent /sɪ'nes(ə)nt/ *adjective* growing old. □ **senescence** *noun*.

••

Semicolon ;

This is used:

1 between clauses that are too short or too closely related to be made into separate sentences; such clauses are not usually connected by a conjunction, e.g.

To err is human; to forgive, divine.
You could wait for him here; on the other hand I could wait in your place; this would save you valuable time.

2 between items in a list which themselves contain commas, if it is necessary to avoid confusion, e.g.

The party consisted of three teachers, who had already climbed with the leader; seven pupils; and two parents.

seneschal /ˈsenɪʃ(ə)l/ *noun* steward of medieval great house.

senile /ˈsiːnaɪl/ *adjective* of old age; mentally or physically infirm because of old age. □ **senile dementia** illness of old people with loss of memory etc. □ **senility** /sɪˈnɪl-/ *noun.*

senior /ˈsiːnɪə/ ● *adjective* higher in age or standing; (placed after person's name) senior to relative of same name. ● *noun* senior person; one's elder or superior. □ **senior citizen** old-age pensioner. □ **seniority** /-ˈɒr-/ *noun.*

senna /ˈsenə/ *noun* cassia; laxative from leaves and pods of this.

señor /senˈjɔː/ *noun* (*plural* **señores** /-rez/) title used of or to Spanish-speaking man.

señora /senˈjɔːrə/ *noun* title used of or to Spanish-speaking esp. married woman.

señorita /senjəˈriːtə/ *noun* title used of or to young Spanish-speaking esp. unmarried woman.

sensation /senˈseɪʃ(ə)n/ *noun* feeling in one's body; awareness, impression; intense feeling, esp. in community; cause of this; sense of touch.

sensational *adjective* causing or intended to cause public excitement etc.; wonderful. □ **sensationalism** *noun*; **sensationalist** *noun & adjective*; **sensationalize** *verb* (also **-ise**) (**-zing** or **-sing**).

sense ● *noun* any of bodily faculties transmitting sensation; sensitiveness of any of these; ability to perceive; (+ *of*) consciousness; appreciation, instinct; practical wisdom; meaning of word etc.; intelligibility, coherence; prevailing opinion; (in *plural*) sanity, ability to think. ● *verb* (**-sing**) perceive by sense(s); be vaguely aware of; (of machine etc.) detect. □ **make sense** be intelligible or practicable; **make sense of** show or find meaning of. □ **sense of humour** see HUMOUR.

senseless *adjective* pointless, foolish; unconscious. □ **senselessly** *adverb*; **senselessness** *noun.*

sensibility *noun* (*plural* **-ies**) capacity to feel; (exceptional) sensitiveness; (in *plural*) tendency to feel offended etc.

■ **Usage** *Sensibility* should not be used in standard English to mean 'possession of good sense'.

sensible /ˈsensɪb(ə)l/ *adjective* having or showing good sense; perceptible by senses; (of clothing etc.) practical; (+ *of*) aware of. □ **sensibly** *adverb.*

sensitive /ˈsensɪtɪv/ *adjective* (often + *to*) acutely affected by external impressions, having sensibility; easily offended or hurt; (often + *to*) responsive to or recording slight changes of condition; Photography responding (esp. rapidly) to light; (of topic etc.) requiring tact or secrecy. □ **sensitively** *noun*; **sensitiveness** *noun*; **sensitivity** /-ˈtɪv-/ *noun* (*plural* **-ies**).

sensitize /ˈsensɪtaɪz/ *verb* (also **-ise**) (**-zing** or **-sing**) make sensitive. □ **sensitization** *noun.*

sensor /ˈsensə/ *noun* device to detect or measure a physical property.

sensory /ˈsensərɪ/ *adjective* of sensation or senses.

sensual /ˈsensjʊəl/ *adjective* of physical, esp. sexual, pleasure; enjoying, giving, or showing this. □ **sensuality** /-ˈæl-/ *noun*; **sensually** *adverb.*

■ **Usage** *Sensual* is sometimes confused with *sensuous.*

sensuous /ˈsensjʊəs/ *adjective* of or affecting senses, esp. aesthetically. □ **sensuously** *adverb*; **sensuousness** *noun.*

■ **Usage** *Sensuous* is sometimes confused with *sensual.*

sent *past & past participle* of SEND.

sentence /ˈsent(ə)ns/ ● *noun* grammatically complete series of words with (implied) subject and predicate (see panel); punishment allotted to person convicted in criminal court; declaration of this. ● *verb* (**-cing**) declare sentence of, condemn.

sententious /senˈtenʃəs/ *adjective* pompously moralizing; affectedly formal; using maxims. □ **sententiousness** *noun.*

sentient /ˈsenʃ(ə)nt/ *adjective* capable of perception and feeling. □ **sentience** *noun*; **sentiently** *adverb.*

sentiment /'sentɪmənt/ *noun* mental feeling; (often in *plural*) opinion; emotional or irrational view(s); tendency to be swayed by feeling; mawkish tenderness.

sentimental /sentɪ'ment(ə)l/ *adjective* of or showing sentiment; showing or affected by emotion rather than reason. □ **sentimentalism** *noun*; **sentimentalist** *noun*; **sentimentality** /-'tæl-/ *noun*; **sentimentalize** *verb* (also **-ise**) (**-zing** or **-sing**); **sentimentally** *adverb*.

sentinel /'sentɪn(ə)l/ *noun* sentry.

sentry /'sentrɪ/ *noun* (*plural* **-ies**) soldier etc. stationed to keep guard. □ **sentry-box** cabin to shelter standing sentry.

sepal /'sep(ə)l/ *noun* division or leaf of calyx.

separable /'sepərəb(ə)l/ *adjective* able to be separated. □ **separability** *noun*.

separate ● *adjective* /'sepərət/ forming unit by itself, existing apart; disconnected, distinct, individual. ● *noun* /'sepərət/ (in *plural*) articles of dress not parts of suits. ● *verb* /'sepəreɪt/ (**-ting**) make separate, sever; prevent union or contact of; go different ways; (esp. as **separated** *adjective*) cease to live with spouse; secede; divide or sort into parts or sizes; (often + *out*) extract or remove (ingredient etc.). □ **separately** *adverb*; **separateness** *noun*; **separator** *noun*.

■ **Usage** *Separate*, *separation*, etc. are not spelt with an *e* in the middle.

separation /sepə'reɪʃ(ə)n/ *noun* separating, being separated; arrangement by which couple remain married but live apart.

separatist /'sepərətɪst/ *noun* person who favours separation, esp. political independence. □ **separatism** *noun*.

sepia /'siːpɪə/ *noun* dark reddish-brown colour or paint; brown tint used in photography.

sepoy /'siːpɔɪ/ *noun historical* Indian soldier under European, esp. British, discipline.

sepsis /'sepsɪs/ *noun* septic condition.

Sept. *abbreviation* September.

sept *noun* clan, esp. in Ireland.

September /sep'tembə/ *noun* ninth month of year.

septet /sep'tet/ *noun* musical composition for 7 performers; the performers; any group of 7.

septic /'septɪk/ *adjective* contaminated with bacteria, putrefying. □ **septic tank** tank in which sewage is disintegrated through bacterial activity.

septicaemia /septɪ'siːmɪə/ *noun* (*US* **septicemia**) blood poisoning.

septuagenarian /septjʊədʒɪ'neərɪən/ *noun* person between 70 and 79 years old.

Septuagesima /septjʊə'dʒesɪmə/ *noun* third Sunday before Lent.

Septuagint /'septjʊədʒɪnt/ *noun* ancient Greek version of Old Testament.

septum /'septəm/ *noun* (*plural* **septa**) partition such as that between nostrils.

Sentence

A sentence is the basic unit of language in use and expresses a complete thought. There are three types of sentence, each starting with a capital letter, and each normally ending with a full stop, a question mark, or an exclamation mark:

Statement: *You're happy.*
Question: *Is it raining?*
Exclamation: *I wouldn't have believed it!*

A sentence, especially a statement, often has no punctuation at the end in a public notice, a newspaper headline, or a legal document, e.g.

Government cuts public spending

A sentence normally contains a subject and a verb, but may not, e.g.

What a mess!   *Where?*   *In the sink.*

sepulchral /sɪˈpʌlkr(ə)l/ *adjective* of tomb or burial; funereal, gloomy.

sepulchre /ˈsepəlkə/ (*US* **sepulcher**) ● *noun* tomb, burial cave or vault. ● *verb* (**-ring**) lay in sepulchre.

sequel /ˈsiːkw(ə)l/ *noun* what follows; novel, film, etc. that continues story of earlier one.

sequence /ˈsiːkwəns/ *noun* succession; order of succession; set of things belonging next to one another; unbroken series; episode or incident in film etc.

sequential /sɪˈkwenʃ(ə)l/ *adjective* forming sequence or consequence. □ **sequentially** *adverb*.

sequester /sɪˈkwestə/ *verb* (esp. as **sequestered** *adjective*) seclude, isolate; sequestrate.

sequestrate /ˈsiːkwɪstreɪt/ *verb* (**-ting**) confiscate; take temporary possession of (debtor's estate etc.). □ **sequestration** *noun*.

sequin /ˈsiːkwɪn/ *noun* circular spangle on dress etc. □ **sequined, sequinned** *adjective*.

sequoia /sɪˈkwɔɪə/ *noun* extremely tall Californian conifer.

sera *plural* of SERUM.

seraglio /səˈrɑːlɪəʊ/ *noun* (*plural* **-s**) harem; *historical* Turkish palace.

seraph /ˈseræf/ *noun* (*plural* **-im** or **-s**) member of highest of 9 orders of angels. □ **seraphic** /səˈræfɪk/ *adjective*.

Serb ● *noun* native of Serbia; person of Serbian descent. ● *adjective* Serbian.

Serbian /ˈsɜːbɪən/ ● *noun* Slavonic dialect of Serbs; Serb. ● *adjective* of Serbs or their dialect.

Serbo-Croat /sɜːbəʊˈkrəʊæt/ (also **Serbo-Croatian** /-krəʊˈeɪʃ(ə)n/) ● *noun* main official language of former Yugoslavia, combining Serbian and Croatian dialects. ● *adjective* of this language.

serenade /serəˈneɪd/ ● *noun* piece of music performed at night, esp. under lover's window; orchestral suite for small ensemble. ● *verb* (**-ding**) perform serenade to.

serendipity /serənˈdɪpɪtɪ/ *noun* faculty of making happy discoveries by accident. □ **serendipitous** *adjective*.

serene /sɪˈriːn/ *adjective* (**-r, -st**) clear and calm; placid, unperturbed. □ **serenely** *adverb*; **serenity** /-ˈren-/ *noun*.

serf *noun historical* labourer not allowed to leave the land on which he worked; oppressed person, drudge. □ **serfdom** *noun*.

serge *noun* durable woollen fabric.

sergeant /ˈsɑːdʒ(ə)nt/ *noun* non-commissioned army or RAF officer next below warrant officer; police officer next below inspector. □ **sergeant major** warrant officer assisting adjutant of regiment or battalion.

serial /ˈsɪərɪəl/ ● *noun* story published, broadcast, or shown in instalments. ● *adjective* of, in, or forming series. □ **serial killer** person who murders repeatedly. □ **serially** *adverb*.

serialize *verb* (also **-ise**) (**-zing** or **-sing**) publish or produce in instalments. □ **serialization** *noun*.

series /ˈsɪərɪːz/ *noun* (*plural* same) number of similar or related things, events, etc.; succession, row, set; *Broadcasting* set of related but individually complete programmes. □ **in series** in ordered succession, (of set of electrical circuits) arranged so that same current passes through each circuit.

serif /ˈserɪf/ *noun* fine cross-line at extremities of printed letter.

serious /ˈsɪərɪəs/ *adjective* thoughtful, earnest; important, requiring thought; not negligible, dangerous; sincere, in earnest; (of music, literature, etc.) intellectual, not popular. □ **seriously** *adverb*; **seriousness** *noun*.

serjeant /ˈsɑːdʒ(ə)nt/ *noun* (in full **serjeant-at-law**, *plural* **serjeants-at-law**) *historical* barrister of highest rank. □ **serjeant-at-arms** official of court, city, or parliament, with ceremonial duties.

sermon /ˈsɜːmən/ *noun* discourse on religion or morals, esp. delivered in church; admonition, reproof.

sermonize *verb* (also **-ise**) (**-zing** or **-sing**) (often + *to*) moralize.

serous /ˈsɪərəs/ *adjective* of or like serum, watery; (of gland etc.) having serous secretion.

serpent /ˈsɜːpənt/ *noun* snake, esp. large; cunning or treacherous person.

serpentine /ˈsɜːpəntaɪn/ ● *adjective* of or like serpent; coiling, sinuous; cunning, treacherous. ● *noun* soft usually dark green rock, sometimes mottled.

SERPS *abbreviation* State Earnings-Related Pension Scheme.

serrated /sə'reɪtɪd/ *adjective* with saw-like edge. □ **serration** *noun*.

serried /'serɪd/ *adjective* (of ranks of soldiers etc.) close together.

serum /'sɪərəm/ *noun* (*plural* **sera** or **-s**) liquid separating from clot when blood coagulates, esp. used for inoculation; watery fluid in animal bodies.

servant /'sɜːv(ə)nt/ *noun* person employed for domestic work; devoted follower or helper.

serve ● *verb* (**-ving**) do service for; be servant to; carry out duty; (+ *in*) be employed in (esp. armed forces); be useful to or serviceable for; meet needs, perform function; go through due period of (apprenticeship, prison sentence, etc.); go through (specified period) of imprisonment etc.; (often + *up*) present (food) to eat; act as waiter; attend to (customer etc.); (+ *with*) supply with (goods); treat (person) in specified way; *Law* (often + *on*) deliver (writ etc.), (+ *with*) deliver writ etc. to; set (ball) in play at tennis etc.; (of male animal) copulate with (female). ● *noun* Tennis etc. service. □ **serve** (**person**) **right** be his or her deserved misfortune. □ **server** *noun*.

service /'sɜːvɪs/ ● *noun* (often in *plural*) work done or doing of work for employer or for community etc.; work done by machine etc.; assistance or benefit given; provision of some public need, e.g. transport or (often in *plural*) water, gas, etc.; employment as servant; state or period of employment; Crown or public department or organization; (in *plural*) the armed forces; ceremony of worship; liturgical form for this; (routine) maintenance and repair of machine etc. after sale; assistance given to customers; serving of food etc., quality of this, nominal charge for this; (in *plural*) motorway service area; set of dishes etc. for serving meal; act of serving in tennis etc., person's turn to serve, game in which one serves. ● *verb* (**-cing**) maintain or repair (car, machine, etc.); provide service for. □ **at** (**person's**) **service** ready to serve him or her; **of service** useful; **service area** area near road supplying petrol,

refreshments, etc.; **service charge** additional charge for service in restaurant etc.; **service flat** one in which domestic service etc. is provided; **service industry** one providing services, not goods; **serviceman**, **servicewoman** person in armed services; **service road** one giving access to houses etc. lying back from main road; **service station** establishment selling petrol etc. to motorists.

serviceable *adjective* useful, usable; durable but plain. □ **serviceability** *noun*.

serviette /sɜːvɪ'et/ *noun* table napkin.

servile /'sɜːvaɪl/ *adjective* of or like slave(s); fawning, subservient. □ **servility** /-'vɪl-/ *noun*.

servitude /'sɜːvɪtjuːd/ *noun* slavery, subjection.

servo- /'sɜːvəʊ/ *combining form* power-assisted.

sesame /'sesəmɪ/ *noun* E. Indian plant with oil-yielding seeds; its seeds.

sesqui- /'seskwɪ/ *combining form* one and a half.

sessile /'sesaɪl/ *adjective* Biology attached directly by base without stalk or peduncle; fixed, immobile.

session /'seʃ(ə)n/ *noun* period devoted to an activity; assembly of parliament, court, etc.; single meeting for this; period during which such meetings are regularly held; academic year. □ **in session** assembled for business, not on vacation. □ **sessional** *adjective*.

set ● *verb* (**-tt-**; *past & past participle* **set**) put, lay, or stand in certain position etc.; apply; fix or place ready; dispose suitably for use, action, or display; adjust hands or mechanism of (clock, trap, etc.); insert (jewel) in ring etc.; lay (table) for meal; style (hair) while damp; (+ *with*) ornament or provide (surface) with; bring into specified state, cause to be; harden, solidify; (of sun, moon, etc.) move towards or below earth's horizon; throw (story etc.) as happening in a certain time or place; (+ *to do*) cause (person) to do specified thing; (+ *present participle*) start (person, thing) doing something; present or impose as work to be done, problem to be solved, etc.; exhibit as model etc.; initiate (fashion etc.); establish (record etc.); determine, decide; appoint, establish; put parts of (broken or dislocated bone, limb, etc.) together for healing; provide (song, words) with music; arrange (type) or type for (book etc.); (of tide, current, etc.) have a certain motion or direction; (of face) assume hard expression; (of eyes etc.) become motionless; have a certain tendency; (of blossom) form into fruit; (of dancer) take position facing partner; (of hunting dog) take rigid attitude indicating presence of game. ● *noun* group of linked or similar things or persons; section of society; collection of objects for specified purpose; radio or television receiver; *Tennis etc.* group of games counting as unit towards winning match; *Mathematics* collection of things sharing a property; direction or position in which something sets or is set; slip, shoot, bulb, etc. for planting; setting, stage furniture, etc. for play, film, etc.; setting of sun, hair, etc.; = SETT. ● *adjective* prescribed or determined in advance; unchanging; fixed; prepared for action; (+ *on, upon*) determined to get, achieve, etc. □ **set about** begin, take steps towards, *colloquial* attack; **set aside** put to one side, keep for future, disregard or reject; **set back** place further back in space or time, impede or reverse progress of, *colloquial* cost (person) specified amount; **set-back** reversal or arrest of progress; **set down** record in writing, allow to alight; **set forth** begin journey, expound; **set in** begin, become established, insert; **set off** begin journey, detonate (bomb etc.), initiate, stimulate, cause (person) to start laughing etc., adorn, enhance, (+ *against*) use as compensating item against; **set on** (cause or urge to) attack; **set out** begin journey, (+ *to do*) intend, exhibit, arrange; **set piece** formal or elaborate arrangement, esp. in art or literature; **set square** right-angled triangular plate for drawing lines at certain angles; **set to** begin doing something vigorously; **set theory** study or use of sets in mathematics; **set-to** (*plural* **-tos**) *colloquial* fight, argument; **set up** place in position or view, start, establish, equip, prepare, *colloquial* cause (person) to look guilty or foolish; **set-up** arrangement

or organization, manner or structure of this, instance of setting person up; **set upon** set on.

sett *noun* (also **set**) badger's burrow, paving-block.

settee /se'ti:/ *noun* sofa.

setter *noun* dog of long-haired breed trained to stand rigid on scenting game.

setting *noun* position or manner in which thing is set; surroundings; period, place, etc. of story, film, etc.; frame etc. for jewel; music to which words are set; cutlery etc. for one person at table; operating level of machine.

settle[1] /'set(ə)l/ *verb* (**-ling**) (often + *down, in*) establish or become established in abode or lifestyle; (often + *down*) regain calm after disturbance, adopt regular or secure way of life, (+ *to*) apply oneself to; (cause to) sit down or come to rest; make or become composed etc.; determine, decide, agree on; resolve (dispute etc.); agree to terminate (lawsuit); (+ *for*) accept or agree to; pay (bill); (as **settled** *adjective*) established; colonize; subside, sink. □ **settle up** pay money owed etc.

settle[2] /'set(ə)l/ *noun* high-backed bench, often with box under seat.

settlement *noun* settling, being settled; place occupied by settlers, small village; political etc. agreement; arrangement ending dispute; terms on which property is given to person; deed stating these; amount or property given.

settler *noun* person who settles in newly developed region.

seven /'sev(ə)n/ *adjective & noun* one more than six. □ **seventh** *adjective & noun.*

seventeen /sevən'ti:n/ *adjective & noun* one more than sixteen. □ **seventeenth** *adjective & noun.*

seventy /'sevənti/ *adjective & noun* (*plural* **-ies**) seven times ten. □ **seventieth** *adjective & noun.*

sever /'sevə/ *verb* divide, break, or make separate, esp. by cutting.

several /'sevr(ə)l/ ● *adjective* a few; quite a large number; *formal* separate, respective. ● *pronoun* a few; quite a large number. □ **severally** *adverb.*

severance /'sevr(ə)ns/ *noun* severing; severed state. □ **severance pay** payment to employee on termination of contract.

severe /sɪ'vɪə/ *adjective* rigorous and harsh; not negligible, worrying; forceful; extreme; exacting; unadorned. □ **severely** *adverb*; **severity** /-'ver-/ *noun*.

sew /səʊ/ *verb* (*past participle* **sewn** or **sewed**) fasten, join, etc. with needle and thread or sewing machine. □ **sewing machine** machine for sewing or stitching.

sewage /'su:ɪdʒ/ *noun* waste matter carried in sewers. □ **sewage farm**, **works** place where sewage is treated.

sewer /'su:ə/ *noun* (usually underground) conduit for carrying off drainage water and waste matter.

sewerage /'su:ərɪdʒ/ *noun* system of or drainage by sewers.

sewing /'səʊɪŋ/ *noun* material or work to be sewn.

sewn *past participle* of SEW.

sex • *noun* group of males or females collectively; fact of belonging to either group; sexual instincts, desires, activity, etc.; *colloquial* sexual intercourse. • *adjective* of or relating to sex or sexual differences. • *verb* determine sex of; (as **sexed** *adjective*) having specified sexual appetite. □ **sex appeal** sexual attractiveness; **sex life** person's sexual activity; **sex symbol** person famed for sex appeal.

sexagenarian /seksədʒɪ'neərɪən/ *noun* person between 60 and 69 years old.

Sexagesima /seksə'dʒesɪmə/ *noun* second Sunday before Lent.

sexism *noun* prejudice or discrimination against people (esp. women) because of their sex. □ **sexist** *adjective & noun*.

sexless *adjective* neither male nor female; lacking sexual desire or attractiveness.

sextant /'sekst(ə)nt/ *noun* optical instrument for measuring angle between distant objects, esp. sun and horizon in navigation.

sextet /seks'tet/ *noun* musical composition for 6 performers; the performers; any group of 6.

sexton /'sekst(ə)n/ *noun* person who looks after church and churchyard, often acting as bell-ringer and grave-digger.

sextuple /'sekstju:p(ə)l/ *adjective* sixfold.

sextuplet /'sekstjʊplɪt/ *noun* each of 6 children born at one birth.

sexual /'sekʃʊəl/ *adjective* of sex, the sexes, or relations between them. □ **sexual intercourse** insertion of man's penis into woman's vagina. □ **sexuality** /-'æl-/ *noun*; **sexually** *adverb*.

sexy *adjective* (-**ier**, -**iest**) sexually attractive or provocative; *colloquial* (of project etc.) exciting. □ **sexily** *adverb*; **sexiness** *noun*.

SF *abbreviation* science fiction.

Sgt. *abbreviation* Sergeant.

sh *interjection* hush.

shabby /'ʃæbɪ/ *adjective* (-**ier**, -**iest**) faded and worn, dingy, dilapidated; poorly dressed; contemptible. □ **shabbily** *adverb*; **shabbiness** *noun*.

shack • *noun* roughly built hut or cabin. • *verb* (+ *up*) *slang* cohabit.

shackle /'ʃæk(ə)l/ • *noun* metal loop or link closed by bolt, coupling link; fetter; (usually in *plural*) restraint. • *verb* (-**ling**) fetter, impede, restrain.

shad *noun* (*plural* same or -**s**) large edible marine fish.

shade • *noun* comparative darkness caused by shelter from direct light and heat; area so sheltered; darker part of picture etc.; a colour, esp. as darker or lighter than one similar; comparative obscurity; slight amount; lampshade; screen moderating light; (in *plural*) esp. *US colloquial* sunglasses; *literary* ghost; (in *plural*, + *of*) reminder of. • *verb* (-**ding**) screen from light; cover or moderate light of; darken, esp. with parallel lines to represent shadow etc.; (often + *away*, *off*, *into*) pass or change gradually. □ **shading** *noun*.

shadow /'ʃædəʊ/ • *noun* shade; patch of shade; dark shape projected by body blocking out light; inseparable attendant or companion; person secretly following another; (with *negative*) slightest trace; insubstantial remnant; shaded part of picture; gloom, sadness. • *verb* cast shadow over; secretly follow and watch. □ **shadow-boxing** boxing against imaginary opponent; **Shadow Cabinet, Minister,** etc., members of opposition party holding posts parallel to those of government. □ **shadowy** adjective.

shady /'ʃeɪdɪ/ adjective (**-ier, -iest**) giving or situated in shade; disreputable, of doubtful honesty.

shaft /ʃɑːft/ noun narrow usually vertical space for access to mine or (in building) for lift, ventilation, etc.; (+ of) ray of (light), stroke of (lightning); handle of tool etc.; long narrow part supporting, connecting, or driving thicker part(s) etc.; archaic arrow, spear, its long slender stem; hurtful or provocative remark; each of pair of poles between which horse is harnessed to vehicle; central stem of feather; column, esp. between base and capital.

shag ● noun coarse tobacco; rough mass of hair; (crested) cormorant. ● adjective (of carpet) with long rough pile.

shaggy adjective (**-ier, -iest**) hairy, rough-haired; tangled. □ **shaggy-dog story** lengthy 'joke' without funny ending. □ **shagginess** noun.

shagreen /ʃæˈɡriːn/ noun kind of untanned granulated leather; sharkskin.

shah /ʃɑː/ noun historical ruler of Iran.

shake ● verb (**-king**; past **shook** /ʃʊk/; past participle **shaken**) move violently or quickly up and down or to and fro; (cause to) tremble or vibrate; agitate, shock, disturb; weaken, impair; colloquial shake hands. ● noun shaking, being shaken; jerk, shock; (**the shakes**) colloquial fit of trembling. □ **shake down** settle or cause to fall by shaking, become comfortably settled or established; **shake hands** (often + with) clasp hands, esp. at meeting or parting or as sign of bargain; **shake off** get rid of, evade; **shake up** mix (ingredients) or restore to shape by shaking, disturb or make uncomfortable, rouse from lethargy etc.; **shake-up** upheaval, reorganization.

shaker noun person or thing that shakes; container for shaking together ingredients of cocktails etc.

Shakespearian /ʃeɪkˈspɪərɪən/ adjective (also **Shakespearean**) of Shakespeare.

shako /'ʃækəʊ/ noun (plural **-s**) cylindrical plumed military peaked cap.

shaky adjective (**-ier, -iest**) unsteady, trembling; infirm; unreliable. □ **shakily** adverb; **shakiness** noun.

shale noun soft rock that splits easily. □ **shaly** adjective.

shall auxiliary verb (3rd singular present **shall**) used to form future tenses.

shallot /ʃəˈlɒt/ noun onion-like plant with cluster of small bulbs.

shallow /'ʃæləʊ/ ● adjective having little depth; superficial, trivial. ● noun (often in plural) shallow place. □ **shallowness** noun.

sham ● verb (**-mm-**) feign; pretend (to be). ● noun imposture, pretence; bogus or false person or thing. ● adjective pretended, counterfeit.

shamble /'ʃæmb(ə)l/ ● verb (**-ling**) walk or run awkwardly, dragging feet. ● noun shambling gait.

shambles plural noun (usually treated as singular) colloquial mess, muddle; butcher's slaughterhouse; scene of carnage.

shambolic /ʃæmˈbɒlɪk/ adjective colloquial chaotic, disorganized.

shame ● noun humiliation caused by consciousness of guilt or folly; capacity for feeling this; state of disgrace or discredit; person or thing that brings disgrace etc.; wrong or regrettable thing. ● verb (**-ming**) bring disgrace on, make ashamed; (+ into, out of) force by shame into or out of. □ **shamefaced** showing shame, bashful.

shameful adjective disgraceful, scandalous. □ **shamefully** adverb; **shamefulness** noun.

shameless adjective having or showing no shame; impudent. □ **shamelessly** adverb.

shammy /'ʃæmɪ/ noun (plural **-ies**) colloquial chamois leather.

shampoo /ʃæmˈpuː/ ● noun liquid for washing hair; similar substance for washing cars, carpets, etc. ● verb (**-poos, -pooed**) wash with shampoo.

shamrock /'ʃæmrɒk/ noun trefoil, as national emblem of Ireland.

shandy /'ʃændɪ/ noun (plural **-ies**) beer with lemonade or ginger beer.

shanghai /ʃænˈhaɪ/ verb (**-hais, -haied, -haiing**) colloquial trick or force (person) to do something, esp. be sailor.

shank *noun* leg, lower part of leg; shaft or stem, esp. joining tool's handle to its working end.

shan't /ʃɑːnt/ shall not.

shantung /ʃænˈtʌŋ/ *noun* soft undressed Chinese silk.

shanty[1] /ˈʃæntɪ/ *noun* (*plural* **-ies**) hut, cabin. □ **shanty town** area with makeshift housing.

shanty[2] /ˈʃæntɪ/ *noun* (*plural* **-ies**) (in full **sea shanty**) sailors' work song.

shape ● *noun* outline; form; specific form or guise; good or specified condition; person or thing seen indistinctly; mould, pattern. ● *verb* (**-ping**) give a certain form to, fashion, create; influence; (usually + *up*) show promise; (+ *to*) make conform to. □ **take shape** assume distinct form, develop.

shapeless *adjective* lacking definite or attractive shape. □ **shapelessness** *noun*.

shapely *adjective* (**-ier, -iest**) of pleasing shape, well-proportioned. □ **shapeliness** *noun*.

shard *noun* broken fragment of pottery, glass, etc.

share /ʃeə/ ● *noun* portion of whole given to or taken from person; each of equal parts into which company's capital is divided, entitling owner to proportion of profits. ● *verb* (**-ring**) have or use with another or others; get, have, or give share of; (+ *in*) participate in; (+ *out*) divide and distribute. □ **shareholder** owner of shares in a company; **share-out** division and distribution.

shark *noun* large voracious sea fish; *colloquial* swindler, extortioner. □ **sharkskin** skin of shark, smooth slightly shiny fabric.

sharp ● *adjective* having edge or point able to cut or pierce; tapering to a point or edge; abrupt, steep, angular; well-defined; severe, intense; pungent, acid; shrill, piercing; harsh; acute, sensitive, clever; unscrupulous; vigorous, brisk; *Music* above true pitch, a semitone higher than note named. ● *noun Music* sharp note; sign (♯) indicating this; *colloquial* swindler, cheat. ● *adverb* punctually; suddenly; at a sharp angle; *Music* above true pitch. □ **sharp practice** barely honest dealings; **sharpshooter**

skilled marksman; **sharp-witted** keenly perceptive or intelligent. □ **sharpen** *verb*; **sharpener** *noun*; **sharply** *adverb*; **sharpness** *noun*.

sharper *noun* swindler, esp. at cards.

shatter /ˈʃætə/ *verb* break suddenly in pieces; severely damage, destroy; (esp. in *passive*) severely upset; (usually as **shattered** *adjective*) *colloquial* exhaust.

shave ● *verb* (**-ving**; *past participle* **shaved** or (as *adjective*) **shaven**) remove (hair, bristles) with razor; remove hair with razor from (leg, head, etc.) or from face of (person); reduce by small amount; pare (wood etc.) to shape it; miss or pass narrowly. ● *noun* shaving, being shaved; narrow miss or escape.

shaver *noun* thing that shaves; electric razor; *colloquial* young lad.

shaving *noun* (esp. in *plural*) thin paring of wood.

shawl *noun* large usually rectangular piece of fabric worn over shoulders etc. or wrapped round baby.

she *pronoun* (as subject of verb) the female person or animal in question.

s/he *pronoun: written representation of* 'he or she'.

sheaf ● *noun* (*plural* **-s** or **sheaves**) bundle of things laid lengthways together and usually tied, esp. reaped corn or collection of papers. ● *verb* make into sheaves.

shear ● *verb* (*past* **sheared**; *past participle* **shorn** or **sheared**) clip wool off (sheep etc.); remove by cutting; cut with scissors, shears, etc.; (+ *of*) strip bare, deprive; distort, be distorted; (often + *off*) break. ● *noun* strain produced by pressure in structure of substance; (in *plural*) (also **pair of shears** *singular*) scissor-shaped clipping or cutting instrument. □ **shearer** *noun*.

sheath /ʃiːθ/ *noun* (*plural* **-s** /ʃiːðz/) close-fitting cover, esp. for blade; condom. □ **sheath knife** dagger-like knife carried in sheath.

sheathe /ʃiːð/ *verb* (**-thing**) put into sheath; encase or protect with sheath.

sheaves *plural of* SHEAF.

shebeen /ʃɪˈbiːn/ *noun esp. Irish* unlicensed drinking place.

shed[1] *noun* one-storeyed building for storage or shelter or as workshop etc.

shed² verb (**-dd-**; past & past participle **shed**) let, or cause to, fall off; take off (clothes); reduce (electrical power load); cause to fall or flow; disperse, diffuse, radiate; get rid of.

she'd /ʃiːd/ she had; she would.

sheen noun lustre, brightness.

sheep noun (plural same) mammal with thick woolly coat, esp. kept for its wool or meat; timid, silly, or easily-led person; (usually in plural) member of minister's congregation. □ **sheep-dip** preparation or place for cleansing sheep of vermin etc.; **sheepdog** dog trained to guard and herd sheep, dog of breed suitable for this; **sheepfold** enclosure for sheep; **sheepshank** knot for temporarily shortening rope; **sheepskin** sheep's skin with wool on.

sheepish adjective embarrassed or shy; ashamed. □ **sheepishly** adverb.

sheer¹ ● adjective mere, complete; (of cliff etc.) perpendicular; (of textile) diaphanous. ● adverb directly, perpendicularly.

sheer² verb swerve or change course; (often + away, off) turn away, esp. from person that one dislikes or fears.

sheet¹ ● noun rectangular piece of cotton etc. as part of bedclothes; broad thin flat piece of paper, metal, etc.; wide expanse of water, ice, flame, etc. ● verb cover (as) with sheet; (of rain etc.) fall in sheets. □ **sheet metal** metal rolled or hammered etc. into thin sheets; **sheet music** music published in separate sheets.

sheet² noun rope at lower corner of sail to control it. □ **sheet anchor** emergency anchor, person or thing depended on as last hope.

sheikh /ʃeɪk/ noun chief or head of Arab tribe, family, or village; Muslim leader.

sheila /ˈʃiːlə/ noun Australian & NZ offensive slang girl, young woman.

shekel /ˈʃek(ə)l/ noun chief monetary unit of Israel; historical weight and coin in ancient Israel etc.; (in plural) colloquial money.

shelduck /ˈʃeldʌk/ noun (plural same or **-s**; masculine **sheldrake**, plural same or **-s**) brightly coloured wild duck.

shelf noun (plural **shelves**) wooden etc. board projecting from wall or forming part of bookcase or cupboard; ledge on cliff face etc.; reef, sandbank. □ **on the shelf** (of woman) considered past marriageable age, put aside; **shelf-life** time for which stored thing remains usable; **shelf-mark** code on book to show its place in library.

shell ● noun hard outer case of many molluscs, tortoise, egg, nut-kernel, seed, etc.; explosive artillery projectile; hollow container for fireworks, cartridges, etc.; light racing boat; framework of vehicle etc.; walls of unfinished or gutted building etc. ● verb remove shell or pod from; fire shells at. □ **come out of one's shell** become less shy; **shellfish** aquatic mollusc with shell, crustacean; **shell out** colloquial pay (money); **shell-shock** nervous breakdown caused by warfare; **shell-shocked** adjective ● **shell-like** adjective.

she'll /ʃiːl/ she will; she shall.

shellac /ʃəˈlæk/ ● noun resin used for making varnish. ● verb (**-ck-**) varnish with shellac.

shelter /ˈʃeltə/ ● noun protection from danger, bad weather, etc.; place providing this. ● verb act or serve as shelter to; shield; take shelter.

shelve verb (**-ving**) put aside, esp. temporarily; put on shelf; provide with shelves; (of ground) slope.

shelving noun shelves; material for shelves.

shepherd /ˈʃepəd/ ● noun (feminine **shepherdess**) person who tends sheep; pastor. ● verb tend (sheep); marshal or guide like sheep. □ **shepherd's pie** minced meat baked with covering of (esp. mashed) potato.

sherbet /ˈʃɜːbət/ noun flavoured effervescent powder or drink.

sherd noun potsherd.

sheriff /ˈʃerɪf/ noun (also **High Sheriff**) chief executive officer of Crown in county, administering justice etc.; US chief law-enforcing officer of county; (also **sheriff-depute**) Scottish chief judge of county or district.

sherry /ˈʃerɪ/ noun (plural **-ies**) fortified wine originally from Spain.

she's /ʃiːz/ she is; she has.

Shetland pony /'ʃetlənd/ *noun* pony of small hardy breed.

shew *archaic* = SHOW.

shiatsu /ʃɪˈætsuː/ *noun* Japanese therapy involving pressure on specific points of body.

shibboleth /'ʃɪbəleθ/ *noun* long-standing formula, doctrine, phrase, etc. espoused by party or sect.

shied *past & past participle* of SHY².

shield /ʃiːld/ ● *noun* piece of defensive armour held in front of body when fighting; person or thing giving protection; shield-shaped trophy; protective plate or screen in machinery etc.; representation of shield for displaying person's coat of arms. ● *verb* protect, screen.

shier *comparative* of SHY¹.

shiest *superlative* of SHY¹.

shift ● *verb* (cause to) change or move from one position to another; remove, esp. with effort; *slang* hurry; *US* change (gear). ● *noun* shifting; relay of workers; period for which they work; device, expedient, trick; woman's loose straight dress; displacement of spectral line; key on keyboard for switching between lower and upper case etc.; *US* gear lever in motor vehicle. □ **make shift** manage, get along; **shift for oneself** rely on one's own efforts; **shift one's ground** alter stance in argument etc.

shiftless *adjective* lacking resourcefulness; lazy.

shifty *adjective* (**-ier, -iest**) *colloquial* evasive, deceitful.

Shiite /'ʃiːaɪt/ ● *noun* member of esp. Iranian branch of Islam opposed to Sunnis. ● *adjective* of this branch.

shillelagh /ʃɪˈleɪlɪ/ *noun* Irish cudgel.

shilling /'ʃɪlɪŋ/ *noun historical* former British coin and monetary unit, worth 1/20 of pound; monetary unit in some other countries.

shilly-shally /'ʃɪlɪʃælɪ/ *verb* (**-ies, -ied**) be undecided, vacillate.

shimmer /'ʃɪmə/ ● *verb* shine tremulously or faintly. ● *noun* tremulous or faint light.

shin ● *noun* front of leg below knee; cut of beef from this part. ● *verb* (**-nn-**) (usually

+ *up, down*) climb quickly using arms and legs. □ **shin-bone** tibia.

shindig /'ʃɪndɪɡ/ *noun* (also **shindy**) *colloquial* lively noisy party; brawl, disturbance.

shine ● *verb* (**-ning**; *past & past participle* **shone** /ʃɒn/ or **shined**) emit or reflect light, be bright, glow; (of sun, star, etc.) be visible; cause to shine; be brilliant, excel; (*past & past participle* **shined**) polish. ● *noun* light, brightness; polish, lustre. □ **take a shine to** *colloquial* take a liking to.

shiner *noun colloquial* black eye.

shingle¹ /'ʃɪŋ(ə)l/ *noun* small rounded pebbles on seashore. □ **shingly** *adjective*.

shingle² /'ʃɪŋ(ə)l/ ● *noun* rectangular wooden tile used on roofs etc.; *archaic* shingled hair. ● *verb* (**-ling**) roof with shingles; *archaic* cut (woman's hair) short and tapering.

shingles /'ʃɪŋ(ə)lz/ *plural noun* (usually treated as *singular*) painful viral infection of nerves with rash, esp. round waist.

Shinto /'ʃɪntəʊ/ *noun* (also **Shintoism**) Japanese religion with worship of ancestors and nature-spirits.

shinty /'ʃɪntɪ/ *noun* (*plural* **-ies**) game resembling hockey; stick or ball for this.

shiny *adjective* (**-ier, -iest**) having shine; (of clothing) with nap worn off.

ship ● *noun* large seagoing vessel; *US* aircraft; spaceship. ● *verb* (**-pp-**) transport, esp. in ship; take in (water) over ship's side etc.; lay (oars) at bottom of boat; fix (rudder etc.) in place; embark; be hired to work on ship. □ **shipmate** fellow member of ship's crew; **ship off** send away; **shipshape** trim, neat, tidy; **shipwreck** *noun* destruction of ship by storm or collision etc., ship so destroyed, *verb* (usually in *passive*) cause to suffer this; **shipwright** shipbuilder, ship's carpenter; **shipyard** place where ships are built.

shipment *noun* goods shipped; act of shipping goods etc.

shipper *noun* person or company that ships goods.

shipping *noun* transport of goods etc.; ships collectively.

shire /ʃaɪə/ *noun* county. □ **shire horse** heavy powerful horse.

shirk *verb* avoid (duty, work, etc.). □ **shirker** *noun*.

shirr *noun* elasticated gathered threads forming smocking. ● *verb* gather (material) with parallel threads. □ **shirring** *noun*.

shirt *noun* upper-body garment of cotton etc., usually with sleeves and collar. □ **in shirtsleeves** not wearing jacket; **shirt dress, shirtwaister** dress with bodice like shirt.

shirty *adjective* (-ier, -iest) *colloquial* annoyed. □ **shirtily** *adverb*; **shirtiness** *noun*.

shish kebab /ʃɪʃ/ *noun* pieces of meat and vegetables grilled on skewer.

shiver[1] /ˈʃɪvə/ ● *verb* tremble with cold, fear, etc. ● *noun* momentary shivering movement; **(the shivers)** attack of shivering. □ **shivery** *adjective*.

shiver[2] /ˈʃɪvə/ ● *noun* (esp. in *plural*) small fragment, splinter. ● *verb* break into shivers.

shoal[1] ● *noun* multitude, esp. of fish swimming together. ● *verb* form shoal(s).

shoal[2] ● *noun* area of shallow water; submerged sandbank. ● *verb* (of water) become shallow.

shock[1] ● *noun* violent collision, impact, etc.; sudden and disturbing emotional effect; acute prostration following wound, pain, etc.; electric shock; disturbance in stability of organization etc. ● *verb* horrify, outrage; cause shock; affect with electric or pathological shock. □ **shock absorber** device on vehicle etc. for absorbing shock and vibration; **shockproof** resistant to effects of shock; **shock therapy** electroconvulsive therapy; **shock wave** moving region of high air pressure caused by explosion etc.

shock[2] *noun* unkempt or shaggy mass of hair.

shocker *noun colloquial* shocking person or thing; sensational novel etc.

shocking *adjective* causing shock, scandalous; *colloquial* very bad. □ **shocking pink** vibrant shade of pink. □ **shockingly** *adverb*.

shod *past & past participle* of SHOE.

shoddy /ˈʃɒdɪ/ *adjective* (-ier, -iest) poorly made; counterfeit. □ **shoddily** *adverb*; **shoddiness** *noun*.

shoe /ʃuː/ ● *noun* foot-covering of leather etc., esp. one not reaching above ankle; protective metal rim for horse's hoof; thing like shoe in shape or use. ● *verb* (**shoes, shoeing**; *past & past participle* **shod**) fit with shoe(s). □ **-shod** having shoes of specified kind; **shoehorn** curved implement for easing heel into shoe; **shoelace** cord for lacing shoe; **shoestring** shoelace, *colloquial* small esp. inadequate amount of money; **shoe-tree** shaped block for keeping shoe in shape.

shone *past & past participle* of SHINE.

shoo ● *interjection* used to frighten animals etc. away. ● *verb* (**shoos, shooed**) utter such sound; (usually + *away*) drive away thus.

shook *past* of SHAKE.

shoot /ʃuːt/ ● *verb* (*past & past participle* **shot**) cause (weapon) to discharge missile; kill or wound with bullet, arrow, etc.; send out or discharge rapidly; come or go swiftly or suddenly; (of plant) put forth buds etc., (of bud etc.) appear; hunt game etc. with gun; film, photograph; *esp. Football* score or take shot at (goal); (often + *up*) *slang* inject (drug). ● *noun* young branch or sucker; hunting party or expedition; land on which game is shot. □ **shooting gallery** place for shooting at targets with rifles etc.; **shooting star** small rapidly moving meteor; **shooting stick** walking stick with foldable seat.

shop ● *noun* place for retail sale of goods or services; act of shopping; place for making or repairing something; *colloquial* place of business etc. ● *verb* (-pp-) go to shop(s) to make purchases; *slang* inform against. □ **shop around** look for best bargain; **shop assistant** person serving in shop; **shop-floor** production area in factory etc., workers as distinct from management; **shopkeeper** owner or manager of shop; **shoplift** steal goods while appearing to shop; **shoplifter** *noun*; **shop-soiled** soiled or faded by display in shop; **shop steward** elected representative of workers in factory etc.; **shopwalker** supervisor in large shop; **talk shop** talk about one's occupation. □ **shopper** *noun*.

shopping *noun* purchase of goods; goods bought. □ **shopping centre** area containing many shops.

shore[1] *noun* land adjoining sea, lake, etc.; (usually in *plural*) country. □ **on shore** ashore; **shoreline** line where shore meets water.

shore[2] *verb* (**-ring**) (often + *up*) support (as if) with prop(s) or beam(s).

shorn *past participle* of SHEAR.

short ● *adjective* measuring little from end to end in space or time, or from head to foot; (usually + *of, on*) deficient, scanty; concise, brief; curt, uncivil; (of memory) unable to remember distant events; (of vowel or syllable) having the lesser of two recognized durations; (of pastry) easily crumbled; (of a drink of spirits) undiluted. ● *adverb* before the natural or expected time or place; abruptly; rudely. ● *noun* short circuit; *colloquial* short drink; short film. ● *verb* short-circuit. □ **short back and sides** short simple haircut; **shortbread**, **shortcake** rich crumbly biscuit or cake made of flour, butter, and sugar; **short-change** cheat, esp. by giving insufficient change; **short circuit** electric circuit through small resistance, esp. instead of through normal circuit; **short-circuit** cause short circuit in, have short circuit, shorten or avoid by taking short cut; **shortcoming** deficiency, defect; **short cut** path or course shorter than usual or normal; **shortfall** deficit; **shorthand** method of rapid writing using special symbols, abbreviated or symbolic means of expression; **short-handed**, **-staffed** understaffed; **shorthorn** animal of breed of cattle with short horns; **short list** list of candidates from whom final selection will be made; **short-list** put on short list; **short-lived** ephemeral; **short-range** having short range, relating to immediate future; **short shrift** curt or dismissive treatment; **short sight** inability to focus except at close range; **short-tempered** easily angered; **short-term** of or for a short period of time; **short-winded** easily becoming breathless. □ **shorten** *verb*.

shortage *noun* (often + *of*) deficiency; lack.

shortening *noun* fat for pastry.

shortly *adverb* (often + *before, after*) soon; curtly.

shorts *plural noun* trousers reaching to knees or higher; *US* underpants.

short-sighted *adjective* having short sight; lacking imagination or foresight. □ **short-sightedly** *adverb*; **short-sightedness** *noun*.

shot[1] *noun* firing of gun etc.; attempt to hit by shooting or throwing etc.; single missile for gun etc.; (*plural* same or **-s**) small lead pellet of which several are used for single charge; (treated as *plural*) these collectively; photograph, film sequence; stroke or kick in ball game; *colloquial* attempt, guess; person of specified skill in shooting; heavy metal ball thrown in shot-put; *colloquial* drink of spirits; injection of drug etc. □ **shotgun** gun for firing small shot at short range; **shotgun wedding** *colloquial* wedding enforced because of bride's pregnancy; **shot-put** athletic contest in which shot is thrown; **shot-putter** *noun*.

shot[2] ● *past & past participle* of SHOOT. ● *adjective* woven so as to show different colours at different angles.

should /ʃʊd/ *auxiliary verb* (3rd singular present **should**) used in reported speech; expressing obligation, likelihood, or tentative suggestion; used to form conditional clause or (in 1st person) conditional mood.

shoulder /ˈʃəʊldə/ ● *noun* part of body to which arm, foreleg, or wing is attached; either of two projections below neck; animal's upper foreleg as joint of meat; (also in *plural*) shoulder regarded as supportive, comforting, etc.; strip of land next to road; part of garment covering shoulder. ● *verb* push with shoulder; make one's way thus; take on (burden, responsibility, etc.). □ **shoulder blade** either flat bone of upper back; **shoulder-length** (of hair etc.) reaching to shoulders; **shoulder pad** pad in garment to bulk out shoulder; **shoulder strap** strap going over shoulder from front to back of garment, strap suspending bag etc. from shoulder.

shouldn't /ˈʃʊd(ə)nt/ should not.

shout /ʃaʊt/ ● *verb* speak or cry loudly; say or express loudly. ● *noun* loud cry calling attention or expressing joy, defiance, approval, etc. □ **shout down** reduce to silence by shouting.

shove /ʃʌv/ ● verb (-ving) push, esp. vigorously or roughly; colloquial put casually. ● noun act of shoving. □ **shove-halfpenny** form of shovelboard played with coins etc. on table; **shove off** start from shore, mooring, etc. in boat, slang depart.

shovel /ˈʃʌv(ə)l/ ● noun spadelike scoop used to shift earth or coal etc. ● verb (-ll-; US -l-) move (as) with shovel. □ **shovelboard** game played esp. on ship's deck by pushing discs over marked surface.

shoveller /ˈʃʌvələ/ noun (also **shoveler**) duck with shovel-like beak.

show /ʃəʊ/ ● verb (past participle **shown** or **showed**) be, or allow or cause to be, seen; manifest; offer for inspection; express (one's feelings); accord, grant (favour, mercy, etc.); (of feelings etc.) be manifest; instruct by example; demonstrate, make understood; exhibit; (often + in, round, etc.) conduct, lead; colloquial appear, arrive. ● noun showing; spectacle, exhibition, display; public entertainment or performance; outward appearance, impression produced; ostentation, mere display; colloquial undertaking, business. □ **good** (or **bad** or **poor**) **show!** colloquial that was well (or badly) done; **showbiz** colloquial show business; **show business** colloquial the entertainment profession; **showcase** glass case or event etc. for displaying goods or exhibits; **showdown** final test or confrontation; **show house, flat** furnished and decorated new house or flat on show to prospective buyers; **showjumping** competitive jumping on horseback; **show off** display to advantage, colloquial act pretentiously; **show-off** colloquial person who shows off; **show-piece** excellent specimen suitable for display; **showroom** room where goods are displayed for sale; **show trial** judicial trial designed to frighten or impress the public; **show up** make or be visible or conspicuous, expose, humiliate, colloquial appear or arrive; **show willing** show willingness to help etc.

shower /ˈʃaʊə/ ● noun brief fall of rain, snow, etc.; brisk flurry of bullets, dust, etc.; sudden copious arrival of gifts, honours, etc.; (in full **shower-bath**) bath in which water is sprayed from above. ● verb descend, send, or give in shower; take shower-bath; (+ upon, with) bestow lavishly. □ **showery** adjective.

showing noun display; quality of performance, achievement, etc.; evidence; putting of case etc.

shown past participle of SHOW.

showy adjective (-ier, -iest) gaudy; striking. □ **showily** adverb; **showiness** noun.

shrank past of SHRINK.

shrapnel /ˈʃræpn(ə)l/ noun fragments of exploded bomb etc.

shred ● noun scrap, fragment; least amount. ● verb (-dd-) tear, cut, etc. to shreds. □ **shredder** noun.

shrew noun small long-snouted mouselike animal; bad-tempered or scolding woman. □ **shrewish** adjective.

shrewd adjective astute; clever. □ **shrewdly** adverb; **shrewdness** noun.

shriek ● noun shrill cry or sound. ● verb make a shriek; say in shrill tones.

shrike noun bird with strong hooked beak.

shrill ● adjective piercing and highpitched. ● verb sound or utter shrilly. □ **shrillness** noun; **shrilly** adverb.

shrimp noun (plural same or **-s**) small edible crustacean; colloquial very small person.

shrine noun sacred or revered place; casket or tomb holding relics.

shrink ● verb (past **shrank**; past participle **shrunk** or (esp. as adjective) **shrunken**) become or make smaller, esp. by action of moisture, heat, or cold; (usually + from) recoil, flinch. ● noun slang psychiatrist. □ **shrink-wrap** wrap (article) in material that shrinks tightly round it.

shrinkage noun process or degree of shrinking; allowance for loss by theft or wastage.

shrivel /ˈʃrɪv(ə)l/ verb (-ll-; US -l-) contract into wrinkled or dried-up state.

shroud /ʃraʊd/ ● noun wrapping for corpse; something which conceals; rope supporting mast. ● verb clothe (corpse) for burial; cover, disguise.

Shrove Tuesday /ʃrəʊv/ noun day before Ash Wednesday.

shrub noun woody plant smaller than tree and usually branching from near ground. □ **shrubby** adjective.

shrubbery noun (plural **-ies**) area planted with shrubs.

shrug ● verb (**-gg-**) draw up (shoulders) momentarily as gesture of indifference, ignorance, etc. ● noun shrugging movement.

shrunk (also **shrunken**) past participle of SHRINK.

shudder /ˈʃʌdə/ ● verb shiver from fear, cold, etc.; feel strong repugnance, fear, etc.; vibrate. ● noun act of shuddering.

shuffle /ˈʃʌf(ə)l/ ● verb (**-ling**) drag or slide (feet) in walking; mix up or rearrange (esp. cards); be evasive; keep shifting one's position. ● noun shuffling action or movement; change of relative positions; shuffling dance. □ **shuffle off** remove, get rid of.

shufti /ˈʃʊftɪ/ noun (plural **-s**) colloquial look, glimpse.

shun verb (**-nn-**) avoid, keep clear of.

shunt ● verb move (train etc.) to another track; (of train) be shunted; redirect. ● noun shunting, being shunted; conductor joining two points in electric circuit for diversion of current; slang collision of vehicles.

shush /ʃʊʃ/ interjection & verb hush.

shut verb (**-tt-**; past & past participle shut) move (door, window, lid, etc.) into position to block opening; become or be capable of being shut; shut door etc. of; become or make closed for trade; fold or contract (book, hand, telescope); bar access to (place). □ **shut down** close, cease working; **shut-eye** colloquial sleep; **shut off** stop flow of (water, gas, etc.), separate; **shut out** exclude, screen from view, prevent; **shut up** close all doors and windows of, imprison, put away in box etc., (esp. in imperative) colloquial stop talking.

shutter ● noun movable hinged cover for window; device for exposing film in camera. ● verb provide or close with shutter(s).

shuttle /ˈʃʌt(ə)l/ ● noun part of loom which carries weft-thread between threads of warp; thread-carrier for lower thread in sewing machine; train, bus, aircraft, etc. used in shuttle service; space shuttle. ● verb (**-ling**) (cause to) move to and fro like shuttle. □ **shuttlecock** cork with ring of feathers, or similar plastic device, struck to and fro in badminton; **shuttle diplomacy** negotiations conducted by mediator travelling between disputing parties; **shuttle service** transport system operating to and fro over short distance.

shy[1] ● adjective (**-er, -est**) timid and nervous in company; self-conscious; easily startled. ● verb (**shies, shied**) (usually + at) (esp. of horse) start back or aside in fright. ● noun sudden startled movement. □ **-shy** showing fear or dislike of. □ **shyly** adverb; **shyness** noun.

shy[2] ● verb (**shies, shied**) throw, fling. ● noun (plural **shies**) throw, fling.

shyster /ˈʃaɪstə/ noun colloquial person who acts unscrupulously or unprofessionally.

SI abbreviation international system of units of measurement (Système International).

si /siː/ noun Music te.

Siamese /saɪəˈmiːz/ ● noun (plural same) native or language of Siam (now Thailand); (in full **Siamese cat**) cat of cream-coloured dark-faced short-haired breed with blue eyes. ● adjective of Siam. □ **Siamese twins** twins joined together at birth.

sibilant /ˈsɪbɪlənt/ ● adjective hissing, sounded with hiss. ● noun sibilant speech sound or letter. □ **sibilance** noun.

sibling /ˈsɪblɪŋ/ noun each of two or more children having one or both parents in common.

sibyl /ˈsɪbɪl/ noun pagan prophetess.

sic adverb used or spelt thus (confirming form of quoted words). [Latin]

sick ● adjective vomiting, disposed to vomit; esp. US ill, unwell; (often + of) colloquial disgusted, surfeited; colloquial (of humour) cruel, morbid, perverted, offensive. ● noun colloquial vomit. ● verb (esp. + up) colloquial vomit. □ **sickbay** place for sick people; **sickbed** invalid's bed; **sick leave** leave granted because of illness; **sick pay** pay given during sick leave.

sicken verb make or become sick, disgusted, etc.; (often + for) show symptoms of illness; (as **sickening** adjective) disgusting, *colloquial* very annoying. □ **sickeningly** *adverb*.

sickle /'sɪk(ə)l/ *noun* short-handled implement with semicircular blade for reaping, lopping, etc.

sickly *adjective* (**-ier, -iest**) liable to be ill, weak; faint, pale; causing sickness; mawkish, weakly sentimental.

sickness *noun* being ill; disease; vomiting, nausea.

side ● *noun* each of inner or outer surfaces of object, esp. as distinct from top and bottom or front and back or ends; right or left part of person's or animal's body; part of object, place, etc. that faces specified direction or that is on observer's right or left; either surface of thing regarded as having two; aspect of question, character, etc.; each of sets of opponents in war, game, etc.; cause represented by this; part or region near edge; *colloquial* television channel; each of lines bounding triangle, rectangle, etc.; position nearer or farther than, or to right or left of, dividing line; line of descent through father or mother; spinning motion given to ball by striking it on side; *slang* swagger, assumption of superiority. ● *adjective* of, on, from, or to side; oblique, indirect; subordinate, subsidiary, not main. ● *verb* (**-ding**) take side in dispute etc.; (+ *with*) be on or join same side as. □ **on the side** as sideline, illicitly, *US* as side dish; **sideboard** table or flat-topped chest with drawers and cupboards for crockery etc.; **sideboards, sideburns** short side-whiskers; **side by side** standing close together, esp. for mutual encouragement; **sidecar** passenger car attached to side of motorcycle; **side drum** small double-headed drum; **side effect** secondary (usually undesirable) effect; **sidekick** *colloquial* close associate; **sidelight** light from side, small light at side of front of vehicle etc.; **sideline** work etc. done in addition to one's main activity, (usually in *plural*) line bounding side of sports pitch etc., space just outside these for spectators to sit; **side-saddle** *noun* saddle for woman riding with both legs on same side of horse, *adverb* sitting thus on horse; **sideshow** minor show

or stall in exhibition, fair, etc.; **sidesman** assistant churchwarden; **sidestep** *noun* step taken sideways, *verb* avoid, evade; **sidetrack** divert from course, purpose, etc.; **sidewalk** *US* pavement; **side-whiskers** hair left unshaven on cheeks; **take sides** support either of (usually two) opposing sides in argument etc.

sidelong ● *adjective* directed to the side. ● *adverb* to the side.

sidereal /saɪ'dɪərɪəl/ *adjective* of or measured or determined by stars.

sideways *adverb* & *adjective* to or from a side; with one side facing forward.

siding *noun* short track by side of railway line for shunting etc.

sidle /'saɪd(ə)l/ *verb* (**-ling**) walk timidly or furtively.

siege /siːdʒ/ *noun* surrounding and blockading of town, castle, etc. □ **lay siege to** conduct siege of; **raise siege** end it.

siemens /'siːmənz/ *noun* (*plural* same) SI unit of electrical conductance.

sienna /sɪ'enə/ *noun* kind of earth used as pigment; its colour of reddish- or yellowish-brown.

sierra /sɪ'erə/ *noun* long jagged mountain chain, esp. in Spain or Spanish America.

siesta /sɪ'estə/ *noun* afternoon nap or rest in hot countries.

sieve /sɪv/ ● *noun* utensil with network or perforated bottom through which liquids or fine particles can pass. ● *verb* (**-ving**) sift.

sift *verb* separate with or cause to pass through sieve; sprinkle through perforated container; closely examine details of, analyse; (of snow, light, etc.) fall as if from sieve.

sigh /saɪ/ ● *verb* emit long deep audible breath in sadness, weariness, relief, etc.; yearn; express with sighs. ● *noun* act of sighing; sound (like that) made in sighing.

sight /saɪt/ ● *noun* faculty of seeing; seeing, being seen; thing seen; range of vision; (usually in *plural*) notable features of a place; device assisting aim with gun or observation with telescope etc.; aim or observation so gained;

colloquial unsightly person or thing; *colloquial* great deal. ● *verb* get sight of; observe presence of; aim (gun etc.) with sight. □ **at first sight** on first glimpse or impression; **on, at sight** as soon as person or thing is seen; **sight-read** read (music) at sight; **sight-screen** *Cricket* large white screen placed near boundary in line with wicket to help batsman see ball; **sightseer** person visiting sights of place; **sightseeing** *noun.*

sighted *adjective* not blind. □ **-sighted** having specified vision.

sightless *adjective* blind.

sign /saɪn/ ● *noun* indication of quality, state, future event, etc.; mark, symbol, etc.; motion or gesture used to convey information, order, etc.; signboard; each of the 12 divisions of the zodiac. ● *verb* write one's name on (document etc.) as authorization; write (one's name) thus; communicate by gesture. □ **signboard** board bearing name, symbol, etc. displayed outside shop, inn, etc.; **sign in** sign register on arrival, get (person) admitted by signing register; **sign language** series of signs used esp. by deaf or dumb people for communication; **sign off** end contract, work, etc.; **sign on** register to obtain unemployment benefit; **sign out** sign register on departing; **signpost** *noun* post etc. showing directions of roads, *verb* provide with signpost(s); **sign up** engage (person), enlist in armed forces; **signwriter** person who paints signboards etc.

signal[1] /'sɪɡn(ə)l/ ● *noun* sign, esp. prearranged one, conveying information or direction; message of such signs; event which causes immediate activity; *Electricity* transmitted impulses or radio waves; sequence of these; device on railway giving instructions or warnings to train drivers etc. ● *verb* (**-ll-**; *US* **-l-**) make signal(s) (to); (often + *to do*) transmit, announce, or direct by signal(s). □ **signal-box** building from which railway signals are controlled; **signalman** railway signal operator.

signal[2] /'sɪɡn(ə)l/ *adjective* remarkable, noteworthy. □ **signally** *adverb.*

signalize *verb* (also **-ise**) (**-zing** or **-sing**) make conspicuous or remarkable; indicate.

signatory /'sɪɡnətərɪ/ ● *noun* (*plural* **-ies**) party that has signed an agreement, esp. a treaty. ● *adjective* having signed such an agreement.

signature /'sɪɡnətʃə/ *noun* person's name or initials used in signing; act of signing; *Music* key signature, time signature; section of book made from one sheet folded and cut. □ **signature tune** tune used esp. in broadcasting to announce a particular programme, performer, etc.

signet /'sɪɡnɪt/ *noun* small seal. □ **signet ring** ring with seal set in it.

significance /sɪɡ'nɪfɪkəns/ *noun* importance; meaning; being significant; extent to which result deviates from hypothesis such that difference is due to more than errors in sampling.

significant /sɪɡ'nɪfɪkənt/ *adjective* having or conveying meaning; important. □ **significant figure** *Mathematics* digit conveying information about a number containing it. □ **significantly** *adverb.*

signify /'sɪɡnɪfaɪ/ *verb* (**-ies**, **-ied**) be sign or symbol of; represent, mean, denote; make known; be of importance, matter. □ **signification** *noun.*

signor /'si:njɔ:/ *noun* (*plural* **-i** /-'njɔ:ri:/) title used of or to Italian man.

signora /si:'njɔ:rə/ *noun* title used of or to Italian esp. married woman.

signorina /si:njɔ'ri:nə/ *noun* title used of or to Italian unmarried woman.

Sikh /si:k/ *noun* member of Indian monotheistic sect.

silage /'saɪlɪdʒ/ *noun* green fodder stored in silo; storage in silo.

silence /'saɪləns/ ● *noun* absence of sound; abstinence from speech or noise; neglect or omission to mention, write, etc. ● *verb* (**-cing**) make silent, esp. by force or superior argument.

silencer *noun* device for reducing noise made by gun, vehicle's exhaust, etc.

silent /'saɪlənt/ *adjective* not speaking; making or accompanied by little or no sound. □ **silently** *adverb.*

silhouette /sɪlu:'et/ ● *noun* dark outline or shadow in profile against lighter background; contour, outline, profile; portrait in profile showing outline only, usually cut from paper or in black on white. ● *verb* (**-tting**) represent or show in silhouette.

silica /ˈsɪlɪkə/ *noun* silicon dioxide, occurring as quartz and as main constituent of sand etc. □ **siliceous** /sɪˈlɪʃəs/ *adjective*.

silicate /ˈsɪlɪkeɪt/ *noun* compound of metal(s), silicon, and oxygen.

silicon /ˈsɪlɪkən/ *noun* non-metallic element occurring in silica and silicates. □ **silicon chip** silicon microchip.

silicone /ˈsɪlɪkəʊn/ *noun* any organic compound of silicon with high resistance to cold, heat, water, etc.

silicosis /sɪlɪˈkəʊsɪs/ *noun* lung disease caused by inhaling dust containing silica.

silk *noun* fine strong soft lustrous fibre produced by silkworms; thread or cloth made from this; (in *plural*) cloth or garments of silk; *colloquial* Queen's Counsel. □ **silk-screen printing** screen printing; **silkworm** caterpillar which spins cocoon of silk; **take silk** become Queen's Counsel.

silken *adjective* of or resembling silk; soft, smooth, lustrous.

silky *adjective* (**-ier**, **-iest**) like silk in smoothness, softness, etc.; suave. □ **silkily** *adverb*.

sill *noun* slab of wood, stone, etc. at base of window or doorway.

silly /ˈsɪlɪ/ ● *adjective* (**-ier**, **-iest**) foolish, imprudent; weak-minded; *Cricket* (of fielder or position) very close to batsman. ● *noun* (*plural* **-ies**) *colloquial* silly person. □ **silliness** *noun*.

silo /ˈsaɪləʊ/ *noun* (*plural* **-s**) pit or airtight structure in which green crops are stored for fodder; tower or pit for storage of grain, cement, etc.; underground storage chamber for guided missile.

silt ● *noun* sediment in channel, harbour, etc. ● *verb* (often + *up*) block or be blocked with silt.

silvan = SYLVAN.

silver /ˈsɪlvə/ ● *noun* greyish-white lustrous precious metal; coins or articles made of or looking like this; colour of silver. ● *adjective* of or coloured like silver. ● *verb* coat or plate with silver; provide (mirror-glass) with backing of tin amalgam etc.; make silvery; turn grey or white. □ **silver birch** common birch with silvery white bark; **silverfish** (*plural* same or **-es**) small silvery wingless insect, silver-coloured fish; **silver jubilee** 25th anniversary of reign; **silver medal** medal awarded as second prize; **silver paper** aluminium foil; **silver plate** articles plated with silver; **silver-plated** plated with silver; **silver sand** fine pure kind used in gardening; **silver screen** (usually **the silver screen**) cinema films collectively; **silverside** upper side of round of beef; **silversmith** worker in silver; **silver wedding** 25th anniversary of wedding.

silvery *adjective* like silver in colour or appearance; having clear soft ringing sound.

simian /ˈsɪmɪən/ ● *adjective* of anthropoid apes; resembling ape, monkey. ● *noun* ape or monkey.

similar /ˈsɪmɪlə/ *adjective* like, alike; (often + *to*) having resemblance. □ **similarity** /-ˈlær-/ *noun* (*plural* **-ies**); **similarly** *adverb*.

simile /ˈsɪmɪlɪ/ *noun* esp. poetical comparison of two things using *like* or *as* (see panel).

similitude /sɪˈmɪlɪtjuːd/ *noun* guise, appearance; comparison or its expression.

simmer /ˈsɪmə/ ● *verb* be or keep just below boiling point; be in state of suppressed anger or laughter. ● *noun* simmering state. □ **simmer down** become less agitated.

simnel cake /ˈsɪmn(ə)l/ *noun* rich fruit cake, usually with almond paste.

simony /ˈsaɪmənɪ/ *noun* buying or selling of ecclesiastical privileges.

simoom /sɪˈmuːm/ *noun* hot dry dust-laden desert wind.

simper /ˈsɪmpə/ ● *verb* smile in silly affected way; utter with simper. ● *noun* such smile.

simple /ˈsɪmp(ə)l/ *adjective* (**-r**, **-st**) easily understood or done, presenting no difficulty; not complicated or elaborate; plain; not compound or complex; absolute, unqualified, straightforward; foolish, feeble-minded. □ **simple-minded** foolish, feeble-minded. □ **simpleness** *noun*.

simpleton /ˈsɪmpəlt(ə)n/ *noun* stupid or gullible person.

simplicity /sɪmˈplɪsɪtɪ/ *noun* fact or condition of being simple.

simplify /ˈsɪmplɪfaɪ/ *verb* (**-ies, -ied**) make simple or simpler. □ **simplification** *noun*.

simplistic /sɪmˈplɪstɪk/ *adjective* excessively or affectedly simple. □ **simplistically** *adverb*.

simply *adverb* in a simple way; absolutely; merely.

simulate /ˈsɪmjʊleɪt/ *verb* (**-ting**) pretend to be, have, or feel; counterfeit; reproduce conditions of (situation etc.), e.g. for training. □ **simulation** *noun*; **simulator** *noun*.

simultaneous /sɪməlˈteɪnɪəs/ *adjective* (often + *with*) occurring or operating at same time. □ **simultaneity** /-təˈneɪɪtɪ/ *noun*; **simultaneously** *adverb*.

sin ● *noun* breaking of divine or moral law; offence against good taste etc. ● *verb* (**-nn-**) commit sin; (+ *against*) offend. □ **sinner** *noun*.

since ● *preposition* throughout or within period after. ● *conjunction* during or in time after; because. ● *adverb* from that time or event until now.

sincere /sɪnˈsɪə/ *adjective* (**-r, -st**) free from pretence, genuine, honest, frank. □ **sincerity** /-ˈser-/ *noun*.

sincerely *adverb* in a sincere way. □ **Yours sincerely** *written before signature at end of informal letter.*

sine *noun* ratio of side opposite angle (in right-angled triangle) to hypotenuse.

sinecure /ˈsaɪnɪkjʊə/ *noun* position that requires little or no work but usually yields profit or honour.

sine die /saɪneɪ ˈdiːeɪ/ *adverb formal* indefinitely. [Latin]

sine qua non /saɪneɪ kwɑː ˈnəʊn/ *noun* indispensable condition or qualification. [Latin]

sinew /ˈsɪnjuː/ *noun* tough fibrous tissue joining muscle to bone; tendon; (in *plural*) muscles, strength; framework of thing. □ **sinewy** *adjective*.

sinful *adjective* committing or involving sin. □ **sinfully** *adverb*; **sinfulness** *noun*.

sing *verb* (*past* **sang**; *past participle* **sung**) utter musical sounds, esp. words in set tune; utter (song, tune); (of wind, kettle, etc.) hum, buzz, or whistle; *slang* become informer; (+ *of*) *literary* celebrate in verse. □ **sing out** shout; **singsong** *noun* session of informal singing, *adjective* (of voice) monotonously rising and falling. □ **singer** *noun*.

singe /sɪndʒ/ ● *verb* (**-geing**) burn superficially; burn off tips or edges of (esp. hair). ● *noun* superficial burn.

single /ˈsɪŋg(ə)l/ ● *adjective* one only, not double or multiple; united, undivided; of or for one person or thing; solitary; taken separately; unmarried; (with negative or in questions) even one. ● *noun* single thing, esp. room in hotel; (in full **single ticket**) ticket for one-way journey; pop record with one piece of music on each side; *Cricket* hit for one run; (usually in *plural*) game with one player on each side. ● *verb* (**-ling**) (+ *out*) choose for special attention. □ **single-breasted** (of coat etc.) with only one vertical row of buttons, and overlapping little at the front; **single-decker** bus with only one

• •

Simile

A simile is a figure of speech involving the comparison of one thing with another of a different kind, using *as* or *like*, e.g.

The water was as clear as glass.
Cherry blossom lay like driven snow upon the lawn.

Everyday language is rich in similes:

with *as*:	as like as two peas	as poor as a church mouse
	as strong as an ox	as rich as Croesus
with *like*:	spread like wildfire	run like the wind
	sell like hot cakes	like a bull in a china shop

• •

deck; **single file** line of people one behind another; **single-handed** without help; **single-handedly** *adverb*; **single-minded** intent on only one aim; **single parent** parent bringing up child or children alone. □ **singly** /'sɪŋglɪ/ *adverb*.

singlet /'sɪŋglɪt/ *noun* sleeveless vest.

singleton /'sɪŋgəlt(ə)n/ *noun* player's only card of particular suit.

singular /'sɪŋgjʊlə/ ● *adjective* unique; outstanding; extraordinary; strange; *Grammar* denoting one person or thing. ● *noun Grammar* singular word or form. □ **singularity** /-'lær-/ *noun* (*plural* **-ies**); **singularly** *adverb*.

Sinhalese /sɪnhə'liːz/ ● *noun* (*plural* same) member of a people from N. India now forming majority of population of Sri Lanka; their language. ● *adjective* of this people or language.

sinister /'sɪnɪstə/ *adjective* suggestive of evil; wicked, criminal; ominous; *Heraldry* on left side of shield etc. (i.e. to observer's right).

sink ● *verb* (*past* **sank** or **sunk**; *past participle* **sunk** or (as *adjective*) **sunken**) fall or come slowly downwards; disappear below horizon; go or penetrate below surface of liquid; go to bottom of sea etc.; settle down; decline in strength and vitality; descend in pitch or volume; cause or allow to sink or penetrate; cause failure of; dig (well), bore (shaft); engrave (die); invest (money); cause (ball) to enter pocket at billiards or hole at golf etc. ● *noun* plumbed-in basin, esp. in kitchen; place where foul liquid collects; place of vice. □ **sinking fund** money set aside for eventual repayment of debt.

sinker *noun* weight used to sink fishing or sounding line.

Sino- /'saɪnəʊ/ *combining form* Chinese.

sinology /saɪ'nɒlədʒɪ/ *noun* study of China and its language, history, etc. □ **sinologist** *noun*.

sinuous /'sɪnjʊəs/ *adjective* with many curves, undulating. □ **sinuosity** /-'ɒs-/ *noun*.

sinus /'saɪnəs/ *noun* either of cavities in skull communicating with nostrils.

sinusitis /saɪnə'saɪtɪs/ *noun* inflammation of sinus.

sip ● *verb* (**-pp-**) drink in small mouthfuls. ● *noun* small mouthful of liquid; act of taking this.

siphon /'saɪf(ə)n/ ● *noun* tube shaped like inverted V or U with unequal legs, used for transferring liquid from one container to another by atmospheric pressure; bottle from which fizzy water is forced by pressure of gas. ● *verb* (often + *off*) conduct or flow through siphon, divert or set aside (funds etc.).

sir /sɜː/ *noun* polite form of address or reference to a man; (**Sir**) title used before forename of knight or baronet.

sire ● *noun* male parent of animal, esp. stallion; *archaic form of address to king*; *archaic* father or other male ancestor. ● *verb* (**-ring**) beget.

siren /'saɪərən/ *noun* device for making loud prolonged signal or warning sound; *Greek Mythology* woman or winged creature whose singing lured unwary sailors on to rocks; dangerously fascinating woman.

sirloin /'sɜːlɔɪn/ *noun* best part of loin of beef.

sirocco /sɪ'rɒkəʊ/ *noun* (*plural* **-s**) Saharan simoom; hot moist wind in S. Europe.

sisal /'saɪs(ə)l/ *noun* fibre from leaves of agave.

siskin /'sɪskɪn/ *noun* small songbird.

sissy /'sɪsɪ/ (also **cissy**) *colloquial* ● *noun* (*plural* **-ies**) effeminate or cowardly person. ● *adjective* (**-ier**, **-iest**) effeminate; cowardly.

sister /'sɪstə/ *noun* woman or girl in relation to her siblings; female fellow member of trade union, sect, human race, etc.; member of female religious order; senior female nurse. □ **sister-in-law** (*plural* **sisters-in-law**) husband's or wife's sister, brother's wife. □ **sisterly** *adjective*.

sisterhood *noun* relationship (as) of sisters; society of women bound by monastic vows or devoting themselves to religious or charitable work; community of feeling among women.

sit *verb* (**-tt-**; *past & past participle* **sat**) support body by resting buttocks on ground, seat, etc.; cause to sit; place in sitting position; (of bird) perch or remain on nest to hatch eggs; (of animal) rest with hind legs bent and buttocks on ground; (of parliament, court, etc.) be in session; (usually + *for*) pose (for portrait); (+ *for*) be MP for (constituency); (often + *for*) take (exam). □ **be sitting pretty** be comfortably placed; **sit back** relax one's efforts; **sit down** sit after standing, cause to sit, (+ *under*) suffer tamely (humiliation etc.); **sit in** occupy place as protest; **sit-in** *noun*; **sit in on** be present as guest etc. at (meeting); **sit on** be member of (committee etc.), *colloquial* delay action about, *slang* repress or snub; **sit out** take no part in (dance etc.), stay till end of, sit outdoors; **sit tight** *colloquial* remain firmly in one's place, not yield; **sit up** rise from lying to sitting, sit firmly upright, defer going to bed, *colloquial* become interested, aroused, etc.; **sit-up** physical exercise of sitting up from supine position without using arms or hands.

sitar /'sɪtɑː/ *noun* long-necked Indian lute.

sitcom /'sɪtkɒm/ *noun colloquial* situation comedy.

site ● *noun* ground chosen or used for town or building; ground set apart for some purpose. ● *verb* (**-ting**) locate, place.

sitter *noun* person who sits for portrait etc.; babysitter.

sitting ● *noun* continuous period spent engaged in an activity; time during which assembly is engaged in business; session in which meal is served. ● *adjective* having sat down; (of animal or bird) still; (of MP etc.) current. □ **sitting-room** room in which to sit and relax.

situ see IN SITU.

situate /'sɪtjʊeɪt/ *verb* (**-ting**) (usually in *passive*) place or put in position, situation, etc.

situation *noun* place and its surroundings; circumstances; position; state of affairs; *formal* paid job. □ **situation comedy** broadcast comedy series involving characters dealing with awkward esp. domestic or everyday situations. □ **situational** *adjective*.

six *adjective & noun* one more than five; *Cricket* hit scoring six runs. □ **hit**, **knock for six** *colloquial* utterly surprise or defeat.

sixpence /'sɪkspəns/ *noun* sum of 6 (esp. old) pence; *historical* coin worth this.

sixpenny /'sɪkspənɪ/ *adjective* costing or worth 6 (esp. old) pence.

sixteen /sɪks'tiːn/ *adjective & noun* one more than fifteen. □ **sixteenth** *adjective & noun*.

sixth ● *adjective & noun* next after fifth; any of 6 equal parts of thing. □ **sixth form** form in secondary school for pupils over 16; **sixth-form college** separate college for pupils over 16; **sixth sense** supposed intuitive or extrasensory faculty.

sixty /'sɪkstɪ/ *adjective & noun* (*plural* **-ies**) six times ten. □ **sixtieth** *adjective & noun*.

sizable = SIZEABLE.

size[1] ● *noun* relative bigness or extent of a thing; dimensions, magnitude; each of classes into which things are divided by size. ● *verb* (**-zing**) sort in sizes or by size. □ **size up** *colloquial* form judgement of.

size[2] ● *noun* sticky solution used for glazing paper and stiffening textiles etc. ● *verb* (**-zing**) treat with size.

sizeable *adjective* (also **sizable**) fairly large.

sizzle /'sɪz(ə)l/ ● *verb* (**-ling**) sputter or hiss, esp. in frying. ● *noun* sizzling sound. □ **sizzling** *adjective & adverb*.

SJ *abbreviation* Society of Jesus.

skate[1] ● *noun* ice-skate; roller-skate. ● *verb* (**-ting**) move, glide, or perform (as) on skates; (+ *over*) refer fleetingly to, disregard. □ **skateboard** *noun* short narrow board on roller-skate wheels for riding on standing up, *verb* ride on skateboard. □ **skater** *noun*.

skate[2] *noun* (*plural* same or **-s**) large edible marine flatfish.

skedaddle /skɪ'dæd(ə)l/ *verb* (**-ling**) *colloquial* run away, retreat hastily.

skein /skeɪn/ *noun* quantity of yarn etc. coiled and usually loosely twisted; flock of wild geese etc. in flight.

skeleton /'skelɪt(ə)n/ ● *noun* hard framework of bones etc. of animal; supporting framework or structure of thing; very thin person or animal; useless or dead remnant; outline sketch. ● *adjective* having only essential or minimum number of people, parts, etc.

□ **skeleton key** key fitting many locks.
□ **skeletal** adjective.

skerry /'skerɪ/ noun (plural **-ies**) Scottish reef, rocky islet.

sketch ● noun rough or unfinished drawing or painting; rough draft, general outline; short usually humorous play. ● verb make or give sketch of; make sketches.

sketchy adjective (**-ier, -iest**) giving only a rough outline; colloquial insubstantial or imperfect, esp. through haste. □ **sketchily** adverb.

skew ● adjective oblique, slanting, set askew. ● noun slant. ● verb make skew; distort; move obliquely.

skewbald /'skju:bɔ:ld/ ● adjective (of animal) with irregular patches of white and another colour. ● noun skewbald animal, esp. horse.

skewer /'skju:ə/ ● noun long pin for holding meat compactly together while cooking. ● verb fasten together or pierce (as) with skewer.

ski /ski:/ ● noun (plural **-s**) each of pair of long narrow pieces of wood etc. fastened under feet for travelling over snow; similar device under vehicle. ● verb (**skis**; **ski'd** or **skied** /ski:d/; **ski-ing**) travel on skis. □ **skier** noun.

skid ● verb (**-dd-**) (of vehicle etc.) slide esp. sideways or obliquely on slippery road etc.; cause (vehicle) to skid. ● noun act of skidding; runner used as part of landing-gear of aircraft. □ **skid-pan** slippery surface for drivers to practise control of skidding; **skid row** US slang district frequented by vagrants.

skiff noun light boat, esp. for rowing or sculling.

skilful /'skɪlfʊl/ adjective (US **skillful**) having or showing skill. □ **skilfully** adverb.

skill noun practised ability, expertness, technique; craft, art, etc. requiring skill.

skilled adjective skilful; (of work or worker) requiring or having skill or special training.

skillet /'skɪlɪt/ noun long-handled metal cooking pot; US frying-pan.

skim verb (**-mm-**) take scum or cream etc. from surface of (liquid); barely touch (surface) in passing over; (often + over) deal with or treat (matter) superficially; (often + over, along) glide lightly; read or look over superficially. □ **skim**, **skimmed milk** milk with cream removed.

skimp verb (often + on) economize; supply meagrely, use too little of.

skimpy adjective (**-ier, -iest**) meagre, insufficient.

skin ● noun flexible covering of body; skin removed from animal, material made from this; complexion; outer layer or covering; film like skin on liquid etc.; container for liquid, made of animal's skin. ● verb (**-nn-**) strip skin from; graze (part of body); slang swindle. □ **skin-deep** superficial; **skin-diver** person who swims near water without diving suit; **skin-diving** noun; **skinflint** miser; **skin-graft** surgical transplanting of skin, skin thus transferred; **skintight** very close-fitting.

skinful noun colloquial enough alcohol to make one drunk.

skinny adjective (**-ier, -iest**) thin, emaciated.

skint adjective slang having no money.

skip¹ ● verb (**-pp-**) move along lightly, esp. by taking two hops with each foot in turn; jump lightly esp. over skipping rope; frisk; gambol; move quickly from one subject etc. to another; omit or make omissions in reading; colloquial not attend etc.; colloquial leave hurriedly. ● noun skipping movement or action. □ **skipping-rope** length of rope turned over head and under feet while jumping it.

skip² noun large container for refuse etc.; container in which men or materials are lowered or raised in mines etc.

skipjack noun (in full **skipjack tuna**) (plural same or **-s**) small Pacific tuna.

skipper /'skɪpə/ ● noun captain of ship, aircraft, team, etc. ● verb be captain of.

skirl ● noun shrill sound of bagpipes. ● verb make skirl.

skirmish /'skɜ:mɪʃ/ ● noun minor battle; short argument etc. ● verb engage in skirmish.

skirt ● noun woman's garment hanging from waist, or this part of complete dress; part of coat etc. that hangs below waist; hanging part at base of hovercraft; (in *singular* or *plural*) border, outlying part; flank of beef etc. ● *verb* go or be along or round edge of. □ **skirting board** narrow board etc. round bottom of room-wall.

skit *noun* light piece of satire, burlesque.

skittish /'skɪtɪʃ/ *adjective* lively, playful; (of horse etc.) nervous, inclined to shy.

skittle /'skɪt(ə)l/ *noun* pin used in game of skittles, in which number of wooden pins are set up to be bowled or knocked down.

skive *verb* (**-ving**) (often + *off*) *slang* evade work; play truant.

skivvy /'skɪvɪ/ *noun* (*plural* **-ies**) *colloquial derogatory* female domestic servant.

skua /'skjuːə/ *noun* large predatory seabird.

skulduggery /skʌl'dʌgərɪ/ *noun* trickery, unscrupulous behaviour.

skulk *verb* lurk or conceal oneself or move stealthily.

skull *noun* bony case of brain; bony framework of head; head as site of intelligence. □ **skull and crossbones** representation of skull over two crossed thigh-bones, esp. on pirate flag or as emblem of death; **skullcap** close-fitting peakless cap.

skunk *noun* (*plural* same or **-s**) black white-striped bushy-tailed mammal, emitting powerful stench when attacked; *colloquial* contemptible person.

sky /skaɪ/ *noun* (*plural* **skies**) (in *singular* or *plural*) atmosphere and outer space seen from the earth. □ **sky blue** bright clear blue; **skydiving** sport of performing acrobatic manoeuvres under free fall before opening parachute; **skylark** *noun* lark that sings while soaring, *verb* play tricks and practical jokes; **skylight** window in roof; **skyline** outline of hills, buildings, etc. against sky; **sky-rocket** *noun* firework shooting into air and exploding, *verb* rise steeply; **skyscraper** very tall building.

slab *noun* flat thickish esp. rectangular piece of solid material; mortuary table.

slack¹ ● *adjective* (of rope etc.) not taut; inactive, sluggish; negligent, remiss; (of tide etc.) neither ebbing nor flowing. ● *noun* slack part of rope etc.; slack period; (in *plural*) casual trousers. ● *verb*

slacken; *colloquial* take a rest, be lazy. □ **slack off** loosen; **slack up** reduce level of activity or speed. □ **slackness** *noun*.

slack² *noun* coal dust, coal fragments.

slacken *verb* make or become slack. □ **slacken off** slack off.

slacker *noun* shirker.

slag ● *noun* refuse left after ore has been smelted etc. ● *verb* (**-gg-**) form slag; (often + *off*) *slang* insult, slander. □ **slag-heap** hill of refuse from mine etc.

slain *past participle* of SLAY.

slake *verb* (**-king**) assuage or satisfy (thirst etc.); cause (lime) to heat and crumble by action of water.

slalom /'slɑːləm/ *noun* downhill ski-race on zigzag course between artificial obstacles.

slam¹ ● *verb* (**-mm-**) shut, throw, or put down violently or with bang; *slang* criticize severely. ● *noun* sound or action of slamming.

slam² *noun* winning of all tricks at cards.

slander /'slɑːndə/ ● *noun* false and damaging utterance about person. ● *verb* utter slander about. □ **slanderous** *adjective*.

slang ● *noun* very informal words, phrases, or meanings, not regarded as standard and often peculiar to profession, class, etc. ● *verb* use abusive language (to). □ **slanging match** prolonged exchange of insults. □ **slangy** *adjective*.

slant /slɑːnt/ ● *verb* slope, (cause to) lie or go obliquely; (often as **slanted** *adjective*) present (news etc.) in biased or particular way. ● *noun* slope, oblique position; point of view, esp. biased one. ● *adjective* sloping, oblique.

slantwise *adverb* aslant.

slap ● *verb* (**-pp-**) strike (as) with palm of hand; lay forcefully; put hastily or carelessly. ● *noun* slapping stroke or sound. ● *adverb* suddenly, fully, directly. □ **slapdash** hasty, careless; **slap-happy** *colloquial* cheerfully casual; **slapstick** boisterous comedy; **slap-up** *colloquial* lavish.

slash ● *verb* cut or gash with knife etc.; (often + *at*) deliver or aim cutting blows; reduce (prices etc.) drastically; criticize harshly. ●noun slashing cut; *Printing* oblique stroke; *slang* act of urinating.

slat noun long narrow strip of wood, plastic, or metal, used in fences, venetian blinds, etc.

slate ●noun fine-grained bluish-grey rock easily split into thin smooth plates; piece of this used esp. in roofing or *historical* for writing on; colour of slate; list of nominees for office etc. ●verb (-ting) roof with slates; *colloquial* criticize severely; *US* make arrangements for (event etc.), nominate for office. ●adjective of (colour of) slate. □ **slating** noun; **slaty** adjective.

slattern /'slæt(ə)n/ noun slovenly woman. □ **slatternly** adjective.

slaughter /'slɔːtə/ ●verb kill (animals) for food etc.; kill (people) ruthlessly or in large numbers; *colloquial* defeat utterly. ●noun act of slaughtering. □ **slaughterhouse** place for slaughter of animals for food. □ **slaughterer** noun.

Slav /slɑːv/ ●noun member of group of peoples of central and eastern Europe speaking Slavonic languages. ●adjective of the Slavs.

slave ●noun person who is owned by and has to serve another; drudge, very hard worker; (+ of, to) obsessive devotee. ●verb (-ving) work very hard. □ **slave-driver** overseer of slaves, hard taskmaster; **slave trade** dealing in slaves, esp. African blacks.

slaver[1] noun *historical* ship or person engaged in slave trade.

slaver[2] /'slævə/ ●verb dribble; drool. ●noun dribbling saliva; flattery; drivel.

slavery /'sleɪvərɪ/ noun condition of slave; drudgery; practice of having slaves.

Slavic /'slɑːvɪk/ adjective & noun Slavonic.

slavish /'sleɪvɪʃ/ adjective like slaves; without originality. □ **slavishly** adverb.

Slavonic /slə'vɒnɪk/ ●adjective of group of languages including Russian, Polish, and Czech. ●noun Slavonic group of languages.

slay verb (past **slew** /sluː/; past participle **slain**) kill. □ **slayer** noun.

sleaze noun *colloquial* sleaziness.

sleazy /'sliːzɪ/ adjective (-ier, -iest) squalid, tawdry. □ **sleazily** adverb; **sleaziness** noun.

sled noun & verb (-dd-) *US* sledge.

sledge ●noun vehicle on runners for use on snow. ●verb (-ging) travel or carry on sledge.

sledgehammer /'sledʒhæmə/ noun large heavy hammer.

sleek ●adjective (of hair, skin, etc.) smooth and glossy; looking well-fed and comfortable. ●verb make sleek. □ **sleekly** adverb; **sleekness** noun.

sleep ●noun condition in which eyes are closed, muscles and nerves relaxed, and consciousness suspended; period of this; rest, quiet, death. ●verb (past & past participle **slept**) be or fall asleep; spend the night; provide sleeping accommodation for; (+ with, together) have sexual intercourse; (+ on) defer (decision) until next day; (+ through) fail to be woken by; be inactive or dead; (+ off) cure by sleeping. □ **sleeping bag** padded bag to sleep in when camping etc.; **sleeping car**, carriage railway coach with beds or berths; **sleeping partner** partner not sharing in actual work of a firm; **sleeping pill** pill to induce sleep; **sleeping policeman** ramp etc. in road to slow traffic; **sleepwalk** walk about while asleep; **sleepwalker** noun □ **sleepless** adjective; **sleeplessness** noun.

sleeper noun sleeping person or animal; beam supporting railway track; sleeping car; ring worn in pierced ear to keep hole open.

sleepy adjective (-ier, -iest) feeling need of sleep; quiet, inactive. □ **sleepily** adverb; **sleepiness** noun.

sleet ●noun snow and rain together; hail or snow melting as it falls. ●verb (after *it*) sleet falls. □ **sleety** adjective.

sleeve noun part of garment covering arm; cover for gramophone record; tube enclosing rod etc. □ **up one's sleeve** in reserve. □ **sleeved** adjective; **sleeveless** adjective.

sleigh /sleɪ/ ●noun sledge, esp. for riding on. ●verb travel on sleigh.

sleight of hand /slaɪt/ noun dexterity, esp. in conjuring.

slender /'slendə/ adjective (-er, -est) of small girth or breadth; slim; slight, scanty, meagre.

slept past & past participle of SLEEP.

sleuth /sluːθ/ colloquial ●noun detective. ●verb investigate crime etc.

slew[1] /sluː/ ●verb (often + round) turn or swing to new position. ●noun such turn.

slew[2] past of SLAY.

slice ●noun thin flat piece or wedge cut from something; share; kitchen utensil with thin broad blade; stroke sending ball obliquely. ●verb (-cing) (often + up) cut into slices; (+ off) cut off; (+ into, through) cut (as) with knife; strike (ball) with slice.

slick ●adjective colloquial skilful, efficient; superficially dexterous, glib; sleek, smooth. ●noun patch of oil etc., esp. on sea. ●verb colloquial make smooth or sleek. □ **slickly** adverb; **slickness** noun.

slide ●verb (past & past participle **slid**) (cause to) move along smooth surface touching it always with same part; move quietly or smoothly; glide over ice without skates; (often + into) pass unobtrusively. ●noun act of sliding; rapid decline; smooth slope down which people or things slide; track for sliding, esp. on ice; part of machine or instrument that slides; mounted transparency viewed with projector; piece of glass holding object for microscope; hair-slide. □ **let things slide** be negligent, allow deterioration; **slide-rule** ruler with sliding central strip, graduated logarithmically for rapid calculations; **sliding scale** scale of fees, taxes, wages, etc. that varies according to some other factor.

slight /slaɪt/ ●adjective small, insignificant; inadequate; slender, frail-looking. ●verb treat disrespectfully, ignore. ●noun act of slighting. □ **slightly** adverb; **slightness** noun.

slim ●adjective (-mm-) not fat, slender; small, insufficient. ●verb (-mm-) (often + down) become slim, esp. by dieting etc.; make slim. □ **slimline** of slender design, not fattening. □ **slimmer** noun; **slimming** noun.

slime noun oozy or sticky substance.

slimy adjective (-ier, -iest) like, covered with, or filled with slime; colloquial disgustingly obsequious. □ **sliminess** noun.

sling[1] ●noun strap etc. used to support or raise thing; bandage supporting injured arm; strap etc. used to throw small missile. ●verb (past & past participle **slung**) suspend with sling; colloquial throw. □ **sling-back** shoe held in place by strap above heel; **sling one's hook** slang go away.

sling[2] noun sweetened drink of spirits (esp. gin) with water.

slink verb (past & past participle **slunk**) (often + off, away, by) move stealthily or guiltily.

slinky adjective (-ier, -iest) (of garment) close-fitting and sinuous.

slip[1] ●verb (-pp-) slide unintentionally or momentarily, lose footing or balance; go with sliding motion; escape or fall because hard to grasp; go unobserved or quietly; make careless or slight mistake; fall below standard; place stealthily or casually; release from restraint or connection; (+ on, off) pull (garment) easily or hastily on or off; escape from, evade. ●noun act of slipping; careless or slight error; pillowcase; petticoat; (in singular or plural) slipway; Cricket fielder behind wicket on off side, (in singular or plural) this position. □ **give (person) the slip** escape from, evade; **slip-knot** knot that can be undone by pull, running knot; **slip-on** (of shoes or clothes) easily slipped on or off; **slipped disc** displaced disc between vertebrae; **slip-road** road for entering or leaving motorway etc.; **slipstream** current of air or water driven backwards by propeller etc.; **slip up** colloquial make mistake; **slip-up** noun; **slipway** ramp for shipbuilding or landing boats.

slip[2] noun small piece of paper, esp. for making notes; cutting from plant for grafting or planting.

slippage noun act or instance of slipping.

slipper noun light loose indoor shoe.

slippery /'slɪpərɪ/ adjective difficult to grasp, stand on, etc., because smooth or wet; unreliable, unscrupulous. □ **slipperiness** noun.

slippy *adjective* (**-ier**, **-iest**) *colloquial* slippery.

slipshod *adjective* careless, slovenly.

slit ● *noun* straight narrow incision or opening. ● *verb* (**-tt-**; *past & past participle* **slit**) make slit in; cut in strips.

slither /ˈslɪðə/ ● *verb* slide unsteadily. ● *noun* act of slithering. □ **slithery** *adjective*.

sliver /ˈslɪvə/ ● *noun* long thin slice or piece. ● *verb* cut or split into slivers.

slob *noun colloquial derogatory* lazy, untidy, or fat person.

slobber /ˈslɒbə/ *verb & noun* slaver. □ **slobbery** *adjective*.

sloe *noun* blackthorn; its small bluish-black fruit.

slog ● *verb* (**-gg-**) hit hard and usually unskilfully; work or walk doggedly. ● *noun* heavy random hit; hard steady work or walk; spell of this.

slogan /ˈsləʊɡən/ *noun* catchy phrase used in advertising etc.; party cry, watchword.

sloop /sluːp/ *noun* small one-masted fore-and-aft rigged vessel.

slop ● *verb* (**-pp-**) (often + *over*) spill over edge of vessel; spill or splash liquid on. ● *noun* liquid spilled or splashed; (in *plural*) dirty waste water, wine, etc.; (in *singular* or *plural*) unappetizing liquid food.

slope ● *noun* inclined position, direction, or state; piece of rising or falling ground; difference in level between two ends or sides of a thing; place for skiing. ● *verb* (**-ping**) have or take slope, slant; cause to slope. □ **slope off** *slang* go away, esp. to evade work etc.

sloppy *adjective* (**-ier**, **-iest**) wet, watery, too liquid; careless, untidy; foolishly sentimental. □ **sloppily** *adverb*; **sloppiness** *noun*.

slosh ● *verb* (often + *about*) splash or flounder; *slang* hit, esp. heavily; *colloquial* pour (liquid) clumsily. ● *noun* slush; act or sound of splashing; *slang* heavy blow.

sloshed *adjective slang* drunk.

slot ● *noun* slit in machine etc. for something (esp. coin) to be inserted; slit, groove, etc. for thing; allotted place in schedule. ● *verb* (**-tt-**) (often + *in*, *into*) place or be placed (as if) into slot;

provide with slot(s). □ **slot machine** machine worked by insertion of coin, esp. delivering small items or providing amusement.

sloth /sləʊθ/ *noun* laziness, indolence; slow-moving arboreal S. American mammal.

slothful *adjective* lazy. □ **slothfully** *adverb*.

slouch /slaʊtʃ/ ● *verb* stand, move, or sit in drooping fashion. ● *noun* slouching posture or movement; *slang* incompetent or slovenly worker etc. □ **slouch hat** hat with wide flexible brim.

slough¹ /slaʊ/ *noun* swamp, miry place. □ **Slough of Despond** state of hopeless depression.

slough² /slʌf/ ● *noun* part that animal (esp. snake) casts or moults. ● *verb* (often + *off*) cast or drop as slough.

Slovak /ˈsləʊvæk/ ● *noun* member of Slavonic people inhabiting Slovakia; their language. ● *adjective* of this people or language.

sloven /ˈslʌv(ə)n/ *noun* untidy or careless person.

Slovene /ˈsləʊviːn/ (also **Slovenian** /-ˈviːnɪən/) ● *noun* member of Slavonic people in Slovenia; their language. ● *adjective* of Slovenia or its people or language.

slovenly ● *adjective* careless and untidy, unmethodical. ● *adverb* in a slovenly way. □ **slovenliness** *noun*.

slow /sləʊ/ ● *adjective* taking relatively long time to do thing(s); acting, moving, or done without speed; not conducive to speed; (of clock etc.) showing earlier than correct time; dull-witted, stupid; tedious; slack, sluggish; (of fire or oven) not very hot; (of photographic film) needing long exposure; reluctant. ● *adverb* slowly. ● *verb* (usually + *down*, *up*) (cause to) move, act, or work with reduced speed or vigour. □ **slowcoach** *colloquial* slow person; **slow motion** speed of film or videotape in which actions etc. appear much slower than usual, simulation of this in real action; **slow-worm** small European legless lizard. □ **slowly** *adverb*; **slowness** *noun*.

sludge *noun* thick greasy mud or sediment; sewage. □ **sludgy** *adjective*.

slug[1] *noun* slimy shell-less mollusc; bullet, esp. irregularly shaped; missile for airgun; *Printing* metal bar for spacing; mouthful of liquor.

slug[2] *US* ● *verb* (**-gg-**) hit hard. ● *noun* hard blow.

sluggard /'slʌgəd/ *noun* lazy person.

sluggish *adjective* inert, slow-moving. □ **sluggishly** *adverb*; **sluggishness** *noun*.

sluice /slu:s/ ● *noun* (also **sluice-gate**, **-valve**) sliding gate or other contrivance for regulating volume or flow of water; water so regulated; (also **sluice-way**) artificial water-channel; place for or act of rinsing. ● *verb* (**-cing**) provide or wash with sluice(s); rinse; (of water) rush out (as if) from sluice.

slum ● *noun* house unfit for human habitation; (often in *plural*) overcrowded and squalid district in city. ● *verb* (**-mm-**) visit slums, esp. out of curiosity. □ **slum it** *colloquial* put up with conditions less comfortable than usual. □ **slummy** *adjective*.

slumber /'slʌmbə/ *verb & noun poetical* sleep.

slump ● *noun* sudden severe or prolonged fall in prices and trade. ● *verb* undergo slump; sit or fall heavily or limply.

slung *past & past participle of* SLING[1].

slunk *past & past participle of* SLINK.

slur ● *verb* (**-rr-**) sound (words, musical notes, etc.) so that they run into one another; *archaic or US* put slur on (person, character); (usually + *over*) pass over lightly. ● *noun* imputation of wrongdoing; act of slurring; *Music* curved line joining notes to be slurred.

slurp *colloquial* ● *verb* eat or drink noisily. ● *noun* sound of slurping.

slurry /'slʌrɪ/ *noun* thin semi-liquid cement, mud, manure, etc.

slush *noun* thawing snow; silly sentimentality. □ **slush fund** reserve fund, esp. for bribery. □ **slushy** *adjective* (**-ier, -iest**).

slut *noun derogatory* slovenly or promiscuous woman. □ **sluttish** *adjective*.

sly *adjective* (**-er, -est**) crafty, wily; secretive; knowing, insinuating. □ **on the sly** secretly. □ **slyly** *adverb*; **slyness** *noun*.

smack[1] ● *noun* sharp slap or blow; hard hit; loud kiss; loud sharp sound. ● *verb* slap; part (lips) noisily in anticipation of food; move, hit, etc. with smack. ● *adverb colloquial* with a smack; suddenly, violently; exactly.

smack[2] (+ *of*) ● *verb* taste of, suggest. ● *noun* flavour or suggestion of.

smack[3] *noun* single-masted sailing boat.

smack[4] *noun slang* heroin, other hard drug.

smacker *noun slang* loud kiss; £1, *US* $1.

small /smɔ:l/ ● *adjective* not large or big; not great in importance, amount, number, etc.; not much; insignificant; of small particles; on small scale; poor, humble; mean; young. ● *noun* slenderest part, esp. of back; (in *plural*) *colloquial* underwear, esp. as laundry. ● *adverb* into small pieces. □ **small arms** portable firearms; **small change** coins, not notes; **small fry** unimportant people, children; **smallholding** agricultural holding smaller than farm; **small hours** night-time after midnight; **small-minded** petty, narrow in outlook; **smallpox** *historical* acute contagious disease with fever and pustules usually leaving scars; **small print** matter printed small, esp. limitations in contract; **small talk** trivial social conversation; **small-time** *colloquial* unimportant, petty. □ **smallness** *noun*.

smarmy /'smɑ:mɪ/ *adjective* (**-ier, -iest**) *colloquial* ingratiating. □ **smarmily** *adverb*; **smarminess** *noun*.

smart ● *adjective* well-groomed, neat; bright and fresh in appearance; stylish, fashionable; *esp. US* clever, ingenious, quickwitted; quick, brisk; painfully severe, sharp, vigorous. ● *verb* feel or give pain; rankle; (+ *for*) suffer consequences of. ● *noun* sharp bodily or mental pain, stinging sensation. ● *adverb* smartly. □ **smartish** *adjective & adverb*; **smartly** *adverb*; **smartness** *noun*.

smarten *verb* (usually + *up*) make or become smart.

smash ● *verb* (often + *up*) break to pieces; bring or come to destruction, defeat, or disaster; (+ *into, through*) move forcefully; (+ *in*) break with crushing blow; hit (ball) hard, esp. downwards. ● *noun* act or sound of

smashing; (in full **smash hit**) very successful play, song, etc. ● *adverb* with smash. □ **smash-and-grab** robbery with goods snatched from broken shop window etc.

smashing *adjective colloquial* excellent, wonderful.

smattering /'smætərɪŋ/ *noun* slight knowledge.

smear /smɪə/ ● *verb* daub or mark with grease etc.; smudge; defame. ● *noun* action of smearing; material smeared on microscope slide etc. for examination; specimen of this. □ **smear test** cervical smear. □ **smeary** *adjective*.

smell ● *noun* sense of odour perception; property perceived by this; unpleasant odour; act of inhaling to ascertain smell. ● *verb* (*past & past participle* **smelt** or **smelled**) perceive or examine by smell; stink; seem by smell to be; (+ *of*) emit smell of, suggest; detect; have or use sense of smell. □ **smelling salts** sharp-smelling substances sniffed to relieve faintness.

smelly *adjective* (**-ier**, **-iest**) strong- or evil-smelling.

smelt[1] *verb* melt (ore) to extract metal; obtain (metal) thus. □ **smelter** *noun*.

smelt[2] *past & past participle* of SMELL.

smelt[3] *noun* (*plural* same or **-s**) small edible green and silver fish.

smilax /'smaɪlæks/ *noun* any of several climbing plants.

smile ● *verb* (**-ling**) have or assume facial expression of amusement or pleasure, with ends of lips turned upward; express by smiling; give (smile); (+ *on*, *upon*) favour. ● *noun* act of smiling; smiling expression or aspect.

smirch *verb & noun* stain, smear.

smirk ● *noun* conceited or silly smile. ● *verb* give smirk.

smite *verb* (**-ting;** *past* **smote;** *past participle* **smitten** /'smɪt(ə)n/) *archaic or literary* hit, chastise, defeat; (in *passive*) affect strongly, seize.

smith *noun* blacksmith; worker in metal, craftsman.

smithereens /smɪðə'riːnz/ *plural noun* small fragments.

smithy /'smɪðɪ/ *noun* (*plural* **-ies**) blacksmith's workshop, forge.

smitten *past participle* of SMITE.

smock ● *noun* loose shirtlike garment, often adorned with smocking. ● *verb* adorn with smocking.

smocking *noun* ornamentation on cloth made by gathering it tightly with stitches.

smog *noun* dense smoky fog. □ **smoggy** *adjective* (**-ier**, **-iest**).

smoke ● *noun* visible vapour from burning substance; act of smoking tobacco etc.; *colloquial* cigarette, cigar. ● *verb* (**-king**) inhale and exhale smoke of (cigarette etc.); do this habitually; emit smoke or visible vapour; darken or preserve with smoke. □ **smoke bomb** bomb emitting dense smoke on bursting; **smoke-free** free from smoke, where smoking is not permitted; **smoke out** drive out by means of smoke, drive out of hiding etc.; **smokescreen** cloud of smoke concealing esp. military operations, ruse for disguising activities; **smokestack** funnel of locomotive or steamship, tall chimney.

smoker *noun* person who habitually smokes tobacco; compartment on train where smoking is permitted.

smoky *adjective* (**-ier**, **-iest**) emitting, filled with, or obscured by, smoke; coloured by or like smoke; having flavour of smoked food.

smolder US = SMOULDER.

smooch /smuːtʃ/ ● *verb* kiss and caress. ● *noun* smooching.

smooth /smuːð/ ● *adjective* having even surface; free from projections and roughness; that can be traversed uninterrupted; (of sea etc.) calm, flat; (of journey etc.) easy; not harsh in sound or taste; conciliatory; slick; not jerky. ● *verb* (often + *out*, *down*) make or become smooth; (often + *out*, *down*, *over*, *away*) get rid of (differences, faults, etc.). □ **smooth touch** noun smoothing touch or stroke. □ **smooth-tongued** insincerely flattering. □ **smoothly** *adverb*; **smoothness** *noun*.

smorgasbord /'smɔːɡəsbɔːd/ *noun* Swedish hors d'oeuvres; buffet meal with various esp. savoury dishes.

smote *past* of SMITE.

smother /'smʌðə/ *verb* suffocate, stifle; (+ *in*, *with*) overwhelm or cover with (kisses, gifts, etc.); extinguish (fire) by heaping with ashes etc.; have difficulty breathing; (often + *up*) suppress, conceal.

smoulder /'sməʊldə/ (*US* **smolder**)
● *verb* burn without flame or internally; (of person) show silent emotion. ● *noun* smouldering.

smudge ● *noun* blurred or smeared line, mark, etc. ● *verb* (**-ging**) make smudge on or with; become smeared or blurred. □ **smudgy** *adjective*.

smug *adjective* (**-gg-**) self-satisfied. □ **smugly** *adverb*; **smugness** *noun*.

smuggle /'smʌg(ə)l/ *verb* (**-ling**) import or export illegally, esp. without paying duties; convey secretly. □ **smuggler** *noun*; **smuggling** *noun*.

smut ● *noun* small piece of soot; spot or smudge made by this; obscene talk, pictures, or stories; fungous disease of cereals. ● *verb* (**-tt-**) mark with smut(s). □ **smutty** *adjective* (**-ier, -iest**).

snack *noun* light, casual, or hasty meal. □ **snack bar** place where snacks are sold.

snaffle /'snæf(ə)l/ ● *noun* (in full **snaffle-bit**) simple bridle-bit without curb. ● *verb* (**-ling**) *colloquial* steal, seize.

snag ● *noun* unexpected obstacle or drawback; jagged projection; tear in material etc. ● *verb* (**-gg-**) catch or tear on snag.

snail *noun* slow-moving mollusc with spiral shell.

snake ● *noun* long limbless reptile; (also **snake in the grass**) traitor, secret enemy. ● *verb* (**-king**) move or twist like a snake. □ **snakes and ladders** board game with counters moved up 'ladders' and down 'snakes'; **snakeskin** *noun* skin of snake, *adjective* made of snakeskin.

snaky *adjective* of or like a snake; sinuous; treacherous.

snap ● *verb* (**-pp-**) break sharply; (cause to) emit sudden sharp sound; open or close with snapping sound; speak irritably; (often + *at*) make sudden audible bite; move quickly; photograph. ● *noun* act or sound of snapping; crisp biscuit; snapshot; (in full **cold snap**) sudden brief period of cold weather; card game in which players call 'snap' when two similar cards are exposed; vigour. ● *adverb* with snapping sound. ● *adjective* done without forethought. □ **snapdragon** plant with two-lipped flowers; **snap-fastener** press-stud; **snap out of** *slang* get out of (mood etc.) by sudden effort; **snapshot** informal or casual photograph; **snap up** accept (offer etc.) hastily or eagerly.

snapper *noun* any of several edible marine fish.

snappish *adjective* curt, ill-tempered.

snappy *adjective* (**-ier, -iest**) *colloquial* brisk, lively; neat and elegant; snappish. □ **snappily** *adverb*.

snare /sneə/ ● *noun* trap, esp. with noose, for birds or animals; trap, trick, temptation; (in *singular* or *plural*) twisted strings of gut, hide, or wire stretched across lower head of side drum to produce rattle; (in full **snare drum**) side drum with snares. ● *verb* (**-ring**) catch in snare, trap.

snarl¹ ● *verb* growl with bared teeth; speak angrily. ● *noun* act or sound of snarling.

snarl² ● *verb* (often + *up*) twist, entangle, hamper movement of (traffic etc.), become entangled. ● *noun* tangle.

snatch ● *verb* (often + *away, from*) seize quickly, eagerly, or unexpectedly; steal by grabbing; *slang* kidnap; (+ *at*) try to seize, take eagerly. ● *noun* act of snatching; fragment of song, talk, etc.; short spell of activity etc.

snazzy /'snæzɪ/ *adjective* (**-ier, -iest**) *slang* smart, stylish, showy.

sneak ● *verb* go or convey furtively; *slang* steal unobserved; *slang* tell tales; (as **sneaking** *adjective*) furtive, persistent and puzzling. ● *noun* mean-spirited, underhand person; *slang* tell-tale. ● *adjective* acting or done without warning, secret. □ **sneak-thief** person who steals without breaking in. □ **sneaky** *adjective* (**-ier, -iest**).

sneaker *noun slang* soft-soled shoe.

sneer ● *noun* derisive smile or remark. ● *verb* (often + *at*) make sneer; utter with sneer. □ **sneering** *adjective*; **sneeringly** *adverb*.

sneeze ● *noun* sudden involuntary explosive expulsion of air from irritated nostrils. ● *verb* (**-zing**) make sneeze.

☐ **not to be sneezed at** *colloquial* worth having or considering.

snick ● *verb* make small notch or cut in; *Cricket* deflect (ball) slightly with bat. ● *noun* such notch or deflection.

snicker /ˈsnɪkə/ *noun & verb* snigger.

snide *adjective* sneering, slyly derogatory.

sniff ● *verb* inhale air audibly through nose; (often + *up*) draw in through nose; smell scent of by sniffing. ● *noun* act or sound of sniffing. ☐ **sniff at** show contempt for; **sniffer-dog** *colloquial* dog trained to find drugs or explosives by scent.

sniffle /ˈsnɪf(ə)l/ ● *verb* (**-ling**) sniff repeatedly or slightly. ● *noun* act of sniffling; (in *singular* or *plural*) cold in the head causing sniffling.

snifter /ˈsnɪftə/ *noun slang* small alcoholic drink.

snigger /ˈsnɪɡə/ ● *noun* half-suppressed laugh. ● *verb* utter snigger.

snip ● *verb* (**-pp-**) cut with scissors etc., esp. in small quick strokes. ● *noun* act of snipping; piece snipped off; *slang* something easily done, bargain.

snipe ● *noun* (*plural* same or **-s**) wading bird with long straight bill. ● *verb* (**-ping**) fire shots from hiding usually at long range; (often + *at*) make sly critical attack. ☐ **sniper** *noun*.

snippet /ˈsnɪpɪt/ *noun* small piece cut off; (usually in *plural*) scrap of information etc., short extract from book etc.

snitch ● *verb slang* steal; (often + *on*) inform on person. ● *noun* informer.

snivel /ˈsnɪv(ə)l/ ● *verb* (**-ll-**; *US* **-l-**) sniffle; weep with sniffling; show maudlin emotion. ● *noun* act of snivelling.

snob *noun* person who despises people with inferior social position, wealth, intellect, tastes, etc. ☐ **snobbery** *noun*; **snobbish** *adjective*; **snobby** *adjective* (**-ier, -iest**).

snood /snuːd/ *noun* woman's loose hairnet.

snook /snuːk/ *noun slang* contemptuous gesture with thumb to nose and fingers spread. ☐ **cock a snook (at)** make this gesture (at), show contempt (for).

snooker /ˈsnuːkə/ ● *noun* game played on oblong cloth-covered table with 1 white, 15 red, and 6 other coloured balls; position in this game where direct shot would give points to opponent. ● *verb* subject (player) to snooker; (esp. as **snookered** *adjective*) *slang* thwart, defeat.

snoop /snuːp/ *colloquial* ● *verb* pry into another's affairs; (often + *about, around*) investigate (often stealthily) transgressions of rules etc. ● *noun* act of snooping. ☐ **snooper** *noun*.

snooty /ˈsnuːtɪ/ *adjective* (**-ier, -iest**) *colloquial* supercilious, snobbish. ☐ **snootily** *adverb*.

snooze /snuːz/ *colloquial* ● *noun* short sleep, nap. ● *verb* (**-zing**) take snooze.

snore ● *noun* snorting or grunting sound of breathing during sleep. ● *verb* (**-ring**) make this sound.

snorkel /ˈsnɔːk(ə)l/ ● *noun* device for supplying air to underwater swimmer or submerged submarine. ● *verb* (**-ll-**; *US* **-l-**) use snorkel.

snort ● *noun* explosive sound made by driving breath violently through nose, esp. by horses, or by humans to show contempt, incredulity, etc.; *colloquial* small drink of liquor; *slang* inhaled dose of powdered cocaine. ● *verb* make snort; *slang* inhale (esp. cocaine); express or utter with snort.

snot *noun slang* nasal mucus.

snotty *adjective* (**-ier, -iest**) *slang* running or covered with nasal mucus; snooty; contemptible. ☐ **snottily** *adverb*; **snottiness** *noun*.

snout /snaʊt/ *noun* projecting nose (and mouth) of animal; *derogatory* person's nose; pointed front of thing.

snow /snəʊ/ ● *noun* frozen vapour falling to earth in light white flakes; fall or layer of this; thing resembling snow in whiteness or texture etc.; *slang* cocaine. ● *verb* (after *it*) snow falls; (+ *in, over, up*, etc.) confine or block with snow. ☐ **snowball** *noun* snow pressed into ball for throwing in play, *verb* throw or pelt with snowballs, increase rapidly; **snow-blind** temporarily blinded by glare from snow; **snowbound** prevented by snow from going out; **snowcap** snow-covered mountain peak; **snowdrift** bank of snow piled up by wind; **snowdrop** spring-flowering plant with white drooping flowers; **snowed under** overwhelmed, esp. with work; **snowflake** each of the flakes in which snow falls; **snow goose** white Arctic goose; **snowline** level above which snow never melts entirely; **snowman** figure made of snow; **snowplough** device for clearing road of snow; **snowshoe** racket-shaped attachment to boot for walking on surface of snow; **snowstorm** heavy fall of snow, esp. with wind; **snow white** pure white. □ **snowy** *adjective* (**-ier, iest**).

SNP *abbreviation* Scottish National Party.

Snr. *abbreviation* Senior.

snub ● *verb* (**-bb-**) rebuff or humiliate in a sharp or cutting way. ● *noun* snubbing, rebuff. ● *adjective* (of nose) short and turned up.

snuff[1] ● *noun* charred part of candle-wick. ● *verb* trim snuff from (candle). □ **snuff it** *slang* die; **snuff out** extinguish (candle), put an end to (hopes etc.).

snuff[2] ● *noun* powdered tobacco or medicine taken by sniffing. ● *verb* take snuff.

snuffle /'snʌf(ə)l/ ● *verb* (**-ling**) make sniffing sounds; speak nasally; breathe noisily, esp. with blocked nose. ● *noun* snuffling sound or speech.

snug ● *adjective* (**-gg-**) cosy, comfortable, sheltered; close-fitting. ● *noun* small room in pub. □ **snugly** *adverb*.

snuggle /'snʌg(ə)l/ *verb* (**-ling**) settle or move into warm comfortable position.

so[1] /səʊ/ ● *adverb* to such an extent, in this or that manner or state; also; indeed, actually; very; thus. ● *conjunction* (often + *that*) consequently, in order that; and then; (introducing question) after that. □ **so-and-so** particular but unspecified person or thing, *colloquial* objectionable person; **so as to** in order to; **so-called** commonly called but often incorrectly; **so long** *colloquial* goodbye; **so so** *colloquial* only moderately good or well.

so[2] = SOH.

soak ● *verb* make or become thoroughly wet through saturation; (of rain etc.) drench; (+ *in*, *up*) absorb (liquid, knowledge, etc.); (+ *in*, *into*, *through*) penetrate by saturation; *colloquial* extort money from; *colloquial* drink heavily.

● *noun* soaking; *colloquial* hard drinker. □ **soakaway** arrangement for disposal of waste water by percolation through soil.

soaking *adjective* (in full **soaking wet**) wet through.

soap ● *noun* cleansing substance yielding lather when rubbed in water; *colloquial* soap opera. ● *verb* apply soap to. □ **soapbox** makeshift stand for street orator; **soap opera** domestic broadcast serial; **soap powder** powdered soap usually with additives, for washing clothes etc.; **soapstone** steatite; **soapsuds** suds.

soapy *adjective* (**-ier, -iest**) of or like soap; containing or smeared with soap; unctuous, flattering.

soar /sɔː/ *verb* fly or rise high; reach high level or standard; fly without flapping wings or using motor power.

sob ● *verb* (**-bb-**) inhale convulsively, usually with weeping; utter with sobs ● *noun* act or sound of sobbing. □ **sob story** *colloquial* story or explanation appealing for sympathy.

sober /'səʊbə/ *adjective* (**-er, -est**) not drunk; not given to drink; moderate, tranquil, serious; (of colour) dull. ● *verb* (often + *down*, *up*) make or become sober. □ **soberly** *adverb*.

sobriety /sə'braɪɪtɪ/ *noun* being sober.

sobriquet /'səʊbrɪkeɪ/ *noun* (also **soubriquet** /'suː-/) nickname.

Soc. *abbreviation* Socialist; Society.

soccer /'sɒkə/ *noun* Association football.

sociable /'səʊʃəb(ə)l/ *adjective* liking company, gregarious, friendly □ **sociability** *noun*; **sociably** *adverb*.

social /'səʊʃ(ə)l/ ● *adjective* of society or its organization, esp. of relations of (classes of) people; living in communities; gregarious. ● *noun* social gathering □ **social science** study of society and social relationships; **social security** state assistance to the poor and unemployed; **social services** welfare services provided by the State, esp. education, health care, and housing; **social work** professional or voluntary work with disadvantaged groups; **social worker** *noun*. □ **socially** *adverb*.

socialism *noun* political and economic theory advocating state ownership and control of means of production, distribution, and exchange; social system based on this. □ **socialist** *noun & adjective*; **socialistic** /-'lɪs-/ *adjective*.

socialite /'səʊʃəlaɪt/ *noun* person moving in fashionable society.

socialize /'səʊʃəlaɪz/ *verb* (also **-ise**) (**-zing** or **-sing**) mix socially; make social; organize in a socialistic way.

society /sə'saɪətɪ/ *noun* (*plural* **-ies**) organized and interdependent community; system and organization of this; (members of) aristocratic part of this; mixing with other people, companionship, company; association, club. □ **societal** *adjective*.

sociology /səʊsɪ'ɒlədʒɪ/ *noun* study of society and social problems. □ **sociological** /-ə'lɒdʒ-/ *adjective*; **sociologist** *noun*.

sock[1] *noun* knitted covering for foot and lower leg; insole.

sock[2] *colloquial* ● *verb* hit hard. ● *noun* hard blow. □ **sock it to** attack or address vigorously.

socket /'sɒkɪt/ *noun* hollow for thing to fit into etc., esp. device receiving electric plug, light bulb, etc.

Socratic /sə'krætɪk/ *adjective* of Socrates or his philosophy.

sod *noun* turf, piece of turf; surface of ground.

soda /'səʊdə/ *noun* any of various compounds of sodium in common use; (in full **soda water**) effervescent water used esp. with spirits etc. as drink. □ **soda fountain** device supplying soda water, shop or counter with this.

sodden /'sɒd(ə)n/ *adjective* saturated, soaked through; stupid, dull, etc. with drunkenness.

sodium /'səʊdɪəm/ *noun* soft silver-white metallic element. □ **sodium bicarbonate** white compound used in baking-powder; **sodium chloride** common salt; **sodium lamp** lamp using sodium vapour and giving yellow light; **sodium nitrate** white powdery compound in fertilizers etc.

sofa /'səʊfə/ *noun* long upholstered seat with raised back and ends. □ **sofa bed** sofa that can be converted into bed.

soffit /'sɒfɪt/ *noun* undersurface of arch, lintel, etc.

soft ● *adjective* not hard, easily cut or dented, malleable; (of cloth etc.) smooth, fine, not rough; mild; (of water) low in mineral salts which prevent lathering; not brilliant or glaring; not strident or loud; sibilant; not sharply defined; gentle, conciliatory, compassionate, sympathetic; feeble, half-witted, silly, sentimental; *colloquial* easy; (of drug) not highly addictive. ● *adverb* softly. □ **have a soft spot for** be fond of; **softball** form of baseball with softer larger ball; **soft-boiled** (of egg) boiled leaving yolk soft; **soft-centred** having soft centre, soft-hearted; **soft drink** non-alcoholic drink; **soft fruit** small stoneless fruit; **soft furnishings** curtains, rugs, etc.; **soft-hearted** tender, compassionate; **soft option** easier alternative; **soft palate** back part of palate; **soft pedal** *noun* pedal on piano softening tone; **soft-pedal** *verb* refrain from emphasizing; **soft sell** restrained salesmanship; **soft soap** *colloquial* persuasive flattery; **soft-spoken** having gentle voice; **soft target** vulnerable person or thing; **soft touch** *colloquial* gullible person, esp. over money; **software** computer programs; **softwood** wood of coniferous tree. □ **softly** *adverb*; **softness** *noun*.

soften /'sɒf(ə)n/ *verb* make or become soft(er); (often + *up*) reduce strength, resistance, etc. of. □ **softener** *noun*.

softie *noun* (also **softy**) (*plural* **-ies**) *colloquial* weak, silly, or soft-hearted person.

soggy /'sɒgɪ/ *adjective* (**-ier**, **-iest**) sodden, waterlogged.

soh *noun* (also **so**) *Music* fifth note of scale in tonic sol-fa.

soil[1] *noun* upper layer of earth, in which plants grow; ground, territory.

soil[2] ● *verb* make dirty, smear, stain; defile; discredit. ● *noun* dirty mark; filth, refuse. □ **soil pipe** discharge-pipe of lavatory.

soirée /'swɑːreɪ/ *noun* evening party.

sojourn /'sɒdʒ(ə)n/ ● *noun* temporary stay. ● *verb* stay temporarily.

sola /'səʊlə/ *noun* pithy-stemmed E. Indian swamp plant. □ **sola topi** sun-helmet made from pith of this.

solace /'sɒləs/ ● *noun* comfort in distress or disappointment. ● *verb* (**-cing**) give solace to.

solan /ˈsəʊlən/ *noun* (in full **solan goose**) large gooselike gannet.

solar /ˈsəʊlə/ *adjective* of or reckoned by sun. □ **solar battery**, **cell** device converting solar radiation into electricity; **solar panel** panel absorbing sun's rays as energy source; **solar plexus** complex of nerves at pit of stomach; **solar system** sun and the planets etc. whose motion is governed by it.

solarium /səˈleərɪəm/ *noun* (*plural* **-ria**) room with sunlamps, glass roof, etc.

sold past & past participle of SELL.

solder /ˈsɒldə/ ● *noun* fusible alloy used for joining metals, wires, etc. ● *verb* join with solder. □ **soldering iron** tool for melting and applying solder.

soldier /ˈsəʊldʒə/ ● *noun* member of army, esp. (in full **common soldier**) private or NCO; *colloquial* bread finger, esp. for dipping in egg. ● *verb* serve as soldier. □ **soldier on** *colloquial* persevere doggedly. □ **soldierly** *adjective*.

soldiery *noun* soldiers collectively.

sole[1] ● *noun* undersurface of foot; part of shoe, sock, etc. below foot, esp. part other than heel; lower surface or base of plough, golf-club head, etc. ● *verb* (**-ling**) provide with sole.

sole[2] *noun* (*plural* same or **-s**) type of flatfish.

sole[3] *adjective* one and only single; exclusive. □ **solely** *adverb*.

solecism /ˈsɒlɪsɪz(ə)m/ *noun* mistake of grammar or idiom; offence against etiquette.

solemn /ˈsɒləm/ *adjective* serious and dignified; formal; awe-inspiring; of cheerless manner; grave. □ **solemnness** *noun*; **solemnity** /səˈlem-/ *noun* (*plural* **-ies**); **solemnly** *adverb*.

solemnize /ˈsɒləmnaɪz/ *verb* (also **-ise**) (**-zing** or **-sing**) duly perform (esp. marriage ceremony); make solemn. □ **solemnization** *noun*.

solenoid /ˈsəʊlənɔɪd/ *noun* cylindrical coil of wire acting as magnet when carrying electric current.

sol-fa /ˈsɒlfɑː/ *noun* system of syllables representing musical notes.

solicit /səˈlɪsɪt/ *verb* (**-t-**) seek repeatedly or earnestly; (of prostitute) accost (man) concerning sexual activity. □ **solicitation** *noun*.

solicitor /səˈlɪsɪtə/ *noun* lawyer qualified to advise clients and instruct barristers.

solicitous /səˈlɪsɪtəs/ *adjective* showing concern; (+ *to do*) eager, anxious. □ **solicitously** *adverb*.

solicitude /səˈlɪsɪtjuːd/ *noun* being solicitous.

solid /ˈsɒlɪd/ ● *adjective* (**-er**, **-est**) of firm and stable shape, not liquid or fluid; of such material throughout, not hollow; alike all through; sturdily built, not flimsy; 3-dimensional; of solids; sound, reliable; uninterrupted; unanimous. ● *noun* solid substance or body; (in *plural*) solid food. ● *adverb* solidly. □ **solid-state** using electronic properties of solids to replace those of valves. □ **solidity** /səˈlɪd-/ *noun*; **solidly** *adverb*; **solidness** *noun*.

solidarity /sɒlɪˈdærɪtɪ/ *noun* unity, esp. political or in industrial dispute; mutual dependence.

solidify /səˈlɪdɪfaɪ/ *verb* (**-ies**, **-ied**) make or become solid.

soliloquy /səˈlɪləkwɪ/ *noun* (*plural* **-quies**) talking without or regardless of hearers; this part of a play. □ **soliloquize** *verb* (also **-ise**) (**-zing** or **-sing**).

solipsism /ˈsɒlɪpsɪz(ə)m/ *noun* theory that self is all that exists or can be known.

solitaire /ˈsɒlɪteə/ *noun* jewel set by itself; ring etc. with this; game for one player who removes pegs etc. from board on jumping others over them; *US* card game for one person.

solitary /ˈsɒlɪtərɪ/ ● *adjective* living or being alone; not gregarious; lonely; secluded; single. ● *noun* (*plural* **-ies**) recluse; *colloquial* solitary confinement. □ **solitary confinement** isolation in separate prison cell.

solitude /ˈsɒlɪtjuːd/ *noun* being solitary; solitary place.

solo /ˈsəʊləʊ/ ● *noun* (*plural* **-s**) piece of music or dance performed by one person; thing done by one person, esp. unaccompanied flight; (in full **solo whist**) type of whist in which one player may oppose the others. ● *verb* (**-es**, **-ed**) perform a solo. ● *adjective & adverb* unaccompanied, alone.

soloist /ˈsəʊləʊɪst/ *noun* performer of solo.

solstice /ˈsɒlstɪs/ *noun* either of two times (**summer, winter solstice**) when sun is farthest from equator.

soluble /ˈsɒljʊb(ə)l/ *adjective* that can be dissolved or solved. □ **solubility** *noun*.

solution /səˈluːʃ(ə)n/ *noun* (means of) solving a problem; conversion of solid or gas into liquid by mixture with liquid; state or substance resulting from this; dissolving, being dissolved.

solve *verb* (**-ving**) answer, remove, or deal with (problem). □ **solvable** *adjective*.

solvency /ˈsɒlvənsɪ/ *noun* being financially solvent.

solvent /ˈsɒlv(ə)nt/ • *adjective* able to pay one's debts; able to dissolve or form solution. • *noun* solvent liquid etc.

somatic /səˈmætɪk/ *adjective* of the body, not of the mind.

sombre /ˈsɒmbə/ *adjective* (also *US* **somber**) dark, gloomy, dismal. □ **sombrely** *adverb*; **sombreness** *noun*.

sombrero /sɒmˈbreərəʊ/ *noun* (*plural* **-s**) broad-brimmed hat worn esp. in Latin America.

some /sʌm/ • *adjective* unspecified amount or number of; unknown, unspecified; approximately; considerable; at least a small amount of; such to a certain extent; *colloquial* a remarkable. • *pronoun* some people or things, some number or amount. • *adverb* *colloquial* to some extent. □ **somebody** *pronoun* some person, some important person; **someday** at some time in the future; **somehow** for some reason, in some way, by some means; **someone** somebody; **something** unspecified or unknown thing, unexpressed or intangible quantity or quality, *colloquial* notable person or thing; **sometime** at some time, former(ly); **sometimes** occasionally; **somewhat** to some extent; **somewhere** (in or to) some place.

somersault /ˈsʌməsɒlt/ • *noun* leap or roll in which one turns head over heels. • *verb* perform somersault.

somnambulism /sɒmˈnæmbjʊlɪz(ə)m/ *noun* sleepwalking. □ **somnambulant** *adjective*; **somnambulist** *noun*.

somnolent /ˈsɒmnələnt/ *adjective* sleepy, drowsy; inducing drowsiness. □ **somnolence** *noun*.

son /sʌn/ *noun* male in relation to his parent(s); male descendant; (+ *of*) male member of (family etc.); male inheritor of a quality etc.; *form of address, esp. to boy.* □ **son-in-law** (*plural* **sons-in-law**) daughter's husband.

sonar /ˈsəʊnɑː/ *noun* system for detecting objects under water by reflected sound; apparatus for this.

sonata /səˈnɑːtə/ *noun* musical composition for one or two instruments in several related movements.

song *noun* words set to music or for singing; vocal music; composition suggestive of song; cry of some birds. □ **for a song** *colloquial* very cheaply; **songbird** bird with musical call; **song thrush** common thrush; **songwriter** writer of (music for) songs.

songster /ˈsɒŋstə/ *noun* (*feminine* **songstress**) singer; songbird.

sonic /ˈsɒnɪk/ *adjective* of or using sound or sound waves. □ **sonic bang, boom** noise made by aircraft flying faster than sound.

sonnet /ˈsɒnɪt/ *noun* poem of 14 lines with fixed rhyme scheme.

sonny /ˈsʌnɪ/ *noun* *colloquial familiar form of address to young boy.*

sonorous /ˈsɒnərəs/ *adjective* having a loud, full, or deep sound; (of speech etc.) imposing. □ **sonority** /səˈnɒr-/ *noun* (*plural* **-ies**).

soon /suːn/ *adverb* in a short time; relatively early; readily, willingly. □ **sooner or later** at some future time. □ **soonish** *adverb*.

soot /sʊt/ *noun* black powdery deposit from smoke.

soothe /suːð/ *verb* (**-thing**) calm; soften, mitigate.

soothsayer /ˈsuːθseɪə/ *noun* seer, prophet.

sooty *adjective* (**-ier, -iest**) covered with soot; black, brownish black.

sop • *noun* thing given or done to pacify or bribe; piece of bread etc. dipped in gravy etc. • *verb* (**-pp-**) (+ *up*) soak up.

sophism /ˈsɒfɪz(ə)m/ *noun* false argument, esp. one meant to deceive.

sophist /ˈsɒfɪst/ *noun* captious or clever but fallacious reasoner. □ **sophistic** /səˈfɪs-/ *adjective*.

sophisticate /sə'fɪstɪkət/ *noun* sophisticated person.

sophisticated /sə'fɪstɪkeɪtɪd/ *adjective* worldly-wise, cultured, elegant; highly developed and complex. □ **sophistication** *noun*.

sophistry /'sɒfɪstrɪ/ *noun* (*plural* **-ies**) use of sophisms; a sophism.

sophomore /'sɒfəmɔː/ *noun US* second-year university or high-school student.

soporific /sɒpə'rɪfɪk/ ● *adjective* inducing sleep. ● *noun* soporific drug or influence. □ **soporifically** *adverb*.

sopping *adjective* drenched.

soppy *adjective* (**-ier**, **-iest**) *colloquial* mawkishly sentimental, silly.

soprano /sə'prɑːnəʊ/ ● *noun* (*plural* **-s**) highest singing voice; singer with this. ● *adjective* having range of soprano.

sorbet /'sɔːbeɪ/ *noun* water-ice; sherbet.

sorcerer /'sɔːsərə/ *noun* (*feminine* **sorceress**) magician, wizard. □ **sorcery** *noun* (*plural* **-ies**).

sordid /'sɔːdɪd/ *adjective* dirty, squalid; ignoble, mercenary. □ **sordidly** *adverb*; **sordidness** *noun*.

sore ● *adjective* painful; suffering pain; aggrieved, vexed; *archaic* grievous, severe. ● *noun* sore place, subject, etc. ● *adverb archaic* grievously, severely. □ **soreness** *noun*.

sorely *adverb* extremely.

sorghum /'sɔːgəm/ *noun* tropical cereal grass.

sorority /sə'rɒrɪtɪ/ *noun* (*plural* **-ies**) *US* female students' society in university or college.

sorrel[1] /'sɒr(ə)l/ *noun* sour-leaved herb.

sorrel[2] /'sɒr(ə)l/ ● *adjective* of light reddish-brown colour. ● *noun* this colour; sorrel animal, esp. horse.

sorrow /'sɒrəʊ/ ● *noun* mental distress caused by loss, disappointment, etc.; cause of sorrow. ● *verb* feel sorrow, mourn. □ **sorrowful** *adjective*.

sorry /'sɒrɪ/ *adjective* (**-ier**, **-iest**) pained, regretful, penitent; feeling pity; wretched.

sort ● *noun* class, kind; *colloquial* person of specified :.ind. ● *verb* (often + *out*, *over*) arrange systematically. □ **of a sort, of sorts** *colloquial* barely deserving the name; **out of sorts** slightly unwell, in low spirits; **sort out** separate into sorts, select from miscellaneous group, disentangle, put into order, solve, *colloquial* deal with or punish.

sortie /'sɔːtɪ/ ● *noun* sally, esp. from besieged garrison; operational military flight. ● *verb* (**sortieing**) make sortie.

SOS *noun* (*plural* **SOSs**) international code-signal of extreme distress; urgent appeal for help.

sot *noun* habitual drunkard. □ **sottish** *adjective*.

sotto voce /sɒtəʊ 'vəʊtʃɪ/ *adverb* in an undertone. [Italian]

sou /suː/ *noun* (*plural* **-s**) *colloquial* very small amount of money; *historical* former French coin of low value.

soubrette /suː'bret/ *noun* pert maidservant etc. in comedy; actress taking this part.

soubriquet = SOBRIQUET.

soufflé /'suːfleɪ/ *noun* light spongy dish made with stiffly beaten egg white.

sough /saʊ, sʌf/ ● *noun* moaning or rustling sound, e.g. of wind in trees. ● *verb* make this sound.

sought /sɔːt/ *past & past participle* of SEEK. □ **sought-after** much in demand.

souk /suːk/ *noun* market-place in Muslim countries.

soul /səʊl/ *noun* spiritual or immaterial part of person; moral, emotional, or intellectual nature of person; personification, pattern; an individual; animating or essential part; energy, intensity; soul music. □ **soul-destroying** tedious, monotonous; **soul mate** person ideally suited to another; **soul music** type of black American music; **soul-searching** introspection.

soulful *adjective* having, expressing, or evoking deep feeling. □ **soulfully** *adverb*.

soulless *adjective* lacking sensitivity or noble qualities; undistinguished, uninteresting.

sound[1] /saʊnd/ ● *noun* sensation produced in ear when surrounding air etc. vibrates; vibrations causing this; what is or may be heard; idea or impression given by words. ● *verb* (cause to) emit sound; utter, pronounce; convey specified impression; give audible signal for; test condition of by sound produced;

□ **sound barrier** high resistance of air to objects moving at speeds near that of sound; **sound effect** sound other than speech or music produced artificially for film, broadcast, etc.; **sounding-board** person etc. used to test or disseminate opinion(s), canopy projecting sound towards audience; **sound off** talk loudly, express one's opinions forcefully; **soundproof** *adjective* impervious to sound, *verb* make soundproof; **sound system** equipment for reproducing sound; **soundtrack** sound element of film or videotape, recording of this available separately; **sound wave** wave of compression and rarefaction by which sound is transmitted in air etc.

sound² /saʊnd/ ● *adjective* healthy, not diseased or rotten, uninjured; correct, well-founded; financially secure; undisturbed; thorough. ● *adverb* soundly. □ **soundly** *adverb*; **soundness** *noun*.

sound³ /saʊnd/ *verb* test depth or quality of bottom of (sea, river, etc.); (often + *out*) inquire (esp. discreetly) into views etc. of (person).

sound⁴ /saʊnd/ *noun* strait (of water).

sounding *noun* measurement of depth of water; (in *plural*) region near enough to shore for sounding; (in *plural*) cautious investigation.

soup /suːp/ ● *noun* liquid food made by boiling meat, fish, or vegetables. ● *verb* (usually + *up*) *colloquial* increase power of (engine), enliven. □ **in the soup** *colloquial* in difficulties; **soup-kitchen** place supplying free soup etc. to the poor; **soup-spoon** large round-bowled spoon. □ **soupy** *adjective* (-ier, -iest).

soupçon /ˈsuːpsɔ̃/ *noun* small quantity, trace.

sour /saʊə/ ● *adjective* having acid taste or smell (as) from unripeness or fermentation; morose, bitter; unpleasant, distasteful; (of soil) dank. ● *verb* make or become sour. □ **sour grapes** resentful disparagement of something coveted; **sourpuss** *colloquial* bad-tempered person. □ **sourly** *adverb*; **sourness** *noun*.

source /sɔːs/ *noun* place from which river or stream issues; place of origination; person, book, etc. providing information. □ **at source** at point of origin or issue.

souse /saʊs/ ● *verb* (-sing) immerse in pickle or other liquid; (as **soused** *adjective*) *colloquial* drunk; (usually + *in*) soak (thing). ● *noun* pickle made with salt; *US* food in pickle; a plunge or drenching in water.

soutane /suːˈtɑːn/ *noun* cassock of RC priest.

south /saʊθ/ ● *noun* point of horizon opposite north; corresponding compass point; (usually **the South**) southern part of world, country, town, etc. ● *adjective* towards, at, near, or facing south; (of wind) from south. ● *adverb* towards, at, or near south; (+ *of*) further south than. □ **southbound** travelling or leading south; **south-east, -west** point midway between south and east or west; **southpaw** *colloquial* left-handed person, esp. boxer; **south-south-east, south-south-west** point midway between south and south-east or south-west. □ **southward** *adjective*, *adverb*, & *noun*; **southwards** *adverb*.

southerly /ˈsʌðəlɪ/ *adjective* & *adverb* in southern position or direction; (of wind) from south.

southern /ˈsʌð(ə)n/ *adjective* of or in south. □ **Southern Cross** constellation with stars forming cross; **southern lights** aurora australis. □ **southernmost** *adjective*.

southerner *noun* native or inhabitant of south.

souvenir /suːvəˈnɪə/ *noun* memento of place, occasion, etc.

sou'wester /saʊˈwestə/ *noun* waterproof hat with broad flap at back; SW wind.

sovereign /ˈsɒvrɪn/ ● *noun* supreme ruler, esp. monarch; *historical* British gold coin nominally worth £1. ● *adjective* supreme; self-governing; royal; (of remedy etc.) effective. □ **sovereignty** *noun* (*plural* -ies).

Soviet /ˈsəʊvɪət/ *historical* ● *adjective* of USSR. ● *noun* citizen of USSR; (**soviet**) elected council in USSR.

sow¹ /saʊ/ *verb* (*past* **sowed**) *past participle* **sown** or **sowed**) scatter (seed) on or in earth, (often + *with*) plant with seed; initiate.

sow² /saʊ/ *noun* adult female pig.

soy *noun* (in full **soy sauce**) sauce made from pickled soya beans.

soya /'sɔɪə/ *noun* (in full **soya bean**) (seed of) leguminous plant yielding edible oil and flour.

sozzled /'sɒz(ə)ld/ *adjective colloquial* very drunk.

spa /spɑː/ *noun* curative mineral spring; resort with this.

space ● *noun* continuous expanse in which things exist and move; amount of this taken by thing or available; interval between points or objects; empty area; outdoor urban recreation area; outer space; interval of time; expanse of paper used in writing, available for advertising, etc.; blank between printed, typed, or written words etc.; *Printing* piece of metal separating words etc. ● *verb* (**-cing**) set or arrange at intervals; put spaces between. □ **space age** era of space travel; **space-age** very modern; **spacecraft** vehicle for travelling in outer space; **spaceman**, **spacewoman** astronaut; **space out** spread out (more) widely; **spaceship** spacecraft; **space shuttle** spacecraft for repeated use; **space station** artificial satellite as base for operations in outer space; **spacesuit** sealed pressurized suit for astronaut in space; **space-time** fusion of concepts of space and time as 4-dimensional continuum.

spacious /'speɪʃəs/ *adjective* having ample space, roomy. □ **spaciously** *adverb*; **spaciousness** *noun*.

spade[1] *noun* long-handled digging tool with rectangular metal blade. □ **spadework** hard preparatory work. □ **spadeful** *noun* (*plural* **-s**).

spade[2] *noun* playing card of suit denoted by black inverted heart-shaped figures with short stems.

spaghetti /spə'getɪ/ *noun* pasta in long thin strands. □ **spaghetti western** cowboy film made cheaply in Italy.

span[1] ● *noun* full extent from end to end; each part of bridge between supports; maximum lateral extent of aeroplane or its wing or of bird's wing etc.; distance between outstretched tips of thumb and little finger; 9 inches. ● *verb* (**-nn-**) extend from side to side or end to end of; bridge (river etc.).

span[2] *past of* SPIN.

spandrel /'spændrɪl/ *noun* space between curve of arch and surrounding rectangular moulding, or between curves of adjoining arches and moulding above.

spangle /'spæŋg(ə)l/ ● *noun* small piece of glittering material, esp. one of many used to ornament dress etc. ● *verb* (**-ling**) (esp. as **spangled** *adjective*) cover (as) with spangles.

Spaniard /'spænjəd/ *noun* native or national of Spain.

spaniel /'spænj(ə)l/ *noun* dog of breed with long silky coat and drooping ears.

Spanish /'spænɪʃ/ ● *adjective* of Spain. ● *noun* language of Spain.

spank *verb & noun* slap, esp. on buttocks.

spanker *noun Nautical* fore-and-aft sail on mizen-mast.

spanking ● *adjective* brisk; *colloquial* striking, excellent. ● *adverb colloquial* very. ● *noun* slapping on buttocks.

spanner /'spænə/ *noun* tool for turning nut on bolt etc. □ **spanner in the works** *colloquial* impediment.

spar[1] *noun* stout pole, esp. as ship's mast etc.

spar[2] ● *verb* (**-rr-**) make motions of boxing; argue. ● *noun* sparring; boxing match. □ **sparring partner** boxer employed to spar with another as training, person with whom one enjoys arguing.

spar[3] *noun* easily split crystalline mineral.

spare /speə/ ● *adjective* not required for ordinary or present use, extra; for emergency or occasional use; lean, thin; frugal. ● *noun* spare part. ● *verb* (**-ring**) afford to give, dispense with; refrain from killing, hurting, etc.; not inflict; be frugal or grudging of. □ **go spare** *colloquial* become very angry; **spare (person's) life** not kill; **spare part** duplicate, esp. as replacement; **spare-rib** closely trimmed rib of esp. pork; **spare time** leisure; **spare tyre** *colloquial* roll of fat round waist; **spare** left over. □ **sparely** *adverb*; **spareness** *noun*.

sparing *adjective* frugal, economical; restrained. □ **sparingly** *adverb*.

spark ● *noun* fiery particle of burning substance; (often + *of*) small amount; flash of light between electric conductors etc.; this for firing explosive mixture in internal-combustion engine;

flash of wit etc.; (also **bright spark**) lively or clever person. ● verb emit spark(s); (often + off) stir into activity, initiate. □ **spark plug**, **sparking plug** device for making spark in internal-combustion engine. □ **sparky** adjective.

sparkle /'spɑːk(ə)l/ ● verb (**-ling**) (seem to) emit sparks; glitter, scintillate; (of wine etc.) effervesce. ● noun glitter; lively quality. □ **sparkly** adjective.

sparkler noun sparkling firework; colloquial diamond.

sparrow /'spærəʊ/ noun small brownish-grey bird. □ **sparrowhawk** small hawk.

sparse /spɑːs/ adjective thinly scattered. □ **sparsely** adverb; **sparseness** noun; **sparsity** noun.

Spartan /'spɑːt(ə)n/ ● adjective of ancient Sparta; austere, rigorous. ● noun native or citizen of Sparta.

spasm /'spæz(ə)m/ noun sudden involuntary muscular contraction; convulsive movement or emotion etc.; (usually + of) colloquial brief spell.

spasmodic /spæz'mɒdɪk/ adjective of or in spasms, intermittent. □ **spasmodically** adverb.

spastic /'spæstɪk/ ● adjective of or having cerebral palsy. ● noun spastic person.

spat[1] past & past participle of SPIT[1].

spat[2] (usually in plural) historical short gaiter covering shoe.

spate noun river-flood; large amount or number (of similar events etc.).

spathe /speɪð/ noun large bract(s) enveloping flower-cluster.

spatial /'speɪʃ(ə)l/ adjective of space. □ **spatially** adverb.

spatter /'spætə/ ● verb splash or scatter in drips. ● noun splash; pattering.

spatula /'spætjʊlə/ noun broad-bladed implement used esp. by artists and in cookery.

spawn ● verb (of fish, frog, etc.) produce (eggs); be produced as eggs or young; produce or generate in large numbers. ● noun eggs of fish, frogs, etc.; white fibrous matter from which fungi grow.

spay verb sterilize (female animal) by removing ovaries.

speak verb (past **spoke**; past participle **spoken** /'spəʊk(ə)n/) utter words in ordinary way; utter (words, the truth, etc.); converse; (+ of, about) mention; (+ for) act as spokesman for; (+ to) speak with reference to or in support of; deliver speech; (be able to) use (specified language) in speaking; convey idea; (usually + to) affect. □ **speak for itself** be sufficient evidence; **speaking clock** telephone service announcing correct time; **speak out** give one's opinion courageously; **speak up** speak (more) loudly.

speaker noun person who speaks, esp. in public; person who speaks specified language; (**Speaker**) presiding officer of legislative assembly; loudspeaker.

spear ● noun thrusting or hurling weapon with long shaft and sharp point; tip and stem of asparagus, broccoli, etc. ● verb pierce or strike (as) with spear. □ **spearhead** noun point of spear, person(s) leading attack or challenge, verb act as spearhead of (attack etc.); **spearmint** common garden mint.

spec[1] noun colloquial speculation. □ **on spec** as a gamble.

spec[2] noun colloquial specification.

special /'speʃ(ə)l/ ● adjective exceptional; peculiar, specific; for particular purpose; for children with special needs. ● noun special constable, train, edition of newspaper, dish on menu, etc. □ **Special Branch** police department dealing with political security; **special constable** person assisting police in routine duties or in emergencies; **special effects** illusions created by props, camera-work, etc.; **special licence** licence allowing immediate marriage without banns; **special pleading** biased reasoning. □ **specially** adverb.

specialist noun person trained in particular branch of profession, esp. medicine; person specially studying subject or area.

speciality /speʃɪ'ælɪtɪ/ noun (plural **-ies**) special subject, product, activity, etc.; special feature or skill.

specialize verb (also **-ise**) (**-zing** or **-sing**) (often + in) become or be specialist; devote oneself to an interest, skill, etc.; (esp. in passive) adapt for particular purpose; (as **specialized** adjective) of a specialist. □ **specialization** noun.

specialty /'speʃəltɪ/ noun (plural -ies) esp. US speciality.

specie /'spiːʃiː/ noun coin as opposed to paper money.

species /'spiːʃɪz/ noun (plural same) class of things having common characteristics; group of animals or plants within genus; kind, sort.

specific /spə'sɪfɪk/ ● adjective clearly defined; relating to particular subject, peculiar; exact, giving full details; archaic (of medicine etc.) for particular disease. ● noun archaic specific medicine; specific aspect. □ **specific gravity** relative density. □ **specifically** adverb; **specificity** /-'fɪs-/ noun.

specification /spesɪfɪ'keɪʃ(ə)n/ noun specifying; (esp. in plural) detailed description of work (to be) done or of invention, patent, etc.

specify /'spesɪfaɪ/ verb (-ies, -ied) name or mention expressly or as condition; include in specifications.

specimen /'spesɪmɪn/ noun individual or sample taken as example of class or whole, esp. in experiments etc.; colloquial usually derogatory person of specified sort.

specious /'spiːʃəs/ adjective plausible but wrong.

speck ● noun small spot or stain; particle. ● verb (esp. as **specked** adjective) mark with specks.

speckle /'spek(ə)l/ ● noun speck, esp. one of many markings. ● verb (-ling) (esp. as **speckled** adjective) mark with speckles.

specs plural noun colloquial spectacles.

spectacle /'spektək(ə)l/ noun striking, impressive, or ridiculous sight; public show; object of public attention; (in plural) pair of lenses in frame supported on nose and ears, to correct defective eyesight.

spectacled adjective wearing spectacles.

spectacular /spek'tækjʊlə/ ● adjective striking, impressive, lavish. ● noun spectacular performance. □ **spectacularly** adverb.

spectator /spek'teɪtə/ noun person who watches a show, game, incident, etc. □ **spectator sport** sport attracting

many spectators. □ **spectate** verb (-ting).

specter US = SPECTRE.

spectra plural of SPECTRUM.

spectral /'spektr(ə)l/ adjective of or like spectres or spectra; ghostly.

spectre /'spektə/ noun (US **specter**) ghost; haunting presentiment.

spectroscope /'spektrəskəʊp/ noun instrument for recording and examining spectra. □ **spectroscopic** /-'skɒp-/ adjective; **spectroscopy** /-'trɒskəpɪ/ noun.

spectrum /'spektrəm/ noun (plural -tra) band of colours as seen in rainbow etc.; entire or wide range of subject, emotion, etc.; arrangement of electromagnetic radiation by wavelength.

speculate /'spekjʊleɪt/ verb (-ting) (usually + on, upon, about) theorize, conjecture; deal in commodities etc. in expectation of profiting from fluctuating prices. □ **speculation** noun; **speculative** /-lətɪv/ adjective; **speculator** noun.

sped past & past participle of SPEED.

speech noun faculty, act, or manner of speaking; formal public address; language, dialect. □ **speech day** annual prize-giving day in school; **speech therapy** treatment for defective speech.

speechify /'spiːtʃɪfaɪ/ verb (-ies, -ied) jocular make speeches.

speechless adjective temporarily silenced by emotion etc.

speed ● noun rapidity; rate of progress or motion; gear on bicycle; relative sensitivity of photographic film to light; slang amphetamine. ● verb (past & past participle **sped**) go or send quickly; (past & past participle **speeded**) travel at illegal or dangerous speed; archaic be or make prosperous or successful. □ **speedboat** fast motor boat; **speed limit** maximum permitted speed on road etc.; **speedway** (dirt track for) motorcycle racing, US road or track for fast vehicles. □ **speeder** noun.

speedometer /spiː'dɒmɪtə/ noun instrument on vehicle indicating its speed.

speedwell /'spiːdwel/ noun small blue-flowered herbaceous plant.

speedy adjective (-ier, -iest) rapid; prompt. □ **speedily** adverb.

speleology /spiːlɪˈɒlədʒɪ/ *noun* the study of caves etc.

spell [1] *verb* (*past & past participle* **spelt** or **spelled**) write or name correctly the letters of (word etc.); (of letters) form (word etc.); result in. □ **spell out** make out letter by letter, explain in detail. □ **speller** *noun.*

spell [2] *noun* words used as charm; effect of these; fascination. □ **spellbound** held as if by spell, fascinated.

spell [3] *noun* (fairly) short period; period of some activity or work.

spelling *noun* way word is spelt; ability to spell.

spelt [1] *past & past participle of* SPELL [1].

spelt [2] *noun* kind of wheat giving very fine flour.

spend *verb* (*past & past participle* **spent**) pay out (money); use or consume (time or energy); use up; (as **spent** *adjective*) having lost force or strength. □ **spendthrift** extravagant person. □ **spender** *noun.*

sperm *noun* (*plural* same or **-s**) spermatozoon; semen. □ **sperm bank** store of semen for artificial insemination; **sperm whale** large whale hunted for spermaceti.

spermaceti /spɜːməˈsetɪ/ *noun* white waxy substance used for ointments etc.

spermatozoon /spɜːmətəˈzəʊən/ *noun* (*plural* **-zoa**) fertilizing cell of male organism.

spermicide /ˈspɜːmɪsaɪd/ *noun* substance that kills spermatozoa. □ **spermicidal** /-ˈsaɪd-/ *adjective.*

spew *verb* (often + *up*) vomit; (often + *out*) (cause to) gush.

sphagnum /ˈsfægnəm/ *noun* (*plural* **-na**) (in full **sphagnum moss**) moss growing in bogs, used as packing etc.

sphere /sfɪə/ *noun* solid figure with every point on its surface equidistant from centre; ball, globe; field of action, influence, etc.; place in society; *historical* each of revolving shells in which heavenly bodies were thought to be set.

spherical /ˈsferɪk(ə)l/ *adjective* shaped like sphere; of spheres. □ **spherically** *adverb.*

spheroid /ˈsfɪərɔɪd/ *noun* spherelike but not perfectly spherical body. □ **spheroidal** /-ˈrɔɪd-/ *adjective.*

sphincter /ˈsfɪŋktə/ *noun* ring of muscle closing and opening orifice.

Sphinx /sfɪŋks/ *noun* ancient Egyptian stone figure with lion's body and human or animal head; (**sphinx**) inscrutable person.

spice ● *noun* aromatic or pungent vegetable substance used as flavouring; spices collectively; piquant quality; slight flavour. ● *verb* (**-cing**) flavour with spice; enhance.

spick and span *adjective* trim and clean; smart, new-looking.

spicy *adjective* (**-ier, -iest**) of or flavoured with spice; piquant, improper. □ **spiciness** *noun.*

spider /ˈspaɪdə/ *noun* 8-legged arthropod, many species of which spin webs esp. to capture insects as food. □ **spider plant** house plant with long narrow leaves.

spidery *adjective* elongated and thin.

spiel /ʃpiːl/ *noun slang* glib speech or story, sales pitch.

spigot /ˈspɪgət/ *noun* small peg or plug; device for controlling flow of liquid in tap.

spike [1] ● *noun* sharp point; pointed piece of metal, esp. forming top of iron railing; metal point on sole of running shoe to prevent slipping; (in *plural*) spiked running shoes; large nail. ● *verb* (**-king**) put spikes on or into; fix on spike; *colloquial* add alcohol to (drink), contaminate. □ **spike (person's) guns** defeat his or her plans.

spike [2] *noun* cluster of flower heads on long stem.

spikenard /ˈspaɪknɑːd/ *noun* tall sweet-smelling plant; *historical* aromatic ointment formerly made from this.

spiky *adjective* (**-ier, -iest**) like a spike; having spikes; *colloquial* irritable.

spill [1] ● *verb* (*past & past participle* **spilt** or **spilled**) allow (liquid etc.) to fall or run out of container, esp. accidentally; (of liquid etc.) fall or run out thus; throw from vehicle, saddle, etc.; (+ *into, out,* etc.) leave quickly; *slang* divulge (information etc.); shed (blood). ● *noun* spilling, being spilt; tumble, esp. from horse or vehicle. □ **spill the beans** *colloquial* divulge secret etc. □ **spillage** *noun.*

spill² *noun* thin strip of wood, paper, etc. for lighting candle etc.

spillikin /'spɪlɪkɪn/ *noun* splinter of wood etc.; (in *plural*) game in which thin rods are removed one at a time from heap without disturbing others.

spilt *past & past participle of* SPILL¹.

spin ● *verb* (**-nn-**); *past* **spun** or **span**; *past participle* **spun** (cause to) turn or whirl round rapidly; make (yarn) by drawing out and twisting together fibres of wool etc.; make (web etc.) by extruding fine viscous thread; (of person's head) be in a whirl; tell or compose (story etc.); toss (coin); (as **spun** *adjective*) made into threads. ● *noun* revolving motion, whirl; rotating dive of aircraft; secondary twisting motion e.g. of ball in flight; *colloquial* brief drive, esp. in car. □ **spin bowler** *Cricket* one who imparts spin to ball; **spin-drier, -dryer** machine for drying clothes by spinning them in rotating drum; **spin-dry** *verb*; **spinning wheel** household implement for spinning yarn, with spindle driven by wheel with crank or treadle; **spin-off** incidental result, esp. from technology; **spin out** prolong; **spin a yarn** tell story.

spina bifida /spaɪnə 'bɪfɪdə/ *noun* congenital spinal defect, with protruding membranes.

spinach /'spɪnɪdʒ/ *noun* green vegetable with edible leaves.

spinal /'spaɪn(ə)l/ *adjective* of spine. □ **spinal column** spine; **spinal cord** cylindrical nervous structure within spine.

spindle /'spɪnd(ə)l/ *noun* slender rod for twisting and winding thread in spinning; pin or axis on which something revolves; turned piece of wood used as banister etc.

spindly *adjective* (**-ier, -iest**) long or tall and thin.

spindrift /'spɪndrɪft/ *noun* spray on surface of sea.

spine *noun* series of vertebrae extending from skull, backbone; needle-like outgrowth of animal or plant; part of book enclosing page-fastening; ridge, sharp projection. □ **spine-chiller** suspense or horror film, story, etc.

spineless *adjective* lacking resoluteness.

spinet /spɪ'net/ *noun historical* small harpsichord with oblique strings.

spinnaker /'spɪnəkə/ *noun* large triangular sail used at bow of yacht.

spinner *noun* spin bowler; person or thing that spins, esp. manufacturer engaged in spinning; spin-drier; revolving bait or lure in fishing.

spinneret /'spɪnəret/ *noun* spinning-organ in spider etc.

spinney /'spɪnɪ/ *noun* (*plural* **-s**) small wood, thicket.

spinster /'spɪnstə/ *noun formal* unmarried woman.

spiny *adjective* (**-ier, -iest**) having (many) spines.

spiraea /spaɪ'rɪə/ *noun* (*US* **spirea**) garden plant related to meadowsweet.

spiral /'spaɪər(ə)l/ ● *adjective* coiled in a plane or as round a cylinder or cone; having this shape. ● *noun* spiral curve; progressive rise or fall. ● *verb* (**-ll-**; *US* **-l-**) move in spiral course; (of prices etc.) rise or fall continuously. □ **spiral staircase** circular staircase round central axis.

spirant /'spaɪərənt/ ● *adjective* uttered with continuous expulsion of breath. ● *noun* spirant consonant.

spire *noun* tapering structure, esp. on church tower; any tapering thing.

spirea *US* = SPIRAEA.

spirit /'spɪrɪt/ ● *noun* person's essence or intelligence, soul; rational being without material body; ghost; person's character; attitude; type of person; prevailing tendency; (usually in *plural*) distilled alcoholic liquor; distilled volatile liquid; courage, vivacity; (in *plural*) mood; essential as opposed to formal meaning. ● *verb* (**-t-**) (usually + *away, off*, etc.) convey mysteriously. □ **spirit gum** quick-drying gum for attaching false hair; **spirit lamp** lamp burning methylated or other volatile spirit; **spirit level** device used to test horizontality.

spirited *adjective* lively, courageous. □ **-spirited** in specified mood. □ **spiritedly** *adverb*.

spiritual /'spɪrɪtʃʊəl/ ● *adjective* of spirit; religious, divine, inspired; refined, sensitive. ● *noun* (also **Negro spiritual**) religious song originally of American blacks. □ **spirituality** /-'æl-/ *noun*; **spiritually** *adverb*.

spiritualism *noun* belief in, and practice of, communication with the dead, esp. through mediums. □ **spiritualist** *noun*; **spiritualistic** /-'lɪs-/ *adjective*.

spirituous /'spɪrɪtʃʊəs/ *adjective* very alcoholic; distilled as well as fermented.

spit¹ ● *verb* (**-tt-**; *past & past participle* **spat** *or* **spit**) eject (esp. saliva) from mouth; do this as gesture of contempt; utter vehemently; (of fire etc.) throw out with explosion; (of rain etc.) fall lightly; make spitting noise. ● *noun* spittle; spitting. □ **spitfire** fiery-tempered person; **spitting distance** *colloquial* very short distance; **spitting image** *colloquial* exact counterpart or likeness.

spit² ● *noun* rod for skewering meat for roasting over fire etc.; point of land projecting into sea; spade-depth of earth. ● *verb* (**-tt-**) pierce (as) with spit. □ **spit-roast** roast on spit.

spite ● *noun* ill will, malice. ● *verb* (**-ting**) hurt, thwart. □ **in spite of** notwithstanding.

spiteful *adjective* malicious. □ **spitefully** *adverb*.

spittle /'spɪt(ə)l/ *noun* saliva.

spittoon /spɪ'tuːn/ *noun* vessel to spit into.

spiv *noun colloquial* man, esp. flashily-dressed one, living from shady dealings. □ **spivvish** *adjective*; **spivvy** *adjective*.

splash ● *verb* (cause to) scatter in drops; wet or stain by splashing; (usually + *across, along, about*, etc.) move with splashing; jump or fall into water etc. with splash; display (news) conspicuously; decorate with scattered colour; spend (money) ostentatiously. ● *noun* act or noise of splashing; quantity splashed; mark of splashing; prominent news feature, display, etc.; patch of colour; *colloquial* small quantity of soda water etc. (in drink). □ **splashback** panel behind sink etc. to protect wall from splashes; **splashdown** alighting of spacecraft on sea; **splash down** *verb*; **splash out** *colloquial* spend money freely.

splat *colloquial* ● *noun* sharp splattering sound. ● *adverb* with splat. ● *verb* (**-tt-**) fall or hit with splat.

splatter /'splætə/ *verb & noun* splash, esp. with continuous noisy action, spatter.

splay ● *verb* spread apart; (of opening) have sides diverging; make (opening) with divergent sides. ● *noun* surface at oblique angle to another. ● *adjective* splayed.

spleen *noun* abdominal organ regulating quality of blood; moroseness, irritability.

splendid /'splendɪd/ *adjective* magnificent; glorious, dignified; excellent. □ **splendidly** *adverb*.

splendiferous /splen'dɪfərəs/ *adjective colloquial* splendid.

splendour /'splendə/ *noun* (*US* **splendor**) dazzling brightness; magnificence.

splenetic /splɪ'netɪk/ *adjective* bad-tempered, peevish.

splenic /'splenɪk/ *adjective* of or in spleen.

splice ● *verb* (**-cing**) join (ropes) by interweaving strands; join (pieces of wood, tape, etc.) by overlapping; (esp. as **spliced** *adjective*) *colloquial* join in marriage. ● *noun* join made by splicing.

splint ● *noun* strip of wood etc. bound to broken limb while it heals. ● *verb* secure with splint.

splinter /'splɪntə/ ● *noun* small sharp fragment of wood, stone, glass, etc. ● *verb* split into splinters, shatter. □ **splinter group** breakaway political group. □ **splintery** *adjective*.

split ● *verb* (**-tt-**; *past & past participle* **split**) break, esp. lengthwise or with grain; break forcibly; (often + *up*) divide into parts, esp. equal shares; (often + *off, away*) remove or be removed by breaking or dividing; (usually + *on, over*, etc.) divide into disagreeing or hostile parties; cause fission of (atom); *slang* leave, esp. suddenly; (usually + *on*) *colloquial* inform; (as **splitting** *adjective*) (of headache) severe; (of head) suffer severe headache. ● *noun* splitting; disagreement, schism; (in *plural*) feat of leaping or sitting with legs straight and pointing in opposite directions. □ **split hairs** make over-subtle distinctions; **split infinitive** one with adverb etc. inserted between *to* and verb (see note below); **split-level** with more than one level; **split personality** condition of alternating personalities; **split pin** metal cotter with its two ends splayed out after passing through hole; **split second** very short time; **split-second** very rapid, (of timing) very accurate; **split up** separate, end relationship.

■ **Usage** Split infinitives, as in *I want to quickly sum up* and *Your job is to really get to know everybody*, are common in informal English, but many people consider them incorrect and prefer *I want quickly to sum up* or *I want to sum up quickly*. They should therefore be avoided in formal English, but note that just changing the order of words can alter the meaning, e.g. *Your job is really to get to know everybody*.

splodge *colloquial* • *noun* daub, blot, smear. • *verb* (**-ging**) make splodge on. □ **splodgy** *adjective*.

splosh *colloquial* • *verb* move with splashing sound. • *noun* splashing sound; splash of water etc.

splotch *noun & verb* splodge. □ **splotchy** *adjective*.

splurge *colloquial* • *noun* sudden extravagance; ostentatious display or effort. • *verb* (**-ging**) (usually + *on*) make splurge.

splutter /ˈsplʌtə/ • *verb* speak or express in choking manner; emit spitting sounds; speak rapidly or incoherently. • *noun* spluttering speech or sound.

spoil • *verb* (*past & past participle* **spoilt** or **spoiled**) make or become useless or unsatisfactory; reduce enjoyment etc. of; decay, go bad; ruin character of by over-indulgence. • *noun* (usually in *plural*) plunder, stolen goods; profit or advantages accruing from success or position. □ **spoilsport** person who spoils others' enjoyment; **spoilt for choice** having excessive number of choices.

spoiler *noun* device on aircraft to increase drag; device on vehicle to improve road-holding at speed.

spoilt *past & past participle* of SPOIL.

spoke[1] *noun* each of rods running from hub to rim of wheel. □ **put a spoke in (person's) wheel** thwart, hinder.

spoke[2] *past* of SPEAK.

spoken *past participle* of SPEAK.

spokesman /ˈspəʊksmən/ *noun* (*feminine* **spokeswoman**) person who speaks for others, representative.

spokesperson /ˈspəʊkspɜːs(ə)n/ *noun* (*plural* **-s** or **spokespeople**) spokesman or spokeswoman.

spoliation /spəʊlɪˈeɪʃ(ə)n/ *noun* plundering, pillage.

spondee /ˈspɒndiː/ *noun* metrical foot of two long syllables. □ **spondaic** /-ˈdeɪɪk/ *adjective*.

sponge /spʌndʒ/ • *noun* sea animal with porous body wall and tough elastic skeleton; this skeleton or piece of porous rubber etc. used in bathing, cleaning, etc.; thing like sponge in consistency, esp. sponge cake; act of sponging. • *verb* (**-ging**) wipe or clean with sponge; (often + *out, away*, etc.) wipe off or rub out (as) with sponge; (often + *up*) absorb (as) with sponge; (often + *on, off*) live as parasite. □ **sponge bag** waterproof bag for toilet articles; **sponge cake, pudding** one of light spongelike consistency; **sponge rubber** porous rubber.

sponger *noun* parasitic person.

spongy *adjective* (**-ier, -iest**) like a sponge, porous, elastic, absorbent.

sponsor /ˈspɒnsə/ • *noun* person who pledges money to charity in return for specified activity by someone; patron of artistic or sporting activity etc.; company etc. financing broadcast in return for advertising; person introducing legislation; godparent at baptism. • *verb* be sponsor for. □ **sponsorship** *noun*.

spontaneous /spɒnˈteɪnɪəs/ *adjective* acting, done, or occurring without external cause; instinctive, automatic, natural. □ **spontaneity** /-təˈneɪɪtɪ/ *noun*; **spontaneously** *adverb*.

spoof /spuːf/ *noun & verb colloquial* parody; hoax, swindle.

spook /spuːk/ • *noun colloquial* ghost. • *verb* *esp. US* frighten, unnerve. □ **spooky** *adjective* (**-ier, -iest**).

spool /spuːl/ • *noun* reel on which something is wound; revolving cylinder of angler's reel. • *verb* wind on spool.

spoon /spuːn/ • *noun* utensil with bowl and handle for putting food in mouth or for stirring etc.; spoonful; spoon-shaped thing, esp. (in full **spoon-bait**) revolving metal fish-lure. ● *verb* (often + *up, out*) take (liquid etc.) with spoon; hit (ball) feebly upwards. □ **spoonbill** wading bird with broad flat-tipped bill; **spoonfeed** feed with spoon, give help etc. to (person) without demanding any effort from recipient. □ **spoonful** *noun* (*plural* **-s**).

spoonerism /'spu:nərız(ə)m/ *noun* (usually accidental) transposition of initial sounds of two or more words.

spoor /spʊə/ *noun* animal's track or scent.

sporadic /spə'rædɪk/ *adjective* occurring only sparsely or occasionally. □ **sporadically** *adverb*.

spore *noun* reproductive cell of ferns, fungi, protozoa, etc.

sporran /'spɒrən/ *noun* pouch worn in front of kilt.

sport ● *noun* game or competitive activity usually involving physical exertion; these collectively; (in *plural*) meeting for competition in athletics; amusement, fun; *colloquial* sportsman, good fellow; person with specified attitude to games, rules, etc. ● *verb* amuse oneself, play about; wear or exhibit, esp. ostentatiously. □ **sports car** low-built fast car; **sports coat, jacket** man's informal jacket; **sports ground** piece of land used for sport; **sportswear** clothes for sports, informal clothes.

sporting *adjective* of or interested in sport; generous, fair. □ **sporting chance** some possibility of success. □ **sportingly** *adverb*.

sportive *adjective* playful.

sportsman /'spɔːtsmən/ *noun* (*feminine* **sportswoman**) person engaging in sport; fair and generous person. □ **sportsmanlike** *adjective*; **sportsmanship** *noun*.

sporty *adjective* (**-ier, -iest**) *colloquial* fond of sport; *colloquial* rakish, showy.

spot ● *noun* small mark differing in colour etc. from surface it is on; pimple, blemish; particular place, locality; particular part of one's body or character; *colloquial* one's (regular) position in organization, programme, etc.; *colloquial* small quantity; spotlight. ● *verb* (**-tt-**) *colloquial* pick out, recognize, catch sight of; watch for and take note of (trains,

talent, etc.); (as **spotted** *adjective*) marked with spots; make spots, rain slightly. □ **in a (tight) spot** *colloquial* in difficulties; **on the spot** at scene of event, *colloquial* in position demanding response or action, without delay, without moving backwards or forwards; **spot cash** money paid immediately after sale; **spot check** sudden or random check; **spotlight** *noun* beam of light directed on small area, lamp projecting this, full publicity, *verb* direct spotlight on; **spot on** *colloquial* precise(ly); **spotted dick** suet pudding containing currants; **spot-weld** join (metal surfaces) by welding at points. □ **spotter** *noun*.

spotless *adjective* absolutely clean, unblemished. □ **spotlessly** *adverb*.

spotty *adjective* (**-ier, -iest**) marked with spots; patchy, irregular.

spouse /spaʊz/ *noun* husband or wife.

spout /spaʊt/ ● *noun* projecting tube or lip for pouring from teapot, kettle, jug, fountain, roof-gutter, etc.; jet of liquid. ● *verb* discharge or issue forcibly in jet; utter at length or pompously. □ **up the spout** *slang* useless, ruined, pregnant.

sprain ● *verb* wrench (ankle, wrist, etc.) causing pain or swelling. ● *noun* such injury.

sprang *past* of SPRING.

sprat *noun* small sea fish.

sprawl ● *verb* sit, lie, or fall with limbs spread out untidily; spread untidily, straggle. ● *noun* sprawling movement, position, or mass; straggling urban expansion.

spray[1] ● *noun* water etc. flying in small drops; liquid intended for spraying; device for spraying. ● *verb* throw as spray; sprinkle (as) with spray; (of tomcat) mark environment with urine to attract females. □ **spray-gun** device for spraying paint etc. □ **sprayer** *noun*.

spray[2] *noun* sprig with flowers or leaves, small branch; ornament in similar form.

spread /spred/ ● *verb* (*past & past participle* **spread**) (often + *out*) open, extend, unfold, cause to cover larger surface, have wide or increasing extent; (cause to) become widely known; cover; (spread (table). ● *noun* act, capability, or extent of spreading; diffusion; breadth; increased girth; difference between two rates, prices, etc.; *colloquial* elaborate meal; paste for spreading on bread etc.; bedspread; printed matter spread over more than one column. □ **spread eagle** figure of eagle with legs and wings extended as emblem; **spread-eagle** place (person) with arms and legs spread out, defeat utterly; **spreadsheet** computer program for handling tabulating figures etc., esp. in accounting.

spree *noun colloquial* extravagant outing; bout of drinking etc.

sprig ● *noun* small branch or shoot; ornament resembling this, esp. on fabric. ● *verb* (**-gg-**) ornament with sprigs.

sprightly /ˈspraɪtlɪ/ *adjective* (**-ier, -iest**) vivacious, lively.

spring ● *verb* (*past* **sprang**; *past participle* **sprung**) rise rapidly or suddenly, leap; move rapidly (as) by action of a spring; (usually + *from*) originate; (cause to) act or appear unexpectedly; *slang* contrive escape (of person from prison etc.); (usually as **sprung** *adjective*) provide with springs. ● *noun* jump, leap; recoil; elasticity; elastic device usually of coiled metal used esp. to drive clockwork or for cushioning in furniture or vehicles; season of year between winter and summer; (often + *of*) early stage of life etc.; place where water, oil, etc. wells up from earth, basin or flow so formed; motive for or origin of action, custom, etc. □ **spring balance** device measuring weight by tension of spring; **springboard** flexible board for leaping or diving from, source of impetus; **spring-clean** *noun* thorough cleaning of house, esp. in spring, *verb* cleanse thus; **spring greens** young cabbage leaves; **spring a leak** develop leak; **spring onion** young onion eaten raw; **spring roll** Chinese fried pancake filled with vegetables etc.; **spring tide** tide with greatest rise and fall; **springtime** season or period of spring.

springbok /ˈsprɪŋbɒk/ *noun* (*plural* same or **-s**) S. African gazelle.

springer *noun* small spaniel.

springy *adjective* (**-ier, -iest**) elastic.

sprinkle /ˈsprɪŋk(ə)l/ ● *verb* (**-ling**) scatter in small drops or particles; (often +

with) subject to sprinkling; (of liquid etc.) fall thus on. ● *noun* (usually + *of*) light shower, sprinkling.

sprinkler *noun* device for sprinkling lawn or extinguishing fires.

sprinkling *noun* small sparse number or amount.

sprint ● *verb* run short distance at top speed. ● *noun* such run; similar short effort in cycling, swimming, etc. □ **sprinter** *noun*.

sprit *noun* small diagonal spar from mast to upper outer corner of sail. □ **spritsail** /ˈsprɪts(ə)l/ sail extended by sprit.

sprite *noun* elf, fairy.

spritzer /ˈsprɪtsə/ *noun* drink of white wine with soda water.

sprocket /ˈsprɒkɪt/ *noun* projection on rim of wheel engaging with links of chain.

sprout /spraʊt/ ● *verb* put forth (shoots etc.); begin to grow. ● *noun* plant shoot; Brussels sprout.

spruce[1] ● *adjective* of trim appearance, smart. ● *verb* (**-cing**) (usually + *up*) make or become smart. □ **sprucely** *adverb*; **spruceness** *noun*.

spruce[2] *noun* conifer with dense conical foliage; its wood.

sprung *past participle* of SPRING.

spry /spraɪ/ *adjective* (**-er, -est**) lively, nimble. □ **spryly** *adverb*.

spud ● *noun colloquial* potato; small narrow spade for weeding. ● *verb* (**-dd-**) (+ *up, out*) remove with spud.

spumante /spuːˈmæntɪ/ *noun* Italian sparkling white wine.

spume /spjuːm/ *noun* & *verb* (**-ming**) froth, foam. □ **spumy** *adjective* (**-ier, -iest**).

spun *past* & *past participle* of SPIN. □ **spun silk** cheap material containing waste silk.

spunk *noun colloquial* mettle, spirit. □ **spunky** *adjective* (**-ier, -iest**).

spur ● *noun* small spike or spiked wheel attached to rider's heel for urging horse forward; stimulus, incentive; spur-shaped thing, esp. projection from mountain (range), branch road or railway, or hard projection on cock's leg. ● *verb* (**-rr-**) prick (horse) with spur;

incite, stimulate. □ **on the spur of the moment** on impulse.

spurge noun plant with acrid milky juice.

spurious /'spjʊərɪəs/ adjective not genuine, fake.

spurn verb reject with disdain or contempt.

spurt ● verb (cause to) gush out in jet or stream; make sudden effort. ● noun sudden gushing out, jet; short burst of speed, growth, etc.

sputnik /'spʊtnɪk/ noun Russian artificial earth satellite.

sputter /'spʌtə/ verb & noun splutter.

sputum /'spju:təm/ noun thick coughed-up mucus.

spy ● noun (plural **spies**) person secretly collecting and reporting information for a government, company, etc.; person watching others secretly. ● verb (**spies**, **spied**) discern, see; (often + on) act as spy. □ **spyglass** small telescope; **spyhole** peep-hole; **spy out** explore or discover, esp. secretly.

sq. abbreviation square.

Sqn. Ldr. abbreviation Squadron Leader.

squab /skwɒb/ ● noun young esp. unfledged pigeon etc.; short fat person; stuffed cushion, esp. as part of car-seat; sofa. ● adjective short and fat.

squabble /'skwɒb(ə)l/ ● noun petty or noisy quarrel. ● verb (**-ling**) engage in squabble.

squad /skwɒd/ noun small group sharing task etc., esp. of soldiers or police officers; team. □ **squad car** police car.

squaddie noun (also **squaddy**) (plural **-ies**) slang recruit, private.

squadron /'skwɒdrən/ noun unit of RAF with 10–18 aircraft; detachment of warships employed on particular service; organized group etc., esp. cavalry division of two troops. □ **squadron leader** RAF officer commanding squadron, next below wing commander.

squalid /'skwɒlɪd/ adjective filthy, dirty; mean in appearance.

squall /skwɔ:l/ ● noun sudden or violent gust or storm; discordant cry, scream. ● verb utter (with) squall, scream. □ **squally** adjective.

squalor /'skwɒlə/ noun filthy or squalid state.

squander /'skwɒndə/ verb spend wastefully.

square /skweə/ ● noun rectangle with 4 equal sides; object of (roughly) this shape; open area enclosed by buildings; product of number multiplied by itself; L- or T-shaped instrument for obtaining or testing right angles; slang conventional or old-fashioned person. ● adjective square-shaped; having or in form of a right angle; angular, not round; designating unit of measure equal to area of square whose side is one of the unit specified; (usually + with) level, parallel; (usually + to) perpendicular; sturdy, squat; arranged; (also **all square**) with no money owed; (of scores) equal; fair, honest; direct; slang conventional, old-fashioned. ● adverb squarely. ● verb (**-ring**) make square; multiply (number) by itself; (usually + to, with) make or be consistent, reconcile; mark out in squares; settle (bill etc.); place (shoulders etc.) squarely facing forwards; colloquial pay, bribe; make scores of (match etc.) equal. □ **square brackets** brackets of the form [ ] (see panel at BRACKET); **square dance** dance with 4 couples facing inwards from 4 sides; **square deal** fair bargain or treatment; **square leg** Cricket fielding position on batsman's leg side nearly opposite stumps; **square meal** substantial meal; **square-rigged** having 4-sided sails set across length of ship; **square root** number that multiplied by itself gives specified number. □ **squarely** adverb.

squash¹ /skwɒʃ/ ● verb crush or squeeze flat or into pulp; (often + into) colloquial force into small space, crowd; belittle, bully; suppress. ● noun crowd, crowded state; drink made of crushed fruit; (in full **squash rackets**) game played with rackets and small ball in closed court. □ **squashy** adjective (**-ier**, **-iest**).

squash² /skwɒʃ/ noun (plural same or **-es**) trailing annual plant; gourd of this.

squat /skwɒt/ ● verb (**-tt-**) sit on one's heels, or on ground with knees drawn up; colloquial sit down; act as squatter. ● adjective (**-tt-**) short and thick, dumpy. ● noun squatting posture; place occupied by squatter(s).

squatter *noun* person who inhabits unoccupied premises without permission.

squaw *noun* N. American Indian woman or wife.

squawk ● *noun* harsh cry; complaint. ● *verb* utter squawk.

squeak ● *noun* short high-pitched cry or sound; (also **narrow squeak**) narrow escape. ● *verb* emit squeak; utter shrilly; (+ *by, through*) *colloquial* pass narrowly; *slang* turn informer.

squeaky *adjective* (**-ier, -iest**) making squeaking sound. □ **squeaky clean** *colloquial* completely clean, above criticism. □ **squeakily** *adverb*; **squeakiness** *noun*.

squeal ● *noun* prolonged shrill sound or cry. ● *verb* make, or utter with, squeal; *slang* turn informer; *colloquial* protest vociferously.

squeamish /ˈskwiːmɪʃ/ *adjective* easily nauseated; fastidious. □ **squeamishly** *adverb*; **squeamishness** *noun*.

squeegee /ˈskwiːdʒiː/ *noun* rubber-edged implement on handle, for cleaning windows etc.

squeeze ● *verb* (**-zing**) (often + *out*) exert pressure on, esp. to extract moisture; reduce in size or alter in shape by squeezing; force or push into or through small or narrow space; harass, pressure; (usually + *out of*) get by extortion or entreaty; press (person's hand) in sympathy etc. ● *noun* squeezing, being squeezed; close embrace; crowd, crowded state; small quantity produced by squeezing; restriction on borrowing and investment. □ **squeeze-box** *colloquial* accordion, concertina.

squelch ● *verb* make sucking sound as of treading in thick mud; move with squelching sound; disconcert, silence. ● *noun* act or sound of squelching. □ **squelchy** *adjective*.

squib *noun* small hissing firework; satirical essay.

squid *noun* (*plural* same or **-s**) 10-armed marine cephalopod.

squidgy /ˈskwɪdʒɪ/ *adjective* (**-ier, -iest**) *colloquial* squashy, soggy.

squiffy /ˈskwɪfɪ/ *adjective* (**-ier, -iest**) *slang* slightly drunk.

squiggle /ˈskwɪg(ə)l/ *noun* short curling line, esp. in handwriting. □ **squiggly** *adjective*.

squint ● *verb* have eyes turned in different directions; (often + *at*) look sidelong. ● *noun* squinting condition; sidelong glance; *colloquial* glance, look; oblique opening in church wall.

squire ● *noun* country gentleman, esp. chief landowner of district; *historical* knight's attendant. ● *verb* (**-ring**) (of man) escort (woman).

squirearchy /ˈskwaɪərɑːkɪ/ *noun* (*plural* **-ies**) landowners collectively.

squirm ● *verb* wriggle, writhe; show or feel embarrassment. ● *noun* squirming movement.

squirrel /ˈskwɪr(ə)l/ ● *noun* bushy-tailed usually tree-living rodent; its fur; hoarder. ● *verb* (**-ll-**; *US* **-l-**) (often + *away*) hoard.

squirt ● *verb* eject (liquid etc.) in jet; be ejected thus; splash with squirted substance. ● *noun* jet of water etc.; small quantity squirted; syringe; *colloquial* insignificant person.

squish *colloquial* ● *noun* slight squelching sound. ● *verb* move with squish; squash. □ **squishy** *adjective* (**-ier, -iest**).

Sr. *abbreviation* Senior.

SRN *abbreviation* State Registered Nurse.

SS *abbreviation* steamship; Saints; *historical* Nazi special police force (*Schutzstaffel*).

SSE *abbreviation* south-south-east.

SSW *abbreviation* south-south-west.

St *abbreviation* Saint.

St. *abbreviation* Street.

st. *abbreviation* stone (weight).

stab ● *verb* (**-bb-**) pierce or wound with knife etc.; (often + *at*) aim blow with such weapon; cause sharp pain to. ● *noun* act or result of stabbing; *colloquial* attempt. □ **stab in the back** *noun* treacherous attack, *verb* betray.

stability /stəˈbɪlɪtɪ/ *noun* being stable.

stabilize /ˈsteɪbɪlaɪz/ *verb* (also **-ise**) (**-zing** or **-sing**) make or become stable. □ **stabilization** *noun*.

stabilizer *noun* (also **-iser**) device to keep aircraft or (in *plural*) child's bicycle steady; food additive for preserving texture.

stable /'steɪb(ə)l/ ● *adjective* (**-r**, **-st**) firmly fixed or established, not fluctuating or changing; not easily upset or disturbed. ● *noun* building for keeping horses; establishment for training racehorses; racehorses of particular stable; people, products, etc. having common origin or affiliation; such origin or affiliation. ● *verb* (**-ling**) put or keep in stable. □ **stably** *adverb*.

stabling *noun* accommodation for horses.

staccato /stə'kɑːtəʊ/ *esp. Music* ● *adverb & adjective* with each sound sharply distinct. ● *noun* (*plural* **-s**) staccato passage or delivery.

stack ● *noun* (esp. orderly) pile or heap; haystack; *colloquial* large quantity; number of chimneys standing together; smokestack; tall factory chimney; stacked group of aircraft; part of library where books are compactly stored. ● *verb* pile in stack(s); arrange (cards, circumstances, etc.) secretly for cheating; cause (aircraft) to fly in circles while waiting to land.

stadium /'steɪdɪəm/ *noun* (*plural* **-s**) athletic or sports ground with tiered seats for spectators.

staff /stɑːf/ ● *noun* stick or pole for walking, as weapon, or as symbol of office; supporting person or thing; people employed in a business etc.; those in authority in a school etc.; group of army officers assisting officer in high command; (*plural* **-s** or **staves**) *Music* set of usually 5 parallel lines to indicate pitch of notes by position. ● *verb* provide (institution etc.) with staff. □ **staff nurse** one ranking just below a sister.

stag *noun* male deer; person who applies for new shares to sell at once for profit. □ **stag beetle** beetle with antler-like mandibles; **stag-party** *colloquial* party for men only.

stage ● *noun* point or period in process or development; raised platform, esp. for performing plays etc. on; (**the stage**) theatrical profession; scene of action; regular stopping place on route; distance between stopping places; section of space rocket with separate engine. ● *verb* (**-ging**) put (play etc.) on stage; organize and carry out. □ **stagecoach** *historical* coach running on regular route; **stage direction** instruction in a play about actors' movements, sound effects, etc.; **stage door** entrance from street to backstage part of theatre; **stage fright** performer's fear of audience; **stage-manage** arrange and control as or like stage manager; **stage manager** person responsible for lighting and mechanical arrangements on stage; **stage-struck** obsessed with becoming actor; **stage whisper** loud whisper meant to be overheard.

stagger /'stægə/ ● *verb* (cause to) walk unsteadily; shock, confuse; arrange (events etc.) so that they do not coincide; arrange (objects) so that they are not in line. ● *noun* staggering movement; (in *plural*) disease, esp. of horses and cattle, causing staggering.

staggering *adjective* astonishing, bewildering. □ **staggeringly** *adverb*.

staging /'steɪdʒɪŋ/ *noun* presentation of play etc.; (temporary) platform; shelves for plants in greenhouse. □ **staging post** regular stopping place, esp. on air route.

stagnant /'stægnənt/ *adjective* (of liquid) motionless, without current; dull, sluggish. □ **stagnancy** *noun*.

stagnate /stæg'neɪt/ *verb* (**-ting**) be or become stagnant. □ **stagnation** *noun*.

stagy /'steɪdʒɪ/ *adjective* (also **stagey**) (**-ier**, **-iest**) theatrical, artificial, exaggerated.

staid *adjective* sober, steady, sedate.

stain ● *verb* discolour or be discoloured by action of liquid sinking in; spoil, damage; colour (wood, etc.) with penetrating substance; treat with colouring agent. ● *noun* discoloration, spot, mark; blot, blemish; dye etc. for staining. □ **stained glass** coloured glass in leaded window etc.

stainless *adjective* without stains; not liable to stain. □ **stainless steel** chrome steel resisting rust and tarnish.

stair *noun* each of a set of fixed indoor steps; (usually in *plural*) such a set. □ **staircase** flight of stairs and supporting structure; **stair-rod** rod securing carpet between two steps; **stairway** staircase; **stairwell** shaft for staircase.

stake ● *noun* stout pointed stick driven into ground as support, boundary mark, etc.; *historical* post to which person was tied to be burnt alive; sum of money etc. wagered on event; (often + *in*) interest or concern, esp. financial; (in *plural*) prize-money, esp. in horse race, such race. ● *verb* (**-king**) secure or support with stake(s); (+ *off*, *out*) mark off (area) with stakes; wager; *US colloquial* support, esp. financially. □ **at stake** risked, to be won or lost; **stake out** *colloquial* place under surveillance; **stake-out** *esp. US colloquial* period of surveillance.

stalactite /'stæləktaɪt/ *noun* icicle-like deposit of calcium carbonate hanging from roof of cave etc.

stalagmite /'stæləgmaɪt/ *noun* icicle-like deposit of calcium carbonate rising from floor of cave etc.

stale ● *adjective* not fresh; musty, insipid, or otherwise the worse for age or use; trite, unoriginal; (of athlete or performer) impaired by excessive training. ● *verb* (**-ling**) make or become stale. □ **staleness** *noun*.

stalemate ● *noun Chess* position counting as draw in which player cannot move except into check; deadlock. ● *verb* (**-ting**) *Chess* bring (player) to stalemate; bring to deadlock.

Stalinism /'staːlɪnɪz(ə)m/ *noun* centralized authoritarian form of socialism associated with Stalin. □ **Stalinist** *noun & adjective*.

stalk[1] /stɔːk/ ● *noun* main stem of herbaceous plant; slender attachment or support of leaf, flower, fruit, etc.; similar support for organ etc. in animal.

stalk[2] /stɔːk/ ● *verb* pursue (game, enemy) stealthily; stride, walk in a haughty way; *formal or rhetorical* move silently or threateningly through (place). ● *noun* stalking of game; haughty gait. □ **stalking-horse** horse concealing hunter, pretext concealing real intentions or actions.

stall[1] /stɔːl/ ● *noun* trader's booth or table in market etc.; compartment for one animal in stable or cowhouse; fixed, usually partly enclosed, seat in choir or chancel of church; (usually in *plural*) each of seats on ground floor of theatre; stalling of engine or aircraft,

condition resulting from this. ● *verb* (of vehicle or its engine) stop because of overload on engine or inadequate supply of fuel to it; (of aircraft or its pilot) lose control because speed is too low; cause to stall. □ **stallholder** person in charge of stall in market etc.

stall[2] /stɔːl/ ● *verb* play for time when being questioned etc.; delay, obstruct.

stallion /'stæljən/ *noun* uncastrated adult male horse.

stalwart /'stɔːlwət/ ● *adjective* strong, sturdy; courageous, resolute, reliable. ● *noun* stalwart person, esp. loyal comrade.

stamen /'steɪmən/ *noun* organ producing pollen in flower.

stamina /'stæmɪnə/ *noun* physical or mental endurance.

stammer /'stæmə/ ● *verb* speak haltingly, esp. with pauses or rapid repetitions of same syllable; (often + *out*) utter (words) in this way. ● *noun* tendency to stammer; instance of stammering.

stamp ● *verb* bring down (one's foot) heavily, esp. on ground, (often + *on*) crush or flatten in this way, walk heavily; impress (design, mark, etc.) on surface, impress (surface) with pattern etc.; affix postage or other stamp to; assign specific character to, mark out. ● *noun* instrument for stamping; mark or design made by this; impression of official mark required to be made on deeds, bills of exchange, etc., as evidence of payment of tax; small adhesive piece of paper as evidence of payment, esp. postage stamp; mark, label, etc. on commodity as evidence of quality etc.; act or sound of stamping foot; characteristic mark, quality. □ **stamp duty** duty imposed on certain kinds of legal document; **stamping ground** *colloquial* favourite haunt; **stamp on** impress (idea etc.) on (memory etc.); **stamp out** produce by cutting out with die etc., put end to.

stampede /stæm'piːd/ ● *noun* sudden flight or hurried movement of animals or people; response of many people at once to a common impulse. ● *verb* (**-ding**) (cause to) take part in stampede.

stance /stɑːns/ *noun* standpoint, attitude; position of body, esp. when hitting ball etc.

stanch /stɑːntʃ, stɔːntʃ/ *verb* (also **staunch** /stɔːntʃ/) restrain flow of (esp. blood); restrain flow from (esp. wound).

stanchion /'stɑːnʃ(ə)n/ *noun* upright post or support.

stand ●*verb* (*past & past participle* **stood** /stʊd/) have, take, or maintain upright or stationary position, esp on feet or base; be situated; be of specified height; be in specified state; set in upright or specified position; move to and remain in specified position, take specified attitude; remain valid or unaltered; *Nautical* hold specified course; endure, tolerate; provide at one's own expense; (often + *for*) be candidate (for office etc.); act in specified capacity; undergo (trial). ●*noun* cessation from progress, stoppage; *Military* (esp. in **make a stand**) halt made to repel attack; resistance to attack or compulsion; position taken up, attitude adopted; rack, set of shelves, etc. for storage; open-fronted stall or structure for trader, exhibitor, etc.; standing-place for vehicles; raised structure to sit or stand on; *US* witness-box; each halt made for performance on tour; group of growing plants. □ **as it stands** in its present condition, in the present circumstances; **stand by** stand nearby, look on without interfering, uphold, support (person), adhere to (promise etc.), be ready for action; **stand-by** (person or thing) ready if needed in emergency etc., readiness for duty etc.; **stand down** withdraw from position or candidacy; **stand for** represent, signify, imply, *colloquial* endure, tolerate; **stand in** (usually + *for*) deputize for; **stand-in** deputy, substitute; **stand off** move or keep away, temporarily dismiss (employee); **stand-off**

half *Rugby* half-back forming link between scrum-half and three-quarters; **standoffish** cold or distant in manner; **stand on** insist on, observe scrupulously; **stand out** be prominent or outstanding, (usually + *against*, *for*), persist in opposition or support; **standpipe** vertical pipe rising from water supply, esp. one connecting temporary tap to mains; **standpoint** point of view; **standstill** stoppage, inability to proceed; **stand to** *Military* stand ready for attack, abide by, be likely or certain to; **stand to reason** be obvious; **stand up** rise to one's feet, come to, remain in, or place in standing position, (of argument etc.) be valid, *colloquial* fail to keep appointment with; **stand-up** (of meal) eaten standing, (of fight) violent, thorough, (of collar) not turned down, (of comedian) telling jokes to audience; **stand up for** support, side with; **stand up to** face (opponent) courageously, be resistant to (wear, use, etc.).

standard /'stændəd/ ●*noun* object, quality, or measure serving as basis, example, or principle to which others conform or should conform or by which others are judged; level of excellence etc. required or specified; ordinary procedure etc.; distinctive flag; upright support or pipe; shrub standing without support, or grafted on upright stem and trained in tree form. ●*adjective* serving or used as standard; of normal or prescribed quality, type, or size. □ **standard-bearer** person who carries distinctive flag, prominent leader in cause; **standard English** most widely accepted dialect of English (see panel); **standard lamp** lamp on tall upright with base; **standard of living** degree of material comfort of person or group; **standard time** uniform time established by law or custom in country or region.

Standard English

Standard English is the dialect of English used by most educated English speakers and is spoken with a variety of accents (see panel at ACCENT). While not *in itself* any better than any other dialect, standard English is the form of English used in all formal written contexts.

standardize *verb* (also **-ise**) (**-zing** or **-sing**) cause to conform to standard. □ **standardization** *noun*.

standing ● *noun* esteem, repute, esp. high; duration. ● *adjective* that stands, upright; established, permanent; (of jump, start, etc.) performed with no run-up. □ **standing order** instruction to banker to make regular payments; **standing orders** rules governing procedure in a parliament, council, etc.; **standing ovation** prolonged applause from audience that has risen to its feet; **standing room** space to stand in.

stank *past of* STINK.

stanza /'stænzə/ *noun* group of lines forming division of poem, etc.

staphylococcus /ˌstæfɪlə'kɒkəs/ *noun* (*plural* **-cocci** /-kaɪ/) bacterium sometimes forming pus. □ **staphylococcal** *adjective*.

staple[1] /'steɪp(ə)l/ ● *noun* shaped piece of wire with two points for fastening papers together, fixing netting to post, etc. ● *verb* (**-ling**) fasten with staple(s). □ **stapler** *noun*.

staple[2] /'steɪp(ə)l/ ● *noun* principal or important article of commerce; chief element, main component; fibre of cotton, wool, etc. with regard to its quality. ● *adjective* main, principal; important as product or export.

star ● *noun* celestial body appearing as luminous point in night sky; large luminous gaseous body such as sun; celestial body regarded as influencing fortunes etc.; conventional image of star with radiating lines or points; famous or brilliant person, leading performer. ● *adjective* outstanding. ● *verb* (**-rr-**) appear or present as leading performer(s); mark, set, or adorn with star(s). □ **starfish** (*plural* same or **-es**) sea creature with 5 or more radiating arms; **star-gazer** *colloquial usually derogatory or jocular* astronomer or astrologer; **starlight** light of stars; **starlit** lit by stars, with stars visible; **Stars and Stripes** US national flag; **star turn** main item in entertainment etc. □ **stardom** *noun*.

starboard /'stɑːbəd/ ● *noun* right-hand side of ship or aircraft looking forward. ● *verb* turn (helm) to starboard.

starch ● *noun* white carbohydrate obtained chiefly from cereals and potatoes; preparation of this for stiffening fabric; stiffness of manner, formality. ● *verb* stiffen (clothing) with starch. □ **starchy** *adjective* (**-ier**, **-iest**).

stare /steə/ ● *verb* (**-ring**) (usually + *at*) look fixedly, esp. in curiosity, surprise, horror, etc. ● *noun* staring gaze. □ **stare (person) in the face** be evident or imminent; **stare out** stare at (person) until he or she looks away.

stark ● *adjective* sharply evident; desolate, bare; absolute. ● *adverb* completely, wholly. □ **starkly** *adverb*.

starkers /'stɑːkəz/ *adjective slang* stark naked.

starlet /'stɑːlɪt/ *noun* promising young performer, esp. film actress.

starling /'stɑːlɪŋ/ *noun* gregarious bird with blackish speckled lustrous plumage.

starry *adjective* (**-ier**, **-iest**) full of stars; starlike. □ **starry-eyed** *colloquial* romantic but impractical, euphoric.

start ● *verb* begin; set in motion or action; set oneself in motion or action; (often + *out*) begin journey etc.; (often + *up*) (cause to) begin operating; (often + *up*) establish; give signal to (competitors) to start in race; (often + *up*, *from*, etc.) jump in surprise, pain, etc.; rouse (game etc.). ● *noun* beginning; starting-place of race etc.; advantage given at beginning of race etc.; advantageous initial position in life, business, etc.; sudden movement of surprise, pain, etc. □ **starting block** shaped block against which runner braces feet at start of race; **starting price** odds ruling at start of horse race.

starter *noun* device for starting vehicle engine etc.; first course of meal; person giving signal to start race; horse or competitor starting in race. □ **for starters** *colloquial* to start with.

startle /'stɑːt(ə)l/ *verb* (**-ling**) shock, surprise.

starve *verb* (**-ving**) (cause to) die of hunger or suffer from malnourishment; *colloquial* feel very hungry; suffer from mental or spiritual want; (+ *of*) deprive of; compel by starvation. □ **starvation** *noun*.

stash *colloquial* ● *verb* (often + *away*) conceal, put in safe place; hoard. ● *noun* hiding place; thing hidden.

state ● *noun* existing condition or position of person or thing; *colloquial* excited or agitated mental condition, untidy condition; political community under one government, this as part of federal republic; civil government; pomp; (**the States**) USA. ● *adjective* of, for, or concerned with state; reserved for or done on ceremonial occasions. ● *verb* (**-ting**) express in speech or writing; fix, specify. □ **lie in state** be laid in public place of honour before burial; **state of the art** current stage of esp. technological development; **state-of-the-art** absolutely up-to-date; **stateroom** state apartment, large private cabin in passenger ship.

stateless *adjective* having no nationality or citizenship.

stately *adjective* (**-ier, -iest**) dignified, imposing. □ **stately home** large historic house, esp. one open to public. □ **stateliness** *noun*.

statement *noun* stating, being stated; thing stated; formal account of facts; record of transactions in bank account etc.; notification of amount due to tradesman etc.

statesman /'steɪtsmən/ *noun* (*feminine* **stateswoman**) distinguished and capable politician or diplomat. □ **statesmanlike** *adjective*; **statesmanship** *noun*.

static /'stætɪk/ ● *adjective* stationary, not acting or changing; *Physics* concerned with bodies at rest or forces in equilibrium. ● *noun* static electricity; atmospherics. □ **static electricity** electricity not flowing as current.

statics *plural noun* (usually treated as *singular*) science of bodies at rest or forces in equilibrium.

station /'steɪʃ(ə)n/ ● *noun* regular stopping place on railway line; person or thing's allotted place, building, etc.; centre for particular service or activity; establishment involved in broadcasting; military or naval base, inhabitants of this; position in life, rank, status; *Australian & NZ* large sheep or cattle farm. ● *verb* assign station to; put in position. □ **stationmaster** official in charge of railway station; **stations of**

the cross *RC Church* series of images representing events in Christ's Passion; **station wagon** *esp. US* estate car.

stationary *adjective* not moving; not meant to be moved; unchanging.

stationer *noun* dealer in stationery.

stationery *noun* writing materials, office supplies, etc.

statistic /stə'tɪstɪk/ *noun* statistical fact or item.

statistical *adjective* of statistics. □ **statistically** *adverb*.

statistics *plural noun* (usually treated as *singular*) science of collecting and analysing significant numerical data; such data. □ **statistician** /stætɪs'tɪʃ(ə)n/ *noun*.

statuary /'stætʃʊərɪ/ ● *adjective* of or for statues. ● *noun* statues collectively; making statues.

statue /'stætʃuː/ *noun* sculptured figure of person or animal, esp. life-size or larger.

statuesque /stætʃʊ'esk/ *adjective* like statue, esp. in beauty or dignity.

statuette /stætʃʊ'et/ *noun* small statue.

stature /'stætʃə/ *noun* height of (esp. human) body; calibre (esp. moral), eminence.

status /'steɪtəs/ *noun* rank, social position, relative importance; superior social etc. position. □ **status quo** /'kwəʊ/ existing conditions; **status symbol** possession etc. intended to indicate owner's superiority.

statute /'stætʃuːt/ *noun* written law passed by legislative body; rule of corporation, founder, etc., intended to be permanent.

statutory /'stætʃʊtərɪ/ *adjective* required or enacted by statute.

staunch[1] /stɔːntʃ/ *adjective* trustworthy, loyal. □ **staunchly** *adverb*.

staunch[2] = STANCH.

stave ● *noun* each of curved slats forming sides of cask; *Music* staff; stanza, verse. ● *verb* (**-ving**; *past & past participle* **stove** /stəʊv/ or **staved**) (usually + *in*) break hole in, damage, crush by forcing inwards. □ **stave off** (*past & past participle* **staved**) avert or defer (danger etc.).

stay[1] ● *verb* continue in same place or condition, not depart or change; (often

+ *at, in, with*) reside temporarily; *archaic or literary* stop, check, (esp. in *imperative*) pause; postpone (judgement etc.); assuage (hunger etc.), esp. for short time. ●*noun* act or period of staying; suspension or postponement of sentence, judgement, etc.; prop, support; (in *plural*) *historical* (esp. boned) corset. □ **stay-at-home** (person) rarely going out; **staying power** endurance; **stay the night** remain overnight; **stay put** *colloquial* remain where it is put or where one is; **stay up** not go to bed (until late).

stay² *noun* rope supporting mast, flagstaff, etc.; supporting cable on aircraft. □ **staysail** sail extended on stay.

stayer *noun* person or animal with great endurance.

STD *abbreviation* subscriber trunk dialling.

stead /sted/ *noun* □ **in (person's, thing's) stead** as substitute; **stand (person) in good stead** be advantageous or useful to him or her.

steadfast /ˈstedfɑːst/ *adjective* constant, firm, unwavering. □ **steadfastly** *adverb*; **steadfastness** *noun*.

steady /ˈstedɪ/ ●*adjective* (**-ier, -iest**) firmly fixed or supported, unwavering; uniform, regular; constant, persistent; (of person) serious and dependable; regular, established. ●*verb* (**-ies, -ied**) make or become steady. ●*adverb* steadily. ●*noun* (*plural* **-ies**) *colloquial* regular boyfriend or girlfriend. □ **steady state** unvarying condition, esp. in physical process. □ **steadily** *adverb*; **steadiness** *noun*.

steak /steɪk/ *noun* thick slice of meat (esp. beef) or fish, usually grilled or fried. □ **steakhouse** restaurant specializing in beefsteaks.

steal ●*verb* (*past* **stole**; *past participle* **stolen** /ˈstəʊl(ə)n/) take (another's property) illegally or without right or permission, esp. in secret; obtain surreptitiously, insidiously, or artfully; (+ *in, out, away, up*, etc.) move, esp. silently or stealthily. ●*noun* US *colloquial* act of stealing, theft; *colloquial* easy task, bargain. □ **steal a march on** gain advantage over by surreptitious means; **steal the show** outshine other performers, esp. unexpectedly.

stealth /stelθ/ *noun* secrecy, secret behaviour.

stealthy *adjective* (**-ier, -iest**) done or moving with stealth. □ **stealthily** *adverb*.

steam ●*noun* gas into which water is changed by boiling; condensed vapour formed from this; power obtained from steam; *colloquial* power, energy. ●*verb* cook (food) in steam; give off steam; move under steam power; (+ *ahead, away*, etc.) *colloquial* proceed or travel fast or with vigour. □ **let off steam** relieve pent-up energy or feelings; **steamboat** steam-driven boat; **steam engine** one worked or propelled by steam; **steam iron** electric iron that emits steam; **steamroller** *noun* heavy slow-moving vehicle with roller, used to flatten new-made roads, crushing power or force, *verb* crush or move forcibly or indiscriminately; **steamship** steam-driven ship; **steam train** train pulled by steam engine; **steam up** cover or become covered with condensed steam, (as **steamed up** *adjective*) *colloquial* angry, excited.

steamer *noun* steamboat; vessel for steaming food in.

steamy *adjective* (**-ier, -iest**) like or full of steam; *colloquial* erotic.

steatite /ˈstɪətaɪt/ *noun* impure form of talc, esp. soapstone.

steed *noun archaic or poetical* horse.

steel ●*noun* strong malleable low-carbon iron alloy, used esp. for making tools, weapons, etc.; strength, firmness; steel rod for sharpening knives. ●*adjective* of or like steel. ●*verb* harden, make resolute. □ **steel band** band playing chiefly calypso-style music on instruments made from oil drums; **steel wool** fine steel shavings used as abrasive; **steelworks** factory producing steel; **steelyard** balance with graduated arm along which weight is moved.

steely *adjective* (**-ier, -iest**) of or like steel; severe, resolute.

steep¹ ●*adjective* sloping sharply; (of rise or fall) rapid; *colloquial* exorbitant, unreasonable, exaggerated, incredible. ●*noun* steep slope, precipice. □ **steepen** *verb*; **steeply** *adverb*; **steepness** *noun*.

steep² ●*verb* soak or bathe in liquid. ●*noun* act of steeping; liquid for steeping. □ **steep in** imbue with, make deeply acquainted with (subject etc.).

steeple /'sti:p(ə)l/ *noun* tall tower, esp. with spire, above roof of church. □ **steeplechase** horse race with ditches, hedges, etc. to jump, cross-country foot race; **steeplejack** repairer of tall chimneys, steeples, etc.

steer[1] *verb* guide (vehicle, ship, etc.) with wheel, rudder, etc.; direct or guide (one's course, other people, conversation, etc.) in specified direction. □ **steer clear of** avoid; **steering column** column on which steering wheel is mounted; **steering committee** one deciding order of business, course of operations etc.; **steering wheel** wheel by which vehicle etc. is steered; **steersman** person who steers ship.

steer[2] *noun* bullock.

steerage *noun* act of steering; *archaic* cheapest part of ship's accommodation.

steering *noun* apparatus for steering vehicle etc.

stegosaurus /stegə'sɔ:rəs/ *noun* (*plural* **-ruses**) large dinosaur with two rows of vertical plates along back.

stela /'sti:lə/ *noun* (*plural* **stelae** /-li:/) (also **stele** /'sti:l/) ancient upright slab or pillar, usually inscribed and sculptured, esp. as gravestone.

stellar /'stelə/ *adjective* of star or stars.

stem[1] • *noun* main body or stalk of plant; stalk of fruit, flower, or leaf; stem-shaped part, e.g. slender part of wineglass; *Grammar* root or main part of noun, verb, etc. to which inflections are added; main upright timber at bow of ship. • *verb* (**-mm-**) (+ *from*) spring or originate from.

stem[2] *verb* (**-mm-**) check, stop.

stench *noun* foul smell.

stencil /'stensɪl/ • *noun* thin sheet in which pattern is cut, placed on surface and printed, inked over, etc.; pattern so produced. • *verb* (**-ll-**; *US* **-l-**) (often + *on*) produce (pattern) with stencil; mark (surface) in this way.

Sten gun *noun* lightweight sub-machine-gun.

stenographer /ste'nɒgrəfə/ *noun esp. US* shorthand typist.

stentorian /sten'tɔ:rɪən/ *adjective* loud and powerful.

step • *noun* complete movement of leg in walking or running; distance so covered; unit of movement in dancing; measure taken, esp. one of several in course of action; surface of stair, stepladder, etc. tread; short distance; sound or mark made by foot in walking etc; degree in scale of promotion, precedence, etc.; stepping in unison or to music; state of conforming. • *verb* (**-pp-**) lift and set down foot or alternate feet in walking; come or go in specified direction by stepping; make progress in specified way; (+ *off*, *out*) measure (distance) by stepping; perform (dance). □ **mind**, **watch one's step** be careful; **step down** resign; **step in** enter, intervene; **stepladder** short folding ladder not leant against wall; **step on it** *colloquial* hurry; **step out** be active socially, take large steps; **stepping-stone** large stone set in stream etc. to walk over, means of progress; **step up** increase, intensify.

step- *combining form* related by remarriage of parent. □ **stepchild**, **stepdaughter**, **stepson** one's husband's or wife's child by previous partner; **stepfather**, **stepmother**, **step-parent** mother's or father's spouse who is not one's own parent; **stepbrother**, **stepsister** child of one's step-parent by previous partner.

stephanotis /stefə'nəʊtɪs/ *noun* fragrant tropical climbing plant.

steppe /step/ *noun* level grassy treeless plain.

stereo /'sterɪəʊ/ • *noun* (*plural* **-s**) stereophonic sound reproduction or equipment; stereoscope. • *adjective* stereophonic; stereoscopic.

stereo- *combining form* solid; 3-dimensional.

stereophonic /sterɪəʊ'fɒnɪk/ *adjective* using two or more channels, to give effect of naturally distributed sound.

stereoscope /'sterɪəskəʊp/ *noun* device for producing 3-dimensional effect by viewing two slightly different photographs together. □ **stereoscopic** /-'skɒp-/ *adjective*.

stereotype /'sterɪəʊtaɪp/ • *noun* person or thing seeming to conform to widely accepted type; such type, idea, or attitude; printing plate cast from mould of composed type. ● verb (**-ping**) (esp. as **stereotyped** adjective) cause to conform to type, standardize; print from stereotype; make stereotype of.

sterile /'sterail/ adjective not able to produce crop, fruit, or young, barren; lacking ideas or originality, unproductive; free from micro-organisms etc. □ **sterility** /stə'rɪl/ noun.

sterilize /'sterɪlaɪz/ verb (also **-ise**) (**-zing** or **-sing**) make sterile; deprive of reproductive power. □ **sterilization** noun.

sterling /'stɜːlɪŋ/ ● adjective of or in British money; (of coin or precious metal) genuine, of standard value or purity; (of person etc.) genuine, reliable. ● noun British money. □ **sterling silver** silver of 92½% purity.

stern[1] adjective severe, grim; authoritarian. □ **sternly** adverb; **sternness** noun.

stern[2] noun rear part, esp. of ship or boat.

sternum /'stɜːnəm/ noun (plural **-na** or **-nums**) breastbone.

steroid /'stɪərɔɪd/ noun any of group of organic compounds including many hormones, alkaloids, and vitamins.

sterol /'sterɒl/ noun naturally occurring steroid alcohol.

stertorous /'stɜːtərəs/ adjective (of breathing etc.) laboured and noisy.

stet verb (**-tt-**) (usually written on proofsheet etc.) ignore or cancel (alteration), let original stand.

stethoscope /'steθəskəʊp/ noun instrument used in listening to heart, lungs, etc.

stetson /'stets(ə)n/ noun slouch hat with wide brim and high crown.

stevedore /'stiːvədɔː/ noun person employed in loading and unloading ships.

stew ● verb cook by long simmering in closed vessel; colloquial swelter; (of tea etc.) become bitter or strong from infusing too long. ● noun dish of stewed meat etc.; colloquial agitated or angry state.

steward /'stjuːəd/ ● noun passengers' attendant on ship, aircraft, or train; official managing meeting, show, etc.; person responsible for supplies of food etc. for college, club, etc.; property manager. □ **stewardship** noun.

stewardess /stjuːə'des/ noun female steward, esp. on ship or aircraft.

stick[1] noun short slender length of wood, esp. for use as support or weapon; thin rod of wood etc. for particular purpose; gear lever, joystick; sticklike piece of celery, dynamite, etc.; (often **the stick**) punishment, esp. by beating; colloquial adverse criticism; colloquial person, esp. when dull or unsociable. □ **stick insect** insect with twiglike body.

stick[2] verb (past & past participle **stuck**) (+ in, into, through) thrust, insert (thing or its point); stab; (+ in, into, on, etc.) fix or be fixed (as) by pointed end; fix or be fixed (as) by adhesive etc.; lose or be deprived of movement or action through adhesion, jamming, etc.; colloquial put in specified position or place, remain; colloquial endure, tolerate; (+ at) colloquial persevere with. □ **get stuck into** slang start in earnest; **stick around** colloquial linger; **sticking plaster** adhesive plaster for wounds etc.; **stick-in-the-mud** colloquial unprogressive or old-fashioned person; **stick it out** colloquial endure to the end; **stick out** (cause to) protrude; **stick out for** persist in demanding; **stick up** be or make erect or protruding upwards, fasten to upright surface, colloquial rob or threaten with gun; **stick up for** support, defend; **stuck for** at a loss for, needing; **stuck with** colloquial unable to get rid of.

sticker noun adhesive label.

stickleback /'stɪk(ə)lbæk/ noun small spiny-backed fish.

stickler /'stɪklə/ noun (+ for) person who insists on something.

sticky adjective (**-ier**, **-iest**) tending or intended to stick or adhere; glutinous, viscous; (of weather) humid; colloquial difficult, awkward, unpleasant, painful. □ **sticky wicket** colloquial difficult situation. □ **stickiness** noun.

stiff ● adjective rigid, inflexible; hard to bend, move, turn, etc.; hard to cope with, needing strength or effort; severe, strong, formal, constrained; (of muscle, person, etc.) aching from exertion, injury, etc.; (of esp. alcoholic drink) strong. ● adverb colloquial utterly, extremely. ● noun slang corpse.

□ **stiff-necked** obstinate, haughty; **stiff upper lip** appearance of firmness or fortitude. □ **stiffen** verb; **stiffly** adverb; **stiffness** noun.

stifle /'staɪf(ə)l/ verb (**-ling**) suppress; feel or make unable to breathe easily; suffocate. □ **stifling** adjective.

stigma /'stɪgmə/ noun (plural **-s** or **stigmata** /-mətə or -'mɑːtə/) shame, disgrace; part of pistil that receives pollen in pollination; (**stigmata**) marks like those on Christ's body after the Crucifixion, appearing on bodies of certain saints etc.

stigmatize /'stɪgmətaɪz/ verb (also **-ise**) (**-zing** or **-sing**) (often + as) brand as unworthy or disgraceful.

stile noun set of steps etc. allowing people to climb over fence, wall, etc.

stiletto /strˈletəʊ/ noun (plural **-s**) short dagger; (in full **stiletto heel**) long tapering heel of shoe; pointed implement for making eyelets etc.

still¹ ● adjective with little or no movement or sound; calm, tranquil; (of drink) not effervescing. ● noun deep silence; static photograph, esp. single shot from cinema film. ● adverb without moving; even now, at particular time; nevertheless; (+ comparative) even, yet, increasingly. ● verb make or become still, quieten. □ **stillbirth** birth of dead child; **stillborn** born dead, abortive; **still life** painting or drawing of inanimate objects. □ **stillness** noun.

still² noun apparatus for distilling spirits etc.

stilt noun either of pair of poles with foot supports for walking at a distance above ground; each of set of piles or posts supporting building etc.

stilted adjective (of literary style etc.) stiff and unnatural.

Stilton /'stɪlt(ə)n/ noun proprietary term strong rich esp. blue-veined cheese.

stimulant /'stɪmjʊlənt/ ● adjective stimulating esp. bodily or mental activity. ● noun stimulant substance or influence.

stimulate /'stɪmjʊleɪt/ verb (**-ting**) act as stimulus to; animate, excite, rouse. □ **stimulation** noun; **stimulative** /-lətɪv/ adjective; **stimulator** noun.

stimulus /'stɪmjʊləs/ noun (plural **-li** /-laɪ/) thing that rouses to activity.

sting ● noun sharp wounding organ of insect, nettle, etc.; inflicting of wound with this; wound itself, pain caused by it; painful quality or effect; pungency, vigour. ● verb (past & past participle **stung**) wound with sting; be able to sting; feel or cause tingling physical pain or sharp mental pain; (+ into) incite, esp. painfully; slang swindle, charge heavily. □ **stinging-nettle** nettle with stinging hairs; **stingray** broad flatfish with stinging tail.

stingy /'stɪndʒɪ/ adjective (**-ier**, **-iest**) niggardly, mean. □ **stingily** adverb; **stinginess** noun.

stink ● verb (past **stank** or **stunk**; past participle **stunk**) emit strong offensive smell; (often +⁀out) fill (place) with stink; (+ out etc.) drive (person) out etc. by stink; colloquial be or seem very unpleasant. ● noun strong offensive smell; colloquial loud complaint, fuss. □ **stink bomb** device emitting stink when opened.

stinker noun slang particularly annoying or unpleasant person; very difficult problem etc.

stinking ● adjective that stinks; slang very objectionable. ● adverb slang extremely and usually objectionably.

stint ● verb (often + on) supply (food, aid, etc.) meanly or grudgingly; (often **stint oneself**) supply (person etc.) in this way. ● noun allotted amount or period of work.

stipend /'staɪpend/ noun salary, esp. of clergyman.

stipendiary /staɪˈpendjərɪ/ ● adjective receiving stipend. ● noun (plural **-ies**) person receiving stipend. □ **stipendiary magistrate** paid professional magistrate.

stipple /'stɪp(ə)l/ ● verb (**-ling**) draw, paint, engrave, etc. with dots instead of lines; roughen surface of (paint, cement, etc.). ● noun stippling; effect of stippling.

stipulate /'stɪpjʊleɪt/ verb (**-ting**) demand or specify as part of bargain etc. □ **stipulation** noun.

stir ● verb (**-rr-**) move spoon etc. round and round in (liquid etc.), esp. to mix ingredients; cause to move, esp. slightly; be or begin to be in motion;

rise from sleep; arouse, inspire, excite; *colloquial* cause trouble by gossiping etc. ●*noun* act of stirring; commotion, excitement. □ **stir-fry** *verb* fry rapidly while stirring, *noun* stir-fried dish; **stir up** mix thoroughly by stirring, stimulate, incite.

stirrup /ˈstɪrəp/ *noun* support for horse-rider's foot, suspended by strap from saddle. □ **stirrup-cup** cup of wine etc. offered to departing traveller, originally rider; **stirrup-pump** hand-operated water-pump with footrest, used to extinguish small fires.

stitch ●*noun* single pass of needle, or result of this, in sewing, knitting, or crochet; particular method of sewing etc.; least bit of clothing; sharp pain in side induced by running etc. ●*verb* sew, make stitches (in). □ **in stitches** *colloquial* laughing uncontrollably; **stitch up** join or mend by sewing.

stoat *noun* mammal of weasel family with brown fur turning mainly white in winter.

stock ●*noun* store of goods etc. ready for sale or distribution; supply or quantity of things for use; equipment or raw material for manufacture, trade, etc.; farm animals or equipment; capital of business; shares in this; reputation, popularity; money lent to government at fixed interest; line of ancestry; liquid made by stewing bones, vegetables, etc.; fragrant garden plant; plant into which graft is inserted; main trunk of tree etc.; (in *plural*) *historical* timber frame with holes for feet in which offenders were locked as public punishment; base, support, or handle for implement or machine; butt of rifle etc.; (in *plural*) supports for ship during building or repair; band of cloth worn round neck. ●*adjective* kept regularly in stock for sale or use; commonly used, hackneyed. ●*verb* have (goods) in stock; provide (shop, farm, etc.) with goods, livestock, etc. □ **stockbroker** member of Stock Exchange dealing in stocks and shares; **stock-car** specially strengthened car used in racing where deliberate bumping is allowed; **Stock Exchange** place for dealing in stocks and shares, dealers working there; **stock-in-trade** requisite(s) of trade or profession;

stock market Stock Exchange, transactions on this; **stockpile** *noun* reserve supply of accumulated stock, *verb* accumulate stockpile (of); **stockpot** pot for making soup stock; **stock-still** motionless; **stocktaking** making inventory of stock; **stock up** (often + *with*) provide with or get stocks or supplies (of); **stockyard** enclosure for sorting or temporary keeping of cattle; **take stock** make inventory of one's stock, (often + *of*) review (situation etc.).

stockade /stɒˈkeɪd/ ●*noun* line or enclosure of upright stakes. ●*verb* (**-ding**) fortify with this.

stockinet /stɒkɪˈnet/ *noun* (also **stockinette**) elastic knitted fabric.

stocking /ˈstɒkɪŋ/ *noun* knitted covering for leg and foot, of nylon, wool, silk, etc. □ **stocking stitch** alternate rows of plain and purl.

stockist *noun* dealer in specified types of goods.

stocky *adjective* (**-ier**, **-iest**) short and strongly built. □ **stockily** *adverb*.

stodge *noun colloquial* heavy fattening food.

stodgy *adjective* (**-ier**, **-iest**) (of food) heavy, filling; dull, uninteresting. □ **stodginess** *noun*.

stoic /ˈstəʊɪk/ *noun* person having great self-control in adversity. □ **stoical** *adjective*; **stoicism** /-ɪsɪz(ə)m/ *noun*.

stoke *verb* (**-king**) (often + *up*) feed and tend (fire, furnace, etc.); *colloquial* fill oneself with food. □ **stokehold** compartment in steamship containing its boilers and furnace; **stokehole** space for stokers in front of furnace.

stoker *noun* person who tends furnace, esp. on steamship.

stole[1] *noun* woman's garment like long wide scarf worn over shoulders; strip of silk etc. worn similarly by priest.

stole[2] *past* of STEAL.

stolen *past participle* of STEAL.

stolid /ˈstɒlɪd/ *adjective* not easily excited or moved; impassive, unemotional. □ **stolidity** /-ˈlɪd-/ *noun*; **stolidly** *adverb*.

stomach /ˈstʌmək/ ●*noun* internal organ in which food is digested; lower front of body; (usually + *for*) appetite, inclination, etc. ● verb (usually in negative) endure. □ **stomach-pump** syringe for forcing liquid etc. into or out of stomach.

stomp ● verb tread or stamp heavily. ● noun lively jazz dance with heavy stamping.

stone ● noun solid non-metallic mineral matter, rock; small piece of this; hard case of kernel in some fruits; hard morbid concretion in body; (plural same) unit of weight (14 lb, 6.35 kg); precious stone. ● verb (-ning) pelt with stones; remove stones from (fruit). □ **Stone Age** prehistoric period when weapons and tools were made of stone; **stone-cold** completely cold; **stone-cold sober** completely sober; **stonecrop** succulent rock plant; **stone-dead** completely dead; **stone-deaf** completely deaf; **stone fruit** fruit with flesh enclosing stone; **stoneground** (of flour) ground with millstones; **stone's throw** short distance; **stonewall** obstruct with evasive answers etc., Cricket bat with excessive caution; **stoneware** impermeable and partly vitrified but opaque ceramic ware; **stonewashed** (esp. of denim) washed with abrasives to give worn or faded look; **stonework** masonry.

stoned adjective slang drunk, drugged.

stony adjective (-ier, -iest) full of stones; hard, rigid; unfeeling, unresponsive. □ **stony-broke** slang entirely without money. □ **stonily** adverb.

stood past & past participle of STAND.

stooge colloquial ● noun person acting as butt or foil, esp. for comedian; assistant or subordinate, esp. for unpleasant work. ● verb (-ging) (+ for) act as stooge for; (+ about, around, etc.) move about aimlessly.

stool /stuːl/ noun single seat without back or arms; footstool; (usually in plural) faeces. □ **stool-pigeon** person acting as decoy, police informer.

stoop ● verb bend down; stand or walk with shoulders habitually bent forward; (+ to do) condescend; (+ to) descend to (shameful act). ● noun stooping posture.

stop ● verb (-pp-) put an end to progress, motion, or operation of; effectively hinder or prevent; discontinue; come

to an end; cease from motion, speaking, or action; defeat; colloquial remain; stay for short time; (often + up) block or close up (hole, leak, etc.); not permit or supply as usual; 'instruct bank to withhold payment on (cheque); fill (tooth); press (violin etc. string) to obtain required pitch. ● noun stopping, being stopped; place where bus, train, etc. regularly stops; full stop; device for stopping motion at particular point; change of pitch effected by stopping string; (in organ) row of pipes of one character, knob etc. operating these; (in camera etc.) diaphragm, effective diameter of lens, device for reducing this; plosive sound. □ **pull out all the stops** make extreme effort; **stopcock** externally operated valve regulating flow through pipe etc.; **stopgap** temporary substitute; **stop off**, **over** break one's journey; **stop press** late news inserted in newspaper after printing has begun; **stopwatch** watch that can be instantly started and stopped, used in timing of races etc.

stoppage noun interruption of work due to strike etc.; (in plural) sum deducted from pay, for tax, etc.; condition of being blocked or stopped.

stopper noun plug for closing bottle etc.

storage /ˈstɔːrɪdʒ/ noun storing of goods etc.; method of, space for, or cost of storing. □ **storage battery**, **cell** one for storing electricity; **storage heater** electric heater releasing heat stored outside peak hours.

store ● noun quantity of something kept ready for use; (in plural) articles gathered for particular purpose, supply of, or place for keeping, these; department store; esp. US shop; (often in plural) shop selling basic necessities; warehouse for keeping furniture etc. temporarily; device in computer for keeping retrievable data. ● verb (-ring) (often + up, away) accumulate for future use; put (furniture etc.) in a store; stock or provide with something useful; keep (data) for retrieval. □ **in store** in reserve, to come, (+ for) awaiting; **storehouse** storage place; **storekeeper** person in charge of stores, US shopkeeper; **storeroom** storage room.

storey /ˈstɔːrɪ/ noun (plural -s) rooms etc. on one level of building.

stork *noun* long-legged usually white wading bird.

storm ● *noun* violent disturbance of atmosphere with high winds and usually thunder, rain, or snow; violent disturbance in human affairs; (+ *of*) shower of missiles or blows; outbreak of applause, hisses, etc.; assault on fortified place. ● *verb* attack or capture by storm; rush violently; rage, be violent; bluster. □ **storm centre** comparatively calm centre of cyclonic storm, centre round which controversy etc. rages; **storm cloud** heavy rain-cloud; **storm troops** shock troops, *historical* Nazi political militia; **take by storm** capture by direct assault, quickly captivate.

stormy *adjective* (**-ier, -iest**) of or affected by storms; (of wind etc.) violent; full of angry feeling or outbursts. □ **stormily** *adverb*.

story /'stɔːrɪ/ *noun* (*plural* **-ies**) account of real or imaginary events; tale, anecdote; history of person, institution, etc.; plot of novel, play, etc.; article in newspaper, material for this; *colloquial* fib. □ **storyteller** person who tells or writes stories, *colloquial* liar.

stoup /stuːp/ *noun* basin for holy water; *archaic* flagon, beaker.

stout /staʊt/ ● *adjective* rather fat, corpulent; thick, strong; brave, resolute, vigorous. ● *noun* strong dark beer. □ **stout-hearted** courageous. □ **stoutly** *adverb*; **stoutness** *noun*.

stove[1] /stəʊv/ *noun* closed apparatus burning fuel or using electricity etc. for heating or cooking. □ **stove-pipe** pipe carrying smoke and gases from stove to chimney.

stove[2] *past & past participle of* STAVE.

stow /stəʊ/ *verb* pack (goods, cargo, etc.) tidily and compactly. □ **stow away** place (thing) out of the way, hide oneself on ship etc. to travel free; **stowaway** person who stows away.

stowage *noun* stowing; place for this.

straddle /'stræd(ə)l/ *verb* (**-ling**) sit or stand across (thing) with legs wide apart; be situated on both sides of; spread legs wide apart.

strafe /strɑːf/ *verb* (**-fing**) bombard; attack with gunfire.

straggle /'stræg(ə)l/ ● *verb* (**-ling**) lack compactness or tidiness; be dispersed or sporadic; trail behind in race etc. ● *noun* straggling group. □ **straggler** *noun*; **straggly** *adjective*.

straight /streɪt/ ● *adjective* not curved, bent, crooked or curly; successive, uninterrupted; ordered, level, tidy; honest, candid; (of thinking etc.) logical; (of theatre, music, etc.) not popular or comic; unmodified, (of a drink) undiluted; *colloquial* (of person etc.) conventional, respectable, heterosexual. ● *noun* straight part, esp. concluding stretch of racetrack; straight condition; *colloquial* conventional person, heterosexual. ● *adverb* in straight line, direct; in right direction; correctly. □ **go straight** (of criminal) become honest; **straight away** immediately; **straight face** intentionally expressionless face; **straight fight** *Politics* contest between two candidates only; **straightforward** honest, frank, (of task etc.) simple; **straight man** comedian's stooge; **straight off** *colloquial* without hesitation. □ **straightness** *noun*.

straighten *verb* (often + *out*) make or become straight; (+ *up*) stand erect after bending.

strain[1] ● *verb* stretch tightly; make or become taut or tense; injure by overuse or excessive demands; exercise (oneself, one's senses, thing, etc.) intensely, press to extremes; strive intensely; distort from true intention or meaning; clear (liquid) of solid matter by passing it through sieve etc. ● *noun* act of straining, force exerted in this; injury caused by straining muscle etc.; severe mental or physical demand or exertion; snatch of music or poetry; tone or tendency in speech or writing.

strain[2] *noun* breed or stock of animals, plants, etc.; characteristic tendency.

strained *adjective* constrained, artificial; (of relationship) distrustful, tense.

strainer *noun* device for straining liquids.

strait *noun* (in *singular* or *plural*) narrow channel connecting two large bodies of water; (usually in *plural*) difficulty, distress. □ **strait-jacket** strong garment with long sleeves for confining violent prisoner etc., restrictive measures; **strait-laced** puritanical.

straitened /'streɪt(ə)nd/ *adjective* of or marked by poverty.

strand[1] ●*verb* run aground; (as **stranded** *adjective*) in difficulties, esp. without money or transport. ●*noun* foreshore, beach.

strand[2] *noun* each of twisted threads or wires making rope, cable, etc.; single thread or strip of fibre; lock of hair; element, component.

strange /streɪndʒ/ *adjective* unusual, peculiar, surprising, eccentric; (often + *to*) unfamiliar, foreign; (+ *to*) unaccustomed; not at ease. □ **strangely** *adverb*; **strangeness** *noun*.

stranger *noun* person new to particular place or company; (often + *to*) person one does not know.

strangle /'stræŋg(ə)l/ *verb* (**-ling**) squeeze windpipe or neck of, esp. so as to kill; hamper or suppress (movement, cry, etc.). □ **stranglehold** deadly grip, complete control. □ **strangler** *noun*.

strangulate /'stræŋgjʊleɪt/ *verb* (**-ting**) compress (vein, intestine, etc.), preventing circulation.

strangulation *noun* strangling, being strangled; strangulating.

strap ●*noun* strip of leather etc., often with buckle, for holding things together etc.; narrow strip of fabric forming part of garment; loop for grasping to steady oneself in moving vehicle. ●*verb* (**-pp-**) (often + *down*, *up*, etc.) secure or bind with strap; beat with strap. □ **straphanger** *slang* standing passenger in bus or train; **straphang** *verb* □ **strapless** *adjective*.

strapping *adjective* large and sturdy.

strata *plural* of STRATUM.

■ **Usage** It is a mistake to use the plural form *strata* when only one stratum is meant.

stratagem /'strætədʒəm/ *noun* cunning plan or scheme; trickery.

strategic /strə'ti:dʒɪk/ *adjective* of or promoting strategy; (of materials) essential in war; (of bombing or weapons) done or for use as longer-term military policy. □ **strategically** *adverb*.

strategy /'strætɪdʒɪ/ *noun* (*plural* **-ies**) long-term plan or policy; art of war; art of moving troops, ships, aircraft, etc.

into favourable positions. □ **strategist** *noun*.

stratify /'strætɪfaɪ/ *verb* (**-ies, -ied**) (esp. as **stratified** *adjective*) arrange in strata, grades, etc. □ **stratification** *noun*.

stratosphere /'strætəsfɪə/ *noun* layer of atmosphere above troposphere, extending to about 50 km from earth's surface.

stratum /'strɑ:təm/ *noun* (*plural* **strata**) layer or set of layers of any deposited substance, esp. of rock; atmospheric layer; social class.

straw *noun* dry cut stalks of grain; single stalk of straw; thin tube for sucking drink through; insignificant thing; pale yellow colour. □ **clutch at straws** try any remedy in desperation; **straw vote, poll** unofficial ballot as test of opinion.

strawberry /'strɔ:bərɪ/ *noun* (*plural* **-ies**) pulpy red fruit having surface studded with yellow seeds; plant bearing this. □ **strawberry mark** reddish birthmark.

stray ●*verb* wander from the right place, from one's companions, etc., go astray; deviate. ●*noun* strayed animal or person. ●*adjective* strayed, lost; isolated, occasional.

streak ●*noun* long thin usually irregular line or band, esp. of colour; strain or trait in person's character. ●*verb* mark with streaks; move very rapidly; *colloquial* run naked in public.

streaky *adjective* (**-ier, -iest**) marked with streaks; (of bacon) with streaks of fat.

stream ●*noun* body of running water, esp. small river; current, flow; group of schoolchildren of similar ability taught together. ●*verb* move as stream; run with liquid; be blown in wind; emit stream of (blood etc.); arrange (schoolchildren) in streams. □ **on stream** in operation or production.

streamer *noun* long narrow strip of ribbon or paper; long narrow flag.

streamline *verb* (**-ning**) give (vehicle etc.) form which presents least resistance to motion; make simple or more efficient.

street *noun* road in city, town, or village; this with buildings on each side.

□ **on the streets** living by prostitution; **streetcar** *US* tram; **street credibility**, **cred** *slang* acceptability within urban subculture; **streetwalker** prostitute seeking customers in street; **streetwise** knowing how to survive modern urban life.

strength *noun* being strong; degree or manner of this; person or thing giving strength; number of people present or available. □ **on the strength of** on basis of.

strengthen *verb* make or become stronger.

strenuous /ˈstrenjʊəs/ *adjective* using or requiring great effort; energetic. □ **strenuously** *adverb*.

streptococcus /streptəˈkɒkəs/ *noun* (*plural* **-cocci** /-kaɪ/) bacterium causing serious infections. □ **streptococcal** *adjective*.

streptomycin /streptəʊˈmaɪsɪn/ *noun* antibiotic effective against many disease-producing bacteria.

stress ● *noun* pressure, tension; quantity measuring this; physical or mental strain; emphasis. ● *verb* emphasize; subject to stress.

stressful *adjective* causing stress.

stretch ● *verb* draw, be drawn, or be able to be drawn out in length or size; make or become taut; place or lie at full length or spread out; extend limbs and tighten muscles after being relaxed; have specified length or extension, extend; strain or exert extremely; exaggerate. ● *noun* continuous extent, expanse, or period; stretching, being stretched; *colloquial* period of imprisonment etc. □ **at a stretch** in one period; **stretch one's legs** exercise oneself by walking; **stretch out** extend (limb etc.), last, prolong; **stretch a point** agree to something not normally allowed. □ **stretchy** *adjective* (**-ier, -iest**).

stretcher *noun* two poles with canvas etc. between for carrying person in lying position; brick etc. laid along face of wall.

strew /struː/ *verb* (*past participle* **strewn** or **strewed**) scatter over surface; (usually + *with*) spread (surface) with scattered things.

'strewth = **'STRUTH**.

striated /straɪˈeɪtɪd/ *adjective* marked with slight ridges or furrows. □ **striation** *noun*.

stricken /ˈstrɪkən/ *archaic past participle* of STRIKE. ● *adjective* affected or overcome (with illness, misfortune, etc.).

strict *adjective* precisely limited or defined, without deviation; requiring complete obedience or exact performance. □ **strictly** *adverb*; **strictness** *noun*.

stricture /ˈstrɪktʃə/ *noun* (usually in *plural*; often + *on*, *upon*) critical or censorious remark.

stride ● *verb* (**-ding**; *past* **strode**; *past participle* **stridden** /ˈstrɪd(ə)n/) walk with long firm steps; cross with one step; bestride. ● *noun* single long step; length of this; gait as determined by length of stride; (usually in *plural*) progress. □ **take in one's stride** manage easily.

strident /ˈstraɪd(ə)nt/ *adjective* loud and harsh. □ **stridency** *noun*; **stridently** *adverb*.

strife *noun* conflict, struggle.

strike ● *verb* (**-king**; *past* **struck**; *past participle* **struck** or *archaic* **stricken**) deliver (blow), inflict blow on; come or bring sharply into contact with; propel or divert with blow; (cause to) penetrate; ignite (match) or produce (sparks etc.) by rubbing; make (coin) by stamping; produce (musical note) by striking; (of clock) indicate (time) with chime etc., (of time) be so indicated; attack suddenly; (of disease) afflict; cause to become suddenly; reach, achieve; agree on (bargain); assume (attitude); find (oil etc.) by drilling; come to attention of or appear to; (of employees) engage in strike; lower or take down (flag, tent, etc.); take specified direction. ● *noun* act of striking; employees' organized refusal to work until grievance is remedied; similar refusal to participate; sudden find or success; attack, esp. from air. □ **on strike** taking part in industrial strike; **strikebreaker** person working or employed in place of strikers; **strike home** deal effective blow; **strike off** remove with stroke, delete; **strike out** hit out, act vigorously, delete; **strike up** start (acquaintance, conversation, etc.), esp. casually, begin playing (tune etc.).

striker *noun* employee on strike; *Football* attacking player positioned forward.

striking *adjective* impressive, noticeable. □ **strikingly** *adverb*.

string ● *noun* twine, narrow cord; length of this or similar material used for tying, holding together, pulling, forming head of racket, etc.; piece of catgut, wire, etc. on musical instrument, producing note by vibration; (in *plural*) stringed instruments in orchestra etc.; (in *plural*) condition or complication attached to offer etc.; set of things strung together; tough side of bean-pod etc. ● *verb* (*past & past participle* **strung**) fit with string(s); thread on string; arrange in or as string; remove strings from (bean-pod etc.). □ **string along** *colloquial* deceive, (often + *with*) keep company (with); **string-course** raised horizontal band of bricks etc. on building; **string up** hang up on strings etc., kill by hanging, (usually as **strung up** *adjective*) make tense.

stringed *adjective* (of musical instrument) having strings.

stringent /ˈstrɪndʒ(ə)nt/ *adjective* (of rules etc.) strict, precise. □ **stringency** *noun*, **stringently** *adverb*.

stringer *noun* longitudinal structural member in framework, esp. of ship or aircraft; *colloquial* freelance newspaper correspondent.

stringy *adjective* (**-ier**, **-iest**) like string, fibrous.

strip[1] ● *verb* (**-pp-**) (often + *of*) remove clothes or covering from, undress; deprive (person) of property or titles; leave bare; (often + *down*) remove accessory fittings of or take apart (machine etc.); remove old paint etc. from with solvent; damage thread of (screw) or teeth of (gearwheel). ● *noun* act of stripping, esp. in striptease; *colloquial* distinctive outfit worn by sports team. □ **strip club** club where striptease is performed; **striptease** entertainment in which performer slowly and erotically undresses.

strip[2] *noun* long narrow piece. □ **strip cartoon** comic strip; **strip light** tubular fluorescent lamp; **tear (person) off a strip** *colloquial* rebuke.

stripe *noun* long narrow band or strip differing in colour or texture from surface on either side of it; *Military* chevron etc. denoting military rank. □ **stripy** *adjective* (**-ier**, **-iest**).

striped *adjective* having stripes.

stripling /ˈstrɪplɪŋ/ *noun* youth not yet fully grown.

stripper *noun* device or solvent for removing paint etc.; performer of striptease.

strive *verb* (**-ving**; *past* **strove** /strəʊv/; *past participle* **striven** /ˈstrɪv(ə)n/) try hard; (often + *with*, *against*) struggle.

strobe *noun colloquial* stroboscope.

stroboscope /ˈstrəʊbəskəʊp/ *noun* lamp producing regular intermittent flashes. □ **stroboscopic** /-ˈskɒp-/ *adjective*.

strode *past* of STRIDE.

stroke ● *noun* act of striking; sudden disabling attack caused esp. by thrombosis; action or movement, esp. as one of series or in game etc.; slightest action; single complete action of moving wing, oar, etc.; whole motion of piston either way; mode of moving limbs in swimming; single mark made by pen, paint brush, etc.; detail contributing to general effect; sound of striking clock; oarsman nearest stern, who sets time of stroke; act or spell of stroking. ● *verb* (**-king**) pass hand gently along surface of (hair, fur, etc.); act as stroke of (boat, crew). □ **at a stroke** by a single action; **on the stroke of** punctually at; **stroke of (good) luck** unexpected fortunate event.

stroll /strəʊl/ ● *verb* walk in leisurely fashion. ● *noun* leisurely walk. □ **strolling players** *historical* actors etc. going from place to place performing.

strong ● *adjective* (**stronger** /ˈstrɒŋɡə/, **strongest** /-ɡɪst/) physically, morally, or mentally powerful; vigorous, robust; performed with muscular strength; difficult to capture, escape from, etc.; (of suspicion, belief, etc.) firmly held; powerfully affecting senses or mind etc.; (of drink, solution, etc.) with large proportion of alcohol etc.; powerful in numbers or equipment etc.; (of verb) forming inflections by vowel change in root syllable. ● *adverb* strongly. □ **come on strong** act forcefully; **going strong** *colloquial* thriving; **strong-arm** using force; **strongbox** strongly made box for valuables; **stronghold** fortress, centre of support for a cause etc.; **strong language** swearing; **strong-minded** determined; **strongroom** strongly built room for valuables; **strong suit** thing in which one excels. □ **strongish** adjective; **strongly** adverb.

strontium /ˈstrɒntɪəm/ noun soft silver-white metallic element. □ **strontium-90** radioactive isotope of this.

strop ● noun device, esp. strip of leather, for sharpening razors; colloquial bad temper. ● verb (**-pp-**) sharpen on or with strop.

stroppy /ˈstrɒpɪ/ adjective (**-ier, -iest**) colloquial bad-tempered, awkward to deal with.

strove past of STRIVE.

struck past & past participle of STRIKE.

structuralism noun doctrine that structure rather than function is important. □ **structuralist** noun & adjective.

structure /ˈstrʌktʃə/ ● noun constructed unit, esp. building; way in which thing is constructed; framework. ● verb (**-ring**) give structure to, organize. □ **structural** adjective; **structurally** adverb.

strudel /ˈstruːd(ə)l/ noun thin leaved pastry filled esp. with apple and baked.

struggle /ˈstrʌg(ə)l/ ● verb (**-ling**) violently try to get free; (often + for, to do) make great efforts under difficulties; (+ with, against) fight against; (+ along, up, etc.) make one's way with difficulty; (esp. as **struggling** adjective) have difficulty in getting recognition or a living. ● noun act or period of struggling; hard or confused contest.

strum ● verb (**-mm-**) (often + on) play on (stringed or keyboard instrument), esp. carelessly or unskilfully. ● noun strumming sound.

strumpet /ˈstrʌmpɪt/ noun archaic prostitute.

strung past & past participle of STRING.

strut ● noun bar in framework to resist pressure; strutting gait. ● verb (**-tt-**) walk in stiff pompous way; brace with strut(s).

'struth /struːθ/ interjection (also **'strewth**) colloquial exclamation of surprise.

strychnine /ˈstrɪkniːn/ noun highly poisonous alkaloid.

stub ● noun remnant of pencil, cigarette, etc.; counterfoil of cheque, receipt, etc.; stump. ● verb (**-bb-**) strike (one's toe) against something; (usually + out) extinguish (cigarette etc.) by pressing lighted end against something.

stubble /ˈstʌb(ə)l/ noun cut stalks of corn etc. left in ground after harvest; short stiff hair or bristles, esp. on unshaven face. □ **stubbly** adjective.

stubborn /ˈstʌbən/ adjective obstinate, inflexible. □ **stubbornly** adverb; **stubbornness** noun.

stubby adjective (**-ier, -iest**) short and thick.

stucco /ˈstʌkəʊ/ ● noun (plural **-es**) plaster or cement for coating walls or moulding into architectural decorations. ● verb (**-es, -ed**) coat with stucco.

stuck past & past participle of STICK[2]. □ **stuck-up** colloquial conceited, snobbish.

stud[1] ● noun large projecting nail, knob, etc. as surface ornament; double button, esp. for use in shirt-front. ● verb (**-dd-**) set with studs; (as **studded** adjective) (+ with) thickly set or strewn with.

stud[2] noun number of horses kept for breeding etc.; place where these are kept; stallion. □ **at stud** (of stallion) hired out for breeding. **stud-book** book giving pedigrees of horses; **stud-farm** place where horses are bred; **stud poker** poker with betting after dealing of cards face up.

student /ˈstjuːd(ə)nt/ noun person who is studying, esp. at place of higher or further education. □ **studentship** noun.

studio /ˈstjuːdɪəʊ/ noun (plural **-s**) workroom of sculptor, painter, photographer, etc.; place for making films, recordings, or broadcasts. □ **studio couch** couch that can be converted into a bed; **studio flat** one-roomed flat.

studious /ˈstjuːdɪəs/ adjective diligent in study or reading; painstaking. □ **studiously** adverb.

study /ˈstʌdɪ/ ● noun (plural **-ies**) acquiring knowledge, esp. from books; (in plural) pursuit of academic knowledge; private room for reading, writing, etc.; piece of work, esp. in painting, done as exercise or preliminary experiment; portrayal, esp. in literature, of character, behaviour, etc.; Music composition designed to develop player's skill; thing worth observing; thing that is or deserves to be investigated. ● verb (-ies, -ied) make study of; scrutinize; devote time and thought to understanding subject etc. or achieving desired result; (as **studied** adjective) deliberate, affected.

stuff ● noun material; fabric; substance or things not needing to be specified; particular knowledge or activity; woollen fabric; nonsense; **(the stuff)** colloquial supply, esp. of drink or drugs. ● verb pack (receptacle) tightly; (+ in, into) force or cram (thing); fill out skin to restore original shape of (bird, animal, etc.); fill (bird, piece of meat, etc.) with mixture, esp. before cooking; (also **stuff oneself**) eat greedily; push, esp. hastily or clumsily; (usually in passive; + up) block up (nose etc.); slang derogatory dispose of. □ **get stuffed** slang derogatory go away, get lost; **stuff and nonsense** something ridiculous or incredible.

stuffing noun padding for cushions etc.; mixture used to stuff food, esp. before cooking.

stuffy adjective (-ier, -iest) (of room etc.) lacking fresh air; dull, uninteresting, conventional, narrow-minded; (of nose etc.) stuffed up. □ **stuffily** adverb; **stuffiness** noun.

stultify /'stʌltɪfaɪ/ verb (-ies, -ied) make ineffective or useless, esp. by routine or from frustration. □ **stultification** noun.

stumble /'stʌmb(ə)l/ ● verb (-ling) accidentally lurch forward or have partial fall; (often + along) walk with repeated stumbles; speak clumsily; (+ on, upon, across) find by chance. ● noun act of stumbling. □ **stumbling block** circumstance causing difficulty or hesitation.

stump ● noun part of cut or fallen tree still in ground; similar part (of branch, limb, tooth, etc.) cut off or worn down; Cricket each of 3 uprights of wicket. ● verb (of question etc.) be too difficult for, baffle; (as **stumped** adjective) at a loss; Cricket put batsman out by touching stumps with ball when he is out of his crease; walk stiffly or clumsily and noisily; US traverse (district) making political speeches. □ **stump up** colloquial produce or pay over (money required).

stumpy adjective (-ier, -iest) short and thick. □ **stumpiness** noun.

stun verb (-nn-) knock senseless; stupefy; bewilder, shock.

stung past & past participle of STING.

stunk past & past participle of STINK.

stunner noun colloquial stunning person or thing.

stunning adjective colloquial extremely attractive or impressive. □ **stunningly** adverb.

stunt[1] verb retard growth or development of.

stunt[2] noun something unusual done to attract attention; trick, daring manoeuvre. □ **stunt man** man employed to take actor's place in performing dangerous stunts.

stupefy /'stjuːpɪfaɪ/ verb (-ies, -ied) make stupid or insensible; astonish. □ **stupefaction** noun.

stupendous /stjuː'pendəs/ adjective amazing; of vast size or importance. □ **stupendously** adverb.

stupid /'stjuːpɪd/ adjective (-er, -est) unintelligent, slow-witted; typical of stupid person; uninteresting; in state of stupor. □ **stupidity** /-'pɪd-/ noun (plural -ies); **stupidly** adverb.

stupor /'stjuːpə/ noun dazed or torpid state; utter amazement.

sturdy /'stɜːdɪ/ adjective (-ier, -iest) robust; strongly built; vigorous. □ **sturdily** adverb; **sturdiness** noun.

sturgeon /'stɜːdʒ(ə)n/ noun (plural same or -s) large edible fish yielding caviar.

stutter /'stʌtə/ verb & noun stammer.

sty[1] /staɪ/ noun (plural **sties**) enclosure for pigs; filthy room or dwelling.

sty[2] /staɪ/ noun (also **stye**) (plural **sties** or **styes**) inflamed swelling on edge of eyelid.

Stygian /'stɪdʒɪən/ adjective literary murky, gloomy.

style /staɪl/ ● noun kind or sort, esp. in regard to appearance and form (of person, house, etc.); manner of writing, speaking, etc.; distinctive manner of person, artistic school, or period; correct way of designating person or thing; superior quality; fashion in dress etc.; implement for scratching or engraving; part of flower supporting

stigma. ● *verb* (**-ling**) design or make etc. in particular style; designate in specified way.

stylish *adjective* fashionable, elegant. □ **stylishly** *adverb*; **stylishness** *noun*.

stylist /ˈstaɪlɪst/ *noun* designer of fashionable styles; hairdresser; stylish writer or performer.

stylistic /staɪˈlɪstɪk/ *adjective* of literary or artistic style. □ **stylistically** *adverb*.

stylized /ˈstaɪlaɪzd/ *adjective* (also **-ised**) painted, drawn, etc. in conventional non-realistic style.

stylus /ˈstaɪləs/ *noun* (*plural* **-luses**) needle-like point for producing or following groove in gramophone record; ancient pointed writing implement.

stymie /ˈstaɪmɪ/ (also **stimy**) ● *noun* (*plural* **-ies**) *Golf* situation where opponent's ball lies between one's ball and the hole; difficult situation. ● *verb* (**stymying** or **stymieing**) obstruct, thwart.

styptic /ˈstɪptɪk/ ● *adjective* serving to check bleeding. ● *noun* styptic substance.

styrene /ˈstaɪriːn/ *noun* liquid hydrocarbon used in making plastics etc.

suave /swɑːv/ *adjective* smooth; polite; sophisticated. □ **suavely** *adverb*; **suavity** *noun*.

sub *colloquial* ● *noun* submarine; subscription; substitute; sub-editor. ● *verb* (**-bb-**) (usually + *for*) act as substitute; sub-edit; lend.

sub- *prefix* at, to, or from lower position; secondary or inferior position; nearly; more or less.

subaltern /ˈsʌbəlt(ə)n/ *noun Military* officer below rank of captain, esp. second lieutenant.

sub-aqua /sʌbˈækwə/ *adjective* (of sport etc.) taking place under water.

subatomic /sʌbəˈtɒmɪk/ *adjective* occurring in, or smaller than, an atom.

subcommittee *noun* committee formed from main committee for special purpose.

subconscious /sʌbˈkɒnʃəs/ ● *adjective* of part of mind that is not fully conscious but influences actions etc. ● *noun* this part of the mind. □ **subconsciously** *adverb*.

subcontinent /ˈsʌbkɒntɪnənt/ *noun* large land mass, smaller than continent.

subcontract ● *verb* /sʌbkənˈtrækt/ employ another contractor to do (work) as part of larger project; make or carry out subcontract. ● *noun* /sʌbˈkɒntrækt/ secondary contract. □ **subcontractor** /-ˈtræktə/ *noun*.

subculture /ˈsʌbkʌltʃə/ *noun* social group or its culture within a larger culture.

subcutaneous /sʌbkjuːˈteɪnɪəs/ *adjective* under the skin.

subdivide /sʌbdɪˈvaɪd/ *verb* (**-ding**) divide again after first division. □ **subdivision** /ˈsʌbdɪvɪʒ(ə)n/ *noun*.

subdue /səbˈdjuː/ *verb* (**-dues**, **-dued**, **-duing**) conquer, suppress; tame; (as **subdued** *adjective*) softened, lacking in intensity.

sub-editor /sʌbˈedɪtə/ *noun* assistant editor; person who prepares material for printing. □ **sub-edit** *verb* (**-t-**).

subheading /ˈsʌbhedɪŋ/ *noun* subordinate heading or title.

subhuman /sʌbˈhjuːmən/ *adjective* (of behaviour, intelligence, etc.) less than human.

subject ● *noun* /ˈsʌbdʒɪkt/ theme of discussion, description, or representation; (+ *for*) circumstance, etc. giving rise to specified feeling, action, etc.; branch of study; word or phrase representing person or thing carrying out action of verb (see panel); person other than monarch living under government; *Philosophy* thinking or feeling entity, conscious self; *Music* theme, leading motif. ● *adjective* /ˈsʌbdʒɪkt/ (+ *to*) conditional on, liable or exposed to; owing obedience to government etc. ● *adverb* /ˈsʌbdʒɪkt/ (+ *to*) conditionally on. ● *verb* /səbˈdʒekt/ (+ *to*) make liable or expose to; (usually + *to*) subdue (person, nation, etc.) to superior will. □ **subjection** *noun*.

subjective /səbˈdʒektɪv/ *adjective* (of art, written history, opinion, etc.) not impartial or literal; *esp. Philosophy* of individual consciousness or perception; imaginary, partial, distorted; *Grammar* of the subject. □ **subjectively** *adverb*; **subjectivity** /sʌbdʒekˈtɪv-/ *noun*.

subjoin /sʌbˈdʒɔɪn/ *verb* add (illustration, anecdote, etc.) at the end.

sub judice /sʌb 'dʒuːdɪsɪ/ *adjective Law* under judicial consideration and therefore prohibited from public discussion. [Latin]

subjugate /'sʌbdʒʊgeɪt/ *verb* (**-ting**) conquer, bring into subjection. □ **subjugation** *noun*; **subjugator** *noun*.

subjunctive /səb'dʒʌŋktɪv/ *Grammar* ● *adjective* (of mood) expressing wish, supposition, or possibility. ● *noun* subjunctive mood or form.

sublease ● *noun* /sʌb'liːs/ lease granted by tenant to subtenant. ● *verb* /sʌb'liːs/ (**-sing**) lease to subtenant.

sublet /sʌb'let/ *verb* (**-tt-**; *past & past participle* **-let**) lease to subtenant.

sub-lieutenant /sʌblef'tenənt/ *noun* officer ranking next below lieutenant.

sublimate ● *verb* /'sʌblɪmeɪt/ (**-ting**) divert energy of (primitive impulse etc.) into socially more acceptable activity; sublime (substance); refine, purify. ● *noun* /'sʌblɪmət/ sublimated substance. □ **sublimation** *noun*.

sublime /sə'blaɪm/ ● *adjective* (**-r**, **-st**) of most exalted kind; awe-inspiring; arrogantly undisturbed. ● *verb* (**-ming**) convert (substance) from solid into vapour by heat (and usually allow to solidify again); make sublime; become pure (as if) by sublimation. □ **sublimely** *adverb*; **sublimity** /-'lɪm-/ *noun*.

subliminal /sʌb'lɪmɪn(ə)l/ *adjective Psychology* below threshold of sensation or consciousness; too faint or rapid to be consciously perceived. □ **subliminally** *adverb*.

sub-machine-gun /sʌbmə'ʃiːngʌn/ *noun* hand-held lightweight machine-gun.

submarine /sʌbmə'riːn/ ● *noun* vessel, esp. armed warship, which can be submerged and navigated under water. ● *adjective* existing, occurring, done, or used below surface of sea. □ **submariner** /-'mærɪnə/ *noun*.

submerge /səb'mɜːdʒ/ *verb* (**-ging**) place, go, or dive beneath water; overwhelm with work, problems, etc. □ **submergence** *noun*; **submersion** *noun*.

submersible /səb'mɜːsɪb(ə)l/ ● *noun* submarine operating under water for short periods. ● *adjective* capable of submerging.

submicroscopic /sʌbmaɪkrə'skɒpɪk/ *adjective* too small to be seen by ordinary microscope.

submission /səb'mɪʃ(ə)n/ *noun* submitting, being submitted; thing submitted; submissive attitude etc.

submissive /səb'mɪsɪv/ *adjective* humble, obedient. □ **submissively** *adverb*; **submissiveness** *noun*.

submit /səb'mɪt/ *verb* (**-tt-**) (often + *to*) cease resistance, yield; present for consideration; (+ *to*) subject or be subjected to (process, treatment, etc.); *Law* argue, suggest.

subnormal /sʌb'nɔːm(ə)l/ *adjective* below or less than normal, esp. in intelligence.

subordinate ● *adjective* /sə'bɔːdɪnət/ (usually + *to*) of inferior importance or rank; secondary, subservient. ● *noun* /sə'bɔːdɪnət/ person working under authority of another. ● *verb* /sə'bɔːdɪneɪt/ (**-ting**) (usually + *to*) make or treat as subordinate. □ **subordinate clause** clause serving as noun, adjective, or

Subject

The subject of a sentence is the person or thing that carries out the action of the verb and can be found by asking the question 'who or what?' before the verb, e.g.

> The goalkeeper *made a stunning save*.
> Hundreds of books *are now available on CD-ROM*.

In a passive construction, the subject of the sentence is in fact the person or thing to which the action of the verb is done, e.g.

> I *was hit by a ball*.
> Has the programme *been broadcast yet?*

adverb within sentence. □ **subordination** noun.

suborn /sə'bɔːn/ verb induce esp. by bribery to commit perjury or other crime.

subpoena /sə'piːnə/ ● noun writ ordering person's attendance in law court. ● verb (past & past participle **-naed** or **-na'd**) serve subpoena on.

sub rosa /sʌb 'rəʊzə/ adjective & adverb in confidence or in secret. [Latin]

subscribe /səb'skraɪb/ verb (**-bing**) (usually + to, for) pay (specified sum) esp. regularly for membership of organization or receipt of publication etc.; contribute to fund, for cause, etc.; (usually + to) agree with (opinion etc.). □ **subscribe to** arrange to receive (periodical etc.) regularly.

subscriber noun person who subscribes, esp. person paying regular sum for hire of telephone line. □ **subscriber trunk dialling** making of trunk calls by subscriber without assistance of operator.

subscript /'sʌbskrɪpt/ ● adjective written or printed below the line. ● noun subscript number etc.

subscription /səb'skrɪpʃ(ə)n/ noun act of subscribing; money subscribed; membership fee, esp. paid regularly.

subsequent /'sʌbsɪkwənt/ adjective (usually + to) following specified or implied event. □ **subsequently** adverb.

subservient /səb'sɜːvɪənt/ adjective servile; (usually + to) instrumental, subordinate. □ **subservience** noun.

subside /səb'saɪd/ verb (**-ding**) become tranquil; diminish; (of water etc.) sink; (of ground) cave in. □ **subsidence** /-'saɪd-, 'sʌbsɪd-/ noun.

subsidiary /səb'sɪdɪərɪ/ ● adjective supplementary; additional; (of company) controlled by another. ● noun (plural **-ies**) subsidiary company, person, or thing.

subsidize /'sʌbsɪdaɪz/ verb (also **-ise**) (**-zing** or **-sing**) pay subsidy to; support by subsidies.

subsidy /'sʌbsɪdɪ/ noun (plural **-ies**) money contributed esp. by state to keep prices at desired level; any monetary grant.

subsist /səb'sɪst/ verb (often + on) keep oneself alive; be kept alive; remain in being, exist.

subsistence noun subsisting; means of supporting life; minimal level of existence, income, etc. □ **subsistence farming** farming in which almost all produce is consumed by farmer's household.

subsoil /'sʌbsɔɪl/ noun soil just below surface soil.

subsonic /sʌb'sɒnɪk/ adjective of speeds less than that of sound.

substance /'sʌbst(ə)ns/ noun particular kind of material; reality, solidity; essence of what is spoken or written; wealth and possessions. □ **in substance** generally, essentially.

substandard /sʌb'stændəd/ adjective of lower than desired standard.

substantial /səb'stænʃ(ə)l/ adjective of real importance or value; large in size or amount; of solid structure; commercially successful; wealthy; largely true; real; existing. □ **substantially** adverb.

substantiate /səb'stænʃɪeɪt/ verb (**-ting**) support or prove truth of (charge, claim, etc.). □ **substantiation** noun.

substantive /'sʌbstəntɪv/ ● adjective actual, real, permanent; substantial. ● noun noun. □ **substantively** adverb.

substitute /'sʌbstɪtjuːt/ ● noun person or thing acting or serving in place of another; artificial alternative to a food etc. ● verb (**-ting**) (often + for) put in place of another; act as substitute for. ● adjective acting as substitute. □ **substitution** noun.

substratum /'sʌbstrɑːtəm/ noun (plural **-ta**) underlying layer.

subsume /səb'sjuːm/ verb (**-ming**) (usually + under) include under particular rule, class, etc.

subtenant /'sʌbtenənt/ noun person renting room or house etc. from its tenant. □ **subtenancy** noun (plural **-ies**).

subtend /sʌb'tend/ verb (of line) be opposite (angle, arc).

subterfuge /'sʌbtəfjuːdʒ/ noun attempt to avoid blame etc., esp. by lying or deceit.

subterranean /sʌbtə'reɪnɪən/ adjective underground.

subtext noun underlying theme.

subtitle /'sʌbtaɪt(ə)l/ ● noun subordinate or additional title of book etc.; caption of cinema film, esp. translating dialogue. ● *verb* (**-ling**) provide with subtitle(s).

subtle /'sʌt(ə)l/ *adjective* (**-r, -st**) hard to detect or describe; (of scent, colour, etc.) faint, delicate; ingenious, perceptive. □ **subtlety** *noun* (*plural* **-ies**); **subtly** *adverb*.

subtract /səb'trækt/ *verb* (often + *from*) deduct (number etc.) from another. □ **subtraction** *noun*.

subtropical /sʌb'trɒpɪk(ə)l/ *adjective* bordering on the tropics; characteristic of such regions.

suburb /'sʌbɜːb/ *noun* outlying district of city.

suburban /sə'bɜːbən/ *adjective* of or characteristic of suburbs; *derogatory* provincial in outlook. □ **suburbanite** *noun*.

suburbia /sə'bɜːbɪə/ *noun usually derogatory* suburbs and their inhabitants etc.

subvention /səb'venʃ(ə)n/ *noun* subsidy.

subversive /səb'vɜːsɪv/ ● *adjective* seeking to overthrow (esp. government). ● *noun* subversive person. □ **subversion** *noun*; **subversively** *adverb*; **subversiveness** *noun*.

subvert /səb'vɜːt/ *verb* overthrow or weaken (government etc.).

subway /'sʌbweɪ/ *noun* underground passage, esp. for pedestrians; *US* underground railway.

subzero /sʌb'zɪərəʊ/ *adjective* (esp. of temperature) lower than zero.

succeed /sək'siːd/ *verb* (often + *in*) have success; prosper; follow in order; (often + *to*) come into inheritance, office, title, or property.

success /sək'ses/ *noun* accomplishment of aim; favourable outcome; attainment of wealth, fame, etc.; successful person or thing. □ **successful** *adjective*; **successfully** *adverb*.

succession /sək'seʃ(ə)n/ *noun* following in order; series of things or people following one another; succeeding to inheritance, office, or esp. throne; right to succeed to one of these, set of people with such right. □ **in succession** one after another; **in succession to** successor of.

successive /sək'sesɪv/ *adjective* following in succession, consecutive. □ **successively** *adverb*.

successor /sək'sesə/ *noun* (often + *to*) person or thing that succeeds another.

succinct /sək'sɪŋkt/ *adjective* brief, concise. □ **succinctly** *adverb*; **succinctness** *noun*.

succour /'sʌkə/ (*US* **succor**) *archaic or formal* ● *noun* help, esp. in time of need. ● *verb* give succour to.

succulent /'sʌkjʊlənt/ ● *adjective* juicy; (of plant) thick and fleshy. ● *noun* succulent plant. □ **succulence** *noun*.

succumb /sə'kʌm/ *verb* (usually + *to*) give way; be overcome; die.

such ● *adjective* (often + *as*) of kind or degree specified or suggested; so great or extreme; unusually, abnormally. ● *pronoun* such person(s) or thing(s). □ **as such** as being what has been specified; **such-and-such** particular but unspecified; **suchlike** *colloquial* of such kind.

suck ● *verb* draw (liquid) into mouth by suction; draw liquid from in this way; roll tongue round (sweet etc.) in mouth; make sucking action or noise; (usually + *down*) engulf or drown in sucking movement. ● *noun* act or period of sucking. □ **suck in** absorb, involve (person); **suck up** (often + *to*) *colloquial* behave in a servile way, absorb.

sucker *noun* person easily duped or cheated; (+ *for*) person susceptible to; rubber etc. cap adhering by suction; similar part of plant or animal; shoot springing from plant's root below ground.

suckle /'sʌk(ə)l/ *verb* (**-ling**) feed (young) from breast or udder.

suckling /'sʌklɪŋ/ *noun* unweaned child or animal.

sucrose /'suːkrəʊz/ *noun* kind of sugar obtained from cane, beet, etc.

suction /'sʌkʃ(ə)n/ *noun* sucking; production of partial vacuum so that external atmospheric pressure forces fluid into vacant space or causes adhesion of surfaces.

Sudanese /suːdə'niːz/ ● *adjective* of Sudan. ● *noun* (*plural* same) native or national of Sudan.

sudden /'sʌd(ə)n/ *adjective* done or occurring unexpectedly or abruptly. □ **all of a sudden** suddenly. □ **suddenly** *adverb*; **suddenness** *noun*.

sudorific /suːdəˈrɪfɪk/ ● adjective causing sweating. ● noun sudorific drug.

suds plural noun froth of soap and water. □ **sudsy** adjective.

sue verb (**sues, sued, suing**) begin lawsuit against; (often + for) make application to law court for compensation etc.; (often + to, for) make plea to person for favour.

suede /sweɪd/ noun leather with flesh side rubbed into nap.

suet /ˈsuːɪt/ noun hard fat surrounding kidneys of cattle and sheep, used in cooking etc. □ **suety** adjective.

suffer /ˈsʌfə/ verb undergo pain, grief, etc.; undergo or be subjected to (pain, loss, punishment, grief, etc.); tolerate. □ **sufferer** noun; **suffering** noun.

sufferance noun tacit permission or toleration. □ **on sufferance** tolerated but not supported.

suffice /səˈfaɪs/ verb (**-cing**) be enough; meet needs of. □ **suffice it to say** I shall say only this.

sufficiency /səˈfɪʃənsɪ/ noun (plural **-ies**) (often + of) sufficient amount.

sufficient /səˈfɪʃ(ə)nt/ adjective sufficing; adequate. □ **sufficiently** adverb.

suffix /ˈsʌfɪks/ ● noun letter(s) added to end of word to form derivative. ● verb add as suffix.

suffocate /ˈsʌfəkeɪt/ verb (**-ting**) kill, stifle, or choke by stopping breathing, esp. by fumes etc.; be or feel suffocated. □ **suffocating** adjective; **suffocation** noun.

suffragan /ˈsʌfrəgən/ noun bishop assisting diocesan bishop.

suffrage /ˈsʌfrɪdʒ/ noun right of voting in political elections.

suffragette /sʌfrəˈdʒet/ noun historical woman who agitated for women's suffrage.

suffuse /səˈfjuːz/ verb (**-sing**) (of colour, moisture, etc.) spread throughout or over from within. □ **suffusion** /-ʒ(ə)n/ noun.

sugar /ˈʃʊgə/ ● noun sweet crystalline substance obtained from sugar cane and sugar beet, used in cookery, confectionery, etc.; Chemistry soluble usually sweet crystalline carbohydrate, e.g. glucose; esp. US colloquial darling (as term of address). ● verb sweeten or coat with sugar. □ **sugar beet** white beet yielding sugar; **sugar cane** tall stout perennial tropical grass yielding sugar; **sugar-daddy** slang elderly man who lavishes gifts on young woman; **sugar loaf** conical moulded mass of hard refined sugar.

sugary adjective containing or resembling sugar; cloying, sentimental. □ **sugariness** noun.

suggest /səˈdʒest/ verb (often + that) propose (theory, plan, etc.); hint at; evoke (idea etc.); (**suggest itself**) (of idea etc.) come into person's mind.

suggestible adjective capable of being influenced by suggestion. □ **suggestibility** noun.

suggestion /səˈdʒestʃ(ə)n/ noun suggesting; thing suggested; slight trace, hint; insinuation of belief or impulse into the mind.

suggestive /səˈdʒestɪv/ adjective (usually + of) conveying a suggestion; (of remark, joke, etc.) suggesting something indecent. □ **suggestively** adverb.

suicidal /suːɪˈsaɪd(ə)l/ adjective (of person) liable to commit suicide; of or tending to suicide; destructive to one's own interests. □ **suicidally** adverb.

suicide /ˈsuːɪsaɪd/ noun intentional self-killing; person who commits suicide; action destructive to one's own interests etc.

sui generis /sjuːaɪˈdʒenərɪs/ adjective of its own kind, unique. [Latin]

suit /suːt, sjuːt/ ● noun set of usually matching clothes consisting usually of jacket and trousers or skirt; clothing for particular purpose; any of the 4 sets into which pack of cards is divided; lawsuit. ● verb go well with (person's appearance); meet requirements of; (**suit oneself**) do as one chooses; be in harmony with; make fitting; be convenient; adapt; (as **suited** adjective) appropriate, well-fitted. □ **suitcase** flat case for carrying clothes, usually with hinged lid.

suitable adjective (usually + to, for) well-fitted for purpose; appropriate to occasion. □ **suitability** noun; **suitably** adverb.

suite /swiːt/ noun set of rooms, furniture, etc.; Music set of instrumental pieces.

suitor /'suːtə/ noun man who woos woman; plaintiff or petitioner in lawsuit.

sulfur US = SULPHUR etc.

sulk ● verb be sulky. ● noun (also **the sulks**) fit of sullen silence.

sulky /'sʌlkɪ/ adjective (-**ier**, -**iest**) sullen and unsociable from resentment or ill temper. □ **sulkily** adverb.

sullen /'sʌlən/ adjective sulky, morose. □ **sullenly** adverb; **sullenness** noun.

sully /'sʌlɪ/ verb (-**ies**, -**ied**) spoil purity or splendour of (reputation etc.).

sulphate /'sʌlfeɪt/ noun (US **sulfate**) salt or ester of sulphuric acid.

sulphide /'sʌlfaɪd/ noun (US **sulfide**) binary compound of sulphur.

sulphite /'sʌlfaɪt/ noun (US **sulfite**) salt or ester of sulphurous acid.

sulphonamide /sʌl'fɒnəmaɪd/ noun (US **sulfonamide**) kind of antibiotic drug containing sulphur.

sulphur /'sʌlfə/ noun (US **sulfur**) pale yellow non-metallic element burning with blue flame and stifling smell. □ **sulphur dioxide** colourless pungent gas formed by burning sulphur in air and dissolving it in water.

sulphuric /sʌl'fjʊərɪk/ adjective (US **sulfuric**) of or containing sulphur with valency of 6. □ **sulphuric acid** dense highly corrosive oily acid.

sulphurous /'sʌlfərəs/ adjective (US **sulfurous**) of or like sulphur; containing sulphur with valency of 4. □ **sulphurous acid** unstable weak acid used e.g. as bleaching agent.

sultan /'sʌlt(ə)n/ noun Muslim sovereign.

sultana /sʌl'tɑːnə/ noun seedless raisin; sultan's wife, mother, concubine, or daughter.

sultanate /'sʌltəneɪt/ noun position of or territory ruled by sultan.

sultry /'sʌltrɪ/ adjective (-**ier**, -**iest**) (of weather) oppressively hot; (of person) passionate, sensual.

sum ● noun total resulting from addition; amount of money; arithmetical problem; (esp. in plural) colloquial arithmetic work, esp. elementary. ● verb

(-**mm**-) find sum of. □ **in sum** briefly, to sum up; **summing-up** judge's review of evidence given to jury, recapitulation of main points of argument etc.; **sum up** (esp. of judge) give summing-up, form or express opinion of (person, situation, etc.), summarize.

sumac /'suːmæk/ noun (also **sumach**) shrub with reddish fruits used as spice; dried and ground leaves of this for use in tanning and dyeing.

summarize /'sʌməraɪz/ verb (also -**ise**) (-**zing** or -**sing**) make or be summary of.

summary /'sʌmərɪ/ ● noun (plural -**ies**) brief account giving chief points. ● adjective brief, without details or formalities. □ **summarily** adverb.

summation /sə'meɪʃ(ə)n/ noun finding of total or sum; summarizing.

summer /'sʌmə/ noun warmest season of year; (often + of) mature stage of life etc. □ **summer house** light building in garden etc. for use in summer; **summer pudding** dessert of soft fruit pressed in bread casing; **summer school** course of lectures etc. held in summer, at university; **summer time** period from March to October when clocks etc. are advanced one hour; **summertime** season or period of summer. □ **summery** adjective.

summit /'sʌmɪt/ noun highest point, top; highest level of achievement or status; (in full **summit conference**, **meeting**, etc.) discussion between heads of governments.

summon /'sʌmən/ verb order to come or appear, esp. in lawcourt; (usually + to do) call on; call together; (often + up) gather (courage, resources, etc.).

summons /'sʌmənz/ ● noun (plural **summonses**) authoritative call to attend or do something, esp. to appear in court. ● verb esp. Law serve with summons.

sumo /'suːməʊ/ noun Japanese wrestling in which only soles of feet may touch ground.

sump noun casing holding oil in internal-combustion engine; pit, well, etc. for collecting superfluous liquid.

sumptuary /'sʌmptʃʊərɪ/ adjective Law regulating (esp. private) expenditure.

sumptuous /'sʌmptʃʊəs/ *adjective* costly, splendid, magnificent. □ **sumptuously** *adverb*; **sumptuousness** *noun*.

Sun. *abbreviation* Sunday.

sun ● *noun* the star round which the earth travels and from which it receives light and warmth; this light or warmth; any star. ● *verb* (**-nn-**) (often **sun oneself**) expose to sun. □ **sunbathe** bask in sun, esp. to tan one's body; **sunbeam** ray of sunlight; **sunblock** lotion protecting skin from sun; **sunburn** inflammation of skin from exposure to sun; **sunburnt** affected by sunburn; **sundial** instrument showing time by shadow of pointer in sunlight; **sundown** sunset; **sunflower** tall plant with large golden-rayed flowers; **sunglasses** tinted spectacles to protect eyes from glare; **sunlamp** lamp giving ultraviolet rays for therapy or artificial suntan; **sunlight** light from sun; **sunlit** illuminated by sun; **sun lounge** room with large windows etc. to receive much sunlight; **sunrise** (time of) sun's rising; **sunroof** opening panel in car's roof; **sunset** (time of) sun's setting; **sunshade** parasol, awning; **sunshine** sunlight, area illuminated by it, fine weather, cheerfulness; **sunspot** dark patch on sun's surface; **sunstroke** acute prostration from excessive heat of sun; **suntan** brownish skin colour caused by exposure to sun; **suntrap** sunny place, esp. sheltered from wind; **sun-up** *esp. US* sunrise.

sundae /'sʌndeɪ/ *noun* ice cream with fruit, nuts, syrup, etc.

Sunday /'sʌndeɪ/ *noun* day of week following Saturday; Christian day of worship; *colloquial* newspaper published on Sundays. □ **month of Sundays** *colloquial* very long period; **Sunday school** religious class held on Sundays for children.

sunder /'sʌndə/ *verb literary* sever, keep apart.

sundry /'sʌndrɪ/ ● *adjective* various, several. ● *noun* (*plural* **-ies**) (in *plural*) oddments, accessories, etc. not mentioned individually. □ **all and sundry** everyone.

sung *past participle* of SING.

sunk *past & past participle* of SINK.

sunken *adjective* that has sunk; lying below general surface; (of eyes, cheeks, etc.) shrunken, hollow.

Sunni /'sʌnɪ/ *noun* (*plural* same or **-s**) one of two main branches of Islam; adherent of this.

sunny *adjective* (**-ier, -iest**) bright with or warmed by sunlight; cheerful. □ **sunnily** *adverb*; **sunniness** *noun*.

sup[1] ● *verb* (**-pp-**) drink by sips or spoonfuls; *esp. Northern English colloquial* drink (alcohol). ● *noun* sip of liquid.

sup[2] *verb* (**-pp-**) *archaic* take supper.

super /'su:pə/ ● *adjective colloquial* excellent, unusually good. ● *noun colloquial* superintendent; supernumerary.

super- *combining form* on top, over, beyond; to extreme degree; extra good or large of its kind; of higher kind.

superannuate /su:pər'ænjʊeɪt/ *verb* (**-ting**) pension (person) off; dismiss or discard as too old; (as **superannuated** *adjective*) too old for work.

superannuation *noun* pension; payment made to obtain pension.

superb /su:'pɜ:b/ *adjective colloquial* excellent; magnificent. □ **superbly** *adverb*.

supercargo /'su:pəka:gəʊ/ *noun* (*plural* **-es**) person in merchant ship managing sales etc. of cargo.

supercharge /'su:pətʃɑ:dʒ/ *verb* (**-ging**) (usually + *with*) charge (atmosphere etc.) with energy, emotion, etc.; use supercharger on.

supercharger *noun* device forcing extra air or fuel into internal-combustion engine.

supercilious /su:pə'sɪlɪəs/ *adjective* haughtily contemptuous. □ **superciliously** *adverb*; **superciliousness** *noun*.

supererogation /su:pərerə'geɪʃ(ə)n/ *noun* doing of more than duty requires.

superficial /su:pə'fɪʃ(ə)l/ *adjective* of or on the surface; lacking depth; swift, cursory; apparent, not real; (esp. of person) of shallow feelings etc. □ **superficiality** /-ʃɪ'æl-/ *noun*; **superficially** *adverb*.

superfluity /su:pə'flu:ɪtɪ/ *noun* (*plural* **-ies**) being superfluous; superfluous amount or thing.

superfluous /su:'pɜ:flʊəs/ *adjective* more than is needed or wanted; useless.

supergrass /'su:pəgrɑːs/ *noun colloquial* police informer implicating many people.

superhuman /su:pə'hju:mən/ *adjective* exceeding normal human capacity or power.

superimpose /su:pərɪm'pəuz/ *verb* (**-sing**) (usually + *on*) place (thing) on or above something else. □ **superimposition** /-pə'zɪʃ(ə)n/ *noun*.

superintend /su:pərɪn'tend/ *verb* manage, supervise (work etc.). □ **superintendence** *noun*.

superintendent /su:pərɪn'tend(ə)nt/ *noun* police officer above rank of chief inspector; person who superintends; director of institution etc.

superior /su:'pɪərɪə/ ● *adjective* higher in rank, quality, etc.; high-quality; supercilious; (often + *to*) better or greater in some respect; written or printed above the line. ● *noun* person superior to another, esp. in rank; head of monastery etc. □ **superiority** /-'ɒr-/ *noun*.

superlative /su:'pɜːlətɪv/ ● *adjective* of highest degree; excellent; *Grammar* (of adjective or adverb) expressing highest or very high degree of quality etc. denoted by simple word. ● *noun Grammar* superlative expression or word; (in *plural*) high praise, exaggerated language.

superman *noun colloquial* man of exceptional powers or achievement.

supermarket /'su:pəmɑːkɪt/ *noun* large self-service store selling food, household goods, etc.

supernatural /su:pə'nætʃər(ə)l/ ● *adjective* not attributable to, or explicable by, natural or physical laws; magical; mystical. ● *noun* (**the supernatural**) supernatural forces etc. □ **supernaturally** *adverb*.

supernova /su:pə'nəuvə/ *noun* (*plural* **-vae** /-viː/ or **-vas**) star that suddenly increases very greatly in brightness.

supernumerary /su:pə'nju:mərəri/ ● *adjective* in excess of normal number; engaged for extra work; (of actor) with non-speaking part. ● *noun* (*plural* **-ies**) supernumerary person or thing.

superphosphate /su:pə'fɒsfeɪt/ *noun* fertilizer made from phosphate rock.

superpower /'su:pəpauə/ *noun* extremely powerful nation.

superscript /'su:pəskrɪpt/ ● *adjective* written or printed above. ● *noun* superscript number or symbol.

supersede /su:pə'siːd/ *verb* (**-ding**) take place of; put or use another in place of. □ **supersession** /-'seʃ-/ *noun*.

supersonic /su:pə'sɒnɪk/ *adjective* of or having speed greater than that of sound. □ **supersonically** *adverb*.

superstar /'su:pəstɑː/ *noun* extremely famous or renowned actor, musician, etc.

superstition /su:pə'stɪʃ(ə)n/ *noun* belief in the supernatural; irrational fear of the unknown or mysterious; practice, belief, or religion based on this. □ **superstitious** *adjective*.

superstore /'su:pəstɔː/ *noun* very large supermarket.

superstructure /'su:pəstrʌktʃə/ *noun* structure built on top of another; upper part of building, ship, etc.

supertanker /'su:pətæŋkə/ *noun* very large tanker.

supertax /'su:pətæks/ *noun* surtax.

supervene /su:pə'viːn/ *verb* (**-ning**) *formal* occur as interruption or change from some state. □ **supervention** *noun*.

supervise /'su:pəvaɪz/ *verb* (**-sing**) oversee, superintend. □ **supervision** /-'vɪʒ(ə)n/ *noun*; **supervisor** *noun*; **supervisory** *adjective*.

superwoman *noun colloquial* woman of exceptional ability or power.

supine /'su:paɪn/ ● *adjective* lying face upwards; inactive, indolent. ● *noun* type of Latin verbal noun.

supper /'sʌpə/ *noun* meal taken late in day, esp. evening meal less formal and substantial than dinner.

supplant /sə'plɑːnt/ *verb* take the place of, esp. by underhand means.

supple /'sʌp(ə)l/ *adjective* (**-r**, **-st**) easily bent, pliant, flexible. □ **suppleness** *noun*.

supplement ● *noun* /'sʌplɪmənt/ thing or part added to improve or provide further information; separate section of newspaper etc. ● *verb* /'sʌplɪment/ provide supplement for. □ **supplemental** /-'ment(ə)l/ *adjective*; **supplementary** /-'mentəri/ *adjective*; **supplementation** *noun*.

suppliant /'sʌplɪənt/ ● *adjective* supplicating. ● *noun* humble petitioner.

supplicate /'sʌplɪkeɪt/ *verb* (**-ting**) *literary* make humble petition to or for. □ **supplicant** *noun*; **supplication** *noun*; **supplicatory** /-kətərɪ/ *adjective*.

supply /sə'plaɪ/ ● *verb* (**-ies, -ied**) provide (thing needed); (often + *with*) provide (person etc. with something); make up for (deficiency etc.). ● *noun* (*plural* **-ies**) provision of what is needed; stock, store; (in *plural*) provisions, equipment, etc. for army, expedition, etc.; person, esp. teacher, acting as temporary substitute. □ **supply and demand** quantities available and required, as factors regulating price. □ **supplier** *noun*.

support /sə'pɔːt/ ● *verb* carry all or part of weight of; keep from falling, sinking, or failing; provide for; strengthen, encourage; give help or corroboration to; speak in favour of; take secondary part to (actor etc.); perform secondary act to (main act) at pop concert. ● *noun* supporting, being supported; person or thing that supports. □ **in support of** so as to support. □ **supportive** *adjective*; **supportively** *adverb*; **supportiveness** *noun*.

supporter *noun* person or thing that supports particular cause, team, sport, etc.

suppose /sə'pəʊz/ *verb* (**-sing**) (often + *that*) assume, be inclined to think; take as possibility or hypothesis; require as condition; (as **supposed** *adjective*) presumed. □ **be supposed to** be expected or required to; (in negative) ought not, not be allowed to; **I suppose so** *expression of hesitant agreement*.

supposedly /sə'pəʊzɪdlɪ/ *adverb* as is generally believed.

supposition /sʌpə'zɪʃ(ə)n/ *noun* what is supposed or assumed.

suppositious /sʌpə'zɪʃəs/ *adjective* hypothetical.

suppository /sə'pɒzɪtərɪ/ *noun* (*plural* **-ies**) solid medical preparation put into rectum or vagina to melt.

suppress /sə'pres/ *verb* put an end to; prevent (information, feelings, etc.) from being seen, heard, or known; *Electricity* partially or wholly eliminate (interference etc.), equip (device) to reduce interference due to it. □ **suppressible** *adjective*; **suppression** *noun*; **suppressor** *noun*.

suppurate /'sʌpjʊreɪt/ *verb* (**-ting**) form or secrete pus; fester. □ **suppuration** *noun*.

supra- *prefix* above.

supranational /suːprə'næʃən(ə)l/ *adjective* transcending national limits.

supremacy /suː'preməsɪ/ *noun* (*plural* **-ies**) being supreme; highest authority.

supreme /suː'priːm/ *adjective* highest in authority or rank; greatest, most important; (of penalty, sacrifice, etc.) involving death. □ **supremely** *adverb*.

supremo /suː'priːməʊ/ *noun* (*plural* **-s**) supreme leader.

surcharge /'sɜːtʃɑːdʒ/ ● *noun* additional charge or payment. ● *verb* (**-ging**) exact surcharge from.

surd ● *adjective* (of number) irrational. ● *noun* surd number.

sure /ʃʊə/ ● *adjective* (often + *of, that*) convinced; having or seeming to have adequate reason for belief; (+ *of*) confident in anticipation or knowledge of; reliable, unfailing; (+ *to do*) certain; undoubtedly true or truthful. ● *adverb colloquial* certainly. □ **make sure** make or become certain, ensure; **sure-fire** *colloquial* certain to succeed; **sure-footed** never stumbling; **to be sure** admittedly, indeed, certainly. □ **sureness** *noun*.

surely *adverb* with certainty or safety; added to statement to express strong belief in its correctness.

surety /'ʃʊərətɪ/ *noun* (*plural* **-ies**) money given as guarantee of performance etc.; person taking responsibility for another's debt, obligation, etc.

surf ● *noun* foam of sea breaking on rock or (esp. shallow) shore. ● *verb* engage in surfing. □ **surfboard** long narrow board used in surfing. □ **surfer** *noun*.

surface /'sɜːfɪs/ ● *noun* the outside of a thing; any of the limits of a solid; top of liquid, soil, etc.; outward or superficial aspect; *Geometry* thing with length and breadth but no thickness. ● *verb* (**-cing**) give (special) surface to (road, paper, etc.); rise or bring to surface; become visible or known; *colloquial* wake up, get up. □ **surface mail** mail not carried by air; **surface tension** tension of surface of liquid, tending to minimize its surface area.

surfeit /'sɜːfɪt/ ● *noun* excess, esp. in eating or drinking; resulting fullness. ● *verb* (**-t-**) overfeed; (+ *with*) (cause to) be wearied through excess.

surfing *noun* sport of riding surf on board.

surge ● *noun* sudden rush; heavy forward or upward motion; sudden increase (in price etc.); sudden but brief increase in pressure, voltage, etc.; surging motion of sea, waves, etc. ● *verb* (**-ging**) move suddenly and powerfully forwards; (of sea etc.) swell.

surgeon /'sɜːdʒ(ə)n/ *noun* medical practitioner qualified to practise surgery; naval or military medical officer.

surgery /'sɜːdʒərɪ/ *noun* (*plural* **-ies**) manual or instrumental treatment of injuries or disorders of body; place where or time when doctor, dentist, etc. gives advice and treatment to patients, or MP, lawyer, etc. gives advice.

surgical /'sɜːdʒɪk(ə)l/ *adjective* of or by surgery or surgeons; used for surgery; (of appliance) worn to correct deformity etc.; (esp. of military action) swift and precise. □ **surgical spirit** methylated spirits used for cleansing etc. □ **surgically** *adverb*.

surly /'sɜːlɪ/ *adjective* (**-ier**, **-iest**) bad-tempered, unfriendly. □ **surliness** *noun*.

surmise /sə'maɪz/ ● *noun* conjecture. ● *verb* (**-sing**) (often + *that*) infer doubtfully; suppose; guess.

surmount /sə'maʊnt/ *verb* overcome (difficulty, obstacle); (usually in *passive*) cap, crown. □ **surmountable** *adjective*.

surname /'sɜːneɪm/ *noun* name common to all members of family.

surpass /sə'pɑːs/ *verb* outdo, be better than; (as **surpassing** *adjective*) greatly exceeding, excelling others.

surplice /'sɜːplɪs/ *noun* loose full-sleeved white vestment worn by clergy etc.

surplus /'sɜːpləs/ ● *noun* amount left over when requirements have been met; excess of income over spending. ● *adjective* exceeding what is needed or used.

surprise /sə'praɪz/ ● *noun* unexpected or astonishing thing; emotion caused by this; catching or being caught unawares. ● *adjective* made, done, etc. without warning. ● *verb* (**-sing**) affect with surprise; (usually in *passive*; + *at*) shock, scandalize; capture by surprise; come upon (person) unawares; (+ *into*) startle, betray, etc. (person) into doing something. □ **surprising** *adjective*; **surprisingly** *adverb*.

surreal /sə'rɪəl/ *adjective* unreal; dreamlike; bizarre.

surrealism /sə'rɪəlɪz(ə)m/ *noun* 20th-c. movement in art and literature aiming to express subconscious mind by dream imagery etc. □ **surrealist** *noun* & *adjective*; **surrealistic** /-'lɪs-/ *adjective*; **surrealistically** /-'lɪs-/ *adverb*.

surrender /sə'rendə/ ● *verb* hand over, relinquish; submit; esp. to enemy; (often **surrender oneself**; + *to*) yield to habit, emotion, influence, etc.; give up rights under (life-insurance policy) in return for smaller sum received immediately. ● *noun* surrendering.

surreptitious /sʌrəp'tɪʃəs/ *adjective* done by stealth; underhand. □ **surreptitiously** *adverb*.

surrogate /'sʌrəgət/ *noun* substitute; deputy, esp. of bishop. □ **surrogate mother** woman who conceives and gives birth to child on behalf of woman unable to do so. □ **surrogacy** *noun*.

surround /sə'raʊnd/ ● *verb* come or be all round; encircle, enclose. ● *noun* border or edging, esp. area between walls and carpet.

surroundings *plural noun* things in neighbourhood of, or conditions affecting, person or thing; environment.

surtax /'sɜːtæks/ *noun* additional tax, esp. on high incomes.

surtitle /'sɜːtaɪt(ə)l/ *noun* caption translating words of opera, projected on to screen above stage.

surveillance /sə'veɪləns/ *noun* close watch undertaken by police etc., esp. on suspected person.

survey ● *verb* /sə'veɪ/ take or present general view of; examine condition of (building etc.); determine boundaries, extent, ownership, etc. of (district etc.). ●noun /'sɜːveɪ/ general view or consideration; surveying of property; result of this; investigation of public opinion etc.; map or plan made by surveying.

surveyor /sə'veɪə/ noun person who surveys land and buildings, esp. professionally.

survival /sə'vaɪv(ə)l/ noun surviving; relic.

survive /sə'vaɪv/ verb (**-ving**) continue to live or exist; live or exist longer than; come alive through or continue to exist in spite of (danger, accident, etc.). □ **survivor** noun.

sus = SUSS.

susceptibility noun (plural **-ies**) being susceptible; (in plural) person's feelings.

susceptible /sə'septəb(ə)l/ adjective impressionable, sensitive; easily moved by emotion; (+ to) accessible or sensitive to; (+ of) allowing, admitting of (proof etc.).

suspect ●verb /səs'pekt/ be inclined to think; have impression of the existence or presence of; (often + of) mentally accuse; doubt innocence, genuineness, or truth of. ●noun /'sʌspekt/ suspected person. ●adjective /'sʌspekt/ subject to suspicion or distrust.

suspend /səs'pend/ verb hang up; keep inoperative or undecided temporarily; debar temporarily from function, office, etc.; (as **suspended** adjective) (of particles or body in fluid) floating between top and bottom. □ **suspended animation** temporary deathlike condition; **suspended sentence** judicial sentence remaining unenforced on condition of good behaviour.

suspender noun attachment to hold up stocking or sock by its top; (in plural) US pair of braces. □ **suspender belt** woman's undergarment with suspenders.

suspense /səs'pens/ noun state of anxious uncertainty or expectation.

suspension /səs'penʃ(ə)n/ noun suspending, being suspended; means by which vehicle is supported on its axles; substance consisting of particles suspended in fluid. □ **suspension bridge** bridge with roadway suspended from cables supported by towers.

suspicion /səs'pɪʃ(ə)n/ noun unconfirmed belief; distrust; suspecting, being suspected; (+ of) slight trace of.

suspicious /səs'pɪʃəs/ adjective prone to or feeling suspicion; indicating or justifying suspicion. □ **suspiciously** adverb.

suss /sʌs/ verb (also **sus**) (**-ss-**) slang (usually + out) investigate, inspect; understand; work out.

sustain /səs'teɪn/ verb bear weight of, support, esp. for long period; encourage, support; endure, stand; (of food) nourish; undergo (defeat, injury, loss, etc.); (of court etc.) decide in favour of, uphold; substantiate, corroborate; keep up (effort etc.). □ **sustainable** adjective.

sustenance /'sʌstɪnəns/ noun nourishment, food; means of support.

suture /'suːtʃə/ ●noun joining edges of wound or incision by stitching; stitch or thread etc. used for this. ●verb (**-ring**) stitch (wound, incision).

suzerain /'suːzəreɪn/ noun historical feudal overlord; archaic sovereign or state having some control over another state that is internally self-governing. □ **suzerainty** noun.

svelte /svelt/ adjective slim, slender, graceful.

SW abbreviation south-west(ern).

swab /swɒb/ ●noun absorbent pad used in surgery; specimen of secretion etc. taken for examination; mop etc. for cleaning or mopping up. ●verb (**-bb-**) clean with swab; (+ up) absorb (moisture) with swab; mop clean (ship's deck).

swaddle /'swɒd(ə)l/ verb (**-ling**) wrap tightly in bandages, wrappings, etc. □ **swaddling-clothes** narrow bandages formerly wrapped round newborn child to restrain its movements.

swag noun slang thief's booty; Australian & NZ traveller's bundle; festoon of flowers, foliage, drapery, etc.

swagger /'swægə/ ●verb walk or behave arrogantly or self-importantly. ●noun swaggering gait or manner.

swain noun archaic country youth; poetical young lover or suitor.

swallow¹ /ˈswɒləʊ/ ● *verb* make or let (food etc.) pass down one's throat; accept meekly or gullibly; repress (emotion); engulf; say (words etc.) indistinctly. ● *noun* act of swallowing; amount swallowed.

swallow² /ˈswɒləʊ/ *noun* migratory swift-flying bird with forked tail. □ **swallow-dive** dive with arms spread sideways; **swallow-tail** deeply forked tail, butterfly etc. with this.

swam *past of* SWIM.

swamp /swɒmp/ ● *noun* piece of wet spongy ground. ● *verb* submerge, inundate; cause to fill with water and sink; overwhelm with numbers or quantity. □ **swampy** *adjective* (**-ier, -iest**).

swan /swɒn/ ● *noun* large web-footed usually white waterfowl with long flexible neck. ● *verb* (**-nn-**) (usually + *about, off*, etc.) *colloquial* move about casually or with superior manner. □ **swansong** person's last work or performance before death, retirement, etc.

swank *colloquial* ● *noun* ostentation, swagger. ● *verb* show off. □ **swanky** *adjective* (**-ier, -iest**).

swap /swɒp/ (also **swop**) ● *verb* (**-pp-**) exchange, barter. ● *noun* act of swapping; thing suitable for swapping.

sward /swɔːd/ *noun literary* expanse of short grass.

swarf /swɔːf/ *noun* fine chips or filings of stone, metal, etc.

swarm¹ /swɔːm/ ● *noun* cluster of bees leaving hive etc. with queen bee to establish new colony; large group of insects, birds, or people; (in *plural*, + *of*) great numbers. ● *verb* move in or form swarm; (+ *with*) be overrun or crowded with.

swarm² /swɔːm/ *verb* (+ *up*) climb (rope, tree, etc.) clasping or clinging with arms and legs.

swarthy /ˈswɔːðɪ/ *adjective* (**-ier, -iest**) dark-complexioned, dark in colour.

swashbuckler /ˈswɒʃbʌklə/ *noun* swaggering adventurer. □ **swashbuckling** *adjective & noun.*

swastika /ˈswɒstɪkə/ *noun* ancient symbol formed by equal-armed cross with each arm continued at a right angle; this with clockwise continuations as symbol of Nazi Germany.

swat /swɒt/ ● *verb* (**-tt-**) crush (fly etc.) with blow; hit hard and abruptly. ● *noun* act of swatting.

swatch /swɒtʃ/ *noun* sample, esp. of cloth; collection of samples.

swath /swɔːθ/ *noun* (also **swathe** /sweɪð/) ridge of cut grass, corn, etc.; space left clear by mower, scythe, etc.

swathe /sweɪð/ *verb* (**-thing**) bind or wrap in bandages, garments, etc.

sway ● *verb* (cause to) move unsteadily from side to side; oscillate irregularly; waver; have influence over. ● *noun* rule, government; swaying motion.

swear /sweə/ *verb* (*past* **swore**; *past participle* **sworn**) state or promise on oath; cause to take oath; *colloquial* insist; (often + *at*) use profane or obscene language; (+ *by*) appeal to as witness or guarantee of oath, *colloquial* have great confidence in. □ **swear in** admit to office etc. by administering oath; **swear off** *colloquial* promise to keep off (drink etc.); **swear-word** profane or obscene word.

sweat /swet/ ● *noun* moisture exuded through pores, esp. when one is hot or nervous; state or period of sweating; *colloquial* state of anxiety; *colloquial* effort, drudgery, laborious task or undertaking; condensed moisture on surface. ● *verb* (*past & past participle* **sweated** or *US* **sweat**) exude sweat; be terrified, suffer, etc.; (of wall etc.) show surface moisture; (cause to) toil or drudge; emit like sweat; make (horse, athlete, etc.) sweat by exercise; (as **sweated** *adjective*) (of goods, labour, etc.) produced by or subjected to exploitation. □ **no sweat** *colloquial* no bother, no trouble; **sweat-band** band of absorbent material inside hat or round head, wrist, etc. to soak up sweat; **sweatshirt** sleeved cotton sweater; **sweatshop** workshop where sweated labour is employed. □ **sweaty** *adjective* (**-ier, -iest**).

sweater *noun* woollen etc. pullover.

Swede *noun* native or national of Sweden; (**swede**) large yellow variety of turnip.

Swedish /ˈswiːdɪʃ/ ● *adjective* of Sweden. ● *noun* language of Sweden.

sweep ● *verb* (*past & past participle* **swept**) clean or clear (room, area, etc.) (as with a broom; (often + *up*) collect or remove (dirt etc.) by sweeping; (+ *aside*, *away*, etc.) dismiss abruptly; (+ *along*, *down*, etc.) drive or carry along with force; (+ *off*, *away*, etc.) remove or clear forcefully; traverse swiftly or lightly; impart sweeping motion to; glide swiftly; go majestically; (of landscape etc.) be rolling or spacious. ● *noun* act or motion of sweeping; curve in road etc.; range, scope; chimney sweep; sortie by aircraft; *colloquial* sweepstake. □ **sweep the board** win all the money in gambling game, win all possible prizes etc.; **sweepstake** form of gambling on horse races etc. in which money staked is divided among those who have drawn numbered tickets for winners.

sweeping *adjective* wide in range or effect; generalized, arbitrary.

sweet ● *adjective* tasting like sugar, honey, etc.; smelling pleasant like perfume, roses, etc., fragrant; melodious; fresh; not sour or bitter; gratifying, attractive; amiable, gentle; *colloquial* pretty; (+ *on*) *colloquial* fond of, in love with. ● *noun* small shaped piece of sugar or chocolate confectionery; sweet dish forming course of meal. □ **sweet-and-sour** cooked in sauce with sugar, vinegar, etc.; **sweetbread** pancreas or thymus of animal, as food; **sweet-brier** single-flowered fragrant-leaved wild rose; **sweetcorn** sweet-flavoured maize kernels; **sweetheart** either of pair of lovers; **sweetmeat** a sweet, a small fancy cake; **sweet pea** climbing garden annual with many-coloured scented flowers; **sweet pepper** fruit of capsicum; **sweet potato** tropical plant with edible tuberous roots; **sweet-talk** flatter in order to persuade; **sweet tooth** liking for sweet-tasting things; **sweet william** garden plant with close clusters of sweet-smelling flowers. □ **sweetish** *adjective*; **sweetly** *adverb*.

sweeten *verb* make or become sweet(er); make agreeable or less painful. □ **sweetening** *noun*.

sweetener *noun* thing that sweetens; *colloquial* bribe.

sweetie *noun* *colloquial* a sweet; sweetheart.

sweetness *noun* being sweet; fragrance. □ **sweetness and light** (esp.

uncharacteristic) mildness and reason.

swell ● *verb* (*past participle* **swollen** /ˈswəʊlən/ or **-ed**) (cause to) grow bigger, louder, or more intense; rise or raise up; (+ *out*) bulge out; (of heart etc.) feel full of joy, pride, etc.; (+ *with*) be hardly able to restrain (pride etc.). ● *noun* act or state of swelling; heaving of sea etc. with unbreaking rolling waves; crescendo; mechanism in organ etc. for gradually varying volume; *colloquial* fashionable or stylish person. ● *adjective colloquial esp. US* fine, excellent.

swelling *noun* abnormally swollen place, esp. on body.

swelter /ˈsweltə/ ● *verb* be uncomfortably hot. ● *noun* sweltering condition.

swept *past & past participle* of SWEEP.

swerve ● *verb* (**-ving**) (cause to) change direction, esp. suddenly. ● *noun* swerving motion.

swift ● *adjective* rapid, quick; prompt. ● *noun* swift-flying long-winged migratory bird. □ **swiftly** *adverb*; **swiftness** *noun*.

swig ● *verb* (**-gg-**) *colloquial* drink in large draughts. ● *noun* swallow of liquid, esp. of large amount.

swill ● *verb* (often + *out*) rinse, pour water over or through; drink greedily. ● *noun* swilling; mainly liquid refuse as pig-food.

swim ● *verb* (**-mm-**; *past* **swam**; *past participle* **swum**) propel body through water with limbs, fins, etc.; perform (stroke) or cross (river etc.) by swimming; float on liquid; appear to undulate, reel, or whirl; (of head) feel dizzy; (+ *in*, *with*) be flooded. ● *noun* act or spell of swimming. □ **in the swim** *colloquial* involved in or aware of what is going on; **swimming bath**, **pool** pool constructed for swimming; **swimming costume** bathing costume; **swimsuit** swimming costume, esp. one-piece for women and girls; **swimwear** clothing for swimming in. □ **swimmer** *noun*.

swimmingly *adverb colloquial* smoothly, without obstruction.

swindle /ˈswɪnd(ə)l/ ● *verb* (**-ling**) (often + *out of*) cheat of money etc.; defraud. ● *noun* act of swindling; fraudulent person or thing. □ **swindler** *noun*.

swine *noun* (*plural* same) *formal or US* pig; *colloquial* (*plural* same or **-s**) disgusting person, unpleasant or difficult thing. □ **swinish** *adjective*.

swing ● *verb* (*past & past participle* **swung**) (cause to) move with to-and-fro or curving motion; sway or hang like pendulum or door etc.; oscillate; move by gripping something and leaping etc.; walk with swinging gait; (+ *round*) move to face opposite direction; (+ *at*) attempt to hit; *colloquial* (of party etc.) be lively; have decisive influence on (voting etc.); *colloquial* be executed by hanging. ● *noun* act, motion, or extent of swinging; swinging or smooth gait, rhythm, or action; seat slung by ropes, chains, etc. for swinging on or in, spell of swinging thus; smooth rhythmic jazz or jazzy dance music; amount by which votes etc. change from one side to another. □ **swing-boat** boat-shaped swing at fairs etc.; **swing-bridge** bridge that can be swung aside to let ships etc. pass; **swing-door** door that swings in either direction and closes by itself when released; **swings and roundabouts** situation allowing equal gain and loss; **swing-wing** (aircraft) with wings that can pivot to point sideways or backwards. □ **swinger** *noun*.

swingeing /ˈswɪndʒɪŋ/ *adjective* (of blow etc.) forcible; huge, far-reaching.

swipe *colloquial* ● *verb* (**-ping**) (often + *at*) hit hard and recklessly; steal. ● *noun* reckless hard hit or attempt to hit.

swirl ● *verb* move, flow, or carry along with whirling motion. ● *noun* swirling motion; twist, curl. □ **swirly** *adjective*.

swish ● *verb* swing (cane, scythe, etc.) audibly through air, grass, etc.; move with or make swishing sound. ● *noun* swishing action or sound. ● *adjective colloquial* smart, fashionable.

Swiss ● *adjective* of Switzerland. ● *noun* (*plural* same) native or national of Switzerland. □ **Swiss roll** cylindrical cake, made by rolling up thin flat sponge cake spread with jam etc.

switch ● *noun* device for making and breaking connection in electric circuit; transfer, changeover, deviation; flexible shoot cut from tree; light tapering rod; *US* railway points. ● *verb* (+ *on, off*)

turn (electrical device) on or off; change or transfer (position, subject, etc.); exchange; whip or flick with switch. □ **switchback** ride at fair etc. with extremely steep ascents and descents, similar railway or road; **switchboard** apparatus for varying connections between electric circuits, esp. in telephony; **switched-on** *colloquial* up to date, aware of what is going on; **switch off** *colloquial* cease to pay attention.

swivel /ˈswɪv(ə)l/ ● *noun* coupling between two parts etc. so that one can turn freely without the other. ● *verb* (**-ll-**; *US* **-l-**) turn (as) on swivel, swing round. □ **swivel chair** chair with revolving seat.

swizz *noun* (also **swiz**) *colloquial* something disappointing; swindle.

swizzle /ˈswɪz(ə)l/ *noun colloquial* frothy mixed alcoholic drink, esp. of rum or gin and bitters; *slang* swizz. □ **swizzle-stick** stick used for frothing or flattening drinks.

swollen *past participle of* SWELL.

swoon /swuːn/ *verb & noun literary* faint.

swoop /swuːp/ ● *verb* (often + *down*) come down with rush like bird of prey; (often + *on*) make sudden attack. ● *noun* act of swooping, sudden pounce.

swop = SWAP.

sword /sɔːd/ *noun* weapon with long blade for cutting or thrusting. □ **put to the sword** kill; **sword dance** dance with brandishing of swords, or steps about swords laid on ground; **swordfish** (*plural* same or **-es**) large sea fish with swordlike upper jaw; **swordplay** fencing, repartee, lively arguing; **swordsman** person of (usually specified) skill with sword; **swordstick** hollow walking stick containing sword blade.

swore *past of* SWEAR.

sworn ● *past participle of* SWEAR. ● *adjective* bound (as) by oath.

swot *colloquial* ● *verb* (**-tt-**) study hard; (usually + *up, up on*) study (subject) hard or hurriedly. ● *noun usually derogatory* person who swots.

swum *past participle of* SWIM.

swung *past & past participle of* SWING.

sybarite /'sɪbəraɪt/ *noun* self-indulgent or luxury-loving person. □ **sybaritic** /-'rɪt-/ *adjective.*

sycamore /'sɪkəmɔː/ *noun* large maple tree, its wood; *US* plane tree, its wood.

sycophant /'sɪkəfænt/ *noun* flatterer, toady. □ **sycophancy** *noun;* **sycophantic** /-'fæn-/ *adjective.*

syllabic /sɪ'læbɪk/ *adjective* of or in syllables. □ **syllabically** *adverb.*

syllable /'sɪləb(ə)l/ *noun* unit of pronunciation forming whole or part of word, usually consisting of vowel sound with consonant(s) before or after (see panel). □ **in words of one syllable** plainly, bluntly.

syllabub /'sɪləbʌb/ *noun* dessert of cream or milk sweetened and whipped with wine etc.

syllabus /'sɪləbəs/ *noun (plural* **-buses** or **-bi** /-baɪ/) programme or outline of course of study, teaching, etc.

syllogism /'sɪlədʒɪz(ə)m/ *noun* form of reasoning in which from two propositions a third is deduced. □ **syllogistic** /-'dʒɪs-/ *adjective.*

sylph /sɪlf/ *noun* elemental spirit of air; slender graceful woman. □ **sylphlike** *adjective.*

sylvan /'sɪlv(ə)n/ *adjective* (also **silvan**) of the woods, having woods; rural.

symbiosis /sɪmbaɪ'əʊsɪs/ *noun (plural* **-bioses** /-siːz/) (usually mutually advantageous) association of two different organisms living attached to one another etc.; mutually advantageous connection between people. □ **symbiotic** /-'ɒt-/ *adjective.*

symbol /'sɪmb(ə)l/ *noun* thing generally regarded as typifying, representing, or recalling something; mark, sign, etc.

representing object, idea, process, etc. □ **symbolic** /-'bɒl-/ *adjective;* **symbolically** /-'bɒl-/ *adverb.*

symbolism *noun* use of symbols; symbols; artistic movement or style using symbols to express ideas, emotions, etc. □ **symbolist** *noun.*

symbolize *verb* (also **-ise**) (**-zing** or **-sing**) be symbol of; represent by symbol(s).

symmetry /'sɪmɪtrɪ/ *noun (plural* **-ies**) correct proportion of parts; beauty resulting from this; structure allowing object to be divided into parts of equal shape and size; possession of such structure; repetition of exactly similar parts facing each other or a centre. □ **symmetrical** /-'met'-/ *adjective;* **symmetrically** /-'met-/ *adverb.*

sympathetic /sɪmpə'θetɪk/ *adjective* of or expressing sympathy; likeable, pleasant; (+ *to*) favouring (proposal etc.). □ **sympathetically** *adverb.*

sympathize /'sɪmpəθaɪz/ *verb* (also **-ise**) (**-zing** or **-sing**) (often + *with*) feel or express sympathy; agree. □ **sympathizer** *noun.*

sympathy /'sɪmpəθɪ/ *noun (plural* **-ies**) sharing of another's feelings; (often + *with*) sharing or tendency to share emotion, sensation, condition, etc. of another person; (in *singular* or *plural*) compassion, commiseration, condolences; (often + *with*) agreement (with person etc.) in opinion or desire. □ **in sympathy** (often + *with*) having, showing, or resulting from sympathy.

symphony /'sɪmfənɪ/ *noun (plural* **-ies**) musical composition in several movements for full orchestra. □ **symphony orchestra** large orchestra playing

---

Syllable

A syllable is the smallest unit of speech that can normally occur alone, such as *a*, *at*, *ta*, or *tat*. A word can be made up of one or more syllables:

> *cat*, *fought*, and *twinge* each have one syllable;
> *rating*, *deny*, and *collapse* each have two syllables;
> *excitement*, *superman*, and *telephoned* each have three syllables;
> *American* and *complicated* each have four syllables;
> *examination* and *uncontrollable* each have five syllables.

symphonies etc. □ **symphonic** /-'fɒn-/ adjective.

symposium /sɪm'pəʊzɪəm/ noun (plural **-sia**) conference, or collection of essays, on particular subject.

symptom /'sɪmptəm/ noun physical or mental sign of disease or injury; sign of existence of something. □ **symptomatic** /-'mæt-/ adjective.

synagogue /'sɪnəgɒg/ noun building for Jewish religious instruction and worship.

sync /sɪŋk/ (also **synch**) colloquial ● noun synchronization. ● verb synchronize. □ **in** or **out of sync** (often + with) according or agreeing well or badly.

synchromesh /'sɪŋkrəʊmeʃ/ ● noun system of gear-changing, esp. in vehicles, in which gearwheels revolve at same speed during engagement. ● adjective of this system.

synchronize /'sɪŋkrənaɪz/ verb (also **-ise**) (**-zing** or **-sing**) (often + with) make or be synchronous (with); make sound and picture (of film etc.) coincide; cause (clocks etc.) to show same time. □ **synchronization** noun.

synchronous /'sɪŋkrənəs/ adjective (often + with) existing or occurring at same time.

syncopate /'sɪŋkəpeɪt/ verb (**-ting**) displace beats or accents in (music); shorten (word) by omitting syllable or letter(s) in middle. □ **syncopation** noun.

syncope /'sɪŋkəpɪ/ noun Grammar syncopation; Medicine fainting through fall in blood pressure.

syncretize /'sɪŋkrətaɪz/ verb (also **-ise**) (**-zing** or **-sing**) attempt to unify or reconcile differing schools of thought. □ **syncretic** /-'kret-/ adjective; **syncretism** noun.

syndicalism /'sɪndɪkəlɪz(ə)m/ noun historical movement for transferring industrial control and ownership to workers' unions. □ **syndicalist** noun.

syndicate ● noun /'sɪndɪkət/ combination of people, commercial firms, etc. to promote some common interest; agency supplying material simultaneously to a number of periodicals etc.; group of people who gamble, organize crime, etc. ● verb /'sɪndɪkeɪt/ (**-ting**) form into syndicate; publish (material) through syndicate. □ **syndication** noun.

syndrome /'sɪndrəʊm/ noun group of concurrent symptoms of disease; characteristic combination of opinions, emotions, etc.

synod /'sɪnəd/ noun Church council of clergy and lay people.

synonym /'sɪnənɪm/ noun word or phrase that means the same as another (see panel).

synonymous /sɪ'nɒnɪməs/ adjective (often + with) having same meaning; suggestive of; associated with.

synopsis /sɪ'nɒpsɪs/ noun (plural **synopses** /-siːz/) summary; outline.

synoptic /sɪ'nɒptɪk/ adjective of or giving synopsis. □ **Synoptic Gospels** those of Matthew, Mark, and Luke.

....

Synonym

A synonym is a word that has the same meaning as, or a similar meaning to, another word:

   cheerful, happy, merry, and *jolly*

are synonyms that are quite close to each other in meaning, as are

   lazy, indolent, and *slothful*

In contrast, the following words all mean 'a person who works with another', but their meanings vary considerably:

colleague	conspirator
collaborator	accomplice
ally	

....

syntax /'sɪntæks/ *noun* grammatical arrangement of words; rules or analysis of this. □ **syntactic** /-'tæk-/ *adjective*.

synthesis /'sɪnθəsɪs/ *noun* (*plural* **-theses** /-siːz/) putting together of parts or elements to make up complex whole; *Chemistry* artificial production of (esp. organic) substances from simpler ones.

synthesize /'sɪnθəsaɪz/ *verb* (also **-ise**) (**-zing** or **-sing**) make synthesis of.

synthesizer *noun* (also **-iser**) electronic, usually keyboard, instrument producing great variety of sounds.

synthetic /sɪn'θetɪk/ ● *adjective* produced by synthesis, esp. to imitate natural product; affected, insincere. ● *noun* synthetic substance. □ **synthetically** *adverb*.

syphilis /'sɪfəlɪs/ *noun* a contagious venereal disease. □ **syphilitic** /-'lɪt-/ *adjective*.

Syrian /'sɪrɪən/ ● *noun* native or national of Syria. ● *adjective* of Syria.

syringa /sɪ'rɪŋgə/ *noun* shrub with white scented flowers.

syringe /sɪ'rɪndʒ/ ● *noun* device for drawing in quantity of liquid and ejecting it in fine stream. ● *verb* (**-ging**) sluice or spray with syringe.

syrup /'sɪrəp/ *noun* (*US* **sirup**) sweet sauce of sugar dissolved in boiling water, often flavoured or medicated; condensed sugar-cane juice; molasses, treacle; excessive sweetness of manner. □ **syrupy** *adjective*.

system /'sɪstəm/ *noun* complex whole; set of connected things or parts; organized group of things; set of organs in body with common structure or function; human or animal body as organized whole; method, scheme of action, procedure, or classification; orderliness; (**the system**) prevailing political or social order, esp. seen as oppressive. □ **get (thing) out of one's system** get rid of (anxiety etc.); **systems analysis** analysis of complex process etc. so as to improve its efficiency, esp. by using computer.

systematic /sɪstə'mætɪk/ *adjective* methodical; according to system; deliberate. □ **systematically** *adverb*.

systematize /'sɪstəmətaɪz/ *verb* (also **-ise**) (**-zing** or **-sing**) make systematic. □ **systematization** *noun*.

systemic /sɪ'stemɪk/ *adjective Physiology* of the whole body; (of insecticide etc.) entering plant tissues via roots and shoots. □ **systemically** *adverb*.

T *noun* □ **to a T** exactly, to a nicety; **T-bone** T-shaped bone, esp. in steak from thin end of loin; **T-junction** junction, esp. of two roads, in shape of T; **T-shirt** short-sleeved casual top; **T-square** T-shaped instrument for drawing right angles.

t. *abbreviation* (also **t**) ton(s); tonne(s).

TA *abbreviation* Territorial Army.

ta /tɑː/ *interjection colloquial* thank you.

tab[1] *noun* small piece of material attached to thing for grasping, fastening, identifying, etc.; *US colloquial* bill; distinguishing mark on officer's collar. □ **keep tabs on** *colloquial* have under observation or in check.

tab[2] *noun* tabulator.

tabard /ˈtæbəd/ *noun* herald's official coat emblazoned with arms of sovereign; woman's or girl's sleeveless jerkin; *historical* knight's short emblazoned garment worn over armour.

tabasco /təˈbæskəʊ/ *noun* pungent pepper; (**Tabasco**) *proprietary term* sauce made from this.

tabby /ˈtæbɪ/ *noun* (*plural* **-ies**) grey or brownish cat with dark stripes.

tabernacle /ˈtæbənæk(ə)l/ *noun historical* tent used as sanctuary by Israelites during Exodus; niche or receptacle, esp. for bread and wine of Eucharist; Nonconformist meeting-house.

tabla /ˈtæblə/ *noun* pair of small Indian drums played with hands.

table /ˈteɪb(ə)l/ ● *noun* flat surface on legs used for eating, working at, etc.; food provided at table; group seated for dinner etc.; set of facts or figures arranged esp. in columns; multiplication table. ● *verb* (**-ling**) bring forward for discussion at meeting etc.; *esp. US* postpone consideration of. □ **at table** taking a meal; **tablecloth** cloth spread over table; **tableland** plateau; **tablespoon** large spoon for serving etc., (also **tablespoonful**) amount held by this; **table tennis** game played with small bats on table divided by net;

tableware dishes etc. for meals; **table wine** wine of ordinary quality; **turn the tables** (often + *on*) reverse circumstances to one's advantage.

tableau /ˈtæbləʊ/ *noun* (*plural* **-x** /-z/) picturesque presentation; group of silent motionless people representing stage scene.

table d'hôte /tɑːbˈlə ˈdəʊt/ *noun* meal from set menu at fixed price.

tablet /ˈtæblɪt/ *noun* small solid dose of medicine etc.; bar of soap etc.; flat slab of stone etc., esp. inscribed.

tabloid /ˈtæblɔɪd/ *noun* small-sized, often popular or sensational, newspaper.

taboo /təˈbuː/ ● *noun* (*plural* **-s**) ritual isolation of person or thing as sacred or accursed; prohibition. ● *adjective* avoided or prohibited, esp. by social custom. ● *verb* (**-oos**, **-ooed**) put under taboo; exclude or prohibit, esp. socially.

tabor /ˈteɪbə/ *noun historical* small drum.

tabular /ˈtæbjʊlə/ *adjective* of or arranged in tables.

tabulate /ˈtæbjʊleɪt/ *verb* (**-ting**) arrange (figures, facts) in tabular form. □ **tabulation** *noun*.

tabulator *noun* device on typewriter etc. for advancing to sequence of set positions in tabular work.

tachograph /ˈtækəɡrɑːf/ *noun* device in vehicle to record speed and travel time.

tachometer /təˈkɒmɪtə/ *noun* instrument measuring velocity or rate of shaft's rotation (esp. in vehicle).

tacit /ˈtæsɪt/ *adjective* implied or understood without being stated. □ **tacitly** *adverb*.

taciturn /ˈtæsɪtɜːn/ *adjective* saying little, uncommunicative. □ **taciturnity** /-ˈtɜːn-/ *noun*.

tack[1] ● *noun* small sharp broad-headed nail; *US* drawing-pin; long stitch for fastening materials lightly or temporarily together; (in sailing) direction, temporary change of direction; course of action or policy. ● *verb* (often + *down* etc.) fasten with tacks; stitch lightly together; (+ *to*, *on*, *on to*) add, append; change ship's course by turning head to wind; make series of such tacks.

tack² *noun* horse's saddle, bridle, etc.

tack³ *noun colloquial* cheap or shoddy material; tat, kitsch.

tackle /'tæk(ə)l/ ● *noun* equipment for task or sport; rope(s), pulley(s), etc. used in working sails, hoisting weights, etc.; tackling in football etc. ● *verb* (**-ling**) try to deal with (problem etc.); grapple with (opponent); confront (person) in discussion; intercept or stop (player running with ball etc.). □ **tackle-block** pulley over which rope runs. □ **tackler** *noun*.

tacky¹ /'tæki/ *adjective* (**-ier**, **-iest**) slightly sticky.

tacky² /'tæki/ *adjective* (**-ier**, **-iest**) *colloquial* in poor taste; cheap, shoddy.

taco /'tækəʊ/ *noun* (*plural* **-s**) Mexican dish of meat etc. in crisp folded tortilla.

tact *noun* adroitness in dealing with people or circumstances; intuitive perception of right thing to do or say. □ **tactful** *adjective*; **tactfully** *adverb*; **tactless** *adjective*; **tactlessly** *adverb*.

tactic /'tæktɪk/ *noun* piece of tactics.

tactical *adjective* of tactics; (of bombing etc.) done in immediate support of military or naval operation; adroitly planning or planned. □ **tactically** *adverb*.

tactics /'tæktɪks/ *plural noun* (also treated as *singular*) disposition of armed forces, esp. in warfare; procedure calculated to gain some end, skilful device(s). □ **tactician** /-'tɪʃ-/ *noun*.

tactile /'tæktaɪl/ *adjective* of sense of touch; perceived by touch. □ **tactility** /-'tɪl-/ *noun*.

tadpole /'tædpəʊl/ *noun* larva of frog, toad, etc. at stage of living in water and having gills and tail.

taffeta /'tæfɪtə/ *noun* fine lustrous silk or silklike fabric.

taffrail /'tæfreɪl/ *noun* rail round ship's stern.

tag ● *noun* label, esp. to show address or price; metal point of shoelace etc.; loop or flap for handling or hanging thing; loose or ragged end; trite quotation, stock phrase. ● *verb* (**-gg-**) furnish with

tag(s); (often + *on*, *on to*) join, attach. □ **tag along** (often + *with*) go along, accompany passively.

tagliatelle /tæljə'teli/ *noun* ribbon-shaped pasta.

tail¹ ● *noun* hindmost part of animal, esp. extending beyond body; thing like tail in form or position, esp. rear part of aeroplane, vehicle, etc., hanging part of back of shirt or coat, end of procession, luminous trail following comet, etc.; inferior, weak, or last part of anything; (in *plural*) *colloquial* tailcoat, evening dress with this; (in *plural*) reverse of coin turning up in toss; *colloquial* person following another. ● *verb* remove stalks of (fruit etc.); *colloquial* follow closely. □ **tailback** long queue of traffic caused by obstruction; **tailboard** hinged or removable back of lorry etc.; **tailcoat** man's coat divided at back and cut away in front; **tailgate** tailboard, rear door of estate car; **tail-light, -lamp** *US* rear light on vehicle etc.; **tail off, away** gradually diminish and cease; **tailpiece** final part of thing, decoration at end of chapter etc.; **tailplane** horizontal aerofoil at tail of aircraft; **tailspin** aircraft's spinning dive, state of panic; **tail wind** one blowing in direction of travel. □ **tailless** *adjective*.

tail² *Law* ● *noun* limitation of ownership, esp. of estate limited to person and his heirs. ● *adjective* so limited.

tailor /'teɪlə/ ● *noun* maker of (esp. men's) outer garments to measure. ● *verb* make (clothes) as tailor; make or adapt for special purpose; work as tailor. □ **tailor-made** made by tailor, made or suited for particular purpose. □ **tailored** *adjective*.

taint ● *noun* spot or trace of decay, corruption, etc.; corrupt condition, infection. ● *verb* affect with taint, become tainted; (+ *with*) affect slightly.

take ● *verb* (**-king**; *past* **took** /tʊk/; *past participle* **taken**) lay hold of; acquire, capture, earn, win; regularly buy (newspaper etc.); occupy; make use of; be effective; consume; use up; carry, accompany; remove, steal; catch, be infected with; be affected by (pleasure etc.); ascertain and record; grasp mentally, understand; accept, submit to; deal with or regard in specified way;

teach, be taught or examined in; submit to (exam); make (photograph); have as necessary accompaniment, requirement, or part. ●*noun* amount taken or caught; scene or film sequence photographed continuously. □ **take after** resemble (parent etc.); **take against** begin to dislike; **take apart** dismantle, *colloquial* defeat, criticize severely; **take away** remove or carry elsewhere, subtract; **take-away** (cooked meal) bought at restaurant for eating elsewhere, restaurant selling this; **take back** retract (statement), convey to original position, carry in thought to past time, return or accept back (goods); **take down** write down (spoken words), dismantle (structure), lower (garment); **take-home pay** employee's pay after deduction of tax etc.; **take in** receive as lodger etc., undertake (work) at home, make (garment etc.) smaller, understand, cheat, include; **take off** remove (clothing), deduct, mimic, begin a jump, become airborne, (of scheme etc.) become successful; **take-off** act of mimicking or becoming airborne; **take on** undertake, acquire, engage, agree to oppose at game, *colloquial* show strong emotion; **take out** remove, escort on outing, get (licence etc.); **take over** succeed to management or ownership of, assume control; **takeover** *noun*; **take to** begin, have recourse to, form liking for; **take up** adopt as pursuit, accept (offer etc.), occupy (time or space), absorb, (often + *on*) interrupt or correct (speaker), shorten (garment), pursue (matter). □ **taker** *noun*.

taking ●*adjective* attractive, captivating. ●*noun* (in *plural*) money taken in business etc.

talc *noun* talcum powder; translucent mineral formed in thin plates.

talcum /'tælkəm/ *noun* talc; (in full **talcum powder**) usually perfumed powdered talc for toilet use.

tale *noun* narrative or story, esp. fictitious; allegation or gossip, often malicious.

talent /'tælənt/ *noun* special aptitude or gift; high mental ability; people of talent; *colloquial* attractive members of opposite sex; ancient weight and money unit. □ **talent-scout, -spotter**

person seeking new talent, esp. in sport or entertainment. □ **talented** *adjective*.

talisman /'tælɪzmən/ *noun* (*plural* **-s**) thing believed to bring good luck or protect from harm.

talk /tɔːk/ ●*verb* (often + *to, with*) converse or communicate verbally; have power of speech; express, utter, discuss; use (language); gossip. ●*noun* conversation; particular mode of speech; short address or lecture; rumour or gossip, its theme; *colloquial* empty boasting; (often in *plural*) discussions, negotiations. □ **talk down** silence by loud or persistent talking, guide (pilot, aircraft) to landing by radio, (+ *to*) speak patronizingly to; **talk into** persuade by talking; **talk of** discuss, express intention of; **talk over** discuss; **talk round** persuade to change opinion etc.; **talk to** rebuke, scold. □ **talker** *noun*.

talkative /'tɔːkətɪv/ *adjective* fond of talking.

talkie *noun colloquial* early film with soundtrack.

talking ●*adjective* that talks or can talk; expressive. ●*noun* action or process of talking. □ **talking of** while we are discussing; **talking point** topic for discussion; **talking-to** *colloquial* scolding.

tall /tɔːl/ ●*adjective* of more than average height; of specified height; higher than surroundings. ●*adverb* as if tall; proudly. □ **taliboy** tall chest of drawers; **tall order** unreasonable demand; **tall ship** high-masted sailing ship; **tall story** *colloquial* extravagant tale.

tallow /'tæləʊ/ *noun* hard (esp. animal) fat melted down to make candles, soap, etc.

tally /'tælɪ/ ●*noun* (*plural* **-ies**) reckoning of debt or score; mark registering number of objects delivered or received; *historical* piece of notched wood for keeping account; identification ticket or label; counterpart, duplicate. ●*verb* (**-ies**, **-ied**) (often + *with*) agree, correspond.

tally-ho /tælɪ'həʊ/ *interjection* huntsman's cry as signal on seeing fox.

Talmud /'tælmʊd/ *noun* body of Jewish civil and ceremonial law. □ **Talmudic** /-'mʊd-/ *adjective*; **Talmudist** *noun*.

talon /'tælən/ *noun* claw, esp. of bird of prey.

talus /'teɪləs/ *noun* (*plural* **tali** /-laɪ/) ankle-bone supporting tibia.

tamarind /'tæmərɪnd/ *noun* tropical evergreen tree; its fruit pulp used as food and in drinks.

tamarisk /'tæmərɪsk/ *noun* seaside shrub usually with small pink or white flowers.

tambour /'tæmbʊə/ *noun* drum; circular frame for stretching embroidery-work on.

tambourine /tæmbə'riːn/ *noun* small shallow drum with jingling discs in rim, shaken or banged as accompaniment.

tame ● *adjective* (of animal) domesticated, not wild or shy; uninteresting, insipid. ● *verb* (**-ming**) make tame, domesticate; subdue. □ **tamely** *adverb*; **tameness** *noun*; **tamer** *noun*.

Tamil /'tæmɪl/ *noun* member of a people inhabiting South India and Sri Lanka; their language. ● *adjective* of this people or language.

tam-o'-shanter /tæmə'ʃæntə/ *noun* floppy woollen beret of Scottish origin.

tamp *verb* ram down tightly.

tamper /'tæmpə/ *verb* (+ *with*) meddle or interfere with.

tampon /'tæmpɒn/ *noun* plug of cotton wool etc. used esp. to absorb menstrual blood.

tan[1] ● *noun* suntan; yellowish-brown colour; bark of oak etc. used for tanning. ● *adjective* yellowish-brown. ● *verb* (**-nn-**) make or become brown by exposure to sun; convert (raw hide) into leather; *slang* thrash.

tan[2] *abbreviation* tangent.

tandem /'tændəm/ ● *noun* bicycle with two or more seats one behind another; vehicle driven tandem. ● *adverb* with two or more horses harnessed one behind another. □ **in tandem** one behind the other, alongside each other, together.

tandoor /'tænduə/ *noun* clay oven.

tandoori /tæn'duərɪ/ *noun* spiced food cooked in tandoor.

tang *noun* strong taste or smell; characteristic quality; part of tool by which blade is held firm in handle. □ **tangy** *adjective* (**-ier**, **-iest**).

tangent /'tændʒ(ə)nt/ *noun* straight line, curve, or surface touching but not intersecting curve; ratio of sides opposite and adjacent to acute angle in right-angled triangle. □ **at a tangent** diverging from previous course or from what is relevant. □ **tangential** /-'dʒenʃ(ə)l/ *adjective*.

tangerine /tændʒə'riːn/ *noun* small sweet-scented fruit like orange, mandarin; deep orange-yellow colour.

tangible /'tændʒɪb(ə)l/ *adjective* perceptible by touch; definite, clearly intelligible, not elusive. □ **tangibility** *noun*; **tangibly** *adverb*.

tangle /'tæŋg(ə)l/ ● *verb* (**-ling**) intertwine or become twisted or involved in confused mass; entangle; complicate. ● *noun* tangled mass or state. □ **tangly** *adjective*.

tango /'tæŋgəʊ/ ● *noun* (*plural* **-s**) (music for) slow South American ballroom dance. ● *verb* (**-goes**, **-goed**) dance tango.

tank *noun* large receptacle for liquid, gas, etc.; heavy armoured fighting vehicle moving on continuous tracks. □ **tank engine** steam engine with integral fuel and water containers. □ **tankful** *noun* (*plural* **-s**).

tankard /'tæŋkəd/ *noun* (contents of) tall beer mug with handle.

tanker *noun* ship, aircraft, or road vehicle for carrying liquids, esp. oil, in bulk.

tanner *noun* person who tans hides.

tannery *noun* (*plural* **-ies**) place where hides are tanned.

tannic /'tænɪk/ *adjective* of tan. □ **tannic acid** yellowish organic compound used in cleaning, dyeing, etc.

tannin /'tænɪn/ *noun* any of several substances extracted from tree-barks etc. and used in tanning etc.

Tannoy /'tænɔɪ/ *noun* proprietary term type of public address system.

tansy /'tænzɪ/ *noun* (*plural* **-ies**) aromatic herb with yellow flowers.

tantalize /'tæntəlaɪz/ *verb* (also **-ise**) (**-zing** or **-sing**) torment with sight of the unobtainable, raise and then dash the hopes of. □ **tantalization** *noun*.

tantamount /'tæntəmaʊnt/ *adjective* (+ *to*) equivalent to.

tantra /'tæntrə/ *noun* any of a class of Hindu or Buddhist mystical or magical writings.

tantrum /'tæntrəm/ *noun* (esp. child's) outburst of bad temper or petulance.

Taoiseach /'ti:ʃəx/ *noun* prime minister of Irish Republic.

tap[1] ●*noun* device by which flow of liquid or gas from pipe or vessel can be controlled; act of tapping telephone; taproom. ●*verb* (**-pp-**) provide (cask) with tap, let out (liquid) thus; draw sap from (tree) by cutting into it; draw supplies or information from; discover and exploit; connect listening device to (telephone etc.). □ **on tap** ready to be drawn off, *colloquial* freely available; **taproom** room in pub serving drinks on tap; **tap root** tapering root growing vertically downwards.

tap[2] ●*verb* (**-pp-**) (+ *at, on, against*, etc.) strike or cause to strike lightly; (often + *out*) make by taps; tap-dance. ●*noun* light blow or rap; tap-dancing; metal attachment on dancer's shoe. □ **tap-dance** *noun* rhythmic dance performed in shoes with metal taps, *verb* perform this; **tap-dancer** *noun*; **tap-dancing** *noun*.

tapas /'tæpæs/ *plural noun* small savoury esp. Spanish dishes.

tape ●*noun* narrow woven strip of cotton etc. for fastening etc.; this across finishing line of race; (in full **adhesive tape**) strip of adhesive plastic etc. for fastening, masking, insulating, etc.; magnetic tape; tape recording; tape-measure. ●*verb* (**-ping**) tie up or join with tape; apply tape to; (+ *off*) seal off with tape; record on magnetic tape; measure with tape. □ **have** (**person, thing**) **taped** *colloquial* understand fully; **tape deck** machine for using audiotape (separate from speakers etc.); **tape machine** device for recording telegraph messages, tape recorder; **tape-measure** strip of tape or thin flexible metal marked for measuring; **tape recorder** apparatus for recording and replaying sounds on magnetic tape; **tape-record** *verb*; **tape recording** *noun*; **tapeworm** tapelike worm parasitic in alimentary canal.

taper /'teɪpə/ ●*noun* wick coated with wax etc. for conveying flame; slender candle. ●*verb* (often + *off*) (cause to) diminish in thickness towards one end, make or become gradually less.

tapestry /'tæpɪstrɪ/ *noun* (*plural* **-ies**) thick fabric in which coloured weft threads are woven to form pictures or designs; (usually wool) embroidery imitating this; piece of this.

tapioca /tæpɪ'əʊkə/ *noun* starchy granular foodstuff prepared from cassava.

tapir /'teɪpə/ *noun* small piglike mammal with short flexible snout.

tappet /'tæpɪt/ *noun* lever etc. in machinery giving intermittent motion.

tar[1] ●*noun* dark thick inflammable liquid distilled from wood, coal, etc.; similar substance formed in combustion of tobacco. ●*verb* (**-rr-**) cover with tar.

tar[2] *noun* *colloquial* sailor.

taramasalata /ˌtærəməsə'lɑːtə/ *noun* (also **taramosalata**) dip made from roe, olive oil, etc.

tarantella /tærən'telə/ *noun* (music for) whirling Southern Italian dance.

tarantula /tə'ræntjʊlə/ *noun* large hairy tropical spider; large black spider of Southern Europe.

tarboosh /tɑː'buːʃ/ *noun* cap like fez.

tardy /'tɑːdɪ/ *adjective* (**-ier, -iest**) slow to act, come, or happen; delaying, delayed. □ **tardily** *adverb*; **tardiness** *noun*.

tare[1] /teə/ *noun* vetch, esp. as cornfield weed or fodder; (in *plural* *Biblical* injurious cornfield weed.

tare[2] /teə/ *noun* allowance made for weight of packing around goods; weight of vehicle without fuel or load.

target /'tɑːgɪt/ ●*noun* mark fired at, esp. round object marked with concentric circles; person, objective, or result aimed at; butt of criticism etc. ●*verb* (**-t-**) single out as target; aim, direct.

tariff /'tærɪf/ *noun* table of fixed charges; duty on particular class of goods; list of duties or customs due.

tarlatan /'tɑːlət(ə)n/ *noun* thin stiff muslin.

Tarmac /'tɑːmæk/ ●*noun* proprietary term tarmacadam; area surfaced with this. ●*verb* (**tarmac**) (**-ck-**) lay tarmacadam on.

tarmacadam /tɑːmə'kædəm/ *noun* bitumen-bound stones etc. used as paving.

tarn *noun* small mountain lake.

tarnish /'tɑːnɪʃ/ ● *verb* (cause to) lose lustre; impair (reputation etc.). ● *noun* tarnished state; stain, blemish.

taro /'tɑːrəʊ/ *noun* (*plural* -**s**) tropical plant with edible tuberous roots.

tarot /'tærəʊ/ *noun* (in *singular* or *plural*) pack of 78 cards used in fortune-telling.

tarpaulin /tɑː'pɔːlɪn/ *noun* waterproof cloth, esp. of tarred canvas; sheet or covering of this.

tarragon /'tærəgən/ *noun* aromatic herb.

tarry¹ /'tɑːrɪ/ *adjective* (-**ier**, -**iest**) of or smeared with tar.

tarry² /'tærɪ/ *verb* (-**ies**, -**ied**) *archaic* linger; stay, wait.

tarsal /'tɑːs(ə)l/ ● *adjective* of the ankle-bones. ● *noun* tarsal bone.

tarsus /'tɑːsəs/ *noun* (*plural* **tarsi** /-saɪ/) bones of ankle and upper foot.

tart¹ *noun* pastry case containing fruit, jam, etc. □ **tartlet** *noun*.

tart² ● *noun slang* prostitute, promiscuous woman. ● *verb* (+ *up*) *colloquial* smarten or dress up, esp. gaudily. □ **tarty** *adjective* (-**ier**, -**iest**).

tart³ *adjective* sharp-tasting, acid; (of remark etc.) cutting, biting. □ **tartly** *adverb*; **tartness** *noun*.

tartan /'tɑːt(ə)n/ *noun* (woollen cloth woven in) pattern of coloured stripes crossing at right angles, esp. denoting a Scottish Highland clan.

Tartar /'tɑːtə/ *noun* member of group of Central Asian people including Mongols and Turks; their Turkic language; (**tartar**) harsh or formidable person. □ **tartar sauce** mayonnaise with chopped gherkins etc.

tartar /'tɑːtə/ *noun* hard deposit that forms on teeth; deposit forming hard crust in wine casks.

tartaric /tɑː'tærɪk/ *adjective* of tartar. □ **tartaric acid** organic acid found esp. in unripe grapes.

tartrazine /'tɑːtrəziːn/ *noun* brilliant yellow dye from tartaric acid, used to colour food etc.

task /tɑːsk/ ● *noun* piece of work to be done. ● *verb* make great demands on. □ **take to task** rebuke, scold; **task force** specially organized unit for task; **taskmaster**, **taskmistress** person who makes others work hard.

Tass *noun* official Russian news agency.

tassel /'tæs(ə)l/ *noun* tuft of hanging threads etc. as ornament; tassel-like flowerhead of plant. □ **tasselled** *adjective* (*US* **tasseled**).

taste /teɪst/ ● *noun* (faculty of perceiving) sensation caused in mouth by contact with substance; flavour; small sample of food etc.; slight experience; (often + *for*) liking, predilection; aesthetic discernment in art, clothes, conduct, etc. ● *verb* (-**ting**) perceive or sample flavour of; eat small portion of; experience; (often + *of*) have specified flavour. □ **taste bud** organ of taste on surface of tongue.

tasteful *adjective* done in or having good taste. □ **tastefully** *adverb*; **tastefulness** *noun*.

tasteless *adjective* flavourless; having or done in bad taste. □ **tastelessly** *adverb*; **tastelessness** *noun*.

taster *noun* person employed to test food or drink by tasting; small sample.

tasting *noun* gathering at which food or drink is tasted and evaluated.

tasty *adjective* (-**ier**, -**iest**) of pleasing flavour, appetizing; *colloquial* attractive. □ **tastiness** *noun*.

tat¹ *noun colloquial* tatty things; junk.

tat² *verb* (-**tt**-) do, or make by, tatting.

ta-ta /tæ'tɑː/ *interjection colloquial* goodbye.

tatter /'tætə/ *noun* (usually in *plural*) rag, irregularly torn cloth, paper, etc. □ **in tatters** *colloquial* torn in many places, ruined.

tattered *adjective* in tatters.

tatting /'tætɪŋ/ *noun* (process of making) kind of handmade knotted lace.

tattle /'tæt(ə)l/ ● *verb* (-**ling**) prattle, chatter, gossip. ● *noun* gossip, idle talk.

tattoo¹ /tə'tuː/ ● *verb* (-**oos**, -**ooed**) mark (skin) by puncturing and inserting pigment; make (design) thus. ● *noun* such design. □ **tattooer** *noun*; **tattooist** *noun*.

tattoo² /tə'tuː/ *noun* evening signal recalling soldiers to quarters; elaboration of this with music and marching etc. as entertainment; drumming, rapping; drumbeat.

tatty /'tætɪ/ *adjective* (-**ier**, -**iest**) *colloquial* tattered; shabby, inferior, tawdry. □ **tattily** *adverb*; **tattiness** *noun*.

taught *past & past participle* of TEACH.

taunt • *noun* insult; provocation. • *verb* insult; provoke contemptuously.

taupe /təʊp/ *noun* grey tinged with esp. brown.

Taurus /'tɔːrəs/ *noun* second sign of zodiac.

taut *adjective* (of rope etc.) tight; (of nerves etc.) tense; (of ship etc.) in good condition. □ **tauten** *verb*; **tautly** *adverb*; **tautness** *noun*.

tautology /tɔː'tɒlədʒɪ/ *noun* (*plural* **-ies**) repetition of same thing in different words. □ **tautological** /-tə'lɒdʒ-/ *adjective*; **tautologous** /-ləgəs/ *adjective*.

tavern /'tæv(ə)n/ *noun* archaic or literary inn, pub.

taverna /tə'vɜːnə/ *noun* Greek restaurant.

tawdry /'tɔːdrɪ/ *adjective* (**-ier**, **-iest**) showy but worthless; gaudy.

tawny /'tɔːnɪ/ *adjective* (**-ier**, **-iest**) of orange-brown colour. □ **tawny owl** reddish-brown European owl.

tax • *noun* money compulsorily levied by state on person, property, business, etc.; (+ *on*, *upon*) strain, heavy demand. • *verb* impose tax on; deduct tax from; make demands on; (often + *with*) charge, call to account. □ **tax avoidance** minimizing tax payment by financial manoeuvring; **tax-deductible** (of expenses) legally deductible from income before tax assessment; **tax disc** licence on vehicle certifying payment of road tax; **tax evasion** illegal non-payment of taxes; **tax-free** exempt from tax; **taxman** *colloquial* inspector or collector of taxes; **taxpayer** person who pays taxes; **tax return** declaration of income etc. for taxation purposes.

taxation /tæk'seɪʃ(ə)n/ *noun* imposition or payment of tax.

taxi /'tæksɪ/ • *noun* (*plural* **-s**) (in full **taxi-cab**) car plying for hire and usually fitted with taximeter. • *verb* (**taxis**, **taxied**, **taxiing** or **taxying**) (of aircraft) go along ground before or after flying; go or carry in taxi. □ **taxi rank** (*US* **taxi stand**) place where taxis wait to be hired.

taxidermy /'tæksɪdɜːmɪ/ *noun* art of preparing, stuffing, and mounting skins of animals. □ **taxidermist** *noun*.

taximeter /'tæksɪmiːtə/ *noun* automatic fare-indicator in taxi.

taxon /'tæks(ə)n/ *noun* (*plural* **taxa**) any taxonomic group.

taxonomy /tæk'sɒnəmɪ/ *noun* classification of living and extinct organisms. □ **taxonomic** /-sə'nɒm-/ *adjective*; **taxonomical** /-sə'nɒm-/ *adjective*; **taxonomist** *noun*.

tayberry /'teɪbərɪ/ *noun* (*plural* **-ies**) hybrid fruit between blackberry and raspberry.

TB *abbreviation* tubercle bacillus; tuberculosis.

tbsp. *abbreviation* tablespoonful.

te /tiː/ *noun* (also **ti**) seventh note of scale in tonic sol-fa.

tea *noun* (in full **tea plant**) Asian evergreen shrub or small tree; its dried leaves; infusion of these leaves as drink; infusion made from other leaves etc.; light meal in afternoon or evening. □ **tea bag** small permeable bag of tea for infusion; **tea break** pause in work for drinking tea; **tea caddy** container for tea; **teacake** light usually toasted sweet bun; **tea chest** light metal-lined wooden box for transporting tea; **tea cloth** tea towel; **tea cosy** cover to keep teapot warm; **teacup** cup from which tea is drunk, amount it holds; **tea leaf** leaf of tea, esp. (in *plural*) after infusion; **teapot** pot with handle and spout, in which tea is made; **tearoom** small unlicensed café; **tea rose** rose with scent like tea; **teaset** set of crockery for serving tea; **teashop** tearoom; **teaspoon** small spoon for stirring tea etc., (also **teaspoonful**) amount held by this; **tea towel** cloth for drying washed crockery etc.; **tea trolley** (*US* **tea wagon**) small trolley from which tea is served.

teach *verb* (*past & past participle* **taught** /tɔːt/) give systematic information, instruction, or training to (person) or about (subject, skill); practise this as a profession; advocate as moral etc. principle; (+ *to do*) instruct to, *colloquial* discourage from. □ **teachable** *adjective*.

teacher *noun* person who teaches, esp. in school.

teaching *noun* teacher's profession; (often in *plural*) what is taught; doctrine.

teak *noun* a hard durable wood.

teal *noun* (*plural* same) small freshwater duck.

team ●*noun* set of players etc. in game or sport; set of people working together; set of draught animals. ●*verb* (usually + *up*) join in team or in common action; (+ *with*) coordinate, match; **team-mate** fellow member of team; **team spirit** willingness to act for communal good; **teamwork** combined effort, cooperation.

teamster /'tiːmstə/ *noun US* lorry driver; driver of team.

tear¹ /teə/ ●*verb* (*past* **tore**; *past participle* **torn**) (often + *up*) pull (apart) with some force; make (hole, rent) thus; undergo this; (+ *away, off, at,* etc.) pull violently; violently disrupt; *colloquial* go hurriedly. ●*noun* hole etc. caused by tearing; torn part of cloth etc. □ **tear apart** search exhaustively, criticize forcefully, divide utterly, distress greatly; **tearaway** *colloquial* unruly young person; **tearing hurry** *colloquial* great hurry; **tear into** *colloquial* severely reprimand, start (activity) vigorously; **tear to shreds** *colloquial* criticize thoroughly.

tear² /tɪə/ *noun* drop of clear salty liquid secreted from eye and shed esp. in grief. □ **in tears** weeping; **teardrop** single tear; **tear duct** drain carrying tears to or from eye; **tear gas** gas causing severe irritation to the eyes.

tearful *adjective* in, given to, or accompanied with tears. □ **tearfully** *adverb*.

tease /tiːz/ ●*verb* (**-sing**) make fun of; irritate; entice sexually while refusing to satisfy desire; pick (wool etc.) into separate fibres; raise nap on (cloth) with teasels etc.; (+ *out*) extract or obtain by careful effort. ●*noun colloquial* person fond of teasing; act of teasing.

teasel /'tiːz(ə)l/ *noun* (also **teazel**, **teazle**) plant with prickly flower heads, used dried for raising nap on cloth; other device used for this.

teaser *noun colloquial* hard question or problem.

teat *noun* nipple on breast or udder; rubber etc. nipple for sucking milk from bottle.

teazel (also **teazle**) = TEASEL.

TEC /tek/ *abbreviation* Training and Enterprise Council.

tec *noun colloquial* detective.

tech /tek/ *noun* (also **tec**) *colloquial* technical college.

technic /'teknɪk/ *noun* (usually in *plural*) technology; technical terms, methods, etc.; technique.

technical *adjective* of the mechanical arts and applied sciences; of a particular subject, craft, etc.; using technical language; specialized; due to mechanical failure; in strict legal sense. □ **technical knockout** referee's ruling that boxer has lost because he is unfit to continue. □ **technically** *adverb*.

technicality /teknɪ'kælɪtɪ/ *noun* (*plural* **-ies**) being technical; technical expression; technical point or detail.

technician /tek'nɪʃ(ə)n/ *noun* person doing practical or maintenance work in laboratory; person skilled in artistic etc. technique; expert in practical science.

Technicolor /'teknɪkʌlə/ *noun proprietary term* process of colour cinematography; (usually **technicolour**) *colloquial* vivid or artificial colour.

technique /tek'niːk/ *noun* mechanical skill in art; method of achieving purpose, esp. by manipulation; manner of execution in music, painting, etc.

technocracy /tek'nɒkrəsɪ/ *noun* (*plural* **-ies**) (instance of) rule or control by technical experts.

technocrat /'teknəkræt/ *noun* exponent or advocate of technocracy. □ **technocratic** /-'kræt-/ *adjective*.

technology /tek'nɒlədʒɪ/ *noun* (*plural* **-ies**) knowledge or use of mechanical arts and applied sciences; these subjects collectively. □ **technological** /-nə'lɒdʒ-/ *adjective*; **technologically** /-nə'lɒdʒ-/ *adverb*; **technologist** *noun*.

tectonic /tek'tɒnɪk/ *adjective* of building or construction; of changes in the earth's crust.

tectonics *plural noun* (usually treated as *singular*) study of earth's large-scale structural features.

teddy /'tedɪ/ *noun* (also **Teddy**) (*plural* **-ies**) (in full **teddy bear**) soft toy bear.

Teddy boy /'tedɪ/ *noun colloquial* 1950s youth with Edwardian-style clothing, hair, etc.

tedious /'ti:dɪəs/ *adjective* tiresomely long, wearisome. □ **tediously** *adverb*; **tediousness** *noun*.

tedium /'ti:dɪəm/ *noun* tediousness.

tee[1] *noun* letter T.

tee[2] ● *noun* cleared space from which golf ball is struck at start of play for each hole; small wood or plastic support for golf ball used then; mark aimed at in bowls, quoits, curling, etc. ● *verb* **(tees, teed)** (often + *up*) place (ball) on tee. □ **tee off** make first stroke in golf, *colloquial* start, begin.

teem[1] *verb* be abundant; (+ *with*) be full of, swarm with.

teem[2] *verb* (often + *down*) pour (esp. of rain).

teen *adjective* teenage.

teenage /'ti:neɪdʒ/ *adjective* of or characteristic of teenagers. □ **teenaged** *adjective*.

teenager /'ti:neɪdʒə/ *noun* person in teens.

teens /ti:nz/ *plural noun* years of one's age from 13 to 19.

teensy /'ti:nzɪ/ *adjective* **(-ier, -iest)** *colloquial* teeny.

teeny /'ti:nɪ/ *adjective* **(-ier, -iest)** *colloquial* tiny.

teepee = TEPEE.

teeter /'ti:tə/ *verb* totter, stand or move unsteadily.

teeth *plural* of TOOTH.

teethe /ti:ð/ *verb* **(-thing)** grow or cut teeth, esp. milk teeth. □ **teething ring** ring for infant to bite on while teething; **teething troubles** initial troubles in an enterprise etc.

teetotal /ti:'təʊt(ə)l/ *adjective* advocating or practising total abstinence from alcohol. □ **teetotalism** *noun*; **teetotaller** *noun*.

TEFL /'tef(ə)l/ *abbreviation* teaching of English as a foreign language.

Teflon /'teflɒn/ *noun proprietary term* non-stick coating for kitchen utensils.

Tel. *abbreviation* (also **tel.**) telephone.

tele- *combining form* at or to a distance; television; by telephone.

telecast /'telɪkɑ:st/ ● *noun* television broadcast. ● *verb* transmit by television. □ **telecaster** *noun*.

telecommunication /,telɪkəmjuːnɪ'keɪʃ(ə)n/ *noun* communication over distances by cable, fibre optics, satellites, radio, etc.; (in *plural*) technology of this.

telefax /'telɪfæks/ *noun* fax.

telegram /'telɪɡræm/ *noun* message sent by telegraph.

telegraph /'telɪɡrɑːf/ ● *noun* (device or system for) transmitting messages to a distance by making and breaking electrical connection. ● *verb* (often + *to*) send message or communicate by telegraph. □ **telegraphist** /tɪ'legrə-/ *noun*.

telegraphic /telɪ'ɡræfɪk/ *adjective* of or by telegraphs or telegrams; economically worded. □ **telegraphically** *adverb*.

telegraphy /tɪ'legrəfɪ/ *noun* communication by telegraph.

telekinesis /,telɪkaɪ'ni:sɪs/ *noun* supposed paranormal force moving objects at a distance. □ **telekinetic** /-'net-/ *adjective*.

telemessage /'telɪmesɪdʒ/ *noun* message sent by telephone or telex and delivered in printed form.

telemetry /tɪ'lemətrɪ/ *noun* process of recording readings of instrument and transmitting them by radio. □ **telemeter** /tɪ'lemɪtə/ *noun*.

teleology /tiːlɪ'ɒlədʒɪ/ *noun* (*plural* **-ies**) *Philosophy* explanation of phenomena by purpose they serve. □ **teleological** /-ə'lɒdʒ-/ *adjective*.

telepathy /tɪ'lepəθɪ/ *noun* supposed paranormal communication of thoughts. □ **telepathic** /telɪ'pæθɪk/ *adjective*; **telepathically** /telɪ'pæθ-/ *adverb*.

telephone /'telɪfəʊn/ ● *noun* apparatus for transmitting sound (esp. speech) to a distance; instrument used in this; system of communication by network of telephones. ● *verb* **(-ning)** send (message) or speak to by telephone; make telephone call. □ **on the telephone** having or using a telephone; **telephone book, directory** book listing telephone subscribers and numbers; **telephone booth, box, kiosk** booth etc. with telephone for public use; **telephone number** number used to call a particular telephone. □ **telephonic** /-'fɒn-/ *adjective*; **telephonically** /-'fɒn-/ *adverb*.

telephonist /tɪ'lefənɪst/ noun operator in telephone exchange or at switchboard.

telephony /tɪ'lefənɪ/ noun transmission of sound by telephone.

telephoto /telɪ'fəʊtəʊ/ noun (plural -s) (in full **telephoto lens**) lens used in telephotography.

telephotography /telɪfə'tɒɡrəfɪ/ noun photographing of distant object with combined lenses giving large image. □ **telephotographic** /-fəʊtə'ɡræf-/ adjective.

teleprinter /'telɪprɪntə/ noun device for sending, receiving, and printing telegraph messages.

teleprompter /'telɪprɒmptə/ noun device beside esp. television camera that slowly unrolls script out of sight of audience.

telesales /'telɪseɪlz/ plural noun selling by telephone.

telescope /'telɪskəʊp/ ● noun optical instrument using lenses or mirrors to magnify distant objects; radio telescope. ● verb (**-ping**) press or drive (sections of tube etc.) one into another; close or be capable of closing thus; compress.

telescopic /telɪ'skɒpɪk/ adjective of or made with telescope; (esp. of lens) able to magnify distant objects; consisting of sections that telescope. □ **telescopic sight** telescope on rifle etc. used for sighting. □ **telescopically** adverb.

teletext /'telɪtekst/ noun computerized information service transmitted to subscribers' televisions.

telethon /'telɪθɒn/ noun long television programme to raise money for charity.

televise /'telɪvaɪz/ verb (**-sing**) transmit by television.

television /'telɪvɪʒ(ə)n/ noun system for reproducing on a screen visual images transmitted (with sound) by radio signals or cable; (in full **television set**) device with screen for receiving these signals; television broadcasting. □ **televisual** /-'vɪʒʊəl/ adjective.

telex /'teleks/ (also **Telex**) ● noun international system of telegraphy using teleprinters and public telecommunication network. ● verb send, or communicate with, by telex.

tell verb (past & past participle **told** /təʊld/) relate in speech or writing; make known, express in words; (often + of, about) divulge information, reveal secret etc.; (+ to do) direct, order; decide about, distinguish; (often + on) produce marked effect or influence. □ **tell apart** distinguish between; **tell off** colloquial scold; **tell-tale** noun person who tells tales, automatic registering device, adjective serving to reveal or betray something; **tell tales** make known person's faults etc.

teller noun person employed to receive and pay out money in bank etc.; person who counts votes; person who tells esp. stories.

telling adjective having marked effect, striking. □ **tellingly** adverb.

telly /'telɪ/ noun (plural **-ies**) colloquial television.

temerity /tɪ'merɪtɪ/ noun rashness, audacity.

temp colloquial ● noun temporary employee, esp. secretary. ● verb work as temp.

temper /'tempə/ ● noun mental disposition, mood; irritation, anger; tendency to become angry; composure, calmness; metal's hardness or elasticity. ● verb bring (clay, metal) to proper consistency or hardness; (+ with) moderate, mitigate.

tempera /'tempərə/ noun method of painting using emulsion e.g. of pigment with egg.

temperament /'tempərəmənt/ noun person's or animal's nature and character.

temperamental /tempərə'ment(ə)l/ adjective regarding temperament; unreliable, moody; colloquial unpredictable. □ **temperamentally** adverb.

temperance /'tempərəns/ noun moderation, esp. in eating and drinking; abstinence, esp. total, from alcohol.

temperate /'tempərət/ adjective avoiding excess, moderate; (of region or climate) mild.

temperature /'temprɪtʃə/ noun measured or perceived degree of heat or cold of thing, region, etc.; colloquial body temperature above normal.

tempest /'tempɪst/ noun violent storm.

tempestuous /tem'pestʃʊəs/ *adjective* stormy, turbulent. □ **tempestuously** *adverb*.

tempi *plural of* TEMPO.

template /'templɪt/ *noun* thin board or plate used as guide in drawing, cutting, drilling, etc.

temple¹ /'temp(ə)l/ *noun* building for worship, or treated as dwelling place, of god(s).

temple² /'temp(ə)l/ *noun* flat part of side of head between forehead and ear.

tempo /'tempəʊ/ *noun* (*plural* **-pos** or **-pi** /-piː/) speed at which music is (to be) played; speed, pace.

temporal /'tempər(ə)l/ *adjective* worldly as opposed to spiritual, secular; of time; of the temples of the head.

temporary /'tempərərɪ/ ● *adjective* lasting or meant to last only for limited time. ● *noun* (*plural* **-ies**) person employed temporarily. □ **temporarily** *adverb*.

temporize /'tempəraɪz/ *verb* (also **-ise**) (**-zing** or **-sing**) avoid committing oneself, so as to gain time; procrastinate; comply temporarily.

tempt *verb* entice, incite to what is forbidden; allure, attract; risk provoking. □ **tempter** *noun*; **tempting** *adjective*; **temptingly** *adverb*; **temptress** *noun*.

temptation /temp'teɪʃ(ə)n/ *noun* tempting, being tempted; incitement, esp. to wrongdoing; attractive thing or course of action.

ten *adjective & noun* one more than nine. □ **the Ten Commandments** rules of conduct given by God to Moses. □ **tenth** *adjective & noun*.

tenable /'tenəb(ə)l/ *adjective* maintainable against attack or objection; (+ *for, by*) (of office etc.) that can be held for period or by (person etc.). □ **tenability** *noun*.

tenacious /tɪ'neɪʃəs/ *adjective* (often + *of*) keeping firm hold; persistent, resolute; (of memory) retentive. □ **tenaciously** *adverb*; **tenacity** /-'næs-/ *noun*.

tenancy /'tenənsɪ/ *noun* (*plural* **-ies**) (duration of) tenant's status or possession.

tenant /'tenənt/ *noun* person who rents land or property from landlord; (often + *of*) occupant of place.

tenantry *noun* tenants of estate etc.

tench *noun* (*plural* same) freshwater fish of carp family.

tend¹ *verb* (often + *to*) be apt or inclined; be moving; hold a course.

tend² *verb* take care of, look after.

tendency /'tendənsɪ/ *noun* (*plural* **-ies**) (often + *to, towards*) leaning, inclination.

tendentious /ten'denʃəs/ *adjective derogatory* designed to advance a particular cause; biased; controversial. □ **tendentiously** *adverb*; **tendentiousness** *noun*.

tender¹ /'tendə/ *adjective* (**tenderer**, **tenderest**) not tough or hard; susceptible to pain or grief; compassionate; delicate, fragile; loving, affectionate; requiring tact; immature. □ **tenderfoot** (*plural* **-s** or **-feet**) novice, newcomer; **tender-hearted** easily moved; **tenderloin** middle part of loin of pork; **tender mercies** harsh treatment. □ **tenderly** *adverb*; **tenderness** *noun*.

tender² /'tendə/ ● *verb* offer, present (services, resignation, payment, etc.); (often + *for*) make tender. ● *noun* offer to execute work or supply goods at fixed price.

tender³ /'tendə/ *noun* person who looks after people or things; supply vessel attending larger one; truck attached to steam locomotive and carrying fuel etc.

tenderize *verb* (also **-ise**) (**-zing** or **-sing**) render (meat) tender by beating etc.

tendon /'tend(ə)n/ *noun* tough fibrous tissue connecting muscle to bone etc.

tendril /'tendrɪl/ *noun* slender leafless shoot by which some climbing plants cling.

tenebrous /'tenɪbrəs/ *adjective literary* dark, gloomy.

tenement /'tenɪmənt/ *noun* room or flat within house or block of flats; (also **tenement house, block**) house or block so divided.

tenet /'tenɪt/ *noun* doctrine, principle.

tenfold *adjective & adverb* ten times as much or many.

tenner /'tenə/ *noun colloquial* £10 or $10 note.

tennis /'tenɪs/ *noun* ball game played with rackets on court divided by net.

□ **tennis elbow** sprain caused by overuse of forearm muscles.

tenon /ˈtenən/ noun wooden projection shaped to fit into mortise of another piece.

tenor /ˈtenə/ ● noun male singing voice between alto and baritone; singer with this; (usually + *of*) general purport, prevailing course of one's life or habits. ● adjective having range of tenor.

tenosynovitis /ˌtenəʊsaɪnəˈvaɪtɪs/ noun repetitive strain injury, esp. of wrist.

tenpin bowling noun game in which ten pins or skittles are bowled at in alley.

tense[1] ● adjective stretched tight; strained; causing tenseness. ● verb (**-sing**) make or become tense. □ **tense up** become tense. □ **tensely** adverb; **tenseness** noun.

tense[2] noun form of verb indicating time of action etc.; set of such forms for various persons and numbers.

tensile /ˈtensaɪl/ adjective of tension; capable of being stretched. □ **tensile strength** resistance to breaking under tension.

tension /ˈtenʃ(ə)n/ noun stretching, being stretched; mental strain or excitement; strained state; stress produced by forces pulling apart; degree of tightness of stitches in knitting and machine sewing; voltage.

tent noun portable shelter or dwelling of canvas etc.

tentacle /ˈtentək(ə)l/ noun slender flexible appendage of animal, used for feeling, grasping, or moving.

tentative /ˈtentətɪv/ adjective experimental; hesitant, not definite. □ **tentatively** adverb.

tenterhooks /ˈtentəhʊks/ plural noun □ **on tenterhooks** in suspense, distracted by uncertainty.

tenuous /ˈtenjʊəs/ adjective slight, insubstantial; oversubtle; thin, slender. □ **tenuity** /-ˈjuːɪtɪ/ noun; **tenuously** adverb.

tenure /ˈtenjə/ noun (often + *of*) holding of property or office; conditions or period of this; guaranteed permanent employment, esp. as lecturer. □ **tenured** adjective.

tepee /ˈtiːpiː/ noun (also **teepee**) N. American Indian's conical tent.

tepid /ˈtepɪd/ adjective lukewarm; unenthusiastic.

tequila /tɪˈkiːlə/ noun Mexican liquor made from agave.

tercel /ˈtɜːs(ə)l/ noun (also **tiercel** /ˈtɪəs(ə)l/) male hawk.

tercentenary /ˌtɜːsenˈtiːnərɪ/ noun (plural **-ies**) 300th anniversary; celebration of this.

tergiversate /ˈtɜːdʒɪvəseɪt/ verb (**-ting**) change one's party or principles; make conflicting or evasive statements. □ **tergiversation** noun; **tergiversator** noun.

term ● noun word for definite concept, esp. specialized; (in *plural*) language used, mode of expression; (in *plural*) relation, footing; (in *plural*) stipulations, charge; price; limited period; period of weeks during which instruction is given or during which law court holds sessions; *Logic* word(s) which may be subject or predicate of proposition; *Mathematics* each quantity in ratio or series, part of algebraic expression; completion of normal length of pregnancy. ● verb call, name. □ **come to terms with** reconcile oneself to; **in terms of** with reference to; **terms of reference** scope of inquiry etc., definition of this. □ **termly** adjective.

termagant /ˈtɜːməgənt/ noun overbearing woman, virago.

terminable /ˈtɜːmɪnəb(ə)l/ ● adjective able to be terminated.

terminal /ˈtɜːmɪn(ə)l/ ● adjective (of condition or disease) fatal; (of patient) dying; of or forming limit or terminus. ● noun terminating thing, extremity; bus or train terminus; air terminal; point of connection for closing electric circuit; apparatus for transmission of messages to and from computer, communications system, etc. □ **terminally** adverb.

terminate /ˈtɜːmɪneɪt/ verb (**-ting**) bring or come to an end; (+ *in*) end in.

termination noun terminating, being terminated; ending; result; induced abortion.

terminology /ˌtɜːmɪˈnɒlədʒɪ/ noun (plural **-ies**) system of specialized terms. □ **terminological** /-nəˈlɒdʒ-/ adjective.

terminus /'tɜːmɪnəs/ *noun* (*plural* **-ni** /-naɪ/ or **-nuses**) point at end of railway or bus route or of pipeline etc.

termite /'tɜːmaɪt/ *noun* antlike insect destructive to timber.

tern *noun* seabird with long pointed wings and forked tail.

ternary /'tɜːnərɪ/ *adjective* composed of 3 parts.

terrace /'terəs/ ● *noun* flat area on slope for cultivation; level paved area next to house; row of houses built in one block of uniform style; terrace house; tiered standing accommodation for spectators at sports ground. ● *verb* (**-cing**) form into or provide with terrace(s). □ **terrace(d) house** house in terrace.

terracotta /terə'kɒtə/ *noun* unglazed usually brownish-red earthenware; its colour.

terra firma /terə 'fɜːmə/ *noun* dry land, firm ground.

terrain /təˈreɪn/ *noun* tract of land, esp. in military or geographical contexts.

terra incognita /terə ɪŋ'kɒgnɪtə/ *noun* unexplored region. [Latin]

terrapin /'terəpɪn/ *noun* N. American edible freshwater turtle.

terrarium /tə'reərɪəm/ *noun* (*plural* **-s** or **-ria**) place for keeping small land animals; transparent globe containing growing plants.

terrestrial /tə'restrɪəl/ *adjective* of or on the earth; earthly; of or on dry land.

terrible /'terɪb(ə)l/ *adjective colloquial* very great, bad, or incompetent; causing or likely to cause terror; dreadful.

terribly *adverb colloquial* very, extremely; in terrible manner.

terrier /'terɪə/ *noun* small active hardy dog.

terrific /tə'rɪfɪk/ *adjective colloquial* huge, intense, excellent; causing terror. □ **terrifically** *adverb*.

terrify /'terɪfaɪ/ *verb* (**-ies, -ied**) fill with terror. □ **terrifying** *adjective*; **terrifyingly** *adverb*.

terrine /tə'riːn/ *noun* (earthenware vessel for) pâté or similar food.

territorial /terɪ'tɔːrɪəl/ ● *adjective* of territory or district. ● *noun* (**Territorial**) member of Territorial Army.

□ **Territorial Army** local volunteer reserve force; **territorial waters** waters under state's jurisdiction, esp. part of sea within stated distance of shore. □ **territorially** *adverb*.

territory /'terɪtərɪ/ *noun* (*plural* **-ies**) extent of land under jurisdiction of ruler, state, etc.; (**Territory**) organized division of a country, esp. if not yet admitted to full rights of a state; sphere of action etc.; province; commercial traveller's sales area; area defended by animal or human, or by team etc. in game.

terror /'terə/ *noun* extreme fear; terrifying person or thing; *colloquial* troublesome or tiresome person, esp. child; terrorism.

terrorist *noun* person using esp. organized violence to secure political ends. □ **terrorism** *noun*.

terrorize *verb* (also **-ise**) (**-zing** or **-sing**) fill with terror; use terrorism against.

terry /'terɪ/ *noun* looped pile fabric used for nappies, towels, etc.

terse /tɜːs/ *adjective* (**-r, -st**) concise, brief; curt. □ **tersely** *adverb*.

tertiary /'tɜːʃərɪ/ *adjective* of third order, rank, etc.

Terylene /'terɪliːn/ *noun proprietary term* synthetic polyester textile fibre.

TESL /'tes(ə)l/ *abbreviation* teaching of English as a second language.

tesla /'tezlə/ *noun* SI unit of magnetic flux density.

tessellated /'tesəleɪtɪd/ *adjective* of or resembling mosaic; finely chequered.

tessellation /tesə'leɪʃ(ə)n/ *noun* close arrangement of polygons, esp. in repeated pattern.

test ● *noun* critical exam or trial of person's or thing's qualities; means, procedure, or standard for so doing; minor exam; *colloquial* test match. ● *verb* put to test; try severely, tax. □ **test card** still television picture outside normal programme hours; **test case** *Law* case setting precedent for other similar cases; **test drive** *noun* drive taken to judge vehicle's performance; **test-drive** *verb* take test drive in; **test match** international cricket or Rugby match, usually in series; **test-tube** thin glass tube closed at one end, used for chemical tests etc.; **test-tube baby** *colloquial* baby conceived elsewhere than in a mother's body. □ **tester** *noun*.

testaceous /tesˈteɪʃəs/ *adjective* having hard continuous shell.

testament /ˈtestəmənt/ *noun* a will; (usually + *to*) evidence, proof; *Biblical* covenant; (**Testament**) division of Bible. □ **testamentary** /-ˈment-/ *adjective*.

testate /ˈtesteɪt/ ● *adjective* having left valid will at death. ● *noun* testate person. □ **testacy** /-təsɪ/ *noun* (*plural* -**ies**).

testator /tesˈteɪtə/ *noun* (*feminine* **testatrix** /-trɪks/) (esp. deceased) person who has made a will.

testes *plural* of TESTIS.

testicle /ˈtestɪk(ə)l/ *noun* male organ that secretes spermatozoa, esp. one of pair in scrotum of man and most mammals.

testify /ˈtestɪfaɪ/ *verb* (-**ies**, -**ied**) (often + *to*) bear witness; give evidence; affirm, declare.

testimonial /testɪˈməʊnɪəl/ *noun* certificate of character, conduct, or qualifications; gift presented as mark of esteem.

testimony /ˈtestɪmənɪ/ *noun* (*plural* -**ies**) witness's statement under oath etc.; declaration, statement of fact; evidence.

testis /ˈtestɪs/ *noun* (*plural* **testes** /-tiːz/) testicle.

testosterone /teˈstɒstərəʊn/ *noun* male sex hormone.

testy /ˈtestɪ/ *adjective* (-**ier**, -**iest**) irascible, short-tempered. □ **testily** *adverb*; **testiness** *noun*.

tetanus /ˈtetənəs/ *noun* bacterial disease causing painful spasm of voluntary muscles.

tetchy /ˈtetʃɪ/ *adjective* (-**ier**, -**iest**) peevish, irritable. □ **tetchily** *adverb*; **tetchiness** *noun*.

tête-à-tête /teɪtɑːˈteɪt/ ● *noun* private conversation between two people. ● *adverb* privately without third person.

tether /ˈteðə/ ● *noun* rope etc. confining grazing animal. ● *verb* fasten with tether. □ **at the end of one's tether** at the limit of one's patience, resources, etc.

tetra- *combining form* four.

tetragon /ˈtetrəgɒn/ *noun* plane figure with 4 sides and angles. □ **tetragonal** /tɪˈtrægən-/ *adjective*.

tetrahedron /tetrəˈhiːdrən/ *noun* (*plural* -**dra** or -**s**) 4-sided triangular pyramid. □ **tetrahedral** *adjective*.

Teutonic /tjuːˈtɒnɪk/ *adjective* of Germanic peoples or languages; German.

text *noun* main part of book; original document, esp. as distinct from paraphrase etc.; passage of Scripture, esp. as subject of sermon; subject, theme; (in *plural*) books prescribed for study; data in textual form, esp. in word processor. □ **textbook** book used in studying, esp. standard book in any subject; **text editor** computing program allowing user to edit text.

textile /ˈtekstaɪl/ ● *noun* (often in *plural*) fabric, esp. woven. ● *adjective* of weaving or cloth; woven.

textual /ˈtekstʃʊəl/ *adjective* of, in, or concerning a text.

texture /ˈtekstʃə/ ● *noun* feel or appearance of surface or substance; arrangement of threads in textile fabric. ● *verb* (-**ring**) (usually as **textured** *adjective*) provide with texture; provide (vegetable protein) with texture like meat. □ **textural** *adjective*.

Thai /taɪ/ ● *noun* (*plural* same or -**s**) native, national, or language of Thailand. ● *adjective* of Thailand.

thalidomide /θəˈlɪdəmaɪd/ *noun* sedative drug found in 1961 to cause foetal malformation when taken early in pregnancy.

than /ðən/ *conjunction* *introducing comparison*.

thane /θeɪn/ *noun* *historical* holder of land from English king by military service, or from Scottish king and ranking below earl; clan-chief.

thank /θæŋk/ ● *verb* express gratitude to; hold responsible. ● *noun* (in *plural*) *colloquial* gratitude; (as *interjection*) *expression of gratitude*. □ **thanksgiving** expression of gratitude, esp. to God; **Thanksgiving (Day)** US national holiday on fourth Thurs. in Nov.; **thanks to** as result of; **thank you** *polite formula expressing gratitude*.

thankful *adjective* grateful, pleased, expressive of thanks.

thankfully *adverb* in a thankful way; let us be thankful that.

■ **Usage** The use of *thankfully* to mean 'let us be thankful that' is common, but it is considered incorrect by some people.

thankless *adjective* not feeling or expressing gratitude; (of task etc.) unprofitable, unappreciated.

that /ðæt/ ● *adjective* (*plural* **those** /ðəʊz/) used to describe the person or thing nearby, indicated, just mentioned, or understood; used to specify the further or less immediate of two. ● *pronoun* (*plural* **those** /ðəʊz/) that one; the one, the person, etc.; /ðət/ (*plural* **that**) who, whom, which (*used to introduce a defining relative clause*). ● *adverb* (+ adjective or adverb) to that degree, so, (with negative) *colloquial* very. ● *conjunction* /ðət/ used to introduce a subordinate clause expressing esp. a statement, purpose, or result. □ **at that** moreover, then; **that is (to say)** in other words, more correctly or intelligibly.

thatch /θætʃ/ ● *noun* roofing of straw, reeds, etc. ● *verb* cover with thatch. □ **thatcher** *noun*.

thaw /θɔː/ ● *verb* (often + *out*) pass from frozen into liquid or unfrozen state; (of weather) become warm enough to melt ice etc.; warm into life, animation, cordiality, etc. ● *noun* thawing; warmth of weather that thaws.

the /ði, ðə, ðiː/ ● *adjective* (called the definite article) *denoting person(s) or thing(s) already mentioned or known about*; *describing as unique*; (+ adjective) *which is, who are, etc.*; (with *the* stressed) *best known*; *used with noun which represents or symbolizes a group, activity, etc.* ● *adverb* (before comparatives in expressions of proportional variation) in or by that degree, on that account.

theatre /ˈθɪətə/ *noun* (*US* **theater**) building or outdoor area for dramatic performances; writing, production, acting, etc. of plays; room or hall for lectures etc. with seats in tiers; operating theatre; scene or field of action.

theatrical /θɪˈætrɪk(ə)l/ ● *adjective* of or for theatre or acting; calculated for effect, showy. ● *noun* (in *plural*) dramatic performances. □ **theatricality** /-ˈkæl-/ *noun*; **theatrically** *adverb*.

thee /ðiː/ *pronoun archaic* (as object of verb) you (singular).

theft /θeft/ *noun* act of stealing.

their /ðeə/ *adjective* of or belonging to them.

theirs /ðeəz/ *pronoun* the one(s) belonging to them.

theism /ˈθiːɪz(ə)m/ *noun* belief in gods or a god. □ **theist** *noun*; **theistic** /-ˈɪstɪk/ *adjective*.

them /ðem, ð(ə)m/ ● *pronoun* (as object of verb) the people or things in question; people in general; people in authority; *colloquial* they. ● *adjective slang or dialect* those.

theme /θiːm/ *noun* subject or topic of talk etc.; *Music* leading melody in a composition; *US* school exercise on given subject. □ **theme park** amusement park based on unifying idea; **theme song, tune** signature tune. □ **thematic** /θɪˈmætɪk/ *adjective*; **thematically** /θɪˈmæt-/ *adverb*.

themselves /ðəmˈselvz/ *pronoun*: emphat. form of THEY or THEM; refl. form of THEM.

then /ðen/ ● *adverb* at that time; after that, next; in that case, accordingly. ● *adjective* such at that time. ● *noun* that time. □ **then and there** immediately and on the spot.

thence /ðens/ *adverb* (also **from thence**) *archaic or literary* from that place, for that reason. □ **thenceforth, thenceforward** from that time on.

theo- *combining form* God or god(s).

theocracy /θɪˈɒkrəsɪ/ *noun* (*plural* **-ies**) form of government by God or a god directly or through a priestly order etc. □ **theocratic** /ðɪəˈkrætɪk/ *adjective*.

theodolite /θɪˈɒdəlaɪt/ *noun* surveying instrument for measuring angles.

theology /θɪˈɒlədʒɪ/ *noun* (*plural* **-ies**) study or system of (esp. Christian) religion. □ **theologian** /θɪəˈləʊdʒ-/ *noun*; **theological** /θɪəˈlɒdʒ-/ *adjective*.

theorem /ˈθɪərəm/ *noun* esp. *Mathematics* general proposition not self-evident but demonstrable by argument; algebraic rule.

theoretical /θɪəˈretɪk(ə)l/ *adjective* concerned with knowledge but not with its practical application; based on theory rather than experience. □ **theoretically** adverb.

theoretician /θɪərəˈtɪʃ(ə)n/ noun person concerned with theoretical part of a subject.

theorist /ˈθɪərɪst/ noun holder or inventor of a theory.

theorize /ˈθɪəraɪz/ verb (also **-ise**) (**-zing** or **-sing**) evolve or indulge in theories.

theory /ˈθɪərɪ/ noun (plural **-ies**) supposition or system of ideas explaining something, esp. one based on general principles; speculative view; abstract knowledge or speculative thought; exposition of principles of a science etc.; collection of propositions to illustrate principles of a mathematical subject.

theosophy /θɪˈɒsəfɪ/ noun (plural **-ies**) philosophy professing to achieve knowledge of God by direct intuition, spiritual ecstasy, etc. □ **theosophical** /θɪəˈsɒf-/ adjective; **theosophist** noun.

therapeutic /θerəˈpjuːtɪk/ adjective of, for, or contributing to the cure of diseases; soothing, conducive to well-being. □ **therapeutically** adverb.

therapeutics plural noun (usually treated as singular) branch of medicine concerned with cures and remedies.

therapy /ˈθerəpɪ/ noun (plural **-ies**) non-surgical treatment of disease etc. □ **therapist** noun.

there /ðeə/ adverb in, at, or to that place or position; at that point; in that respect; used for emphasis in calling attention; used to indicate the fact or existence of something. ● noun that place. ● interjection expressing confirmation, triumph, etc.; used to soothe a child etc. □ **thereabout(s)** near that place, amount, or time; **thereafter** formal after that; **thereby** by that means or agency; **therefore** for that reason, accordingly, consequently; **therein** formal in that place or respect; **thereof** formal of that or it; **thereto** formal to that or it, in addition; **thereupon** in consequence of that, directly after that.

therm /θɜːm/ noun unit of heat, former UK unit of gas supplied.

thermal /ˈθɜːm(ə)l/ ● adjective of, for, producing, or retaining heat. ● noun rising current of warm air. □ **thermal unit** unit for measuring heat. □ **thermally** adverb.

thermionic valve /θɜːmɪˈɒnɪk/ noun device giving flow of electrons in one direction from heated substance, used esp. in rectification of current and in radio reception.

thermo- combining form heat.

thermodynamics /θɜːməʊdaɪˈnæmɪks/ plural noun (usually treated as singular) science of relationship between heat and other forms of energy. □ **thermodynamic** adjective.

thermoelectric /θɜːməʊɪˈlektrɪk/ adjective producing electricity by difference of temperatures.

thermometer /θəˈmɒmɪtə/ noun instrument for measuring temperature, esp. graduated glass tube containing mercury or alcohol.

thermonuclear /θɜːməʊˈnjuːklɪə/ adjective relating to nuclear reactions that occur only at very high temperatures; (of bomb etc.) using such reactions.

thermoplastic /θɜːməʊˈplæstɪk/ ● adjective becoming plastic on heating and hardening on cooling. ● noun thermoplastic substance.

Thermos /ˈθɜːməs/ noun (in full **Thermos flask**) proprietary term vacuum flask.

thermosetting /θɜːməʊsetɪŋ/ adjective (of plastics) setting permanently when heated.

thermosphere /ˈθɜːməsfɪə/ noun region of atmosphere beyond mesosphere.

thermostat /ˈθɜːməstæt/ noun device for automatic regulation of temperature. □ **thermostatic** /-ˈstæt-/ adjective; **thermostatically** /-ˈstæt-/ adverb.

thesaurus /θɪˈsɔːrəs/ noun (plural **-ri** /-raɪ/ or **-ruses**) dictionary of synonyms etc.

these plural of THIS.

thesis /ˈθiːsɪs/ noun (plural **theses** /-siːz/) proposition to be maintained or proved; dissertation, esp. by candidate for higher degree.

Thespian /ˈθespɪən/ ● adjective of drama. ● noun actor or actress.

they /ðeɪ/ pronoun (as subject of verb) the people or things in question; people in general; people in authority.

they'd /ðeɪd/ they had; they would.

they'll /ðeɪəl/ they will; they shall.

they're /ðeə/ they are.

they've /ðeɪv/ they have.

thiamine /ˈθaɪəmɪn/ *noun* (also **thiamin**) B vitamin found in unrefined cereals, beans, and liver.

thick /θɪk/ ● *adjective* of great or specified extent between opposite surfaces; (of line etc.) broad, not fine; closely set; crowded; (usually + *with*) densely filled or covered; firm in consistency; made of thick material; muddy, impenetrable; *colloquial* stupid; (of voice) indistinct; (of accent) marked; *colloquial* intimate. ● *noun* thick part of anything. ● *adverb* thickly. □ **a bit thick** *colloquial* unreasonable, intolerable; **in the thick of** in the busiest part of; **thickhead** *colloquial* stupid person; **thickheaded** *adjective*; **thickset** heavily or solidly built, set or growing close together; **thick-skinned** not sensitive to criticism; **through thick and thin** under all conditions, in spite of all difficulties. □ **thickly** *adverb*; **thickness** *noun*.

thicken *verb* make or become thick(er); become more complicated.

thickener *noun* substance used to thicken liquid.

thickening *noun* thickened part; = THICKENER.

thicket /ˈθɪkɪt/ *noun* tangle of shrubs or trees.

thief /θiːf/ *noun* (*plural* **thieves** /θiːvz/) person who steals, esp. secretly.

thieve /θiːv/ *verb* (**-ving**) be a thief; steal. □ **thievery** *noun*.

thievish *adjective* given to stealing.

thigh /θaɪ/ *noun* part of leg between hip and knee. □ **thigh-bone** femur.

thimble /ˈθɪmb(ə)l/ *noun* metal or plastic cap worn to protect finger and push needle in sewing.

thimbleful *noun* (*plural* **-s**) small quantity, esp. of drink.

thin /θɪn/ ● *adjective* (**-nn-**) having opposite surfaces close together, of small thickness or diameter; (of line etc.) narrow, fine; made of thin material; lean, not plump; not dense or copious; of slight consistency; weak, lacking an important ingredient; (of excuse etc.) transparent, flimsy. ● *adverb* thinly. ● *verb* (**-nn-**) make or become thin(ner); (often + *out*) make or become less dense, crowded, or numerous. □ **thin**

on the ground few; **thin on top** balding; **thin-skinned** sensitive to criticism. □ **thinly** *adverb*; **thinness** *noun*.

thine /ðaɪn/ *archaic* ● *pronoun* yours (singular). ● *adjective* your (singular).

thing /θɪŋ/ *noun* any possible object of thought or perception including people, material objects, events, qualities, ideas, utterances, and acts; *colloquial* one's special interest; (**the thing**) *colloquial* what is proper, fashionable, needed, important, etc.; (in *plural*) personal belongings, clothing, or equipment; (in *plural*) affairs, circumstances. □ **have a thing about** *colloquial* be obsessed by or prejudiced about.

thingummy /ˈθɪŋəmɪ/ *noun* (*plural* **-ies**) (also **thingumabob** /-məbɒb/, **thingumajig** /-mədʒɪg/) *colloquial* person or thing whose name one forgets or does not know.

think /θɪŋk/ ● *verb* (*past & past participle* **thought** /θɔːt/) be of opinion; (+ *of, about*) consider; exercise mind; form ideas, imagine; have half-formed intention. ● *noun colloquial* act of thinking. □ **think better of** change one's mind about (intention) after reconsideration; **think out** consider carefully, devise; **think over** reflect on; **think-tank** *colloquial* group of experts providing advice and ideas on national or commercial problems; **think twice** avoid hasty action etc.; **think up** *colloquial* devise.

thinker *noun* person who thinks in specified way; person with skilled or powerful mind.

thinking ● *adjective* intelligent, rational. ● *noun* opinion, judgement.

thinner *noun* solvent for diluting paint etc.

third /θɜːd/ *adjective & noun* next after second; any of 3 equal parts of thing. □ **third degree** severe and protracted interrogation by police etc.; **third man** *Cricket* fielder near boundary behind slips; **third party** another party besides the two principals; **third-party insurance** insurance against damage or injury suffered by person other than the insured; **third-rate** inferior, very poor; **Third World** developing countries of Africa, Asia, and Latin America. □ **thirdly** *adverb*.

thirst /θɜːst/ ● noun (discomfort caused by) need to drink; desire, craving. ● verb feel thirst.

thirsty /ˈθɜːstɪ/ adjective (-ier, -iest) feeling thirst; (of land, season, etc.) dry, parched; (often + for, after) eager; colloquial causing thirst. □ **thirstily** adverb; **thirstiness** noun.

thirteen /θɜːˈtiːn/ adjective & noun one more than twelve. □ **thirteenth** adjective & noun.

thirty /ˈθɜːtɪ/ adjective & noun (plural -ies) three times ten. □ **thirtieth** adjective & noun.

this /ðɪs/ ● adjective (plural **these** /ðiːz/) used to describe the person or thing nearby, indicated, just mentioned, or understood; used to specify the nearer or more immediate of two; the present (morning, week, etc.). ● pronoun (plural **these** /ðiːz/) this one. ● adverb (+ adjective or adverb) to this degree or extent.

thistle /ˈθɪs(ə)l/ noun prickly plant, usually with globular heads of purple flowers; this as Scottish national emblem. □ **thistledown** down containing thistle-seeds. □ **thistly** adjective.

thither /ˈðɪðə/ adverb archaic or formal to that place.

tho' = THOUGH.

thole /θəʊl/ noun (in full **thole-pin**) pin in gunwale of boat as fulcrum for oar; each of two such pins forming rowlock.

thong /θɒŋ/ noun narrow strip of hide or leather.

thorax /ˈθɔːræks/ noun (plural **-races** /-rəsɪz/ or **-raxes**) part of the body between neck and abdomen. □ **thoracic** /-ˈræs-/ adjective.

thorn /θɔːn/ noun sharp-pointed projection on plant; thorn-bearing shrub or tree. □ **thornless** adjective.

thorny adjective (-ier, -iest) having many thorns; (of subject) problematic, causing disagreement.

thorough /ˈθʌrə/ adjective complete, unqualified, not superficial; acting or done with great care etc. □ **thoroughbred** adjective of pure breed, high-spirited, noun such animal, esp. horse; **thoroughfare** public way open at both ends, esp. main road; **thoroughgoing** thorough, complete. □ **thoroughly** adverb; **thoroughness** noun.

those plural of THAT.

thou[1] /ðaʊ/ pronoun archaic (as subject of verb) you (singular).

thou[2] /ðaʊ/ noun (plural same or **-s**) colloquial thousand; one thousandth.

though /ðəʊ/ (also **tho'**) ● conjunction in spite of the fact that; even if; and yet. ● adverb colloquial however, all the same.

thought[1] /θɔːt/ noun process, power, faculty, etc. of thinking; particular way of thinking; sober reflection, consideration; idea, notion; intention, purpose; (usually in plural) one's opinion.

thought[2] past & past participle of THINK.

thoughtful adjective engaged in or given to meditation; giving signs of serious thought; considerate. □ **thoughtfully** adverb; **thoughtfulness** noun.

thoughtless adjective careless of consequences or of others' feelings; caused by lack of thought. □ **thoughtlessly** adverb; **thoughtlessness** noun.

thousand /ˈθaʊz(ə)nd/ adjective & noun (plural same) ten hundred; (**thousands**) colloquial large number. □ **thousandth** adjective & noun.

thrall /θrɔːl/ noun literary (often + of, to) slave; slavery.

thrash /θræʃ/ verb beat or whip severely; defeat thoroughly; move or fling (esp. limbs) violently. □ **thrash out** discuss to conclusion.

thread /θred/ ● noun spun-out cotton, silk, glass, etc.; length of this; thin cord of twisted yarns used esp. in sewing and weaving; continuous aspect of thing; spiral ridge of screw. ● verb pass thread through (needle); put (beads) on thread; arrange (material in strip form, e.g. film) in proper position on equipment; pick (one's way) through maze, crowded place, etc. □ **threadbare** (of cloth) so worn that nap is lost and threads showing, (of person) shabby, (of idea etc.) hackneyed; **threadworm** parasitic threadlike worm.

threat /θret/ noun declaration of intention to punish or hurt; indication of something undesirable coming; person or thing regarded as dangerous.

threaten /ˈθret(ə)n/ verb use threats towards; be sign or indication of (something undesirable); (+ to do) announce one's intention to do (undesirable thing); give warning of infliction of (harm etc.); (as **threatened** adjective) (of species etc.) likely to become extinct.

three /θriː/ adjective & noun one more than two. □ **three-cornered** triangular, (of contest etc.) between 3 people etc.; **three-dimensional** having or appearing to have length, breadth, and depth; **three-legged race** race for pairs with right leg of one tied to other's left leg; **threepence** /'θrepəns/ sum of 3 pence; **threepenny** /'θrepənɪ/ costing 3 pence; **three-piece** (suit or suite) consisting of 3 items; **three-ply** (wool etc.) having 3 strands, (plywood) having 3 layers; **three-point turn** method of turning vehicle in narrow space by moving forwards, backwards, and forwards again; **three-quarter** Rugby any of 3 or 4 players just behind half-backs; **the three Rs** reading, writing, and arithmetic.

threefold adjective & adverb three times as much or many.

threesome noun group of 3 people.

threnody /'θrenədɪ/ noun (plural -**ies**) song of lamentation.

thresh verb beat out or separate grain from (corn etc.). □ **thresher** noun.

threshold /'θreʃəʊld/ noun plank or stone forming bottom of doorway; point of entry; limit below which stimulus causes no reaction.

threw past of THROW.

thrice adverb archaic or literary 3 times.

thrift noun frugality, economical management. □ **thrifty** adjective (-**ier**, -**iest**).

thrill ● noun wave or nervous tremor of emotion or sensation; throb, pulsation. ● verb (cause to) feel thrill; quiver or throb (as) with emotion.

thriller noun sensational or exciting play, story, etc.

thrips noun (plural same) insect harmful to plants.

thrive verb (-**ving**; past **throve** or **thrived**; past participle **thriven** /'θrɪv(ə)n/ or **thrived**) prosper; grow vigorously.

thro' = THROUGH.

throat noun gullet, windpipe; front of neck; literary narrow passage or entrance.

throaty adjective (-**ier**, -**iest**) (of voice) hoarsely resonant.

throb ● verb (-**bb-**) pulsate; vibrate with persistent rhythm or with emotion. ● noun throbbing, violent beat or pulsation.

throe noun (usually in plural) violent pang. □ **in the throes of** struggling with the task of.

thrombosis /θrɒm'bəʊsɪs/ noun (plural -**boses** /-siːz/) coagulation of blood in blood vessel or organ.

throne ● noun ceremonial chair for sovereign, bishop, etc.; sovereign power. ● verb (-**ning**) enthrone.

throng ● noun (often + of) crowd, esp. of people. ● verb come in multitudes; fill (as) with crowd.

throstle /'θrɒs(ə)l/ noun song thrush.

throttle /'θrɒt(ə)l/ ● noun (lever etc. operating) valve controlling flow of steam or fuel in engine; throat. ● verb (-**ling**) choke, strangle; control (engine etc.) with throttle. □ **throttle back**, **down** reduce speed of (engine etc.) by throttling.

through /θruː/ (also **thro'**, US **thru**) ● preposition from end to end or side to side of; between, among; from beginning to end of; by agency, means, or fault of; by reason of; US up to and including. ● adverb through something; from end to end; to the end. ● adjective (of journey etc.) done without change of line, vehicle, etc.; (of traffic) going through a place to its destination; (of road) open at both ends. □ **be through** colloquial (often + with) have finished, cease to have dealings; **through and through** thoroughly, completely; **throughput** amount of material put through a manufacturing etc. process or a computer.

throughout /θruː'aʊt/ ● preposition right through; from end to end of. ● adverb in every part or respect.

throve past of THRIVE.

throw /θrəʊ/ ● verb (past **threw** /θruː/; past participle **thrown**) propel through space; force violently into specified position or state; turn or move (part of body) quickly or suddenly; project (rays, light, etc.); cast (shadow); bring to the ground; colloquial disconcert; (+ on, off, etc.) put (clothes etc.) carelessly or hastily on, off, etc.; cause (dice) to fall on table etc., obtain (specified number) thus; cause to pass or extend suddenly to another state or position; move (switch, lever); shape (pottery) on wheel; have (fit, tantrum, etc.); give (a party). ●*noun* throwing, being thrown; distance a thing is or may be thrown; (**a throw**) *slang* each, per item. □ **throw away** discard as unwanted, waste, fail to make use of; **throw-away** to be thrown away after (one) use, deliberately underemphasized; **throw back** (usually in *passive*; + *on*) compel to rely on; **throwback** (instance of) reversion to ancestral character; **throw in** interpose (word, remark), include at no extra cost, throw (football) from edge of pitch where it has gone out of play; **throw-in** throwing in of football from edge of pitch; **throw off** discard, contrive to get rid of, write or utter in offhand way; **throw open** (often + *to*) cause to be suddenly or widely open, make accessible; **throw out** put out forcibly or suddenly, discard, reject; **throw over** desert, abandon; **throw up** abandon, resign from, vomit, erect hastily, bring to notice.

thrum ●*verb* (**-mm-**) play (stringed instrument) monotonously or unskilfully; (often + *on*) drum idly. ●*noun* such playing; resultant sound.

thrush[1] *noun* kind of songbird.

thrush[2] *noun* fungus infection of throat, esp. in children, or of vagina.

thrust ●*verb* (*past & past participle* **thrust**) push with sudden impulse or with force; (+ *on*) impose (thing) forcibly on; (+ *at, through*) pierce, stab, lunge suddenly; make (one's way) forcibly; (as **thrusting** *adjective*) aggressive, ambitious. ●*noun* sudden or forcible push or lunge; forward force exerted by propeller or jet etc.; strong attempt to penetrate enemy's line or territory; remark aimed at person; stress between parts of arch etc.; (often + *of*) theme, gist.

thud /θʌd/ ●*noun* low dull sound as of blow on non-resonant thing. ●*verb* (**-dd-**) make thud; fall with thud.

thug /θʌɡ/ *noun* vicious or brutal ruffian. □ **thuggery** *noun*; **thuggish** *adjective*.

thumb /θʌm/ ●*noun* short thick finger on hand, set apart from other 4; part of glove for thumb. ●*verb* soil or wear with

thumb; turn over pages (as) with thumb; request or get (lift) by sticking out thumb. □ **thumb index** set of lettered grooves cut down side of book etc. for easy reference; **thumbnail** *noun* nail of thumb, *adjective* concise; **thumbscrew** instrument of torture for squeezing thumbs; **thumbs up**, **down** indication of approval or rejection; **under** (**person's**) **thumb** dominated by him or her.

thump /θʌmp/ ●*verb* beat heavily, esp. with fist; throb strongly; (+ *at, on*, etc.) knock loudly. ●*noun* (sound of) heavy blow.

thumping *adjective colloquial* huge.

thunder /'θʌndə/ ●*noun* loud noise accompanying lightning; resounding loud deep noise; strong censure. ●*verb* sound with or like thunder; move with loud noise; utter loudly; (+ *against* etc.) make violent threats. □ **thunderbolt** flash of lightning with crash of thunder, unexpected occurrence or announcement, supposed bolt or shaft as destructive agent; **thunderclap** crash of thunder; **thundercloud** electrically charged cumulus cloud; **thunderstorm** storm with thunder and lightning; **thunderstruck** amazed. □ **thunderous** *adjective*; **thundery** *adjective*.

thundering *adjective colloquial* huge.

Thur. *abbreviation* (also **Thurs.**) Thursday.

thurible /'θjʊərɪb(ə)l/ *noun* censer.

Thursday /'θɜːzdeɪ/ *noun* day of week following Wednesday.

thus /ðʌs/ *adverb formal* in this way, like this; accordingly, as a result or inference; to this extent, so.

thwack ●*verb* hit with heavy blow. ●*noun* heavy blow.

thwart /θwɔːt/ ●*verb* frustrate, foil. ●*noun* rower's seat.

thy /ðaɪ/ *adjective* (also **thine**, esp. before vowel) *archaic* your (singular).

thyme /taɪm/ *noun* herb with aromatic leaves.

thymol /'θaɪmɒl/ *noun* antiseptic made from oil of thyme.

thymus /'θaɪməs/ *noun* (*plural* **thymi** /-maɪ/) ductless gland near base of neck.

thyroid /'θaɪrɔɪd/ noun thyroid gland. □ **thyroid cartilage** large cartilage of larynx forming Adam's apple; **thyroid gland** large ductless gland near larynx secreting hormone which regulates growth and development; extract of this.

thyself /ðaɪ'self/ pronoun archaic: emphat. form of THOU[1] or THEE; refl. form of THEE.

ti = TE.

tiara /tɪ'ɑ:rə/ noun jewelled ornamental band worn on front of woman's hair; 3-crowned diadem formerly worn by pope.

tibia /'tɪbɪə/ noun (plural **tibiae** /-bɪiː/) inner of two bones extending from knee to ankle.

tic noun (in full **nervous tic**) spasmodic contraction of muscles, esp. of face.

tick[1] ● noun slight recurring click, esp. of watch or clock; colloquial moment; small mark (✓) to denote correctness etc. ● verb make sound of tick; (often + off) mark with tick. □ **tick off** colloquial reprimand; **tick over** (of engine) idle, function at basic level; **tick-tack** kind of manual semaphore used by racecourse bookmakers; **tick-tock** ticking of large clock etc.

tick[2] noun parasitic arachnid or insect on animals.

tick[3] noun colloquial financial credit.

tick[4] noun case of mattress or pillow; ticking.

ticker noun colloquial heart; watch, US tape machine. □ **ticker-tape** paper strip from tape machine, esp. as thrown from windows to greet celebrity.

ticket /'tɪkɪt/ ● noun piece of paper or card entitling holder to enter place, participate in event, travel by public transport, etc.; notification of traffic offence etc.; certificate of discharge from army or of qualification as ship's master, pilot, etc.; price etc. label; esp. US list of candidates put forward by group, esp. political party, principles of party; (**the ticket**) colloquial what is needed. ● verb (**-t-**) attach ticket to.

ticking noun strong usually striped material to cover mattresses etc.

tickle /'tɪk(ə)l/ ● verb (**-ling**) touch or stroke lightly so as to produce laughter and spasmodic movement; excite agreeably, amuse; catch (trout etc.) by rubbing it so that it moves backwards into hand. ● noun act or sensation of tickling.

ticklish /'tɪklɪʃ/ adjective sensitive to tickling; difficult to handle.

tidal /'taɪd(ə)l/ adjective related to, like, or affected by tides. □ **tidal wave** exceptionally large ocean wave, esp. one caused by underwater earthquake, widespread manifestation of feeling etc.

tidbit US = TITBIT.

tiddler /'tɪdlə/ noun colloquial small fish, esp. stickleback or minnow; unusually small thing.

tiddly[1] /'tɪdlɪ/ adjective (**-ier, -iest**) colloquial slightly drunk.

tiddly[2] /'tɪdlɪ/ adjective (**-ier, -iest**) colloquial little.

tiddly-wink /'tɪdlɪwɪŋk/ noun counter flicked with another into cup; (in plural) this game.

tide ● noun regular rise and fall of sea due to attraction of moon and sun; water as moved by this; time, season; trend of opinion, fortune, or events. ● verb (**-ding**) (**tide over**) temporarily provide with what is needed. □ **tide-mark** mark made by tide at high water, colloquial line of dirt round bath, or on person's body between washed and unwashed parts; **tideway** tidal part of river.

tidings /'taɪdɪŋz/ noun archaic or jocular (treated as singular or plural) news.

tidy /'taɪdɪ/ ● adjective (**-ier, -iest**) neat, orderly; (of person) methodical; colloquial considerable. ● noun (plural **-ies**) receptacle for odds and ends. ● verb (**-ies, -ied**) (often + up) make (oneself, room, etc.) tidy; put in order. □ **tidily** adverb; **tidiness** noun.

tie ● verb (**tying**) attach or fasten with cord etc.; form into knot or bow; (often + down) restrict, bind; (often + with) make same score as another competitor; bind (rafters etc.) by crosspiece etc.; Music unite (notes) by tie. ● noun cord etc. used for fastening; strip of material worn round collar and tied in knot at front; thing that unites or restricts people; equality of score, draw, or dead heat among competitors; match between any pair of players or teams; rod or beam holding parts of structure together; *Music* curved line above or below two notes of same pitch that are to be joined as one. □ **tie-break, -breaker** means of deciding winner when competitors have tied; **tie-dye** method of producing dyed patterns by tying string etc. to keep dye from parts of fabric; **tie-pin** ornamental pin to hold necktie in place; **tie up** fasten with cord etc., invest (money etc.) so that it is not immediately available for use, fully occupy (person), bring to satisfactory conclusion; **tie-up** connection, association.

tied *adjective* (of dwelling house) occupied subject to tenant's working for house's owner; (of public house etc.) bound to supply only particular brewer's liquor.

tier /tɪə/ *noun* row, rank, or unit of structure, as one of several placed one above another. □ **tiered** *adjective*.

tiercel = TERCEL.

tiff *noun* slight or petty quarrel.

tiger /'taɪgə/ *noun* large Asian animal of cat family, with yellow-brown coat with black stripes; fierce, formidable, or energetic person. □ **tiger-cat** any moderate-sized feline resembling tiger; **tiger lily** tall garden lily with dark-spotted orange flowers.

tight /taɪt/ ● *adjective* closely held, drawn, fastened, fitting, etc.; impermeable, impervious; tense, stretched; *colloquial* drunk; *colloquial* stingy; (of money or materials) not easily obtainable; stringent, demanding; presenting difficulties; produced by or requiring great exertion or pressure. ● *adverb* tightly. □ **tight corner** difficult situation; **tight-fisted** stingy; **tight-lipped** restraining emotion, determinedly reticent; **tightrope** high tightly stretched rope or wire on which acrobats etc. perform. □ **tighten** *verb*; **tightly** *adverb*; **tightness** *noun*.

tights *plural noun* thin close-fitting stretch garment covering legs, feet, and lower torso.

tigress /'taɪgrɪs/ *noun* female tiger.

tilde /'tɪldə/ *noun* mark (~) placed over letter, e.g. Spanish *n* in *señor*.

tile ● *noun* thin slab of concrete, baked clay, etc. for roofing, paving, etc. ● *verb* (**-ling**) cover with tiles. □ **tiler** *noun*.

tiling *noun* process of fixing tiles; area of tiles.

till¹ ● *preposition* up to, as late as. ● *conjunction* up to time when; so long that.

■ **Usage** In all senses, *till* can be replaced by *until*, which is more formal in style.

till² *noun* money-drawer in bank, shop, etc., esp. with device recording amount and details of each purchase.

till³ *verb* cultivate (land).

tillage *noun* preparation of land for growing crops; tilled land.

tiller /'tɪlə/ *noun* bar by which boat's rudder is turned.

tilt ● *verb* (cause to) assume sloping position or heel over; (+ *at*) thrust or run at with weapon; (+ *with*) engage in contest. ● *noun* tilting; sloping position; (of medieval knights etc.) charging with lance against opponent or mark. □ (**at**) **full tilt** at full speed, with full force.

tilth *noun* tillage, cultivation; cultivated soil.

timber /'tɪmbə/ *noun* wood for building, carpentry, etc.; piece of wood, beam, esp. as rib of vessel; large standing trees; (as *interjection*) tree is about to fall.

timbered *adjective* made (partly) of timber; (of land) wooded.

timbre /'tæmbə/ *noun* distinctive character of musical sound or voice apart from its pitch and volume.

timbrel /'tɪmbr(ə)l/ *noun* *archaic* tambourine.

time ● *noun* indefinite continuous progress of past, present, and future events etc. regarded as a whole; more or less definite portion of this, historical or other period; allotted or available portion of time; definite or fixed point or portion of time; (**a time**) indefinite period; occasion; moment etc. suitable for purpose; (in *plural*) (after numeral etc.) *expressing multiplication*; lifetime; (in *singular* or *plural*) conditions of life or of period; *slang* prison sentence; apprenticeship; date or expected date of childbirth or death; measured amount of time worked; rhythm or measure of musical composition. ● *verb* (**-ming**) choose time for, do at chosen or appropriate time; ascertain time taken by. □ **at the same time** simultaneously, nevertheless; **at times** now and then; **from time to time** occasionally; **in no time** rapidly, in a moment; **in time** not late, early enough, eventually, following time of music etc.; **on time** punctually; **time-and-motion** measuring efficiency of industrial etc. operations; **time bomb** one designed to explode at pre-set time; **time capsule** box etc. containing objects typical of present time, buried for future discovery; **time-honoured** esteemed by tradition or through custom; **timekeeper** person who records time, watch or clock as regards accuracy; **timekeeping** keeping of time, punctuality; **time-lag** interval between cause and effect; **time off** time used for rest or different activity; **timepiece** clock, watch; **time-server** person who adapts his or her opinions to suit prevailing circumstances; **time-share** share in property under time-sharing scheme; **time-sharing** use of holiday home by several joint owners at different times of year, use of computer by several people for different operations at the same time; **time sheet** sheet of paper for recording hours worked; **time-shift** move from one time to another; **time signal** audible indication of exact time of day; **time signature** *Music* indication of rhythm; **time switch** one operating automatically at preset time; **timetable** *noun* table showing times of public transport services, scheme of lessons, etc., *verb* include or arrange in such schedule; **time zone** range of longitudes where a common standard time is used.

timeless *adjective* not affected by passage of time. □ **timelessness** *noun*.

timely *adjective* (**-ier, -iest**) opportune, coming at right time. □ **timeliness** *noun*.

timer *noun* person or device that measures time taken.

timid /'tɪmɪd/ *adjective* (**-er, -est**) easily alarmed; shy. □ **timidity** /-'mɪd-/ *noun*; **timidly** *adverb*.

timing *noun* way thing is timed; regulation of opening and closing of valves in internal-combustion engine.

timorous /'tɪmərəs/ *adjective* timid, frightened. □ **timorously** *adverb*.

timpani /'tɪmpənɪ/ *plural noun* (also **tympani**) kettledrums. □ **timpanist** *noun*.

tin ● *noun* silvery-white metal used esp. in alloys and in making tin plate; container of tin or tin plate, esp. for preserving food; tin plate. ● *verb* (**-nn-**) preserve (food) in tin; cover or coat with tin. □ **tin foil** foil of tin, aluminium, or tin alloy, used to wrap food; **tin hat** *colloquial* military steel helmet; **tin-opener** tool for opening tins; **tin-pan alley** world of composers and publishers of popular music; **tin plate** sheet steel coated with tin; **tinpot** cheap, inferior; **tinsnips** clippers for cutting sheet metal; **tin-tack** tack[1] coated with tin.

tincture /'tɪŋktʃə/ ● *noun* (often + *of*) slight flavour or tinge; medicinal solution of drug in alcohol. ● *verb* (**-ring**) colour slightly, tinge, flavour; (often + *with*) affect slightly.

tinder /'tɪndə/ *noun* dry substance readily taking fire from spark. □ **tinder-box** *historical* box with tinder, flint, and steel for kindling fires.

tine *noun* prong, tooth, or point of fork, comb, antler, etc.

ting ● *noun* tinkling sound as of bell. ● *verb* cause to emit this.

tinge /tɪndʒ/ ● *verb* (**-ging**) (often + *with*; often in *passive*) colour slightly. ● *noun* tendency to or trace of some colour; slight admixture of feeling or quality.

tingle /'tɪŋg(ə)l/ ● *verb* (**-ling**) feel or cause slight pricking or stinging sensation. ● *noun* tingling sensation.

tinker /'tɪŋkə/ ● *noun* itinerant mender of kettles, pans, etc.; *Scottish & Irish* Gypsy; *colloquial* mischievous person or animal. ● *verb* (+ *at, with*) work in amateurish or desultory way; work as tinker.

tinkle /'tɪŋk(ə)l/ ● *verb* (**-ling**) (cause to) make short light ringing sounds. ● *noun* tinkling sound.

tinnitus /'tɪnɪtəs/ *noun Medicine* condition with ringing in ears.

tinny *adjective* (**-ier, -iest**) like tin; flimsy; (of sound) thin and metallic.

tinsel /ˈtɪns(ə)l/ *noun* glittering decorative metallic strips, threads, etc.; superficial brilliance or splendour. □ **tinselled** *adjective*.

tint ● *noun* a variety of a colour; tendency towards or admixture of a different colour; faint colour spread over surface. ● *verb* apply tint to, colour.

tintinnabulation /tɪntɪnæbjʊˈleɪʃ(ə)n/ *noun* ringing of bells.

tiny /ˈtaɪnɪ/ *adjective* (**-ier**, **-iest**) very small.

tip¹ ● *noun* extremity, esp. of small or tapering thing; small piece or part attached to end of thing. ● *verb* (**-pp-**) provide with tip. □ **tiptop** *colloquial* first-rate, of highest excellence.

tip² ● *verb* (**-pp-**) (often + *over*, *up*) (cause to) lean or slant; (+ *into* etc.) overturn, cause to overbalance, discharge contents of (container etc.) thus. ● *noun* slight push or tilt; place where refuse is tipped.

tip³ ● *verb* (**-pp-**) give small present of money to, esp. for service; name as likely winner of race or contest; strike or touch lightly. ● *noun* small present of money given esp. for service; piece of private or special information, esp. regarding betting or investment; piece of advice. □ **tip-off** a hint, warning, etc.; **tip off** give warning, hint, or inside information to.

tippet /ˈtɪpɪt/ *noun* cape or collar of fur etc.

tipple /ˈtɪp(ə)l/ ● *verb* (**-ling**) drink intoxicating liquor habitually or repeatedly in small quantities. ● *noun colloquial* alcoholic drink. □ **tippler** *noun*.

tipster /ˈtɪpstə/ *noun* person who gives tips about horse racing etc.

tipsy /ˈtɪpsɪ/ *adjective* (**-ier**, **-iest**) slightly drunk; caused by or showing intoxication.

tiptoe /ˈtɪptəʊ/ ● *noun* the tips of the toes. ● *verb* (**-toes**, **-toed**, **-toeing**) walk on tiptoe or stealthily. ● *adverb* (also **on tiptoe**) with heels off the ground.

TIR *abbreviation* international road transport (*transport international routier*).

tirade /taɪˈreɪd/ *noun* long vehement denunciation or declamation.

tire¹ /taɪə/ *verb* (**-ring**) make or grow weary; exhaust patience or interest of; (in *passive*; + *of*) have had enough of.

tire² *US* = TYRE.

tired *adjective* weary, ready for sleep; (of idea) hackneyed. □ **tiredly** *adverb*; **tiredness** *noun*.

tireless *adjective* not tiring easily, energetic. □ **tirelessly** *adverb*; **tirelessness** *noun*.

tiresome *adjective* tedious; *colloquial* annoying. □ **tiresomely** *adverb*.

tiro /ˈtaɪərəʊ/ *noun* (also **tyro**) (*plural* **-s**) beginner, novice.

tissue /ˈtɪʃuː/ *noun* any of the coherent collections of cells of which animals or plants are made; tissue-paper; disposable piece of thin absorbent paper for wiping, drying, etc.; fine woven esp. gauzy fabric; (often + *of*) connected series (of lies etc.). □ **tissue-paper** thin soft paper for wrapping etc.

tit¹ *noun* any of various small birds.

tit² *noun* □ **tit for tat** blow for blow, retaliation.

Titan /ˈtaɪt(ə)n/ *noun* (often **titan**) person of superhuman strength, intellect, or importance.

titanic /taɪˈtænɪk/ *adjective* gigantic, colossal.

titanium /taɪˈteɪnɪəm/ *noun* dark grey metallic element.

titbit /ˈtɪtbɪt/ *noun* (*US* **tidbit**) dainty morsel; piquant item of news etc.

titchy /ˈtɪtʃɪ/ *adjective* (**-ier**, **-iest**) *colloquial* very small.

tithe /taɪð/ *historical* ● *noun* one-tenth of annual produce of land or labour taken as tax for Church. ● *verb* (**-thing**) subject to tithes; pay tithes.

Titian /ˈtɪʃ(ə)n/ *adjective* (of hair) bright auburn.

titillate /ˈtɪtɪleɪt/ *verb* (**-ting**) excite, esp. sexually; tickle. □ **titillation** *noun*.

titivate /ˈtɪtɪveɪt/ *verb* (**-ting**) *colloquial* smarten; put finishing touches to. □ **titivation** *noun*.

title /ˈtaɪt(ə)l/ *noun* name of book, work of art, etc.; heading of chapter etc.; title-page; caption or credit in film etc.; name denoting person's status; championship in sport; legal right to ownership of property; (+ *to*) just or recognized claim to. □ **title-deed** legal document constituting evidence of a right;

title-holder person holding (esp. sporting) title; **title-page** page at beginning of book giving title, author, etc.; **title role** part in play etc. from which its title is taken.

titled *adjective* having title of nobility or rank.

titmouse /'tɪtmaʊs/ *noun* (*plural* **titmice**) small active tit.

titrate /taɪ'treɪt/ *verb* (**-ting**) ascertain quantity of constituent in (solution) by adding measured amounts of reagent. □ **titration** *noun*.

titter /'tɪtə/ ● *verb* laugh covertly, giggle. ● *noun* covert laugh.

tittle /'tɪt(ə)l/ *noun* particle, whit.

tittle-tattle /'tɪt(ə)ltæt(ə)l/ *noun & verb* (**-ling**) gossip, chatter.

tittup /'tɪtəp/ ● *verb* (**-p-** or **-pp-**) go friskily or jerkily, bob up and down, canter. ● *noun* such gait or movement.

titular /'tɪtjʊlə/ *adjective* of or relating to title; existing or being in name only.

tizzy /'tɪzɪ/ *noun* (*plural* **-ies**) *colloquial* state of nervous agitation.

TNT *abbreviation* trinitrotoluene.

to /tə/, before vowel tʊ, when stressed tu:/ ● *preposition* in direction of; as far as, not short of; according to; compared with; involved in, comprising; *used to introduce indirect object of verb etc.*, *to introduce or as substitute for infinitive, or to express purpose, consequence, or cause*. ● *adverb* in normal or required position or condition; (of door) nearly closed. □ **to and fro** backwards and forwards, (repeatedly) from place to place; **to-do** fuss, commotion; **toing and froing** constant movement to and fro, great or dispersed activity.

toad *noun* froglike amphibian breeding in water but living chiefly on land; repulsive person. □ **toadflax** plant with yellow or purple flowers; **toad-in-the-hole** sausages baked in batter; **toadstool** fungus (usually poisonous) with round top and slender stalk.

toady /'təʊdɪ/ ● *noun* (*plural* **-ies**) sycophant. ● *verb* (**-ies**, **-ied**) (+ *to*) behave servilely to, fawn on. □ **toadyism** *noun*.

toast ● *noun* sliced bread browned on both sides by radiant heat; person or thing in whose honour company is requested to drink; call to drink or instance of drinking thus. ● *verb* brown by heat, warm at fire etc.; drink to the health or in honour of. □ **toasting-fork** long-handled fork for toasting bread etc.; **toastmaster**, **toastmistress** person announcing toasts at public occasion; **toast rack** rack for holding slices of toast at table.

toaster *noun* electrical device for making toast.

tobacco /tə'bækəʊ/ *noun* (*plural* **-s**) plant of American origin with leaves used for smoking, chewing, or snuff; its leaves, esp. as prepared for smoking.

tobacconist /tə'bækənɪst/ *noun* dealer in tobacco.

toboggan /tə'bɒgən/ ● *noun* long light narrow sledge for sliding downhill, esp. over snow. ● *verb* ride on toboggan.

toby jug /'təʊbɪ/ *noun* jug or mug in shape of stout man in 3-cornered hat.

toccata /tə'kɑːtə/ *noun Music* composition for keyboard instrument, designed to exhibit performer's touch and technique.

tocsin /'tɒksɪn/ *noun* alarm bell or signal.

today /tə'deɪ/ ● *adverb* on this present day; nowadays. ● *noun* this present day; modern times.

toddle /'tɒd(ə)l/ ● *verb* (**-ling**) walk with young child's short unsteady steps; *colloquial* walk, stroll, (usually + *off*, *along*) depart. ● *noun* toddling walk.

toddler *noun* child just learning to walk.

toddy /'tɒdɪ/ *noun* (*plural* **-ies**) sweetened drink of spirits and hot water.

toe ● *noun* any of terminal projections of foot or paw; part of footwear that covers toes; lower end or tip of implement etc. ● *verb* (**toes**, **toed**, **toeing**) touch with toe(s). □ **on one's toes** alert; **toecap** (reinforced) part of boot or shoe covering toes; **toe-hold** slight foothold, small beginning or advantage; **toe the line** conform, esp. under pressure; **toenail** nail of each toe.

toff *noun slang* upper-class person.

toffee /'tɒfɪ/ *noun* firm or hard sweet made of boiled butter, sugar, etc.; this substance. □ **toffee-apple** toffee-coated apple; **toffee-nosed** *slang* snobbish, pretentious.

tofu /'təʊfuː/ noun curd of mashed soya beans.

tog[1] colloquial ● noun (in plural) clothes. ● verb (-gg-) (+ out, up) dress.

tog[2] noun unit of thermal resistance of quilts etc.

toga /'təʊɡə/ noun historical ancient Roman citizen's loose flowing outer garment.

together /tə'ɡeðə/ ● adverb in(to) company or conjunction; simultaneously; one with another; uninterruptedly. ● adjective colloquial well-organized, self-assured, emotionally stable. □ **togetherness** noun.

toggle /'tɒɡ(ə)l/ noun short bar used like button for fastening clothes; Computing key or command which alternately switches function on and off.

toil ● verb work laboriously or incessantly; make slow painful progress. ● noun labour; drudgery. □ **toilsome** adjective.

toilet /'tɔɪlɪt/ noun lavatory; process of washing oneself, dressing, etc. □ **toilet paper** paper for cleaning oneself after using lavatory; **toilet roll** roll of toilet paper; **toilet water** dilute perfume used after washing.

toiletries /'tɔɪlɪtriːz/ plural noun articles or cosmetics used in washing, dressing, etc.

toilette /twɑː'let/ noun process of washing oneself, dressing, etc.

toils /tɔɪlz/ plural noun net, snare.

token /'təʊkən/ ● noun symbol, reminder, mark; voucher; thing equivalent to something else, esp. money. ● adjective perfunctory, chosen by tokenism to represent a group. □ **token strike** brief strike to demonstrate strength of feeling.

tokenism noun granting of minimum concessions.

told past & past participle of TELL.

tolerable /'tɒlərəb(ə)l/ adjective endurable; fairly good. □ **tolerably** adverb.

tolerance /'tɒlərəns/ noun willingness or ability to tolerate; permitted variation in dimension, weight, etc.

tolerant /'tɒlərənt/ adjective disposed to tolerate others; (+ of) enduring or patient of.

tolerate /'tɒləreɪt/ verb (-ting) allow the existence or occurrence of without authoritative interference; endure; find or treat as endurable; be able to take or undergo without harm. □ **toleration** noun.

toll[1] /təʊl/ noun charge to use bridge, road, etc.; cost or damage caused by disaster etc. □ **toll-gate** barrier preventing passage until toll is paid.

toll[2] /təʊl/ ● verb (of bell) ring with slow uniform strokes, ring (bell) thus; announce or mark (death etc.) thus; (of bell) strike (the hour). ● noun tolling or stroke of bell.

toluene /'tɒljuːiːn/ noun colourless liquid hydrocarbon used in manufacture of explosives etc.

tom noun (in full **tom-cat**) male cat.

tomahawk /'tɒməhɔːk/ noun N. American Indian war-axe.

tomato /tə'mɑːtəʊ/ noun (plural **-es**) glossy red or yellow fleshy edible fruit; plant bearing this.

tomb /tuːm/ noun burial-vault; grave; sepulchral monument. □ **tombstone** memorial stone over grave.

tombola /tɒm'bəʊlə/ noun kind of lottery.

tomboy /'tɒmbɔɪ/ noun girl who enjoys rough noisy recreations. □ **tomboyish** adjective.

tome noun large book or volume.

tomfool /tɒm'fuːl/ ● noun fool. ● adjective foolish. □ **tomfoolery** noun.

Tommy /'tɒmɪ/ noun (plural **-ies**) colloquial British private soldier.

tommy-gun /'tɒmɪɡʌn/ noun submachine-gun.

tomorrow /tə'mɒrəʊ/ ● adverb on day after today; in future. ● noun the day after today; the near future.

tomtit noun tit, esp. blue tit.

tom-tom /'tɒmtɒm/ noun kind of drum usually beaten with hands.

ton /tʌn/ noun measure of weight equalling 2,240 lb (**long ton**) or 2,000 lb (**short ton**); metric ton; unit of measurement of ship's tonnage; (usually in plural) colloquial large number or amount; slang speed of 100 m.p.h., score of 100.

tonal /'təʊn(ə)l/ adjective of or relating to tone or tonality.

tonality /təˈnælɪtɪ/ *noun* (*plural* **-ies**) relationship between tones of a musical scale; observance of single tonic key as basis of musical composition; colour scheme of picture.

tone ● *noun* sound, esp. with reference to pitch, quality, and strength; (often in *plural*) modulation of voice to express emotion etc.; manner of expression in writing or speaking; musical sound, esp. of definite pitch and character; general effect of colour or of light and shade in picture; tint or shade of colour; prevailing character of morals, sentiments, etc.; proper firmness of body, state of (good) health. ● *verb* (**-ning**) give desired tone to; alter tone of; harmonize. □ **tone-deaf** unable to perceive differences in musical pitch; **tone down** make or become softer in tone; **tone up** make or become stronger in tone. □ **toneless** *adjective*; **tonelessly** *adverb*; **toner** *noun*.

tongs *plural noun* implement with two arms for grasping coal, sugar, etc.

tongue /tʌŋ/ ● *noun* muscular organ in mouth used in tasting, swallowing, speaking, etc.; tongue of ox etc. as food; faculty or manner of speaking; particular language; thing like tongue in shape. ● *verb* (**-guing**) use tongue to articulate (notes) in playing wind instrument. □ **tongue-in-cheek** ironic(ally); **tongue-tied** too shy to speak; **tongue-twister** sequence of words difficult to pronounce quickly and correctly.

tonic /ˈtɒnɪk/ ● *noun* invigorating medicine; anything serving to invigorate; tonic water; *Music* keynote. ● *adjective* invigorating. □ **tonic sol-fa** musical notation used esp. in teaching singing; **tonic water** carbonated drink with quinine.

tonight /təˈnaɪt/ ● *adverb* on present or approaching evening or night. ● *noun* the evening or night of today.

tonnage /ˈtʌnɪdʒ/ *noun* ship's internal cubic capacity or freight-carrying capacity; charge per ton on freight or cargo.

tonne /tʌn/ *noun* 1,000 kg.

tonsil /ˈtɒns(ə)l/ *noun* either of two small organs on each side of root of tongue.

tonsillectomy /tɒnsəˈlektəmɪ/ *noun* (*plural* **-ies**) surgical removal of tonsils.

tonsillitis /tɒnsəˈlaɪtɪs/ *noun* inflammation of tonsils.

tonsorial /tɒnˈsɔːrɪəl/ *adjective* usually *jocular* of hairdresser or hairdressing.

tonsure /ˈtɒnʃə/ ● *noun* shaving of crown or of whole head as clerical or monastic symbol; bare patch so made. ● *verb* (**-ring**) give tonsure to.

too *adverb* to a greater extent than is desirable or permissible; *colloquial* very; in addition; moreover.

took *past of* TAKE.

tool /tuːl/ ● *noun* implement for working on something by hand or by machine; thing used in activity; person merely used by another. ● *verb* dress (stone) with chisel; impress design on (leather); (+ *along, around*, etc.) *slang* drive or ride esp. in a casual or leisurely way.

toot /tuːt/ ● *noun* sound (as) of horn etc. ● *verb* sound (horn etc.); give out such sound.

tooth /tuːθ/ *noun* (*plural* **teeth**) each of a set of hard structures in jaws of most vertebrates, used for biting and chewing; toothlike part or projection, e.g. cog of gearwheel, point of saw or comb, etc.; (often + *for*) taste, appetite; (in *plural*) force, effectiveness. □ **fight tooth and nail** fight fiercely; **get one's teeth into** devote oneself seriously to; **in the teeth of** in spite of, contrary to, directly against (wind etc.); **toothache** pain in teeth; **toothbrush** brush for cleaning teeth; **toothpaste** paste for cleaning teeth; **toothpick** small sharp stick for removing food lodged between teeth. □ **toothed** *adjective*; **toothless** *adjective*.

toothsome *adjective* (of food) delicious.

toothy *adjective* (**-ier, -iest**) having large, numerous, or prominent teeth.

tootle /ˈtuːt(ə)l/ *verb* (**-ling**) toot gently or repeatedly; (usually + *around, along*, etc.) *colloquial* move casually.

top[1] ● *noun* highest point or part; highest rank or place, person occupying this; upper end, head; upper surface, upper part; cover or cap of container etc.; garment for upper part of body; utmost degree, height; (in *plural*) *colloquial* person or thing of best quality; (esp. in *plural*) leaves etc. of plant grown chiefly for its root; *Nautical* platform round head of lower mast. ● *adjective* highest in position, degree, or importance. ● *verb* (**-pp-**) furnish with top, cap, etc.; be higher or better than, surpass, be at or reach top of; *slang* kill, hit golf ball above centre. □ **on top of** fully in command of, very close to, in addition to; **top brass** *colloquial* high-ranking officers; **topcoat** overcoat, final coat of paint etc.; **top dog** *colloquial* victor, master; **top drawer** *colloquial* high social position or origin; **top dress** apply fertilizer on top of (earth) without ploughing it in; **top-flight** of highest rank of achievement; **top hat** tall silk hat; **top-heavy** overweighted at top; **topknot** knot, tuft, crest, or bow worn or growing on top of head; **topmast** mast on top of lower mast; **top-notch** *colloquial* first-rate; **top secret** of utmost secrecy; **topside** outer side of round of beef, side of ship above waterline; **topsoil** top layer of soil; **top up** complete (amount), fill up (partly empty container); **top-up** addition, amount that completes or quantity that fills something. □ **topmost** *adjective*.

top² *noun* toy spinning on point when set in motion.

topaz /ˈtəʊpæz/ *noun* semiprecious transparent stone, usually yellow.

tope *verb* (**-ping**) *archaic or literary* drink alcohol to excess, esp. habitually. □ **toper** *noun*.

topi /ˈtəʊpɪ/ *noun* (also **topee**) (*plural* **-s**) hat, esp sun-helmet.

topiary /ˈtəʊpɪərɪ/ ● *adjective* of or formed by clipping shrubs, trees, etc. into ornamental shapes. ● *noun* topiary art.

topic /ˈtɒpɪk/ *noun* subject of discourse, conversation, or argument.

topical *adjective* dealing with current affairs, etc. □ **topicality** /-ˈkæl-/ *noun*.

topless *adjective* without a top; (of garment) leaving breasts bare; (of woman) bare-breasted; (of place) where women go or work bare-breasted.

topography /təˈpɒgrəfɪ/ *noun* detailed description, representation, etc. of features of a district; such features. □ **topographer** *noun*; **topographical** /tɒpəˈgræf-/ *adjective*.

topology /təˈpɒlədʒɪ/ *noun* study of geometrical properties unaffected by changes of shape or size. □ **topological** /tɒpəˈlɒdʒ-/ *adjective*.

topper *noun colloquial* top hat.

topping *noun* thing that tops, esp. sauce on dessert etc.

topple /ˈtɒp(ə)l/ *verb* (**-ling**) (often + *over, down*) (cause to) fall as if top-heavy; overthrow.

topsy-turvy /tɒpsɪˈtɜːvɪ/ *adverb & adjective* upside down; in utter confusion.

toque /təʊk/ *noun* woman's close-fitting brimless hat.

tor *noun* hill, rocky peak.

torch *noun* battery-powered portable lamp; thing lit for illumination; source of heat, light, or enlightenment. □ **carry a torch for** have (esp. unreturned) love for.

tore *past of* TEAR¹.

toreador /ˈtɒrɪədɔː/ *noun* bullfighter, esp. on horseback.

torment ● *noun* /ˈtɔːment/ (cause of) severe bodily or mental suffering. ● *verb* /tɔːˈment/ subject to torment, tease or worry excessively. □ **tormentor** /-ˈmen-/ *noun*.

torn *past participle of* TEAR¹.

tornado /tɔːˈneɪdəʊ/ *noun* (*plural* **-es**) violent storm over small area, with whirling winds.

torpedo /tɔːˈpiːdəʊ/ ● *noun* (*plural* **-es**) cigar-shaped self-propelled underwater or aerial missile that explodes on hitting ship. ● *verb* (**-es, -ed**) destroy or attack with torpedo(es); make ineffective. □ **torpedo boat** small fast warship armed with torpedoes.

torpid /ˈtɔːpɪd/ *adjective* sluggish, apathetic; numb; dormant. □ **torpidity** /-ˈpɪd-/ *noun*.

torpor /ˈtɔːpə/ *noun* torpid condition.

torque /tɔːk/ *noun* twisting or rotary force, esp. in machine; *historical* twisted metal necklace worn by ancient Gauls and Britons.

torrent /ˈtɒrənt/ *noun* rushing stream of liquid; downpour of rain; (in *plural*) (usually + *of*) violent flow. □ **torrential** /təˈrenʃ(ə)l/ *adjective*.

torrid /ˈtɒrɪd/ *adjective* intensely hot; scorched, parched; passionate, intense.

torsion /ˈtɔːʃ(ə)n/ *noun* twisting. □ **torsional** *adjective*.

torso /'tɔːsəʊ/ noun (plural **-s**) trunk of human body; statue of this.

tort noun breach of legal duty (other than under contract) with liability for damages. □ **tortious** /'tɔːʃəs/ adjective.

tortilla /tɔː'tiːjə/ noun thin flat originally Mexican maize cake eaten hot.

tortoise /'tɔːtəs/ noun slow-moving reptile with horny domed shell. □ **tortoiseshell** mottled yellowish-brown turtle-shell, cat or butterfly with markings resembling tortoiseshell.

tortuous /'tɔːtʃʊəs/ adjective winding; devious, circuitous. □ **tortuously** adverb.

torture /'tɔːtʃə/ ● noun infliction of severe bodily pain, esp. as punishment or means of persuasion; severe physical or mental pain. ● verb (**-ring**) subject to torture. □ **torturer** noun; **torturous** adjective.

Tory /'tɔːrɪ/ colloquial ● noun (plural **-ies**) member of Conservative party. ● adjective Conservative. □ **Toryism** noun.

tosa /'təʊsə/ noun dog of a mastiff breed.

tosh noun colloquial rubbish, nonsense.

toss ● verb throw up, esp. with hand; roll about, throw, or be thrown, restlessly or from side to side; throw lightly or carelessly; throw (coin) into air to decide choice etc. by way it falls, (often + for) settle question or dispute with (person) thus; (of bull etc.) fling up with horns; coat (food) with dressing etc. by shaking it. ● noun tossing; fall, esp. from horseback. □ **toss one's head** throw it back, esp. in anger, impatience, etc.; **toss off** drink off at a draught, dispatch (work) rapidly or easily; **toss up** verb toss coin; **toss-up** noun doubtful matter, tossing of coin.

tot[1] noun small child; dram of liquor.

tot[2] verb (**-tt-**) (usually + up) add, mount. □ **tot up to** amount to.

total /'təʊt(ə)l/ ● adjective complete, comprising the whole; absolute, unqualified. ● noun whole sum or amount. ● verb (**-ll-**; US **-l-**) (often + to, up to) amount to; calculate total of. □ **totality** /-'tæl-/ noun (plural **-ies**); **totally** adverb.

totalitarian /təʊtælɪ'teərɪən/ adjective of one-party government requiring complete subservience to state. □ **totalitarianism** noun.

totalizator /'təʊtəlaɪzeɪtə/ noun (also **totalisator**) device showing number and amount of bets staked on race when total will be divided among those betting on winner; this betting system.

totalize /'təʊtəlaɪz/ verb (also **-ise**) (**-zing** or **-sing**) combine into a total.

tote[1] noun slang totalizator.

tote[2] verb (**-ting**) esp. US colloquial carry, convey. □ **tote bag** large and capacious bag.

totem /'təʊtəm/ noun natural object (esp. animal) adopted esp. among N. American Indians as emblem of clan or individual; image of this. □ **totem-pole** post with carved and painted or hung totem(s).

toto see IN TOTO.

totter /'tɒtə/ ● verb stand or walk unsteadily or feebly; shake, be about to fall. ● noun unsteady or shaky movement or gait. □ **tottery** adjective.

toucan /'tuːkən/ noun tropical American bird with large bill.

touch /tʌtʃ/ ● verb come into or be in physical contact with; (often + with) bring hand etc. into contact with; cause (two things) to meet thus; rouse tender or painful feelings in; strike lightly; (usually in negative) disturb, harm, affect, have dealings with, consume, use; concern; reach as far as; (usually in negative) approach in excellence; modify; (as **touched** adjective) colloquial slightly mad; (usually + for) slang request and get money etc. from (person). ● noun act of touching; sense of feeling; small amount, trace; (**a touch**) slightly; Music manner of playing keys or strings, instrument's response to this; artistic, literary, etc. style or skill; slang act of requesting and getting money etc. from person; Football part of field outside touchlines. □ **touch-and-go** critical, risky; **touch at** Nautical call at (port etc.); **touch down** (of aircraft) alight; **touchdown** noun; **touchline** side limit of football etc. pitch; **touch off** explode by touching with match etc., initiate (process) suddenly; **touch on, upon** refer to or mention briefly or casually, verge on; **touch-paper** paper impregnated with nitre for igniting fireworks etc.; **touchstone** dark schist or jasper for testing alloys by marking it with them, criterion; **touch-type** type without looking at keys; **touch-typist** noun; **touch up** give finishing touches to, retouch, *slang* molest sexually; **touch wood** touch something wooden to avert ill luck; **touchwood** readily inflammable rotten wood.

touché /tuːˈʃeɪ/ *interjection acknowledging justified accusation or retort, or hit in fencing.* [French]

touching ● *adjective* moving, pathetic. ● *preposition literary* concerning. □ **touchingly** *adverb.*

touchy *adjective* (**-ier**, **-iest**) apt to take offence, over-sensitive. □ **touchily** *adverb;* **touchiness** *noun.*

tough /tʌf/ ● *adjective* hard to break, cut, tear, or chew; able to endure hardship, hardy; stubborn, difficult; *colloquial* acting sternly, (of luck etc.) hard; *colloquial* criminal, violent. ● *noun* tough person, esp. ruffian. □ **toughen** *verb;* **toughness** *noun.*

toupee /ˈtuːpeɪ/ *noun* hairpiece to cover bald spot.

tour /tʊə/ ● *noun* holiday journey or excursion including stops at various places; walk round, inspection; spell of military or diplomatic duty; series of performances, matches, etc. at different places. ● *verb* (often + *through*) go on a tour; make a tour of (country etc.). □ **on tour** (esp. of sports team, theatre company, etc.) touring; **tour operator** travel agent specializing in package holidays.

tour de force /tʊə də ˈfɔːs/ *noun* (*plural* **tours de force** same pronunciation) outstanding feat or performance. [French]

tourer *noun* car or caravan for touring in.

tourism *noun* commercial organization and operation of holidays.

tourist *noun* holiday traveller; member of touring sports team. □ **tourist class** lowest class of passenger accommodation in ship, aeroplane, etc.

tourmaline /ˈtʊəməliːn/ *noun* mineral with unusual electric properties and used as gem.

tournament /ˈtʊənəmənt/ *noun* large contest of many rounds; display of military exercises; *historical* pageant with jousting.

tournedos /ˈtʊənədəʊ/ *noun* (*plural* same /-dəʊz/) small thick piece of fillet of beef.

tourney /ˈtʊənɪ/ ● *noun* (*plural* **-s**) tournament. ● *verb* (**-eys**, **-eyed**) take part in tournament.

tourniquet /ˈtʊənɪkeɪ/ *noun* device for stopping flow of blood through artery by compression.

tousle /ˈtaʊz(ə)l/ *verb* (**-ling**) make (esp. hair) untidy; handle roughly.

tout /taʊt/ ● *verb* (usually + *for*) solicit custom persistently, pester customers; solicit custom of or for; spy on racehorses in training. ● *noun* person who touts.

tow[1] /təʊ/ ● *verb* pull along by rope etc. ● *noun* towing, being towed. □ **in tow** being towed, accompanying or in the charge of a person; **on tow** being towed; **towpath** path beside river or canal originally for horse towing boat.

tow[2] /təʊ/ *noun* fibres of flax etc. ready for spinning. □ **tow-headed** having very light-coloured or tousled hair.

towards /təˈwɔːdz/ *preposition* (also **toward**) in direction of; as regards, in relation to; as a contribution to, for; near.

towel /ˈtaʊəl/ ● *noun* absorbent cloth, paper, etc. for drying after washing etc. ● *verb* (**-ll-**; *US* **-l-**) rub or dry with towel.

towelling *noun* thick soft absorbent cloth used esp. for towels.

tower /ˈtaʊə/ ● *noun* tall structure, often part of castle, church, etc.; fortress etc. with tower; tall structure housing machinery etc. ● *verb* (usually + *above*, *up*) reach high, be superior; (as **towering** *adjective*) high, lofty, violent. □ **tower block** tall building of offices or flats; **tower of strength** person who gives strong emotional support.

town /taʊn/ *noun* densely populated area, between city and village in size; London or the chief city or town in area; central business area in neighbourhood. □ **go to town** *colloquial* act or work with energy or enthusiasm; **on the town** *colloquial* enjoying urban night-life; **town clerk** *US & historical* official in charge of records etc. of town; **town gas** manufactured gas for domestic etc. use; **town hall** headquarters of local government, with public meeting rooms etc.; **town house** town residence, esp. one of terrace;

town planning planning of construction and growth of towns; **township** *South African* urban area for occupation by black people, *US & Canadian* administrative division of county, or district 6 miles square, *Australian & NZ* small town; **townspeople** inhabitants of town.

townie /ˈtaʊnɪ/ *noun* (also **townee** /-ˈniː/) *derogatory* inhabitant of town.

toxaemia /tɒkˈsiːmɪə/ *noun* (*US* **toxemia**) blood poisoning; increased blood pressure in pregnancy.

toxic /ˈtɒksɪk/ *adjective* poisonous; of poison. □ **toxicity** /-ˈsɪs-/ *noun*.

toxicology /tɒksɪˈkɒlədʒɪ/ *noun* study of poisons. □ **toxicological** /-kəˈlɒdʒ-/ *adjective*; **toxicologist** *noun*.

toxin /ˈtɒksɪn/ *noun* poison produced by living organism.

toy ● *noun* plaything; thing providing amusement; diminutive breed of dog etc. ● *verb* (usually + *with*) amuse oneself, flirt, move thing idly. □ **toy boy** *colloquial* woman's much younger boyfriend; **toyshop** shop selling toys.

trace[1] ● *verb* (**-cing**) find signs of by investigation; (often + *along, through, to,* etc.) follow or mark track, position, or path of; (often + *back*) follow to origins; copy (drawing etc.) by marking its lines on superimposed translucent paper; mark out, delineate, or write, esp. laboriously. ● *noun* indication of existence of something, vestige; very small quantity; track, footprint; mark left by instrument's moving pen etc. □ **trace element** chemical element occurring or required, esp. in soil, only in minute amounts. □ **traceable** *adjective*.

trace[2] *noun* each of two side-straps, chains, or ropes by which horse draws vehicle. □ **kick over the traces** become insubordinate or reckless.

tracer *noun* bullet etc. made visible in flight by flame etc. emitted; artificial radioisotope which can be followed through body by radiation it produces.

tracery /ˈtreɪsərɪ/ *noun* (*plural* **-ies**) decorative stone openwork, esp. in head of Gothic window; lacelike pattern.

trachea /trəˈkiːə/ *noun* (*plural* **-cheae** /-ˈkiːiː/) windpipe.

tracing *noun* traced copy of drawing etc.; act of tracing. □ **tracing-paper** translucent paper for making tracings.

track ● *noun* mark(s) left by person, animal, vehicle, etc.; (in *plural*) such marks, esp. footprints; rough path; line of travel; continuous railway line; racecourse, circuit, prepared course for runners; groove on gramophone record; single song etc. on gramophone record, CD, or magnetic tape; band round wheels of tank, tractor, etc. ● *verb* follow track of; trace (course, development, etc.) from vestiges. □ **in one's tracks** *colloquial* where one stands, instantly; **make tracks** *colloquial* depart; **make tracks for** *colloquial* go in pursuit of or towards; **track down** reach or capture by tracking; **tracker dog** police dog tracking by scent; **track events** running-races; **track record** person's past achievements; **track shoe** runner's spiked shoe; **track suit** warm outfit worn for exercising etc. □ **tracker** *noun*.

tract[1] *noun* (esp. large) stretch of territory; bodily organ or system.

tract[2] *noun* pamphlet, esp. containing propaganda.

tractable /ˈtræktəb(ə)l/ *adjective* easily managed; docile. □ **tractability** *noun*.

traction /ˈtrækʃ(ə)n/ *noun* hauling, pulling; therapeutic sustained pull on limb etc. □ **traction-engine** steam or diesel engine for drawing heavy load.

tractor /ˈtræktə/ *noun* vehicle for hauling farm machinery etc.; traction-engine.

trad *colloquial* ● *noun* traditional jazz. ● *adjective* traditional.

trade ● *noun* buying and selling; this between nations etc.; business merely for profit (as distinct from profession); business of specified nature or time; skilled handicraft; (**the trade**) people engaged in specific trade; *US* transaction, esp. swap; (usually in *plural*) trade wind. ● *verb* (**-ding**) (often + *in, with*) engage in trade, buy and sell; exchange; *US* swap; (usually + *with, for*) have transaction. □ **trade in** exchange (esp. used article) in part payment for another; **trade mark** device or name legally registered to represent a company or product, distinctive characteristic; **trade name** name by which a thing is known in a trade, or given by manufacturer to a product, or under which a business trades; **trade off** exchange as compromise; **trade-off** balance, compromise; **trade on** take advantage of; **tradesman**, **tradeswoman** person engaged in trade, esp. shopkeeper; **trade(s) union** organized association of workers in trade, profession, etc. formed to further their common interests; **trade-unionist** member of trade union; **trade wind** constant wind blowing towards equator from NE or SE. □ **trader** noun.

tradescantia /trædɪs'kæntɪə/ noun (usually trailing) plant with large blue, white, or pink flowers.

trading noun engaging in trade. □ **trading estate** area designed for industrial and commercial firms; **trading post** store etc. in remote region; **trading-stamp** token given to customer and exchangeable in quantity usually for goods.

tradition /trə'dɪʃ(ə)n/ noun custom, opinion, or belief handed down to posterity; handing down of these.

traditional adjective of, based on, or obtained by tradition; (of jazz) in style of early 20th c. □ **traditionally** adverb.

traditionalism noun respect or support for tradition. □ **traditionalist** noun & adjective.

traduce /trə'dju:s/ verb (**-cing**) slander. □ **traducement** noun; **traducer** noun.

traffic /'træfɪk/ ●noun vehicles moving on public highway, in air, or at sea; (usually + in) trade, esp. illegal; coming and going of people or goods by road, rail, air, sea, etc.; dealings between people etc.; (volume of) messages transmitted through communications system. ●verb (**-ck-**) (often + in) deal, esp. illegally; barter. □ **traffic island** raised area in road to divide traffic and provide refuge for pedestrians; **traffic jam** traffic at standstill; **traffic light(s)** signal controlling road traffic by coloured lights; **traffic warden** person employed to control movement and parking of road vehicles. □ **trafficker** noun.

tragedian /trə'dʒi:dɪən/ noun author of or actor in tragedies.

tragedienne /trədʒi:dɪ'en/ noun actress in tragedies.

tragedy /'trædʒɪdɪ/ noun (plural **-ies**) serious accident, sad event; play with tragic unhappy ending.

tragic /'trædʒɪk/ adjective disastrous, distressing, very sad; of tragedy. □ **tragically** adverb.

tragicomedy /trædʒɪ'kɒmədɪ/ noun (plural **-ies**) drama or event combining comedy and tragedy.

trail ●noun track or scent left by moving person, thing, etc.; beaten path, esp. through wild region; long line of people or things following behind something; part dragging behind thing or person. ●verb draw or be drawn along behind; (often + behind) walk wearily; follow trail of, pursue; be losing in contest; (usually + away, off) peter out; (of plant etc.) grow or hang over wall, along ground, etc.; hang loosely. □ **trailing edge** rear edge of aircraft's wing.

trailer noun set of extracts from film etc. shown in advance to advertise it; vehicle pulled by another; US caravan.

train ●verb (often + to do) teach (person etc.) specified skill, esp. by practice; undergo this process; bring or come to physical efficiency by exercise, diet, etc.; (often + up, along) guide growth of (plant); (usually as **trained** adjective) make (mind etc.) discerning through practice etc.; (often + on) point, aim. ●noun series of railway carriages or trucks drawn by engine; thing dragged along behind or forming back part of dress etc.; succession or series of people, things, events, etc.; group of followers, retinue. □ **in train** arranged, in preparation; **train-bearer** person holding up train of another's robe etc.; **train-spotter** person who collects numbers of railway locomotives. □ **trainee** /-'ni:/ noun.

trainer noun person who trains horses, athletes, etc.; aircraft or simulator used to train pilots; soft running shoe.

training /'treɪnɪŋ/ noun process of teaching or learning a skill etc.

traipse colloquial ●verb (**-sing**) tramp or trudge wearily. ●noun tedious journey on foot.

trait /treɪ/ noun characteristic.

traitor /'treɪtə/ noun (feminine **traitress**) person guilty of betrayal or disloyalty. □ **traitorous** adjective.

trajectory /trə'dʒektəri/ *noun* (*plural* **-ies**) path of object moving under given forces.

tram *noun* (also **tramcar**) electrically powered passenger road vehicle running on rails. □ **tramlines** rails for tram, *colloquial* either pair of parallel lines at edge of tennis etc. court.

trammel /'træm(ə)l/ ● *noun* (usually in *plural*) impediment, restraint; kind of fishing net. ● *verb* (**-ll-**; *US* **-l-**) hamper.

tramp ● *verb* walk heavily and firmly; go on walking expedition; walk laboriously across or along; (often + *down*) tread on, stamp on; live as tramp. ● *noun* itinerant vagrant or beggar; sound of person or people walking or marching; long walk; *slang* derogatory promiscuous woman.

trample /'træmp(ə)l/ *verb* (**-ling**) tread under foot; crush thus. □ **trample on** tread heavily on, treat roughly or with contempt.

trampoline /'træmpəli:n/ ● *noun* canvas sheet connected by springs to horizontal frame, used for acrobatic exercises. ● *verb* (**-ning**) use trampoline.

trance /trɑ:ns/ *noun* sleeplike state; hypnotic or cataleptic state; such state as supposedly entered into by medium; rapture, ecstasy.

tranny /'træni/ *noun* (*plural* **-ies**) *colloquial* transistor radio.

tranquil /'træŋkwɪl/ *adjective* serene, calm, undisturbed. □ **tranquillity** /-'kwɪl-/ *noun*; **tranquilly** *adverb*.

tranquillize *verb* (also **-ise**; *US* also **tranquilize**) (**-zing** or **-sing**) make tranquil, esp. by drug etc.

tranquillizer *noun* (also **-iser**; *US* also **tranquilizer**) drug used to diminish anxiety.

trans- *prefix* across, beyond; on or to other side of; through.

transact /træn'zækt/ *verb* perform or carry through (business etc.).

transaction /træn'zækʃ(ə)n/ *noun* piece of commercial or other dealing; transacting of business; (in *plural*) published reports of discussions and lectures at meetings of learned society.

transatlantic /trænzət'læntɪk/ *adjective* beyond or crossing the Atlantic; American; *US* European.

transceiver /træn'si:və/ *noun* combined radio transmitter and receiver.

transcend /træn'send/ *verb* go beyond or exceed limits of; excel, surpass.

transcendent *adjective* excelling, surpassing; transcending human experience; (esp. of God) existing apart from, or not subject to limitations of, material universe. □ **transcendence** *noun*; **transcendency** *noun*.

transcendental /trænsen'dent(ə)l/ *adjective* a priori, not based on experience, intuitively accepted; abstract, vague. □ **Transcendental Meditation** meditation seeking to induce detachment from problems, anxiety, etc.

transcontinental /ˌtrænzkɒntɪ'nent(ə)l/ *adjective* extending across a continent.

transcribe /træn'skraɪb/ *verb* (**-bing**) copy out; write out (notes etc.) in full; record for subsequent broadcasting; *Music* adapt for different instrument etc. □ **transcriber** *noun*; **transcription** /-'skrɪp-/ *noun*.

transcript /'trænskrɪpt/ *noun* written copy.

transducer /trænz'dju:sə/ *noun* device for changing a non-electrical signal (e.g. pressure) into an electrical one (e.g. voltage).

transept /'trænsept/ *noun* part of cross-shaped church at right angles to nave; either arm of this.

transfer ● *verb* /træns'fɜ:/ (**-rr-**) convey, remove, or hand over (thing etc.); make over possession of (thing, right, etc.) to person; move, change, or be moved to another group, club, etc.; change from one station, route, etc. to another to continue journey; convey (design etc.) from one surface to another. ● *noun* /'trænsfɜ:/ transferring, being transferred; design etc. (to be) conveyed from one surface to another; football player etc. who is transferred; document effecting conveyance of property, a right, etc. □ **transferable** /-'fɜ:rəb(ə)l/ *adjective*; **transference** /'trænsfərəns/ *noun*.

transfigure /træns'fɪgə/ *verb* (**-ring**) change appearance of, make more elevated or idealized. □ **transfiguration** *noun*.

transfix /træns'fɪks/ *verb* paralyse with horror or astonishment; pierce with sharp implement or weapon.

transform /træns'fɔ:m/ *verb* change form, appearance, character, etc. of, esp. considerably; change voltage etc. of (alternating current). □ **transformation** /-fə'meɪ-/ *noun*.

transformer *noun* apparatus for reducing or increasing voltage of alternating current.

transfuse /træns'fju:z/ *verb* (**-sing**) transfer (blood or other liquid) into blood vessel to replace that lost; permeate. □ **transfusion** *noun*.

transgress /trænz'gres/ *verb* infringe (law etc.); overstep (¹limit laid down); sin. □ **transgression** *noun*; **transgressor** *noun*.

transient /'trænzɪənt/ *adjective* of short duration; passing. □ **transience** *noun*.

transistor /træn'zɪstə/ *noun* semiconductor device capable of amplification and rectification; (in full **transistor radio**) portable radio using transistors.

transistorize *verb* (also **-ise**) (**-zing** or **-sing**) equip with transistors rather than valves.

transit /'trænzɪt/ *noun* going; conveying, being conveyed; passage, route; apparent passage of heavenly body across meridian of place or across sun or planet. □ **in transit** (while) going or being conveyed.

transition /træn'zɪʒ(ə)n/ *noun* passage or change from one place, state, condition, style, etc. to another. □ **transitional** *adjective*; **transitionally** *adverb*.

transitive /'trænsɪtɪv/ *adjective* (of verb) requiring direct object expressed or understood.

transitory /'trænzɪtərɪ/ *adjective* not lasting; brief, fleeting.

translate /træn'sleɪt/ *verb* (**-ting**) (often + *into*) express sense of in another language or in another form; be translatable; interpret; move or change, esp. from one person, place, or condition to another. □ **translatable** *adjective*; **translation** *noun*; **translator** *noun*.

transliterate /trænz'lɪtəreɪt/ *verb* (**-ting**) represent (word etc.) in closest corresponding characters of another script. □ **transliteration** *noun*.

translucent /trænz'lu:s(ə)nt/ *adjective* allowing light to pass through, semitransparent. □ **translucence** *noun*.

transmigrate /trænzmaɪ'greɪt/ *verb* (**-ting**) (of soul) pass into different body. □ **transmigration** *noun*.

transmission /trænz'mɪʃ(ə)n/ *noun* transmitting, being transmitted; broadcast programme; device transmitting power from engine to axle in vehicle.

transmit /trænz'mɪt/ *verb* (**-tt-**) pass or hand on, transfer; communicate or be medium for (ideas, emotions, etc.); allow (heat, light, sound, etc.) to pass through. □ **transmissible** *adjective*; **transmittable** *adjective*.

transmitter *noun* person or thing that transmits; equipment used to transmit radio etc. signals.

transmogrify /trænz'mɒgrɪfaɪ/ *verb* (**-ies, -ied**) *jocular* transform, esp. in magical or surprising way. □ **transmogrification** *noun*.

transmute /trænz'mju:t/ *verb* (**-ting**) change form, nature, or substance of; *historical* change (base metals) into gold. □ **transmutation** *noun*.

transom /'trænsəm/ *noun* horizontal bar in window or above door; (in full **transom window**) window above this.

transparency /træns'pærənsɪ/ *noun* (*plural* **-ies**) being transparent; picture (esp. photograph) to be viewed by light passing through it.

transparent /træns'pærənt/ *adjective* allowing light to pass through and giving maximum visibility possible; (of disguise, pretext, etc.) easily seen through; (of quality etc.) obvious; easily understood. □ **transparently** *adverb*.

transpire /træns'paɪə/ *verb* (**-ring**) (of secret, fact, etc.) come to be known; happen; emit (vapour, moisture) or be emitted through pores of skin etc. □ **transpiration** /-spɪ-/ *noun*.

■ **Usage** The use of *transpire* to mean 'happen' is considered incorrect by some people.

transplant ● *verb* /træns'plɑ:nt/ plant elsewhere; transfer (living tissue or organ) to another part of body or to another body. ●*noun* /'trænsplɑːnt/ transplanting of organ or tissue; thing transplanted. □ **transplantation** *noun*.

transport ●*verb* /træns'pɔːt/ take to another place; *historical* deport (criminal) to penal colony; (as **transported** *adjective*) (usually + *with*) affected with strong emotion. ●*noun* /'trænspɔːt/ system of transporting, means of conveyance; ship, aircraft, etc. used to carry troops, military stores, etc.; (esp. in *plural*) vehement emotion. □ **transportable** /-'pɔːt-/ *adjective*.

transportation /trænspɔː'teɪʃ(ə)n/ *noun* (system of) conveying, being conveyed; *US* means of transport; *historical* deporting of criminals.

transporter *noun* vehicle used to transport other vehicles, heavy machinery, etc. □ **transporter bridge** bridge carrying vehicles etc. across water on suspended moving platform.

transpose /træns'pəʊz/ *verb* (**-sing**) cause (two or more things) to change places; change position of (thing) in series or (word(s)) in sentence; *Music* write or play in different key. □ **transposition** /-pə'zɪʃ(ə)n/ *noun*.

transsexual /træns'seksʊəl/ (also **transexual**) ●*adjective* having physical characteristics of one sex and psychological identification with the other. ●*noun* transsexual person; person who has had sex change.

transship /træns'ʃɪp/ *verb* (**-pp-**) transfer from one ship or conveyance to another. □ **transshipment** *noun*.

transubstantiation /trænsəbstænʃɪ'eɪʃ(ə)n/ *noun* conversion of Eucharistic elements wholly into body and blood of Christ.

transuranic /trænzjʊ'rænɪk/ *adjective Chemistry* (of element) having higher atomic number than uranium.

transverse /'trænzvɜːs/ *adjective* situated, arranged, or acting in crosswise direction. □ **transversely** *adverb*.

transvestite /trænz'vestaɪt/ *noun* man deriving pleasure from dressing in women's clothes. □ **transvestism** *noun*.

trap ●*noun* device, often baited, for catching animals; arrangement or trick to catch (out) unsuspecting person; device for releasing clay pigeon to

be shot at or greyhound at start of race etc.; curve in drainpipe etc. that fills with liquid and forms seal against return of gas; two-wheeled carriage; trapdoor; *slang* mouth. ●*verb* (**-pp-**) catch (as) in trap; catch (out) using trick etc.; furnish with traps. □ **trapdoor** door in floor, ceiling, or roof.

trapeze /trə'piːz/ *noun* crossbar suspended by ropes as swing for acrobatics etc.

trapezium /trə'piːzɪəm/ *noun* (*plural* **-s** or **-zia**) quadrilateral with only one pair of sides parallel; *US* trapezoid.

trapezoid /'træpɪzɔɪd/ *noun* quadrilateral with no sides parallel; *US* trapezium.

trapper *noun* person who traps wild animals, esp. for their fur.

trappings /'træpɪŋz/ *plural noun* ornamental accessories; (esp. ornamental) harness for horse.

Trappist /'træpɪst/ ●*noun* monk of order vowed to silence. ●*adjective* of this order.

trash ●*noun* esp. *US* worthless or waste stuff, rubbish; worthless person(s). ●*verb slang* wreck, vandalize. □ **trash can** *US* dustbin. □ **trashy** *adjective* (**-ier**, **-iest**).

trauma /'trɔːmə/ *noun* (*plural* **traumata** /-mətə/ or **-s**) emotional shock; physical injury, resulting shock. □ **traumatic** /-'mæt-/ *adjective*; **traumatize** *verb* (also **-ise**) (**-zing** or **-sing**).

travail /'træveɪl/ *literary* ●*noun* laborious effort; pangs of childbirth. ●*verb* make laborious effort, esp. in childbirth.

travel /'træv(ə)l/ ●*verb* (**-ll-**, *US* **-l-**) go from one place to another; make journey(s), esp. long or abroad; journey along or through, cover (distance); *colloquial* withstand long journey; act as commercial traveller; move or proceed as specified; *colloquial* move quickly; pass from point to point; (of machine or part) move or operate in specified way. ●*noun* travelling, esp. abroad; (often in *plural*) spell of this; range, rate, or mode of motion of part in machinery. □ **travel agency** agency making arrangements for travellers; **travelling salesman** commercial traveller; **travel-sick** nauseous owing to motion in travelling.

travelled *adjective* (*US* **traveled**) experienced in travelling.

traveller *noun* (*US* **traveler**) person who travels or is travelling; commercial traveller. □ **traveller's cheque** cheque for fixed amount, cashed on signature for equivalent in other currencies; **traveller's joy** wild clematis.

travelogue /'trævəlɒg/ *noun* film or illustrated lecture about travel.

traverse ● *verb* /trə'vɜːs/ (**-sing**) travel or lie across; consider or discuss whole extent of. ● *noun* /'trævəs/ sideways movement; traversing; thing that crosses another. □ **traversal** *noun.*

travesty /'trævɪstɪ/ ● *noun* (*plural* **-ies**) grotesque parody, ridiculous imitation. ● *verb* (**-ies, -ied**) make or be travesty of.

trawl ● *verb* fish with trawl or seine or in trawler; catch by trawling; (*often* + *for, through*) search thoroughly. ● *noun* trawling; (in full **trawl-net**) large wide-mouthed fishing net dragged by boat along sea bottom.

trawler *noun* boat used for trawling.

tray *noun* flat board with raised rim for carrying dishes etc.; shallow lidless box for papers or small articles, sometimes forming drawer in cabinet etc.

treacherous /'tretʃərəs/ *adjective* guilty of or involving violation of faith or betrayal of trust; not to be relied on, deceptive. □ **treacherously** *adverb;* **treachery** *noun.*

treacle /'triːk(ə)l/ *noun* syrup produced in refining sugar; molasses. □ **treacly** *adjective.*

tread /tred/ ● *verb* (*past* **trod**; *past participle* **trodden** or **trod**) (*often* + *on*) set one's foot down; walk on; (*often* + *down, in, into*) press (down) or crush with feet; perform (steps etc.) by walking. ● *noun* manner or sound of walking; top surface of step or stair; thick moulded part of vehicle tyre for gripping road; part of wheel or sole of shoe etc. that touches ground. □ **treadmill** device for producing motion by treading on steps on revolving cylinder, similar device used for exercise, monotonous routine work; **tread water** maintain upright position in water by moving feet and hands.

treadle /'tred(ə)l/ *noun* lever moved by foot and imparting motion to machine.

treason /'triːz(ə)n/ *noun* violation of allegiance to sovereign (e.g. plotting assassination) or state (e.g. helping enemy).

treasonable *adjective* involving or guilty of treason.

treasure /'treʒə/ ● *noun* precious metals or gems; hoard of them; accumulated wealth; thing valued for rarity, workmanship, associations, etc.; *colloquial* beloved or highly valued person. ● *verb* (**-ring**) value highly; (*often* + *up*) store up as valuable. □ **treasure hunt** search for treasure, game in which players seek hidden object; **treasure trove** treasure of unknown ownership found hidden.

treasurer *noun* person in charge of funds of society etc.

treasury /'treʒərɪ/ *noun* (*plural* **-ies**) place where treasure is kept; funds or revenue of state, institution, or society; (**Treasury**) (offices and officers of) department managing public revenue of a country. □ **Treasury bench** government front bench in parliament; **treasury bill** bill of exchange issued by government to raise money for temporary needs.

treat ● *verb* act, behave towards, or deal with in specified way; apply process or medical care or attention to; present or handle (subject) in literature or art; (*often* + *to*) provide with food, drink, or entertainment at one's own expense; (*often* + *with*) negotiate terms; (*often* + *of*) give exposition. ● *noun* event or circumstance that gives great pleasure; meal, entertainment, etc. designed to do this; (**a treat**) *colloquial* extremely good or well. □ **treatable** *adjective.*

treatise /'triːtɪz/ *noun* literary composition dealing esp. formally with subject.

treatment *noun* process or manner of behaving towards or dealing with person or thing; medical care or attention.

treaty /'triːtɪ/ *noun* (*plural* **-ies**) formal agreement between states; agreement between people, esp. for purchase of property.

treble /'treb(ə)l/ ● *adjective* threefold, triple; 3 times as much or many; high-pitched. ● *noun* treble quantity or thing; (voice of) boy soprano; high-pitched instrument; high-frequency sound of radio, record player, etc. ● *verb* (**-ling**) multiply or be multiplied by 3. □ **trebly** *adverb*.

tree ● *noun* perennial plant with woody self-supporting main stem and usually unbranched for some distance from ground; shaped piece of wood for various purposes; family tree. ● *verb* (**trees, treed**) cause to take refuge in tree. □ **treecreeper** small creeping bird feeding on insects in tree-bark; **tree-fern** large fern with upright woody stem; **tree surgeon** person who treats decayed trees in order to preserve them.

trefoil /'trefɔɪl/ *noun* plant with leaves of 3 leaflets; 3-lobed ornamentation, esp. in tracery windows.

trek ● *verb* (**-kk-**) make arduous journey, esp. (*historical*) migrate or journey by ox-wagon. ● *noun* such journey; each stage of it. □ **trekker** *noun*.

trellis /'trelɪs/ *noun* (in full **trellis-work**) lattice of light wooden or metal bars, esp. support for climbing plants.

tremble /'tremb(ə)l/ ● *verb* (**-ling**) shake involuntarily with emotion, cold, etc.; be affected with extreme apprehension; quiver. ● *noun* trembling, quiver. □ **trembly** *adjective* (**-ier, -iest**).

tremendous /trɪ'mendəs/ *adjective* colloquial remarkable, considerable, excellent; awe-inspiring, overpowering. □ **tremendously** *adverb*.

tremolo /'tremələʊ/ *noun* (*plural* **-s**) tremulous effect in music.

tremor /'tremə/ *noun* shaking, quivering; thrill (of fear, exultation, etc.); (in full **earth tremor**) slight earthquake.

tremulous /'tremjʊləs/ *adjective* trembling. □ **tremulously** *adverb*.

trench ● *noun* deep ditch, esp. one dug by troops as shelter from enemy's fire. ● *verb* dig trench(es) in; make series of trenches (in) so as to bring lower soil to surface. □ **trench coat** lined or padded waterproof coat, loose belted raincoat.

trenchant /'trentʃ(ə)nt/ *adjective* incisive, terse, vigorous. □ **trenchancy** *noun*; **trenchantly** *adverb*.

trencher /'trentʃə/ *noun* historical wooden etc. platter for serving food.

trencherman /'trentʃəmən/ *noun* eater.

trend ● *noun* general direction and tendency. ● *verb* turn away in specified direction; have general tendency. □ **trend-setter** person who leads the way in fashion etc.

trendy colloquial often derogatory ● *adjective* (**-ier, -iest**) fashionable. ● *noun* (*plural* **-ies**) fashionable person. □ **trendily** *adverb*; **trendiness** *noun*.

trepan /trɪ'pæn/ historical ● *noun* surgeon's cylindrical saw for making opening in skull. ● *verb* (**-nn-**) perforate (skull) with trepan.

trepidation /trepɪ'deɪʃ(ə)n/ *noun* fear, anxiety.

trespass /'trespəs/ ● *verb* (usually + *on, upon*) enter unlawfully (on another's land, property, etc.); encroach. ● *noun* act of trespassing; archaic sin, offence. □ **trespasser** *noun*.

tress *noun* lock of hair; (in *plural*) hair.

trestle /'tres(ə)l/ *noun* supporting structure for table etc. consisting of two frames fixed at an angle or hinged or of bar with two divergent pairs of legs; (in full **trestle-table**) table of board(s) laid on trestles; (in full **trestle-work**) open braced framework to support bridge etc.

trews *plural noun* close-fitting usually tartan trousers.

tri- *combining form* three (times).

triad /'traɪæd/ *noun* group of 3 (esp. notes in chord). □ **triadic** /-'æd-/ *adjective*.

trial /'traɪəl/ *noun* judicial examination and determination of issues between parties by judge with or without jury; test; trying thing or person; match held to select players for team; contest for horses, dogs, motorcycles, etc. □ **on trial** being tried in court of law, being tested; **trial run** preliminary operational test.

triangle /'traɪæŋg(ə)l/ *noun* plane figure with 3 sides and angles; any 3 things not in straight line, with imaginary lines joining them; implement etc. of this shape; Music instrument of steel rod bent into triangle, struck with small steel rod; situation involving 3 people. □ **triangular** /-'æŋgjʊlə/ *adjective*.

triangulate /traɪ'æŋgjʊleɪt/ *verb* (**-ting**) divide (area) into triangles for surveying purposes. □ **triangulation** *noun*.

triathlon /traɪ'æθlən/ *noun* athletic contest of 3 events. □ **triathlete** *noun*.

tribe *noun* (in some societies) group of families under recognized leader with blood etc. ties and usually having common culture and dialect; any similar natural or political division; *usually derogatory* set or number of people, esp. of one profession etc. or family. □ **tribesman**, **tribeswoman** member of tribe. □ **tribal** *adjective.*

tribulation /trɪbjʊˈleɪʃ(ə)n/ *noun* great affliction.

tribunal /traɪˈbjuːn(ə)l/ *noun* board appointed to adjudicate on particular question; court of justice.

tribune /trɪˈbjuːn/ *noun* popular leader, demagogue; (in full **tribune of the people**) *Roman History* officer chosen by the people to protect their liberties.

tributary /ˈtrɪbjʊtərɪ/ ● *noun* (*plural* **-ies**) stream etc. that flows into larger stream or lake, *historical* person or state paying or subject to tribute. ● *adjective* that is a tributary.

tribute /ˈtrɪbjuːt/ *noun* thing said or done or given as mark of respect or affection etc.; (+ *to*) indication of (some praiseworthy quality); *historical* periodic payment by one state or ruler to another, obligation to pay this.

trice *noun* □ **in a trice** in an instant.

triceps /ˈtraɪseps/ *noun* muscle (esp. in upper arm) with 3 points of attachment.

triceratops /traɪˈserətɒps/ *noun* large dinosaur with 3 horns.

trichinosis /trɪkɪˈnəʊsɪs/ *noun* disease caused by hairlike worms.

trichology /trɪˈkɒlədʒɪ/ *noun* study of hair. □ **trichologist** *noun.*

trichromatic /traɪkrəˈmætɪk/ *adjective* 3-coloured.

trick ● *noun* thing done to deceive or outwit; illusion; knack; feat of skill or dexterity; unusual action learned by animal; foolish or discreditable act; hoax, joke; idiosyncrasy; cards played in one round, point gained in this. ● *verb* deceive by trick; swindle; (+ *into*) cause to do something by trickery; take by surprise.

trickery *noun* deception, use of tricks.

trickle /ˈtrɪk(ə)l/ ● *verb* (**-ling**) (cause to) flow in drops or small stream; come or go slowly or gradually. ● *noun* trickling flow. □ **trickle charger** *Electricity* device for slow continuous charging of battery.

trickster /ˈtrɪkstə/ *noun* deceiver, rogue.

tricky *adjective* (**-ier**, **-iest**) requiring care and adroitness; crafty, deceitful. □ **trickily** *adverb;* **trickiness** *noun.*

tricolour /ˈtrɪkələ/ *noun* (*US* **tricolor**) flag of 3 colours, esp. French national flag.

tricot /ˈtriːkəʊ/ *noun* knitted fabric.

tricycle /ˈtraɪsɪk(ə)l/ *noun* 3-wheeled pedal-driven vehicle.

trident /ˈtraɪd(ə)nt/ *noun* 3-pronged spear.

Tridentine /traɪˈdentaɪn/ *adjective* of traditional RC orthodoxy.

triennial /traɪˈenɪəl/ *adjective* lasting 3 years; recurring every 3 years.

trifle /ˈtraɪf(ə)l/ ● *noun* thing of slight value or importance; small amount; (**a trifle**) somewhat; dessert of sponge cakes with custard, cream, etc. ● *verb* (**-ling**) talk or act frivolously; (+ *with*) treat frivolously, flirt heartlessly.

trifling *adjective* unimportant; frivolous.

trigger /ˈtrɪgə/ ● *noun* movable device for releasing spring or catch and so setting off mechanism, esp. of gun; event etc. that sets off chain reaction. ● *verb* (often + *off*) set (action, process) in motion, precipitate. □ **trigger-happy** apt to shoot on slight provocation.

trigonometry /trɪgəˈnɒmɪtrɪ/ *noun* branch of mathematics dealing with relations of sides and angles of triangles, and with certain functions of angles. □ **trigonometric** /-nəˈmet-/ *adjective;* **trigonometrical** /-nəˈmet-/ *adjective.*

trike *noun colloquial* tricycle.

trilateral /traɪˈlætər(ə)l/ *adjective* of, on, or with 3 sides; involving 3 parties.

trilby /ˈtrɪlbɪ/ *noun* (*plural* **-ies**) soft felt hat with narrow brim and indented crown.

trilingual /traɪˈlɪŋgw(ə)l/ *adjective* speaking or in 3 languages.

trill ● *noun* quavering sound, esp. quick alternation of notes; bird's warbling; pronunciation of letter *r* with vibrating tongue. ● *verb* produce trill; warble (song); pronounce (*r* etc.) with trill.

trillion /ˈtrɪljən/ *noun* (*plural* same) million million; million million million;

(trillions) *colloquial* large number. □ **trillionth** *adjective & noun*.

trilobite /'traɪləbaɪt/ *noun* kind of fossil crustacean.

trilogy /'trɪlədʒɪ/ *noun* (*plural* **-ies**) set of 3 related novels, plays, operas, etc.

trim • *verb* (**-mm-**) make neat or tidy or of required size or shape, esp. by cutting away irregular or unwanted parts; (+ *off*, *away*) cut off; ornament; adjust balance of (ship, aircraft) by arranging cargo etc.; arrange (sails) to suit wind. • *noun* state of readiness or fitness; ornament, decorative material; trimming of hair etc. • *adjective* (**-mm-**) neat; in good order, well arranged or equipped.

trimaran /'traɪməræn/ *noun* vessel like catamaran, with 3 hulls side by side.

trimming *noun* ornamental addition to dress, hat, etc.; (in *plural*) *colloquial* usual accompaniments.

trinitrotoluene /traɪnaɪtrə'tɒljʊiːn/ *noun* (also **trinitrotoluol** /-'tɒljʊɒl/) a high explosive.

trinity /'trɪnɪtɪ/ *noun* (*plural* **-ies**) being 3; group of 3; (**the Trinity**) the 3 persons of the Christian Godhead. □ **Trinity Sunday** Sunday after Whit Sunday.

trinket /'trɪŋkɪt/ *noun* trifling ornament, esp. piece of jewellery.

trio /'triːəʊ/ *noun* (*plural* **-s**) group of 3; musical composition for 3 performers; the performers.

trip • *verb* (**-pp-**) (often + *up*) (cause to) stumble, esp. by catching foot; (+ *up*) (cause to) commit fault or blunder; run lightly; make excursion to place; operate (mechanism) suddenly by knocking aside catch etc.; *slang* have drug-induced hallucinatory experience. • *noun* journey or excursion, esp. for pleasure; stumble, blunder, tripping, being tripped up; nimble step; *slang* drug-induced hallucinatory experience; device for tripping mechanism etc. □ **trip-wire** wire stretched close to ground to operate alarm etc. if disturbed.

tripartite /traɪ'pɑːtaɪt/ *adjective* consisting of 3 parts; shared by or involving 3 parties.

tripe *noun* first or second stomach of ruminant, esp. ox, as food; *colloquial* nonsense, rubbish.

triple /'trɪp(ə)l/ • *adjective* of 3 parts, threefold; involving 3 parties; 3 times as much or as many. • *noun* threefold number or amount; set of 3. • *verb* (**-ling**) multiply by 3. □ **triple crown** winning of 3 important sporting events; **triple jump** athletic contest comprising hop, step, and jump. □ **triply** *adverb*.

triplet /'trɪplɪt/ *noun* each of 3 children or animals born at one birth; set of 3 things, esp. of notes played in time of two.

triplex /'trɪpleks/ *adjective* triple, threefold.

triplicate • *adjective* /'trɪplɪkət/ existing in 3 examples or copies; having 3 corresponding parts; tripled. • *noun* /'trɪplɪkət/ each of 3 copies or corresponding parts. • *verb* (**-ting**) /'trɪplɪkeɪt/ make in 3 copies; multiply by 3. □ **triplication** *noun*.

tripod /'traɪpɒd/ *noun* 3-legged or 3-footed stand, stool, table, or utensil.

tripos /'traɪpɒs/ *noun* honours exam for primary degree at Cambridge University.

tripper *noun* person who goes on pleasure trip.

triptych /'trɪptɪk/ *noun* picture etc. with 3 panels usually hinged vertically together.

trireme /'traɪriːm/ *noun* ancient Greek warship, with 3 files of oarsmen on each side.

trisect /traɪ'sekt/ *verb* divide into 3 (usually equal) parts. □ **trisection** *noun*.

trite *adjective* hackneyed. □ **tritely** *adverb*; **triteness** *noun*.

tritium /'trɪtɪəm/ *noun* radioactive isotope of hydrogen with mass about 3 times that of ordinary hydrogen.

triumph /'traɪʌmf/ • *noun* state of victory or success; great success or achievement; supreme example; joy at success. • *verb* gain victory, be successful; *Roman History* ride in triumph; (often + *over*) exult.

triumphal /traɪ'ʌmf(ə)l/ *adjective* of, used in, or celebrating a triumph.

■ **Usage** *Triumphal*, as in *triumphal arch*, should not be confused with *triumphant*.

---

triumphant /traɪ'ʌmf(ə)nt/ *adjective* victorious, successful; exultant. □ **triumphantly** *adverb*.

■ **Usage** See note at TRIUMPHAL.

triumvirate /traɪˈʌmvərət/ *noun* ruling group of 3 men.

trivalent /traɪˈveɪlənt/ *adjective Chemistry* having a valency of 3. □ **trivalency** *noun.*

trivet /ˈtrɪvɪt/ *noun* iron tripod or bracket for pot or kettle to stand on.

trivia /ˈtrɪvɪə/ *plural noun* trifles, trivialities.

trivial /ˈtrɪvɪəl/ *adjective* of small value or importance; concerned only with trivial things. □ **triviality** /-ˈæl-/ *noun* (*plural* **-ies**); **trivially** *adverb.*

trivialize *verb* (also **-ise**) (**-zing** or **-sing**) make or treat as trivial, minimize. □ **trivialization** *noun.*

trochee /ˈtrəʊkiː/ *noun* metrical foot of one long followed by one short syllable. □ **trochaic** /trəˈkeɪɪk/ *adjective.*

trod *past & past participle* of TREAD.

trodden *past participle* of TREAD.

troglodyte /ˈtrɒɡlədaɪt/ *noun* cave dweller.

troika /ˈtrɔɪkə/ *noun* Russian vehicle drawn by 3 horses abreast.

Trojan /ˈtrəʊdʒ(ə)n/ ● *adjective* of ancient Troy. ● *noun* native or inhabitant of ancient Troy; person who works, fights, etc. courageously. □ **Trojan Horse** person or device planted to bring about enemy's downfall.

troll[1] /trəʊl/ *noun* supernatural cave-dwelling giant or dwarf in Scandinavian mythology.

troll[2] /trəʊl/ *verb* fish by drawing bait along in water.

trolley /ˈtrɒlɪ/ *noun* (*plural* **-s**) table, stand, or basket on wheels or castors for serving food, carrying luggage etc., gathering purchases in supermarket, etc.; low truck running along rails; (in full **trolley-bus**) wheel attached to pole etc. for collecting current from overhead electric wire to drive vehicle. □ **trolley bus** electric bus using trolley-wheel.

trollop /ˈtrɒləp/ *noun* disreputable girl or woman.

trombone /trɒmˈbəʊn/ *noun* brass wind instrument with sliding tube. □ **trombonist** *noun.*

troop /truːp/ ● *noun* assembled company, assemblage of people or animals; (in *plural*) soldiers, armed forces; cavalry unit commanded by captain; artillery unit; group of 3 or more Scout patrols. ● *verb* (+ *in, out, off,* etc.) come together or move in a troop. □ **troop the colour** transfer flag ceremonially at public mounting of garrison guards; **troop-ship** ship for transporting troops.

trooper *noun* private soldier in cavalry or armoured unit; *Australian & US* mounted or State police officer; cavalry horse; troop-ship.

trope *noun* figurative use of word.

trophy /ˈtrəʊfɪ/ *noun* (*plural* **-ies**) cup etc. as prize in contest; memento of any success.

tropic /ˈtrɒpɪk/ *noun* parallel of latitude 23° 27′ N. (**tropic of Cancer**) or S. (**tropic of Capricorn**) of Equator; (**the Tropics**) region lying between these.

tropical *adjective* of or typical of the Tropics.

troposphere /ˈtrɒpəsfɪə/ *noun* layer of atmosphere extending about 8 km upwards from earth's surface.

trot ● *verb* (**-tt-**) (of person) run at moderate pace; (of horse) proceed at steady pace faster than walk; traverse (distance) thus. ● *noun* action or exercise of trotting; (**the trots**) *slang* diarrhoea. □ **on the trot** *colloquial* in succession, continually busy; **trot out** *colloquial* introduce (opinion etc.) repeatedly or tediously.

troth /trəʊθ/ *noun archaic* faith, fidelity; truth.

trotter *noun* (usually in *plural*) animal's foot, esp. as food; horse bred or trained for trotting.

troubadour /ˈtruːbədʊə/ *noun* singer, poet; French medieval poet singing of love.

trouble /ˈtrʌb(ə)l/ ● *noun* difficulty, distress, vexation, affliction; inconvenience, unpleasant exertion; cause of this; perceived failing; malfunction; disturbance; (in *plural*) public disturbances. ● *verb* (**-ling**) cause distress to, disturb; be disturbed; afflict, cause pain etc. to; subject or be subjected to inconvenience or unpleasant exertion. □ **in trouble** likely to incur censure or punishment, *colloquial* pregnant and unmarried; **troublemaker** person who habitually causes trouble; **troubleshooter** mediator in dispute, person who traces and corrects faults in machinery etc.

troublesome *adjective* causing trouble, annoying.

trough /trɒf/ *noun* long narrow open receptacle for water, animal feed, etc.; channel or hollow like this; elongated region of low barometric pressure.

trounce /traʊns/ *verb* (**-cing**) inflict severe defeat, beating, or punishment on.

troupe /truːp/ *noun* company of actors, acrobats, etc.

trouper *noun* member of theatrical troupe; staunch colleague.

trousers /ˈtraʊzəz/ *plural noun* two-legged outer garment from waist usually to ankles. □ **trouser suit** woman's suit of trousers and jacket.

trousseau /ˈtruːsəʊ/ *noun* (*plural* **-s** or **-x** /-z/) bride's collection of clothes etc.

trout /traʊt/ *noun* (*plural* same or **-s**) fish related to salmon.

trove /trəʊv/ *noun* treasure trove.

trowel /ˈtraʊəl/ *noun* flat-bladed tool for spreading mortar etc.; scoop for lifting small plants or earth.

troy *noun* (in full **troy weight**) system of weights used for precious metals etc.

truant /ˈtruːənt/ ● *noun* child who does not attend school; person who avoids work etc. ● *adjective* idle, wandering. ● *verb* (also **play truant**) be truant. □ **truancy** *noun* (*plural* **-ies**).

truce *noun* temporary agreement to cease hostilities.

truck [1] *noun* lorry; open railway wagon for freight.

truck [2] *noun* □ **have no truck with** avoid dealing with.

trucker *noun* *esp. US* long-distance lorry driver.

truckle /ˈtrʌk(ə)l/ ● *noun* (in full **truckle-bed**) low bed on wheels, stored under another. ● *verb* (**-ling**) (+ to) submit obsequiously to.

truculent /ˈtrʌkjʊlənt/ *adjective* aggressively defiant. □ **truculence** *noun*, **truculently** *adverb*.

trudge ● *verb* (**-ging**) walk laboriously; traverse (distance) thus. ● *noun* trudging walk.

true ● *adjective* (**-r**, **-st**) in accordance with fact or reality; genuine; loyal, faithful; (+ *to*) accurately conforming to (type, standard); correctly positioned or balanced, level; exact, accurate. ● *adverb archaic* truly; accurately; without variation. □ **out of true** out of alignment.

truffle /ˈtrʌf(ə)l/ *noun* rich-flavoured underground fungus; sweet made of soft chocolate mixture.

trug *noun* shallow oblong garden-basket.

truism /ˈtruːɪz(ə)m/ *noun* self-evident or hackneyed truth.

truly /ˈtruːlɪ/ *adverb* sincerely; really; loyally; accurately. □ **Yours truly** *written before signature at end of informal letter; jocular* I, me.

trump [1] ● *noun* playing card(s) of suit temporarily ranking above others; (in *plural*) this suit; *colloquial* helpful or excellent person. ● *verb* defeat with trump; *colloquial* outdo. □ **come** or **turn up trumps** *colloquial* turn out well or successfully, be extremely successful or helpful; **trump card** card belonging to, or turned up to determine, trump suit, *colloquial* valuable resource; **trump up** fabricate, invent (accusation, excuse, etc.).

trump [2] *noun archaic* trumpet-blast.

trumpery /ˈtrʌmpərɪ/ ● *noun* worthless finery; rubbish. ● *adjective* showy but worthless, trashy, shallow.

trumpet /ˈtrʌmpɪt/ ● *noun* brass instrument with flared mouth and bright penetrating tone; trumpet-shaped thing; sound (as) of trumpet. ● *verb* (**-t-**) blow trumpet; (of elephant) make trumpet; proclaim loudly. □ **trumpeter** *noun*.

truncate /trʌŋˈkeɪt/ *verb* (**-ting**) cut off top or end of; shorten. □ **truncation** *noun*.

truncheon /ˈtrʌntʃ(ə)n/ *noun* short club carried by police officer.

trundle /ˈtrʌnd(ə)l/ *verb* (**-ling**) roll or move, esp. heavily or noisily.

trunk *noun* main stem of tree; body without limbs or head; large luggage-box with hinged lid; *US* boot of car:

elephant's elongated prehensile nose; (in *plural*) men's close-fitting shorts worn for swimming etc. □ **trunk call** long-distance telephone call; **trunk line** main line of railway, telephone system, etc.; **trunk road** important main road.

truss •*noun* framework supporting roof, bridge, etc.; supporting surgical appliance for hernia etc. sufferers; bundle of hay or straw; cluster of flowers or fruit. •*verb* tie up (fowl) for cooking; (often + *up*) tie (person) with arms to sides; support with truss(es).

trust •*noun* firm belief that a person or thing may be relied on; confident expectation; responsibility; *Law* arrangement involving trustees, property so held, group of trustees; association of companies for reducing competition. •*verb* place trust in, believe in, rely on; (+ *with*) give (person) charge of; (often + *that*) hope earnestly that a thing will take place; (+ *to*) consign (thing) to (person); (+ *in*) place reliance in; (+ *to*) place (esp. undue) reliance on. □ **in trust** (of property) managed by person(s) on behalf of another; **trustworthy** deserving of trust, reliable. □ **trustful** *adjective*.

trustee /trʌsˈtiː/ *noun* person or member of board managing property in trust with legal obligation to administer it solely for purposes specified. □ **trusteeship** *noun*.

trusting *adjective* having trust or confidence. □ **trustingly** *adverb*.

trusty •*adjective* (**-ier**, **-iest**) *archaic or jocular* trustworthy. •*noun* (*plural* **-ies**) prisoner given special privileges for good behaviour.

truth /truːθ/ *noun* (*plural* **truths** /truːðz/) quality or state of being true; what is true.

truthful *adjective* habitually speaking the truth; (of story etc.) true. □ **truthfully** *adverb*; **truthfulness** *noun*.

try •*verb* (**-ies**, **-ied**) attempt, endeavour; test (quality), test by use or experiment test qualities of; make severe demands on; examine effectiveness of for purpose; ascertain state of fastening of (door etc.); investigate and decide (case, issue) judicially, (often + *for*) subject (person) to trial; (+ *for*) apply or compete for, seek to attain. •*noun*

(*plural* **-ies**) attempt; *Rugby* touching-down of ball by player behind opposing goal line, scoring points and entitling player's side to a kick at goal. □ **try one's hand** (often + *at*) have attempt; **try it on** *colloquial* test how much unreasonable behaviour etc. will be tolerated; **try on** put (clothes etc.) on to test fit etc.; **try-on** *colloquial* act of trying it on or trying on clothes etc., attempt to deceive; **try out** put to the test, test thoroughly; **try-out** experimental test.

trying *adjective* annoying, exasperating; hard to bear.

tryst /trɪst/ *noun archaic* meeting, esp. of lovers.

tsar /zɑː/ *noun* (also **czar**) (*feminine* **tsarina** /-ˈriːnə/) *historical* emperor of Russia. □ **tsarist** *noun & adjective*.

tsetse /ˈtsetsɪ/ *noun* African fly feeding on and transmitting disease.

tsp. *abbreviation* (*plural* **tsps.**) teaspoonful.

TT *abbreviation* teetotal(ler); tuberculin-tested; Tourist Trophy.

tub •*noun* open flat-bottomed usually round vessel; tub-shaped (usually plastic) carton; *colloquial* bath; *colloquial* clumsy slow boat. •*verb* (**-bb-**) plant, bathe, or wash in tub. □ **tub-thumper** *colloquial* ranting preacher or orator.

tuba /ˈtjuːbə/ *noun* (*plural* **-s**) low-pitched brass wind instrument.

tubby /ˈtʌbɪ/ *adjective* (**-ier**, **-iest**) short and fat. □ **tubbiness** *noun*.

tube •*noun* long hollow cylinder; soft metal or plastic cylinder sealed at one end; hollow cylindrical bodily organ; *colloquial* London underground; cathode ray tube, esp. in television; (**the tube**) *esp. US colloquial* television; *US* thermionic valve; inner tube. •*verb* (**-bing**) equip with tubes; enclose in tube.

tuber /ˈtjuːbə/ *noun* short thick rounded root or underground stem of plant.

tubercle /ˈtjuːbək(ə)l/ *noun* small rounded swelling on part or in organ of body, esp. as characteristic of tuberculosis. □ **tubercle bacillus** bacterium causing tuberculosis. □ **tuberculous** /-ˈbɜːkjʊləs/ *adjective*.

tubercular /tjuˈbɜːkjʊlə/ *adjective* of or affected with tuberculosis.

tuberculin /tjuˈbɜːkjʊlɪn/ *noun* preparation from cultures of tubercle bacillus used in diagnosis and treatment of tuberculosis. □ **tuberculin-tested** (of milk) from cows shown to be free of tuberculosis.

tuberculosis /tjʊbɜːkjʊˈləʊsɪs/ noun infectious bacterial disease marked by tubercles, esp. in lungs.

tuberose /ˈtjuːbərəʊz/ noun plant with creamy-white fragrant flowers.

tuberous /ˈtjuːbərəs/ adjective having tubers; of or like a tuber.

tubing noun length of tube; quantity of or material for tubes.

tubular /ˈtjuːbjʊlə/ adjective tube-shaped; having or consisting of tubes.

TUC abbreviation Trades Union Congress.

tuck • verb (often + in, up) draw, fold, or turn outer or end parts of (cloth, clothes, etc.) close together, push in edges of bedclothes around (person); draw together into small space; stow (thing) away in specified place or way; make stitched fold in (cloth etc.). • noun flattened fold sewn in garment etc.; colloquial food, esp. cakes and sweets. □ **tuck in** colloquial eat heartily; **tuck shop** shop selling sweets etc. to schoolchildren.

tucker /ˈtʌkə/ • noun Australian & NZ slang food. • verb (esp. in passive; often + out) US & Australian colloquial tire.

Tudor /ˈtjuːdə/ adjective of royal family of England from Henry VII to Elizabeth I; of this period (1485–1603); of the architectural style of this period.

Tues. abbreviation (also **Tue.**) Tuesday.

Tuesday /ˈtjuːzdeɪ/ noun day of week following Monday.

tufa /ˈtjuːfə/ noun porous rock formed round mineral springs; tuff.

tuff noun rock formed from volcanic ash.

tuft noun bunch of threads, grass, feathers, hair, etc. held or growing together at base. □ **tufted** adjective; **tufty** adjective.

tug • verb (**-gg-**) (often + at) pull hard or violently; tow (vessel) by tugboat. • noun hard, violent, or jerky pull; sudden emotion; (also **tugboat**) small powerful boat for towing ships. □ **tug of war** trial of strength between two sides pulling opposite ways on a rope.

tuition /tjuːˈɪʃ(ə)n/ noun teaching; fee for this.

tulip /ˈtjuːlɪp/ noun bulbous spring-flowering plant with showy cup-shaped flowers; its flower. □ **tulip-tree** tree with tulip-like flowers.

tulle /tjuːl/ noun soft fine silk etc. net for veils and dresses.

tumble /ˈtʌmb(ə)l/ • verb (**-ling**) (cause to) fall suddenly or headlong; fall rapidly in amount etc.; roll, toss; move or rush in headlong or blundering fashion; (often + to) colloquial grasp meaning of; fling or push roughly or carelessly; perform acrobatic feats, esp. somersaults; rumple, disarrange. • noun fall; somersault or other acrobatic feat. □ **tumbledown** falling or fallen into ruin, dilapidated; **tumble-drier, -dryer** machine for drying washing in heated rotating drum; **tumble-dry** verb.

tumbler noun drinking glass without handle or foot; acrobat; part of mechanism of lock.

tumbrel /ˈtʌmbr(ə)l/ noun (also **tumbril**) historical open cart in which condemned people were carried to guillotine during French Revolution.

tumescent /tjʊˈmes(ə)nt/ adjective swelling. □ **tumescence** noun.

tumid /ˈtjuːmɪd/ adjective swollen, inflated; pompous. □ **tumidity** /-ˈmɪd-/ noun.

tummy /ˈtʌmɪ/ noun (plural **-ies**) colloquial stomach.

tumour /ˈtjuːmə/ noun (US **tumor**) abnormal or morbid swelling in the body.

tumult /ˈtjuːmʌlt/ noun uproar, din; angry demonstration by mob, riot; conflict of emotions etc. □ **tumultuous** /tjʊˈmʌltʃʊəs/ adjective.

tumulus /ˈtjuːmjʊləs/ noun (plural **-li** /-laɪ/) ancient burial mound.

tun noun large cask; brewer's fermenting-vat.

tuna /ˈtjuːnə/ noun (plural same or **-s**) large edible marine fish; (in full **tuna-fish**) its flesh as food.

tundra /ˈtʌndrə/ noun vast level treeless Arctic region with permafrost.

tune • noun melody; correct pitch or intonation. • verb (**-ning**) put (musical instrument) in tune; (often + in) adjust (radio etc.) to desired frequency etc.; adjust (engine etc.) to run smoothly. □ **change one's tune** voice different opinion, become more respectful; **tune up** bring instrument(s) to proper pitch; **tuning-fork** two-pronged steel fork giving particular note when struck.

tuneful *adjective* melodious, musical. □ **tunefully** *adverb.*

tuneless *adjective* unmelodious, unmusical. □ **tunelessly** *adverb.*

tuner *noun* person who tunes pianos etc.; part of radio or television receiver for tuning.

tungsten /'tʌŋst(ə)n/ *noun* heavy steel-grey metallic element.

tunic /'tju:nɪk/ *noun* close-fitting short coat of police or military uniform; loose often sleeveless garment.

tunnel /'tʌn(ə)l/ ● *noun* underground passage dug through hill, or under river, road, etc.; underground passage dug by animal. ● *verb* (**-ll-**; *US* **-l-**) (+ *through, into*) make tunnel through (hill etc.); make (one's way) so. □ **tunnel vision** restricted vision, *colloquial* inability to grasp wider implications of situation etc.

tunny /'tʌnɪ/ *noun* (*plural* same or **-ies**) tuna.

tuppence = TWOPENCE.

tuppenny = TWOPENNY.

Tupperware /'tʌpəweə/ *noun proprietary term* range of plastic containers for food.

turban /'tɜ:bən/ *noun* man's headdress of fabric wound round cap or head, worn esp. by Muslims and Sikhs; woman's hat resembling this.

turbid /'tɜ:bɪd/ *adjective* muddy, thick, not clear; confused, disordered. □ **turbidity** /-'bɪd-/ *noun.*

■ **Usage** *Turbid* is sometimes confused with *turgid.*

turbine /'tɜ:baɪn/ *noun* rotary motor driven by flow of water, gas, etc.

turbo- *combining form* turbine.

turbocharger /'tɜ:bəʊtʃɑ:dʒə/ *noun* (also **turbo**) supercharger driven by turbine powered by engine's exhaust gases.

turbojet /'tɜ:bəʊdʒet/ *noun* jet engine in which jet also operates turbine-driven air-compressor; aircraft with this.

turboprop /'tɜ:bəʊprɒp/ *noun* jet engine in which turbine is used as in turbojet

and also to drive propeller; aircraft with this.

turbot /'tɜ:bət/ *noun* (*plural* same or **-s**) large flatfish valued as food.

turbulent /'tɜ:bjʊlənt/ *adjective* disturbed, in commotion; (of flow of air etc.) varying irregularly; riotous, restless. □ **turbulence** *noun*; **turbulently** *adverb.*

tureen /tjʊə'ri:n/ *noun* deep covered dish for soup.

turf *noun* (*plural* **-s** or **turves**) short grass with surface earth bound together by its roots; piece of this cut from ground; slab of peat for fuel; (**the turf**) horse racing, racecourse. ● *verb* cover (ground) with turf; (+ *out*) *colloquial* expel, eject. □ **turf accountant** bookmaker. □ **turfy** *adjective.*

turgid /'tɜ:dʒɪd/ *adjective* swollen, inflated; (of language) pompous, bombastic. □ **turgidity** /-'dʒɪd-/ *noun.*

■ **Usage** *Turgid* is sometimes confused with *turbid.*

Turk *noun* native or national of Turkey.

turkey /'tɜ:kɪ/ *noun* (*plural* **-s**) large originally American bird bred for food; its flesh. □ **turkeycock** male turkey.

Turkish ● *adjective* of Turkey. ● *noun* language of Turkey. □ **Turkish bath** hot-air or steam bath followed by massage etc., (in *singular* or *plural*) building for this; **Turkish carpet** thick-piled woollen carpet with bold design; **Turkish delight** kind of gelatinous sweet; **Turkish towel** one made of cotton terry.

turmeric /'tɜ:mərɪk/ *noun* E. Indian plant of ginger family; its rhizome powdered as flavouring or dye.

turmoil /'tɜ:mɔɪl/ *noun* violent confusion; din and bustle.

turn ● *verb* move around point or axis, give or receive rotary motion; change from one side to another, invert, reverse; give new direction to, take new direction, aim in certain way; (+ *into*) change in nature, form, or condition to; (+ *to*) set about, have recourse to, consider next; become; (+ *against*) make or become hostile to; (+ *on, upon*) face hostilely; change colour; (of milk) become sour; (of stomach) be nauseated; cause (milk) to become sour or (stomach) to be nauseated; (of head) become giddy; translate; move to other side of, go round; pass age or time of; (+ *on*) depend on; send, put, cause to go; remake (sheet, shirt collar, etc.); make (profit); divert (bullet); shape (object) in lathe; give (esp. elegant) form to. ● *noun* turning, rotary motion; changed or change of direction or tendency; point of turning or change; turning of road; change of direction of tide; change in course of events; tendency, formation; opportunity, obligation, etc. that comes successively to each of several people etc.; short walk or ride; short performance on stage, in circus, etc.; service of specified kind; purpose; *colloquial* momentary nervous shock; *Music* ornament of principal note with those above and below it. □ **in turn** in succession; **take (it in) turns** act alternately; **turncoat** person who changes sides; **turn down** reject, reduce volume or strength of (sound, heat, etc.) by turning knob, fold down; **turn in** hand in, achieve, *colloquial* go to bed, incline inwards; **turnkey** *archaic* jailer; **turn off** stop flow or working of by means of tap, switch, etc., enter side road, *colloquial* cause to lose interest; **turn on** start flow or working of by means of tap, switch, etc., *colloquial* arouse, esp. sexually; **turn out** expel, extinguish (light etc.), dress, equip, produce (goods etc.), empty, clean out, (cause to) assemble, prove to be the case, result, (usually + *to be*) be found; **turnout** number of people who attend meeting etc., equipage; **turn over** reverse position of, cause (engine etc.) to run, (of engine) start running, consider thoroughly, (+ *to*) transfer care or conduct of (person, thing) to (person); **turnover** turning over, gross amount of money taken in business, rate of sale and replacement of goods, rate at which people enter and leave employment etc., small pie with pastry folded over filling; **turnpike** *US & historical* road on which toll is charged; **turnstile** revolving gate with arms; **turntable** circular revolving plate or platform; **turn to** begin work; **turn turtle** capsize; **turn up** increase (volume or strength of) by turning knob etc.,

discover, reveal, be found, happen, arrive, shorten (garment etc.), fold over or upwards; **turn-up** turned-up end of trouser leg, *colloquial* unexpected happening.

turner *noun* lathe-worker.

turnery *noun* objects made on lathe; work with lathe.

turning *noun* road branching off another, place where this occurs; use of lathe; (in *plural*) chips or shavings from this. □ **turning circle** smallest circle in which vehicle can turn; **turning point** point at which decisive change occurs.

turnip /ˈtɜːnɪp/ *noun* plant with globular root; its root as vegetable.

turpentine /ˈtɜːpəntaɪn/ *noun* resin from any of various trees; (in full **oil of turpentine**) volatile inflammable oil distilled from turpentine and used in mixing paints etc.

turpitude /ˈtɜːpɪtjuːd/ *noun formal* depravity, wickedness.

turps *noun colloquial* oil of turpentine.

turquoise /ˈtɜːkwɔɪz/ ● *noun* opaque semiprecious stone, usually greenish-blue; this colour. ● *adjective* of this colour.

turret /ˈtʌrɪt/ *noun* small tower, esp. decorating building; usually revolving armoured structure for gun and gunners on ship, fort, etc.; rotating holder for tools in lathe etc. □ **turreted** *adjective*.

turtle /ˈtɜːt(ə)l/ *noun* aquatic reptile with flippers and horny shell. □ **turtle-neck** high close-fitting neck on knitted garment.

turtle-dove /ˈtɜːt(ə)ldʌv/ *noun* wild dove noted for soft cooing and affection for its mate.

tusk *noun* long pointed tooth, esp. projecting beyond mouth as in elephant, walrus, or boar. □ **tusked** *adjective*.

tussle /ˈtʌs(ə)l/ *noun & verb* (**-ling**) struggle, scuffle.

tussock /ˈtʌsək/ *noun* clump of grass etc.

tut = TUT-TUT.

tutelage /ˈtjuːtɪlɪdʒ/ *noun* guardianship; being under this; tuition.

tutelary /ˈtjuːtɪlərɪ/ *adjective* serving as guardian or protector; of guardian.

tutor /'tjuːtə/ ● *noun* private teacher; university teacher supervising studies or welfare of assigned undergraduates. ● *verb* act as tutor (to). □ **tutorship** *noun*.

tutorial /tjuː'tɔːrɪəl/ ● *adjective* of tutor or tuition. ● *noun* period of tuition for single student or small group.

tutti /'tʊtɪ/ *Music* ● *adjective & adverb* with all instruments or voices together. ● *noun* (*plural* -s) tutti passage.

tut-tut /tʌt'tʌt/ (also **tut**) ● *interjection expressing rebuke or impatience.* ● *noun* such exclamation. ● *verb* (-tt-) exclaim thus.

tutu /'tuːtuː/ *noun* (*plural* -s) dancer's short skirt of stiffened frills.

tuxedo /tʌk'siːdəʊ/ *noun* (*plural* -s or -es) *US* (suit including) dinner jacket.

TV *abbreviation* television.

twaddle /'twɒd(ə)l/ *noun* silly writing or talk.

twain *adjective & noun* archaic two.

twang ● *noun* sound made by plucked string of musical instrument, bow, etc.; nasal quality of voice. ● *verb* (cause to) emit twang. □ **twangy** *adjective*.

tweak ● *verb* pinch and twist; jerk; adjust finely. ● *noun* such action.

twee *adjective* (**tweer** /'twiːə/, **tweest** /'twiːɪst/) *derogatory* affectedly dainty or quaint.

tweed *noun* rough-surfaced woollen cloth usually of mixed colours; (in *plural*) clothes of tweed.

tweedy *adjective* (-ier, -iest) of or dressed in tweed; heartily informal.

tweet ● *noun* chirp of small bird. ● *verb* make this noise.

tweeter *noun* loudspeaker for high frequencies.

tweezers /'twiːzəz/ *plural noun* small pair of pincers for picking up small objects, plucking out hairs, etc.

twelfth *adjective & noun* next after eleventh; any of twelve equal parts of thing. □ **Twelfth Night** evening of 5 Jan.

twelve /twelv/ *adjective & noun* one more than eleven.

twenty /'twentɪ/ *adjective & noun* (*plural* -ies) twice ten. □ **twentieth** *adjective & noun*.

twerp *noun slang* stupid or objectionable person.

twice *adverb* two times; on two occasions; doubly.

twiddle /'twɪd(ə)l/ ● *verb* (-ling) twist or play idly about. ● *noun* act of twiddling. □ **twiddle one's thumbs** make them rotate round each other, have nothing to do.

twig[1] *noun* very small branch of tree or shrub.

twig[2] *verb* (-gg-) *colloquial* understand, realize.

twilight /'twaɪlaɪt/ *noun* light from sky when sun is below horizon, esp. in evening; period of this; faint light; period of decline. □ **twilight zone** decrepit urban area, undefined or intermediate area.

twilit /'twaɪlɪt/ *adjective* dimly illuminated (as) by twilight.

twill *noun* fabric woven with surface of parallel diagonal ridges. □ **twilled** *adjective*.

twin ● *noun* each of closely related pair, esp. of children or animals born at a birth; counterpart. ● *adjective* forming, or born as one of, twins. ● *verb* (-nn-) join closely, (+ *with*) pair; bear twins; link (town) with one abroad for social and cultural exchange. □ **twin bed** each of pair of single beds; **twin set** woman's matching cardigan and jumper; **twin town** town twinned with another.

twine ● *noun* strong coarse string of twisted strands of fibre; coil, twist. ● *verb* (-ning) coil, twist; form (string etc.) by twisting strands.

twinge /twɪndʒ/ *noun* sharp momentary local pain.

twinkle /'twɪŋk(ə)l/ ● *verb* (-ling) shine with rapidly intermittent light; sparkle; move rapidly. ● *noun* sparkle or gleam of eyes; twinkling light; light rapid movement. □ **twinkly** *adjective*.

twirl ● *verb* spin, swing, or twist quickly and lightly round. ● *noun* twirling; flourish made with pen.

twist ● *verb* change the form of by rotating one end and not the other or the two ends opposite ways; undergo such change; wrench or distort by twisting; wind (strands etc.) about each other, form (rope etc.) thus; (cause to) take spiral form; (+ *off*) break off by twisting; misrepresent meaning of (words); take winding course; *colloquial* cheat; (as **twisted** *adjective*) perverted; dance the twist. ●*noun* twisting, being twisted; thing made by twisting; point at which thing twists; *usually adjective* peculiar tendency of mind, character, etc.; unexpected development; (**the twist**) 1960s dance with twisting hips. □ **twisty** *adjective* (**-ier**, **-iest**).

twister *noun colloquial* swindler.

twit [1] *noun slang* foolish person.

twit [2] *verb* (**-tt-**) reproach, taunt, usually good-humouredly.

twitch ●*verb* quiver or jerk spasmodically; pull sharply at. ●*noun* twitching; *colloquial* state of nervousness. □ **twitchy** *adjective* (**-ier**, **-iest**).

twitter /'twɪtə/ ●*verb* (esp. of bird) utter succession of light tremulous sounds; utter or express thus. ●*noun* twittering; *colloquial* tremulously excited state.

two /tu:/ *adjective & noun* one more than one. □ **two-dimensional** having or appearing to have length and breadth but no depth, superficial; **two-edged** having both good and bad effect, ambiguous; **two-faced** insincere; **two-handed** with 2 hands, used with both hands or by 2 people; **twopence** /'tʌpəns/ sum of 2 pence, (esp. with negative) *colloquial* thing of little value; **twopenny** /'tʌpənɪ/ costing twopence, *colloquial* cheap, worthless; **two-piece** (suit etc.) comprising 2 matching parts; **two-ply** (wool etc.) having 2 strands, (plywood) having 2 layers; **two-step** dance in march or polka time; **two-stroke** (of internal-combustion engine) having power cycle completed in one up-and-down movement of piston; **two-time** *colloquial* be unfaithful to, swindle; **two-tone** having two colours or sounds; **two-way** involving or operating in two directions, (of radio) capable of transmitting and receiving signals.

twofold *adjective & adverb* twice as much or many.

twosome *noun* two people together.

tycoon /taɪ'ku:n/ *noun* business magnate.

tying *present participle* of TIE.

tyke /taɪk/ *noun* (also **tike**) objectionable or coarse man; small child.

tympani = TIMPANI.

tympanum /'tɪmpənəm/ *noun* (*plural* **-s** or **-na**) middle ear; eardrum; vertical space forming centre of pediment; space between lintel and arch above door etc.

type /taɪp/ ●*noun* sort, class, kind; person, thing, or event exemplifying class or group; *colloquial* person, esp. of specified character; object, idea, or work of art serving as model; small block with raised character on upper surface for printing; printing types collectively; typeset or printed text. ●*verb* (**-ping**) write with typewriter; typecast; assign to type, classify. □ **-type** made of, resembling, functioning as; **typecast** cast (performer) repeatedly in similar roles; **typeface** inked surface of type, set of characters in one design; **typescript** typewritten document; **typesetter** compositor, composing machine; **typewriter** machine with keys for producing printlike characters; **typewritten** produced thus.

typhoid /'taɪfɔɪd/ *noun* (in full **typhoid fever**) infectious bacterial fever attacking intestines.

typhoon /taɪ'fu:n/ *noun* violent hurricane in E. Asian seas.

typhus /'taɪfəs/ *noun* an acute infectious fever.

typical /'tɪpɪk(ə)l/ *adjective* serving as characteristic example; (often + *of*) characteristic of particular person or thing. □ **typicality** /-'kæl-/ *noun*; **typically** *adverb*.

typify /'tɪpɪfaɪ/ *verb* (**-ies**, **-ied**) be typical of; represent by or as type. □ **typification** *noun*.

typist /'taɪpɪst/ *noun* (esp. professional) user of typewriter.

typo /'taɪpəʊ/ *noun* (*plural* **-s**) *colloquial* typographical error.

typography /taɪ'pɒgrəfɪ/ *noun* printing as an art; style and appearance of printed matter. □ **typographer** *noun*; **typographical** /-pə'græf-/ *adjective*; **typographically** /-pə'græf-/ *adverb*.

tyrannical /tɪ'rænɪk(ə)l/ *adjective* acting like or characteristic of tyrant.

tyrannize /ˈtɪrənaɪz/ *verb* (also **-ise**) (**-zing** or **-sing**) (often + *over*) treat despotically.

tyrannosaurus /tɪrænəˈsɔːrəs/ *noun* (*plural* **-ruses**) very large carnivorous dinosaur with short front legs and powerful tail.

tyranny /ˈtɪrənɪ/ *noun* (*plural* **-ies**) cruel and arbitrary use of authority; rule by tyrant; period of this; state thus ruled. □ **tyrannous** *adjective*.

tyrant /ˈtaɪərənt/ *noun* oppressive or cruel ruler; person exercising power arbitrarily or cruelly.

tyre /ˈtaɪə/ *noun* (*US* **tire**) rubber covering, usually inflated, placed round vehicle's wheel for cushioning and grip.

tyro = TIRO.

tzatziki /tsætˈsiːkɪ/ *noun* Greek dish of yoghurt with cucumber and garlic.

Uu

U [1] □ **U-boat** *historical* German submarine; **U-turn** U-shaped turn of vehicle to face in opposite direction, reversal of policy.

U [2] *abbreviation* (of film classified as suitable for all) universal.

UB40 *abbreviation* card for claiming unemployment benefit; *colloquial* unemployed person.

ubiquitous /juːˈbɪkwɪtəs/ *adjective* (seemingly) present everywhere simultaneously; often encountered. □ **ubiquity** *noun*.

UCCA /ˈʌkə/ *abbreviation* Universities Central Council on Admissions.

UDA *abbreviation* Ulster Defence Association.

udder /ˈʌdə/ *noun* baglike milk-producing organ of cow etc.

UDI *abbreviation* unilateral declaration of independence.

UDR *abbreviation* Ulster Defence Regiment.

UEFA /juːˈeɪfə/ *abbreviation* Union of European Football Associations.

UFO /ˈjuːfəʊ/ *noun* (also **ufo**) (*plural* **-s**) unidentified flying object.

ugh /əx, ʌɡ/ *interjection expressing disgust etc.*

Ugli /ˈʌɡlɪ/ *noun* (*plural* **-lis** or **-lies**) *proprietary term* mottled green and yellow citrus fruit.

ugly /ˈʌɡlɪ/ *adjective* (**-ier**, **-iest**) unpleasant to eye, ear, mind, etc.; discreditable; threatening, dangerous; morally repulsive. □ **ugly duckling** person lacking early promise but blossoming later. □ **uglify** *verb* (**-ies**, **-ied**); **ugliness** *noun*.

UHF *abbreviation* ultra-high frequency.

uh-huh /ˈʌhʌ/ *interjection colloquial* yes.

UHT *abbreviation* ultra heat treated (esp. of milk, for long keeping).

UK *abbreviation* United Kingdom.

Ukrainian /juːˈkreɪnɪən/ ● *noun* native, national, or language of Ukraine. ● *adjective* of Ukraine.

ukulele /juːkəˈleɪlɪ/ *noun* small guitar with 4 strings.

ulcer /ˈʌlsə/ *noun* (often pus-forming) open sore on or in body; corrupting influence. □ **ulcerous** *adjective*.

ulcerate /ˈʌlsəreɪt/ *verb* (**-ting**) form into or affect with ulcer. □ **ulceration** *noun*.

ullage /ˈʌlɪdʒ/ *noun* amount by which cask etc. falls short of being full; loss by evaporation or leakage.

ulna /ˈʌlnə/ *noun* (*plural* **ulnae** /-niː/) longer bone of forearm, opposite thumb; corresponding bone in animal's foreleg or bird's wing. □ **ulnar** *adjective*.

ulster /ˈʌlstə/ *noun* long loose overcoat of rough cloth.

Ulsterman /ˈʌlstəmən/ *noun* (*feminine* **Ulsterwoman**) native of Ulster.

ult. *abbreviation* ultimo.

ulterior /ʌlˈtɪərɪə/ *adjective* not admitted; hidden, secret.

ultimate /ˈʌltɪmət/ ● *adjective* last, final; fundamental, basic. ● *noun* (**the ultimate**) best achievable or imaginable;

final or fundamental fact or principle. □ **ultimately** adverb.

ultimatum /ʌltɪˈmeɪtəm/ noun (plural **-s**) final statement of terms, rejection of which could cause hostility etc.

ultimo /ˈʌltɪməʊ/ adjective of last month.

ultra /ˈʌltrə/ ● adjective extreme, esp. in religion or politics. ● noun extremist.

ultra- combining form extreme(ly), excessive(ly); beyond.

ultra-high /ʌltrəˈhaɪ/ adjective (of frequency) between 300 and 3000 megahertz.

ultramarine /ʌltrəməˈriːn/ ● noun (colour of) brilliant deep blue pigment. ● adjective of this colour.

ultrasonic /ʌltrəˈsɒnɪk/ adjective of or using sound waves pitched above range of human hearing. □ **ultrasonically** adverb.

ultrasound /ˈʌltrəsaʊnd/ noun ultrasonic waves.

ultraviolet /ʌltrəˈvaɪələt/ adjective of or using radiation just beyond violet end of spectrum.

ultra vires /ʌltrə ˈvaɪəriːz/ adverb & adjective beyond one's legal power or authority. [Latin]

ululate /ˈjuːljʊleɪt/ verb (**-ting**) howl, wail. □ **ululation** noun.

um interjection representing hesitation or pause in speech.

umbel /ˈʌmb(ə)l/ noun flower-cluster with stalks springing from common centre. □ **umbellate** adjective.

umbelliferous /ʌmbəˈlɪfərəs/ adjective (of plant, e.g. parsley or carrot) bearing umbels.

umber /ˈʌmbə/ ● noun (colour of) dark brown earth used as pigment. ● adjective umber-coloured.

umbilical /ʌmˈbɪlɪk(ə)l/ adjective of navel. □ **umbilical cord** cordlike structure attaching foetus to placenta.

umbilicus /ʌmˈbɪlɪkəs/ noun (plural **-ci** /-saɪ/ or **-cuses**) navel.

umbra /ˈʌmbrə/ noun (plural **-s** or **-brae** /-briː/) shadow cast by moon or earth in eclipse.

umbrage /ˈʌmbrɪdʒ/ noun offence taken.

umbrella /ʌmˈbrelə/ noun collapsible cloth canopy on central stick for protection against rain, sun, etc.; protection, patronage; coordinating agency.

umlaut /ˈʊmlaʊt/ noun mark (¨) over vowel, esp. in German, indicating change in pronunciation; such a change.

umpire /ˈʌmpaɪə/ ● noun person enforcing rules and settling disputes in game, contest, etc. ● verb (**-ring**) (often + for, in, etc.) act as umpire (in).

umpteen /ˈʌmptiːn/ adjective & noun colloquial very many. □ **umpteenth** adjective & noun.

UN abbreviation United Nations.

un- prefix added to adjectives, nouns, and adverbs, meaning: not; non-; reverse of, lack of; added to verbs, verbal derivatives, etc. to express contrary or reverse action, deprivation or removal from. For words starting with un- that are not found below, the root-words should be consulted.

unaccountable /ʌnəˈkaʊntəb(ə)l/ adjective without explanation, strange; not answerable for one's actions. □ **unaccountably** adverb.

unadopted /ʌnəˈdɒptɪd/ adjective (of road) not maintained by local authority.

unadulterated /ʌnəˈdʌltəreɪtɪd/ adjective pure; complete, utter.

unaffected /ʌnəˈfektɪd/ adjective (usually + by) not affected; free from affectation. □ **unaffectedly** adverb.

unalloyed /ʌnəˈlɔɪd/ adjective complete, pure.

un-American /ʌnəˈmerɪkən/ adjective uncharacteristic of Americans; contrary to US interests, treasonable.

unanimous /juːˈnænɪməs/ adjective all in agreement; (of vote etc.) by all without exception. □ **unanimity** /-nəˈnɪm-/ noun, **unanimously** adverb.

unannounced /ʌnəˈnaʊnst/ adjective not announced, without warning.

unanswerable /ʌnˈɑːnsərəb(ə)l/ adjective that cannot be answered or refuted.

unapproachable /ʌnəˈprəʊtʃəb(ə)l/ adjective inaccessible; (of person) unfriendly, aloof.

unassailable /ʌnəˈseɪləb(ə)l/ adjective that cannot be attacked or questioned.

unassuming /ʌnəˈsjuːmɪŋ/ adjective not pretentious, modest.

unattached /ʌnəˈtætʃt/ adjective not engaged, married, etc.; (often + to) not attached to particular organization etc.

unaware /ʌnə'weə/ • *adjective* (usually + *of, that*) not aware; unperceptive. • *adverb* unawares.

unawares /ʌnə'weəz/ *adverb* unexpectedly; inadvertently.

unbalanced /ʌn'bælənst/ *adjective* emotionally unstable; biased.

unbeknown /ʌnbɪ'nəʊn/ *adjective* (also **unbeknownst** /-'nəʊnst/) (+ *to*) without the knowledge of.

unbend /ʌn'bend/ *verb* (*past & past participle* **unbent**) straighten; relax; become affable.

unbending /ʌn'bendɪŋ/ *adjective* inflexible; firm, austere.

unblushing /ʌn'blʌʃɪŋ/ *adjective* shameless; frank.

unbosom /ʌn'bʊzəm/ *verb* disclose (thoughts etc.); (**unbosom oneself**) disclose one's thoughts etc.

unbounded /ʌn'baʊndɪd/ *adjective* infinite.

unbridled /ʌn'braɪd(ə)ld/ *adjective* unrestrained, uncontrolled.

uncalled-for /ʌn'kɔːldfɔː/ *adjective* (of remark etc.) rude and unnecessary.

uncanny /ʌn'kæni/ *adjective* (**-ier, -iest**) seemingly supernatural, mysterious. □ **uncannily** *adverb*; **uncanniness** *noun*.

uncapped /ʌn'kæpt/ *adjective* Sport (of player) not yet awarded his or her cap or never having been selected to represent his or her country.

unceremonious /ʌnserɪ'məʊnɪəs/ *adjective* abrupt, discourteous; informal. □ **unceremoniously** *adverb*.

uncertain /ʌn'sɜːt(ə)n/ *adjective* not certain; unreliable; changeable. □ **in no uncertain terms** clearly and forcefully. □ **uncertainly** *adverb*; **uncertainty** *noun* (*plural* **-ies**).

uncharted /ʌn'tʃɑːtɪd/ *adjective* not mapped or surveyed.

uncle /'ʌŋk(ə)l/ *noun* parent's brother or brother-in-law. □ **Uncle Sam** *colloquial* US government.

unclean /ʌn'kliːn/ *adjective* not clean; unchaste; religiously impure.

uncomfortable /ʌn'kʌmftəb(ə)l/ *adjective* not comfortable; uneasy. □ **uncomfortably** *adverb*.

uncommon /ʌn'kɒmən/ *adjective* unusual, remarkable. □ **uncommonly** *adverb*.

uncompromising /ʌn'kɒmprəmaɪzɪŋ/ *adjective* stubborn; unyielding. □ **uncompromisingly** *adverb*.

unconcern /ʌnkən'sɜːn/ *noun* calmness; indifference, apathy. □ **unconcerned** *adjective*.

unconditional /ʌnkən'dɪʃən(ə)l/ *adjective* not subject to conditions, complete. □ **unconditionally** *adverb*.

unconscionable /ʌn'kɒnʃənəb(ə)l/ *adjective* without conscience; excessive.

unconscious /ʌn'kɒnʃəs/ • *adjective* not conscious. • *noun* normally inaccessible part of mind affecting emotions etc. □ **unconsciously** *adverb*; **unconsciousness** *noun*.

unconsidered /ʌnkən'sɪdəd/ *adjective* not considered; disregarded; not premeditated.

unconstitutional /ʌnkɒnstɪ'tjuːʃən(ə)l/ *adjective* in breach of political constitution or procedural rules.

uncooperative /ʌnkəʊ'ɒpərətɪv/ *adjective* not cooperative.

uncork /ʌn'kɔːk/ *verb* draw cork from (bottle); vent (feelings).

uncouple /ʌn'kʌp(ə)l/ *verb* (**-ling**) release from couples or coupling.

uncouth /ʌn'kuːθ/ *adjective* uncultured, rough.

uncover /ʌn'kʌvə/ *verb* remove cover or covering from; disclose.

uncrowned /ʌn'kraʊnd/ *adjective* having status but not name of.

unction /'ʌŋkʃ(ə)n/ *noun* anointing with oil etc. as religious rite or medical treatment; oil etc. so used; soothing words or thought; excessive or insincere flattery; (pretence of) deep emotion.

unctuous /'ʌŋktʃʊəs/ *adjective* unpleasantly flattering; greasy. □ **unctuously** *adverb*.

uncut /ʌn'kʌt/ *adjective* not cut; (of book) with pages sealed or untrimmed; (of film) not censored; (of diamond) not shaped; (of fabric) with looped pile.

undeniable /ʌndɪ'naɪəb(ə)l/ *adjective* indisputable; certain. □ **undeniably** *adverb*.

under /'ʌndə/ • *preposition* in or to position lower than; below; beneath; inferior to, less than; undergoing, liable to;

controlled or bound by; classified or subsumed in. ● *adverb* in or to lower condition or position. ● *adjective* lower.

underachieve /ˌʌndərəˈtʃiːv/ *verb* (-ving) do less well than might be expected, esp. academically. □ **underachiever** *noun*.

underarm *adjective & adverb Cricket etc.* with arm below shoulder level.

underbelly *noun* (*plural* **-ies**) under surface of animal etc., esp. as vulnerable to attack.

underbid /ˌʌndəˈbɪd/ *verb* (-dd-; *past & past participle* **-bid**) make lower bid than; *Bridge etc.* bid too little (on).

undercarriage *noun* wheeled retractable landing structure beneath aircraft; supporting framework of vehicle etc.

undercharge /ˌʌndəˈtʃɑːdʒ/ *verb* (-ging) charge too little to.

underclothes *plural noun* (also **underclothing**) clothes worn under others, esp. next to skin.

undercoat *noun* layer of paint under another; (in animals) under layer of hair etc.

undercook /ˌʌndəˈkʊk/ *verb* cook insufficiently.

undercover /ˌʌndəˈkʌvə/ *adjective* surreptitious; spying incognito.

undercroft *noun* crypt.

undercurrent *noun* current below surface; underlying often contrary feeling, force, etc.

undercut ● *verb* /ˌʌndəˈkʌt/ (-tt-; *past & past participle* **-cut**) sell or work at lower price than; strike (ball) to make it rise high; undermine. ● *noun* /ˈʌndəkʌt/ underside of sirloin.

underdeveloped /ˌʌndədɪˈveləpt/ *adjective* immature; (of country etc.) with unexploited potential.

underdog *noun* oppressed person; loser in fight etc.

underdone /ˌʌndəˈdʌn/ *adjective* undercooked.

underemployed /ˌʌndərɪmˈplɔɪd/ *adjective* not fully occupied.

underestimate ● *verb* /ˌʌndərˈestɪmeɪt/ (-ting) form too low an estimate of. ● *noun* /ˌʌndərˈestɪmət/ estimate that is too low. □ **underestimation** *noun*.

underexpose /ˌʌndərɪkˈspəʊz/ *verb* (-sing) expose (film) for too short a time. □ **underexposure** *noun*.

underfed /ˌʌndəˈfed/ *adjective* malnourished.

underfelt *noun* felt laid under carpet.

underfloor /ˌʌndəˈflɔː/ *adjective* (esp. of heating) beneath floor.

underfoot /ˌʌndəˈfʊt/ *adverb* (also **under foot**) under one's feet; on the ground.

underfunded /ˌʌndəˈfʌndɪd/ *adjective* provided with insufficient money.

undergarment *noun* piece of underclothing.

undergo /ˌʌndəˈgəʊ/ *verb* (3rd singular present **-goes**; *past* **-went**; *past participle* **-gone** /-ˈgɒn/) be subjected to, endure.

undergraduate /ˌʌndəˈgrædʒʊət/ *noun* person studying for first degree.

underground ● *adverb* /ˌʌndəˈgraʊnd/ beneath the ground; in(to) secrecy or hiding. ● *adjective* /ˈʌndəgraʊnd/ situated underground; secret, subversive; unconventional. ● *noun* /ˈʌndəgraʊnd/ underground railway; secret subversive group or activity.

undergrowth *noun* dense shrubs etc., esp. in wood.

underhand *adjective* secret, deceptive; *Cricket etc.* underarm.

underlay¹ ● *verb* /ˌʌndəˈleɪ/ (*past & past participle* **-laid**) lay thing under (another) to support or raise. ● *noun* /ˈʌndəleɪ/ thing so laid (esp. under carpet).

underlay² *past of* UNDERLIE.

underlie /ˌʌndəˈlaɪ/ *verb* (-lying; *past* **-lay**; *past participle* **-lain**) lie under (stratum etc.); (esp. as **underlying** *adjective*) be basis of, exist beneath superficial aspect of.

underline /ˌʌndəˈlaɪn/ *verb* (-ning) draw line under (words etc.); emphasize.

underling /ˈʌndəlɪŋ/ *noun usually derogatory* subordinate.

undermanned /ˌʌndəˈmænd/ *adjective* having insufficient crew or staff.

undermine /ˌʌndəˈmaɪn/ *verb* (-ning) injure or wear out insidiously or secretly; wear away base of; make excavation under.

underneath /ˌʌndəˈniːθ/ ● *preposition* at or to lower place than; below; on inside of. ● *adverb* at or to lower place; inside.

●*noun* lower surface or part. ●*adjective* lower.

undernourished /ʌndə'nʌrɪʃt/ *adjective* insufficiently nourished. □ **undernourishment** *noun*.

underpants *plural noun* undergarment for lower part of torso.

underpass *noun* road etc. passing under another; subway.

underpay /ʌndə'peɪ/ *verb (past & past participle* **-paid**) pay too little to (person) or for (thing). □ **underpayment** *noun*.

underpin /ʌndə'pɪn/ *verb* (**-nn-**) support from below with masonry etc.; support, strengthen.

underprivileged /ʌndə'prɪvɪlɪdʒd/ *adjective* less privileged than others; having below average income, rights, etc.

underrate /ʌndə'reɪt/ *verb* (**-ting**) have too low an opinion of.

underscore /ʌndə'skɔː/ *verb* (**-ring**) underline.

undersea *adjective* below sea or its surface.

underseal *verb* seal underpart of (esp. vehicle against rust etc.).

under-secretary /ʌndə'sekrətərɪ/ *noun* (*plural* **-ies**) subordinate official, esp. junior minister or senior civil servant.

undersell /ʌndə'sel/ *verb (past & past participle* **-sold**) sell at lower price than (another seller).

undershirt *noun esp. US* vest.

undershoot /ʌndə'ʃuːt/ *verb (past & past participle* **-shot**) land short of (runway etc.).

undershot *adjective* (of wheel) turned by water flowing under it; (of lower jaw) projecting beyond upper jaw.

underside *noun* lower side or surface.

undersigned /ʌndə'saɪnd/ *adjective* whose signature is appended.

undersized /'ʌndə'saɪzd/ *adjective* smaller than average.

underspend /ʌndə'spend/ *verb (past & past participle* **-spent**) spend less than (expected amount) or too little.

understaffed /ʌndə'stɑːft/ *adjective* having too few staff.

understand /ʌndə'stænd/ *verb (past & past participle* **-stood**) comprehend, perceive meaning, significance, or cause of; know how to deal with; (often +

that) infer, take as implied. □ **understandable** *adjective;* **understandably** *adverb.*

understanding ●*noun* intelligence; ability to understand; individual's perception of situation; agreement, esp. informal. ●*adjective* having understanding or insight; sympathetic. □ **understandingly** *adverb.*

understate /ʌndə'steɪt/ *verb* (**-ting**) express in restrained terms; represent as being less than it really is. □ **understatement** *noun.*

understudy /'ʌndəstʌdɪ/ ●*noun* (*plural* **-ies**) person ready to take another's role when required, esp. in theatre. ●*verb* (**-ies**, **-ied**) study (role etc.) for this purpose; act as understudy to.

undersubscribed /ʌndəsəb'skraɪbd/ *adjective* without sufficient subscribers, participants, etc.

undertake /ʌndə'teɪk/ *verb* (**-king**; *past* **-took**; *past participle* **-taken**) agree to perform or be responsible for; engage in; (usually + *to do*) promise; guarantee, affirm.

undertaker /'ʌndəteɪkə/ *noun* professional funeral organizer.

undertaking /ʌndə'teɪkɪŋ/ *noun* work etc. undertaken; enterprise; promise; /'ʌn-/ professional funeral management.

undertone *noun* subdued tone; underlying quality or feeling.

undertow *noun* current below sea surface contrary to surface current.

underused /ʌndə'juːzd/ *adjective* not used to capacity.

undervalue /ʌndə'vælju/ *verb* (**-ues**, **-ued**, **-uing**) value insufficiently; underestimate.

underwater /ʌndə'wɔːtə/ ●*adjective* situated or done under water. ●*adverb* under water.

underwear *noun* underclothes.

underweight /ʌndə'weɪt/ *adjective* below normal weight.

underwent *past* of UNDERGO.

underwhelm /ʌndə'welm/ *verb jocular* fail to impress.

underworld *noun* those who live by organized crime; mythical home of the dead.

underwrite /ˈʌndəˈraɪt/ *verb* (**-ting**; *past* **-wrote**; *past participle* **-written**) sign and accept liability under (insurance policy); accept (liability) thus; undertake to finance or support; engage to buy all unsold stock in (company etc.). □ **underwriter** /ˈʌn-/ *noun*.

undesirable /ʌndɪˈzaɪərəb(ə)l/ ● *adjective* unpleasant, objectionable. ● *noun* undesirable person. □ **undesirability** *noun*.

undies /ˈʌndɪz/ *plural noun colloquial* (esp. women's) underclothes.

undo /ʌnˈduː/ *verb* (*3rd singular present* **-does**; *past* **-did**; *past participle* **-done**; *present participle* **-doing**) unfasten; annul; ruin prospects, reputation, or morals of.

undoing *noun* (cause of) ruin; reversing of action etc.; unfastening.

undone /ʌnˈdʌn/ *adjective* not done; not fastened; *archaic* ruined.

undoubted /ʌnˈdaʊtɪd/ *adjective* certain, not questioned. □ **undoubtedly** *adverb*.

undreamed /ʌnˈdriːmd, ʌnˈdremt/ *adjective* (also **undreamt** /ʌnˈdremt/) (often + *of*) not thought of, never imagined.

undress /ʌnˈdres/ ● *verb* take off one's clothes; take clothes off (person). ● *noun* ordinary dress, esp. as opposed to (full-dress) uniform; naked or scantily clad state.

undressed /ʌnˈdrest/ *adjective* no longer dressed; (of food) without dressing; (of leather) untreated.

undue /ʌnˈdjuː/ *adjective* excessive, disproportionate. □ **unduly** *adverb*.

undulate /ˈʌndjʊleɪt/ *verb* (**-ting**) (cause to) have wavy motion or look. □ **undulation** *noun*.

undying /ʌnˈdaɪɪŋ/ *adjective* immortal; never-ending.

unearth /ʌnˈɜːθ/ *verb* discover by searching, digging, or rummaging.

unearthly /ʌnˈɜːθlɪ/ *adjective* supernatural; mysterious; *colloquial* very early.

unease /ʌnˈiːz/ *noun* nervousness, anxiety.

uneasy /ʌnˈiːzɪ/ *adjective* (**-ier**, **-iest**) disturbed or uncomfortable in body or mind. □ **uneasily** *adverb*; **uneasiness** *noun*.

unemployable /ʌnɪmˈplɔɪəb(ə)l/ *adjective* unfit for paid employment.

unemployed /ʌnɪmˈplɔɪd/ *adjective* out of work; not used.

unemployment /ʌnɪmˈplɔɪmənt/ *noun* lack of employment. □ **unemployment benefit** state payment made to unemployed worker.

unencumbered /ʌnɪnˈkʌmbəd/ *adjective* (of estate) having no liabilities; free, not burdened.

unequivocal /ʌnɪˈkwɪvək(ə)l/ *adjective* not ambiguous, plain, unmistakable. □ **unequivocally** *adverb*.

UNESCO /juːˈneskəʊ/ *abbreviation* (also **Unesco**) United Nations Educational, Scientific, and Cultural Organization.

uneven /ʌnˈiːv(ə)n/ *adjective* not level; of variable quality; (of contest) unequal. □ **unevenly** *adverb*.

unexceptionable /ʌnɪkˈsepʃənəb(ə)l/ *adjective* entirely satisfactory.

■ **Usage** *Unexceptionable* is sometimes confused with *unexceptional*.

unexceptional /ʌnɪkˈsepʃən(ə)l/ *adjective* normal, ordinary.

■ **Usage** *Unexceptional* is sometimes confused with *unexceptionable*

unfailing /ʌnˈfeɪlɪŋ/ *adjective* not failing, constant, reliable. □ **unfailingly** *adverb*.

unfaithful /ʌnˈfeɪθfʊl/ *adjective* not faithful, esp. adulterous. □ **unfaithfulness** *noun*.

unfeeling /ʌnˈfiːlɪŋ/ *adjective* unsympathetic, harsh.

unfit /ʌnˈfɪt/ *adjective* (often + *for*, *to do*) not fit, unsuitable; in poor health.

unflagging /ʌnˈflæɡɪŋ/ *adjective* tireless, persistent.

unflappable /ʌnˈflæpəb(ə)l/ *adjective colloquial* impe~turbable.

unfledged /ʌnˈfledʒd/ *adjective* inexperienced; not fledged.

unfold /ʌnˈfəʊld/ *verb* open out; reveal; become opened out; develop.

unforgettable /ʌnfəˈɡetəb(ə)l/ *adjective* memorable, wonderful.

unfortunate /ʌnˈfɔːtʃənət/ ● *adjective* unlucky; unhappy; regrettable. ● *noun* unfortunate person. □ **unfortunately** *adverb*.

unfounded /ʌnˈfaʊndɪd/ *adjective* (of rumour etc.) without foundation.

unfreeze /ʌnˈfriːz/ verb (**-zing**; past **unfroze**; past participle **unfrozen**) (cause to) thaw; derestrict (assets etc.).

unfrock /ʌnˈfrɒk/ verb defrock.

unfurl /ʌnˈfɜːl/ verb unroll, spread out.

ungainly /ʌnˈgeɪnlɪ/ adjective awkward, clumsy.

unget-at-able /ʌngetˈætəb(ə)l/ adjective colloquial inaccessible.

ungodly /ʌnˈgɒdlɪ/ adjective impious, wicked; colloquial outrageous.

ungovernable /ʌnˈgʌvənəb(ə)l/ adjective uncontrollable, violent.

ungracious /ʌnˈgreɪʃəs/ adjective discourteous, grudging.

ungrateful /ʌnˈgreɪtfʊl/ adjective not feeling or showing gratitude. □ **ungratefully** adverb.

ungreen /ʌnˈgriːn/ adjective harmful to environment; not concerned with protection of environment.

unguarded /ʌnˈgɑːdɪd/ adjective incautious, thoughtless; not guarded.

unguent /ˈʌŋgwənt/ noun ointment, lubricant.

ungulate /ˈʌŋgjʊlət/ ● adjective hoofed. ● noun hoofed mammal.

unhallowed /ʌnˈhæləʊd/ adjective unconsecrated; not sacred; wicked.

unhand /ʌnˈhænd/ verb rhetorical or jocular take one's hands off, release (person).

unhappy /ʌnˈhæpɪ/ adjective (**-ier**, **-iest**) miserable; unfortunate; disastrous. □ **unhappily** adverb; **unhappiness** noun.

unhealthy /ʌnˈhelθɪ/ adjective (**-ier**, **-iest**) in poor health; harmful to health; unwholesome; slang dangerous. □ **unhealthily** adverb.

unheard-of /ʌnˈhɜːdɒv/ adjective unprecedented.

unhinge /ʌnˈhɪndʒ/ verb (**-ging**) take (door etc.) off hinges; (esp. as **unhinged** adjective) derange, disorder (mind).

unholy /ʌnˈhəʊlɪ/ adjective (**-ier**, **-iest**) profane, wicked; colloquial dreadful, outrageous.

unhorse /ʌnˈhɔːs/ verb (**-sing**) throw (rider) from horse.

uni /ˈjuːnɪ/ noun (plural **-s**) esp. Australian & NZ colloquial university.

uni- combining form having or composed of one.

Uniate /ˈjuːnɪət/ ● adjective of Church in E. Europe or Near East acknowledging papal supremacy but retaining its own liturgy etc. ● noun member of such Church.

unicameral /juːnɪˈkæmər(ə)l/ adjective having one legislative chamber.

UNICEF /ˈjuːnɪsef/ abbreviation United Nations Children's Fund.

unicellular /juːnɪˈseljʊlə/ adjective consisting of a single cell.

unicorn /ˈjuːnɪkɔːn/ noun mythical horse with single straight horn.

unicycle /ˈjuːnɪsaɪk(ə)l/ noun one-wheeled cycle used by acrobats etc.

unification /juːnɪfɪˈkeɪʃ(ə)n/ noun unifying, being unified. □ **Unification Church** religious organization funded by Sun Myung Moon. □ **unificatory** adjective.

uniform /ˈjuːnɪfɔːm/ ● adjective unvarying; conforming to same standard or rule; constant over a period. ● noun distinctive clothing worn by members of same organization etc. □ **uniformed** adjective; **uniformity** /-ˈfɔːm-/ noun; **uniformly** adverb.

unify /ˈjuːnɪfaɪ/ verb (**-ies**, **-ied**) make or become united or uniform.

unilateral /juːnɪˈlætər(ə)l/ adjective done by or affecting one side only. □ **unilaterally** adverb.

unilateralism noun unilateral disarmament. □ **unilateralist** noun & adjective.

unimpeachable /ʌnɪmˈpiːtʃəb(ə)l/ adjective beyond reproach.

uninviting /ʌnɪnˈvaɪtɪŋ/ adjective unattractive, repellent.

union /ˈjuːnjən/ noun uniting, being united; whole formed from parts or members; trade union; marriage; concord; university social club or debating society. □ **Union flag, Jack** national flag of UK.

unionist noun member of trade union, advocate of trade unions; (usually **Unionist**) supporter of continued union between Britain and Northern Ireland. □ **unionism** noun.

unionize verb (also **-ise**) (**-zing** or **-sing**) organize in or into trade union. □ **unionization** noun.

unique /juːˈniːk/ adjective being the only one of its kind; having no like, equal, or parallel; remarkable. □ **uniquely** adverb.

■ **Usage** The use of *unique* to mean 'remarkable' is considered incorrect by some people.

unisex /ˈjuːnɪseks/ adjective (of clothing etc.) designed for both sexes.

unison /ˈjuːnɪs(ə)n/ noun concord; coincidence in pitch of sounds or notes.

unit /ˈjuːnɪt/ noun individual thing, person, or group, esp. for calculation; smallest component of complex whole; quantity chosen as standard of measurement; smallest share in unit trust; part with specified function in complex mechanism; fitted item of furniture, esp. as part of set; subgroup with special function; group of buildings, wards, etc. in hospital; single-digit number, esp. 'one'. □ **unit cost** cost of producing one item; **unit trust** company investing contributions from many people in various securities.

Unitarian /juːnɪˈteərɪən/ noun member of religious body maintaining that God is one person not Trinity. □ **Unitarianism** noun.

unitary /ˈjuːnɪtəri/ adjective of unit(s); marked by unity or uniformity.

unite /jʊˈnaɪt/ verb (**-ting**) join together, esp. for common purpose; join in marriage; (cause to) form physical or chemical whole. □ **United Kingdom** Great Britain and Northern Ireland; **United Nations** (treated as *singular* or *plural*) international peace-seeking organization; **United States** = United States of America.

unity /ˈjuːnɪti/ noun (plural **-ies**) oneness, being one; interconnecting parts making a whole, the whole made; solidarity, harmony between people etc.; the number 'one'.

universal /juːnɪˈvɜːs(ə)l/ ● adjective of, belonging to, or done etc. by all; applicable to all cases. ● noun term, characteristic, or concept of general application. □ **universal coupling, joint** one transmitting rotary power by a shaft at any angle; **universal time** Greenwich Mean Time. □ **universality** /-ˈsæl-/ noun, **universally** adverb.

universe /ˈjuːnɪvɜːs/ noun all existing things; Creation; all humankind.

university /juːnɪˈvɜːsɪti/ noun (plural **-ies**) educational institution of advanced learning and research, conferring degrees; members of this.

unkempt /ʌnˈkempt/ adjective dishevelled, untidy.

unknown /ʌnˈnəʊn/ ● adjective (often + to) not known, unfamiliar. ● noun unknown thing, person, or quantity. □ **unknown quantity** mysterious or obscure person or thing; **Unknown Soldier, Warrior** unidentified soldier symbolizing nation's dead in war.

unlawful /ʌnˈlɔːfʊl/ adjective illegal, not permissible. □ **unlawfully** adverb.

unleaded /ʌnˈledɪd/ adjective (of petrol etc.) without added lead.

unleash /ʌnˈliːʃ/ verb free from leash or restraint; set free to pursue or attack.

unleavened /ʌnˈlev(ə)nd/ adjective made without yeast etc.

unless /ʌnˈles/ conjunction if not; except when.

unlettered /ʌnˈletəd/ adjective illiterate.

unlike /ʌnˈlaɪk/ ● adjective not like, different. ● preposition differently from.

unlikely /ʌnˈlaɪkli/ adjective (**-ier, -iest**) improbable; (+ to do) not expected; unpromising.

unlisted /ʌnˈlɪstɪd/ adjective not included in list, esp. of Stock Exchange prices or telephone numbers.

unload /ʌnˈləʊd/ verb remove load from (vehicle etc.); remove (load) from vehicle etc.; remove ammunition from (gun); colloquial get rid of.

unlock /ʌnˈlɒk/ verb release lock of; release or disclose by unlocking; release feelings etc. from.

unlooked-for /ʌnˈlʊktfɔː/ adjective unexpected.

unlucky /ʌnˈlʌki/ adjective (**-ier, -iest**) not fortunate or successful; wretched; bringing bad luck; ill-judged. □ **unluckily** adverb.

unman /ʌnˈmæn/ verb (**-nn-**) deprive of courage, self-control, etc.

unmannerly /ʌnˈmænəli/ adjective ill-mannered.

unmask /ʌnˈmɑːsk/ verb remove mask from; expose true character of; remove one's mask.

unmentionable /ʌnˈmenʃənəb(ə)l/
● *adjective* unsuitable for polite conversation. □ *noun* (in *plural*) *jocular*
undergarments.

unmistakable /ʌnmɪˈsteɪkəb(ə)l/ *adjective* clear, obvious, plain. □ **unmistak-
ably** *adverb*.

unmitigated /ʌnˈmɪtɪɡeɪtɪd/ *adjective* not
modified; absolute.

unmoved /ʌnˈmuːvd/ *adjective* not
moved; constant in purpose;
unemotional.

unnatural /ʌnˈnætʃər(ə)l/ *adjective* contrary to nature; not normal; lacking
natural feelings; artificial, forced.
□ **unnaturally** *adverb*.

unnecessary /ʌnˈnesəsərɪ/ *adjective* not
necessary; superfluous. □ **unnecessarily** *adverb*.

unnerve /ʌnˈnɜːv/ *verb* (**-ving**) deprive of
confidence etc.

unobjectionable /ʌnəbˈdʒekʃənəb(ə)l/
adjective acceptable.

unobtrusive /ʌnəbˈtruːsɪv/ *adjective* not
making oneself or itself noticed. □ **unobtrusively** *adverb*.

unofficial /ʌnəˈfɪʃ(ə)l/ *adjective* not officially authorized or confirmed.
□ **unofficial strike** strike not ratified
by trade union.

unpack /ʌnˈpæk/ *verb* open and empty;
take (thing) from package etc.

unpalatable /ʌnˈpælətəb(ə)l/ *adjective* (of
food, suggestion, etc.) disagreeable,
distasteful.

unparalleled /ʌnˈpærəleld/ *adjective*
unequalled.

unparliamentary /ʌnpɑːləˈmentərɪ/ *adjective* contrary to proper parliamentary
usage. □ **unparliamentary language**
oaths, abuse.

unpick /ʌnˈpɪk/ *verb* undo sewing of.

unplaced /ʌnˈpleɪst/ *adjective* not placed
as one of the first 3 in race etc.

unpleasant /ʌnˈplez(ə)nt/ *adjective* disagreeable. □ **unpleasantly** *adverb*; **un-
pleasantness** *noun*.

unplug /ʌnˈplʌɡ/ *verb* (**-gg-**) disconnect
(electrical device) by removing plug
from socket; unstop.

unplumbed /ʌnˈplʌmd/ *adjective* not
plumbed; not fully explored or
understood.

unpopular /ʌnˈpɒpjʊlə/ *adjective* not
popular, disliked. □ **unpopularity**
/-ˈlær-/ *noun*.

unpractised /ʌnˈpræktɪst/ *adjective* (*US*
unpracticed) not experienced or
skilled; not put into practice.

unprecedented /ʌnˈpresɪdentɪd/ *adjective* having no precedent, unparalleled.

unprepossessing /ʌnpriːpəˈzesɪŋ/ *adjective* unattractive.

unprincipled /ʌnˈprɪnsɪp(ə)ld/ *adjective*
lacking or not based on moral
principles.

unprintable /ʌnˈprɪntəb(ə)l/ *adjective* too
offensive or indecent to be printed.

unprofessional /ʌnprəˈfeʃ(ə)l/ *adjective* contrary to professional standards;
unskilled, amateurish.

unprompted /ʌnˈprɒmptɪd/ *adjective*
spontaneous.

unputdownable /ʌnpʊtˈdaʊnəb(ə)l/ *adjective colloquial* compulsively readable.

unqualified /ʌnˈkwɒlɪfaɪd/ *adjective* not
qualified or competent; complete.

unquestionable /ʌnˈkwestʃənəb(ə)l/
adjective that cannot be disputed or
doubted. □ **unquestionably** *adverb*.

unquote /ʌnˈkwəʊt/ *interjection* used in
dictation etc. to indicate closing quotation marks.

unravel /ʌnˈræv(ə)l/ *verb* (**-ll-**; *US* **-l-**)
make or become unknitted, unknotted,
etc.; solve (mystery etc.); undo (knitted
fabric).

unreal /ʌnˈrɪəl/ *adjective* not real; imaginary; *slang* incredible.

unreasonable /ʌnˈriːzənəb(ə)l/ *adjective*
excessive; not heeding reason. □ **unreasonably** *adverb*.

unregenerate /ʌnrɪˈdʒenərət/ *adjective*
obstinately wrong or bad.

unrelenting /ʌnrɪˈlentɪŋ/ *adjective* not
abating; merciless.

unreliable /ʌnrɪˈlaɪəb(ə)l/ *adjective*
erratic.

unrelieved /ʌnrɪˈliːvd/ *adjective* monotonously uniform.

unremarked /ʌnrɪˈmɑːkt/ *adjective* not
mentioned or remarked on.

unremitting /ʌnrɪˈmɪtɪŋ/ *adjective* incessant. □ **unremittingly** *adverb*.

unremunerative /ʌnrɪˈmjuːnərətɪv/ *adjective* unprofitable.

unrequited /ˌʌnrɪˈkwaɪtɪd/ *adjective* (of love etc.) not returned.

unreserved /ˌʌnrɪˈzɜːvd/ *adjective* without reservation. □ **unreservedly** /-dlɪ/ *adverb*.

unrest /ʌnˈrest/ *noun* disturbance, turmoil, trouble.

unrivalled /ʌnˈraɪv(ə)ld/ *adjective* (*US* **unrivaled**) having no equal.

unroll /ʌnˈrəʊl/ *verb* open out from rolled-up state; display, be displayed.

unruffled /ʌnˈrʌf(ə)ld/ *adjective* calm.

unruly /ʌnˈruːlɪ/ *adjective* (**-ier, -iest**) undisciplined, disorderly. □ **unruliness** *noun*.

unsatisfactory /ˌʌnsætɪsˈfæktərɪ/ *adjective* poor, unacceptable.

unsaturated /ʌnˈsætʃəreɪtɪd/ *adjective* Chemistry (of fat) containing double or triple molecular bonds and therefore capable of combining with hydrogen.

unsavoury /ʌnˈseɪvərɪ/ *adjective* (*US* **unsavory**) disgusting; (esp. morally) offensive.

unscathed /ʌnˈskeɪðd/ *adjective* uninjured, unharmed.

unschooled /ʌnˈskuːld/ *adjective* uneducated, untrained.

unscientific /ˌʌnsaɪənˈtɪfɪk/ *adjective* not scientific in method etc. □ **unscientifically** *adverb*.

unscramble /ʌnˈskræmb(ə)l/ *verb* (**-ling**) decode, interpret (scrambled transmission etc.).

unscreened /ʌnˈskriːnd/ *adjective* (esp. of coal) not passed through screen; not checked, esp. for security or medical problems; not having screen; not shown on screen.

unscrew /ʌnˈskruː/ *verb* unfasten by removing screw(s), loosen (screw).

unscripted /ʌnˈskrɪptɪd/ *adjective* (of speech etc.) delivered impromptu.

unscrupulous /ʌnˈskruːpjʊləs/ *adjective* without scruples; unprincipled. □ **unscrupulously** *adverb*; **unscrupulousness** *noun*.

unseasonal /ʌnˈsiːzən(ə)l/ *adjective* not typical of the time or season.

unseat /ʌnˈsiːt/ *verb* remove from (esp. parliamentary) seat; dislodge from horseback etc.

unseeing /ʌnˈsiːɪŋ/ *adjective* unobservant; blind. □ **unseeingly** *adverb*.

unseemly /ʌnˈsiːmlɪ/ *adjective* (**-ier, -iest**) indecent; unbecoming.

unseen /ʌnˈsiːn/ ● *adjective* not seen; invisible; (of translation) to be done without preparation. ● *noun* unseen translation.

unselfish /ʌnˈselfɪʃ/ *adjective* concerned about others; sharing. □ **unselfishly** *adverb*; **unselfishness** *noun*.

unsettled /ʌnˈset(ə)ld/ *adjective* restless, disturbed; open to further discussion; liable to change; not paid.

unsex /ʌnˈseks/ *verb* deprive of qualities of one's (esp. female) sex.

unshakeable /ʌnˈʃeɪkəb(ə)l/ *adjective* firm; obstinate.

unsightly /ʌnˈsaɪtlɪ/ *adjective* ugly. □ **unsightliness** *noun*.

unskilled /ʌnˈskɪld/ *adjective* lacking or (of work) not needing special skills.

unsociable /ʌnˈsəʊʃəb(ə)l/ *adjective* disliking company.

■ **Usage** *Unsociable* is sometimes confused with *unsocial*.

unsocial /ʌnˈsəʊʃ(ə)l/ *adjective* not social; not suitable for or seeking society; outside normal working day; antisocial.

■ **Usage** *Unsocial* is sometimes confused with *unsociable*.

unsolicited /ˌʌnsəˈlɪsɪtɪd/ *adjective* voluntary.

unsophisticated /ˌʌnsəˈfɪstɪkeɪtɪd/ *adjective* artless, simple, natural.

unsound /ʌnˈsaʊnd/ *adjective* unhealthy; rotten; weak; unreliable.

unsparing /ʌnˈspeərɪŋ/ *adjective* lavish; merciless.

unspeakable /ʌnˈspiːkəb(ə)l/ *adjective* that words cannot express; indescribably bad. □ **unspeakably** *adverb*.

unstable /ʌnˈsteɪb(ə)l/ *adjective* (**-r, -st**) likely to fall; not stable emotionally; changeable.

unsteady /ʌnˈstedɪ/ *adjective* (**-ier, -iest**) not firm; changeable; not regular. □ **unsteadily** *adverb*; **unsteadiness** *noun*.

unstick /ʌnˈstɪk/ *verb* (*past & past participle* **unstuck**) separate (thing stuck to another). □ **come unstuck** *colloquial* fail.

unstinting /ʌnˈstɪntɪŋ/ *adjective* lavish; limitless. □ **unstintingly** *adverb*.

unstressed /ʌnˈstrest/ *adjective* not pronounced with stress.

unstring /ʌnˈstrɪŋ/ *verb* (*past & past participle* **unstrung**) remove string(s) of (bow, harp, etc.); take (beads etc.) off string; (esp. as **unstrung** *adjective*) unnerve.

unstructured /ʌnˈstrʌktʃəd/ *adjective* without structure; informal.

unstudied /ʌnˈstʌdɪd/ *adjective* easy, natural, spontaneous.

unsung /ʌnˈsʌŋ/ *adjective* not celebrated, unrecognized.

unswerving /ʌnˈswɜːvɪŋ/ *adjective* constant, steady. □ **unswervingly** *adverb*.

unthinkable /ʌnˈθɪŋkəb(ə)l/ *adjective* unimaginable, inconceivable; *colloquial* highly unlikely or undesirable.

unthinking /ʌnˈθɪŋkɪŋ/ *adjective* thoughtless; unintentional, inadvertent. □ **unthinkingly** *adverb*.

untidy /ʌnˈtaɪdɪ/ *adjective* (**-ier, -iest**) not neat or orderly. □ **untidily** *adverb*; **untidiness** *noun*.

until /ənˈtɪl/ *preposition & conjunction* = TILL¹.

■ **Usage** *Until*, as opposed to *till*, is used especially at the beginning of a sentence and in formal style, as in *Until you told me, I had no idea* or *He resided there until his decease.*

untimely /ʌnˈtaɪmlɪ/ *adjective* inopportune; premature.

untiring /ʌnˈtaɪərɪŋ/ *adjective* tireless.

unto /ˈʌntʊ/ *preposition archaic* to.

untold /ʌnˈtəʊld/ *adjective* not told; immeasurable.

untouchable /ʌnˈtʌtʃəb(ə)l/ ● *adjective* that may not be touched. ● *noun* Hindu of group believed to defile higher castes on contact.

untoward /ʌntəˈwɔːd/ *adjective* inconvenient, unlucky; awkward, refractory; unseemly.

untrammelled /ʌnˈtræm(ə)ld/ *adjective* not hampered.

untruth /ʌnˈtruːθ/ *noun* being untrue; lie.

unused *adjective* /ʌnˈjuːzd/ not in use, never used; /ʌnˈjuːst/ (+ *to*) not accustomed.

unusual /ʌnˈjuːʒ(ə)l/ *adjective* not usual; remarkable. □ **unusually** *adverb*.

unutterable /ʌnˈʌtərəb(ə)l/ *adjective* inexpressible; beyond description. □ **unutterably** *adverb*.

unvarnished /ʌnˈvɑːnɪʃt/ *adjective* not varnished; plain, direct, simple.

unveil /ʌnˈveɪl/ *verb* uncover (statue etc.) ceremonially; reveal (secrets etc.).

unversed /ʌnˈvɜːst/ *adjective* (usually + *in*) not experienced or skilled.

unwarrantable /ʌnˈwɒrəntəb(ə)l/ *adjective* (also **unwarranted**) unjustified.

unwashed /ʌnˈwɒʃt/ *adjective* not washed or clean. □ **the great unwashed** *colloquial* the rabble.

unwell /ʌnˈwel/ *adjective* ill.

unwholesome /ʌnˈhəʊlsəm/ *adjective* detrimental to moral or physical health; unhealthy-looking.

unwieldy /ʌnˈwiːldɪ/ *adjective* (**-ier, -iest**) cumbersome or hard to manage owing to size, shape, etc.

unwilling /ʌnˈwɪlɪŋ/ *adjective* reluctant. □ **unwillingly** *adverb*; **unwillingness** *noun*.

unwind /ʌnˈwaɪnd/ *verb* (*past & past participle* **unwound**) draw out or become drawn out after having been wound; *colloquial* relax.

unwitting /ʌnˈwɪtɪŋ/ *adjective* not knowing, unaware; unintentional. □ **unwittingly** *adverb*.

unwonted /ʌnˈwəʊntɪd/ *adjective* not customary or usual.

unworldly /ʌnˈwɜːldlɪ/ *adjective* spiritual; naïve.

unworthy /ʌnˈwɜːðɪ/ *adjective* (**-ier, -iest**) (often + *of*) not worthy or befitting; discreditable, unseemly. □ **unworthiness** *noun*.

unwritten /ʌnˈrɪt(ə)n/ *adjective* not written; (of law etc.) based on tradition or judicial decision, not on statute.

up ● *adverb* towards or in higher place or place regarded as higher, e.g. the north, a capital; to or in erect or required position; in or into active condition; in stronger position; (+ *to, till*, etc.) to specified place, person, or time;

higher in price; completely; completed; into compact, accumulated, or secure state; having risen; happening, esp. unusually. ● *preposition* upwards and along, through, or into; at higher part of. ● *adjective* directed upwards. ● *noun* spell of good fortune. ● *verb* (**-pp-**) *colloquial* start (abruptly or unexpectedly) to speak or act; raise. □ **on the up (and up)** *colloquial* steadily improving; **up against** close to, in(to) contact with, *colloquial* confronted with; **up-and-coming** *colloquial* (of person) promising, progressing; **up for** available for or standing for (sale, office, etc.); **upstate** *US* (in, to, or of) provincial, esp. northern, part of a state; **upstream** *adverb* against flow of stream etc., *adjective* moving upstream; **up to** until, below or equal to, incumbent on, capable of, occupied or busy with; **uptown** *US* (in, into, or of) residential part of town or city; **upwind** in the direction from which the wind is blowing.

upbeat ● *noun* Music unaccented beat. ● *adjective colloquial* optimistic, cheerful.

upbraid /ʌp'breɪd/ *verb* (often + *with*, *for*) chide, reproach.

upbringing *noun* child's rearing.

up-country /ʌp'kʌntrɪ/ *adjective & adverb* inland.

update ● *verb* /ʌp'deɪt/ (**-ting**) bring up to date. ● *noun* /'ʌpdeɪt/ updating; updated information etc.

up-end /ʌp'end/ *verb* set or rise up on end.

upfront /ʌp'frʌnt/ *colloquial* ● *adverb* (usually **up front**) at the front; in front; (of payments) in advance. ● *adjective* honest, frank, direct; (of payments) made in advance.

upgrade /ʌp'greɪd/ *verb* (**-ding**) raise in rank etc.; improve (equipment etc.).

upheaval /ʌp'hi:v(ə)l/ *noun* sudden esp. violent change or disturbance.

uphill ● *adverb* /ʌp'hɪl/ up a slope. ● *adjective* /'ʌphɪl/ sloping up; ascending; arduous.

uphold /ʌp'həʊld/ *verb* (*past & past participle* **upheld**) support; maintain; confirm. □ **upholder** *noun*.

upholster /ʌp'həʊlstə/ *verb* provide (furniture) with upholstery. □ **upholsterer** *noun*.

upholstery *noun* covering, padding, springs, etc. for furniture; upholsterer's work.

upkeep *noun* maintenance in good condition; cost or means of this.

upland /'ʌplənd/ *noun* (usually in *plural*) higher parts of country. ● *adjective* of these parts.

uplift ● *verb* /ʌp'lɪft/ raise; (esp as **uplifting** *adjective*) elevate morally or emotionally. ● *noun* /'ʌplɪft/ elevating influence; support for breasts etc.

up-market /ʌp'mɑːkɪt/ *adjective & adverb* of or to more expensive sector of market.

upon /ə'pɒn/ *preposition* on.

■ *Usage* Upon is usually more formal than *on*, but it is standard in *once upon a time* and *upon my word*.

upper /'ʌpə/ ● *adjective* higher in place; situated above; superior in rank etc. ● *noun* part of shoe or boot above sole. □ **on one's uppers** *colloquial* extremely short of money; **upper case** capital letters; **the upper crust** *colloquial* the aristocracy; **upper-cut** hit upwards with arm bent; **the upper hand** dominance, control; **Upper House** higher legislative assembly, esp. House of Lords.

uppermost ● *adjective* highest, predominant. ● *adverb* on or to the top.

uppity /'ʌpɪtɪ/ *adjective* (also **uppish**) *colloquial* self-assertive, arrogant.

upright /'ʌpraɪt/ ● *adjective* erect, vertical; (of piano) with vertical strings; honourable, honest. ● *noun* upright post or rod, esp. as structural support; upright piano.

uprising *noun* insurrection.

uproar *noun* tumult, violent disturbance.

uproarious /ʌp'rɔːrɪəs/ *adjective* very noisy; provoking loud laughter; very funny. □ **uproariously** *adverb*.

uproot /ʌp'ruːt/ *verb* pull (plant etc.) up from ground; displace (person); eradicate.

upset ● *verb* /ʌp'set/ (**-tt-**; *past & past participle* **upset**) overturn; disturb temper, digestion, or composure of; disrupt. ● *noun* /'ʌpset/ overturning, surprising result. ● *adjective* /ʌp'set, 'ʌp-/ disturbed.

upshot *noun* outcome, conclusion.

upside down /ʌpsaɪd 'daʊn/ *adverb & adjective* with upper and lower parts reversed, inverted; in(to) total disorder.

upstage /ʌp'steɪdʒ/ ● *adjective & adverb* nearer back of theatre stage. ● *verb* (**-ging**) move upstage to make (another actor) face away from audience; divert attention from (person) to oneself.

upstairs ● *adverb* /ʌp'steəz/ to or on an upper floor. ● *adjective* /'ʌpsteəz/ situated upstairs. ● *noun* /ʌp'steəz/ upper floor.

upstanding /ʌp'stændɪŋ/ *adjective* standing up; strong and healthy; honest.

upstart ● *noun* newly successful, esp. arrogant, person. ● *adjective* that is an upstart; of upstarts.

upsurge *noun* upward surge.

upswept *adjective* (of hair) combed to top of head.

upswing *noun* upward movement or trend.

uptake *noun colloquial* understanding; taking up (of offer etc.).

uptight /ʌp'taɪt/ *adjective colloquial* nervously tense, angry; *US* rigidly conventional.

upturn ● *noun* /'ʌptɜːn/ upward trend, improvement. ● *verb* /ʌp'tɜːn/ turn up or upside down.

upward /'ʌpwəd/ ● *adverb* (also **upwards**) towards what is higher, more important, etc. ● *adjective* moving or extending upwards. □ **upwardly** *adverb*.

uranium /jʊ'reɪnɪəm/ *noun* radioactive heavy grey metallic element, capable of nuclear fission and used as source of nuclear energy.

urban /'ɜːbən/ *adjective* of, living in, or situated in city or town. □ **urban guerrilla** terrorist operating in urban area.

urbane /ɜː'beɪn/ *adjective* suave; elegant. □ **urbanity** /-'bæn-/ *noun*.

urbanize /'ɜːbənaɪz/ *verb* (also **-ise**) (**-zing** or **-sing**) make urban, esp. by destroying rural quality of (district). □ **urbanization** *noun*.

urchin /'ɜːtʃɪn/ *noun* mischievous, esp. ragged, child; sea urchin.

Urdu /'ʊədu:/ *noun* Persian-influenced language related to Hindi, used esp. in Pakistan.

urea /jʊə'riːə/ *noun* soluble nitrogenous compound contained esp. in urine.

ureter /jʊə'riːtə/ *noun* duct carrying urine from kidney to bladder.

urethra /jʊə'riːθrə/ *noun* (*plural* **-s**) duct carrying urine from bladder.

urge /ɜːdʒ/ ● *verb* (**-ging**) (often + *on*) drive forcibly, hasten; entreat or exhort earnestly or persistently; (often + *on, upon*) advocate (action, argument, etc.) emphatically. ● *noun* urging impulse or tendency; strong desire.

urgent /'ɜːdʒ(ə)nt/ *adjective* requiring immediate action or attention; importunate. □ **urgency** *noun*; **urgently** *adverb*.

uric acid /'jʊərɪk/ *noun* constituent of urine.

urinal /jʊə'raɪn(ə)l/ *noun* place or receptacle for urinating by men.

urinary /'jʊərɪnərɪ/ *adjective* of or relating to urine.

urinate /'jʊərɪneɪt/ *verb* (**-ting**) discharge urine. □ **urination** *noun*.

urine /'jʊərɪn/ *noun* waste fluid secreted by kidneys and discharged from bladder.

urn *noun* vase with foot, used esp. for ashes of the dead; large vessel with tap, in which tea etc. is made or kept hot.

urology /jʊə'rɒlədʒɪ/ *noun* study of the urinary system. □ **urological** /-rə'lɒdʒ-/ *adjective*.

ursine /'ɜːsaɪn/ *adjective* of or like a bear.

US *abbreviation* United States.

us /ʌs, əs/ *pronoun* used by speaker or writer to refer to himself or herself and one or more others as object of verb; used for ME by sovereign in formal contexts or by editorial writer in newspaper; *colloquial* we.

USA *abbreviation* United States of America.

usable /'juːzəb(ə)l/ *adjective* that can be used.

USAF *abbreviation* United States Air Force.

usage /'juːsɪdʒ/ *noun* use, treatment; customary practice, established use (esp. of language).

use ● *verb* /juːz/ (**using**) cause to act or serve for purpose; bring into service; treat in specified way; exploit for one's own ends; (as **used** *adjective*) secondhand. ● *noun* /juːs/ using, being used;

right or power of using; benefit, advantage; custom, usage. □ **in use** being used; **make use of** use, benefit from; **used to** /juːst/ *adjective* accustomed to, *verb* used before other verb to describe habitual action (e.g. *I used to live here*); **use up** consume, find use for (leftovers etc.).

■ **Usage** The usual negative and question forms of *used to* are, for example, *You didn't use to go there* and *Did you use to go there?* Both are, however, rather informal, so it is better in formal language to use *You used not to go there* and a different expression such as *Were you in the habit of going there?* or *Did you go there when you lived in London?*

---

useful *adjective* that can be used to advantage; helpful, beneficial; *colloquial* creditable, efficient. □ **usefully** *adverb*; **usefulness** *noun*.

useless *adjective* serving no purpose, unavailing; *colloquial* feeble, ineffectual. □ **uselessly** *adverb*; **uselessness** *noun*.

user *noun* person who uses a thing. □ **user-friendly** (of computer, program, etc.) easy to use.

usher /'ʌʃə/ ● *noun* person who shows people to their seats in cinema, church, etc.; doorkeeper of court etc. ● *verb* act as usher to; (usually + *in*) announce, show in.

usherette /ʌʃə'ret/ *noun* female usher, esp. in cinema.

USSR *abbreviation historical* Union of Soviet Socialist Republics.

usual /'juːʒəl/ *adjective* customary; habitual. □ **as usual** as is (or was) usual. □ **usually** *adverb*.

usurer /'juːʒərə/ *noun* person who practises usury.

usurp /juː'zɜːp/ *verb* seize (throne, power, etc.) wrongfully. □ **usurpation** /juːzə'p-/ *noun*; **usurper** *noun*.

usury /'juːʒərɪ/ *noun* lending of money at interest, esp. at exorbitant or illegal rate; interest at this rate. □ **usurious** /juːʒʊərɪəs/ *adjective*.

utensil /juː'tens(ə)l/ *noun* implement or vessel, esp. for kitchen use.

uterus /'juːtərəs/ *noun* (*plural* **uteri** /-raɪ/) womb. □ **uterine** /-raɪn/ *adjective*.

utilitarian /juːtɪlɪ'teərɪən/ ● *adjective* designed to be useful rather than attractive; of utilitarianism. ● *noun* adherent of utilitarianism.

utilitarianism *noun* doctrine that actions are justified if they are useful or benefit majority.

utility /juː'tɪlɪtɪ/ ● *noun* (*plural* **-ies**) usefulness; useful thing, public utility. ● *adjective* basic and standardized. □ **utility room** room for domestic appliances, e.g. washing machine, boiler, etc.; **utility vehicle** vehicle serving various functions.

utilize /'juːtɪlaɪz/ *verb* (also **-ise**) (**-zing** or **-sing**) turn to account, use. □ **utilization** *noun*.

utmost /'ʌtməʊst/ ● *adjective* farthest, extreme; greatest. ● *noun* the utmost point, degree, etc. □ **do one's utmost** do all that one can.

Utopia /juː'təʊpɪə/ *noun* imagined perfect place or state. □ **Utopian**, **utopian** *adjective*.

utter[1] /'ʌtə/ *adjective* complete, absolute. □ **utterly** *adverb*; **uttermost** *adjective*.

utter[2] /'ʌtə/ *verb* emit audibly; express in words; *Law* put (esp. forged money) into circulation.

utterance *noun* uttering; thing spoken; power or manner of speaking.

UV *abbreviation* ultraviolet.

uvula /'juːvjʊlə/ *noun* (*plural* **uvulae** /-liː/) fleshy part of soft palate hanging above throat. □ **uvular** *adjective*.

uxorious /ʌk'sɔːrɪəs/ *adjective* excessively fond of one's wife.

Vv

V¹ noun (also **v**) (Roman numeral) 5.

V² abbreviation volt(s).

v. abbreviation verse; versus; very; verb; vide.

vac noun colloquial vacation.

vacancy /'veɪkənsɪ/ noun (plural **-ies**) being vacant; unoccupied post, place, etc.

vacant adjective not filled or occupied; not mentally active, showing no interest. □ **vacant possession** ownership of unoccupied house etc. □ **vacantly** adverb.

vacate /və'keɪt/ verb (**-ting**) leave vacant, cease to occupy.

vacation /və'keɪʃ(ə)n/ noun fixed holiday period, esp. in law courts and universities; US holiday; vacating, being vacated.

vaccinate /'væksɪneɪt/ verb (**-ting**) inoculate with vaccine to immunize against disease. □ **vaccination** noun.

vaccine /'væksiːn/ noun preparation used for inoculation, originally cowpox virus giving immunity to smallpox.

vacillate /'væsɪleɪt/ verb (**-ting**) fluctuate in opinion or resolution. □ **vacillation** noun; **vacillator** noun.

vacuous /'vækjʊəs/ adjective expressionless; unintelligent. □ **vacuity** /və'kjuːɪtɪ/ noun; **vacuously** adverb.

vacuum /'vækjʊəm/ ● noun (plural **-s** or **vacua**) space entirely devoid of matter; space or vessel from which air has been completely or partly removed by pump etc.; absence of normal or previous content; (plural **-s**) colloquial vacuum cleaner. ● verb colloquial clean with vacuum cleaner. □ **vacuum brake** brake worked by exhaustion of air; **vacuum cleaner** machine for removing dust etc. by suction; **vacuum flask** vessel with double wall enclosing vacuum so that contents remain hot or cold; **vacuum-packed** sealed after partial removal of air; **vacuum tube** tube containing near-vacuum for free passage of electric current.

vagabond /'vægəbɒnd/ ● noun wanderer, esp. idle one. ● adjective wandering, having no settled habitation or home.

vagary /'veɪgərɪ/ noun (plural **-ies**) caprice, eccentric act or idea.

vagina /və'dʒaɪnə/ noun (plural **-s** or **-nae** /-niː/) canal joining womb and vulva of female mammal. □ **vaginal** adjective.

vagrant /'veɪgrənt/ ● noun person without settled home or regular work. ● adjective wandering, roving. □ **vagrancy** noun.

vague /veɪg/ adjective uncertain, ill-defined; not clear-thinking, inexact. □ **vaguely** adverb; **vagueness** noun.

vain adjective conceited; empty, trivial; unavailing, useless. □ **in vain** without result or success, lightly or profanely. □ **vainly** adverb.

vainglory /veɪn'glɔːrɪ/ noun extreme vanity, boastfulness. □ **vainglorious** adjective.

valance /'væləns/ noun short curtain round bedstead, above window, etc.

vale noun (archaic except in place names) valley.

valediction /vælɪ'dɪkʃ(ə)n/ noun formal bidding farewell; words used in this. □ **valedictory** adjective & noun (plural **-ies**).

valence /'veɪləns/ noun valency.

valency /'veɪlənsɪ/ noun (plural **-ies**) combining-power of an atom measured by number of hydrogen atoms it can displace or combine with.

valentine /'væləntaɪn/ noun (usually anonymous) letter or card sent as mark of love on St Valentine's Day (14 Feb.); sweetheart chosen on that day.

valerian /və'lɪərɪən/ noun any of various kinds of flowering herb.

valet /'vælɪt/ ● noun gentleman's personal servant. ● verb (**-t-**) act as valet (to).

valetudinarian /vælɪtjuːdɪ'neərɪən/ ● noun person of poor health or unduly anxious about health. ● *adjective* of a valetudinarian.

valiant /'væljənt/ *adjective* brave. □ **valiantly** *adverb*.

valid /'vælɪd/ *adjective* (of reason, objection, etc.) sound, defensible; legally acceptable, not yet expired. □ **validity** /və'lɪd-/ *noun*.

validate /'vælɪdeɪt/ *verb* (**-ting**) make valid, ratify. □ **validation** *noun*.

valise /və'li:z/ *noun US* small portmanteau.

Valium /'vælɪəm/ *noun proprietary term* the tranquillizing drug diazepam.

valley /'vælɪ/ *noun* (*plural* **-s**) low area between hills, usually with stream or river.

valour /'vælə/ *noun* (*US* **valor**) courage, esp. in battle. □ **valorous** *adjective*.

valuable /'væljʊəb(ə)l/ ● *adjective* of great value, price, or worth. ● *noun* (usually in *plural*) valuable thing.

valuation /væljʊ'eɪʃ(ə)n/ *noun* estimation (esp. by professional valuer) of thing's worth; estimated value.

value /'vælju:/ ● *noun* worth, desirability, or qualities on which these depend; worth as estimated; amount for which thing can be exchanged in open market; equivalent of thing; (in full **value for money**) something well worth money spent; ability of a thing to serve a purpose or cause an effect; (in *plural*) one's principles, priorities, or standards; *Music* duration of note; *Mathematics* amount denoted by algebraic term. ● *verb* (**-ues, -ued, -uing**) estimate value of; have high or specified opinion of. □ **value added tax** tax levied on rise in value of services and goods at each stage of production; **value judgement** subjective estimate of worth etc. □ **valueless** *adjective*.

valuer *noun* person who estimates or assesses values.

valve *noun* device controlling flow through pipe etc., usually allowing movement in one direction only; structure in organ etc. allowing flow of blood etc. in one direction only; thermionic valve; device to vary length of tube in trumpet etc.; half-shell of oyster, mussel, etc.

valvular /'vælvjʊlə/ *adjective* having valve(s); having form or function of valve.

vamoose /və'mu:s/ *verb US slang* depart hurriedly.

vamp¹ ● *noun* upper front part of boot or shoe. ● *verb* (often + *up*) repair, furbish, or make by patching or piecing together; improvise musical accompaniment.

vamp² *colloquial* ● *noun* woman who uses sexual attraction to exploit men. ● *verb* allure or exploit (man).

vampire /'væmpaɪə/ *noun* supposed ghost or reanimated corpse sucking blood of sleeping people; person who preys on others; (in full **vampire bat**) bloodsucking bat.

van¹ *noun* covered vehicle or closed railway truck for transporting goods etc.

van² *noun* vanguard, forefront.

vanadium /və'neɪdɪəm/ *noun* hard grey metallic element used to strengthen steel.

vandal /'vænd(ə)l/ *noun* person who wilfully or maliciously damages property. □ **vandalism** *noun*.

vandalize /'vændəlaɪz/ *verb* (also **-ise**) (**-zing** or **-sing**) destroy or damage wilfully or maliciously (esp. public property).

vane *noun* weather vane; blade of windmill, ship's propeller, etc.

vanguard /'vænɡɑːd/ *noun* foremost part of advancing army etc.; leaders of movement etc.

vanilla /və'nɪlə/ *noun* tropical fragrant climbing orchid; extract of its fruit (**vanilla-pod**), or synthetic substitute, used as flavouring.

vanish /'vænɪʃ/ *verb* disappear; cease to exist. □ **vanishing point** point at which receding parallel lines appear to meet.

vanity /'vænɪtɪ/ *noun* (*plural* **-ies**) conceit about one's attainments or appearance; futility, unreal thing. □ **vanity bag, case** woman's make-up bag or case.

vanquish /'væŋkwɪʃ/ *verb literary* conquer, overcome.

vantage /'vɑːntɪdʒ/ *noun* advantage, esp. in tennis; (also **vantage point**) place giving good view.

vapid /'væpɪd/ *adjective* insipid, dull, flat. □ **vapidity** /və'pɪd-/ *noun*.

vapor *US* = VAPOUR.

vaporize /'veɪpəraɪz/ *verb* (also **-ise**) (**-zing** or **-sing**) change into vapour. □ **vaporization** *noun*.

vaporous /'veɪpərəs/ *adjective* in the form of or consisting of vapour.

vapour /'veɪpə/ *noun* (*US* **vapor**) moisture or other substance diffused or suspended in air, e.g. mist, smoke; gaseous form of substance. □ **vapour trail** trail of condensed water from aircraft etc.

variable /'veərɪəb(ə)l/ ● *adjective* changeable, adaptable; apt to vary, not constant; *Mathematics* (of quantity) indeterminate, able to assume different numerical values. ● *noun* variable thing or quantity. □ **variability** *noun*.

variance /'veərɪəns/ *noun* (usually after *at*) difference of opinion; dispute; discrepancy.

variant ● *adjective* differing in form or details from standard; having different forms. ● *noun* variant form, spelling, type, etc.

variation /veərɪ'eɪʃ(ə)n/ *noun* varying; departure from normal kind, standard, type, etc.; extent of this; thing that varies from type; *Music* theme in changed or elaborated form.

varicose /'værɪkəʊs/ *adjective* (esp. of vein etc.) permanently and abnormally dilated.

variegated /'veərɪgeɪtɪd/ *adjective* with irregular patches of different colours; having leaves of two or more colours. □ **variegation** *noun*.

variety /və'raɪətɪ/ *noun* (*plural* **-ies**) diversity; absence of uniformity; collection of different things; class of things differing from rest in same general class; member of such class; (+ *of*) different form of thing, quality, etc.; *Biology* subdivision of species; series of dances, songs, comedy acts, etc.

various /'veərɪəs/ *adjective* different, diverse; several. □ **variously** *adverb*.

■ **Usage** *Various* (unlike *several*) is not a pronoun and therefore cannot be used with *of*, as (wrongly) in *Various of the guests arrived late.*

varnish /'vɑːnɪʃ/ ● *noun* resinous solution used to give hard shiny transparent coating. ● *verb* coat with varnish; conceal with deceptively attractive appearance.

varsity /'vɑːsɪtɪ/ *noun* (*plural* **-ies**) *colloquial* university.

vary /'veərɪ/ *verb* (**-ies**, **-ied**) be or become different; be of different kinds; modify, diversify.

vascular /'væskjʊlə/ *adjective* of or containing vessels for conveying blood, sap, etc.

vas deferens /væs 'defərenz/ *noun* (*plural* **vasa deferentia** /veɪsə defə'renʃɪə/) sperm duct of testicle.

vase /vɑːz/ *noun* vessel used as ornament or container for flowers.

vasectomy /və'sektəmɪ/ *noun* (*plural* **-ies**) removal of part of each vas deferens, esp. for sterilization.

Vaseline /'væsɪliːn/ *noun* *proprietary term* type of petroleum jelly used as ointment etc.

vassal /'væs(ə)l/ *noun* humble dependant; *historical* holder of land by feudal tenure.

vast /vɑːst/ *adjective* immense, huge. □ **vastly** *adverb*; **vastness** *noun*.

VAT *abbreviation* value added tax.

vat *noun* tank, esp. for holding liquids in brewing, dyeing, and tanning.

Vatican /'vætɪkən/ *noun* palace or government of Pope in Rome.

vaudeville /'vɔːdəvɪl/ *noun* esp. *US* variety entertainment.

vault /vɔːlt/ ● *noun* arched roof; vaultlike covering; underground room as place of storage; underground burial chamber; act of vaulting. ● *verb* leap or spring, esp. using hands or pole; spring over in this way; (esp. as **vaulted** *adjective*) make in form of vault, provide with vault(s).

vaunt /vɔːnt/ *verb & noun* *literary* boast.

VC *abbreviation* Victoria Cross.

VCR *abbreviation* video cassette recorder.

VD *abbreviation* venereal disease.

VDU *abbreviation* visual display unit.

veal *noun* calf's flesh as food.

vector /'vektə/ *noun* *Mathematics & Physics* quantity having both magnitude and direction; carrier of disease.

veer /vɪə/ *verb* change direction, esp. (of wind) clockwise; change in opinion, course, etc.

vegan /'viːgən/ ● *noun* person who does not eat animals or animal products. ● *adjective* using or containing no animal products.

vegetable /'vedʒtəb(ə)l/ ● *noun* plant, esp. edible herbaceous plant. ● *adjective* of, derived from, or relating to plant life or vegetables as food.

vegetarian /vedʒɪ'teərɪən/ ● *noun* person who does not eat meat or fish. ● *adjective* excluding animal food, esp. meat. □ **vegetarianism** *noun*.

vegetate /'vedʒɪteɪt/ *verb* (**-ting**) lead dull monotonous life; grow as plants do.

vegetation /vedʒɪ'teɪʃ(ə)n/ *noun* plants collectively; plant life.

vegetative /'vedʒɪtətɪv/ *adjective* concerned with growth and development rather than sexual reproduction; of vegetation.

vehement /'viːəmənt/ *adjective* showing or caused by strong feeling, ardent. □ **vehemence** *noun*, **vehemently** *adverb*.

vehicle /'viːɪk(ə)l/ *noun* conveyance used on land or in space; thing or person as medium for thought, feeling, or action; liquid etc. as medium for suspending pigments, drugs, etc. □ **vehicular** /vɪ'hɪkjʊlə/ *adjective*.

veil /veɪl/ ● *noun* piece of usually transparent material attached to woman's hat or otherwise forming part of headdress, esp. to conceal or protect face; piece of linen etc. as part of nun's headdress; thing that hides or disguises. ● *verb* cover with veil; (esp. as **veiled** *adjective*) partly conceal. □ **beyond the veil** in the unknown state of life after death; **draw a veil over** avoid discussing; **take the veil** become nun.

vein /veɪn/ *noun* any of tubes carrying blood to heart; (in general use) any blood vessel; rib of leaf or insect's wing; streak of different colour in wood, marble, cheese, etc.; fissure in rock filled with ore; specified character or tendency, mood. □ **veined** *adjective*.

Velcro /'velkrəʊ/ *noun proprietary term* fastener consisting of two strips of fabric which cling when pressed together.

veld /velt/ *noun* (also **veldt**) *South African* open country.

veleta /və'liːtə/ *noun* ballroom dance in triple time.

vellum /'veləm/ *noun* fine parchment, originally calfskin; manuscript on this; smooth writing paper imitating vellum.

velociraptor /vɪ'lɒsɪræptə/ *noun* small carnivorous dinosaur with short front legs.

velocity /vɪ'lɒsɪtɪ/ *noun* (*plural* **-ies**) speed, esp. of inanimate things.

velour /və'lʊə/ *noun* (also **velours** same pronunciation) plushlike fabric.

velvet /'velvɪt/ ● *noun* soft fabric with thick short pile on one side; furry skin on growing antler. ● *adjective* of, like, or soft as velvet. □ **on velvet** in advantageous or prosperous position; **velvet glove** outward gentleness cloaking firmness or inflexibility. □ **velvety** *adjective*.

velveteen /velvɪ'tiːn/ *noun* cotton fabric with pile like velvet.

Ven. *abbreviation* Venerable.

venal /'viːn(ə)l/ *adjective* able to be bribed; involving bribery; corrupt. □ **venality** /-'næl-/ *noun*.

■ **Usage** *Venal* is sometimes confused with *venial*.

vend *verb* offer (esp. small wares) for sale. □ **vending machine** slot machine selling small items. □ **vendor** *noun*.

vendetta /ven'detə/ *noun* blood feud; prolonged bitter quarrel.

veneer /vɪ'nɪə/ ● *noun* thin covering of fine wood; (often + *of*) deceptively pleasing appearance. ● *verb* apply veneer to (wood etc.).

venerable /'venərəb(ə)l/ *adjective* entitled to deep respect on account of age, character, etc.; *title of archdeacon*.

venerate /'venəreɪt/ *verb* (**-ting**) regard with deep respect. □ **veneration** *noun*.

venereal /vɪ'nɪərɪəl/ *adjective* of sexual desire or intercourse; of venereal disease. □ **venereal disease** disease contracted by sexual intercourse with infected person.

Venetian /vɪ'niːʃ(ə)n/ ● noun native, citizen, or dialect of Venice. ● adjective of Venice. □ **venetian blind** window-blind of adjustable horizontal slats.

vengeance /'vendʒ(ə)ns/ noun punishment inflicted for wrong to oneself or to one's cause. □ **with a vengeance** to extreme degree, thoroughly, violently.

vengeful /'vendʒfʊl/ adjective seeking vengeance, vindictive.

venial /'viːnɪəl/ adjective (of sin or fault) pardonable, not mortal. □ **veniality** /-'æl-/ noun.

■ **Usage** Venial is sometimes confused with venal.

venison /'venɪs(ə)n/ noun deer's flesh as food.

Venn diagram noun diagram using overlapping and intersecting circles etc. to show relationships between mathematical sets.

venom /'venəm/ noun poisonous fluid of esp. snakes; malignity, virulence of feeling, language, or conduct. □ **venomous** adjective; **venomously** adverb.

venous /'viːnəs/ adjective of, full of, or contained in veins.

vent[1] ● noun opening for passage of air etc.; outlet, free expression; anus, esp. of lower animal. ● verb give vent or free expression to.

vent[2] noun slit in garment, esp. in back of jacket.

ventilate /'ventɪleɪt/ verb (-ting) cause air to circulate freely in (room etc.); air (question, grievance, etc.). □ **ventilation** noun.

ventilator noun appliance or aperture for ventilating room etc.; apparatus for maintaining artificial respiration.

ventral /'ventr(ə)l/ adjective of or on abdomen.

ventricle /'ventrɪk(ə)l/ noun cavity in body; hollow part of organ, esp. brain or heart.

ventricular /ven'trɪkjʊlə/ adjective of or shaped like ventricle.

ventriloquism /ven'trɪləkwɪz(ə)m/ noun skill of speaking without moving the lips. □ **ventriloquist** noun.

venture /'ventʃə/ ● noun risky undertaking; commercial speculation. ● verb (-ring) dare, not be afraid; dare to go,

make, or put forward; take risks, expose to risk, stake. □ **Venture Scout** senior Scout.

venturesome adjective disposed to take risks.

venue /'venjuː/ noun appointed place for match, meeting, concert, etc.

Venus fly-trap /'viːnəs/ noun insectivorous plant.

veracious /və'reɪʃəs/ adjective formal truthful, true. □ **veracity** /-'ræs-/ noun.

veranda /və'rændə/ noun (sometimes partly covered) platform along side of house.

verb noun word used to indicate action, event, state, or change (see panel).

verbal adjective of words; oral, not written; of a verb; (of translation) literal. □ **verbally** adverb.

verbalize verb (also **-ise**) (**-zing** or **-sing**) put into words.

verbatim /vɜː'beɪtɪm/ adverb & adjective in exactly the same words.

verbena /vɜː'biːnə/ noun (plural same) plant of genus of herbs and small shrubs with fragrant flowers.

verbiage /'vɜːbɪɪdʒ/ noun derogatory unnecessary number of words.

verbose /vɜː'bəʊs/ adjective using more words than are needed. □ **verbosity** /-'bɒs-/ noun.

verdant /'vɜːd(ə)nt/ adjective (of grass, field, etc.) green, lush. □ **verdancy** noun.

verdict /'vɜːdɪkt/ noun decision of jury; decision, judgement.

verdigris /'vɜːdɪgriː/ noun greenish-blue substance that forms on copper or brass.

verdure /'vɜːdjə/ noun literary green vegetation or its colour.

verge[1] noun edge, border; brink; grass edging of road etc.

verge[2] verb (**-ging**) (+ on) border on; incline downwards or in specified direction.

verger /'vɜːdʒə/ noun caretaker and attendant in church; officer carrying staff before dignitaries of cathedral etc.

verify /'verɪfaɪ/ verb (**-ies**, **-ied**) establish truth or correctness of by examination etc.; fulfil, bear out. □ **verification** noun.

verily /'verɪlɪ/ adverb archaic truly, really.

verisimilitude /verɪsɪˈmɪlɪtjuːd/ *noun* appearance of being true or real.

veritable /ˈverɪtəb(ə)l/ *adjective* real, rightly so called.

verity /ˈverɪtɪ/ *noun* (*plural* -**ies**) true statement; *archaic* truth.

vermicelli /vɜːmɪˈtʃelɪ/ *noun* pasta in long slender threads.

vermicide /ˈvɜːmɪsaɪd/ *noun* drug used to kill intestinal worms.

vermiform /ˈvɜːmɪfɔːm/ *adjective* worm-shaped. □ **vermiform appendix** small blind tube extending from caecum in man and some other mammals.

vermilion /vəˈmɪljən/ ● *noun* brilliant scarlet pigment made esp. from cinnabar; colour of this. ● *adjective* of this colour.

vermin /ˈvɜːmɪn/ *noun* (usually treated as *plural*) mammals and birds harmful to game, crops, etc.; parasitic worms or insects; vile people.

verminous *adjective* of the nature of or infested with vermin.

vermouth /ˈvɜːməθ/ *noun* wine flavoured with aromatic herbs.

vernacular /vəˈnækjʊlə/ ● *noun* language or dialect of country; language of particular class or group; homely speech. ● *adjective* (of language) of one's own country, not foreign or formal.

vernal /ˈvɜːn(ə)l/ *adjective* of or in spring.

vernier /ˈvɜːnɪə/ *noun* small movable scale for reading fractional parts of subdivisions on fixed scale of measuring instrument.

veronica /vəˈrɒnɪkə/ *noun* speedwell.

verruca /vəˈruːkə/ *noun* (*plural* **verrucae** /-siː/ or -**s**) wart or similar growth, esp. on foot.

versatile /ˈvɜːsətaɪl/ *adjective* turning easily or readily from one subject or occupation to another, skilled in many subjects or occupations; having many uses. □ **versatility** /-ˈtɪl-/ *noun*.

verse *noun* poetry; stanza of poem or song; each of short numbered divisions of Bible.

versed /vɜːst/ *adjective* (+ *in*) experienced or skilled in.

versicle /ˈvɜːsɪk(ə)l/ *noun* short sentence, esp. each of series in liturgy said or sung by minister or priest, answered by congregation.

Verb

A verb says what a person or thing does, and can describe:

    an action, e.g. *run, hit*
    an event, e.g. *rain, happen*
    a state, e.g. *be, have, seem, appear*
    a change, e.g. *become, grow*

Verbs occur in different forms, usually in one or other of their tenses. The most common tenses are:

the simple present tense:	*The boy walks down the road.*
the continuous present tense:	*The boy is walking down the road.*
the simple past tense:	*The boy walked down the road.*
the continuous past tense:	*The boy was walking down the road.*
the perfect tense:	*The boy has walked down the road.*
the future tense:	*The boy will walk down the road.*

Each of these forms is a finite verb, which means that it is in a particular tense and that it changes according to the number and person of the subject, as in

I am	*you walk*
we are	*he walks*

An infinitive is the form of a verb that usually appears with 'to', e.g.

    to wander, to look, to sleep.

versify /'vɜːsɪfaɪ/ verb (-ies, -ied) turn into or express in verse; compose verses. □ **versification** noun.

version /'vɜːʃ(ə)n/ noun account of matter from particular point of view; particular edition or translation of book etc.

verso /'vɜːsəʊ/ noun (plural -s) left-hand page of open book, back of printed leaf.

versus /'vɜːsəs/ preposition against.

vertebra /'vɜːtɪbrə/ noun (plural -brae /-briː/) each segment of backbone. □ **vertebral** adjective.

vertebrate /'vɜːtɪbrət/ ● adjective having backbone. ● noun vertebrate animal.

vertex /'vɜːteks/ noun (plural -tices /-tɪsiːz/ or -texes) highest point, top, apex; meeting-point of lines that form angle.

vertical /'vɜːtɪk(ə)l/ ● adjective at right angles to horizontal plane; in direction from top to bottom of picture etc.; of or at vertex. ● noun vertical line or plane. □ **vertical take-off** take-off of aircraft directly upwards. □ **vertically** adverb.

vertiginous /vɜː'tɪdʒɪnəs/ adjective of or causing vertigo.

vertigo /'vɜːtɪgəʊ/ noun dizziness.

vervain /'vɜːveɪn/ noun any of several verbenas, esp. one with small blue, white, or purple flowers.

verve noun enthusiasm, energy, vigour.

very /'verɪ/ ● adverb in high degree; (+ own or superlative adjective) in fullest sense. ● adjective real, properly so called etc. □ **very good, well** formula of consent or approval; **very high frequency** 30–300 megahertz (in radio); **Very Reverend** title of dean.

vesicle /'vesɪk(ə)l/ noun small bladder, blister, or bubble.

vespers /'vespəz/ plural noun evening church service.

vessel /'ves(ə)l/ noun hollow receptacle, esp. for liquid; ship or boat, esp. large one; duct or canal holding or conveying blood, sap, etc.

vest ● noun undergarment worn on upper part of body; US & Australian waistcoat. ● verb (+ with) bestow (powers, authority, etc.) on; (+ in) confer (property or power) on (person) with immediate fixed right of future possession. □ **vested interest** personal interest in state of affairs, usually with expectation of gain, Law interest (usually in land or money held in trust) recognized as belonging to person.

vestal virgin /'vest(ə)l/ noun virgin consecrated to Vesta, Roman goddess of hearth and home, and vowed to chastity.

vestibule /'vestɪbjuːl/ noun lobby, entrance hall.

vestige /'vestɪdʒ/ noun trace, evidence; slight amount, particle; Biology part or organ now atrophied that was well-developed in ancestors. □ **vestigial** /-'tɪdʒɪəl/ adjective.

vestment /'vestmənt/ noun ceremonial garment worn by priest etc.

vestry /'vestrɪ/ noun (plural -ies) room or part of church for keeping vestments etc. in.

vet ● noun colloquial veterinary surgeon. ● verb (-tt-) make careful and critical examination of (scheme, work, candidate, etc.).

vetch noun plant of pea family largely used for fodder.

veteran /'vetərən/ noun old soldier or long-serving member of any group; US ex-serviceman or -woman. □ **veteran car** one made before 1905.

veterinarian /vetərɪ'neərɪən/ noun formal veterinary surgeon.

veterinary /'vetərɪnərɪ/ adjective of or for diseases and injuries of animals. □ **veterinary surgeon** person qualified to treat animals.

veto /'viːtəʊ/ ● noun (plural -es) right to reject measure etc. unilaterally; rejection, prohibition. ● verb (-oes, -oed) reject (measure etc.); forbid.

vex verb annoy, irritate; archaic grieve, afflict.

vexation /vek'seɪʃ(ə)n/ noun vexing, being vexed; annoying or distressing thing.

vexatious /vek'seɪʃəs/ adjective causing vexation; Law lacking sufficient grounds for action and seeking only to annoy defendant.

vexed adjective (of question) much discussed.

VHF abbreviation very high frequency.

via /'vaɪə/ preposition by way of, through.

viable /ˈvaɪəb(ə)l/ *adjective* (of plan etc.) feasible, esp. economically; (esp. of foetus) capable of living and surviving independently. □ **viability** *noun*.

viaduct /ˈvaɪədʌkt/ *noun* long bridge carrying railway or road over valley.

vial /ˈvaɪəl/ *noun* small glass vessel.

viands /ˈvaɪəndz/ *plural noun formal* articles of food.

viaticum /vaɪˈætɪkəm/ *noun* (*plural* **-ca**) Eucharist given to dying person.

vibes /vaɪbz/ *plural noun colloquial* vibrations; esp. feelings communicated; vibraphone.

vibrant /ˈvaɪbrənt/ *adjective* vibrating; resonant; (often + *with*) thrilling; (of colour) bright and striking. □ **vibrancy** *noun*.

vibraphone /ˈvaɪbrəfəʊn/ *noun* percussion instrument with motor-driven resonators under metal bars giving vibrato effect.

vibrate /vaɪˈbreɪt/ *verb* (**-ting**) move rapidly to and fro; (of sound) throb, resonate; (+ *with*) quiver; swing to and fro, oscillate. □ **vibratory** *adjective*.

vibration *noun* vibrating; (in *plural*) mental (esp. occult) influence, atmosphere or feeling communicated.

vibrato /vɪˈbrɑːtəʊ/ *noun* tremulous effect in musical pitch.

vibrator *noun* device that vibrates, esp. instrument used in massage or sexual stimulation.

viburnum /vaɪˈbɜːnəm/ *noun* shrub with pink or white flowers.

vicar /ˈvɪkə/ *noun* incumbent of C. of E. parish where in former times incumbent received stipend rather than tithes; *colloquial* any member of the clergy.

vicarage *noun* vicar's house.

vicarious /vɪˈkeərɪəs/ *adjective* experienced indirectly; acting or done etc. for another; deputed, delegated. □ **vicariously** *adverb*.

vice[1] *noun* immoral conduct; particular form of this; bad habit. □ **vice ring** group of criminals organizing prostitution; **vice squad** police department concerned with prostitution.

vice[2] *noun* (*US* **vise**) clamp with two jaws for holding an object being worked on.

vice- *combining form* person acting in place of; person next in rank to.

vice-chancellor /vaɪsˈtʃɑːnsələ/ *noun* deputy chancellor (esp. administrator of university).

viceregal /vaɪsˈriːg(ə)l/ *adjective* of viceroy.

vicereine /ˈvaɪsreɪn/ *noun* viceroy's wife; woman viceroy.

viceroy /ˈvaɪsrɔɪ/ *noun* ruler on behalf of sovereign in colony, province, etc.

vice versa /vaɪs ˈvɜːsə/ *adverb* with order of terms changed, other way round.

Vichy water /ˈviːʃiː/ *noun* effervescent mineral water from Vichy in France.

vicinity /vɪˈsɪnɪtɪ/ *noun* (*plural* **-ies**) surrounding district; (+ *to*) nearness to. □ **in the vicinity (of)** near (to).

vicious /ˈvɪʃəs/ *adjective* bad-tempered, spiteful; violent; corrupt. □ **vicious circle** self-perpetuating, harmful sequence of cause and effect. □ **viciously** *adverb*; **viciousness** *noun*.

vicissitude /vɪˈsɪsɪtjuːd/ *noun literary* change, esp. of fortune.

victim /ˈvɪktɪm/ *noun* person or thing destroyed or injured; prey, dupe; creature sacrificed to a god etc.

victimize *verb* (also **-ise**) (**-zing** or **-sing**) single out for punishment or unfair treatment; make (person etc.) a victim. □ **victimization** *noun*.

victor /ˈvɪktə/ *noun* conqueror, winner of contest.

Victoria Cross /vɪkˈtɔːrɪə/ *noun* highest decoration for conspicuous bravery in armed services.

Victorian /vɪkˈtɔːrɪən/ • *adjective* of time of Queen Victoria; prudish, strict. • *noun* person of this time.

Victoriana /vɪktɔːrɪˈɑːnə/ *plural noun* articles, esp. collectors' items, of Victorian period.

victorious /vɪkˈtɔːrɪəs/ *adjective* conquering, triumphant; marked by victory. □ **victoriously** *adverb*.

victory /ˈvɪktərɪ/ *noun* (*plural* **-ies**) success in battle, war, or contest.

victual /ˈvɪt(ə)l/ • *noun* (usually in *plural*) food, provisions. • *verb* (**-ll-**; *US* **-l-**) supply with victuals; lay in supply of victuals; eat victuals.

victualler /'vɪtlə/ *noun* (*US* **victualer**) person who supplies victuals; (in full **licensed victualler**) publican licensed to sell alcohol.

vicuña /vɪ'kju:nə/ *noun* S. American mammal with fine silky wool; cloth made from its wool; imitation of this.

vide /'vi:deɪ/ *verb* (in *imperative*) see, consult. [Latin]

videlicet /vɪ'deliset/ *adverb* that is to say; namely.

video /'vɪdɪəʊ/ ● *adjective* relating to recording or reproduction of moving pictures on magnetic tape; of broadcasting of these. ● *noun* (*plural* **-s**) such recording or broadcasting; *colloquial* video recorder; *colloquial* film on videotape. ● *verb* (**-oes, -oed**) record on videotape. □ **video cassette** cassette of videotape; **video game** computer game played on television screen; **video nasty** *colloquial* horrific or pornographic video film; **video (cassette) recorder** apparatus for recording and playing videotapes.

videotape ● *noun* magnetic tape for recording television pictures and sound. ● *verb* (**-ping**) record on this.

vie /vaɪ/ *verb* (**vying**) (often + *with*) contend, compete, strive for superiority.

Vietnamese /vjetnə'mi:z/ ● *adjective* of Vietnam. ● *noun* (*plural* same) native, national, or language of Vietnam.

view /vju:/ ● *noun* range of vision; what is seen, scene, prospect, picture etc. of this; opinion; inspection by eye or mind. ● *verb* look at; survey visually or mentally; form mental impression or opinion of; watch television. □ **in view of** considering; **on view** being shown or exhibited; **viewdata** news and information service from computer source, connected to TV screen by telephone link; **viewfinder** part of camera showing field of photograph; **viewpoint** point of view; **with a view to** with hope or intention of.

viewer *noun* television-watcher; device for looking at film transparencies etc.

vigil /'vɪdʒɪl/ *noun* keeping awake during night etc., esp. to keep watch or pray; eve of festival or holy day.

vigilance *noun* watchfulness; caution. □ **vigilant** *adjective*.

vigilante /vɪdʒɪ'lænti/ *noun* member of self-appointed group for keeping order etc.

vignette /vi:'njet/ *noun* short description, character sketch; illustration not in definite border; photograph etc. with background shaded off.

vigour /'vɪgə/ *noun* (*US* **vigor**) activity and strength of body or mind; healthy growth; animation. □ **vigorous** *adjective*; **vigorously** *adverb*.

Viking /'vaɪkɪŋ/ *noun* Scandinavian raider and pirate of 8th–11th c.

vile *adjective* disgusting; depraved; *colloquial* abominably bad. □ **vilely** *adverb*; **vileness** *noun*.

vilify /'vɪlɪfaɪ/ *verb* (**-ies, -ied**) speak ill of, defame. □ **vilification** *noun*.

villa /'vɪlə/ *noun* country house, mansion; rented holiday home, esp. abroad; detached or semi-detached house in residential district.

village /'vɪlɪdʒ/ *noun* group of houses etc. in country district, larger than hamlet and smaller than town.

villager *noun* inhabitant of village.

villain /'vɪlən/ *noun* wicked person; chief wicked character in play, story, etc.; *colloquial* criminal, rascal.

villainous *adjective* wicked.

villainy *noun* (*plural* **-ies**) wicked behaviour or act.

villein /'vɪlɪn/ *noun historical* feudal tenant entirely subject to lord or attached to manor. □ **villeinage** *noun*.

vim *noun colloquial* vigour, energy.

vinaigrette /vɪnɪ'gret/ *noun* salad dressing of oil and wine vinegar.

vindicate /'vɪndɪkeɪt/ *verb* (**-ting**) clear of suspicion; establish merits, existence, or justice of. □ **vindication** *noun*; **vindicator** *noun*; **vindicatory** *adjective*.

vindictive /vɪn'dɪktɪv/ *adjective* tending to seek revenge. □ **vindictively** *adverb*; **vindictiveness** *noun*.

vine *noun* trailing or climbing woody-stemmed plant, esp. bearing grapes.

vinegar /'vɪnɪgə/ *noun* sour liquid produced by fermentation of wine, malt, cider, etc. □ **vinegary** *adjective*.

vineyard /'vɪnjɑːd/ *noun* plantation of grapevines, esp. for wine-making.

vingt-et-un /vɛ̃teɪˈœ̃/ *noun* = PONTOON[1]. [French]

vino /ˈviːnəʊ/ *noun slang* wine, esp. of inferior kind.

vinous /ˈvaɪnəs/ *adjective* of, like, or due to wine.

vintage /ˈvɪntɪdʒ/ ●*noun* season's produce of grapes, wine from this; grape-harvest, season of this; wine of high quality from particular year and district; year etc. when thing was made, thing made etc. in particular year etc. ●*adjective* of high or peak quality; of a past season. □ **vintage car** car made 1917–1930.

vintner /ˈvɪntnə/ *noun* wine merchant.

vinyl /ˈvaɪnɪl/ *noun* any of group of plastics made by polymerization.

viol /ˈvaɪəl/ *noun* medieval stringed instrument similar in shape to violin.

viola[1] /vɪˈəʊlə/ *noun* instrument like violin but larger and of lower pitch.

viola[2] /ˈvaɪələ/ *noun* any plant of genus including violet and pansy, esp. cultivated hybrid.

viola da gamba /vɪəʊlə də ˈgæmbə/ *noun* viol held between player's legs.

violate /ˈvaɪəleɪt/ *verb* (**-ting**) disregard, break (oath, law, etc.); treat profanely; break in on, disturb; rape. □ **violation** *noun*, **violator** *noun*.

violence /ˈvaɪələns/ *noun* being violent; violent conduct or treatment; unlawful use of force. □ **do violence to** act contrary to, outrage.

violent /ˈvaɪələnt/ *adjective* involving great physical force; intense, vehement; (of death) resulting from violence or poison. □ **violently** *adverb*.

violet /ˈvaɪələt/ ●*noun* plant with usually purple, blue, or white flowers; bluish-purple colour at opposite end of spectrum from red; paint, clothes, or material of this colour. ●*adjective* of this colour.

violin /vaɪəˈlɪn/ *noun* high-pitched instrument with 4 strings played with bow. □ **violinist** *noun*.

violoncello /vaɪələnˈtʃeləʊ/ *noun* (*plural* -**s**) *formal* cello.

VIP *abbreviation* very important person.

viper /ˈvaɪpə/ *noun* small venomous snake; malignant or treacherous person.

virago /vɪˈrɑːgəʊ/ *noun* (*plural* -**s**) fierce or abusive woman.

viral /ˈvaɪər(ə)l/ *adjective* of or caused by virus.

virgin /ˈvɜːdʒɪn/ ●*noun* person who has never had sexual intercourse; (**the Virgin**) Christ's mother Mary. ●*adjective* not yet used etc.; virginal. □ **the Virgin birth** doctrine of Christ's birth from virgin mother. □ **virginity** /vəˈdʒɪn-/ *noun*.

virginal ●*adjective* of or befitting a virgin. ●*noun* (usually in *plural*) legless spinet in box.

Virginia creeper /vəˈdʒɪnɪə/ *noun* vine cultivated for ornament.

Virgo /ˈvɜːgəʊ/ *noun* sixth sign of zodiac.

virile /ˈvɪraɪl/ *adjective* having masculine vigour or strength; sexually potent; of man as distinct from woman or child. □ **virility** /-ˈrɪl-/ *noun*.

virology /vaɪˈrɒlədʒɪ/ *noun* study of viruses.

virtual /ˈvɜːtʃʊəl/ *adjective* being so for practical purposes though not strictly or in name. □ **virtual reality** computer-generated images, sounds, etc. that appear real to the senses. □ **virtually** *adverb*.

virtue /ˈvɜːtʃuː/ *noun* moral goodness; particular form of this; chastity, esp. of woman; good quality; efficacy. □ **by** or **in virtue of** on account of, because of.

virtuoso /vɜːtʃʊˈəʊsəʊ/ *noun* (*plural* -**si** /-siː/ or -**sos**) highly skilled artist, esp. musician. □ **virtuosity** /-ˈɒs-/ *noun*.

virtuous /ˈvɜːtʃʊəs/ *adjective* morally good; *archaic* chaste. □ **virtuously** *adverb*.

virulent /ˈvɪrʊlənt/ *adjective* poisonous; (of disease) violent; bitterly hostile. □ **virulence** *noun*; **virulently** *adverb*.

virus /ˈvaɪərəs/ *noun* microscopic organism able to cause diseases; computer virus.

visa /ˈviːzə/ *noun* endorsement on passport etc., esp. allowing holder to enter or leave country.

visage /ˈvɪzɪdʒ/ *noun literary* face.

vis-à-vis /viːzɑːˈviː/ ●*preposition* in relation to; in comparison with. ●*adverb* opposite. [French]

viscera /ˈvɪsərə/ *plural noun* internal organs of body. □ **visceral** *adjective*.

viscid /ˈvɪsɪd/ *adjective* glutinous, sticky.

viscose /ˈvɪskəʊz/ *noun* viscous form of cellulose used in making rayon etc.; fabric made from this.

viscount /ˈvaɪkaʊnt/ *noun* British nobleman ranking between earl and baron.

viscountess /ˈvaɪkaʊntɪs/ *noun* viscount's wife or widow; woman holding rank of viscount.

viscous /ˈvɪskəs/ *adjective* glutinous, sticky; semifluid; not flowing freely. □ **viscosity** /-kɒs-/ *noun* (*plural* **-ies**).

visibility /vɪzɪˈbɪlɪtɪ/ *noun* being visible; range or possibility of vision as determined by light and weather.

visible /ˈvɪzɪb(ə)l/ *adjective* able to be seen, perceived, or discovered; in sight; apparent, open, obvious. □ **visibly** *adverb.*

vision /ˈvɪʒ(ə)n/ *noun* act or faculty of seeing, sight; thing or person seen in dream or trance; thing seen in imagination; imaginative insight; foresight, good judgement in planning; beautiful person etc.; TV or cinema picture, esp. of specified quality.

visionary ● *adjective* given to seeing visions or to fanciful theories; having vision or foresight; not real, imaginary; unpractical. ● *noun* (*plural* **-ies**) visionary person.

visit /ˈvɪzɪt/ ● *verb* (**-t-**) go or come to see (person, place, etc.); stay temporarily with or at; (of disease, calamity, etc.) attack; (often + *upon*) inflict punishment for (sin). ● *noun* act of visiting, temporary stay with person or at place; (+ *to*) occasion of going to doctor etc.; formal or official call.

visitant /ˈvɪzɪt(ə)nt/ *noun* visitor, esp. ghost etc.

visitation /vɪzɪˈteɪʃ(ə)n/ *noun* official visit of inspection; trouble etc. seen as divine punishment.

visitor *noun* person who visits; migrant bird.

visor /ˈvaɪzə/ *noun* movable part of helmet covering face; shield for eyes, esp. one at top of vehicle windscreen.

vista /ˈvɪstə/ *noun* view, esp. through avenue of trees or other long narrow opening; mental view of long succession of events.

visual /ˈvɪʒʊəl/ *adjective* of or used in seeing. □ **visual display unit** device

displaying data of computer on screen. □ **visually** *adverb.*

visualize *verb* (also **-ise**) (**-zing** or **-sing**) imagine visually. □ **visualization** *noun.*

vital /ˈvaɪt(ə)l/ ● *adjective* of or essential to organic life; essential to existence, success, etc.; full of life or activity; fatal. ● *noun* (in *plural*) vital organs, e.g. lungs and heart. □ **vital statistics** those relating to number of births, marriages, deaths, etc., *jocular* measurements of woman's bust, waist, and hips. □ **vitally** *adverb.*

vitality /vaɪˈtælɪtɪ/ *noun* animation, liveliness; ability to survive or endure.

vitalize *verb* (also **-ise**) (**-zing** or **-sing**) endow with life; make lively or vigorous. □ **vitalization** *noun.*

vitamin /ˈvɪtəmɪn/ *noun* any of various substances present in many foods and essential to health and growth.

vitaminize *verb* (also **-ise**) (**-zing** or **-sing**) introduce vitamins into (food).

vitiate /ˈvɪʃɪeɪt/ *verb* (**-ting**) impair, debase; make invalid or ineffectual.

viticulture /ˈvɪtɪkʌltʃə/ *noun* cultivation of grapes.

vitreous /ˈvɪtrɪəs/ *adjective* of or like glass.

vitrify /ˈvɪtrɪfaɪ/ *verb* (**-ies**, **-ied**) change into glass or glassy substance, esp. by heat. □ **vitrification** *noun.*

vitriol /ˈvɪtrɪəl/ *noun* sulphuric acid or sulphate; caustic speech or criticism. □ **vitriolic** /-ˈɒl-/ *adjective.*

vitro see IN VITRO.

vituperate /vaɪˈtjuːpəreɪt/ *verb* (**-ting**) criticize abusively. □ **vituperation** *noun;* **vituperative** /-rətɪv/ *adjective.*

viva[1] /ˈvaɪvə/ *colloquial* ● *noun* (*plural* **-s**) viva voce. ● *verb* (**vivas**, **vivaed**, **vivaing**) viva-voce.

viva[2] /ˈviːvə/ ● *interjection* long live. ● *noun* cry of this as salute etc. [Italian]

vivacious /vɪˈveɪʃəs/ *adjective* lively, animated. □ **vivacity** /vɪˈvæsɪtɪ/ *noun.*

vivarium /vaɪˈveərɪəm/ *noun* (*plural* **-ria** or **-s**) glass bowl etc. for keeping animals for scientific study; place for keeping animals in (nearly) their natural conditions.

viva voce /vaɪvə ˈvəʊtʃɪ/ ● *adjective* oral. ● *adverb* orally. ● *noun* oral exam.

viva-voce *verb* (**-vocees**, **-voceed**, **-voceing**) examine orally.

vivid /'vɪvɪd/ *adjective* (of light or colour) bright, strong, intense; (of memory, description, etc.) lively, incisive, graphic. □ **vividly** *adverb*; **vividness** *noun*.

vivify /'vɪvɪfaɪ/ *verb* (**-ies**, **-ied**) give life to, animate.

viviparous /vɪ'vɪpərəs/ *adjective* bringing forth young alive.

vivisect /'vɪvɪsekt/ *verb* perform vivisection on.

vivisection /vɪvɪ'sekʃ(ə)n/ *noun* surgical experimentation on living animals for scientific research. □ **vivisectionist** *noun*.

vixen /'vɪks(ə)n/ *noun* female fox; spiteful woman.

viz. *abbreviation* videlicet.

vizier /vɪ'zɪə/ *noun historical* high official in some Muslim countries.

V-neck *noun* V-shaped neckline on pullover etc.

vocabulary /və'kæbjʊlərɪ/ *noun* (*plural* **-ies**) words used by language, book, branch of science, or author; list of these; person's range of language.

vocal /'vəʊk(ə)l/ *adjective* of or uttered by voice; speaking one's feelings freely. □ **vocal cords** voice-producing part of larynx. □ **vocally** *adverb*.

vocalist *noun* singer.

vocalize *verb* (also **-ise**) (**-zing** or **-sing**) form (sound) or utter (word) with voice; articulate, express. □ **vocalization** *noun*.

vocation /vəʊ'keɪʃ(ə)n/ *noun* divine call to, or sense of suitability for, career or occupation; employment, trade, profession. □ **vocational** *adjective*.

vocative /'vɒkətɪv/ ● *noun* case of noun used in addressing person or thing. ● *adjective* of or in this case.

vociferate /və'sɪfəreɪt/ *verb* (**-ting**) utter noisily; shout, bawl. □ **vociferation** *noun*.

vociferous /və'sɪfərəs/ *adjective* noisy, clamorous; loud and insistent in speech. □ **vociferously** *adverb*.

vodka /'vɒdkə/ *noun* alcoholic spirit distilled esp. in Russia from rye etc.

vogue /vəʊg/ *noun* (**the vogue**) prevailing fashion; popular use. □ **in vogue** in fashion. □ **voguish** *adjective*.

voice ● *noun* sound formed in larynx and uttered by mouth, esp. in speaking, singing, etc.; ability to produce this; use of voice, spoken or written expression, opinion so expressed, right to express opinion; *Grammar* set of verbal forms showing whether verb is active or passive. ● *verb* (**-cing**) express; (esp. as **voiced** *adjective*) utter with vibration of vocal cords. □ **voice-over** commentary in film by unseen speaker.

void ● *adjective* empty, vacant; not valid or binding. ● *noun* empty space, sense of loss. ● *verb* invalidate; excrete.

voile /vɔɪl/ *noun* thin semi-transparent fabric.

vol. *abbreviation* volume.

volatile /'vɒlətaɪl/ *adjective* changeable in mood, flighty; unstable; evaporating rapidly. □ **volatility** /-'tɪl-/ *noun*.

vol-au-vent /'vɒləʊvɒ̃/ *noun* small round case of puff pastry with savoury filling.

volcanic /vɒl'kænɪk/ *adjective* of, like, or produced by volcano.

volcano /vɒl'keɪnəʊ/ *noun* (*plural* **-es**) mountain or hill from which lava, steam, etc. escape through earth's crust.

vole *noun* small plant-eating rodent.

volition /və'lɪʃ(ə)n/ *noun* act or power of willing. □ **of one's own volition** voluntarily.

volley /'vɒlɪ/ ● *noun* (*plural* **-s**) simultaneous firing of a number of weapons; bullets etc. so fired; (usually + *of*) torrent (of abuse etc.); *Tennis, Football, etc.* playing of ball before it touches ground. ● *verb* (**-eys**, **-eyed**) return or send by volley. □ **volleyball** game for two teams of 6 hitting large ball by hand over net.

volt /vəʊlt/ *noun* SI unit of electromotive force. □ **voltmeter** instrument measuring electric potential in volts.

voltage *noun* electromotive force expressed in volts.

volte-face /vɒlt'fɑːs/ *noun* (*plural* **voltes-face** same pronunciation) complete change of position in one's attitude or opinion.

voluble /'vɒljʊb(ə)l/ *adjective* speaking or spoken fluently or with continuous flow of words. □ **volubility** *noun*; **volubly** *adverb*.

volume /'vɒljuːm/ *noun* single book forming part or all of work; solid content, bulk; space occupied by gas or liquid; (+ *of*) amount or quantity of; quantity or power of sound; (+ *of*) moving mass of (water, smoke, etc.).

voluminous /və'luːmɪnəs/ *adjective* (of drapery etc.) loose and ample; written or writing at great length.

voluntary /'vɒləntrɪ/ ● *adjective* done, acting, or given willingly; unpaid; (of institution) supported or built by charity; brought about by voluntary action; (of muscle, limb, etc.) controlled by will. ● *noun* (*plural* **-ies**) organ solo played before or after church service. □ **voluntarily** *adverb*.

volunteer /vɒlən'tɪə/ ● *noun* person who voluntarily undertakes task or enters military etc. service. ● *verb* (often + *to*) undertake or offer voluntarily; (often + *for*) be volunteer.

voluptuary /və'lʌptʃʊərɪ/ *noun* (*plural* **-ies**) person who seeks luxury and sensual pleasure.

voluptuous /və'lʌptʃʊəs/ *adjective* of, tending to, occupied with, or derived from, sensuous or sensual pleasure; (of woman) curvaceous and sexually desirable. □ **voluptuously** *adverb*.

vomit /'vɒmɪt/ ● *verb* (**-t-**) eject (contents of stomach) through mouth, be sick; (of volcano, chimney, etc.) eject violently, belch forth. ● *noun* matter vomited from stomach.

voodoo /'vuːduː/ ● *noun* religious witchcraft as practised esp. in W. Indies. ● *verb* (**-doos**, **-dooed**) affect by voodoo; bewitch.

voracious /və'reɪʃəs/ *adjective* greedy in eating, ravenous; very eager. □ **voraciously** *adverb*; **voracity** /-'ræs-/ *noun*.

vortex /'vɔːteks/ *noun* (*plural* **-texes** or **-tices** /-tɪsiːz/) whirlpool, whirlwind; whirling motion or mass; thing viewed as destructive or devouring.

votary /'vəʊtərɪ/ *noun* (*plural* **-ies**; *feminine* **votaress**) (usually + *of*) person dedicated to service of god or cult; devotee of a person, occupation etc.

vote ● *noun* formal expression of choice or opinion by ballot, show of hands, etc.; (usually **the vote**) right to vote; opinion expressed by vote; votes given by or for particular group. ● *verb* (**-ting**) (often + *for*, *against*) give vote; enact etc. by majority of votes; *colloquial* pronounce by general consent; (often + *that*) suggest, urge. □ **vote down** defeat (proposal etc.) by voting; **vote in** elect by voting; **vote with one's feet** *colloquial* indicate opinion by one's presence or absence.

voter *noun* person voting or entitled to vote.

votive /'vəʊtɪv/ *adjective* given or consecrated in fulfilment of vow.

vouch /vaʊtʃ/ *verb* (+ *for*) answer or be surety for.

voucher *noun* document exchangeable for goods or services; receipt.

vouchsafe /vaʊtʃ'seɪf/ *verb* (**-fing**) *formal* condescend to grant; (+ *to do*) condescend.

vow /vaʊ/ ● *noun* solemn, esp. religious, promise. ● *verb* promise solemnly; *archaic* declare solemnly.

vowel /'vaʊəl/ *noun* speech sound made by vibrations of vocal cords, but without audible friction; letter(s) representing this.

■ **Usage** The (written) vowels of English are customarily said to be *a*, *e*, *i*, *o*, and *u*, but *y* can be either a consonant (as in *yet*) or a vowel (as in *by*), and combinations of these six, such as *ee* in *keep*, *ie* in *tied*, *ou* in *pour*, and *ye* in *rye*, are just as much vowels.

vox pop *noun colloquial* popular opinion as represented by informal comments.

vox populi /vɒks 'pɒpjʊlaɪ/ *noun* public opinion, popular belief. [Latin]

voyage /'vɔɪdʒ/ ● *noun* journey, esp. long one by sea or in space. ● *verb* (**-ging**) make voyage. □ **voyager** *noun*.

voyeur /vwɑː'jɜː/ *noun* person who derives sexual pleasure from secretly observing others' sexual activity or organs; (esp. covert) spectator. □ **voyeurism** *noun*; **voyeuristic** /-'rɪs-/ *adjective*.

vs. *abbreviation* versus.

VSO *abbreviation* Voluntary Service Overseas.

VTOL /'viːtɒl/ *abbreviation* vertical take-off and landing.

vulcanite /'vʌlkənaɪt/ *noun* hard black vulcanized rubber.

vulcanize /'vʌlkənaɪz/ *verb* (also **-ise**) (**-zing** or **-sing**) make (rubber etc.) stronger and more elastic by treating with sulphur at high temperature. □ **vulcanization** *noun*.

vulgar /'vʌlgə/ *adjective* coarse; of or characteristic of the common people; in common use, prevalent. □ **vulgar fraction** fraction expressed by numerator and denominator (e.g. ½), not decimally (e.g. 0.5); **the vulgar tongue** native or vernacular language. □ **vulgarity** /-'gær-/ *noun* (*plural* **-ies**); **vulgarly** *adverb*.

vulgarian /vʌl'geərɪən/ *noun* vulgar (esp. rich) person.

vulgarism *noun* vulgar word or expression.

vulgarize /'vʌlgəraɪz/ *verb* (also **-ise**) (**-zing** or **-sing**) make vulgar; spoil by popularizing. □ **vulgarization** *noun*.

Vulgate /'vʌlgeɪt/ *noun* 4th-c. Latin version of Bible.

vulnerable /'vʌlnərəb(ə)l/ *adjective* easily wounded or harmed; (+ *to*) open to attack, injury, or criticism. □ **vulnerability** *noun*.

vulpine /'vʌlpaɪn/ *adjective* of or like fox; crafty, cunning.

vulture /'vʌltʃə/ *noun* large carrion-eating bird of prey; rapacious person.

vulva /'vʌlvə/ *noun* (*plural* **-s**) external female genitals.

vv. *abbreviation* verses.

vying *present participle* of VIE.

Ww

W *abbreviation* (also **W.**) watt(s); west(ern).

w. *abbreviation* wicket(s); wide(s); with.

wacky /'wækɪ/ *adjective* (**-ier, -iest**) *slang* crazy.

wad /wɒd/ • *noun* lump of soft material to keep things apart or in place or to block hole; roll of banknotes. • *verb* (**-dd-**) stop up or fix with wad; line, stuff, or protect with wadding.

wadding *noun* soft fibrous material for stuffing quilts, packing fragile articles in, etc.

waddle /'wɒd(ə)l/ • *verb* (**-ling**) walk with short steps and swaying motion. • *noun* such walk.

wade • *verb* (**-ding**) walk through water, mud, etc., esp. with difficulty; (+ *through*) go through (tedious task, book, etc.); (+ *into*) *colloquial* attack (person, task). • *noun* spell of wading. □ **wade in** *colloquial* make vigorous attack or intervention.

wader *noun* long-legged waterfowl; (in *plural*) high waterproof boots.

wadi /'wɒdɪ/ *noun* (*plural* **-s**) rocky watercourse in N. Africa etc., dry except in rainy season.

wafer /'weɪfə/ *noun* very thin light crisp biscuit; disc of unleavened bread used in Eucharist; disc of red paper stuck on legal document instead of seal. □ **wafer-thin** very thin.

waffle[1] /'wɒf(ə)l/ *colloquial* • *noun* aimless verbose talk or writing. • *verb* (**-ling**) indulge in waffle.

waffle[2] /'wɒf(ə)l/ *noun* small crisp batter cake. □ **waffle-iron** utensil for cooking waffles.

waft /wɒft/ • *verb* convey or be conveyed smoothly (as) through air or over water. • *noun* whiff.

wag[1] • *verb* (**-gg-**) shake or wave to and fro. • *noun* single wagging motion. □ **wagtail** small bird with long tail.

wag[2] *noun* facetious person.

wage • *noun* (in *singular* or *plural*) employee's regular pay, esp. paid weekly. • *verb* (**-ging**) carry on (war etc.).

waged *adjective* in regular paid employment.

wager /'weɪdʒə/ *noun & verb* bet.

waggish *adjective* playful, facetious. □ **waggishly** *adverb*.

waggle /'wæg(ə)l/ *verb* (**-ling**) *colloquial* wag.

wagon /'wægən/ *noun* (also **waggon**) 4-wheeled vehicle for heavy loads; open railway truck. □ **on the wagon** *slang* abstaining from alcohol; **wagon-load** as much as wagon can carry.

wagoner *noun* (also **waggoner**) driver of wagon.

waif *noun* homeless and helpless person, esp. abandoned child; ownerless object or animal.

wail ● *noun* prolonged plaintive inarticulate cry of pain, grief, etc.; sound resembling this. ● *verb* utter wail; lament or complain persistently.

wain *noun* *archaic* wagon.

wainscot /'weɪnskət/ *noun* (also **wainscoting**) boarding or wooden panelling on room-wall.

waist *noun* part of human body between ribs and hips; narrowness marking this; circumference of waist; narrow middle part of anything; part of garment encircling waist; *US* bodice, blouse; part of ship between forecastle and quarterdeck. □ **waistband** strip of cloth forming waist of garment; **waistcoat** usually sleeveless and collarless waist-length garment; **waistline** outline or size of waist.

wait ● *verb* defer action until expected event occurs; await (turn etc.); (of thing) remain in readiness; (usually as **waiting** *noun*) park briefly; act as waiter or attendant; (+ *on, upon*) await convenience of, be attendant to. ● *noun* act or period of waiting; (usually + *for*) watching for enemy; (in *plural*) archaic street singers of Christmas carols. □ **waiting-list** list of people waiting for thing not immediately available; **waiting-room** room for people to wait in, esp. at surgery or railway station.

waiter *noun* (*feminine* **waitress**) person who serves at hotel or restaurant tables.

waive *verb* (**-ving**) refrain from insisting on or using.

waiver *noun* *Law* (document recording) waiving.

wake[1] ● *verb* (**-king**; *past* **woke**; *past participle* **woken** /'wəʊk(ə)n/) (often + *up*) (cause to) cease to sleep or become alert; *archaic* (except as **waking** *adjective* & *noun*) be awake; disturb with noise; evoke. ● *noun* (chiefly in Ireland) vigil beside corpse before burial, attendant lamentations and merrymaking; (usually in *plural*) annual holiday in (industrial) N. England.

wake[2] *noun* track left on water's surface by moving ship etc.; turbulent air left by moving aircraft. □ **in the wake of** following, as result of.

wakeful *adjective* unable to sleep; sleepless; vigilant. □ **wakefully** *adverb*; **wakefulness** *noun*.

waken /'weɪkən/ *verb* make or become awake.

walk /wɔːk/ ● *verb* move by lifting and setting down each foot in turn, never having both feet off the ground at once; (of quadruped) go with slowest gait; travel or go on foot, take exercise thus; traverse (distance) in walking; tread floor or surface of; cause to walk with one. ● *noun* act of walking, ordinary human gait; slowest gait of animal; person's manner of walking; distance walkable in specified time; excursion on foot; place or track meant or fit for walking. □ **walkabout** informal stroll by royal person etc., Australian Aboriginal's period of wandering; **walking frame** tubular metal frame to assist elderly or disabled people in walking; **walking stick** stick carried for support when walking; **walk off with** *colloquial* steal, win easily; **walk of life** one's occupation; **walk-on part** short or non-speaking dramatic part; **walk out** depart suddenly or angrily, stop work in protest; **walk-out** *noun*; **walk out on** desert; **walkover** easy victory; **walk the streets** be prostitute; **walkway** passage or path for walking along. □ **walkable** *adjective*.

walker *noun* person etc. that walks; framework in which baby can walk unaided; walking frame.

walkie-talkie /wɔːkɪ'tɔːkɪ/ *noun* portable two-way radio.

Walkman /'wɔːkmən/ *noun* (*plural* **-s**) *proprietary term* type of personal stereo.

wall /wɔːl/ ● *noun* continuous narrow upright structure of usually brick or stone, esp. enclosing or dividing a space or supporting a roof; thing like wall in appearance or effect; outermost layer of animal or plant organ, cell, etc. ● *verb* (esp. as **walled** *adjective*) surround with wall; (usually + *up*, *off*) block with wall; (+ *up*) enclose within sealed space. □ **go to the wall** fare badly in competition; **up the wall** *colloquial* crazy, furious; **wallflower** fragrant garden plant, *colloquial* woman not dancing because partnerless; **wall game** Eton form of football; **wallpaper** *noun* paper for covering interior walls of rooms, *verb* decorate with wallpaper; **wall-to-wall** fitted to cover whole floor, *colloquial* ubiquitous.

wallaby /ˈwɒləbɪ/ *noun* (*plural* **-ies**) small kangaroo-like marsupial.

wallah /ˈwɒlə/ *noun slang* person connected with a specified occupation or thing.

wallet /ˈwɒlɪt/ *noun* small flat case for holding banknotes etc.

wall-eye *noun* eye with whitish iris or outward squint. □ **wall-eyed** *adjective*.

wallop /ˈwɒləp/ *colloquial* ● *verb* (**-p-**) thrash, beat. ● *noun* whack; beer.

wallow /ˈwɒləʊ/ ● *verb* roll about in mud etc.; (+ *in*) indulge unrestrainedly in. ● *noun* act of wallowing; place where animals wallow.

wally /ˈwɒlɪ/ *noun* (*plural* **-ies**) *slang* foolish or incompetent person.

walnut /ˈwɔːlnʌt/ *noun* tree with aromatic leaves and drooping catkins; its nut; its timber.

walrus /ˈwɔːlrəs/ *noun* (*plural* same or **walruses**) long-tusked amphibious arctic mammal. □ **walrus moustache** long thick drooping moustache.

waltz /wɔːls/ ● *noun* ballroom dance in triple time; music for this. ● *verb* dance waltz; (often + *in*, *out*, *round*, etc.) *colloquial* move easily, casually, etc.

wampum /ˈwɒmpəm/ *noun* strings of shell-beads formerly used by N. American Indians for money, ornament, etc.

wan /wɒn/ *adjective* (**-nn-**) pale, weary-looking. □ **wanly** *adverb*.

wand /wɒnd/ *noun* fairy's or magician's magic stick; staff as sign of office etc.; *colloquial Music* conductor's baton.

wander /ˈwɒndə/ *verb* (often + *in*, *off*, etc.) go from place to place aimlessly; meander; diverge from path etc.; talk or think incoherently, be inattentive or delirious. □ **wanderlust** eagerness to travel or wander, restlessness. □ **wanderer** *noun*.

wane ● *verb* (**-ning**) (of moon) decrease in apparent size; decrease in power, vigour, importance, size, etc. ● *noun* process of waning. □ **on the wane** declining.

wangle /ˈwæŋg(ə)l/ *colloquial* ● *verb* (**-ling**) contrive to obtain (favour etc.). ● *noun* act of wangling.

wannabe /ˈwɒnəbɪ/ *noun slang* avid fan who apes person admired; anyone wishing to be someone else.

want /wɒnt/ ● *verb* (often + *to do*) desire; wish for possession of; need; (+ *to do*) *colloquial* should; (usually + *for*) lack; be without or fall short by; (as **wanted** *adjective*) (of suspected criminal etc.) sought by police. ● *noun* lack, deficiency; poverty, need.

wanting *adjective* lacking (in quality or quantity), unequal to requirements; absent.

wanton /ˈwɒnt(ə)n/ ● *adjective* licentious; capricious, arbitrary; luxuriant, wild. ● *noun literary* licentious person. □ **wantonly** *adverb*.

wapiti /ˈwɒpɪtɪ/ *noun* (*plural* **-s**) large N. American deer.

war /wɔː/ ● *noun* armed hostility, esp. between nations; specific period of this; hostility between people; (often + *on*) efforts against crime, poverty, etc. ● *verb* (**-rr-**) (as **warring** *adjective*) rival, fighting; make war. □ **at war** engaged in war; **go to war** begin war; **on the warpath** going to war, *colloquial* seeking confrontation; **war crime** crime violating international laws of war; **war cry** phrase or name shouted to rally troops, party slogan; **war dance** dance performed by primitive peoples before battle or after victory; **warhead** explosive head of missile; **warhorse** *historical* trooper's horse, *colloquial* veteran soldier; **war memorial** monument to those killed in (a) war; **warmonger** /-mʌŋgə/ person who promotes war; **warpaint** paint put on body esp. by N. American Indians before battle, *colloquial* make-up; **warship** ship used in war.

warble /'wɔːb(ə)l/ ● verb (**-ling**) sing in a gentle trilling way. ● noun warbling sound.

warbler noun bird that warbles.

ward /wɔːd/ noun separate division or room of hospital etc.; administrative division, esp. for elections; minor etc. under care of guardian or court; (in plural) corresponding notches and projections in key and lock; archaic guardianship. □ **ward off** parry (blow), avert (danger etc.); **wardroom** officers' mess in warship.

warden /'wɔːd(ə)n/ noun supervising official; president or governor of institution; traffic warden.

warder /'wɔːdə/ noun (feminine **wardress**) prison officer.

wardrobe /'wɔːdrəʊb/ noun large cupboard for storing clothes; stock of clothes; theatre's costume department. □ **wardrobe master, mistress** person in charge of theatrical wardrobe.

wardship noun tutelage.

ware noun things of specified kind made usually for sale; (usually in plural) articles for sale.

warehouse ● noun building in which goods are stored; wholesale or large retail store. ● verb (**-sing**) store in warehouse.

warfare /'wɔːfeə/ noun waging war, campaigning.

warlike adjective hostile; soldierly; military.

warlock /'wɔːlɒk/ noun archaic sorcerer.

warm /wɔːm/ ● adjective of or at fairly high temperature; (of person) with skin at natural or slightly raised temperature; (of clothes) affording warmth; hearty, enthusiastic; sympathetic, friendly, loving; colloquial dangerous, hostile; colloquial (in game) near object sought, near to guessing; (of colour) reddish or yellowish, suggesting warmth; (of scent in hunting) fresh and strong. ● verb make or become warm. ● noun act of warming; warmth. □ **warm-blooded** (of animals) having blood temperature well above that of environment; **warm-hearted** kind, friendly; **warming-pan** historical flat closed vessel holding hot coals for warming beds; **warm up** make or become warm, prepare for performance etc. by practising, reach temperature for efficient working, reheat (food); **warm-up** noun. □ **warmly** adverb; **warmth** noun.

warn /wɔːn/ verb (often + of, that) inform of impending danger or misfortune; (+ to do) advise (person) to take certain action; (often + against) inform (person) about specific danger. □ **warn off** tell (person) to keep away (from).

warning noun what is said or done or occurs to warn person.

warp /wɔːp/ ● verb make or become distorted, esp. through heat, damp, etc.; make or become perverted or strange; haul (ship etc.) by rope attached to fixed point. ● noun warped state; mental perversion; lengthwise threads in loom; rope used in warping ship.

warrant /'wɒrənt/ ● noun thing that authorizes an action; written authorization, money voucher, etc.; written authorization allowing police to carry out search or arrest; certificate of service rank held by warrant officer. ● verb serve as warrant for, justify; guarantee. □ **warrant officer** officer ranking between commissioned and non-commissioned officers.

warranty /'wɒrənti/ noun (plural **-ies**) undertaking as to ownership or quality of thing sold etc., often accepting responsibility for repairs needed over specified period; authority, justification.

warren /'wɒrən/ noun network of rabbit burrows; densely populated or labyrinthine building or district.

warrior /'wɒriə/ noun person skilled in or famed for fighting.

wart /wɔːt/ noun small round dry growth on skin; protuberance on skin of animal, surface of plant, etc. □ **wart-hog** African wild pig. □ **warty** adjective.

wary /'weəri/ adjective (**-ier, -iest**) on one's guard, circumspect; cautious. □ **warily** adverb; **wariness** noun.

was 1st & 3rd singular past of BE.

wash /wɒʃ/ ● verb cleanse with liquid; (+ out, off, away, etc.) remove or be removed by washing; wash oneself or one's hands (and face); wash clothes, dishes, etc.; (of fabric or dye) bear washing without damage; bear scrutiny, be believed or acceptable; (of river etc.) touch; (of liquid) carry along in specified direction; sweep, move, splash; (+ *over*) occur without affecting (person); sift (ore) by action of water; brush watery colour over; *poetical* moisten. ● *noun* washing, being washed; clothes for washing or just washed; motion of agitated water or air, esp. due to passage of vessel or aircraft; kitchen slops given to pigs; thin, weak, inferior, or animals' liquid food; liquid to spread over surface to cleanse, heal, or colour. □ **washbasin** basin for washing one's hands etc.; **washboard** ribbed board for washing clothes, this as percussion instrument; **wash down** wash completely, (usually + *with*) accompany or follow (food); **washed out** faded, pale, *colloquial* exhausted; **washed up** *esp. US slang* defeated, having failed; **wash one's hands of** decline responsibility for; **wash out** clean inside of by washing, *colloquial* cause to be cancelled because of rain; **wash-out** *colloquial* complete failure; **washroom** *esp. US* public toilet; **washstand** piece of furniture for holding washbasin, soap-dish, etc.; **wash up** wash (dishes etc.) after use, *US* wash one's face and hands, (of sea) carry on to shore. □ **washable** *adjective*.

washer *noun* person or thing that washes; flat ring placed between two surfaces or under plunger of tap, nut, etc. to tighten joint or disperse pressure.

washerwoman *noun* laundress.

washing *noun* clothes etc. for washing or just washed. □ **washing machine** machine for washing clothes; **washing powder** soap powder or detergent for washing clothes; **washing-up** washing of dishes etc., dishes etc. for washing.

washy *adjective* (**-ier, -iest**) too watery or weak; lacking vigour.

wasn't /ˈwɒz(ə)nt/ was not.

Wasp /wɒsp/ *noun* (also **WASP**) *US usually derogatory* middle-class white American [Anglo-Saxon] Protestant.

wasp /wɒsp/ *noun* stinging insect with black and yellow stripes. □ **wasp-waist** very slender waist.

waspish *adjective* irritable, snappish.

wassail /ˈwɒseɪl/ *archaic* ● *noun* festive drinking. ● *verb* make merry.

wastage /ˈweɪstɪdʒ/ *noun* amount wasted; loss by use, wear, or leakage; (also **natural wastage**) loss of employees other than by redundancy.

waste ● *verb* (**-ting**) use to no purpose or for inadequate result or extravagantly; fail to use; (often + *on*) give (advice etc.) without effect; (in *passive*) fail to be appreciated or used properly; wear away; make or become weak; devastate. ● *adjective* superfluous, no longer needed; uninhabited, not cultivated. ● *noun* act of wasting; waste material; waste region; diminution by wear; waste pipe. □ **go, run to waste** be wasted; **wasteland** land not productive or developed, spiritually or intellectually barren place or time; **waste paper** used or valueless paper; **waste pipe** pipe carrying off waste material; **waste product** useless by-product of manufacture or organism.

wasteful *adjective* extravagant; causing or showing waste. □ **wastefully** *adverb*.

waster *noun* wasteful person; *colloquial* wastrel.

wastrel /ˈweɪstr(ə)l/ *noun* good-for-nothing person.

watch /wɒtʃ/ ● *verb* keep eyes fixed on; keep under observation, follow observantly; (often + *for*) be in alert state, be vigilant; (+ *over*) look after, take care of. ● *noun* small portable timepiece for wrist or pocket; state of alert or constant attention; *Nautical* usually 4-hour spell of duty; *historical* (member of) body of men patrolling streets at night. □ **on the watch for** waiting for (anticipated event); **watchdog** dog guarding property, person etc. monitoring others' rights etc.; **watching brief** brief of barrister who follows case for client not directly concerned; **watchman** man employed to look after empty building etc. at night; **watch out** (often + *for*) be on one's guard; **watch-tower** tower for observing prisoners, attackers, etc.; **watchword** phrase summarizing guiding principle. □ **watcher** *noun* (also *in combination*).

watchful *adjective* accustomed to watching; on the watch. □ **watchfully** *adverb*; **watchfulness** *noun*.

water /ˈwɔːtə/ ●*noun* transparent colourless liquid found in seas and rivers etc. and in rain etc.; sheet or body of water; (in *plural*) part of sea or river; (often **the waters**) mineral water at spa etc.; state of tide; solution of specified substance in water; transparency and lustre of gem; (usually in *plural*) amniotic fluid. ●*verb* sprinkle or soak with water; supply (plant or animal) with water; secrete water; (as **watered** *adjective*) (of silk etc.) having irregular wavy finish; take in supply of water. □ **make water** urinate; **water-bed** mattress filled with water; **water biscuit** thin unsweetened biscuit; **water buffalo** common domestic Indian buffalo; **water cannon** device giving powerful water-jet to disperse crowd etc.; **water chestnut** corm from a sedge, used in Chinese cookery; **water-closet** lavatory that can be flushed; **watercolour** pigment mixed with water and not oil, picture painted or art of painting with this; **watercourse** stream of water, bed of this; **watercress** pungent cress growing in running water; **water-diviner** dowser; **water down** dilute, make less forceful or horrifying; **waterfall** stream or river falling over precipice or down steep hill; **waterfowl** bird(s) frequenting water; **waterfront** part of town adjoining river etc.; **waterhole** shallow depression in which water collects; **water-ice** flavoured and frozen water and sugar; **watering-can** portable container for watering plants; **watering-place** pool where animals drink, spa or seaside resort; **water jump** jump over water in steeplechase etc.; **water level** surface of water, height of this, water table; **water lily** aquatic plant with floating leaves and flowers; **waterline** line where surface of water touches ship's side; **waterlogged** saturated or filled with water; **water main** main pipe in water supply system; **waterman** boatman plying for hire; **watermark** faint design made in paper by maker; **water-meadow** meadow periodically flooded by stream; **water melon** large dark green melon with red pulp and watery juice; **water-mill** mill worked by waterwheel; **water pistol** toy pistol shooting jet of water; **water polo** game played by swimmers with ball like football; **water-power** mechanical force from weight or motion of water; **waterproof** *adjective* impervious to water, *noun* such garment or material, *verb* make waterproof; **water-rat** water vole; **water rate** charge for use of public water supply; **watershed** line between waters flowing to different river basins, turning point in events; **waterside** edge of sea, lake, or river; **water-ski** ski (esp. one of pair) on which person is towed across water by motor boat; **waterspout** gyrating column of water and spray between sea and cloud; **water table** plane below which ground is saturated with water; **watertight** so closely fastened or fitted that water cannot leak through, (of argument etc.) unassailable; **water tower** tower with elevated tank to give pressure for distributing water; **water vole** aquatic vole; **waterway** navigable channel; **waterwheel** wheel driven by water to drive machinery or to raise water; **water-wings** inflated floats used to support person learning to swim; **waterworks** establishment for managing water supply, *colloquial* shedding of tears, *colloquial* urinary system.

watery *adjective* containing too much water; too thin in consistency; of or consisting of water; vapid, uninteresting; (of colour) pale; (of sun, moon, or sky) rainy-looking; (of eyes) moist.

watt /wɒt/ *noun* SI unit of power.

wattage *noun* amount of electrical power expressed in watts.

wattle[1] /ˈwɒt(ə)l/ *noun* interlaced rods and sticks used for fences etc.; Australian acacia with fragrant golden yellow flowers. □ **wattle and daub** network of rods and twigs plastered with clay or mud as building material.

wattle[2] /ˈwɒt(ə)l/ *noun* fleshy appendage hanging from head or neck of turkey etc.

wave ●*verb* (**-ving**) move (hand etc.) to and fro in greeting or as signal; show sinuous or sweeping motion; give such motion to; direct (person) or express (greeting etc.) by waving; give undulating form to, have such form. ●*noun*

moving ridge of water between two
depressions; long body of water curling
into arch and breaking on shore; thing
compared to this; gesture of waving;
curved shape in hair; temporary occurrence or heightening of condition or
influence; disturbance carrying motion, heat, light, sound, etc. through
esp. fluid medium; single curve in this.
□ **wave aside** dismiss as intrusive or
irrelevant; **waveband** radio wavelengths between certain limits; **wave
down** wave to (vehicle or driver) to
stop; **wavelength** distance between
successive crests of wave, this as distinctive feature of radio waves from a
transmitter, *colloquial* person's way of
thinking.

wavelet *noun* small wave.

waver /'weɪvə/ *verb* be or become unsteady or irresolute, begin to give way.

wavy *adjective* (**-ier, -iest**) having waves
or alternate contrary curves. □ **wavi-
ness** *noun*.

wax[1] ● *noun* sticky pliable yellowish
substance secreted by bees as material
of honeycomb; this bleached and purified for candles, modelling, etc.; any
similar substance. ● *verb* cover or treat
with wax; remove hair from (legs etc.)
using wax. □ **waxwork** object, esp. lifelike dummy, modelled in wax, (in *plural*)
exhibition of wax dummies.

wax[2] *verb* (of moon) increase in apparent size; grow larger or stronger; become.

waxen *adjective* smooth or pale like wax;
archaic made of wax.

way ● *noun* road, track, path, street;
course, route; direction; method,
means; style, manner; habitual course
of action; normal course of events;
distance (to be) travelled; unimpeded
opportunity or space to advance; advance, progress; specified condition or
state; respect, sense. ● *adverb colloquial*
far. □ **by the way** incidentally; **by way
of** by means of, as a form of, passing
through; **give way** yield under pressure, give precedence; **in the way, in
(person's) way** forming obstruction
(to); **lead the way** act as guide or
leader; **make one's way** go, prosper;
make way for allow to pass, be superseded by; **out of the way** not forming

obstruction, disposed of, unusual, remote; **pay its** or **one's way** cover costs,
pay one's expenses as they arise;
under way in motion or progress; **way
back** *colloquial* long ago; **wayfarer** traveller, esp. on foot; **waylay** lie in wait
for, stop to accost or rob; **way of life**
principles or habits governing one's
actions; **way-out** *colloquial* unusual, eccentric; **wayside** (land at) side of road.

wayward /'weɪwəd/ *adjective* childishly
self-willed; capricious. □ **wayward-
ness** *noun*.

WC *abbreviation* water-closet; West Central.

W/Cdr. *abbreviation* Wing Commander.

we /wiː/ *pronoun* used by speaker or
writer to refer to himself or herself and
one or more others as subject of *verb*;
used for I by sovereign in formal
contexts or by editorial writer in newspaper.

weak *adjective* lacking in strength,
power, vigour, resolution, or number;
unconvincing; (of verb) forming inflections by suffix. □ **weak-kneed** *colloquial*
lacking resolution; **weak-minded**
mentally deficient, lacking resolution.
□ **weaken** *verb*.

weakling *noun* feeble person or animal.

weakly ● *adverb* in a weak way. ● *adjective*
(**-ier, -iest**) sickly, not robust.

weakness *noun* being weak; weak
point; self-indulgent liking.

weal[1] ● *noun* ridge raised on flesh by
stroke of rod or whip. ● *verb* raise weals
on.

weal[2] *noun literary* welfare.

wealth /welθ/ *noun* riches; being rich;
abundance.

wealthy *adjective* (**-ier, -iest**) having
abundance, esp. of money.

wean *verb* accustom (infant or other
young mammal) to food other than
mother's milk; (often + *from, away
from*) disengage (from habit etc.) by
enforced discontinuance.

weapon /'wepən/ *noun* thing designed,
used, or usable for inflicting bodily
harm; means for gaining advantage in
a conflict.

weaponry *noun* weapons collectively.

wear /weə/ ● *verb* (*past* **wore**; *past participle*
worn) have on one's person as cloth-
ing, ornament, etc.; exhibit (expression

etc.); *colloquial* (usually in negative) tolerate; (often + *away*, *down*) damage or deteriorate gradually by use or attrition; make (hole etc.) by attrition; (often + *out*) exhaust; (+ *down*) overcome by persistence; (+ *well* etc.) endure continued use or life; (of time) pass, esp. tediously. ●*noun* wearing, being worn; things worn; fashionable or suitable clothing; (in full **wear and tear**) damage from continuous use. □ **wear out** use or be used until useless, tire or be tired out. □ **wearer** *noun*.

wearisome /'wɪərɪsəm/ *adjective* tedious, monotonous.

weary /'wɪərɪ/ ● *adjective* (**-ier**, **-iest**) very tired, intensely fatigued; (+ *of*) tired of; tiring, tedious. ● *verb* (**-ies**, **-ied**) make or become weary. □ **wearily** *adverb*; **weariness** *noun*.

weasel /'wiːz(ə)l/ *noun* small ferocious reddish-brown flesh-eating mammal.

weather /'weðə/ ● *noun* atmospheric conditions at specified place or time as regards heat, cloudiness, humidity, sunshine, wind, and rain etc. ● *verb* expose to or affect by atmospheric changes, season (wood); be discoloured or worn thus; come safely through (storm etc.); get to windward of. □ **make heavy weather of** *colloquial* exaggerate difficulty of; **under the weather** *colloquial* unwell, depressed; **weather-beaten** affected by exposure to weather; **weatherboard** board attached at bottom of door to keep out rain, each of series of overlapping horizontal boards on wall; **weathercock** weather vane in form of cock, inconstant person; **weather forecast** prediction of likely weather; **weather vane** revolving pointer on church spire etc. to show direction of wind.

weave[1] ● *verb* (**-ving**; *past* **wove** /wəʊv/; *past participle* **woven**) form (fabric) by interlacing threads, form (threads) into fabric, esp. in loom; (+ *into*) make (facts etc.) into story or connected whole; make (story etc.) thus. ● *noun* style of weaving.

weave[2] *verb* (**-ving**) move repeatedly from side to side; take intricate course.

weaver *noun* person who weaves fabric; (in full **weaver-bird**) tropical bird building elaborately woven nest.

web *noun* woven fabric; amount woven in one piece; complex series; cobweb or similar tissue; membrane connecting toes of aquatic bird or other animal; large roll of paper for printing. □ **web-footed** having toes connected by web. □ **webbed** *adjective*.

webbing *noun* strong narrow closely woven fabric for belts etc.

weber /'veɪbə/ *noun* SI unit of magnetic flux.

Wed. *abbreviation* (also **Weds.**) Wednesday.

wed *verb* (**-dd-**; *past & past participle* **wedded** or **wed**) *usually formal or literary* marry; unite; (as **wedded** *adjective*) of or in marriage; (+ *to*) obstinately attached to (pursuit etc.).

we'd /wiːd/ we had; we should; we would.

wedding /'wedɪŋ/ *noun* marriage ceremony. □ **wedding breakfast** meal etc. between wedding and departure for honeymoon; **wedding cake** rich decorated cake served at wedding reception; **wedding ring** ring worn by married person.

wedge ● *noun* piece of tapering wood, metal, etc., used for forcing things apart or fixing them immovably etc.; wedge-shaped thing. ● *verb* (**-ging**) secure or force open or apart with wedge; (+ *in*, *into*) pack or force (thing, oneself) in or into. □ **thin end of the wedge** *colloquial* small beginning that may lead to something more serious.

wedlock /'wedlɒk/ *noun* married state. □ **born in** or **out of wedlock** born of married or unmarried parents.

Wednesday /'wenzdeɪ/ *noun* day of week following Tuesday.

wee *adjective* (**weer** /'wiːə/, **weest** /'wiːɪst/) *esp. Scottish* little; *colloquial* tiny.

weed ● *noun* wild plant growing where it is not wanted; lanky and weakly person or horse; (**the weed**) *slang* marijuana, tobacco. ● *verb* rid of weeds or unwanted parts; (+ *out*) sort out and remove (inferior or unwanted parts etc.), rid of inferior or unwanted parts etc.; remove or destroy weeds.

weeds *plural noun* (in full **widow's weeds**) *archaic* deep mourning worn by widow.

weedy *adjective* (**-ier, -iest**) weak, feeble; full of weeds.

week *noun* 7-day period reckoned usually from Saturday midnight; any 7-day period; the 6 days between Sundays; the 5 days Monday to Friday, period of work then done. □ **weekday** day other than (Saturday or) Sunday; **weekend** Saturday and Sunday.

weekly ● *adjective* done, produced, or occurring once a week. ● *adverb* once a week. ● *noun* (*plural* **-ies**) weekly newspaper or periodical.

weeny /'wiːnɪ/ *adjective* (**-ier, -iest**) *colloquial* tiny.

weep ● *verb* (*past & past participle* **wept**) shed tears; (often + *for*) lament over; be covered with or send forth throes, exude liquid; come or send forth in drops; (as **weeping** *adjective*) (of tree) have drooping branches. ● *noun* spell of weeping.

weepie *noun colloquial* sentimental or emotional film, play, etc.

weepy *adjective* (**-ier, -iest**) *colloquial* inclined to weep, tearful.

weevil /'wiːvɪl/ *noun* destructive beetle feeding esp. on grain.

weft *noun* threads woven across warp to make fabric.

weigh /weɪ/ *verb* find weight of; balance in hand (as if) to guess weight of; (often + *out*) take definite weight of (substance), measure out (specified weight); estimate relative value or importance of; (+ *with, against*) compare with; be of specified weight or importance; have influence; (often + *on*) be heavy or burdensome (to); raise (anchor). □ **weighbridge** weighing machine for vehicles; **weigh down** bring down by weight, oppress; **weigh in** (of boxer before contest, or jockey after race) be weighed; **weigh-in** *noun*; **weigh in with** *colloquial* advance (argument etc.) confidently; **weigh up** *colloquial* form estimate of; **weigh one's words** carefully choose words to express something.

weight /weɪt/ ● *noun* force on a body due to earth's gravitation; heaviness of body; quantitative expression of a body's weight, scale of such weights; body of known weight for use in weighing or weight training; heavy body, esp. used in mechanism etc.; load, burden; influence, importance; preponderance (of evidence etc.). ● *verb* attach a weight to, hold down with a weight; impede, burden. □ **pull one's weight** do fair share of work; **weightlifting** sport of lifting heavy objects; **weight training** physical training using weights. □ **weightless** *adjective*.

weighting *noun* extra pay in special cases.

weighty *adjective* (**-ier, -iest**) heavy; momentous; deserving attention; influential, authoritative.

weir /wɪə/ *noun* dam across river to retain water and regulate its flow.

weird /wɪəd/ *adjective* uncanny, supernatural; *colloquial* queer, incomprehensible. □ **weirdly** *adverb*; **weirdness** *noun*.

welch = **welsh**.

welcome /'welkəm/ ● *noun* kind or glad greeting or reception. ● *interjection* expressing such greeting. ● *verb* (**-ming**) receive with welcome. ● *adjective* gladly received; (+ *to*) cordially allowed or invited to. □ **make welcome** receive hospitably.

weld ● *verb* join (pieces of metal or plastic) using heat, usually from electric arc; fashion into effectual or homogeneous whole. ● *noun* welded joint. □ **welder** *noun*.

welfare /'welfeə/ *noun* well-being, happiness; health and prosperity (of person, community, etc.); (**Welfare**) financial support from state. □ **welfare state** system of social services controlled or financed by government, state operating this; **welfare work** organized effort for welfare of poor, disabled, etc.

welkin /'welkɪn/ *noun poetical* sky.

well[1] ● *adverb* (**better, best**) in satisfactory way; with distinction; in kind way; thoroughly, carefully; with heartiness or approval; probably, reasonably; to considerable extent; *slang* extremely. ● *adjective* (**better, best**) in good health; in satisfactory state or position, advisable. ● *interjection* expressing astonishment, resignation, etc., or introducing speech. □ **as well** in addition, advisable, desirable, reasonably; **as well as** in addition to; **well-adjusted** mentally and emotionally stable; **well-advised** prudent; **well and truly** decisively, completely; **well-appointed** properly equipped or fitted out; **well away** having made considerable progress, *colloquial* fast asleep or drunk; **well-balanced** sane, sensible; **well-being** happiness, health, prosperity; **well-born** of noble family; **well-bred** having or showing good breeding or manners; **well-built** big, strong, and shapely; **well-connected** related to good families; **well-disposed** (often + *towards*) friendly, sympathetic; **well-earned** fully deserved; **well-founded** based on good evidence; **well-groomed** with carefully tended hair, clothes, etc.; **well-heeled** *colloquial* wealthy; **well-informed** having much knowledge or information; **well-intentioned** having or showing good intentions; **well-judged** opportunely, skilfully, or discreetly done; **well-known** known to many; **well-meaning, -meant** well-intentioned; **well-nigh** almost; **well off** rich, fortunately situated; **well-read** having read (and learnt) much; **well-spoken** articulate or refined in speech; **well-to-do** prosperous; **well-tried** often tested with good result; **well-wisher** person who wishes another well; **well-worn** much used, trite.

well² ● *noun* shaft sunk in ground to obtain water, oil, etc.; enclosed space resembling well-shaft, e.g. central space in building for staircase, lift, light, or ventilation; source; (in *plural*) spa; inkwell; railed space in law court. ● *verb* (+ *out, up*) rise or flow as water from well. □ **well-head, -spring** source.

we'll /wiːl/ we shall; we will.

wellington /'welɪŋt(ə)n/ *noun* (in full **wellington boot**) waterproof rubber boot usually reaching knee.

welly /'welɪ/ *noun* (*plural* **-ies**) *colloquial* wellington.

Welsh ● *adjective* of Wales. ● *noun* language of Wales; (**the Welsh**) (treated as *plural*) the Welsh people. □ **Welshman, Welshwoman** native of Wales; **Welsh rarebit** dish of melted cheese etc. on toast.

welsh *verb* (also **welch** /welʃ/) (of loser of bet, esp. bookmaker) evade an obligation; (+ *on*) fail to carry out promise to (person), fail to honour (obligation).

welt ● *noun* leather rim sewn to shoe-upper for sole to be attached to; weal; ribbed or reinforced border of garment; heavy blow. ● *verb* provide with welt; raise weals on, thrash.

welter /'weltə/ ● *verb* roll, wallow; (+ *in*) be soaked in. ● *noun* general confusion; disorderly mixture.

welterweight /'weltəweɪt/ *noun* amateur boxing weight (63.5–67 kg).

wen *noun* benign tumour on skin.

wench *noun* jocular girl, young woman.

wend *verb* □ **wend one's way** go.

went *past* of GO¹.

wept *past & past participle* of WEEP.

were *2nd singular past, plural past,* and *past subjunctive* of BE.

we're /wɪə/ we are.

weren't /wɜːnt/ were not.

werewolf /'weəwʊlf/ *noun* (*plural* **-wolves**) *Mythology* human being who changes into wolf.

Wesleyan /'wezlɪən/ ● *adjective* of Protestant denomination founded by John Wesley. ● *noun* member of this denomination.

west ● *noun* point of horizon where sun sets at equinoxes; corresponding compass point; (usually **the West**) European civilization, western part of world, country, town, etc. ● *adjective* towards, at, near, or facing west; (of wind) from west. ● *adverb* towards, at, or near west; (+ *of*) further west than. □ **go west** *slang* be killed or wrecked etc.; **westbound** travelling or leading west; **West End** fashionable part of London; **west-north-west, west-south-west** point midway between west and north-west or south-west. □ **westward** *adjective, adverb, & noun;* **westwards** *adverb.*

westering /'westərɪŋ/ *adjective* (of sun) nearing the west.

westerly /'westəlɪ/ ● *adjective & adverb* in western position or direction; (of wind) from west. ● *noun* (*plural* **-ies**) wind from west.

western /'west(ə)n/ ● *adjective* of or in west. ● *noun* film or novel about cowboys in western N. America. □ **westernize** *verb* (also **-ise**) (**-zing** or **-sing**); **westernmost** *adjective.*

westerner noun native or inhabitant of west.

wet ● adjective (-tt-) soaked or covered with water or other liquid; (of weather) rainy; (of paint) not yet dried; used with water; colloquial feeble. ● verb (-tt-; past & past participle **wet** or **wetted**) make wet; urinate in or on. ● noun liquid that wets something; rainy weather; colloquial feeble or spiritless person; colloquial liberal Conservative; colloquial drink. □ **wet blanket** gloomy person discouraging cheerfulness etc.; **wet-nurse** noun woman employed to suckle another's child, verb act as wet-nurse to, colloquial treat as if helpless.

wether /'weðə/ noun castrated ram.

we've /wiːv/ we have.

Wg. Cdr. abbreviation Wing Commander.

whack colloquial ● verb hit forcefully; (as **whacked** adjective) tired out. ● noun sharp or resounding blow; slang share.

whacking colloquial ● adjective large. ● adverb very.

whale ● noun (plural same or **-s**) large fishlike marine mammal. ● verb (-ling) hunt whales. □ **whalebone** elastic horny substance in upper jaw of some whales.

whaler noun whaling ship or seaman.

wham interjection colloquial: expressing forcible impact.

wharf /wɔːf/ ● noun (plural **wharves** /wɔːvz/ or **-s**) quayside structure for loading or unloading of moored vessels. ● verb moor (ship) at wharf; store (goods) on wharf.

what /wɒt/ ● interrogative adjective used in asking someone to specify one or more things from an indefinite number. ● adjective (usually in exclamation) how great, how remarkable. ● relative adjective the or any … that. ● interrogative pronoun what thing(s); what did you say? ● relative pronoun the things which; anything that. □ **whatever** anything at all that, no matter what, (with negative or in questions) at all, of any kind; **what for?** colloquial for what reason?; **what have you** colloquial anything else similar; **whatnot** unspecified thing; **what not** colloquial other similar things; **whatsoever** whatever; **know what's what** colloquial have common sense,

know what is useful or important; **what with** colloquial because of.

wheat noun cereal plant bearing dense 4-sided seed-spikes; its grain used for flour etc. □ **wheat germ** wheat embryo extracted as source of vitamins; **wheatmeal** flour from wheat with some bran and germ removed.

wheatear /'wiːtɪə/ noun small migratory bird.

wheaten adjective made of wheat.

wheedle /'wiːd(ə)l/ verb (-ling) coax by flattery or endearments; (+ **out**) get (thing) from person or cheat (person) of thing by wheedling.

wheel ● noun circular frame or disc revolving on axle and used to propel vehicle or other machinery; wheel-like thing; motion as of wheel; movement of line of men etc. with one end as pivot; (in plural) slang car. ● verb turn on axis or pivot; swing round in line with one end as pivot; (often + **about, around**) (cause to) change direction or face another way; push or pull (wheeled thing, or its load or occupant); go in circles or curves. □ **wheel and deal** engage in political or commercial scheming; **wheelbarrow** small cart with one wheel at front and two handles; **wheelbase** distance between axles of vehicle; **wheelchair** disabled person's chair on wheels; **wheel-spin** rotation of vehicle's wheels without traction; **wheels within wheels** intricate machinery, colloquial indirect or secret agencies; **wheelwright** maker or repairer of wheels.

wheelie noun slang manoeuvre on bicycle or motorcycle with front wheel off the ground.

wheeze ● verb (-zing) breathe or utter with audible whistling sound. ● noun sound of wheezing; colloquial clever scheme. □ **wheezy** adjective (-ier, -iest).

whelk noun spiral-shelled marine mollusc.

whelp ● noun young dog, puppy; archaic cub; ill-mannered child or youth. ● verb give birth to puppies.

when ● interrogative adverb at what time. ● relative adverb (time etc.) at or on which. ● conjunction at the or any time that; as soon as; although; after which, and then, but just then. ● *pronoun* what time; which time. □ **whenever, whensoever** at whatever time, on whatever occasion, every time that.

whence *archaic or formal* ● *interrogative adverb* from what place. ● *relative adverb* (place etc.) from which. ● *conjunction* to the place from which.

where /weə/ ● *interrogative adverb* in or to what place; in what direction; in what respect. ● *relative adverb* (place etc.) in or to which. ● *conjunction* in or to the or any place, direction, or respect in which; and there. ● *interrogative pronoun* what place. ● *relative pronoun* the place in or to which. □ **whereabouts** *interrogative adverb* approximately where, *noun* person's or thing's location; **whereas** in contrast or comparison with the fact that, taking into consideration the fact that; **whereby** by what or which means; **wherefore** *archaic* for what or which reason; **wherein** *formal* in what or which; **whereof** *formal* of what or which; **whereupon** immediately after which; **wherever** anywhere at all that, no matter where; **wherewithal** /-wɪðɔːl/ *colloquial* money etc. needed for a purpose.

wherry /'werɪ/ *noun* (*plural* **-ies**) light rowing boat, usually for carrying passengers; large light barge.

whet *verb* (**-tt-**) sharpen; stimulate (appetite etc.). □ **whetstone** stone for sharpening cutting-tools.

whether /'weðə/ *conjunction introducing first or both of alternative possibilities.*

whew /hwjuː/ *interjection expressing astonishment, consternation, or relief.*

whey /weɪ/ *noun* watery liquid left when milk forms curds.

which ● *interrogative adjective used in asking someone to specify one or more things from a definite set of alternatives.* ● *relative adjective* being the one just referred to, and this or these. ● *interrogative pronoun* which person(s) or thing(s). ● *relative pronoun* which thing(s). □ **whichever** any which, no matter which.

whiff *noun* puff of air, smoke, etc.; smell; (+ *of*) trace of; small cigar.

Whig *noun historical* member of British political party succeeded by Liberals. □ **Whiggery** *noun*; **Whiggish** *adjective*; **Whiggism** *noun*.

while ● *noun* period of time. ● *conjunction* during the time that, for as long as, at the same time as; although, whereas. ● *verb* (**-ling**) (+ *away*) pass (time etc.) in leisurely or interesting way. ● *relative adverb* (time etc.) during which. □ **for a while** for some time; **in a while** soon; **once in a while** occasionally.

whilst /waɪlst/ *adverb & conjunction* while.

whim *noun* sudden fancy, caprice.

whimper /'wɪmpə/ *verb* make feeble, querulous, or frightened sounds. ● *noun* such sound.

whimsical /'wɪmzɪk(ə)l/ *adjective* capricious, fantastic. □ **whimsicality** /-'kæl-/ *noun*; **whimsically** *adverb*.

whimsy /'wɪmzɪ/ *noun* (*plural* **-ies**) whim.

whin *noun* (in *singular* or *plural*) gorse. □ **whinchat** small songbird.

whine ● *noun* long-drawn complaining cry (as) of dog or child; querulous tone or complaint. ● *verb* (**-ning**) emit or utter whine(s); complain.

whinge /wɪndʒ/ *verb* (**-geing** or **-ging**) *colloquial* complain peevishly.

whinny /'wɪnɪ/ ● *noun* (*plural* **-ies**) gentle or joyful neigh. ● *verb* (**-ies, -ied**) emit whinny.

whip ● *noun* lash attached to stick, for urging on or for punishing; person appointed by political party to control its discipline and tactics in Parliament; whip's written notice requesting member's attendance; food made with whipped cream etc.; whipper-in. ● *verb* (**-pp-**) beat or urge on with whip; beat (eggs, cream, etc.) into froth; take or move suddenly or quickly; *slang* steal, excel, defeat; bind with spirally wound twine; sew with overcast stitches. □ **whipcord** tightly twisted cord; **(the) whip hand** advantage, control; **whiplash** sudden jerk; **whipper-in** huntsman's assistant who manages hounds; **whipping boy** scapegoat; **whip-round** *colloquial* informal collection of money among group of people; **whipstock** handle of whip.

whippersnapper /'wɪpəsnæpə/ *noun* small child; insignificant but presumptuous person.

whippet /'wɪpɪt/ *noun* crossbred dog of greyhound type, used for racing.

whippoorwill /'wɪpʊəwɪl/ *noun* N. American nightjar.

whirl ●*verb* swing round and round, revolve rapidly; (+ *away*) convey or go rapidly in car etc.; send or travel swiftly in orbit or curve; (of brain etc.) seem to spin round. ●*noun* whirling movement; state of intense activity or confusion. □ **give it a whirl** *colloquial* attempt it; **whirlpool** circular eddy in sea, river, etc.; **whirlwind** *noun* whirling mass or column of air, *adjective* very rapid.

whirligig /'wɜːlɪɡɪɡ/ *noun* spinning or whirling toy; merry-go-round; revolving motion.

whirr ●*noun* continuous buzzing or softly clicking sound. ●*verb* (**-rr-**) make this sound.

whisk ●*verb* (+ *away*, *off*) brush with sweeping movement, take suddenly; whip (cream, eggs, etc.); convey or go lightly or quickly; wave (object). ●*noun* whisking movement; utensil for whipping eggs, cream, etc.; bunch of twigs, bristles, etc. for brushing or dusting.

whisker /'wɪskə/ *noun* (usually in *plural*) hair on cheeks or sides of face of man; each of bristles on face of cat etc.; *colloquial* small distance. □ **whiskered** *adjective*; **whiskery** *adjective*.

whisky /'wɪskɪ/ *noun* (*Irish & US* **whiskey**) (*plural* **-ies** or **-eys**) spirit distilled esp. from malted barley.

whisper /'wɪspə/ ●*verb* speak using breath instead of vocal cords; talk or say in barely audible tone or confidential way; rustle, murmur. ●*noun* whispering speech or sound; thing whispered.

whist *noun* card game, usually for two pairs of opponents. □ **whist drive** whist-party with players moving on from table to table.

whistle /'wɪs(ə)l/ ●*noun* clear shrill sound made by forcing breath through lips contracted to narrow opening; similar sound made by bird, wind, missile, etc.; instrument used to produce such sound. ●*verb* (**-ling**) emit whistle; give signal or express surprise or derision by whistling; (often + *up*) summon or give signal to thus; produce (tune) by whistling; (+ *for*) seek or desire in vain. □ **whistle-stop** *US* small unimportant town on railway; politician's brief pause for electioneering speech on tour.

Whit ●*noun* Whitsuntide. ●*adjective* of Whitsuntide. □ **Whit Sunday** 7th Sunday after Easter, commemorating Pentecost.

whit *noun* particle, least possible amount.

white ●*adjective* of colour produced by reflection or transmission of all light; of colour of snow or milk; pale; of the human racial group having light-coloured skin; albino; (of hair) having lost its colour; (of coffee) with milk or cream. ●*noun* white colour, paint, clothes, etc.; (in *plural*) white garments worn in cricket, tennis, etc.; (player using) lighter-coloured pieces in chess etc.; egg white; whitish part of eyeball round iris; white person. □ **white ant** termite; **whitebait** small silvery-white food-fish; **white cell** leucocyte; **white-collar** (of worker or work) non-manual, clerical, professional; **white corpuscle** leucocyte; **white elephant** useless possession; **white feather** symbol of cowardice; **white flag** symbol of surrender; **white goods** large domestic electrical equipment; **white heat** degree of heat making metal glow white, state of intense anger or passion; **white-hot** *adjective*; **white hope** person expected to achieve much; **white horses** white-crested waves; **white lead** mixture containing lead carbonate used as white pigment; **white lie** harmless or trivial untruth; **white magic** magic used for beneficent purposes; **white meat** poultry, veal, rabbit, and pork; **White Paper** government report giving information; **white pepper** pepper made by grinding husked berry; **white sauce** sauce of flour, melted butter, and milk or cream; **white slave** woman entrapped for prostitution; **white spirit** light petroleum as solvent; **white sugar** purified sugar; **white tie** man's white bow tie as part of full evening dress; **whitewash** *noun* solution of chalk or lime for whitening walls etc., means of glossing over faults, *verb* apply whitewash (to), gloss over, clear of blame; **white wedding** wedding where bride wears formal white dress; **whitewood** light-coloured wood, esp. prepared for staining etc. □ **whiten** *verb*; **whitener** *noun*; **whiteness** *noun*; **whitish** *adjective*.

whither /'wɪðə/ *archaic* ● *interrogative adverb* to what place. ● *relative adverb* (place etc.) to which.

whiting¹ /'waɪtɪŋ/ *noun* (*plural* same) small edible sea fish.

whiting² /'waɪtɪŋ/ *noun* ground chalk used in whitewashing etc.

whitlow /'wɪtləʊ/ *noun* inflammation near fingernail or toenail.

Whitsun /'wɪts(ə)n/ ● *noun* Whitsuntide. ● *adjective* of Whitsuntide.

Whitsuntide *noun* weekend or week including Whit Sunday.

whittle /'wɪt(ə)l/ *verb* (**-ling**) (often + *at*) pare (wood etc.) by cutting thin slices or shavings from surface; (often + *away*, *down*) reduce by repeated subtractions.

whiz (also **whizz**) ● *noun* sound made by object moving through air at great speed. ● *verb* (**-zz-**) move with or make a whiz. □ **whiz-kid** *colloquial* brilliant or highly successful young person.

WHO *abbreviation* World Health Organization.

who /huː/ ● *interrogative pronoun* what or which person(s), what sort of person(s). ● *relative pronoun* (person or persons) that. □ **whoever, whosoever** the or any person(s) who; no matter who.

whoa /wəʊ/ *interjection* used to stop or slow horse etc.

who'd /huːd/ who had; who would.

whodunit /huːˈdʌnɪt/ *noun* (also **whodunnit**) *colloquial* detective story, play, or film.

whole /həʊl/ ● *adjective* uninjured, unbroken, intact, undiminished; not less than; all, all of. ● *noun* complete thing; all of a thing; (+ *of*) all members etc. of. □ **on the whole** all things considered; **wholefood** food not artificially processed or refined; **wholehearted** completely devoted, done with all possible effort or sincerity; **wholeheartedly** *adverb*; **wholemeal** meal or flour made from whole grains of wheat.

wholesale /'həʊlseɪl/ ● *noun* selling in large quantities, esp. for retail by others. ● *adjective & adverb* by wholesale; on a large scale. ● *verb* (**-ling**) sell wholesale. □ **wholesaler** *noun*.

wholesome *adjective* promoting physical, mental, or moral health; prudent.

wholly /'həʊllɪ/ *adverb* entirely, without limitation; purely.

whom /huːm/ *pronoun* (as object of verb) who. □ **whomever** (as object of verb) whoever; **whomsoever** (as object of verb) whosoever.

whoop /huːp, wuːp/ ● *noun* cry expressing excitement etc.; characteristic drawing-in of breath after cough in whooping cough. ● *verb* utter whoop. □ **whooping cough** /'huːpɪŋ/ infectious disease, esp. of children, with violent convulsive cough.

whoopee /wʊˈpiː/ *interjection* expressing wild joy. □ **make whoopee** /'wʊpɪ/ *colloquial* make merry, make love.

whoops /wʊps/ *interjection colloquial apology for obvious mistake.*

whop *verb* (**-pp-**) *slang* thrash, defeat.

whopper *noun slang* big specimen; great lie.

whopping *adjective colloquial* huge.

whore /hɔː/ *noun* prostitute; *derogatory* promiscuous woman. □ **whorehouse** brothel.

whorl /wɜːl/ *noun* ring of leaves etc. round stem; one turn of spiral.

whortleberry /'wɜːt(ə)lberɪ/ *noun* (*plural* **-ies**) bilberry.

who's /huːz/ who is; who has.

■ **Usage** Because it has an apostrophe, *who's* is easily confused with *whose*. They are each correctly used in *Who's there?* (= Who is there?), *Who's taken my pen?* (= Who has taken my pen?), and *Whose book is this?* (= Who does this book belong to?).

whose /huːz/ ● *interrogative, pronoun, & adjective* of whom. ● *relative adjective* of whom or which.

why /waɪ/ ● *interrogative adverb* for what reason or purpose. ● *relative adverb* (reason etc.) for which. ● *interjection expressing surprise, impatience, reflection, or protest.* □ **whys and wherefores** reasons, explanation.

WI *abbreviation* West Indies; Women's Institute.

wick *noun* strip or thread feeding flame with fuel.

wicked /ˈwɪkɪd/ *adjective* (**-er**, **-est**) sinful, immoral; spiteful; playfully malicious; *colloquial* very bad; *slang* excellent. □ **wickedly** *adverb*; **wickedness** *noun*.

wicker /ˈwɪkə/ *noun* plaited osiers etc. as material for chairs, baskets, etc. □ **wickerwork** wicker, things made of wicker.

wicket /ˈwɪkɪt/ *noun Cricket* 3 upright stumps with bails in position defended by batsman, ground between the two wickets, state of this, batsman's being got out; (in full **wicket-door**, **-gate**) small door or gate, esp. beside or in larger one. □ **wicket-keeper** fielder close behind batsman's wicket.

wide ● *adjective* having sides far apart, broad, not narrow; (following measurement) in width; extending far, not restricted; liberal, not specialized; open to full extent; (+ *of*) not within reasonable distance of, far from. ● *adverb* to full extent; far from target etc. ● *noun* wide ball. □ **-wide** extending over whole of; **wide awake** fully awake, *colloquial* wary or knowing; **wide ball** *Cricket* ball judged by umpire to be beyond batsman's reach; **wide-eyed** surprised, naïve; **widespread** widely distributed. □ **widen** *verb*.

widely *adverb* far apart; extensively; by many people; considerably.

widgeon /ˈwɪdʒ(ə)n/ *noun* (also **wigeon**) kind of wild duck.

widow /ˈwɪdəʊ/ ● *noun* woman who has lost her husband by death and not married again. ● *verb* make into widow or widower; (as **widowed** *adjective*) bereft by death of spouse. □ **widow's peak** V-shaped growth of hair on forehead. □ **widowhood** *noun*.

widower /ˈwɪdəʊə/ *noun* man who has lost his wife by death and not married again.

width *noun* measurement from side to side; large extent; liberality of views etc.; piece of material of full width. □ **widthways** *adverb*.

wield /wiːld/ *verb* hold and use, control, exert.

wife *noun* (*plural* **wives**) married woman, esp. in relation to her husband. □ **wifely** *adjective*.

wig *noun* artificial head of hair.

wigeon = WIDGEON.

wiggle /ˈwɪg(ə)l/ *colloquial* ● *verb* (**-ling**) move from side to side etc. ● *noun* wiggling movement; kink in line etc. □ **wiggly** *adjective* (**-ier**, **-iest**).

wight /waɪt/ *noun archaic* person.

wigwam /ˈwɪgwæm/ *noun* N. American Indian's hut or tent.

wilco /ˈwɪlkəʊ/ *interjection colloquial:* expressing compliance or agreement.

wild /waɪld/ ● *adjective* in original natural state; not domesticated, cultivated, or civilized; unrestrained, disorderly; tempestuous; intensely eager, frantic; (+ *about*) *colloquial* enthusiastically devoted to; *colloquial* infuriated; random, ill-aimed, rash. ● *adverb* in a wild way. ● *noun* wild place, desert. □ **like wildfire** with extraordinary speed; **run wild** grow or stray unchecked or undisciplined; **wild card** card having any rank chosen by its player, person or thing usable in different ways; **wildcat** *noun* hot-tempered or violent person, *adjective* (of strike) sudden and unofficial, reckless, financially unsound; **wild-goose chase** foolish or hopeless quest; **wildlife** wild animals collectively; **Wild West** western US in lawless times. □ **wildly** *adverb*; **wildness** *noun*.

wildebeest /ˈwɪldəbiːst/ *noun* (*plural* same or **-s**) gnu.

wilderness /ˈwɪldənɪs/ *noun* desert, uncultivated area; confused assemblage.

wile ● *noun* (usually in *plural*) stratagem, trick. ● *verb* (**-ling**) lure.

wilful /ˈwɪlfʊl/ *adjective* (*US* **willful**) intentional, deliberate; obstinate. □ **wilfully** *adverb*.

will[1] *auxiliary verb* (*3rd singular present* **will**) *used to form future tenses; expressing request as question;* be able to; have tendency to; be likely to.

will[2] ● *noun* faculty by which person decides what to do; fixed desire or intention; will-power; legal written directions for disposal of one's property etc. after death; disposition towards others. ● *verb* try to cause by will-power; intend, desire; bequeath by will. □ **at will** whenever one wishes; **will-power** control by purpose over impulse; **with a will** vigorously.

willing /ˈwɪlɪŋ/ *adjective* ready to consent or undertake; given etc. by willing person. □ **willingly** *adverb*; **willingness** *noun*.

will-o'-the-wisp /wɪləðə'wɪsp/ *noun* phosphorescent light seen on marshy ground; elusive person.

willow /'wɪləʊ/ *noun* waterside tree with pliant branches yielding osiers. □ **willowherb** plant with leaves like willow; **willow-pattern** conventional Chinese design of blue on white china etc.

willowy *adjective* lithe and slender; having willows.

willy-nilly /wɪlɪ'nɪlɪ/ *adverb* whether one likes it or not.

wilt ● *verb* wither, droop; lose energy. ● *noun* plant disease causing wilting.

wily /'waɪlɪ/ *adjective* (**-ier, -iest**) crafty, cunning.

wimp *noun* *colloquial* feeble or ineffectual person. □ **wimpish** *adjective*.

wimple /'wɪmp(ə)l/ *noun* headdress covering neck and sides of face, worn by some nuns.

win ● *verb* (**-nn-**; *past & past participle* **won** /wʌn/) secure as result of fight, contest, bet, etc.; be victor, be victorious in. ● *noun* victory in game etc. □ **win the day** be victorious in battle, argument, etc.; **win over** gain support of; **win through, out** overcome obstacles.

wince ● *noun* start or involuntary shrinking movement of pain etc. ● *verb* (**-cing**) give wince.

winceyette /wɪnsɪ'et/ *noun* lightweight flannelette.

winch ● *noun* crank of wheel or axle; windlass. ● *verb* lift with winch.

wind[1] /wɪnd/ ● *noun* air in natural motion; breath, esp. as needed in exertion or playing wind instrument; power of breathing easily; empty talk; gas generated in bowels etc.; wind instruments of orchestra etc.; scent carried by the wind. ● *verb* exhaust wind of by exertion or blow; make (baby) bring up wind after feeding; detect presence of by scent. □ **get wind of** begin to suspect; **get, have the wind up** *colloquial* become, be, frightened; **in the wind** *colloquial* about to happen; **put the wind up** *colloquial* frighten; **take the wind out of (person's) sails** frustrate by anticipation; **windbag** *colloquial* person who talks a lot but says little of value; **wind-break** thing that breaks force of

wind; **windcheater** windproof jacket; **windfall** fruit blown down by wind, unexpected good fortune, esp. legacy; **wind instrument** musical instrument sounded by air-current; **wind-jammer** merchant sailing ship; **windmill** mill worked by action of wind on sails, toy with curved vanes revolving on stick; **windpipe** air-passage between throat and lungs; **windscreen** screen of glass at front of car etc.; **windscreen wiper** rubber etc. blade to clear windscreen of rain etc.; **windshield** *US* windscreen; **wind-sock** canvas cylinder or cone on mast to show direction of wind; **windswept** exposed to high winds; **wind-tunnel** enclosed chamber for testing (models or parts of) aircraft etc. in winds of known velocities.

wind[2] /waɪnd/ ● *verb* (*past & past participle* **wound** /waʊnd/) go in spiral, crooked, or curved course; make (one's way) thus; wrap closely, coil; provide with coiled thread etc.; surround (as) with coil; wind up (clock etc.). ● *noun* bend or turn in course. □ **wind down** lower by winding, unwind, approach end gradually; **winding-sheet** sheet in which corpse is wrapped for burial; **wind up** *verb* coil whole of, tighten coiling or coiled spring of, *colloquial* increase intensity of, *colloquial* provoke to anger etc., bring to conclusion, arrange affairs of and dissolve (company), cease business and go into liquidation, *colloquial* arrive finally; **wind-up** *noun* conclusion, *colloquial* attempt to provoke.

windlass /'wɪndləs/ *noun* machine with horizontal axle for hauling or hoisting.

window /'wɪndəʊ/ *noun* opening, usually with glass, in wall etc. to admit light etc.; the glass itself; space for display behind window of shop; window-like opening; transparent part in envelope showing address; opportunity for study or action. □ **window-box** box placed outside window for cultivating plants; **window-dressing** art of arranging display in shop window etc., adroit presentation of facts etc. to give falsely favourable impression; **window-pane** glass pane in window; **window-seat** seat below window, seat next to window in aircraft etc.; **window-shop** look at goods in shop windows without buying anything.

windsurfing noun sport of riding on water on sailboard. □ **windsurf** verb; **windsurfer** noun.

windward /'wɪndwəd/ • adjective & adverb on or towards side from which wind is blowing. • noun this direction.

windy adjective (-ier, -iest) stormy with or exposed to wind; generating or characterized by flatulence; colloquial wordy; colloquial apprehensive, frightened. □ **windiness** noun.

wine • noun fermented grape juice as alcoholic drink; fermented drink resembling this made from other fruits etc.; colour of red wine. • verb (-ning) drink wine; entertain with wine. □ **wine bar** bar or small restaurant where wine is main drink available; **wine cellar** cellar for storing wine, its contents; **wineglass** glass for wine, usually with stem and foot; **winepress** press in which grape juice is extracted for wine; **wine waiter** waiter responsible for serving wine.

wing • noun each of the limbs or organs by which bird etc. flies; winglike part supporting aircraft; projecting part of building; Football etc. forward player at either end of line, side part of playing area; (in plural) sides of theatre stage; extreme section of political party; flank of battle array; part of vehicle over wheel; air-force unit of several squadrons. • verb travel or traverse on wings; wound in wing or arm; equip with wings; enable to fly, send in flight. □ **on the wing** flying; **take under one's wing** treat as protégé; **take wing** fly away; **wing-case** horny cover of insect's wing; **wing-chair** chair with side-pieces at top of high back; **wing-collar** man's high stiff collar with turned-down corners; **wing commander** RAF officer next below group captain; **wing-nut** nut with projections to turn it by; **wingspan** measurement right across wings. □ **winged** adjective.

winger noun Football etc. wing player.

wink • verb (often + at) close and open one eye quickly, esp. as signal; close eye(s) momentarily; (of light) twinkle; (of indicator) flash on and off. • noun act of winking; colloquial short sleep. □ **wink at** purposely avoid seeing, pretend not to notice.

winkle /'wɪŋk(ə)l/ • noun edible sea snail. • verb (-ling) (+ out) extract with difficulty.

winning • adjective having or bringing victory; attractive. • noun (in plural) money won. □ **winning post** post marking end of race. □ **winningly** adverb.

winnow /'wɪnəʊ/ verb blow (grain) free of chaff etc.; (+ out, away, from, etc.) rid grain of (chaff etc.); sift, examine.

winsome /'wɪnsəm/ adjective attractive, engaging. □ **winsomely** adverb; **winsomeness** noun.

winter /'wɪntə/ • noun coldest season of year. • verb (usually + at, in) spend the winter. □ **winter garden** garden of plants flourishing in winter; **wintergreen** kind of plant remaining green all winter; **winter sports** sports practised on snow or ice; **wintertime** season or period of winter.

wintry /'wɪntrɪ/ adjective (-ier, -iest) characteristic of winter; lacking warmth. □ **wintriness** noun.

winy adjective (-ier, -iest) wine-flavoured.

wipe • verb (-ping) clean or dry surface of by rubbing; rub (cloth) over surface; spread (liquid etc.) over surface by rubbing; (often + away, off, etc.) clear or remove by wiping; erase, eliminate. • noun act of wiping; piece of specially treated cloth for wiping. □ **wipe out** utterly destroy or defeat, clean inside of; **wipe up** dry (dishes etc.), take up (liquid etc.) by wiping.

wiper noun windscreen wiper.

wire • noun metal drawn out into thread or slender flexible rod; piece of this; length of this used for fencing or to carry electric current etc.; colloquial telegram. • verb (-ring) provide, fasten, strengthen, etc. with wire; (often + up) install electrical circuits in; colloquial telegraph. □ **get one's wires crossed** become confused; **wire-haired** (of dog) having stiff wiry hair; **wire netting** netting made of meshed wire; **wire-tapping** tapping of telephone wires; **wire wool** mass of fine wire for scouring; **wireworm** destructive larva of a kind of beetle.

wireless noun radio; radio receiving set.

wiring *noun* system or installation of electrical circuits.

wiry *adjective* (**-ier, -iest**) sinewy, untiring; like wire, tough and coarse.

wisdom /'wɪzdəm/ *noun* experience, knowledge, and the power of applying them; prudence, common sense; wise sayings. □ **wisdom tooth** hindmost molar usually cut at age of about 20.

wise¹ /waɪz/ *adjective* having, showing, or dictated by wisdom; prudent, sensible; having knowledge; suggestive of wisdom; *US colloquial* alert, crafty. □ **be, get wise to** *colloquial* be, become, aware of; **wisecrack** *colloquial noun* smart remark, *verb* make wisecrack; **wise guy** *colloquial* know-all; **wise man** wizard, esp. one of the Magi; **wise up** *esp. US colloquial* inform, get wise. □ **wisely** *adverb*.

wise² /waɪz/ *noun archaic* way, manner, degree.

-wise /waɪz/ *combining form added to nouns to form adjectives and adverbs:* in the manner or direction of (e.g. *clockwise, lengthwise*); with reference to (e.g. *weatherwise*).

wiseacre /'waɪzeɪkə/ *noun* person who affects to be wise.

wish ● *verb* (often + *for*) have or express desire or aspiration; want, demand; express one's hopes for; *colloquial* foist. ● *noun* desire, request, expression of this; thing desired. □ **wishbone** forked bone between neck and breast of fowl; **wish-fulfilment** tendency of unconscious wishes to be satisfied in fantasy; **wishing-well** well at which wishes are made.

wishful *adjective* (often + *to do*) desiring. □ **wishful thinking** belief founded on wishes rather than facts.

wishy-washy /'wɪʃɪwɒʃɪ/ *adjective colloquial* feeble or poor in quality or character; weak, watery.

wisp *noun* small bundle or twist of straw etc.; small separate quantity of smoke, hair, etc.; small thin person. □ **wispy** *adjective* (**-ier, -iest**).

wisteria /wɪ'stɪərɪə/ *noun* (also **wistaria** /-teər-/) climbing plant with purple, blue, or white hanging flowers.

wistful /'wɪstful/ *adjective* yearning, mournfully expectant or wishful. □ **wistfully** *adverb*; **wistfulness** *noun*.

wit *noun* (in *singular* or *plural*) intelligence, understanding; (in *singular*) imaginative and inventive faculty; amusing ingenuity of speech or ideas; person noted for this. □ **at one's wit's** or **wits' end** utterly at a loss or in despair; **have** or **keep one's wits about one** be alert; **out of one's wits** mad; **to wit** that is to say, namely.

witch *noun* woman supposed to have dealings with Devil or evil spirits; old hag; fascinating girl or woman. □ **witchcraft** use of magic, bewitching charm; **witch-doctor** tribal magician of primitive people; **witch, wych hazel** N. American shrub, astringent lotion from its bark; **witch-hunt** campaign against people suspected of unpopular or unorthodox views.

witchery /'wɪtʃərɪ/ *noun* witchcraft.

with /wɪð/ *preposition expressing instrument or means used, company, parting of company, cause, possession, circumstances, manner, agreement, disagreement, antagonism, understanding, regard.* □ **with it** *colloquial* up to date, alert and comprehending; **with that** thereupon.

withdraw /wɪð'drɔː/ *verb* (*past* **-drew**; *past participle* **-drawn**) pull or take aside or back; discontinue, cancel, retract; remove, take away; take (money) out of an account; retire or go apart; (as **withdrawn** *adjective*) unsociable. □ **withdrawal** *noun*.

withe = WITHY.

wither /'wɪðə/ *verb* (often + *up*) make or become dry and shrivelled; (often + *away*) deprive of or lose vigour or freshness; (esp. as **withering** *adjective*) blight with scorn etc. □ **witheringly** *adverb*.

withers /'wɪðəz/ *plural noun* ridge between horse's shoulder-blades.

withhold /wɪð'həʊld/ *verb* (*past & past participle* **-held**) refuse to give, grant, or allow; hold back, restrain.

within /wɪ'ðɪn/ ● *adverb* inside; indoors; in spirit. ● *preposition* inside; not beyond or out of; not transgressing or exceeding; not further off than.

without /wɪ'ðaʊt/ ● *preposition* not having, feeling, or showing; free from; in absence of; with neglect or avoidance of; *archaic* outside. ● *adverb archaic or literary* outside, out of doors.

withstand /wɪð'stænd/ *verb* (*past & past participle* **-stood**) oppose, hold out against.

withy /'wɪðɪ/ *noun* (*plural* **-ies**) tough flexible shoot, esp. of willow.

witless *adjective* foolish; crazy.

witness /'wɪtnɪs/ ● *noun* eyewitness; person giving sworn testimony; person attesting another's signature to document; (+ *to*, *of*) person or thing whose existence etc. attests or proves something. ● *verb* be eyewitness of; be witness to (signature etc.); serve as evidence or indication of; give or be evidence. □ **bear witness to** attest truth of, state one's belief in; **witness-box** (*US* **-stand**) enclosed space in law court from which witness gives evidence.

witter /'wɪtə/ *verb* (often + *on*) *colloquial* chatter annoyingly or on trivial matters.

witticism /'wɪtɪsɪz(ə)m/ *noun* witty remark.

wittingly /'wɪtɪŋlɪ/ *adverb* consciously, intentionally.

witty *adjective* (**-ier**, **-iest**) showing verbal wit. □ **wittily** *adverb*; **wittiness** *noun*.

wives *plural* of WIFE.

wizard /'wɪzəd/ ● *noun* sorcerer, magician; person of extraordinary powers. ● *adjective slang* wonderful. □ **wizardry** *noun*.

wizened /'wɪz(ə)nd/ *adjective* shrivelled-looking.

WNW *abbreviation* west-north-west.

WO *abbreviation* Warrant Officer.

woad *noun* plant yielding blue dye; this dye.

wobble /'wɒb(ə)l/ ● *verb* (**-ling**) sway from side to side; stand or go unsteadily, stagger; waver, vacillate. ● *noun* wobbling motion. □ **wobbly** *adjective* (**-ier**, **-iest**).

woe *noun* affliction, bitter grief; (in *plural*) calamities. □ **woebegone** dismal-looking.

woeful *adjective* sorrowful; causing or feeling affliction; very bad. □ **woefully** *adverb*.

wok *noun* bowl-shaped frying-pan used in esp. Chinese cookery.

woke *past* of WAKE[1].

woken *past participle* of WAKE[1].

wold /wəʊld/ *noun* high open uncultivated land or moor.

wolf /wʊlf/ ● *noun* (*plural* **wolves** /wʊlvz/) wild animal related to dog; *slang* man who seduces women. ● *verb* (often + *down*) devour greedily. □ **cry wolf** raise false alarm; **keep the wolf from the door** avert starvation; **wolfhound** dog of kind used originally to hunt wolves; **wolfsbane** an aconite; **wolf-whistle** man's whistle to attractive woman. □ **wolfish** *adjective*.

wolfram /'wʊlfrəm/ *noun* tungsten; tungsten ore.

wolverine /'wʊlvəri:n/ *noun* N. American animal of weasel family.

wolves *plural* of WOLF.

woman /'wʊmən/ *noun* (*plural* **women** /'wɪmɪn/) adult human female; the female sex; *colloquial* wife, girlfriend.

womanhood *noun* female maturity; womanliness; womankind.

womanish *adjective derogatory* effeminate, unmanly.

womanize *verb* (also **-ise**) (**-zing** or **-sing**) (of man) be promiscuous. □ **womanizer** *noun*.

womankind *noun* (also **womenkind**) women in general.

womanly *adjective* having or showing qualities associated with women. □ **womanliness** *noun*.

womb /wu:m/ *noun* organ of conception and gestation in female mammals.

wombat /'wɒmbæt/ *noun* burrowing plant-eating Australian marsupial.

women /'wɪmɪn/ *plural* of WOMAN. □ **women's libber** *colloquial* supporter of women's liberation; **women's liberation, lib** *colloquial* movement for release of women from subservient status; **women's rights** human rights of women giving equality with men.

womenfolk *noun* women in general; women in family.

won *past & past participle* of WIN.

wonder /'wʌndə/ ● *noun* emotion, esp. admiration, excited by what is unexpected, unfamiliar, or inexplicable;

strange or remarkable thing, specimen, event, etc. ● *adjective* having amazing properties etc. ● *verb* be filled with wonder; (+ *that*) be surprised to find that, be curious to know. □ **no** or **small wonder** it is not surprising; **wonderland** fairyland, place of surprises or marvels.

wonderful *adjective* very remarkable or admirable. □ **wonderfully** *adverb*.

wonderment *noun* surprise, awe.

wondrous /'wʌndrəs/ *poetical* ● *adjective* wonderful. ● *adverb* wonderfully.

wonky /'wɒŋkɪ/ *adjective* (**-ier, -iest**) *slang* crooked; unsteady; unreliable.

wont /wəʊnt/ ● *adjective archaic or literary* (+ *to do*) accustomed. ● *noun formal or jocular* custom, habit.

won't /wəʊnt/ will not.

wonted /'wəʊntɪd/ *adjective* habitual, usual.

woo *verb* (**woos, wooed**) court, seek love of; try to win; seek support of; coax, importune.

wood /wʊd/ *noun* hard fibrous substance of tree; this for timber or fuel; (in *singular* or *plural*) growing trees occupying piece of ground; wooden cask for wine etc.; wooden-headed golf club; ball in game of bowls. □ **out of the wood(s)** clear of danger or difficulty; **wood anemone** wild spring-flowering anemone; **woodbine** honeysuckle; **woodchuck** N. American marmot; **woodcock** game bird related to snipe; **woodcut** relief cut on wood, print made from this; **woodcutter** person who cuts timber; **woodland** wooded country; **woodlouse** small land crustacean with many legs; **woodman** forester; **woodpecker** bird that taps tree trunks to find insects; **woodpigeon** dove with white patches round neck; **wood pulp** wood fibre prepared for papermaking; **woodwind** wind instrument(s) of orchestra made originally of wood; **woodwork** making of things in wood, things made of wood; **woodworm** beetle larva that bores in wood, resulting condition of wood.

wooded *adjective* having woods.

wooden /'wʊd(ə)n/ *adjective* made of wood; like wood; stiff, clumsy; expressionless. □ **woodenly** *adverb*; **woodenness** *noun*.

woody *adjective* (**-ier, -iest**) wooded; like or of wood.

woof¹ /wʊf/ ● *noun* gruff bark of dog. ● *verb* give woof.

woof² /wuːf/ *noun* weft.

woofer /'wuːfə/ *noun* loudspeaker for low frequencies.

wool /wʊl/ *noun* fine soft wavy hair forming fleece of sheep etc.; woollen yarn, cloth, or garments; wool-like substance. □ **wool-gathering** absentmindedness; **the Woolsack** Lord Chancellor's seat in House of Lords.

woollen /'wʊlən/ (*US* **woolen**) ● *adjective* made (partly) of wool. ● *noun* woollen fabric; (in *plural*) woollen garments.

woolly ● *adjective* (**-ier, -iest**) bearing or like wool; woollen; indistinct; confused. ● *noun* (*plural* **-ies**) *colloquial* woollen (esp. knitted) garment.

woozy /'wuːzɪ/ *adjective* (**-ier, -iest**) *colloquial* dizzy; slightly drunk.

word /wɜːd/ ● *noun* meaningful element of speech, usually shown with space on either side of it when written or printed; speech as distinct from action; one's promise or assurance; (in *singular* or *plural*) thing said, remark, conversation; (in *plural*) text of song or actor's part; (in *plural*) angry talk; news, message; command. ● *verb* put into words, select words to express. □ **word-blindness** dyslexia; **word for word** in exactly the same words, literally; **the Word (of God)** the Bible; **word of mouth** speech (only); **word-perfect** having memorized one's part etc. perfectly; **word processor** computer software or hardware for storing text entered from keyboard, incorporating corrections, and producing printout; **word-process** *verb*; **word processing** *noun*.

wording *noun* form of words used.

wordy *adjective* (**-ier, -iest**) using or expressed in (too) many words.

wore *past* of WEAR.

work /wɜːk/ ● *noun* application of effort to a purpose, use of energy; task to be undertaken; thing done or made by work, result of action; employment, occupation, etc., esp. as means of earning money; literary or musical composition; actions or experiences of specified kind; (in *plural*) operative part of clock etc.; **(the works)** *colloquial* all that is available or needed, full treatment; (in *plural*) operations of building or repair; (in *plural*; often treated as *singular*) factory; (usually in *plural* or *in combination*) defensive structure. ● *verb* be engaged in activity; be employed in certain work; make efforts; be craftsman in (material); operate or function, esp. effectively; operate, manage, control; put or keep in operation or at work, cause to toil; cultivate (land); produce as result; *colloquial* arrange; knead, hammer, bring to desired shape or consistency; do, or make by, needlework etc.; (cause to) make way or make (way) slowly or with difficulty; gradually become (loose etc.) by motion; artificially excite; purchase with labour instead of money; obtain money for by labour; (+ *on, upon*) influence; be in motion or agitated, ferment. □ **get worked up** become angry, excited, or tense; **workaday** ordinary, everyday, practical; **work-basket** basket for sewing materials; **workbench** bench for manual work, esp. carpentry; **workbox** box for tools, needlework, etc.; **workday** day on which work is usually done; **work experience** temporary experience of employment for young people; **workforce** workers engaged or available, number of these; **workhouse** *historical* public institution for the poor; **work in** find place for; **workload** amount of work to be done; **workman** man employed to do manual labour, person who works in specified manner; **workmanlike** showing practised skill; **workmanship** degree of skill in doing task or of finish in product; **workmate** person working alongside another; **work off** get rid of by work or activity; **work out** *verb* solve (sum) or find (amount) by calculation, understand (problem, person, etc.), be calculated, have result, provide for all details of, engage in physical exercise; **workout** *noun* session of physical exercise; **work over** examine thoroughly, *colloquial* treat with violence; **workshop** room or building in which goods are manufactured, place or meeting for concerted activity; **work-shy** disinclined to work; **workstation** location of stage in manufacturing process,

computer terminal; **worktop** flat (esp. kitchen) surface for working on; **work to rule** follow official working rules exactly to reduce efficiency as protest; **work-to-rule** *noun*; **work up** bring gradually to efficient or advanced state, advance gradually, elaborate or excite by degrees, mingle (ingredients), learn (subject) by study.

workable *adjective* that can be worked, will work, or is worth working. □ **workability** *noun*.

worker *noun* manual or industrial etc. employee; neuter bee or ant; person who works hard.

working ● *adjective* engaged in work; while so engaged; functioning, able to function. ● *noun* activity of work; functioning; mine, quarry; (usually in *plural*) mechanism. □ **working capital** capital used in conducting a business; **working class** social class employed for wages, esp. in manual or industrial work; **working-class** *adjective*; **working day** workday, part of day devoted to work; **working knowledge** knowledge adequate to work with; **working lunch** lunch at which business is conducted; **working order** condition in which machine works; **working party** committee appointed to study and advise on some question.

world /wɜːld/ ● *noun* the earth, planetary body like it; the universe, all that exists; time, state, or scene of human existence; **(the, this world)** mortal life; secular interests and affairs; human affairs, active life; average, respectable, or fashionable people or their customs or opinions; all that concerns or all who belong to specified class or sphere of activity; vast amount. ● *adjective* of or affecting all nations. □ **out of this world** *colloquial* extremely good etc.; **think the world of** have very high regard for; **world-class** of standard considered high throughout world; **world-famous** known throughout the world; **world music** pop music incorporating ethnic elements; **world war** one involving many important nations; **world-weary** bored with human affairs; **worldwide** *adjective* occurring or known in all parts of the world; *adverb* throughout the world.

worldly *adjective* (**-ier, -iest**) temporal, earthly; experienced in life, sophisticated, practical. □ **worldly-wise** prudent in one's dealings with world.

worm /wɜːm/ ● *noun* any of several types of creeping invertebrate animal with long slender body and no limbs; larva of insect; (in *plural*) internal parasites; insignificant or contemptible person; spiral of screw. ● *verb* crawl, wriggle; (**worm oneself**) insinuate oneself (into favour etc.); (+ *out*) obtain (secret etc.) by cunning persistence; rid (dog etc.) of worms. □ **worm-cast** convoluted mass of earth left on surface by burrowing earthworm; **wormeaten** eaten into by worms, decayed, dilapidated.

wormwood /ˈwɜːmwʊd/ *noun* plant with bitter aromatic taste; bitter humiliation, source of this.

wormy *adjective* (**-ier, -iest**) full of worms; wormeaten.

worn ● *past participle* of WEAR. ● *adjective* damaged by use or wear; looking tired and exhausted.

worry /ˈwʌrɪ/ ● *verb* (**-ies, -ied**) be anxious; harass, importune, be trouble or anxiety to; shake or pull about with teeth; (as **worried** *adjective*) uneasy. ● *noun* (*plural* **-ies**) thing that causes anxiety or disturbs tranquillity; disturbed state of mind, anxiety. □ **worry beads** string of beads manipulated with fingers to occupy or calm interest. □ **worrier** *noun*.

worse /wɜːs/ ● *adjective* more bad; in or into worse health or worse condition. ● *adverb* more badly; more ill. ● *noun* worse thing(s); (**the worse**) worse condition. □ **the worse for wear** damaged by use, injured; **worse off** in a worse (esp. financial) position. □ **worsen** *verb*.

worship /ˈwɜːʃɪp/ ● *noun* homage or service to deity; acts, rites, or ceremonies of this; adoration, devotion; (**His, Her, Your Worship**) *title used of or to* mayor, magistrate, etc. ● *verb* (**-pp-**) adore as divine, honour with religious rites; idolize; attend public worship; be full of adoration. □ **worshipper** *noun*.

worshipful *adjective* (also **Worshipful**) *archaic* honourable, distinguished (esp. in old titles of companies or officers).

worst /wɜːst/ ● *adjective* most bad. ● *adverb* most badly. ● *noun* worst part or possibility. ● *verb* get the better of, defeat. □ **at** (**the**) **worst** in the worst possible case; **do your worst** *expression of defiance*; **get the worst of it** be defeated; **if the worst comes to the worst** if the worst happens.

worsted /ˈwʊstɪd/ *noun* fine woollen yarn; fabric made from this.

wort /wɜːt/ *noun* infusion of malt before it is fermented into beer.

worth /wɜːθ/ ● *adjective* of value equivalent to; such as to justify or repay; possessing property equivalent to. ● *noun* value; equivalent of money etc. in commodity etc. □ **worth it** (*colloquial*), **worth** (**one's**) **while**, **worthwhile** worth the time or effort spent.

worthless *adjective* without value or merit. □ **worthlessness** *noun*.

worthy /ˈwɜːðɪ/ ● *adjective* (**-ier, -iest**) deserving respect, estimable; entitled to recognition; (usually + *of*) deserving; (+ *of*) adequate or suitable for the dignity etc. of. ● *noun* (*plural* **-ies**) worthy person; person of some distinction.

would *auxiliary verb* (*3rd singular present* **would**) *used in reported speech or to form conditional mood; expressing habitual past action, request as question, or probability.* □ **would-be** desiring or aspiring to be.

wouldn't /ˈwʊd(ə)nt/ would not.

wound[1] /wuːnd/ ● *noun* injury done by cut or blow to living tissue; pain inflicted on feelings, injury to reputation. ● *verb* inflict wound on.

wound[2] *past & past participle* of WIND[2]. □ **wound up** excited, tense, angry.

wove *past* of WEAVE[1].

woven *past participle* of WEAVE[1].

wow /waʊ/ ● *interjection expressing astonishment or admiration.* ● *noun slang* sensational success. ● *verb slang* impress greatly.

WP *abbreviation* word processor.

WPC *abbreviation* woman police constable.

w.p.m. *abbreviation* words per minute.

WRAC *abbreviation historical* Women's Royal Army Corps.

wrack *noun* seaweed cast up or growing on seashore; destruction.

WRAF *abbreviation historical* Women's Royal Air Force.

wraith /reɪθ/ *noun* ghost; spectral appearance of living person supposed to portend that person's death.

wrangle /'ræŋg(ə)l/ ● *noun* noisy argument or dispute. ● *verb* (**-ling**) engage in wrangle.

wrap ● *verb* (**-pp-**) (often + *up*) envelop in folded or soft encircling material; (+ *round*, *about*) arrange or draw (pliant covering) round (person). ● *noun* shawl, scarf, etc.; wrapper; *esp. US* wrapping material. □ **under wraps** in secrecy; **wraparound**, **wrapround** (esp. of clothing) designed to wrap round, curving round at edges; **wrap-over** *adjective* (of garment) overlapping when worn, *noun* such garment; **wrapped up in** engrossed or absorbed in; **wrap up** *colloquial* finish off (matter), put on warm clothes.

wrapper *noun* cover for sweet, book, posted newspaper, etc.; loose enveloping robe or gown.

wrapping *noun* (esp. in *plural*) material used to wrap, wraps, wrappers. □ **wrapping paper** strong or decorative paper for wrapping parcels.

wrasse /ræs/ *noun* (*plural* same or **-s**) brilliant-coloured edible sea fish.

wrath /rɒθ/ *noun literary* extreme anger. □ **wrathful** *adjective*.

wreak *verb* (usually + *upɒn*) give play to (vengeance etc.); cause (damage etc.).

wreath /riːθ/ *noun* (*plural* **-s** /riːðz/) flowers or leaves wound together into ring, esp. as ornament for head or door or for laying on grave etc.; curl or ring of smoke, cloud, or soft fabric.

wreathe /riːð/ *verb* (**-thing**) encircle (as with or like wreath; (+ *round*) wind (one's arms etc.) round (person etc.); move in wreaths.

wreck ● *noun* sinking or running aground of ship; ship that has suffered wreck; greatly damaged building, thing, or person. ● *verb* seriously damage (vehicle etc.); ruin (hopes etc.); cause wreck of (ship).

wreckage *noun* wrecked material; remnants of wreck; act of wrecking.

wrecker *noun* person or thing that wrecks or destroys, esp. (*historical*) person who tries from shore to bring about shipwreck for plunder or profit.

Wren *noun* member of WRNS.

wren *noun* small usually brown short-winged songbird.

wrench ● *noun* violent twist or oblique pull or tearing off; tool for gripping and turning nuts etc.; painful uprooting or parting etc. ● *verb* twist or pull violently round or sideways; (often + *off*, *away*, etc.) pull with wrench.

wrest *verb* wrench away from person's grasp; (+ *from*) obtain by effort or with difficulty.

wrestle /'res(ə)l/ ● *noun* contest in which two opponents grapple and try to throw each other to ground; hard struggle. ● *verb* (**-ling**) have wrestling match; (often + *with*) struggle; (+ *with*) do one's utmost to deal with. □ **wrestler** *noun*.

wretch *noun* unfortunate or pitiable person; reprehensible person.

wretched /'retʃɪd/ *adjective* (**-er**, **-est**) unhappy, miserable; unwell; of bad quality, contemptible; displeasing. □ **wretchedly** *adverb*; **wretchedness** *noun*.

wriggle /'rɪg(ə)l/ ● *verb* (**-ling**) twist or turn body with short writhing movements; make wriggling motions; (+ *along*, *through*, etc.) go thus; be evasive. ● *noun* wriggling movement. □ **wriggly** *adjective*.

wring ● *verb* (*past & past participle* **wrung**) squeeze tightly; (often + *out*) squeeze and twist, esp. to remove liquid; break by twisting; distress, torture; extract by squeezing; (+ *out*, *from*) obtain by pressure or importunity. ● *noun* act of wringing. □ **wringing** (**wet**) so wet that water can be wrung out; **wring one's hands** clasp them as gesture of grief; **wring the neck of** kill (chicken etc.) by twisting neck.

wringer *noun* device for wringing water from washed clothes etc.

wrinkle /'rɪŋk(ə)l/ ● *noun* crease in skin or other flexible surface; *colloquial* useful hint, clever expedient. ● *verb* (**-ling**) make wrinkles in; form wrinkles. □ **wrinkly** *adjective* (**-ier**, **-iest**).

wrist *noun* joint connecting hand and forearm; part of garment covering wrist. □ **wrist-watch** small watch worn on strap etc. round wrist.

wristlet *noun* band or ring to guard, strengthen, or adorn wrist.

writ *noun* formal written court order to do or not do specified act.

write *verb* (**-ting**; *past* **wrote**; *past participle* **written** /'rɪt(ə)n/) mark paper or other surface with symbols, letters, or words; form or mark (such symbols etc.); form or mark symbols of (word, document, etc.); fill or complete with writing; put (data) into computer store; (esp. in *passive*) indicate (quality or condition) by appearance; compose for reproduction or publication; (usually + *to*) write and send letter; convey (news etc.) by letter; state in book etc.; (+ *into*, *out of*) include or exclude (character, episode) in or from story. □ **write down** record in writing; **write in** send suggestion etc. in writing, esp. to broadcasting service; **write off** *verb* cancel (debt etc.), acknowledge as lost, completely destroy, (+ *for*) order or request by post; **write-off** *noun* thing written off, esp. vehicle etc. so damaged as not to be worth repair; **write up** *verb* write full account of; **write-up** *noun* written or published account, review.

writer *noun* person who writes, esp. author. □ **writer's cramp** muscular spasm due to excessive writing.

writhe /raɪð/ *verb* (**-thing**) twist or roll oneself about (as) in acute pain; suffer mental torture.

writing *noun* written words etc.; handwriting; (usually in *plural*) writer's works. □ **in writing** in written form.

written *past participle* of WRITE.

WRNS *abbreviation historical* Women's Royal Naval Service.

wrong ● *adjective* mistaken, not true, in error; unsuitable, less or least desirable; contrary to law or morality;

amiss, out of order. ● *adverb* in wrong manner or direction, with incorrect result. ● *noun* what is morally wrong; unjust action. ● *verb* treat unjustly; mistakenly attribute bad motives to. □ **go wrong** take wrong path, stop functioning properly, depart from virtuous behaviour; **in the wrong** responsible for quarrel, mistake, or offence; **wrongdoer** person who behaves immorally or illegally; **wrongdoing** *noun*; **wrong-foot** *colloquial* catch off balance or unprepared; **wrong-headed** perverse and obstinate; **wrong side** worse or undesirable or unusable side; **wrong way round** in opposite of normal orientation or sequence. □ **wrongly** *adverb*; **wrongness** *noun*.

wrongful *adjective* unwarranted, unjustified. □ **wrongfully** *adverb*.

wrote *past* of WRITE.

wroth /rəʊθ/ *adjective archaic* angry.

wrought /rɔːt/ *archaic past & past participle* of WORK. □ **wrought iron** form of iron suitable for forging or rolling, not cast.

wrung *past & past participle* of WRING.

WRVS *abbreviation* Women's Royal Voluntary Service.

wry /raɪ/ *adjective* (**-er**, **-est**) distorted, turned to one side; contorted in disgust, disappointment, or mockery; (of humour) dry and mocking. □ **wryneck** small woodpecker able to turn head over shoulder. □ **wryly** *adverb*; **wryness** *noun*.

WSW *abbreviation* west-south-west.

wt *abbreviation* weight.

wych hazel /wɪtʃ/ witch hazel.

WYSIWYG /'wɪzɪwɪg/ *adjective indicating that text on computer screen and printout correspond exactly* (what you see is what you get).

Xx

X¹ *noun* (also **x**) (Roman numeral) 10; first unknown quantity in algebra; unknown or unspecified number, person, etc.; cross-shaped symbol, esp. used to indicate position or incorrectness, to symbolize kiss or vote, or as signature of person who cannot write. □ **X-ray** *noun* electromagnetic radiation of short wavelength able to pass through opaque bodies, photograph made by X-rays, *verb* photograph, examine, or treat with X-rays.

X² *adjective* (of film) classified as suitable for adults only.

xenophobia /zenəˈfəʊbɪə/ *noun* hatred or fear of foreigners.

Xerox /ˈzɪərɒks/ ● *noun* proprietary term type of photocopier; copy made by it. ● *verb* (**xerox**) make Xerox of.

Xmas /ˈkrɪsməs, ˈeksməs/ *noun colloquial* Christmas.

xylophone /ˈzaɪləfəʊn/ *noun* musical instrument of graduated wooden or metal bars struck with small wooden hammers.

Yy

Y *noun* (also **y**) second unknown quantity in algebra; Y-shaped thing.

yacht /jɒt/ ● *noun* light sailing vessel for racing or cruising; larger usually power-driven vessel for cruising. ● *verb* race or cruise in yacht. □ **yachtsman**, **yachtswoman** person who yachts.

yah /jɑː/ *interjection* of derision, defiance, etc.

yahoo /jɑːˈhuː/ *noun* bestial person.

Yahweh /ˈjɑːweɪ/ *noun* Jehovah.

yak *noun* long-haired Tibetan ox.

yam *noun* tropical or subtropical climbing plant; edible starchy tuberous root of this; *US* sweet potato.

yang *noun* (in Chinese philosophy) active male principle of universe (compare YIN).

Yank *noun colloquial often derogatory* American.

yank *verb & noun colloquial* pull with jerk.

Yankee /ˈjæŋkɪ/ *noun colloquial* Yank; *US* inhabitant of New England or of northern States.

yap ● *verb* (**-pp-**) bark shrilly or fussily; *colloquial* talk noisily, foolishly, or complainingly. ● *noun* sound of yapping.

yard¹ *noun* unit of linear measure (3 ft, 0.9144 m.); this length of material; square or cubic yard; spar slung across mast for sail to hang from; (in *plural*, + *of*) *colloquial* a great length. □ **yard-arm** either end of ship's yard; **yardstick** standard of comparison, rod a yard long usually divided into inches etc.

yard² *noun* piece of enclosed ground, esp. attached to building or used for particular purpose; *US & Australian* garden of house.

yardage *noun* number of yards of material etc.

yarmulke /ˈjɑːməlkə/ *noun* (also **yarmulka**) skullcap worn by Jewish men.

yarn ● *noun* spun thread for weaving, knitting, etc.; *colloquial* story, traveller's tale, anecdote. ● *verb colloquial* tell yarns.

yarrow /ˈjærəʊ/ *noun* perennial plant, esp. milfoil.

yashmak /ˈjæʃmæk/ *noun* veil concealing face except eyes, worn by some Muslim women.

yaw ● *verb* (of ship, aircraft, etc.) fail to hold straight course, go unsteadily. ● *noun* yawing of ship etc. from course.

yawl *noun* kind of sailing boat; small fishing boat.

yawn ●*verb* open mouth wide and inhale, esp. when sleepy or bored; gape, be wide open. ●*noun* act of yawning.

yaws /jɔːz/ *plural noun* (usually treated as *singular*) contagious tropical skin disease.

yd *abbreviation* (*plural* **yds**) yard (measure).

ye /jiː/ *pronoun archaic* (as subject of verb) you (plural).

yea /jeɪ/ *archaic* ●*adverb* yes. ●*noun* 'yes' vote.

yeah /jeə/ *adverb colloquial* yes.

year /jɪə/ *noun* time occupied by one revolution of earth round sun, approx. 365¼ days; period from 1 Jan. to 31 Dec. inclusive; period of 12 calendar months; (in *plural*) age, time of life; (usually in *plural*) *colloquial* very long time. □ **yearbook** annual publication bringing information on some subject up to date.

yearling *noun* animal between one and two years old.

yearly ●*adjective* done, produced, or occurring once every year; of or lasting a year. ●*adverb* once every year.

yearn /jɜːn/ *verb* be filled with longing, compassion, or tenderness. □ **yearning** *noun & adjective.*

yeast *noun* greyish-yellow fungus, got esp. from fermenting malt liquors and used as fermenting agent, to raise bread, etc.

yeasty *adjective* (**-ier, -iest**) frothy; in ferment; working like yeast.

yell ●*noun* sharp loud cry; shout. ●*verb* cry, shout.

yellow /'jeləʊ/ ●*adjective* of the colour of lemons, buttercups, etc.; having yellow skin or complexion; *colloquial* cowardly. ●*noun* yellow colour, paint, clothes, etc. ●*verb* turn yellow. □ **yellow-belly** *colloquial* coward; **yellow card** card shown by referee to football-player being cautioned; **yellow fever** tropical virus fever with jaundice etc.; **yellowhammer** bunting of which male has yellow head, neck, and breast; **Yellow Pages** *proprietary term* telephone directory on yellow paper, listing and classifying business subscribers; **yellow streak**

colloquial trace of cowardice. □ **yellowish** *adjective*; **yellowness** *noun*; **yellowy** *adjective.*

yelp ●*noun* sharp shrill bark or cry as of dog in excitement or pain. ●*verb* utter yelp.

yen[1] *noun* (*plural* same) chief monetary unit of Japan.

yen[2] *colloquial* ●*noun* intense desire or longing. ●*verb* (**-nn-**) feel longing.

yeoman /'jəʊmən/ *noun esp. historical* man holding and farming small estate; member of yeomanry force. □ **Yeoman of the Guard** member of bodyguard of English sovereign.

yeomanry *noun* (*plural* **-ies**) group of yeomen; *historical* volunteer cavalry force in British army.

yes ●*adverb indicating affirmative reply to question, statement, request, command, etc.*; (**yes?**) indeed?, is that so?, what do you want? ●*noun* utterance of word yes. □ **yes-man** *colloquial* weakly acquiescent person.

yesterday /'jestədeɪ/ ●*adverb* on the day before today. ●*noun* the day before today.

yesteryear /'jestəjɪə/ *noun archaic or rhetorical* last year; the recent past.

yet ●*adverb* up to now or then; (with negative or in questions) so soon as, or by, now or then; again, in addition; in the remaining time available; (+ *comparative*) even; nevertheless. ●*conjunction* but nevertheless.

yeti /'jetɪ/ *noun* supposed manlike or bearlike Himalayan animal.

yew *noun* dark-leaved evergreen coniferous tree; its wood.

YHA *abbreviation* Youth Hostels Association.

Yiddish /'jɪdɪʃ/ ●*noun* language used by Jews in or from Europe. ●*adjective* of this language.

yield /jiːld/ ●*verb* produce or return as fruit, profit, or result; concede, give up; (often + *to*) surrender, submit, defer; (as **yielding** *adjective*) soft and pliable, submissive; (+ *to*) give right of way to. ●*noun* amount yielded or produced.

yin *noun* (in Chinese philosophy) passive female principle of universe (compare YANG).

yippee /jɪˈpiː/ *interjection expressing delight or excitement.*

YMCA *abbreviation* Young Men's Christian Association.

yob /jɒb/ *noun* (also **yobbo**, *plural* **-s**) *slang* lout, hooligan. □ **yobbish** *adjective.*

yodel /ˈjəʊd(ə)l/ ● *verb* (**-ll-**; *US* **-l-**) sing with melodious inarticulate sounds and frequent changes between falsetto and normal voice, in manner of Swiss mountain-dwellers. ● *noun* yodelling cry.

yoga /ˈjəʊgə/ *noun* Hindu system of meditation and asceticism; system of physical exercises and breathing control used in yoga.

yoghurt /ˈjɒgət/ *noun* (also **yogurt**) rather sour semi-solid food made from milk fermented by added bacteria.

yogi /ˈjəʊgɪ/ *noun* (*plural* **-s**) devotee of yoga.

yoke ● *noun* wooden crosspiece fastened over necks of two oxen etc. and attached to plough or wagon to be pulled, (*plural* same or **-s**) pair (of oxen etc.); object like yoke in form or function, e.g. wooden shoulder-piece for carrying pair of pails, top part of garment from which rest hangs; sway, dominion, servitude; bond of union, esp. of marriage. ● *verb* (**-king**) put yoke on; couple or unite (pair); link (one thing) to (another); match or work together.

yokel /ˈjəʊk(ə)l/ *noun* country bumpkin.

yolk /jəʊk/ *noun* yellow inner part of egg.

Yom Kippur /jɒm ˈkɪpə/ *noun* most solemn religious fast day of Jewish year, Day of Atonement.

yon *adjective & adverb literary & dialect* yonder.

yonder /ˈjɒndə/ ● *adverb* over there, at some distance in that direction, in place indicated. ● *adjective* situated yonder.

yore *noun* □ **of yore** a long time ago.

york *verb Cricket* bowl out with yorker.

yorker *noun Cricket* ball that pitches immediately under bat.

Yorkist /ˈjɔːkɪst/ ● *noun historical* follower of House of York, esp. in Wars of the Roses. ● *adjective* of House of York.

Yorkshire pudding /ˈjɔːkʃə/ *noun* baked batter usually eaten with roast beef.

Yorkshire terrier /ˈjɔːkʃə/ *noun* small long-haired blue and tan kind of terrier.

you /juː/ *pronoun* the person(s) or thing(s) addressed; one, a person.

you'd /juːd/ you had; you would.

you'll /juːl/ you will; you shall.

young /jʌŋ/ ● *adjective* (**younger** /ˈjʌŋgə/, **youngest** /ˈjʌŋgɪst/) not far advanced in life, development, or existence, not yet old; immature, inexperienced, youthful; of or characteristic of youth. ● *noun* offspring, esp. of animals. □ **youngish** *adjective.*

youngster *noun* child, young person.

your /jɔː/ *adjective* of or belonging to you.

you're /jɔː/ you are.

yours /jɔːz/ *pronoun* the one(s) belonging to you.

yourself /jɔːˈself/ *pronoun* (*plural* **yourselves**): *emphatic & reflexive form of* YOU.

youth /juːθ/ *noun* (*plural* **-s** /juːðz/) being young; early part of life, esp. adolescence; quality or condition characteristic of the young; young man; (treated as *plural*) young people collectively. □ **youth club** place for young people's leisure activities; **youth hostel** any of chain of cheap lodgings where (esp. young) holiday-makers can stay for the night.

youthful *adjective* young or still having characteristics of youth. □ **youthfulness** *noun.*

you've /juːv/ you have.

yowl /jaʊl/ ● *noun* loud wailing cry (as) of cat or dog in distress. ● *verb* utter yowl.

yo-yo /ˈjəʊjəʊ/ *noun* (*plural* **yo-yos**) toy consisting of pair of discs with deep groove between them in which string is attached and wound, and which can be made to fall and rise.

yr. *abbreviation* year(s); younger; your.

yrs. *abbreviation* years; yours.

YTS *abbreviation* Youth Training Scheme.

yuan /juːˈɑːn/ *noun* (*plural* same) chief monetary unit of China.

yucca /ˈjʌkə/ *noun* white-flowered plant with swordlike leaves, often grown as house plant.

yuck /jʌk/ *interjection* (also **yuk**) *slang* expression of strong distaste.

yucky *adjective* (also **yukky**) **(-ier, -iest)** *slang* messy, repellent; sickly, sentimental.

Yugoslav /'juːgəslɑːv/ *historical* ● *adjective* of Yugoslavia. ● *noun* native or national of Yugoslavia. □ **Yugoslavian** /-'slɑːv-/ *adjective & noun.*

yuk = YUCK.

yukky = YUCKY.

yule *noun* (in full **yule-tide**) *archaic* festival of Christmas. □ **yule-log** large log burnt at Christmas.

yummy /'jʌmɪ/ *adjective* **(-ier, -iest)** *colloquial* tasty, delicious.

yuppie /'jʌpɪ/ *noun* (also **yuppy**) (*plural* **-ies**) *colloquial usually derogatory* young ambitious professional person working in city.

YWCA *abbreviation* Young Women's Christian Association.

Zz

zabaglione /zæbə'ljəʊnɪ/ *noun* Italian dessert of whipped and heated egg yolks, sugar, and wine.

zany /'zeɪnɪ/ *adjective* **(-ier, -iest)** comically idiotic; crazily ridiculous.

zap *verb* **(-pp-)** *slang* kill, destroy; attack; hit hard.

zeal *noun* fervour, eagerness; hearty persistent endeavour. □ **zealous** /'zeləs/ *adjective.*

zealot /'zelət/ *noun* extreme partisan, fanatic.

zebra /'zebrə, 'ziː-/ *noun* (*plural* same or **-s**) African black and white striped horse-like animal. □ **zebra crossing** striped street-crossing where pedestrians have precedence.

Zeitgeist /'tsaɪtgaɪst/ *noun* spirit of times. [German]

Zen *noun* form of Buddhism emphasizing meditation and intuition.

zenith /'zenɪθ/ *noun* point of heavens directly overhead; highest point (of power, prosperity, etc.).

zephyr /'zefə/ *noun* *literary* mild gentle breeze.

zero /'zɪərəʊ/ ● *noun* (*plural* **-s**) figure 0, nought, nil; point on scale of thermometer etc. from which positive or negative quantity is reckoned; (in full **zero-hour**) hour at which planned, esp. military, operation is timed to begin, crucial moment; lowest or earliest point. ● *adjective* no, not any. ● *verb* **(zeroes, zeroed)** adjust (instrument etc.) to zero. □ **zero in on** take aim at, focus attention on; **zero-rated** on which no VAT is charged.

zest *noun* piquancy; keen interest or enjoyment, relish, gusto; outer layer of orange or lemon peel.

zigzag /'zɪgzæg/ ● *adjective* with abrupt alternate right and left turns. ● *noun* zigzag line, thing having sharp turns. ● *adverb* with zigzag manner or course. ● *verb* **(-gg-)** move in zigzag course.

zilch *noun* *esp. US slang* nothing.

zillion /'zɪljən/ *noun* (*plural* same) *colloquial* indefinite large number; (**zillions**) very large number.

Zimmer frame /'zɪmə/ *noun proprietary term* kind of walking frame.

zinc *noun* greyish-white metallic element.

zing *colloquial* ● *noun* vigour, energy. ● *verb* move swiftly, esp. with shrill sound.

zinnia /'zɪnɪə/ *noun* garden plant with showy flowers.

zip ● *noun* light sharp sound; energy, vigour; (in full **zip-fastener**) fastening device of two flexible strips with interlocking projections, closed or opened by sliding clip along them. ● *verb* **(-pp-)** (often + *up*) fasten with zip-fastener; move with zip or at high speed.

zipper *noun* *esp. US* zip-fastener.

zircon /'zɜːkən/ *noun* translucent varieties of zirconium silicate cut into gems.

zirconium /zəˈkəʊnɪəm/ *noun* grey metallic element.

zit *noun esp. US slang* pimple.

zither /ˈzɪðə/ *noun* stringed instrument with flat soundbox, placed horizontally and played by plucking.

zloty /ˈzlɒtɪ/ *noun* (*plural* same or **-s**) chief monetary unit of Poland.

zodiac /ˈzəʊdɪæk/ *noun* belt of heavens including all apparent positions of sun, moon, and planets as known to ancient astronomers, and divided into 12 equal parts (**signs of the zodiac**).

zombie /ˈzɒmbɪ/ *noun* corpse said to have been revived by witchcraft; *colloquial* dull or apathetic person.

zone ● *noun* area having particular features, properties, purpose, or use; well-defined region of more or less beltlike form; area between two concentric circles; encircling band of colour etc.; *archaic* girdle, belt. ● *verb* (**-ning**) encircle as or with zone; arrange or distribute by zones; assign as or to specific area. □ **zonal** *adjective*.

zonked /zɒŋkt/ *adjective slang* (often + *out*) exhausted; intoxicated.

zoo *noun* zoological garden.

zoological /zəʊəˈlɒdʒɪk(ə)l, zuːə-/ *adjective* of zoology. □ **zoological garden(s)** public garden or park with collection of animals for exhibition and study.

■ **Usage** See note at ZOOLOGY.

zoology /zəʊˈɒlədʒɪ, zuːˈɒl-/ *noun* scientific study of animals. □ **zoologist** *noun*.

■ **Usage** The second pronunciation given for *zoology*, *zoological*, and *zoologist* (with the first syllable pronounced as in *zoo*), although extremely common, is considered incorrect by some people.

zoom ● *verb* move quickly, esp. with buzzing sound; cause aeroplane to mount at high speed and steep angle; (often + *in*, *in on*) (of camera) change rapidly from long shot to close-up (of). ● *noun* aeroplane's steep climb. □ **zoom lens** lens allowing camera to zoom by varying focal length.

zoophyte /ˈzəʊəfaɪt/ *noun* plantlike animal, esp. coral, sea anemone, or sponge.

zucchini /zuːˈkiːnɪ/ *noun* (*plural* same or **-s**) *esp. US & Australian* courgette.

zygote /ˈzaɪɡəʊt/ *noun Biology* cell formed by union of two gametes.

New Words Survey

aftermarket /ˈɑːftəˌmɑːkɪt/ n. **1** market in spare parts and components. **2** *Stock Exch.* market in shares after their original issue.

agroforestry /ˌægrəʊˈfɒrɪstrɪ/ n. agriculture incorporating the cultivation and conservation of trees.

air bag n. safety device that fills with air or nitrogen on impact to protect the occupants of a vehicle in a collision.

air bridge n. *Brit.* portable bridge or walkway put against an aircraft door.

airdrop –n. dropping of supplies etc. by parachute. –v. (**-dropped, -dropping**) drop (supplies etc.) by parachute.

alcoholic soft drink n. a traditionally soft drink such as lemonade, which contains alcohol.

aloe vera /ˈvɪərə/ n. **1** Caribbean aloe yielding a gelatinous substance used esp. in cosmetics as an emollient. **2** this substance. [modern Latin, = true aloe]

alternative energy n. energy fuelled in ways that do not harm the environment.

anchorperson n. (*pl.* **-s** or **-people**) anchorman or anchorwoman (used as a neutral alternative).

angel dust n. *slang* the hallucinogenic drug phencyclidine hydrochloride.

animatronics /ˌænɪməˈtrɒnɪks/ n.pl. (treated as *sing.*) technique of making and operating lifelike robots. □ **animatronic** *adj.* [blend of ANIMATED, ELECTRONICS]

authoring /ˈɔːθərɪŋ/ n. creation of programs, databases, etc. for computer applications.

bailout /ˈbeɪlaʊt/ n. financial assistance given to a failing business, economy, etc. to save it from collapse.

balsamic vinegar n. a dark, sweet, Italian vinegar, matured in wooden barrels.

Balti /ˈbɔːltɪ, ˈbælti/ n. type of Pakistani curry, usu. cooked and served in a dish like a shallow wok.

basehead n. *US slang* person who habitually takes either of the drugs freebase or crack. [blend of FREEBASE, HEAD]

BBFC *abbr.* British Board of Film Classification (formerly *British Board of Film Censors*).

bean-counter n. orig. *US colloq. derog.* accountant.

bells and whistles n.pl. esp. *Computing* attractive additional features; gimmicks. [allusion to old fairground organs]

bhaji /ˈbɑːdʒɪ/ n. (*pl.* **-s**) **1** Indian dish of fried vegetables. **2** small flat cake or ball of vegetables, fried in batter (*onion bhaji*). [Hindi *bhājī* fried vegetables]

biocide /ˈbaɪəˌsaɪd/ n. **1** poisonous substance, esp. a pesticide. **2** destruction of life.

biodiversity /ˌbaɪəʊdaɪˈvɜːsɪtɪ/ n. diversity of plant and animal life.

biogas /ˈbaɪəʊˌɡæs/ n. gaseous fuel, esp. methane, produced by fermentation of organic matter.

biohazard /ˈbaɪəʊˌhæzəd/ n. risk to human health or the environment arising from biological work, esp. with micro-organisms.

biome /ˈbaɪəʊm/ n. **1** large naturally occurring community of flora and fauna adapted to the particular conditions in which they occur, e.g. tundra. **2** geographical region containing such a community.

biopic /ˈbaɪəʊˌpɪk/ n. *colloq.* biographical film. [blend of BIOGRAPHY, PICTURE]

bird-strike n. collision between a bird and an aircraft.

body bag n. bag for carrying a corpse from the scene of warfare, an accident, etc.

body piercing n. piercing of holes in parts of the body other than the ear lobes.

boot camp *n.* (esp. in the US) institution for young offenders, having a tough quasi-military regime.

bozo /'bəʊzəʊ/ *n.* (*pl.* -s) esp. *US slang* stupid or insignificant person.

breakfast television *n.* early-morning television.

bridge-building *n.* promotion of friendly relations, esp. between countries. □ **bridge-builder** *n.*

broadband *attrib. adj.* relating to or using signals over a broad range of frequencies, esp. in high-capacity telecommunications.

brown goods *n.pl. Brit.* household goods such as television sets and audio equipment.

bubble wrap *n.* plastic wrapping material in sheets containing numerous small air-filled bladders.

buffer zone *n.* zone separating potential belligerents.

bull bar *n.* metal bar or framework on a vehicle to protect it in the event of collision with a large animal.

bullet train *n.* high-speed passenger train, esp. in Japan.

cafetière /kæf'tjeə(r)/ *n. Brit.* coffee pot with a plunger that pushes the grounds to the bottom. [French]

camera-ready *adj.* (of copy) in a form suitable for immediate photographic reproduction.

cantina *n.* bar or wine shop. [Spanish and Italian]

carjacking *n.* hijacking of a car. □ **carjack** *v.* **carjacker** *n.*

cash cow *n. colloq.* a business, or part of one, that provides a steady cash flow.

CAT /kæt/ *abbr.* **1** computer-assisted [or -aided] testing. **2** *Med.* computerized axial tomography (*CAT scanner*)

charbroil /'tʃɑːbrɔɪl/ *v.* grill (meat etc.) on a rack over charcoal. [blend of CHARCOAL, BROIL]

cherry-pick *v.* (also *absol.*) pick (the best) from a group.

chromosome map *n.* plan showing the relative positions of genes along the length of a chromosome.

ciabatta /tʃə'bɑːtə/ *n.* (*pl.* -s) type of moist aerated Italian bread made with olive oil. [Italian dialect word, =slipper (from its shape)]

Citizen's Charter *n. Polit.* a document guaranteeing citizens redress where a public service fails to meet standards.

City Technology College *n.* type of secondary school, set up mainly in towns and cities through partnerships between the Government and business and concentrating on technology and science.

command economy *n.* = PLANNED ECONOMY.

constructive dismissal *n.* the changing of an employee's job or working conditions with the aim of forcing resignation.

coulis /'kuːlɪ/ *n.* (*pl.* same) fruit purée thin enough to pour. [French from *couler* flow]

coursework *n.* work done during a course of study, esp. when counting towards a student's final assessment.

crawl space *n.* underfloor space giving access to ducts.

CRC *abbr. Printing* camera-ready copy.

Creutzfeldt–Jakob disease /ˌkrɔɪtsfelt'jækɒb/ *n.* type of spongiform encephalopathy affecting human beings, characterized by progressive dementia. [*Creutzfeldt* and *Jakob*, names of physicians]

crisis management *n.* practice of taking managerial action only when a crisis has developed.

cross-subsidize *v.* (also *-ise*) subsidize out of the profits of another business or activity. □ **cross-subsidy** *n.*

cruise control *n.* device which automatically maintains a motor vehicle at a chosen speed.

cryonics /kraɪ'ɒnɪks/ *n.* deep-freezing of the bodies of those who have died of an incurable disease, in the hope of a future cure. □ **cryonic** *adj.*

cutesy /'kjuːtsɪ/ *adj. colloq.* dainty or quaint in an affected degree.

cyberspace /'saɪbəˌspeɪs/ *n.* notional environment in which electronic communication occurs; virtual reality.

dark matter *n.* hypothetical nonluminous material in space, not detected, but predicted by many cosmological theories.

date rape n. rape of a girl or woman by a person with whom she is on a date.

dialogue box n. (*US* **dialog box**) *Computing* small area on-screen in which the user is prompted to provide information, select commands, etc.

differently abled adj. euphem. disabled.

disempower /ˌdɪsɪmˈpaʊə(r)/ v. remove the power to act from (a person, group, etc.) □ **disempowerment** n.

distance learning n. education by correspondence course or from broadcasts, telephone tutorials, etc.

dork n. slang **1** penis. **2** stupid or contemptible person.

double whammy n. (pl. -ies) colloq. twofold blow or setback.

down time n. time during which a machine, esp. a computer is out of action or unavailable for use.

dream ticket n. ideal pair of candidates standing together.

drophead n. Brit. adjustable fabric roof of a car.

dry slope n. ski slope covered with a plastic material which simulates snow.

ecocide /ˈiːkə(ʊ)ˌsaɪd/ n. destruction of the natural environment.

eco-friendly /ˌiːkəʊˈfrendlɪ/ adj. not harmful to the environment.

eco-label /ˈiːkəʊˌleɪb(ə)l/ n. label identifying manufactured products that satisfy certain environmental conditions □ **eco-labelling** n.

ecotourism /ˌiːkəʊˈtʊərɪz(ə)m/ n. tourism directed towards exotic natural environments, esp. intended to support conservation efforts. □ **ecotourist** n.

edutainment /ˌedjʊˈteɪnm(ə)nt/ n. entertainment with an educational aspect.

electroporation /ɪˌlektrəʊpəˈreɪʃ(ə)n/ n. Biol. action or process of introducing DNA or chromosomes into the cells of bacteria etc. using a pulse of electricity to open the pores in the cell membranes briefly. [Greek *poros* passage, pore]

encephalopathy /enˌsefəˈlɒpəθɪ, en-ˌkef-/ n. (pl. -ies) disease of the brain.

EPROM /ˈiːprɒm/ n. Computing read-only memory whose contents can be erased and replaced by a special process. [*erasable programmable ROM*]

Euro-MP n. member of the European Parliament.

Euro-sceptic /ˈjʊərəʊˌskeptɪk/ n. person who is not enthusiastic about increasing the powers of the European Union.

face-off n. direct confrontation.

factory shop n. (also **factory outlet**) shop in which goods are sold directly by the manufacturers at a discount.

false colour n. colour introduced during the production of an image to aid interpretation and not present in the object.

fandom /ˈfændəm/ n. the world of fans and enthusiasts, esp. of fans of science fiction magazines.

fantasy football n. (also **fantasy cricket** etc.) competition in which participants select imaginary teams from among the players in a league etc. and score points according to the actual performance of their players.

fanzine /ˈfænziːn/ n. magazine for fans, esp. those of science fiction, sport, or popular music. [blend of FANATIC, MAGAZINE]

fartlek /ˈfɑːtlek/ n. Athletics method of training for middle- and long-distance running, mixing fast with slow work. [Swedish]

fasciitis /ˌfæsɪˈaɪtɪs/ n. Med. inflammation of the thin sheath of fibrous tissue enclosing a muscle etc.

feel-good attrib. adj. that creates a feeling of well-being in people (a feel-good film).

fly-drive attrib. adj. designating a holiday which combines the cost of a return flight and that of car rental.

freebase n. slang cocaine purified by heating with ether, and inhaled or smoked.

freeze-frame –n. (also attrib.) facility of stopping a videotape etc. in order to view a motionless image. –v. use freeze-frame on (an image etc.).

fruitarian /fruːˈteərɪən/ n. person who eats only fruit.

funboard n. type of windsurfing board that is less stable but faster than a standard board.

G7 *attrib. adj.* designating a group of seven leading industrialized nations.

gas field *n.* area yielding natural gas.

General National Vocational Qualification *n.* (in the UK) general qualification for students undertaking specific training or higher education, set at various levels.

glass ceiling *n.* unacknowledged barrier to personal advancement.

global village *n.* the world considered as a single community linked by telecommunications.

go-by *n. colloq.* snub; slight (*gave him the go-by*).

golden handcuffs *n.pl. colloq.* promise of future benefits, e.g. pensions or share options, for those who stay with a company.

golden parachute *n. colloq.* financial compensation guaranteed to executives dismissed as a result of a merger or takeover.

grant aid *n.* grant by central government to local government or an institution.

greening *n.* **1** planting of trees etc. in urban or desert areas. **2** process of becoming or making aware of or sensitive to ecological issues.

grey market *n.* unofficial trade esp. in unissued shares or in scarce goods.

gridlock *n.* **1** traffic jam affecting a whole network of intersecting streets. **2** state of unresolved conflict. □ **gridlocked** *adj.*

groupware *n. Computing* software designed to facilitate collective working.

growbag *n.* (also **Gro-bag** *propr.*) bag containing potting compost for growing plants in, e.g. tomatoes.

guest beer *n. Brit.* **1** [in a tied public house] beer offered in addition to those produced by the brewery. **2** (in a free house) beer available only temporarily.

hackette /hæˈket/ *n. colloq.* usu. *derog.* female journalist.

hate mail *n.* usu. anonymous letters of hostility towards the recipient.

HDTV *abbr.* high-definition television.

heli-skiing /ˈheliˌskiːɪŋ/ *n.* skiing in which transport up the mountain is by helicopter.

Hib *n. Med* a bacterium causing infant meningitis (often *attrib.*: *Hib vaccine*).

high-five *n. US slang* gesture of celebration or greeting in which two people slap each other's palms with their arms outstretched over their heads.

home shopping *n.* shopping carried out from home using catalogues, satellite TV channels, etc.

hospital trust *n.* (in the UK) trust consisting of a National Health Service hospital or hospitals no longer under local authority control.

hotting *n. slang* practice of driving recklessly in a stolen car. □ **hotter** *n.*

hot tub *n.* bath of hot aerated water used for recreation or physical therapy.

hot-wire *v.* esp. *US slang* start the engine of (a car etc.) by bypassing the ignition switch.

house-sit *v.* live in and look after a house while its owner is away. □ **housesitter** *n.*

humongous /hjuːˈmʌŋgəs/ *adj.* (also **humungous**) *slang* huge, enormous.

hyperinflation /ˌhaɪpərɪmˈfleɪʃ(ə)n/ *n.* monetary inflation at a very high rate.

hyperspace /ˈhaɪpəspeɪs/ *n.* space of more than three dimensions, esp. (in science fiction) a notional space-time continuum in which motion and communication at speeds greater than that of light are supposedly possible.

hypo-allergenic /ˌhaɪpəʊˌæləˈdʒenɪk/ *adj.* having little tendency, or a specially reduced tendency, to cause an allergic reaction.

ibuprofen /ˌaɪbjuːˈprəʊf(ə)n/ *n.* an analgesic and anti-inflammatory drug.

image processing *n.* analysis and manipulation of an image. □ **image processor** *n.*

induction loop *n.* loop of wire around an area in a building etc., producing an electromagnetic signal received directly by hearing aids.

infomercial /ˌɪnfəˈmɜːʃ(ə)l/ *n.* (also **informercial**) esp. *US* advertising film, esp. on television, which is informative and purportedly objective.

infotainment /ˌɪnfəˈteɪmm(ə)nt/ *n.* broadcast material intended both to entertain and to inform.

ink-jet printer n. printer in which the characters are formed by minute jets of ink.

INSET /'ɪnset/ n. (often attrib.) training during term-time for teachers in British state schools. [in-service education and training]

intermediate technology n. technology suitable for use in developing countries.

Internet /'ɪntəˌnet/ n. international computer network linking computers from educational institutions, government agencies, industry, etc.

in-your-face adj. (also **in your face** predic.) slang aggressively blatant or provocative.

ion exchange n. exchange of ions of the same charge between a usu. aqueous solution and a solid, used in water-softening etc. □ **ion-exchanger** n.

jailbait n. (collect) slang girl, or girls, under the age of consent.

jetfoil /'dʒetfɔɪl/ n. type of passenger-carrying hydrofoil.

jet ski –n. (pl. -s) jet-propelled vehicle like a motorbike, for riding across water. –v. (**jet-ski**) (-skies, -skied, -skiing) ride on a jet ski.

keratotomy /ˌkerə'tɒtəmɪ/ n. Med. surgical operation involving cutting into the cornea of the eye, esp. (in full **radial keratotomy**) to correct myopia.

kick-down n. Brit device for changing gear in a motor vehicle by full depression of the accelerator.

killer cell n. Physiol. white blood cell which destroys infected or cancerous cells.

kiss-off n. esp. US slang an abrupt or rude dismissal.

laserdisc /'leɪzəˌdɪsk/ n. disc on which signals and data are recorded to be reproduced by directing a laser beam on to the surface.

laser printer n. printer in which a laser is used to form a pattern of dots on a photosensitive drum corresponding to the pattern of print required.

leader board n. scoreboard, esp. at a golf course, showing the names etc. of the leading competitors.

lean-burn adj. of or designating an internal-combustion engine designed to run on a lean mixture to reduce pollution.

light pollution n. excessive brightening of the night sky by street lights etc.

line manager n. manager to whom an employee is directly responsible.

lip-sync n. (also **-synch**) (in film acting etc.) movement of a performer's lips in sychronization with a pre-recorded soundtrack.

logic bomb n. Computing set of instructions incorporated into a program so that if a particular logical condition is satisfied they will be carried out, usu. with harmful effects.

lounge lizard n. colloq. idler in fashionable society.

luvvy /'lʌvɪ/ n. (also **luvvie**) (pl. -ies) Brit. colloq. actor or actress, esp. one who is particularly effusive or affected.

machine translation n. translation carried out by a computer.

magic bullet n. colloq any highly specific medicine or other cure.

maglev /'mæglev/ n. (usu. attrib.) transport system in which trains glide above a track, supported by magnetic repulsion. [magnetic levitation]

magnetic resonance imaging n. form of medical imaging using the nuclear magnetic resonance of protons in the body.

market maker n. Brit. member of the Stock Exchange granted certain privileges and trading to prescribed regulations.

megastore /'megəˌstɔː(r)/ n. large shop selling many different types of goods.

messenger RNA n. the form of RNA in which genetic information transcribed from DNA as a sequence of bases is transferred to a ribosome.

middle ground n. **1** the thought, area, or path tending to moderation and compromise. **2** people regarded as holding moderate views.

minibar /'mɪnɪˌbɑː(r)/ n. selection of mainly alcoholic drinks placed in a hotel room for the use of guests and charged on the bill if used.

mission statement n. declaration made by a company etc. of its general principles of operation.

mixed media –*n.* use of a variety of mediums in an entertainment, work of art, etc. –*attrib. adj.* (also **mixed-media**) = MULTIMEDIA.

mobile phone *n.* (also **mobile telephone**) portable radio telephone.

moleskin *n.* **1** skin of a mole used as fur. **2 a** a kind of cotton fustian with its surface shaved before dyeing. **b** (in *pl.*) clothes, esp. trousers, made of this.

monounsaturated /ˌmɒnəʊʌnˈsætʃə‚reɪtɪd/ *adj. Chem.* (of a compound, esp. a fat) saturated except for one multiple bond.

multitasking /ˌmʌltɪˈtɑːskɪŋ/ *n. Computing* execution of a number of tasks at the same time. □ **multitask** *v.*

nanotechnology /ˌnænə(ʊ)tekˈnɒlədʒɪ/ *n.* branch of technology that deals with dimensions and tolerances of less than 100 nanometres, esp. the manipulation of individual atoms and molecules. □ **nanotechnological** /-nəˈlɒdʒɪk(ə)l/ *adj.* **nanotechnologist** *n.*

narrowcast esp. *US* –*v.* (*past* and *past part.* -**cast** or -**casted**) transmit (a television programme etc.), esp. by cable, to an audience targeted by interests or location. –*n.* transmission or programme of this kind. □ **narrowcasting** *n.*

National Vocational Qualification *n.* (in the UK) a qualification in a vocational subject set at five levels.

nation state *n.* sovereign state of which most of the citizens or subjects are united also by factors such as a language, common descent, etc., which define a nation.

negative equity *n.* indebtedness arising when the market value of a property falls below the outstanding amount of a mortgage secured on it.

new man *n.* man who rejects sexist attitudes and the traditional male role.

news-gatherer *n.* person who researches news items, esp. for broadcast or publication. □ **news-gathering** *n.*

nip and tuck –*n. colloq.* cosmetic surgical operation. –*adv. US* neck and neck.

no-fly zone *n.* zone in which aircraft are forbidden to fly.

non-invasive /ˌnɒnɪnˈveɪsɪv/ *adj.* **1** (of a medical procedure) not requiring incision into the body or the removal of tissue. **2** (of an infection etc.) not tending to spread.

nuclear magnetic resonance *n.* absorption of electromagnetic radiation by certain nuclei in an external magnetic field, used mainly as an analytical technique and in body imaging for diagnosis.

oceanarium /ˌəʊʃəˈneərɪəm/ *n.* (*pl.* -**s** or -**ria**) large sea-water aquarium for keeping sea animals.

otter-board *n.* device for keeping the mouth of a trawl net open.

out-of-body experience *n.* sensation of being outside one's body, esp. of floating and being able to observe oneself from a distance.

Pacific Rim *n.* (usu. prec. by *the*) countries and regions bordering the Pacific Ocean, esp. the small nations of eastern Asia.

packet switching *n.* method of data transmission in which parts of a message are sent independently by the optimum route for each part and then reassembled.

pacy /ˈpeɪsɪ/ *adj.* (also **pacey**) (-**cier**, -**ciest**) fast-moving.

paintball *n.* game in which participants simulate military combat using air-guns to shoot capsules of paint at each other. □ **paintballer** *n.*

pakora /pəˈkɔːrə/ *n.* piece of cauliflower, carrot, or other vegetable, coated in seasoned batter and deep-fried. [Hindi]

palmtop *n.* computer small and light enough to be held in one hand.

parador /ˈpærədɔː(r)/ *n.* (*pl.* -**s** or **paradores** /ˌpærəˈdɔːrez/) hotel' owned and administered by the Spanish government. [Spanish]

paragliding /ˈpærəˌɡlaɪdɪŋ/ *n.* sport resembling hang-gliding, using a wide parachute-like canopy attached to the body by a harness. □ **paraglide** *v.* **paraglider** *n.*

party-poop *n.* (also **party-pooper**) esp. *US slang* person who throws gloom over social enjoyment. □ **party-pooping** *n.*

party popper *n.* device which rapidly ejects a paper streamer, used as an amusement at parties.

payback period *n.* length of time required for an investment to pay for itself in terms of profits or savings.

people carrier *n.* motor vehicle of the size and shape of a small minibus but with approximately eight seats which may swivel, be removable, or convert into a table.

performance art *n.* a kind of visual art in which the activity of the artist forms a central feature. □ **performance artist** *n.*

permaculture /ˈpɜːməˌkʌltʃə(r)/ *n.* development of agricultural ecosystems intended to be complete and self-sustaining.

photochemical smog /ˌfəʊtəʊˈkemɪk(ə)l/ *n.* a condition of the atmosphere caused by the action of sunlight on pollutants, resulting in haze and high levels of ozone and nitrogen oxide.

photodegradable /ˌfəʊtəʊdɪˈɡreɪdəb(ə)l/ *adj.* capable of being decomposed by the action of light, esp. sunlight.

photo session *n.* session in which a photographer takes photographs of a person for use in advertising etc.

pill-popper *n. colloq.* **1** person who takes pills freely. **2** drug addict. □ **pill-popping** *n. & attrib. adj.*

pin-down *n.* action or policy of putting children in care into solitary confinement for long periods of time.

placeman *n.* person appointed to a position chiefly to implement the political policies of a higher authority.

planned economy *n.* an economy in which production, prices, incomes, etc. are determined centrally by government.

pooper scooper /ˈpuːpə(r)/ *n.* (also **poop scoop**) *colloq.* implement for clearing up (esp. dog) excrement.

Popemobile /ˈpəʊpməˌbiːl/ *n.* bulletproof vehicle with a raised viewing area, used by the Pope on official visits.

pork barrel *n.* (hyphenated when *attrib.*) *US colloq.* **1** source of government funds for projects designed to win votes (*disapproved of pork-barrel funding*)

2 the funds themselves. □ **pork-barrelling** *n.*

post-traumatic stress disorder /ˌpəʊs(t)trɔːˈmætɪk/ *n. Med.* condition of persistent mental and emotional stress occurring after injury or severe psychological shock.

power-assisted *adj.* (esp. of steering and brakes in a motor vehicle) employing an inanimate source of power to assist manual operation.

power-broker *n.* esp. *N. Amer.* person who exerts influence or affects the equilibrium of political power by intrigue. □ **power-broking** *n.*

price-sensitive *adj.* **1** (of a product) whose sales are greatly influenced by its price. **2** (of information) that would affect prices if it were made public.

pro-choice /prəʊˈtʃɔɪs/ *adj.* favouring the right of a woman to choose to have an abortion.

rail gun *n.* electromagnetic projectile launcher used esp. an an anti-missile weapon.

rainbow coalition *n.* political alliance of minority peoples and other disadvantaged groups.

rat-run *n. colloq.* route on minor roads used by traffic to avoid congestion at peak periods.

remote sensing *n.* scanning of the earth by satellite or high-flying aircraft.

reskill /riːˈskɪl/ *v.* teach, or equip with, new skills.

ribosome /ˈraɪbəˌsəʊm/ *n. Biochem.* each of the minute particles consisting of RNA and associated proteins found in the cytoplasm of living cells, concerned with the synthesis of proteins. □ **ribosomal** *adj.*

ripstop *–attrib. adj.* (of fabric, clothing, etc.) woven so that a tear will not spread. *–n.* ripstop fabric

road rage *n.* overhead metal bar strengthening the frame of a vehicle (esp. in racing) and protecting the occupants if the vehicle overturns.

roll bar *n.* overhead metal bar strengthening the frame of a vehicle (esp. in racing) and protecting the occupants if the vehicle overturns.

Rollerblade *–n. propr.* each of a pair of boots fitted with small wheels for roller skating in the manner of ice skating. –v. (**rollerblade**) skate using such boots. □ **rollerblader** n.

roll-out n. **1 a** official wheeling out of a new aircraft or spacecraft. **b** official launch of a new product. **2** part of a landing during which an aircraft travels along the runway losing speed.

roo bar n. = BULL BAR.

rootsy /'ruːtsɪ/ adj. colloq. (of music) uncommercialized, full-blooded, esp. showing traditional origins.

rumble strip n. series of raised strips across a road or along its edge to make vehicles vibrate, warning drivers of speed restrictions or of the edge of the road.

running light n. each of a set of small lights on a motor vehicle that remain illuminated while the vehicle is running.

salaryman n. (in Japan) white-collar worker.

saturation bombing n. Mil. intensive aerial bombing.

scratch card n. game card having one or several sections coated in a waxy substance which may be scratched away to reveal a possible prize.

scrunch-dry v. dry (hair) while scrunching it.

self-build /self'bɪld/ n. (often attrib.) building of homes by their future owners (self-build cooperative) □ **self-builder** n.

seronegative /ˌsɪərəʊ'neɡətɪv/ adj. Med. giving a negative result in a test of blood serum e.g. for presence of a virus.

seropositive /ˌsɪərəʊ'pɒzɪtɪv/ adj. Med. giving a positive result in a test of blood serum e.g. for presence of a virus.

set-aside n. policy of taking land out of production to reduce crop surpluses.

short-termism n. concentration on short-term projects etc. for immediate profit at the expense of long-term security.

signature dish n. speciality dish created by and associated with a particular chef.

six-pack n. pack of six cans of beer held together with a plastic fastener.

slaphead n. slang derog. person with very short hair or very little hair.

slapper n. Brit. slang offens. promiscuous woman.

smart card n. plastic card with a built-in microprocessor, esp. as a credit or other bank card for the instant transfer of funds etc.

snakeboard –n. flexible type of skateboard. –v. ride on a snakeboard. □ **snakeboarder** n. **snakeboarding** n.

snowboard n. wide ski used for sliding downhill on snow. □ **snowboarder** n. **snowboarding** n.

soft-top n. **1** motor vehicle roof that is soft and can be folded back. **2** vehicle having such a roof.

sonogram /'səʊnəɡræm/ n. **1** graph representing a sound, showing the distribution of energy at different frequencies. **2** esp. Med. visual image produced from an ultrasound examination. [Latin sonus sound]

space blanket n. light metal-coated sheet designed to retain heat.

speed merchant n. colloq. motorist who enjoys driving fast.

spongiform encephalopathy n. slow viral encephalopathy in which the brain becomes spongy.

squall line n. Meteorol. narrow band of high winds along a cold front.

stand-to n. Mil. action or state of standing to; readiness for action or attack.

step aerobics n.pl. type of aerobics involving stepping up on to and down from a portable block.

store card n. credit card issued by a store to its customers.

styrofoam /'staɪrəˌfəʊm/ n. esp. US a kind of expanded polystyrene.

summiteer /ˌsʌmɪ'tɪə(r)/ n. **1** participant in a summit meeting. **2** climber who has completed an ascent to a summit.

supermodel /'suːpəˌmɒd(ə)l/ n. highly-paid model employed in high-profile glamour modelling.

superstate /'suːpəˌsteɪt/ n. powerful political state, esp. one formed from a federation of nations.

sweatpants n.pl. loose thick esp. cotton trousers with an elasticated or

drawstring waist, worn for sports or leisurewear.

swipe card *n.* credit card etc. on which magnetically encoded information is stored to be read by an electronic device.

switchgear *n.* **1** switching equipment used in the transmission of electricity. **2** switches or electrical controls in a motor vehicle.

tanga /'tæŋgə/ *n. Brit.* pair of briefs consisting of small panels connected with strings. [Portuguese]

targa /'tɑːgə/ *n.* [often *attrib.*] type of convertible sports car with a roof hood or panel that can be removed. [Italian, = shield, name originally of a model of Porsche]

taxiway *n.* route along which an aircraft taxies to or from a runway.

T-bar *n.* (in full **T-bar lift**) type of ski lift in the form of a series of inverted T-shaped bars for towing skiers uphill.

team player *n.* person who plays or works well as a member of a team and is not solely concerned with his or her own glory.

telecommute /,telɪkə'mjuːt/ *v.* work from home, communicating by telephone, telex, modem, etc. □ **telecommuter** *n.*

telecottage /'telɪ,kɒtɪdʒ/ *n.* centre fitted with office equipment (computer, photocopier, fax machine, etc.) for people working freelance or at a distance from an employer etc.

telepoint /'telɪ,pɔɪnt/ *n.* **1** place where a cordless telephone may be connected to the telephone network. **2** system providing or using such places.

telepresence /'telɪ,prez(ə)ns/ *n.* **1** use of virtual reality technology esp. for remote control of machinery or for apparent participation in distant events. **2** sensation of being elsewhere created in this way.

teleshopping /'telɪ,ʃɒpɪŋ/ *n.* ordering of goods by customers using a telephone or direct computer link.

televiewer /'telɪ,vjuːə(r)/ *n.* person who watches television. □ **televiewing** *adj.*

telework /'telɪ,wɜːk/ *v.* = TELECOMMUTE. □ **teleworker** *n.*

throw-over *attrib. adj.* that can be thrown over (esp. a bed, sofa) as a decorative cover.

tie-back *n.* decorative strip of fabric or cord for holding a curtain back from the window.

top-down *attrib. adj.* **1** proceeding from the general to the particular, or from the top downwards. **2** hierarchical.

Total Quality Management *n.* (in industry) a systematic approach to improving the quality of products and customer service etc., while reducing costs.

touch screen *n.* VDU screen that displays data, esp. information to customers, when it is touched.

TQM *abbr.* Total Quality Management.

trackball *n. Computing* small ball that is rotated in a holder to move a cursor on a screen.

trade-weighted *adj.* (esp. of exchange rates) weighted according to the importance of the trade with the various countries involved.

transfer RNA *n.* RNA conveying an amino acid molecule from the cytoplasm to a ribosome for use in protein synthesis.

triage /'triːɑːʒ/ *n.* **1** act of sorting according to quality. **2** assignment of degrees of urgency to decide the order of treatment of wounds, illnesses, etc. [French]

uplighter *n.* light placed or designed to throw illumination upwards.

uprate /ʌp'reɪt/ *v.* **1** increase the value of (a pension, benefit, etc.). **2** upgrade.

upward mobility *n.* social or professional advancement.

vanity publisher *n.* publisher who publishes only at the author's expense. □ **vanity publishing** *n.*

videoconference *n.* use of television sets linked by telephone lines etc. to enable a group of people to communicate with each other in sound and vision. □ **videoconferencing** *n.*

videofit *n.* reconstructed picture of a person (esp. one sought by the police) built up on a computer screen by selecting and combining facial features according to witnesses' descriptions (cf. PHOTOFIT).

videophone *n.* telephone device transmitting a visual image as well as sound.

voluntary-controlled *adj.* (usu. *attrib.* (in the UK) designating a voluntary school fully funded by the local authority.

voluntary school *n.* (in the UK) school which, though not established by the local education authority, is funded mainly or entirely by it, and which encourages a particular set of usu. religious beliefs.

whammy /'wæmɪ/ *n.* (*pl.* **-ies**) esp. *US colloq.* **1** evil or unlucky influence. **2** (esp. in phr. **double whammy**) blow or setback.

whiteboard *n.* board with a white surface, used esp. for classroom presentations using felt-tip pens.

white-knuckle *attrib. adj.* (esp. of a fairground ride) designed to cause excitement or tension.

widget /'wɪdʒɪt/ *n. colloq.* any gadget or device. [perhaps an alteration of GADGET]

wind farm *n. Ecol* group of energy-producing windmills or wind turbines.

wordsearch *n.* grid-shaped puzzle of letters in columns, containing several hidden words written in any direction.

workfare /'wɜːkfeə(r)/ *n.* welfare system which requires some work from or training of those receiving benefits.

world order *n.* (esp. in phr. **new world order**) system controlling events in the world, esp. an international set of arrangements for preserving global political stability.

World Wide Web *n.* (prec. by *the*) **1 a** set of standards for the representation and distribution of hypertext documents. **b** software operating according to these standards. **2** information accessible by such means.

yuppify /'jʌpɪfaɪ/ *v.* (**-ies**, **ied**) (esp. as **yuppified** *adj.*) *colloq.* make typical of or suitable for yuppies. □ **yuppification** /-fɪ'keɪʃ(ə)n/ *n.*

zydeco /-zaɪdɪˌkəʊ/ *n.* a kind of Afro-American dance music originally from southern Louisiana. [Louisiana Creole]

American dry

1 pint = 33.60 cu. in.	= 0.550 litre
1 quart = 2 pints	= 1.101 litres
1 peck = 8 quarts	= 8.81 litres
1 bushel = 4 pecks	= 35.3 litres

American liquid

1 pint = 16 fluid oz.	= 0.473 litre
= 28.88 cu. in	
1 quart = 2 pints	= 0.946 litre
1 gallon = 4 quarts	= 3.785 litres

Avoirdupois weight

1 grain	= 0.065 gram
1 dram	= 1.772 grams
1 ounce = 16 drams	= 28.35 grams
1 pound = 16 ounces	= 0.4536 kilogram
= 7,000 grains	(0.45359237 exactly)
1 stone = 14 pounds	= 6.35 kilograms
1 quarter = 2 stones	= 12.70 kilograms
1 hundredweight = 4 quarters	= 50.80 kilograms
1 (long) ton = 20 hundredweight	= 1.016 tonnes
1 short ton = 2,000 pounds	= 0.907 tonne

2 Metric, with British equivalents

Linear measure

1 millimetre	= 0.039 inch
1 centimetre = 10 mm	= 0.394 inch
1 decimetre = 10 cm	= 3.94 inches
1 metre = 10 dm	= 1.094 yards
1 decametre = 10 m	= 10.94 yards
1 hectometre = 100 m	= 109.4 yards
1 kilometre = 1,000 m	= 0.6214 mile

Square measure

1 square centimetre	= 0.155 sq. inch
1 square metre = 10,000 sq. cm	= 1.196 sq. yards
1 are = 100 sq. metres	= 119.6 sq. yards
1 hectare = 100 ares	= 2.471 acres

1 square kilometre = 0.386 sq. mile
= 100 hectares

Cubic measure

1 cubic centimetre = 0.061 cu. inch
1 cubic metre = 1.308 cu. yards
= 1,000,000 cu. cm

Capacity measure

1 millilitre = 0.002 pint (British)
1 centilitre = 10 ml = 0.018 pint
1 decilitre = 10 cl = 0.176 pint
1 litre = 10 dl = 1.76 pints
1 decalitre = 10 l = 2.20 gallons
1 hectolitre = 100 l = 2.75 bushels
1 kilolitre = 1,000 l = 3.44 quarters

Weight

1 milligram = 0.015 grain
1 centigram = 10 mg = 0.154 grain
1 decigram = 10 cg = 1.543 grain
1 gram = 10 dg = 15.43 grain
1 decagram = 10 g = 5.64 drams
1 hectogram = 100 g = 3.527 ounces
1 kilogram = 1,000 g = 2.205 pounds
1 tonne (metric ton) = 1,000 kg = 0.984 (long) ton

3 Temperature

Fahrenheit: Water boils (under standard conditions) at 212° and
freezes at 32°.
Celsius or Centigrade: Water boils at 100° and freezes at 0°.
Kelvin: Water boils at 373.15 K and freezes at 273.15 K.

Celsius	Fahrenheit
—17.8°	0°
—10°	14°
0°	32°
10°	50°
20°	68°
30°	86°
40°	104°
50°	122°
60°	140°
70°	158°
80°	176°
90°	194°
100°	212°

To convert Celsius into Fahrenheit: multiply by 9, divide by 5, and
add 32.
To convert Fahrenheit into Celsius: subtract 32, multiply by 5,
and divide by 9.